CUBA IN TRANSITION

Volume 12

Papers and Proceedings of the

Twelfth Annual Meeting
of the
Association for the Study of the Cuban Economy (ASCE)

Coral Gables, Florida
August 1–3, 2002

(ISBN 0-9649082-1-2)

Cuba in Transition volumes may be purchased from:

Association for the Study of the Cuban Economy
P.O. Box 0567
McLean, Virginia 22101-0567

Email: antoniog@att.net

Information on availability of volumes and book order forms are available at www.ascecuba.org.

PREFACE

This volume of *Cuba in Transition* brings together papers and selected commentaries presented at the Twelfth Annual Meeting of the Association of the Study of the Cuban Economy, which took place August 1-3, 2002, in Coral Gables, Florida. As with previous volumes, this collection of papers and commentaries covers a wide range of topics related to Cuba's economy and society: the current economic situation, macroeconomics, foreign investment, the external sector, tourism, agriculture, transition issues, governance and the role of civil society, legal issues, and demography.

The theme for the Twelfth Annual Meeting was "The State, Institutions and the Market Economy." As the world enters the 21st Century, we have learned that where there is no state, there can be no development. The state must lay the foundation for the market to flourish. We also have learned that private property cannot exist without a governmental apparatus, ready and able to secure not only individuals rights—such as free speech and social justice—but also people's individual holdings. In short, institutions and the rule of law are central to the development process. At the Twelfth Meeting, we heard several important presentations on this key relationship from invited experts and meeting participants. We also held a special half-day session on August 3, entitled "Renovaciones o reincidencias: La democracia cubana en el nuevo siglo," which brought together prominent speakers to discuss the constitutional basis for a democratic Cuba and related issues. We will issue the papers and discussions at this session as the second volume of the ASCE Occasional Studies.

On behalf of the Board of Directors of ASCE, I would like to take this opportunity to thank Jorge Pérez-López and Joseph L. Scarparci for preparing and editing this volume of *Cuba in Transition*. I also would like to thank the Institute for Cuban and Cuban-American Studies of the University of Miami for its cooperation at the annual meeting and its generous contribution in support of this volume's publication.

Beatriz C. Casals
ASCE President

IN MEMORIAM

Evaldo A. Cabarrouy (1945–2002)

On August 8, 2002, Evaldo A. Cabarrouy, Professor of Economics and Finance at the University of Puerto Rico, Rio Piedras Campus, passed away unexpectedly in Puerto Rico. The recipient of a Ph.D. in Economics from the University of Texas, Evaldo was a long-term member and supporter of ASCE, as well an esteemed friend and colleague. He joined the University of Puerto Rico in 1985, after serving as director of the MBA Program at the Universidad del Turabo. He also was a Visiting Professor at the Bildner Center for Western Hemisphere Studies under the City University of New York-University of Puerto Rico Academic Exchange Program during the 2001-2002 academic years. From 1990 to 1991, he was Program Economic Advisor to the U.S. Agency for International Development in El Salvador and in 1992 Advisor to the Governor of Puerto Rico on economic development. Earlier in his career, he was a Latin American Teaching Fellow, a Fullbright Scholar in Colombia, and a participant in the U.S. Information Agency Overseas Speakers Program. Evaldo's research on Cuba centered on fiscal and monetary issues and more recently on the role of small and medium enterprises. He presented several papers at the annual meetings and frequently served as discussant or session chair. Evaldo had just participated in the Twelfth Annual Meeting of the Association a few days before his untimely death. Evaldo also maintained strong collegial relationships with economists in Cuba. Those of us who study the Cuban economy and knew Evaldo will miss not only his professional contributions, but also his friendship, generosity and good humor. May our esteemed colleague rest in peace.

TABLE OF CONTENTS

ASSOCIATION FOR THE STUDY
OF THE CUBAN ECONOMY (ASCE)

Twelfth Annual Meeting
Omni Colonnade Hotel, Coral Gables, Florida
August 1–3, 2002

Conference Program

Current Economic and Political Situation

Carlos N. Quijano, ASCE President

Marta Beatriz Roque, Instituto Cubano de Economistas Independientes

Oscar Espinosa Chepe, Independent Journalist

Pablo Alfonso, *El Nuevo Herald*

Marifeli Pérez-Stable, Florida International University

The State, Institutions and the Market Economy

The Role of Private Institutions in the Transition Econmy
Guy Pfeffermann, Director and Chief Economic Advisor, International Finance Corporation

Transparency and Governance: Recent Experiences in Transition Economies
Miguel Schloss, Transparency International

Macroeconomics

Update on Cuban Dollarization
Roberto Orro, H. Calero Consulting Group

Parasitismo Económico y su Impacto en el Tránsito hacia el Mercado.
Manuel García Díaz, Universidad de Granada

Lecciones de la crisis Argentina para Cuba
Rolando Castañeda, IDB (retired)

Educational Investment and Human Capital Creation in Cuba
Manuel Madrid-Aris, Florida International University

Discussants: Ernesto Hernández-Catá, IMF, and Joaquín Pujol, IMF (retired)

Educational and Legal Issues and the Transition (co-sponsored by the Institute for Cuban and Cuban American Studies, University of Miami)

The Role of Education in Promoting Cuba's Integration into the International Society: Lessons in Transition from Post-Communist States of Central and Eastern Europe
Andy Gómez, University of Miami

Rehabilitando la educación en una Cuba en proceso de cambio
Graciella Cruz-Taura, Florida Atlantic University

Overview of the Dollar Market for High Value Foods in Cuba
    James E. Ross, University of Florida
Discussants: William Trumbull, West Virginia University, and Matthew McPherson, West Virginia University

Coloquio Constitucional Sobre la Tercera República

El Hombre para el Estado o el Estado para el Hombre
    Alberto Luzárraga, Cuban American Research Group
Privatizando el Socialismo
    Manuel Pérez Torres, Entrepreneur, founder of MT1 Software
Challenges for a Transitional Judicial System in a Post-Castro Cuba
    Mario Díaz Cruz III, Dorsey & Whitney LLP, New York, New York
Discussant: Luis J. Pérez, Akerman Senterfitt, Miami

Student Panel

An Evaluation of Four Decades of Cuban Healthcare
    Felipe E. Sixto, Florida International University
Discussant: Antonio Gayoso, Investment and Economics, LLC
Revolutionary Leaders, Ideology and Change
    Erin Ennis, Catholic University of America
Discussant: Edward Gonzalez, UCLA Emeritus and member of Adjunct Staff, RAND
A Taste of Capitalism: The Rise and Fall of Havana's Private Restaurants (*Paladares*)
    Ted Henken, Tulane University
Discussant: Juan Carlos Espinosa

Tourism

The Tourism Sector During the Republic: Performance, Policy and the Public Debate
    María Dolores Espino, St. Thomas University
Trinidad's Tourism Debacle: Between "Glocal" Heritage and National Economic Development
    Joseph Scarpaci, Virginia Tech
Impact of September Eleven on Tourism Activities in Cuba and the Caribbean
    Nicolás Crespo, Phoenix Hospitality and Consulting Corp., and Charles Suddaby, Charles Suddaby and Associates
Discussants: Marifeli Pérez-Stable, FIU, and Art Padilla, North Carolina State University

Constitutions, Property Rights and Public Choice

Economic Implications of the 1940 Constitution: Lessons for the Future
    Jorge A. Sanguinetty, DevTech Systems
Discussant: Joaquín Pujol, IMF (retired)
The U.S. Constitution and Private Property: Reflections for Cuba
    Juan A.B. Belt, Inter-American Development Bank
Discussant: Alberto Luzárraga, Cuban American Research Group
A Public Choice Model of the Incentives of Castro as Authoritarian
    Gary M. Shiffman, Greenberg Traurig
Discussant: Nicolás Sánchez, College of the Holy Cross

Cuba and the Overseas Community

Cuba's Future Economic Crisis: The Aging Population and the Social Safety Net
    Sergio Díaz-Briquets, Casals and Associates
Discussant: Lisandro Pérez, FIU

Legal Dollars and Illegal Parties: The Political Logic of Cuba's Uneven Liberalization
>   Javier Corrales, Amherst College

Discussant: Holly Ackerman, University of Miami

Transition Issues

Cuba in an Unending Special Period
>   Jorge F. Pérez-López, U.S. Department of Labor

Discussant: Gary Maybarduk, U.S. Department of State

The Cuban Transition in the Light of the Lessons of Ten Years of Experience in the Former Soviet Bloc
>   Ernesto Betancourt, Consultant

Discussant: Marta Beatriz Roque, Instituto Cubano de Economistas Independientes

Social Entrepreneurship and Economic Development: Lessons for a Post-Castro Cuba
>   Fernando Alvarez, Berkley Center for Entrepreneurial Studies, NYU-Stern School of Business

Discussant: José Ramón de la Torre, Chapman School of Business, FIU

SESIÓN ESPECIAL
Renovaciones o Reincidencias: La Democracia Cubana en el Nuevo Siglo

Apertura

Carlos N. Quijano

Ponentes

Rafael Rojas

Carlos Alberto Montaner

Néstor Carbonell Cortina

Luis Aguilar León

Comentaristas

Antonio Gayoso

Jorge A. Sanguinetty

Alberto Luzárraga

Orlando Gutiérrez

CUBA: LA CRISIS SE PROFUNDIZA

Oscar Espinosa Chepe

Estimados compatriotas y amigos: Ante todo quiero expresarles mi agradecimiento por la invitacin a participar en la Reunión Anual de la Asociación para el Estdio de la Economía Cubana, y poder contribuir con mi modesto aporte al desarrollo de los debates.

En el período transcurrido desde la celebración de la anterior reunión en agosto del 2001, la situación económica, política y social de Cuba se ha deteriorado significativamente, con evidentes tendencias al agravamiento.

Las autoridades cubanas enfrentadas al derrumbe económico ocasionado por la pérdida de las subvenciones procedentes del bloque soviético, se vieron forzadas a iniciar determinadas reformas en los años 1993 y 1994, con el objetivo de paliar la crisis.

No obstante sus limitaciones, los cambios tuvieron un impacto positivo sobre la economía debido a la existencia de un gran potencial productivo subutilizado. Esto se aprecia en que la caída del PIB se detuvo; y a partir de 1995 se inició una modesta recuperación que, hacia inicios del 2002, había logrado disminuir hasta un 13,0% la brecha existente con respecto a los niveles de 1989, lo cual en 1993 llegó a un 35,0%, de acuerdo con las controvertidas estadísticas oficiales.

A pesar de ello, desde hacía años se percibían señales de problemas en la recuperación económica debido esencialmente al paulatino agotamiento de los efectos movilizadores de las mencionadas reformas, apreciables en primer lugar en las dificultades para obtener financiamiento externo.

En el 2001, se anunció oficialmente un crecimiento del PIB del 3,0% frente al 5,0% previsto. Pero este aumento carece de sustentación. La producción azucarera de la zafra 2000-2001 fue de 3,3 millones de toneladas, una cantidad inferior al 13,0% de lo obtenido en la anterior. Por otra parte, sólo llegaron 555 turistas más que en el 2000, para un total de 1 774 541. El ingreso bruto generado por la actividad en el año fue de 1846,2 millones de dólares, un 5,2% inferior al obtenido en el 2001. El plan establecía una meta de 2 millones de turistas, que debían haber aportado 2230,9 millones de dólares.

La desaceleración económica a escala mundial, agravada por los sucesos terroristas del 11 de septiembre, además de incidir negativamente en la llegada de los turistas, provocó una reducción de los ingresos por concepto de remesas y las inversiones extranjeras; mientras las exportaciones fueron afectadas por la disminución de los precios de los principales rubros.

A esto se unió la cancelación por Rusia de los acuerdos de arrendamiento de la Base de Lourdes, con lo que se perdió una entrada annual de más de 200 millones de dólares; un monto superior a las exportaciones de la industria del tabaco en los últimos años.

Ello motivó la reducción sustancial de la capacidad de compra en el exterior, lo cual necesariamente tiene que haber impactado en todos los sectores económicos nacionales en mayor o menor medida.

Asimismo, a principios de noviembre del 2001 azotó la Isla el huracán Michelle, que ocasionó severos daños a la infraestructura económica; destruyó miles de viviendas; e infligió considerables pérdidas a la agricultura.

1

Según cifras oficiales sobre el comportamiento de la economía el pasado año, la agricultura decreció en 1,7% y la producción industrial sólo tuvo un engrosamiento del 0,5%. Como se apuntara anteriormente, el turismo, la actividad económica más importante en la actualidad, disminuyó en términos de valor en un 5,2%.

Entonces, cabe preguntar, ¿dónde radica el crecimiento proclamado del PIB en el 2001? Quizás en el supuesto 7,9% de aumento de los servicios comunales, sociales y personales anunciados por las autoridades, referido a "progresos" en la educación, salud pública y cultura que nada tienen que ver con la realidad.

En lo relativo al nivel de vida de la población, se pudo apreciar desde inicios del año una contracción de la oferta, tanto a través del racionamiento, como en la cadena de tiendas que comercializan en moneda nacional. Ese fenómeno se advirtió también en los establecimientos de ventas en divisas.

En los últimos meses del año, la cotización del peso cubano convertible o el dólar subió de 22 unidades del peso cubano corriente a 27 unidades en las casas de cambio oficiales. Eso representó para los cubanos sin acceso a la moneda estadounidense, adquirir el peso convertible a precios incrementados en un 22,7% para poder comparar artículos esenciales en las tiendas de venta en divisas.

Producto de la inyección de dinero a la circulación monetaria causada por la depreciación del peso, así como de los efectos negativos del huracán Michelle sobre la economía, los precios de muchas mercancías comercializadas en moneda nacional se incrementaron notablemente en los últimos meses del 2001, incluidos una variedad de rubros ofertados en establecimientos estatales. Ejemplo de eso pudo apreciarse en los Mercados Agropecuarios de la Habana, los llamados "Topados," pertenecientes a entidades gubernamentales, donde de noviembre a diciembre los precios de las hortalizas, como promedio, crecieron 33,4%, las viandas 20,7%, las frutas 20,6% y los granos 21,5%. Estas realidades hacen poco creíble la información oficial de que el Indice de Precios al Consumidor (IPC) descendió el pasado año (-1,4%).

Los problemas observados en la economía cubana en el año 2001, se han recrudecido en el 2002 con mucha más fuerza. El Plan para este año estableció un magro crecimiento del 3,0% en el PIB. Incluso si se cumpliera, alejaría aun más la fecha para alcanzar los niveles productivos precrisis. Sin embargo, con los limitados datos sobre el comportamiento de la economía en el primer semestre que ya se poseen, puede preverse que será muy difícil llegar a ese propósito, e incluso existe la posibilidad de un decrecimiento.

Las cifras brindadas sobre el turismo muestran que los arribos en el primer cuatrimestre han sido inferiores en un 14,0% en relación con igual etapa del año precedente. Hay que tener en cuenta que de enero a abril históricamente llega a Cuba el 33,0% del total de los turistas del año, por lo cual puede vaticinarse que será muy difícil alcanzar los niveles del 2001, aun cuando exista cierto grado de recuperación.

Adicionalmente debe apuntarse que el ingreso bruto por turista decrece desde 1996. Entonces ese indicador fue de 1328 dólares, pero descendió paulatinamente hasta situarse a 1098 dólares en el 2000 y 1040 en el 2001. Las razones de esta continuada caída pudieran encontrarse fundamentalmente en dos factores: la llegada de turistas de muy bajos ingresos, y una oferta de productos y servicios retringida, con precios no acordes a su calidad.

En ello puede haber jugado un papel importante una forzada política de sustitución de insumos importados, dirigida a incrementar el consumo de productos nacionales, que no satisfacen las exigencias de los turistas.

En cuanto a la zafra azucarera, se ha informado que llegó a 3 610 000 toneladas; ligeramente superior a la anterior que fue de algo más de 3,5 millones. La misma comenzó a finales de noviembre y los últimos centrales estuvieron moliendo hasta principios de junio, prolongándose por 8 meses.

Aunque no se ha ofrecido información acerca de los parámetros productivos alcanzados, se estima que el rendimiento industrial obtenido no rebasó siquiera el 11,0%, y la utilización de las capacidades de molienda quedó muy por debajo del 70,0%. En cuanto a los rendimiento agrícolas, se mantienen como promedio alrededor de 35 toneladas por hectárea; uno de los peores del mundo.

En realidad, la zafra fue afectada por el huracán Michelle pues, al atravesar el centro de la Isla, revolcó y acostó la caña en ese territorio, lo que dificultó la mecanización de la cosecha. Sin embargo, esto pudiera haberse resuelto en gran medida, a través del incremento del trabajo manual.

Al pobre volumen de azúcar producido y el alto nivel de ineficiencia prevaleciente en esta zafra, se agrega que los precios del producto en el mercado mundial se encuentran altamente deteriorados; a menos de 6 centavos de dólares estadounidenses la libra. Como consecuencia, los resultados económicos obtenidos pueden haber sido los peores de los últimos años. Oficialmente se estima un descenso en el valor exportado de 120 millones de dólares respecto al año pasado, sólo por los efectos de los precios.

La elevada ineficiencia de la industria azucarera cubana desde hace mucho tiempo, unida a un contexto económico muy complejo, llevó al Gobierno al cierre definitivo de 71 centrales de los 156 existentes. Esta medida se ha tratado de justificar aduciendo los bajos precios del azúcar en el mercado mundial.

Sin embargo, es bien conocido que aunque efectivamente las cotizaciones del azúcar se encuentran muy bajas, sin perspectivas reales de mejoramiento, los motivos del desastre de la agricultura se hallan en la falta de previsión de la política seguida al no desarrollarse la producción de derivados de la caña de azúcar, como se efectuó en muchos países.

A ello se unió un constante aumento de la ineficiencia en la producción azucarera, tanto en el aspecto agrícola como en el industrial. Su colapso no está dado por los bajos precios del azúcar en el mercado internacional, sino por políticas de desarrollo absolutamente erradas, que soslayaron las tendencias del mercado y, al mismo tiempo, por la caída de la eficiencia.

El Gobierno cubano ha acrecentado la censura sobre la información económica desde el 2001. Pero resulta claro que han existido problemas en la agricultura, no sólo a consecuencia del huracán Michelle, sino también por la carencia de muchos recursos, en particular combustible. La cosecha tabacalera alcanzó 37,9 millones de toneladas, un monto similar a la del 2000.

En el resto de los sectores no ha habido serias dificultades con los abastecimientos. Se aprecia que la capacidad de pago del país se ha constreñido extraordinariamente, al punto de existir serias dificultades para poder hacer frente a las obligaciones dimanadas del acuerdo petrolero con Venezuela.

Esto llevó a un incremento de precios en las tiendas de venta en divisas a principios de junio; medida desesperada del Gobierno para recaudar por esa vía las divisas que con urgencia necesitaba.

Hay que resaltar que los incrementos de precios no sólo se observan en el sector dolarizado de la economía. Además se aprecian en los establecimientos de venta en moneda nacional y en el mercado negro. En la propia ciudad de La Habana, en los Mercados Agropecuarios Estatales, conocidos como Mercados Topados, durante el mes de julio con respecto a igual mes del 2001 se observaron fuertes incrementos de las cotizaciones para los productos ofertados. En las viandas, un 20,0% como promedio; en los granos, un 23,0%; en las hortalizas, un 66,0%; en los cítricos y frutas, con un surtido muy limitado, un 20,0%; y en la carne de cerdo, un 7,0%.

En el Mercado Agropecuario No Estatal, donde rige la ley de la oferta y demanda, los precios también has ascendido, aunque debe reslatarse que la calidad de los artículos es superior y la variedad mucho más amplia.

Estos aumentos estan dados no sólo por menores disponibilidades de productos, sino también por un crecimiento de la liquidez monetaria en poder de la población (efectivo en circulación y ahorro). El efectivo en circulación, de acuerdo a datos oficiales, ascendió a 6 486,3 millones de pesos en el 2001. Esa cifra fue superior en 1 395,8 millones al monto del año precedente y 1 931,3 millones más que en 1993 cuando estuvo presente un gran excedente monetario.

Por su parte, el ahorro ascendió a 5 988,2 millones de pesos, comprendidos en esta cifra las cuentas de ahorro a la vista (4 842,1 millones); depósitos a plazo (1

118,0 millones) y cuentas corrientes (28,1 millones). Un volumen en su conjunto superior en 553,2 millones a los niveles existentes en el 2000.

Debido al deterioro de la economía, el Gobierno anunció la minoración de las inversiones en el 2001, sin dar cifras sobre lo ejecutado ni acerca de las metas del 2002. En ello seguramente ha influido la disminución de las inversiones extranjeras. Sobre la base de información publicada por el Banco Central de Cuba, la inversión directa en el 2001 cayó a 38,9 millones, de 448,1 millones en el 2000.

La formación bruta de capital en el 2000 representó el 9,7% del PIB, a precios corrientes; prácticamente la tercera parte del 26,3% logrado en 1989, de acuerdo a fuentes oficiales. Ahora, lejos de contenerse el proceso de descapitalización presente en la economía desde hace años, éste se acelerará con consecuencias funestas para el desarrollo del país.

En lo referente al comercio exterior, la situación del intercambio de bienes se sigue deteriorando. En el 2000, el déficit llegó a 3153,1 millones de dólares. Para el 2001 fue informado un saldo negativo de 3120,3 millones, ligeramente inferior al año precedente, cuestión que sorprende si se tiene en cuenta la disminución de las disponibilidades de azúcar para la venta al exterior y el deterioro generalizado en los precios de los principales rubros exportables. De todas formas por cada dólar de mercancía exportada se continúan importando tres: una situación económicamente insostenible en las actuales condiciones que augura superiores dificultades para el país en los meses venideros.

Asimismo, la estructura de las importaciones se ha mantenido como antes de 1959, cuando los productos de la industria azucarera, el tabaco torcido y en rama, el níquel y los productos de la pesca tenían una posición dominante.

El níquel, con una producción que reabasó las 76,000 toneladas el pasado año, ha mostrado avances debido a la inversión extranjera. No obstante, atraviesa una coyuntura negativa en cuanto a sus precios en el mercado mundial.

Como puede comprenderse, la situación financiera externa de la nación es muy difícil, y sin acceso a la ayuda de las organizaciones crediticias internacionales, con las cuales las autoridades de La Habana siempre se han negado a cooperar.

La deuda externa al cierre del 2001 ascendió a 10,893,0 millones de dólares, según informaciones aportadas por el Banco Central de Cuba, sin incluir las obligaciones contraídas con los países del extinto bloque soviético, de las cuales sólo las relativas a la URSS tienen un monto de 20,8 miles de millones de rublos transferibles, moneda de cuenta utilizada cuando fueron contraídas las deudas. Este rublo equivalía a 1,11 dólares, pero nunca alcanzó la pretendida transferibilidad.

La estructura monetaria de la deuda externa cubana esta compuesta fundamentalmente por divisas diferentes al dólar norteamericano, y con la depreciación de éste en los últimos tiempos, esencialmente frente al euro, resulta previsible un importante incremento de las obligaciones financieras cubanas expresadas en dólares.

A este complejo panorama económico se añade el deterioro continuado de los sistemas de educación, salud pública y seguridad social, que habían alcanzado niveles relativamente altos. En la educación, aunque el Gobierno efectúa esfuerzos por evitarlo, prosigue la fuga de personal docente debido a los bajos salarios, pésimas condiciones de trabajo, y la sobrecarga de actividades extraescolares, fundamentalmente de carácter político.

Para contrarrestar esa situación, se han iniciado campañas para la formación emergente de profesores, con jóvenes extraídos de la enseñanza preuniversitaria que son preparados en pocos meses. Como se comprenderá, eso no será una solución, pues dicho personal deficientemente preparado cuando se enfrente a las difíciles condiciones escolares, probablemente también desertará de sus labores.

Asimismo, en el curso escolar recién concluido comenzó un ciclo de clases por televisión para lo cual fueron distribuidos miles de equipos por todo el país. Aunque en principio pudiera ser una vía para complementar la enseñanza de las distintas asignaturas, con la carencia de personal calificado que sirva de guía a los alumnos, es muy poco probable que los beneficios conseguidos mediante este nuevo método sean relevantes; al margen de que se conoce que muchos de los materiales transmitidos a los alumnos no tienen por objetivo elevar el nivel cultural, sino el adoctrinamiento político.

En la salud pública, al tiempo que se mantiene la escasez de medicamentos, materiales quirúrgicos y de aseo, no hay suficiente personal paramédico, especialmente enfermeros, a consecuencia de la fuga masiva, en busca de mejores condiciones en otras actividades. La solución que se ha querido brindar es similar a la aplicada en el caso de los maestros, o sea la preparación como enfermeros de cientos de jóvenes en cursos emergentes, sin tomar en consideración el verdadero problema: la falta de motivación de los trabajadores de la salud pública.

En lo que respecta a la seguridad social, la pensión promedio mensual en el 2000 era de 102 pesos. En el 2001, se decidió aumentarla casuísticamente a las personas que ganan menos de 100 pesos, ante la gran depreciación que sufrió la moneda nacional ese año. De todas formas puede concluirse que la inmensa mayoría de los jubilados cubanos reciben mensualmente una pensión inferior a 5 dólares. Para que se tenga una idea de la trágica situación por la que atraviesan muchos jubilados, puede señalarse que un paquete de huevos de 30 unidades cuesta 3,60 dólares en las tiendas de venta en divisas, o sea equivalente a 97,20 pesos.

En cuanto al empleo, se anunció una tasa de paro del 4,1% de la población económicamente activa en el 2001, y existen planes para reducirla aun más en el 2002. Para ello, se ha enviado decenas de miles de jóvenes desocupados a estudiar, pagándosele un estipendio. A los efectos de las estadísticas, no se consideran sin ubicación laboral.

Como se comprenderá, esta forma de "empleo" es controversial, además de tener efectos negativos sobre la ya complicada situación financiera interna, pues de esa forma se sigue inyectando dinero a la circulación monetaria sin un respaldo productivo. A la vez, habría que preguntarse qué pasará cuando estos jóvenes concluyan sus cursos, y no haya puestos de trabajo que ofrecer.

El salario promedio mensual fue de 245 pesos en el 2001, aproximadamente 9,07 dólares al cambio vigente desde octubre de ese año; un incremento del 4,7% respecto al existente en el 2000 y considerablemente mayor al supuesto aumento anunciado de la productividad (1,6%).

Por otra parte, se mantiene sin divulgar la cifra de subempleo, que según analistas podría estimarse, conservadoramente, cercana al 20,0% de la población económicamente activa.

Todo ello ha sucedido dentro de una economía crecientemente dolarizada, que ha fragmentado a la sociedad entre ciudadanos con acceso y sin acceso al dólar. Eso obliga a los segundos a conseguir la ansiada moneda de cualquier manera, lo que provoca la proliferación de muchas actividades ilícitas, particularmente el robo de bienes y artículos de centros de trabajo, al aprovecharse del descontrol existente.

Lamentablemente, ante la profundización de la crisis, el Gobierno ha optado por el inmovilismo y el atrincheramiento en sus posiciones. Incluso medidas de apertura tomadas a mediados de los años 90, como es el caso del trabajo por cuenta propia, son afectadas mediante la constante elevación de los impuestos; la aplicación de astronómicas multas; el retiro de licencias con el menor pretexto; la no entrega de nuevos permisos en muchos oficios; y la creación de restricciones y prohibiciones en un clima de total inseguridad.

Si a fines de 1995 poseían licencias 208 500 personas (sin incluir a los arrendadores de viviendas y otras actividades aprobadas con posterioridad), al concluir el 2001 solo quedaban 153 800 trabajadores por cuenta propia, comprendidas todas las categorías, de acuerdo a informaciones publicadas por el Banco Central de Cuba.

El descenso del trabajo por cuenta propia (TPCP) también se aprecia en la diminución de los aportes al presupuesto nacional, y la pérdida continuada de su peso específico en los ingresos totales del presupuesto. En 1997, el TPCP aportó al presupuesto 205,7 millones de pesos, lo que representó el 2,4% del total de sus ingresos. En el 2000, fue 135,4 millones de pesos para un 1,2%.

A todas las dificultades señaladas se agrega un continuado aislamiento internacional de Cuba, esencialmente en el marco de la relaciones con los países latinoamericanos. Diferencias con Argentina, Perú, Uruguay, Costa Rica y hasta México, con el cual las autoridades cubanas tuvieron históricamente buenos vínculos, hacen prever un distanciamiento con probables consecuencias muy negativas para la economía y la sociedad cubana en su conjunto.

Mientras en el continente americano se desarrolla y fortalece una corriente hacia la integración, y paso a paso se desmontan las barreras comerciales entre los países de la región, y de éstos con otros bloques económicos del resto del mundo, Cuba se mantiene apartada de dicho proceso. Ello tendrá efectos funestos para sus relaciones comerciales y de todo tipo en el futuro.

En conclusión puede afirmarse que las tendencias económicas negativas del 2001 se mantienen en el 2002, en condiciones más deplorables, y sin advertirse una reacción positiva por parte de las autoridades cubanas con vista a formular cambios que faciliten un reacomodo.

El Período Especial, como eufemísticamente se llama a la abarcadora crisis iniciada a principios de los años 90, ha entrado en una segunda etapa, cargada de precariedad y con consecuencias imprevisibles para el pueblo cubano.

Estimados compatriotas y amigos: Deseo reiterar mi agradecimiento por propiciar mi participación en esta XII Reunión Annual de la Asociación para el Estudio de la Economía Cubana, así como mis más sinceros deseos de que este encuetro resulte muy fructífero. Nuestra patria lo necesita.

CUBA: UNA VISIÓN PERIODÍSTICA

Pablo Alfonso

LO POLÍTICO

En los últimos dos meses ha ocurrido en Cuba un interesante proceso político, cuyas consecuencias finales todavía están por vislumbrarse: Me refiero al Proyecto Varela auspiciado por la mayoría de los grupos opositores internos y a la Enmienda Constitucional, impulsada por el gobierno, que declaró *irrevocable* al socialismo cubano.

Con toda seguridad todos ustedes han estado al tanto, en mayor o menor grado, de ambos acontecimientos y no voy a entrar en detalles sobre ellos. Sin embargo, creo que es importante apuntar que los mismos han generado una nueva dinámica en la relación gobierno-oposición interna.

Oposición Interna

El Proyecto Varela significó para la oposición interna un cambio cualitativo en su tradicional quehacer político. Independientemente de su contenido, el cual podemos o no compartir, total o parcialmente, no hay dudas que esta iniciativa sirvió para movilizar en torno a un *proyecto político concreto* a los grupos opositores de la isla.

La mayoría de los grupos opositores internos se han caracterizado hasta ahora por una actitud *defensiva,* cuya principal actividad ha sido la denuncia de la situación política y las violaciones a los derechos humanos.

El Proyecto Varela, respaldado por más de 11,000 ciudadanos que lo avalaron con su firma, y en cuyo proceso intervinieron decenas de activistas en todo el país, supone la existencia de una capacidad organizativa y movilizadora de la oposición de la cual hasta ahora no existían evidencias.

Su principal particularidad es que se trata de un proyecto político que intenta utilizar la propia institucionalidad del régimen como un mecanismo de cambio.

Su presentación ante la Asamblea Nacional sorprendió al gobierno que no estaba preparado para enfrentar ese tipo de reto. Habría que señalar, además, que su coincidencia con la visita del ex-presidente Jimmy Carter a Cuba, contribuyó a su repercusión nacional e internacional, y aumentó el desconcierto inicial del gobierno.

La Enmienda Constitucional Irrevocable

Aunque el gobierno alegó oficialmente que las enmiendas constituían una respuesta al presidente de Estados Unidos, George W. Bush, la mayoría de los analistas coinciden que las mismas estaban dirigidas, esencialmente, contra el Proyecto Varela.

La reacción del gobierno ante el reto institucional planteado por el Proyecto Varela fue cambiar las reglas del juego, para protegerse. Ese cambio representa una actitud defensiva. De hecho es la primera vez que el gobierno pierde la ofensiva en la dinámica política interna, independientemente de que mantenga con firmeza las riendas del poder.

El proceso que concluyó con la Enmienda Constitucional irrevocable tiene visos de cierta improvisación. El ejemplo más claro es el término *socialismo intocable* elegido inicialmente y bajo el cual se recogieron los millones de firmas. Al final, tuvo que ser cambiado por *irrevocable* que tiene una connotación menos dramática.

En las sesiones de la Asamblea Nacional hubo algunas curiosas advertencias sobre el término *intocable* y sobre el proceso mismo, que pueden ilustrar más esa improvisación. Un ejemplo.

> Vale recordar que la Unión Soviética fue disuelta, aunque el 75% de la población había apoyado en un referendo su no disolución apenas unos meses antes de que esto se consumara. (Felipe Pérez Roque, Ministro de Relaciones Exteriores.)

Antes de agotar este punto quiero llamar la atención sobre un aspecto institucional del mismo. Reconozco que puede resultar un vano ejercicio esotérico, entrar en consideraciones legales y constitucionales del régimen cubano, pero aún las más férreas dictaduras se comportan dentro de determinadas reglas de juego. Cuando éstas se alteran o se cambian, no es por capricho.

El Artículo 137 de la Constitución vigente faculta a la Asamblea Nacional para introducir reformas o enmiendas como las acordadas en días pasados. Por lo tanto para adoptar esos acuerdos, bastaba con reunir a la Asamblea.

Las movilizaciones populares y las masivas recogidas de firmas, previas a la reunión de la Asamblea, parecieran destinadas a enfrentar a los diputados ante un hecho consumado.

Aparentemente el gobierno llevó a cabo una especie de referendo, al revés, donde invirtió los términos del proceso. Primero fue la movilización popular, y la recogida de firmas, a modo de votación y después la presentación de las enmiendas ante la Asamblea.

Comparto con ustedes otra reflexión personal. La Asamblea Nacional, según la Constitución vigente debe celebrar, cada año, dos períodos ordinarios de sesiones. El primero estaba señalado para el pasado cinco de julio, pero fue pospuesto, sin mayores explicaciones, hasta nuevo aviso. El segundo se celebra habitualmente a mediados o fines de diciembre. Sin embargo, hace algunos días Fidel Castro convocó a elecciones generales para todos los niveles, incluidos los diputados a la Asamblea Nacional.

¿Significa ésto que la Asamblea Nacional ya no se reunirá más hasta que sean electos nuevos diputados? Si esto fuera así, ¿por qué el régimen viola las reglas de su propio juego, es decir, la Constitución vigente, que establece celebrar dos sesiones anuales de la Asamblea?

Dentro de este vistazo político hay que tener en cuenta que el próximo Congreso del Partido Comunista de Cuba debe celebrarse antes de que concluya este año. Por lo pronto ya se han dado todos los pasos iniciales para el evento y elegido a los nuevos dirigentes políticos en todas las instancias de base, municipales y provinciales. En ese proceso no se han producido cambios significativos de dirigentes y es previsible que tampoco ocurran en el Congreso, que pudiera celebrarse el próximo mes de octubre.

LO ECONÓMICO

El año 2002 comenzó bajo el signo de desastre que dejó el huracán Michelle, que afectó a más de la mitad del país en noviembre último, dejando pérdidas calculadas en 1,800 millones de dólares.

La previsión oficial de crecimiento del Producto Interno Bruto (PIB) para este año es del 3%, cifra que se mantiene todavía como meta, a pesar de la crítica situación que se reporta en tres sectores claves de la economía: el turismo, la industria azucarera y el sector energético.

Turismo

Los planes de alcanzar la cifra de dos millones de turistas para este año parecen, nuevamente, inalcanzables.

En 2001 el turismo sólo creció 0,03%, o sea sólo 555 turistas más que el año anterior. Un total de 1.774.000 turistas produjeron ingresos brutos por valor de 1.952 millones de dólares, según datos oficiales.

La tasa de ocupación de las capacidades turísticas alcanzó el 68.9%, en comparación con el 74,2% alcanzado en el 2000. La industria turística registró un decrecimiento de 5,2% en sus ingresos brutos—comparado con el año 2000—de acuerdo con cifras del Informe Económico 2001, del Banco Central de Cuba.

Este año el primer millón de turistas se alcanzó el pasado domingo, un mes más tarde que en el 2001.

Para el primer trimestre de este año, el turismo había bajado un 14%, según datos del ministro de Turismo, Ibrahim Ferradaz.

Industria Azucarera

La ineficiencia operativa y los bajos precios del mercado han obligado al gobierno a anunciar una profunda reestructuración azucarera, que pone fin al llamado plan de recuperación de esa importante industria nacional.

Según cifras oficiales, en la última zafra el costo de producción de una tonelada de azúcar fue de 359 pesos, muy por encima del nivel planificado de 260 pesos por tonelada.

De los 156 ingenios azucareros que hay en el país, sólo 71 quedarán produciendo azúcar, 14 seran utilizados en la producción de derivados y 7 convertidos en museos destinados al turismo.

Unos 100.000 trabajadores, de los 400.000 que emplea la agroindustria azucarera, serán destinados a otras áreas del sector agrícola.

La Comisión Nacional de Reestructuración Azucarera, ha dicho que a esos trabajadores se les pagarán sus salarios, tomando en cuenta el promedio devengado el año anterior, hasta tanto sean reubicados en sus nuevas labores.

Cuba tiene un area de dos millones de hectáreas dedicadas a la siembra de caña y aproximadamente la mitad de esos terrenos, tendrán que reconvertirse para dedicarlos a productos alimenticios varios, ganadería vacuna, porcina y avícola, según los planes.

Otro de los serios problemas que confronta la reestructuración de esta industria son los bateyes de los 64 ingenios desmantelados. Ellos representan, en la práctica, 64 poblaciones o comunidades rurales cuya vida económica, social y cultural giraba en torno al ingenio.

El gobierno ha prometido mantener en esos bateyes los servicios educacionales, de salud, comercio y el resto de las actividades socio culturales, aunque no ha explicado cómo lo va a lograr.

Sector Energético

El corte del suministro petrolero de Venezuela desde abril—unos 53,000 barriles diarios—obligó al gobierno a hacer millonarios desembolsos adicionales para adquirir combustibles en otros mercados distantes y con altos precios de entrega inmediata.

Esos problemas incidieron en un alza de precios decretada a fines de mayo que afecta a una amplia gama de productos de las tiendas en dólares, donde concurre la población para completar la pequeña canasta básica subsidiada.

El aumento de precios, coincidió con un plan del gobierno para reducir en un 10% el consumo eléctrico en compañías y entidades estatales. En diciembre del 2001 el gobierno había implantado ya una reducción del consumo en todos sus organismos estatales, pero según las informaciones publicadas, ante la llegada del verano se hizo necesario reducir aún más su uso.

"Para junio-octubre es necesario un mayor control y disminución de las importaciones de combustible para la generación, lo que indica producir con menos recursos energéticos," indicaba una nota publicada en *Granma*.

Precisamente para hoy, primero de agosto, se ha anunciado la reanudación de los embarques de crudo venezolano, suspendidos desde abril último.

De acuerdo con declaraciones del presidente de PDVSA, Alí Rodríguez, Cuba y Venezuela habrían alcanzado un acuerdo para refinanciar unos 142 millones de dólares por concepto de facturas petroleras; acuerdo que habría facilitado la reanudación de los embarques.

Según cifras divulgadas por PDVSA, Venezuela ha vendido a Cuba en los útimos dos años 25,58 millones de barriles de crudo como parte del acuerdo petrolero que suscribieron ambos países en octubre del 2000, y que otorga a la isla condiciones preferenciales de financiamiento, que incluyen un plazo de pago de 15 años, dos años de gracia, una tasa de interés de 2%, y un cálculo del precio del barril entre 15 y 30 dólares.

Otras Consideraciones Económicas

- El peso cubano se devaluó 22,7% en el último trimestre del 2001, fundamentalmente por los efectos de los atentados del 11 de septiembre en Estados Unidos, la caída del turismo y de los precios internacionales de los productos de exportación cubanos y el alza de los que importa. El tipo de cambio no ha variado este año y se mantiene en 26 pesos por dólar para la venta y 27 para la compra, a diferencia de los 21 pesos a que se cotizaba en octubre del 2001.

- Desde el pasado primero de junio, comenzó a circular oficialmente el euro, como forma de pago en los principales centros turísticos del país. Con esta medida circulan ahora en el país cuatro tipos de moneda: el peso, el peso convertible, el dólar y el euro. La circulación del euro fue autorizada por el gobierno alegando que más del 55% de los turistas que visitan Cuba proceden de la Unión Europea; además la isla realiza casi el 40% de su comercio exterior con miembros de la UE y más de la mitad de las empresas mixtas que operan en Cuba, cuentan con capital procedente de esas naciones.

- En junio de 2002, la UE, el socio comercial e inversionista más importante de Cuba, dirigió al gobierno un documento de 11 páginas, exponiendo las serias dificultades que enfrentan sus empresarios en la isla. Según el documento los inversionistas en Cuba están afectados por las rigurosas regulaciones legales que rigen su actividad comercial; los excesivos impuestos, las dificultades para contratar la fuerza laboral y una ineficiente burocracia estatal que dificultan la actividad empresarial y productiva, entre otros problemas.

CONCLUSION

En una larga entrevista concedida en La Habana a la agencia Reuters, el director del Centro para el Estudio de la Economía Cubana de la Universidad de La Habana, Juan Triana, reconoció que Cuba enfrenta su peor crisis financiera desde el colapso de la Unión Soviética.

"Este año es el más difícil que hemos tenido desde los inicios de los años 90, pero el que diga que la Cuba de hoy está en la misma situación de los años 90 desconoce todo lo que hemos hecho en 12 años de transformación," dijo Triana.

Quisiera concluir estos comentarios con las razones por las cuales, según Triana, la economía cubana está en mejores condiciones que hace una década para superar su actual crisis. Cito textualmente:

> Desde entonces, hemos recuperado casi todo el terreno que perdimos y lo más importante es que la economía ha cambiado su estructura de manera sustancial. Hoy, más del 50 por ciento de los ingresos por exportaciones (de unos 4.000 millones de dólares en 2001) viene del sector de los servicios, básicamente turismo, y la otra parte en bienes. En los años 90 el azúcar era preponderante y hoy no es así. El níquel ahora registra unos ingresos similares y productos no tradicionales como los cítricos y los medicamentos suponen un 20 por ciento de las ganancias por exportaciones. Cuba también depende menos de las importaciones de combustible y alimentos que en el pasado.

Dejo a la consideración de ustedes, los especialistas, la confirmación de esas aseveraciones, que, sin dudas, pueden servir para condimentar el debate.

THE STATE, INSTITUTIONS AND THE MARKET ECONOMY: INSTITUTIONS FOR THE PRIVATE SECTOR IN TRANSITION ECONOMIES

Guy Pfeffermann

The institutional underpinning of successful market economies is a topic that is receiving increasing attention in the economics profession. When asked why living standards improve in some countries and not in others, until about ten years ago most economists would, I think, have focused mainly on the availability of educated people, the state of health, economic diversification and, of course, "getting prices right" and the quality of macroeconomic policy. However, attention to institutional factors was never absent from development discussions. Indeed, the "Washington Consensus," a list of policies which would stimulate healthy economic development, which is much maligned today and unfairly so, quite explicitly encompasses institutional factors. It recommends the abolition of regulations that impede the entry of new firms or restrict competition, as well as a legal system that provides secure property rights and makes them available to the informal sector.[1] To me, the only unfortunate thing about the Washington Consensus is its name.

What I find astonishing is how little attention the economics profession has paid to the role which pri-

vate enterprises play in fomenting development. Most of the economics literature takes it for granted that firms will respond automatically to macroeconomic and price incentives. Yet private firms play the major role in producing goods and services, including many of the basic goods that we need to survive, as well as to thrive; in creating jobs and incomes; in capturing, applying and transmitting useful knowledge; in generating consumer surplus, and so forth. The International Finance Corporation published a booklet entitled *Paths Out of Poverty*, that articulates the role of private enterprise in developing countries,[2] and a forthcoming book sponsored by IFC and the World Bank will focus on the role private firms play in fostering economic mobility in developing countries.[3]

But times are changing, and Nicholas Stern, the World Bank's Chief Economist, made the quality of the investment climate one of the main pillars of economic growth and poverty reduction, the other being empowerment policies such as making clean water, health and education services available to poor people.[4] One of the reasons Stern focuses on the invest-

---

1. *The Political Economy of Policy Reform.* John Williamson, Editor, Institute for International Economics, Washington DC, 1994 (pp. 26-28).

2. *Paths Out of Poverty—The Role of Private Enterprise in Developing Countries.* IFC, Washington DC, 2000.

3. *Pathways Out of Poverty—Private Firms and Economic Mobility in Developing Countries.* Guy Pfeffermann and Gary S. Fields, Eds., 2002.

4. "A Strategy for Development." Nicholas Stern, World Bank, May 2001.

ment climate is his own experience of dealing with former communist countries when he was Chief Economist of the European Bank for Reconstruction and Development. In these countries, perhaps more visibly than in others, there can be no sustained economic development without a growing and dynamic private sector. All this may seem obvious to you, but it isn't to all economists. Indeed, what Joseph Stiglitz has been writing conveys deep reservations about the role of private firms in development.[5] None of this is to minimize the role of the state. Indeed, it is hard to conceive of a good investment climate without strong and effective public management.

In the next few minutes I will present to you some new empirical evidence about the institutional dimensions of private sector development. I will then zero in on some of the lessons that have been learned in the process of transition from centrally planned to market economies. Any similarity between the countries I mention and an unnamed country that might possibly be on your mind is coincidental. Needless to say, I am speaking in my personal capacity.

My first point is that doing business in developing and transition countries can be exceedingly frustrating.

The World Bank conducted a worldwide survey of businesses, focusing mainly on their interface with public officials.[6] Executives of about ten thousand firms, mostly small and medium-sized enterprises, were interviewed in 80 countries and West Bank & Gaza. This included local firms as well as firms with foreign ownership. The survey asked how problematic were a set of constraints for the growth and operation of their firm. The leading constraints vary by region. In Latin America, for example, the four top perceived obstacles to doing business were (1) taxes and tax regulations; (2) policy instability; (3) street crime; and (4) lack of financing. In European transition countries, taxes and tax regulations came first al-

so, followed by lack of financing; inflation; and policy instability. Responses were similar in the former Soviet Union, except that policy instability was considered more problematic than inflation.

About two-thirds of firms in Central Europe, Latin America and the former Soviet Union report that the government is inefficient in delivering services. Worldwide, the majority of firms express negative opinions for public health, parliament, and public works/roads, while over 40 percent negatively evaluate the courts, police, education services, and central government leadership. The most positive ratings go to the postal, telephone and electric power services. Executives spend an inordinate amount of their valuable time, dealing with public officials. This is obviously related to corruption, which about half the executives interviewed in the former Soviet Union and in Central Europe regard as a serious impediment to doing business. A good number of former communist countries have dysfunctional taxation systems (something that Russia has been taking steps to ameliorate). Not uncommonly, there are so many different taxes on the books that honest firms would end up paying in taxes more than their total earnings. Unsurprisingly, firms are driven into illegality, and hence are particularly vulnerable to demands by corrupt officials.

Perhaps most important, econometric analyses of the survey results demonstrate that these institutional obstacles reduce sales growth as well as investment significantly. In other words, improving the interface between government and business enhances the abilities of firms to produce what people need.

So far, we have looked at perceptions by existing businesses. These are the businesses that "made it" to begin with. Many entrepreneurs were not so lucky and never even made it to the starting post. Regimes that discourage the launching of new enterprises are particularly harmful to economic and social develop-

---

5. See notably *Globalization and Its Discontents*. Joseph Stiglitz, W.W. Norton & Company, 2002.

6. "Voices of the Firms." Andrew Stone, Daniel Kaufmann and Geeta Batra. Forthcoming, World Bank. The survey data can be found at: http://www.worldbank.org/privatesector/ic/icresources.htm and users can apply an interactive web tool to explore the data at http://info.worldbank.org/governance/wbes/.

ment. New enterprises are more productive than old ones.[7] They outperform old enterprises in sales, exports, investment, and employment. In the Czech Republic, Hungary, Lithuania, and Poland, new enterprises grew very rapidly, and now account for half or more of employment (equal to the average in the European Union) and between 55 and 65 percent of value added. Conversely, in Kazakhstan, Russia and Ukraine, which have seen modest or no growth in new enterprises, the share of employment has stayed at or below 20 percent and the share of value added between 20 and 30 percent. The latter countries favor old established firms, which are draining resources, such as credit, away from potential new and far more productive firms.[8]

Foreign investors too face very different establishment costs in different countries. According to recent World Bank research,[9] foreign firms wishing to operate in the 32 countries surveyed had to face up to 29 administrative procedures in order to enter the market, up to 125 to secure a land site, and up to 26 in order to commence operations. The time required in order to secure all these permits was between 200 and 1,300 business days. Looking at the transition countries surveyed, it took 702 business days in Bulgaria to get permission to enter and secure land, and 634 in Romania. In contrast, this took 75 days in Slovenia, one of the more successful transition economies.

More often than not, governments which make life difficult for new enterprises are acting on behalf of powerful established firms, public or private, which have "captured" policy-makers. The Worldwide Business Environment Survey suggests that in half of the countries in transition, the policies, laws, and regulations are reported by firm executives to have been shaped to a large extent by firms that have made corrupt payments. The impact of such state capture on the business and investment climate is very large. Firms in countries that avoided state capture grew much faster and invested significantly more than firms in countries subject to state capture. Equally important, firms that are "captors" benefited dramatically from their insider status, although not by virtue of their competitiveness.[10]

The most exhaustive study so far of privatization and enterprise restructuring in transition countries offers conclusions that may be very useful to future transition countries.[11] Privatization to outsiders, for example strategic investors (as opposed to incumbent state enterprise managers and workers), has a large positive impact on enterprise restructuring. Privatization to workers did not enhance restructuring in Eastern Europe and had negative effects in the former Soviet Union. Hardened budgets—i.e., reduction or elimination of government subsidies to state enterprises—are also significant in explaining the extent of restructuring. Another lesson (not from this study, but from experience) is that small firms, such as restaurants, dry cleaning establishments, etc., should be privatized very rapidly.

A lesson emerges very clearly from all these transition experiences. Just as nature abhors a vacuum, so it goes for institutions. Once a centrally-planned regime comes to an end, unless new rules of the game are introduced *and enforced* very swiftly, an institutional vacuum will develop which is most likely to be filled by a combination of rent-seeking oligarchs tied to the new government and mafia enforcers. It is then most difficult and in some cases until now impossible to get rid of these parasitic surrogates for market institutions. In other words, both economic reforms and institutional reforms should be carried quickly after transition. This is what was achieved in

---

7. See *Transition—The First Ten Years*. World Bank, 2002.

8. From *Transition—The First Ten Years*. op.cit.

9. "Administrative Barriers to Foreign Investment in Developing Countries." World Bank Policy Research Working Paper Number 2848, by Jacques Morisset and Olivier Lumenga Neso, May 2002.

10. See *Pathways Out of Poverty*, chapter by Geeta Batra, Daniel Kaufmann and Andrew H.W. Stone.

11. "Enterprise Restructuring in Transition: A Quantitative Survey." Simeon Djankov and Peter Murrell, *Journal of Economic Literature,* forthcoming.

Poland, one of the most successful transition countries. Specifically:

- Prices should be freed as quickly as possible, as was done for example in Poland and Vietnam; maintenance of unrealistic raw materials and energy prices not only drained tens of billions of dollars out of Russia, but discouraged enterprise creation big time;

- Land and real estate ownership should be established as rapidly as possible; restitution claims are best dealt with in cash compensation (or treasury bills), and not in the actual physical assets (land, housing, plant) reclaimed by former owners; unless this is done, the ownership of assets may remain in doubt for years, blocking most new investment, and possibly causing years of lost production, capital flight, high unemployment and social turmoil. Hungary provides a good model of how cash compensation can be achieved quickly; and

- Elementary political good sense suggests that opposition to the market economy should be minimized. There are many ways of doing so, for example: giving employees of privatized or re-privatized firms minority shareholdings at concessional prices; gearing social policies toward preserving advantages that a mixed economy may not provide—so, for example, the women of East Germany lost free child care and therefore find it harder to continue working, not to mention lost reproductive rights ; the same goes for the access of poor persons to basic services such as clean water provision, health and education. A well-educated and healthy work force is an invaluable asset to private enterprise in our globalized economy, as well as to society at large.

Before concluding I would like to touch on what I consider a very important facet of transition, and one which is not often being considered by economists. I am speaking of psychological transition. As the Germans found out after the Wall came down in 1989, the psychological make-up of East Germans who grew up under communism is very different (and in some respects remains so to this day) from that of West Germans. Possibly, some of these differences existed before the communist occupation of East Germany and East Berlin, but mostly, the differences arose as a result of forty years of communist rule. Two signals characteristics of communist socialization are relevant to the transition to market institutions, and they are two sides of the same coin: risk aversion, and the expectation of maximum security, however dismal the standard of living. Risk aversion translates into a bureaucratic mind-set. Employees tended to wait until they were told what to do. Party cadres tried to maintain a monopoly of initiative and organizational skills. At the same time, the regime provided job security, child care, as noted earlier, and other basic benefits, albeit often at minimal levels. Twelve years after reunification, these attitudes still linger with older people in the Eastern states of Germany, many of whom are now saying: "it wasn't so bad back then after all."

In the words of a former East German spy, a member of the party elite, "We always ask whether someone is from east or west. Then all is revealed. The typical West German is to us arrogant. The typical East German is to them lazy. It has not changed. The psychological divide remains deep… But we are not lazy. Germans in the east are still waiting for orders. They have to be told what to do. One bad thing we did was to take initiative away from people."[12]

Such psychological differences are of course hard to manage. A number of foreign businesses in Eastern European transition countries and in Russia only hired very young staff who had never worked under communism. Demography solves the problem eventually, as young people who did not grow up under communism grow in numbers and eventually replace their older compatriots. Until that demographic transition takes hold, the task of government is to avoid a sense of marginalization on the part of the

---

12. "Life after the Stasi." Jim Hoagland, *Washington Post,* July 18, 2002. The cited East German is Edgar Uher, now a successful entrepreneur.

current majority who never experienced anything except the old regime.

In conclusion, rapid growth and poverty-reduction are possible only when private enterprise operates in a good investment climate. Besides good macroeconomic policies, this requires a firm institutional roadbed, which, in turn, supposes the existence of an administratively competent and relatively un-corrupt government. Some good things most communist systems produced were excellent education (by international standards) and, in many countries, good basic health services for the vast majority of the population. Good health and education (essential elements of "empowerment") are invaluable assets on which post-communist governments can build. Yet the development experiences of transition countries were quite varied: some, like Estonia, have managed very well and are on the point of joining the European Union. Others have failed to bank on their human capital, partly because they did not reform their private sector institutions in depth. Perhaps most important, a transition government must try to avoid institutional vacuum which invites state capture by parasitic elements of society. Whatever the pace of transition, the process is painful and can take a lot of time, but the alternative is worse.

COMBATING CORRUPTION: FROM WORDS TO DEEDS

Miguel Schloss

SUMMARY AND CONCLUSIONS

The Trends and Underlying Forces

"If the causes of violent conflict are not addressed …the inhuman and barbaric behavior that fuels war will continue"

— The Hon. Jeff Radebe

The Cold War, in which superpowers sought to maintain a global balance of power without resorting to nuclear arms, masked many local, intrastate conflicts by internationalizing them. What in actuality were civil wars among indigenous groups contending for local power were turned into "virtual" international conflicts fought by proxy. Externally financed economic growth and outside support for authoritarian regimes concealed deeply rooted internal ethnic, religious, social, and economic cleavages. With the end of the Cold War, this virtual bubble burst, leaving an unprecedented number of civil wars. Of the 108 violent conflicts between 1989 and 1998, 92 were considered to be intrastate. Consequently, peacekeeping and peace building have taken on new prominence as tasks for the United Nations. In the first 45 years of its existence, the UN spent 23 percent of its budget, or about US$3.6 billion, on peacekeeping. In the past 10 years this has increased dramatically; 77 percent of the UN budget (roughly US$12.1 billion per year) has been allocated to maintaining peace within rather than across national borders.

Unlike interstate conflict, which often mobilizes national unity and strengthens societal cohesiveness, violent conflict within a state can be caused by and/or weakens its social fabric. It divides the population by undermining interpersonal and communal trust, destroying the norms and values that underlie cooperation and collective action for the common good, and increasing the likelihood of communal strife. Often overlooked is the governance element triggering or sustaining such conflicts: governments run for private benefit, and societies, clans, or families having to fare for public goods (support of the weak, education, etc.)—the exact obverse of a functional society. This damages in turn the values and social relations that bond communities together, as well as the bridges between civil society and the state which impedes the ability of either communal groups or the state to recover after hostilities cease.

Oftentimes, such conflicts are fueled or sustained through corrupt and illegal practices, such as trafficking high-value diamonds, drugs and other forms of using what would otherwise generate "public resources" for private aims (arms, militia, or just siphoning funds to private accounts of local leaders). It would be nice if, by simply curtailing such funds (i.e. acting though the *supply side*, so to speak), one could dry-up the supply of resources that fuel such efforts. However, for the present, money-laundering arrangements and anti-corruption conventions among countries are in their infancy, their reach of institutions still limited and untested, and enforcement arrangements too cumbersome to make much of a dent on the problem. Accordingly, a more determinate and coherent effort needs to be done to address the *demand side* of such funds, and with it the underlying drivers of the conflicts, to resolve the problems in more fundamental ways.

16

The Incentives and the "Levers for Change"

"Things should be made as simple as possible, but not any simpler"

—Albert Einstein

These relations, predominantly based on kinship, ethnicity, and religion, are largely protectionist, defense mechanisms that form a safety net for basic survival. While surely these conflicts oftentimes are driven by other causes—raw power, ambitions of warlords, simple prejudice and other such factors— the above discussion sheds light on some economic dimensions of conflict and illustrate how issues of governance affect social cohesion. They can magnify or even drive people into violent conflict with several conditioning factors, such as inequality, indignity and exclusion.

Each conflict should be properly understood when shaping the structure of peace building interventions (relief, reconstruction, and reconciliation) after hostilities cease. Initially, one must observe the institutional build-up that can take place organically, coping mechanisms to provide to civil society that governments are unable to provide. Because the nature and causes of war are situation-specific and peculiar to each country's unique condition, efforts for relief, reconstruction, and reconciliation need to take note of these differences.

Both bonding and bridging efforts within civil society require a move toward welfare and social protection and, to an increasing extent, growth and development. As conflicts begin to wane, traditional types of social organizations, such as pagoda and funeral associations in Cambodia, associations of widows and orphans in Rwanda, Mayan women's associations in Guatemala, or even private local entrepreneurs in Somalia have sprung up to provide public services, caring for vulnerable groups or act as catalysts for the peace processes.

By the same token, new forms of civil society can be shaped to underpin more advanced forms of public sector institutional development. In Guatemala, for example, networks of civil society organizations such as a confederation that constituted the Chapter in Formation of Transparency International (TI)

helped monitor actions of public institutions, such as Congress and other aspects of nation building.

More broadly, strong societies with inclusionary institutions and social policies as manifested in conflict-mediating institutions, such as efficient and non-corrupt bureaucracy, are more likely to be able to prevent or withstand the socioeconomic and political shocks associated with internal conflicts. Accordingly, step-by-step efforts need to be oriented towards:

- Building, **empowering** and enabling an active **civil society** that protects the rights of the individual and of groups while engaging and holds emerging state institutions accountable to the rule of law, including actions that: (a) ensure freedom of information; (b) provide for publicly driven hearing or similar arrangements for drafting laws, regulations or other vehicles of governmental acts; (c) develop media, civil society organizations, etc.; and (d) build checks and balances to ensure independent and effective judiciary, decentralization with accountability, and support the above-mentioned civil society oversight arrangements.

- Starting **build-up of public administration** and public finance through setting up the rudiments of: (a) meritrocratic civil service; (b) transparent, monetized public sector with adequate remuneration; and (c) associated accountability in expenditures (by setting up independent treasury, audit, procurement functions and processes)

- **Establishing accountability of political process and finance** through: (a) disclosure of parliamentary or equivalent legislature votes; (b) transparency in party financing; (c) asset declaration, conflict of interest rules and/or similar actions to build transparency of associated sections of political processes.

- **Establishing mediating mechanisms**, requiring as limited institutional-intensive arrangements as possible to facilitate an enabling environment for the development of movements and entrepreneurs, however fledging, though competition and entry through: (a) competitive restructuring of monopolies; (b) regulatory simplification; and (c) reducing discretionary powers of public authorities to the maximum extend practical

- **Supporting** local efforts **through global institutions**, by building up the transparency of their transactions, including their tax and royalty payments, imports and exports, and their business standards and associated internal control arrangements.

WHAT WE KNOW ABOUT TACKLING CORRUPTION

The Issue

"Power corrupts. Absolute power corrupts absolutely"

— Lord Acton

Corruption is a complex phenomenon and in many cases is the consequence of more deep-seated problems of policy distortion, institutional incentives, and governance. Therefore, it cannot be addressed by simple legal acts proscribing corruption. In fact, in virtually all countries, local laws forbid corrupt behavior. Yet, in more cases than is readily admitted, effective efforts to combat corruption have been limited. The reason is that, by definition, in many developing and transition economies, the judiciary, legal enforcement institutions, police, and other legal bodies are unreliable because the rule of law is often fragile and therefore can be captured by corrupt interests. This is particularly the case in zones of conflict.

But corruption is not limited to these economies. In developed countries, tax incentives, standards of conduct, and general attitudes often lend themselves to providing the resources for corruption. Indeed, "the abuse of public office for private gain," as corruption is generally defined, takes place in rich and poor countries and must be tackled as much in the places where payments originate as where they are received. However, where public governance arrangements are

weak or non-existent, such as in war areas, conditions are prone for corruption.

Implications

"There is no such thing as a free lunch"

— Milton Friedman

"Money doesn't talk, it swears"

— Bob Dylan

In the final analysis, corruption is as much a moral as a governance and development issue. It can distort entire decision-making processes on investment projects and other commercial transactions and the very social fabric of societies. Some fairly robust statistical evidence shows that higher corruption is associated with: (i) higher (and more costly) public investment; (ii) lower government revenues; (iii) lower expenditures on operations and maintenance; and (iv) ensuing lower quality of public infrastructure.[1] The evidence also shows that corruption increases public investment by making it more expensive while reducing its productivity—not to mention the loss of resources to the countries resulting from uneconomic investments.[2]

By the same token, not only the size, but also the composition and associated quality of public investment programs are affected by levels of corruption. By and large, corrupt administrations tend to spend less on education and other social expenditures because expensive infrastructure or the maintenance of large defense (including arms) expenditures outlays crowd out spending on education and other investments in people.[3] This suggests that corruption tends to mortgage future generations, since economic growth over the long haul is directly related with educational attainment. The secondary effects of policy distortions can be equally staggering, since they produce multiplying effects throughout the economy, as discussed later on in this paper.[4] This is particularly

---

1. Vito Tanzi and Hamit Davaodi, "Corruption, Public Investment, and Growth,"IMF Working Paper 97/139 (1977).

2. Dieter Frisch, "Les effets de la corruption sur le developpement," TI Working Papers Series, No 7 (1995); D. Kaufmann, "Corruption: The Facts," *Foreign Policy* (Summer 1997).

3. Paolo Mauro, "Corruption Causes, Consequences and Agenda for Future Research," *Finance & Development* (March 1998)

4. Miguel Schloss, "Does Petroleum Procurement and Trade Matter,? *Finance & Development* (March 1993).

serious when generation of savings and surpluses are already far short of the investment requirements in that continent.

In all, these are the vehicles through which corruption lowers economic growth. An implication is that economists should be more restrained in their praise of high public sector investment and stresses the importance of placing much greater attention on corruption as well as on the quality and composition of public expenditures. The issue of corruption, and its attendant effects of efficient and effective resource use, needs accordingly a much higher place in the policy debate among all concerned.

By the late 1980s and early 1990s, most countries in Latin America adopted structural adjustment, economic liberalization, and "modernization" policies, aimed at coping with and preventing economic crises by developing building blocks to improve the agility and effectiveness of public sector management. A mixed reform record has brought about recognition that the problems were more fundamental than they were thought of originally and that a "second generation" of reform is needed. Similar actions have started in much of Africa and Asia.

In light of a growing recognition of the complexities of the reform processes, an increasing number of countries is beginning to tackle broader and deeper institutional issues, such as decentralization/sub-national government reform, judicial reform, and anti-corruption efforts. Some countries are going beyond these issues and are tackling issues such as "voice"/ participation; "exit"/competition; restructuring of enforcement mechanisms of internal rules and regulations. Work in these new areas requires stronger, broader and deeper commitments for sustainable implementation and, with it, increasing demands on TI Chapters (such as is occurring in Argentina, Chile, Paraguay or some countries with serious civil records such as Colombia or Guatemala).

The Roots of Corruption & Corrective Action (The Demand Side)

"One of the reasons why governmental corruption has grown to be pervasive...is primarily because much

effort has been spent to remedy the problem rather than understand it"

— Olowu 1992

Clearly, a more comprehensive approach is needed than the popular road of issuing declarations, policy statements or even legislation. More importantly, to assure better results, a greater focus is needed on the underlying causes of corruption and on mutually supporting mechanisms between governments, business practices in the private sector, and civil society.

But corruption is not limited to these economies. In developed countries, tax incentives, standards of conduct, and general attitudes often lend themselves to providing the resources for corruption. Indeed, "the abuse of public office for private gain," as corruption is generally defined, takes place in rich and poor countries and must be tackled as much in the places where payments originate as where they are received.

To assist governments, the business community and other interested parties debate on the issue, Transparency International (TI) has been publishing an increasingly comprehensive **Corruption Perceptions Index (CPI).** This index is a "poll of polls" drawing upon numerous distinct surveys of expert and general public views of the extent of corruption in countries around the world. Recent data show that the bulk of countries, including those in the Latin America region, have poor scores—ratings of less than 50%— thereby strongly suggesting that corruption is a serious issue, deserving much higher attention in the policy agenda of this region.

In this regard, it should be understood that bribery encompasses payoffs for a variety of illicit activities: (i) getting around licenses, permits and signatures; (ii) acquiring monopolistic power—entry barriers to competitors; (iii) access to public goods, including legal or uneconomic awards of public procurement contracts; (iv) access to the use of public physical assets or their outright stripping and appropriation; (v) access to preferential financial assets—credit; (vi) illegal trade in goods banned for security and health considerations, such as drugs and nuclear materials; (vii) illicit financial transactions, such as money laundering and insider trading; (viii) influencing admin-

Figure 1. Corruption Perception by Regions

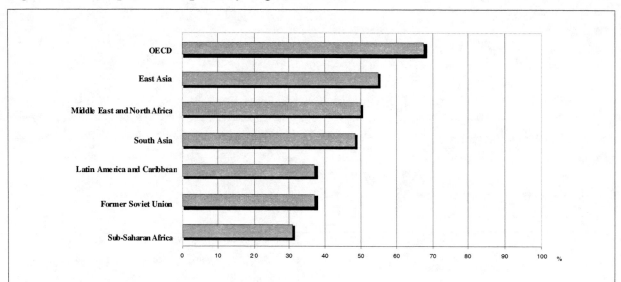

Figure 2. Corruption and Regulatory Discretion

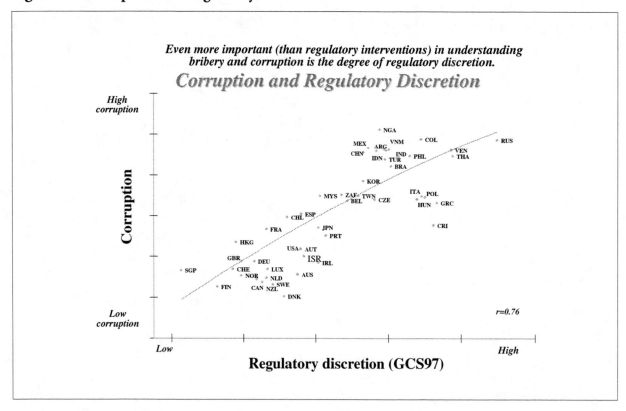

istrative or legislative actions; and (ix) influencing judicial decisions.

In all these cases, corruption occurs when economic opportunities for it prevail and political will to combat it is lacking. In a way, corruption is a symptom of fundamental economic and political problems. Ad-

dressing them effectively therefore requires dealing with the underlying economic, political, and institutional causes. At the root of many of the problems, often times one can find excessive discretionary powers.

Figure 3. Bribery vs. Civil Service Professionalism

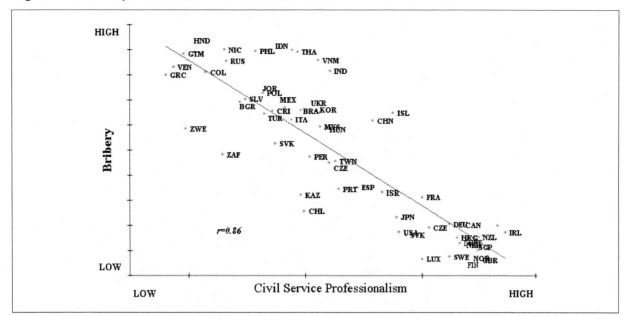

Figure 4. Time Management Spent with Bureaucrats and Frequency of Bribery

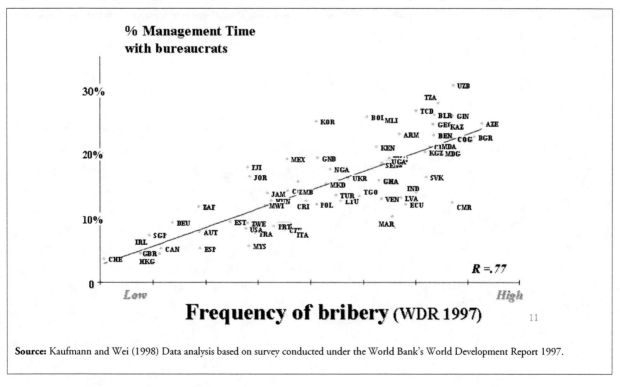

Source: Kaufmann and Wei (1998) Data analysis based on survey conducted under the World Bank's World Development Report 1997.

For this reason, reducing opportunities for discretion is often an important element for **prevention**. These typically include liberalization policies such as reductions of trade restrictions, subsidies, price controls, and directed credit, that have been undertaken in a growing number of countries in Latin America, as well as more recently in Africa and Asia.

Conversely, it stands to reason that the higher the professional levels in civil service on the sheer existence of a credible public administration (a particular

Figure 5. Corruption and the Rule of Law

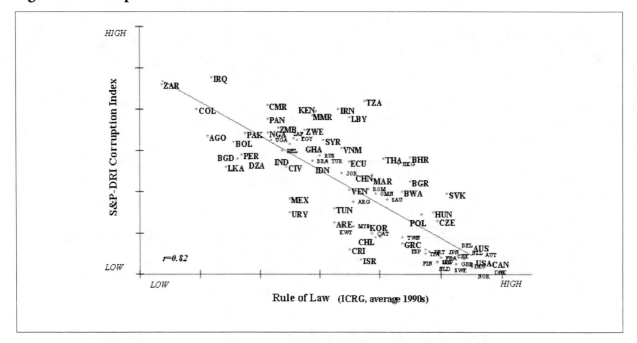

neuralgic issue in zones of conflict), the lower are the perceived levels of corruption.

Quite apart of the wastefulness of corruption expenditures and associated misallocation of resources, valuable management time gets siphoned off through time spent with public officials.

Accordingly, on the **enforcement** side, weak institutions often require the help of independent oversight commissions with powers to investigate and, at times, prosecute or adjudicate, as has been instituted in Chile, Hong Kong, Singapore, and Botswana. This can be a particular promising avenue to dialog, or avoid as much as practical judicial systems, which tend to be cumbersome and slow in producing corrective action, given their underlying adversarial process arrangements. More generally, and not surprisingly, corruption perceptions tend to be higher, the weaker the rule of law in the countries concerned. Almost by definition, this factor makes zones of conflict easy prey for corruption.

Finally, proper **interface** needs to be formed between civil society, the private sector, and governments to help assess the issues and develop support for combating corruption and to develop more effective ways of doing business. More than in any other field, cor-

ruption is not an area that lends itself to technocratic solutions developed by a few and executed by many; long-term and sustainable development requires a real stake of all concerned and often needs home-grown and tailor-made solutions.

Most civil societies are new and weak. The former have decision-making procedures and clear lines of communications; civil society has none of these. Governments and private companies have authorities to please and schedules to be followed; civil societies have nothing of the sort—and yet must respond organically to people's concerns. For the most part, there is a mismatch between civil society's capacity to perform its role and those of Government and private sector.

That being said, a number of regions have already started to undertake positive strides ahead in a number of key areas. In the United States, the United Kingdom, and many of the western democracies there is a long record of and experience built on transparency in decision-making and involvement of civil society. More generally, though, the more pluralistic the societies, the lower the levels of corruption.

Figure 6. Controlling Bribery and Civil Liberties

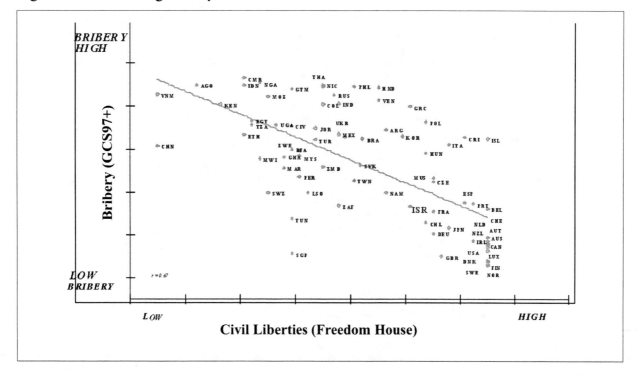

Also in a growing number of countries such as in Latin America, aside from the structural reforms under way, there is a growing civil society, including some twenty TI Chapters in various stages of formation, which are engaged in a growing number of strategic activities.

The Roots of Corruption & Corrective Action (The Supply Side)

"To lead people, walk behind them"

— Lao Tzu

The **Bribe Payers Index (BPI)** ranks the leading exporting countries in terms of the degree to which their companies are perceived to be paying bribes abroad. The BPI indicates that corruption is widely seen as playing a significant role in international commerce. The data provides a disturbing picture of the degree to which leading exporting countries are perceived to be using corrupt practices.

Business executives and professionals in leading emerging market countries see international bribe paying to be greatest in the public works and construction sectors, followed by the arms industry.

Particularly disturbing is the high corruption associated with resource-based industries—the economic bedrock for many developing countries.[5] Take the case, for instance of petroleum, where countries like Nigeria, Indonesia, Algeria, Mexico export anywhere between US $2 to 35 billion, depending on oil output volumes and prices—and yet their performance in terms of GDP growth is significantly lower than countries in the same income per capita levels. Where has that money gone that there is so little to show for? It thus is not surprising that petroleum producing countries tend to fall in the lower percentile categories of governance ratings, where corruption figures high.

But the secondary effects, downstream, are equally devastating though much more widespread. Petroleum products play a pivotal role in Sub-Saharan Africa's economic development. Their purchase absorbs

5. Carlos Leite and Jens Weidemann, "Does Mother Nature Corrupt?," *Natural Resources, Corruption, and Economic Growth,* IMF working Paper 99/85 (1999).

Figure 7. Bribery in Business Sectors

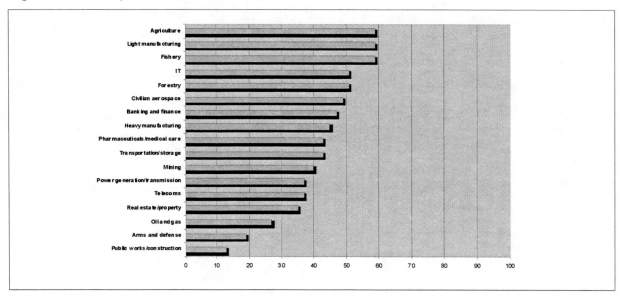

Figure 8. Ominous Correlations: Oil Economies

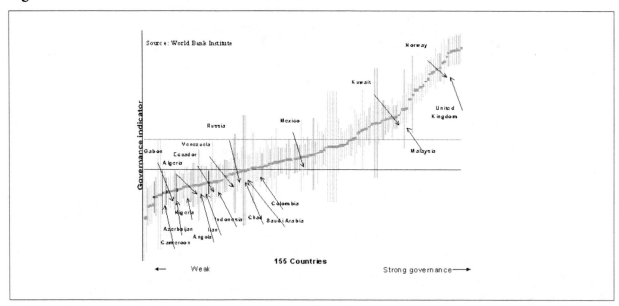

20-35 percent of export ratings for the bulk of the countries in the region, and generates approximately 40 percent of tax revenues—thus constituting the single largest item in the balance of payments and fiscal revenues for most countries in this region. Although the primary energy balance is currently dominated by household consumption of fuel wood, petroleum products are the most important source of commercial energy, supplying approximately 70 percent of commercial requirements; and they are likely

to be the fastest growing portion of the region's energy balance as the continent's modernization unfolds.

As the region becomes more developed, the demand for energy will also grow, thus setting up a vicious circle: Economic growth will be needed to pay for the expanding oil bill, and more imported fuel will be needed to generate economic growth. These countries must make fundamental policy choices with respect to the petroleum industry if they are to escape this self-defeating cycle.

Except for Angola, Cameroon, Congo, Gabon, and Nigeria, all countries of sub-Saharan Africa are net importers of crude oil or petroleum products. Data comparing per capita GDP to oil imports show that the lower the per capita GDP, the higher the percentage of net imports represented by petroleum. Greater efficiency in procuring and distributing petroleum products would reduce the amount of funds these countries devote to paying their oil bills, thus freeing those resources for the other uses and potentially reducing the poverty level do these countries.

And yet massive resources "disappear" from the way the business is conducted. If corrected, savings of about US$ 1.4 billion a year at 1989-90 prices. This amount is greater than total World Bank annual disbursements of adjustment policy loans, and close to 50 per cent higher that the net disbursement to the entire region combined. These savings represent the difference between the actual cost of supplying petroleum products to consumers and benchmark cost corresponding to procuring these products from world markets under competitive conditions.

As one reviews transaction throughout the supply chain, fully half of resources cost could be recuperated at the point of procurement, some 40 % at the refining stage, and the remainder through inland distribution. Moreover, the greater losses are associated with discretionary power and monopoly arrangements.

The inescapable conclusion is that hydrocarbons procurement and distribution must be opened to the discipline of greater competition. Indeed, the experience recorded in other regions (Western Europe, southeast Asia, and Latin America) that have allowed numerous available suppliers to compete in their markets suggests that a policy change in Africa along these lines would provide significant benefits to the continent, in the form of more efficient and corruption free petroleum procurement and trade.

Going beyond the production and distribution of natural resources industries by multinational companies, corruption is of growing concern to donors, nongovernmental organizations, governments, businesses more generally, and citizens, in developing and industrial countries alike. Fortunately, the opportunities to address corruption are also greater than they have ever been. New global standards of behavior are emerging, driven partly by changing attitudes toward transnational bribery in industrial countries and partly by heightened awareness in developing countries of the costs of corruption. But much more work is needed to develop institutionally binding industry standards. These could be furthered through more effective inter and industry standards, and proper coalition building with relevant civil society organizations.

Governments. Quite apart of economic and public sector reforms along the lines noted above, a number of initiatives have been taken at the international levels that are bound to have constructive repercussions in many countries.

- Twenty-five countries signed the landmark Inter-American Convention Against Corruption in March 1996, two years after the issue of corruption was put on the agenda of the Summit of the Americas by the leaders of the Western Hemisphere. The convention requires countries that have not already done so to criminalize transnational bribery and all illicit enrichment. Other provisions include building commitments to provide greater mutual assistance laws and to establish a framework for cooperation on extradition. In addition, the convention encourages countries to adopt a wide range of laws and regulations to prevent corruption. These measures include conflict of interest rules, disclosure of assets of high public officials and their families, establishment of national organizations for the oversight of such laws, protection of whistleblowers, and open government procurement.

- Similarly, in late 1997, thirty-four countries signed the OECD Convention on Bribery of Foreign Public Officials in International Business Transactions. The purpose of the convention is to criminalize corruption of foreign officials and to end the tax deductibility of bribes, thereby removing the associated fiscal incentives. This is a historic first step forward, and one that provides a sound, though limited, framework for an international anti-bribery system.

- Multilateral development banks have similarly begun to play their role in their respective areas of expertise and responsibility. The IMF has started to restrict its operations in countries where the level of corruption is deemed to negatively affect in a material way their economic performance. The World Bank has initiated a more comprehensive program. First, it introduces sanctions on firms and governments engaged in corrupt practices. Under this arrangement, it would ban firms that offer bribes from future Bank financed procurement worldwide. It would also cancel loans to governments whose officials solicited bribes. Lastly, the World Bank the reoriented its disbursement procedures to strengthen borrower accountability for sound procurement and financial management.

While these are undoubtedly important steps, their proper implementation is key to deliver on the promise of accountable governments and hospitable business environments. Nothing, of course, prevents countries from developing their own action without a common framework in the region. After all, effective action on the fight against corruption will require more than acting through criminal law and sending people to prison.

On the multilateral development institutions front, additional actions are also being taken; the Inter-American Development Bank has started to tighten procurement guidelines and enhance support for public sector reform programs. It would be desirable that organizations, such as the World Trade Organization, review their programs to see how they could underpin more forcefully efforts to combat corruption. The World Bank needs to strengthen its working arrangements with relevant civil society institution, and sharpen its country assistance strategies by mainstreaming anti-corruption efforts in its policy, public sector reform, projects, and other lending, as well as its economic and sector work.

Private Sector. There are differences of opinion about the value of corporate anti-corruption programs and associated codes of conduct. Given the many parties involved, the "going alone" practices have proven to be particularly ineffective. Coalition-building approaches with relevant constituencies is thus indispensable. Many in the business community believe that self-regulation is the right solution and that it is preferable to government regulation. Others argue that self-regulation is a sham and only government action can be expected to curb corruption. When seen, however, as a component of a comprehensive anti-corruption program, they could provide a stimulus to more business-like and effective economic activity. They are not a substitute for government regulations: both are needed and each reinforces the other.

A wave of global, sectoral and professional codes has emerged to respond to these concerns. Some are listed below:

- Global Business Codes
  - International Chamber of Commerce (ICC) Rules of Conduct to Combat Extortion and Bribery 1996
  - Pacific Basic Economic Council (PBEC) Charter
  - Draft TI/SAI Business Principles for Countering Bribery
  - MNC Corporate Codes
- Sectorial Codes
  - Wolfsberg Global Anti-Money-Laundering Guidelines for Private Banking
  - Voluntary Anti-Bribery Code for the Mining Sector?
- Professional Codes
  - FIDIC code (consulting engineers)
  - IBA code (layers)
  - IFAC code (accountants)

A "best practices" study undertaken by Transparency International USA in 1996 of anti-corruption programs used by major American companies[6] stressed

---

6. Transparency International-USA, "Corporate Anti-Corruption Programs, a Survey of Best Practices," (1996).

that whether a code of conduct is only a piece of paper or it controls corporate behavior, depends on the compliance program the company uses. Unequivocal commitment by top management is essential. Among the key elements of such codes, the study highlighted:

- A clear policy statement that the company prohibits employees and third parties representing the company from offering anything of value, directly or indirectly, to a government official to influence or reward an action.

- Detailed guidelines regarding gifts and entertainment, travel expenses and strict compliance with applicable laws and regulations regarding corporate political contributions and their disclosure.

- The existence of a system of internal controls and record keeping that ensures that company books accurately reflect its transactions, overseen by an audit committee, composed of outside directors and associated internal reporting.

The key in evaluating the role of corporate anti-bribery codes of conduct is their interplay with government programs. The effectiveness of corporate codes is enhanced by governmental measures. Similarly, corporate codes reinforce the effectiveness of government anti-bribery programs. The main elements to build such synergy are:

- The threat of penalties through criminal law is a potent influence. Managers tend to be concerned about their personal exposure to large fines and prison terms, and such provisions have been found useful in turning off extortion by local or foreign officials by making refusals to pay credible. The synergy between government enforcement and corporate compliance programs is further enhanced by U.S. Justice Department's sentencing guidelines. These provide more lenient treatment for companies that conduct proper compliance programs. The sentencing guidelines provide a strong incentive for companies to establish compliance programs and usually include auditing and monitoring arrangements, enforcement of disciplinary mechanisms, and appropriate response and due diligence after

detection. This approach exists in the United States, and several European countries, Australia, and Canada have or are in the process of adopting similar legislation.

- The tax treatment of bribes can also make a major difference in corporate behavior. When the tax laws treat bribes as tax-deductible, the message is that foreign bribes are considered a legitimate business expense—if not a subsidized activity by government. Denying tax deductibility for bribes requires corporations to distinguish between proper and improper business expenses. This means that relevant corporate managers will be carefully scrutinized, as they can be exposed to liability for tax fraud.

Civil Society. A growing number of structures, institutions, and associations—outside state apparatus and profit-making businesses—are evolving for the joint and proactive pursuit of shared interests. Chambers of commerce, professional and religious associations and various forms of non-governmental organizations are becoming players, shaping opinions, building coalitions, providing testimonies and monitoring government and enterprises.

What legitimates civil society organizations is a concern about issues that are not adequately represented in the normal political process and a focus on problems that often go beyond the limited reach or capabilities of the nation-state, where market forces are unlikely to result in desired results. Moreover, their rules do not arise out of self-interest or profit-orientation, but from people or organizations that are committed to the public interest in a specific area, such as corruption.

In the end, though, civil societies are the stakeholders and the ultimate affected parties of corruption—and thus must be engaged constructively to get the support and buy-in for the necessary reforms. Only in this way can the necessary policy and institutional changes become viable and sustainable. Countries that have been hospitable and supportive of civil society bodies—through hearing arrangements in their regulatory and legislative procedures and involving them in oversight institutions—have in fact enabled

Figure 9.   Unofficial Economy and Corruption Index
   (Unofficial economy as percent of GDP)

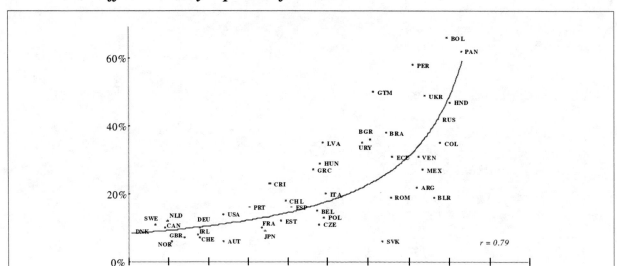

the organic and internally driven evolution of policies and institutions.

As the argument goes, if civil society gets involved as a partner and its efforts at monitoring the state are encouraged, this would contribute to the eventual elimination of corruption.[7] However, the issue of partnership is a complex one. Governments, multilateral development institutions and private sector institutions are for the most part established and strong.

Moving to Action

"Everything is in the execution"

— Napoleon

A growing number of countries have started to take actions that one way or another address some of the issues referred to before. Institutional and civil service reforms in the form of privatization, salary reforms. Disclosure of assets has been introduced in countries ranging from Bolivia and Ecuador to Georgia and others. Economic policies are being revamped through deregulation, de-licensing, tax ad-

ministration reforms changes in custom administrations in Latvia, Ecuador, Albania and many others. Financial controls and changes in public procurement arrangements have been introduced in Georgia, Ecuador and Bolivia, to mention a few. Public and civil society oversight arrangements are enhanced through ombudsmen offices, private sector monitoring arrangements, diagnostic surveys with civil society involvement in Ecuador, Albania and others. So are legal and judicial reforms, including changes in Supreme Court organization, changes in judicial procedures, new competency and selection arrangements of judges, introduction of mediation and arbitration procedures in Bolivia, Chile, Albania and others.

In the end, these reforms are not so much about laws and top-down changes, but more about empowerment, transparency, scrutiny, changes in incentives. More broadly, a combination of actions on prevention, enforcement, and support of the local community could help in overcoming the problems. Many of the corrective actions are associated with deregula-

7. Transparency International, "The Corrpution Fighters' Tool Kits" (October 2001); "Herramientas para Control Ciudadano de la Corrupción" (Octubre 2001).

tion and depolitization of economic activities, generation of information and data for greater transparency and associated accountability, build-up of appropriate legal institutions or set-up of parallel ones—or self-regulating bodies where this is not possible, and development of coalitions to promote coherent actions among different players in a society.

In the end, though, any effort has to be underpinned by some form of diagnosis of the specific problem, an ensuing prioritization and sequencing of interventions, and monitoring of impact. Whatever course is taken, experience suggests that focus has to be on minimum, critical mass of interventions—at times a few initial examples—to get some early gains for later replication.

Leveling the Playing Field

"Sunlight is the best disinfectant"

— Latin American aphorism

Where such interface is poor, there is a tendency to "crowd out" the economy into the informal sector and with it the levels of corruption.

For this reason, TI has been set-up to facilitate the intervention between different groups, particularly civil society with governments and the private sector.

As effective action can only be sustained through the presence of institutions that can catalyze the various interest groups in a non-partisan manner, TI has been established as a not-for-profit and non-governmental organization to counter corruption in international business transactions. Over the years, it has fostered National Chapters to build alliances, enhance awareness, create support for actions to combat corruption, help overcome resistance of those with a stake in the status quo, and mobilize people and expertise behind meaningful action—and in the end, to improve the interface between governments, businesses, and civil society for effective governance.

If experience elsewhere is to serve as a guide for effective anti-corruption efforts, then a purely technocratic approach to the subject will not be feasible or sustainable. Thus, the process of reaching correction actions will be as important as their content. Indeed, in this field, more than anywhere else, the wide rami-

fications of change can only take place as a result of the dialogue that is internally driven—in each country, in each situation. Only home-grown strategies developed in full partnership with civil society have any chance of success. The means, of course, the technical assistance and other efforts usually provided by the donor community have to move from introducing standard "best practice" to "good fit," tailor-made solutions—better designed to meet local institutional and cultural concerns. In the end, it is for each society to find answers to its own challenges. Others can assist, present a menu of options and practices (see illustration in Annex I), and inform the process, from which local anti-corruption coalitions—the primary actors—must find and force their own solutions and associated strategies for reform.

CUBA, AND THE MISSING GOVERNANCE LINK FOR TRANSITION

"Ahead of us are Darwinian shakeouts in every market place with no consolation prize for losing companies and nations"

— John W. Welsh

In sorting out the issues and their solutions, it is difficult not to sound a bit trite. There are binding limits as to the specificity of conclusions one can reach without first hand information on Cuba's state of affairs. Strictly speaking, there are a variety of methods and approaches to diagnose the problems, analyze the feasibility of recommendations with a rigorous assessment of political realities and constraints to reform. For instance, surveys have been developed and carried out in many countries that can help diagnose the extent and source of institutional dysfunction in a country, set reform priorities, and inform policy dialogue. They can, among other things, also help quantify the economic and social costs of corruption, and institutional distortions, and evaluate the quality of public service delivery and of the business environment—and ultimately the corrective actions to be taken. Nothing of this is available in the case of Cuba.

That being said, judging from the experience of economies in Eastern European and Central Asian countries, special attention will be needed on issues of internal governance during the transition process. Otherwise, Cuba may easily fall prey—given the lack of market-driven institutions—to insiders and nomenklatura managers, very much as has been the experience of Russia when it rushed into privatizing public monopolies, rather than focusing in creating the checks-and-balances and oversight vehicles to build competition. In this regard, Cuba will start off the process with a public sector that has very low levels of accountability, a poor regulatory framework, although with a reasonably professional public sector, stability and rule of law (see Annex II).[8] Under the circumstances, six areas merit special attention.

First, corruption and institutional rigidities fuel illicit and unproductive activities, and is a bewilderingly complex issue with deep vested interests. There are thus binding limits to actions aimed at or limiting the "supply" side of corruption through various forms of control arrangements. Actions aimed at the *underlying incentives* driving corruption (i.e. the "demand side") and reducing opportunities for discretion, with their attendant associated governance arrangements are bound to work better, and provide in the longer-term more promising avenues to help develop accountable, effective, efficient and responsive administrations.

Second, corruption and governance issues are problems whose solutions can only be homegrown. Fighting corruption and restructuring government is thus the business of everyone: governments, private sector, and civil society. An alliance between all of them is a true test of a country's commitment to the subject. More than anywhere else, in transition economies, the solutions have to be rooted in the *build-up of constituencies* that are willing to persist in the build up of institutions, and hold accountable public administrations. Ideally, a well grounded survey of areas of vulnerabilities, as mentioned above, could turn the policy debate away from a focus on individuals towards institutions, allow the establishment of baselines against which progress in reform efforts can be

measured, and encourage attention by the executive, parliamentary scrutiny, and greater participation of civil society to stimulate the demand for better governance and measures against corruption. The buildup of a vibrant and independent private sector and civil society will thus be one of the crucial steps in Cuba's transition.

Third, living in an age of *vanishing* political *borders*, rapidly coalescing transnational global culture, and growing economic integration, an isolated existence is no longer a viable option—at least not without a prohibitive cost in economic development as increasingly evident in Cuba. International standards, such as those being adopted by major enterprises, international conventions such as those agreed by the OECD and the Americas, and guidelines adopted by international lending institutions are becoming an integral part of the global scene of increased transparency and growing concern on corruption. No country is immune to these global trends. It is thus incumbent upon all countries and institutions to deal with these issues—or world economic development will bypass those who prefer to remain on the old course. Technology changes, growing information flows, and the attendant increases in competition are forcing businesses to provide superior goods and services at competitive prices. Bribes may "sell" obsolete and high-priced goods—but at the cost of losing competitive edge. In the end, success will only come to those able to thrive through their ability to develop knowledge in every field of their business, to innovate for superior performance. The key for them is transparency and accountability—and their success is rooted on being better, not just good.

Fourth, improved enterprise performance must be at the heart of any successful transition from a command to a market-oriented economy. The standard pattern in the transition economies has been to seek to improve companies by heightening competition and enhancing corporate governance in various ways: by privatizing state-owned firms; by allowing and en-

---

8. Daniel Kaufmann, Aart Kray, Pablo Zoido, "Governance Matters II." World Bank Policy Research Working Paper 2772 (February 2002).

couraging new firms and competition between existing firms; and by withdrawing government subsidies so that firms must face their own profits and losses, or what the literature refers to as a hard budget constraint. The ability of reforms to improve corporate performance appears highly sensitive to the institutional environment and initial conditions in which the policies were introduced—and Cuba's starting point is for the most part weak in terms of initial conditions of the enterprises involved, the institutional and legal framework, especially the corporate governance structure; the relationship between the very small private sector and the state; and the competitiveness of product markets.

Fifth, similarly, the widely accepted legitimacy of the entire *interface between Government and enterprise* sectors needs to be addressed. The economies of Central Europe were led by legitimate governments elected on platforms of reform, while the reformers in Russia and many of the CIS countries represented a small but powerful political group that was advising the president, but was opposed by much of the parliamentary and civil service structure. Moreover, governments in Russia and other CIS countries had to make compromises in introducing policies to build internal political support for reform, perhaps because they faced more deeply entrenched managerial interests. It is unclear the extent to which the vested interests in Cuba have been institutionalized. To the extent that they are, this could result in reforms that may be less conducive to improved enterprise performance and restructuring, notably with respect to privatization methods, corporate governance, competition, and subsidies.

Sixth, concerning issues of process, the same applies to overall public sector management. Many governments (and Cuba may not be an exception) have found to their dismay in recent years that secretive decision-making by small elites can no longer be sustained. Contrary to the claims often made by central banks, government officials, and even some in international organizations that decision making on technical or complex subjects is best left to experts, without informed participation by all those affected, policy decisions will fail to take into account important information and interests and will lack legitimacy that only public voice can bring. Transparency plays many beneficial roles in both market and governance. All indications are that it increases the efficiency with which markets operate and may reduce the likelihood of financial crises. On governance, transparency is logically necessary for accountability; such accountability is the political equivalent of the efficiency generated between firms. Since political authorities are monopolies, "competition" occurs between ideas and use of resources, rather than organizations. But a culture of transparency will not come solely as the result of hectoring—or even conditionality applied by the international financial institutions. It requires thinking beyond disclosure standards that are being so widely discussed to question the incentives facing public sector activities.

In sum, corruption is a highly sensitive issue. There is nothing right about it. It is wrong in principle, wrong in practice, and wrong wherever and whenever it occurs. Transparency and changes in incentives are the best antidotes. But, as all indicators suggest, Cuba is a long way from a transparent level playing field. Different organizations and different countries draw different lines in the sand in different places. And the deeper truth is that legitimate investment and corruption do not mix. Corruption destroys billions of scarce dollars every year. It is the dry rot undermining aid. It distorts development, it frightens away genuine foreign investors, and it perverts societies. The road to reform, competition, and modernization seems to be the only hope for a revitalized Cuba, and it passes through an open incentive structure, and the build-up of associated governance arrangements to guarantee the competition of ideas, products, services and opportunities.

ANNEX I
ANATOMY OF ANTI-CORRUPTION PROGRAMS

Below is a wide (but not exhaustive) list of steps that might be part of an anti-corruption program. Not all steps are appropriate in every setting, and not all are steps that can or should be taken. It is essential to diagnose an individual setting and consider proposed solutions carefully and to work closely with allies in the government and with other partners to coordinate strategies and identify individual activities that complement each other.

Prevention

1. Economic reform (to tailor the role of the state and the design of economic policies to institutional capability)

    - Liberalization and deregulation where possible (to move toward a smaller more efficient government)

    - Privatization of parastatals in competitive sectors

    - A new look at tax and regulatory policy (to match policies to enforcement capabilities to the extent possible)

    - Opening of trade regimes to create "competition" and pressure for reform

2. Administrative Reform

    - Preparation of an inventory of proper "checks and balances" in the public sector

    - Establishment of "competing bureaucracies" (either horizontally—within one level of government, or vertically—among different levels of government) to deliver similar services where possible.

    - Assignment of responsibilities (including devolution to subnational governments) with institutional capacity in mind

    - Identification and support of "pockets of excellence"

3. Civil Service Reform

    - Move toward merit-based processes in civil service recruitment, performance-evaluation, promotion and termination

    - Establishment of reasonable salary levels and gradation

4. Budget Reform and Financial Management

    - Review/audit of government procurement practices

    - Service delivery surveys (as an audit device for budget execution)

    - Bypassing of government agencies: direct donor funding of community-level service delivery projects or private infrastructure projects

    - Accounting, disclosure and auditing standards for public and private sector institutions

    - Prudential regulations, bankruptcy arrangements and other oversight mechanisms for financial intermediation

5. Reform in Tax and Customs Organization

    - Functional organization of departments (across types of taxes)

    - Establishment of benchmarks for performance

    - Increasing data availability and transparency

    - Strengthening of taxpayer appeals mechanisms (both internal and external to the revenue departments)

Enforcement

1. Procurement

    - Inclusion of "no-bribery-pledge" in bidding documents (not an end in itself; will make a difference only if there is political support for underlying reforms)

    - Encouraging alternative legal institutions (to conventional public rule of law institutions) for settlement of disputes, mediation, etc.

2. Legal and Judicial Reform

    - Review of anti-corruption and conflict-of-interest legislation to ensure adequacy.

    - Steps towards heightened independence of the judiciary

    - Strengthening incentives and building skills of public prosecutors

    - Review of administrative law (to strengthen transparency and public input to regulatory rulemaking)

- Set-up of a special anti-corruption agency
- Disclosure of higher-level civil servants' and/or politicians income or tax return

Interfacing

1. Societal Support Action

   - Awareness raising and collaborative problem-identification through workshops
   - Generating and disseminating information and data
   - Review of libel legislation (to strengthen the watchdog role of the press)
   - Journalist training and support
   - Identification and support of "local champions" (including NGOs)

   - Collective action by international and domestic institutions, involving political leadership, business communities, financial institutions and NGOs

2. Political Process

   - Review of campaign finance laws
   - Support for political party formation and voice
   - Support for constitutional reform (to strengthen civil liberties)

3. Self-Regulating Arrangements

   - Issuance of codes of conduct of enterprises
   - Establishment of review boards or oversight committee
   - Sentencing guidelines reflecting enterprises self-corrective behavior

ANNEX II
GOVERNANCE INDICATORS: THE PLACE OF CUBA

Governance can be depicted as the traditions and institutions by which authority in a country is exercised. This includes (1) the process by which governments are selected, monitored and replaced, (2) the capacity of the government to effectively formulate and implement sound policies, and (3) the respect of citizens and the state for institutions that govern economic and social interactions among them.

The first two governance clusters are intended to capture the first part of the above-mentioned definition of governance: the process by which those in authority are selected and replaced. The first of these constitutes "Voice and Accountability," and includes in it a number of indicators measuring various aspects of the political process, civil liberties and political rights. These indicators measure the extent to which citizens of a country are able to participate in the selection of governments. Also included in this category are indicators measuring the independent of the media, which serves an important role in monitoring those in authority and holding them accountable for their actions. (See Figure 10)

The second governance cluster is labeled "Political Stability." This index combines several indicators that measure perceptions of the likelihood that the government in power will be destabilized or overthrown by unconstitutional and/or violent means, including terrorism. This index captures the idea that the quality of governance in a country is compromised by the likelihood of wrenching changes in government, which not only has a direct effect on the continuity of policies, but also at a deeper level undermines the ability of all citizens to peacefully select and replace those in power. (See Figure 11)

The next two clusters summarize various indicators of the ability of the government to formulate and implement sound policies. "Government Effectiveness" combines perceptions of the quality of public service provision, the quality of the bureaucracy, the competence of civil servants, the independence of the civil service from political pressures, and the credibility of the government's commitment to policies. The main focus of this index is on "inputs" required for the government to be able to produce and implement good policies and deliver public goods. (See Figure 12)

The second, referred to as "Regulatory Quality," is more focused on the policies themselves. It includes measures of the incidence of market-unfriendly policies such as price controls, inadequacy of bank supervision, as well as perceptions of the burdens imposed by excessive regulation in areas such as foreign trade and business development. (See Figure 13)

Figure 10. Voice and Accountability–2001

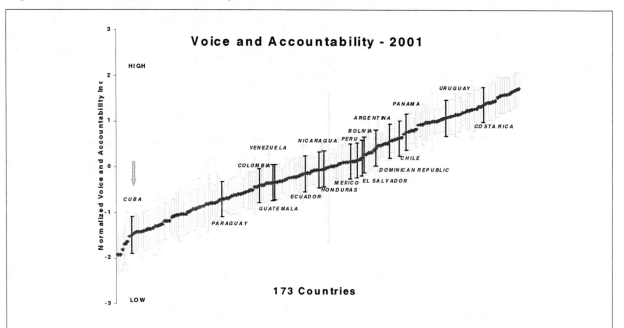

Source for Data: http://www.worldbank.org/wbi/governance/govdata2001.htm. This chart shows estimates of Voice and Accountability for 173 countries during 2000/01, with selected countries indicated for illustrative purposes. The vertical bars show the likely range of Governance indicators, and the midpoints of these bars show the most likely value for each country. The length of these ranges varies with the amount of information available for each country.

Source: "Governance Matters II: updated Indicators for 2000-01" by Daniel Kaufmann, Aart Kraay and Pablo Zoido-Lobaton, Jan 2002.

Figure 11. Political Stability and Lack of Violence – 2001 (Latin American Countries)

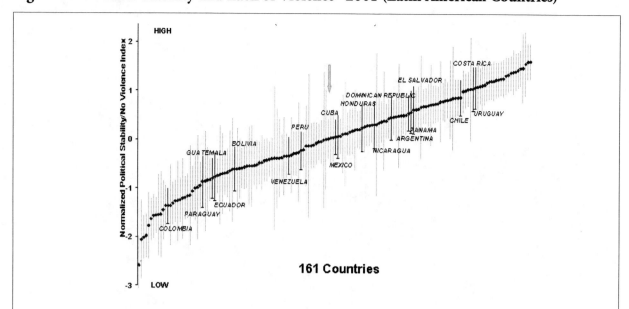

Source for Data: http://www.worldbank.org/wbi/governance/govdata2001.htm. This chart shows estimates of political stability and lack of violence for 161 countries during 2000/01, with selected countries indicated for illustrative purposes. The vertical bars show the likely range of Governance indicators, and the midpoints of these bars show the most likely value for each country. The length of these ranges varies with the amount of information available for each country.

Source: "Governance Matters II: updated Indicators for 2000-01" by Daniel Kaufmann, Aart Kraay and Pablo Zoido-Lobaton, Jan. 2002.

Figure 12. Government Effectiveness – 2001

Source for Data: http://www.worldbank.org/wbi/governance/govdata2001.htm. This chart shows estimates of government effectiveness for 159 countries during 2000/01, with selected countries indicated for illustrative purposes. The vertical bars show the likely range of Governance indicators, and the midpoints of these bars show the most likely value for each country. The length of these ranges varies with the amount of information available for each country

Source: "Governance Matters II: updated Indicators for 2000-01" by Daniel Kaufmann, Aart Kraay and Pablo Zoido-Lobaton, Jan. 2002.

Figure 13. Regulatory Quality – 2001 *(Latin American Countries)*

Regulatory Quality - 2001
(Latin American Countries)

168 Countries

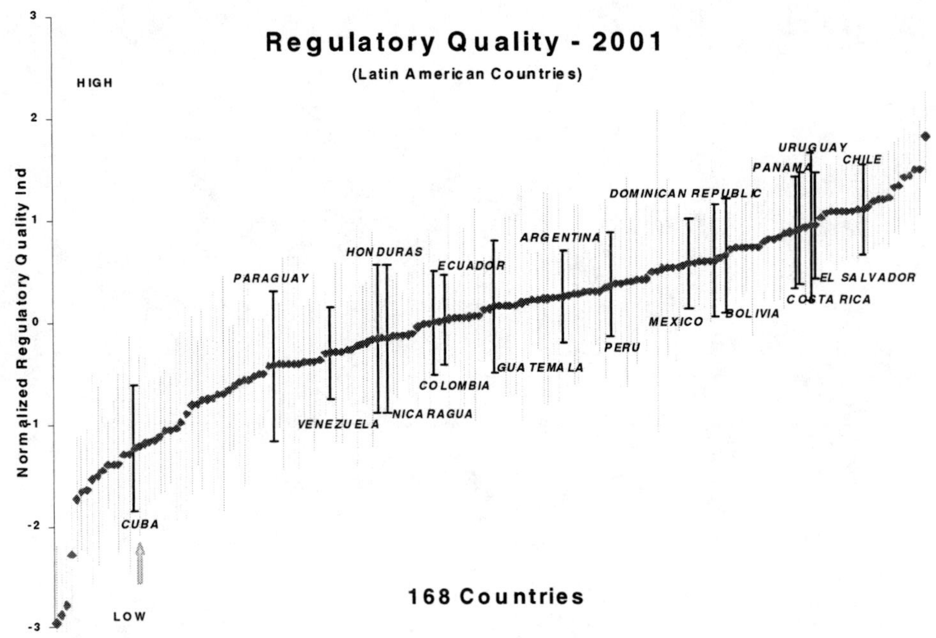

Source for Data: http://www.worldbank.org/wbi/governance/govdata2001.htm. This chart shows estimates of Regulatory Quality for 168 countries during 2000/01, with selected countries indicated for illustrative purposes. The vertical bars show the likely range of Governance indicators, and the midpoints of these bars show the most likely value for each country. The length of these ranges varies with the amount of information available for each country.

Source: "Governance Matters II: updated Indicators for 2000-01" by Daniel Kaufmann, Aart Kraay and Pablo Zoido-Lobaton, Jan. 2002.

The last two clusters summarize in broad terms the respect of citizens and the state for the institutions that govern their interactions. "Rule of Law" includes several indicators that measure the extent to which agents have confidence in and abide by rules of the society. These include perceptions of the incidence of both violent and non-violent crime, the effectiveness and predictability of the judiciary, and the enforceability of contracts. Together, these indicators measure the success of a society in developing an environment in which fair and predictable rules form the basis for economic and social interactions. (See Figure 14)

The final cluster, referred as "Control of Corruption," measures perceptions of corruption, conventionally defined as the exercise of public power for private gain. Despite this straightforward focus, the particular aspect of corruption measured by various sources differs somewhat, ranging from the frequency of "additional payments to get things done," the effects of corruption on the business environment, to measuring "grand corruption" in the political arena or in the tendency of elites forms to engage in "state capture". The presence of corruption is often a manifestation of a lack of respect of both the corrupter (typically a private citizen or firm) and the corrupted (typically a public official) for the rules that govern their interactions, and hence represents a failure of governance. (See Figure 15)

Figure 14. Rule of Law – 2001 *(Latin American Countries)*

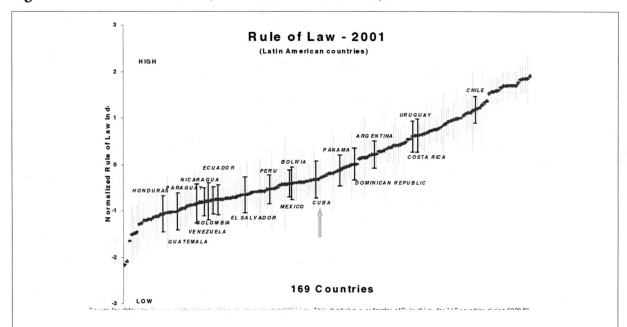

Source for Data: http://www.worldbank.org/wbi/governance/govdata2001.htm. This chart shows estimates of Rule of Law for 169 countries during 2000/01, with selected countries indicated for illustrative purposes. The vertical bars show the likely range of Governance indicators, and the midpoints of these bars show the most likely value for each country. The length of these ranges varies with the amount of information available for each country.

Source: "Governance Matters II: updated Indicators for 2000-01" by Daniel Kaufmann, Aart Kraay and Pablo Zoido-Lobaton, Jan. 2002.

Figure 15. Control of Corruption – 2001 *(Latin American Countries)*

Source for Data: http://www.worldbank.org/wbi/governance/govdata2001.htm. This chart shows estimates of Rule of Law for 169 countries during 2000/01, with selected countries indicated for illustrative purposes. The vertical bars show the likely range of Governance indicators, and the midpoints of these bars show the most likely value for each country. The length of these ranges varies with the amount of information available for each country.

Source: "Governance Matters II: updated Indicators for 2000-01" by Daniel Kaufmann, Aart Kraay and Pablo Zoido-Lobaton, Jan. 2002.

UPDATE ON CUBAN DOLLARIZATION

Roberto Orro

In May 1997, the Cuban government officially announced the creation of the Central Bank of Cuba, as part of a package of financial sector reforms. As pointed out in a recent study by ECLA, the Central Bank of Cuba inherited from the former National Bank of Cuba the exclusive responsibility for issuing money as well as the faculty to formulate and implement monetary policy, manage foreign currency reserves, oversee the functioning of the payment system, work as the state banker and oversee the financial institutions operating in Cuba. ECLA concludes that the new legislation incorporates into the Central Bank most of the monetary functions carried out by modern central banks.[1]

Nonetheless, it is recognized in the same document that the system of dollar payments tends to be spread all over the planned economy, which is in contradiction with the goals previously announced for the Central Bank.[2] Actually, one of the main features of the Cuban economy is the contradiction between the existence of a Central Bank and the ongoing dollarization of the economy. Neither the long stability of the peso against the dollar nor the economic recovery over the last five years have prevented the dollar from becoming the preferred mean of exchange. Although domestic savings are almost negligible, the dollar has also gained ground in this important economic factor.

After legalizing the holding of dollar balances in 1993, the Cuban authorities have never hidden their misgivings about opening this door the citizenry. Once in a while, a prominent member of the economic cabinet states that the Cuban peso should be restored as the only mean of exchange. However, the reasons behind anti-dollar statements seem to be political rather than economic. The elite is afraid that dollarization would continue to zap the basis of its power; they fear that the dollar could sever the traditional tie between political loyalty and economic welfare.

The government has kept a tight monetary discipline and undertaken some measures to foster the domestic use of the Cuban peso as well, while promoting the use of the dollar throughout the public sector. Indeed, a distinctive feature of the Cuban dollarization is its sponsorship and promotion by the Cuban government. Such a policy has resulted in monetary and exchange rate dualism, which hampers efficient resource allocation and introduces harmful distortions into the price system. However, instead of reviving the Cuban peso, the authorities have decided to end the dualism system by spreading the use of the dollar all over the planned sector.

This paper is intended to update the an earlier by Kildegaard and Orro[3] on Cuban dollarization with the latest economic developments on the island. Al-

---

1. Economic Comission for Latin America (2000), *La Economía Cubana: Reformas Estructurales y Desempeño en los 90*, México, Fondo de Cultura Económica, p. 171.

2. ECLA, *La Economía Cubana,* p. 166.

3. Kildegaard and Orro (1999).

though the current paper continues on the same spirit of the earlier one, it offers a more thorough analysis of the reasons compelling the Cuban government to bolster dollarization. The paper is divided into two parts. The first part explains the reasons for the Cuban government's fostering of dollarization and describes recent developments in this process. The second part presents our point of view on the advantages for Cuba of maintaining and enhancing dollarization. Finally we present the conclusions

WHY DOES THE CUBAN GOVERNMENT BOLSTER DOLLARIZATION?

Despite the fact that the roots of dollarization in Cuba stretch back to the 1980s, when the government set up a commercial network in dollars, the phenomenon blossomed after the liberalization of the use of dollars in 1993.[4] In 1994, Cuba was undergoing its worst economic crisis ever. Production of consumption goods had fallen sharply fell and the devaluation of the Cuban peso in the black market seemed to be bottomless. The domestic currency had been almost driven out as a mean of exchange by the dollar. At that time, the population had already defied the remaining restrictions imposed by the authorities regarding the exchange of dollars. The number of citizens using dollars rose every day because of remittances and a thriving black market linking Cubans with foreign tourists. Finally, the authorities realized that such authoritarian policy was pointless and decided to overrule the restrictions keeping ordinary citizens from trading and buying with dollars.

The curtailment of Soviet subsidies and the desperate need for new sources of revenues in foreign currency pushed structural reforms in the economy during the 1990s. Within the new economic model, tourism ceased to play second fiddle and became the engine of the economy. Since the very beginning of the reform process, it was clear that the tourist sector would rely on foreign investment, so that the government could prevent its foreign partners from taking

exchange risks. Investors would have never accepted operating and dealing in Cuban pesos, a currency that can barely hold a flimsy equilibrium against the dollar. That is why the authorities chose to use the American currency as an exclusive tool of payment and unit of account for the tourist sector.

The state monopoly over the tourist sector and foreign trade, as well as the absence of government debt, led to another interesting feature of the Cuban economy: there is not need for seigniorage whatsoever. Unlike other developing countries that heavily rely on inflationary tax, the Cuban government can rule it out. Moreover, indiscriminate monetary issue can only bring disadvantages. Among the possibilities stemming from government ownership/co-ownership of the tourist and foreign trade networks, the Cuban authorities have the power to fix high markup prices on the consumption goods sold in the dollarized network. Of course, revenues from tourism should be shared with foreign partners but, on the Cuban side, only the government is entitled to participate in this business.

From the economic point of view, dollarization has not added any new problem or distortion not existing when Cuba was inserted in the inefficient system of economic relations centered on the Soviet Union. The monetary dualism and the co-existence of two exchange rates drag on the resource allocation and affect the purchase power of the population but not significantly more than the former planning and economic control mechanisms did.

The Cuban authorities have recognized the bias connected with the exchange rate dualism. The population buys dollars at around 20 pesos per dollar (a rate set by the market) but the government sets a rate of 1 to 1 for many transactions within the planned sector. When an exporter needs to buy inputs from a domestic firm, it needs to first exchange dollars for pesos at the official rate. Likewise, importer firms are

---

4. It is noteworthy that the term dollarization means the use of a foreign currency to carry out the three functions of money: mean of exchange, unit of account, and store of value. Dollarization is usually mistaken for currency substitution, which only refers to the use of a foreign currency as mean of exchange. Although currency substitution is often the last stage of dollarization, the opposite ocurred in Cuba: accounts in dollars are still very unusual.

entitled to buy dollars at the very advantageous and unrealistic official rate. But such an arbitrary parity is not a recent phenomenon. It started long before the reform program of the 1990s.

The dynamics of the Cuban economy, featuring an increasing insertion into the world market, has minimized the negative impact of monetary dualism. During the first years of the economic restructuring, only those sectors directly linked to foreign markets were able to compute financial balances in foreign currencies. In contrast, sectors weakly connected with external trade were more likely to suffer from distortions. As the external trade shifted from the former Soviet Union to western markets, the number of firms allowed to operate in dollars rose remarkably. It is noteworthy that the authorities have chosen an heterodox path to solve the conflict between the Cuban peso and the dollar, by enhancing the use of the dollar within the state economy. Government-owned exporting firms are allowed to buy domestic inputs in dollars and salary compensations in dollars has been implemented in many public enterprises. At the same time, state firms have been encouraged to maintain equilibrium in their transactions in foreign currencies, through the implementation of a mechanism known as foreign currency balance sheet.[5]

This behavior is the best choice for the Cuban authorities. Scrambling to rescue the Cuban peso does not seem to be a viable choice. The Cuban economy has always been remarkably open, so even the government needs to import a substantial amount of consumption and capital goods. The government has a permanent need for dollars and the idea of embarking on a new adventure, where the dollars previously collected would be traded for pesos and then reconverted into dollars, does not appear very alluring. It is easier by far to operate in dollars and ensure that no losses are incurred in exchanges from one currency to the other.

It has been alleged that dollarization hinders the development of the tradable goods sector. But the development of the Cuban external sector over the

1990s rebuts this assertion. First, it should be noted that the devaluation game, which has not proved to be very effective in other countries, will not necessarily provide competitiveness in an economy with a well educated labor force earning miserable salaries. And second, in open economies heavily relying on tourism, even non-tradable goods, like real estate, turn into tradable ones.

While expanding the dollar's scope, the authorities refuse to take the peso out of circulation. It is a wise decision as the domestic currency guarantees—thanks to the absolute power of the state to set prices and salaries—some protection against external shocks. Those who state that dollarization dampens competitiveness forget that the Cuban peso is still circulating and is a powerful tool in the hands of the authorities to absorb negative external shocks. The Cuban workers' salaries in pesos are entirely fixed by the government, so it has no domestic liability in dollars. Indeed, the population can buy dollars in a free but very limited market, which only reflects the purchasing parity between some domestic and foreign consumption goods. The government is not committed to defend this parity, and, in the event of some adverse external shock, it does not have any obligation to maintain a predetermined level of salaries in dollars.

Monetary dualism provides another subtle and profitable option to the government. As every single Cuban worker in joint ventures must be hired through the state, the latter charges foreign partners an amount in dollars for each worker employed. Most of these dollars are converted into pesos at the rate of one to one, and then delivered to the workers in the form of salaries, along with a small compensation either in dollars or baskets of consumer goods.

The concept of monetary policy has adopted a peculiar form in Cuba. It is not used to smooth economic cycles by manipulating interest rates, but rather to ensure that salaries do not fall down to the point of deterring citizens from working, as it happened at the beginning of the 1990s. The interest rate is a variable

---

5. ECLA, *La Economía Cubana*.

quite divorced from the capital investment process, which is centrally determined and subject to the stunted domestic saving and some resources provided by foreign partners. As the path followed by the authorities to eliminate monetary dualism implies bringing public firms into the dollar's world, we do not expect the investment process to rely on the Cuban peso in the short run.

The political costs attached to dollarization spur sporadic statements by members of the elite about the necessity to restore the Cuban peso as the unique currency. But such statements are rather the result of the government's concern that dollarization is wiping out the traditional bonds between political loyalty, reliability and wealth. The authorities grunt and complain when they see how many ordinary citizens, not linked to the communist party at all, are able to buy in shopping centers and go to restaurants formerly reserved for tourists or highly ranked public officials. In spite of these statements, the government has confirmed in public its commitment to dollarization. Without any doubt, the government is empowered to make illegal the holding of dollars but this option would be extremely costly: the foreign exchange black market would return and prisons will be filled up again with citizens accused and convicted of dealing with dollars.

Some measures taken by the government to prop up the Cuban peso (for example, restaurants and cafeterias selling products in Cuban pesos) have been seen as an attempt to revive and restore the purchasing power of the domestic currency. Whoever has attended these places would question such assertion. Only consumption goods made in Cuba are sold there (like Tropicola, a Cuban soda) at prices set on the basis of their equivalence in dollars. In this "domestic network," the government refuses to sell imported goods, not even an imported pin, which is solid evidence of its aversion to exchange risks.[6]

As the objective function governing the Cuban economy is the optimization of the benefits of the State,

the government would unlikely bet on the domestic currency. In spite of its protracted stability against the dollar, the Cuban peso does not yield interest and its international demand is null. The only way for the Cuba peso to gain some quality is through capital and money markets. But Cuba has no conditions to set up such markets, given the government's reluctance to liberalize the investment process: not even real estate and car markets are allowed.

Although the Central Bank undertook some measures intended to encourage remittances and other payments in euros, the authorities are quite far from being willing to abandon the dollar or return to the peso. It is noteworthy that dollarization means a foreign currency—dollar, euro, whatever—driving out the domestic currency. Because of the persistence of the embargo, it is easier and less costly for the Cuban authorities to operate in euros rather than in dollars.

In August 2001, the Central Bank enacted regulations barring the circulation of fractional dollar currency in the country, while making it clear they would never make the dollar illegal again. Popularly known as *chavito*, in Cuba circulates a convertible peso, a currency quite different from the Cuban peso and unambiguously equivalent to the U.S dollar. The government has been fostering this currency in order to lessen costs stemming from using a foreign currency. In the scenario of complete substitution of the U.S dollar by the convertible peso, Cuba would be taking another step toward a currency board resembling the orthodox board that the British colonies used to have in the XIX century, and different from new fashion systems like the one implemented in Argentina.[7]

Cuban policymakers have stated their interest in finding a fair exchange rate for the peso. But, while reading CEPAL's works, it looks that the problem is reduced to some analysis and estimations, where the multiple barriers set by the government do not matter at all. How can the policymakers find the actual value of the Cuban peso when even real state and car

---

6. This statment is based on the personal experiences of the author during his regular visits to Cuba since 1997.

7. For insights on the history of currency boards, see Hanke, Jonung and Schuler (1993).

sales are forbidden, bank savings are unlinked from investment, and the government halts the development of the private sector? Anyhow, if such parity were found, nothing could be done to offset dollarization and the authorities would likely be the first ones repudiating the Cuban peso.

Within the current Cuban political framework, it is unthinkable that the government can build even the simplest money market and issue public debt instruments. Notwithstanding the long stability the Cuban peso has enjoyed, political and economic uncertainty is still hanging over the island. As another interesting feature of the economy, direct investment is—and will be as long as the current system lasts—the prevailing modality of investment in Cuba. In absence of capital and money markets and constitutional warranties backing up investment in financial assets, there is only room for a limited number of projects, which can be controlled by foreign businessmen until they are sure that the transformation of their money into physical assets has been completed. It is extremely improbable that an investor would accept to buy a bond issued by a government with a long and well-known record of defaults on external debt.[8]

DOLLARIZATION AS A VIABLE CHOICE IN THE FUTURE

Cuba is still far away from being market economy country. However, sooner than later the country will start a decisive economic reform and the topic of exchange rate and monetary policy will necessarily be discussed.

The prospective exercise implies, as in other many cases, the never-ending debate between predetermined rules and monetary authorities with discretionary power. There is a plethora of works on the Cuban economy addressing this topic, most of them written based on the transition experiences of Latin America and Western Europe. Nonetheless, it is worth mentioning that many of those studies were written before the financial reform in 1997. They also relied on the assumption—not always explicit—that the political and economic transition would begin on ground where the model inherited from the former Soviet Union prevailed.[9] Even though the Cuban economy is still subordinated to politics and the need for preservation of the Communist party, there have been many significant changes that are paving the road for a transformation to a market economy regime. Such changes, and on doubt others, will constitute the initial conditions in the future and will influence transition policies.

The debate on how feasible it is to let the U.S dollar replace domestic currencies has gained worldwide relevance. The collapse of the Mexican peso in 1994, the Asian financial crisis in 1997 and the shattered Argentinian currency board have prompted the search for safer and more viable options. Meanwhile, the good performance of the euro bolsters the arguments of advocates of exchange rate unification throughout the American continent.[10]

The evolution of dollarization has bound the possible scenarios for Cuba in the future, but dollarization should not be seen as a policy of last resort to halt inflation and restore macroeconomic equilibrium.[11] Actually, the country has enjoyed a long period of exchange rate stability and inflation is under control. The choices left to Cuba for the future are uprooting dollarization—which would likely lead to a floating currency—or completing the process started by the communist authorities. Before making the final decision, policymakers should remember that a floating exchange rate behaves poorly under dollarization. Snatching away the U.S dollar is a necessary condition for floating system to work and the costs linked to such compulsory option should be also taken into account.

---

8. It is clear that confiscation is by far more costly than faulting on debt. The first choice entails many political and economic costs unbearable for the government.

9. See Pérez (1994), Sanguinetty (1994) and Lasaga (1995),

10. See Summers (1999), http://www.senate.gov/~banking/99_04hrg/042299/summers.htm.

11. Calvo and Vegh (1992).

Nowadays, as a result of the transformations that have occurred since the end of the Soviet era, reverting dollarization would be extremely costly. The current political system does not seem to be on the verge of collapse. It should be expected that dollarization will continue to take root in Cuban society and the cost of reversing this process will get even higher.

Raising interest rate, one of the traditional recipes to reverse dollarization, would be totally ineffective. Even more radical is the option of compulsory conversion of deposits in dollars into domestic currency. This point deserves more attention. Cuban domestic saving is very small. Therefore, the relevant issue would be the prohibition to open new accounts in dollars, instead of conversion itself. As the authorities have allowed the citizenry to open accounts denominated in dollars, the cost attached to an authoritarian measure such as prohibiting deposits in dollars, would be unbearable for a democratic regime.

For every Cuban citizen, the U.S dollar has become something highly coveted. Access to dollars allows Cubans to alleviate their precarious economic situation and escape the society's basement, sadly reserved for those who do not have relatives abroad or any other way to obtain dollars. The lifting of prohibitions on the population to hold dollars was somehow seen by the average Cuban as a triumph over a government historically reluctant to make even the smaller concession. The authorization to hold dollars opened to Cubans the doors of the dollarized network and other places usually reserved for tourists and members of the elite. It is absurd to believe that the Cuban people would embrace the idea of reverting dollarization in order to guarantee and protect the monetary independence of the nation. For Cubans, holding dollars is the true independence, so taking away the U.S. currency would be unacceptable.

What happened in Cuba after the tragic events of September 11th can help us to figure out the implications of a compulsory conversion of dollars into Cuban pesos. Fears spurred by the attack stormed the exchange rate market and the price of the dollar went up from 22 to 27 pesos.[12] What would happen if there were rumors that the government would again forbid the holding of dollars by the Cuban citizens? Speculation, black market and illegal traffic of dollars would return. In spite of the absence of economic and political relationships with the U.S, the flow of money, information and people between both countries is intense. It is plausible to expect tighter ties even in the short run, so any compulsory measure in the exchange rate field will be unlikely to succeed.

If dislodging dollarization is not feasible, a floating system would be very vulnerable. When a floating system coexists with large holdings of foreign currency, the economy is left without nominal anchor. The monetary authority has no control over money supply in that the monetary aggregates should include holdings of foreign currency valued in terms of domestic currency.[13]

Another crucial factor is the link between dollarization and inflation. When the economic agents have the choice to shift from domestic to foreign currency at low cost, money demand becomes more elastic.[14] Therefore, the inflation rate maximizing seigniorage in dollarized economies is higher. Moreover, there is enough empirical evidence on inflation turning more volatile in economies with currency substitution.[15] It is clear that hardly any benefit should be expected from inflation in Cuba.

In highly dollarized economies a fixed exchange rate seems to be the best choice. But there is a plethora of crisis and financial collapses associated to fixed exchange rates and even the former advocates of this system are now looking for a safer option. Even the currency boards have not escaped from speculative

---

12. This is not official information. It was provided to the author by relatives and friends living in the island.

13. See Karaken and Wallace (1981), and Girton and Roper (1981).

14. Ramírez Rojas (1986).

15. Calvo and Vegh (1992).

attacks. The recent developments in Argentina have proved that currency boards are not a miraculous solution for emerging markets.[16]

What would be the main obstacles to maintain and complete dollarization in Cuba? Finding a lender of last resort is the greatest challenge. To solve this problem, some economists suggest an agreement with the monetary authority of the country issuing the utilized currency. The latter would mean that Cuba should enter into an agreement with the U.S. Federal Reserve. But the Fed has rejected the role of lender of last resort to other countries and banks, so this problem remains a great concern. The fact that the Cuban economy is considerably smaller than other Latin American economies like Mexico and Argentina, and the need for the U.S. to react to the growing influence of the euro, might make easier to overcome misgivings from the U.S side. A possible option to ease this problem is to impose larger reserve requirements and longer maturity terms over bank deposits. Foreign banks undoubtedly will play a key role in the future Cuban banking system. Hence, branches confronting liquidity problems could rely on their headquarters, at least partially, to help them through difficult times.

One of the main objections against dollarization is that it constraints the scope of policymakers to play an active role in the economy. But the question is how large would such scope would be in any event? It is clear that even in the best possible scenario, Cuban policymakers would be have a small range to maneuver. A factor to take into account is the absence of the money demand history needed to make decisions and undertake monetary policy. A second factor is the problems that will surely arise in forming a staff capable of designing, championing and carrying out the policy.

Notwithstanding the commitment of the future administration to democracy and a market economy, it will have to work in a country marked by more than half century of authoritarian regimes. Executing an exchange regime—whether floating or fixed—where the central bank enjoys discretionary power, also affordable to the government, would complicate the extremely hard task of building a democratic society. In such a frail political context, the classic problem of dynamic inconsistency tends to get worse.[17]. A quick review of history immediately reveals that the independence of central banks rarely occurs in countries with new and weak democracies. It is only after suffering financial crisis and bitter lessons that this independence is reached. Even if it arises from democratic elections, the future government of Cuba will have to go through many setbacks to take on the heavy burden of repressing dollarization and building a sound and independent monetary authority.

Flexible exchange rates are seen as powerful tool to soften adverse shocks in external trade. This feature might be very important in larger economies with high volatility in exchange terms, which is not precisely the Cuban case, where the radical transformation of the export sector has laid the ground for sustainable growth. Tourism is a superior good with a clear upward trend over time. This sector is not exempted from fluctuations, but not as much as sugar, Cuba's main export until the past decade. Of course, there still remains vulnerability stemming from the need for imported oil. But the U.S. is also an oil importing country, so any measure taken by this country to reduce oil prices will also benefit Cuba. Although Cuba and the U.S. have no diplomatic relations and the U.S. embargo has not been lifted yet, the Cuban economy shows clear signs of moving along with the U.S economic cycle. Every effort by the U.S. to reactivate its economy will have positive, indirect—but remarkable—repercussions on the Cuban goods and services export sectors.

The only advantage of a flexible system, if any, is as tool to bolster competitiveness. But we do not believe this is the best way for Cuba to seek competitiveness. In a country with a good potential for growth and a well-educated labor force—although not as much as

---

16. Chown (1999), http://www.riia.org/briefingpapers/bp57.html.

17. Kidland and Prescott (1977)

the Cuban government boasts—productivity gains should be sought through a reform program aimed at achieving better resource allocation and providing incentives to private sector.

CONCLUSIONS

Notwithstanding the protracted macroeconomic stability enjoyed by Cuba, dollarization has not cast any sign of reversion. The creation of the Central Bank in 1997 has not prevented the dollar from spreading throughout the economy.

The state monopoly over the economy is a very important factor explaining the coexistence of two currencies, as the Cuban peso is just left to play the role of shock absorber. The power to fix prices and salaries enables the government to have income in dollars and expenditures in Cuban pesos. So why should it end a practice that only yields benefits?

The time when the collapse of the current political system seemed imminent is gone. The authorities have succeeded in jumping off from the Soviet ship and boarding a western one, with the dollar becoming a useful vehicle to dismantle the legacy of the former Soviet Union. The expansion and deeper rooting of the U.S currency throughout the economy will go on as long as the current political system lasts.

Sooner rather than later, Cuba will take the path of democracy and market economy. When this happens, the U.S currency will be an inseparable part of the economy and society, and the best choice left to the new authorities will be to complete the process begun by the communist authorities and dollarize the entire economy.

REFERENCES

Calvo, G. and Vegh, C. (1992) "Currency Substitution in Developing Countries: An Introduction." *Revista de Análisis Económico*, 7.

CEPAL (2000) *La Economía Cubana Reformas Estructurales y Desempeño en los 90*. Fondo de Cultura Económica, México, DF.

Chown, J. (1999) *Currency Boards or Dollarization—Solutions or Traps?* http://www.riia.org/briefing-papers/bp57.html

Girton, L. and Roper D. (1981) "Theory and Implications of Currency Substitution." *Journal of Money, Credit and Banking*, Vol. 13, pp. 12-30.

Hanke, S., Jonung, L. and Schuler, K. (1993) *Russian Currency and Finance: A Currency Board Approach to Reform*. Routledge.

Kareken, J. and Wallace, N. (1981) "On the Indeterminacy of Equilibrium Exchange Rates." *Quarterly Journal of Economics*, Vol. 96, pp. 207-222.

Kildegaard, A. and Orro, R. (1999) "Dollarization in Cuba and Implications for the Future Transition." *Cuba in Transition—Volume 9*, Association for the Study of Cuban Economy.

Kydland, F. and Prescott, E..C. (1977) "Rulers Rather than Discretion: The Inconsistency of Optimal Plans." *Journal of Political Economy*, 85.

Lasaga, M. (1995) "Financing the Economic Reconstruction of Cuba." *Cuba in Transition—Volume 5*, Association for the Study of Cuban Economy.

Pérez, L. (1994) "The Implications of Currency Substitution Experiences in Latin America and in Europe for Cuba." *Cuba in Transition—Volume 4*. Association for the Study of Cuban Economy.

Ramírez-Rojas, L. (1985) "Currency Substitution in Argentina, México and Uruguay." *IMF Staff Papers*, Vol. 32, pp. 629-667.

Sanguinetty, J. (1994) "Monetary Dualism as an Instrument Towards a Market Economy: The Cuban Case." *Cuba in Transition—Volume 4*, Association for the Study of Cuban Economy.

Summers, L. (1999) *Testimony before the Senate Banking, Housing and Urban Affairs Committee*, April.

PARASITISMO ECONÓMICO Y SU IMPACTO EN EL TRÁNSITO HACIA EL MERCADO

Manuel García Díaz

Durante los más de 40 años de gobierno castrista las estructuras del sistema productivo han sufrido importantes cambios. El estudio de tales estructuras materiales es crucial para trazar la política económica de la transición hacia el mercado. Desde los años 50, gracias a los trabajos de Alienes, se conoce el carácter decisivo de las exportaciones en la economía cubana.

En el presente trabajo, utilizando las estadísticas oficiales del gobierno cubano (publicadas por el gobierno o por la CEPAL), el autor analiza las más importantes características estructurales del comercio exterior de la Isla bajo el gobierno castrista. Tal análisis muestra cómo se han comportado dichas características con posterioridad al año 1959 y, especialmente, devela en qué sentido y en qué medida las exportaciones mantienen su carácter de variable decisiva de la economía cubana. Sobre tal base, y mostrando las interrelaciones entre las variables Importaciones y Exportaciones, se demuestra que la estructura productiva ha variado de modo que el incremento de 1 dólar de exportaciones requiere incrementar las importaciones en más de 1 dólar. Se demuestra así que una de las mayores y más graves distorsiones que ha sufrido la economía cubana durante estos años es que ha devenido en una economía parasitaria. No es una cuestión referida a un sector o rama, sino al sistema en su conjunto. Este aspecto resulta fundamental para la política económica de tránsito hacia el mercado, ya que la liberalización de los mismos y la simple acción de sus leyes eliminarían tal parasitismo, pero ello, de no tomarse medidas que lo

impidan, pudiera conllevar, con toda probabilidad, la paralización casi total de la economía cubana.

LAS EXPORTACIONES Y EL INGRESO NACIONAL

Estudios anteriores de la economía cubana han develado su alta dependencia en relación con el comercio exterior. Desde mediados del siglo XX, gracias a los trabajos de D. Julián Alienes, se conoce tal característica. Al menos desde principios del siglo, cuando se desarrolló el gigantesco complejo agro-industrial azucarero, la economía de la Isla ha sido dependiente, en muy alto grado, de las exportaciones. Así lo constata Alienes que califica a la exportación como "variable decisiva en la economía cubana" (1951, págs. 272-310). Otro destacado economista cubano escribía más recientemente; "La economía cubana, cualquiera sea su nivel de desarrollo, dependerá siempre del comercio exterior. Lo fundamental consiste en cambiar su estructura exportadora de modo que la dependencia resulte fuerte y flexible a la vez..." (Figueras, 1994, pág. 3).

Pero ¿en qué sentido y en qué medida depende la economía de las exportaciones y, en general, del comercio exterior? Para determinarlo, comenzaremos por correlacionar el Ingreso Nacional Creado, como variable dependiente, con las Exportaciones, como variable predictora. Para ello hemos empleado el modelo lineal general con la forma:

$$YC = a + bX + \zeta \qquad (1)$$

donde: X = Exportaciones.

Tabla 1.   Estructura de las Exportaciones de Bienes *(millones de pesos)*

Grupo de Productos	1960 Valor	1960 %	1975 Valor	1975 %	1989 Valor	1989 %
Azúcar y Derivados	482,9	79,4	2.651,8	89,8	3.948,5	73,2
Productos de la Minería	22,9	3,8	139,9	4,7	497,7	9,2
Tabaco y Manufacturas	55,6	9,1	52,8	1,8	83,6	1,6
Productos de la Pesca	2,1	0,3	52,2	1,8	128,8	2,4
Otros	44,8	7,4	55,5	1,9	733,4	13,6

Fuente: Tabla elaborada por el autor con datos de Junta Central de Planificación (1977) y Comité Estatal de Estadísticas (1990).

YC = Ingreso Nacional Creado.

Los datos que hemos utilizado son los del período 1960-89.[1] Los resultados de los cálculos de la regresión de la ecuación (1) de estimación del Ingreso Nacional Creado con las Exportaciones como variable predictora son:

$$YC = 3.631,8 + 1,786X \qquad (1a)$$

R = 0,988.

R cuadrado = 0,976.

R cuadrado corregida = 0,975.

El estadístico F de Fisher-Snedecor (para un intervalo de confianza del 95%) muestra que la probabilidad de rechazo de la hipótesis es menor que 0,000. Igual resultado se obtiene para el estadístico T de Student para la constante (con un intervalo de confianza del 95%) y para el estadístico T de Student para b (con un intervalo de confianza del 95%), obteniéndose para ambos una probabilidad de rechazo de la hipótesis menor que 0,000.

Estos resultados muestran una alta bondad del ajuste de la ecuación (1a) a la realidad. Reflejan, de manera muy elocuente, que el papel de las exportaciones en la economía cubana es tan decisivo que de su volumen depende el volumen del Ingreso Nacional Creado.

Debido a tal tremenda dependencia, la concentración de las exportaciones en unos pocos productos pudiera ser un elemento generador de conflictos, dado su carácter de variable exógena. Sin embargo, la estructura de las exportaciones cubanas durante el período 1960-89 muestran, como se ve en los 3 momentos que aparecen en la tabla N⁰ 1 (1960, 1975 y 1989), que solamente tres productos cubren más del 80% de ellas.

El azúcar, entre 1960 y 1975, gana mucho peso debido al incremento de su precio (82.82 $/T en 1960 y 484,88 $/T en 1975), ya que a precios constantes decreció 2,2% (1975 respecto a 1960).[2] En el siguiente período, entre 1975 hasta 1989, pierde peso, a pesar de que incrementan tanto su precio (que llega a los casi 550 $/T en 1989) como los volúmenes físicos exportados, pues de 5,7 MT en 1975 se pasa a exportar 7,1 MT en 1989. Su pérdida de peso se debe al crecimiento más rápido de las exportaciones de los demás productos, pues más que se triplican las exportaciones de productos de la minería, se duplican los productos de la pesca y se multiplican por 13 las exportaciones de "otros productos," renglón que lo forman, principalmente, productos primarios y manufacturas ligeras.

No obstante tales crecimientos, todavía las exportaciones del país en el año 1989 dependían en tres cuartas partes de la economía azucarera, situación similar a los tiempos anteriores a 1958 (Ver Alienes, 1951, pág. 327).

La estructura de las exportaciones de bienes durante la década de los 90 sufre un cambio radical como resultado de la catástrofe económica que padece el país agudizada por la brusca desaparición de sus principales mercados. Las cifras son las que aparecen en la Tabla N⁰ 2.

---

1. Ver en el Anexo las características de las series temporales utilizadas en los distintos modelos que aquí se desarrollan.

2. Cálculos realizados por el autor en base a los datos de Comité Estatal de Estadísticas (1990).

Tabla 2. **Exportaciones de Bienes en el Año 1999[a]** *(millones de dólares)*

Producto	Valor	%	1999/1989
Azúcar y Derivados	462	30,5	0,117
Productos de la Minería	394	26,1	0,792
Tabaco y Manufacturas	172	11,4	2,057
Otros	484	32	0,561

Fuente: Tabla elaborada por el autor con datos de Comité Estatal de Estadísticas (1990) y CEPAL (2001)

a. La fuente no detalla los productos de la pesca que se exportan, por lo cual aparecen dentro de "Otros."

A los productos del azúcar, minería y tabaco habría que agregar, como uno de los principales productos de las exportaciones actuales, los ingresos netos provenientes de la actividad turística, que en el año 1999 generó unos ingresos brutos que ascendieron a 1.901 millones de dólares (CEPAL, 2001, Cuba, Cuadro Nº 7).

Los problemas que han aquejado a la economía cubana en los últimos años, debido a las variaciones de los precios del azúcar y del níquel, y más recientemente, a la reducción del flujo de turistas como consecuencia del 11 de septiembre, confirman la peligrosidad que conlleva para la economía del país la concentración de las exportaciones en tan pocos productos.

EL MULTIPLICADOR DEL COMERCIO EXTERIOR

Los anteriores cálculos nos han servido, sobre todo, para comprobar la altísima dependencia del desarrollo económico de la Isla de una variable exógena. Veamos ahora otra característica del comercio exterior que resulta fundamental para el desarrollo económico del país: el multiplicador del comercio exterior *k*.

Como sabemos,

$$k = \frac{1}{\alpha + \mu}$$

donde: α = propensión marginal al ahorro,

μ = propensión marginal a la importación.

Calculemos la propensión marginal al consumo. Para ello, hemos construido el correspondiente conjunto de datos para el período 1960-89 (ver el Anexo), para las siguientes variables:[3]

1. Ingreso Nacional Disponible, que es igual al Ingreso Nacional Creado (valor agregado neto en los sectores de la esfera productiva) más las importaciones menos las exportaciones;

2. Consumo, que es igual al consumo privado (consumo, por parte de la población, de bienes y servicios destinados a la venta) más el consumo del sector público (consumo, por los sectores de la esfera no productiva [sector público], de bienes y servicios destinados a la venta).

Utilizaremos el modelo lineal general

$$C = c + \chi YD + \zeta \qquad (2)$$

donde: C = Consumo,

YD = Ingreso Nacional Disponible,

χ = Propensión Marginal al Consumo.

Los resultados obtenidos son los siguientes:

C = 1.299,969 + 0,688YD   (2a)
R = 0,991.
R cuadrado = 0,982.
R cuadrado corregida = 0,981.

El estadístico F de Fisher-Snedecor (para un intervalo de confianza del 95%) muestra que la probabilidad de rechazo de la hipótesis es menor que 0,000. Igual resultado se obtiene para el estadístico T de Student para la constante (con un intervalo de confianza del 95%) y para el estadístico T de Student para b (con un intervalo de confianza del 95%), obteniéndose para ambos una probabilidad de rechazo de la hipótesis menor que 0,000.

De donde resulta:

Propensión Marginal al Consumo χ = 0,688.
Propensión Marginal al Ahorro α = 0,312
Multiplicador de las inversiones k_i = 3,205.

---

3. Tenemos la alternativa de calcular la propensión marginal al consumo a partir del consumo per cápita. La propensión marginal a consumir, en este caso, es ligeramente inferior (0,632) a la que aparece en los cálculos que siguen (0,688).

Por su lado, el volumen de las importaciones debe depender del volumen del Ingreso Nacional Creado. Correlacionemos ambas variables mediante el modelo lineal general

$$M = d + \mu YC + \zeta \tag{3}$$

donde: M = Importaciones,

YC = Ingreso Nacional Creado,

μ = Propensión Marginal a las Importaciones

De manera similar a lo hecho en las ecuaciones (1) y (2), hemos utilizado los datos para el período 1960-1989 (ver Anexo).

Los resultados obtenidos, que aparecen a continuación, nos revelan la existencia de una alta correlación entre ambas variables:

$$M = -2.601 + 0,713YC \tag{3a}$$
R = 0,981.
R cuadrado = 0,962.
R cuadrado corregida = 0,961.

El estadístico F de Fisher-Snedecor (para un intervalo de confianza del 95%) muestra que la probabilidad de rechazo de la hipótesis es menor que 0,000. Igual resultado se obtiene para el estadístico T de Student para la constante (con un intervalo de confianza del 95%) y para el estadístico T de Student para b (con un intervalo de confianza del 95%), obteniéndose para ambos una probabilidad de rechazo de la hipótesis menor que 0,000.

De donde la Propensión Marginal a la Importación $\mu = 0,713$.[4] Como $\alpha = 0,312$ y $\mu = 0,713$, tenemos que el valor del multiplicador del comercio exterior para la economía cubana es

$$k = 0,9756$$

Este resultado es totalmente anómalo. ¡Un valor del multiplicador del comercio exterior menor que la unidad! Es posible demostrar que el multiplicador de la política fiscal puede tener valores muy bajos, incluso por debajo de 1, en el caso de que sea muy pequeña la sensibilidad a los cambios del tipo de interés. Pero, este no es el caso. Se trata del multiplicador del comercio exterior. ¿Por qué puede ocurrir esto? La propensión marginal a la importación es tan grande que, en combinación con tan baja propensión marginal al consumo, provoca que el incremento de la renta que se filtra hacia las importaciones determina que el efecto multiplicador de las inversiones sea menor que la unidad.

EL MULTIPLICADOR DEL COMERCIO EXTERIOR CON REPERCUSIONES EXTERNAS

Este valor tan bajo del multiplicador tiene otras consecuencias sobre la economía nacional: reduce la influencia de las relaciones externas en el crecimiento económico. De lo que hemos visto no se puede llegar aún a la conclusión de que un incremento de 1 peso de la inversión provoca un crecimiento de la producción menor que 1 peso. En efecto, de la misma forma que las importaciones generan una filtración del efecto multiplicador hacia el extranjero, las exportaciones provocan una filtración desde el extranjero hacia el país. Es la denominada repercusión externa. Para percibirla debemos analizar la interdependencia macroeconómica de la economía cubana con el "resto del mundo." Para ello estudiaremos el proceso de ajuste-ingreso de la economía cubana con el resto del mundo.[5]

Consideraremos un mundo de dos países, Cuba y resto del mundo.[6] Partimos de la condición de equilibrio interno en un país:

---

4. Si se calcula la Propensión Marginal a la Importación a partir de las Importaciones por habitante, recibiríamos 0,802 como valor de tal variable.

5. En el caso de la Cuba actual no tiene sentido hablar de ajuste-precio, pues el peso cubano no es convertible, ni se cotiza ni se comercia en los mercados internacionales de divisas. Asimismo, pienso que durante el período de transición hacia el mercado, tampoco será posible recurrir al mecanismo de ajuste-precio durante un largo lapso de tiempo. La causa de ello es la siguiente. El proceso de dolarización de la economía cubana, tal como se produjo, significó la virtual liquidación del peso cubano en el mercado interior. En esas condiciones, las devaluaciones que pueda sufrir el peso no deben tener influencia en la Balanza de Pagos.

6. Una explicación más detallada del modelo puede verse en Chacholiades (1990).

$$I + X = S(Y) + M(Y) \qquad (4)$$

donde: I = Inversión,

X = Exportación,

S = Ahorro,

M = Importaciones,

Y = Ingreso Nacional.

Denominemos con el subíndice c a las variables de Cuba y con o las del resto del mundo. Luego:

$$I_c + X_c = S_c(Y_c) + M_c(Y_c) \qquad (5a)$$

$$I_o + X_o = S_o(Y_o) + M_o(Y_o) \qquad (5b)$$

Como $X_c = M_o$ y $X_o = M_c$

$$I_c + M_o(Y_o) = S_c(Y_c) + M_c(Y_c) \qquad (6a)$$

$$I_o + M_c(Y_c) = S_o(Y_o) + M_o(Y_o) \qquad (6b)$$

De estas ecuaciones se pueden deducir las curvas de reacción de ambos países al variar el ingreso nacional del otro. Para Cuba, esta ecuación es el conjunto de valores de Y_c para los cuales se cumple la ecuación (6a) para un conjunto de valores de Y_o. Lo mismo para el resto del mundo. Es evidente que, en un mismo plano, el punto de intersección de ambas curvas es el punto de las rentas de equilibrio para ambos países.

De ese modelo pueden deducirse, para los dos países, los multiplicadores del comercio exterior con repercusiones externas. Para Cuba:

$$k_{cc} = k_c/(1 - k_c \cdot k_o \cdot \mu_c \cdot \mu_o) \qquad (7)$$

sería el multiplicador del comercio exterior con repercusiones externas de Cuba ante el incremento de la inversión en Cuba, y

$$k_{oc} = (k_c \cdot k_o \cdot \mu_c)/(1 - k_c \cdot k_o \cdot \mu_c \cdot \mu_o) \qquad (8)$$

el multiplicador del comercio exterior con repercusiones externas del resto del mundo ante un cambio en la inversión en Cuba, donde:

$$k = 1/(1 - \chi + \mu)$$ es multiplicador del comercio exterior.

μ = Propensión marginal a la importación.

χ = Propensión marginal al consumo.

Veamos ahora las consecuencias para Cuba de los valores tan altos de la propensión marginal a la importación. Como ya calculamos antes,

$$\chi_c = 0,688$$
$$\mu_c = 0,713$$
$$k_c = 0,976$$

Supongamos que, para el resto del mundo, se obtienen los siguientes valores:

$$\chi_o = 0,92$$
$$\mu_o = 0,29$$

luego,

$$k_o = 2,703$$

Con estos valores obtenemos:

$$k_{cc} = 2,147$$

Pero este valor está determinado por la altísima propensión marginal a la importación. De modo que, si suponemos que se reduce hasta el 0,5 la propensión marginal a la importación de Cuba, que es todavía una cifra alta, aunque similar a la que estimó Alienes para los años 50, tendríamos que:

$$k_c = 1,23$$
$$k_{cc} = 2,375$$

Es decir, en este último caso, por cada peso de incremento en la Inversión en Cuba, se obtiene un incremento del ingreso nacional igual a 2,375 pesos, una proporción 11% mayor que en la actualidad,[7] a pesar de tan baja propensión marginal al consumo. Si suponemos para esta última un valor "más normal," digamos, 0,85. entonces

$$k_c = 1,538$$
$$k_{cc} = 3,87$$

¡Más del 80% mayor que en la actualidad!

---

7. Puede demostrarse que el multiplicador k_{oc}, que muestra la influencia de un cambio de la inversión en Cuba en el resto del mundo, también tendrá un valor positivo.

La altísima propensión marginal a la importación, en combinación con la tan reducida propensión marginal al consumo, constituye, probablemente, uno de los más graves problemas que padece hoy la economía cubana, en lo que se refiere a la estructura material de la economía, pues constituye un gigantesco lastre para un país que depende de la exportación para crecer.

¿Qué es lo que mantiene una tan baja propensión marginal al consumo? ¿Qué es lo que ha provocado una tan alta propensión marginal a la importación? ¿Con cuáles otras variables interaccionan estas y cómo lo hacen de modo que se produzca tan anómalo comportamiento económico?

La respuesta a la primera pregunta es evidente: el monopolio estatal de las capacidades de producción y, mediante el racionamiento, de la distribución del producto, en combinación con el monopolio del comercio exterior e interior, le permitió al gobierno reducir a mínimos el consumo personal. Si bien es cierto que con ello se pudiera crear un cierto potencial de fuente nacional de ahorro, lo que evidentemente se logró fue provocar, con el empobrecimiento material de la población, un estímulo muy negativo sobre la productividad del trabajador. Con esto último se neutralizaba el potencial de crecimiento de la producción que pudiera aportar tal fuente nacional de ahorro.

Dar respuesta a las preguntas segunda y tercera es una tarea un poco más compleja. Ante todo, hay que admitir que, para el caso de la Cuba actual, resulta imposible (más bien, absurdo) utilizar el modelo IS-LM para intentar dar respuesta a estas preguntas. Ello se debe a que las variables que intervienen en el mecanismo del equilibrio simultáneo del mercado de bienes y del mercado monetario no son operativas en el medio ambiente cubano desde 1960 hasta la fecha.

Veamos (Tabla Nº 3) cuál ha sido la dinámica de algunos de los principales macro-indicadores de la economía cubana entre 1960 y 1989. Mientras que el consumo personal por habitante creció, en términos reales, al raquítico tipo del 1,6% promedio anual (3,6% anual a precios corrientes), las importaciones y

Tabla 3. Dinámica de Macro-Indicadores 1960-1989

Macro-Indicador	Tipo de Crecimiento Promedio Anual (%)
Producto Social Global (a precios constantes)	4,1
Producto Social Global per cápita (a precios constantes)	2,6
Ingreso Nacional Creado (a precios constantes)	4,4
Ingreso Nacional Creado (a precios corrientes)	5,0
Ingreso Nacional Creado per cápita (a precios constantes)	3,1
Consumo Personal (a precios constantes)	3,1
Consumo Personal per cápita (a precios constantes)	1,6
Importaciones Totales (a precios corrientes)	9,5
Exportaciones totales (a precios corrientes)	7,8
Exportaciones de Azúcar (a precios constantes)	0,8

Fuente: Tabla elaborada por el autor con datos de JUCEPLAN (1977) y Comité Estatal de Estadísticas (1990)

exportaciones crecieron, respectivamente, al 9,5% y al 7,8% promedio anual. Durante 29 años crecieron las importaciones más rápido que las exportaciones en 1,7 puntos anuales, que acumulados en los 29 años significa que las importaciones crecieron un 63% más que las exportaciones. Eso llevó a que, si en 1960 se importaron 0,2655 pesos para producir 1 peso de ingreso nacional, en 1989, para producir la misma cantidad de ingreso nacional se importaron 0,6366 centavos ¡se multiplicaron en 2,4 veces las importaciones para producir 1 peso de ingreso nacional! Se importaba para exportar, y mientras más se exportaba, menos quedaba para la demanda final interna. Si a ello se le suma el hecho de que el volumen físico de las exportaciones de azúcar (75-80% del total de exportaciones) creció durante ese período a una tasa promedio anual del 0,8%, se completa un cuadro rayano con el absurdo: se importaba para exportar y el producto que constituía el 80% de la exportación apenas crecía. Esto pudiera explicar, en parte, las causas de que el valor del multiplicador del comercio exterior sea inferior a la unidad, pero sobre todo, nos indica que hay que buscar la causa en la relación entre importaciones y estructura productiva.

Tabla 4. Estructura de las Importaciones *(millones de pesos)*

Grupo de Productos	1958		1975		1989	
	Valor	%	Valor	%	Valor	%
Bienes de Consumo	303,5	39,1	413,2	13,3	843,8	10,4
Bienes Intermedios	265,3	34,1	1.963,7	63,1	5.427,7	66,8
Bienes de Capital	208,3	26,8	736,2	23,6	1.852,7	22,8

Fuente: Tabla elaborada por el autor con datos de Comité Estatal de Estadísticas (1990).

LAS IMPORTACIONES

Anteriormente calculamos la Propensión Marginal a la Importación, para la cual obtuvimos un valor de 0,713. Resalta tan altísimo valor, y resulta preocupante, ya que es el factor determinante, con toda seguridad, de una altísima elasticidad-ingreso de las importaciones. En efecto, aplicando la fórmula

Elasticidad-ingreso de las importaciones = (dM/M)/(dYC/YC)

para el promedio de Importaciones e Ingreso Nacional Creado en el decenio 1980-89, se obtiene un valor de este indicador superior a 1,35.

En los años 50 los cálculos realizados por Alienes (1951) arrojaban que la propensión marginal a la importación tenía un valor aproximado a 0,50. ¿A qué se debe que haya crecido hasta 0,71? Examinemos la estructura de las importaciones. Para ello utilizaremos la clasificación alternativa por productos que aparece en el *Anuario Estadístico de Cuba 1989*, según la cual se clasifican las importaciones en:

- Bienes de consumo;
- Bienes intermedios;
- Bienes de capital.

Como el año 1960 no aparece clasificado de tal manera, tomaremos, como año inicial, el de 1958.

La estructura de las importaciones ha sufrido un cambio radical; mientras que las importaciones de bienes de consumo han crecido durante los 31 años al tipo promedio anual del 3,4%, las de bienes de capital lo han hecho al 7,3% anual y la de bienes intermedios crecen al 10,2% anual. Esos datos comparan con el del ingreso nacional creado, que creció, entre 1960 y 1989, al tipo promedio anual del 4,4%, con una diferencia de casi 6 puntos porcentuales de la importación de bienes intermedios.

A los fines de poder determinar la cuantía en que dependen del ingreso nacional creado la importación de bienes de consumo y la de bienes para el consumo intermedio, hemos calculado para esas variables las ecuaciones del modelo lineal general, correlacionándolas con el Ingreso Nacional Creado (ver Anexo), y hemos obtenido los siguientes resultados:

$$BC = -145,8 + 0,0069YC \qquad (9)$$

$$BI = -2.356,7 + 0,549YC \qquad (10)$$

donde: BC = Importaciones de bienes de consumo.
BI = Importaciones de bienes intermedios.
YC = Ingreso Nacional Creado.

Tabla 5. Bondad del Ajuste de las Ecuaciones 9 y 10

	Ecuación 9 (BC)	Ecuación 10 (BI)
R	0,987	0,993
R cuadrado	0,974	0,986
R cuadrado corregida	0,970	0,984
F de Fisher-Snedecor (intervalo de confianza del 95%)	< 0,000	< 0,000
T de Student para la constante (intervalo de confianza del 95%)	0,026	< 0,000
T de Student para b (intervalo de confianza del 95%)	< 0,000	< 0,000

El resultado es muy revelador y, como se ve en la Tabla 5, las ecuaciones 9 y 10 se ajustan muy bien al comportamiento real. La propensión marginal a la importación de bienes intermedios en el período se elevaba a 0,549, es decir, para incrementar en un peso el ingreso nacional creado había que importar adicionalmente 55 centavos de bienes intermedios. Eso llevó a que en 1989 se importaron 42 centavos de bienes intermedios por peso de ingreso nacional creado (5.428 M pesos de importaciones sobre 12.791 de Ingreso Nacional Creado), mientras que en el año 1960 se consumían 19 centavos de bienes intermedios y capital importados por peso de ingreso nacional creado (ver JUCEPLAN 1977). Las causas pueden ser dos: primero, un cambio considerable en la estructura de la producción, en favor de actividades intensivas en bienes intermedios de importación; segundo, un decrecimiento de la eficiencia en la utilización de bienes intermedios.

Entre 1960 y 1989 no se produjeron cambios estructurales de magnitudes tales que permitan justificar tal aumento, pues tanto la industria como la agricultura mantuvieron sus proporciones en el total del producto (46-48% y 16-17%, respectivamente). Los únicos cambios notables se produjeron en la construcción y en el comercio. El primero de ellos, alto consumidor de bienes intermedios, pasa del 4% al 9%, pero su volumen es relativamente pequeño en comparación con el incremento de las importaciones de bienes intermedios. El comercio reduce su participación y, además, no es un alto consumidor de bienes intermedios.

Las ecuaciones halladas son muy importantes, ya que se corresponden con la estructura de las capacidades de producción de bienes para la venta creada hasta 1989. A partir de 1990, salvo en el sector del Turismo, prácticamente no se han hecho nuevas inversiones en sectores de la producción para la venta.[8]

Este aspecto estructural, que muestran las ecuaciones (9) y (10), resulta muy importante y útil en lo referido al análisis que estamos realizando, ya que permite concluir que el estrangulamiento de la economía por parte de las importaciones hay que buscarlo en la producción, concretamente en la estructura productiva, y no en el consumo de la población.

INTERDEPENDENCIA ENTRE IMPORTACIONES Y EXPORTACIONES

De las ecuaciones calculadas tomemos las de exportaciones e importaciones:

$$YC = 3.631,8 + 1,786X \qquad (1a)$$

$$M = -2.601 + 0,713YC \qquad (2a)$$

Sustituyendo YC en una de las dos ecuaciones llegamos al siguiente resultado:

$$M = -11 + 1.273X \qquad (11)$$

Esta relación muestra el gravísimo problema estructural de la economía cubana actual: para incrementar un dólar de exportación, hay que importar 1,273 dólares. La extraordinariamente alta propensión marginal a las importaciones hace que estas hayan devenido en el principal factor estrangulador de la economía del país. Deviene así en variable principal de la economía cubana por ser el eslabón más débil en la cadena del desarrollo económico, ya que para producir y exportar la economía cubana necesita de una fuente exógena de divisas sin contrapartida, como créditos frescos o las remesas. Debido a los problemas con el pago de la deuda externa, la fuente de créditos frescos se ha ido reduciendo paulatinamente y en la actualidad son cantidades muy reducidas (sujetas al pago de créditos anteriores). De tal modo, quedan solamente las remesas como fuente principal de transferencias sin contrapartida.

Si esto es cierto, entonces tendrá que existir una correlación muy fuerte entre las exportaciones y las transferencias, es decir, existirá una ecuación

$$X = e + fTR + \zeta \qquad (12)$$

donde TR son las transferencias y X las exportaciones, con un alto valor del coeficiente de correlación. Para comprobarlo, tomaremos los valores correspondientes, entre los años 1993 y 2000, del cuadro 20 de CEPAL (2001). Al calcular el modelo obtenemos los siguientes resultados:

$$X = 564,9 + 4,38TR \qquad (12a)$$
R = 0,952.
R cuadrado = 0,905.
R cuadrado corregida = 0,89.

El estadístico F de Fisher-Snedecor (para un intervalo de confianza del 95%) muestra que la probabilidad de rechazo de la hipótesis es menor que 0,000. Simi-

---

8. Las grandes inversiones extranjeras se han dirigido a la compra de instalaciones ya existentes, como las fábricas de níquel del norte de Oriente (ver UNCTAD 2001, Country Fact Sheet: Cuba).

lares resultados se obtienen para el estadístico T de Student para la constante (con un intervalo de confianza del 95%), con una probabilidad de rechazo de la hipótesis igual a 0,214; y para el estadístico T de Student para b (con un intervalo de confianza del 95%) menor que 0,000.

Según nuestras ecuaciones (1a), (2a) y (12a), para un nivel de transferencias de 850 millones de dólares (igual al nivel estimado para el año 2000), se obtendrían los siguientes estimados:

> Exportaciones = 4.287,9 M de $.
> Ingreso Nacional Creado[9] =
> 11.290 M de Pesos (a precios de 1981).
> Importaciones = 5,447,8 M de $.

Según el cuadro 20 de CEPAL (2001) las Exportaciones (estimaciones de CEPAL) reales ascendieron a 4.807 M de $, y las Importaciones a 5.587 M de $. Pero, si las Transferencias (sin contrapartida) desaparecen, entonces los valores estimados serían:

> Exportaciones = 564,9 M de $.
> Ingreso Nacional Creado =
> 4.640,7 M de pesos (a precios de 1981).
> Importaciones = 797,8 M de $.

En los marcos de las condiciones político-económicas actuales, y teniendo en cuenta la poca disposición que muestra el gobierno cubano para liberalizar los mercados, poco puede esperarse en cuanto a la eliminación de tan grave anomalía. Parece que el parasitismo económico es un mal endémico del actual régimen.

PARASITISMO Y TRANSICIÓN

Se puede, entonces, tener la casi absoluta certeza de que, cuando comience el período de transición de la economía cubana hacia el mercado, la variable económica más importante será la importación, y lo será durante un tiempo. Ello será así por ser esta variable el principal factor estrangulador de las exportaciones, de las cuales depende el desarrollo del país. A medida que esta situación anómala se corrija, las exportacio-

nes recuperarán el papel de variable económica decisiva.

La política económica en relación con las importaciones será de primera importancia para el gobierno que emprenda la transición hacia una economía de mercado, por, al menos, dos razones. Primera, es determinante en la creación de condiciones para el desarrollo económico. Y segunda, si no se corrige la situación actual, la paralización masiva de actividades será irrefrenable.

Por supuesto, como consecuencia del proceso de transición hacia el mercado se deberán crear las condiciones que posibiliten el desarrollo económico normal de la Isla. Sin embargo, todo intento de generar desarrollo económico en Cuba pasa, indefectiblemente, por el incremento de las exportaciones. Pero, dada la interdependencia entre exportaciones e importaciones, limitar el esfuerzo en el crecimiento de las primeras, lejos de resolver el problema, lo complicaría aún más. Como paso previo hay que reducir drásticamente la propensión marginal a las importaciones. El análisis realizado ha mostrado que el nudo gordiano de esta cuestión radica en el consumo de bienes intermedios importados.

La segunda razón parece ser más acuciante, debido a la situación del empleo que heredará el gobierno que inicie la transición al mercado.

En efecto, el desempleo en Cuba es uno de los problemas más críticos de la actualidad. Será heredado por el gobierno que inicie la transición hacia el mercado. El gobierno cubano ha logrado evitar, mediante artificios, que este fenómeno aparezca en su real magnitud. Decenas de miles de personas están ocupando puestos de trabajo innecesarios. Es probable que el desempleo reconocido, más el desempleo latente, alcance la cifra de más de 700 mil personas. Este desempleo latente, con toda probabilidad, devendrá en desempleo efectivo una vez se emprenda el camino del mercado, pues no hay razón alguna para mantenerlo, y si muchas para liberar a la producción de bienes y servicios de tan pesado lastre.

---

9. En términos del Sistema de Balances.

Como muestra la experiencia de otros países del "socialismo real" que han emprendido la ruta de las reformas mercantiles, las medidas de liberalización adoptadas han conllevado que actividades, que sobrevivían gracias a las subvenciones del estado, no pudieron rebasar las exigencias del mercado. Hay que contar con que las medidas de liberalización de los mercados y de eliminación de las subvenciones a actividades que no son rentables ni necesarias en una sociedad normal, provocarán el cierre de muchas instalaciones de producción de bienes y servicios, y con ello, se incrementará el desempleo. Por tanto, es altamente probable que el gobierno de transición, tendrá que enfrentar un paro masivo, del cual será culpado, y que generará gran inestabilidad social.

Por ello, evitar la paralización en gran escala de actividades económicas deviene en elemento crucial para que el tránsito no aparezca como generador de desempleo masivo. Si se liberalizan los mercados interior y exterior sin haber corregido la anómala propensión marginal a las importaciones, las consecuencias que provocaría, que hoy recaen sobre el país en su conjunto, sobre todo, sobre los consumidores, tendrían que ser asumidas por las empresas. El consumo de bienes intermedios, desmesuradamente alto, tendrá su reflejo en la salud financiera de las empresas. Luego, las propias leyes del mercado se encargarán de sacarlas del juego. Pero, por las cifras con que contamos, este es un fenómeno que afecta al aparato productivo en su conjunto. Luego, emprender el tránsito sin prever este peligro y sin tomar medidas que tiendan a eliminarlo, pudiera provocar la paralización total del sistema productivo.

Hay que determinar cuáles son las actividades que provocan tal consumo de bienes intermedios. Una vez identificados los productos y actividades que generan tales desmesurados consumos intermedios, hay que implementar medidas que coadyuven a la sustitución de importaciones en ellos y a incrementar la eficiencia en la utilización de los bienes intermedios, en particular los importados. Posiblemente, será necesario practicar políticas proteccionistas, sin que, de

antemano, se pueda descartar la conveniencia de otorgar subvenciones a determinadas actividades productivas.

CONCLUSIONES

El análisis realizado ha mostrado que el principal problema de la economía cubana actual, en lo que se refiere a la estructura material, es la estrangulación que sufre por la interacción y dependencia entre las importaciones, las exportaciones y las transferencias de divisas sin contrapartida. De tal manera, la economía cubana actual puede representarse, de forma sintética, por el siguiente sistema de ecuaciones:

$$YC = 3.631,8 + 1,786X$$
$$M = -2.601 + 0,713YC$$
$$X = 564,9 + 4,38TR$$

Donde:

YC = Ingreso Nacional Creado,
X = Exportaciones totales,
M = Importaciones totales,
TR = Transferencias ingresadas
        sin contrapartida.

Cada dólar de transferencias sin contrapartida provoca el crecimiento de 4,38 dólares de exportaciones; el incremento de 1 dólar adicional de exportaciones provoca un crecimiento de 1,786 dólares de ingreso nacional creado; y el incremento de un dólar de éste último requiere incrementar las importaciones en 0,713 dólares. En resumen, incrementar un dólar de exportación requiere un incremento de las importaciones de más de 1,27 dólares. Estas relaciones revelan que, por su estructura material actual, la economía cubana posee la siguiente característica fundamental: requiere un flujo de ingreso de divisas sin contrapartida a los fines de poder producir para exportar, de lo cual depende el Ingreso Nacional Creado.

En resumen, *la economía cubana ha devenido en una economía parasitaria*, condición que, muy probablemente, mantendrá hasta el momento en que se emprenda la transición al mercado.

ANEXO
SOBRE LAS ESTADÍSTICAS

Uno de los mayores obstáculos con que tropezamos los que intentamos trabajar con la información estadística de la economía de Cuba, es la poca homogeneidad de las series temporales disponibles. Hasta 1989, en virtud de la alineación de Cuba con el campo del socialismo "real" y, desde 1972, su condición de miembro del Consejo de Ayuda Mutua Económica (CAME), el gobierno cubano adoptó, como sistema estadístico nacional, el vigente en aquellos países, el conocido como Sistema de Balances. Una de las consecuencias en Cuba de la caída del Muro de Berlín y de la desintegración de la Unión Soviética, fue que el sistema estadístico vigente hasta ese momento ha dejado de tener razón de ser, pues todos los organismos a los que Cuba debe tributar información económica utilizan el Sistema de Cuentas Nacionales. Así, nos encontramos que las series estadísticas disponibles a partir de 1993 (algunas incluyendo datos de años anteriores) están elaboradas siguiendo los conceptos y métodos del Sistema de Cuentas Nacionales.

A lo anterior hay que agregar que en los años que van desde 1959 hasta 1975 los Anuarios Estadísticos no fueron publicados para todos los años y, además de que los publicados no coincidían conceptual y metodológicamente ni con el Sistema de Contabilidad Nacional ni con el mencionado Sistema de Balances, entre ellos se perciben diferencias metodológicas y de procedimientos que los invalidan para ser utilizados para conformar el tramo correspondiente de la serie temporal del período. No existe, por tanto, publicación oficial de la autoridad estadística del país que permita la construcción de series temporales completas desde 1959 hasta la fecha.

Ante la necesidad de contar con series estadísticas con el suficiente nivel de confiabilidad para realizar estudios del período a partir de 1960, el Instituto de Investigaciones Económicas de la Junta Central de Planificación encaró, como el primero de sus trabajos, la reconstrucción de las series estadísticas cubanas desde 1960 hasta 1975. Este trabajo fue publicado en el año 1977 con la clasificación de Secreto, con el título

"Reconstrucción y Análisis de las Series Estadísticas de la Economía Cubana 1960-1975," y sirvió de base de datos principal para la elaboración, a partir de ese año, de la Estrategia de Desarrollo hasta el año 2000. Se reconstruyeron las series siguiendo la metodología del Sistema de Balances, excepto en el hecho, que determina otra diferencia metodológica entre los tres tramos, de que la clasificación de la producción de las empresas se hizo bajo el criterio institucional, debido a que la documentación existente imposibilitaba clasificar las actividades de las empresas por el método de la actividad principal, como es usual. Esto significa que la producción (y todos los demás datos estadísticos) de las empresas, independientemente de su actividad principal, se contabilizaban por el sector que correspondía a la institución (ministerio u otro tipo de organismo central del estado) al que se subordinaban administrativamente. Es decir, si una empresa constructora se subordinaba durante el período al Ministerio de la Industria Azucarera, su producción se contabilizaba como Producción de Azúcar. Evidentemente, ello puede inducir errores. Sin embargo, tales hechos contables no son significativos, pues los casos mayores sujetos a tal tipo de clasificación errónea se encuentran en las empresas constructoras subordinadas al Ministerio de la Agricultura y en las empresas de la industria mecánica subordinadas al Ministerio de la Industria Azucarera. En ambos casos, su volumen es insignificante en comparación con el volumen total de producción de cada uno de ellos, respectivamente, la producción agrícola y la producción azucarera.

Resumiendo, existen tres tramos de las series temporales de las estadísticas económicas oficiales de Cuba:

- 1960-75, contenidas en el mencionado trabajo de la Junta Central de Planificación, publicadas con el título "Reconstrucción y Análisis de las Series Estadísticas de la Economía Cubana: 1960-1975," y elaboradas siguiendo los conceptos y métodos del Sistema de Balances;

- 1975–89, expuestas en los Anuarios Estadísticos de Cuba, publicados por el Comité Estatal de Estadísticas, también elaboradas siguiendo los conceptos y métodos del Sistema de Balances;

- 1990–2000, publicadas por el Gobierno cubano en publicaciones propias o en los documentos de CEPAL. Estas series han sido elaboradas siguiendo los patrones del Sistema de Cuentas Nacionales.

Varias fueron las razones que han determinado que en el presente trabajo el autor se inclinara hacia la utilización de variables correspondientes al Sistema de Balances, es decir, las series estadísticas de los dos primeros tramos 1959-75 y 1975-89. La primera, es que las proporciones fundamentales actuales de la economía cubana se formaron, sobre la base de la estructura heredada en 1959, en los años 1960–90, debido a la magnitud de inversiones ejecutadas en ese período. Además, consideramos que para el cálculo de las magnitudes y proporciones estructurales que nos interesan no se deben utilizar los datos posteriores a 1990 hasta el 2000 debido a que están muy determinados por la catástrofe sufrida por la economía del país con la desaparición de la Unión Soviética y el CAME.[10] Una tercera causa es que el autor fue, entre 1975 y 1986, miembro de la Comisión de Implantación del Sistema de Dirección y Planificación de la Economía primero y, posteriormente, Vicepresidente de la Junta Central de Planificación donde dirigía, entre otras actividades, las del Instituto de Investigaciones Económicas. En los marcos de la Comisión se elaboró el Sistema Estadístico Nacional que se aplicó entre 1975 y 1990; en la Junta Central de Planificación, como ya se dijo, se realizó el trabajo de reconstrucción de las estadísticas económicas del tramo 1959-75. Por tanto, conoce con detalle y profundidad los conceptos y principios metodológicos del Sistema de Balances y del contenido de sus indicadores, sus similitudes y diferencias con los correspondientes del Sistema de Contabilidad Nacional, así como los defectos y virtudes de tales series cronológicas; incluso conoció de las manipulaciones a que fueron sometidas las series temporales de los dos primeros tramos.

A los fines de que los resultados de los cálculos realizados sobre la base de las series 1960-89 pudieran ser útiles para analizar la situación en los últimos años, se tomaron variables que fueran homogéneas en todos los tramos (como lo son las importaciones y exportaciones) o que, para aquellas que no son homogéneas en los tres tramos, pudieran utilizarse como valores aproximados de los macro-indicadores correspondientes al Sistema de Cuentas Nacionales. No es ocioso recordar que las magnitudes y proporciones estructurales que nos interesan no son los valores absolutos de las variables (o sus valores aproximados) sino las propensiones marginales asociadas a ellas, en particular los de la propensión marginal a la importación y la propensión marginal al consumo, que son las que determinan los valores de los multiplicadores de la inversión y del comercio exterior.

Las variables utilizadas en el modelo son:

X = Exportaciones.
M = Importaciones.
BC = Importaciones de bienes de consumo.
BI = Importaciones de bienes intermedios.

Las anteriores cuatro variables son homogéneas para los tres tramos de la serie temporal. Se utilizaron, además, las siguientes:

- **YC = Ingreso Nacional Creado.** Se ha tomado al indicador del mismo nombre en el Sistema de Balances, es decir, al valor agregado neto en las ramas de producción de bienes y servicios destinados a la venta. Es un valor aproximado del Producto Interior Neto del Sistema de Cuentas Nacionales, pues se diferencia de éste en que no incluye los Gastos de Gobierno (Producción del Gobierno). Considero que esta variable, en el caso de la Cuba actual, al excluir los gastos de gobierno, refleja mejor el volumen de producción nacional porque la producción pública en el caso de Cuba estaba tergiversada (sobrevaluada) por dos razones: la primera es el altísimo nivel de subvención de que era beneficiaria, proveniente

---

10. A lo cual hay que añadir que estos datos provocan la percepción de que han sido manipulados con el aparente fin de ocultar la verdadera magnitud de la catástrofe económica sufrida por el país.

de la Unión Soviética y de otros países socialistas. En segundo lugar, la política populista de empleo, que llevó a la práctica de sobredimensionar el Sector Público (los servicios del gobierno). Esto último era posible gracias, por supuesto, a la altísima subvención recibida. Luego, al no considerar los gastos de gobierno como parte del Ingreso Nacional Creado, logramos evitar (al menos parcialmente) el que las subvenciones aparezcan como parte del Producto Interno Bruto y, consecuentemente, del Ingreso Nacional Creado.

- **YD = Ingreso Nacional Disponible.** Se ha tomado el indicador del mismo nombre en el Sistema de Balances. Es un buen valor aproximado de la variable Renta Nacional Neta Disponible del Sistema de Cuentas Nacionales. Es igual al Ingreso Nacional Creado más Importaciones menos Exportaciones. Aquí, nuevamente, nos tenemos que referir a las subvenciones recibidas del exterior. Como quedó implícito al referirnos al contenido de este indicador, no incluimos las "Transferencias de divisas sin contrapartida," por lo que puede pensarse que estamos dejando de incluir las subvenciones que, evidentemente, forman parte del Ingreso Nacional Disponible. En el caso de Cuba no ocurre esto, ya que las subvenciones que recibía de la Unión Soviética y de otros países socialistas se materializaban no en un flujo de divisas que entraba en el país, sino en líneas de créditos que permitían adquirir bienes y servicios, en particular bienes de equipo, para la producción y las inversiones. De tal manera, estas subvenciones entraban al país en forma de importaciones por encima de la capacidad real de importación del país. Luego, al considerar las importaciones estamos incluyendo el valor de tales subvenciones. De tal manera, si sumamos en el Ingreso Nacional Disponible el valor nominal de

las subvenciones lo que haríamos en realidad sería duplicarlas.

- **C = Consumo.** Valor aproximado de la variable "Consumo Nacional Final" en el Sistema de Cuentas Nacionales. Se forma por la suma del consumo privado (consumo, por parte de la población, de bienes y servicios destinados a la venta) y del consumo de bienes y servicios por el sector público. La diferencia con el indicador correspondiente del Sistema de Cuentas Nacionales es que no incluye los salarios del sector público. Dados los factores "políticos" que han determinado tanto el volumen de los trabajadores del sector público en Cuba como de sus salarios, lo cual ha conllevado que éste sea uno de los principales factores de la hiperinflación que sufre el país, pueden hacer pensar (y así lo hace el autor) que su exclusión, lejos de restar precisión a los cálculos, contribuye en el sentido contrario.

- **TR = Transferencias sin contrapartida,** variable que solamente se utiliza para los cálculos durante en el período 1993–2000, y que se toma de las series estadísticas publicadas en CEPAL (2000 y 2000a).

La compatibilidad en cuanto a la valoración a precios constantes está garantizada. Ello se debe a que para todo el período 1960-1989, en los casos de variables que debían tomarse a precios constantes, se han valorado a precios de 1981; por otro lado, las estadísticas oficiales del gobierno cubano para los años 1990–2000 (tanto las propias como las publicadas por CEPAL) se valoran a precios de 1981.

Por último, a continuación presentamos las series temporales (en millones de pesos) de las variables Ingreso Nacional Creado, Ingreso Nacional Disponible y Consumo, que son las utilizadas en nuestros cálculos. Las demás, pueden ser encontradas en los Anuarios Estadísticos editados por el Comité Estatal de Estadísticas y en las publicaciones de la CEPAL.

Año	Ingreso Nacional Creado (YC)	Ingreso Nacional Disponible (YD)	Consumo (C)
1960	3.068	3.526	3.794
1961	3.116	3.636	3.710
1962	3.333	4.077	3.852
1963	3.340	4.498	4.074
1964	3.779	4.950	4.281
1965	3.950	4.704	4.334
1966	3.914	4.890	4.548
1967	4.310	5.242	4.782
1968	4.120	5.237	4.863
1969	4.093	5.321	4.949
1970	4.497	5.579	5.190
1971	4.645	6.015	5.725
1972	5.038	6.436	6.391
1973	5.653	7.409	6.446
1974	6.185	8.197	6.762
1975	8.112	9.341	7.150
1976	8.356	9.893	7.462
1977	8.413	9.925	7.458
1978	9.466	10.054	7.864
1979	9.620	10.075	8.182
1980	9.853	11.047	8.816
1981	11.504	12.297	9.416
1982	12.176	12.263	9.689
1983	12.926	12.757	9.948
1984	13.695	14.080	10.437
1985	13.952	14.527	10.690
1986	12.857	13.560	10.952
1987	12.284	12.889	10.715
1988	12.764	13.355	10.924
1989	12.791	13.658	11.027

BIBLIOGRAFÍA

Alienes Urosa, J. (1951), *Características Fundamentales de la Economía Cubana*, Ed. P. Fernández y Cía., La Habana.

Chacholiades, M. (1993), *Economía Internacional*, 2º Edición, Ed. McGraw-Hill, Madrid.

Comisión Económica para América Latina CEPAL (2000), *Cuba: Evolución Económica Durante 1999*, Internet.

Comisión Económica para América Latina CEPAL (2000a), *La Economía Cubana: Reformas Estructurales y Desempeño en los Noventa* (Segunda Edición), Ed Fondo de Cultura Económica, México.

Comisión Económica para América Latina CEPAL (2001), *Estudio Económico de América Latina y el Caribe 2000-2001*, Internet.

Comisión Económica para América Latina CEPAL (2001a), *Cuba: Evolución Económica Durante 2000*, Internet.

Comité Estatal de Estadísticas (1990). *Anuario Estadístico de Cuba 1989*, Ed. Comité Estatal de Estadísticas de Cuba, La Habana.

Figueras, M. A. (1994), *Aspectos Estructurales de la Economía Cubana*, Ed. Ciencias Sociales, La Habana.

Junta Central de Planificación (1977), *Reconstrucción y Análisis de las Series Estadísticas de la Economía Cubana 1960-1975*, Dos Tomos, Ed. JUCEPLAN, La Habana.

United Nations Conference for Trade and Development (UNCTAD), (2001) *World Investment Report 2001: Promoting Linkages*, United Nations, New York y Ginebra.

LECCIONES DE LA EXPERIENCIA DE REFORMAS Y DE LA CRISIS ARGENTINA PARA LA TRANSICIÓN CUBANA: IMPORTANCIA DEL PROYECTO VARELA

Rolando H. Castañeda[1]

Since the launch of the Convertibility Plan in 1991, the Argentine economy has been undergoing a massive transformation. The main feature of this program, supported by the World Bank Group, IDB and IMF, was the establishment of a currency board arrangement. This was part of a sweeping set of reforms that altered the monetary system, improved fiscal and tax policies, liberalized trade, and reformed the public sector, including a rapid privatization program and changes to the social security system.

…Argentina has experienced strong average economic growth in the 1990s. The size of the economy expanded from $141 billion in 1990 to $282 billion in 1999, despite being hit by external shocks and two severe recessions. Argentina has now one of the world's lowest inflation rates and productivity has rapidly increased, responding to the new economic signals. The banking system has been strengthened through improvements in regulation and supervision, privatization, restructuring and consolidation. The role of the state has been changed, mainly as a result of privatization and decentralization to the provinces of health and education. Tax reforms removed many distortions and reduced tax handles and a new federal public sector financial management system was implemented. Poverty quickly fell from the peak of 41 percent reached in 1989-90.

— World Bank (2000, p. i)

Argentina was the spoiled child of the Washington Consensus. The IMF, the World Bank, and the IDB too…looked fondly on Argentina's success in halting inflation and on the steps it took to open its economy to foreign investment and deregulate and privatize…. the official creditors paid too little attention to public borrowing, worried too little about tax evasion…[Argentina] enjoyed the benefits of the spoiled child's excessive borrowing through much of the decade.

— Nancy Birdsall (2002, p. 3)

La cita anterior del Country Assistance Strategy del Banco Mundial de setiembre del 2000 muestra que la comunidad financiera internacional consideró la conducción de la política económica argentina durante los años noventa a modo de un paradigma estelar a imitar por los países en desarrollo sobre cómo insertarse a la globalización y al nuevo orden internacional. Standard & Poor's clasificó la deuda argentina de A-3, los bonos argentinos constituían el 25% del índice de J. P. Morgan y el país tuvo un diferencial favorable respecto al índice básico de la tasa de interés para los países emergentes hasta 2000 (ver Cuadro 1 al final del trabajo). Renombrados economistas (entre ellos Dornbusch, 2000 y Becker, 1996) destacaron la caja de convertibilidad y el impulso privatizador del gobierno de Menem, y recomendaron imitar dicho modelo al resto de América latina para lograr estabilidad y crecimiento. La regulación y supervisión

---

1. Las opiniones expresadas son de la exclusiva responsabilidad del autor y no reflejan sus vínculos institucionales presentes ni pasados.

bancaria prudenciales argentinas se consideraban entre las mejores de los países emergentes.

La Asamblea Anual del FMI y del Banco Mundial de octubre de 1998, encomió al presidente Carlos Menem y lo presentó rodeado por el entonces presidente de los E.U.A., William Clinton, el secretario del Tesoro, Robert Rubin, y el director gerente del FMI, Michel Camdessus. Sin embargo, al igual que ocurre con las estrellas reales, a partir de 1999 la economía argentina, después de brillar en el firmamento económico regional por algunos años, agotó su energía, los efectos positivos de la caja de convertibilidad y de la confianza de los inversionistas externos, se detuvo y comenzó a contraerse. Actualmente el país se ha aproximado a un límite crítico de manera peligrosa, a partir del cual podría producirse un colapso y generar un hoyo negro en el espacio regional. En términos generales, los desafíos de estabilización, reformas estructurales e institucionales, así como los costos privados y sociales asociados al proceso de ajuste que Argentina enfrenta son formidables en el corto y mediano plazo.

El propósito de este ensayo es derivar algunas lecciones relevantes para evitar una crisis similar una vez que Cuba comience con decisión su transición hacia una economía de mercado. Algunas de las características y problemas que presenta su economía—bajo comercio exterior, tasa de cambio fija, déficit fiscales crónicos, elevado endeudamiento externo, y las marcadas debilidades de la pequeña y mediana empresa, de la sociedad civil y de las instituciones—son similares a los que Argentina mostraba en 2001. Antes de extraer esas lecciones conviene revisar qué sucedió realmente en Argentina y ampliar en las semejanzas de los problemas de ambos países.

El ensayo tiene seis secciones. La primera sección revisa lo ocurrido en la economía argentina en 1990-2001 y la situación en 2002. La segunda expone algunas consecuencias principales de la crisis argentina. La tercera analiza las posibles causas de la crisis argentina. La cuarta sección presenta una apreciación críti-

ca de los errores de diseño y ejecución de política económica argentina con objeto de obtener lecciones para la transición cubana. La quinta expone las características y la evolución macroeconómica de Cuba en 1990-2001 y la situación en 2002. Finalmente, la sexta sección hace algunas observaciones finales sobre cómo evitar una crisis tipo argentina y cómo mejorar el proceso de reformas en la transición cubana, y sobre la importancia de las propuestas del Proyecto Varela.

ARGENTINA: CARACTERÍSTICAS Y EVOLUCIÓN MACROECONÓMICA EN 1990-2001 Y SITUACIÓN EN 2002

La economía argentina se caracterizó por un elevado crecimiento del PIB real de aproximadamente un 57% en 1991-1998 (ver Cuadro 1), después que superó con base en el Plan de Convertibilidad y de la "revolución productiva," la contracción sufrida en la década de los ochenta, aproximadamente 1.3% anual, y controló las hiperinflaciones de 1989 y 1990, de 4,924% y 1,344% anual, respectivamente.

Dicho plan se fundamentó en el establecimiento de la caja de convertibilidad el 1 de abril de 1991;[2] mediante el cual se autorizaban al dólar y al peso respaldado 1 a 1 por el dólar (garantizado por la Constitución Política) como los medios de pagos de la economía, lo que sirvió de una fuerte ancla al nivel de precios. También contribuyeron la reforma del estado que privatizó y dio en concesiones muchas empresas estatales; el programa de apertura comercial; y la reforma del sector fiscal orientada a reducir el gasto público y a implantar la reforma tributaria consistente en sustituir los impuestos al comercio exterior por los del valor agregado y sobre los ingresos. Una parte pequeña del crecimiento en 1990-1998 es atribuible a la recuperación de la contracción de la década de los ochenta. Más tarde, el país sufrió una recesión incesante en el trienio 1999-2001 que dura todavía. En 2002 se espera una contracción entre el 15% y 20% del PIB real.

---

2. La caja de convertibilidad argentina no fue ortodoxa ya que otorgaba poderes al Banco Central para fijar reservas y otras regulaciones a los bancos comerciales, con algún grado de libertad para integrar parte de las reservas con títulos públicos.

La inflación, medida por los precios al consumidor, se redujo del 84% en 1991 al 1.6% en 1995. Con posterioridad, los precios al consumidor se mantuvieron casi constantes o disminuyeron levemente hasta 2001, ver Cuadro 1. En 2002 se espera una inflación del 80%.

El déficit fiscal financiero en relación con el PIB aumentó con algunas fluctuaciones del 0.1% en 1992 al 3.9% en 2001. A principios de la década de los noventa el gobierno central logró aumentar sus ingresos como resultado de las masivas privatizaciones y concesiones de empresas públicas, lo que implicó una disminución posterior de los ingresos provenientes de las mismas. A partir de 1994 los ingresos fiscales también disminuyeron como consecuencia de la privatización del seguro social, al pasarse del sistema de cuenta única fiscal a cuentas individuales de capitalización de los asegurados, depositados en instituciones privadas, lo cual significó una reducción neta de los ingresos fiscales, equivalente al 3.2% del PIB en 2001.[3]

Dado que una parte central de la deuda pública se colocó externamente y a mediano plazo, la deuda fiscal bruta externa en relación con el PIB aumentó del 31.8% en 1992 al 57.7% en el 2001 como resultado del sostenido y creciente déficit fiscal, a pesar de que el país fue beneficiario de la reestructuración de la deuda externa y de los bonos Brady el 7 de abril de 1993. El pago neto de intereses al exterior en relación con las exportaciones de bienes y servicios aumentó progresivamente del 10.2% en 1992 al 18.1% en 2001. Además, el perfil de la deuda tenía muchos vencimientos de corto plazo.

La tasa de cambio real efectiva fluctuó en 1992-1996 y se apreció posteriormente en forma continua a medida que el real se depreció, los socios del Mercosur fueron flexibilizando sus monedas, y el euro y las monedas asiáticas se depreciaron con respecto al dólar. Según Perry y Serven (2002, p. 24) la tasa de cambio real de equilibrio se apreció aproximadamente un 55% entre 1997 y 2001. Según Calvo et al. (2002, p. 13) la tasa de cambio real habría que depreciarla en

46% para lograr el equilibrio en la cuenta corriente de la balanza de pagos a fin de compensar la situación surgida en 1998-2001.

La tasa de crecimiento de las exportaciones de bienes y servicios de Argentina fue de 8.1% en 1992-2001, en contraste con 9.8% de los siete países mayores de América latina y el Caribe y 11.5% de los países de ingreso intermedio en el mundo. De hecho las exportaciones de bienes y servicios prácticamente se estancaron después de 1998 (ver Cuadro 1). Argentina no logró diversificar su oferta exportable, centrada en productos primarios, durante el periodo de expansión económica. Argentina exportaba el 11.5% del PIB en 2001, la menor proporción entre los países mayores e intermedios de América latina. En 2000 el 24% del comercio exterior fue con Brasil, el 14% con otros países de América latina, el 13% con los E.U.A., el 25% con Europa y el 24% con el resto del mundo. Argentina tenía la menor proporción de sus exportaciones a los E.U.A. entre los países mayores e intermedios de América latina en 2000.

La tasa de inversión interna bruta en relación con el PIB aumentó del 17.4% en 1992 21.1% en 1998, pero sufrió una caída del 32% en 1999-2001, y sólo alcanzó 15.6% en 2001. Un factor que explica el descenso después de 1998 fue el alto nivel de las tasas de interés real activas que estuvieron asociadas al elevado y creciente riesgo país, el cual se incrementó paulatinamente por el mayor déficit fiscal y el resultante mayor nivel de endeudamiento externo respecto al PIB. El diferencial de la tasa de interés de Argentina que llegó a ser menor 446 puntos que el índice de los países emergentes, se fue reduciendo y se revirtió hasta superar dicho índice 3,586 puntos a finales del 2001 (ver Cuadro 1).

Los depósitos del sistema bancario, salvo en 1995, crecieron sostenidamente hasta 2000. Sin embargo, las variables monetarias y crediticias del sistema bancario se deterioraron drásticamente en 2001. El total de depósitos del sistema financiero (M3) se redujo US$21.9 mil millones en 2001, aproximadamente 23%, mientras las reservas internacionales se contra-

---

3. Carmelo Mesa-Lago ha analizado este tema con detenimiento en diversas ocasiones.

jeron US$12 mil millones. El sistema bancario sufrió pérdidas continuas y crecientes a partir de 1998 debido al aumento de cartera de préstamos atrasados determinado por la recesión. Los préstamos atrasados como porcentaje del total de préstamos aumentaron del 6.0% en 1998 al 10.2% en 2001. La tasa de retorno sobre el capital de los bancos comerciales fue de –2.2%, –6.7% y –9.4% en 1998, 1999 y 2000, respectivamente.

Los activos de los bancos extranjeros pasaron del 15% del total de activos de los bancos comerciales en 1994 al 73% en 2000. La creciente participación de la banca extranjera influyó en que la pequeña y mediana empresa perdieran acceso a la banca comercial. Este es un fenómeno similar al experimentado en varios países de Europa central con la creciente participación de la banca extranjera.

La tasa de desempleo urbana aumentó continuamente hasta alcanzar al 17.5% en 1995, luego descendió levemente con la expansión del trienio 1996-1998, pero creció nuevamente con la recesión del trienio 1999-2001. La mayoría de los analistas atribuye el aumento del desempleo en los noventa al anquilosado mercado laboral y al aumento de la participación laboral. Mientras el costo del capital disminuyó por la apertura externa rápida, los costos indirectos de la mano de obra se mantuvieron elevados. Por ejemplo, hay tributación para desempleo e indemnización por despidos; es difícil despedir a los empleados; el periodo de prueba para los nuevos empleados es muy corto; la legislación sobre trabajadores temporales y a tiempo parcial es confusa con lo cual se utilizan pocos trabajadores temporales y a tiempo parcial *de jure*; las convenciones colectivas de trabajo son sectoriales y los contratos de trabajo no caducan hasta que se negocia otro nuevo. Por ello, se desarrolló un mercado laboral informal donde se empleaban trabajadores temporales y a tiempo parcial *de facto*. En resumen, la legislación y prácticas laborales vigentes protegen mucho al trabajador empleado, pero dificultan y hacen muy costosa la contratación de nuevos empleados. Se estima que los costos laborales no salariales de Argentina son un 50% de los costos salariales, mientras que son un 33% en los países desarrollados.

La tasa de productividad laboral aumentó rápidamente en 1990-1995 con muchas reestructuraciones, pero después se estancó. Los salarios privados se mantuvieron más o menos constantes en 1996-2001 (ver Cuadro 1).

En 1999 el presidente De la Rúa llegó al poder después de una campaña electoral basada en atender a "los heridos del modelo," acabar con la corrupción, e impulsar un programa alternativo para reactivar la economía y pulverizar el desempleo. Sin embargo, en enero del 2000, las autoridades aumentaron significativamente los impuestos (el "impuestazo") a fin de enfrentar cuatro problemas básicos: eliminar el déficit fiscal; detener la contracción de la actividad económica y el empleo; paralizar la reducción de los depósitos en los bancos y la pérdida de reservas. Es decir, se inició una consolidación fiscal expansionaria que es muy difícil lograr, especialmente cuando se basa en el aumento de los impuestos en vez de la reducción del gasto fiscal, y que ha sido exitosa en muy pocos países en los noventa, Dinamarca e Irlanda.

Como preludio de la crónica de una muerte anunciada, en 2001 el gobierno aplicó nuevos impuestos en abril en un intento de cumplir con el nuevo acuerdo con el FMI, entre ellos, el impuesto a los movimientos financieros ("el impuesto al cheque"). Asimismo, emitió señales inconsistentes con el régimen cambiario vigente al enviar una nueva ley cambiaria al Congreso ("Ley de Convertibilidad Ampliada") el 17 de abril, que fue aprobada el 25 de junio, para modificar la igualdad del peso con el dólar por una igualdad del peso con una canasta consistente en 50% por el dólar y 50% por el euro; sustituyó al independiente presidente del banco central el 25 de abril; y otorgó un trato preferencial a las exportaciones a la vez que impuso aranceles "temporales" a las importaciones el 15 de junio de 2001, bajo el llamado "factor de convergencia" para acercarse al valor de la nueva paridad cambiaria, lo que equivalió a una devaluación fiscal de aproximadamente el 8%.

Posteriormente, pasó una ley de déficit cero para el gobierno central el 30 de julio que incluyó una reducción del 13% de las pensiones del seguro social y de los salarios de los empleados públicos superiores a US$500 mensuales, y limitó las extracciones de los depósitos de ahorros a US$250 semanales ("el corralito") y las transferencias al exterior el 1 de diciembre. Se estima que los bancos comerciales extranjeros extrajeron fuertes cantidades de dólares antes que el FMI anunciara el 5 de diciembre del 2001 que no desembolsaría el tramo por US$1.3 mil millones que estaba pendiente.

El 23 de diciembre de 2001, la cesación de pagos de la deuda, excepto con las instituciones financieras multilaterales de desarrollo, la mayor en la historia mundial, se agregó a la doble inconvertibilidad de la moneda y al congelamiento de los depósitos bancarios. El 9 de enero de 2002, la devaluación del peso, el establecimiento del control de cambios y la imposición de una "pesificación asimétrica"[4] terminó por quebrar la estructura contractual (dolarizada) e institucional vigente, generando significativas transferencias de riqueza de acreedores y ahorristas a deudores, cuantiosas pérdidas patrimoniales de los bancos comerciales, y una enorme incertidumbre y desconfianza sobre el derecho de propiedad y el cumplimiento de las reglas de juego futuras.

Después de la ley de déficit cero, en un país que es federal, los gobiernos provinciales comenzaron a emitir cuasi-dineros para cumplir con sus obligaciones ordinarias (por ejemplo, las llamadas letras de cancelación de obligaciones provinciales, LECOPS), los cuales pasaron de AR$2.1 mil millones en diciembre del 2001 a AR$5.2 mil millones en marzo del 2002. También existen los patacones, los porteños, entre otros cuasi-dineros.

Los costos de salida de la caja de convertibilidad eran explícitamente elevados, lo cual en la visión de sus defensores era su principal virtud. Las autoridades se aferraron al régimen, con el apoyo de las instituciones multilaterales de desarrollo, pero éste colapsó caóticamente, por el retiro masivo de depósitos del sistema financiero y trastornó el sistema de pagos del país. Argentina pasó de ser el paradigma del libre mercado a un sistema ultra regulado en el que casi toda operación comercial está controlada o directamente prohi-

bida. El "corralito" reflejó lo insostenible de la convertibilidad y su imposición le puso fin. La salida de la caja de convertibilidad fue desordenada. Las políticas económicas del gobierno del presidente Duhalde profundizaron la caída que se venía dando y generaron nuevos problemas.

CONSECUENCIAS DE LA CRISIS

Argentina tuvo cinco presidentes entre diciembre de 2001 y enero del 2002 y posteriormente tuvo que adelantar las elecciones presidenciales previstas para octubre de 2003 a marzo de 2003. El país enfrenta una crisis económica, financiera, política y social de grandes proporciones, ya que requiere revertir problemas fundamentales, que están sujetos a incertidumbres, riesgos e histéresis. Tales como restablecer el crédito externo, así como la confianza de la población en el sistema bancario y financiero y en el sistema de seguridad social. Hay que renegociar el nivel y las condiciones de la elevada deuda externa, la descongelación de las cuentas bancarias, la recapitalización de los bancos quebrados, hay cuasi-dineros en circulación, salarios y pensiones no pagados, y un muy elevado nivel de desempleo. Hay altos niveles de pobreza en un país rico en recursos naturales y capital humano y con una elevada capacidad de producción inutilizada. Muchos jóvenes y profesionales están emigrando. La recuperación será ardua y demorada.

La intensificación de la contracción de la actividad económica y del empleo se vio agudizada durante el segundo semestre de 2001 y particularmente en diciembre por la paralización del sistema de pagos y la imposición de controles administrativos generalizados. Sin un cambio significativo de política económica es difícil remover los controles bancarios y cambiarios establecidos para reprimir desequilibrios fundamentales. Si bien, la flotación del peso debería restablecer la competitividad externa de los bienes transables alentando la recuperación de la economía, la expansión de los bienes transables toma tiempo y requiere financiamiento de capital de trabajo y de inversiones que el sistema bancario-crediticio en crisis

---

4. Los depósitos en dólares se pesificaron a US$1=AR$1.4 y los préstamos bancarios en dólares se pesificaron US$1=AR$1. Con este medida el patrimonio de los bancos comerciales cayó en aproximadamente US$17.5 mil millones.

no es capaz de aportar y que muchos empresarios no están dispuestos a efectuar, al menos de momento. Como consecuencia de la pesificación asimétrica los exportadores ya no cuentan con líneas de prefinanciación ni internas ni externas; tampoco cuentan con ningún otro tipo de crédito que les permita financiar una readecuación de sus plantas. Por ello, el proceso de recuperación tomará tiempo al igual que en la crisis asiática, aunque las condiciones actuales de Argentina son más difíciles que las de esos países al inicio de sus crisis, ya que ninguno de ellos suspendió el pago de la deuda externa.

A los países asiáticos (Corea del Sur, Filipinas, Indonesia, Malasia y Tailandia) les tomó un promedio de tres años volver a la situación inicial después de su crisis: Hubo dos años de recesión y uno de recuperación. Ulteriormente, la recuperación ha continuado a pesar del lento crecimiento de la economía mundial. Las recuperaciones de Indonesia y Tailandia, que tenían condiciones iniciales más arduas, tomaron unos cinco años.

En Argentina muchas de las empresas de servicios públicos se privatizaron o se otorgaron en concesiones mediante el mecanismo de financiación de proyectos.[5] Esto hace que muchas de ellas estén quebradas *de facto*, ya que sus ingresos ahora son en pesos, en vez de dólares como eran antes de fines del 2001, pero sus obligaciones financieras son en dólares, algunas de ellas en bonos colocados en los mercados internacionales. Muchas de esas empresas posiblemente vuelvan a ser estatizadas, independientemente que las tarifas de los servicios públicos se ajusten.

La crisis es de tal magnitud que Caballero y Dornbusch (2002a y 2002b) propusieron, con base en la experiencia austríaca después de la I Guerra Mundial, que se establezcan administraciones de interventores externos en las áreas fiscal, monetaria y de regulación bancaria, basadas en reglas aceptadas por las autoridades argentinas, para restablecer la credibilidad y permitir que la economía funcione apropiadamente. Estas medidas deberían ser complementadas por otras destinadas a combatir la corrupción y proteger los derechos de propiedad.

En las condiciones actuales de Argentina, el manejo económico hacia el cual debe propenderse es claro, pero requiere de importantes acuerdos políticos: La regularización del sistema de pagos y de los sistemas bancario y financiero, eliminando los cuasi–dineros de circulación; unas finanzas públicas ordenadas que incluyan, entre otros aspectos, un balance cercano al equilibrio, un nuevo acuerdo entre el gobierno central y las provincias para atender los gastos sociales y un mejor sistema de administración tributaria; un sistema ordenado de flotación cambiaria que mantenga la competitividad externa; una flexibilización del mercado de trabajo; una regla estable para la fijación de la política monetaria, que garantice bajos niveles de inflación y eventualmente de desempleo; una renegociación de la deuda externa y restablecer la estructura contractual e institucional que se quebró.

En estos momentos estamos pendientes de conocer si Argentina finalmente, como Chile y México lo hicieron antes, podrá manejar los efectos de la flotación sin destruir lo positivo del pasado, tornándose más competitiva y dinámica. Hasta ahora no se le ve por buen camino. Sorprende la obsesión por más préstamos de los organismos multilaterales de desarrollo mientras hacen lo imposible por aterrar a los inversionistas privados. La incapacidad para abordar una solución al problema del sistema financiero y la ruptura de todos los contratos, por leyes y más leyes, es un mal presagio. Su destino alternativo es entrar en una inercia de crecimiento bajo su potencial, acentuada por debilidades institucionales crónicas, como ha sido el caso de Venezuela después de la crisis financiera de los noventa.

---

5. O sea una empresa se constituye con un capital social de aproximadamente un 30% de los activos y una deuda del 70% de los activos para adquirir los activos o disfrutar de la corriente de ingresos que se deriva de la actividad privatizada o concesionada por un periodo relativamente largo de años.

If, a decade ago, Argentina had known what it knows now, would it have chosen a currency board? Probably not.

— Economic focus Dollar mad?, *The Economist*, October 27, 2001, p. 72.

CAUSAS DE LA CRISIS

Algunos economistas atribuyen la crisis a la rigidez del sistema monetario-cambiario (Blanchard, 2001; Krugman, 2001; Larrain y Velasco, 2001; Rodrik, 2002; Weisbrot y Barker, 2002a). Otros a la incapacidad de ordenar las cuentas fiscales (Mussa, 2002);[6] otros a algunos errores básicos de política económica, particularmente en 2000 y 2001, tanto nacionales como de los organismos financieros internacionales o de ambos (Calvo et al, 2002; Hanke, 2002; Sachs, 2002; y Stiglitz, 2002). Otros a las reformas de mercado realizadas (Campodonico, 2002; Weisbrot y Barker, 2002a); otros a la forma como las reformas de mercado se realizaron, especialmente la privatización, la desregulación, el descuido por la pequeña y mediana empresa y por la sociedad civil (Campodonico, 2002; Eiras y Shaefer, 2002; Barker y Weisbrot, 2002, Zamagni, 2002); otros a la debilidad de las instituciones fundamentales, que se traduce en un elevado grado de corrupción y clientelismo (Eiras y Shaefer, 2002). Otros a una serie de "shocks" externos simultáneos, o sea, a algo así como mala suerte (Birdsall, 2002). Estas diferentes opiniones han hecho difícil la aceptación general de soluciones a la crisis, ya que es muy diferente si la crisis se debió a malas políticas, malas instituciones o mala suerte.

A continuación se analizan las causas principales de la crisis, distinguiendo entre los factores directos determinantes de ella de otros factores importantes que han influido en un menor crecimiento de la economía, pero que no contribuyeron directamente a desatar la crisis.

La recaída de la economía en 1995, vinculada al llamado "efecto tequila," mostró la vulnerabilidad estructural, o la insuficiencia de grados de libertad de la caja de convertibilidad ante "shocks externos" (apreciación del dólar, depreciaciones cambiarias de sus socios comerciales y la política monetaria restrictiva en los E.U.A.), dada la rigidez de los precios y salarios, así como del régimen laboral. Los depósitos de los bancos comerciales se redujeron 20%, se detuvo la entrada neta de capitales y el PIB cayó 2.8%. No obstante, las preocupaciones sobre el sistema cambiario se disiparon cuando Argentina adoptó medidas para fortalecer y mejorar la situación de los bancos comerciales en particular y del sector financiero en general, aunque no del sector fiscal, y cuando la economía enfrentó un entorno externo más favorable. Parte del fortalecimiento y consolidación del sector bancario se debió a los mayores requerimientos de liquidez y a la mayor participación de la banca extranjera, lo que se percibió como que ésta podría actuar de prestamista de última instancia ante nuevos shocks externos.

La economía creció nuevamente en 1996-1998. Sin embargo, en 1999-2001 se vio afectada significativamente como consecuencia de los efectos de las crisis asiática y rusa, la depreciación del real brasileño en un 50% (Brasil era entonces el principal socio comercial), la fuerte depreciación de las monedas asiáticas, la apreciación del dólar y la política monetaria restrictiva de los E.U.A.

Argentina no comparte un área de moneda óptima con los E.U.A., ya que posee un comercio limitado, no tiene completa movilidad de factores y está sujeta a diferentes shocks. Adicionalmente, tiene su comercio exterior mayoritario con países (Brasil, otros miembros del Mercosur y Europa) cuyas monedas fluctúan con respecto al dólar. Argentina es una economía relativamente cerrada con un importante sector de no transables; por lo tanto, puede beneficiarse sustancialmente de variaciones en su tasa de cambio

---

6. La representante del Banco Mundial en Argentina, Myrna Alexander, tiene una opinión similar. Ella señaló en una entrevista: "hay que preguntarle al ex ministro de Economía Roque Fernández y al Fondo Monetario Internacional por qué se financió el aumento del gasto público en el país. Ahora sabemos que hubo falta de control político de los gastos del Estado"…"El mejor momento para salir de la convertibilidad era 1997, después de un año de crecimiento y luego de superar muy bien la crisis del efecto tequila, pero lamentablemente en ese momento, nadie habló de ello." *La Nación*, 23 de julio del 2002.

externa nominal para ajustar la relación entre los bienes transables y los bienes no transables.

La caja de convertibilidad tuvo efectos directos negativos sobre el sector real y efectos directos positivos sobre el sector financiero. Los efectos directos negativos provinieron de una tasa de cambio sobrevaluada y una tasa de interés mayor[7] que determinaron un menor crecimiento del PIB debido a la menor competitividad de los bienes transables y a la menor inversión. Los efectos directos positivos provinieron de la mayor confianza en el sistema monetario y financiero y en la estabilidad de precios, particularmente después de los periodos hiperinflacionarios de 1989 y 1990, lo que permitió la remonetización. La convertibilidad ganó credibilidad con relación a la permanencia de la paridad cambiaria.

La pérdida de competitividad cambiaria debió ser compensada por la disminución, o corrección a la baja, de los precios y salarios,[8] pero éstos se mantuvieron más o menos constantes, impidiendo el ajuste requerido o haciéndolo lento y determinando la recesión (ver Cuadro 1). También las normas rígidas del régimen laboral impidieron el ajuste de las empresas.

La explicación anterior de la crisis descansa en los desequilibrios causados por la rigidez del régimen cambiario (caja de convertibilidad)[9] y la de los precios, salarios y del régimen laboral, pero dependió también de otro factor simultáneo importante: los desequilibrios causados el creciente déficit fiscal.

En la primera mitad de la década y a pesar del elevado crecimiento, los ingresos extraordinarios de las privatizaciones y concesiones ocultaron déficits fiscales endémicos. En la segunda mitad de la década, los déficits fiscales fueron financiados con mayor endeudamiento, tanto interno como externo (ver Cuadro 1), a medida que los ingresos extraordinarios desaparecieron y que fue necesario además enfrentar la pérdida de ingresos fiscales por la privatización del seguro social y la descentralización administrativa. Las privatizaciones y concesiones de las empresas públicas brindaron US$49 mil millones al Gobierno entre 1991-1999. El proceso de descentralización de los gastos sociales (educación, salud, saneamiento, agua potable, etc.) a las provincias en país federal fue patético, ya que se le traspasaron las obligaciones de los gastos a las provincias sin darle suficientes ingresos, lo cual desató un proceso permanente de negociaciones para financiar esos gastos que culminó en "presupuestos blandos" y la emisión de cuasi-dineros a partir del déficit cero de 2001.

El creciente déficit fiscal determinó una perversa trampa dinámica de endeudamiento y de especulación contra la caja de convertibilidad, que se vio agudizada en el contexto del empeoramiento del mercado financiero internacional para los países emergentes y cuando la tasa de interés de EUA subió a partir de 1999. Así, el déficit fiscal se expandió por los requerimientos de la mayor deuda externa en relación con el PIB, y por las mayores tasas de interés asociadas al creciente riesgo país y al nivel de las tasas internacionales. A la vez la mayor tasa de interés deprimió la tasa de inversión.

Si bien los niveles del déficit fiscal y del endeudamiento externo en relación con el PIB en 2001 no eran tan elevados en términos internacionales (Calvo e Izquierdo, 2002 y Weisbrot y Barker, 2002a), sí tenían tendencias claramente expansivas, habiendo aumentado el déficit fiscal del 0.1% en 1992 al 3.5% en

---

7. El promedio de la prima de riesgo país fue de 600 puntos básicos en el quinquenio 1996-2000. La tasa de interés promedia de los bonos de E.U.A. a diez años del período fue aproximadamente 5%. Por lo tanto, la tasa de interés de los bonos argentinos, determinante principal de la tasa de interés en el país, resultó del 11%.

8. Los beneficios del patrón oro en el siglo XIX y principios del siglo XX (1815-1914) se exageran. Se le atribuye el crecimiento mundial y no se tiene en cuenta que dicho periodo se caracterizó por grandes innovaciones técnicas, el crecimiento del comercio internacional, por las revoluciones del transporte y las comunicaciones, la paz mundial y la libre movilidad de las personas. La época del patrón oro mostró que la flexibilidad de una economía endeudada internacionalmente es limitada aún con precios y salarios flexibles, ya que las deudas no son flexibles y su peso relativo se eleva rápidamente cuando hay deflación. Además, la deflación es un proceso muy difícil, especialmente cuando hay un elevado desempleo inicial y los precios y salarios se ajustan lentamente.

9. Algunos autores han denominado a las cajas de convertibilidad como píldoras de envenenamiento.

2001 y el endeudamiento público externo del 31.8% en 1992 al 57.7% en 2001, respectivamente (ver Cuadro 1). En 1994 un empleado público ganaba un 16% más que un empleado privado, en 2000 ganaba un 21% más (ver Cuadro 1). Sus dinámicas expansivas si eran incompatibles con el régimen cambiario vigente y la solvencia del sistema bancario y financiero que clasificaba "sin riesgos" los bonos públicos. Varios economistas (entre ellos Krueger, 2002 y Rogoff, 2002) han señalado que Argentina debió acumular superávits en su periodo de expansión para seguir políticas compensatorias en su periodo de contracción.

En el contexto anterior (tasa de cambio sobrevaluada, deuda y déficit fiscales crecientes) ocurrieron algunos errores de política económica significativos en 2000 y 2001. El régimen de convertibilidad estaba concebido precisamente para restringir los grados de libertad de la política económica. Con esto, cada medida heterodoxa tuvo dos efectos: uno de poder reactivador y otro de menor credibilidad al "ablandar" las estrictas reglas vigentes.

El acuerdo de rescate por US$40 mil millones con el FMI [10] y los otros organismos financieros internacionales (Banco Mundial y BID) en diciembre del 2000 para mantener la caja de convertibilidad y evitar la crisis, el llamado blindaje financiero, descansó en el aumento de los impuestos y la reducción del gasto público en un momento de recesión interna. En agosto del 2001 hubo otro paquete financiero del FMI por US$8 mil millones. Dicha política fiscal implicó un circulo vicioso no sólo de corto plazo al profundizar la recesión y el déficit fiscal por la menor actividad económica que determinó cuando se requería reactivar la demanda agregada, sino que también tuvo connotaciones negativas sobre la oferta agregada y sobre el crecimiento económico a mediano y largo plazo al desalentar la inversión, debido al elevado nivel de impuestos ya existente. Además, el blindaje hizo endeudarse aún más al país para mantener una tasa de cambio que el mercado consideraba baja y allanó la fuga de capitales.

La renuncia al uso de una política monetaria activa y la independencia del banco central habían desempeñado un papel central en la credibilidad en la caja de convertibilidad y en la eliminación de la hiperinflación a partir de 1991. Sin embargo, en 2001 las autoridades cometieron el error de seguir una política monetaria expansiva al modificar las normas sobre las reservas bancarias, después que despidieron a Pedro Pou, el independiente presidente del banco central, quien la había mantenido neutral. Ello acentuó la reducción de los depósitos y precipitó la fuga de capitales.

El "megacanje" de la deuda externa que el ministro Cavallo realizó para modificar el perfil de vencimiento de la deuda en julio del 2001, tuvo un efecto negativo al aumentar la tasa de interés y afectar el sistema financiero (los bancos y los fondos de pensiones). No es apropiado efectuar esos canjes en medio de una crisis especulativa; Argentina había perdido reservas internacionales por 40% en enero-julio y 25% sólo en julio del 2001, respectivamente.

Argentina fue el país que más avanzó a escala mundial en el proceso de privatización y en otorgar en concesiones empresas públicas y de servicios público en la década de los noventa. Sin embargo, algunas privatizaciones y concesiones dejaron bastante que desear, en especial las de telecomunicaciones. Básicamente transformaron monopolios públicos en monopolios privados al no disponerse del marco regulador y supervisor apropiado, con lo cual la economía no se benefició de la mayor flexibilidad y competitividad que esta significativa transformación le debía otorgar. Por el contrario, ciertas tarifas de servicios públicos básicos aumentaron sin mejorar la calidad de los servicios prestados y/o debían ajustarse periódicamente mediante indexaciones, haciendo la economía menos competitiva internacionalmente.

Campodonico (2002) considera que las reformas de mercado realizadas determinaron la vulnerabilidad externa de la economía y definieron la crisis. Destaca primordialmente la rápida apertura de la economía al comercio externo y a los movimientos de capital. La

---

10. Un programa de rescate de US$50 mil millones había sacado a México de la crisis de 1995.

rápida apertura al comercio hizo quebrar a muchas empresas manufactureras que no pudieron ajustarse de inmediato en un momento que se carecía de crédito para la pequeña y mediana empresa. Los movimientos de capital netos a Argentina, que incluyeron inversiones directas e inversiones de cartera de gran escala, cesaron prácticamente en 1999 después de los efectos de las crisis asiática y rusa. Fueron US$53 mil millones en 1991 a 1999, US$1.8 mil millones en 2000 y -US$13 mil millones en 2001. Calvo (2002) destaca el llamado riesgo de la globalización ("globalization hazard") a las fuertes fluctuaciones y los "sudden stops" experimentados por los movimientos de capital a América latina. Varios economistas han expresado sus criticas a la apertura a los movimientos de capital de corto plazo, o al menos a la apertura "prematura" a los mismos, o sea antes que la estabilización se consolide.[11]

Zamagni (2002) señala que las reformas descuidaron las pequeñas y medianas empresas (PYMES) que tienen un papel fundamental para el desarrollo nacional directamente como la estructura permanente de la economía y fuente de empleo y producción, así como la sociedad civil organizada que desempeña una tarea esencial en el desarrollo institucional y de la gobernabilidad presionado a los partidos políticos y al gobierno. Para mantener PYMES pujantes se necesita una política industrial que las fomente y aliente, especialmente en lo referente a actualización tecnológica, innovación y competitividad; la gran empresa transnacional suele emigrar cuando las condiciones internas no son las apropiadas, "No se puede concebir un de-

sarrollo permanente cuando los empresarios no son responsables del país donde viven." La sociedad civil debe participar activamente en la construcción del proyecto de sociedad para darle estabilidad y contrabalancear el poder político, especialmente cuando los partidos políticos tradicionales están en crisis, y hay una gran ineficiencia en la prestación de los servicios sociales públicos.[12]

Entre otros factores que se han señalado como determinantes de la crisis y que han contribuido a un menor crecimiento, está la corrupción existente que impide el funcionamiento de un sistema legal efectivo y una adecuada protección del derecho de propiedad y aumenta los costos de transacción, así como el clientelismo político que determina una baja efectividad del gasto público, que le resta competitividad y flexibilidad a la economía. Los abundantes trámites administrativos dificultan la entrada a nuevas actividades y facilitan la corrupción. Argentina ocupa la posición 50 de 75 países en cuanto al número de trámites (12) y al tiempo requerido para establecer un negocio, 71 días (Djankov et al, 2000, Cuadro III).

Según Transparencia Internacional (2001), Argentina mostró un índice de percepción de corrupción de 3.5 en 2001, ocupando la posición 72 entre 124 países y la posición 11 entre 18 países regionales. Si bien el país tiene que avanzar mucho en esta área fundamental, es difícil atribuir su crisis a la corrupción. Otros países que tienen un mayor grado de corrupción no han atravesado una crisis de la magnitud argentina, aunque sin duda éste un factor agravante de

---

11. La importancia de este tema, así como otros muchos sobre intensidad y secuencia de las reformas, buscando crear momentum y efectividad, había sido destacada por McKinnon (1991), pero no recibió la debida atención. La rápida reversión y volatilidad de los flujos de capital de corto plazo llevó a prominentes economistas a cuestionar los beneficios netos de la apertura de la cuenta de capital de corto plazo (Bhagwati, 1998a, 1998b; Krugman, 1998, 1999; Stiglitz, 1998). Krugman recomendó a Malasia establecer controles de cambios en medio de la crisis asiática. Actualmente, hay consenso, incluyendo al FMI, en cuanto a que la liberación de los movimientos de capital de corto plazo en presencia de una tasa de cambio fija y de sistemas bancarios y financieros débiles, conduce a crisis cambiarias y financieras. "The IMF and the U.S. Treasury did not encourage countries to liberalize short-term flows through the banking sector, which is what turned out to be the Achilles Heel during the Asian crisis. And many countries liberalize for their own reasons rather than as a consequence of external prodding-Thailand for instance was keen to have Bangkok emerge as international financial sector like Singapore. Nevertheless, as a result of the criticism by Stiglitz and others, the IMF is more vocal in pointing out the risks of rapid capital account liberalization. While such cautionary notes have always been present in IMF advice on capital account liberalization, today they are much more likely to be given greater prominence." Thomas C. Dawson, Director, External Relations Department, IMF, *A Speech to the MIT Club of Washington*, de 13 de junio del 2002.

12. Stefano Zamagni, Entrevista a *La Nación*, 4 de agosto del 2002.

sus problemas y determinante de un menor crecimiento económico a largo plazo.[13]

El factor mala suerte, o sea el entorno internacional y los shocks externos adversos en 1999-2001, sin duda también contribuyeron a desatar la crisis. Sin embargo, otros países latinoamericanos se vieron afectados adversamente por los mismos factores y pudieron superarlos sin crisis similares. Por ello, no se debe considerar el factor mala suerte, como lo hace Birdsall (2002, p.4), como un factor principal determinante de la crisis. Como Carlos Díaz-Alejandro señalaba las interacciones no lineales entre políticas nacionales arriesgadas y deficientes y shocks externos extraordinarios y persistentes conduce a severas crisis, tanto en su alcance como en su duración, que ni las políticas erróneas ni los shocks podrían generar en forma aislada.

En resumen, la crisis económica y financiera fue causada por errores de diseño de las políticas económicas de estabilización, crecimiento y cambios institucionales, que se vieron reforzados por la mala conducción de la política económica en 2000 y 2001, desatando la crisis y creando problemas innecesarios para la recuperación. Entre los errores de diseño y ejecución se destacan la inconsistente y funesta combinación de caja de convertibilidad, con déficits fiscales y deuda externa crecientes, en el contexto de precios, salarios y mercado laboral inflexibles que contribuyeron a una tasa de cambio apreciada y tasas de interés muy elevadas para alentar la competitividad externa y la inversión. También contribuyeron, entre otros factores, la forma en que se realizaron las privatizaciones y las concesiones, la descentralización administrativa, el descuido de las PYMES y la escasa participación de la sociedad civil en las reformas realizadas, así como la corrupción y clientelismo existentes.

A menudo una reforma mal hecha es todavía más perjudicial que la falta de reformas.

— Mario Vargas Llosa, "Queremos ser Pobres," *Diario Las Américas*, 7 de julio del 2002, p. 4-A.

LECCIONES DE LA EXPERIENCIA DE REFORMAS Y CRISIS ARGENTINA PARA PAÍSES COMO CUBA CON ECONOMÍAS RELATIVAMENTE CERRADAS, DÉFICITS FISCALES CRÓNICOS, TASA DE CAMBIO FIJA, ALTAMENTE ENDEUDADOS E INSTITUCIONES DÉBILES

Argentina eligió diversas iniciativas de economía política en 1990-2001. Se cuenta con experiencias positivas y negativas de estabilización, reformas estructurales y cambios institucionales, que deben ser analizadas en detalle. A continuación se señalan algunas de las principales que no son todas las que merecen destacarse, pero seguramente se encuentran entre las que no hay que olvidar:

- En general Argentina no puso suficiente énfasis en la consistencia general, la dinámica y la sostenibilidad de las reformas en el tiempo, y puso más énfasis en mantener la convertibilidad (instrumento) que en lograr el crecimiento sostenido (objetivo). La consistencia general, la dinámica y la sostenibilidad de las políticas macroeconómicas aplicadas son esenciales.[14] La inconsistencia e insostenibilidad de las políticas del dólar fijo, precios y salarios nominales relativamente rígidos, crecientes déficits fiscales y endeudamiento externo, contrastan con la armonía de los cuatro pilares macroeconómicos de países como Chile: Tipo de cambio flotante, superávit fiscal estructural, metas de inflación y endeudamiento externo bajos. Es necesario establecer esta combinación virtuosa, en particular una tasa de cambio

---

13. En la región Chile tiene un índice de 7.5, seguido por Trinidad y Tobago 5.3, Uruguay 5.1, Costa Rica 4.5, Perú 4.1, Brasil 4.0, Colombia 3.8, México 3.7, Panamá 3.7, El Salvador 3.6 y Argentina 3.5. Después le siguen República Dominicana 3.1, Guatemala 2.9, Venezuela 2.8, Honduras 2.7, Nicaragua 2.4, Ecuador 2.3 y Bolivia 2.0 (www.transparency.org/cpi/2001).

14. En un estudio realizado para Chile, Gallego y Loayza (2002) encontraron que una variable auxiliar llamada "complementariedad de políticas" explica casi un tercio del aumento del crecimiento de la economía chilena en 1986-1998 en relación con 1971-1985. Gallego y Loayza, consideran que esta variable refleja la interacción positiva o sinergia entre los factores que promueven el crecimiento y su alto valor revela que existe un premio considerable a realizar en forma conjunta y coherente reformas y liberalización de mercados, más allá de la suma del sólo efecto positivo independiente de cada política en particular. Tal especie de respaldo virtuoso se aprecia también en otros países con elevado crecimiento en los últimos años, como Corea del Sur, Holanda, Irlanda y Tailandia.

real competitiva y el manejo presupuestario disciplinado, pilares de la competitividad externa y de la estabilización económica para flexibilizar la economía y reducir la vulnerabilidad externa.

- La secuencia y la asimetría con que Argentina aplicó las reformas tuvieron consecuencias significativas. Debió haber un mayor énfasis o priorización inicial en lograr y consolidar la estabilización—que es una condición necesaria para el apropiado funcionamiento del sistema económico—con medidas para eliminar el déficit fiscal y los presupuestos "blandos" de las provincias. En este sentido, la privatización de la seguridad social y la descentralización administrativa fueron prematuras y contribuyeron a aumentar el déficit fiscal. Posteriormente en 2001, se utilizaron medidas tardías, muy drásticas y traumáticas, para reducir el déficit fiscal y lograr la estabilización, las cuales acentuaron las incertidumbres, la contracción de la producción, el descontento social y desataron la crisis. Es muy difícil realizar consolidaciones fiscales expansionarias, o sea reducir el gasto y aumentar los impuestos cuando hay recesión. Desde el inicio de las reformas, es imprescindible lograr y mantener no sólo una inflación baja sino un equilibrio creíble en las cuentas fiscales mediante una combinación apropiada de políticas fiscal, tasa de cambio y endeudamiento externo (McKinnon, 1991 y Sachs, 1996).

- Es fundamental preservar la flexibilidad de los precios y los salarios relativos internacionalmente,[15] para mantener la competitividad externa vía la tasa de cambio externa, cuando los precios y los salarios nominales no se ajustan automática y

rápidamente hacia la baja, de modo de brindar prioridad al crecimiento económico orientado al exterior y reducir el grado de vulnerabilidad externa. Si se analizan las experiencias de Chile, México y Brasil,[16] el resultado final de una tasa de cambio flexible ha sido positivo, a pesar de lo difícil y complejo que fue devaluar o depreciar a mitad del proceso de reformas. La clave consistió en entender que si bien era necesario cambiar la estrategia hacia una de dólar flexible con mayores o menores intervenciones del banco central, los elementos esenciales de una economía competitiva y moderna, como son la apertura al comercio externo, un mercado financiero operativo y el respeto a los contratos, no sólo se mantendrían, sino que se reforzarían y consolidarían.

- La solución para impedir emisiones monetarias inflacionarias no es mantener la paridad cambiaria fija en un contexto de precios, salarios nominales y mercado de trabajo relativamente rígidos, lo que constituye un callejón sin salida, sino tener una política monetaria con metas de inflación y de tasa de desempleo determinadas por un banco central independiente que no preste al gobierno central, ajustando la tasa de interés cuando la inflación supere las metas establecidas.[17] La caja de convertibilidad de Argentina y los bajos niveles de inflación no impidieron déficits fiscales, ni una deuda pública creciente, ni una tasa de cambio apreciada, es decir, expusieron las limitaciones de una estabilización basada en una tasa de cambio fija.[18]

- Hay que promover permanentemente un desarrollo competitivo y eficiente del sector bancario y financiero en términos de liquidez, solvencia,

---

15. Tal como Friedman (1968) señaló, es mucho más fácil ajustar la tasa de cambio ante shocks externos que modificar miles de precios y salarios (contratos laborales), particularmente si éstos tienen inflexibilidades nominales.

16. Brasil tenía una tasa de cambio fija del real con el dólar, pero no las ataduras constitucionales de Argentina.

17. Los países que utilizan metas de inflación han sido en general exitosos en lograrlas a menores costos en términos de niveles de producción, por ello este régimen de política monetaria se considera muy exitoso. Actualmente lo utilizan, entre otros, Brasil, Colombia, Chile, México y Perú en América latina. Nueva Zelandia, Chile, Canadá e Israel estuvieron entre los países pioneros en utilizarla en 1990-1992. (Mishkin y Schmidt-Hebbel, 2001).

18. Israel y Polonia lograron estabilizaciones exitosas con base en la utilización temporal de la tasa de cambio en la década de los noventa.

calidad de activos, reservas y márgenes de intermediación decrecientes para proteger su solidez y la confianza pública. Y así posibilitar el pleno y oportuno cumplimiento de los contratos y compromisos adquiridos con los depositantes, acreedores internos y externos. La banca extranjera tiene ventajas en términos de eficiencia y de disminuir la vulnerabilidad del sector bancario, pero no impide las crisis financieras, ni suele financiar las PYMES.

- El desarrollo y consolidación de las PYMES es muy importante para el crecimiento económico sostenible y la expansión de una clase media pujante, tal como lo muestran las diferentes experiencias (positivas y negativas) de Argentina, Europa central, los países de la antigua Unión Soviética, China y Vietnam en la década de los noventa. Para ello se necesita una clara política de transformación productiva que facilite el establecimiento, desarrollo y orientación de las PYMES hacia el exterior, por ejemplo, con mecanismos que apoyen las exportaciones en las áreas de información, financiamiento y seguros.

- La privatización y las concesiones de empresas públicas tienen profundas implicaciones sobre la economía y el comportamiento social y político. Si las privatizaciones y las concesiones no se hacen apropiadamente se eliminan muchas de sus ventajas microeconómicas (mejorar la utilización y asignación de los recursos); más aún tienen efectos perversos con condiciones de histéresis o irreversibles, que paralizan el proceso de reformas al establecer dudas sobre la legitimidad del mismo y dar la apariencia que el Estado está dominado o capturado por unos pocos intereses privados. La liberalización de precios a monopolios naturales o a monopolios en mercados imperfectos carentes de una adecuada competitividad sin las correspondientes regulaciones o sin la segmentación de las grandes empresas para crear competencia puede tener el efecto de reducir la producción, contribuir al aumento de precios e ignorar la protección de los consumidores. En Argentina hubo mucho énfasis en la liberalización y desregulación de las empresas públicas privatizadas y concesionadas, pero no en el establecimiento de las regulaciones y supervisión prudenciales para que se desarrollaran mercados competitivos y funcionaran apropiadamente. Además, lamentablemente se las utilizó para financiar el gasto público y postergar la disciplina fiscal.

- La descentralización fiscal tiene significativos alcances sobre la economía y el comportamiento fiscal y político. Si la descentralización no se hace apropiadamente se eliminan muchos de sus beneficios microeconómicos (mejor asignación y control del gasto) y puede tener costos macroeconómicos (aumentar el déficit fiscal), más aún puede haber efectos perversos con condiciones de histéresis, que paralizan el proceso de reformas al determinar presupuestos "blandos". La descentralización fiscal traspasó el problema del déficit del gobierno central a los gobiernos provinciales en un área que el país le otorgaba mucha importancia—como son los gastos sociales en educación, salud, agua potable y saneamiento—sin suficientes mecanismos ni procedimientos adecuados de control del gasto. En Argentina hubo mucho énfasis en la descentralización administrativa, pero no en el establecimiento de los mecanismos para eliminar y controlar efectivamente el déficit fiscal.

- La liberalización financiera "prematura" a los flujos de capital de corto plazo, o sea antes de consolidar la estabilización, creó una serie de inconsistencias, tensiones y dilemas, ya que dichos flujos son procíclicos, e hizo la economía argentina vulnerable a la volatilidad de las crisis financieras externas e internas, tanto en frecuencia como en intensidad. Así, la insuficiente estabilización, junto a una apertura a los movimientos de capitales externos, condujo a una situación de tasa de cambio baja (apreciada) y tasas de interés elevadas con los consecuentes efectos adversos sobre la pérdida de competitividad de los bienes transables, y bajos niveles de inversión y de ahorro.[19] De igual forma alentó a las instituciones financieras a endeudarse en divisas, prestar en moneda nacional y favoreció el consumo de origen importado. Tasas cambiarias mayores y más realistas, así como tasas de interés menores, o sea macroprecios mejor alineados, constituyen un entorno más propicio para el crecimiento y la apertura externa y hubieran tenido efectos positivos sobre los bienes transables, las tasas de ahorro e inversión y el nivel de actividad económica. Antes de la crisis de 2001, dada la tasa de cambio apreciada y las claras perspectivas de un ajuste cambiario, la apertura a los movimientos de corto plazo facilitó la fuga de capitales.

- La apertura al comercio exterior rápida y drástica—eliminando las restricciones cuantitativas y estableciendo tarifas arancelarias bajas y menos diferenciadas—puede ser inadecuada. Especialmente, cuando las empresas tienen escaso tiempo para ajustarse, brindar una respuesta efectiva y realizar una reestructuración apropiada, en particular cuando las PYMES tienen problemas de acceso al crédito, lo que determina que muchas empresas quiebren. Un mecanismo más eficiente y efectivo es reducir los aranceles progresivamente con límites precisos en el tiempo, como lo hizo Chile al final de la década de los setenta.

- Es importante establecer y desarrollar instituciones sólidas que estimulen la oferta agregada para corregir errores, evitar omisiones y reducir los costos de transacción en áreas donde hay significativas externalidades al brindar a los agentes económicos un clima de incentivos más propicio para las nuevas actividades. Tales como: Proporcionar garantías efectivas de que los derechos de propiedad privada y los contratos serán respetados; que la justicia es independiente e igual para todos; que los impuestos no se despilfarran; que

la corrupción es la excepción y no la regla; que un banco central verdaderamente independiente vela por la estabilidad económica, que hay flexibilidad en el mercado de trabajo para la contratación de nuevos empleados (p.e. contratos temporales o empleos de tiempo parcial) y que existe libre entrada y salida efectiva de personas y empresas a las nuevas actividades en término de simplificación de procedimientos administrativos. El papel de la sociedad civil es estratégico en establecer y desarrollar estas instituciones. Si no hay instituciones apropiadas, o sea si no se realizan reformas de segunda generación, se producen crisis de "segunda generación."

- Hay que evitar que los bancos internacionales de desarrollo (el Banco Mundial y el BID) utilicen sus recursos para apoyar programas de estabilización del FMI, mediante préstamos de rápido desembolso, que le corresponden a esa institución. Cuando los préstamos del FMI, aún por encima de las cuotas acostumbradas, no son suficientes, hay problemas fundamentales que requieren ajustes substanciales de inmediato, ya sea en la tasa de cambio o en el nivel y términos de endeudamiento externo.[20]

- Los deficientes desarrollo político y de la gobernabilidad suelen convertirse en severos obstáculos para el progreso económico y social. La economía no es independiente de la política. Es necesario avanzar en las reformas políticas fundamentales consensuadas mediante la sociedad civil para que el desarrollo y las instituciones en este ámbito faciliten *mutatis mutandis* la dinámica y eficiencia del proceso de apertura y competencia económica asociado. En el caso argentino fue notario el sometimiento del poder judicial al poder

---

19. Ello agudizó el efecto Balassa-Samuelson, o sea la tendencia a apreciarse de la moneda nacional debido a la diferencia en los aumentos de productividad de los bienes transables en contraste con los bienes no transables (ECE, 2001, No 1, pp. 227-239). En Argentina la productividad de los bienes transables aumentó al 7% anual en 1990-1998, mientras que la de los bienes no transables sólo aumentó al 2% anual (World Bank, página web, 2000).

20. Es paradójico que las instituciones financieras internacionales reciban el pago completo de la deuda pública externa, mientras los bancos comerciales, los proveedores y otros acreedores externos tengan que aceptar una pérdida en la deuda, cuando fueron esas instituciones las que contribuyeron al endeudamiento externo al mantener una tasa de cambio artificialmente elevada. Aquí se da el problema de riesgo moral ("moral hazard") tan comentado en la literatura económica, o de prestar sin riesgos de pérdidas, lo que alienta los malos préstamos. Además, se establece un clima contrario para la inversión privada en los países emergentes.

ejecutivo, el cambio constitucional para permitir un segundo mandato a Menem, la diferencia entre las promesas electorales y las realidades de gobierno, particularmente en 1999-2001; la ausencia de consenso político para eliminar el déficit fiscal crónico y para flexibilizar el mercado de trabajo; así como las políticas inconsistentes de mantener el gasto público a la vez que los ingresos fiscales se reducían por la privatización del seguro social y la descentralización administrativa. En el gobierno de Duhalde en 2002 se destacan los severos conflictos entre el ejecutivo y el legislativo y entre el ejecutivo y el poder judicial. El proceso de reformas estructurales se realizó sin la participación activa de la sociedad civil y se detuvo a mediados de la década cuando el énfasis del presidente Menem fue lograr un segundo y tercer mandatos, que eran inconstitucionales. Sin embargo, debe señalarse que poco antes de la crisis de 2001, el ejecutivo logró que el legislativo le aprobara poderes especiales y varias medidas de emergencia, el llamado Plan de Competitividad, en un plazo relativamente breve.

• Por último, aunque no menos importante, Argentina muestra los enormes costos sociales y riesgos políticos de la aplicación de políticas económicas que mantienen a amplios sectores de la población pobres y excluidos, o sea con elevado desempleo y subempleo, e insuficiente protección social. Esta situación social adversa puede desatar o exacerbar situaciones de violencia (protestas y desordenes públicos0 ante medidas impopulares, como ocurrió poco antes de la renuncia del ministro Cavallo y el presidente De la Rúa en diciembre del 2001. La ruptura del tejido social tiene efectos económicos adversos. Por ello, es imprescindible brindar significativa atención a los temas de cohesión social, atendiendo a que no halla ciudadanos totalmente desamparados en una sociedad que practicó resultados socioeconómicos mínimos por generaciones. Se requiere un nuevo orden institucional o contrato social más humano y solidario que logre efectos positivos sobre el desarrollo democrático y socioeconómico mediante una activa participación de la sociedad civil en las reformas realizadas.

CUBA: CARACTERÍSTICAS Y EVOLUCIÓN MACROECONÓMICA EN 1990-2001 Y SITUACIÓN EN 2002

A partir de las reformas parciales adoptadas en 1993-1994, la economía cubana experimentó una recuperación continua del PIB real del 32.3% en 1994-2001, aproximadamente un 4.1% anual, pero la misma ha sido insuficiente para alcanzar los niveles del PIB real logrados en 1989 (ver Cuadro 2 al final del trabajo). Recientemente, Jorge Pérez-López (2002) llamó la década de los noventa como la década perdida desde el punto de vista del crecimiento económico.

En 1989-1995 Cuba experimentó una inflación, medida por el deflactor implícito del PIB, que aumentó el nivel de precios internos en 57.1% a la tasa de cambio oficial vigente (US$1=CU$1). La inflación estuvo asociada al creciente déficit fiscal en 1989-1994, financiado con emisión monetaria. El déficit fiscal acumulado como porcentaje del PIB en 1989-1994 fue equivalente al 104.7%.

Hay evidencia de que las presiones inflacionarias reprimidas aumentaron en 1990-2001 debido a la expansión del excedente monetario asociado al déficit fiscal crónico.[21] En 1990 Cuba tenía un efectivo en circulación de CU$2,341 millones, una liquidez monetaria de CU$4,986 millones y un PIB a precios corrientes CU$20,879 millones; en 2001 tenía un efectivo en circulación de CU$5,782 millones, una liquidez monetaria de CU$12,000 millones y un PIB a precios corrientes CU$31,220 millones. O sea, mientras el efectivo en circulación y la liquidez aumentaron 147% y 141% respectivamente, los precios (medidos por el deflactor del PIB) aumentaron 59% y el PIB real se contrajo 6.3%. Existe una significativa diferencia entre los precios agrícolas libres y oficiales (Alvarez, 2001). Adicionalmente, la tasa de cambio "extraoficial" promedio anual se mantuvo en US$1=CU$19 o más a partir de 1996, con una me-

---

21. Al respecto la liquidez monetaria como porcentaje del PIB aumentó del 24% en 1990 al 38% en 2001.

dia de CU$22 en 1996-2002, habiendo aumentado de CU$21 en 2000 a CU$26 en 2001, o aproximadamente 23.8%.

La escasa competitividad externa de Cuba, resultado de su ineficiente organización económica, inadecuados precios relativos y una tasa de cambio sobrevaluada, se refleja en la baja relación de las exportaciones de bienes y servicios al PIB (14.9% en 2001). En 2001 las exportaciones de bienes y servicios eran todavía el 78% del nivel de 1989, lo que ha determinado la escasez crónica de divisas. La tasa de crecimiento de las exportaciones de bienes y servicios en un periodo de recuperación, ha sido del 9.1% anual en 1994-2001, pero en realidad 8.4% anual, ya que el componente importado de bienes y servicios del turismo es muy elevado, 78%.[22]

Los trabajadores por cuenta propia o microempresarios que llegaron a 208,500 personas en 1995 se han reducido continuamente hasta 153,800 personas en 2001 debido a la constante elevación y alto nivel impositivo, la aplicación de abultadas multas, el retiro de licencias y el establecimiento de restricciones y prohibiciones que empujan a la clandestinidad o abstenerse del registro formal. El sistema impositivo "Restringe la entrada de nuevas empresas al sector y lleva a otras a la quiebra, reduce la producción, eleva los precios para los ciudadanos cubanos, disminuye el empleo en el sector y probablemente contrae la generación de ingresos" (Ritter, 2000, p. 161).

La tasa de inversión bruta con relación al PIB se mantuvo en un dígito entre 1992 y 2001, determinando un bajo potencial de crecimiento de la economía a largo plazo. Parte importante de ese nivel es atribuible a la estabilización seguida por el gobierno de recortar los gastos de capital para reducir el déficit fiscal. La economía cubana logró estabilizarse con base en la reducción de la tasa de inversión en 1990-2001, así como la economía argentina se estabilizó con base en la caja de convertibilidad. Ambos procesos de estabilización disminuyeron la inflación, pero redujeron las posibilidades de crecimiento, lo cual muestra una clara confusión de los medios con los fi-

nes de la política económica. Las importaciones de maquinaria y transporte (bienes de capital) que eran US$2,718 millones y el 36.7% de las importaciones totales en 1990 se redujeron a US$1,202 millones y el 24.9% de las importaciones totales en 2000.

El nivel del déficit fiscal fue en promedio del 2.3% del PIB durante 1994-2001. El déficit del seguro social explica la mayor parte del mismo (ver Cuadro 2). Después que el déficit fiscal había aumentado hasta el 30.4% del PIB en 1993—cuando los gastos fiscales se mantuvieron constantes mientras los ingresos se redujeron por la contracción económica—el gobierno emprendió un severo recorte de subsidios a las empresas, aumentó los precios sin ajustar los salarios, ni siquiera parcialmente hasta 1999, y disminuyó rigurosamente la inversión.

La deuda externa en moneda convertible, que está en moratoria desde 1986, aumentó de US$6.1 mil millones en 1989 a US$11.0 mil millones en 2001, como consecuencia del crónico déficit en la cuenta corriente de la balanza de pagos, la acumulación de pagos vencidos de interés y la depreciación de algunas monedas con respecto al dólar en el cual la deuda cubana está denominada. Sin embargo, la relación de la deuda al PIB, que llegó a aumentar al 52.9% del PIB en 1993, disminuyó al 35.1% del PIB en 2001 por el estancamiento del principal de la deuda externa y la recuperación parcial de la economía.

En 2001 los intereses de la deuda externa convertible serían del orden del 23% de las exportaciones de bienes y servicios (bajo el supuesto de una tasa de interés promedia del 10% para la deuda), relación que es mayor que el nivel de Argentina en 2001 cuando entró en crisis económica, y del 35% (bajo el supuesto de una tasa de interés promedia del 15%). Evidentemente, Cuba tiene un problema de solvencia económica, además de liquidez.

Según la CEPAL (2002), el gobierno decidió postergarlas reformas económicas adicionales que estaba contemplando debido a la coyuntura económica desfavorable que el país enfrenta, lo cual se deriva del

---

22. El turismo a Cuba es una especie de maquila con un bajo componente de valor agregado nacional.

menor turismo después de los acontecimientos del 11 de setiembre del 2001, del menor envío de remesas, los daños causados por el huracán Michelle de noviembre del 2001,[23] la caída de los precios del azúcar, del níquel y del nivel de la inversión extranjera, y el cierre de la base rusa de Lourdes que brindaba un ingreso anual de US$200 millones.

OBSERVACIONES FINALES SOBRE CÓMO EVITAR UNA CRISIS TIPO ARGENTINA EN LAS REFORMAS Y TRANSICIÓN CUBANAS. IMPORTANCIA DEL PROYECTO VARELA.

Es importante señalar que si bien no se conocen los eventos que puedan ocurrir en Cuba en los próximos años y que es prácticamente imposible trazar un programa en todos sus detalles, la formulación y ejecución de un programa de reformas pragmáticas de mercado es la única alternativa posible. Ya sea que el país adopte como meta un modelo socialista de mercado á la China y Vietnam o un modelo de una economía social de mercado á la Europa central (Polonia, Hungría, Eslovenia).

Con ese fin, el país deberá lograr un consenso político de las reformas a realizar para superar su situación de pobreza y reinsertarse al proceso de globalización y la sociedad del conocimiento y la informática de los cuales puede obtener excelentes beneficios en términos de bienes y servicios, tecnología, mercados y financiamiento externo, para lo cual requiere a su vez superar los desafíos que dichos procesos presentan. El consenso deberá incluir a toda la población en el proceso de reformas, compensando a los que se vean afectados adversamente por el mismo a través de la red de seguridad social. Tratar de imponer reformas sin consenso político y con exclusión social, aprovechando las llamadas ventanas de oportunidad, terminan restándole apoyo al proceso que es continuo y requiere ser fomentado permanentemente, y determinan una alta vulnerabilidad ante shocks externos en vez de su irreversibilidad, como lamentablemente Argentina lo muestra.

El Proyecto Varela recién planteado por la oposición propone cambios sociales, económicos y políticos básicos que tienen una gran trascendencia para el futuro inmediato y de largo plazo de Cuba. Específicamente, el Proyecto propone la libertad de asociación a fin de que se puedan constituir entidades de la sociedad civil, la autorización de la pequeña y mediana empresa y la contratación directa de trabajadores para facilitar la recuperación de la economía y superar los niveles alcanzados en 1989, la elección directa de los funcionarios públicos en el ámbito central y provincial de forma de desarrollar una democracia participativa real; y la liberación de los presos políticos para comenzar la postergada reconciliación nacional.

Las experiencias recientes de Argentina, de los países de Europa central y la antigua Unión Soviética, nos enseñan que las entidades de la sociedad civil juegan un papel decisivo en el desarrollo institucional necesario que es fundamental para transformar efectivamente a la sociedad y establecer un proyecto nacional de país con respaldo ciudadano. Las PYMES son decisivas en una economía socialista estancada, no sólo como fuente directa de crecimiento económico y de empleo sino también para facilitar indirectamente la reestructuración de las grandes empresas estatales. Las PYMES han desempeñado un papel fundamental en el crecimiento económico de China, Vietnam y los países exitosos de Europa central. La democracia participativa es fundamental para que la economía responda efectivamente a los intereses ciudadanos y desarrolle los incentivos apropiados para efectuar los cambios consensuales que se requieren para modernizar las instituciones nacionales.

Cuba deberá desarrollar un programa de reformas de mercado consistente y sostenible en el tiempo, el cual deberá sustentarse en dos pilares macroeconómicos fundamentales: (1) lograr y consolidar una estabilización que permita que el sistema económico funcione adecuadamente como asignador de recursos en el tiempo y (2) mantener una tasa de cambio externa competitiva que facilite abrirse al exterior, crecer orientado a los mercados externos y hacer frente con flexibilidad a los shocks externos. Estas dos medidas esenciales deberán complementarse con el desarrollo

---

23. Los daños a la infraestructura económica, las viviendas y la agricultura fueron estimados en 6% del PIB (CEPAL, 2002, p. 8)

de un banco central independiente que establezca metas de inflación y tasas de desempleo, y por otras medidas para fomentar la pequeña y mediana empresa, la sociedad civil y el desarrollo institucional.

La dolarización propuesta por algunos economistas para alentar la estabilidad y contribuir al crecimiento tiene importantes fortalezas y debilidades. Por un lado, facilita la estabilización rápidamente, pero, por otro, requiere una importante disciplina fiscal y de endeudamiento externo, y no permite ajustes fáciles ni rápidos ante la pérdida de competitividad externa ni ante shocks externos debido a la inflexibilidad cambiaria, lo que limita el crecimiento a largo plazo. Edwards y Magendzo (2002) encontraron que los países que han adoptado la dolarización tienen mayor estabilidad, pero menor crecimiento y la misma volatilidad ante shocks externos.

Por ello, dejar flexible el tipo de cambio es una buena medida para que sea el mercado, y no una decisión administrativa, el que fije el precio de equilibrio, modulado por las intervenciones del Banco Central. El financiamiento externo es insuficiente para resolver los déficits estructurales de la balanza de pagos, más bien es útil para resolver desequilibrios transitorios en los flujos de divisas.

La privatización y la concesión de empresas de servicios públicos, que son fundamentales para la modernización y competitividad externa del país, deberán ser precedidas del establecimiento de un marco regulador y supervisor prudencial que aliente la competencia, la expansión de la inversión y de la producción de los servicios públicos, y que proteja al consumidor.

Asimismo, la importante liberalización de los mercados bancario y financiero deberá ser antecedida por el establecimiento de un marco regulador y supervisor prudencial que asegure la liquidez y solvencia, y aliente la eficiencia de las instituciones bancarias y financieras.

La descentralización administrativa que es importante para acercar los gastos públicos a los beneficiarios finales, con sus importantes efectos en términos de eficiencia de resultados y control, deberá realizarse cuidadosamente para evitar que las transferencias de gastos sin las transferencias equivalentes de ingresos desaten "presupuestos blandos" en áreas sociales prioritarias, con sus nefastos efectos fiscales.

Finalmente, deberán establecerse instituciones esenciales que permitan que la economía de mercado pueda funcionar y desarrollarse apropiadamente, disminuyendo los gastos de transacción, tales como: Garantizar la propiedad privada y el cumplimiento de los contratos; permitir la libre entrada y salida a nuevas actividades, simplificando los trámites administrativos; asegurar la independencia del poder judicial y crear mecanismos para resolver conflictos comerciales por el arbitraje y la mediación; flexibilizar el mercado de trabajo para que se permita la contratación de empleados temporales y a tiempo parcial *de jure y no de facto* en nuevas actividades en un momento que debe aumentar el desempleo y no brindar prioridad al mantenimiento de empleos en actividades que han quedado obsoletas y son insostenibles.

REFERENCIAS

José Alvarez, "Rationed Products and Something Else: Food Availability and Distribution in 2000 Cuba," en *Cuba in Transition—Volume 11*, Miami, Florida: 2001, pp305-322.

Jagdish Bhagwati (a), "The Capital Myth," *Foreign Affairs*, Vol. 77, No. 1998.

Jagdish Bhagwati (b), "Why Free Capital Mobility May Be Hazardous to Your Health. Lessons from the Latest Financial Crisis," comentarios en la reunión del NBER sobre controles de capitales de noviembre de 1998.

Dean Barker y Mark Weisbrot, *The Role of Social Security Privatization in Argentina's Economic Crisis,* Center for Economic and Policy Research, 16 de abril del 2002.

Gary S. Becker, "Argentina helps Lead the Way in Privatizing Social Security," en Project Syndicate, de diciembre de 1996, http://www.project-syndicate.org/home/home.php4.

Nancy Birdsall, *What Went Wrong in Argentina?,* Center for Global Development, 29 de enero del 2002

Olivier Blanchard, *Beware of Symbols,* en Project Syndicate, 14 de diciembre del 2001.

Ricardo Caballero y Rudiger Dornbusch (a), Argentina: Rescue Plan that Works, 3 de marzo del 2002, página web del profesor Rudiger Bornbusch.

Ricardo Caballero y Rudiger Dornbusch (b), The Battle for Argentina, 4 de abril del 2002, página web del profesor Rudiger Dornbusch..

Guillermo A. Calvo, *The Real Hazard of Globalization,* en Project Syndicate, Febrero del 2002, http://www.project-syndicate.org/home/home.php4.

Guillermo A. Calvo, Alejandro Izquierdo y Ernesto Talvi, *Sudden Stops, the Real Exchange Rate and Fiscal Sustainability: Argentina's Lessons,* IDB Working paper 469, abril del 2002.

Guillermo Calvo y Alejandro Izquierdo, *What Went Wrong in Argentina?,* en Project Syndicate, 13 de marzo del 2002, http://www.project-syndicate.org/home/home.php4.

Humberto Campodonico, Argentina: Sheer Neoliberal Lunacy, en *Third World Resurgence Magazine,* Issue No. 137-138, enero–febrero del 2002.

Comisión Económica para América Latina y el Caribe (CEPAL, a), *Estudio de América Latina y el Caribe, 2000-2001: Argentina* (p.103-113), diciembre de 2001.

Comisión Económica para América Latina y el Caribe (CEPAL, b), *The Cuban Economy, Strucutural Reforms and Economic Performance in the 1990s,* LC/MEX/R.746/Rev. 1, 6 de diciembre de 2001.

Comisión Económica para América Latina y el Caribe (CEPAL), *Cuba: Evolución Económica durante 2001,* LC/MEX/L.465, 21 de mayo de 2002.

Simeon Djankov, Rafael la Porta, Florencio Lopez-de-Silanes y Andres Shleifer, *The Regulation of Entry,* National Bureau of Economic Research, Working Paper, 7892, setiembre del 2000.

Rudiger Dornbusch, *A New Currency Strategy for Mexico,* en Project Syndicate, 13 de noviembre de 2000, http://www.project-syndicate.org/home/home.php4.

Sebastian Edwards e I. Igal Magendzo, *Dollarization, Inflation and Growth,* Noviembre del 2001.

Ana I. Eiras y Brett D. Shaefer, *La Crisis en Argentina: Una Ausencia de Capitalismo,* The Heritage Foundation, Setiembre del 2001.

Milton Friedman, "The Role of Monetary Policy, *American Economic Review,* Vol. 58, 1968, pp. 1-7.

Francisco Gallego y Norman Loayza, "La Epoca Dorada del Crecimiento en Chile: Explicaciones y Proyecciones," *Revista Economía Chilena,* Vol 5, No 1, abril, 2002.

Stephen Hanke, *Argentina: The U.S. Role,* excerpt of congressional testimony presented before the U.S. Congress on March 5, 2002.

Anne Krueger, "Crisis Prevention and Resolution: Lessons from Argentina," IMF, 17 de julio de 2002.

Paul Krugman, *Curfews on Capital Flight, What are the Options?,* 1998, página web de Paul Krugman,

Paul Krugman, "A Latin Tragedy," *New York Times,* 15 de julio del 2001.

Paul Krugman, "Argentina's Money Mania," *New York Times,* 12 de enero del 2002.

Felipe Larrain and Andres Velasco, *Argentina and the Soft Underbelly of Hard Money,* en Project Syndicate, 8 de setiembre del 2001, http://www.project-syndicate.org/home/home.php4.

Ronald McKinnon, *The Order of Economic Liberalization*, Baltimore; The John Hopkins, University Press, 1991

Frederic S. Mishkin y Klaus Schmidt-Hebbel, *One Decade of Inflation Targeting in the World, What Do We Know and What Do We Need to Know?*, National Bureau of Economic Research, Working Paper, 8397, julio del 2001

Michael Mussa, *Argentina and the Fund: From Triumph to Tragedy*, Institute for International Economics, 3 de enero del 2002.

Jorge Pérez-López, "The Cuban Economy in an Unending Special Period," 2002, en este volumen.

Guillermo Perry y Luis Serven, *The Anatomy of a Multiple Crisis: Why Was Argentina Special and What Can We Learn From It?*, World Bank, 10 de mayo de 2002,

Archibald R. M. Ritter, El sistema impositivo para la microempresa en Cuba, *Revista de la Cepal*, No. 71, agosto del 2000, pp. 145-162.

Dani Rodrik, *Reform in Argentina*, 3 de enero del 2002.

Kenneth Rogoff, "Managing the World Economy", en *The Economist*, Agosto 3-9, 2002, pp. 62-63.

Jeffrey Sachs, "Transition at Mid-Decade" en *American Economic Review*, Vol. 86, No. 2, May, 1996, pp. 128-133.

Jeffrey Sachs, 2002, *The IMF is Bleeding Argentina to Death*, en Project Syndicate, 24 de abril del 2002, http://www.project-syndicate.org/home/home.php4.

Joseph Stiglitz, *Lessons form Argentina*, en Project Syndicate, 8 de enero del 2002, http://www.project-syndicate.org/home/home.php4.

Mark Weisbrot y Dean Barker (a), *What Happened to Argentina?*, Center for Economic and Policy Research, 3 de enero del 2002.

Mark Weisbrot y Dean Barker(b), *When "Good Parents" Go Bad*, Center for Economic and Policy Research, 20 de abril del 2002.

World Bank, *Argentina: Country Assistance Strategy*, 8 de setiembre del 2000

World Bank, *El Desafío de la Productividad Argentina en el Nuevo Milenio*, pagina web.

Cuadro 1. Argentina: Indicadores Económicos Seleccionados, 1989-2001 a/

	1989	1990	1991	1992	1993	1994	1995	1996	1997	1998	1999	2000	2001
Tasa de variación anual del PIB real	-6.9	-1.8	9.9	8.9	5.9	5.8	-2.8	5.5	8.1	3.9	-3.4	-0.5	-4.4
Tasa de variación anual del consumo privado real						6.0	-4.4	5.5	9.0	3.5	-2.0	-0.7	-5.7
Tasa de variación anual de la inversión real						13.5	-13.1	9.0	17.5	6.7	-12.7	-6.8	-15.8
Tasa de variación anual de las importaciones de b y s reales						21.4	-9.7	17.4	26.9	8.4	-11.3	0.0	-13.9
Tasa de variación anual de las exportaciones de b y s reales						15.3	22.9	7.4	12.5	10.4	-1.3	2.6	2.9
PIB en miles de millones US$			213.4	215.5	236.5	257.4	258.0	272.1	292.9	298.9	283.5	284.2	268.7
Exportaciones de bienes y servicios millones de US$				15,325	16,341	19,364	24,897	28,302	30,834	31,046	27,857	31,093	30,856
Exportaciones/PIB (%)				7.1	6.9	7.5	9.7	10.4	10.5	10.4	9.8	10.9	11.5
Diferencial de la tasa de Argentina con la tasa básica de los países emergentes a fines del año	4,923.8	1,343.9					-169	-43	-42	-446	-271	-98	3,586
Indice de la bolsa de valores MERVA a fines de año		317	798	427	583	460	519	649	687	429	550	417	295
Tasa de variación anual precios al consumidor			84.0	17.5	7.4	3.9	1.6	0.1	0.3	0.7	-1.8	-0.7	-1.6
Remuneración media real				101.7	100.4	101.1	100.0	99.9	99.3	99.0	100.1	101.6	101.6
Tasa de variación anual remuneración media real					-1.3	0.7	-1.1	-0.1	-0.6	-0.3	1.1	1.5	0.0
Tasa de desempleo urbano			6.5	7.0	9.6	11.5	17.5	17.2	14.9	12.9	14.3	15.1	17.5
Resultado fiscal financiero/PIB (%)			-1.2	-0.1	1.5	-0.3	-0.6	-1.9	-1.5	-1.4	-1.7	-2.4	-3.9
Tasa de interés real activa					3.1	5.7	14.0	10.3	8.7	9.6	12.4	12.2	24.2
Inversión interna bruta como % del PIB			14.3	17.4	19.1	20.5	18.3	18.9	20.5	21.1	19.1	17.9	15.8
Deuda bruta sobre el PIB			32.7	31.8	34.3	33.3	38.3	40.3	42.6	47.3	51.0	51.8	57.7
Intereses netos sobre las exportaciones				10.2	10.5	11.2	12.5	13.7	14.0	17.7	21.8	18.1	
Pagos de intereses sobre el PIB (%)					1.2	1.2	1.6	1.7	2	2.2	2.9	3.4	3.6
Déficit por privatización del seguro social sobre el PIB (%)						0.5	1.1	1.2	1.3	1.6	1.9	2.6	3.2
Variación de las reservas internacionales			1,880	3,274	4,250	682	-102	3,882	3,273	3,438	1,201	-439	-12,083
M1/ (%)PIB			3.1	5.4	7.0	7.4	7.1	8.0	8.6	8.6	8.9	9.1	6.1
M3 en miles de millones de US$										90.3	92.4	96.5	74.6
Sueldo anual promedio de un empleado privado						12,103	12,220	12,012	11,856	11,999	12,181	12,246	12,090
Sueldo anual promedio de un empleado público						14,049	13,845	13,211	13,953	14,329	14,936	14,875	14,609
Relación sueldos públicos/sueldos privados						1.16	1.13	1.10	1.18	1.19	1.23	1.21	1.21

a/ Fuentes: Pagina web del Ministerio de Economía; CEPAL, 2001a, Cuadro 1; Barker y Weisbrot, 2002, Krueger, 2002.

Cuadro 2. Cuba: Indicadores Económicos Seleccionados, 1989-2001

	1989	1990	1991	1992	1993	1994	1995	1996	1997	1998	1999	2000	2001
PIB millones CU$ a/, a1/	20,795	20,879	17,554	16,382	16,617	20,375	23,025	24,481	24,675	25,863	27,597	29,903	31,220
Producción azucarera en millones de toneladas f/, i1/	7.3	8.1	7.4	6.9	4.1	3.9	3.1	4.4	4.2	3.2	3.7	3.9	3.5
Exportaciones de bienes y servicios mill. de US$ c/, a1/	5,993	5,940	3,563	2,522	1,968	2,542	2,926	3,707	3,974	4,132	4,311	4,798	4,667
Exportaciones b y s/PIB (%)	28.8	28.4	20.3	15.4	11.8	12.5	12.7	15.1	16.1	16.0	15.6	16.0	14.9
Deflator implícito del PIB (1981=100), a/, a1/	99.2	102.6	95.3	98.7	115.9	141.3	155.8	153.9	151.3	156.7	157.4	161.4	163.6
Tasa de crecimiento del deflactor implícito		3.4	-7.1	3.6	17.4	21.9	10.3	-1.2	-1.7	3.6	0.4	2.5	1.4
Tipo de cambio extraoficial a/, a1/	nd	7.0	20.0	35.0	78.0	95.0	32.1	19.2	23.0	21.0	20.0	21.0	26.0
Indice PIB real (1989=100)	100	97.1	87.9	79.2	68.4	68.8	70.5	75.9	77.8	78.7	83.6	88.4	91.0
Inversión interna bruta millones CU$ de 1981 b/, b1/	5,234	5,085	2,752	1,147	692	705	954	1,172	1,382	1,614	1,697	1,854	1,892
Inversión interna bruta como % del PIB b/, b1	25.0	25.0	14.9	6.9	4.8	4.9	6.5	7.4	8.2	9.8	nd	nd	9.9
Tasa de variación anual del PIB real		-2.9	-9.5	-9.9	-13.6	0.6	2.5	7.6	2.5	1.2	6.2	5.7	3.0
Salario medio mensual CU$ d/	188	187	185	182	182	185	194	202	206	206	nd	nd	nd
Salario medio mensual real, 1990=100 a/	104.5	100	97.4	86.6	78.1	60.1	55.7	56.9	58.1	57.3	nd	nd	nd
Tasa de desempleo e/, a1/	7.9	7.3	7.7	6.1	6.2	6.7	7.9	7.6	7.0	6.6	6.0	5.5	4.1
Resultado fiscal millones de CU$ f/, c1/	-1,404	-1,958	-3,765	-4,869	-5,051	-1,421	-766	-571	-459	-560	-612	-672	-738
Resultado fiscal/PIB (%)	-6.8	-9.4	-21.4	-29.7	-30.4	-7.0	-3.3	-2.3	-1.9	-2.2	-2.2	-2.2	-2.0
Déficit del seguro social millones de CU$ f, c1/	-418	-473	-560	-675	-527	-651	-696	-671	-565	-680	-671	-605	-622
Déficit del seguro social como % del PIB	-2.0	-2.3	-3.2	-4.1	-3.2	-3.2	-3.0	-2.7	-2.3	-2.6	-2.4	-2.0	-2.0
Déficit del seguro social como % del déficit total	29.8	24.2	14.9	13.9	10.4	45.8	90.9	117.5	123.1	121.4	109.6	90.0	84.3
Liquidez monetaria millones de CU$ g/, d1/	4,163	4,986	6,563	8,361	11,043	9,944	9,251	9,534	9,441	9,710	9,902	10,490	12,000
Liquidez monetaria como % del PIB	20.0	23.9	37.4	51.0	66.5	48.8	40.2	38.9	38.3	37.5	35.9	35.1	38.4
Deuda externa bruta moneda convertible en millones US$ a/, h/, e1/	6,093	6,807	6,495	6,405	8,785	9,083	10,504	10,465	10,146	11,209	11,078	10,961	10,961
Deuda externa bruta sobre el PIB	29.3	32.6	37.0	39.1	52.9	44.6	45.6	42.7	41.1	43.3	40.1	36.7	35.1
Intereses netos como % de las exportaciones (supuesto tasa de interés del 10%)	10.2	11.5	18.2	25.4	44.6	35.7	35.9	28.2	25.5	27.1	25.7	22.8	23.5
Intereses netos como % de las exportaciones (supuesto tasa de interés del 15%)	15.3	17.2	27.3	38.1	67.0	53.6	53.8	42.3	38.3	40.7	38.5	34.3	35.2

Fuentes: CEPAL, 2001b: a/ Cuadro A.1, b/ Cuadro A.2, c/ Cuadro A-3, d/ Cuadro A. 47, e/ Cuadro A. 46, f/ Cuadro A.13, g/ Cuadro A.26, h/ Cuadro A.43, i/Cuadro A.92.
CEPAL, 2002: a1/ Cuadro 1, b1/ Cuadro 2, c1/ Cuadro 20, d1/ Cuadro 22, e1/ Cuadro 18, f1/ Cuadro 7

THE ROLE OF EDUCATION IN PROMOTING CUBA'S INTEGRATION INTO THE INTERNATIONAL SOCIETY: LESSONS IN TRANSITION FROM THE POST-COMMUNIST STATES OF CENTRAL AND EASTERN EUROPE

Andy S. Gomez

The evanescence of communism in Central and Eastern Europe in 1989-91 is considered the end of the twentieth century, just as World War I, which led to the Russian Revolution in 1917, is presented as its beginning. During the first thirty years of that period, from the start of World War I to the end of World War II, there was remarkable political turmoil in Europe: leftist revolutions, coups d'etat, military dictatorships, fascist regimes and civil wars. Yet this period might be placed as a relatively short parenthesis within a longer process dominated by significant progress in economic growth, political liberalization, and democratization, which have developed since the early nineteenth century.

Ultimately, the Soviet empire broke up into a myriad of nationalities and sovereign states. In August of 1991, in order to preserve the union, a group of politicians and bureaucrats performed a parody of a coup d'etat against the communist leader Mikhail Gorbachev, which also failed unexpectedly. Soon thereafter, on Christmas Day, the Union of Soviet Socialist Republics proceeded peacefully to dissolve itself.

The surprise at discovering the previously unsuspected fragility of one to the two world superpowers detracted attention from the exemplariness of the transition processes. Never before had a number of such large and quick political transformations been attained with so high a rate of success and so low a level of violent conflict. From the late 1980's on, major political and economic transformations were introduced in a total of twenty-eight countries. In a considerable majority of them, significant degrees of civil liberties and political competition to elect each of the new country's leader was established. This was mostly accomplished by creating and encouraging the expansion of an infrastructure that would help develop a civil society (create institutions) that would support these changes and transitions to a more democratic form of government in most of these countries.

The proliferation of old and new states now occupying the region of Eastern Europe and the Baltic Republics has created a tapestry of diversity in educational provisions, as in most other areas of civic life. Schopflin (1993) identifies three models of post-communist society that is worth mentioning. They are:

- **Traditional Society.** Defined by the area's rural past, its ideas strongly collectivist, negatively egalitarian or hierarchical, anti-intellectual, distrustful of politics and due to its lack of political sophistication, vulnerable to manipulation by populist demagogues. Recurring "revisionist" trends in Russia and its former states seem to go along with this definition.

- **Socialist Society.** This is where communist influence is still to be reckoned with. It is a society where the state is still considered the best guarantor of both individual and collective well-being.

It has a sizeable intelligentsia and upper echelons who have converted political power into economic power under post-communism. This is where the phenomenon of "Chauvino-Communism" emerged, where highly placed functionaries salvage political power by a rapid conversion to nationalism while often embracing market principles.

- **Liberal Society.** This is characterized by it openness to new ideas, to the market, to new initiatives, technology and a flexible political system based on compromise and openness to change. This system is the most difficult route to follow because it represents the total antithesis of what happened before. When it fails to deliver on its promises the consequences are extreme.

It will take sometime for the "new changes" introduced to rearrange themselves in patterns that seem appropriate to their changed environment. Of the institutions central to the perpetuation of the communist regime, education was the most jealously guarded because it represented the process of ideological transfer, without which the state had no claim on his citizenry. Communist societies such as Cuba, consider "ideas" weapons in the class struggle. They stress the function of education in particular in facilitating political indoctrination of the population and value education as a way to bring social equality. There is no question that the legacy of forty years of Soviet domination and central planning has been a major inhibitor in the restructuring of the education systems in these nations. What is emerging from the efforts of politicians looking at the West, and local leaders uncertain of their mandate is a disquieting mixture of radical progressivism on the one hand and historical nostalgia on the other.

CHALLENGES FACING TRANSITION

Transition from a non-democratic regime by agreement between different political actors is a rational game. If rulers are unable to maintain their unchallenged domination and the opposition is not powerful enough to impose its preferred regime alternative, two possible outcomes can result. The first is a civil war; that is, a confrontation between groups sustaining incompatible political alternatives in which they

will fight to eliminate each other. Eventually, one of the sides can become a single, absolute winner in what is usually called "revolution or counterrevolution." Yet choosing a strategy of frontal conflict carries the risk of becoming an absolute loser, as well as the cost of significant destruction on both sides.

The second possible outcome is a compromise of national actors with different regime preferences on an intermediate formula between dictatorship and democracy. In order to be agreeable, a compromise must be reached which includes the calling of a multiparty election, which does not secure an absolute winner. On the other side, the ruler(s) can rely upon their advantage as an incumbent(s) to turn the compromise into a lasting "semi-democratic" regime, which would allow the ruler(s) not to be expelled from power or even, to recover some of their previously challenged positions. On the other side, the democratic opposition can envision the agreement as a merely transitory stage, giving it some chance of gaining power and introducing further reforms, which can lead to the eventual establishment of a democratic regime.

All of these scenarios cannot take place without having an educated and well-informed populace that can at least comprehend the purposes and principles behind all of these possible transitional scenarios.

The phrase "nations in transition" or "countries in transition," as it is currently used in the literature, usually refers to the former communist countries (Birzea, 1994). However, the concept of "educational transition" discussed in this paper is not confined to transformations in the education system of communist countries since 1989. It is equally applicable to other countries that have experienced a transformation in their education system following a political transition from an authoritarian regime to a democratic government.

In order to fully understand the processes of educational transition, it is necessary first to establish exactly what is meant by the phrase "educational transition." What is the nature of education transition in countries moving from authoritarian rule to democratic government? The concept of "education transitions" will be defined and the process described in board, non-country specific terms, with the help of the model depicted in Figure 1, which is offered as a tool to assist in the description and explanation of the educational transition processes which have occurred following recent political transitions.

Figure 1. Process of Educational Transition From Authoritarian Rule to Democratic Government

PHASE V:	IMPLEMENTATION AT SCHOOL LEVEL Micro-level Transition
PHASE IV:	EDUCATIONAL LEGISLATION Macro-level Transition
PHASE III:	PROVINCIAL ELECTIONS Nature Of Future Educational System Clearer
PHASE II:	NATIONAL ELECTIONS National Policy Formulations
PHASE I:	INTERIM PHASE Uncertainty Prevails
PRE-PHASE:	Ideological Collapse Anti-authoritarian Climate
AUTHORITARIAN SYSTEM:	PREVAILING IDEOLOGY Threatened

The model was created by a small group of research scholars in Oxford, England (Oxford Studies in Comparative Education) in 1995. The group's intention was to create a model, which would undergo considerable modification according to the situations in each country.

The beginning stage of the model intends to contrast certain states or conditions or education systems as they move from authoritarianism to democracy. This led the group to develop a list of descriptors and their opposites as reflected in the table below.

The model introduced in Figure 1 lays out the process of educational transition in countries moving from authoritarian rule to democratic government. The term "transition" is used in common discourse to refer to changes in such areas as age, occupation and social status. The tendency to equate changes and transition in this way, and to view life as "but a constant succession of changes in transition" (Birzea, 1994) has prompted certain scholars to define transi-

tions as a "permanent state of discontinuity in personal and communal life" (Adams, Birzea, 1994). However, the concept of transitions with which this paper is concerned is a far more complex phenomenon, and one which cannot simply be equated with change, where change is defined as no more than a variation, an alteration or the substitution of one thing for another.

Similarly, the standard use of the word "reform" fails to capture the essences of the transition processes addressed later in this paper, and thus the use "change" and "reform" interchangeably with "transition" in this context is to distort the essence of political, social and economic transformations which have occurred in many of the Soviet bloc countries since 1989. The educational transition processes in these countries following the collapse of the incumbent totalitarian regimes transpired not because of the simple change in government, but because of the wholesale transformation or transition of the prevailing political system. The educational transition process is not exemplified by the passage from one class to the next within a school, or even the graduation from one level to another within the education system as a whole. It is a far more complex concept, which as Badat has explained, is clearly related to the broader political arena (Badat, 1995). That is not to argue that every political change is accompanied by a change in the education system.

Unlike political transition, educational transition is neither easy nor simple to delimit. It may be relatively straightforward to identify the process of political transition as the primary catalyst, but to determine both a finite start and the end to the educational transition process is somewhat more difficult. With respect to its beginning, it can be argued that this coincides with the ideological collapse and that the process of educational transition, though passive at first, becomes active with the start of Phase I or the interim phase. Its end-point is even more of a challenge to delimit.

To summarize the nature of the educational transition process, it is important to emphasize that wholesale educational transition has its roots in the prevailing political climate and not in legislative reforms pertaining to education (Birzea, 1994). This reality is clearly represented in the model presented. Another very important feature of educational transition is that it is a process, which takes a considerable length of time. Like the political transformation from authoritarianism to democracy, it does not occur instantaneously and involves the passage over time from a starting point that is certain to an end-point, which is, in the beginning, almost always relatively unknown.

TEACHING CIVIC EDUCATION FOR A DEMOCRATIC TRANSITION

The ideas of liberty, democracy and constitutionalism have risen in the world as the bastions of totalitarian communism crumbled and collapsed. The newly empowered citizens of these countries have tried to build democratic foundations for their evolving nation-states. In their daunting pursuit of liberty, they have understood that new curricula for their schools are as important as new constitutions for their governments. Among other educational goals, they have recognized that schools must teach young citizens the theory and practices of constitutional democracy if they would develop and sustain free societies and free governments.

Regardless of their differences in history, culture, and resources, all people interested in teaching constitutional democracy authentically and effectively must address general educational elements pertaining to civic knowledge, civic skills and civic virtues. These general and basic categories of civic education may be treated differently by educators of different countries according to their specific needs. But there are certain themes within each category that should apply to everyone. They are the criteria by which we define civic education for constitutional democracy. These criteria are: civic knowledge, civic skills, civic virtues and the role of the teacher.

Civic Knowledge

The first objective of civic education is to teach thoroughly the meaning of the most basic ideas, so that students will know what a constitutional democracy is and what it is not. If students would be prepared to act as citizens of a constitutional democracy, they must know how to distinguish this type of government from other types. The label, constitutional democracy, has often been used by regimes with showcase constitutions proclaiming popular governments and individual rights, which have meant little or nothing to the regime's victims of tyranny. The so called "people's democracies" of former communist countries are tragic twentieth-century examples of the bogus use of a political label.

Through their civic education in schools, students should develop defensible criteria by which to think critically and evaluate the extent to which their government and other governments of the world do or do not function authentically as constitutional democracies. A few key concepts necessary to a deep understanding of constitutional democracy must be taught and learned. These are:

- Rule of law

- Limited government

- Representative government

- Individual rights

- Popular sovereignty

- Political participation

- Civil society

Students must learn how these key concepts of democratic political theory are institutionalized and practiced in their own country in comparison to other nation-states of the world. Finally, students must pursue inquires about the transitional, generic, perennial problems of any constitutional democracy, such as: (a) how to combine liberty with order, majority rule with minority rights; and (b) private rights with the public good.

Everyone must understand that a constitutional democracy will fail if (a) the government has too much power or too little power; or (b) the government over-emphasizes majority rule at the expense of minority rights or vice-versa.

How to practically and effectively address these dilemmas is the ultimate challenge of citizenship in a constitutional democracy and the determiner of the political system's destiny.

Civic Skills

Core knowledge must be applied effectively to civic life if it would serve the needs of citizens and their "civitas." Thus, a central facet of civic education for constitutional democracy is development of intellectual skills and participatory skills, which enable citizens to think and act on behalf of their individual rights and the common good. Intellectual skills empower citizens to identify, describe and explain information and ideas pertinent to public issues and to make and defend decisions on these issues. Participatory skills empower citizens to influence public policy decisions and to hold accountable their representative in government. The development of civic skills requires intellectual active learning by students inside and outside the classroom. Students are continually challenged to use information and ideas, individually and collectively, to analyze case studies, respond to public issues, and resolve political problems.

Civic Virtues

A third generic category of democratic civic education pertains to virtues. These are traits of character necessary to presentation and improvement of a constitutional democracy. If citizens would enjoy the privileges and rights of their polity, they must take responsibility for them, which requires a certain measure of civic virtue.

Civic virtues, such as self-discipline, civility, compassion, tolerance, and respect of the worth and dignity of all individuals are indispensable to the proper functioning of civil society and constitutional government. These characteristics must be nurtured through various social agencies, including school, in a healthy constitutional democracy.

The Democratic Teacher

As educational reformers in former communist countries have begun to build new education programs for transition that will support democratic values, they have turned to the "Western World" for assistance in overcoming an imposing array of obstacles left by the communist system. These obstacles include the lack of classroom instructional materials, teachers with little or no understanding of democracy and no formal training in appropriate pedagogical techniques. However, transitional reforms moved forward. There are three general components of democratic civic education, which transcends political boundaries and cultures. They are:

- Core concepts that denote essential knowledge.
- Intellectual and participatory skills that enable practical application of civic knowledge.
- Virtues that dispose citizens to act for the good of their community.

The effective democratic teacher develops lessons and learning activities for students that emphasize and intertwine the three generic components of civic education in a classroom environment compatible with the theory and practices of constitutional democracy and liberty.

The democratic teacher, for example, emphasizes interactive learning tasks in which students are challenged to take responsibility for their achievement of educational objectives. The democratic teacher encourages and protects free and open expression of ideas in an atmosphere of academic freedom.

Further, the democratic teacher establishes and applies rules fairly, according to principles of equal protection and due process for each individual. This is recognition that true liberty is inextricably connected with just rules, and that equal right to freedom of individuals depends upon an equitable rule of law for all members of the community. Finally, the democratic teacher creates a classroom environment in which the worth and dignity of each person is respected.

CASE STUDIES

Three countries in particular are worth mentioning in terms of their success in developing and implementing their respective education transitions projects. As we will see, their projects focused on providing training and skills for their citizens in the development of a democratic system. These countries are the Czech Republic, Latvia and Poland.

Czech Republic

On January 1, 1993, the establishment of separate Czech and Slovak Republics marked the start of separate democratic reform movements. After more than forty years of Soviet communist ideology as the central theme in teacher education and curriculum development, Czech educational reformers turned to various western sources for assistance in reforming civic education. For example, the Center for Civic Education in California has worked closely with Czech reformers to establish national educational standards for the teaching and learning of civics and government. This project was funded by the U.S. Department of Education.

Briefly, the intent of the project is to revise the existing social studies curricular framework for secondary schools (ages 17 to 18) by taking particular aim at overarching objectives for civic education reform started in 1989. These objectives include the elimination of Marxist-Leninist perspectives in the historical, philosophical, and social science content of the curriculum; the re-introduction of the study of religion into the curriculum; a renewed study of Czech history, culture, heritage, and geography; and a pedagogical shift from transmitting information to passive students in order to prompt inquiry and active learning. Accompanying each lesson is a teacher's manual that presents a rationale and suggestions for further use of the teaching methods employed in the new lessons.

As originally designed, the project included a core component known as the "Curriculum Development Workshop." The workshop provided training and practice for teachers on how to implement these concepts into the curriculum. The other two components were a partnership program linked to the workshop (U.S. teachers and Czech teachers) and the evaluation of the product by both parties. The evaluation provided the opportunity to access the effectiveness of the program in a timely manner that allowed for changes (if needed) to be developed and implemented.

The Curriculum Development Workshop met weekly on the University of Iowa campus. A selected group of Czech teachers took part in a twelve-week workshop. The workshop focused on the main task which was to develop a set of lessons based on the active learning strategies that foster democratic skills and attitudes. The content of the lessons centered on five key concepts derived from the existing social sciences curriculum. These were:

- State and Government Policy.

- Constitutional and local law.

- Citizenship and Human Rights.

- Free Market Economics.

- The Czech Republic in a Global Community.

By the end of the workshop, the Czech teachers had written 61 lessons on 20 topics related to both the civic education reform objectives and the five key concepts of the social studies curriculum noted earlier. These lessons introduced teaching strategies rarely practiced before in the Czech Republic, such as role playing, simulations, educational games, decision trees, civic writing, and cooperative learning. Additionally, some lessons highlighted content areas new to Czech social studies courses including aids awareness, industrial pollution, and civic activism.

Four years later the same teachers involved in the development of the new curriculum conducted a workshop in the Czech Republic and invited educators from the United States to participate. The aim of the workshop was to review, evaluate and prepare new material for schools. At the same time, the Czech teachers conducted a workshop with Czech researchers on the methods of data collection and analysis required for a systematic evaluation of the new lessons. This component of the project focused on an evaluation of knowledge, skill, and attitude outcomes commonly associated with life in a democracy.

Given forty-three years of totalitarian communism, it is unreasonable to expect complete educational reform to result from one curriculum development project. However, the new education reform represents the kind of project that combines the educational expertise of a developed democracy with the contextual understanding of a transitional democracy in an effort to reform civic education through classroom practice. As Czech teachers continue to implement new curricula for democratic citizenship education, the greater the hope for a democratic citizenry becomes a reality in the Czech Republic.

Latvia

Knowing the close connection between well-educated citizens and democratic well being, many Latvians decided to reform their existing curriculum and teaching methods of their schools. They replaced the "Soviet-era" courses on citizenship with new teaching materials and methods suitable for citizenship in a "true" constitutional democracy. They also looked to the "West" for assistance which came initially from the World Federation of Free Latvians, an international organizations that nurtured the spirit of national independence and liberty during the long and difficult Soviet occupation of their homeland.

The American Latvian Association, a component of the World Federation of Free Latvians started a civic education project. Financial support for the project was provided by the National Endowment for Democracy, an agency of the Federal Government of the USA. The project started in 1993. Its purpose was to design and develop materials for new courses in the following areas:

• Civic Education

• Constitutional Law

• Rights and Responsibilities of Citizens

• Institutions of Government

These new courses were targeted at the upper-primary levels of school (8th and 9th graders). The introductory courses emphasized the interactions of citizens with the new constitutional government. More importantly, the teaching method adopted emphasized active learning instead of passive reception of information. The lessons required students to acquire and apply information and ideas to problems and issues rather than merely receive and repeat them. The teachers also adopted the use of higher-level cognitive operations involved in the organization, implementation, and evaluation of the subject matter. Various kinds of work group were used to teach skills of democratic participation and decision-making, such as: role playing, simulations, and political problem solving skills. All three of these ideas were accompanied by materials including a teacher handbook on civics, a student handbook on civics and testing materials.

From the beginning, the staff of the project considered the education of teachers to be a critical component of their work. Unless teachers understood the content and pedagogy of civic education for democracy, the core mission of the project would go unfulfilled. Therefore, starting in 1994, the project staff conducted more than 100 seminars and workshops for teachers in schools throughout Latvia. More than 800 teachers participated in these workshops the first year alone. These workshops were based on lessons and teaching methods developed in the teacher and student handbooks. Thus, by 1996, civic education had become part of the teacher education at three major universities in Latvia.

In its short life, the project has been very productive in promoting civic education for democracy in Latvia. Its mission its far from being finished. Challenges of the present and future include further promotion and development throughout Latvian society of knowledge, skills, and attitudes necessary for effective and responsible citizenship in the constitutional democracy of the country.

Poland

One of the largest, most comprehensive projects of transition is the "Education for Democratic Citizenship in Poland," a cooperative effort of the Polish Ministry of National Education in local control schools in Warsaw, Poland. The project is often cited as a model of how to construct a long-term multi-dimensional approach to civic education reform.

The project started in 1991. The plan called for a set of distinct but related activities that would respond to specific, urgent problems identified by the Poles, such as the desperate need for new teaching materials. The overall goals of the project was to institutionalize civic education in all schools in Poland for the next decade as well as to build a national dialogue among Polish educators on the meaning of democratic citizenship and civic education with American educators.

To start, the National Endowment for Democracy funded a smaller-project, which involved twenty-five polish educators in developing curriculum guides and support materials. The guides presented the rationale, goals, objectives, and content outlines for primary and secondary school civic curriculum. For example, one supporting book presents 16 sample lessons plans illustrating topics and goals set forth in the curriculum guide. A second book consists of 36 readings on political life, citizenship, and human rights by prominent Polish scholars and political activists.

Another project was the "Primary School Civics Course," funded by the Pew Charitable Trusts. In this case, Polish university professors prepared detailed syllabus for a two-semester course on the principles of democracy as they applied to the organization and operations of schools. The syllabus was organized around topics. These were:

- Student rights and Responsibilities.
- Schools and the Local Community.
- The Role of Schools in a Democratic Society.

The syllabus included goals, detailed explanations, suggested readings, and sample teaching strategies for each topic.

In December 1993, a group of prominent educators and scholars across Poland met in Warsaw to critique and discuss the materials developed for these projects. The outcome of these meetings were very useful in the sense that new ideas were introduced and the curriculum and teaching methods were adopted according to the needs of the rapidly changing Polish society.

This program has been very successful from the point of view of integrating individuals and organizations within a democratic society. However, like the other cases, the program was reformed several times to address the rapidly changing needs of the Polish citizens and their governmental institutions.

What occurred in the Czech Republic, Latvia and Poland will not take place in Cuba. Why? First and foremost Fidel Castro has no intentions of retiring, sharing power, or even passing his authority to anyone including his brother Raúl while he is still alive. In the last several years, Fidel and Raúl have taken steps to plan for the day Fidel will no longer be around to govern Cuba. The initial plan can be de-

fined as measures that would centralize the authority of the regime under the leadership of his brother Raúl who lacks his older brother's charisma and leadership qualities. This will also help preserve the ideological values of the revolution. The plan can be defined more of a "succession of power" rather than a "transition" like those that took place in Eastern Europe.

POLICY RECOMMENDATIONS

There are a number of lessons that can be learned from Central and Eastern Europe. However, the Czech Republic has been the one country at the forefront in having its education system play a key and active role in their transition.

The government of the Czech Republic in 2001 approved "The National Program of Development Education." The document is part of their strategy to further expend social and economic development in the country. The main focus of the plan is the development of the human and social capital by focusing on the creation of a "new" value system that emphasizes democratic citizenship and the quality of everyday life for its citizens. This was the first project adopted by the new government after the political changes of 1989 that focused on systematic reform.

The adopted strategy was an effort to upgrade the level of education and human resource development across all ages of society with the sole purpose of creating a strong civil society that could sustain a democratic society for years to come.

The creation of political and economic conditions for permanent change in attitudes towards investment in education was the main strategy behind the plan. These were:

- The implementation of a system of lifelong learning for all citizens.
- The adaptation of an educational system that takes into consideration the "everyday" needs of the "new" society and the "individual."
- The development of a system to monitor and evaluate the effectiveness of the plan. The promotion of internal reforms and openness of the edu-

cational institutions to deal with these new set of needs.

- Change the role and professional standards of the academic community at all levels.

- Transition from a centralized system of management to a decentralized system with specific accountability standards and measures.

Each strategic concept was characterized by the following aims and provisions:

- The implementation of a flexible system of life-long learning: The idea was to saturate and initiate educational needs in children, youth and adults in order to develop a civil society that could support a democratic form of government and a free economic system.

- The adaptation of an educational system that takes into consideration the "everyday" needs of society. The goal was to increase the quality and practical function of the education system in preparation for the demands a new system of government will place on its citizens. At the same time meet the demands of professional and technical training that would create individuals with employable skills that would sustain a developing economy.

- Development of a system that would monitor and evaluate the effectiveness of the plan. The idea was to monitor the input and output (product) of the education system to assure that the "new" citizens needs were been met.

- Promotion of internal reforms and openness of the educational institutions. The plan called for an autonomous system that would allow institutions to experiment with "new" educational techniques. The system also encouraged collaboration between the public and private sectors. Specifically along the lines of training, research and development.

- Change the role and professional standards of the academic community. Support and reward (financially) the academic community for designing academic programs that met the needs of society and that would be coordinated with the business sector. At the same time, the plan called

for strengthening the social and professional status of teachers and academics.

- Transition from a centralized system of educational management to a decentralized and flexible system that can react to the needs of its citizens quicker. This would be accomplished by having the active participation of the public and private sectors of civil society in the process of planning, organizing, implanting and evaluation. The plan also called for very specific accountability measures.

CONCLUSION

In summary, education reconstruction in a post-Communist country will continue to face many problems and obstacles. The key will be focused on the following: (a) physical reconstruction; (b) ideological reconstruction; (c) psychological reconstruction; (d) provision of materials and curricular reconstruction; and (e) human resources.

UNESCO's unit for educational rehabilitation and reconstruction speaks of reconstruction as a more or less protected process with short, medium and long-term goals. Emergency programs, concerned with basic requirements needed to get the education system working again, respond to the most urgent needs, both for the infrastructural and material, and for the human component. Priorities must be determined, as efforts will be directed toward basic needs. UNESCO argues that reconstruction must not be carried out piecemeal, but must be carefully planned implemented. Agencies concerned with reconstruction should ideally be formulating plans for intervention in education long before it is possible to put programs in place.

For the medium and longer-term reconstruction, UNESCO speaks of a "master plan" for the education system, which will emerge from the needs analysis based on the following dimensions and components. These are:

- Environmental

- Organizational

- Infrastructural

- Material and Financial

- Human
- Institutional
- Pedagogical
- Curricular

Effective planning for all aspects of educational reconstruction and capacity building will depend on the creation of organizational frameworks at the national, local and institutional levels.

Finally, the toughest challenge facing any post-communist country in its transition will be ideological and psychological reconstruction. These two issues need to be further explored and researched. However, they are worth mentioning in this paper. Ideological reconstruction in democratization is seen as a major concept in reforming authoritarian, totalitarian, autocratic systems and the attitudes of individuals and encouraging the replacement of previous structures and values. A vital aspect in the democratization of education is the encouragement of critical, independent and creative thinking. UNESCO strongly believes that to accomplish this task, the "new" education system in a transition should: (a) educate children and adults with a sense of openness and comprehension toward other people, their diverse cultures and histories and their fundamental shared humanity; and (b) teach them the importance of refusing violence and adopting peaceful means for resolving disagreements and conflicts.

A common feature of post-conflict situations is the presence of various psychological problems ranging from demoralization to severe trauma. The need for urgent psychological reconstruction has been recognized by a number of international agencies, as a key to any form for a successful transition.

In the confusion and deprivation, which often characterize post-crisis situations, it is not uncommon for those affected to experience lack of confidence, low morale and frequently, nostalgia for the past. The reestablishment of morale and restoration of confidence is an arduous process that often creates a feeling of nostalgia for past practices and lifestyles as, for example, in many post-Soviet bloc countries where teachers and student continued to find the implementation of new policies, practices, and teaching and learning styles with which they are unfamiliar particularly difficult to cope with.

The uncertainty, insecurity and instability that follow periods of crises inevitably result in stress, anxiety and depression, conditions which often lead to physical illness in both adults and children. There is a widespread need for special rehabilitation programs designed to assist children traumatized by crises, especially following violence or the loss of a family member as a result of conflict. There are numerous examples of programs used by countries going through transition to help identify and treat trauma sufferers. However, it is important to recognize that psychological reconstruction, especially in the case of trauma is a long-term process. At the same time, trauma represents a serious obstacle where educational processes in schools are concerned. Regular schooling is important in the establishment of the secure, caring environment deemed by psychologist to be the most effective means of relieving psychological repercussions for children. However, we must not forget that psychological support for the teachers is also very important.

It is important in any transition to listen to individual needs and develop plans of actions, which are flexible and can be adopted to various ideological and psychological conditions. If this is not done from the beginning, then the transition process will be superficial and will eventually fail.

BIBLIOGRAPHY

Badat, Saleem (1995). "Educational Politics in the Transition Period." *Comparative Education*, 31, pp. 141-159.

Bahmueller, Charles F., general editor. *Civitas: A Framework for Civic Education*. Calabasas, CA: Center for Civic Education, 1991.

Birzea, Cesar (1994). *Educational Policies of the Countries in Transition.* Strasbourg: Council of Europe.

Broadfoot, P., Brock, C. & Tulasiewicz, W. (1981). *Politics and Educational Change.* London: Croom Helm.

Broclawik, Krysztof., and others. *Schools and Democratic Society: A Course Syllabus for Poland's Future Teachers.* Columbus, OH: The Mershon Center, 1992.

Dalin, Per (1978). *Limits to Educational Change.* London: Macmillan Press.

Darvas, Peter & Tibbitts, Felisa (1992). "Educational Change in Central Eastern Europe: Tradition, Context, and New Actors- The Case of Hungary," in A. Tjeldvoll (Ed.). *Education in East/Central Europe: Report of the OSLO Seminar.* Buffalo: State University of New York.

Kandel, I.L. (1948). *Education in an Era of Transition.* London: Evans Brothers.

Melosik, Zbyszko, "Poland in the 1990's: The Role of Education in Creating a Participatory Society," *Social Education* 55 (March 1991): 191-193.

O'Donnell, G. & Schmitter, P. (1986). *Transitions from Authoritarian Rule.* Baltimore: Johns Hopkins University Press.

Remy, Richard, and Jacek Strzemieczny, eds. *Civic Education for Democracy in Poland.* Washington, DC: National Council for the Social Studies in association with the ERIC Clearinghouse for Social Studies/Social Science Education, forthcoming in 1996.

Salter, Brian & Tapper, T. (1981). *Education Politics and The State. The Theory and Practice of Educational Change.* London: Grant McIntyre.

Schopflin, George (1993). *Politics in Eastern Europe 1945-1992.* Oxford: Blackwell.

Weiler, Hans N. (9178). "Education and Development: From the Age of Innocence to the Age of Scepticism," *Comparative Education*, 14, pp. 179-198.

REHABILITANDO LA EDUCACIÓN EN LA CUBA QUE TRANSITA

Graciella Cruz-Taura[1]

En cuarenta y tres años, el sistema educacional cubano ha cumplido con los objetivos para la sobrevivencia política de una sociedad unipartidista de corte leninista.[2] La escuela alfabetiza a toda la población, instruyéndola en una opción ideológica. El estudiante es guiado hacia organizaciones de masa que facilitan la movilización cuando el régimen paternalista lo determina necesario. Sin embargo, el sistema no ha podido cumplir con el objetivo de crear al hombre nuevo socialista, el que entre otras motivaciones solidarias, contribuiría al desarrollo de la economía nacional.

El derrumbe del bloque de países comunistas ha obligado a Cuba a participar en la economía global en condiciones para las que la población cubana no fue preparada. Si Cuba aspira a una transición pacífica hacia un mundo interconectado, la educación cubana necesita liberarse de la metodología marxista y ofrecer a la población programas de educación cívica y capacitación laboral acordes al nuevo orden global. Este estudio ofrece recomendaciones para la rehabilitación de la educación en Cuba.

A primera vista, todo parece estar bien en el sistema educacional cubano. Un estudio de la UNESCO compara a estudiantes del tercero y cuarto grado en varios países de Latinoamérica y los niños cubanos le llevan la cabeza a todos los demás.[3] Visitantes internacionales son llevados a algunas escuelas modelos, como la Lenín en La Habana, y no pueden menos que quedar muy bien impresionados.[4] La continuidad de una política educacional da al sistema ciertos elementos de triunfo. Sus rasgos principales aparecen en el Cuadro 1.

Lo que no explican las apariencias es por qué el régimen está graduando "maestros emergentes" sin los años de preparación superior que antes exigía. Durante un discurso a la Asamblea de Balance del Parti-

1. Este estudio preliminar forma parte del que la autora realiza sobre la educación cubana para el Cuba Transition Project, proyecto del Instituto para Estudios Cubanos y Cubanoamericanos de la Universidad de Miami, bajo la dirección del Dr. Jaime Suchlicki, auspiciado por la United States Agency for International Development. La autora agradece a ASCE la oportunidad de presentar esta ponencia y poder mejorarla con los comentarios críticos de sus participantes. Los conceptos aquí expresados son criterio de la autora y no necesariamente coinciden con los de la agencia patrocinadora.

2. De los muchos estudios de la educación cubana revolucionaria, vale destacar Nikolái Kolésnikov, *Cuba: Educación popular y preparación de los cuadros nacionales 1959-1982* (Moscú: Editorial Progreso, 1983) que incluye esquemas excelentes de los organogramas de las estructuras educativas cubanas. Las estadísticas oficiales aparecen cada año en el *Anuario Estadístico*. Para un análisis de estas cifras, véase Benigno E. Aguirre y Roberto J. Vichot, "The Reliability of Cuba's Educational Statistics," *Comparative Education Review* 42:2 (mayo 1998): 118-38.

3. UNESCO Laboratorio Latinoamericano de Evaluación de la Calidad de la Educación, *Primer estudio internacional comparativo sobre lenguaje, matemáticas, y factores asociados en tercero y cuarto grado* (Santiago de Chile: UNESCO, 1998).

4. Lavinia Gasparini, *The Cuban Education System: Lessons and Dilemmas* (Washington: Banco Mundial, 2000) y Ronald A. Lindahl, "Evaluating the Cuban System: A Goal-Fulfillment Critique," *International Education* 29:2 (primavera 2000): 5-20.

Cuadro 1.

Componentes Básicos del Sistema Educacional Cubano

Acceso masivo
Formación marxista-leninista del hombre nuevo
Principio de estudio y trabajo
Burocracia centralizada
Preferencia científica y técnica
Promoción por perfil ideológico
Participación comunitaria vía organizaciones de masa

do de Ciudad de La Habana a comienzos de julio de 2002, Castro se refirió a los más de 4,500 maestros emergentes en la ciudad y aseguró que ya "86,000 jóvenes, que no estudiaban ni trabajaban [estaban] incorporados a las Escuelas de Superación Integral." También habló de los "miles de trabajadores sociales y profesores para la enseñanza de Computación… crea[ndo] más de 12 000 empleos."[5] El por qué no estudian en un sistema gratuito tantos jóvenes que tampoco trabajan sugiere causas más profundas entre las que resaltan la dolarización de la economía, el turismo, y la falta de valores.

El sistema educacional de Cuba se ciñe a la pedagogía marxista que le impide liberalizar los métodos y el contenido pedagógicos, así como proveer a la población de una educación mejor orientada al desarrollo de una economía auto-sostenible. Esta última deficiencia resulta aún más notable cuando se considera el esfuerzo del gobierno revolucionario por más de cuatro décadas por aumentar la productividad laboral y diversificar la economía. La evidencia disponible de los países de Europa Oriental, cuyos sistemas educacionales Cuba ha emulado, nos demuestran las limitaciones impuestas por los imperativos ideológicos. Estos sistemas también tuvieron éxito al ampliar la disponibilidad de escolaridad a toda la población y desarrollar programas superiores en las ciencias exactas. Sin embargo, fracasaron en la calidad de la instrucción masiva y en el aprovechamiento de los presupuestos tan generosos que le fueron asignados. Así mismo, el sistema cubano padece la mala administración de una burocracia excesiva y centralizada que demuestra serle fiel al partido único pero que no parece conocer la eficiencia.

La carencia de eficiencia no sería tan trágica si el graduado cubano pudiera aprovechar la educación recibida para ganarse la vida. Pero la correlación entre la educación vocacional y las necesidades del mercado laboral nunca ha operado en la economía cubana. En medio de alabanzas a los logros, el mismo Castro se quejaba de que el éxito educacional no se reflejaba en la economía desde la época de la Ofensiva Revolucionaria en los años 60. Esta situación se ha intensificado durante el Período Especial, cuando los sueldos en pesos no alcanzan para adquirir la canasta de consumo familiar, que es más accesible a cualquier partícipe en el sector turístico, lo que no requiere mucha preparación. Los profesionales abandonan sus puestos para participar en la economía del dólar. Cuando es un maestro el que abandona el aula, ya sea permanentemente o por faltar con frecuencia, la educación sufre directamente. Cuando estudiantes de las secundarias y centros de educación superior deciden buscarse unos dólares en las zonas turísticas en lugar de asistir a clases, el impacto sacude la razón de ser de la educación.

Para el simposio internacional Pedagogía '99, el Ministerio de Educación elaboró un documento muy detallado, en el que se perfila la preocupación por el problema educacional/laboral del país:

> La Educación Técnica y Profesional tiene el encargo social de formar trabajadores aptos para un mundo laboral en continuo cambio, donde se requiere periódicamente reciclar, reconvertir o actualizar las habilidades específicas. [...] Para ello el Comité Ejecutivo del Consejo de Ministros normó mediante acuerdo de ese órgano, las tareas que de forma conjunta acometen los organismos de la Administración Central del Estado y la Educación Técnica y Profesional, las que se materializan mediante planes de trabajo conjuntos en: la entrega a los centros politécnicos, según las disponibilidades, de la base material de estudio especializada,[...] la actualización de los perfiles ocupacionales de los planes de estudio existentes en correspondencia con los calificadores de ocupaciones; [...]Además, la capacitación técnica a los trabajadores se realiza por diferentes vías bajo la rectoría metodológica del Mi-

---

5. Reynold Rassi y Alberto Núñez, "Para este país no hay nada imposible: Presidió Fidel la Asamblea de Balance…" *Granma* (8 julio 2002): 1.

nisterio de Educación. Desde hace varios años la Educación Técnica y Profesional le ha concedido gran importancia a la formación de perfil amplio, la obtención de la calificación obrera en todas las especialidades [...] se ha reducido el número de especialidades a 93 de más de 400 en los años setenta.[6]

Recientemente, los programas que graduan *enfermeros emergentes, maestros emergentes,* y *médicos del alma,* en su mayoría estudiantes que apenas completaron el noveno grado, también revelan la preocupación del gobierno por integrar a la población de menos de 27 años a la vida laboral, así como por mantener los altos índices de trabajadores de la educación y la salud pública en que el régimen se apoya para propaganda y legitimidad. Sin embargo, el grado de calificación para desempeñar estas profesiones que puedan poseer estos egresados determinará el éxito de esta iniciativa. Está en tela de juego que la mayoría esté capacitada para ejercer después de instruirse en programas de menos de un año de duración.

La ideología determina el currículo en Cuba, mandato que limita el contenido y las experiencias del alumnado. El potencial de aprendizaje del alumno disminuye en base a procesos inadecuados. Estos procesos incluyen poca motivación en la relación maestro-alumno, uso frecuente de sustitutos, maestros emergentes, o alumnos sin supervisión profesional, y aulas en mal estado. Las dificultades económicas han engavetado muchos planes para llevar computadoras a las aulas. En documentos oficiales, el gobierno asegura que la educación es tarea de toda la sociedad pero toda relación de padres con las escuelas continua canalizada através de organizaciones oficiales, ahogando cualquier esfuerzo comunitario para complementar la educación infantil y para exigir mejores servicios de las autoridades.

Si las mismas medidas que toma el régimen nos indican que la escuela cubana adolece, también dentro de Cuba han surgido voces independientes pidiendo la rehabilitación del sistema educacional. En particular, el Colegio de Pedagogos Independientes de Cuba, fundado en 1996, ha publicado manifiestos a favor de un nuevo orden escolar.[7] Los escritos de Dagoberto Valdés, del Centro de Formación Cívica y Religiosa de Pinar del Río, también se basan en la necesidad de introducir otras perspectivas a la educación en la Isla.[8]

RECOMENDACIONES

Generales

Mantener y mejorar (y en algunos casos, activar) aquellos componentes del actual sistema educacional de Cuba que contribuyen al desarrollo del individuo y de la cultura:

- Mantener el acceso gratuito a la escuela para toda la población de ambos sexos hasta el noveno grado, en todo el territorio nacional urbano y rural.

- Proveer de programas de Educación Especial a estudiantes con deficiencias físicas, mentales, o emocionales.

- Basar el ingreso a cualquier institución o programa educacional en el expediente académico, sin consideración de raza, edad, sexo, religión, o afiliación política.

- Proporcionar educación vocacional y técnica a la población de edad laboral.

- Proporcionar el componente nutritivo de desayuno y/o almuerzo escolar.

- Facilitar la salud pública con exámenes de vista, oído, vacunaciones, y programas de información para la salud que no sólo incluyan conocimientos positivos (e.g. nutrición, sexualidad, ejercicio)

6. Pedagogía '99, *La educación en Cuba: Encuentro por la unidad de los educadores latinoamericanos* (La Habana: Ministerio de Educación, 1999), págs. 38-39.

7. "Declaración de Principios del Colegio de Pedagogos de Cuba," en http://www.bpicuba.org/cultura.declara.htm (13 junio 1999); y "Reflexiones" (manuscrito, noviembre 2001).

8. Véanse "La educación: El derecho a elegir cómo ser," en http:///www.vitral.org./ (editorial, marzo-abril 1998); Dagoberto Valdés Hernández, *Un proyecto de educación cívica, pluralismo, y participación para Cuba* (Caracas: Fundación Konrad Adenauer, 1997); y Adolfo Fernández Saínz, "La nueva escuela," en http://www.ecograficos.com/cubacatolica/articulo_12.html (julio 2002).

pero aquéllos de lacra social (e.g. alcoholismo, drogadicción, SIDA, enfermedades venéreas).

- Mantener los programas de educación física.

- Mantener la calidad en programas de orientación científica y biotecnológica, así como en los de lenguas extranjeras. Desarrollar y mejorar programas en las industrias que requieren mayor fuerza laboral, como la agropecuaria, la turística, y la de la construcción.

- Desarrollar planes para cursos de computación.

Recomendaciones Administrativas

Legalizar la educación privada y/o religiosa: Una sociedad abierta facilita opciones a sus ciudadanos. La competencia entre varias alternativas educacionales conlleva a mejores maestros y mejores escuelas, lo que resulta en mejores alumnos estudiando con profesores más calificados y mejor pagados. Toda institución o programa de estudios que conceda títulos deberá satisfacer lo requisitos establecidos por el Ministerio de Educación.

Reducir la burocracia: La responsabilidad fiscal y la eficiencia obligan a reducir las nóminas del sistema educacional cubano. Aparte del elaborado organigrama del Ministerio de Educación, los Ministerios de Educación Superior, Cultura, y Salud Pública están directamente involucrados en el proceso educacional, a lo que hay que agregar dependencias educacionales del Ministerio de las Fuerzas Armadas y del Partido Comunista, entre otros. Haría falta que un nuevo Ministerio de Educación marcara las pautas y requisitos para todos los programas titulares de un país de 11,200,000 habitantes. Esto permitiría una política ministerial transparente de toda la empresa educacional desde pre-escolar hasta la universidad, más aproximada a las necesidades nacionales, y con más determinación para procurar los fondos que le permitirían cumplir con su misión.

Revisar contratos y salarios de docentes: La demanda de maestros calificados debe reflejarse en los contratos laborales. Estos deben especificar la preparación y experiencia que se requieren de todo maestro licenciado. Docentes actualmente alejados de las aulas podrían ser reinstituidos al obtener certificación temporaria hasta rendir cursos en un período de tiempo para reactivar sus licencias. Así mismo, a los maestros emergentes se les deben ofrecer programas de superación pedagógica. Los sueldos de maestros deben compensar los años de preparación, títulos, especializaciones, y años de servicio. Suplementos, como bonos y vivienda, pueden servir de incentivos para destacarse en plazas rurales.

Exigir profesionalismo: Tal y como está documentado que ocurre en todos los sectores de la sociedad cubana, los cargos administrativos en el sector de la educación dependen del perfil político del designado; títulos profesionales y experiencia en la enseñanza no son requisitos para dirigir una escuela o un programa de estudios. Con el fin de exigir profesionalismo, se deben establecer requisitos mínimos que incluyan experiencia docente (en las aulas) antes de ser candidato a una plaza de director o subdirector.

Disposiciones con requisitos para designaciones y evaluaciones de todo el personal docente y administrativo ya existen, según publicaciones oficiales, pero la práctica demuestra que no están en vigor. El servicio comunitario vía actividades partidistas no debe aparecer en ninguna evaluación profesional. Un paso importante para la aplicación objetiva de las disposiciones sería la recertificación de todo el personal docente, otorgando certificados temporarios por dos o tres años a todos aquellos que no estuviesen calificados. Durante dicho período de gracia estarían disponibles cursos de superación pedagógica en horarios nocturnos, de fin de semana, o de verano, para ayudar a aquéllos que tengan verdadera vocación de maestros y deseen continuar en sus puestos pero con las credenciales y el sueldo correspondientes.

El informe del 2002 enviado por el Colegio de Pedagogos Independientes de Cuba a la Comisión de Derechos Humanos de las Naciones Unidas en Ginebra documenta más de 300 casos de maestros que fueron despedidos (o reasignados a plazas fuera de su capacitación) por motivos ideológicos. Estos casos necesitan ser revisados por una comisión escolar que verifique que las causas alegadas por los cesantes fueron arbitrarias y no por descalificaciones morales o profesionales. Aquéllos despedidos por razones arbitrarias deberán ser restituidos a sus plazas. Los que lleven años sin desempeñar sus carreras de maestros, también deben recibir certificados temporarios mientras asistan a cursos de pedagogía.

Expedientes escolares: Todo expediente escolar debe documentar el progreso académico e intelectual del estudiante. La evaluaciones cognitivas y sicológicas deben limitarse a la información, que según las pautas establecidas, es útil a los educadores para aconsejar, anivelar, y establecer metas razonables para cada estudiante, individualmente. Ningún expediente debe incluir información de carácter político referente al estudiante o a su familia, ni referencias a la participación de éstos en actividades extracurriculares. El récord familiar de actividad revolucionaria (membresía en el Partido Comunista u organizaciones de masa) o su ausencia (caso de hijos de presos políticos o activistas religiosos), así como comentarios contrarrevolucionarios hechos por el estudiante o su participación en grupos (e.g., pioneros, Juventud Comunista) actualmente forman parte del expediente escolar, pero deben desaparecer del mismo.

Recomendaciones para la relación escuela-familia

Involucrar a los padres en las decisiones escolares: Para ser una sociedad abierta, Cuba necesita recuperar el papel de la familia en las educación de los hijos. La patria potestad compartida por ambos padres debe incluir la autoridad para elegir el tipo de educación que se desea para los hijos, incluyendo las alternativas de matricularlos en escuelas religiosas, privadas, con o sin entrenamiento militar, y con o sin pupilaje e internado. La actual crisis de valores que caracteriza a la juventud cubana es agudizada por la política comunista que separa al niño de la familia, con requisitos como la escuela al campo.

Actualmente toda la participación de los padres y de la comunidad en las escuelas es canalizada atravéz de organizaciones de masa dirigidas por miembros del partido único. Hasta los consejos de padres reacaen bajo las estructuras partidistas.

Proveer servicios sociales: La escuela debe proveer a la comunidad de servicios sociales, tales como grupos de apoyo para padres y alumnos. Las escuelas cubanas tienen este componente pero se limita a lo ideológico. Estos programas refuerzan la imagen de que el ré-

gimen revolucionario protege al pueblo, a diferencia del trabajador en la sociedad capitalista.

Todo cambio crea ansiedad, aún cuando el que lo experimenta percibe que será por un futuro mejor. La ansiedad es más profunda cuando se trata de transitar del paternalismo de un régimen totalitario para enfrentar los riesgos que conlleva tomar decisiones en una sociedad abierta. El individuo tiene que aceptar las consecuencias del éxito o del fracaso.

Padres y estudiantes necesitan tomar decisiones laborales y profesionales teniendo en cuenta posibles consecuencias. Las decisiones deben basarse no sólo en las metas del individuo sino cosiderando las del bienestar de la comunidad y de la nación. Como resultado de la propaganda comunista, existe mucha confusión entre los conceptos *patria* y *gobierno*. Bajo el comunismo, al cubano se le ha inculcado que amar la patria requiere devoción incondicional al gobierno. El nuevo ciudadano necesita distinguir y discutir ideas que cuestionen o desafíen las ideas oficialistas y hacerlo en un ambiente de respeto hacia el vecino discrepante. Necesita comprender que la propaganda puede promover odio y furia hacia los que disientan, aún dentro de la familia o fuera del territorio nacional. El ciudadano cubano necesita tomar conciencia de que la educación debe liberar, lejos de hacer temer la persecución.

Lanzar una campaña de información: Una campaña nacional por los medios masivos debe promover (1) el valor de una ciudadanía educada y (2) las oportunidades educacionales para toda la población que aspire a carreras y empleos en una economía en desarrollo. Una campaña de servicio público debe poner énfasis en presentar al ciudadano informado que sabe cuáles son sus derechos y respeta a la oposición. La transición desplaza a muchos de sus empleos por lo que hace falta anunciar nuevos campos y carreras, centros de estudio y becas disponibles, así como oportunidades de trabajo.

Conseguir apoyo para iniciativas educacionales através de organizaciones no-gubernamentales: El lustro pasado Cuba ha visto el desarrollo de una red de organizaciones no gubernamentales (ONG), lo que a su vez ha ayudado a organizaciones independientes, como la red de Bibliotecas Independientes de Cuba, a promover la reforma educacional.[9] Estas entidades han proporcionado otras alternativas al cubano al facilitarle lecturas censuradas.

Anterior a estas iniciativas de los noventa, década que experimentó el aumento de periodistas y bibliotecas independientes, entre otros grupos, el acceso al libro prohibido a menudo sólo era posible atravéz de las actividades de las iglesias, a pesar de las restricciones que se les aplicaban. Aunque muy pocos cubanos enviaban a sus hijos a la catequesis católica o se matriculaban en el seminario protestante, la evidencia indica que estas instituciones fueron el único respiro, libre de la prensa oficialista, para el pueblo; Oswaldo Payá del Proyecto Varela y Dagoberto Valdés de la revista *Vitral* son productos de esa época. Es por esto que hoy, a pesar de las continuas restricciones, el desarrollo de la sociedad civil tiene nexos con las iglesias (de varias denominaciones) que desarrollan proyectos de trabajo social en la Isla. Es importante que todo plan de reformas incorpore a estas organizaciones para asistir en la rehabilitación de la educación.

El Ministerio de Educación ha suscrito varios acuerdos con ONG internacionales para proyectos educacionales. Muchos de éstos han permitido al régimen continuar llevando becarios de otras partes del mundo a estudiar en la Isla, particularmente del África. Proyectos con fundaciones internacionales o con entidades del sistema de Naciones Unidas (e. g. UNESCO, UNICEF, OEI) proporcionan asistencia al sistema cubano.[10] Es fundamental que estos nexos continúen durante la transición.

Recomendaciones Curriculares

Eliminar el monopolio del pensamiento y lenguaje marxistas-leninistas en los materiales educacionales de las escuelas cubanas: Con la excepción de algunos cursos a nivel universitario en historia, filosofía, o metodología de las ciencias sociales, no es necesario que todo curso desde el preescolar hasta el posgrado deba estar relacionado con el pensamiento

marxista-leninista. Este es el caso en Cuba en todas las materias, a expensas de que el estudiante no pueda explorar otra perspectiva.

Desde los materiales para enseñar a leer a párvulos hasta la educación superior, libros de textos nuevos deben reemplazar los existentes. Por razones de tiempo y recursos, acuerdos con casas editoriales en la América Latina y España pueden apurar este proceso en muchas materias. Los educadores cubanos deben concentrarse en escribir libros de texto relacionados directamente con Cuba, como historia y literatura.

Cuba posee suficientes educadores capacitados, tanto en el sistema como cesantes o jubilados, para seleccionar textos y para preparar a los maestros que han de utilizarlos en las clases. Muchos de estos maestros están activos en el sistema, pero los recursos de jubilados o cesantes (como los miembros del Colegio de Pedagogos Independientes) deben utilizarse.

Incorporar suplemento de educación cívica en todos los niveles de enseñanza: Los planes educacionales deben incluir, no como materia separada sino integral a toda actividad, la enseñanza del respeto a los derechos y la propiedad ajenos, la tolerancia, el conocimiento de los derechos civiles y de los principios democráticos.

Propocionar entrenamiento para docentes en los nuevos contenidos y metodologías: Los maestros cubanos necesitan recibir instrucción pedagógica para poder ejercer el magisterio de acuerdo a los cambios curriculares. Estos cursos pueden ser parte de los requisitos para obtener (o mantener) certificados.

Siguiendo el ejemplo de programas de rehabilitación en Europa Oriental, estos cursos deben ser impartidos por maestros cubanos que se han destacado en la profesión, los que recibirían entrenamiento adecuado en cursos especiales en Cuba o en el extranjero. La selección de estos catedráticos para maestros debe servir de prueba a una política ministerial que no considere el perfil político, dando oportunidad a aquellos acti-

---

9. http://www.cubanet.org/bibliotecas.htm y Marion Loyd, "Independent Libraries in Cuba Defy Government's Lock on Information," *The Chronicle of Higher Education* 47:39(8 junio 2001): A40-A42.

10. Pedagogía '99, págs. 66-67.

vos que lo merecen como a los que el sistema rechazó por razones ideológicas.

Desarrollar la educación electrónica y a distancia:
La investigación a todos los niveles y la competencia en el nuevo orden global exigen una tecnología correspondiente, que sólo comienza con cursos de computación.

Los cursos a distancia pueden proporcionar entrenamiento en áreas de Cuba donde el acceso a un centro de educación para adultos no es fácil. Para los maestros que aspiren a revalidar su certificación o a prepararse para los cambios en la enseñanza, los cursos por la Internet pueden servir de alternativa cuando se les dificulte asistir a un curso tradicional. Para los maestros rurales, la ayuda en la preparación de clases y la superación propia contribuirá cualitativamente.

Aunar esfuerzos con los de otras entidades nacionales en pos de reformas: Los programas de educación deben formar parte de todo el plan de reconstrucción nacional. Las reformas serán exitosas a largo plazo si alivian la situación social, moral, y cultural. A corto plazo, la reforma educacional necesita enseñar al cubano a reactivar la economía, dirigiéndolo a nuevas áreas y empresas en desarrollo, siempre contribuyendo a mejorar su productividad. Los programas de capacitación y educación de adultos deben satisfacer la demanda del mercado laboral. En particular, las industrias turística, agropecuaria, y de la construcción precisan coordinar planes y programas de entrenamiento con las instituciones que las provean de trabajadores.

Es por eso que los proyectos para el desarrollo económico del país deben incluir la descripción de un componente educacional, e.g. entrenamiento, cuyo coste debe calcularse en el presupuesto para dicho proyecto. En la medida que Cuba logre asistencia interna-

cional, los fondos destinados a la educación serán garantizados como un porcentaje de cada préstamo o donación.

Establecer una Junta de Supervisión: Reformas de la magnitud que requiere el sistema educacional cubano exigen inspección y evaluación no sólo de los administradores del sistema sino de un grupo de ciudadanos independientes. El Ministro de Educación debe establecer una junta independiente que revise los cambios que se van incorporando al sistema y evalúe la eficiencia, los gastos, y el tiempo en base a los resultados que las reformas causan. Esta Junta de Supervisión necesita representar a los distintos sectores de la sociedad cubana. Entre ellos, no sólo especialistas en pedagogía pero representantes de la industria y el comercio deben contribuir a la evaluación de un sistema educativo que necesita rehabilitarse.

Estas recomendaciones tienen en cuenta la historia de la educación en Cuba antes y después de la Revolución de 1959, la experiencia de los países del bloque soviético que por una década han lidiado por rehabilitar sus respectivos sistemas, y las condiciones en Cuba tras una década de Período Especial. Las publicaciones académicas y de organizaciones internacionales sobre la reforma de la educación en distintas partes del mundo también han sido útiles para diagnosticar los problemas y debilidades del caso cubano y explorar soluciones.[11] Muchas de estas recomendaciones podrían contribuir por si solas a mejorar aspectos de la situación actual de la educación; algunas sólo bastarían con que un gobierno aplicase las mismas reglas que ya tiene promulgadas. Si lo que se desea no es una mejoría sino una sanación, entonces sólo un programa reformista que parta de la premisa de que el sistema educativo debe desechar el marxismo-leninismo, parece prometer un panorama más alentador para la Cuba que transita.

---

11. Una extensa bibliografía acompaña el estudio de la educación que prepara la autora para el *Cuba Transition Project*. Para de detalles de la publicación, véase http://ctp.iccas.miami.edu.

ALTERNATIVE RECOMMENDATIONS FOR DEALING WITH EXPROPRIATED U.S. PROPERTY IN POST-CASTRO CUBA

Matías F. Travieso-Díaz, Esq.

INTRODUCTION

This paper examines one of the most important bilateral issues that will need to be addressed by the United States and a future Cuban Government—the resolution of the outstanding claims of U.S. nationals[1] for the uncompensated expropriation of their assets in the early years of the Cuban Revolution.

The paper assumes that resolution of the U.S. claims issue will not be practicable while the current socialist regime is in power in Cuba. While Cuban officials have periodically expressed a willingness to discuss settlement of the claims issue with the United States,[2] such willingness is usually expressed in the context of setting off those claims against Cuba's alleged right to recover hundreds of billions of dollars in damages from the United States due to the U.S. trade embargo and other acts of aggression against Cuba.[3] To date, the Cuban government has given no indication that it is prepared to negotiate in good faith and without preconditions a potential settlement of the U.S. expropriation claims with this country.

---

1. The term "U.S. nationals" means in the claims context those natural persons who were citizens of the United States at the time their properties in Cuba were seized by the Cuban Government, or those corporations or other entities organized under the laws of the United States and 50% or more of whose stock or other beneficial interest was owned by natural persons who were citizens of the United States at the time the entities' properties in Cuba were taken. *See* 22 U.S.C. § 1643a(1). Individuals and entities meeting this definition were eligible to participate in the Cuban Claims Program established by Congress in 1964 to determine the amount and validity of their claims against the Government of Cuba for the uncompensated taking of their properties after January 1, 1959. *See* 22 U.S.C. § 1643.

2. *See, e.g., Alarcon: Nation 'U.S. Protectorate' With Helms Burton Bill*, PRENSA LATINA, Nov. 1, 1995, *available in* F.B.I.S. (LAT-95-215), Nov. 7, 1995, at 1 (hereinafter "ALARCON").

3. This position is expressly set forth in Cuba's Law 80 of 1996, the "Law on the Reaffirmation of Cuban Dignity and Sovereignty," whose Art. 3 reads in relevant part:

   Art. 3.—The claims for compensation for the expropriation of U.S. properties in Cuba nationalized through that legitimate process, validated by Cuban law and international law referred to in the preceding article, may be part of a negotiation process between the Government of the United States and the Government of the Republic of Cuba, on the basis of equality and mutual respect.

   The indemnification claims due to the nationalization of said properties shall be examined together with the indemnification to which the Cuban state and the Cuban people are entitled as a result of the damages caused by the economic blockade and the acts of aggression of all nature which are the responsibility of the Government of the United States of America.

   Ley Número 80: Ley de Reafirmación de la Dignidad y Soberanía Cubanas," *Gaceta Oficial* (December 24, 1996, Extraordinary Edition). An English language translation appears at 36 I.L.M. 472 (1997). For the complete text of Law 80 online *see* http://www.cubavsbloqueo.cu/cubavsbloqueo/leyantidoto.htm.

The expropriation of U.S. assets in Cuba was one of the leading causes of the deterioration in relations between the two countries in the early 1960s and the imposition of the U.S. embargo on trade with Cuba, which remains in place to this date.[4] The expropriation claims issue is widely recognized as an obstacle to the re-establishment of normal relations between the United States and Cuba.

While this bilateral issue is being discussed by the governments of both countries, Cuba will also need to prepare itself to address the expropriation claims of Cuban nationals, whether the claimants are on the island or abroad. Resolving the claims by Cuban nationals is a separate issue from addressing the claims of U.S. nationals, but the two processes have so many political and economic interconnections that one cannot be easily addressed in isolation from the other.[5] The facts surrounding both sets of expropriations are similar, as is Cuba's failure to provide compensation to either group of claimants. Both categories of claimants will also compete for the very limited resources that the Cuban government will have at its disposal at the time it is called upon to provide remedies to the claimants. In addition, Cuba may need, for internal political reasons, to give roughly equivalent relief to Cuban nationals and U.S. claimants.[6] Indeed, one of the potential alternatives discussed in this paper is to have some U.S. na-

tionals opt out of the formal U.S.-Cuba settlement process and seek resolution of their claims under Cuba's domestic claim resolution program. Therefore, both groups of claimants must receive due consideration when seeking solutions to the claims issue.

There is also little doubt that once Cuba starts making a transition to a free-market economy, it will need to provide a remedy to those whose property was seized by the Revolutionary Government after 1959 and have not yet received compensation for the taking. Such an assumption is based on the requirements of international and Cuban law, fundamental notions of fairness, and the evident political necessity to settle property disputes before Cuba can achieve stability.

The resolution of outstanding U.S. expropriation claims is also a pre-condition to major foreign capital flow into Cuba. As long as property titles remain unsettled, foreigners are going to perceive investing in Cuba as a rather risky proposition and may be discouraged from stepping into the country.[7]

There are two additional reasons why resolution of the outstanding property claims of U.S. nationals must be one of the first orders of business of a transition government in Cuba. First, U.S. laws require resolution of U.S. nationals' expropriation claims before the embargo on trade with Cuba is lifted and

---

4. The trade embargo was officially imposed by President Kennedy in February 1962. *See* Proclamation 3447, 27 Fed. Reg. 1085 (1962), 3 C.F.R., 1059-63 Comp., at 157. Previously, authorization had been suspended for most industrial export licenses to Cuba. 43 DEPT. STATE BULL. 715 (1960). President Eisenhower had also reduced the quota of Cuban sugar in the U.S. market to zero. Proclamation No. 3383, effective December 21, 1960, 25 Fed. Reg. 13131. Additional trade restrictions were imposed by other laws enacted in the 1960-1962 period. Therefore, by the time President Kennedy proclaimed a total trade embargo, trade between the U.S. and Cuba was already essentially cut off. For a Cuban perspective on the history of the embargo, *see* http://www.cubagob.cu/.

5. *See* Matías F. Travieso-Díaz, *Some Legal and Practical Issues in the Resolution of Cuban Nationals' Expropriation Claims Against Cuba*, 16 U. PA. J. INT'L BUS. L. 217 (1995), for a discussion of the potential resolution of expropriation claims by Cuban nationals.

6. *See* Matías F. Travieso-Díaz and Steven R. Escobar, *Cuba's Transition to a Free-Market Democracy: A Survey of Required Changes to Laws and Legal Institutions*, 5 DUKE J. COMP. & INT'L L. 379, 412 (1995); Rolando H. Castañeda and George P. Montalván, *Economic Factors in Selecting an Approach to Expropriation Claims in Cuba*, presented at the Shaw, Pittman, Potts & Trowbridge Workshop on "Resolution of Property Claims in Cuba's Transition," Washington, D.C. 16 (Jan. 1995) (on file with author) (hereinafter "CASTAÑEDA AND MONTALVÁN").

7. All countries in Eastern Europe that have implemented schemes to settle expropriation claims have experienced a great deal of uncertainty over property rights. This uncertainty has discouraged potential investors and has delayed privatization efforts. Cheryl W. Gray et al., EVOLVING LEGAL FRAMEWORKS FOR PRIVATE SECTOR DEVELOPMENT IN CENTRAL AND EASTERN EUROPE (World Bank Discussion Paper No. 209) 4 (1993) (hereinafter "Gray et al."). While it appears inevitable that the claims resolution process will have some impact on Cuba's economic transition, the rapid development of a claims resolution plan would help minimize this impact.

foreign aid can resume;[8] and second, apart from any legal requirements, resolution of U.S. nationals' expropriation claims have been since the days of President Kennedy's administration one of the stated U.S. conditions for the normalization of relations between the U.S. and Cuba.[9] These factors demand the speedy negotiation of an agreement between the U.S. and Cuba about resolving the expropriation claims of U.S. nationals.

The discussion that follows discusses and comments on several potential claim resolution alternatives that can be implemented to address the expropriation claims of U.S. nationals. This paper, however, does not offer a specific proposal on how the outstanding property claims of U.S. nationals should be handled. Several such proposals to do this have already been developed.[10] The viability of any proposed program will ultimately be determined by the circumstances

under which a settlement of outstanding claims is undertaken, including the economic and political conditions in which Cuba finds itself when the government decides to deal with the problem.

HISTORICAL SUMMARY

Synopsis of Cuba's Expropriations

Cuba seized the properties of U.S. and other foreign nationals on the island starting in 1959, with the bulk of the expropriations taking place in the second half of 1960.[11] The process started in 1959 with the takeover of agricultural and cattle ranches under the Agrarian Reform Law;[12] reached a critical stage in July 1960 with the promulgation of Law 851, which authorized the expropriation of the property of U.S. nationals;[13] was carried out through several resolutions in the second half of 1960, again directed mainly against properties owned by U.S. nationals, although those of other foreign nationals were also

---

8. Section 620(a)(2) of the Foreign Assistance Act of 1961, 22 U.S.C. § 2370 (a)(2) (1988) (amended in 1994) prohibits U.S. assistance to Cuba until Cuba has taken "appropriate steps under international law standards to return to United States nationals, and to entities no less than 50 percent beneficially owned by United States citizens, or provide equitable compensation to such citizens and entities for property taken from such citizens and entities on or after January 1, 1959, by the government of Cuba." Also, the LIBERTAD Act includes as a precondition to declaring that a "democratically elected government" is in power in Cuba (thereby authorizing the provision of significant economic aid to Cuba and the lifting of the U.S. trade embargo) that Cuba has made "demonstrable progress in returning to United States citizens (and entities which are 50 percent or more beneficially owned by United States citizens) property taken by the Cuban Government from such citizens and entities on or after January 1, 1959, or providing full compensation for such property in accordance with international law standards and practice." *See* Cuban Liberty and Democratic Solidarity (LIBERTAD) Act of 1996, Pub. L. No. 104-114, 110 Stat. 785 (Mar. 12, 1996), *codified as* 22 U.S.C. Chapter 69A, (hereinafter "the Helms-Burton Law"), §§ 202(b)(2)(B), 204(c), 206(6). The Helms-Burton Law further expresses the "sense of Congress" that the satisfactory resolution of property claims by a Cuban Government recognized by the United States "remains an essential condition for the full resumption of economic and diplomatic relations between the United States and Cuba." *Id.,* § 207.

9. *See, e.g.*, Lisa Shuchman, *U.S. Won't Ease Embargo Against Cuba, Official Says,* PALM BEACH POST, Apr. 29, 1994, at 5B (quoting Dennis Hays, then Coordinator of Cuban Affairs, U.S. Department of State, as saying that before the U.S. lifts the trade embargo against Cuba, the expropriation of American-owned property by the Cuban Government will have to be addressed); Frank J. Prial, *U.N. Votes to Urge U.S. to Dismantle Embargo on Cuba,* N.Y. TIMES, Nov. 25, 1992, at A1 (quoting Alexander Watson, then Deputy U.S. Representative to the United Nations, as stating in an address to the General Assembly of the United Nations that the United States chooses not to trade with Cuba because "among other things Cuba, 'in violation of international law, expropriated billions of dollars worth of private property belonging to U.S. individuals and has refused to make reasonable restitution.' ")

10. See, e.g., Nicolás Sánchez, *A Proposal for the Return of Expropriated Cuban Properties to their Original Owners,* in CUBA IN TRANSITION—PAPERS AND PROCEEDINGS OF THE FOURTH ANNUAL MEETING OF THE ASSOCIATION FOR THE STUDY OF THE CUBAN ECONOMY 350 (1994); Kern Alexander and Jon Mills, *Resolving Property Claims in a Post-Socialist Cuba,* 27 GEORGETOWN INT'L L. J. 137 (1995) (hereinafter KERN & MILLS).

11. For a detailed description of the process by which Cuba expropriated the assets of U.S. nationals, see Michael W. Gordon, THE CUBAN NATIONALIZATIONS: THE DEMISE OF PROPERTY RIGHTS IN CUBA 69-108 (1975) (hereinafter "THE CUBAN NATIONALIZATIONS").

12. Ley de Reforma Agraria, *published in* Gaceta Oficial, June 3, 1959 ("AGRARIAN REFORM LAW").

13. Law 851 of Nationalization of July 6, 1960, *published in* Gaceta Oficial, July 7, 1960.

taken;[14] and continued through 1963, when the last U.S. companies still in private hands were expropriated.[15] In a parallel process, most assets owned by Cuban nationals, except for small parcels of land, homes, and personal items were seized at various times between 1959 and 1968.[16]

The laws issued by the Cuban Government to expropriate the holdings of U.S. nationals contained undertakings by the state to provide compensation to the owners.[17] Nevertheless, in almost no case was compensation paid.

The expropriation claims by nationals of other countries were considerably smaller than those of U.S. and Cuban nationals, and for the most part have been settled through agreements between Cuba and the respective countries (e.g., Spain, France, Switzerland, United Kingdom and Canada).[18] Claims have been settled at a fraction of the assessed value of the expropriated assets.[19]

The U.S. Claims Certification Program

In 1964, the U.S. Congress amended the International Claims Settlement Act to establish a Cuban Claims Program, under which the Foreign Claims Settlement Commission of the United States ("FCSC") was given authority to determine the validity and amount of claims by U.S. nationals against the Government of Cuba for the taking of their property since January 1, 1959.[20] The Cuban Claims Program of the FCSC was active between 1966 and 1972. During that time, it received 8,816 claims by U.S. corporations (1,146) and individual citizens (7,670).[21] It certified 5,911 of those claims, with an aggregate amount of $1.8 billion;[22] denied 1,195 claims, with an aggregate amount of $1.5 billion; and

---

14. Resolution No. 1, August 6, 1960, *published in* Gaceta Oficial, August 6, 1960; Resolution No. 2, September 17, 1960, *published in* Gaceta Oficial, September 17, 1960; Laws 890 and 891 of October 13, 1960, *published in* Gaceta Oficial, October 13, 1960; Resolution No. 3, October 24, 1960. For a listing of laws, decrees and resolutions by means of which Cuba's expropriations of the assets of U.S. nationals were implemented, see FOREIGN CLAIMS SETTLEMENT COMM'N, FINAL REPORT OF THE CUBAN CLAIMS PROGRAM 78-79 (1972) (hereinafter "1972 FCSC REPORT").

15. THE CUBAN NATIONALIZATIONS, at 105-106.

16. For a summary of Cuba's expropriations of the assets of its nationals, see Nicolás J. Gutiérrez, Jr., *The De-Constitutionalization of Property Rights: Castro's Systematic Assault on Private Ownership in Cuba,* presented at the American Bar Association's 1994 Annual Meeting, New Orleans, La. (1994), *reprinted in* 1 LATIN AM. BUS. L. ALERT 5 (1994).

17. Law 851 of July 6, 1960, which authorized the nationalization of the properties of U.S. nationals, provided for payment for those expropriations by means of 30-year bonds yielding two percent interest, to be financed from the profits Cuba realized from sales of sugar in the U.S. market in excess of 3 million tons at no less than 5.75 cents per pound. The mechanism set up by this law was illusory because the U.S. had already virtually eliminated Cuba's sugar quota, *see* Proclamation No. 3355, 25 Fed. Reg. 6414 (1960) (reducing Cuba's sugar quota in the U.S. market by 95%). Nonetheless, the inclusion of this compensation scheme in the law was acknowledgment by Cuba of its obligation to indemnify the U.S. property owners for the takings.

18. Cuba has entered into settlement agreements with five foreign countries for the expropriation of the assets of their respective nationals in Cuba: France, on March 16, 1967; Switzerland, March 2, 1967; United Kingdom, October 18, 1978; Canada, November 7, 1980; and Spain, January 26, 1988. *See* http://www.cubavsbloqueo.cu/. *See also,* Michael W. Gordon, The Settlement of Claims for Expropriated Foreign Private Property Between Cuba and Foreign Nations other than the United States, 5 LAW. AM. 457 (1973).

19. The Spanish claims, for example, were valued at $350 million but were ultimately settled for about $40 million. Even this limited amount was not paid until 1994, six years after the claims were settled and three decades after the claims accrued. *Cuba to Compensate Spaniards for Property Seizures,* REUTERS TEXTLINE, February 15, 1994, *available in* LEXIS, World Library, Txtlne File.

20. 22 U.S.C. §1643 *et seq.* (1988) (amended in 1994).

21. 1972 FCSC REPORT, Exhibit 15.

22. *Id.* The value of the certified Cuban claims exceeds the combined certified amounts of all other claims validated by the FCSC for expropriations of U.S. nationals' assets by other countries (including the Soviet Union, China, East Germany, Poland, Czechoslovakia, Hungary, Vietnam, and others). FOREIGN CLAIMS SETTLEMENT COMM'N 1994 ANNUAL REPORT 146 (1994) (hereinafter "1994 FCSC REPORT"). The total amount certified by the FCSC is almost double the $956 million book value of all U.S. investments in Cuba through the end of 1959, as reported by the U.S. Department of Commerce. Jose F. Alonso and Armando M. Lago, *A First Approximation of the Foreign Assistance Requirements of a Democratic Cuba, in* ASCE-3 at 168, 201. The valuation of the U.S. nationals' expropriation claims has never been established in an adversary proceeding. The FCSC certification process involved administrative hearings in which only the claimants introduced evidence on the extent and value of their losses. *See* 45 C.F.R. Part 531.

dismissed without consideration (or saw withdrawn) 1, 710 other claims.[23]

Of the $1.8 billion in certified claims, over 85% (about $1.58 billion) corresponded to 898 corporate claimants, and the rest (about $220 million) was spread among 5,013 individual claimants.[24] There were only 131 claimants—92 corporations and 39 individuals—with certified claims of $1 million or more; only 48 claimants, all but five of them corporations, had certified claims in excess of $5 million.[25] These figures show that the U.S. claimants fall into two general categories: a small number of claimants (mostly corporations) with large claims, and a large number of claimants (mainly individuals) with small claims.

Although the Cuban Claims Act did not expressly authorize the inclusion of interest in the amount allowed, the FCSC determined that simple interest at a 6% rate should be included as part of the value of the claims it certified. Applying such interest rate on the outstanding $1.8 billion principal yields a present value, as of April 2002, of approximately $6.4 billion.[26] This amount does not include the value of the claims that were disallowed for lack of adequate proof, nor those that were not submitted to the FCSC during the period specified in the statute.

LEGAL BASES FOR U.S. NATIONALS' EXPROPRIATION CLAIMS

The expropriation claims by U.S. nationals are based on well established principles of international law that recognize the sovereign right of states to expropriate the assets of foreign nationals in the states' territory, but require "prompt, adequate and effective" compensation to aliens whose property is expropriated.[27] The "prompt, adequate and effective" compensation formulation was coined in 1938 by U.S. Secretary of State Cordell Hull.[28] Under current practice, the "prompt" element of the Hull formula means payment without delay.[29] The "adequate" element means that the payment should reflect the "fair market value" or "value as a going concern" of the expropriated property.[30] The "effective" element is satisfied when the payment is made in the currency of

---

23. 1972 FCSC REPORT, Exhibit 15.

24. *Id.*

25. *Id.* at 413.

26. *Id.* at 76. The interest rate, if any, that should be applied to the amounts certified by the FCSC would most likely be subject to negotiation between the United States and Cuba.

27. Shanghai Power Co. v. United States, 4 Cl. Ct. 237, 240 (Ct. Cl. 1983), *aff'd mem.,* 765 F.2d 59 (Fed. Cir. 1984), *cert. denied,* 474 U.S. 909 (1985); RESTATEMENT (SECOND) OF FOREIGN RELATIONS LAW §§ 185-90 (1965). It has been held by U.S. courts that Cuba's expropriations of the assets of U.S. nationals violated international law because Cuba failed to provide adequate compensation, and because it carried the expropriations out in a discriminatory manner against U.S. nationals and conducted them for purposes of retaliation against the U.S. government. Banco Nacional de Cuba v. Sabbatino, 193 F.Supp. 375, 384 (S.D.N.Y. 1961), *aff'd,* 307 F.2d 845 (2d Cir. 1962), *rev'd on other grounds,* 376 U.S. 398 (1964); Banco Nacional de Cuba v. Farr, 272 F.Supp. 836, 838 (S.D.N.Y. 1965), *aff'd,* 383 F.2d 166, 184-85 (2d Cir. 1967), *cert. denied,* 390 U.S. 956 (1968). *See generally,* THE CUBAN NATIONALIZATIONS at 109-152.

28. A shorthand sometimes used for the Hull formula is that of "just compensation," meaning "in the absence of exceptional circumstances . . . an amount equivalent to the value of the property taken . . . paid at the time of the taking . . . and in a form economically usable by the foreign national." Patrick M. Norton, *A Law of the Future or a Law of the Past? Modern Tribunals and the International Law of Expropriation,* 85 A.J.I.L. 474, 475 (1991);RESTATEMENT (THIRD) OF FOREIGN RELATIONS LAW § 712 (1987).

29. Ibrahim F. I. Shihata, Legal Treatment of Foreign Investment: The World Bank Guidelines 163 (1993) (hereinafter "LEGAL TREATMENT OF FOREIGN INVESTMENT").

30. Alan C. Swan & John F. Murphy, Cases and Materials on the Regulation of International Business and Economic Relations 774-76 (1991) (hereinafter "SWAN & MURPHY"). Shihata explains the "adequacy" element of compensation as follows:

> Compensation will be deemed 'adequate' if it is based on the fair market value of the taken asset as such value is determined immediately before the time at which the taking occurred or the decision to take the asset became publicly known.

LEGAL TREATMENT OF FOREIGN INVESTMENT at 61. Shihata goes on to define fair market value as the amount that a willing buyer would normally pay to a willing seller after taking into account the nature of the investment, the circumstances in which it would operate in the future and its specific characteristics, including the period in which it has been in existence, the proportion of tangible assets in the total investment and other relevant factors. *Id.* at 161-162.

the alien's home country; in a convertible currency (as designated by the International Monetary Fund); or in any other currency acceptable to the party whose property is being expropriated.[31] Cuba has clearly failed to satisfy its obligations under international law with respect to providing compensation for the properties it seized from U.S. nationals.[32]

Domestic Cuban law in effect at the time of the takings also dictates that the U.S. property owners (like their Cuban national counterparts) should receive adequate compensation for the expropriations. It is unclear whether under Cuban law the claims of U.S. citizens, supported under international as well as Cuban law principles, should have priority over those of Cuban nationals, whose rights rest solely or mainly upon Cuban law. The distinction, if any, may as a practical matter be inconsequential because, as discussed earlier, political considerations dictate that the claims of both groups should be addressed fairly and in a similar manner.

ALTERNATIVE RECOMMENDATIONS FOR DEALING WITH U.S. NATIONALS' CLAIMS

Any proposal for the resolution of the U.S. nationals' expropriation claims against Cuba must recognize the objectives that a claims resolution program needs to achieve the fundamental differences between the various types of property subject to claims, and the practical limitations that will be encountered by the Cuban government as it seeks to provide remedies to both U.S. and domestic expropriation victims. The interaction between these factors adds a significant degree of complexity to the problem.

There are also fundamental differences among the property interests covered by the claims, which suggest that certain remedies may be better suited for some types of property than for others. For example, restitution of residential property may be extremely difficult, both from the legal and political standpoints;[33] monetary compensation may be an inadequate remedy where the property is unique, such as in the case of beach-front real estate in a resort area.

Cuba will also be confronted with political, as well as financial, limitations to its ability to provide certain remedies. A settlement that involves huge financial obligations over a long period of time may be resisted politically by, among others, the generation that came of age after the expropriations were carried out.[34]

In the discussion that follows, I will seek to identify how these factors come into play with regard to the different remedies that may be provided.

Cuban Claims Settlement Precedents

It is instructive to examine the precedent of the settlement agreements that Cuba has negotiated with other countries for the expropriation of the assets of their nationals. According to a Cuban summary, those agreements have five important facts in common: (1) they were negotiated over long periods of time; (2) none of the agreements adhered to the "Hull Formula", and in particular none implemented the "adequacy" standard, in that they were lump sum, country-to-country settlements that did not take into account either individually or collectively the amounts claimed by the nationals for the loss of their properties; (3) the payments were made in installments, rather than all at once; (4) the payment was in either the currency of the country advancing the claims or, as was the case with Spain and Switzer-

---

31. *Id.* at 163.

32. It has been the conclusion of U.S. courts and legal scholars that at least some of the expropriations of the assets of U.S. nationals, such as those arising from Law 851 of July 6, 1960, were contrary to international law on the additional grounds that they were ordered in retaliation against actions taken by the U.S. to eliminate Cuba's sugar quota, and because they discriminated against U.S. nationals.

33. *See* Juan C. Consuegra-Barquín, *Cuba's Residential Property Ownership Dilemma: A Human Rights Issue Under International Law,* 46 RUTGERS L.R. 873 (1994) (hereinafter "CONSUEGRA-BARQUIN") (discussing the difficulties that a Cuban transition government will face in seeking to provide remedies for residential property expropriations.)

34. *See* Emilio Cueto, *Property Claims of Cuban Nationals,* presented at the Shaw, Pittman, Potts & Trowbridge Workshop on "Resolution of Property Claims in Cuba's Transition," Washington, D.C. 9-12 (Jan. 1995) (on file with author) (hereinafter "CUETO").

land, in trade goods as well as currency; and (5) all agreements were negotiated between Cuba and the state that representing the claimants, without claimant participation.[35]

While these precedents are not controlling, they are indicative of the kinds of terms that Cuba may seek if monetary compensation is the standard used for the negotiations. Clearly, an agreement with the United States patterned after these historical precedents would provide only a fraction—perhaps a small fraction—of the amounts sought by the claimants.

Alternative 1: Government-to-Government Negotiations

Discussion of Alternative. The President of the United States has wide, but not plenary, power to settle claims against foreign governments for the uncompensated taking of property belonging to U.S. citizens.[36] The U.S. Department of State, under authority delegated by the President, acts on behalf of U.S. claimants in the negotiation of their claims with an expropriating foreign country.[37] Under the "doctrine of espousal," the negotiations conducted by the Department of State are binding on the claimants, and the settlement that is reached constitutes their sole remedy.[38]

In most agreements negotiated in the past, the United States and the expropriating country have arrived at a settlement involving payment by the expropriating country to the United States of an amount that is a fraction of the total estimated value of the confiscated assets.[39] The settlement proceeds are then distributed among the claimants in proportion to their losses. In most cases, the settlement does not include accrued interest, although a 1992 settlement with Germany over East Germany's expropriations of the assets of U.S. nationals did include the payment of simple interest at the approximate annual rate of 3% from the time the U.S. properties were taken.[40]

Under standard practice, U.S. claimants may not "opt out" of the settlement reached by the U.S. Government. Dissatisfied claimants are barred from pursuing their claims before U.S. courts or in the settling country.[41]

Comments on Government-to-Government Negotiations Alternative. The above described traditional settlement agreement would not appear, in itself, to be adequate to satisfy the needs of the parties in the Cuban situation. The amount of the outstanding certified claims by U.S. nationals is so large that it would likely outstrip Cuba's ability to pay a significant portion of the principal, let alone interest. In addition, Cuba's transition government will be burdened already by a very large external debt: Cuba owes over $11 billion to international private and public lenders in the West, and has defaulted on its

---

35. *See* http://www.cubavsbloqueo.cu/.

36. Dames & Moore v. Regan, 453 U.S. 654, 688, 101 S. Ct. 2972, 69 L. Ed. 918 (1981); Shanghai Power Co. v. United States, *supra*, 4 Cl. Ct. at 244-245. The President's authority is limited by the rarely-exercised power of Congress to enact legislation requiring that a settlement seen as unfavorable be renegotiated. Dames & Moore v. Regan, *supra*, 453 U.S. at 688-689 and n.13.

37. *See id.*, 453 U.S. at 680 and n.9, for a listing of ten settlement agreements reached by the U.S. Department of State with foreign countries between 1952 and 1981.

38. *Id.*, 453 U.S. at 679-680; Asociacion de Reclamantes v. United States, 735 F.2d 1517, 1523 (D.C. Cir. 1984); RICHARD B. LILLICH AND BURNS H. WESTON, INTERNATIONAL CLAIMS: THEIR SETTLEMENT BY LUMP SUM AGREEMENTS 6 (1975).

39. For example, the U.S. settled its nationals' claims against the People's Republic of China for $80.5 million, which was about 40% of the $197 million certified by the FCSC. Shanghai Power Co. v. United States, *supra*, 4 Cl. Ct. at 239; XVIII I.L.M. 551 (May 1979).

40. Letter from Ronald J. Bettauer, Assistant Legal Adviser for International Claims and Investment Disputes, U.S. Department of State, to claimants (May 29, 1992); Agreement Between the Government of the United States of America and the Government of the Federal Republic of Germany Concerning the Settlement of Certain Property Claims, May 13, 1992, TIAS 11959 (hereinafter German Agreement).

41. *See,* Shanghai Power Co. v. United States, *supra*.

loan obligations.[42] Also, Cuba owes Russia, as successor to the Soviet Union, 15 to 20 billion U.S. dollars in loans that it has never repaid.[43] Any additional obligations to U.S. claimants would only exacerbate Cuba's debt situation.

Thus, a traditional settlement involving the payment of money, even if payment is spread out over time, would be likely to place Cuba in difficult financial straits. Such a settlement could also have adverse political repercussions.[44]

This is not to say that, even if other settlement alternatives were considered (see *infra*), there would be no need for a lump sum payment by Cuba. Such a payment (in the order of, say, $200 million) could be set aside to satisfy the claims of those for whom other alternative remedies would not be desirable or practicable. Lump sum settlement proceeds could, for example, provide limited monetary compensation to all claimants to the extent of their certified losses involving residential and small farm properties.[45] Alternatively, a lump sum payment of $200 million would provide over 50% principal recovery (but no interest) to the 5,013 certified claimants who are individuals.[46]

One potential source of funds for such lump payments could be blocked Cuban assets under the control of the U.S. Government. However, some if not all of these assets are likely to be unavailable because they have been made eligible, through legislation passed in 1996 and 2000, for recovery by those raising claims of personal injury or death as the result of actions by the Cuban Government.[47] Therefore, Cuba will need to identify some other source of funds to satisfy the lump sum payment portion of any settlement of U.S. national expropriation claims.

---

42. *See,* http://www.odci.gov/cia/publications/factbook/geos/cu.html. Cuba's external debt is a staggering 58% of the country's Gross Domestic Product. *Id.*

43. *Id.*

44. *See* CUETO at 9-12, 34-36.

45. Residential property and small farms are good candidates for a compensation remedy because such a remedy avoids the potential need to dispossess current occupants to those properties, who may have acquired legal rights to them and whose eviction might be politically untenable; *see* CONSUEGRA-BARQUIN. In addition, owners of residential or small farming property in a foreign country may be generally less likely to desire restitution of those assets almost forty years after they were taken.

46. A 50% level of recovery would exceed that in most "lump sum" settlements negotiated by the U.S. under the International Claims Settlement Act programs. *See* 1994 FCSC REPORT at 146.

47. The Foreign Sovereign Immunities Act, 28 U.S.C. § 1602 *et seq.*, protects, subject to specified exceptions, the property of foreign states or their agencies and instrumentalities from damages claims by private parties. One of the exceptions to this immunity permits suits against certain foreign states (including Cuba) for terrorist acts or provision of material support thereto. 28 U.S.C. §1605(a)(7). Under that provision (known as the Terrorist Act Exception) and a counterpart provision in the criminal code, U.S. nationals have the right to recover treble damages, plus attorneys' fees, for injuries to person, property or business incurred as a result of international terrorism. However, the Terrorist Act Exception also allows the President to waive the ability to execute any judgments that are obtained in such a suit against blocked assets of the foreign government. 28 U.S.C. §1610(f)(3).

In 2000, however, Congress enacted the "Victims of Trafficking and Violence Protection Act of 2000," Public Law 106-386 (approved October 28, 2000), whose section 2002(a) allows plaintiffs holding certain judgments against Cuba to recover against blocked Cuban assets. The legislation was intended to permit recovery of judgments awarded to the families of the Brothers to the Rescue pilots whose planes were shot down by Cuba in 1996. See Jonathan Groner, Payback Time for Terror Victims, Legal Times, June 7, 2000, available online at http://www.law.com/cgi-bin/gx.cgi/AppLogic+FTContentServer?pagename=law/View&c=Article&cid=ZZZ6C54V59C&live=true &cst=1&pc=0&pa=0&s=News&ExpIgnore=true&showsummary=0; see also, Alejandre v. Republic of Cuba, 996 F.Supp. 1239 (S.D. Fl., 1997). The Alejandre court allowed the recovery of $187 million in compensatory and punitive damages which, under the 2000 legislation, could be recovered against Cuba's blocked assets, whose value was pegged in 1993 at approximately $112 million. *See* Department of Treasury, Office of Foreign Assets Control, Annual Report to the Congress on Assets in the United States Belonging to Terrorist Countries or International Terrorist Organizations, April 19, 1993, available online at http://www.fas.org/irp/congress/1993_cr/h930503-terror.htm. Therefore, the Cuban blocked assets under control by the U.S. government would probably not be available to provide payment to expropriation claimants.

Alternative Methods not Involving Government-to-Government Negotiations

Whether as part of a government-to-government settlement, or independently of it, U.S. claimants could be authorized to obtain relief directly from Cuba for their expropriation claims. This relief could be the result of private, individual negotiations with the Cuban Government or through participation by the U.S. claimants in Cuba's formal claim resolution program. This section examines those alternatives.

Alternative 2: Direct Negotiations Between the Claimants and the Cuban Government

Discussion of Alternative. It would be possible for the United States and Cuba to arrive at a negotiated settlement that allowed alternative remedies beyond the up-front payment of money, and which included the possibility that individual claimants would waive their right to receive a share of the lump sum settlement proceeds and instead negotiate directly with the Cuban Government for restitution of their expropriated assets, investment concessions, payments in commodities other than cash, or compensation by means of Cuban Government obligations.[48] While there is no direct precedent for such a procedure and the courts have ruled that individual claimants have no right to negotiate directly with the debtor government,[49] in the case of Cuba, such a flexible settlement may prove to be in the best interest of all parties.[50]

Comments on Direct Claimant Negotiations with Cuba. A direct settlement between a U.S. claimant and Cuba, if successful, should satisfy the claimant in that it would represent the best resolution that he was able to obtain through bargaining with Cuba. Such a settlement attempt, however, might not be successful. Therefore, if the direct negotiations alternative were authorized, the United States and Cuba would have to agree on a mechanism for assuring that those claimants who waived the right to be represented by the U.S. Government in the negotiations with Cuba received a fair and equitable treatment by Cuba, and that if such negotiations failed the claimant would not be left without a remedy.

One way of protecting the rights of the U.S. claimants who choose to negotiate directly with Cuba could be for the Cuban Government to agree to submit to binding international arbitration any claim that it was unable to settle with a U.S. national. Historically, however, arbitration of disputes between private citizens and states has resulted in inconsistent decisions on key issues. In **Saudi Arabia v. Arabian American Oil Co.** (ARAMCO), reprinted in 27 ILR 117 (1958), for example, the arbitration tribunal refused to apply the law of Switzerland where the tribunal was located, even though Saudi Arabia had agreed to have the seat of the tribunal in Switzerland. By contrast, the arbitrator in **Saphire International Petroleum v. National Iranian Oil Co.**, reprinted in 35 ILR 136 (1963), decided that the legal system of the place of arbitration would govern the arbitration. Likewise, inconsistent results on this issue were achieved in three other arbitrations between Libya and the nationals of foreign states that arose out of

---

48. In November 2000, a task force of former U.S. Government officials and other public figures established by the Council on Foreign Relations issued a report that recommended a number of initiatives to prepare for a transition in bilateral relations between the United States and Cuba. The task force, headed by former Assistant Secretaries of State for Inter-American Affairs Bernard W. Aronson and William D. Rogers, recommended among other steps resolving expropriation claims by licensing American claimants to negotiate settlements directly with Cuba, including equity participation in Cuban enterprises. *See* http://www.cfr.org/Public/media/pressreleases2000_112900.html. The U.S. Government has not authorized such direct negotiations in the past.

49. *See* Dames & Moore v. Regan, *supra*.

50. There are indications that at least some major U.S. claimants would be interested in alternative methods to settle their claims. *Amstar Says, Let's Make a Deal*, CUBA NEWS, Jan. 1996, at 6. There is also some precedent for such flexibility. The U.S. settlement agreement with Germany, for example, allows U.S. nationals to forego their portions of the settlement amount and instead pursue their claims under Germany's program for the resolution of claims arising from East Germany's expropriations. German Agreement, *supra*, Art. 3; 57 Fed. Reg. 53175, 53176 (November 6, 1992).

the nationalization of Libyan oil in the early 1970s.[51] This lack of uniformity and predictability in the outcomes underscores the need to establish clearly and in advance the legal regime for the arbitration of disputes between U.S. citizens and the Cuban government.

Predictability of applicable rules could be achieved if the United States and Cuba agreed in advance to a procedure analogous to that used by the Iran-U.S. Claims Tribunal ("Tribunal") set up to resolve the expropriation claims of U.S. nationals against Iran.[52] The Tribunal has three jurisdictional grants of power: (1) it may hear the "claims of nationals of the United States against Iran and claims of nationals of Iran against the United States;"[53] (2) it may hear "official claims of the United States and Iran against each other arising out of contractual arrangements between them;"[54] and (3) it may hear disputes between the United States and Iran regarding the interpretation or performance of any provision of the General Declaration[55] or the claims of their nationals.[56] One important aspect of the Tribunal's framework is the adoption of The United Nations Commission on International Trade Law's ("UNCITRAL")

Arbitration Rules, which are designed to address international commercial arbitration.[57] This choice of rules allowed supervisory jurisdiction to the courts of the Netherlands where the Tribunal sits.[58]

The Tribunal has taken the view that the claims of nationals are the claims of a private party on one side and a Government or Government-controlled entity on the other.[59] In accord with this view, the procedures set up by the Tribunal require exhaustion of local remedies and provide that the private claimants themselves will present their claims to the Tribunal.[60] The nationals themselves file the claims and present them, and also decide whether to withdraw or accept any settlement offer.

One of the most innovative structural elements of the Tribunal is that a Security Account held in trust by the Algerian Government—consisting of a portion of frozen Iranian assets—has been established for the purpose of guaranteeing that the awards of the Tribunal are capable of being satisfied. This Account is only available to satisfy the claims of U.S. nationals, and cannot be used for awards in favor of

---

51. *British Petroleum Exploration Co. v. Libyan Arab Republic*, reprinted in 53 ILR 297 (1973) (deciding that the municipal procedural law would govern the arbitration); Texaco Overseas Petroleum & California Asiatic Oil Co. v. Libya, reprinted in 17 ILM 1 (1978) (holding that local law was not to be applied to the arbitration); *Libyan American Oil Co. v. Libyan Arab Republic,* 20 ILM 1 (1981) (leaving unclear whether the arbitration was governed by the international legal system or the place of arbitration).

52. *See* NORTON at 482-486.

53. Declaration of the Government of the Democratic and Popular Republic of Algeria Concerning The Settlement of Claims by the Government of the United States of America and the Government of the Islamic Republic of Iran, 19 January 1981 ("Claims Settlement Declaration"), Art. II(1).

54. *Id.*, Art. II(2)

55. Declaration of the Government of the Democratic and Popular Republic of Algeria dated 19 January 1981 ("General Declaration"). *See*, Claims Settlement Declaration, Art. II(3).

56. *Id.*, Art. VI(4).

57. *See* United Nations United Nations Commission on International Trade Law Arbitration Rules (1976), ("UNCITRAL rules"), *available online* at http://www.jus.uio.no/lm/un.arbitration.rules.1976

58. Article VI of the Claims Settlement Declaration allows the Tribunal to be located in The Hague "or any other place agreed by Iran and the United States." Whether the Netherlands was the most advantageous place for the Tribunal was debated internally within the United States government. See Symposium on the Settlement with Iran, 13 Law. Am.1, 46 (1981).

59. *See Islamic Republic of Iran and United States,* (Case A18) (Dual Nationality), Dec. 32-A18-FT (Langergren, Holtzman (CO), Kashani (DO), Riphagen (CO), Aldrich, Shafeiei (DO), Mangard, Ansari (DO), & Mosk (CO), arbs., Apr. 6, 1984), 5 IRAN-U.S. C.T.R. 251 (1984 I).

60. Claims for less than $250,000 may be presented by the government of a national according to a supplemental clause. Claims Settlement Declaration, Art. III(3).

Iranian nationals or Iranian governmental counter-claims.[61]

The structure of the Tribunal is thus largely self-contained in both its procedural operation and its ability to satisfy successful claims.[62] However, there are areas in which the Tribunal's relationship to the external world may need to be considered. For example, should the Security Account become depleted, enforcement of Tribunal decisions would become a significant issue.

The main area of potential divergence between the Tribunal and a counterpart tribunal set up to adjudicate disputes between a U.S. claimant and Cuba would be that, in the case of Iran, significant assets of that country were frozen in the United States and were made available to satisfy arbitration awards in favor of private claimants. As discussed above, no such funds are likely to exist in the case of Cuba, so provisions would have to be made to set up an independent source of funds available to satisfy Tribunal awards—else a victory by a U.S. claimant in arbitration could prove pyrrhic because no funds might be available from which to satisfy the award.

Alternative 3: Participation in Cuba's Claim Resolution Program

Assuming that it was not feasible to have direct negotiations between U.S. claimants and Cuba, another alternative could be to allow U.S. nationals to participate in Cuba's domestic claims resolution program. Under such a program, there would be several alternative forms of compensation that could be made available to the claimant (as well as to Cuban claimants). These alternative remedies are discussed next.

Restitution Methods: Direct Restitution. Restitution of the actual property that was confiscated ("direct restitution") would be the solution that many U.S. corporate claimants might prefer, assuming such a choice was available under Cuba's claims resolution program.[63] Some types of expropriated property, e.g. large industrial installations, may lend themselves readily to direct restitution since the identity of the former owners is likely to be uncontested and the extent of the ownership rights may be easy to establish.[64]

Restitution, however, may in many instances prove difficult to implement even for readily identifiable property because the ability to grant restitution of the actual property seized by the Cuban Government

---

61. General Declaration, para. 7 ("All funds in the Security Account are to be used for the sole purpose of the payments of . . . claims against Iran . . .").

62. For example, the UNCITRAL rules provide for the appointment of an authority to resolve disputes over the Tribunal's composition. UNCITRAL Rules, Art. 9-12.

63. Restitution has been used as the remedy of choice for expropriations in many countries in Central and Eastern Europe, including Germany, Czechoslovakia, the Baltic republics, Bulgaria and Romania. On the other hand, Hungary, Russia and all other former republics of the USSR (with the exception of the Baltic republics) have expressly refused to grant restitution of property expropriated during the communist era. Frances H. Foster, *Post-Soviet Approaches to Restitution: Lessons for Cuba, in* CUBA IN TRANSITION: OPTIONS FOR ADDRESSING THE CHALLENGE OF EXPROPRIATED PROPERTIES (hereinafter OPTIONS) 93 (JoAnn Klein, ed., 1994).

The former Czechoslovakia is a good example of the restitution approach. Czechoslovakia implemented an aggressive, across-the-board restitution program, under which it enacted a series of restitution laws that distinguished between "small" property (such as small businesses and apartment buildings), "large" property, and agricultural lands and forests, with each type of property being subject to somewhat different procedures and remedies. The restitution of "small" property was governed by the Small Federal Restitution Law, which provided for direct restitution to original owners. GRAY ET AL. at 49. The Large Federal Restitution Law governed the restitution of "large" property (industries and associated real estate), and again provided for the return of the property to its former owners, except in situations where the property was in use by natural persons or foreign entities, in which case restitution was barred and compensation had to be paid instead. GELPERN at 337-38 (1993). Likewise, for agricultural land and forests, the Federal Land Law provided presumptive restitution of lands to the original owners. Where neither the land originally expropriated nor a substantially similar parcel in the locality was available, financial compensation was provided as an alternative remedy. *Id.*

64. The top twenty U.S. claimants, in terms of amounts certified by the FCSC, are all corporations. Their combined claims add up to $1.25 billion, or 70% of the total certified. Most of the corporations owned sugar mills and other industrial installations that would be readily identifiable.

may be negated by a variety of circumstances. The property may have been destroyed or substantially deteriorated; it may have been subject to transformation, merger, subdivision, improvement, or other substantial changes; it may have been devoted to a use that may not be easily reversed or which may have substantial public utility; or its character or use may be such that the state decides not to return to its former owners. In such cases, some form of compensation would need to be granted.

In addition, in the last decade, Cuba (through state-owned enterprises) has entered into a number of joint ventures with foreign, non-U.S. investors. Many of these ventures involve property that was expropriated from U.S. and Cuban nationals. In deciding whether to provide direct restitution of those properties to the U.S. claimants, the Cuban Government will have to balance the rights and interests of the former owners against those of third parties who have invested in Cuba. Likewise, the rights of any other leaseholders, occupants, or other users of the property would also have to be taken into account.

Where direct restitution is the appropriate remedy, a number of matters will have to be worked out between Cuba and the U.S. claimants. For example, Cuba may want to impose restrictions or requirements on the claimants' use of the property, or on their ability to transfer title for a certain period of time after restitution. Also, a potentially complex valuation process may need to be undertaken if the property has been improved since being expropriated. In some instances, an agreement will need to be reached in advance on the recovering owner's responsibility for the environmental reclamation of the property, to the extent that ecological impacts from operation of the facility have occurred or are expected to occur in the future. Many other issues are likely to come up in individual cases.

Cuba may also decide to impose a "transfer tax" or equivalent fee on the restitution transaction. The purposes of such tax would be to raise funds for other aspects of the program, and to ensure that settlement of the claim by restitution does not leave a claimant in a better position than that of other claimants who have availed themselves of other forms of recovery, such as partial compensation.

Substitutional Restitution. There may be instances in which direct restitution will be impractical, but both Cuba and the U.S. claimant will still wish to apply a restitution type of remedy. Such circumstances may dictate restitution of substitute property (that is, the transfer to the claimant of other property, equivalent in value to the one confiscated). Where restitution of substitute property is proposed, it will be necessary to set rules on, among other things, how the equivalence of the properties is to be established.

Substitutional restitution may be appropriate, for example, in cases where the confiscated property is farmland that has been conveyed to co-operatives or divided among small farmers. Rather than dispossessing the current occupants, Cuba may offer to convey to the U.S. claimants agricultural or other lands in state hands that may be equivalent to those expropriated.

Comment on Restitution Methods. Direct and substitutional restitution programs implemented in certain Eastern European countries have been criticized on economic grounds.[65] Some analysts have concluded that the use of restitution in Cuba would be fraught with perils.[66] The restitution of properties to U.S. claimants has also been opposed because it "would be tantamount to insisting that nationalistic feelings in Cuba due to foreign ownership of the country's principal assets never had a basis in fact."[67] Despite these concerns and criticisms, restitution—

---

65. Gray et al. summarize the restitution experience in Eastern Europe as follows:

   Restitution-in-kind is complex and leaves many problems in its wake. The legal precedence typically given restitution over privatization has created great uncertainty among potential investors and has complicated privatization, particularly in the case of small business and housing. It is also leading to many disputes that are beginning to clog the courts. In Romania, for example, restitution of agricultural land has led to more than 300,000 court cases. GRAY ET AL at 4. They level the same criticism against the programs instituted in Czechoslovakia. *Id.* at 49.

whether direct or substitutional— is likely to be an important ingredient in the mix of remedies granted to U.S. claimants under Cuba's claims settlement program. It will be inappropriate in many instances, and even where appropriate, its use should be tempered by the realization that restitution will often be a slow and difficult process, and one subject to contentious disputes among a variety of claimants, including former owners and their successors, current occupants, and others.[68] In addition, if a variety of remedies are offered, care must be taken to assure that those availing themselves of the restitution alternative are neither better nor worse off than those receiving other types of remedy.

Issuance of State Obligations

Discussion of Alternative. A number of Eastern European countries have used state-issued instruments, which will be generally referred to here as "vouchers," to provide full or partial compensation to expropriation claimants.[69] The vouchers may not be redeemed for cash, but can be used, among other things, as collateral for loans; to pay (fully or in part) for property sold by the state, including shares in privatized enterprises; to purchase real estate put up for sale by the state; to be exchanged for annuities; or as investment instruments.[70]

---

66. For example, in evaluating the potential implementation of a restitution program in Cuba in light of the experiences in the Baltic republics, one commentator writes:

> Furthermore, the preceding study suggests that restitution could serve as a major brake on overall Cuban national economic modernization. It could delay the establishment of stable, marketable legal title to assets, a critical requirement for both privatization and domestic and foreign investment. Moreover, it could drain an already depleted Cuban national treasury. A Baltic-style restitution program would obligate the Cuban State either to turn over state and collective property gratuitously or to pay equivalent compensation. In the Cuban case this would be particularly onerous because of the sheer enormity of U.S. claims for "prompt, adequate and effective" compensation for expropriated property.

Finally, Estonia, Latvia, and Lithuania indicate that restitution could have a severe socioeconomic impact on current Cuban citizens. As in these three states, the Cuban government has heavily subsidized the living expenses of its population. It has prevented its citizens from significant acquisition of assets and, until recently, legally prohibited them from accumulating hard currency. Thus, if Cuba should elect to return property to former owners (many of whom are foreign corporations or émigrés) and to introduce free market mechanisms, its present population would be at a competitive disadvantage. *See* FOSTER at 113 (footnotes omitted).

67. CASTAÑEDA & MONTALVÁN at 14. These concerns reflect apprehension over a return to the significant role played by U.S. investors in the Cuban economy at the time of the 1959 Revolution, when U.S. investments in Cuba amounted to roughly one-third of the capital value of Cuba's industrial plant. *See* Eric N. Baklanoff, EXPROPRIATIONS OF U.S. INVESTMENTS IN CUBA, MEXICO, AND CHILE 27 and n. 43 (1975). At that time, U.S. owned enterprises dominated or played leading roles in the agricultural, mining, manufacturing, petroleum, and utility industries. *Id.* at 12-31.

68. In the former Czechoslovakia, for example, restitution led to numerous disputes between original owners and current occupants, as well as disputes between competing claimants, resulting in clogged courts. GRAY ET AL. at 49.

69. Hungary has used compensation vouchers as the sole means of indemnifying expropriation claimants. Katherine Simonetti et al., *Compensation and Resolution of Property Claims in Hungary, in* OPTIONS at 61, 69 (hereinafter "SIMONETTI"). The means of compensation are interest-bearing transferable securities or "vouchers" known as Compensation Coupons, issued by a Compensation Office charged with the administration of the claims program.

interest rate set by the central bank.

70. *Id.* at 69-72. In Hungary, vouchers can be used also to purchase farmland in auctions held by the state; however, only former owners of land may use their vouchers for that purpose.

The voucher system provides a potential way of resolving many of the U.S. nationals' expropriation claims in Cuba, particularly those of former owners of small and medium enterprises who may not be interested in recovering the properties they once owned because of the obsolescence or physical deterioration of the facilities.[71] The system recognizes the limits of the country's ability to pay compensation claims, and avoids the dislocation costs and disputes associated with direct restitution systems. As with restitution remedies, an issue that would need to be resolved at the outset would be the compensation to be offered in proportion to loss.

The system has potentially great flexibility, for the vouchers could be used for a variety of purposes, some of which may be more attractive than others to individual claimants. Also, in addition to vouchers, other issued instruments could be used as means of compensating U.S claimants. These include annuities, bonds, promissory notes, stock certificates in privatized enterprises, and other debt or equity instruments.

Comments on Issuance of State Obligations

There are several potential drawbacks to a system of vouchers or other state-issued instruments.[72] The instruments will fluctuate in value, and are likely to depreciate if Cuba's economic recovery falters.[73] In addition, to the extent the instruments are used as income-generating devices (e.g., for the collection of annuities), the rate of return is likely to be very low.[74] Also, the basic underpinning of a voucher system is confidence in the state's ability to make good on its commitments. Therefore, the security, transferability, and marketability of the compensation instruments is a serious concern that the Cuban Government will need to overcome in order for the remedy to have acceptability with the claimants.

Other Compensation Mechanisms

Discussion of Alternative. Other remedies that might be utilized in Cuba, and have not yet been tried elsewhere, could consist of economic incentives to invest in the country. These remedies could include, for example, giving credits on taxes and duties to the extent of all or part of the claim amount; granting the ability to exchange the claim for other investment opportunities, such as management contracts, beneficial interests in state-owned enterprises, or preferences in government contracting; and conferring other benefits. Each claimant might be interested in a different "package," so *ad-hoc*, case-by-case negotiations would need to be conducted, at least to resolve the most significant claims.[75]

Comments on Other Compensation Mechanisms

While allowing some creativity in the development of claims resolution arrangements suitable for individual claimants, the ability to create ad-hoc resolutions could potentially complicate the claims process to the point of making it unwieldy. An even more significant risk is that a perception could easily develop that there is a lack of fairness and transparency in the process, since comparing the economic benefit of a "deal" to another might be difficult and open to a variety of interpretations. Thus, care will have to be exercised if this alternative is utilized.

---

71. A Cuban economist has included the issuance of vouchers as an option for providing compensation to U.S. corporate claimants. Pedro Monreal, *"Las Reclamaciones del Sector Privado de los Estados Unidos Contra Cuba: Una Perspectiva Académica,"* paper presented at the Shaw, Pittman, Potts & Trowbridge Workshop on "Resolution of Property Claims in Cuba's Transition," Washington, D.C. 5 (Jan. 1995) (on file with author). The alternative proposed by this economist would require the claimant to invest in Cuba an amount equal to the value of the coupons it received.

72. *See* CUETO at 26-28 for a brief discussion of some of the valuation and financing issues that will surface if Cuba seeks to implement a voucher compensation scheme. See also, CASTAÑEDA AND MONTALVÁN at 14-16.

73. This was experienced, for example, in the Czech and Slovak republics. Heather V. Weibel, *Avenues for Investment in the Former Czechoslovakia: Privatization and the Historical Development of the New Commercial Code*, 18 DEL. J. CORP. L. 889, 920 (1993).

74. The experience in Hungary has been that vouchers used to collect annuities have yielded very disappointing results. SIMONETTI at 78.

75. A. R. M. Ritter, Financial Aspects of Normalizing Cuba's International Relations: The Debt and Compensation Issues, in TRANSITION IN CUBA at 559-560.

CONCLUSIONS AND RECOMMENDATIONS
Conclusions

There will come a time when the U.S. and Cuba will set out to negotiate a settlement of the expropriation claims of U.S. nationals against Cuba. The date of such an event is uncertain, but it is most likely that the negotiations will be held while Cuba is besieged by a depressed economy and an unstable political situation.

The conditions under which the settlement will be negotiated will greatly restrict the remedies that Cuba will be able to offer the U.S. claimants. Certainly, the traditional way of settling expropriation claims (i.e., Cuba's payment of a lump sum of money to the U.S. government to be distributed pro-rata among all claimants) will not be adequate, given Cuba's inability to pay a significant portion of the amounts it owes. Lump-sum compensation should be given to the U.S. nationals to the extent funds are available, but should be substituted with (for those claimants wishing to opt out of the lump-sum settlement) a variety of other remedies to be negotiated by the claimants with Cuba, including restitution of the expropriated assets, compensation through state-issued instruments, and other means. While the eventual solution reached in each case is likely to only grant partial recovery to the claimant, the results in most cases would probably be more beneficial to the claimants than a lump-sum distribution.

The types of remedies available to U.S. nationals opting to participate in a parallel Cuban domestic claims program would of necessity have to be few in number, relatively straightforward in execution, and demand little in the way of up-front cash outlays by the state. The results of a domestic Cuban process are likely to leave many dissatisfied. Therefore, both the Cuban government and the claimants should be prepared to exhibit flexibility in working towards as fair and reasonable a resolution of the claims as can be achieved under the circumstances.

Recommendations

As the discussion in this paper suggests, the U.S. government needs to make a number of important policy decisions to prepare itself to discuss with Cuba the potential resolution of the claims issue. For example, the U.S. Government will need to decide whether to organize its settlement approach around the traditional "espousal" principle and preclude claimants from engaging in separate negotiations with Cuba, or whether it will adopt a more flexible approach that allows claimants to be represented by the U.S. Government or pursue other avenues to obtain redress.

These and other policy issues should be examined in the near term by a multi-agency task force, perhaps with the assistance of outside experts. The task force's mandate should be to identify what policy issues will need to be addressed by the U.S. Government in the process of negotiating a resolution of the claims issue with Cuba, recommend solutions to those issues, and propose legislation to be enacted if the proposed issue resolution requires appropriations or some other form of legislative action.

All countries in Eastern Europe that have implemented schemes to settle expropriation claims have experienced a great deal of uncertainty over property rights. This uncertainty has discouraged potential investors and has delayed privatization efforts. While it appears inevitable that the claims resolution process will have some impact on Cuba's economic transition, the rapid development of a claims resolution plan would help minimize this impact.

LET THERE BE CANDY FOR EVERYONE: REFORM, REGULATION, AND RENT-SEEKING IN THE REPUBLIC OF CUBA, 1902-1952

Mary Speck

When Dr. Ramón Grau San Martin returned to the Cuban presidency in 1944, he seemed to be fulfilling the dreams of a generation of Cuban nationalists who first broke into politics as the student revolutionaries of 1933. Grau, the archrival of military powerbroker and president General Fulgencio Batista, represented the aspirations of those who clamored for agrarian reform, the nationalization of public services, and the end of "economic individualism."[1] Unlike his ill-starred presidency in 1933, brought down after only four-months by a combination of U.S. pressure, business opposition, and labor unrest, Grau's new regime began as Cuba rode a wave of World War II-engendered prosperity. Sugar prices, the barometer of Cuba's highly open economy, were the highest since 1924 and would continue to soar as the allies struggled to feed a devastated Europe. Grau, who had previously governed during the depths of the depression, could now oversee the sharing out of an economic boom. He promised to make good the Authentic Party slogan, "Cuba for Cubans." "To govern is to distribute," he told his followers. "Let there be candy for everyone."[2]

But Grau, the martyr of the generation of 1933, would be remembered for redistribution of a different sort. He would go down in the annals of contemporary Cuban history as one of the most corrupt presidents in the five decades between independence and Batista's 1952 *golpe de estado*. Cuban historians have dismissed the fashionable physician turned populist politician as a "caricature" of the revolutionary, whose government "surpassed the corrupt politics reigning in Cuba since [the withdrawal of U.S. troops in] 1902."[3] A British historian condemns him as the leader who "did more than any other single man to kill the hope of democratic practice in Cuba."[4] The collapse of Cuban democracy in the 1950s had multiple causes but key among them was the political corruption that undermined the island's republican institutions. General Fulgencio Batista would take up the standard of the fight against graft

---

1. See E. Vignier and G. Alonso, *La corrupción política y administrativa en Cuba: 1944-1952* (Havana: Editorial de Ciencias Sociales, 1973), 4.

2. Quoted in Jorge I. Domínguez, *Cuba: Order and Revolution* (Cambridge: Harvard University Press, Belknap Press, 1978), 108.

3. Vignier and Alonso, *Corrupción*, 29.

4. Hugh Thomas, *Cuba or The Pursuit of Freedom* (New York: Harper & Row, 1971), 737.

and gangsters when he overthrew Grau's successor, Carlos Prio, in 1952. Less than seven years later, Batista himself would fall, his own government mortally weakened by the violence and venality of his supporters.

Historians sometimes write as if there were two Ramón Grau San Martins and two *Auténtico* parties: the idealistic reformers of 1933 and the corrupt politicians of the 1940s. Reform is said to have died in 1933, along with the hope of founding a government that was willing and able to defend national interests. Thus, the *Auténticos* who returned to power in 1944 could only do so by betraying the "historical mandate" of 1933.[5] The "frustration" of Cuban nationalist aspirations during the Republic, the shattering of reformers' dreams of social justice on the rock of U.S pro-business policies, becomes the key to understanding the triumph of "radical nationalism" after the 1959 revolution. For some historians, Grau's ouster meant the end of reform for the next quarter century. A popular textbook of modern Latin American history simply dismisses as unimportant the twenty-five years of Cuban history leading up to the Cuban revolution. "Cuban politics saw little change between 1934 and 1959," write Thomas Skidmore and Peter Smith. "What had happened to the revolutionary fervor of 1933? Where was the coalition that had so frightened Washington? It had gone the way of all Cuban nationalist movements—rendered impotent by the unbeatable alliance of Cuban elites, their political and military handmaidens, and Uncle Sam."[6]

But the Revolution of 1933 survived the ouster of Grau and his radical student supporters. 1933 was not the end, but the beginning of a new era of reform, designed to protect Cuban labor and regulate Cuban business. Between 1933 and 1958, the Cuban government "extended its regulatory and distributive activity enormously," writes political scientist Jorge

Domínguez.[7] By the time Grau returned to power in 1944 an extensive system of economic controls was already in place, which began in the sugar sector but were extended to much of the rest of the economy. Those industries not subject to government regulation were controlled by mandatory business and professional organizations, which lobbied for government favors and often restricted new entries. At the center of this regulatory regime was the president, who distributed favors and mediated disputes. The Cuban Congress, like many Latin American legislatures, was relatively weak, with some power to distribute patronage, but little control over the president, who legislated by decree.

The scandals of the Grau administration—such as the alleged pilfering of $174 million in pension funds deposited in the public treasury—were merely the most spectacular manifestations of a system rife with possibilities for rent-seeking, influence peddling, and outright theft. The idealistic reformers of the 1930s had worked to create a state that would protect Cuban workers, Cuban business people, and Cuban bureaucrats from the ravages of worldwide depression. But they also created a complex system of quotas and subsidies, price controls and wage guarantees, licenses and permits—that pitted powerful interest groups against each other in competition for government-dispensed privileges.

REGULATION AND RENT SEEKING

Corruption, of course, did not appear first in the decades before the Cuban revolution. It had deep roots in Cuba's colonial history. Spanish bureaucrats were accustomed, and expected, to supplement meager official stipends with payoffs and kickbacks. Such "fee for service" corruption may even have had some positive effects by allowing entrepreneurs to "grease the wheels" of a sluggish Colonial bureaucracy.[8] In the first two decades of the Republic, corruption was still "patrimonial" in nature: public office was sought

---

5. Louis A. Pérez, *Cuba: Between Reform and Revolution* (New York: Oxford University Press, 1995), 287.

6. Thomas E. Skidmore and Peter H. Smith, *Modern Latin America,* 4th ed. (New York: Oxford University Press, 1997), 272.

7. Domínguez, *Cuba,* 90.

8. See Nathaniel Leff, "Economic Development Through Bureaucratic Corruption," *American Behavioral Scientist* 8 (1964).

largely for private gain.[9] Contemporary newspapers printed lurid accounts of graft in public works contracts. Public payrolls were swollen with *botellas,* literally bottles, meaning fictitious jobs that were never actually filled. The lottery became notorious as a source of income to be portioned out among political supporters. Such corruption had little impact on the private business community. Because there was little state regulation of the economy, interest groups had little reason to lobby for government benefits.

The stakes changed, however, with the economic and social reforms that began in the late 1920s. Ever increasing state regulation and control over key sectors, such as the sugar industry, exacerbated the corruption already endemic in Cuban public affairs, turning both politics and business into a fierce struggle for government favors. Corruption from the 1930s on took the form not only of outright kickbacks, bribes, and graft but also of what economists call a "rent-seeking" mentality that pervaded Cuban society. Instead of concentrating on innovations to improve products or develop new products, Cuban workers, farmers, and industrialists had to compete to secure political benefits and protection. Ironically, reforms originally designed to shield both business and labor from depression in the 1930s, ended up heightening what a 1951 World Bank report called the "high level of economic insecurity which affects all groups in Cuba."[10] In a largely stagnant economy, competition to protect one's share of national production through public policy was fierce. Instead of "creative destruction," Cuba's cycle of export booms and busts had

intensified, in the World Bank's words, "the natural 'defensive' impulses of economic groups against new methods of production which appear to offer competition or to threaten opportunities for jobs or profits."[11]

Rent-seeking, defined as "the political activity of individuals and groups who devote scarce resources to the pursuit of monopoly rights granted by governments," can both exacerbate political factionalism and inhibit economic growth.[12] Rent-seeking ranges from outright bribery to costly lobbying for import quotas or licenses, tariff exemptions and other tax privileges, price supports or controls, and government credit or direct subsidies. Competition for government benefits diverts time and resources that might otherwise be devoted to productive activities, resulting in a welfare loss to the economy as a whole. Innovation is discouraged as both entrepreneurs and workers focus instead on winning government favors and blocking the efforts of their competitors to do the same. Economist Anne Krueger has described how protectionist policies in developing nations can create a "vicious circle" of ever-increasing regulation that stifles economic growth. Mancur Olson, in *The Rise and Decline of Nations,* argued that the rent-seeking behavior of interest groups—or "distributional coalitions"—could accelerate the economic decline of advanced industrial states, such as Great Britain after World War II.[13] The fight to distribute, rather than create, wealth can become a zero-sum game as growth stalls. To survive, businesses, banks, and la-

---

9. Domínguez calls Cuban politics in the early Republic "neopatrimonial" after Max Weber's definition of the patrimonial political system as one where "all government authority and the corresponding economic rights tend to be treated as privately appropriated economic advantages." See Domínguez, *Cuba,* 35-36.

10. International Bank for Reconstruction and Development, *Report on Cuba* (Washington, D.C.: International Bank for Reconstruction and Development, 1951), 66. Hereafter referred to as World Bank, *Report.*

11. World Bank, *Report.*

12. William C. Mitchell and Michael C. Munger, "Economic Models of Interest Groups: An Introductory Survey," *American Journal of Political Science* 35, no. 2 (May 1991), 525. See also Anne O. Krueger, "The Political Economy of the Rent Seeking Society," *The American Economic Review* 64, no. 3 (June 1974), 291-303; and "Virtuous and Vicious Circles in Economic Development," *The American Economic Review* 83, no. 2 (May 1993), 351-355; Kevin M. Murphy, Andrei Shleifer, Robert W. Vishny, "Why is Rent-Seeking so Costly to Growth?" *The American Economic Review* 83, no. 2 (May 1993), 409-414; and, Andrei Shleifer, Robert W. Vishny, "Corruption," *The Quarterly Journal of Economics* 108, no. 3 (Aug. 1993), 599-617.

13. Mancur Olson, *The Rise and Decline of Nations* (New Haven, Conn.: Yale University Press, 1982).

bor unions must focus their energies on cultivating political contacts, whether licit or illicit.

BITTER SWEET

Cuba before the revolution was in many ways an economic success story. The exportation of sugar, a commodity that requires huge investments in industry and infrastructure, had created a highly capitalized economy with far more wealth per person than the rest of the Caribbean and probably more than any other tropical nation.[14] By the end of the 1920s, Cuba's per-capita income was the third highest in Latin America, after Argentina's and Chile's, and was nearly three times that of Mexico and Brazil. In terms of both human and physical infrastructure, Cuba had far outstripped its neighbors. Social indicators such as literacy, infant mortality and life expectancy, were well above the norm in the Caribbean and Central America, comparable only to the levels achieved by the relatively wealthy countries of Latin America's Southern Cone.[15] Despite the country's dependence on agricultural exports, over half of the population lived in urban areas.[16] And Cuba had a well-developed transportation system. The island had regular steamboat service between major coastal cities by the 1820s and completed its first railroad in 1837, before the mother country of Spain and before any of its independent but politically tumultuous neighbors in Central or South America. By the mid-twentieth century, Cuba had more kilometers of railroad per person than the United States.[17] It also ranked among the top nations of Latin America in terms of cars, television sets, and telephones per capita.[18]

While such statistics do not mean that all, or even most, Cubans enjoyed the benefits of economic growth, they do suggest that pre-revolutionary Cuba was far from a "banana republic," nor was it underdeveloped compared to most of Latin American or even southern Europe. Sugar had not created an enclave economy, where the exportation of commodities benefited only a tiny elite tied to foreign interests. It had provided the island with substantial physical and human capital. But the statistics mask flaws that made Cuban economic growth highly inequitable and difficult to sustain. By 1950, sugar had long ceased to be the dynamic industry that once attracted massive immigration and investment. Nor had dynamic new industries emerged to take advantage of the infrastructure that sugar had created. Unemployment, both chronic and seasonal due to the agricultural cycle, was a serious political and economic problem. While Havana had grown into an elegant metropolis, much of the countryside languished with high rates of disease and malnutrition. And even Havana's wealth had been created largely by the parents and grandparents of its 1950 residents. "[T]he present per capita income of about $300 is only slightly above that of the early 1920s," wrote the World Bank in 1951. "It is largely the result of the [World War II] sugar boom which brought back into full use equipment installed in the first quarter of the century [...] Cuba's present standard of living, therefore, depends mainly on an industry which stopped growing many years ago."[19]

---

14. Henry Christopher Wallich, *Monetary Problems of an Export Economy: The Cuban Experience, 1914-1947,* Harvard Economic Studies, vol. 88 (Cambridge: Harvard University Press, 1950), 3.

15. See GDP estimates gathered by Angus Maddison in *Two Crises: Latin America and Asia, 1929-38 and 1973-83* (Paris: OECD, 1985), Table A.1. According to Maddison, in 1929 Argentina's per capita income was U.S. $415, Chile's was $250 and Cuba's was $238. Mexico and Brazil both had per capita incomes of about $85. Life expectancy at birth was more than 40 years, second only to Argentina, and the literacy rate was 70 percent. See Cuban Economic Research Project, *A Study on Cuba* (Miami: University of Miami Press, 1965), 208. Hereafter referred to in footnotes as CERP, *Study.*

16. According to the census of 1931, 51.36 percent of the population lived in cities of more than one thousand inhabitants. CERP, *Study,* 305.

17. Cuba had nearly 3.4 kilometers of railroad per 1,000 persons; the United States had about 2.4 kilometers per 1,000 persons. World Bank, *Report,* 241.

18. See CERP, *Study,* 579, 582-583.

19. World Bank, *Report,* 7.

Cubans were well aware of the dangers of depending on one primary export crop. In boom times, as in busts, Cubans leaders realized that sugar alone could not guarantee prosperity. Since 1898, rulers of the island, including U.S. occupiers, had decried the dangers of a one-crop economy. Even before independence, Cuba's national hero, the poet José Martí, whose words were (and are) quoted like the Bible by politicians of every stripe, had called an over reliance on plantation agriculture "suicidal." Since the mid-1920s, diversification of Cuban agriculture and industry had been a fundamental tenet of public policy, supported in principle by the sugar industry itself. And yet entrepreneurs, who had aggressively undercut their international competitors during the early twentieth century, would prove by and large incapable of developing successful new products for the domestic and world markets. National leaders who had once hailed sugar as the source of the island's relative affluence now condemned it as an Achilles' heal that was jeopardizing the nation's stability and independence.

In the late nineteenth century, when the island of Cuba seemed poised to dominate the United States'—and the world's—sugar market, a leading autonomist had famously said, in effect, "Without sugar, there is no country."[20] By the late 1920s, the formula had been reversed and an eminent professor of economics would warn: "Either the Republic must demolish [sugar] cane or cane will demolish the Republic."[21] In both eras, sugar was identified with nationhood—or the lack of it. Heavy U.S. investment in the sugar industry from the mid teens to the early twenties only exacerbated the feeling that Cuba had lost control of the source of its political and eco-nomic sovereignty. Sugar had brought unprecedented prosperity in the first two decades of the century followed by the ruin of many sugar planters and mill owners in the financial crash of 1921. It was transforming the social and economic landscape of the country in ways that many found distasteful and even dangerous. Thus Fernando Ortiz, a multifaceted intellectual who was most famous for his works on Afro-Cuban culture, compared sugar unfavorably with tobacco in *Cuban Counterpoint*. Ortiz is lyrical in his portrayal of tobacco as the product of independent Cuban farmers who took an artisan's pride in the quality of their leaf. Sugar, on the other hand, was the undifferentiated output of huge factories owned by foreign capital and manned by a rural proletariat.[22] Ramiro Guerra, an historian who had tremendous influence over Cuban scholarship and public policy, warned that vast foreign-owned latifundia were taking over the Cuban countryside, eliminating or impoverishing Cuba's small farmers, shrinking its domestic market and placing the island at the mercy of international markets.[23] The distinguished historian Herminio Portell Vilá, author of a multi-volume history of Cuban relations with Spain and the United States, would call the sugar industry a "Frankenstein," a deformed vestige of Cuba's "colonial economy."[24]

U.S. PROTECTIONISM

So why did sugar remain central to the Cuban economy, long after it had ceased to be an engine of export-led economic growth? Much of the post-Revolutionary historiography of the Cuban Republic has focused on U.S. interests, which are assumed to have sought "control" of the island's resources. According to one sweeping assertion, U.S. trade and investment

---

20. Rafael Fernández de Castro, a reformer and advocate of autonomy from Spain. His actual words were: "Sin azúcar no se concibe la isla de Cuba y sin el consumo de ese producto por los Estados Unidos no se concibe nuestra existencia como pueblo culto." Quoted in Julio Le Riverend, *Historia Económica de Cuba* (Havana: Editorial de Ciencias Sociales, 1985), 538.

21. José Comallonga, cited in J. Alvarez Díaz, et. al., *Cuba: Geopolítica y Pensamiento Económico* (Miami: Duplex Paper Products of Miami for the Colegio de Economistas de Cuba en el Exilio, 1964), 289.

22. Fernando Ortiz, *Cuban Counterpoint: Tobacco and Sugar* (Durham, N.C.: Duke University Press, 1995).

23. Ramiro Guerra y Sánchez, *Azúcar y Población en las Antillas* (Havana: Editorial de Ciencias Sociales, 1970). This was first published in 1927.

24. Herminio Portell Vilá, *La industria azucarera y su futuro* (Havana: Molina y Cía, 1942), 20. Pamphlet reprinted from *Revista Bimestre Cubana* 50, no. 2 (July-Dec. 1942).

"excluded Cubans from agriculture and mining, utilities and transportation, trade and commerce, industry and manufacture, banking and finance."[25] Cuban Marxists asserted that the U.S. capital condemned Cuba to an economy where foreigners owned the export industry and foreign companies flooded the rest of the economy with imports.[26] Explicitly, or implicitly, many U.S. historians still accept the premise of William Appleman William's influential tome, *The Tragedy of American Diplomacy*, which argued that the United States was impelled to intervene in Latin America by the drive to increase U.S. trade and investment.[27] "Defense of capital interests served as the cornerstone of U.S. policy," says a 1986 history of Cuba. These interests demanded, above all, "a docile working class, a passive peasantry, a compliant bourgeoisie, and a subservient political elite."[28]

U.S. economic policy did, of course, influence the course of Cuban development, but not because of any inexorable need by U.S. capitalists to penetrate—or in today's terms "globalize"—the island's economy. Economic interpretations of U.S. foreign policy often fail to take into account the complex and conflicting interests of U.S. exporters, farmers, industrialists, bankers, and foreign investors. Perhaps nowhere is this clearer than in U.S.-Cuban relations, where the interests of U.S. investors in the island's sugar industry clashed repeatedly with those of sugar producers in the United States and its foreign territories. Moreover, the United States at the turn of the century was far from committed to "globalization." "In the Gilded Age, America's industrial, commercial, and agricultural economy diversified, establishing the United States as one of the giants on the world scene," writes political scientist Judith Goldstein. Nonetheless, U.S. trade policies, instead

of projecting U.S. economic might by promoting commerce, turned progressively more defensive:

> It was during this period of increasing American competitiveness and relatively more open European markets that the United States moved to institutionalize trade protections. Ironically, policy during this period ran counter to America's apparent interests; as the United States became increasingly competitive on world markets and more interested in world trade, American policy became increasingly more autarkic.[29]

It was Cuban exporters who sought most eagerly to penetrate the U.S. market, not vice versa. Cuba in the first quarter of the twentieth century was poised to become the "world's sugar bowl." Its land was ideal for sugar cane cultivation. Its sugar mills boasted the latest technology. Cuba's very efficiency as a low-cost producer, however, became a threat to competitors abroad. Sugar was—and is—one of the most highly protected commodities on the international market. (Unfortunately for Cuba, another highly protected commodity was the island's other major export, tobacco). Many European nations, and some Latin American nations, such as Mexico and Argentina, also set up protective barriers to stimulate the domestic production of sugar. There was nothing natural about the world's "overproduction" of sugar from the 1920s on; it was the result of deliberate government policy.

Among the biggest losers in the tariff battles waged in the U.S. Congress during the early twentieth century were the sugar producers of Cuba, both foreign and domestic. Congress barely passed the Reciprocity Treaty of 1902 after a long and heated debate and despite intense lobbying by beet producers from key Western States. Instead of the free trade advocated by Cuban business and political leaders, it granted Cuba

25. Pérez, *Cuba*, 213.

26. See, for example, Jorge Ibarra, *Prologue to Revolution: Cuba, 1898-1958* (Boulder, Colo.: Lynne Rienner Publishers, Inc., 1998), and Oscar Pino Santos, *El asalto a Cuba por la oligarquía financiera Yanqui* (Havana: Casa de las Américas, 1973).

27. William Appleman Williams, *The Tragedy of American Diplomacy, 2nd ed.* (New York: Dell Publishing Co., 1972).

28. Louis A. Pérez, Jr., *Cuba under the Platt Amendment, 1902-1934* (Pittsburgh, Pa.: University of Pittsburgh Press, 1986), xv-xvi.

29. Judith Goldstein, *Ideas, Interests, and American Trade Policy* (Ithaca: Cornell University Press, 1993), 8. See also Cynthia A. Hody, *The Politics of Trade: American Political Development and Foreign Economic Policy* (Hanover, N.H.: University Press of New England, 1996) on the institutional impediments to international economic cooperation.

only a 20 percent reduction on the already high over-all tariff.

Cuban and U.S. mill owners and cane planters on the island again joined forces with U.S. sugar refiners, soft drink and candy manufacturers to lobby against the Hawley-Smoot Tariff of 1929—and lost. The domestic sugar industry in the United States, also hard hit by low commodity prices, proved politically more powerful. Although sugar producers in Cuba were given a preferential tariff rate in the Reciprocity Treaty of 1934, it came with ropes attached. The Sugar Act of 1934, also known as the Jones-Costigan Act, allocated quotas to the different geographical areas that supplied the U.S. market. Moreover, the quotas were based on U.S. market share during 1931, 1932 and 1933, years when Cuba's exports had been drastically reduced by the Hawley-Smoot tariff. For the high cost sugar beet producers in the American West, such quotas were a godsend. But for sugar mill owners in Cuba, who had invested heavily to expand production in the 1920s, quotas, though preferable to the prohibitive tariff rates imposed in 1929, were still an unhappy compromise.

U.S. trade policies not only limited the growth of Cuban sugar exports, they discouraged the growth of other export industries, as well. High tariffs on finished tobacco products (and militant Cuban unions) encouraged U.S. cigar makers in Havana to shut down their factories and re-open them in New Jersey.[30] Would-be exporters of winter vegetables and citrus fruits also faced tariff barriers supported by strong domestic lobbies. It did not matter that many of these small farmers were U.S. citizens, lured to the island shortly after independence by land developers who promised that Cuba would soon become the United States' "winter garden."[31] Well-organized fruit growers in Florida and California made sure that tariffs were high enough to discourage foreign imports, including those raised by their compatriots

in Cuba. By the 1920s, the few foreign-born agricultural colonists who remained on the island produced their fruits and vegetables mainly for the Cuban domestic market.[32]

Despite the limits of the reciprocity treaty, the Cuban economy grew rapidly in the first decades after independence. Until about 1925, both large and small mills, whether foreign or domestically owned, increased their output. But much of the capacity created by the sugar industry in the 1920s was not used until the Second World War. And sugar, once viewed as a source of wealth, became, according to its critics, an economic albatross.

COORDINATED PRODUCTION

By the late 1930s, the future of Cuba's once dynamic sugar industry was in doubt. Efforts to form an international cartel had not only failed to raise sugar prices but encouraged non-cartel members to increase their production. The United States quota system assured Cuban producers of a stable, but not a growing, market. The complex internal system of controls and quotas imposed by the Cuban government from the 1930s on was a response to the industry's dismal international prospects. With a limited external market, many mills faced certain bankruptcy and tens of thousands of workers faced unemployment. Reorganization of the industry would have been economically painful, and, for a country still reeling from Machado's overthrow, politically disastrous. Just as U.S. beet sugar producers had demanded import quotas to protect themselves from foreign competition, Cuban producers demanded internal quotas to protect themselves from internal competition. Decree 522, promulgated in 1936, followed a year later by the Law of Sugar Coordination, set up an elaborate regulatory system designed to guarantee the survival of the island's smaller (and generally least efficient) mills, along with independent sugar planters or colonos. Small mills were guaranteed minimum basic

---

30. See CERP, *Study,* 265. On Cuban unions and U.S. tobacco manufacturers, see Jean Stubbs, *Tabaco en la periferia: El complejo agro-industrial cubano y su movimiento obrero, 1860-1959* (Havana: Editorial de Ciencias Sociales, 1989), 47.

31. See for example *The Cuba Review,* 4 (February 1906), 22. *The Cuba Review,* published by the Munson Steam Ship Line, originally promoted U.S. colonization of the island. By the mid-1910s, however, the magazine covered mainly the sugar industry.

32. Cuba, *Census of the Republic of Cuba, 1919* (Havana, n.d.), 60-61.

quotas, while larger mills were limited to their average production in 1934 and 1935 (when most were operating well below capacity). Sugar planters or *colonos* in turn won cane quotas to preserve their share of the cane sold to mills, and also secured restrictions on the amount of "administration cane" large mill owners could grow on their own property. *Colonos* also won the so-called "right of permanent occupancy," which meant that as long they met their cane quota and paid their rent (whose amount was tied to the price of sugar), they could never be evicted. And just to be sure no mill owner or cane grower ever went into bankruptcy, the act extended a moratorium on agricultural loans. A final provision of the Act tied wages to sugar prices, although, in reality, sugar worker salaries were allowed to rise with prices, but not to fall as fast or as far.

As José Antonio Guerra (son of historian Ramiro Guerra) wrote in 1942, the system was designed to freeze the status quo in place:

> Our system of sugar production control is organized to distribute and maintain the industry in all of the areas where it existed before the restrictions [on sugar production] began, and to prevent the displacement, not just of mills, but, more importantly, of planters. This policy rests on the fundamental principle of recognizing and respecting as inviolable in each region, the existing interests in each area, namely, the interests of the industrial unit, the mill, the colonia, the land-owner, the workers, the local merchants, the transport systems, and the municipality which derives its basic income from the activity of the local sugar mill.[33]

The economic polices that emerged beginning in the 1930s were geared, not toward growth, but toward protecting Cuban jobs and Cuban businesses. In the words of the World Bank, Cuban economic policies focused on "preserving the status quo and on regulating the division of a fixed national production, rather than on innovation to enlarge the total product."[34] They succeeded. Cuba had about the same number of active mills in 1959 as it had had two decades earlier. But the result was an industry operating well below capacity until the outbreak of World War II.

Mills were discouraged from economizing by reducing the length of the harvest or improving the productivity of labor. Labor legislation made it difficult to dismiss workers for any reason, including "*tecnificación.*" Sugar unions also protested against rising "*intensivismo*" in sugar factories. In 1950, mills that managed to produce their quotas in less time were forced to pay their workers "*superproducción*" to compensate them for hours lost.[35] Efficiency was also discouraged in the agricultural sector. Growers had little incentive to improve the quality of their cane because their payments (a percentage of the sugar manufactured from their cane, paid in kind or in currency) were based, not on the yield of their individual crops, but on the average yield of the entire cane crop processed at their local mill. In order to equalize payments to *colonos* with poor land, the percentage payment declined as yield increased. (After 1949, this provision was dropped and colonos received uniform payments, independent of yield). There was little reward for raising yield by planting better varieties of cane, cutting cane only when mature, or delivering it promptly to the mill. [36]

The Sugar Stabilization Institute, known by its Spanish acronym, ICEA, was in charge of enforcing sugar regulations. ICEA was essentially a legal cartel, governed by a board comprising 12 mill owners, 6 growers, the head of the sugar workers union and a government delegate. The Cuban president appointed the owners and growers from lists submitted by their respective associations. The institute negotiated international contracts and allocated production and crop quotas. But it was the Cuban president who

---

33. José Antonio Guerra, Appendix to Guerra, *Azúcar y Población*, 258.

34. World Bank, *Report*, 779.

35. Oscar Zanetti, *Dinámica del estancamiento: El cambio tecnológico en la industria azucarera cubana entre 1926 y 1958* (Havana: Instituto de Historia de Cuba, 1996), 32.

36. CERP, 339-345.

brokered disputes between mill owners and growers, workers and management, intervening to prevent mill owners from using their greater influence in ICEA to the detriment of powerful growers or unions.

The attempt to create risk-free capitalism—at least for domestic producers—was not limited to the sugar sector. Quotas were extended to two other important products, tobacco and coffee. Nor were imports allowed to bring unbridled competition to the island's domestic market. Most industries were organized in manufacturers' associations that secured tax advantages, subsidies, and protective tariff barriers against finished products while lobbying for low tariffs on imported inputs. The result was a complex system of taxes and tariffs, riddled with exemptions. Manufacturers did not hesitate to join forces with labor when threatened with technologies that might raise productivity and thus displace workers by putting inefficient enterprises out of business. Attempts to mechanize cigar production beginning as early as the 1920s were repeatedly thwarted by a powerful alliance of small manufacturers and skilled workers. Candy manufacturers who invested in modern machines during the 1940s had to run them at the lowest possible speed so as not to put their rivals out of business and displace workers. Textile factories faced potent opposition from their competitors and their workers as they tried to raise productivity in the 1940s and 50s. Measures designed to protect employment discouraged the creation of new jobs. A self-regulatory commission, created to defend Cuba's shoe industry from the competition of cheap imports and the even cheaper products of local "cottage" manufacturers, went so far as to outlaw the establishment of new factories.

The financial system also faced regulations designed principally to protect Cuban borrowers from the risk of bankruptcy. After the crash of 1921, the government instituted a moratorium on debt repayments that was extended and expanded in 1933 and 1934 and eventually enshrined in the Constitution of 1940. The fact that foreigners controlled the banking sector did not hinder the government's willingness or ability to impose onerous regulations. "Had there been domestic banks, their influence and public concern for their solvency might have caused the moratorium laws [...] to be less sweeping," wrote a North American economist in 1950. "Since the foreign banks can hardly fail, the government need not be too considerate with them."[37] But the moratoria did not just affect foreign bankers. Many Cubans had invested their savings in real estate mortgages, which offered safety and a relatively high return. Under the moratoria, such domestic capital was frozen and the returns either eliminated or substantially reduced. Cubans seeking safety and higher returns had to export their savings abroad, further reducing the supply of local capital.

Capital flight was just one of the many costs of economic controls. Elaborate regulations inevitably inspired expensive efforts to evade them. Having the best lawyers became as important as employing the best engineers. It might even be considered a prerequisite. Restrictions on the employment of foreign technicians and professionals (including Cubans trained abroad) could only be circumvented through a lengthy appeals process. If lawyers could not help, there were less formal ways to grease the wheels of Cuba's cumbersome bureaucracy. The World Bank's 1951 report decried the high cost of implementing (and bypassing) economic controls. "Whatever the merits of the controls themselves, they have been only partially effective," the World Bank wrote:

> Enforcement of many of them requires a small army of inspectors, clerks and officials of various kinds. Few of these are paid enough to be attracted to their positions for reasons of salary alone. The island's factory operators and businessmen, knowing this, seldom hesitate to offer what seems to them a more advantageous deal than compliance with the law. Often the result is not control at all, but simply a higher cost of production through extra cash outlays to officials for their 'cooperation.'[38]

---

37. Wallich, *Monetary Problems*, 166.

This low level corruption is considered by some analysts to be even more harmful than high-level kleptocracy. Bureaucrats may "overfish" and thus deplete a "commons" to seek private gains, they argue.[39] If new bureaucrats want a share in the rents, there is an incentive to create new rules and regulations so as to extract still more rents. Whether because of bureaucratic desires to maximize their income, or simply the ever more complicated task of satisfying competing interests, rules governing the sugar sector proliferated in the 1930s and 40s. Before 1915, the industry was basically unregulated. From 1915 to 1924, there were 43 new laws, decrees or administrative regulations enacted concerning the sugar sector, most of which were temporary measures dealing with World War I (when the government negotiated the sale of Cuba's crop to the United States) and the 1921 crash, which left many mills and planters bankrupt. From 1925 to 1934, there were 159 new laws and rules, many of which were also temporary measures, dealing with Cuba's attempt to form an international cartel, which required limiting domestic production through the country's first quota system. Then from 1935-1944, there were 325 new rules, fixing wages, prices, rents, railroad tariffs, quotas for exports, quotas for domestic consumption, and quotas for Cuban sugar refiners; governing labor unions, cooperatives, and the obligatory associations of sugar manufacturers, growers and technicians; encouraging (with little success) the cultivation of non-sugar crops and providing debt relief. Additional legislation placed new taxes on the sugar industry to pay for it all. During the next seven years of *Auténtico* rule, the government added 190 more sugar regulations, an average of about 27 a year.[40]

Labor legislation became even more complex. From 1902 to 1924, the government published some 177 rules, concerning such things as child and female labor, housing, accident insurance, Sunday rest, and port workers. After the mid-twenties, the pace of rulemaking increased. From 1925 to 1934, there were 185 new labor laws and regulations. Then after the mid-1930s, new labor laws began multiplying rapidly: from 1935-1944, there were 881 new rules. During the governments of Grau and Carlos Prio, from 1945-1952, policymakers added another 766 rules.[41] Labor legislation had become a complex web of benefits, wage controls, job guarantees, un-and underemployment subsidies, arbitration procedures, health and safety regulations plus measures designed to regulate (and, if necessary, repress) labor unions and professional associations. All these new rules, of course, were multiplied by the daily bureaucratic rulings on the requests of individual producers to trade quotas, hire or fire workers, renovate facilities, import machinery and more.

ROVING BANDITRY

In addition to the myriad opportunities such complex rules offered for low-level graft, the Republic had a history of illicit enrichment at the highest reaches of government. The accuracy of the charges leveled by the Republic's unbridled press at virtually every administration after 1902 is difficult to judge. Only Cuba's first President, Tomás Estrada Palma (1902-1906), was widely praised for his fiscal (and personal) frugality, although his party's efforts to purge the bureaucracy and manipulate votes to assure its total control of elected posts, both nationally and locally, led to the August Revolution of 1906. The outrage expressed by opposition politicians out of office does not seem to have deterred them once in of-

38. World Bank, *Report*, 178

39. See Mancur Olson, "Dictatorship, Democracy and Development," *American Political Science Review* 87 (1993): 567-575; Shleifer and Vishny, "Corruption."

40. Calculated from the list compiled by Milo A. Borges, *Compilación Ordenada y Completa de la Legislación Cubana, 1899-1950*, vol. 3 (Havana: Editorial Lex, 1952) and Mariano Sánchez Roca, *Compilación Ordenada y Completa de la Legislación Cubana, 1951-1958*, vol. 4 (Havana: Editorial Lex, 1960). Borges lists laws, decree-laws, accords, and ministerial resolutions both chronologically and by subject. I have used his subject categories, while taking care not to double count items that may appear in several categories.

41. Ibid. This includes some sugar legislation.

fice. General José Miguel Gómez, a provincial caudillo known as *El Tiburón* (The Shark), led the Liberal revolt against Palma. But during his own presidency (1909-1913), he allegedly multiplied government jobs for his friends, popularly called "cuneros" or foundlings. "*El Tiburón se baña, pero salpica,*" went a popular saying.[42] A Cuban contemporary called him a "ruined planter who made himself a millionaire from night to morning and not by the sweat of his brow."[43] His private secretary, who later wrote a tell-all book, said Gómez was worth $8 million on leaving office, largely consisting of stock he was allowed to buy at considerably below market prices.[44]

General Mario Menocal (1913-1921), another Liberation Army officer turned politician, was a wealthy man before winning the presidency, having served as the general manager who built the U.S.-owned *Chaparra* sugar mill, then the world's largest. Nonetheless, Menocal's success in business did not prevent him from distributing lucrative contracts and privileges to his extended family, including the coveted export and import permits required during trade restrictions imposed during World War I. Most notoriously, contemporaries accused Menocal of securing millions in loans from the National Bank to build his own sugar mill, which he completed while president.[45] He sold the *Palma* mill, very opportunely, to U.S. investors a few years later. In late 1920, sugar prices, which had spiraled in the aftermath of World War I, collapsed, bringing urban and rural real estate values with them. The crash ruined many mill-owners, both U.S. and Cuban, as well as the country's banking system. Menocal, however, seems to have escaped unscathed. He was said to be worth $1 million

on taking office and $30 or $40 million when he left.[46]

And so it went. A special U.S. envoy, sent to straighten out the island's finances, micromanaged the government of Alfredo Zayas (1921-1925) from behind the scenes, forcing him to accept the appointment of the so-called "honest cabinet." As soon as Zayas managed to negotiate a desperately needed $5 million loan with J.P. Morgan, however, he summarily dismissed the ministers approved by Washington. Zayas supposedly pocketed between $2 million to $14 million before his term ended.[47] His successor Gerardo Machado (1925-1933) allegedly bestowed millions on his followers in Congress by distributing lottery collectorships (an investment which helped him to secure the constitutional revision he needed to seek a second term) and accumulated millions more himself by awarding public works contracts to companies in which he had a substantial interest. Fulgencio Batista, who dominated a series of unstable governments after Machado's presidency until assuming the presidency himself in 1940, allegedly amassed as much as $20 million through graft from public works projects, much of which was converted into urban property.[48]

Estimates of ill-gotten gains such as these, generally provided by political enemies, may be highly exaggerated. Nevertheless, the presidents of Cuba's short-lived republic seem to have resembled the "roving bandits" described by Mancur Olson: weak kleptocratic leaders who sought to maximize their short-term profits, paying little attention to the long-term consequences. Moreover, the public perception that top-level officials were corrupt encouraged dishonesty throughout the government. "Corruption at the

---

42. The shark takes a bath, but he splashes, meaning that Gómez made sure his friends shared in his enjoyments.

43. Ramón Vasconcelos, whose 1916 book (*El general Gómez y la sedición de mayo*) is cited in Charles E. Chapman, *A History of the Cuban Republic: A Study in Hispanic American Politics* (New York: The MacMillan Co., 1927), 286.

44. Lt. Col. Avelino Sanjenís, quoted by Chapman, *History*, 289.

45. This was a private bank, although it held government deposits.

46. Chapman, *History*, 395.

47. Leland H. Jenks, *Our Cuban Colony: A Study in Sugar* (New York: Vanguard Press, 1928), 247.

48. This is an estimate by Carlos Rafael Rodríguez, a Communist Party leader who served in Batista's cabinet, given to historian Hugh Thomas. Thomas, *Cuba*, 736.

top creates expectations among bureaucrats that they should share in the wealth and reduces the moral and psychological constraints on lower level officials," as Susan Rose-Ackerman has written. "Low-level malfeasance that can be kept under control by an honest ruler may become endemic with a dishonest ruler."[49]

One of the tragedies of Ramón Grau San Martín's presidency is that on assuming office he seemed to promise a new style of government, which would be both populist and transparently honest. Well aware that battling corruption had become a key political issue, Grau made public his own income and assets, ordering his cabinet to do the same. Despite this auspicious beginning, scandals and escalating violence by warring political gangsters marred his rule and tainted that of his handpicked successor, Carlos Prío.

The high-level thievery of Grau and his associates seems to have been unprecedented in scope and audacity. In 1948, his education minister and close friend José Manuel Alemán fled to Miami, where U.S. officials discovered $20 million in cash, stuffed in his suitcase.[50] Then a shortfall of some $40 million was discovered at the start of Prío's government in the social security and private pension funds deposited with the Cuban treasury, primarily by the powerful sugar workers' union. As the World Bank noted wryly in its 1951 report, "the government of that time levied a forced loan on non-governmental pension funds lodged with them, without any formal ac-

knowledgment of debt and, therefore, without paying the retirement funds any interest for use of their money."[51] In 1950, ex-president Grau himself was charged with misusing $174 million. But his trial was indefinitely—and in the end definitively—delayed after gunmen invaded the courthouse and stole all documents relevant to the case.

The tragic climax to the *Auténtico* Party's seven-year rule came in March 1952 when Grau's old nemesis, General Batista, seized power in a coup. Seven years later, Batista himself would be overthrown by Fidel Castro and his followers. Castro would later publicly embrace socialism and make opposition to U.S. imperialism the ideological keystone of his regime.

But the politics of post-revolutionary Cuba, forged in the heat of the Cold War, should not obscure the history of the Republic's last years. As political scientist Jorge Domínguez has pointed out, "by the 1940s and early 1950s, nationalism had declined in appeal as an ideology," largely as a result of the reforms that had given Cubans—whether businessmen or bureaucrats—control of the economy.[52] Shortsighted and selfish as U.S. policies toward Cuba may have been since independence, the final unraveling of the Republic obeyed a largely internal dynamic. Well-intentioned reform, ever more-complex regulation, endemic rent-seeking and high-level corruption not only undermined a once dynamic economy but helped discredit democratic rule.

---

49. Susan Rose Ackerman, *Corruption and Government: Causes, Consequences, and Reform* (Cambridge: Cambridge University Press, 1999), 120.

50. Thomas, *Cuba*, 758, citing Arthur Gardner, who in 1948 worked for the U.S. Treasury. He later became ambassador to Cuba.

51. World Bank, *Report*, 487.

52. Domínguez, *Cuba*, 115.

CORRUPCIÓN ACTUAL EN CUBA: HERENCIA Y VICIO

Ricardo A. Puerta[1]

A partir de 1959, se instala en Cuba un Gobierno Revolucionario que cambia el sistema imperante, de capitalista a socialista. Podrá argumentarse que ni el antiguo ni el nuevo régimen eran "lo que dicen los libros." Pero sobre el tema de la corrupción hay más consenso. Los analistas aceptan, tanto los de antes como los del presente, que el antiguo régimen, el pre-fidelista, era corrupto. Y entonces surgen varias preguntas de interés: ¿En qué consistía esa corrupción? ¿Qué sucedió con ella en el fidelismo? ¿La erradicaron? ¿Tiene el fidelismo una corrupción que le es propia? Y si la tiene….¿Cómo se manifiesta? ¿Cómo se explica?

El presente trabajo no entra en detalles sobre las primeras tres preguntas, las cuales tienen que ver con la corrupción heredada. Sólo nos adentramos en el análisis de las tres últimas: la corrupción que le es propia. La trataremos en cinco epígrafes. Después de situar y definir el tema en la introducción, analizamos la evidencia del tipo de corrupción que existe en Cuba, sus modalidades, agentes y actos frecuentes. El tercer epígrafe expone la explicación oficial de la corrupción y la cuestiona, señalando otras causas intrínsecas en la institucionalidad del fidelismo. A continuación, se señalan las diversas expresiones de anti-corrupción que se perciben dentro y fuera del gobierno, sus acentos, *modus operandi* y efectividad. El trabajo concluye con unos comentarios sobre el material que proyectamos hacia el futuro de Cuba.

Una nota del autor. Si bien el tema de la corrupción en Cuba, seduce—por "la razón y pasión" que despierta lo cubano—al espulgarlo, nos deja ansiosos... queriendo saber más sobre el tema. En su análisis, buscamos respuestas más completas y no tan fragmentarias como las que, hasta ahora, conocemos. Además, la corrupción es un tema peculiar de investigación. Manifiesta una lacra social, ilegal, prohibida, inmoral, que públicamente nadie la propone o defiende, ni siquiera los corruptos. Opera bajo un enigma atrayente, válido en el resto de los países del mundo, pero en el caso cubano se torna aún más fascinante. En la Isla, "todo es político," y por lo tanto, la corrupción, es "de interés nacional," "razón de Estado," y para muchos hasta "un problema de seguridad personal y nacional." Es una urgencia gelatinosa.

INTRODUCCIÓN

La corrupción, según Transparencia Internacional,[2] se entiende como el "abuso del poder público para el provecho personal." Decir que la corrupción que hay hoy en Cuba está causada por el sistema imperante, conlleva dos negaciones que son falsas:

1. Que la corrupción NO existe en países de "economía de mercado" o no socialistas.

2. Que en Cuba dicho mal NO existía en los gobiernos republicanos anteriores al fidelismo.

---

1. Sin el apoyo brindado a la investigación de campo sobre este tema por el Centro de Estudios para una Opción Nacional (CEON) este trabajo no hubiera sido posible. El CEON es una organización no-gubernamental (ONG), orientada al diagnóstico y fomento de una transición en Cuba, con sede en Miami, Florida. Material aquí incluido es parte de un estudio más amplio sobre "Corrupción, transparencia y rendimiento de cuentas en Cuba," a publicarse próximamente por el CEON.

La corrupción es un mal universal, está globalizada. No tiene tinte político, ni religioso, ni geográfico, ni racial. No es exclusiva de los países pobres ni ricos, del Sur o del Norte, de cultura occidental u oriental. Pero al mismo tiempo, no existe de igual forma en todos los países. Tiene grados y modalidades en naciones tan disímiles como Estados Unidos y Haití, Alemania y Rusia, Chile y Paraguay, Japón y Angola.

La corrupción tiene efectos negativos en la vida de las naciones. Socava el imperio de la ley. Equivale a un impuesto invisible que encarece los negocios y pasa sus costos sociales a los más débiles, que según estudios reconocidos son los menos habilitados para soportarla. La corrupción incide negativamente en el desarrollo económico, la democratización, las libertades sociales y la estabilidad política.

En el caso cubano, el fidelismo no "inventó" la corrupción en Cuba. La Cuba republicana antes de 1959 nunca estuvo exenta de actos de corrupción, conocidos en su conjunto como peculado. Ninguno de los gobiernos de Cuba desde 1902 a 1959, electos o golpistas, se distinguió por una gestión pública clara, y menos aún, por el manejo honesto de los recursos de la nación.[3] El patrimonialismo, padrinazgo y clientelismo burocrático estaban tan insertos en la Cuba republicana, que la promesa de acabar radicalmente con estos vicios fue una de las causas que impulsó el fidelismo al poder.[4]

Sin embargo, todavía es posible afirmar que hay en la actualidad cierto tipo de corrupción propia al régimen fidelista, en concreto, dos modalidades: la corrupción heredada del antiguo régimen, que el castrismo reprodujo y amplió; y la corrupción creada por las prácticas e instituciones singulares del régimen.

LA CORRUPCIÓN EN CUBA[5]

La corrupción en Cuba existe en forma generalizada. En Cuba existe una cultura del robo. Está fomentada a través del mismo Estado cubano—ubicuo y monopólico—manejado desde un comando central, personalizado en su Máximo Líder, con una instancia operativa próxima: el Grupo de Apoyo del Comandante. A dicha comandancia responden las jerarquías de mando de los sectores estratégicos del país; en especial, seguridad, economía, cultura, Partido, relaciones exteriores y los "proyectos mascota" del Comandante.

La corrupción generalizada puede dividirse en mayor y menor. La mayor es propia de la *nomenklatura*: los miembros de la alta dirigencia política, administrativa y empresarial del país. Nos referimos, concretamente, al Jefe de Gobierno, Ministros, jerarcas del Partido y militares de alto rango al frente de sectores claves de la economía—comercio exterior, turismo, empresas industriales y el azúcar. Desde los años 70, Fidel Castro, en persona, entre uno de sus proyectos mascota, maneja las altas finanzas dolarizadas del régimen, a través de las Reservas del Comandante. A dichas cuentas fueron a parar fondos soviéticos que cubrían las operaciones militares cubanas en Africa y

---

2. Definición según Transparencia Internacional (TI), organización no gubernamental, única en el mundo que se dedica a la lucha exclusiva contra la corrupción. Anualmente publica un informe en el que instituciones y analistas evalúan la situación de corrupción por países. 102 países aparecen investigados en el Informe del 2002. Cuba ni siquiera aparece entre ellos. Las naciones que no están en la lista, casi la mitad de los estados de la tierra, se sospecha que sus administraciones son aún más corruptas que las investigadas. Diario *El Heraldo*, Tegucigalpa, Honduras (29 de agosto, 2002).

3. Ni el gobierno de Don Tomás Estrada Palma se liberó de este flagelo. El peculado le apareció cuando pagó pensiones a los veteranos de la Guerra de Independencia, utilizando el fondo de 35 millones de dólares (Préstamo Speyer), obtenido de Estados Unidos en 1903. Beals (1933) , pág. 198.

4. Hay dos discursos de Fidel Castro "La historia me absolverá" (1953) y el del 1ro. de enero de 1959, en Santiago de Cuba, donde menciona la corrupción varias veces. Además, el Partido Ortodoxo, fundado por Eduardo Chibás en 1947, tenía como lema "Vergüenza contra dinero." En él militó Castro en su etapa electoralista y nunca pudo ganar una elección dentro ni fuera del Partido.

5. Agradezco las críticas y sugerencias hechas al autor por el Profesor Richard Lotspeich de la Universidad Estatal de Indiana, comentarista de nuestro Panel "Combatiendo la Corrupción" en la reunión de ASCE. No sólo fueron valiosos sus comentarios durante el panel, sino aún más las elaboradas notas escritas que le entregó al autor al final del Panel. Sin embargo, el autor es el único responsable por la incorporación de los aportes del Profesor Lotspeich a esta versión final del trabajo.

las actividades subversivas de la empresa CIMEX, creada en 1979 y después reemplazada por el Departamento de Moneda Convertible (MC)[6] que dirigía Tony de la Guardia, condenado y fusilado en la Causa Ochoa.

El empresariado militar tiene su ámbito de operaciones dentro de la *nomenklatura*. Manejan los negocios estatales del socialismo, como si fueran propios, por eso también se les conoce como los "burgosocialistas." Lo de burgués les cae no sólo por su condición de "capitán de empresa," sino también por sus estilos de vida, propios de la burguesía, la cual practican en medio de las carestías reinantes. También se les conoce "los cuentapropistas de la *nomenklatura*."

Los actos más frecuentes de corrupción mayor son la aceptación de sobornos pagados por inversionistas extranjeros en Cuba, cobro por residencia cubana a criminales internacionales, narcotráfico a través de puertos y pistas cubanas, falsificación de dólares, ventas de visados, de salidas ilegales del país,[7] soborno a funcionarios y representantes artísticos para actuar cobrando en dólares,[8] saqueo y comercio de obras culturales del patrimonio nacional o de colecciones de la alta burguesía que "huyó de Cuba," contrabando de mercancías y valores, blanqueo de dinero negro, disfrute gratuito de servicios dolarizados de salud, venta de excepciones legales, etc. Estas prácticas se patentizan en los casos del General Ochoa y los

hermanos de la Guardia; en los "empayamamientos" de Efigenio Amejeiras, Carlos Aldana y "Robertico" Robaina; y en *la limpieza* hecha en el sector turístico en 1999, cuando cayeron Mirta Rosa, Directora de Publicitur, Manuel Limonta, Director del Centro de Biotecnología, José Manuel Manresa, Director de Cubalse, Luis Manuel Cantillo, Presidente de Rumbos,[9] Andrés Soberón, Jefe de la División Hotelera de Cubanacán y un grupo de generales del ejército cubano.

Todos ellos tienen algo en común al tratarse de cubanos. Cada vez que un destacado personaje del gobierno pierde la protección de la dirigencia, es defenestrado de su cargo. Y entre los rumores que circulan por la calle sobre su "caída" está el "descontrol económico" y "problemas morales"—con frecuencia reconocidos oficialmente—o el "mal manejo de los recursos" –que pocas veces aparece en el comunicado oficial circulado al efecto. Aún antes que la renuncia o el despido se hicieran públicos, ya "la calle" conocía el caso. El ahora "en desgracia" llevaba años de lujos y excesos, impropios para el Período Especial. Sin embargo, el oficialismo da otra razón pública sobre las purgas. Se hacen, dicen, para "salvaguardar los principios revolucionarios."

En Cuba también se cometen actos corruptos de pequeña escala, la llamada corrupción menor. Esta en la calle, el vecindario, los colectivos de trabajadores, or-

---

6. En Cuba se conocía por MC. Surge para "luchar contra el bloqueo," para "buscar divisas" "por medios legales e ilegales." Entre sus prácticas estaban el secuestro de empresarios acaudalados y personajes pudientes, extorsiones, chantajes, falsificación de dólares, la "conexión africana" (contrabando de marfil, joyas, pieles de cebra, tigres, etc.), equipos electrónicos y tráfico de drogas. El MC era popularmente conocido en Cuba por "Marihuana y Cocaína."

7. La salida ilegal de Cuba por avión con destino a un país latinoamericano o europeo, o por lancha "rápida" con entrega el mismo día en costas de Estados Unidos, esta costando por persona de cinco mil a diez mil dólares ($5,000-$10,000), o su equivalente en otra moneda dura. El monto total depende del número de parientes involucrados en una misma salida, la condición financiera del que paga y el rango socio-político de los transportados. Además, mientras menos probabilidades tengan los candidatos para salir legalmente de Cuba, el transporte ilegal les cuesta más.

8. "Sobornar a funcionarios y representantes artísticos para poder actuar en lugares donde puedas obtener dólares se ha convertido en una práctica común", dijo el guitarrista Yimi Alonso, integrante del Trio Ruvela. "Es una actitud de sobrevivencia." Citado por Cancio (2001).

9. La compañía turística Rumbos fue la más salpicada por el escándalo. Rumbos era una compañía turística que gestionaba tiendas, cafeterías, alojamientos y multitud de ofertas opcionales que iban desde el paracaidismo al golf. El detonante tuvo que ver con las actividades de una agencia mexicana, asentada en Cuba, dedicada a promover el turismo sexual, manejada por la esposa del entonces canciller cubano Robertico Robaina. Rumbos fue la empresa cubana que ganó el premio más importante de la convención de turismo, celebrada en la isla en mayo de 1999, y, un mes antes, su sección de La Habana fue declarada "Colectivo Proeza Laboral" por sus aportes a la economía nacional. Vicent (1999).

ganismos y empresas, en la economía de resistencia, en los cuentapropistas y agricultores independientes, en el mercado negro.[10] Es la versión popular y cotidiana de la corrupción generalizada. Aparece asociada con "la lucha diaria por la comida," en medio de la libreta "que ya cumple 40 años,"[11] con sus propios mecanismos de supervivencia, casi todos informales, a los cuales el cubano medio esta forzado a recurrir para "resolver." Exige el "trapicheo," "buscarse la vida," "bisneo," "fachando," "sociolismo" y de otros procesos de invención popular que son necesarios para adquirir bienes y servicios de la vida diaria: alimentación y bebida, vestido y calzado, medicinas, equipos domésticos de consumo duradero, vivienda, transporte y servicios públicos locales y domiciliarios, incluyendo la televisión por cable.

La corrupción menor tiene sus propios agentes: maceta, merolico, chulos, jinetero, guajimene, conecte, ratero, pícaro, listero, colero, etc., cada uno con valores elásticos y funciones específicas. Pero todos ellos comparten algo en común: para sus insumos se abastecen de los activos del Estado, por robo violento, indiferencia o contubernio de sus supervisores, quienes por dejadez o complicidad "son también parte del negocio."

Lo robado se "bisnea" en el mercado negro. Los productos de la comida diaria criolla son los más demandados: arroz, frijoles, carne de cerdo, carne de res, de pollo, huevos, plátano, yuca, malanga, etc. El "cubano de a pie" también "compra" en el mercado negro manteca, aceite, mariscos, ron, cerveza, medicinas y hasta gasolina, o servicio de cantina a domicilio (pagada en dólares en Miami). A veces los productos robados no se consumen, sino que sirven "de moneda" para traficar en trueque. El trueque se ha convertido en una forma popular de hacer negocios en Cuba. Conlleva el rechazo de la moneda nacional—el peso cubano—como medio en transacciones de intercam-

bio. Pero a su vez, al negociar se rechaza si hay dólares o euros de por medio.

Los mercados ilegales son también los preferidos para "adquirir" bienes y servicios tan diversos como la baja en el servicio militar obligatorio, consultas médicas con medicinas garantizadas, comprar una computadora con impresora, máquina de faxes, dentaduras postizas, lograr inscripción en escuelas técnicas y del nivel medio de prestigio para que el estudiante "no sea becado" y se pueda quedar en casa, acceso a lugares turísticos "exclusivos" para "trabajadores destacados," u obtener uniformes de escuela porque el anual "no lo dan" o "no alcanza." En este último caso, como parte del servicio, la tienda "entrega a domicilio," dependiendo del "conecte."

Ciertos negocios ilegales suceden también en zonas aledañas a las "vendutas" y "candongas."[12] Nos referimos a "almacenes alquilados" por jubilados o pensionistas que viven en casas subutilizadas. Los vendedores de esos mercados, "en días muertos," alquilan espacios en estos "almacenes" y guardan allí sus mercaderías y estantes. Dentro del alquiler que pagan va incluida "la tajada" para el inspector del gobierno, quien al recibirla se compromete a no actuar contra los "ilegales."

En las empresas con controles administrativos débiles o inexistentes, es donde prolifera más la corrupción menor. Ello abarca a la gran mayoría de las empresas cubanas, más las estatales, en comparación con cooperativas, mixtas o privadas. Es de conocimiento público que "a más injerencia estatal, más corrupción en la empresa." Los actos corruptos más frecuentes en las empresas son: robo, fraude, desfalcos y saqueo de materias primas, de productos intermedios o terminados, de equipos y herramientas, y de dinero en efectivo. El beneficio personal equivale al uso, o al trueque o venta de lo ilegal en el mercado negro. Lo

---

10. Según el Índice de Libertad Económica, el mercado negro en Cuba opera a "un nivel de actividad muy alto. Es mayor que su economía legal. Hasta las actividades económicas básicas (la venta de leche y pan, los servicios de transporte y la vivienda, entre otros) se desarrollan en el mercado negro. Cuba es uno de los principales centros abastecedores de drogas ilegales y existe un contrabando considerable de bienes de consumo. La situación del mercado negro de divisas es similar." O'Driscoll et. al. (2002), pág. 187

11. Cada día lo que da la libreta es menos en productos y en cantidades. Escasamente alcanza para cubrir una semana al mes.

12. Término importado de Angola, subproducto de las campañas internacionalistas.

expropiado al Estado no es un robo, sino una compensación al "salario de hambre" que reciben. Cuando estas transacciones se hacen con la anuencia de las autoridades de la empresa o del barrio, se dice que están amparadas por el sociolismo: término de perspectiva humana que está por encima de lo político. Se refiere a la trama de relaciones de compañerismo, amistad o parentesco valoradas a costa de la "ideología oficial." Es conducta cotidiana en el colectivo de trabajo y en el vecindario. Engalana lo que el gobierno llama "conducta impropia."

Pero el pueblo también se ampara en el "sociolismo" para actuar en la "economía de resistencia." En este contexto, el término justifica los delitos cometidos por el cubano para "sobrevivir," en esta "nueva era" "sin comunismo real," el mismo que antes nos "servía de muleta y nos aguantaba a todos." El sociolismo se rige por el principio de "hoy por mí y mañana por ti." Desde siempre se dijo en Cuba que "quien tiene un amigo tiene un central (azucarero)." Y dada las carencias existentes, y ante la imposibilidad de conseguir lo necesario por medios legales, la casi totalidad de los cubanos—incluyendo a los mandos medios y bajos del régimen—se ven obligados a apoyarse en amistades, amigos, conocidos, etc. para sobrevivir, aún en lo ilegal.[13]

La corrupción es el eje integrador de los diferentes mercados: estatales y privados, legales, ilegales y alegales.[14] Mientras más informal y voluminoso sea un mercado, la corrupción menor y mayor tiene más probabilidades de articularse en el mismo. La articulación se da en complicidad con las autoridades. Por el control que ejercen los órganos cubanos de orden y seguridad sobre los ciudadanos—todavía con bastante éxito—es imposible que sus agentes de calle y archivo no sepan quiénes son los promotores, operadores, financieros y beneficiarios de la corrupción menor y mayor, a menos que ellos mismos no sean

también parte del negocio, y en cierto aspecto, sus garantes. Es en la articulación de la corrupción menor y mayor donde el volumen y los montos traficados a nivel de calle se agregan, y se vuelven económicamente atractivos. En la articulación también se decide a quiénes toca penalizar en la línea de operaciones, a nivel de calle, por "excesos," "violación de reglas," etc. o a veces por "efectos demostrativos," "para darle a alguien una lección, aviso o un escarmiento." Es también en la articulación donde el mercado ilegal se vuelve mercado alegal, término referido a lo ilegal que el oficialismo conoce y tolera.

CAUSAS

Carlos Lage, Vice-Presidente de Cuba dió la versión oficial sobre la corrupción reinante, cuando en mayo del 2001 afirmó: "La corrupción es intrínseca al sistema capitalista, y pudiera decirse, es la savia que lo alimenta, pero es totalmente contraria al socialismo"…Y la que sin duda hay … viene del "legado" y "males del capitalismo."[15]

La tesis de Lage se reduce a un juego de palabras que no sobrevive un análisis social serio. La misma historia del régimen lo desautoriza. El enriquecimiento ilícito no apareció en "la Cuba socialista" sólo de herencia o con las medidas "capitalistas" introducidas en los años 90, como oficialmente se dice. Desde los mismos orígenes del gobierno fidelista, hay corrupción propia, contrario a su insistente prédica. Por ejemplo, la "dolce vita" de los "revolucionarios cubanos" de la década del 60, apareció en Cuba casi "al tomar los barbudos el poder" en 1959. Se hizo visible en "la nueva clase" cuando se apropió de las mansiones, joyas y yates que habían dejado en la Isla "los ladrones, asesinos y esbirros de Batista, prófugos de la justicia revolucionaria." Todas esas propiedades, que sumaban millones de pesos —o dólares de aquella época porque aún ambos eran equivalentes—si de verdad fueron mal habidas por sus presuntos

---

13. Fundación Liberal José Martí (1992).

14. "Alegal" se refiere a lo ilegal que el oficialismo sabe, tolera y fomenta. Implica dejadez, connivencia, complicidad y contubernio de la autoridad legal o administrativa con los delitos reinantes y conocidos. Es sabido además, que los organismos de seguridad en Cuba acumulan datos "comprometedores..." y sacan la "tarjeta" cuando deciden "pasar la cuenta..." por razones políticas. Ni los de arriba, ni los de abajo se libran de este acoso y arbitrariedad.

15. Vicent (2001).

dueños... ¿por qué no se subastaron en venta pública, y con los fondos generados, combatir la pobreza u otras lacras heredadas del antiguo régimen? Si los fondos robados eran del erario público... ¿por qué se convirtieron en uso o dominio privado de ciertos dirigentes revolucionarios?

¿Otro "legado"? El tráfico de drogas con la tutela del Estado cubano—hecho inexistente antes de 1959—apareció en Cuba a fines de los setenta, cuando hacía una década que el antiguo régimen había caído y cuando el fidelismo ya estaba en su "etapa de institucionalización." La presencia de la droga en la Isla antes de 1959, sin embargo, era distinta [negocio y consumo a nivel personal o de grupo, sin el apoyo oficioso de personas y recursos que son parte de la estructura de poder, v.g., las fuerzas armadas y sus equipos e instalaciones]. Tan fuerte estaba, que fomentaba campañas internacionalistas para "liberar pueblos hermanos explotados por el imperialismo." Sin embargo, como afirma uno de los agentes operativos de aquellos años, hoy exilado en París, "entre los revolucionarios, aquello (el tráfico de drogas) no chocaba porque era una forma más de hacerle la guerra al imperialismo."[16]

¿Otro legado? Darle santuario de residencia en Cuba a poderosos delincuentes internacionales—buscados por la justicia de sus países y por Estados Unidos—es otro invento socialista. Al respecto, hay seis casos muy conocidos de reciente historia:

1. Robert Vesco, norteamericano, estafador financiero ("asilo humanitario" en Cuba);

2. Jaime Guillot Lara, mexicano, traficante notorio ("residente protegido" y vecino de Vesco en Cuba);

3. Carlos Lehder, colombiano, traficante internacional de drogas (regaló al Gobierno cubano dos aviones "a cambio de servicios" recibidos);

4. Amado Carrillo Fuentes, el Señor de los Cielos, poderoso narcotraficante mexicano (pagó cinco millones de dólares a Fidel Castro para usar la Isla como refugio de amor y negocios);

5. Alejandro Bernal, uno de los mayores proveedores de droga a los carteles de México (gozó de acceso privilegiado a la Isla y lavó millones de dólares a través de inversiones allí);

6. Carlos Salinas de Gortari, ex Presidente de México, mentor y cómplice de su hermano. Este último cumple una larga condena en su país por malversación de fondos públicos, lavado de dinero y transacciones internacionales ilegales.

Según el discurso oficial, la corrupción también está ligada al "economicismo," término que popularizó el Che Guevara en la década de los 60, cuando favorecía los incentivos morales sobre los materiales en la formación "del hombre nuevo." Traído a los tiempos actuales, el economicismo sugiere preferencia por el mercado, rechazo a la emulación y al trabajo voluntario, reconocimiento del derecho que tiene el trabajador de recibir pago en efectivo por el trabajo realizado, apego del ahorro, derecho de poseer, acumular bienes y poder disponer de ellos a voluntad, y a heredar, a acumular un patrimonio, poder invertirlo, recibir renta o dividendos por lo invertido; y al consumo de bienes y servicios, según el poder adquisitivo del comprador. Como se ve, el economicismo, en argot fidelista, equivale a uno de los varios anti-sistemas que flotan en el ambiente, en este caso, la alternativa liberal capitalista. Para el fidelismo, la corrupción está ligada a los anti-sistemas, a su sustituto, evolución o restauración. Mientras tanto, la gente expresa y pugna por otro tipo de economía, por un cambio económico interno.

Pero hay otras causas en la institucionalidad del régimen que explican la corrupción generalizada que hay en Cuba. "Los de arriba" justifican sus privilegios en Cuba como "contrapeso legítimo a una vida ....llena de riesgos." Una compensación por los "sacrificios patrios," por estar "dedicados a la vida pública." Y aquí entra la sabiduría popular con su racionalidad: si esto reclaman los que disfrutan de "una renta moralmente cuestionable derivada de su posición jerárquica" ¿por qué "los de abajo" no pueden hacer lo mismo, y aprovecharse de las oportunidades de

---

16. Masetti (1999).

corrupción que tienen a la mano, en su vecindario, organizaciones de masa y centros de trabajo? Consecuentemente, "los de abajo" usan la corrupción también como un pago extra—siempre incompleto—por los sacrificios que ellos padecen a diario bajo el régimen socialista: racionamiento, trabajo "voluntario" sin paga, bajos salarios, apagones frecuentes, falta de higiene por la falta de agua, jabón y detergentes, etc. La dirigencia no sólo pide al pueblo esos sacrificios, sino que ha declarado por reforma constitucional al actual socialismo inalterable; aún cuando 11,020 cubanos de la Isla, amparados en un derecho de la Constitución socialista vigente, solicitaron—mediante su firma e identificación personal—un referéndum para decidir si socialismo actual debe o no continuar. Nos referimos al Proyecto Varela, de amplio conocimiento fuera y dentro de la Isla, sobre todo, después de la visita a Cuba de Jimmy Carter, ex Presidente de los Estados Unidos.

Hay además, otras causas de la corrupción muy distintas a las que menciona Lage. Las redes que generan esta lacra en Cuba se alimentan del llamado "triángulo de la corrupción": abuso del poder, ética laxa y debilidad institucional. Analicemos, brevemente, cada uno de estos aspectos en el caso cubano:

Abusos del Poder

Los abusos del poder están dados en la misma operatividad propia del régimen. Abusos que suceden por el centralismo y personalismo en las decisiones de gobierno. La injerencia del Ejecutivo es permanente en los otros dos poderes del Estado—Legislativo y Judicial—garantizada por la impunidad que goza la cúpula burocrática, partidista y empresarial cubana. Con tres agravantes:

- La prensa nacional no sirve de "cuarto poder" para informar, vigilar y denunciar los abusos, a menos que el comunicado de ese tipo provenga de la dirigencia.

- No hay en el sistema un espacio público donde la sociedad civil cubana pueda exigir transparencia,[17] monitorear el desempeño del gobierno o pedirle rendición de cuentas.

- Las facciones internas que hay en el Partido Comunista, en las burocracias estatales o empresariales—disidencia real y oposición potencial desde el poder—no pueden salir a la opinión pública por sí mismas, a no ser que convenga a la coyuntura política que al momento vive la dirigencia, y sea autorizada por ésta.

Ética Permisiva

En cuanto a la ética permisiva, hay dos elementos importantes a analizar. Primero, si hay o no una ética establecida, a lo largo de casi cinco décadas de poder. La historia nos confirma que la ética del sistema ha cambiado tantas veces de principios fundacionales, que al momento no se sabe cuál es. Después de tantos bandazos es muy difícil saber cual es "la buena." En este sentido, el fidelismo sacrifica principios éticos con tal de mantenerse en el poder. Aquí la autobiografía del líder carismático se confunde con la historia del régimen. Empezó bajando de La Sierra Maestra, acompañado de miles de nobles barbudos, llenos de anécdotas heroicas, dando ejemplos de fe y caridad cristiana.

Antes del primer año estaban expropiando bienes mal habidos de los criminales y ladrones del antiguo régimen, y eso tenía la simpatía de casi todo el pueblo cubano. Pero no se quedaron ahí, siguieron expropiando también a dueños de bienes bien habidos—empresas y residencias—cuyo único delito era haber acumulado atractivos patrimonios, ajenos al batistato. Así el Estado cubano llegó a acumular un apetecible botín de viviendas y negocios, supuestamente recuperados "al robo y latrocinio" del antiguo régimen, y se lo repartieron entre ellos mismos. La base material de los fidelistas, como nueva clase en el poder, fue posible en Cuba a partir de este gran robo y piñata nacional. El Estado patrimonial del régimen batistia-

---

17. Transparencia supone claridad y honestidad en las transacciones públicas y suficiente información a la ciudadanía acerca del proceso en que se producen. Supone la eliminación de barreras del conocimiento sobre el destino de las partidas presupuestarias, de las transacciones públicas y de la adjudicación de licitaciones, y exige la eliminación de los criterios políticos e ideológicos al decidir dichas licitaciones. Avila (2001).

no nunca fue tan rico y variado como el botín que amontonó el régimen fidelista, mediante las expropiaciones legales e ilegales que realizó.

Cuando el Máximo llegó a los pocos meses a la cúspide del Gobierno Revolucionario, después de un golpe de estado—único en la historia por haberse realizado desde un programa televisado—contra el entonces Presidente del Gobierno Revolucionario, Manuel Urrutia, consolidó su liderato moral, no sólo en la Isla, sino también en las naciones del Tercer Mundo. Pero esto no duró mucho. De líder moral de los países no alineados, en menos de una década, pasó a ser el garante de los intereses geopolíticos de la Unión Soviética en varios continentes. Mientras tanto, a nivel nacional adoptó el estalinismo, como modelo autoritario de gobierno de una revolución que empezó "tan cubana como las palmas." La sovietización del proceso cubano brinda tres garantías a su dirigencia: (1) el alcance del poder total; (2) la protección contra una acción definitiva de los norteamericanos; (3) los beneficios del *rubloducto* ("los logros sociales de la revolución y las victorias internacionalistas cubanas"). Aún así, los analistas del caso cubano, sostienen con fundamento que la relación Cuba-URSS fue siempre tensa y, a ratos, contestataria [Mikoyán / 1962; Crisis de Octubre/1962; Microfacción/1967-68; No-Alineados-Afganistán/1979]. Sospechamos que el Gobierno cubano se olió la perestroika y esto provoca el giro de 1986, que se conoce como *la rectificación de errores y tendencias negativas* (lo que trajo la purga de Humberto Pérez y su grupo). Todo esto muestra además que en Cuba sus líderes han estado siempre montados en un cachumbambé político.

Lo expuesto son sólo pinceladas del fidelismo. Demuestran el trueque de principios por metas políticas de un régimen que ha mantenido a tres generaciones de cubanos en una turbulencia ética.

Hay muchos más datos, con igual o mayor grado de persuasión, que los antes expuestos. Desgraciadamente son inapropiados en un trabajo de esta extensión. Sin embargo, podríamos sistematizar todos ellos, aún los no expuestos, con un postulado básico y su coro-

lario, ambos válidos para cualquier época o momento del fidelismo: el mayor opositor del Fidel de hoy, es el Fidel de ayer." Corolario: la sustentación del poder es la única idea fuerza que Fidel ha probado tener y manejado con éxito en casi cinco décadas de vida política. Evidencia: Es el único Jefe de Gobierno que sobrevive la Guerra Fría: ésta se acabó pero él no. Ello demuestra su excepcional capacidad de maniobra, es decir, su gran permisividad ética, donde la corrupción es una carta táctica más dentro del juego. Para el que convierte "derrotas en victoria," los límites morales están siempre abiertos. Sólo él... mañoso...los define.

El papel de la corrupción en la construcción del sistema se ve claramente ejemplificado en el internacionalismo fidelista en Africa, Asia y Latinoamérica. Al igual que otras grandes tragedias de la humanidad, ésta empezó por el idealismo. Miles de jóvenes cubanos fueron enviados de "misioneros fidelistas" a países del Tercer Mundo, en diversos cometidos, desde terroristas, soldados y guerrilleros—para eliminar "enemigos"—hasta "voluntarios" en labores humanitarias—como los médicos cubanos que curaban (y siguen curando) en comunidades en donde nunca antes ha llegado un doctor.

Pero las numerosas misiones, en más de 50 países del mundo, acabaron santificando—no a los humanitarios—sino a los "*killers*," a "los asesinos," agentes llenos de furor y delirio, con previa autorización dada por la dirigencia cubana para transgredir la estrecha frontera entre lo operativo y lo delictivo. Su máxima regla le servía de conciencia: "contra el imperialismo, todo está permitido."[18] Entre los "*killers*" de alta intensidad en el pasado, se encuentran el Che Guevara, los hermanos de la Guardia y el General Ochoa; y entre los más recientes y de baja intensidad, están Roberto Robaina y el actual canciller cubano, Felipe Pérez Roque. Todos epítomes del internacionalismo fidelista, en diferentes grados.

Debilidad Institucional

Es un error creer que Cuba tiene un Estado fuerte porque es monopólico y centralizado. La aparente

---

18. Masetti (1999).

fortaleza del Estado cubano no descansa en eso, sino en la efectividad de sus aparatos de orden y seguridad. En el control que ejerce sobre la población disidente, opositora, activistas de derechos humanos, etc.—y en la vigilancia continua que también practica sobre sus simpatizantes, para prevenir que se vuelvan desleales o neutrales. La capacidad de esos aparatos está demostrada por sus respuestas rápidas contra cualquier acción moral contestataria (protestas callejeras, huelgas de hambre públicas, etc.) o mitigadora frente a males naturales (huracanes, inundaciones, epidemias, etc.).

Pero los aparatos de orden y seguridad no son todo el Estado cubano, sino una parte del mismo. El tamaño del Estado cubano no implica fortaleza, sino todo lo contrario. Está hipertrofiado. Está sobredimensionado en centralismos e injerencias. Arrastra muchas y diversas funciones (regulador, fiscalizador, productor, comprador, vendedor, contratista, inversionista, empleador, empresario, propietario, etc.), magnificadas por el carácter excluyente y omnipresente de la ideología oficial.[19] En contraste, su desempeño es bajo para lo que dispone (patrimonio) y maneja (presupuesto y personal). Resultando en una gestión real incompetente, que por inepta, obtiene rendimientos muy bajos. Es, sin duda, el principal reproductor de la desorganización a nivel nacional, y por ende, de la corrupción.

La debilidad institucional está asociada con las políticas económicas que impulsa el gobierno. Cuba es un país Estadocentrista, donde la unidad política organizada a nivel nacional maneja directamente empresas (Estado empresario), y hace todo lo posible por controlar (Estado rector) el resto de las empresas que operan en el país fuera de su propiedad directa. Por ello, propiamente hablando, en Cuba no hay empresa privada. Todas las empresas de propiedad no estatal que operan en sociedad o con dependencia económica del Estado, bien para lograr sus insumos (Estado vendedor), medios de producción—mano de obra y activos fijos (Estado contratista)—o para sus productos (Estado comprador).

Como opera con una sociedad civil emergente y reprimida padece de baja legitimidad. No le rinde cuentas a las "bases duras" de la sociedad cubana—las sociales, públicas no gubernamentales. Su legitimidad real está reducida a las "bases blandas" de la sociedad cubana—las sociales, públicas gubernamentales: la dirigencia, Partido único, organizaciones de masas, prensa y otros medios de comunicación.

Por eso, Cuba es un sistema de capitalismo de Estado. Cualquier otra variante de capitalismo o socialismo en la Isla, es de enclave o secundario en el sistema global. Dentro de tal modelo, el principal mercado interno de Isla es el Gobierno, y ninguna empresa "privada" o de otro tipo puede ignorar "la plaza gubernamental, como la primaria en sus operaciones, a menos que lo haga ilegalmente. Considerando esto, lo que sigue parece irónico, pero es cierto. Aún cuando Cuba es un país de economía reprimida y de alto riesgo para la inversión,[20] todavía llegan a la Isla inversionistas extranjeros y multinacionales que buscan

---

19. Conlleva la identificación de términos que no pueden ser unívocos, tales como Patria y socialismo, Estado y Gobierno, autoridad y poder, legalidad y moralidad, cubano y revolucionario. Este papel, centralista y abarcador de la ideología produce una sensación de cansancio ante las repetidas orientaciones y consignas. Conferencia de Obispos Católicos de Cuba, "El amor todo lo espera" (1995), página 410.

20. Por ejemplo, el Foro Económico Mundial utiliza 8 criterios para determinar, en una escala, la competitividad de un país: el grado de apertura económica, el papel del Estado en la economía, la eficiencia del sistema financiero como intermediario de recursos hacia el sector productivo, la calidad de la infraestructura económica (carretera, ferrocarriles, telecomunicaciones, transporte aéreo), la aplicación de tecnologías modernas, la gestión a nivel de empresas, la competitividad en el mercado de trabajo y el marco legal e institucional para los negocios. Según estos criterios, Cuba resulta como un país de baja competitividad. Citado por Castañeda (1999), págs. 229-230. Hay que señalar que el Índice de Libertad Económica (ILE) mencionado a continuación se mide a la inversa: cuanto más alto es el puntaje en determinado factor, mayor es el nivel de interferencia del gobierno en la economía y menor el nivel de libertad económica de un país. A mayor puntaje menos libertad económica. Cuba se encuentra en la posición mundial número 153 de 161 países estudiados en 2002, con un puntaje de 4.75, mínimo de 1.75 (que corresponde a Hong Kong) y máximo de 5.00 (que corresponde a Corea del Norte). Cuba mantiene la peor posición entre las 26 economías de América Latina y el Caribe. El puntaje se obtiene de medir 50 variables independientes que se subdividen e 10 factores generales de libertad económica. Las 50 variables se agrupan en 10 categorías: política comercial, carga impositiva del gobierno, intervención del gobierno en la economía, política monetaria, flujos de capital e inversión extranjera, actividad bancaria y financiera, salarios y precios, derechos de propiedad, regulaciones y mercado negro. O'Driscoll, et. al. (2002)

aprovecharse de la mano de obra, los recursos primarios o del paisaje nacional; especialmente en los sectores de la nueva dinámica económica: turismo, tecnologías de punta e industrias exportadoras. Todo lo que produzca ganancias en divisas o en moneda dura, es de prioridad tanto para estos inversionistas como para los dirigentes, burócratas y empresarios nacionales.[21] En este "encuentro de intereses," expresado en moneda dura, la corrupción es parte del negocio, un bien negociable.

Cuba es una economía de un mercado monopólico: el Gobierno. Como monopolio al fin, lo normado tiene aplicación casuística. Hay tres principios vigentes en la normativa cubana que no pueden olvidarse: (1) lo que no está autorizado, está prohibido; (2) las normas y regulaciones son tantas para un caso, que nunca pueden aplicarse del todo; y (3) los distintos momentos ideológicos del régimen han producido conjuntos normativos diferentes, algunos contradictorios. La libertad de aplicación está, por lo tanto, en la inconsistencia de la norma. Ello nutre la **doble moral** que es elemento fundamental de la conducta de supervivencia de la población y promueve un gran campo de **discrecionalidad** en los distintos niveles de la vida nacional y sus actores:

- en los dirigentes—dependiendo de la importancia del caso ("estratégico") y su cuantía (monto),

- en los burócratas (administradores y funcionarios), al adaptar la normativa, siempre sobra y falta algo;

- en el cliente, quien difícilmente conoce y entiende el modelo ("idiosincrático") cubano, que demanda paciencia (emocional y financiera) y capacidad para moverse "al ritmo criollo" hasta resolver o abandonar el caso.

Todo esto incita a la "creatividad socialista" y a la informalidad, ambas cultivos propicios para la corrupción.

Comentemos brevemente las principales causas que promueven la corrupción dentro de la debilidad institucional del régimen cubano:

La política económica no busca el bienestar del pueblo sino comandar súbditos, cuyos estómagos y esperanzas estén a la disposición y control de los dirigentes para recibir de ellos seguridad. Esto hace que más cubanos, sin una base económica propia, dependan enteramente del Estado.

Externamente, Cuba no esta inserta en los mercados internacionales. A pesar que mantiene relaciones diplomáticas con 178 países, y comerciales con 166 de ellos, Cuba no participa en los grandes acuerdos comerciales ni financieros regionales o internacionales, mas bien se ha quedado realizando intercambios puntuales y de corto plazo, en parte, por incumplimientos de compromisos adquiridos de mediano o largo plazo.

La política económica del régimen ha seguido un movimiento pendular interno: liberar o regular mercados, sin que ninguna apertura haya durado más de diez años consecutivos y sin que el Gobierno haya dejado de ser el principal mercado nacional. Bajo este "estira y encoge," los cambios económicos carecen en Cuba de la holgura necesaria para enfrentarlos con visión y prudencia. En tal sentido, por *falta de tiempo*, el afectado no puede compensar lo que pierde por el cambio, ni aprovecharse de lo nuevo que el cambio le trae. Los cambios pendulares impiden el crecimiento económico sostenido en todos los cubanos, pero principalmente en los que ya se decidieron a no de-

---

21. Dentro del empresariado cubano se destaca el complejo militar industrial y de servicios. Esta integrado (por miles) de ex miembros de alto rango de las fuerzas armadas y de los cuerpos de inteligencia cubanos. Entre sus (cientos de) instituciones y empresas incluye: Ministerios (de Azúcar, Pesca, Marina Mercante, y de Transporte y Puertos), Corporación Civil de Aviación, Instituto Nacional de Reservas del Estado, Plan Turquino-Manatí, Banca Metropolitana, Habanos S.A., Gaviota, Grupo de Electrónica de Cuba, CIMEX, CUBANACAN, TECNOTEC, Geo-Cuba, Unión Militar Industrial, Granjas y Plantas Cítricas, Zonas Exportadoras-Procesadoras, Comisión Estatal de Perfeccionamiento Empresarial, y el Departamento Ideológico del Comité Central del Partido Comunista de Cuba. Mastrapa III (2000), Págs. 437-438. Detrás del empresariado militar esta el "Grupo de Raúl Castro," quien personalmente lo dirige, e incluye más de un centenar de profesionales y técnicos cubanos, graduados de las mejores universidades de Europa, Canadá y América Latina. Este Grupo viene operando en Cuba desde principios de 1980. Uno de sus lemas favoritos es: "el problema político, militar e ideológico de este país es buscar comida," frase lapidaria dicha por Raúl Castro en 1994.

pender económicamente del Estado. Los cuentapropistas[22] y agricultores independientes funcionan en Cuba dentro de una lógica de mercado, y cuando sea necesario, al margen de la economía. Por lo tanto, son los mejores ejemplos para medir el efecto de los vaivenes de la política económica del régimen.

Existe una indefinición entre los diferentes tipos de empresas (estatales, mixtas y privadas) en cuanto a límites autorizados, dominios, acciones y decisiones. La indefinición deja un espacio abierto y límites imprecisos en cuanto a la propiedad y gestión de las empresas. Ello posibilita el centralismo y voluntarismo de la dirigencia y la arbitrariedad de los burócratas.

"A nivel de cola y calle" es de conocimiento popular que los dirigentes del Estado cubano gozan de privilegios por ocupar los puestos que ejercen. Y que esos privilegios los tienen los funcionarios de los ministerios, de las empresas estatales y del Partido, mediante la realización de actos corruptos, involucrándose en "hechos y negocios ilícitos, inmoralidades y otras faltas e irregularidades." Lo prueban sus estilos de vida[23] ante los sueldos bajos que reciben, dato que el pueblo también sabe por experiencia. Y frente a las conocidas violaciones hechas a la "moral revolucionaria"… el pueblo se pregunta… ¿de dónde sale la plata para la buena vida en Cuba?

Los poderes discrecionales que tienen los dirigentes en la toma de decisiones son tan extraordinarios como los privilegios que gozan. Los más aprovecha-

dos de esta holgura subjetiva son aquellos que aprueban autorizaciones, licencias, permisos, certificados, acreditaciones, pasaportes, visas, etc. También incluye a empresarios estatales que disponen de "áreas o asuntos propios para hacer negocios, dejando campo abierto para "el pícaro y el gerente" trabajando para intereses comunes. Todos estos burócratas están protegidos por la impunidad reinante, que se mantiene en sus dos dimensiones: por el descontrol o ausencia de una supervisión administrativa que deberían hacer y no hacen las instancias. Y por la complicidad de las autoridades del orden y seguridad, y del poder judicial—jueces y magistrados—con la alta dirigencia cubana.

En este sentido, Cuba es un Estado de decretos y burócratas (dirigentes), no un Estado de leyes, y menos de derecho. La voluntad arbitraria de los dirigentes y burócratas es soberana en las instancias decisorias, la norma es la no-norma,[24] y lo que ayer era válido, hoy ya no lo es. En las instancias no decisorias, el funcionario esta sujeto a un sistema de comando central. Por ejemplo, en inversiones extranjeras, un negociador oficial del gobierno no tiene la última palabra, ni siquiera para los puntos de agenda que negocia. El oficial podrá abrir, levantar datos y diagnosticar el caso, pero sólo decide su jefe, el inmediato, y el de más arriba, y así, hasta satisfacer los varios niveles, según el monto de lo negociado. A medida que los montos de inversión sean mayores, más arriba hay que ir en la jerarquía burocrática buscando la una decisión "fi-

---

22. Si bien en 1968 no se llamaban cuentapropistas, los pequeños y medianos empresarios fueron "eliminados" por la Ofensiva Revolucionaria del Gobierno de ese año; en reacción, se creó un sector informal de pequeñas y medianas empresas en la economía cubana que *nunca* el régimen ha podido eliminar. En 1986 vuelven a sufrir otra arremetida del Gobierno como parte del proceso de Rectificación de Errores y Tendencias Negativas. Y partir de los 90, el Gobierno a reconocerlos legalmente, como "cuentapropistas," aunque la mayoría, hasta hoy sigue "alegal e ilegalmente." El "estira y encoje" con los agricultores independientes empezó en 1959 y aún no termina. Como "clase incómoda" del fidelismo, los pequeños agricultores *nunca* han aceptado producir colectivamente, como reiteradamente les ha "impuesto" el gobierno cubano. Por su parte, el sistema "los tiene agarrados" en cuanto a insumos, ventas de cosecha y financiamiento. Mientras tanto, los agricultores maniobran dentro y fuera del sistema, desde sus conucos, medios de producción "elásticos" (usan muchos de productores colectivizados y cooperativistas). Prefieren el mercado negro para "moverse." Los Congresos de la Asociación Nacional de Pequeños Agricultores (ANAP) reflejan el forcejeo mutuo.

23. "Todos tienen uno o más automóviles. Y sus viviendas son superiores, en calidad y confort, a las del cubano promedio. De igual forma, sus hijos disfrutan de vacaciones en Varadero. No le faltan alimentos, que por supuesto, no compran en cualquier mercado. La carne de res, el pollo, el camarón, el café, la cerveza de marca, y los rones de exportación siempre están a su alcance. Si antes el partido comunista criticaba, mordazmente, al militante o funcionario que tenía amantes, hoy no se puede ser un buen dirigente sin ser un buen amante, o presumir de ello." Colás (2001).

24. Agradezco a Maria Cristina Herrera el aporte de este término, su dinámica y el efecto en el sistema.

nal," al extremo, que ciertos proyectos, "pertenecen" *a priori* al Comandante. Ello explica porqué una propuesta de empresa mixta, tome hasta tres años para aprobarse.

Además, con excepción de la ocasional vigilancia y monitoreo realizados por los disidentes y opositores al régimen, sobre el desempeño de los organismos y empresas estatales, no existe en Cuba ningún otro guardián sensor, instalado en el gobierno, que responda directamente a instancia alguna de la sociedad civil, sociedad política (partidos y movimientos políticos), o la prensa.

ACCIONES DE ANTI-CORRUPCIÓN[25]

La lucha contra la corrupción en Cuba ya tiene una normativa que le sirve de referente para sus acciones. La vigente Constitución Socialista de Cuba reconoce el derecho que tiene toda persona a reclamar y obtener la correspondiente reparación e indemnización cuando sufre daño o perjuicio causado indebidamente por funcionarios o agentes del Estado con motivo del ejercicio de las funciones propias de sus cargos. Asimismo, los elegidos en los órganos representativos de poder tienen el deber de rendir cuenta de su actuación y pueden ser revocados de sus cargos en cualquier momento.[26] "Hace unos años (en 1997) fue elaborado y aprobado el Código de Ética de los Cuadros del Estado Cubano, que fue precedido por todo un proceso de estudio, discusión y validación de sus preceptos entre todos aquellos que ocupan alguna responsabilidad de dirección, tanto en el ámbito empresarial, como público en Cuba." [27]

Además, la dirigencia del actual régimen, a nombre del Estado cubano, es signataria de declaraciones, acuerdos, tratados y convenios internacionales que crean compromisos y responsabilidades en sus autoridades y administradores para combatir la corrupción. Están específicamente rubricados por Fidel Castro como Jefe del Gobierno o sus representantes, por ejemplo, las declaraciones de las Cumbres Iberoame-

ricanas de Presidentes y Jefes de Estado y los eventos mundiales, donde Cuba ha participado, bajo los auspicios de las agencias y programas de las Naciones Unidas.

Pero el marco base por excelencia para encauzar la lucha contra la corrupción por un Estado en específico, esta dado por la Declaración Universal de los Derechos Humanos, aprobada y proclamada por la Asamblea General de las Naciones Unidas, el 10 de diciembre de 1948, y ratificada por Cuba en esa fecha.

Pero la normativa encauza, pero no define acciones. A finales de abril de 2001, el Gobierno cubano creó el Ministerio de Auditoría y Control, bajo la dirección de Lina Pedraza, Ministra, y de los viceministros Gladys Bejarano, Liliana Ezquerra, Amando Diez y Reynol Pérez. En el acto de presentación del nuevo Ministerio, efectuado el 1ro. de junio de 2001 en la Escuela del MINBAS, Carlos Lage, miembro del Consejo de Estado y Vicepresidente de la República, expresó que el organismo recién constituido tiene como objetivos:

- …conducir (el)…funcionamiento de la Administración del Estado,

- … (guiar la) ….conducta de los cuadros..,

- ….preservar la disciplina administrativa..,

- …y promover la integridad de las administraciones, sus dirigentes y funcionarios".

En ninguno de los cuatro objetivos del nuevo Ministerio esta el control y la prevención de la corrupción existente. Esas dos funciones siguen bajo la responsabilidad de "los organismos y las empresas." En este sentido, el Fiscal General de la República y el Ministerio del Interior colaborarán con el Ministerio de Auditoría y Control, cada uno desde sus respectivas capacidades, para llevar ante la justicia revolucionaria a los presuntos corruptos.

---

25. Los datos y citas para esta sección están extraídos, en su mayoría, de Lee (2001) y Vicent (2001). Por razones de espacio, las fuentes no se distinguen en el texto.

26. Artículos 26 y 28, inciso c) de la Constitución de la República de Cuba, 1992

27. Citado por Columbié (2001)

Durante la ceremonia, Lage señaló que no hay casos de corrupción "en la dirección de los ministerios." Ni negó, ni reconoció que haya corrupción en el resto de los cuadros o en las líneas de operación y de servicio al público de los organismos. Y en cuanto a ellos señaló que "todavía están presentes y afloran (en los organismos estatales) viejos y malos hábitos, falta de agilidad en las respuestas (y) se delegan facultades sin garantizar el imprescindible control."

En la lista de peticiones fue amplio y predicante. Dijo: "se requiere fortalecer los órganos de trabajo colectivos y asegurar que sean en ellos donde se adopten las decisiones más importantes." Que de ahora en adelante el combate a la corrupción sea "una tarea constante de todos" y que "seamos capaces de promover, fomentar y consolidar el hábito del control y un clima de máxima honradez en cada colectivo de trabajadores." "Necesitamos cuadros capaces y eficientes pero, ante todo, austeros y modestos. No pueden faltar la austeridad y la modestia y ni siquiera dar lugar a apreciaciones equivocadas. Hay que velar porque esos valores predominen donde trabajamos y vivimos, exigiéndonos a nosotros y a nuestros ciudadanos."

En resumen, el Ministerio de Auditoría y Control, a pesar de su nombre, ni prevendrá, ni controlará la corrupción. Ello sigue bajo la responsabilidad de cada Ministerio y colectivo de trabajadores. Esta estrategia es la misma que hasta ahora se venía ensayando, sin éxito, para controlar la corrupción. Su ineficacia se demuestra en el hecho de que en vez de disminuir, la corrupción aumenta en las empresas, a pesar del mo-

nitoreo y apoyo del Sistema de Perfeccionamiento Empresarial,[28] que empezó a final de los 80.

En tal sentido, el Estado cubano mantiene su estrategia de ser "juez y parte" para el control de la corrupción, aunque el agente contralor sigue por fuera del Ministerio "de Anti-Corrupción," en cada organismo y empresa. De hecho, el Ministerio nace en una coyuntura que no puede obviarse: "La creación del Ministerio tiene lugar en medio de una fuerte ofensiva ideológica y política por recuperar y revitalizar la pureza revolucionaria.[29] Funcionarios cubanos admiten que las reformas aperturistas, introducidas a partir de 1993, aunque escasas y tímidas, han provocado desigualdades y conductas como el "amiguismo," el "egoísmo" y el "acomodamiento," que favorecen las conductas corruptas."

Pero la percepción popular esta más al tanto de lo que sucede en el país que Lage. En la calle se insiste que "ahora, en el 2001, con el nivel ciertamente más deshogado, la figura del crimen económico: hurto de mercancías, desvío de recursos, mal uso de fondos.... alcanza cotas verdaderamente alarmantes... Aquí hay que robar para vivir..."[30] Y aunque la corrupción "sea contraria al socialismo," como insistió Lage en su discurso al inaugurar el Ministerio, lo será sólo en los libros, porque en el socialismo real la corrupción está disparada y por la libre.

Dentro de la sociedad civil cubana—en especial a través de disidentes, activistas de derechos humanos y opositores del gobierno—continúan las denuncias de actos corruptos, donde aparecen incriminados dirigentes, autoridades, administradores y miembros de empresas, Partido y organismos, de niveles locales,

---

28. En junio de 2001, el diario *Juventud Rebelde*, citando a la antigua Oficina Nacional de Auditoría: "en pleno año 2000, cuando la economía cubana se juega el todo por el todo para seguir recuperándose y perfeccionando su perfil, es insólito que aún el 54% de las entidades auditadas presenta malo o deficientes resultados en el control de sus recursos y el registro de sus hechos económicos." Citado por Vicent (2001) y por Díaz Castro (2001).

29. El Período Especial aún vigente descansa en un postotalitarismo carismático—Mujal León y Saavedra (1997)—... un "híbrido que no se iguala con el totalitarismo o alguna forma de autoritarismo. Combina el componente autocrático postotalitario con la exacerbación del líder carismático del totalitarismo, un naciente pluralismo económico; una economía dual (funcionamiento en moneda nacional y dólares); un partido comunista con signos de debilitamiento, en el que se incrementa la distancia entre sus corrientes moderadas y duras; el gobierno basado en el *decretismo*; un desplazamiento del marxismo leninismo ortodoxo y el retorno al discurso nacionalista y al anti-norteamericano; unas condiciones más limitadas para la capacidad de movilización del sistema que pierde legitimidad y se refugia en el carisma de su jefe como la principal base de sustentación." Citado por Alvarez García y González Núñez (2001).

30. Garve (2001).

municipales o provinciales. Los medios nacionales de comunicación pasan por alto estas denuncias, pero circulan algo en Cuba a través de las agencias de noticias de los periodistas independientes, y más aún desde el extranjero. Con frecuencia estas denuncias llegan a la Isla por la radio y otros medios. Los denunciantes describen el acto corrupto, identifican por nombres y cargos a los implicados, analizan las causas de lo ocurrido y solicitan una acción firme y concreta de las autoridades contra los presuntos malhechores. Estas acciones oficiales se piden a nivel de donde se cometió el acto. Estas respuestas de las autoridades se esperan del Ministerio o entidad sectorial o municipal correspondiente, la Fiscalía y el Ministerio del Interior. Con rareza se pide al Ministerio "de Anti-Corrupción" que haga algo; más bien destacan su inercia ante lo denunciado.[31] La denuncia, casi siempre, queda sin respuesta, demostrando con ello la impunidad rampante: ni enjuiciamiento ni penalidad para los corruptos en Cuba. Mientras los personajes denunciados sean de más alto rango, la impunidad es mayor.

CONCLUSIONES

El peculado lo heredó el fidelismo del antiguo régimen. El Estado patrimonial—con sus correlatos de padrinazgo y clientelismo burocrático—no nació en 1959, cuando el fidelismo tomó el poder en Cuba. Pero fue incapaz de erradicar dichas lacras, y agregó las propias con el avance de "las medidas revolucionarias." El "nuevo sistema" generalizó la corrupción a través de los organismos, las empresas y el Partido, cuyas burocracias están gobernadas centralmente, desde la cúspide del Gobierno, por un Ejecutivo que interviene en el resto de los poderes del Estado. Gobernantes y gobernados, "los de arriba" y "los de abajo," todos necesitan de la corrupción—mayor y menor— para subsistir y progresar bajo el socialismo cubano, "el propio sistema te empuja a eso."[32]

Al autor se le ha hecho difícil lograr más evidencias sobre articulación de la corrupción mayor y menor en el actual régimen. Reconoce que dicha articulación integra los tres tipos de mercados existentes en la Isla: legal, alegal e ilegal. Sin embargo, la investigación que sustenta el presente trabajo no ha logrado encontrar el "eslabón perdido" de la corrupción generalizada (actos concretos donde estén articuladas la corrupción menor y mayor). Para ello sólo se presenta una prueba indirecta (inercia de los órganos de orden y seguridad); por lo tanto, hacen faltan pruebas directas de dicha articulación.

Las acciones de anti-corrupción necesitan ser enriquecidas con más experiencias gubernamentales que respondan a distintos referentes. Entre los posibles referentes están reglamentos, guías, manuales y otros documentos, encaminados a prevenir o corregir actos de corrupción.

Con respecto a las acciones gubernamentales de anti-corrupción hace falta también documentar más ejemplos. Nos referimos a casos específicos del Ministerio de Auditoría y Control, del Fiscal General de la República o del Ministerio del Interior, así como los proyectos y programas de educación ciudadana realizados por los organismos no-gubernamentales del Gobierno cubano, conocidos como GONGOS (GOvernmental-NONGovermental OrganizationS) por sus siglas en inglés.

La actual corrupción en Cuba está reproducida y amparada por el mismo Estado del actual régimen cubano: Estado monopólico, hipertrofiado, débil e impune. Bajo estas condiciones, la corrupción coincide con la ubicuidad, el centralismo y la injerencia estatal, principalmente en la economía y la cultura. Y también con la protección oficial que disfrutan sus dirigentes por no tener que responder públicamente por sus actos. Así seguirá mientras el Estado cubano mantenga su perfil actual. Sólo una transición al mer-

---

31. Hasta los mismos funcionarios del régimen se quejan de las respuestas débiles del Gobierno. Jorge Luis Pino, Jefe de la Unidad de Enfrentamiento al Delito Económico del Departamento Técnico de Investigaciones (DTI) de la Provincia de Villa Clara, pidió actuar con mayor energía ante estos problemas y puso como ejemplo que a nivel nacional el 85% de los transgresores sólo han sido amonestados o se les ha rebajado el sueldo, en una reunión de análisis del tema en el territorio. Rey (2002).

32. Garve (2001).

cado y a la democracia[33] podrá conducir a Cuba a una situación menos propensa a la corrupción. Otra alternativa sería que el régimen actual "se perfeccione," como proponen algunos de sus dirigentes, lo cual implicaría "más de lo mismo," arrastrando las lacras que le son consustanciales.

En tal sentido, la transición[34] es un hecho seguro en el futuro más inmediato que remoto de Cuba, aunque de fecha impredecible. Para disponer de las condiciones más favorables para su inicio, es necesario seguir denunciando actos corruptos, tal y como lo han venido haciendo los disidentes externos al poder—periodistas independientes, activistas de derechos humanos y los opositores al régimen—que están fuera del gobierno. También es necesario que los disidentes internos—reformistas y aperturistas—que están dentro del Gobierno, sigan fomentando en los organismos y empresas del Estado proyectos y programas de transparencia y anti-corrupción, amparados en la legalidad socialista. Instituciones y programas estatales ya existentes—como el Sistema de Perfeccionamiento Empresarial, la Fiscalía y los Ministerios del Interior y el de Auditoria y Control—a pesar de sus limitaciones, son esfuerzos que eventualmente podrían coadyuvar para acciones más amplias y efectivas.

Cierto potencial también existe en el movimiento municipalista cubano, cuyas tradiciones y luchas descentralizadoras representan un capital social difícil de encontrar en otros movimientos civilistas. Eventualmente, ya en una era de transición hacia un sistema democrático, ambos grupos—disidentes externos e internos—y grupos como el municipalista, podrían converger en una gran causa nacional, con objetivos comunes de transparencia y anti-corrupción. Por su naturaleza civilista, esta causa todavía permite diferencias político partidistas entre sus líderes, simpatizantes y activistas.

BIBLIOGRAFÍA

Alberto F. Alvarez García y Gerardo González Núñez. *Intelectuales vs. Revolución.* (El caso del Centro de Estudios sobre América/CEA). Talleres de Des Livres et des Copies. Montreal, Canadá. Mayo, 2001

Victor Rolando Arroyo. "Se apoderan funcionarios de vehículos donados para enfermos." UPECI, *Cubanet.* Noticias. 16 de Abril, 2002.

Victor Rolando Arroyo. "Malversación millonaria en empresas estatales de Pinar del Río." UPECI, *Cubanet.* Noticias. 26 de Octubre, 2001.

Marlin Oscar Avila. *Creando transparencia a través de la iniciativa ciudadana.* Centro de Investigación y Promoción de los Derechos Humanos/CIPRODEH. Tegucigalpa, Honduras. 28 de Agosto, 2001

Vanessa Bauza. "Borrowing reform ideas from capitalism." Havana Bureau. *South Florida Sun Sentinel.* 14 Octubre, 2001.

Carleton Beals. *The Crime of Cuba.* J. B. Lippincott Co. Filadelfia y Londres. 1933.

---

33. Centeno y Rands, dos estudiosos de transiciones declaran: "hemos descubierto que la transición que sigue una vía socialdemócrata, en la que se combinan las fuerzas del mercado, las prestaciones asistenciales, la participación democrática y el imperio de la ley, supone la opción más rápida y segura para alcanzar un nuevo orden político y económico. El capitalismo necesita un Estado y la democracia precisa de justicia social." Centeno y Rands (2002), pág. 216.

34. Los escenarios de transición de Cuba empiezan con la muerte de Fidel y Raúl en vida. ¿Cuál serían los escenarios si Raúl muriera antes que Fidel? Esta opción es plausible debido a la edad y salud de Raúl.

Juan F. Benemelis. *Las guerras secretas de Fidel Castro*. Fundación Elena Mederos. Rodes Printing, Miami, Florida. 2002.

Ernesto F. Betancourt. "El trujillismo, etapa final del castrismo II." *El Nuevo Herald*. 16 de Marzo, 2002.

Wilfredo Cancio. "Artistas recurren al soborno para sobrevivir en la Isla." *El Nuevo Herald*. 8 de Agosto, 2001.

Carta de Cuba. "La Isla. Fraude, basura y población." *El Nuevo Herald*. 25 de Febrero, 2002.

Rolando H. Castañeda. "Cuba y los antiguos países socialistas de Europa: la importancia de los aspectos institucionales y de economía política en la transición del socialismo a una economía de mercado." *Cuba in Transition—Volume 9*. Association for the Study of the Cuban Economy/ASCE. Washington. 1999. Págs. 224-243.

Miguel Angel Centeno y Tania Rands. "El mundo que han perdido. Una evaluación de las transformaciones en Europa Oriental." *Encuentro*. Asociación Encuentro de la Cultura Cubana. Num. 25. Verano 2002. Madrid, España. Páginas 215-243.

Ramón Humberto Colás. "Corrupción de todo tipo en Cuba, a pesar de lo que dice Pérez Roque." Nueva Prensa Cubana. Reproducido en *Diario Las Américas*, Miami, FL. 31 de mayo de 2001 y por *Disidente*, Año 16, número 168. Puerto Rico. Edición Internacional, página 18.

Mariela Columbié Santana. "La ética y los valores en el Sector Público como un imperativo de nuestros pueblos." Revista *Probidad*. <contacto@probidad.org>. Edición Quince. Julio-Agosto, 2001.

Conferencia de Obispos Católicos de Cuba. "El amor todo lo espera" en *La voz de la Iglesia en Cuba: 100 Documentos Episcopales*. Obra Nacional de la Buena Prensa, A.C. México, D.F. Documento #87, Páginas 399-418. 1995

Amarilis Cortina Rey. "Cien desempleados por corrupción en la fábrica de cerveza Hatuey." Cuba-Verdad. *Cubanet*. Noticias. 18 de Abril, 2002

Tania Díaz Castro. "La corrupción y sus raíces incurables." UPECI. *Cubanet*. Noticias. 5 de Octubre, 2001.

Haroldo Dilla, Gerardo González y Ana Teresa Vincentelli. *Participación popular y desarrollo en los municipios cubanos*. Centro de Estudios de América (CEA). La Habana, Cuba. 1993

Oscar Espinosa Chepe. "El cuentapropismo continúa reduciéndose." *Cubanet*. Noticias. 18 de Marzo, 2002

José Luis Fernández. "Cómo llego y se mantuvo en el poder Fidel Castro." *La Voz de Cuba Libre*. Año IV, No. 81. 15 Marzo, 2001.

Rui Ferreira. "El Contacto es la clave para irse de Cuba." *El Nuevo Herald*. 10 de Agosto, 2001.

José Antonio Fornaris. "Batalla perdida de antemano." Cuba Verdad. *Cubanet*. Noticias. 29 de enero, 2002

Alejandro de la Fuente. "¿En los márgenes de la nación? El caso del Realengo 18." Ensayo que forma parte de un libro a publicarse por el *Instituto de Estudios Cubanos* en 2003.

Fundación Liberal José Martí. *Diccionario Secreto de la Revolución Cubana*. Servicio de Documentación. Gráficas Rógar. Madrid, España. 1992

Juan Carlos Garcell. "Expulsan de sus cargos a veinte funcionarios cubanos por 'irregularidades y violaciones.'" APLO. *Cubanet*. Noticias. 16 Noviembre, 2001.

Luis Manuel García. "Trata de cubanos." *Encuentro en la red*. Economía. Año III, Edición 290. 30 de Enero, 2002.

Luis Garve. "El pícaro, el gerente y la corrupción." CPI. *Cubanet*. 26 de junio, 2001,

Normando Hernández, CPIC. "Funcionario de Las Tunas 'desvía' materiales de construcción para ampliar su casa." *Cubanet*. Noticias. 2 de Abril, 2002.

Diario El Heraldo. "Honduras sigue en los últimos lugares en el índice de corrupción." Tegucigalpa, Honduras. 29 de Agosto, 2002.

Susana Lee. "Tenemos el inexcusable deber de aplastar todas las manifestaciones de corrupción." *Granma.* 2 de Junio, 2001.

Felix López. "Un año para soluciones audaces, integrales y revolucionarias." *Diario Granma.* Nacionales. 30 de Enero, 2002.

Jorge Masseti. *El furor y el delirio.* (Itinerario de un hijo de la Revolución Cubana). Tusquets Editores S.A. Barcelona, España. 1999.

Hector Maseda. "El hombre nuevo o corrupción al por mayor." Grupo Decoro. *Cubanet.* Noticias. 20 de Marzo, 2002.

Hector Maseda. "¿Hasta dónde llevarán a Don Liborio?" Grupo Decoro. *Cubanet.* Noticias. 5 Noviembre, 2001.

Armando Mastrapa III. "Soldiers and Businessmen: The FAR during the Special Period" en *Cuba in Transition—Volume 10.* Association for the Study of the Cuban Economy/ASCE. Washington. Págs. 428-441, 2000.

Ramón Guillermo Medina. "Funcionario del Poder Popular lucra con vehículo del Estado." Cuba-Verdad. *Cubanet.* Noticias. 21 Noviembre, 2001.

Eusebio Mujal León y Jorge Saavedra. "El postotalitarismo carismático y el cambio de régimen: Cuba en perspectiva comparada." *Encuentro.* Asociación Encuentro de la Cultura Cubana. Num. 25. Madrid, España. Otoño-invierno, 1997. Páginas 115-123.

Movimiento Sindical Independiente de Cuba. "Corrupción estatal deja sin empleo a trabajadores." Lux Info-Press. *Cubanet.* 1 Julio, 2002.

Gerald P. O'Driscoll, Jr., Kim R. Holmes & Mary Anastasia O'Grady *Índice de Libertad Económica 2002.* The Heritage Foundation y Dow Jones & Co, Inc. 2002.

Jorge Olivera Castillo. "Muerte sin entierro." *Encuentro en la red.* Sociedad. Año III, Edición 359. 7 Mayo, 2002.

Andrés Oppenheimer. *Crónicas de héroes y bandidos.* Grijalbo. México. 1998.

Isabel Rey. "La isla del facho." *Encuentro en la red.* Economía. Año III, Edición 320. 13 Marzo, 2002.

Gerardo Reyes. "Un poderoso narco pagó millones a Cuba." *El Nuevo Herald.* 10 de diciembre, 2001.

The Economist. "The worm that never dies." 2 Marzo, 2002. pág. 11.

The Economist. "The short arm of the law." 2 Marzo, 2002. pág. 85.

USAID. "Anti-corruption Resources: What is corruption." *Democracy and Governance Home.* Anti-corruption Index. Internet. www.usaid.gov/democracy/anticorrupotion/corruption.

Mauricio Vicent. "Cuba destituye a varios altos cargos vinculados a empresas que promocionan el turismo sexual". *El País.* Internacional. Digital. No.1134. Madrid, España. 11 de junio, 1999.

Mauricio Vicent. "Un nuevo ministerio combatirá la contaminación capitalista en Cuba." Estadística de la noticia. Edición impresa internacional. Internet, 6 de junio de 2001.

COMBATING CORRUPTION IN POST-CASTRO CUBA

Sergio Díaz-Briquets and Jorge Pérez-López[1]

The Cuban transition from a totalitarian state to a more politically open form of government with a market-oriented economy will entail a vast transformation of the country's institutions. While daunting, this process offers many opportunities. Cuba can learn from the experiences—positive and negative—of other nations that have gone through similar processes and adopt institutional structures suited to curbing corruption and creating an environment where the private sector can flourish while developing a lean and efficient government capable of delivering quality services.

This paper offers an inventory and description of policy initiatives found or believed to be effective in other national settings in combating corruption and promoting transparency/accountability that may be relevant to a Cuba in transition. These initiatives may provide guidance to a transition government in the island. They may also provide guidance to the international development community, likely to be a key player in Cuba's transition and economic recovery.

A TRANSPARENCY/ACOUNTABILITY STRATEGY

A priority for the architects of the Cuban transition should be to build into the process a transparency/accountability strategy that avoids the eruption of corruption that occurred in the transitions in the former Soviet Union and Eastern Europe and that followed the electoral defeat of the Sandinista government in Nicaragua. Two forms of corruption have been prevalent in these societies:

- *Administrative corruption* arises from the use of public office for private gain. This form of corruption was endemic in socialist countries with state ownership of the means of production and centrally planned economies. Examples of administrative corruption include bribes, "grease payments," and misdirection of public property by state officials to their own benefit or that of their families.

- *State capture* refers to the activities of individuals or groups to influence the formation of laws, decrees, regulations and other government policies (i.e., the basic rules of the game) to their own advantage by means of the illicit and non-transparent provision of private benefits to public officials. This form of corruption arises primarily early in transitions when legal frameworks are not yet in place. For example, an oligarch at the head of a powerful financial or industrial group could buy off legislators to erect barriers to entry in a particular sector.

A transparency/accountability strategy must address both administrative corruption as well as state capture and be comprehensive enough to encompass short-, medium- and long-term interventions, so as

---

1. This paper is based on the authors' longer paper, "Alternative Recommendations on Dealing with Corruption in a Post-Castro Cuba," prepared for the Cuba Transition Project, University of Miami, September 2002. The paper expresses only the personal views of the authors.

to minimize corruption during and after the transition.

The design of anti-corruption transition strategies has a strong temporal dimension. For purposes of this paper, we define the short term to coincide with the onset of the transition, the time period (1 to 2 years) when first generation reforms are implemented. [2] On the transparency/accountability front, the focus during this stage of reform should be on minimizing the illegal acquisition of national assets by corrupt public officials and others in position of authority or with insider knowledge. At the same time, the basic foundations must begin to be set for a transparent and honestly-managed public sector, and for the minimization of opportunities for corruption at the interstices where the private and public sectors meet.

The mid- and long-term coincide roughly with the time period when second generation reforms are implemented. The transparency/accountability strategy during this period should focus on creating a modern public sector with transparent, efficient and customer-oriented dependencies, grounded in a legal system respectful of human rights, equipped with appropriate control institutions, and under the oversight of a free and independent media. At the same time, efforts should be made to empower an educated citizenry to assure their overview rights are respected and to demand that the national government complies with international obligations to curb corruption.

SHORT TERM MEASURES

Cuba will benefit from what has been learned in other transition economies, and from what the international development community has to offer in terms of technical advice and financial support. The international development community can assist Cuba early in the transition process by establishing techni-

cal consultative bodies to assist with the development and monitoring of liberalization policies. A privatization board jointly staffed by Cuban nationals and expatriate consultants experienced in the design and management of such programs, for example, could ensure at least a minimum of transparency during the privatization of state-owned assets.

While combating corruption has not been at the forefront of the priorities of policy makers during this crucial period of the early transition, properly designed, transparent and well implemented liberalization, privatization and competitive procurement policies can help control corruption and check oligarchs' attempts to capture the state. Also very important during this period will be vigilance by the international community—an expected key source of reconstruction and emergency assistance—to prevent corrupt officials from appropriating foreign assistance funds.

Liberalization

Some macroeconomic reforms and deregulation can contribute to the expansion of markets and reductions in rents. Lowering and eliminating tariffs, quotas and other barriers to international trade as well as eliminating exchange rate restrictions, price controls and unwarranted permit requirements will strip government officials of discretion and of the power to extract bribes. At the same time, removing such controls reduces transaction costs, eliminates supply bottlenecks and fosters competition. If unchecked, domestic interests will attempt to slow down or build in exemptions for their industries wielding infant industry arguments and painting doomsday unemployment scenarios.

Privatization

In addition to salutary economic efficiency effects, privatization removes the state from economic activi-

---

2. First generation or Type I reforms typically include macroeconomic stabilization, price liberalization, encouragement of new firms, and the dismantling of the institutions of the socialist system (including the break up of state-owned enterprises and selected privatization actions). Second generation or Type II reforms typically involve the development and enforcement of laws, regulations and institutions that would ensure the successful market-oriented economy, among them completing the privatization of large and medium size enterprises; establishment and enforcement of a market-oriented legal system and accompanying institutions; further in-depth development of a viable commercial banking sector and the appropriate regulatory infrastructure; labor market regulations; and institutions related to public unemployment and retirement systems. The illustrative list of measures is drawn from Svejnar (2002:5).

ties and reduces opportunities for corruption in sales, procurement, employment and financing. To ensure the integrity of privatization, transparency measures must be an integral part of such processes. Privatization must also be accompanied by regulatory and commercial frameworks that promote competition and protect consumers and investors. In the absence of such frameworks, privatization merely shifts rent seeking from governments to the private sector.

During the early stages of the transition, large-scale privatization of state-owned enterprises is unlikely as much work is necessary to prepare the ground for such action. Before large-scale privatization of state-owned enterprises can occur, it will be essential to put in place a basic institutional framework to make the process transparent and accessible facilitate and maximize returns to the nation.

A more likely vehicle to promote competition in the early stages of the transition is the stimulation of small and medium size enterprises (SMEs). Essential for the creation of SMEs is a macroeconomic environment that promotes stabilization and growth. Based on the experience of the reforming countries in Central and Eastern Europe, among the policies that can promote SMEs early in the transition are an economic stabilization program that imposes hard budget constraints and minimizes state subsidies; efficient markets that foster competition through deregulation and liberalization of markets and prices; sound and transparent fiscal policies and fair and effective taxation (Gayoso 1999:62). A fair and efficient taxation system can dissuade companies to go underground (that is, into the informal sector) to evade taxes and raise sufficient revenue to allow the state to provide essential services. Also important is to establish as streamlined a system of licensing of SMEs as possible in order to accelerate their establishment, encourage their legal status (critical in the longer term for the establishment of a taxation system), and reduce the opportunity for administrative corruption (bribes, "grease" payments) that officials who issue permits might demand.

MEDIUM TO LONG TERM MEASURES

Transparency International (TI), a non-governmental organization that leads the global fight against corruption, has proposed a model "National Integrity System" or transparency/accountability strategy for governments to promote "the public interest rather than the private interests of those in control." The challenge for countries embracing democracy, including countries in transition, is (Pope 2000:33):

> to move away from a system which is essentially top down: one in which an autocratic ruling elite gives orders which are followed, to a greater or lesser degree, by those down the line. The approach is to move instead to a system of "horizontal accountability"; one in which power is dispersed, where none has a monopoly, and where each is separately accountable.

Several interconnected and mutually supporting elements are necessary for an integrity system to come into fruition. It begins with the standard separation of power (executive, legislative, and judicial) that check the power of rulers in democratic systems, complemented by active citizen involvement and institutions specifically charged with preventing corruption. An integral part is an independent and free media and an informed citizenry willing to provide continuous oversight over how public funds are managed and spent. Equally important are a legal infrastructure to prevent and punish corrupt acts, a professional civil service capable of effectively and honestly running government operations, and specialized official entities (e.g., Comptroller General Office, Ombudsman, investigation agencies, Anti-corruption commissions) with a partial or full focus on corruption.

Although the specific components of an integrity system and how they function may vary from country to country—according to form of government, legal tradition, and so on—the ultimate goal is to have them operate as part of a coherent whole that, through its combined actions, interferes with the ability of dishonest individuals to exploit corruption opportunities. If they do, the system should be capable of detecting and punishing corrupt acts.

A Coherent Legal Infrastructure

It is beyond the scope of this paper to dwell in detail on the legal infrastructure that will be necessary for transparent and honest government. The constitutional and legal foundations of a future Cuba are complex problems whose elucidation will be partly determined by the country's legal traditions, the nature of the transition, and the leadership of the nation. These domestic legal foundations could build upon transnational legal instruments that could support national anti-corruption initiatives (more on this below).

Domestic legal anti-corruption measures generally fall into preventive and curative instruments. The former refer to "a set of upstream rules and norms of good behavior (codes of conduct, manifestos, declarations) conducive to a corruption-free society." The latter consist of "anti-corruption laws proper (general or specific legislative enactment), whose purpose is to provide appropriate remedies, including criminal sanctions and penalties, procedural rules, and institutional mechanisms, as needed, to combat acts of corruption that have already occurred" (Ofosu-Amaah, Soopramanien, and Uprety 1999:3).

A comprehensive legal framework would include organic laws that structure and regulate the public sector and may encompass explicit or implicit transparency/accountability elements, such as civil service laws and associated ethical standards for public servants, and laws regulating how state resources are managed and controlled. Of particular relevance to preventing or reversing state capture are initiatives that promote transparency both with regard to the degree of openness of the state's decision-making processes and of the disclosure of interactions that could influence such decisions. Among the specific initiatives to enhance transparency that may be relevant to a Cuba in transition are (e.g., USAID 1999):

- Sunshine laws that require government officials to hold certain meetings in public, promoting accountability and transparency in government decision making. Particularly important is public access to meetings discussing budgetary issues and leading to decisions regarding the use of public property as is reliance on public hearings to inform citizens about public policy issues and to obtain citizen input regarding the development of laws, rules and regulations.

- Freedom of access to information, a cornerstone of democratic government, is based on two elementary principles: citizens have a right to know how they are governed and the higher the level of opacity, the greatest the opportunity for mischief. For example, citizens should have a right to know the text of draft legislation being considered by the government, views put forth by parties regarding legislation, and the voting record of elected officials.

- Public financial disclosure is a set of rules that requires government officials with certain degree of decision-making power to disclose periodically the extent and nature of their assets not only to prevent illicit enrichment while holding power but also to identify potential conflict of interest in decision-making.

- Whistleblower legislation that affords employees the right "to challenge workplace corruption and mismanagement" since "secrecy and silence through intimidation and fear are the ultimate objectives and methods underlying organizational reprisal techniques" is a sharp surgical instrument to expose and prosecute public and private corruption (Keshet and Devine 2002).

- Ombudsmen offices, when properly organized and managed, and truly independent of the government organizations they monitor, can contribute to good governance by allowing citizens to raise concerns about government issues and for government offices to respond to those concerns (Pope 2000:83-94).

The domestic legal framework should also devote special attention to issues related to drug trafficking, money laundering and human trafficking. Following the dismantling of Cuba's police state and the opening and increasing integration of Cuba to the global economy, these types of illicit activities are likely to increase significantly unless effective preventive and prosecutorial measures are put in place.

International Legal Instruments

The international community has adopted several legal instruments to minimize public sector bribery and other illicit practices, recognizing that "international cooperation can help engender both the will to fight corruption and the capability to do so" (Klitgaard 1998:5). Since bribery often involves illegal payments by transnational corporations to public officials in the country where the corrupt act occurs, international instruments tend to complement each other by criminalizing bribe payment by foreign firms and/or penalizing bribe acceptance by public officials or politicians in countries where paid. International cooperation is also often needed to investigate, prosecute and punish corrupt individuals (or to recover ill-gotten assets) even when the offense is committed solely within a country's borders without involvement of an offender from another country.

Of particular relevance for a post-transition Cuba are anti-corruption conventions developed by the Organization for Economic Cooperation and Development (OECD) and by the Organization of American States (OAS).

• The Convention on Combating Bribery of Foreign Public Officials in International Business Transactions, adopted by the OECD in 1997 (OECD 1998). It is intended to prevent bribe payments by private entities of signatory countries conducting business abroad.

• The Inter-American Convention Against Corruption (ICAC), adopted in 1996 under the auspices of the OAS. The focus of the ICAC is on curbing corruption at home. It requires signatory countries to develop standards of conduct for public officials, strengthen control systems, and promote civil society involvement in the prevention of corruption (OAS 1998).

A Cuba in transition should promptly become a signatory to the OECD Convention and the ICAC (both instruments are open to signature by non-members of the OECD and the OAS, respectively) and other relevant international agreements. It should also adopt the necessary legal enabling mechanisms to comply with domestic enforcement and international cooperation obligations embodied by these international instruments.

A Professional Civil Service

An essential component, or pillar, of a long-term transparency/accountability strategy is a well-trained, professional civil service capable of efficiently discharging its obligations to the nation and the public, while safeguarding the national patrimony. Developing such a professional civil service will require many years of effort. The first order of business will be to establish the foundation for the development of a professional and non-political civil service that operates according to transparent and non-ambiguous rules, makes decisions without favoritism, and makes remuneration and advancement decisions based on merit rather than political favoritism or nepotism. Civil servants should be tenured and compensated adequately to reduce the corruption temptation. The latter will be a major challenge during the early years of Cuba's transition as its weak economy must address numerous financial demands simultaneously. The actions of the professional civil service should be subject to scrutiny by civil society and by the media.

The upper echelons of socialist Cuba's civil service is by definition thoroughly politicized—Communist party *apparatchiks* and their families and friends control the top government positions. Furthermore, Cuba's civil service is bloated, notorious for its inefficiency, poorly attuned to modern managerial concepts, enmeshed in a tradition of secrecy and lack of transparency, oblivious to the notion of customer service, and poorly paid.

While the transition away from socialism will lead to a substantial reduction in the number of civil servants as more satisfying and better-remunerated employment opportunities open up in the private sector, a painful process of retrenchment lies ahead. Political sensitivities to some extent will determine which public officials will be retained and which will be let go, but as much as possible these decisions should be made according to skill criteria and managerial need. In doing so, Cuba will undoubtedly benefit from the experience of other countries that have embarked on major modernizations of their civil services. These international experiences offer various reform models that Cuba could consider. They also provide a record of how these complex reform programs could be best implemented as well as off-the-shelf training curricula that with relative ease could be adapted to local conditions to upgrade skills and instill transparency and values of service to the public among Cuban civil service officials.

Financial Management, Control and Audit

Effective management of the national economy was not a policy priority of socialist Cuba. Generous Soviet subsidies, which lasted through the end of the 1980s, served to mask the regime's inefficiency and misuse of resources. During a period in the mid-1960s, Cuba went so far as to abolish the Ministry of Finance, operate without a national budget, and eliminate accounting and financial control systems, doing away with concepts such as cost of goods sold and interest payments; the study of economics as well as the career of public accountant disappeared from the university during this period (Batista Odio 1986:239-240).

In the 1970s, some of these policies gradually began to be reversed as attempts were made—under Soviet prodding—to regain a modicum of economic efficiency. In 1995, President Fidel Castro, noting that an important factor behind the demise of the Soviet Union had been widespread corruption, called for measures to improve accounting and audit procedures, as well as to reduce black market activities (Reuters 2001). In May 2001, the Cuban government announced the creation of a new Ministry for Audit and Control (Creado el Ministerio 2001) and, at about the same time, the government established a code of ethics for public officials and announced improvement in government accounting practices (Reuters 2001; Columbié Santana 2001).

To fulfill its functions adequately and prevent corruption, a Supreme Audit Institution (SAI)[3]—the functional equivalent of Cuba's current Ministry for Audit and Control—must be guaranteed political and financial independence. This can only be assured if the SAI is accountable not to an overtly centralized and dictatorial executive, but rather to a powerful legislature in a political system with appropriate checks and balances (Pope 2000:75-82).

A post-transition Cuba must guard against the temptation of recreating historical control institutions that have been found elsewhere to fail to control corruption and instead have engendered political deals to cover it, such as the traditional Court of Accounts (Tribunal de Cuentas). The underlying principles behind a Court of Accounts are in conflict with those of a modern SAI. While the latter provides an independent audit function, promotes financial control improvements, and disseminates audit findings, it is not responsible for making legal determinations or prosecuting wrongdoing, the province of the former. That a Court of Accounts is empowered to render judgements and prosecute wrongdoing creates grave conflicts (and the opportunity for cover ups) in the political process that underlies the appointment of its members. Furthermore, the fairness of the Court's decisions are always open to question since its ruling cannot be appealed based on its own audit findings absent independent review.

A SAI can blossom when it provides oversight in a country with sound financial management practices. Since the 1980s, many Latin American countries, at the urging of the U.S. Agency for International Development and with financial support from the World Bank and the Inter-American Development Bank, have embarked on long-term and ambitious efforts to develop Integrated Financial Management Systems (IFMS). An IFMS (Wesberry 2001b:97) consists of:

> an interrelated set of subsystems, which plan, process, and report on resources, quantifying them in financial terms. The basic subsystems normally are accounting, budgeting, cash management, debt management, and their related internal controls. Other subsystems sometimes included in an IFMS are collection and receivable management, acquisitions and supply management, information management, tax and customs administrations, and retirement or social security system administration, together with their own internal

---

3. In many countries this function is performed by the Office of the Comptroller General.

controls. One of the most important elements of internal control is an independent and professional internal audit function, which constitutes an integral part of IFMS.

The strength of an IFMS in deterring corruption lies in its ability to generate a "common, single, reliable database to and from which all data flows," since all data users must submit information to a shared accounting system. As Wesberry (2001b:98-99) notes (see also, Pope 2000:221-234), modern IFMS, dependent on powerful high-technology tools and computing equipment, help prevent corruption in many ways. They provide multilevel budgetary control, permit spotlighting weaknesses, allow for internal validation of integrity, and make feasible the control over resources. Further, IFMS promote transparency, require the use of consistent policies, decentralize authority and accountability, reduce the need for accountants, give immediate audit capabilities, are capable of disclosing patterns of corrupt practices, and facilitate computer assisted auditing.

Although the advantage of an IFMS for a post-transition Cuba—both for efficiency in government and curbing corruption—is beyond dispute, it will probably take a decade or more and tens of millions of dollars to make such a system fully functional. An IFMS national in scope requires the development and implementation of accounting and auditing standards, the initial and ongoing training of financial management personnel, and the acquisition and installation of modern computer systems linking all branches of government, from the central government to the municipalities. Fortunately, technological advances, particularly the development of microcomputers and the steady decline in the cost of computing power as technology advances, makes feasible the gradual introduction of modern financial management practices, perhaps focusing first on key organizations (i.e., ministries). Also to Cuba's advantage is the considerable experience and knowledge the international financial institutions have accumulated through the technical support and financial assistance they have offered to many countries in the design and introduction of IFMS.

Code of Ethics for Public Officials

The literature on public sector ethics suggests that for codes of conduct to be effective, they must be implemented in national settings characterized by political openness and transparency—two ingredients lacking in Cuba today. In order to work properly, codes of ethics must be set in a national environment where the actions of the highest authorities can be discussed and challenged openly. Codes of ethics appear to work best when "an improper act of a professional nature can be questioned by peers, and the professional group may take actions according to the mores of the group" (Ofusu-Amaah, Soopramanien, and Uprety 1999:16).

In 1997, Cuba enacted a *Código de Etica de los Cuadros del Estado Cubano* (Columbié Santana 2001:7). Reflecting the ideological dogma of the totalitarian state, this code of ethics relies on the same principles that over more than four decades have failed to limit corruption in socialist Cuba, and does not address lack of transparency, individual accountability, and the inability to challenge the upper reaches of the political leadership.

Once a transition occurs, codes of ethics may have an important role to play in limiting corruption, particularly if institutional mechanisms and enforceable laws serve to control abuses of power. Among other things, public servants should be protected from political pressures, decision-making processes made transparent and open to scrutiny, and adequate accounting mechanisms adopted (Pope 2000:175-194).

Public Procurement Procedures

Few areas of government activity offer more opportunities for corruption than public sector or government procurement. In pre-Castro's Cuba, allegations of public sector procurement corruption were common and often the source of political disputes. Since 1959, comparable accusations have become relatively infrequent, mostly due to the centralized nature of the totalitarian state, absence of domestic private firms, and rigid media censorship. In addition, international public sector procurement in socialist Cuba is conducted behind closed doors, outside public scrutiny, and according to whatever rules are found expedient to satisfy political or national security goals, or simply the interests of the ruling elite.

With a transition to a market-oriented economy, Cuba would do well to adhere to accepted international norms regarding public procurement. There is a growing global movement to reform public procurement procedures to accelerate economic growth, make government more efficient, and rein in public spending. The impetus for change has been the realization that corruption in public sector procurement creates many economic distortions that interfere with the development process. Key remedies appear to be in the areas of greater transparency and clear rules whereby government contracts are awarded to bidders.

Several basic principles define a fair and efficient procurement process (Pope 2002:206-207). It should be economical, that is, through the procurement process, the government should acquire those goods and services that offer the best combination of quality and price. It should also be fair and impartial; bid winners should be chosen on the bases of qualifications and merit. Transparency is of the essence. Bidders should respond to specifications that are announced publicly. The process should have a complexity commensurate with the nature of the goods or services being purchased and, most importantly, should be accountable to the public. The bases for all decisions should be justified and recorded. Public sector procurement should be made as transparent as possible so that "institutions, processes, and decisions are made accessible to the general public or to representatives of the public so that processes and decisions can be monitored, reviewed, commented upon, and influenced by the stakeholders" (Wiehen 2001:86).

Establishing a market-oriented public sector procurement system in a post transition Cuba may be facilitated by the adoption of recommended norms proposed by international organizations. Examples are those embodied in the International Competitive Bidding (ICB) principles of the World Bank and the Model Law on Procurement of Goods, Construction and Services of the United Nations Commission on International Law (UNCITRAL). These recom-

mended norms, however, should not be adopted uncritically but rather tailored to the national context in which they are to operate and always seeking to maximize, within that national context, efficiency and anti-corruption objectives. Procurement reforms, in Cuba as elsewhere, as Rose-Ackerman (1999:59) has observed, "highlight the tradeoffs between avoiding corruption and giving officials the flexibility to make decisions in the light of their own knowledge. Discretion increases corrupt incentives, but critics of elaborate procurement codes point to their excessive rigidity."

When appropriate, past procurement experience should serve as a selection criterion provided sufficient information is available to allow as many bidders as possible to participate in public competitions. Related to the above is the need to prevent firms to use information to collude to rig prices. Rose-Ackerman also recommends the use of price benchmarking (for comparable goods and services available in the marketplace) whenever possible to simplify purchases and acquire the best products and services at the lowest price. A basic principle for the design of an integrity-focused procurement system is that the more accountable and transparent it is, the more discretion it could allow public officials to have (Rose-Ackerman 1999:64).

In summary, a post-transition Cuba should design and implement public sector procurement procedures guided by the principles of transparency and accountability by public officials. Bidding competitions should, following Wesberry (2001a:86) "describe clearly and fairly what is to be purchased; publicize the opportunity to make offers to supply; establish fair criteria for selection decision-making; receive offers (bids) from responsible suppliers; compare them and determine which is best, according to the predetermined rules for selection." Contracts should be awarded to selected bidders with no price reduction demands or changes in winning offers. The establishment of modern and transparent procurement procedures should be part of a broader civil service reform process whose ultimate intent is an efficient and responsive state.

Citizen Oversight

There is broad consensus in the transparency/anti-corruption community that without a vibrant and vigilant civil society, legal and technical measures by themselves are insufficient to stem corruption. Involving civil society in the fight against corruption is at the center of most anti-corruption efforts today. This is the case, for example, with the independent anti-corruption commissions—with a three-pronged mandate: prevention, investigation, and public education (see below)—established in several countries. The rationale behind this mandate is that the three domains are mutually supportive: a well-educated and vigilant public provides crucial input for preventive and investigative functions, while effective prevention and investigation encourage citizen involvement. Other more focused approaches, popular in Latin America, rest on the notion that the citizenry has to be educated and mobilized to provide oversight on how the government sector allocates and utilizes public resources. Social auditing—also known as social control in Honduras, *veedurías* in Colombia, and score card in India—entails mobilizing citizens to provide oversight over particular types of projects, generally at the community level.

While citizen oversight initiatives are part and parcel of the right of association citizens enjoy in a democratic society, and should rightfully have a role to play in limiting corruption in a post-transition Cuba, the history of the country suggests that they should be designed cautiously. More than four decades of government-inspired and -controlled mass organizations[4] will surely leave a sour taste among many Cubans. They are likely to see citizen oversight institutions as akin to the totalitarian-inspired mass organizations created by the Castro government as instruments for social and political control. Interestingly, in the former Soviet Union, whistleblower programs advocated in the West have been found to

be politically contentious, given the country's totalitarian past. To succeed in a post-Castro Cuba, future social auditing programs must be provided with very clear and specific legal mandates and promoted strictly on a voluntary basis.

Current thinking in developing circles is emphatic in the belief that one of the most effective ways to curb corruption is to redistribute political power and spending authority away from central governments and toward local or municipal governments. Citizens are more aware of and have a more direct stake in how local governments deliver services and manage resources, and also have greater ability to influence the decision-making process and more closely monitor performance. Thus, governments around the developing world, particularly in Latin America, have amended their constitutions and other legal instruments to gradually increase the amount of financial resources and responsibilities flowing from central to local governments, especially municipalities. Aside from efficiency and equity reasons, the goal is to shift power away from highly centralized governments that historically have been responsive to powerful urban-based political constituencies while largely neglecting more marginal segments of the national population.[5]

A long-term transparency/anti-corruption strategy must consider the devolution of political and financial management to communities, with the proviso that policies must be instituted to help develop the institutional local capability to manage and monitor public spending. Initiatives of this nature must be accompanied by legal instruments designed to encourage community participation in decision-making and granting unrestricted oversight rights to individuals and citizen groups over how local government decisions are made and financial resources managed. It should be obvious that aside from its beneficial effects in controlling corruption, decentralization of fi-

---

4. The reference here is to the official mass organizations, such as the Committees for the Defense of the Revolution (CDR), the Federation of Cuban Women (FMC), the Cuban Workers' Central (CTC) and the Union of Communist Youth (UJC). These mass organizations, among others, are explicitly mentioned in Article 7 of the Socialist Constitution of 1976.

5. This has been the case even in highly centralized Cuba, where in recent years municipalities have been granted a greater say over the management of social services (Dilla 2001).

nancial and management authority will result in the deepening of democratic governance by encouraging citizen involvement in all facets of political life.

Coalition Building

Citizen oversight is most effective in combating corruption when broad sectors of society join forces to do so. While the efforts provided or led by individual citizens often are crucial, collective actions instigated or embraced by citizen group organizations coalescing around particular goals or professional interests can have multiplier effects that greatly enhance the impact of anti-corruption initiatives. Most obvious are those social benefits that could accrue from actions individually taken by professional associations —accountants, auditors, lawyers, engineers, physicians, educators—labor unions, media, business associations, and others to curb corruption. These could include, for example, the adoption of professional or business codes of ethics, ethics training, or peer oversight monitoring mechanisms to ensure proper conduct.

The business sector has a key role to play in the implementation of transparency/anti-corruption initiatives. Private sector firms often bear the negative impact of public sector corruption, while others, perversely, benefit from it. Most reputable businesses would prefer to operate in a competitive, corruption-free environment, but often they are deterred from doing so by a "prisoner's dilemma": firms unwilling to pay bribes or provide other favors to corrupt officials often lose business to firms not likewise constrained. But if the private sector becomes organized and works together with civil society, this situation can be changed. Business associations that adhere to ethical principles can have a major impact on corruption by assisting their members in rejecting bribery and other shady deals. Such associations could enact and help enforce business ethics codes, assist individual firms comply with procurement procedures and rules to prevent the payment of bribes, and serve as a conduit for an ongoing transparency-promotion dialogue between the private and public sectors (OECD 1999).

Even more significant is the coming together of different social sectors to achieve common goals, as when professional associations lend their technical expertise to civil society organizations to monitor the manner in which public sector projects are designed and managed, or funds spent. The cooperation principle is implicit in many social auditing schemes, for example when professional associations provide expertise to citizen watchdog groups, or when firms agree to public procurement bidding principles monitored by citizens' organizations. If a true commitment exists to adopt ethical and transparent values, the broader the coalition to gradually expand an integrity framework, the better.

In Cuba's case, such lofty cooperation will not be achieved overnight. Many developments will have to come together to erode the country's ingrained corruption tradition and begin to create a culture of honesty and transparency. How will independent professional and partisan interest groups be organized and operate? Will economic growth be sufficient to allow individuals to satisfy their families' needs without having to steal from each other or the state? Will Cubans gradually adopt commonly-shared civic and probity values, consistent with good governance and market principles? Will they overcome the behavioral legacy left by an economy of scarcity? When will they come to realize that the right to associate freely, without coercion or political manipulation, is a fundamental precondition to control corruption and to ensure Cuba's democratic governance? These are major questions indeed. They call attention once again to the priority a post-transition Cuba must assign to promoting equitable economic growth, establish transparent government institutions, and promote education in civic values.

Building Public Awareness

Discounting the ignorance about democratic governance issues to which the population of Cuba has been subjected throughout more than four decades of socialist rule could be very costly. Modern concepts of transparency and accountability are unknown to most Cubans, who have lived under socialism for more than forty years. They have been taught that the paternalistic state is not to be questioned, and are only familiar with the information provided by the state media. To most Cubans, the concept that public servants are accountable to the citizenry is foreign, as is the very notion of transparency—the right of citizens to know how government decisions are made.

These basic principles are second nature to citizens of democratic societies, but will come as a revelation to many Cubans. This is not surprising, as unfortunately even today in many countries in Latin America and other developing regions, basic rights of access to information and public accountability do not fully exist. As in Cuba, in some countries the state budget and how it is derived are treated as state secrets, programmatic and spending decisions are still made in the dark, and public officials act as if they were accountable to no one. These are most fertile grounds for corruption to flourish.

Once the transition begins, a systematic and long-term effort must be made to educate the citizens of Cuba regarding their right to know and to monitor how government operates. These efforts must begin at a very elementary level and include concepts such as transparency and accountability as part of a broader national effort to inculcate in the population basic knowledge about basic democratic governance principles and how a market economy operates. Governance education must also pay attention to the awe in which most Cubans regard the State: they must be taught that actions by public officials could and should be challenged when warranted without fear of retribution. These are obviously long-term education efforts that should be conducted through every possible means: the mass media, school curricula, civic organizations and by government itself.

A National Anti-Corruption Commission

An important policy decision for a post-transition Cuban government will be whether to establish an anti-corruption commission as a vehicle for the private and public sectors, as well as civil society, to collaborate in the development, implementation, and monitoring of a national transparency/accountability strategy. Such commissions have been established in several countries under different formats to provide a forum for representatives of government, business and civil society to meet regularly to identify, discuss, and make recommendations regarding transparency/

anti-corruption issues. Some national commissions serve as consultative or policy making bodies exclusively, while others have a more formal and broader mandate that might include an investigative role (e.g., the well-known Hong Kong Independent Commission Against Corruption or the more recent Independent Corrupt Practices and Other Related Offenses Commission, ICPC, in Nigeria). In functioning democracies with transparent and efficient public sectors and routine citizen oversight of government activities, such commissions are unnecessary and redundant. The opposite appears to be the case in countries with a history of authoritarian rule and lacking a transparency tradition.

In a transition Cuba, a consultative and policy anti-corruption commission, composed of business and civil society members with an integrity reputation to protect and honest and politically-influential government officials committed to a transparency agenda, could serve to maintain the corruption issue in the limelight and to effectively mobilize public opinion. Equipped with a small but well-qualified staff, and with assured funding from general government revenues (or from international sources, if needed), an anti-corruption commission could serve as a channel for ongoing government-business-civil society dialogue and as a transmission belt for citizen input. While functionally limited to act as a consultation and recommendation body, the commission could be legally empowered to review government policies and programs and required to make its recommendations public. In establishing a transparency/accountability commission, several decisions would be critical: the number and composition of its membership, criteria for selection of the membership and persons responsible for the selection, term of service of members, process for filling vacancies, and rules of procedure of the commission.

If vested with the proper authority and a trusted membership, a transparency/accountability commission could serve as a highly visible forum in a Cuba in transition for dialogue, citizen education, and development of policy-oriented recommendations. It could further serve as a confidence building body for a citizenry not familiar with the proper management of the state and its interaction with the public and private sector business interests.

CONCLUDING REMARKS

Corruption occurs in the dark and takes advantage of emerging opportunities. Corruption abhors transparency, sunshine and accountability. To control corruption, particularly during transitions when large changes are occurring and policies are in flux, it is essential to be constantly on the lookout for creative new approaches to beat the system, and be prepared to fine-tune control mechanisms.

Rather than focusing on isolated anti-corruption mechanisms, the goal of a broad transparency/accountability or integrity system—such as the one that we propose for a Cuba in transition and beyond—is to center attention on mutually supportive relationships. As Pope notes (2000:37), "what is the benefit of a sound and 'clean' Judiciary ready to uphold the Rule of Law, if there is corruption in the police, investigators, prosecutors or the legal profession? The Judges would simply not receive the cases they should hear; they would then sit in splendid isolation—honest, capable, yet able to achieve little."

The international financial institutions and the bilateral development agencies can play an important role in preventing corruption in a post-transition Cuba. First, they can implement transparency/accountability policies to prevent corruption within their programs. Second, they can assist in financing government- and civil society-sponsored anti-corruption initiatives, including projects to strengthen the rule of law, financial control and accountability mechanisms, and citizen oversight. Third, a post-transition Cuba should benefit from the technical transparency/accountability support and financing likely to be provided by the international donor community. Finally, the international development community should prod a future Cuban government to adopt a proactive transparency/accountability strategy.

While it may never be possible to totally eradicate corruption in Cuba—or anywhere else for that matter—the toolbox available today to combat it is growing exponentially. Transparency, accountability, vigilance and preparing for the worse may well be the best deterrents to prevent the scourge of corruption from derailing the long-awaited transition in the island.

REFERENCES

Batista Odio, Carlos Alberto. 1986. "Particularidades más importantes de los presupuestos cubanos en los últimos 30 años." In Academia de Ciencias de Cuba, Instituto de Filosofía, *Jornada Científica Internacional XXX Aniversario del Ataque al Cuartel Moncada* (La Habana: Editorial de Ciencias Sociales).

Columbié Santana, Mariela. 2001. "La ética y los valores en el Sector Público como un imperativo de nuestros pueblos." *Revista Probidad Digital*, July 15.

"Creado el Ministerio de Auditoría y Control." 2001. *Granma Digital*, May 3.

Dilla, Haroldo. 2001. "Municipios, crisis y reforma económica en Cuba." *Encuentro de la Cultura Cubana*, 23, pp. 199-206.

Gayoso, Antonio. 1999. "The Role of Small and Medium Size Enterprise in Cuba's Future." In *Cuba in Transition—Volume 9*, pp. 60-72. Washington: Association for the Study of the Cuban Economy

Keshet, Jasmin and Tom Devine. 2002. "The Significance of Whistleblowers to Challenge Corruption." www.respondanet.com/english.

Klitgaard, Robert. 1998. "International Cooperation Against Corruption." *Finance and Development* (March), pp. 3-6.

Ofosu-Amaah, W. Paatii, Raj Soopramanien, and Kishor Uprety. 1999. *Combating Corruption: A Comparative Review of Selected Legal Aspects of State Practice and Major International Initiatives.* Washington: The World Bank.

Organization for Economic Cooperation and Development (OECD). 1998. *Convention on Combating Bribery of Foreign Public Officials in International Business Transaction.* DAFFE/IME/BR(97)20. Paris.

Organization for Economic Cooperation and Development (OECD). 1999. *Fighting Corruption in Developing Countries and Emerging Economies: The Role of the Private Sector, Final Report.* Washington: Washington Conference on Corruption.

Organization of American States (OAS). 1998. *Inter-American Convention against Corruption.* OEA/Ser.A STI/2. Washington, DC.

Pope, Jeremy. 2000. *Confronting Corruption: The Elements of a National Integrity System.* Berlin: Transparency International.

Reuters. 2001. "Cuba crea el nuevo ministerio anticorrupción." *El Nuevo Herald Digital*, May 4.

Rose-Ackerman, Susan. 1999. *Corruption and Government: Causes, Consequences and Reform.* Cambridge: Cambridge University Press.

Svejnar, Jan. 2002. "Transition Economies: Performance and Challenges." *Journal of Economic Perspectives* 16:1 (Winter), pp. 3-28.

U.S. Agency for International Development (USAID). 1999. *A Handbook on Fighting Corruption.* Washington: USAID, Center for Democracy and Governance.

Wesberry, Jim. 2001a. "Combating Fraud in Procurement and Contracting." In World Bank Institute, *Improving Governance and Controlling Corruption.* Washington: The World Bank, pp. 83-90.

Wesberry, Jim. 2001b. "Sound Financial Management to Counteract Corruption." In World Bank Institute, *Improving Governance and Controlling Corruption.* Washington: The World Bank, pp. 95-106.

Wiehen, Michael H. 2001. "Transparency in Procurement." In Lara M., Gabriel and Rick Stapenhurst (with Mary Thomas), editors. *The Role of Bilateral Donors in Fighting Corruption.* Washington: The World Bank Institute, pp. 85-93.

FOREIGN INVESTMENT IN CUBA: RECENT DEVELOPMENTS AND ROLE IN THE ECONOMY

Paolo Spadoni[1]

Since the early 1990s, Cuba has suffered debilitating blows that resulted from the demise of the Soviet Union and the disappearance of the economic and financial system in which the island was inserted (Council for Mutual Economic Assistance, or CMEA). The termination of traditional trade partnerships with the Soviet Bloc and the loss of the favorable and stable terms under which most of its trade took place left Cuba without markets for its traditional exports (mainly sugar, tobacco, and nickel) and drastically reduced its import capacity (in particular oil). With the real GDP plummeting by more than 40% between 1990 and 1993, Cuban authorities were forced to develop a strategy of reinsertion into the global economy aimed at seeking new markets, sources of financing, and technology.

Cuba's response to the deteriorating economic situation was the implementation in September 1990 of an economic austerity program called "special period in time of peace." The program consisted of a series of measures intended to conserve energy and raw materials, stimulate food production, expand markets for exports and imports, introduce some management and selective structural reforms, and accelerate the development of international tourism. However, the main novelty was the opening of the island to foreign private capital, a significant change for a socialist country whose economy had previously been under exclusive Cuban state control and ownership. Cuban authorities conceived the promotion of foreign investment as a way to stimulate the diversification of exports, acquisition of raw materials, import substitution, insertion into new markets, introduction of modern practices of management, and acquisition of technology.[2]

President Fidel Castro and other senior officials have never concealed their intention to keep foreign ownership and capital in the communist island at a minimum level. They keep saying that foreign investment is a complementary measure aimed at strengthening and improving the country's state-run socialist system, not destroy it. Nevertheless, an increasing number of foreign firms have entered the Cuban market since 1993, mostly attracted by the opportunity to get a foothold in the Cuban economy before the lifting of the embargo, take advantage of the lack of U.S. competition, and make good levels of profit in a country that has set a brand new business and economic path.

What begun as investments in a handful of hotel and oil exploration joint ventures in the early 1990s has grown into a significant and varied presence in al-

---

1. This paper is mostly based on field research conducted in Cuba during the summer of 2002. The Department of Food and Resource Economics at the University of Florida supported the field research trip and the preparation of this paper. The author alone is responsible for the content and interpretations.

2. Pérez Villanueva, Omar Everleny. *El Papel de la Inversion Extranjera Directa en las Economias Subdesarrolladas. El Caso Cubano.* Ph.D. Dissertation, Universidad de la Habana (1998), p. 98.

most all sectors of the Cuban economy, from mining and tourism to financial services, manufacturing, construction, food processing and agriculture. While it cannot be argued that foreign investment plays a fundamental role in the Cuban economy, it appears evident that foreign capital has helped Cuba to increase production of oil and generation of electricity, find new markets for its main exports (apart from sugar) such as nickel and tobacco, and boost international tourism from Canada and the countries of the European Union. Joint ventures for the construction and exploitation of new hotels in the island and management expertise provided through administration contracts have transformed tourism, at least in gross terms, as the country's biggest generator of foreign exchange.

In addition, thanks to foreign direct investment and the recent promotion of new forms of investment such as cooperative productions (specific agreements between small and mid-size companies aimed to take advantage of functioning installations and facilities), domestic supplies to the tourist industry and to the internal market in hard currency have increased. Since the legalization of dollar holdings in August 1993, dollar transactions in government-owned retail stores have taken a prominent role in the Cuban economy. These transactions are mainly triggered by remittances sent from the United States coupled with increasing shortages of products in the domestic market in local currency. Some 60% of all Cubans are estimated to have occasional or regular access to dollars, absent which they would not be able to purchase many goods that are not available in the peso market.[3]

Any attempt to carry out a comprehensive analysis of foreign investment in Cuba is hindered by the lack of reliable and detailed information on the activities of foreign firms and their contribution in terms of capital. Due to what Cubans call the "U.S. economic blockade" against the island, public disclosure of data on the presence of foreign capital in Cuba is practically limited to statistics on the number of international economic associations (Asociaciones Económicas con Capital Extranjero, or AECEs)[4] by year, by sector, and by country. This method of reporting the level of foreign investment in the country offers no information on the value or strategic importance of the deals involved. Nevertheless, this paper utilizes the best available information from a variety of sources (some of them confidential) in order to provide a detailed overview of foreign business activities in Cuba, with a particular attention on recent developments and new strategies implemented by the Cuban government. It begins with an analysis of the evolution of foreign direct investment (FDI) in the island and the main results of international economic associations in 2001 (a few AECEs signed in the first half of 2002 and expansion plans of existing investors are also reported). It continues with an examination of new forms of investment that have assumed growing importance in the last few years, such as cooperative production agreements with overseas firms. Finally, it uses some indicators of AECEs and other accessible data to give a sense of what foreign investment represents to the Cuban economy.

FOREIGN DIRECT INVESTMENT IN CUBA

With the demise of the former Soviet Union in the early 1990s and the plunge of its economy, Cuba's need to find alternative financing, technology, and markets for its products grew more urgent. As a result, the government moved actively to seek new long-shunned foreign investment and the first handful of joint ventures were signed in the hotel industry and oil exploration under Decree Law 50 of 1982. Regarding the latter, the limit of 49% for the foreign

---

3. The Economist Intelligence Unit (EIU). "External shocks squeeze growth." *Country Briefing* (June 18, 2002).

4. The term *international economic association* (or simply *economic association*) refers to the following: joint activities by one or more national investors and one or more foreign investors for the production of goods, the offering of services, or both, for profit, either as joint ventures or international economic-associations contracts. *Joint ventures* have a legal status distinct from that of any one of either of the parties; the proportions of capital stock which should be contributed by the foreign investor and the national investor are agreed upon by both partners and defined as part of the authorization. *International economic association contracts* do not imply a legal entity separate from those of the contracting parties; each contracting party makes its own contribution and maintains control over it.

share of joint ventures and the low level of investment protection for overseas companies were certainly major dissuading factors for capital inflows. Cuban statutory guarantees fell considerably short of providing the level of investment protection foreign companies would demand. According to Article 24 of Decree-Law 50, if the Cuban government unilaterally terminated the activities of a joint venture, the Cuban National Bank simply guaranteed to foreign investors the ability to repatriate the proceeds of their share after liquidation. In addition, it was clear that the intention of the Cuban government was to maintain the most important sectors of the economy in national hands.[5]

The opening to foreign investment and international tourism, matched by increasing interest but also growing complaints from foreign companies, led the government to draw up updated and more attractive legislation in 1995. Law 77 of 1995, while repeating some of the basic aspects of the Decree Law 50 of 1982, set out specific guarantees for foreign firms by establishing full protection and security against expropriation and opened all sectors of the Cuban economy (except public health, education services, and armed forces) to foreign investment. It also abolished the limit of 49% of foreign shares for joint ventures and authorized for the first time the possibility of 100% wholly foreign owned investments. Finally, in an attempt to speed up and streamline the approval process of new agreements, the law required the approval or denial of an investment within 60 days of the presentation of the formal request.

After 1993, Cuba intensified the promotion of foreign investment. Through visits to foreign countries, participation in international investment events, and meetings with potential investors, Cuban officials have been very active in publicizing the advantages of business activities in the island.[6] As a result, the number of international economic associations has grown steadily and expanded to different sectors of the Cuban economy such as mining, construction, light and food industry, agriculture, and services. What's more important, small joint ventures with relatively low amount of foreign capital invested gave way, to some degree, to larger associations (such as joint ventures with Canada's Sherritt International in the nickel sector and Italy's STET in telecommunications) with large foreign capital investments as well as new and more modern operations.

An important change of policy toward foreign investment occurred in 1998 when the Cuban authorities declared their preference for economic associations that involved higher amounts of capital and loan financing. In fact, as a result of banking reforms and continued economic recovery, Vice President Carlos Lage announced that year the intention of the government to pursue a strategy of encouraging foreign investment in large development projects while limiting investments in smaller projects, unless they included the introduction of new technologies or new export markets. He added that Cuba's government-operated banks were in a position to provide small amounts of capital.[7] For instance, in 2000, direct investment agreements mainly included large projects in oil, energy, construction, and telecommunications, for which Cuba was unable to provide financing.[8] The government has also continued to promote joint ventures in the tourist sector for the construction of hotels and resorts for international tourism.

Cuba's increased selectivity on foreign investment is demonstrated by data on authorized and dissolved international economic associations (Figure 1). Between 1988 and 2001, a total of 555 AECEs were formed in Cuba, most of them joint ventures; at the

5. Confidential Report for the Embassy of Japan in Havana. "Investment Opportunities in Cuba." Unpublished (March 31, 1999), p.10.

6. Pérez-López, Jorge F. "Foreign Investment in Cuba in the Second Half of the 1990s." Paper presented at International Symposium organized by Carleton University and the University of Havana, September 28-30, 1999.

7. U.S.-Cuba Trade and Economic Council, "Foreign Investment Policy Change." *Economic Eye on Cuba* (February 16, 1998 to February 22, 1998). http://www.cubatrade.org/eyeonr.html#4.

8. EIU. "Foreign investment focuses on large projects." *Country Briefing* (February 12, 2001).

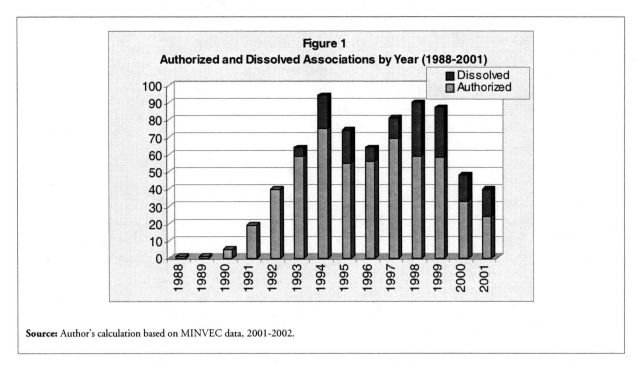

Figure 1
Authorized and Dissolved Associations by Year (1988-2001)

Source: Author's calculation based on MINVEC data, 2001-2002.

end of 2001, 400 remained active.[9] The number of dissolved AECEs is 155, approximately 28% of the total constituted. The number of active associations, which had been increasing at an annual average rate of around 28% between 1993 and 1997, rose by just 6% per year between 1998 and 2001. This is not surprising, considering that almost 60% of dissolutions occurred in the last 4 years. However, it should be noted that the number of authorizations steadily declined during the same period. Interestingly, the Cuban Ministry of Foreign Investment (MINVEC) reports that other 72 international economic associations operating in Cuba are in the process of dissolution. Therefore, unless a significant number of new agreements are signed in 2002 (or perhaps most of the contracts of the AECEs subject to dissolution are renewed), it is possible that the total number of active AECEs will begin to decrease for the first time since 1988.

Many international economic associations formed in the early 1990s dissolved because of the termination of the contract between the Cuban state and the overseas investor. These were mostly small and medium size AECEs whose profits have been disappointing, in part because of the lack of adequate financing. In fact, although changing priorities of the Cuban authorities toward foreign investment might have played a role in this development, it is not a secret that the Cuban partner in joint ventures is often unable to live up to its payment committments. Other international associations dissolved because of the withdrawal of the foreign partner. The existing restrictions on the operation of enterprises, excessive bureaucratic practices, and failures to achieve the planned results seem to be the most common causes.

A number of foreign firms involved in oil and mining exploration activities have stopped their operations in recent years. In the oil sector, the only positive oil exploration and production results have been those of the Canadian companies Sherritt International and Pebercan Corporation, which are drilling wells in Cuba's northern coast. In 2001, these firms produced around 68% of Cuba's total national oil output.[10] On the other hand, France's Total (the first

9. In July 2002, Cuba's Vice-Minister of Foreign Investment Ernesto Sentí reported that the number of active international associations in Cuba had reached 412. See AP. "Prometen facilitar inversiones" (July 18, 2002).

10. The percentage is calculated from EIU data. See EIU. "Foreign partners report output growth." *Cuba Country Report* (May 1, 2002).

western oil company to sign an exploration contract with Cuba in 1990) halted its operations on the island in 1994, Britain's British Borneo and France's Geopetrole in 1997, Britain's Premier Oil in 1998,[11] and Brazil's Petrobras in June 2001. In the mining sector, several Canadian companies that explored for precious and base metals (gold, silver, copper, and zinc) reportedly interrupted their operations in the last few years because of the sudden fall of international prices of those metals.[12] For instance, Northern Orion Exploration Ltd. had a joint venture with Cuba's Geominera in a gold-silver mine at Delita in the Isle of Youth, but because of low gold prices the partners agreed to halt the work in 1998. CaribGold Resources, which had signed in 1993 a joint venture with Geominera to explore and develop deposits of gold and base metals in the province of Camagüey, terminated its activities in early 1998.[13]

In spite of the increasing number of dissolutions and the lower rate of authorizations of AECEs, Cuban authorities argue that foreign investment is in a process of consolidation. In February 2002, Minister Marta Lomas stated: "While Cuba is often blamed for trying to slow down foreign investment, what is happening in reality is the opposite. The country has been concentrating on businesses with results."[14] Indeed, many foreign investors are engaging in profitable operations and expanding their interests in the Caribbean island. It is true that some major foreign companies have had problems in 2001 (especially those in the tourist sector such as Spain's Sol Meliá), but none of them have pulled out of the country. For instance Brazil's Petrobras, after ending its oil explorations, said the decision was temporary and that it was still interested in prospecting for oil in deep-water areas in the Gulf of Mexico. Not even those com-

panies that have been targeted or sanctioned by the Helms-Burton law of 1996 have divested themselves of their Cuban holdings.[15] In short, 400 international economic associations remain active in Cuba and someone must be making money.

At the end of 2001, the greatest percentage of economic associations with foreign capital was linked to basic industry (mainly mining, oil, and energy), followed by tourism, construction and light industry manufacturing (Figure 2). From previous years, there is a reduction of AECEs in basic industry and, to a lesser extent, in the metalworking and food industries. This supports the aforementioned argument that a number of associations involved in oil and mining exploration contracts have halted their operations recently. On the other hand, joint ventures in tourism, sugar, and communications were on the rise. Developments in the sugar sectors are very important, and will be analyzed in the next section.

Estimating the value of foreign direct investment in Cuba to date is not easy, mainly because the government refuses to provide updated overall figures. The secrecy is justified by the authorities of the island as a protective measure against the U.S. economic sanctions. Even the Havana embassies of the major investing countries are unable to give complete figures because, according to them, investments in Cuba are often channeled through third countries or offshore financial centers, thus escaping registration by the real country of origin.[16]

The Economic Commission for Latin America and the Caribbean (CEPAL) estimates that, since the authorization of the first joint venture in 1988 until 2001, the total amount of committed foreign invest-

11. Confidential Report (1999), pp.40-41.

12. Interview with news correspondent stationed in Havana (July 3, 2002).

13. "Poor Prices, Exploration Results Cause Demise of Joutel Resources." *Cuba News*, 7:1 (January 1999).

14. Economics Press Service. "Inversión Extranjera. Menos de lo esperado, pero…" (February 15, 2002).

15. The law is the U.S. latest package of economic sanctions against the communist island. It aims to complicate Cuba's opening to foreign investment by targeting those foreign companies that "traffic" in American properties expropriated during the early days of the revolution. For further details see: Spadoni, Paolo. "The Impact of the Helms-Burton Legislation on Foreign Investment in Cuba." In *Cuba in Transition—Volume 11* (Washington: Association for the Study of the Cuban Economy, 2001), pp.18-36.

16. Confidential Report (1999), pp.3-4.

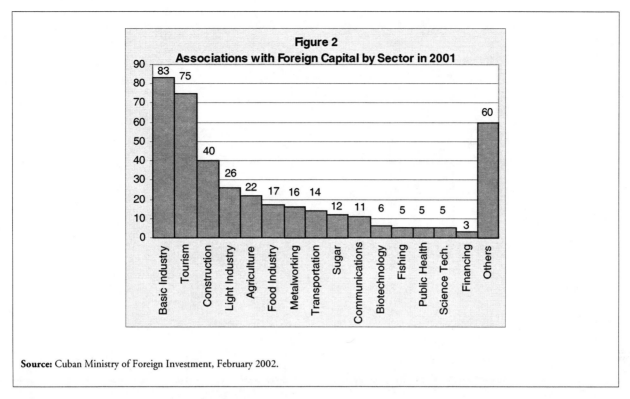

Source: Cuban Ministry of Foreign Investment, February 2002.

Table 1.   Foreign Direct Investment in Cuba in $U.S. million (1993-2001)

Year	1993	1994	1995	1996	1997	1998	1999	2000	2001	Total
Direct Investment	54.0	563.4ª	4.7	82.1	442.0	206.6	178.2	448.1	38.9(a)	1,964

Source: Cuban Central Bank, May 2002.

a.   1994 data are cumulative to that year. (a) Preliminary estimate

ment is $5.4 billion, of which around half has already been delivered.[17] The latest balance of payments data of the Cuban Central Bank puts accumulated foreign direct investment (delivered FDI) at $1,964 million (Table 1). The 2002 economic report has revised data for 2000 from $399.9 million to $448.1 million, while FDI for the year 2001 is just $38.9 million.[18] The latter is a very disappointing result that comes on top of declines in tourism (gross revenues have decreased for the first time since 1991), exports, and other hard currency revenues such as remittances. Sectors with a significant presence of foreign capital are tourism, energy, oil, mining, telecommunications, and construction.

In terms of the number of foreign direct investments, countries of the European Union as a group account for more than 50% of the total (Figure 3). International economic associations with Canadian partners have declined, while those with Chinese and Latin American companies are on the rise. Spain continues to be the main investor in the island (104 joint venture agreements signed), followed by Canada (70), Italy (57), and France (18).

17. CEPAL. "Cuba: Evolución Económica Durante 2001" (June 6, 2002), p.5.

18. The value of delivered FDI for 2001 has generated controversy because it contradicts previous figures announced by governmental sources. In fact, in December 2001 it was reported that FDI amounted to an estimated $200 million. See Triana Cordoví, Juan. "La Economía Cubana en el 2001, una Perspectiva Global." La Habana, Centro de Estudios de la Economía Cubana (April 2002), p.14. Also see EIU. "Data given on trade & investment partners." *Country Report Cuba* (February 11, 2002).

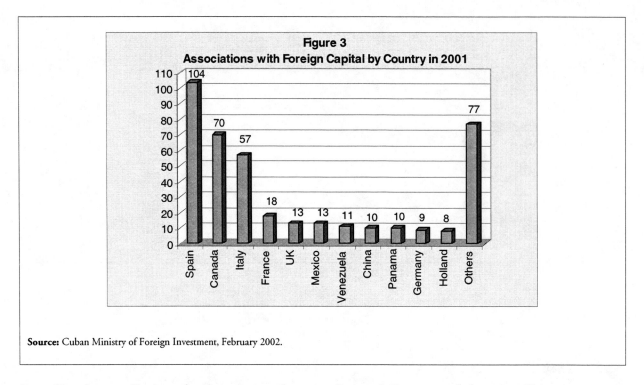

Figure 3
Associations with Foreign Capital by Country in 2001

Source: Cuban Ministry of Foreign Investment, February 2002.

Regarding the contribution of each country and sector to the total amount of FDI in Cuba, the only data available are those of the U.S.-Cuba Trade and Economic Council as of March 1999. The total value of committed/delivered FDI through AECEs was estimated by this source at $1,767.2 million. Leading countries are Canada ($600 million), Mexico ($450 million), Italy ($387 million) and Spain ($100 million). Leading sectors are telecommunications ($650 million), mining ($350 million), and tourism ($200 million).[19]

FDI IN 2001 AND 2002

FDI results in 2001 were mixed. On the one hand, the number of authorizations for international economic associations was the lowest since 1991, while the amount of foreign capital delivered to the country plummeted to levels unseen in recent years. On the other hand, the main economic indicators of associations with foreign capital showed progress from the previous year, and there is still interest among foreign companies to invest in the island.[20]

The Cuban Ministry of Foreign Investment reports that 24 new international economic associations were authorized in 2001, of which 13 operated abroad.[21] The number of dissolved enterprises for the year is 16. The majority of new AECEs were linked to tourism (7), construction (7), and sugar (5). The most active foreign companies were from Spain, Canada, Brazil, Italy, and China (Figure 4). In terms of foreign capital invested, the most important agreements signed in 2001 were in the tourist sector, perhaps with the exception of an important joint venture in the sugar industry. The most significant agreements were the following:

• A joint venture between the Cuban company Cubanacán and the Spanish groups Inversiones Hoteleras Bahía del Duque and Sol Meliá for the construction of five hotels (with a total of 1,150 rooms) in the zone of Bacunayagua, between the

19. See U.S.-Cuba Trade and Economic Council. http://www.cubatrade.org

20. Interview with news correspondent stationed in Havana (July 3, 2002).

21. It is reported that a total of 72 international economic associations operated abroad at the end of 2001, mainly in construction, biotechnology and pharmaceutical. See EIU. *Country Report on Cuba* (February 11, 2002).

Figure 4. Authorized AECEs by Sector and by Country in 2001: Total 24[a]

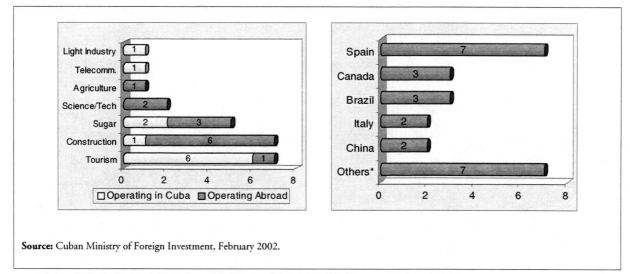

Source: Cuban Ministry of Foreign Investment, February 2002.

a. *Others include: Holland (1), Belarus (1), Ukraine (1), Mexico (1), Uruguay (1), Portugal (1).

Cuban western provinces of Havana and Matanzas. The total investment is estimated at more than $200 million.[22]

- A joint venture (Desarrollo Turístico Bacunayagua S.A) between Cubanacán and the Spanish firm Valle Yumurí S.A. to build a new resort in the province of Matanzas.

- A joint venture (Shangai Sun Cuba, Ltd.) between Cubanacán and the Chinese government-owned firm Suntime for the construction of two hotels: a five-star hotel with 700 rooms in Shangai, China, and another one in the tourist area Marina Hemingway in the western part of the Ciudad de la Habana province.[23]

- A joint venture between the Cuban company Gran Caribe and the Spanish groups Globalian and Blau Hotels to open three or four hotels in Cuba.[24]

- A joint venture (Santa Lucía S.A.) between Gran Caribe and the Spanish group Grubarges Inversiones for the construction, management, and marketing of a three-star hotel of 720 rooms in a seaside resort in the province of Camagüey. The project is estimated at $62 million.[25]

Developments in the sugar industry deserve special mention. The sector, which employs about a half-million workers, is currently undergoing significant transformations. Due to falling international prices and low production, gross revenues from sugar exports plummeted from $4.3 billion in 1989-90 to

22. "Millions in Cuban Hotels," *Prensa Latina* (May 28, 2001).

23. Interestingly, the Cuban group Habaguanex S.A. and the state-run Chinese firm Construction and Engineering Corporation (CS-GEG) had signed a joint venture in 2000 for the construction of a hotel in Havana's sea-front Malecón. The operation was halted in 2001 without explanation from the Cuban authorities. Unofficial Cuban sources argue that several projects presented by the Chinese company failed to meet the architectural standards required by the Cuban government for new hotels in the colonial district known as "Old Havana." Interview with an economist of the Centro de Estudios de la Economía Cubana, Havana (June 11, 2002). However, given the good status of the relationship between Havana and Beijing and the increasing financing provided by the latter to Cuba in recent years, it is conceivable that the Cuban authorities simply gave China a better deal. The hotel in the tourist area Marina Hemingway is a bigger and more important project. Interview with news correspondent posted in Havana, June 13, 2002.

24. EIU. "First-half tourism results encouraging." *Country Briefing* (August 31, 2001). 24

25. "Constitution of the mixed company Santa Lucia S.A." *Granma Internacional* (November 7, 2001).

$441 million in 2001-02.[26] Therefore, the Cuban government has implemented a wide program of restructuring of the whole industry aimed to modernize its facilities, reduce production costs, diversify the range of products made from sugar cane, and boost exports and revenues. Priority is given to by-products such as alcohol, animal feeds, "bagasse" (cane residue), and ingredients for the biotechnology and the pharmaceutical sector. With the dismantling of inefficient sugar mills, a significant number of workers will be allocated to other activities. It is also reported that more than 3 million acres of land used for sugar cane will now be used for livestock breeding, various crops (citrus and vegetable), and reforestation.[27]

The island's authorities have made clear they are actively seeking foreign partners to invest in sugar derivatives. Several joint ventures have been reported so far with investors from Spain, Mexico, Canada, Italy, and France. The main novelty in 2001 is the creation of five new joint ventures of which at least three are in the area of raw sugar production or refining. But we must remember that Cuba will continue to produce sugar and hopes to maintain a production at around four million tons per year. A joint venture (Compañía Azucarera Internacional S.A.) has been formed between Cubazúcar and an unknown foreign partner to market Cuban sugar in the world market. It is the first time since 1959 that a foreign firm is allowed to manage production and, therefore, to be directly involved in sugar exports. The company appears to be one of those that already financed sugar output.[28] Cuban authorities have also announced the creation of Corporación Financiera Azucarera S.A,

an entity that will provide financial services to the sugar industry.[29] Finally, three new joint ventures have been created with Ukraine (Urcaribeimpex), Belarus (Belatinsajar), and Brazil (Tecnagro). The first two entities will refine and sell Cuban sugar in the Ukraine and Belarus and will also sell sugar in Russia. As part of the deal, Cuba will also receive technical equipment (tractor engines and tires) for the sugar harvest. Tecnagro will provide automation services to Brazil's sugar industry.[30]

As reported in the previous section, only $38.9 million in foreign direct investment was delivered to Cuba in 2001. While Cuban authorities justified the decline arguing that it mirrored a general trend throughout Latin America, some investors said the business climate is much worse in Cuba. According to a European businessman, "they (Cubans) insist you be partner with a state-run company, that you hire workers at high rates through government-run labor agencies and then you run-up against the bureaucracy and the U.S. embargo and threats to boot."[31]

An additional problem, perhaps reflecting the concerns among foreign investors, is that a significant amount of pledged foreign capital has not been delivered yet. Apart from the joint ventures authorized in the tourist sector in 2001,[32] we should remember that agreements involving large amounts of capital were signed in 2000. In fact, Minister of Foreign Investment Marta Lomas declared that in 2000, the total number of contracts with foreign partners was 33, compared to 58 agreements signed a year before. But she added that the amount of foreign capital com-

---

26. Eaton, Tracey. "Sweet sorrows for Cuba restructuring of sugar industry leaves workers with a bitter taste." *The Dallas Morning News* (July 9, 2002).

27. Oramas, Joaquín. "Alternatives in the sugar industry." *Granma Internacional* (July 4, 2002).

28. Although Cuba generally does not reveal joint venture partners (citing the four-decade old U.S. embargo and the more recent Helms-Burton law), business and diplomatic sources in Havana said that Paris-registered Pacol, S.A., a firm connected to the British sugar trader E.D. & F Man, is behind the deal. Frank, Mark. "New Cuban sugar exporter has mystery partner." *Reuters*, March 7, 2002.

29. "Creadas en Cuba dos importantes compañías azucareras," *Opciones* (June 20, 2002).

30. "Cuba promueve inversiones extranjeras en industria azucarera," EFE (July 21, 2001).

31. "Foreign investment in Cuba plummeted to $38.9 million in 2001 from $488 million the year before," Reuters. (July 8, 2002).

32. Construction of new hotels can take up to 2-3 years to be completed. Therefore, foreign capital pledged in 2001 might begin to be delivered in 2002.

mitted was twice that for 1999.[33] For instance, Spain's Inversiones Ibersuizas and Swiss-based Holderbank (one of the biggest cement companies in the world) signed an agreement with the Cuban state in 2000 for the construction of a cement plant in Santiago de Cuba, which involves investments for $150 million.[34]

In December 1999, the Spanish/French company Altadis purchased 50% of the shares of Habanos S.A., the company that markets Cuban tobacco products internationally; foreign investment in this operation has been estimated at around $476 million. If we analyze data on foreign direct investment in 2000 ($448.1 million), we can fairly assume that the agreement with Altadis accounts for most of the inflows. In fact, it is reported that the Spanish-French company paid the Cuban government $439 million in 2000, with the remaining $38 million dependent of Habanos reaching unspecified earning targets in 2001-2004.[35] Therefore, in the light of the low amount of FDI reported in 2001, it appears clear that a significant part of the capital pledged in 2000 has not been delivered to the country.

In evaluating the performance of FDI in Cuba, it is important to acknowledge that the government has been looking in recent years not only for large investments but also for soft credit (highly concessional loan financing) provided by foreign partners.[36] In fact, because of the collapse of the former Soviet Union and the economic pressure of the U.S. embargo against the island, Cuba has had to rely almost exclusively on expensive short-term credit to halt the deep economic recession of the early 1990s. With the exception of China, the attempts of the Cuban government have generated little results so far.

During the last few years, China has been the only foreign country that has provided a considerable amount of loan financing to Cuba at highly concessional terms (Figure 5). The Cuban Ministry of Foreign Investment reports that, between 1990 and 2001, China provided soft credit to the island of $123.8 million, mostly in the areas of education ($41.9 million), tourism ($24 million), and agriculture ($15.6 million). More than half of that amount has been granted in the last four years.[37] Chinese companies have invested in Cuba's fishing, agriculture, food and textile industries. In addition, Chinese president Jiang Zemin pledged around $385 million in loan to Cuba in April 2001. Over the next five years, China will lend Havana money (mainly in the form of soft credit) to modernise telecommunications ($200 million), build a hotel ($24 million), and promote cultural and information programs ($150 million).[38]

---

33. "Inversión Extranjera: ¿Opción Válida?" *Economics Press Service* (March 31, 2001).

34. Vicent, Mauricio. "Los tropezones Cubanos del capital extranjero." *El País* (July 24, 2000).

35. EIU. "Foreign investment flows remain opaque." *Country Report Cuba* (May 4, 2001).

36. An interesting formula to obtain soft credit that might set a precedent for future agreements is the one used by the Cuban government with the Brazilian company Souza Cruz. In April 1995, the latter signed a joint venture (BrasCuba S.A.) with Cuba's Unión del Tabaco. With an initial investment of $7 million, BrasCuba renovated an existing cigarette factory in Havana and started producing and selling several brands of cigarettes for the domestic market as well as for external markets. For about four years, brands produced by BrasCuba (Hollywood, Popular, Monterrey, and Vegas) competed in the domestic dollar market with other wholly-owned government brands such as Partagás and Montecristo. In 1999, the authorities of the island renegotiated the agreement with Souza Cruz. The government withdrew from the dollar market its own brands and practically gave BrasCuba the monopoly of cigarettes in dollar stores and for exports (a new brand, Romeo y Julieta, was launched early that year). In exchange, Souza Cruz granted a soft credit to the government for the construction of a big cigarette factory in Holguin. The latter produces a new brand of cigarettes (Criollo) for the domestic market in local currency and has announced the introduction of three other brands such as Titanes, Aroma, and Flor de Aroma. Interview with news correspondent stationed in Havana, July 3, 2002.

37. Cuban official sources (MINVEC) report that, through projects of cooperation at the governmental level, Cuba received a total of $14.6 million in soft credit in 2001, of which $8.4 million are from Spain (Basque region) and $6 million from China. In addition, Cuba received a total of $82.6 million in donations, mostly from Spain ($21.1 million), European Union ($12.9 million), United States ($9.2 million), and Italy ($6.4 million).

38. "China to lend Cuba $400 million," *BBC News* (April 13, 2001). See also EIU, "China promises financing," *Country Report Cuba* (May 4, 2001).

Figure 5.   Credit from China by Year and by Sector, 1990-2001

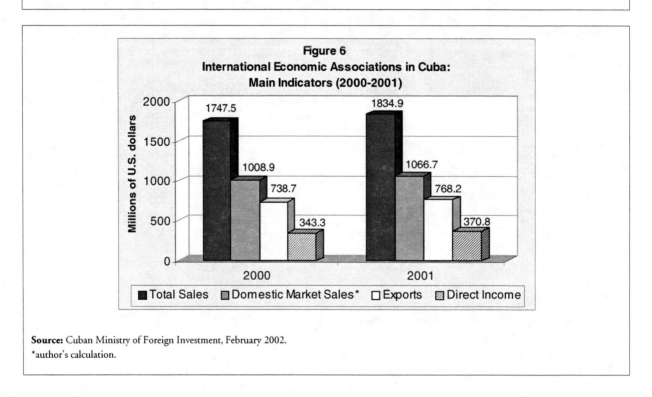

Source: Cuban Ministry of Foreign Investment, February 2002.

Source: Cuban Ministry of Foreign Investment, February 2002.
*author's calculation.

In contrast with the low number of authorizations of new AECEs and the meager amount of delivered FDI in 2001, positive aspects should be underlined. First of all, the main indicators of international economic associations have shown a constant progress since the opening to foreign investment in the early 1990s. This development appears to confirm that the Cuban authorities have been concentrating over the years on investments with results.

The trends of the main indicators of international economic associations in 2001 were positive. Total

sales of AECEs increased by 5% over the previous year and reached $1,834.9 million. Sales in the domestic market ($1,066.7 million) rose by almost 6% and exports generated through AECEs ($768.2) by 4%. Finally, direct income or "ingresos al país" from international economic associations (which refers to the profits of the Cuban partners in AECEs plus revenues from workers' salaries) peaked at $370.8 million, an increase of 8% from 2000 (Figure 6). The Cuban Ministry of Foreign Investment also reports that net profits of all AECEs grew by 19%.

Another important aspect of foreign investment in Cuba is that, in spite of the critical international context created by the September 11 attacks and the extensive damages caused by hurricane Michelle in November 2001, there is still interest among foreign firms to engage in business activities in the island. Some existing investors are expanding their interests in Cuba while negotiations with new partners continue. For instance Juan Fleites Melo, vice-president of Cubapetróleo (CUPET) declared in October 2001 that Cuba was planning to sign new risk exploration contracts in the oil sector. He did not reveal the name of the firms involved, but said they are from Europe and Asia. He also added that some potential investors could feel the pressure of the U.S. economic embargo while others are simply waiting for the results of drilling by Spain's Repsol YPF.[39] The latter, one of the biggest oil companies in the world, signed a contract with CUPET in 2000 for oil exploration in Cuban waters in the Gulf of Mexico and has indicated an interest in the modernization of the oil refinery in Cienfuegos.[40]

Some of the new agreements signed in the first half of 2002 are:

- In the tourism sector, the Italian group Mosaico and the Cuban chain Horizontes Hoteles have formed a joint venture (Toscuba S.A.) for the construction of a four-star hotel with 292 rooms in Trinidad. The hotel will be managed by Spain's Sol Meliá, which is already involved in 22 administration contracts in the Cuban tourist sector.[41] In addition, the Canadian company Leasure Canada has announced plans to build an 850-room waterfront hotel in Western Havana in a joint venture with Cuba's Gran Caribe.[42] Fi-

nally, the Cuban group Cubanacán has announced the construction of six new hotels through joint ventures with foreign investors in 2002, although it did not specify the year of approval of the agreements. Important companies involved in these projects are Canada's Wilton Properties and Jamaica's Sandals Resorts.[43]

- In the agricultural sector, the Cuban company Cítricos del Caribe S.A. has signed a joint venture with the Spanish wine distributor Palacio de Arganza for the construction of a plant in Ceiba del Agua (province of Havana) that will make wine for the domestic market using Cuban grapes. The investment is estimated at $2.5 million.[44]

- In the food industry, the Cuban corporation Coralsa has signed a joint venture (Central Lechera de La Habana S.A.) with Spain's Corporación Alimentaria Peñasanta for the processing and production of sterilized milk in plastic bottles.[45]

Although most of the agreements signed in 2002 do not involve large amounts of investment (except for some in the tourist sector), it is significant that new foreign companies are entering the Cuban market.

Regarding existing foreign investors, it is reported that the Cuban-Chilean joint venture Rio Zaza S.A., specialized in the production and marketing of natural juices and milk products, has begun selling more than 40 new food products in Cuban retail shops. Prior to 2001, most of the company's products were exported or sold to the tourism industry. Rio Zaza now sells to retailers that serve the local peso market as well as hard currency stores. The joint venture had

---

39. Frank, Mark. "Cuba optimista sobre sus posibilidades petroleras," *Reuters* (October 24, 2001).

40. EIU. "Oil production booms & foreign investment grows." *Country Report Cuba* (February 1, 2001)

41. Hosteltur. "Cuba: La cadena Horizontes y un grupo italiano crean empresa mixta para la construcción de un hotel que administrará Sol Meliá," (May 24, 2002)

42. Like other investors, Leisure Canada has explicitly stated that its aim is to meet demand from U.S. visitors once the current travel ban is lifted. EIU. "Hotel investments keep coming." *Country Report Cuba* (August 1, 2002).

43. Pasic, Djenita. "Early bird gets Cuban cash?" *International Communiqué* (Spring 2002).

44. "Empresa mixta cubano-española apuesta por producir vinos en Cuba," EFE (June 8, 2002).

45. "CAPSA suscribe con gobierno cubano creación empresa lactea mixta," EFE (March 1, 2002).

revenues of about $24 million in 2001 (an increase of 20% over 2000 sales) and announced it will spend up to $3 million to modernize its packaging operations and diversify its products.[46] The Canadian brewing company Cerbuco, which makes beer under the brand names Cristal, Bucanero, and Mayabe, has announced it has extended to 30 years a joint venture (Cervecería Bucanero S.A.) with the Cuban corporation Coralsa and plans to triple its beer production in Cuba. It also intends to build a new brewery and expand the company's existing brewery located in Holguín (Eastern Cuba).[47] Finally, the Spanish firm Pescanova, which had extended in 2001 its contract with the Cuban company Caribex for the commercialization of lobsters, announced in May 2002 it will invest around $30 million in six shrimp farms in Cuba.[48]

A final comment is that the prospects for further foreign direct investment in Cuba remain uncertain. In the short run, it is conceivable that the slowdown in the world economy exacerbated by the September 11 attacks on the United States will limit the ability of the Cuban government to attract a significant amount of FDI. In fact, with export prices of nickel, sugar and tobacco down, along with a fall in tourism and remittances from abroad, some potential investors may refrain from entering the Cuban market. If we add to this the growing complaints among existing investors regarding the restrictions on the operations of enterprises and the inability of the Cuban government to meet its payments commitments, the future appears grim.[49] Nevertheless, with the economic situation expected to improve in 2003, and

tourism to recover from its current downturn, it is likely that foreign direct investment will pick up. The agreements signed in the first half of 2002 in the tourist sector and the aforementioned expansion plans show that some investors have already bet on a recovery. According to the Economist Intelligence Unit, the flow of net FDI in 2002-2003 is estimated to be about $250 to $300 million, largely as a result of new investments in energy and tourism.[50]

NEW FORMS OF INVESTMENT

Cuba's increased selectivity toward foreign direct investment and its preference for large projects in recent years do not mean that small and medium businesses have been halted. They are simply being provided for through other mechanisms such as cooperative production agreements, regulated by Cuba's Executive Committee of the Council of Ministers on December 6, 2000 (Agreement N.3827). As with joint ventures, the government says the objectives of these agreements with foreign partners are to obtain capital, new technology and know-how, substitute imports, and gain access to markets. Furthermore, in addition to the increasing number of management contracts in the tourist sector (promoted since the opening to foreign investment in the early 1990s), Cuban authorities have encouraged administration contracts in industrial sectors with foreign partners. This demonstrates that the search for technology and markets is accompanied by a growing awareness of the value of management expertise.

Cooperative production aims to solve three major complaints raised by investors in Cuba, while committing state property in those activities that do not

---

46. "Chilean-Cuban joint food-processing venture expands," *CubaNews* (March 2002).

47. EIU. "Beer joint venture to expand production." *Country Report Cuba* (May 1, 2002).

48. ATD 3000. "Pescanova invertirá 33 millones en Cuba." (May 3, 2002).

49. As proof of Cuba's financing problems and the downturn in tourism after September 11, in its 2001 year-end report Spain's Sol Meliá (the leader in Cuba's tourist sector with equity interests in 4 hotels and 22 management contracts) revealed that Cuba had been one of the most affected destinations in the Caribbean. The company's results in the first quarter of 2002 show a 33.2% decrease in management fees from Cuba in comparison with the same period a year before. This is mainly due to the slowdown of the German and Canadian feeder markets, especially in the Varadero region. At any rate, Sol Meliá has an expansion plan for its Cuba division that includes the incorporation of 4 new hotels under management contract. For further details see Sol Meliá. "2001 Preliminary Year-End Results." http://www.solmelia.com/solmelia/english/accionistas/resultados/4quarter_01.pdf Also See Sol Meliá. "2002 First Quarter Results." http://www.solmelia.com/solmelia/english/accionistas/resultados/1quarter_02.pdf

50. EIU. "Outlook for 2002-03: External Sector." *Country Report Cuba* (September 12, 2002).

necessitate significant capital for their development. In spite of Law 77, foreign investors keep complaining about the length of negotiations, excessive bureaucratic practices, and expensive dollar payments to Cuban workers recruited by a state-entity (while the government pays them in Cuban pesos).[51] As compared to an international economic association, the approval of a cooperative production arrangements is much more simple and faster (between one and three months), and the documentation required is less rigorous.[52] In fact, while the former must be authorized by the Executive Committee of the Council of Ministers or by a government commission designated for that purpose, the latter is simply approved by the Ministry overseeing the Cuban entity.

Cooperative production agreements can take many forms. For instance, instead of purchasing equity, a foreign investor can provide capital and sell on credit raw material, technology, and know-how to its Cuban partner in exchange for a fixed sum per product produced (royalty), or buy the finished product outright for export. These agreements are not too different from international economic association contracts regulated by Law 77. The main novelty,

however, is that in cooperative productions the work force is paid directly by the government in local currency, and the foreign partner pays no taxes. With foreign companies avoiding to pay for labor in dollars, business operations contemplated by these agreements have been characterized by some investors as a sort of "maquila," in the style of U.S. assembly plants on the Mexican border.[53] There is also a possibility that a foreign firm is engaged in both a cooperative production and an administration contract, thus having the control of an enterprise and a share of its revenues.

Sometimes, a cooperative production arrangement might represent the first step toward the creation of an international economic association. For example, the aforementioned milk processing joint venture, Central Lechera de La Habana S.A. (signed in 2001), commenced operations in 2000 as a cooperative production arrangement.[54] This is a way for the Cuban government to test the seriousness of a foreign company as well as its capacity to provide new markets and technological assistance. It is also a necessary process to increase the efficiency of existing installations and facilities. As noted by Jesus Pérez Othón,

---

51. Cuba's labor code for AECEs has been denounced by several international labor organizations. Criticism mainly focuses on the system of payment of Cuban workers hired by foreign companies along with discriminatory practices of recruitment due to patronage, cronyism, and conformity of workers' ideas and behavior to official ideology. The issue has gained importance since the opening to foreign investment in early 1990s and especially after the 1993 legalization of hard currency holdings and the expansion of state-owned dollar stores previously reserved for foreigners. Cuban workers in AECEs receive their wages in domestic currency at the official exchange rate of 1 peso per dollar. However, due to generalized shortages of goods available through the normal distribution system, they are increasingly compelled to buy dollars at the unofficial exchange rate (which is currently 26 pesos per dollar) in order to purchase the products they need in stores that deal only with foreign currency. In this regard, two Cuban exile groups (the Cuban Committee for Human Rights and the Independent Federation of Electric, Gas, and Water Plants of Cuba) filed a lawsuit in 1999 against 40 foreign companies accusing them to be part of an illegal scheme by the Cuban government to deprive Cuban workers of most of their salary. According to the lawsuit, foreign companies pay their workers up to $450 dollar a month each. However, the employment agency pays the same workers an equivalent of $5 dollar a month, while the government keeps the rest. See Morton, Peter. "Two Canadian companies in Cuba lawsuit," *The National Post* (June 29,1999). Cuban authorities defend their labor code and justify the high charge made to foreigners by claiming that: 1) direct dollar payments by foreign companies to their workers would create too much difference between the latter and the rest of the Cuban work force; 2) direct payments in domestic currency by foreign companies should also include the cost of benefits for medical assistance, education, and housing that is instead assumed by the Cuban government; 3) it is fair for foreign companies to pay their workers more than in other emerging markets because Cuban workers are more efficient and qualified. Interview with economist of Instituto Nacional de Investigaciones Económicas, Havana (June 7, 2001); interview with economist of Centro de Estudios de la Economía Cubana, Havana (June 7, 2001).

52. The MINVEC reports that the average time of negotiations for AECE in 2001 has been 10.8 months, as compared to 11.1 months in 2000. However, this is still longer than elsewhere in Latin America.

53. Frank, Mark. "Cuba adopts two-track foreign investment policy," *Reuters* (August 26, 2001).

54. See U.S. Cuba Trade and Economic Council. "Dairy Joint Venture with CAPSA of Spain expects revenues of US$4.7 million in 2002/2003." *Economic Eye on Cuba* (April 1-7, 2002).

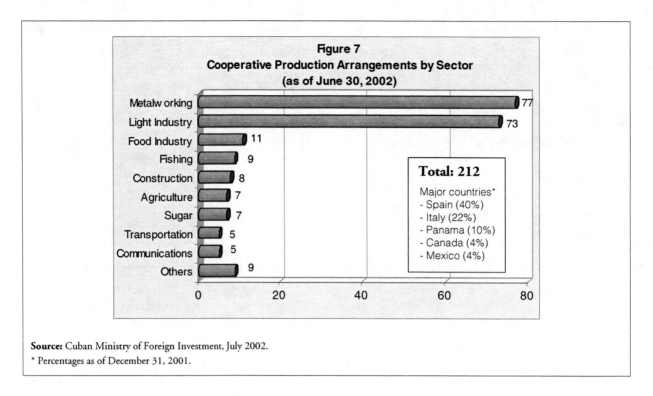

Figure 7
Cooperative Production Arrangements by Sector
(as of June 30, 2002)

Total: 212
Major countries*
- Spain (40%)
- Italy (22%)
- Panama (10%)
- Canada (4%)
- Mexico (4%)

Source: Cuban Ministry of Foreign Investment, July 2002.
* Percentages as of December 31, 2001.

Minister of Light Industry, "sometimes you have 90% of the equipment, but without that vital 10% you can't make a new product that will succeed in the world market."[55]

Following the Agreement N.3827 of December 2000, the Cuban Ministry of Foreign Investment passed Resolution N.37 in 2001, which regulates the whole process of registration, control, and supervision of cooperative production arrangements. At the end of June 2002, there were 212 cooperative production ventures in Cuba (Figure 7). Not surprisingly, they are mostly linked to labor-intensive sectors such as metal/machinery (77 agreements signed) and light industry (73), with smaller numbers in food industry (11), fishing (9), construction (8), agriculture

(7), and sugar (7). There were also 9 administration contracts in industrial sectors, 7 in metalworking/machinery and 2 in the aviation sector. In the first half of 2002, 14 new cooperative production agreements were approved, thus demonstrating the willingness of small and mid-size companies to take advantage of new modalities of doing business in the communist island.[56] Spain is Cuba's main partner, with around 40% of the total number of cooperative production agreements. Other major investors are from Italy (22%), Panama (10%), Canada (4%), and Mexico (4%).[57]

Estimating the flow of capital provided by foreign partners through cooperative productions is very difficult, given the lack of detailed statistics. Neverthe-

---

55. Pagés, Raisa. "Light Industry. Not just conquering markets, but maintaining them," *Granma Internacional* (July 13, 2001).

56. For instance, as part of the program of restructuring of the sugar industry, Cuba signed two new cooperative production agreements in June 2002. The Spanish company Compañia Elaboradora de Caucho (COECA) will provide technological assistance for the installation of a new plant that produces rubber parts for the sugar and agricultural industries. See "Una empresa española aportará a Cuba tecnologia punta para la fabricación de piezas de caucho," Europa Press (June 20, 2002). Another Spanish firm, Dilsa, will supply automotive equipment to the Cuban company TransMinaz to renew technology related to transportation and to save fuel in the sugar industry. See "Empresas de Cuba y España colaborarán en sector del azúcar," EFE (June 22, 2002).

57. According to figures released by MINVEC in April 2002, the total number of cooperative production arrangements at the end of 2001 was 198. Spain was the most active investor with 79 agreements signed, followed by Italy (43), Panama (20), Canada (9), and Mexico (8).

less, it is reported that the sharp decline of delivered FDI in 2001 is not only due to concerns about Cuba's business climate among foreign companies (and because 2000 data were inflated by the agreement with the Spanish/French company Altadis), but also to the promotion of new forms of investment such as cooperative production agreements. Investment financing provided under such contracts is not considered as foreign direct investment and appears in the balance of payments under "other capital flows, net." The figure in this category, which also includes short-term financing, increased significantly in 2001 as compared to the previous year.[58]

THE ROLE OF FOREIGN INVESTMENT IN THE CUBAN ECONOMY

It has been claimed by some scholars that foreign investment plays a negligible, or at least very limited role in the Cuban economy.[59] Criticism mainly focuses on the total amount of FDI delivered to the country, which is significantly lower than in other emerging markets in Latin America. In fact, even smaller Caribbean islands such as Dominican Republic, Trinidad and Tobago, and Jamaica have been more successful than Cuba in attracting foreign investment in recent years. However, the significance of foreign capital in Cuba cannot be measured from a simple quantitative comparison with other countries.[60]

First, it must be remembered that the U.S. 40-year economic embargo against the island, reinforced with the enactment of the Helms-Burton law in 1996, has created a riskier and more uncertain business environment and complicated Cuba's access to external financing for important sectors of the econo-

my.[61] Second, Cuban authorities make no secret they resorted to foreign investment in the early 1990s out of necessity, and essentially against their will. By their own admission, the country is not moving towards the creation of a market economy and the development of a real and substantial private sector. In August 2000, Carlos Lage said: "The government policy is aimed at establishing a state economy, not one in which transnational companies may arrive and lead to the disappearance of nationally-owned enterprises, and in which foreign capital makes national wealth emigrate toward rich countries. The economy will be regulated so that the benefits of investment go to society."[62] Third, and more important, the Cuban economy and its business environment present characteristics that are very different from any other country of the region. Therefore, quantitative comparisons with other Latin American countries based on delivered FDI have a limited value.

While the role of foreign capital in the Cuban economy is not fundamental, there are some indicators that show it is nevertheless quite important. In the light of these indicators, Cuba's reiterated claims that overseas investments are a complementary measure for the economic development of the country appear at least questionable. For instance, since 1995 export revenues (goods and services) generated through international economic associations have grown steadily, reaching $768.2 million in 2001. What's more important, their share in Cuba's total value of exports of goods and services has also increased (Figure 8). In 2001, AECEs accounted for approximately 16.5% of the country's total dollar revenues from all sources. If we consider that FDI in Cuba between 1991 and 2000 represented just 8% of the gross fixed

58. EIU. "Outlook for 2002-03: External Sector." *Country Report Cuba* (September 12, 2002).

59. For instance, María Werlau argues that the flow of FDI into Cuba in the last decade has been very disappointing both in overall cumulative terms as well as in comparison with other countries. She adds that FDI in Cuba today remains little more than an instrument of economic survival, subservient to the imperatives of maintaining political control. See Werlau, María. "A Commentary on Foreign Investment in Cuba." In *Cuba in Transition—Volume 11* (Washington: Association for the Study of the Cuban Economy, 2001), pp. 290-292.

60. Pérez Villanueva, Omar Everleny. *Estabilidad Macroeconómica y Financiamento Externo: La Inversión Extranjera Directa en Cuba.* Havana: Centro de Estudios de la Economía Cubana (CEEC), April 2000, pp.25-26.

61. Spadoni, "The Impact of the Helms-Burton Legislation on Investment in Cuba," p. 30.

62. "No official market economy for Cuba," *Caribbean and Central America Report* (August 22, 2000).

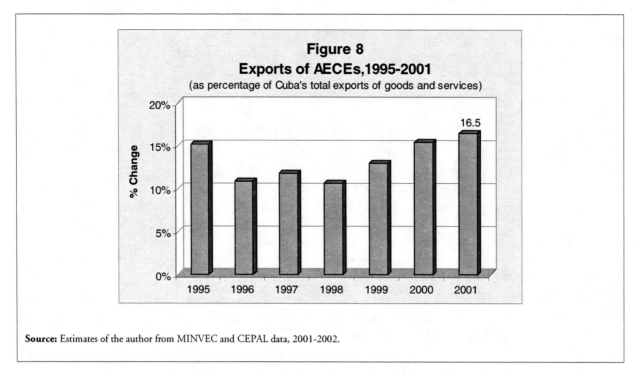

Figure 8
Exports of AECEs,1995-2001
(as percentage of Cuba's total exports of goods and services)

Source: Estimates of the author from MINVEC and CEPAL data, 2001-2002.

capital formation[63] (capital created for the production of goods and services), the performance of AECEs appears remarkable.

In addition, it must be noted that export revenues generated by AECEs are derived to a great extent from products rather than services. The latter may include the sales of joint ventures in the tourist sector (where dollar revenues are mostly linked to management contracts rather than AECEs) and international telephone calls. Today, exports of goods are certainly less important for the Cuban economy than during the 1980s, but they are still a precious source of hard-currency for the country. The U.S.-Cuba Trade and Economic Council reports that AECEs accounted for approximately 50% of Cuba's revenues from all product exports in 2001.[64] According to my findings, this percentage seems to be somewhat inflated. Even assuming that all export revenues of AECEs in 2001 are from products, their share would be around

46%.[65] At any rate, we can fairly say that foreign participation plays a significant role in the country's total export earnings from goods. Moreover, if we add exports from free trade zone ($26.3 million in 2001) and especially those generated through cooperative production agreements, the importance of foreign investment is even more pronounced.

Other indicators shed light on the role of FDI in the Cuban economy. It is reported that, by the end of 1997, joint ventures with foreign capital already accounted for the following shares of economic activity: 100% of oil exploration; 100% of metal mining; 100% of the production of lubricants; 100% of the production of soap, perfumes, personal hygiene products, and industrial cleaners; 100% of telephone services (wire and cellular); 100% of the export of rum; 70% of the production of citrus fruits, juices, and concentrates; 50% of the production of nickel; 50% of the production of cement; 10% of all rooms

---

63. Pérez Villanueva, Omar Everleny. "La Inversión Extranjera Directa en Cuba: Evolución y Perspectivas." In *Cuba. Reflexiones Sobre su Economía*. Universidad de La Habana (2002), p.73.

64. U.S.-Cuba Trade and Economic Council. "Five largest U.S. dollar export revenue sectors have foreign participation." *Economic Eye on Cuba* (April 1-7, 2002).

65. The percentage is calculated from the latest data of the Cuban Central Bank, according to which Cuba's total earnings from product exports in 2001 was $1,661.5 million.

for international tourism, plus an additional 39% under administration contracts with foreign firms.[66]

Since 1997, the importance of foreign capital has grown even more. In the oil sector, Cuban authorities announced that, as of December 2000, foreign companies had invested a total of $446.6 million.[67] Crude oil extracted through exploration activities with overseas firms (along with the introduction of top level technologies) has enabled the Cuban government to increase domestic production of electricity and natural gas. For instance, the Energas plant constructed with the Canadian company Sherritt in 2000 (cost of the project around $150 million) uses the natural gas released during oil extraction for producing electricity. In 2001, more than 70% of the country's electricity was generated with domestic fuel.[68] It is reported that total foreign investment in nickel amounts to over $400 million, supporting production increases from 26,900 tons in 1994 to 76,500 tons in 2001. Just one plant (Pedro Soto Alba), operated through a joint venture between Cuba's General Nickel Co. S.A. and Canada's Sherritt International, produced a record 32,360 tons in 2001 (42% of the total production).[69] In the cement sector, FDI has taken a prominent role thanks to the involvement of Spain's Inversiones Ibersuizas and Swiss-based Holderbank. In tourism, 26 joint ventures in the hotel industry had 15,600 rooms under development and 3,700 in operation in 2000, just 11% of the 35,000 available rooms in Cuba. However, there were 17,000 rooms under management contracts with foreign firms that represented around 48% of the total.[70] Finally, with new agreements such as those of Compañía Azucarera, Altadis, and Pescanova (see above), foreign participation has a substantial influence over the production and marketing for the five largest export sectors (in terms of gross U.S. dollar revenues) such as sugar, nickel, tobacco, rum, and fishing.[71] According to the Cuban Central Bank, these sectors accounted in 2001 for more than 32% of Cuba's total dollar revenues from all sources.

Foreign investment has not only helped Cuba to find new markets for its main products but also increased the competitiveness of Cuban production and, therefore, the contribution of import substitution to overall economic expansion. If we analyze the evolution of the sales of international economic associations since 1995, we can see that the share of exports has been decreasing whereas the domestic market has gained importance (Figure 9). While in 1995 exports represented approximately two-thirds of the sales of AECEs, in 2001 they have dropped to around 42%. Meanwhile domestic market sales have grown steadily, accounting for about 58% of total AECE sales in 2001. Of course, we are left without knowing the composition of these sales and their impact on import substitution. However, if in the last two years international economic associations have sold in the domestic market goods and services worth more than $2 billion ($1008.9 million in 2000 and $1066.7 million in 2001), it is conceivable that such an impact has not been negligible.

In the oil sector, foreign capital has doubled Cuba's refinery capacity and allowed the country to save more than $410 million in oil imports during 2000.[72] In addition, the proportion of domestically-produced goods provided to the tourist industry has increased from 12% in 1990 to 67% in 2001. Ten

---

66. Pérez Villanueva, Omar Everleny. *La Inversión Extranjera Directa en Cuba. Peculiaridades.* La Habana: Centro de Estudios de la Economía Cubana (March 1999), p.119.

67. See "El efecto del bloqueo solo en los ingresos azucareros ascienden a mas de $6400 miliones." Informe de Cuba al Secretario General de la ONU. *Granma Internacional* (July 21, 2001).

68. Molina, Gabriel. "Island to produce 90% of its own electricity by year's end." *Granma Internacional* (April 27, 2001).

69. "Sherritt reports mixed results," *CubaNews.* (March 2002).

70. Figueras Pérez, Miguel Alejandro. "El Turismo Internacional y la Formación de Clusters Productivos en la Economía Cubana." In *Cuba. Reflexiones Sobre su Economía.* Universidad de La Habana (2002), p.109.

71. U.S.-Cuba Trade and Economic Council, "Five largest dollar export revenue sectors have foreign participation" (2002).

72. Pérez Villanueva, Omar Everleny. "La Inversión Extranjera Directa en Cuba," (2002), p.86.

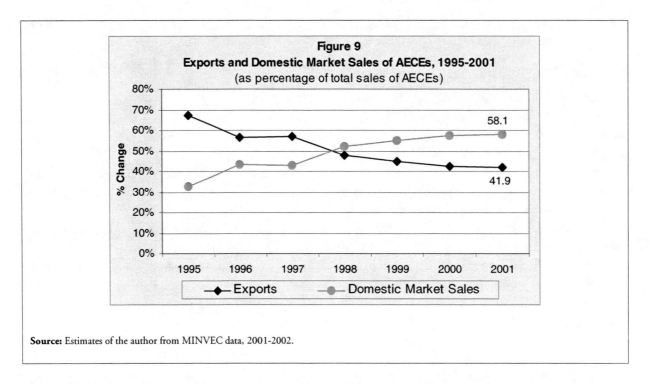

Figure 9
Exports and Domestic Market Sales of AECEs, 1995-2001
(as percentage of total sales of AECEs)

Source: Estimates of the author from MINVEC data, 2001-2002.

years ago, practically all products used by hotels and restaurants had to be imported. The development of mixed enterprises in tourism has stimulated the formation of new joint ventures in other sectors (in particular food industry, agriculture, and services) to supply them at low cost. As noted by Figueras Pérez, a significant number of joint ventures with foreign capital and technology supply a wide range of products to the tourist sector such as mineral waters, soft drinks, alcoholic beverages, processed meat, omnibuses, air conditioners, and telephone and electronic equipment.[73] Finally, the share of domestic goods sold to the network of dollar stores has grown from 47% in 1999 to 55% in 2001, mainly because of foreign direct investment and cooperative production arrangements in the food processing and light manufacturing industry. For instance, it is reported that 16 joint ventures in food industry produced just 6% of its total production in 2000, but played an important role in terms of participation in the domestic dollar

market. That year, sales in dollar stores from food processing ($200 million) and light manufacturing ($137 million) accounted for more than 50% of domestically produced total sales in these outlets.[74]

This section has provided some evidence for the role played by foreign capital in the Cuban economy. However, while having a significant impact on total exports as well as on supplies to the tourist industry and dollar stores, foreign investment cannot be objectively considered as the most important factor for the economic development of the country. For instance, since the legalization of dollar holdings in 1993, the domestic dollar market has expanded rapidly on account of growing remittances (estimated at about $720 million in 2000 by CEPAL). Between 1994 and 2000, sales in Cuba's dollar stores have increased from $200 million to $1.25 billion.[75] In the light of this development, several scholars contend that remittances have been the single most important

---

73. Figueras Pérez, Miguel Alejandro. "El turismo internacional y la formación de clusters productivos," (2002), p. 112.

74. Domestically produced sales in dollar stores in 2000 have been estimated at $600 million. See EIU. "Hard currency sales boost light industry." *Country Report Cuba* (February 1, 2001).

75. See Conas. *Cuba: Inversiones y Negocios*. La Habana (April 2000), p.33. Also see EIU, "Hard currency sales boost light industry" (2001).

factor in reactivating the Cuban economy in the second half of the 1990s.

Pedro Monreal, an academic from the island, argues that Cuba has become in recent years increasingly dependent on remittances and donations from abroad. He specifies that, in strict terms, the Cuban economy cannot be qualified as an economy that depends fundamentally on remittances because other important activities such as tourism and mining have emerged. Nevertheless, he concludes that the importance of money sent from abroad is beyond dispute. In fact, in net terms, remittances are the biggest source of foreign exchange for the country, more than tourism and sugar.[76] This appears to be the case. Most people analyze data on revenues from tourism ($1,856 million in 2001)[77] and believe that the tourist industry is the main generator of hard currency. However, it must be noted that these are gross figures. In net terms, revenues are significantly lower. In March 2001, Carlos Lage estimated the cost per dollar of gross income from tourist activities at $0.76.[78] This indicator is very high and refers only to the direct cost in dollar, not the indirect cost incurred by the state in the tourist sector. We must consider that domestically produced goods for tourism have an imported (indirect) component in dollars, which implies that the cost per dollar of gross income would be even higher. Direct and indirect cost per dollar have been estimated by some economists at more than $0.80, which would mean for the country a net result of just $0.20 for every dollar of gross income from tourist activities.[79]

CONCLUSION

From the analysis presented in this paper, we can conclude that recent results of foreign investment in Cuba have been mixed. Although Cuban authorities argue that the opening to foreign capital is somewhat consolidating, recent trends on authorized international economic associations and the flow of delivered FDI to the country are worrisome. The number of new economic associations with overseas partners has been decreasing, while the amount of foreign capital delivered plummeted in 2001. Even more important, a significant amount of capital pledged by foreign companies in the last two years has not been delivered yet, perhaps reflecting the growing complaints among investors for the existing restrictions on the operation of enterprises.

However, there are some positive aspects that should be underlined. The number of international economic associations has shown steady growth since the opening to foreign investment in the early 1990s, thus supporting Cuba's claims that the government has been successful in attracting foreign investment. In 2001, exports and domestic market sales of international associations increased from the previous year. Moreover, in spite of the critical international context created by September 11 (with negative effects on tourism and remittances from abroad) and the extensive damages caused by hurricane Michelle in November 2001, there is still interest among foreign firms to engage in business activities on the island. Tourism still offers some of the brightest investment opportunities in Cuba, as demonstrated by several agreements signed in 2001 and during the first half of 2002. Cuban authorities are also giving priority to investments in energy, oil, and sugar by-products. The main novelty of 2001 was the approval of joint ventures in raw sugar production and refining, as part of a wide process of restructuring of the sugar industry.

A major contention of this study is that foreign investment plays an important role in the Cuban economy, certainly more than Castro's government is willing to admit. Foreign investment has helped Cuba find new markets for its main products, increased the competitiveness of Cuban production, and stimulated import substitution. Overseas compa-

---

76. Monreal, Pedro. "Las Remesas Familiares en la Economía Cubana." *Encuentro de la Cultura Cubana*, 14 (Otoño de 1999), p. 50.

77. See Oficina Nacional de Estadísticas (ONE). *Estadísticas Seleccionadas 2001*. La Habana (April 2002)

78. Declaration of Carlos Lage on Cuban National Television (Noticiero Nacional de la Television Cubana) (March 18, 2001).

79. "Cuba: economía y turismo," Economics Press Service, No. 10 (May 31, 2001).

nies have a substantial influence over the production and marketing of Cuba's most important export sectors. Additionally, international economic associations and new forms of investment such as cooperative production agreements have boosted domestic supply to the tourist industry and to the increasingly important internal market in hard currency.

FOREIGN INVESTMENT IN CUBA: PROSPECTS AND PERILS

Matias F. Travieso-Diaz and Charles P. Trumbull IV [1]

One of the few sources of foreign capital available to Cuba is direct foreign investment. Cuba receives virtually no aid from foreign governments or international organizations.[2] Cuba is also unable to borrow from multinational lending institutions because of its history of defaults on foreign loans and other factors.[3] The loans that Cuba is able to obtain are in the nature of pre-financing of crops (mainly sugar and tobacco), are secured by the crops, and are granted for short periods of time and at very high rates of interest.[4] Cuba derives significant amounts of foreign currency by way of remittances from individuals abroad to relatives and friends in Cuba. However, remittances do not provide the benefits in employment, asset development and transfer of technology and know-how derived from foreign investment.[5]

Thus, the most important means within the control of the Cuban government to obtain foreign capital is foreign direct investment ("FDI").[6] Even though firmly adhering to a socialist political and economic framework, Cuba has taken a series of measures to promote FDI in the country, and representatives of the Cuban government express frequently the national interest in attracting foreign capital to boost

---

1. This paper is based in part on information gathered by Mr. Trumbull during a research trip to Cuba in December 2001. All interviews cited in the text were conducted by Mr. Trumbull. Some of the material in this paper appeared in Matías Travieso-Díaz and Jorge Pérez-López, *La Inversión Extranjera en Cuba: Pasado, Presente y Futuro*, in *La Actual Economía Cubana a Debate*, Universidad de Granada, 2001 (hereinafter "Debate").

2. The Central Intelligence Agency ("CIA") reports that the total aid received by Cuba in 1997 was only 46 million dollars. CIA, The World Factbook 1999—Cuba, http://www.odci.gov/publications/factbook/cu.html/#econ.

3. The unwillingness of international lending institutions to make credit facilities available to Cuba is due in part to the effects of the "Helms-Burton Law," Cuban Liberty and Democratic Solidarity (LIBERTAD) Act of 1996, Pub. L. No. 104-114, 110 Stat. 785, *codified at 22 U.S.C. Chapter 69A*. Section 104(b) of the Helms-Burton Law requires that the United States reduce its contributions to international organizations such as the World Bank or the InterAmerican Development Bank in the same amount as any loans or other forms of credit or aid that these institutions grant Cuba. In addition, Cuba is not currently a member of the International Monetary Fund.

4. Carmelo Mesa-Lago, *The Cuban Economy in 1997-98: Performance and Policies*, in *Cuba in Transition—Volume 8* 1, 3-4 (Aug. 1998) (hereinafter "Mesa Lago 1998").

5. Information from the annual reports from the Cuban Central Bank indicates that remittances from abroad (mostly from Cuban Americans) amounted to U.S. $820 million in 1998. Banco Central de Cuba, *Informe Económico 1998* (Havana, April 1999).

6. FDI is defined as the establishment of a permanent relationship between an actor (the investor) and his object (a commercial operation) in which the actor seeks to exert direct influence in the behavior of the object. Through FDI, the actor acquires a direct financial interest in some aspect of the economy of a foreign nation, with the intention of controlling the management of the acquired interest. Lars Oxelheim, *Introduction*, in *The Global Race For Foreign Direct Investment* 11 (Lars Oxelheim ed., 1993) (hereinafter "The Global Race For Foreign Direct Investment.")

the economy and continue coping with the economic crisis that has afflicted the country since the disappearance of the Socialist bloc.[7]

Cuba's efforts to attract foreign investment have resulted in the inflow of substantial amounts of foreign capital by way of FDI. However, as will be discussed below, foreign investment has been affected by the country's political and economic program, which serves as a constant brake to the possibility of capital influx.

TYPES OF FOREIGN INVESTMENT CURRENTLY ALLOWED IN CUBA

An important step towards the development of a foreign investment regime took place on September 5, 1995, when Cuba's National Assembly approved the current Foreign Investment Law, Law No. 77 of 1995 ("Law 77").[8] Law 77 retained many of the restrictions and impediments to FDI imposed by its predecessor.[9] However, a number of the changes instituted in Law 77 represented steps forward that liberalized somewhat the investment regime in the country.[10]

Law 77 identifies three permissible types of foreign investment: joint ventures ("*empresas mixtas*"), international economic associations, and companies with totally foreign capital.[11] On December 6, 2000 the Executive Committee of Cuba's Council of Ministers officially recognized two new forms of FDI: production contracts ("*contratos de producción cooperada de bienes o la prestación de servicios*") and management contracts ("*contratos de administración productiva*").[12] Although all forms of FDI are often lumped together in discussions on foreign investment in Cuba, it is important to keep in mind the attributes, structure and purposes of each.

Joint Ventures

A joint venture is a legal entity consisting of one or more Cuban parties and one or more foreign investors. The contributions of each participant and the breakdown in stock ownership are agreed upon before governmental approval is granted, and are reflected in the joint venture agreement and the decree approving the joint venture. The Cuban party generally supplies real estate and labor, while the foreign investor provides capital, technical resources, and know-how (both technical and managerial). The joint venture is legally independent from the investing entities, and must register with the Cuban Chamber of Commerce to attain official status.[13] Profits earned by the joint venture are distributed to the investors according to their respective ownership share.

The following true example illustrates how joint ventures are formed. Community Bicycle Network ("CBN") is a Canadian non-profit organization that specializes in bicycle skills training, bicycle repair,

---

7. As is well known, Cuba's need to attract FDI is a direct consequence of the disappearance of Socialism in Eastern Europe. Prior to 1990, Cuba depended on the Socialist bloc (mainly the Soviet Union) for 81% of its exports and 85% of its imports, and for the financing of the economy through loans and subsidies. The demise of the Socialist bloc had a catastrophic impact on Cuba, which suddenly lost is markets, its sources of supply, and its credit and financing mechanisms.

8. *Ley Número 77 de la Inversión Extranjera*, Gaceta Oficial, September 6, 1995. For an online English translation of Law 77, *see* http://www.latintrade.com/newsite/content/cprofiles/data-ext.cfm?d=2001&c=9.

9. Decree-Law 50 of February 15, 1982 ("Law 50").

10. Law 77 has been analyzed in a number of studies, *see e.g.*, René Burguet Rodríguez, *Ley de la inversión extranjera en Cuba* (Madrid: Consultoría Jurídica Internacional, 1995); Juan Vega Vega, *Cuba: Inversiones extranjeras a partir de 1995* (Madrid: Ediciones Endymion, 1997); Dídac Fábregas i Guillén, *La Ley de la inversión extranjera y la situación económica actual de Cuba* (Barcelona: Viena, S.L., 1998); Debate.

11. Law 77, Art. 12.

12. Foreign Trade No. 4/2001: Cuba (hereinafter "Foreign Trade"). These forms of investment were officially endorsed because they were shown in practice to provide "favorable economic results for each of the contracting parties," thus meriting legal recognition. *Id.*

13. Resolution No. 26 of the Cuban Chamber of Commerce, issued on December 5, 1995, created a Registry of enterprises with foreign participation. Being listed in that Registry is a prerequisite to doing business in Cuba. Resolución No. 26—Reglamento del Registro de Inversiones Extranjeras, Cámara de Comercio de la República de Cuba, Gaceta Oficial (Dec. 15, 1995), p. 504-506.

and cycling promotion.[14] CBN decided to invest in Cuba and contacted the Cuban firm Fénix, which provides transportation in the historic section of Havana. CBN and Fénix agreed to form a joint venture under the name Bicicletas Cruzando Fronteras ("Bicicletas"). CBN would own 49% of the joint venture and Fénix would own 51%. The joint venture agreement stipulates that Fénix will provide the building and workspace for Bicicletas (valued at $100,000), the manual labor (15 workers, each valued at $500/month) for one year, and $10,000 cash. Thus, the total Cuban initial investment is $200,000. CBN is obliged to invest an equivalent amount (minus 1%) in hard currency, bicycle parts, specialists, and tools. After both parties agree on the terms of investment, the Executive Committee of the Council of Ministers must approve the joint venture. Only then will Bicicletas be able to start operations.[15]

Economic Associations

The formation of international economic associations ("IEAs") does not require the establishment of a legal entity separate from the contracting investors. IEAs are normally established because the contracting parties can meet a common objective through co-operation. Each party agrees to make specific contributions to the IEA, but no capital is set aside. The parties must, however, agree to a profit sharing arrangement and a tax payment plan. The two most common forms of IEAs are production contracts and management contracts (the two forms of FDI formally sanctioned by the Cuban government in December 2000).

Production Contracts: Production contracts are an increasingly common mechanism for channeling FDI into Cuba. Their attractiveness lies in part in the fact that, as noted above, the foreign investor does not have to turn over capital to the enterprise or share its management with a potentially inept Cuban counterpart. The respective roles of the parties are specified in Resolution 37/2001 as follows:

> The foreign party supplies finances, prime materials, material resources, technology, or technological assistance in exchange for a set price agreed upon by both parties, with the intention that the Cuban counterpart produce commercial goods or services for the interior or exterior of the island.[16]

These contracts appear to be particularly suitable for labor-intensive industries. Production contracts allow Cuban companies with a labor surplus to gain access to capital and technology and increase the productivity of their labor force.[17]

According to Conas,[18] the government now encourages prospective investors to negotiate a production contract with a Cuban business partner before seeking to set up a joint venture. Production contracts are usually of short duration (typically a year) and allow both parties a relatively low-risk "trial run" before they commit to forming a more permanent venture. A production contract also gives the foreign investor an opportunity to familiarize himself with the business environment in Cuba prior to committing significant resources to operations in the country.[19]

Management Contracts: Management contracts are most common in, but not limited to, the tourism sector. Since the enactment of Law 50, the Cuban government has acknowledged that foreign firms would be more capable and efficient in the administration of hotels and other tourism facilities than the

---

14. CBN receives local donations, sponsorships, and grants from the Canadian government. Although CBN is a non-profit organization, the joint venture it formed in Cuba was expected to generate a profit for the Cuban government.

15. Bicicletas Cruzando Fronteras is in fact a joint venture that is preparing to begin operations in Havana. Although the company has been in negotiations with the Cuban government for over a year, to the last of the authors' knowledge it is still waiting for permission to operate.

16. Foreign Trade.

17. Interview with Mark Frank, independent journalist living in Cuba, December 17, 2001.

18. Conas (Consultores Asociados, S.A.), a state-owned consulting firm that advises foreign investors. *See, e.g.,* http://www.infocom.etecsa.cu/new/conas/conase.html.

19. Interview with Lic. Amado Guntin, Conas' Gerente Jurídico, December 24, 2001 (hereinafter "Guntin").

government or state-owned enterprises. Thus, management contracts have been in use since the re-introduction of FDI in Cuba.

The formation of a management contract is described in Resolution 37/2001:

> A state entity contracts a foreign entity to manage one or more lines of production, service, or any part of the activity that these lines may carry out, for a determined period of time, with remuneration based on the results of the activity agreed upon.

> The Ministry of Tourism must approve all hotel administration contracts. The Ministry of Foreign Investment and Economic Cooperation (MINVEC) approves contracts for Administration of Production.[20]

According to Resolution 37/2001, the objective of management contracts is to achieve greater efficiency and earnings from the installation or activity that they are to manage. At the onset of the contract goals and indicators are set to measure the performance of the foreign administrator.[21]

Generally, the foreign administrator acts in the name of its Cuban counterpart; however, this requirement can be waived in appropriate cases. For example, the Meliá Cohiba hotel in Havana is 100% Cuban-government owned; however, it operates under Meliá's name.[22]

Cuban Branches of Foreign Companies

Foreign companies (e. g., Mercedes-Benz, Castrol, Bank of Canada, Mexicana Air, etc.) are allowed to set up commercial branches in Cuba without participation or investment from a Cuban partner.[23] These branches typically operate as sales offices from which goods and services are sold in hard currency to the government, enterprises involving foreign investors, or the general population. Currently there are over eight hundred Cuban branches of international companies registered with the Cuban Chamber of Commerce.[24]

Totally Foreign-Owned Companies

Law 77 allows the establishment of enterprises that are totally owned by foreign investors, although this modality of FDI is disfavored and is quite rare.[25] This type of enterprise is established through its registration with the Chamber of Commerce once its establishment is authorized by the Cuban government.[26]

SOME FEATURES OF CUBA'S FOREIGN INVESTMENT STRUCTURE

Law 77 incorporates several features that serve to make investment more attractive to foreign investors. Following is a summary description of these features.

Establishment of an Agency to Process Investment Proposals

Law 77 created the Ministry of Foreign Investment and Economic Cooperation ("MINVEC") as the agency responsible for, inter alia, the receipt, processing and distribution among other appropriate government agencies of foreign investment applications and the ultimate submittal of foreign investment proposals to the Executive Committee of the Council of Ministers for approval.[27]

---

20. Resolution 37/2001, *supra*, Art. 7.

21. *Id.*, Art. 8.

22. Interview with Cuban economist (name withheld by request), December 14, 2001 (hereinafter "Cuban Economist").

23. *Sucursales de Compañías Extranjeras Regulaciones Laborales y Permiso de Trabajo,* Colección Jurídica No. 18, Cámara de Comercio, Havana.

24. *Id.*

25. *Juventud Rebelde, entrevista a Ibrahim Ferradaz* by Marta Veloz, Apr. 21, 1999, http://www.fut.es/~mpgp/amigos177.htm (hereinafter "Veloz"). From the start, the Cuban government cautioned that very few enterprises would be allowed to operate based on 100% foreign ownership. Douglas Farah, *Socialist Cuba Alters Course to Spur Foreign Investment,* Washington Post, Sep. 6, 1995, p. A25.

26. Law 77, Art. 15(2).

27. *Id.*, Art. 23(6). MINVEC Resolution No. 116/95, issued on November 1, 1995, provides details on the process for submitting a foreign investment application, including the documentation that is required and the process for the negotiations between the prospective investor and the MINVEC. Resolución No. 116/95, Ministerio para la Inversión Extranjera y la Colaboración Económica, Gaceta Oficial (Dec. 11, 1995), p. 488-490.

Nominally Simplified Approval Process

Law 77 allows approval of foreign investment proposals to be delegated to an outside Commission in order to expedite the approval process. This delegation option, however, is not available for most investments of any significance.[28]

Law 77 also requires that the approval decision be reached within 60 days of the submittal of the investment application.[29] No mechanisms are set forth in the Law to enforce this deadline, and the Law does not provide for default approval of the application in the case of governmental failure to act within the allotted time.

Moreover, the Law is silent on the most dilatory step of the investment approval process, which is the period of negotiations between the prospective investor and its Cuban counterpart, and between the investors and the Cuban government agencies reviewing the proposal. This negotiation and review process is well recognized as being protracted and onerous.[30]

Ability to Import and Export

Enterprises involving foreign investors have the right to contract directly for the purchase and sale of goods abroad, a function that prior to the enactment of Law 77 was reserved for the state.[31]

Ability to Repatriate Earnings and Sale Proceeds

Foreign investors are allowed to repatriate, in freely convertible currency, earnings, proceeds from the sale of the enterprise, salaries of foreign employees, and any compensation received in the event of government expropriation.[32]

Tax Regime

The tax regime for enterprises that include foreign investors was established by the 1994 Tax Code and left largely unmodified by Law 77.[33] Enterprises including foreign investors are subject to a 30% tax on net profits and a 25% payroll tax to cover employment benefits provided by the state.[34] There are no taxes on gross receipts or individual income by the foreign investor. The Minister of Finance, in consultation with the MINVEC, can declare an enterprise involving foreign investors temporarily exempt from some or all applicable taxes.[35] Law 77 also allows the Cuban customs administration to waive the applicable duties on goods imported by the enterprise in appropriate cases.[36]

Guarantees Against Expropriation

Law 77 contains express guarantees against the uncompensated expropriation of the property of foreign investors, and commits the state to protect investors from claims by third parties founded on the expropriation of their assets by Cuba, in the event those

---

28. Art. 21 of Law 77 reserves to the Executive Committee of the Council of Ministers the approval decision with respect to the following types of investment: (1) those in which the total value of the investment (including the Cuban component) exceeds U.S. $10 million; (2) enterprises with 100% foreign capital; (3) investments in public services such as transportation, telecommunications, water systems, electric power, or other public works; (4) those involving the exploitation of natural resources; (5) those requiring the conveyance of state property or state rights; and (6) those in which the Cuban participant is one of the commercial enterprises set up by the armed forces.

29. Law 77, Art. 23 (e)(6).

30. Gary Maybarduk, *The State of the Cuban Economy 1998-99*, in *Cuba in Transition—Volume 9* 9 (Aug. 1999) (hereinafter "Maybarduk"); Veloz.

31. Law 77, Art. 29.

32. Law 77, Art. 3, 4, 6 & 8.

33. Law No. 74—Del Sistema Tributario, Gaceta Oficial (Aug. 5, 1994). Law 77 established a new tax on the earnings of enterprises that exploit natural resources. The tax can be as high as 50%, depending on the resource being exploited. Law 77, Art. 39(b).

34. *Id.*, Art. 39(a), (c). Other taxes that may be applicable to foreign investors include personal property and sales taxes, taxes on the use of public services, title registration and conveyance taxes, and advertising taxes.

35. *Id.*, Art. 43.

36. *Id.*, Art. 41.

claims are upheld by the Cuban courts.[37] The compensation to be paid under these provisions is to be in freely convertible currency, although the amount and terms of payment are left to negotiation by the parties or, in case of disputes, by an experienced international organization chosen jointly by the investor and the MINVEC.[38]

Decrees and Regulations that Facilitate Foreign Investment

Cuba has issued several decrees and regulations which are not specifically directed at foreign investment but which tend to facilitate the foreign investment process. These include, for example, the establishment of free-trade zones[39] and the institution of banking reforms.[40] The banking reforms separated the functions of the central bank from those of the commercial banking system, providing a more suitable framework for the operation of commercial banks and financial institutions, thereby facilitating the operations of enterprises including foreign investors.

Investment Protection Treaties

Cuba has signed more than fifty bilateral investment treaties ("BITs") with other countries, intended to protect foreign investment.[41] The BITs address four topics: (1) conditions for the approval of foreign investments, (2) state treatment of foreign investors, (3) expropriation, and (4) resolution of disputes between the foreign investor and the host country. The BITs that Cuba has negotiated generally follow the international norms and standards for such agreements.

CURRENT STATUS OF FOREIGN INVESTMENT

A total number of 540 enterprises with foreign participation have been established in Cuba.[42] Of those, 400 remain in operation.[43] Spain has the largest number of investors (97); Canada follows with 75; Italy is next with 55; and 18 enterprises have French investors.[44] Of the existing enterprises, 83 are involved in basic industry, 75 are in tourism, and 40 are in constru8ction.[45] The total number of compa-

---

37. *Id.*, Art. 3, 5.

38. *Id.*, Art. 3.

39. *See* Decreto-Ley No. 165—Ley Sobre Zonas Francas y Parques Industriales (June 3, 1996), *available online at* http://www.camaracuba.cubaweb.cu/download/Dl165sp.zip, Procedimiento para la presentación de la solicitud de otorgamiento de una concesión administrativa respecto a una zona franca y su tramitación, MINVEC (October 24, 1996); Procedimiento para la autorización del establecimiento de operadores en las instalaciones de las zonas francas, MINVEC (October 24, 1996), MINVEC Resolution No. 66/96, (October 24, 1996).

40. *Central Bank of Cuba established*, Granma International Electronic Edition, no. 25 (1997). Legislative Decree No. 172 established the Central Bank of Cuba, and Legislative Decree No. 173 set forth regulations governing the operation of commercial banks.

41. For a detailed discussion of Cuba's BITs, *see* Matías F. Travieso-Díaz and Jorge Pérez-López, *The Contribution of BITs to Cuba's Foreign Investment Program*, 32 Georgetown L. & Pol. Int'l Bus. J. 529 (2001). Capital-exporting countries negotiate BITs to protect the economic interests of their nationals and create mechanisms for the resolution of investment disputes, so as to reduce the possibility of arbitrary action by the host country. United Nations Conference on Trade and Development, *Bilateral Investment Treaties in the mid-1990s* (Geneva: UNCTAD, 1998), p. 10.

42. Omar Everleny Pérez Villanueva, *La Inversión Extranjera Directa en Cuba: Evolución y Perspectivas*, Centro de Estudios de la Economía Cubana, Universidad de la Habana, 2001 (hereinafter "Pérez").

43. Paolo Spadoni, "Foreign Investment in Cuba: Recent Developments and the Role in the Economy," in this volume. According to Spadoni, the number of enterprises in operation may have reached 412 by the summer of 2002 (hereinafter "Spadoni").

44. *Id.*

45. *Id.*

nies has grown slowly in the last five years, roughly at the rate of 30 per year.

As noted earlier, the amount of FDI in Cuba is relatively small. Foreign investment to date totals only $1.9 billion.[46] In addition, most investors bring in limited amounts of capital; seventy-five percent of all investment is less than $5 million. Potential reasons for these phenomena are examined below.

Despite the relatively small amount of foreign investment, the presence of foreign capital has benefited the Cuban economy. Between 1992 and 2000, enterprises with foreign investors exported $757.5 million worth of goods.[47] In the past two years joint ventures have produced about 15% of all Cuban exports.[48] In 2000, the total accumulated sales of goods and services reached $1.748 billion.[49]

The tourism sector has been the greatest success story in Cuba's drive to selectively attract FDI. Until 2001, tourism in Cuba had been increasing at an annual rate of 18%. In the year 2000, 1.8 million tourists visited the island, spending about $2 billion.[50] After disappointing tourist arrivals in 2001 and the first quarter of 2002, the Cuban government scaled down expectations, but predicts that Cuba will receive between 5 and 7 million tourists by 2010.[51] If the U.S. embargo prohibitions on tourist travel to

Cuba end, tourist arrivals could easily surpass these predictions.[52] The government promotes foreign investment in eight main tourist areas: Havana, Varadero, Santiago de Cuba, Isla de la Juventud, Costa Sur Central, Holguín, and Jardines del Rey. Potential investments include hotels, golf courses, marinas, aquatic centers, spas, and other recreational facilities.[53]

Telecommunications is another area of potential growth for FDI. Over the past five years Cuba has placed telecommunications and information technology as top development priorities. However, Cuba does not have the capital to invest in the new technology required to improve telecommunications. Thus, the government is actively seeking foreign capital in the telecommunications sector, specifically to support the growth of information technology activities, expand and rehabilitate sensing equipment and electronic devices, develop an international phone service company, and install fiber optic cables.[54]

INTERNAL OBSTACLES TO THE GROWTH OF FOREIGN INVESTMENT IN CUBA

Cuba has a number of advantages that make it potentially attractive to foreign investors. Cubans are generally well educated, and illiteracy is almost non-existent. The country has the highest percentage of

---

46. *See* Oficina Nacional de Estadísticas, Anuario Estadístico de Cuba, August 2001 (hereinafter "Anuario Estadístico"). Foreign investment figures vary widely, in part because many estimates include projected or proposed investments in addition to those in place. Carmelo Mesa-Lago, *The Cuban Economy in 1999-2001: Evaluation of Performance and Debate on the Future* in *Cuba in Transition—Volume 11* 1, 4 (Aug. 2001) (hereinafter "Mesa-Lago 2001"). The total amount of FDI reported by official Cuban sources in 1998 was $2.2 billion, whereas a similar estimate given in mid-1995 was $2 billion. Compare Mesa Lago 1998, p. 4 with, e.g., *Cuba Reports Foreign Investment Exceeding $2 Bn*, Reuters, July 10, 1995. The lack of growth of foreign investment in the last few years is consistent with the information that is received informally from potential investors who have given up in their plans to invest in Cuba due to the difficulties encountered in trying to do so. Maybarduk, 1, 8-9.

47. Pérez.

48. *Id.*

49. *Id.*

50. Mesa-Lago 2001.

51. "Tourism Continues to Grow, but Profits Lag," Jason Freer. Cuba Today: Spring, 2001.

52. As of this writing, Congress was considering legislation that would prevent the Treasury Department from using funds to enforce the existing ban on tourist travel to Cuba, although President Bush has threatened to veto any such legislation if enacted. *House Votes to End Some Cuba Restrictions,* New York Times, July 24, 2002.

53. *Cuba: Foreign Investment Opportunities*, MINVEC, Centro de Promoción de Inversiones, Havana 2001 (hereinafter "Opportunities").

54. *Id.*

university graduates in Latin America. Seven out of 100 workers hold a university degree.[55]

Cuba also has a low crime rate. Although theft occurs, Cuba is virtually free of violent crime. Havana boasts one of the lowest murder rates per capita and the smallest number of unsolved murders of metropolitan cities in the world. The high degree of personal safety could provide an incentive for potential investors, particularly in comparison to other Latin American countries.

Cuba's geographic location also makes it a natural gateway for trade between Latin America and North America. The territories of both Mexico and the United States are approximately 100 miles from Cuba. In addition, Cuba has in place some of the infrastructure required for it to serve as an international trade gateway. There are 21 airports on the island, 9 of which have international terminals. José Martí Airport currently handles 17,000 tons of cargo a year and is being upgraded to handle almost three times that amount. Additionally, Cuba has a large number of harbors that can handle international maritime traffic, and a national highway system that connects one end of the island to the other.[56]

Yet, as noted above, the amount of foreign investment that has actually entered Cuba is limited and the rate of investment appears to be slowing, rather than increasing. This slowdown in investment is occurring even though a resolution adopted by the Fifth Congress of the Cuban Communist Party in October 1997 called for greater promotion of foreign investment, particularly in projects that would contribute to the achievement of the national develop-

ment plans,[57] and the fact that Cuban government officials have sought to implement this resolution by actively pursuing foreign investors and extolling the advantages of investing in Cuba.

The main reason for this relative lack of success is that investing in Cuba remains an arduous, frustrating and risky proposition. Many of the problems that will be described in this section are also highlighted in a report released in the summer of 2002 by the European Programme of Cooperation, apparently sent to the Cuban government in hopes of improving the relationship between the European investors and the Cuban government.[58] This report will be referenced below as appropriate.

Government's Restrictive Approach To Foreign Investment

Foreign investment is highly regulated and only welcome in certain areas of the economy. The Center for Investment Promotion at MINVEC openly declares, "FDI is regarded as a complement for local development efforts and is, therefore, focused on the search for new external markets, competitive technologies, and financing."[59] The Minister of the MINVEC has likewise announced that Cuba will be more selective in the future in accepting foreign partners.[60]

The government only allows investors who meet certain criteria. Marta Lomas, Minister of MINVEC, confirms Cuba's selective approach to FDI. She claims that "authorities first identify what foreign investment the island wants, and then who will be the investor." [61] Investors must be able to contribute financial support, technology, and new markets in order to be authorized to invest.[62] Also, the Cuban gov-

---

55. Timothy Ashby, *IT in the Land of Salsa, Rum, and Fidel,* World Trade: July, 2001 (hereinafter "Ashby").

56. *Id.*

57. *Resolución económica: V Congreso del Partido Comunista de Cuba* (Havana: Editora Política, 1997), p. 25.

58. European Programme of Cooperation, "The Legal and Administrative Framework for Foreign Trade and Investment by European Companies in Cuba" (July 2002), *available online at* http://www.cubatraderpublications.com/euletter/index.com (hereinafter "EU Report").

59. *See* Opportunities.

60. Andrew Cawthorne, *La Habana se ha Hecho más Selectiva en la Búsqueda de Inversionistas,* El Nuevo Herald, May 15, 1999.

61. Radio Habana Cuba broadcast, January 3, 2001.

62. Interview with Lic. Roberto Yebra Muñoz, Investment Promoter at MINVEC, on Dec 12, 2001 (hereinafter "Yebra").

ernment will not allow foreign investment that directly competes with state owned enterprises, but only investment that will benefit Cuban companies as well as the investor.[63] In short, the decision as to which investments are acceptable or desired are made entirely by the government, and not by the demands of the market.

The investment process is especially difficult for investors who have a particular project in mind. Cuban enterprises can only operate in accordance with defined "social objectives" (corporate purposes), established by the government to avoid competition between state-owned enterprises.[64] A foreign investor can only form a joint venture with a Cuban company that has social objectives compatible with the proposed investment. This is a problem for the foreign investor, who must find a Cuban company that is allowed to engage in the desired business.[65] Thus, for instance, in the CBN example discussed above, the investors from CBN were informed, after they had made the initial investment, that Fénix was not currently permitted to rent bicycles, since the rental of bicycles was not one of Fénix's social objectives. Thus, before bicycle rental operations can begin, Fénix has to get approval from the Council of Ministers to add the rental of bicycles to its social objectives. The issue is further complicated by the fact that Habaguanex, another enterprise controlled by the Office of the Historian, has bicycle part sales as a social objective. Thus, approving Fénix's proposal would mean allowing Bicicletas Cruzando Fronteras to compete indirectly with Habaguanex.[66]

The restrictive definition of the social objective of Cuba's state owned companies also limits the possibility of expansion of joint ventures and other arrangements with foreign investors. Assume, for example, that CBN and Fénix decided after starting operations that Bicicletas could be more profitable if it sold refurbished bicycles to the government. Assume also that a second state-owned enterprise or joint venture already sold bicycles to the state. In all likelihood, the government would not allow the CBN-Fénix joint venture to amend its charter so that it could sell bicycles to state institutions, even if it could do so at a lower price than the enterprise currently doing so. Thus, the rigidity of the enterprise structure in Cuba would preclude a transaction in which the state derived a benefit in the acquisition of bicycles at lower prices and a state-owned enterprise increased its profit margin, again with a beneficial impact on the state. The difference in interests between the foreign investor (who is concerned with making a profit) and the Cuban government (which desires to uphold socialist objectives) creates conflicts within the operation of the joint venture. The EU Report on investment points this out as follows: "The interests in strategic objectives of the two partners often do not coincide and this results in the artificial associations and in lack of clarity in the development of the firm."[67]

Bureaucratic Impediments

The second main barrier to foreign investment is the arduous process needed to obtain the Cuban government's authorization of any investment. Even with the help of a government-owned consultant such as Conas, this process normally takes one year and can take up to 18 months.[68] There is no guarantee that the government will accept the proposed investment even after this period of time.

The process starts with the preparation of a letter of introduction and document package that the foreign investor must submit to MINVEC. Prior to any fur-

---

63. *Id.*

64. Guntin.

65. *Id.*

66. Approval of the expansion of Fénix's social purpose remained pending as of December 2001.

67. *See* EU Report.

68. Interview with two Cuban government officials on 12-28-01, names withheld by request (hereinafter "Two Government Officials").

ther action, MINVEC will review the letter of introduction and decide whether the investment is in an area of the economy prioritized for investment, whether it conflicts with the business of existing state-owned enterprises or other enterprises involving foreign investors, and whether the investor is solvent and his business plan is economically feasible.[69] MINVEC will also verify that invested funds are from legitimate sources, and that the proposed investment does not put the foreign investor at risk of litigation in the United States under the Helms-Burton law.[70]

If this first step is successful and MINVEC approves the presentation letter, the Cuban counterpart is authorized to begin negotiations with the foreign investor. Those negotiations can take many months. When the parties have reached an agreement, the foreign investor and its Cuban counterpart jointly prepare a feasibility study of the proposed enterprise. This study, often 100 pages long, must include every detail pertinent to the set-up and management of the company: foreign contribution, Cuban contribution, number of workers, workers' salaries, projected production rates, prices of the products, costs of inputs, type of materials used for construction, location of the enterprise, possible effects on the environment, etc. [71]

The feasibility study must include any information that is likely to be required by the government agencies with potential jurisdiction over the venture. The Ministry of Finances and Prices, for example, will request the prices of any goods that will be sold commercially within the Cuban market.[72] (The Ministry of Finances and Prices seeks this information in order to limit the enterprise's ability to compete with state-owned enterprises selling similar products.) Likewise, the Ministry of Labor will request an employment worksheet ("*plantilla de trabajo*") for any project that utilizes Cuban labor. This plantilla must specify exactly how many workers will be employed, what their functions will be, and how much they will be paid.[73] The Ministry of Labor regulates salaries of all national workers, and workers in joint ventures or economic associations cannot, without special permission, earn more than their counterparts in state-owned enterprises.

The foreign investor sends the feasibility study to MINVEC, which will submit the study with its recommendations to a Governmental Commission, a committee made up of all relevant government ministers and agency heads.[74] Law 77 is vague on which ministries and agencies are relevant to a proposed investment. It simply states, "Once the request is accepted by the MINVEC, it shall be submitted for consultation to all corresponding agencies and institutions, in order to obtain their report on matters pertinent to them."[75]

The Governmental Commission has sixty days to accept or reject the investment proposal based on the feasibility study.[76] Proposals are rarely accepted on the first submission; the Commission may reject the proposal altogether, or may identify problems or deficiencies and send it back to the investor.[77] Any participating minister can send the feasibility study back to the investor and request that specified changes be made. If the investor addresses the problems, the

---

69. The EU Report points out that the Cuban government does not provide the same financial guarantee that it demands of foreign investors. This places extra costs and burden on the foreign investor, while decreasing the risk for the Cuban government. EU Report.

70. Two Government Officials, *supra.*

71. *Id.*

72. *Id.*

73. *Id.*

74. Law 77, Art. 23(e)(4).

75. *Id.*

76. *Id.*, Art. 23(e)(6).

77. Two Government Officials.

study goes back to the Government Commission, which again has sixty days to rule on the proposal.

If the Commission accepts the investment proposal, it forwards the proposal and a recommendation of approval to the Executive Committee of the Council of Ministers which includes President Fidel Castro, Armed Forces Minister Raúl Castro, the First Vice President (Carlos Lage), and any members of the Council of Ministers appointed by Fidel Castro.[78] The Executive Committee has the ultimate power to accept or reject the proposed investment. If the Executive Committee accepts the investment, it drafts an official decree authorizing formation of the enterprise.[79] The foreign investor, the Cuban counterpart, and a representative of the Executive Committee then sign a document establishing the enterprise. The enterprise is registered with the Chamber of Commerce and is then able to begin operations.

This cumbersome process, which involves the approval of numerous ministries and agency heads, up to President Castro himself, impedes investment process and discourages all but the most determined investors.

Labor Regime

As noted above, Law 77 allows a foreign investor to hire foreign personnel to fill managerial and technical positions. On the other hand, the Cuban labor force may not be hired directly by the investor or by the enterprise formed by the investor and its Cuban counterpart. Law 77 retains the system, established under Law 50, which requires that Cuban labor be provided by the state through a contracting agency designated by the MINVEC.[80] The law, however, allows in exceptional cases that an enterprise with foreign participation contract with all or some of its employees directly, if the decree approving formation of the enterprise so specifies. There is also a residual clause in the labor provisions of Law 77, which states that the decree authorizing formation of the enterprise may establish a labor regime that differs from that established in the law.[81] This provision could, if so desired, provide further flexibility than that granted by the law itself. However, neither of these two clauses appears to have been invoked to date.

Law 77 and its regulations are currently being implemented as follows.[82] During the preparation of the feasibility study, the foreign investor and its Cuban counterpart of a joint venture determine the number of workers needed. They then contact an employment agency designated by the MINVEC. This employment agency is often a subsidiary of a state-owned enterprise in the sector of the economy that is the subject of the foreign investment, possibly the same enterprise that is partnering with the foreign investor. Cubanacán, for example, is a Cuban armed

---

78. *See* http://www.cubagob.cu for a listing of the members of Cuba's Council of Ministers.

79. Law 77, Art. 24.

80. *See id.,* Art. 31-35. The provisions of the law are further elaborated in Resolution No. 3/96 of the Ministry of Labor, issued in March 1996, which established regulations for the employment of workers in enterprises with foreign participation operating in Cuba. *Resolución No. 3/96, Ministerio de Trabajo y Seguridad Social—Reglamento sobre el régimen laboral en la inversión extranjera,* Gaceta Oficial (May 24, 1996), p. 266-272.

81. Law 77, Art. 33(1), states: "Workers in joint ventures who are Cuban or permanent residents in Cuba, with the exception of the members of the management or administration, are contracted by an employing entity proposed by the Ministry of Foreign Investment and Economic Cooperation, and authorized by the Ministry of Labor and Social Security."

82. The following description of the implementation of the labor provisions of Law 77 is based on a number of interviews held in Cuba and abroad in December 2001. *See* n.2, *supra.* The interviewees included employees of joint ventures, employees of state-owned enterprises, foreign investors, government officials, Cuban economists, and independent journalists. Mr. Trumbull had no acquaintance with most of the workers interviewed, and none of the interviews were set up by state officials. Interviewees were told that the interviews were confidential and would only be used for academic purposes. Interviews with investors included one investor who is enjoying moderate success, one who is frustrated with the investment process, and one who has completely pulled out of Cuba. Two of the government officials interviewed requested that their names and affiliations not be revealed. While the total number of interviews (20) was relatively small the views expressed were generally consistent with other sources of information available to the authors. In addition, there was substantial uniformity in the factual information provided by the interviewees, which included workers, journalists, other independent observers, foreign investors, government officials, and members of the public.

forces enterprise engaged in tourism activities.[83] Over the past decade, Cubanacán has formed a number of joint ventures with foreign companies.[84] Cubanacán has also set up a number of smaller, specialized companies serving specific aspects of the tourism industry. One of these smaller companies is an employment agency. This agency supplies labor to all joint ventures formed by foreign investors that enter into contracts with Cubanacán.

The MINVEC-designated employment agency and the joint venture determine a monthly wage in U.S. dollars for each worker category to be paid to the agency. In the CBN example discussed above, CBN agreed to pay the employment agency $460/month for each mechanic, $500/month for a sales representative, and $550/month for a general manager.[85] This wage is increased by a 25% payroll tax, which is to be paid directly by the enterprise (in reality, by the foreign investor) to the employment agency, also in U.S. dollars. The employment agency pays the workers a salary in Cuban pesos that is comparable to the national average for that type of work set by the Labor Ministry. Thus, each mechanic receives about 200 pesos/month, a sales representative gets 300 pesos/month, and the general manager receives 400 pesos/month.[86]

The employment agency is responsible for all aspects of the hiring, employment conditions, and termination of the Cuban worker. Each employment agency has a "*bolsa de trabajo,*" or employment register listing available workers. Whenever an enterprise with foreign investor participation needs Cuban workers, the employment agency sets up interviews between the management of the joint venture and selected workers from the pool of available workers listed in the bolsa de trabajo. The foreign investor and the Cuban counterpart make the ultimate decision on who, among the workers selected from the pool, they want to have hired.[87] It is unclear how large the pool of potential workers is or how it is established. However, based on an earlier arrangement established in 1990 for workers in the tourism sector, workers are selected for incorporation into the pool on the basis of their "moral qualities" as much as, if no more than, their ability to perform the required work tasks.[88]

The enterprise can also hire workers that are not part of the pool in the bolsa de trabajo. If a foreign investor wishes to hire a Cuban who is not associated with the employment agency, the investor must contact the employment agency and notify it that he wants to contract a particular worker. The employment agency will run a background check on the worker to determine that he does not have a serious criminal record and is in "good moral standing."[89] Then, the employment agency will hire the worker and the en-

---

83. Information on Cubanacán is available at http://www.cubanacan.cu.

84. The Sol Palmeras hotel, for example, is operated by a joint venture between Cubanacán and a Spanish conglomerate. María Dolores Espino, *Cuban Tourism During the Special Period"* in *Cuba in Transition—Volume 10* 360, 362 (Aug. 2000).

85. One criticism included in the EU Report is that the Cuban employment agencies sometimes overstate the position of Cuban workers in order to overcharge the foreign investor. Thus, a "storekeeper" becomes the "head of store."

86. These numbers are rough estimates based on conversations with Cuban workers.

87. Interviews with various foreign investors as well as Lic. Roberto Yebra at the MINVEC Center for Economic Promotion and Lic. Amado Guntin at Conas.

88. *"Resolución No. 15/90 del Comité Estatal de Trabajo y Seguridad Social,"* Gaceta Oficial (September 15, 1990). *See* Jorge F. Pérez-López, *Cuba's Thrust to Attract Foreign Investment: A Special Labor Regime for Joint Ventures in International Tourism,* Inter-American Law Review 24:2 (Winter 1992-93), p. 221-279, for a comparative analysis of the labor regime established for the tourism sector against the provisions of the Cuban Labor Code.

89. The Vice President of Cuba's employment agency ACOREC ("Agencia de Contratación a Representaciones Comerciales") stated that an employment agency does not consider whether a worker is a member of the Communist party when deciding if a worker is in good moral standing. (Interview 12-24-01). However, the charge is often made that party loyalty is a virtually indispensable prerequisite to obtaining employment in enterprises involving foreign participation. Thus, employment is granted on the basis of loyalty to the government rather than personal merit, in violation of Convention 111 of the International Labor Organization ("ILO"), which guarantees non-discrimination in employment. Pax Christi Netherlands, *Cuba: A Year After the Pope* (Utrecht: Pax Christi Netherlands, February 1999), p. 23. The politically based discrimination in which the Cuban government engages in the training and employment of workers has been the subject of frequent condemnation before the Experts Committee on the Application of Conventions and Recommendations of the ILO. See http://www.ilo.org.

terprise can contract for his services with the agency. In no event can the enterprise contract directly with a worker.[90]

Employers' opinions vary regarding the usefulness of the employment agencies. David McMillan, president of Venezia Hospitality International, writes, "my general experience with employment agencies has been positive."[91] Employment agencies can help foreign investors who are not familiar with the Cuban economy or Cuban labor force find employees who are, at least, adequate and dependable.

On the other hand, many foreign investors have discovered that the workers obtained through the bolsa de trabajo are not always the most qualified for a particular job. For example, the CBN investors that set up the Bicicletas Cruzando Fronteras enterprise claim that none of the workers interviewed through the bolsa de trabajo had any previous experience working with bicycles, and none were eager to work as bicycle mechanics. However, all workers interviewed were unemployed and needed work. The investor decided to hire the workers out of the bolsa de trabajo because he did not have the time or connections to find better workers.[92]

Nevertheless, it is possible to circumvent this restriction. One foreign investor who owns a small travel agency in Havana has chosen to hire all workers outside of the employment agency's bolsa de trabajo. He has been traveling to Cuba for over twenty years, has many Cuban friends, and is familiar with the socialist

ways of doing business. He initially had to register his company with HAVANATUR, the state enterprise that controls tour operator activities in Cuba, and get his labor through that agency. Subsequently, he was able to hand-pick seven employees whom he knew and trusted. He gave their names to HAVANATUR's employment agency, which then hired them and leased them back to the investor.[93]

These examples illustrate that the more experience a foreign investor has in Cuba, the more likely it is that he will be able to secure a qualified and dependable work force by looking outside the bolsa de trabajo to meet its labor needs.

Branches of foreign companies operating in Cuba have slightly different requirements regarding the supply of Cuban labor. Branches of foreign companies are required by labor regulations to obtain labor through the Cuban employment agency ACOREC, which specializes in providing labor to foreign company branches operating in Cuba.[94] The foreign firm office has an initial 1-2 month trial period in which it is free to ask for termination of the new employee without notice. If the firm decides to keep the worker, it can contract with ACOREC for that worker for a period of up to 5 years.[95] The foreign firm must designate what each worker's job will be, the hours of employment, and his responsibilities.

Unlike other employment agencies that are willing to negotiate employee contracts with the joint venture, ACOREC has an established, non-negotiable list of

---

90. Art. 34 of Law 77 provides that: (1) the employment relationship is between the worker and the state employment agency, and the enterprise with foreign participation is not a party to that relationship; (2) the state agency is responsible for paying the worker's salary; (3) the state agency is responsible for firing and replacing those workers whose performance is deficient; and (4) any labor grievances are to be raised before the state agency, although the enterprise utilizing the worker's services is financially responsible for the costs associated with the resolution of such grievances. Under this arrangement, the enterprise's only recourse against inadequate workers is to return them to the employment agency if their work is unsatisfactory.

91. David McMillan, *Cuban Workers in the Tourism Sector*, Cuba Today, National Policy Association, Spring 2001.

92. Interview with CBN representative, 12-20-01.

93. Interview with foreign investor on 12-14-01. The Report includes this complaint. "The system of staff selection is controlled by the employment agencies who try to impose their candidates (frequently not suitable professionally) and make it difficult to hire candidates identified by the foreign investor."

94. Resolución No. 32/99 1998, *Sucursales de Compañías Extranjeras: Regulaciones Laborales y Permiso de Trabajo* (hereinafter "Sucursales").

95. *Id.*

charges for different categories of workers.[96] ACOREC charges from $425/month for a general laborer to $1000/month for a legal consultant, supervisor, engineer, or vice-president. Workers employed by ACOREC receive a salary, in pesos, equivalent to the national average for that category of worker. Thus, Cuban branches of foreign firms may have to pay more for each worker than enterprises including foreign investors do, yet the workers in those branches may not get paid as much as their counterparts working in joint ventures or economic associations, since the salaries of the latter are to some extent negotiable and may be higher than the official rate.[97] Another state agency, CUBALSE, S.A. ("Cuba al Servicio de Extranjeros, S.A.") provides Cuban personnel to foreign entities, particularly foreign embassies and other offices of foreign governments and international organizations.

Whatever agency is used to obtain workers for the enterprise, one feature is common: the foreign investor has to pay the employment agency in U.S. dollars for the labor of Cuban workers. The employment agency pays each worker a salary in pesos based on the average national salary for the worker's profession. Often, even applying the official 1 dollar equal to 1 peso rate, the Cuban worker receives even less in pesos than what the foreign investor pays the employment agency in U.S. dollars. Thus since the actual rate of exchange is 26 pesos to a dollar, the worker may receive less than 4 cents out of each dollar of his salary paid by the investor.

Criticisms Leveled Against Cuba's Labor Regime for Enterprises Including Foreign Investors: Cuba's labor policy has been called exploitative by inde-pendent organizations within Cuba as well as international organizations such as the UN Human Rights Watch and the International Labor Organization ("ILO").[98] According to labor rights organizations, Cuba violates the standards of labor established by the ILO and ratified by the Cuban government. Article 2 of Convention 87 of the ILO, adopted in 1948, declares, "Workers and employers, without distinction whatsoever, shall have the right to establish and, subject only to the rules of the organization concerned, to join organizations of their own choosing without previous authorization." Cuba's practices have also been denounced by Cuban American labor organizations.[99]

Cuba is also in violation of Convention 95 of the ILO.[100] Article 5 of this convention, adopted in 1949, states, "Wages shall be paid directly to the worker concerned except as may be otherwise provided by national laws or regulations, collective agreement or arbitration award or where the worker concerned has agreed to the contrary." Article 9 declares, "Any deduction of wages with a view to insuring a direct or indirect payment for the purpose of obtaining or retaining employment, made by a worker to an employer or his representative or to any intermediary, shall be prohibited." Contrary to this Convention, the Cuban government prohibits direct employment by foreign firms. As discussed above, foreign investors must contract Cuban workers through a state employment agency. The investor pays the worker's salary to the employment agency in US dollars, and the employment agency pays him or her a small fraction of this money in Cuban pesos. This "confiscation" of wages is done without the

---

96. ACOREC employs over 2000 Cubans working in over 600 foreign companies. Interview with Vice President of ACOREC, December 23, 2001 (hereinafter "ACOREC VP").

97. A Canadian investor indicated that her feasibility study towards approval of her proposed investment had been rejected because she proposed to pay a mechanic 250 pesos/month instead of the state-mandated salary of 129 pesos. Before the feasibility study could be approved, she had to explain why the mechanic deserved to be paid almost double the national average mechanic salary. Interview with foreign investor, December 13, 2001.

98. *See, e.g.,* http://www.ilo.org, http://www.hrw.org/reports/1999/cuba/Cuba996-01.htm#P392_35421.

99. *See, e.g.,* "Report of the Violations of the International Labor Organization's Standards and Conventions by Cuba," Confederación Obrera Nacional Independiente de Cuba. 2000-2001.

100. Cuba ratified this convention on September 24, 1959.

consent of the worker, and is, as many critics claim, a clear violation of Convention 95 of the ILO.

The entire labor regime for enterprises involving foreign investors has been widely denounced, especially by Cuban-American scholars and academics within the United States.[101] One analyst has written, "The Cuban government entity that hires the workers is a company with an illicit purpose. It has been created only to harm and defraud a third party, namely the Cuban work force."[102] Another points out that "Cuban workers feel exploited and resent the unjust and inhumane control of the Cuban government over their lives. They blame the deplorable contractual agreements structured by the Cuban government—with the 'complicity' of foreign investors—for their ignominious existence."[103]

U.S. based analysts advocate that the Cuban government commit to and implement principles of ethical investment in the country.[104] A number of ethical investment principles have been developed for Cuba, chief among them the "Arcos principles" first defined in 1994 and named after a well-known Cuban dissident, before U.S. enterprises are allowed to do business in Cuba. These principles call on foreign investors to: respect the dignity of the Cuban people and the due process of law; provide equal rights and non-discrimination of the Cuban people in access to and use of facilities and in the purchase of goods and services, especially those normally reserved for foreign visitors or residents; engage in equal and fair hiring and employment practices, with non-discrimination for reasons based on political considerations, sex, race, religion or age; promote fair labor standards and the right of Cuban workers to form labor unions and to receive fair wages; and improve the quality of employees' lives outside the work-place in such areas as: occupational safety and health, culture, and environmental protection.[105]

Cuba's Response to International Criticism: The Cuban government acknowledges that its indirect employment system may seem exploitative when judged in the context of a capitalist framework. However, it argues that within the socialist system it is necessary and just. There are three main arguments the Cuban government makes in support of its system for providing labor to enterprises involving foreign investors.

First, the Cuban labor code guarantees certain rights to Cuban workers, and the use of a Cuban employment agency protects these rights. All workers receive one month of paid vacation per year, paid sick leave with the guarantee to return to work, and paid maternity leave from the seventh month of pregnancy through the first six months of the baby's life. Additionally, employment agencies guarantee equal payment for men and women, and equal opportunities for all races.[106] The Cuban government further cites poor labor conditions in the Caribbean and claims that the existing labor policy protects Cuban workers from similar exploitation.

Second, indirect employment helps preserve Cuba's social welfare system. Employment agencies provide a constant source of hard currency for the Cuban

---

101. *See, e.g.,* Efrén Córdoba, *Régimen laboral,* in *40 Años de Revolución: El legado de Castro* (Miami: Ediciones Universal, 1999), p. 167; Alberto Luzárraga, *Cuba Socialista—La Nulidad de los Contratos de Inversión Extranjera por Causa Ilícita—Defraudar al Trabajador,* http://www.amigospais-guaracabuya.org/oagal004.html.

102. Luzárraga, *supra.*

103. Guillermo Cueto, *Cuban Sweat for Sale,* Cuba Today, Fall 2000, Vol., No. 2. Cuban-American labor experts also criticize harshly Cuba's general labor practices, claiming that the Cuban government exploits the Cuban work force. They point out that "Cuba has the lowest wages of any country in Latin America, including Haiti." They add that Cuba has the longest workweek of any country (48 hours) and that the Cuban government has refused to abolish child labor. Efrén Córdova and Eduardo García Moure, *Modern Slavery: Labor Conditions in Cuba,* Institute for Cuban and Cuban American Studies, University of Miami (April 2000).

104. *See, e.g.,* "Principles for Private Sector Investment in Cuba," National Policy Association Cuba Working Group, Summer 2000 Vol. 1 No. 1, available online at http://www.npa1.org.

105. The complete text of the Arcos principles is available online at http://www.sigloxxi.org/arcos-i.htm.

106. ACOREC VP.

government. About 30,000 Cubans work in joint ventures and foreign firms.[107] Enterprises with foreign investment pay an average of $500/month per worker. Thus, the government collects $15 million per month in hard currency from the employment of Cuban workers by enterprises involving foreign investors.[108]

Third, the Cuban government requires that each sector of the economy contribute a certain amount of money to support the social welfare system.[109] For sectors in which foreign investment is allowed, much of this money is collected in hard currency through the employment agencies. The government invests this money in health care, education, and other governmental purposes. Thus, the Cuban government argues, the money that the government keeps away from the worker is reinvested for the good of the entire population.[110]

Finally, the Cuban government views indirect employment as the only form of employment compatible with socialist goals. The Cuban government states that it cannot allow a system of employment that promotes inequality between Cubans working in the joint venture sector (.7% of the working population) and the public sector work force (77.5% of the population).[111] The average monthly salary paid by

the state to Cuban workers is approximately 250 pesos, less than $10/month.[112] If workers under joint ventures were allowed to earn $500/month, a great inequality would arise between the two classes of workers. This disparity could lead to discontentment among state workers, social unrest, and a decline in productivity. The government claims that maintaining wage equilibrium between the state and private sector is the only way to keep the fabric of society from tearing apart.[113]

Evaluation of Cuba's Position: Cuba's arguments appear unpersuasive. Regardless of the government's attempted justification, the state pockets over 95% of the value of the work provided by workers employed by enterprises with foreign investors. It is clear that such confiscation is in direct violation of international conventions accepted throughout the world, as well as Cuba's own Labor Code.[114] While it may be true that the end of indirect employment could cause social upheaval, this result would only demonstrate the inherent flaws in the socialist system. As to the financing of social welfare programs, the state could, for example, finance social welfare by further opening the economy to foreign investment and collecting taxes on the income of enterprises involving foreign investors.[115] The State could also privatize state-owned enterprises, and allow the ongoing *perfeccio-*

---

107. According to the Anuario Estadístico de Cuba, 26,800 Cubans worked in joint ventures. An additional 2000 workers worked for foreign firms.

108. According to Promoters at MINVEC all prices for Cuban labor are negotiated between the foreign investor and the corresponding employment agency. Information provided by several interviewees indicates that the average salary paid for a joint venture worker is $375-$475, and the average price for a worker in a foreign firm is $500-$700.

109. Interview with Cuban worker on 12-10-01, name withheld by request.

110. ACOREC VP.

111. Anuario Estadístico de Cuba.

112. *Informe de la Economía,* Granma (Havana), December 23, 2000.

113. ACOREC VP.

114. *See* ILO Convention 95 on worker salaries, Art. 5 and 6. This practice violates the principle of wage integrity against government confiscation, contained in Cuba's Labor Code.

115. It should be noted that, despite the government's boasts about providing social welfare, per capita expenditures for social services is significantly lower than those in several other Latin American countries. In 1997, Cuba spent only $457/person on social welfare, a 26.3% decrease from 1990 levels. Argentina, Uruguay, Panama, Costa Rica, Brasil, and Chile all spent more money per capita than did Cuba. Rolando Castañeda, *Cuba y América Latina: Consideraciones sobre el Nivel de la Evolución del Indice de Desarrollo Humano y del Gasto Social en la Decada de los Noventa,* in *Cuba in Transition—Volume 10* 234 (Aug. 2000). Since 1997 social welfare spending has increased, but only slightly. According to a Cuban source, the government has chosen to invest most of the earnings from joint venture enterprises back into key economic sectors rather than spend the money on increasing social welfare programs. Cuban Economist.

namiento empresarial process to become a true enterprise reform movement.[116] In short, the state could do many things to bridge the inequality that now exists between the salaries paid in state enterprises and those involving foreign investors rather than retaining it.

Worker Views:[117] Despite the governmental confiscation of most of their salaries, Cuban workers in enterprises involving foreign investors feel that they are still better off than workers in state-owned enterprises. Workers in joint ventures and branches of foreign companies enjoy better working conditions than in state-owned enterprises. For example, the offices of the branches of foreign companies are usually air-conditioned, a rarity in Cuba. Workers receive perks such as free clothing, food, and transportation to and from work.

Most importantly, workers receive under-the-table bonuses in dollars from foreign investors. These payments are widely made but rarely talked about because unregulated bonuses are illegal, since the government controls and dictates workers' salaries. However, the government knows that workers' salaries are inadequate. Thus, in order to keep workers productive (and often to prevent them from stealing), foreign investors commonly pay the Cuban employees a "stimulus" bonus.[118]

A foreign investor from CBN indicated that she noticed a bit of petty theft of tools and supplies in the first few months of operations in Cuba. To curb further losses, she started paying each employee a bonus of $10/month, essentially doubling their salary. Another foreign investor paid workers in U.S. dollars for all extra or overtime work they did. (Since all employee duties and work hours must be set prior to the authorization is issued to the enterprise, the foreign investor cannot require Cuban workers to do tasks outside of their prescribed duties.) Arrangements such as these provide an additional source of hidden costs to the foreign investor, but allow him an opportunity to enhance worker compensation by paying a dollar supplement in a quasi-legal manner. Thus, if a foreign manager wants a worker to perform work outside regular scheduled hours, it is advantageous for both the foreign investor and the Cuban worker that the worker be paid directly in dollars rather than having the dollars go to the employment agency.[119] Workers in enterprises involving foreign investors know that they can receive stimulus payments in dollars in a number of ways, particularly if they are honest, competent, and dedicated. This understanding fuels the desire among Cubans to work in enterprises that involve foreign investors.

In reality, workers employed by enterprises with foreign participation generally receive two salaries: an official salary paid by the employment agency in Cuban pesos and an unofficial salary paid directly by the employer in U.S. dollars and in consumer goods. If one takes into account both salaries, the average joint-venture worker earns substantially more than the average worker in the state sector does. Cuban workers' opinions also vary on the fairness of the "confiscation" of their wages by the state. Some workers point out that they do not need much money each month to live on.[120] They receive rationed food, transportation, clothing, free health care and education, and subsidized prices for other goods and services.

A Cuban sailor who worked for several years on a foreign-owned boat remarked, "You cannot blindly compare salaries in Cuba with salaries in other countries. Yes, it will look like exploitation. But, one has to know the system, and the history of that system.

---

116. See Matías F. Travieso-Díaz, *Cuba's Perfeccionamiento Empresarial Law: A Step Towards Privatization?* 23 U. Pa. J. Intern'l Econ. Law 119 (2002).

117. The information in this section is based interviews with employees in the Bank of Canada, Cubacel, ACOREC, Sol Meliá and other enterprises.

118. Interviews with Cuban Economist and Two Government Officials.

119. Interview with a former investor in Cuba who has since stopped all investment in Cuba.

120. Interviews with employees at CubaLinda, the Bank of Canada, and Sol Meliá.

In Cuba, we have a social obligation that you don't have in other countries." A worker in a foreign owned tourist agency had a similar opinion. "As a person, I think that the system is unjust. But, as a Cuban I think it is necessary." A Cuban representative at the Bank of Canada pointed out that the majority of Cubans would like to suffer the "exploitation" to which he is subject. Although his salary is in Cuban pesos, his job provides him with many perks. He eats at the cafeteria every day for free.[121] The Bank of Canada buys him clothes, and provides him a $30,000 sports utility vehicle and a credit card to buy gasoline. He has lived all around the world, and claims that he still prefers to live in Cuba. "I am fine. I live well. I prefer to help my country than take all the money for myself. One has to have a revolutionary mentality." None of the workers interviewed said that he felt exploited by working through the employment agencies.

This attitude of workers in joint ventures may seem counter-intuitive. It is possible that these workers resent that the government confiscates 95% of their wages, but are not willing to talk for fear of losing their jobs. However, Cuban workers do not necessarily view labor economics as workers in capitalist countries do. Cuban workers are paid a nominal salary, which is not determined by the value of their output, and receive a number of subsidized goods and services that do not cover their basic necessities. Nevertheless, workers do not feel entitled to receive compensation commensurate with their contribution, possibly because no worker in the state sector receives such pay, or (less likely) because they believe that an egalitarian socialist state is fairer than a capitalist state. They also may not regard the money paid by the foreign investor for their labor as rightfully theirs.

Thus, the question of exploitation is a complex one, at least from the employees' perspective. Workers in foreign investments are better off than their state-sector colleagues. They do not have to steal, hustle, or work on the black market to make a living as do many other Cubans. They have free education, health care, and subsidized goods and services. Yet, they do not have the freedoms that workers in other countries have, even those working under poor labor conditions. Cuban workers in joint ventures are dependent on the state. The state decides who will do what work, how much he will be paid, and how long he will work. The state rewards those who are loyal to the state, and punishes those who are not. The Cuban work force is merely a means used to further the goals of the state.

Problems Posed by Cuba's Labor Regime: Regardless of the views of the Cuban government and the workers, there is no question that the current labor regime constitutes an impediment to foreign investment in the country. First, as noted above, investors have to pay a dual salary for the right to use Cuban labor: an official salary to the employment agency, and an under-the-table payment directly to the worker. At a minimum, the need to provide a two-salary method of compensation increases operating costs for enterprises involving foreign investors and makes their enterprises in Cuba less profitable and competitive. In addition, the foreign investor is not guaranteed to get personnel who are qualified to perform in accordance with the job's requirements, and have little control over labor relations. Finally, investors are subject to international criticism as aiding and abetting the workers' exploitation, creating image concerns for some investors. Taken together, these problems translate into a disincentive to do business in Cuba. The EU Report sums up the problems by saying: "The numerous general and specific difficulties in this sphere put up the price of the labor force to a point which makes them a major hindrance to greater flows of foreign investment."[122]

CONCLUSION: THE FUTURE OF FOREIGN INVESTMENT

Despite its initial successes in the early and mid 1990s, Cuba has not been able to secure foreign investment to the degree that the country requires and

---

121. The Bank of Canada pays $3/day for each employee's lunch.

122. See EU Report.

is capable of attracting. The main reason for this failure is the contradictory attitude of the Cuban government towards investment, the obstacles and restrictions that are placed before a prospective investor, and the ominous shadow of U.S. sanctions and other external factors. In all, investing in Cuba must surely be seen by most foreign entrepreneurs as a perilous task.

On the other hand, the current environment in Cuba is not favorable to the entry of foreign investment. While some of the adverse factors are external (particularly the poor relations between Cuba and the United States), the greater and most significant obstacles to investment are internal and can be overcome by the implementation of suitable government initiatives.

Despite the current deficiencies and problems, foreign investment should continue to play an important role in the economic development of Cuba, both in the immediate future and once the country adopts a more welcoming attitude to foreign capital. For investment to realize its full potential, however, it will

be necessary that both the laws and the government attitudes change towards a regime that regulates, but at the same time fosters, foreign investment.

This is not to say that elimination of the internal obstacles to foreign investment will be easy. Some of the contradictions caused by Cuba's adherence to a socialist program while seeking to implement limited capitalistic measures cannot be remedied without reorientation of the government's thinking of the role of the state in the country's economic activity. (This is particularly true with respect to the labor issue, as evidenced by the arguments raised by the government in support of the current framework for the use of Cuban labor by enterprises including foreign investors.) On the other hand, to the extent that the reluctance by investors to enter the Cuban market is based on the perception that Cuba raises too many obstacles and restrictions to FDI, such a perception could be ameliorated without great difficulty and in a relatively short period of time were Cuba inclined to do so.

197

LAS NEGOCIACIONES INTERNACIONALES ACTUALES DE CUBA

Francisco León

El gobierno cubano dio muestras de su capacidad negociadora internacional en el Mundo de la Guerra Fría superando a sus socios del Campo Socialista en logro de favores de la Unión Soviética; manteniendo, a la vez, un reconocimiento como actor independiente de los países llamados no alineados. El fin del orden internacional bipolar puso a prueba esa capacidad al multiplicar las instancias y actores negociadores, así como las oportunidades de reinserción internacional del país. En balance las oportunidades de reinserción más plena han sido rechazadas y las crisis económicas han sido recurrentes, a pesar, de los éxitos parciales del programa de estabilización (1994-95) y de la estrategia de diversificación de relaciones y la descentralización de su gestión.

En el nuevo milenio la posibilidad de continuar negociaciones diferenciadas con sus contrapartes comerciales se ha reducido al aumentar la interdependencia entre ellas con:

- La aceleración de la transición de Rusia a una economía de mercado, su incorporación al Club de París y sus coincidencias crecientes de posiciones en materia de seguridad con los Estados Unidos de Norteamérica-EUA;

- El uso de la cláusula democrática y el respeto de los derechos humanos por la Unión Europea-UE y los países de América Latina y el Caribe-ALC;

- La creciente diferenciación en la importancia de sus socios comerciales; y

- La globalización y regionalización de las reglas de juego resultantes de los acuerdos de la OMC, el ALCA, UE-ALC y entre países de ALC.

Los márgenes de negociación con que cuenta el gobierno cubano se han estrechado pero continua su interés y el de las contrapartes en esas negociaciones. En general, por la importancia internacional del país y, la posibilidad de influir en el proceso de sucesión política por el costo de la pérdida de las oportunidades actuales para quienes asuman el nuevo gobierno en Cuba.

En este trabajo abordaré: (1) el escenario negociador 1990-2000; (2) la emergencia del nuevo escenario negociador en el primer bienio del Tercer Milenio; y, finalmente, (3) las perspectivas e impacto de las principales negociaciones.

EL ESCENARIO NEGOCIADOR, 1990-2000

Durante la primera década posterior a la Guerra Fría y el fin del Campo Socialista, el gobierno cubano:

- Enfrentó el desafío de reforzar las relaciones políticas y comerciales con los organismos de integración y los países europeos, latinoamericanos y caribeños, y, la urgencia de normalizar las relaciones con EUA;

- Compartió con Rusia el interés por salvar algo de las relaciones comerciales y el apoyo logístico en materia de seguridad desarrollados en las décadas anteriores; y,

- Buscó reforzar el refuerzo del apoyo de los países no alineados en las instancias multilaterales, especialmente, de Naciones Unidas. Así como de los movimientos de solidaridad con Cuba en numerosos países.

La adaptación al cambiante e inseguro escenario supuso, además, la adopción de medidas impuestas por las condiciones económicas y militares en que quedaba el país y, sugeridas por la capacidad de movilización y negociación internacional del gobierno. Así, la retirada de las tropas de Angola y otros países africanos, fue completada a mediados de 1991 poniendo fin a la denominada Operación Carlota. Mientras, internamente, se organizaba y desarrollaba la estrategia Guerra de Todo el Pueblo, para desalentar una eventual invasión de EUA. Complementariamente, utilizó alternativas de reemplazo de la solidaridad socialista participando en esquemas de integración regional de nuevo cuño como la Asociación de Estados del Caribe, y, en el Grupo de Sao Paulo, que reunió a las organizaciones políticas y sociales opuestas al orden panamericano y mundial emergente y del que el liderazgo cubano fuera uno de sus gestores.

No obstante esos esfuerzos tuvieron que dar prioridad y un espacio más amplio a los cambios económicos requeridos por la sobrevivencia del régimen y la población. En especial, al agravarse la crisis y alcanzar los desequilibrios macro-económicos niveles que comprometían la continuidad del régimen y superado las carencias de la población las de los peores años de la década de 1980s.

Estos cambios, comenzaron antes del fin del CAME y de la Unión Soviética al introducir las autoridades modalidades de inversión extranjera mediante la asociación empresarial y promover la diversificación de las fuentes de ingresos externos aumentando el turismo de países occidentales. Sin embargo, estas medidas reformistas tuvieron, en reacción obligada a las circunstancias, que ser sobrepasadas por otras como la libre circulación de divisas, la reforma agraria y la negociación bilateral de la deuda externa en monedas de libre convertibilidad. Las cuales introdujeron el dualismo en la economía y niveles de inequidad que rompieron los cánones establecidos en los 1970s y 1980s.

El gobierno cubano adoptó para su reinserción económica internacional una estrategia de diversificación de relaciones internacionales y la descentralización de su gestión (E. Álvarez 2000) a numerosas empresas de nueva creación. La cual contrasta con la centralizada y concentrada que caracterizó el periodo de pertenencia al CAME, donde las reglas eran uniformes y los actores involucrados eran pocos. La nueva estrategia representó un complejo y variado esfuerzo de negociación bilateral, incluyendo prácticamente la totalidad de los países industrializados con excepción de EUA. Los países con los cuales mantiene relaciones es el más alto de su historia (165) y con ellos había suscrito en 1999: 141 convenios bilaterales, 100 comerciales y 30 de protección recíproca de inversiones. (E. Álvarez 2000: 18-19 y M. Fernández 2000: 246)

La posición negociadora cubana se benefició en lo político de la influencia de la reciente y exitosa participación europea y latinoamericana en el proceso de Paz de Centroamérica, en que cooperaron a que se impusiera la posición de dejar la conducción y la posterior democratización a los actores nacionales. Y, en lo económico, por el interés de los empresarios e inversionistas de los países europeos por instalarse en la Isla. Aprovechando, la demanda en divisas generada por el creciente flujo de recursos aportados a la economía por las remesas familiares y el turismo y, las ventajas otorgadas al capital extranjero por el gobierno cubano y la ausencia de las empresas de EUA. A la espera del momento en que el mayor acceso a mercados y financiamiento y de turismo con la normalización de relaciones EUA-Cuba, valorizaran sus inversiones y las posibilidades de incrementar sus actividades.

En lo político, la confianza en que el liderazgo cubano iba a ser capaz de realizar la transición a la democracia y las libertades civiles dio paso en la segunda mitad de los 1990s al establecimiento de condiciones exigidas a sus avances hacia la democracia y el respeto de los derechos humanos consagrada en la Posición Común adoptada (1996) por la UE y el consenso del Grupo de Río que se traduciría en la votación anual progresivamente más adversa en la Comisión de Derechos Humanos de Naciones Unidas en Ginebra.

En este accionar, concertado o coincidente, la UE y ALC han tenido en Canadá un asociado en esta suerte de apoyo crítico. Y, el aporte de estos tres socios, en inversiones, tecnología, comercio y flujos turísticos, si bien, han cooperado a la sobrevivencia del régimen y la economía, han ido minando la legitimidad política internacional del régimen y no han permitido la transformación, el crecimiento sostenido y la reducción de la vulnerabilidad externa de la economía. En efecto, el rechazo del gobierno cubano a las exigencias políticas de la UE y ALC ha dado lugar a una situación paradojal en la cual:

- Ha podido negociar bilateralmente la deuda externa pero, no ha logrado un acuerdo global para acceder a créditos a mediano y largo plazo de los gobiernos y la banca de esos países;

- Sigue siendo el único país de ALC que no tiene un acuerdo de cooperación con la UE y, miembro de la Asociación África, Caribe y Pacífico que no beneficia del Acuerdo de Cotonoú; e,

- Ingresó a ALADI, pero carece de la opción de acceder a ser miembro y a los beneficios de los acuerdos de integración comercial regional—MERCOSUR, CAN, CARICOM y MCCA—y, a la participación en las negociaciones del ALCA.

La posición negociadora cubana respondió a algunas dificultades y supuestos que cómo constantes influyeron en el desarrollo de la misma en los 1990s, en particular:

- **La difícil adaptación a su realidad de "pequeña economía" no integrada a bloques regionales:** Durante el periodo 1990-2000, autoridades y críticos del régimen tendieron a considerar el tamaño de la economía al fin del CAME y la Unión Soviética como el referente normativo y la situación posterior como temporal. Y, en particular, las autoridades aspiraban a mantener el poder de negociación política internacional que hizo posible esos volúmenes de comercio exterior

y de inversiones. No fue hasta fines de ese periodo que las metas de producción, exportaciones e importaciones comenzaron a ser revisadas a la baja[1] al tener que aceptar su nueva realidad política-militar internacional y tener que competir con otras pequeñas economías de la Cuenca del Caribe como República Dominicana y Costa Rica. Al competir con ellas, Cuba comprueba la dificultad de hacerlo al no estar beneficiada de la Iniciativa EUA para la Cuenca del Caribe y de los Acuerdos de Cotonoú con la UE ni integrada a CARICOM y el MCCA.

- **La continuidad de las relaciones con Rusia debido a ventajas mutuas y a pesar de las diferencias ideológicas:** En tres ocasiones (1992, 1997 y 2000) Rusia y Cuba intentaron recuperar las inversiones en la Isla en beneficio mutuo y, restablecieron el intercambio de azúcar y petróleo a precios de mercado mundial. (O. Gridchina 1998 y Granma 2001a y b) Aunque ambos mostraron volvió de respetar los acuerdos, el contexto internacional hizo difícil su cumplimiento. Hasta la visita del Presidente Putin a la Isla (diciembre de 2000) el valor estratégico de la Isla parecía continuar, el nivel de importaciones de bienes de capital de Rusia volvió a incrementarse y, volvió a ser discutida la continuidad de macro proyectos inconclusos en el campo de la industria, la energía y la minería. Pero, muy pronto, a comienzos del 2001, Rusia revisa la prioridad estratégica de la Isla teniendo en cuenta las nuevas tecnologías de vigilancia por satélites y replantea en sus negociaciones con Cuba la utilización de la estación de Lourdes, la permanencia de su personal militar a cargo y el pago del alquiler por la operación. Abriendo así el camino a una revisión de las ventajas mutuas en sus relaciones con la Isla, provocando una airada reacción del gobierno (octubre de 2001) y, dando inicio a un distanciamiento entre ambos gobiernos.

---

1. El caso más notorio ha sido el de las exportaciones azucareras donde la meta pasó de los 7 a los 5 millones de toneladas durante la década.

- **La prioridad a la normalización de las relaciones con EUA:** Las autoridades en EUA apostaron por la caída del régimen cubano e inscribieron en la ley Helms Burton la prohibición a comerciar con los bienes incautados en 1960s, el modelo de transición democrática aceptable, que incluye la no presencia de Fidel y Raúl Castro en el poder. No obstante, el liderazgo cubano reconoció el papel dominante de su enemigo en el orden internacional emergente y, la necesidad de normalizar las relaciones con un vecino geográficamente cercano y determinante de su reinserción internacional. Su posición, en consecuencia, combinó el refuerzo de su lugar en la política interna y la re-inserción progresiva en la economía de EUA con la diversificación de sus relaciones internacionales para mantener su poder de negociación bilateral con tan poderoso vecino.

La normalización ha sido esquiva. Pocos dudan de la oportunidad con que: la dirigencia cubana comenzó a deslindar su posición de la de los movimientos definidos como "terroristas" (fines 1990s), abrió el diálogo con la UE, insistió en el contacto con EUA post 11 de Septiembre, continuó su reinserción progresiva en la economía y mantuvo un lugar permanente y desproporcionado a su importancia internacional en la política, incluida de seguridad, interna de EUA. De este modo ha sido capaz de lograr una relativa neutralización de las políticas de desestabilización de la Administración en Washington, pero no las presiones por alinearlo internacionalmente y limitar su capacidad de control de la oposición política interna.

En el escenario negociador cubano 1990-2000, el grupo de apoyo crítico ALC-Canadá-UE, EUA y Rusia constituyen los tres frentes/contrapartes del gobierno isleño. No obstante, estos no han sido coincidentes en sus posiciones, más bien se han alternado en sus momentos de acercamiento-distanciamiento. En el primer quinquenio ALC-Canadá-UE jugaron por el acercamiento, EUA por el distanciamiento y Rusia comenzó cercano a los primeros pero terminó junto a EUA. Y, en el segundo, ALC-Canadá-UE fueron coincidiendo progresivamente en el distanciamiento hasta cerrar posiciones a partir de 1998, mientras se producía un progresivo acercamiento con

EUA y Rusia osciló entre el distanciamiento (1995-1997) y el acercamiento posterior. La situación es aún más compleja si hacemos intervenir los actores internos, así en el caso de la UE:

- La Comisión, el Parlamento y el Consejo europeos han tardado años en alinearse en una u otra posición; y,

- Los empresarios y otros actores (partidos políticos, ONGs, comunidades autónomas regionales, etc.) han jugado, por lo general, a la posición opuesta sin por ello, dejar de contar con el apoyo de sus gobiernos nacionales y de los organismos de la UE.

Esta complejidad del proceso de negociación al no coincidir las posiciones en los principales frentes/contrapartes durante los 1990s, ha hecho más ardua la gestión de las relaciones internacionales al gobierno cubano. Un país en condiciones de vulnerabilidad política y económica tan extremas ha tenido muy escasas posibilidades de rechazar apoyos internacionales ni prescindir de su diversificación por débil que fuera la confiabilidad de estos; logrando ellos ventajas superiores a las habituales. Entre ellos los apoyos nacionales de los países "enemigos" de EUA como Irak, Irán o Libia; de socios ocasionales en ALC como el Perú de Fujimori algunos años y la Venezuela de Chávez más recientemente; y, de asociaciones de países como los del CARICOM y la APC, que nunca pudieron ser totales por la propia dependencia de los mismos de UE y EUA. Adicionalmente, no siendo posible al gobierno cubano mantener una política de alianzas consistente, los cambios en el escenario internacional pueden acarrear aguas inesperadas al molino del apoyo y de las sanciones por acciones similares. Así las relaciones con grupos utilizando la violencia como arma política permite su cooperación en el proceso de paz en Colombia o, le dificulta las relaciones políticas con algunos países miembros de la UE.

La vulnerabilidad política-económica extrema, en varios momentos del periodo 1990-actual sirve para explicar la magnificación en la prensa cubana de las visitas externas de mandatarios o personalidades o el apoyo externo a la economía. No obstante, con ello junto a vender, internamente, la imagen de apoyo internacional y la esperanza de la pronta solución de los problemas de abastecimiento de la población e insuficiencia de créditos externos, el gobierno refuerza la conciencia de vulnerabilidad externa del país en la ciudadanía.

LA EMERGENCIA DE UN NUEVO ESCENARIO NEGOCIADOR EN EL PRIMER BIENIO DEL TERCER MILENIO

El cambio de escenario

El nuevo Milenio ha estado marcado por la aceleración y el incremento de los eventos imprevisibles en el orden internacional. (M. Naim 2002) La coincidencia de la crisis económica con la de seguridad mundiales ha llevado a los grandes poderes nacionales como EU y UE y, a quiénes aspiran a mantener esa posición como Rusia a concentrar su atención en un número cada vez más reducido de problemas y de actores nacionales. Aumentando la incertidumbre para las economías emergentes y los pequeños estados de ser marginados, mantenidos temporalmente en "lista de espera" (stand by) o pasar al centro de la atención mundial. Siendo difícil determinar, o no existir, los criterios generales para merecer uno u otro tratamiento. Como puede observarse al comparar tres economías emergentes con crisis económicas y políticas pero desigualmente importantes en la crisis mundial de seguridad como Argentina, Pakistán y Turquía. La marginación o puesta en lista de espera por las grandes potencias de la primera, contrasta con la atención preferente de las dos últimas.

Este cambio en el funcionamiento del sistema internacional afecta a Cuba y la capacidad negociadora de su gobierno, principalmente por:

- Convertirse la ventaja de ser un país relevante para EUA, Rusia y UE en la década pasada en desventaja al aumentar la aleatoriedad de su marginalidad/importancia internacional;

- Haber pasado el Caribe de zona de seguridad estratégica mundial a regional, en particular, por efecto del cambio en la tecnología de seguridad de rastreo desde puntos fijos a por satélite; y,

- La menor capacidad de respuesta militar cubana como consecuencia del debilitamiento económico y, las diferencias con su principal abastecedor de equipos y suministros, Rusia.

El debilitamiento de la capacidad negociadora del gobierno cubano contrasta con las exigencias crecientes que generan los desafíos que enfrenta, lo cual se aprecia al comparar ambos escenarios. En particular:

- En el escenario negociador precedente el gobierno cubano representaba a una economía pequeña y vulnerable pero a un país relevante política y en términos de seguridad para EUA, UE y Rusia. En cambio, en el emergente, a la pequeñez de su economía se añade el impacto de la crisis mundial sobre la misma y, la pérdida de importancia como país, para ellos. La opción de centrar sus esfuerzos internos y capacidad negociadora externa en superar o minimizar su fragilidad económica no es más viable; pues tiene que conceder igual prioridad merecer la atención de, al menos, uno de esos tres poderes mundiales.

- En el escenario precedente el desafío a su capacidad negociadora consistía en enfrentar la multiplicidad de instancias y de actores en y con quienes negociar, en el emergente es establecer la agenda de negociaciones y manejarse ante los eventos capaces de influir en ella y los resultados de las negociaciones. La aceleración e incremento de dificultad de previsión de los cambios en el orden mundial aumenta la magnitud de ese desafío y la dificultad de acotar la agenda y de adecuarse a sus frecuentes cambios determinados externamente. Y,

- En el escenario anterior el objetivo era mantener su participación en el sistema internacional con posterioridad a la Guerra Fría, a sabiendas que no sería posible hacerlo al mismo nivel. En cambio, en el emergente, la aspiración a una participación mundial se mantiene solo como componente simbólico,[2] concentrando los esfuerzos en lograrlo en el Caribe y Latinoamérica.

---

2. Por ejemplo pretendiendo un liderazgo en el movimiento anti-globalización y, usando el capital humano en salud para participar en campañas mundiales—como el SIDA—o en el fortalecimiento de los sistemas de salud de países de menor desarrollo.

Este breve análisis permite entender como las relaciones de poder en el nuevo escenario obligan al gobierno cubano a adoptar la agenda de los otros y, a los medios para lograr entrar en ella. Quedándole solo como opciones de consideración EUA y UE que tienen una agenda regional caribeña, latinoamericana y continental americana. En el caso del primero por ser el poder regional; y, la segunda por deuda histórica (Caribe), intereses políticos y económicos (AL y EUA) y su participación en el Triángulo Atlántico.[3] Las negociaciones del gobierno cubano con los organismos de integración y países de ALC, en ese contexto, buscan mejorar su posición en la que tienen con EUA y UE, sea obteniendo apoyo político o un acuerdo comercial que favorezca puntualmente su economía. O sea, no es un frente autónomo de negociación como en los 1990s cuando fue barajada la opción de incorporarse a algún acuerdo de integración. En particular MERCOSUR.

Finalmente con Rusia la opción es temporal y menor, pues busca minimizar los costos de la marginación de su centro de interés. En particular, para el suministro de armas, equipos y piezas de repuesto y petróleo y, en las ventas de azúcar.

Las negociaciones UE-Cuba

En el escenario emergente el interés de la UE en Cuba esta vinculado a su política hacia el Caribe (CARICOM y República Dominicana) y, muy especialmente, a la negociación regionalizada establecida con los países APC en el Acuerdo de Cotonoú. (23-6-2000) La inclusión de Cuba, como ya anteriormente la de República Dominicana y Haití, darían otra dimensión política, económica y poblacional a la región Caribe. Lo cual facilita el objetivo del Acuerdo: la reinserción competitiva de micro y pequeñas economías en la mundial, apoyadas financiera y técnicamente con recursos de la Unión durante la transición (2002-2008) de un tratamiento comercial de excepción a las reglas de la OMC. Las exigencias de avanzar hacia la democracia y el respeto de los derechos humanos se mantiene pero la UE (Consejo y Comisión) decide (Agosto-Septiembre-2001) e inicia 1-2 de Diciembre un diálogo político con Cuba, retomando su línea de negociación condicionada (1992-1996) anterior a la adopción de la Posición Común.

La política europea hacia el Caribe se inscribe en un rediseño más global orientado a adecuar las estructuras de la Unión a los desafíos de su ampliación y la biregionalización de sus relaciones con las economías emergentes y de menor desarrollo en África, ALC, Sur y Sudeste de Asia, y el Mediterráneo. Combinando el cambio en las prioridades y la asignación de recursos en las políticas internas, comenzando por la Agrícola Común-PAC,[4] con el de sus posiciones en las negociaciones en la OMC y las biregionales. Este cambio de posición con respecto a los subsidios y el acceso de los productos agrícolas a la producción y el mercado europeos, respectivamente; ya pudo observarse con anterioridad en la propuesta hecha al MERCOSUR (agosto de 2001) y en la Conferencia de la OMC en Doha-Qatar (noviembre de 2001).

La UE, como era de esperar, encontró una dura oposición de los países de la ACP, especialmente los del Caribe, a aceptar la regionalización de las negociaciones, a pesar del incentivo de 22 billones de Euros disponibles para apoyar la transición a condiciones de competitividad mundial. Los países del Caribe entendieron, finalmente, que esa condición era similar a la que la UE había adoptado biregionalmente con el resto de AL estableciendo su tradicional triple nivel (país, Acuerdo de Integración, ALC) en sus negociaciones. Reforzando sus vínculos con AL,[5] en especial con los de la Cuenca del Caribe (F. León 2002b) y su

---

3. EUA-UE-ALC.

4. La Comisión acordó introducir ante el Parlamento y el Consejo una reducción 2003-2005 del 20 % de los fondos de la PAC, que suman más del 50% de su presupuesto, modificando el subsidio a productos del agro por uno global a las empresas en función de su modernización y los aportes al desarrollo rural y la protección ambiental. Uno de los objetivos de este cambio es facilitar las negociaciones de la UE en la OMC, donde puede mejorar su posición con la reducción de las tarifas de las importaciones agrícolas.

5. En la XXIII Conferencia de Jefes de Estados y de Gobierno del CARICOM (Georgetown, Guyana 3-5 de julio de 2002) acordó utilizar el borrador de acuerdo de libre comercio entre Trinidad Tobago y Costa Rica para iniciar una negociación más general con ese país de todos los miembros. Y, discutió que para lograr el objetivo de expandirse más allá de sus confines geográficos, Belice, Guyana y Suriname deben servir como puertas de acceso para incrementar el comercio con Latinoamérica.

conformidad con la negociación regionalizada acordada por los países del Caribe y la UE en la Segunda Cumbre UE-ALC (22-24 de mayo de 2002) en Madrid.

Para el gobierno cubano la nueva posición UE en las negociaciones con el Caribe y con el país representa un contexto regional favorable y una oportunidad para salir del impasse creado a partir de la adopción de la Posición Común en 1996. Y, aunque reiteró su oposición a las condicionantes políticas que se le imponían continuo negociando con la UE. En ese contexto, tal y como capitalizando sus relaciones con el Caribe desde los 1980s y una política de presencia renovada en África desde fines de los noventa[6] había logrado su ingreso como 78vo miembro de la ACP (14 de diciembre de 2000), anunció a través del Ministro de Relaciones Exteriores (agosto de 2001) su intención de ingresar al Acuerdo de Cotonoú. (J. Oramas 2001) Comenzando, a partir de ese momento, una estrategia de presión para lograrlo, cuyo primer éxito fue la declaración de apoyo de los Cancilleres de la ACP. En la cual pedían, considerando los resultados de las reuniones Troika Comunitaria-Gobierno cubano (1-2 de diciembre de 2001) a la Habana, entre otros:

- A la Unión Europea... traducir este espíritu en una revisión sustantiva de su Posición Común en aras de tratar a Cuba de manera justa e imparcial.

- Su firme esperanza de que tal revisión de la Posición Común de la UE conduzca al acceso de Cuba al Acuerdo de Asociación ACP-UE, Acuerdo de Cotonoú, sin ningunas condicionantes especiales o injustas. E,

- Instruye al Presidente del Consejo de Ministros ACP y al Secretario General del Grupo ACP transmitir a la UE... la posición del Grupo ACP según consta en esta resolución.[7]

La intención de las autoridades cubanas era de lograr que sus negociaciones con la UE estuvieran sujetas a las normas comunes a los países ACP y no a la Posición Común sobre Cuba, lo que facilitaría su participación en los Acuerdos de Cotonoú y la firma del de Cooperación. El portavoz de la Comisión, sin embargo, manifestó que los avances hechos por Cuba en materia de derechos humanos y políticos eran insuficientes para modificar la esencia de la Posición Común. No obstante ello, el gobierno cubano continuó recabando apoyo en las instancias de la UE (Consejo, Comisión, Parlamento) y en los países miembros confiado en lograr el acuerdo de los 15 miembros del Consejo de la UE e ingresar a Cotonoú en 2001. Aunque postergó la presentación de su candidatura para ese ingreso.

El periodo de la Presidencia española de la UE (enero-junio de 2002) fue, como vaticinaron algunos especialistas (J. Roy 2001), poco propicio para la continuidad del diálogo político iniciado en la Habana en diciembre del año anterior bajo la Presidencia belga. Las declaraciones del Jefe de Gobierno español en Praga (3 de diciembre de 2001) en que anticipó que la UE mantendría la Posición Común sobre Cuba porque no había razones suficientes para modificarla, anticiparon el final poco feliz de las gestiones cubanas. Sin embargo, es exagerado sostener que una Presidencia de tan corta duración ni un país sea capaz de determinar las decisiones del Consejo, la Comisión y el Parlamento de la UE.

El camino hacia el entendimiento con la UE era difícil pues tenía que vencer la prueba de la Revisión Anual de la situación de derechos humanos en Cuba en la 58ava Comisión de Naciones Unidas en Ginebra en marzo. Donde, como es sabido nuevamente, el gobierno cubano fue mal evaluado en una votación donde no participó EUA y la mayoría de países que apoyaron esa conclusión eran europeos y latinoameri-

---

6. Desde 1982 el CARICOM estableció una Comisión bilateral con Cuba y desde comienzos del 2000, ella es invitada a participar en algunas de sus reuniones internas y con otros países. Con República Dominicana las relaciones se oficializaron y reforzaron en los 1990s con un beneficioso comercio para la balanza externa de ese país y el abastecimiento alimenticio cubano. Finalmente, con África la cooperación militar de los 1980s ha dado paso a la humanitaria en educación y, especialmente, en salud.

7. Resolución sobre el acceso de Cuba al Acuerdo de Asociación ACP-UE del Consejo de Ministros de ACP, reunido en Bruselas el 6 y 7 de diciembre de 2001.

canos. Lo cual provocó críticas inusualmente duras y poco diplomáticas de las autoridades cubanas a los países miembros de la UE[8] y a los latinoamericanos, especialmente al Presidente de Uruguay. Y, era un signo de que la evaluación de los avances cubanos en el tema por la UE en junio tendría un tenor similar, como efectivamente resultó.

En una entrevista al diario *El País*, el Vicepresidente Carlos Lage durante su estancia en Madrid representando a Cuba en la Cumbre UE-ALC en mayo de 2002 esbozaría, el análisis que, posteriormente contendría la Nota Diplomática (27 de junio de 2002) comunicada a través de su Embajada en la Habana por el Gobierno Cubano a la Presidencia española. En particular, al acusar a la UE de "hacer planteamientos sobre asuntos internos que se aplican solo a Cuba, lo que supone un doble rasero y una doble moral." (J. M. Larraya 2001) En la Nota, adicionalmente, hay fuertes recriminaciones al gobierno español por continuar sirviendo los intereses de EUA al obstaculizar el diálogo político UE-Cuba, como en 1996 al promover la aprobación de la Posición Común. Pero sin dejar de reconocer que esa decisión es de los 15 países y compromete a la Comisión y al Consejo UE, a la cual acusa de inconsistencia en materia de derechos humanos al negarse a aprobar un conjunto de resoluciones de Naciones Unidas sobre el tema.

Aún en ese contexto, las presiones/buenos oficios de los gobiernos de los países ACP, especialmente, del Caribe sobre la UE para lograr la admisión "por vía rápida" (fast track) de Cuba al Acuerdo de Cotonoú continuaron. Y, nuevamente, en la Cumbre ACP de Fidji (17-19 de julio de 2002) insistieron recibiendo de parte del Comisario para Asuntos Económicos y el Comercio-UE Pascal Lamy, la negativa fundamentada en que: el país candidato no satisfacía los principios básicos del Acuerdo en materia de democracia y derechos humanos.[9] Lo que constituyó, a decir del

jefe de la delegación cubana una humillación y una bofetada a Cuba.

Mientras todo ello ocurría, en el frente interno, los empresarios de los países UE con actividades en la Isla creyeron oportuno sintetizar en un documento de trabajo, entregado al gobierno a través de las representaciones diplomáticas de sus países en la Habana, los obstáculos que el marco administrativo y legal de su comercio exterior e inversiones representa para operar en forma competitiva con otros países del Caribe. Documento que las representaciones diplomáticas apoyaron como una demostración del interés de sus gobiernos en Cuba y en su futuro. Entre las principales quejas y demandas destacamos:

- La falta de seguridad jurídica y de un marco legal estable y transparente que, en particular, al no ser uniforme concede ventajas a unas empresas sobre otras.

- El control estatal de la distribución interna de los productos y del mercado de trabajo y, el uso de los impuestos como forma de sancionar la conducta de las empresas más que como medio de recaudación fiscal. Y,

- Las deficiencias del sistema financiero, en particular, respecto a las firmas de asociación estado-empresa extranjera a las cuales virtualmente no financia. Complementado por las dificultades que las firmas estatales tienen para cumplir sus obligaciones de pago incrementando el riesgo para las extranjeras de operar en el país.

Las diferencias políticas y económicas UE-Cuba y las presiones/condicionantes de la primera se mantienen buscando impulsar el comienzo de las reformas políticas y una segunda fase de las económicas en la Isla. Al quedar fuera del Acuerdo de Cotonoú, el gobierno cubano pierde los medios técnicos y financieros específicos para la región del Caribe puestos a disposición por la UE para facilitar la transición de estas peque-

---

8. En la Nota diplomática a la Presidencia española el gobierno cubano sostiene que las consultas multilaterales sobre la materia con las contrapartes europeas acordadas durante la visita de la Troika comunitaria en diciembre de 2001, no habían sido convocadas por la Comisión, el Consejo y la Troika de la UE. Lo cual, de ser cierto, era otra señal igualmente negativa de parte de la UE.

9. De acuerdo a la versión dada a la prensa por la delegada de Barbados que encabezó el Grupo del Caribe en esa Cumbre. (P. O´Connor 2002)

ñas economías a condiciones más competitivas en su mercado y en el mundial. Una ayuda que, hasta el presente, el ALCA no ha considerado para los pequeños estados y economías.

Este tratamiento, especialmente apreciado por esos beneficiarios, resulta aún más atractivo para Cuba que esta excluida del acceso a préstamos de mediano y largo plazo y, ha carecido en 1989-2002 de un calendario de transición a la competitividad internacional y, en un mercado mayor al del antiguo CAME como es la UE. En adición, como nunca ha tenido acceso privilegiado al mercado europeo, la Isla no perdería derechos como el resto del Caribe sino que participaría en la negociación y de los beneficios de las nuevas condiciones de hacerlo. Este hecho cambiaría la perspectiva de los inversionistas, particularmente europeos, que anticipando las reglas de acceso a mercado y de subsidios emergentes seleccionan países desde donde exportar a la UE los productos que actualmente gozan de protección. Entre ellos hay varios, como el azúcar, en los cuales Cuba puede tener o recuperar competitividad internacional. La aspiración del gobierno cubano, sin embargo, es aún mayor pues incluye acceder también al acuerdo de Cooperación que discutió infructuosamente a mediados de la década pasada, con lo cual tendría acceso a otros organismos de financiamiento de la UE para países de economías emergentes[10] y de menor desarrollo.

La carrera del gobierno cubano fue, como en las pruebas ciclistas, "contra el reloj" y su pretensión se estrelló contra la oposición de la UE a su entrada al Acuerdo de Cotonoú. Y, consiguientemente no estará presente en el inicio de las negociaciones UE-Caribe (27 de septiembre de 2002) del Acuerdo de Asociación Económica-Economic Partnership Agreement-EPA.

Finalmente, la negativa de la UE de cambiar las normas de la Posición Común por las de la ACP y la iniciativa de los empresarios y las embajadas europeas en la Habana refuerzan la decisión de mantener la espe-

cificidad en las negociaciones con Cuba. Lo cual no anula, pero si limita, los avances que el gobierno cubano puede hacer con los países miembros, individualmente considerados y, con las instancias sub-nacionales (estados, comunidades autónomas, etc.) de los mismos.

Las negociaciones EUA-Cuba

Durante los 1990s Cuba ha evolucionado hacia el patrón caribeño de economía y de relaciones con EUA: importancia de las comunicaciones telefónicas, viajes y remesas familiares; concentración de su población emigrante y de la influencia política en una o unas pocas ciudades; y, papel estratégico en el tráfico de drogas, la inmigración ilegal y la protección ambiental de la cuenca marítima común. Manteniendo, importantes diferencias: dependencia comercial marginal; y, conflictividad asociada a la oposición entre regímenes políticos e ideológicos. Estando en el centro de la discusión si el régimen cubano continua o no siendo un peligro para la seguridad de EUA. Estos cambios, aunque influyentes, no tienen el peso en la configuración del nuevo escenario de las relaciones EUA-Cuba que la emergencia del sistema unipolar de seguridad, de ordenamiento político y la economía mundiales. El papel dominante de EUA, previsible desde el fin de la Guerra Fría, solo concretaría en el Nuevo Milenio.

Aunque no existen negociaciones pues los contactos formales son puntuales,[11] la normalización de las relaciones entre ambos países evoluciona, principalmente, bajo la influencia de los grupos de presión, a favor y contra de la misma. Su análisis se simplifica cuando el interés de estos actores esta centrado en la adopción o derogación de medidas de normalización, como fue el caso con la suspensión del embargo de alimentos y medicinas en junio de 2000. Y, posteriormente, del levantamiento de la prohibición de los viajes turísticos a la Isla.

La dinámica de las relaciones ha sido comandada por la influencia crítica que desde las elecciones presiden-

---

10. Incluyendo, eventualmente, el Banco Europeo de Fomento y Reconstrucción que apoya la transición a una economía de mercado de los antiguos países socialistas de Europa y Asia.

11. La única instancia es la establecida a fines de 1994 para regular la migración ilegal de cubanos.

ciales ha logrado la comunidad cubana en EUA gracias a la importancia decisiva del estado de la Florida en esas y otras elecciones, como las de Noviembre 2002 para gobernadores de varios estados y congresistas. Y, los cambios de política exterior en la Administración del actual Presidente Bush desde el 11-9, en particular, que se han traducido en las presiones de Washington para obtener el alineamiento del gobierno cubano en la lucha contra el terrorismo. Donde los gestos de la Habana han sido, declarar que está dispuesta a permitir la libre inspección de sus instalaciones capaces de producir armas biológicas de destrucción masiva; y, contactos para intercambiar información útil en la prevención de actos terroristas. A este respecto, la Administración EUA no ha aceptado las ofertas cubanas de establecer un canal formal para tratar de estos asuntos, como existe en materia de inmigración ilegal desde 1995, por lo que han debido seguir otros canales. El argumento último de la Casa Blanca es que la información suministrada no ha sido confiable. En el caso de la oferta de permitir la inspección, esta fue obtenida por la mediación informal del ex Presidente Carter durante su viaje a la Isla. El intercambio de información sobre actividades terroristas puede facilitarse gracias a la activación (2001), por el gobierno cubano, de la membresía en la INTERPOL.

Los cambios en la posición de la Habana en las negociaciones con EUA responden al supuesto de que la estrategia de Washington, a mediano y largo plazo, es el levantamiento gradual del embargo económico pero continuando las actividades de desestabilización del régimen. El liderazgo político de la Isla, habría cedido al argumento que el fin gradual del embargo puede ser la modalidad más favorable para lograr mantener el régimen y el avance de la reinserción internacional de la economía. Sus medios más usados incluyen, la batalla de opinión pública en EUA sobre la obsolescencia de la política exterior y las concesiones a los grupos de interés económico interesados en el comercio con la Isla. En lo político, el gobierno cubano se defiende alegando la legitimidad de sus acti-

vidades, incluidas las de espionaje contra EUA, como respuesta a las actividades terroristas permitidas desde el territorio de ese país; y, trata de vincular a su oposición política interna de su enemigo. Y, en lo económico, hace compras al contado a grupos empresariales interesados en realizar exportaciones para lograr su apoyo en la normalización de las esas relaciones.

La compra de medicamentos y, particularmente, de productos agrícolas y agroindustriales ha logrado influir favorablemente en los intereses económicos y los medios políticos de estados, como los del Medio Oeste y los productores arroceros del Sur, cuyos votos pueden ser decisivos para el levantamiento de la prohibición de los viajes turísticos por el Congreso y el Presidente. El monto estimado de las compras cubanas ha variado, recientemente, al prometer el Presidente Castro a los empresarios y políticos[12] que participaron en la Feria de productos agrícolas en la Habana (26-30 de septiembre) que está dispuesto a usar no solo el ingreso por viajes turísticos sino también de remesas familiares procedentes de EUA. De los algo más de cien ahora comprados, o prometido comprar, podrían pasar a varios cientos de millones de dólares. Tanto como lo permitan otras compras en el exterior vitales para la economía cubana como las petroleras.

Es importante analizar, además, la repercusión de la autorización de los viajes turísticos y las mayores compras de medicinas y productos del agro de EUA en sus relaciones con los actuales abastecedores (Canadá, y los países de ALC y los miembros la UE), dado el margen importante de intervención en el comercio exterior que tiene un régimen como el cubano. El incremento del número de turistas procedentes de EUA beneficiará tanto al régimen como a las empresas extranjeras que operan en las actividades turísticas y de producción para abastecer la demanda interna de estas. Los ingresos fiscales y los de las empresas estatales serán mayores, pero también las utilidades de las extranjeras. Y, estas últimas se verán en la necesidad de invertir adicionalmente en la Isla para

---

12. Un reciente análisis de la Cuba Policy Foundation, Washington, D.C., muestra que participaron compañías de 33 estados, que eligen 66 senadores, y 104 distritos congresionales. De los distritos 49 son republicanos y 55 demócratas.

captar ese creciente flujo turístico. En cambio, la proporción de las compras a los actuales abastecedores canadienses, europeos y latinoamericanos, mermarán. En resumen, el gobierno cubano gana un arma importante para incrementar sus inversiones extranjeras y, aumenta su poder de negociación con los abastecedores de medicinas y de productos del agro que fueron favorecidos por prohibición de las importaciones de EUA.

Muchos defensores y detractores de la normalización de las relaciones EUA-Cuba coinciden en el impacto negativo que la falta de acceso al mayor mercado del mundo tiene para la economía cubana y, el efecto corrosivo que las medidas de acción/reacción de las partes en conflicto tienen en la equidad social y el bienestar de la población cubana.[13] No es difícil, sin embargo, identificar opciones abiertas al gobierno cubano para enfrentar el embargo menos negativas para la equidad y más dinamizadoras del crecimiento económico en la Isla, en particular, de las remesas familiares. Pero ellas, como sería autorizar empresas privadas empleando asalariados, requerirían de reformas que son resistidas por el liderazgo político isleño. En particular, por servir de base a un desarrollo de la sociedad civil al reducir el control estatal de los mercados de trabajo y de bienes. La apuesta de los que en EUA piensan que el levantamiento gradual del embargo favorecería la transición a la democracia, el respeto de los derechos humanos y la economía de mercado, es de que el régimen tendrá que hacer reformas en esa dirección para enfrentar la creciente inequidad, la modernización de su economía y responder a las exigencias de los cambios en las reglas del comercio regional y mundial.

Las negociaciones Rusia/Cuba

Mientras en los 1990s Rusia intentaba tener una contribución relevante y aprovechar de la reinserción internacional cubana para la suya propia; en la presente década, al transformarse sus relaciones con EUA y la UE, ha dado pasos para ayudar en la eliminación de algunos de los puntos en conflicto entre EUA y Cuba, que fueron producto de su alineamiento y la cooperación de la Unión Soviética durante la Guerra Fría. Entre ellas, el proyecto de la planta termonuclear de Juraguá (Cienfuegos) y la estación de Lourdes. Simultáneamente con buscar, gracias a su incorporación al grupo de países miembros del Club de París, de usar de esa condición para obligar a Cuba a negociar su deuda con ella. Contribuyendo en mayo 2001 al fracaso de las conversaciones entre el gobierno cubano y los otros países acreedores miembros del Club.

La reinserción política, en seguridad y económica internacional de Rusia hace que sus relaciones con Cuba sean cada vez más asimétricas. Esta depende de la ex-potencia desde en aspectos críticos de seguridad como la renovación de equipos y armamentos hasta el mantenimiento de la flota de aviación comercial. Mientras que sus aportes son crecientemente marginales, como en el caso del azúcar, salvo cuando le permite a Moscú fortalecer sus relaciones con EUA y con UE.

La combinación de la asimetría de las relaciones y su importancia como parte de las relaciones de Rusia con EUA y UE hacen que sus negociaciones con Cuba tengan lugar en un clima de desconfianza sino de conflictividad, pero el gobierno cubano no puede obviarlas. El argumento cubano del interés de terceros en reemplazar a Rusia ha surtido poco efecto, como ha podido comprobarse en el caso de la eventual utilización de la base de Lourdes por China.

Desde el virulento intercambio de notas diplomáticas después del anuncio del fin del contrato por el uso de la base de Lourdes y la retirada de las tropas rusas estacionadas en Cuba, ambos gobiernos han adoptado un enfoque pragmático en sus relaciones. Ya en diciembre de 2001, La Habana re-iniciaba los vuelos de Cubana de Aviación a Moscú donde la flota aérea tiene su mantenimiento y, las compras de azúcar por Rusia se han mantenido. No obstante, el deterioro de las relaciones, fruto de la mutua desconfianza, continua. El reciente anuncio (octubre de 2002) de los Presidentes Putin y Lagos, durante la visita del último a Moscú y San Petersburgo, de que Rusia utiliza-

---

13. Entre las excepciones puede verse W. Trumbull 2001.

ría a Chile como base de sus operaciones empresariales en América Latina, un lugar que a comienzos de los 1990s fue prometido a Cuba, es la muestra más reciente de las consecuencias del deterioro de las relaciones Rusia-Cuba.

Nota sobre las relaciones ALC-Cuba

En la presente década las relaciones regionales latinoamericanas y caribeñas han ganado en consistencia al coordinarse el funcionamiento del sistema panamericano (OEA) y el de generación de consensos ALC a través del Grupo de Río (GR). Este proceso ha respondido, en buena parte, a la triple negociación en que enfrentan los países para la creación del ALCA, la de los acuerdos de asociación económica con la UE y las que tienen lugar en la OMC en la actual ronda de Doha. Cuba al estar excluida del sistema panamericano y no haber aceptado la cláusula democrática del GR, no participa a esas negociaciones; salvo en las de las Naciones Unidas donde es miembro del GRULA.

Sus negociaciones en ALC son bilaterales y, a lo sumo siguen patrones comunes como los establecidos en la ALADI. Como los demás países miembros participan a las negociaciones del ALCA, al concluir (2005) este proceso los acuerdos bilaterales de Cuba con países miembros de la ALADI no podrán contener cláusulas que contravengan las reglas del acuerdo hemisférico. (P. Da Motta y M. Halperin) Con lo cual los bilaterales con Cuba estarán condicionados por los del ALCA.

El único de los esquemas de formación de consensos regionales en el que participa Cuba es la Asociación de Estados del Caribe, formada por las pequeñas economías del Caribe y Centroamérica más Colombia, México y Venezuela. El éxito del gobierno cubano en obtener el apoyo del Caribe, contrasta con las discretas/conflictivas con los centroamericanos. Con Colombia siguen en lo económico un patrón bilateral poco diferente que con otros países suramericanos y, en lo político están marcados por el apoyo del gobierno cubano en las negociaciones de paz, el cual ha continuado con el nuevo gobierno del Presidente Álvaro Uribe. Finalmente, con México y Venezuela las relaciones son más importantes, sea por la solidaridad de décadas y el carácter integral de las mexicanas y, la

especial modalidad establecida con Venezuela desde fines de 1990s. No obstante, en ambos casos las relaciones conocen un impasse. Con México a raíz del conflicto surgido en torno a la invitación a la Conferencia de Naciones Unidas en Monterrey, muy personalizado en el Canciller Castañeda, del cual el último episodio ha sido el cambio del embajador mexicano en la Habana en septiembre de 2002. En el caso de Venezuela por la crisis de gobernabilidad que enfrenta el Presidente Hugo Chávez que hace peligrar la posibilidad de terminar su mandato, crisis esta en la que las relaciones con Cuba y, en especial con entre ambos Presidentes, son un factor en el conflicto entre gobierno y oposición. Las relaciones con México y Venezuela ocupan un lugar e insumen un tiempo importante en política internacional del gobierno, entre otras, por no tener el gobierno alternativa que compense ventajas del acuerdo logrado en financiamiento y abastecimiento petrolero con pago parcial en servicios. Y en el de México porque, ajeno a que pueda ser reemplazado como alternativa de las importaciones de EUA que siguen prohibidas y de abastecimiento petrolero, a ningún país turístico del Caribe, como Cuba, le conviene tener malas relaciones con la segunda potencia regional, después de EUA, en esa actividad.

La posible elección de Luis Ignacio Lula da Silva como Presidente de Brasil el 27 de Octubre próximo constituye una nueva oportunidad de establecer relaciones de cooperación y comerciales más amplias con la principal economía de ALC. Es de esperar que las experiencias mexicana y venezolana sirvan de lección a la dirigencia cubana para no repetir los mismos errores con Brasil, en particular, el quedar envuelto en el conflicto oposición gobierno.

PERSPECTIVAS E IMPACTO DE LAS NEGOCIACIONES

Perspectivas

Las negociaciones con la UE orientadas a lograr la participación en el Acuerdo de Cotonoú y el de Cooperación y, el proceso encaminado a lograr el levantamiento de la prohibición de viajes turísticos de ciudadanos de EUA, siguen marcadas por exigencia de una transición a la democracia, el respeto de los derechos humanos con énfasis en los civiles y, la economía de mercado, la cual es rechazada por el gobierno. Aunque UE y EUA usan parámetros diferentes para juzgar los avances en ese proceso, en ambos casos, las exigencias están establecidas en la Posición Común y la ley Helms Burton, aprobadas por el Consejo UE y por el Congreso y el Presidente EU, respectivamente. La solución al impasse entre UE, EUA y Cuba que genera sus posiciones sobre las exigencias políticas, ha entrado en una fase de contradicciones. Junto a las declaraciones de apertura del gobierno cubano al comienzo del diálogo político con la UE y, en la concepción y desarrollo de la "mediación sui generis" como de la visita del ex-Presidente Carter a la Isla. El mismo gobierno, levanta el muro de la reforma constitucional para prolongar simbólicamente el régimen más allá del proceso de sucesión del liderazgo político actual, volviendo más de una década después a una postura que recuerda a los habitantes de la antigua Numancia prefiriendo, en el caso de la dirigencia cubana, el aislamiento a la reinserción internacional.

Mi hipótesis de trabajo es que esta contradicción es resultante del doble desafío, político y económico, que tienen que enfrentar el gobierno y el régimen para su viabilidad. El político donde el gobierno, no es más capaz de garantizarla militarmente; y, ante la incapacidad de aislar la población de la influencia externa, tiene que recurrir a la movilización política y reafirmación ideológica para legitimar y dar eficacidad al control de las organizaciones de masas y del Partido Comunista para sostener el régimen. Y el económico donde, al no aceptar las reformas exigidas en las negociaciones para su reinserción en la economía mundial, es incapaz de obtener los recursos y realizar los cambios requeridos a su viabilidad. En lo fundamental, poniendo fin a la economía dual (estatal peso/joint venture divisa) y sus consecuencias: inequidad social, incremento de la población pobre/vulnerable y, ausentismo/baja productividad laboral.

Atrapado en esta contradicción, el gobierno trata de conciliar la rigidez de su estrategia política y en las negociaciones internacionales abriendo algunas ventanas al pragmatismo. En particular:

- Combinando la rigidez en las negociaciones UE con el pragmatismo en los acuerdos bilaterales con los países miembros y los inversionistas y

empresarios extranjeros. Introduciendo los cambios económicos en forma sostenida (F. León 2002 a) pero aparentando mantener las reglas de juego socialistas. Y,

- Alentando a los grupos favorables a la normalización de las relaciones en EUA con la esperanza en la eficacia de los cambios graduales en el régimen político a la del embargo. Y con medidas para generar seguridad en los intereses económicos que los ingresos que generen las remesas y los viajes turísticos serán utilizados para comprarles alimentos y medicinas.

Consciente de la marginalidad creciente de Cuba en las negociaciones internacionales, el gobierno confía en su capacidad de mantener su importancia en la política interna EUA y, la presión de los inversionistas y empresarios europeos en sus países para mantener a la Isla en la agenda de decisiones nacionales. Las evidencias en los últimos meses indican, sin embargo, como el riesgo a aumentado exponencialmente tanto como el desgaste de su habilidad para situarse en la opinión pública y los centros de decisiones. Cuba esta lejos de ocupar la atención de Argentina de los países e inversionistas europeos y norteamericanos. Y, el apoyo de los congresistas de estados donde hay empresas interesadas en la venta de alimentos y medicinas en EUA, es decisiva para lograr la aprobación en el Congreso de la autorización de los viajes turísticos, aumentar los ingresos por ese concepto y, consiguientemente, la importancia de la Isla en las exportaciones agrícolas del país. Sin embargo, el manejo de las relaciones quedará en manos del Ejecutivo, para el cual Cuba es marginal como elemento en su guerra al terrorismo y como aporte a la solución de la inestabilidad del crecimiento económico del país. Y, algo similar ocurre en Rusia y en los países relevantes para el gobierno cubano en ALC. Los comunistas rusos tienen otras prioridades en su lucha contra el Presidente Putin y, los dirigentes del PRI y el PRD que negociar con el Presidente Fox para dedicar más de unos pocos días a las denuncias de Fidel Castro y sus ministros.

Impactos

Mi hipótesis de trabajo privilegia la unificación de las condiciones de negociación y el proceso de sucesión del liderazgo político en la determinación de los impactos de las negociaciones internacionales cubanas. Para resolver su problema económico básico, la reprogramación de la deuda externa y lograr el acceso a prestamos de mediano y largo plazo de las instituciones financieras internacionales.

El estado cubano, cualquiera sea el gobierno que la represente, tiene que tener en cuenta a todos sus acreedores miembros del Club de París y a EUA. Las soluciones al diferendo sobre ambas deudas son ahora interdependientes, porque Cuba tiene que poner sobre la mesa del Club de Paris toda su deuda. Y, de otra parte, la dinámica del proceso de sucesión política es la que determinará quiénes son los dirigentes cubanos-actuales y potenciales-tenidos en cuenta en las negociaciones. Lo cual explica la eliminación de candidatos que, como el canciller Robaina, se salgan de los canales del Partido y de la línea de mando establecida por el Presidente Castro para hacer avanzar sus aspiraciones a sucederlo en la cima del poder.

Al producirse la unificación de la deuda externa (2001) en medio de la crisis económica que afecta a Cuba, como al resto del Caribe, la situación se agravó dada la vulnerabilidad de corto plazo de la economía. En efecto, desde mediados 2001, el gobierno cubano debió plantear la necesidad de que se constituyera un consorcio de bancos e instituciones acreedoras para renegociar el pago de su deuda a corto plazo (proveedores e instituciones financieras), que constituye un 40% (CEPAL 2002) del total. Esta negociación conjunta no ha tenido lugar, obligando a arreglos bilaterales limitados por la reducida capacidad de pago del país, con la consiguiente suspensión de los suministros por parte de algunos importantes proveedores internacionales, como sucede con el petróleo venezolano.

En un contexto de unificación de la deuda externa no es más un problema del gobierno de turno sino que a todos los participantes pues comprometen al estado cubano y; por ende, la posición adoptada tiene que ser una política de estado. Esta situación emergente, costará mucho aceptar al gobierno, acostumbrado a pensar que es el único poder y a la permanencia sin límites de los dirigentes. Desde junio de 2000, con el desmayo sufrido por el Presidente Castro en un acto público en El Cotorro, Provincia Habana, la eventualidad de un fin abrupto a su continuidad en las riendas del gobierno aceleró el proceso de sucesión. Haciendo más necesario el consenso en la posición negociadora lo cual se advirtió en la mayor uniformidad en las declaraciones de los miembros del gobierno. No dudo, que también haya contribuido al redoblado control y la dureza del ataque a los opositores, dentro y fuera del país, como a los aspirantes con posibilidades sucesorias que gozaban de apoyos en los medios políticos de los países acreedores de la deuda externa.

A su vez, la exigencia a negociar con un gobierno democráticamente elegido, que esta detrás de la exigencia al pluralismo político y a las elecciones libres, de UE y EUA; muestra el interés en que los acuerdos respondan a una posición y compromiso de estado y, no de un partido. Para los hombres de estado europeos y estadounidenses las relaciones internacionales conducentes a acuerdos durables y viables exigen del libre juego del pluralismo político. El mismo que es resistido por la dirigencia cubana actual, al igual que lo es por europeos y norteamericanos su adhesión a la democracia directa preconizada por la dirigencia cubana, y reiterada, en Junio pasado, con la recolección de firmas para hacer prácticamente imposible el cambio de régimen en el marco de la actual constitución.

BIBLIOGRAFÍA

Elena Álvarez, 2000, "Descentralización y diversificación en la Economía Cubana: Nuevas bases para la cooperación internacional." *Cuba: Investiga-* *ción Económica*, Año 6, Número 1, Enero-Marzo, pp.-23

CEPAL, 2001, *Balance Preliminar de las Economías de América Latina y el Caribe*, Santiago de Chile, Diciembre.

Pedro da Motta y Marcelo Halperin, 2001, "Definición de una Estrategia para la Preservación de las Preferencias Intra-ALADI en el Acuerdo que establecería el ALCA," Montevideo: ALADI, 26 de Marzo.

Marcelo Fernández F., 2000, "Cuba: Recuperación económica y apertura. Nuevas reflexiones sobre 'el período especial,'" *Revista Bimestre Cubana*, Época III, Número 12, Enero Junio, pp. 235-249.

Granma, 2001a, "Declaración Oficial del Gobierno de la República de Cuba," Octubre 18.

Granma, 2001b, Editorial "Párrafo Infame," Octubre 27.

Olga V. Gridchina, 1998, "Cuba-Rusia: ¿Reanimación de las relaciones económicas?" En Eduardo Cuenca García, Coordinador, *Enfoque sobre la Reciente Economía Cubana*, Madrid: Agualarga Editores, pp 139-149.

Carlos Lage, 2002, " Entrevista," *El País*, Mayo 21.

José Miguel Larraya, 2001, "Carlos Lage, Vicepresidente de Cuba: El futuro político del país pasa por un partido más fuerte," *El País Internacional*, Mayo 16.

Francisco León, 2002a, "Reformas económicas y negociaciones internacionales: La coyuntura actual," en Mauricio de Miranda, editor (en preparación).

Francisco León, 2002b, "El Caribe en la Construcción de la de una relación biregional estratégica UE-ALC," en José María Alsina, Ed., *Conferencia Preparatoria de la Segunda Cumbre UE-ALC*, Madrid: Tribuna Americana, Casa América (en prensa).

José Mayo, 2002, Entrevista al Ministro de Gobierno Ricardo Cabrisas. "La Isla está preparada para enfrentar la crisis económica internacional," *Granma*, 8 de Enero.

Moisés Naim, 2002, "A virulent new strain of crisis," *The Financial Times*, May 13.

Peter O'Connor, 2002, " Europe Excludes Cuba From Aid Funds," The Associated Press, July 19.

Joaquín Oramas, 2001, "Dipuesta Cuba a ingresar a la Convención de Cotonú," *Granma Internacional*, 24 de Agosto.

Joaquín Roy, 2001, "Cuba y la Unión Europea," *Diario Montañés*, España, Agosto 31.

William N. Trumbull, 2001, "Imperfect Methodology But the Right Results? The USITC Report on the Economic Impact of U. S. Sanctions with Respect to Cuba," *Cuba in Transition—Volume 11*, ASCE, pp 105-110.

SELECTED ASPECTS OF CUBA'S INTELLECTUAL PROPERTY LAWS

Jesús (Jay) Sanchelima

The main purpose of this paper is to address selective topics of Cuba's intellectual property laws, to compare them with U.S. laws, when applicable, and to address potential effects on U.S. intellectual property (IP) rights.

CURRENT CUBAN INTELLECTUAL PROPERTY LEGISLATION

Patents and Utility Models

Cuban patent laws are codified in Decree 68 of May 14, 1983.[1] In its introductory paragraphs, it is specified that the new laws are intended to replace the former laws considered obsolete. The new laws were necessary to conform to Cuba's current development, the construction of socialism, and the fact that Cuba is a developing country and a member of the socialist community.[2] These prefatory words should alert an intellectual property lawyer that the social policies intended to be advanced are different. Hence, results may be unpredictable in litigation unless the practitioner takes these objectives into consideration. Which brings us to the fact that the U.S. embargo or blockade[3] makes many of these consider-

ations a mere academic exercise from a commercial standpoint at this time. Furthermore, and as in most developing countries, patent litigation is not common in Cuban courts keeping the enforceability of patent laws under a question mark.

On the other hand, there may be practical interest in the prior references that could be generated in that country (patents, publications, reduction to practice, etc.).[4] Cubans are resourceful, educated, and exposed to cutting-edge technology in certain areas. As it is described below, several multi-party treaties join this republic with other industrialized nations providing for reciprocal rights that affect us more directly.

The competent national authority administering the patent and trademark laws was the Oficina Nacional de Invenciones, Información Técnica y Marcas (ONIITEM), which is now the Oficina de Marcas y Patentes de Cuba.

The restrictions upon Cuban citizens under the communist form of government prevents them from availing themselves of the incentives extended by the

---

1. The 1983 law replaced the previous decree-law of April 4, 1936, which in turn replaced several military orders dating back to the U.S. military intervention from 1898 to 1902.

2. The socialist community no longer exists as such today. The characteristics of Cuba's development are quite different from those of 1983. The development of socialism has probably reached its maximum point, since there is nothing else for Cubans to socialize. Ironically enough, it may be that de-socialization has begun for selected industries, but only foreigners are allowed to participate. Then, the only assertion that remains true is that Cuba is a developing country.

3. The U.S. has maintained that its foreign policy towards Cuba is a bilateral matter, an embargo. Cuba has taken the position that U.S. extraterritorial acts constitute a violation of international law and that its actions constitute a blockade. The international community has sided with Cuba, according to the votes taken on the issue in the United Nations since 1992.

4. 35 U.S.C. §§102, 103, provide that certain activities abroad can bar patentability in the United States.

characteristic exclusive rights extended by intellectual property grants. Rather, the inventors are required to go through their employers or labor centers, and the authors cannot freely negotiate their copyrighted work, even if they take the initiative to register it or even promote it. It is through state-owned corporations that most of the business activity takes place. Again, Cuba's commercial activity may not be of consequence, but its research undertakings have gone beyond those of comparable countries, specially, in biotechnology and other cutting-edge areas.

It is reasonable to assume that with the attention patent laws have received in the international business arena, the indifference towards Cuba's laws and inventive activity should not be discarded even if the U.S. embargo is not lifted. American industries will suddenly find a Caribbean Taiwan a few miles off its shores.

Trademarks

In May 2000, the then-current intellectual property law[5] was repealed, in part, to accommodate the new Decree-law 203 for Trademarks and other Distinct Signs.[6] This legislation[7] is quite advanced by all standards even though Cuba has a closed market inherent of a communist-centralized economy.[8] It is noteworthy that the new legislation recognizes fragrances, sounds, colors, and three-dimensional objects as protectable marks. This is particularly interesting for a country where there is practically no advertising media and the commercial impression on the consumer is not an experience for most Cubans.[9]

The new law also adds provisions for preliminary relief (even ex parte) and customs-enforcement measures. These new provisions are intended to bring the country in line with the requirements of the World Trade Organization (Trade-Related Aspects of Intellectual Property, TRIPS). The preliminary relief could take the form of a temporary restraining order or seizure. These orders can last up to 20 days. A judicial action needs to be instituted before their expiration if the applicant wants to maintain continuity in its effect. The preliminary relief can also be obtained through an *ex parte* application.[10] Similarly, preliminary customs injunctive relief is valid for 10 days and, for good cause, extended for another 10 days. In both instances, a bond needs to be posted to guarantee any damages in the event the proceedings were not justified. These procedures are similar to those used in most countries to fight piracy. There have been no cases yet using these new provisions, to the best of the author's knowledge.

The test for deciding whether a mark is registrable over other previously registered marks or applications is not clear. The new law uses different terms in connection with this keystone issue in trademark law. The United States test basically includes a determination of whether purchasers are likely to be confused as to the source of goods or services. The U.S. Patent and Trademark Office, in its administrative examinations, follows this test with relatively minor variations.[11] The new Cuban trademark law uses different language for this concept. In Article 42 (e), a mark registration owner is granted the right to exclude others who use designations that could cause the regis-

---

5. Decree-law No. 68 of May 14, 1983 of Inventions, Scientific Discoveries, Industrial Models, Marks and Marks of Geographic Origin.

6. Decree-law 293 of May 2, 2000.

7. Decree-laws are different from laws in that the former are not approved by the entire parliamentary body but rather by the State Council, which is a sub-set of the full assembly.

8. There has been a proliferation of state and mixed state/private enterprises. However, their creation and limitations still respond to a centralized economic system. After the triumph of the revolutionary government in 1959, all private enterprises were nationalized with the exception of some small tracts of land kept by farmers/workers.

9. With the exception of those in high positions who have traveled abroad, there is practically no consumer culture in Cuba.

10. Chapter 2, Title X of decree-law 203.

11. In re E. I. du Pont de Nemours & Co. , 476 F.2d 1357, 177 U.S.P.Q. 563 (CCPA 1973).

trant an economic harm and it is understood that probability for likelihood of confusion is presumed for identical marks used for identical services or goods. In Article 57, the words "risk of confusion" are used in the context of a registration annulment proceeding. Article 17(d) also refers to risk of confusion or association for. In the U.S. (common law) legal system with its characteristic significant deference to judicial precedents the different words could be tantamount to a quagmire (judicial second-guessing of legislative intent with no debate record). In civil code countries, this is not important since the codified laws are interpreted *de novo* for each case. This author believes, however, that the subtle differences between possibilities and probabilities will not preoccupy Cuban jurists in this field, at least not for a while.

Another interesting aspect of the new trademark law can be found in Chapter V, Sections Two and Three. Section Two refers to a procedure for annulment of mark registrations based, *inter alia,* on the existence of superior relative rights of third parties such as the owners of previously filed applications or registered marks, or even famous marks that became notorious prior to the junior mark. Section Three deals with cancellation procedures and is primarily concerned with general rights of the consumers, such as injecting terms in the public domain or the characterization of genericness. Section Two, dealing primarily with private rights, does not have a statute of limitation while there is a statute of limitation under Section Three. This contrasts with U.S. trademark laws where the consumer (not represented in the typical litigation proceeding) has superior rights *vis-á-vis* the property rights of the mark owner. This may be a leg-islative lapse in a society that is primarily concerned with collectivism over private property rights.

Cuba is a member of most, if not all, treaties that relate to the protection of intellectual property rights.[12] Membership in these treaties is a source of much-needed hard currency for the embargoed/blocked country.[13] But beyond that, it has been instrumental in injecting trademark concepts to executives in state-owned companies and especially those entities concerned with exports. Until a few years ago, Cuba did not police its marks or did it reluctantly. This has changed with well-publicized U.S. cases like those involving the marks Havana Club, Cohiba and others. The old thinking, and still kept by many Cuban jurists, is that it is an exercise in futility to try to enforce Cuban trademark rights in the United States. However, this attitude has changed lately as Cuban executives become more knowledgeable on intellectual property matters.

The cases litigated in Cuba typically do not progress beyond the trial level. And most of them involve appeals from administrative registration refusals. Many cases involve facts relating to consumer expectations that have not occurred in four decades.[14] One of these cases involved the American mark "Kool Aid."[15] The Cuban Intellectual Property Office sought to cancel the registration for non-use and, on appeal, the court[16] excused the non-use based on *force majeure* (the U.S. economic blockade) and reversed the administrative decision of the Office.

In sum, it remains to be seen how the Cuban Intellectual Property Office will apply the new trademark law and the courts interpret and enforce it.

---

12. Cuba is a member of the Paris Convention, the General Inter-American Convention, the World Intellectual Property Organization (WIPO), the Madrid Agreement, the Madrid Protocol, among others.

13. The controversy of whether the U.S. embargo/blockade laws are bilateral or unilateral measures has been debated for many years in many *fora*.

14. After the triumph of the revolutionary government in 1959, private enterprise was nationalized with the exception of some small tracts of lands kept by the farmers/workers.

15. Kraft Foods, Inc. v. Oficina Cubana de la Propiedad Intelectual, Judgment No. 428, 2a Sala, Civil and Adm. Provincial Tribunal, August 31, 1998.

16. All appeals from the Cuban Patent and Trademark Office are reviewed by the Provincial Court for La Habana.

Copyrights

Current Cuban copyright laws are found in Law No. 14 of December 28, 1977,[17] assigning to the Ministry of Culture the responsibility of implementing and administering it. Decree No. 20 of February 21, 1978 created the National Center for Copyrights (Centro Nacional de Derecho de Autor, or CENDA) and several resolutions issued by the Ministry of Culture implement certain practices and regulations described below. Law No. 14 was enacted by the National Assembly of People's Power (Asamblea Nacional del Poder Popular)[18] based on Article 39[19] of the Cuban Constitution. The Cuban Constitution was promulgated in 1976 and amended in 1992. Chapter V of the Constitution deals with Education and Culture, and in part states that the State promotes and orients education, culture and science in all of its manifestations.[20] This Chapter also states that creative artistic creation is free provided its contents are not contrary to the Revolution.[21]

INTERNATIONAL TREATIES

Cuba is a member of most multilateral international treaties in effect relating to intellectual property law. Its international commitments include: Paris Convention for the Protection of Intellectual Property, Locarno Agreement on Industrial Designs Classification,[22] Patent Cooperation Treaty (PCT),[23] Strasbourg Agreement on Patent Classification,[24] World Intellectual Property Organization (WIPO), Budapest Agreement on Microorganism,[25] Madrid Arrangement (trademarks),[26] Madrid Protocol (trademarks),[27] Lisbon Agreement on Appellations of Origin,[28] Santiago Convention of 1923 (trademarks),[29] Nice Agreement on Classification of Goods and Services,[30] Vienna Agreement on Classification

---

17. Revoking the colonial Spanish Law of Intellectual Property of January 10, 1879 (the 1879 Law) and its Regulation of September 3, 1880, for Implementing the Intellectual Property Law (the 1880 Regulation). Other related and revoked laws are Articles 392 and 554 of the Social Defense Code (Código de Defensa Social) providing criminal sanctions for the violation of the copyright laws. Article 554, in particular, has striking similarities with Section 43(a) of the Lanham Act. 15 U.S.C. §1125(a), including copyrighted work in the protection and possible incarceration of up to one year.

18. The National Assembly of People's Power is Cuba's one-chamber legislative body.

19. There is an error in the official text of the law, which makes reference to Article 38 when it should be Article 39. This was confirmed with legal personnel at CENDA.

20. Article 39 of the Cuban Constitution, as amended in 1992.

21. *Id.* Article 39.

22. Locarno Agreement Establishing an International Classification for Industrial Designs, Locarno Agreement (1968), amended in 1979 (Locarno Union) signed on October 9, 1998.

23. Patent Cooperation Treaty (PCT) (Washington, 1970), amended in 1979 and modified in 1984 (PCT Union) signed on July 16, 1996.

24. Strasbourg Agreement Concerning the International Patent Classification, Strasbourg Agreement (1971), amended in 1979 (IPC Union) signed on November 9, 1996.

25. Budapest Treaty on the International Recognition of the Deposit of Microorganisms for the Purposes of Patent Procedure, Budapest Treaty (1977), modified in 1980 (Budapest Union) signed on February 19, 1994.

26. Madrid Agreement Concerning the International Registration of Marks, Stockholm (1967), and amended in 1979, entered into on December 6, 1989.

27. Protocol Relating to the Madrid Agreement Concerning the International Registration of Marks, Madrid Protocol (1989) (Madrid Union) joined on December 26, 1995.

28. Lisbon Agreement for the Protection of Appellations of Origin and their International Registration, Lisbon Agreement (1958), revised at Stockholm (1967), and amended in 1979 (Lisbon Union).

29. Convention for the Protection of Commercial, Industrial, and Agricultural Trade-Marks and Commercial Names, signed at Santiago, Chile, April 28, 1923, 33 LTS 47, ratified 88 LTS 324.

30. Nice Agreement Concerning the International Classification of Goods and Services for the Purposes of the Registration of Marks. Nice Agreement (1957), revised at Stockholm (1967) and at Geneva (1977), and amended in 1979 (Nice Union) entered into on December 26, 1995.

of the Figurative Elements of Marks,[31] Nairobi Treaty on the Protection of the Olympic Symbol,[32] Pan-American Convention of 1929 (trademarks),[33] Buenos Aires Convention of 1910 (patents),[34] Universal Copyright Convention (UCC) and Berne Convention for the Protection of Literary and Artistic Works.[35] Additionally, Cuba has signed the following treaties that are not in force yet: Geneva Act of the Hague Agreement Concerning the International Registration of Industrial Designs (Geneva, 1999), Patent Law Treaty (Geneva, 2000).

If we look at Table 1, it can be readily seen that Cuba's international involvement in multilateral intellectual property treaties surpasses, by far, that of the United States.

This is also understandable since many of these international treaties provide a source of hard currency to the signatory states, and sometimes even without requiring any filings. For instance, under the PCT, designated countries are entitled to a portion of the fees paid. WIPO regularly distributes these fees and provides technical support to Patent and Trademark Offices in developing countries.

Therefore, and in view of the limited internal use for the characteristic exclusive rights granted by intellectual property grants, it is clear that the incentives for accepting these major commitments respond to short-term needs for hard currency, technical support and compliance with the applicable provisions of TRIPS (WTO). The longer-term benefits of stimulating inventors, authors and business persons to invent, create and improve on the quality of their goods and services is as distant as in any of the other similarly situated developing countries in the region. One exception, however, could be the biotechnology field, to which the state has devoted extraordinary resources.

CONCLUSION

In sum, it can be said that Cuba has had intellectual property laws in its books since its colonial days and judging by its membership in most multilateral international treaties in this field, it has created an impressive infrastructure for the protection of intellectual property rights. However, the enforcement of these rights remains as a question mark in the event that its economy is liberalized. Other developing countries with free market economies also have advanced IP laws, but piracy is rampant and lack of intellectual property culture and respect prevent their enforcement. These developing countries are driven by different forces than those driving the developed countries in enforcing IP laws. But, whether foreign countries enforce their laws or not, the intertwined network of international commitments transmit important effects and limitations in our organic laws that need to be taken into consideration.

---

31. Vienna Agreement Establishing an International Classification of the Figurative Elements of Marks, Vienna Agreement (1973), amended in 1985 (Vienna Union) signed on July 18, 1997.

32. Nairobi Treaty on the Protection of the Olympic Symbol, signed on October 21, 1984.

33. General Inter-American Convention for Trade Mark and Commercial Protection, with Protocol on the Inter-American Registration of Trade-Marks, and Final Act of the Pan American Trade Mark Conference, signed at Washington, February 20, 1929, 124 LTS 357.

34. Convention on the Protection of Patents of Invention, Designs and Industrial Models, adopted by the Fourth International American Conference, signed in Buenos Aires on August 20, 1910, 155 LTS 179.

35. Berne Convention for the Protection of Literary and Artistic Works joined on February 20, 1997.

Table 1.   Intellectual Property Multilateral Agreements to Which Cuba is a Party

Treaty	Date of Cuba's Accession	Date of U.S. Accession	Formal Name of Treaty
Paris Union	11/17/1904	5/30/1997	Paris Convention for the Protection of Industrial Property, Paris Convention (1993), revised at Brussels (1900), Washington (1911), The Hague (1925), London (1934), Lisbon (1958) and Stockholm (1967), and amended in 1979.
Locarno Union	10/9/1998		Locarno Agreement Establishing an International Classification for Industrial Designs, Locarno Agreement (1968), amended in 1979.
PCT Union	7/16/1996	1/24/1978	Patent Cooperation Treaty (PCT), Washington (1970), amended in 1979 and modified in 1984.
IPC Union	11/9/1996	10/7/1985	Strasbourg Agreement Concerning the International Patent Classification, Strasbourg Agreement (1971), amended in 1979.
Budapest Union	2/19/1994	8/19/1980	Budapest Treaty on the International Recognition of the Deposit of Microorganisms for the Purposes of Patent Procedure, Budapest Treaty (1977), modified in 1980.
Madrid Arrangement	12/9/1998		Madrid Agreement Concerning the International Registration of Marks, Stockholm (1967), amended in 1979.
Madrid Union	12/26/1995		Protocol Relating to the Madrid Agreement Concerning the International Registration of Marks, Madrid Protocol (1989).
Lisbon Union	9/25/1966		Lisbon Agreement for the Protection of Appellation of Origin and their International Registration, Lisbon Agreement (1958), revised at Stockholm (1967), and amended in 1979.
Santiago Convention	1923	1923	Convention for the Protection of Commercial, Industrial, and Agricultural Trade-Marks and Commercial Names, signed at Santiago de Chile, April 28, 1923, 33 LTS 47, ratified 88 LTS 324.
Nice Union	12/26/1995		Nice Agreement Concerning the International Classification of Goods and Services for the Purposes of the Registration of Marks, Nice Agreement (1957), revised at Stockholm (1967), and amended in 1979.
Vienna Union	7/18/1997		Vienna Agreement Establishing an International Classification of the Figurative Elements of Marks, Vienna Agreement (1973), amended in 1985.
Nairobi Treaty	10/21/1994		Nairobi Treaty on the Protection of the Olympic Symbol.

Table 1. **Intellectual Property Multilateral Agreements to Which Cuba is a Party (Continued)**

Treaty	Date of Cuba's Accession	Date of U.S. Accession	Formal Name of Treaty
Pan/American Convention	9/20/1929	2/20/1929	General Inter-American Convention for Trade Mark and Commercial Protection, with Protocol on the Inter-American Registration of Trade-Marks, and Final Act of the Pan American Trade Mark Conference, signed at Washington, February 29, 1929.
Buenos Aires Convention	8/20/1910	8/20/1910	Convention on the Protection of Patents of Invention, Designs and Industrial Models, adopted by the Fourth International American Conference, signed at Buenos Aires on August 20, 1910, 155 LTS 179.
Washington Convention	1946	1946	The Washington Convention (1946) for the Protection of Scientific, Literary and Artistic Works.
UCC	1955	9/16/1955	Universal Copyright Convention, as revised at Paris on July 24, 1971.
Berne Convention	2/20/1997	3/1/1989	Berne Convention for the Protection of Literary and Artistic Works.

HAVANA CLUB IN THE WTO:
HEREIN OF INTERNATIONAL LAW AND AMERICAN POWER

Alan Swan

There has risen today a relatively new voice in American policy making circles. A voice that degrades international law and trumpets the virtues of unilateralism. Much of the academic writing in support of this viewpoint is a singular concatenation of confused concepts. Much of it is pure isolationism wrapped in the flag of Constitutional preservation. And much of it is unadulterated arrogance—the view that because our power is so great we can unilaterally, if we apply our power effectively, get other nations to do pretty much what we want without having to tie ourselves down with treaties and other reciprocal obligations that only limit our sovereignty. A reinvented Hobessian state of nature.

This is neither the time nor place to take on the whole of the unilateralist mindset. Here I have only one fundamental and very practical point to make. The problem is that the unilateralists don't understand one of the most potent sources of American power; our international legal obligations, particularly our treaties.

Few treaties comprehensive enough to be important to the preservation of world order—whether they deal with national security, trade, other economic matters, the environment, human rights, disarmament or any other subject—can be at all effective without the active support and participation of the United States. That's the first elementary lesson that comes with power—we're needed. The second elementary lesson is that if needed we can more often than not turn treaty commitments to our advantage—they can become a direct complement to and extension of the more immediate military and economic instruments of our national power. In particular they can legitimate and hence command adherence by other Nations to those principles of international conduct that serve our own long-term national interests—which is, of course, the ultimate object of having power. And this is precisely the lesson to emerge in very practical terms from litigation between the European Union and the United States in the World Trade Organization (WTO), litigation which, with a touch of poetic justice, starts in a law suit over rights to an American trademark for Cuban rum—Havana Club.

So, I begin with a brief description of the Havana Club litigation. It involved an infringement claim brought by a joint venture between the Cuban government and Pernod, a French company—what I'll call the Cuban-Pernod Group—against Bacardi. Ultimately the U.S. courts dismissed the claim largely on the strength of §211 of the 1998 Omnibus Appropriations Act. This led the European Union to challenge the validity of §211 in the WTO on the ground that the U.S. statute violated the TRIPS agreement. (TRIPS stands for Trade Related Intellectual Property Rights and is one of the basic agreements under the WTO umbrella.)

Before getting into the details of the WTO case, however, I want to talk briefly about the importance of the TRIPS to the global economic and ultimately political interests of the United States. Only against that background can one begin to fully appreciate not only why the U.S. may rightfully claim to have won a very substantial victory in the §211 case, but also why that victory illustrates how important our international legal entanglements can be to the preservation even extension of America's capacity to influence events in the world in which we live æ America's power.

How did this occur? It occurred because the underlying policy rationale used by the U.S. to support its core legal contention in the case was given full recognition by the WTO's Appellate Body. That underlying policy, in turn, is and will continue to be vital to preserving the safety and integrity of U.S foreign investments around the globe. Yet, it is a policy much contested by other nations. Its recognition, arguably its endorsement, by the WTO Appellate Body, therefore, represents a major step toward legitimating the U.S. position; one more example of how American power can be and often is utterly dependent for its preservation upon international law.

HAVANA CLUB IN THE U.S. COURTS

Now let me turn to the Havana Club litigation in the U.S. courts, a story well known to many of you perhaps better than I. Up until 1960, Cuban rum marketed under the Havana Club label was sold world wide including sales to the U.S. by JASA, a Cuban company owned by the Arechabala family. In 1960 JASA was confiscated by the Cuban government and the exportation of rum taken over by Cubaexport, a Government enterprise, which could not, of course, sell to the U.S. because of the trade embargo.

In 1976, Cubaexport registered the Havana Club trademark with the U.S. Patent and Trademark Office. Then in 1993, after the fall of the Soviet Union, Cubaexport entered into a 50/50 joint venture with Pernod a French company. In 1995, Cubaexport obtained from the U.S. Treasury Department's, Office of Foreign Assets Control (OFAC), a license to assign the U.S Havana Club trademark to its several subsidiaries. While OFAC subsequently rescinded the license, the reasons for its initial issuance have interesting implications.

Because they could not sell Cuban run into the U.S. market at the time, what the Cuban-Pernod Group was doing when they first registered the Havana Club mark with the U.S. Trademark office, then renewed that registration and received the OFAC license, was protecting their future position in that market anticipating that the legal barrier would someday be lifted. At the time, American companies were doing the same thing; preserving their future position in the Cuban market. Over 400 U.S. companies had registered their trademarks in Cuba even though they could not then export their products to Cuba. Quite plainly actions by OFAC and the U.S. Trademark Office were carefully crafted to avoid any retaliatory action by the Cuban government against those American companies.

Also, by protecting the Cuban-Pernod claim to the Havana Club mark, OFAC was preserving the commercial value of that claim for future use as a potentially major addition to any pool of Cuban assets turned over to the United States for the settlement of American claims against Cuba; an advantage completely dissipated by the enactment of §211 and the failure of the United States to honor the Cuban-Pernod rights.

Finally, in 1997, the Arechebala family sold out all of its interests in Havana Club to Bacardi who, in anticipation of that sale commenced, in 1995, to sell a small quantity of Bahamian rum to the United States under the Havana Club trademark. Whereupon the Cuban-Pernod Group sued Bacardi for trademark infringement

Before the infringement issue was tried, but well after the litigation had commenced, Congress enacted §211 of the 1998 Omnibus Appropriation Act, and on the strength of that statute the Cuban-Pernod infringement claim was dismissed. This occurred in 1999. Late the same year the European Union filed a claim with the WTO alleging that §211 violated the TRIPS agreement.

TRIPS AND THE GLOBAL PROTECTION OF U.S. INTELLECTUAL PROPERTY

At this point let me turn to the agreement on Trade-Related Aspects of International Property Rights (TRIPS) and its importance to the United States. Understand that we have never had, nor is there today, a truly international patent or international trademark or copyright. Intellectual property rights still remain creatures of national or what international lawyers call "municipal law." There have long been in place, however, a number of treaties setting out procedures by which a patent, trademark or copyright owner in one country signatory to one of these treaties could perfect his rights to a patent, trademark or copyright under the national law of another signatory. These treaties also laid-down certain minimum substantive standards that the national intellectual property laws of each signatory had to meet and then established two very critical principles of nondiscrimination: the "national treatment" and the Most Favored Nation, or MFN, principle.

This cooperative system was built upon two principal treaties: the Paris Convention of 1884, governing patents and trademarks, and the 1886 Berne Convention, governing copyrights.

While the system worked reasonably well for the industrialized countries that had well developed research and inventive capabilities, there was nothing it in for countries that did not have inventions, ideas and distinctive product names and marks to protect. Their optimal strategy was to import products and various copyrighted media, do the reverse engineering, replicate the technology, affix the traditional names and trademarks, copy the books, the artwork, the other media all without obtaining permission from or paying royalties to the owners of these valuable properties. In this category were most of the nations in the world. Almost all the signatories to the Paris and Berne Conventions were industrialized countries. The developing countries, including those with some of the World's most promising markets— China, India, Korea, Brazil, Mexico and others— not only shunned the treaties, but steadfastly refused to enact even the most rudimentary intellectual property laws of their own. At one point before negotiation of the WTO agreements, the U.S. Department of Commerce estimated that U.S. companies were losing in excess of $4 billion a year in royalties they would otherwise earn if the Paris-Berne system were in effect worldwide.

Quite naturally, when it came to the Uruguay Round of Multilateral Trade Negotiations, the United States, the European Union and Japan pushed hard for the establishment of a credible system of intellectual property rights protection to which all nations would have to adhere if they wanted to participate in the world trading system. This led to the negotiation of the TRIPS Agreement which: (1) incorporated most of the important provisions of the Paris and Berne Conventions; (2) added some additional procedural and substantive undertakings to which national law had to conform; and (3) reinforced the "national treatment" and MFN provisions in those earlier treaties. Most significantly, there was no escape. Any nation that wanted to benefit from the WTO trade rules would have to adhere to the TRIPS Agreement. As of January 1, there were 144 such nations.

Yet, as one might expect the transition has not been easy for some developing countries. You are all aware, I am sure, of the African drug issue. Then there is the disgraceful way in which the United States and the Europeans have reneged on their promise to liberalize imports of agricultural goods, textiles and garments from developing countries in exchange for TRIPS. So adjustments will be made. But the adjustments won't change the fact that the core TRIPS regime is a vital addition to the arsenal of American economic power in the World; a regime critical to the retention by the United States of its current dominant position in the world of high technology.

THE WTO LITIGATION

Now, bear with me. Against this background let me take you through the §211 case as it played out in the WTO dispute settlement process. The provisions of §211 at issue were:

- First, a provision prohibiting OFAC from issuing any license to register or otherwise deal in a trademark similar to a mark used in a business confiscated by the Castro government unless the original owner of the mark expressly consented thereto.

- Second, two separate subsections of §211 barring the U.S. courts from enforcing or otherwise recognizing any rights to a trademark confiscated by the Cuban government, if those rights were asserted by the Cuban government, a Cuban national or successor-in-interest (e.g., Pernod) without the consent of the original owner.

As one can readily see each of these provisions effectively barred the Cuban-Pernod Group from asserting any rights against Bacardi for infringement of the Havana Club trademark in the U.S. courts. Certainly, the Arechebala interests had never consented to the assertion of those rights. This, in turn, led the European Union to contend that the United States had violated the following provisions of the TRIPS Agreement:

1. A provision taken from Article 6 of the Paris Convention requiring all trademarks duly registered in a country of origin (e.g., Cuba) to be "accepted for filing and protected as is" in all other signatory countries (e.g., the United States), subject only to such exceptions as were expressly listed in that provision. There was no express exception for confiscated trademarks.

   The Europeans argued, of course, that this provision, contrary to §211, required the United States to honor the Cuban-Pernod Group's claims under the Havana Club trademark as registered in Cuba. In response, the United States argued that a fundamental structural principle of the TRIPS Agreement was that questions relating to the "ownership" of trademarks had been left to national law and were not controlled by TRIPS or the other treaties. Article 6 of the Paris Convention, in other words, had to be construed narrowly as pertaining only to questions of form, not to questions of ownership. §211 pertained to ownership, not form. Stated another way, according to the United States, Article 6 only required that a trademark duly registered in one signatory not be rejected by another merely for a failure to meet the latter's requirements as to "form." It did not require the latter to recognize ownership rights conferred by the first country; the country of origin because ownership was strictly a matter for the second country's own national law—including, for the United States, §211. Ultimately the U.S. won on this point.

The interesting point for our purposes, however, is why it won—a matter to which I shall return shortly.

2. Next the EU cited Article 15 of the TRIPS which stipulates that any sign or combination of signs, including names, numerals, pictures, etc, capable of "distinguishing goods and services" was to be "capable of constituting a trademark" and hence "eligible for registration as a trademark."

   This provision, the EU argued, was mandatory. Anything "capable" of being a trademark, such as the Havana Club label, had to be treated *in all respects* by the WTO members as a valid subsisting trademark. Again, the United States met this contention by emphasizing the overall structural principle; questions of ownership were left to national law not to the treaties. To be consistent with that principle, Article 15 could only be read as saying that if a sign was physically "capable" of being a trademark it had to be treated by every WTO member as legally "eligible" for recognition as a trademark, but without prejudice to the right of each member to determine under its national law who owned the mark. This is precisely what §211 did. It assigned ownership of a confiscated mark to the original owner as against the confiscating power or its successors-in-interest. Again, the United States won on this point, but again the intriguing question is why it won.

3. The European Union next turned to Article 16 of the TRIPS agreement granting to the "owner" of every trademark registered in a member State the "exclusive right to prevent all third parties not having the owner's consent from using" the mark in connection with trading goods or services similar to those in respect of which the trademark was registered.

   Again relying upon the preclusive right of national law to determine ownership, the United States responded with the rather obvious point that since under §211 the Cuban-Pernod Group could not qualify as "owners" of the Havana Club mark, they had no Article 16 rights of which they could be deprived. Again the United States won its point.

Although it lost on two other points, both the result of careless drafting that Congress can easily remedy, it is clear that the United States won a singular victory in the §211 case. The key to that victory was unequivocally the decision by the Appellate Body that issues of trademark ownership were, under the law of the treaties, to be left to national law and not controlled by TRIPS or the other applicable treaties, subject only to national treatment and MFN.

Now, mark the next point well, for it is the most important point. Adoption of that rule was decisively, in my judgment, the result of a fundamental policy decision by the Appellate Body. National law control over trademark ownership was absolutely essential to preserving for trademarks the broader principle that under international law no nation was required to honor rights in or claims to property that had been expropriated or otherwise taken from its citizens by another nation without adequate compensation; the so-called doctrine of State Responsibility for alien property. There was no such exception for confiscated trademarks in the rules of recognition found in TRIPS or the other treaties. If there was to be any such rule for trademarks, questions of trademark ownership had, as a matter of treaty law, to be taken out of the hands of the treaties and left to national law—to laws such as §211. A point repeatedly acknowledged by the Appellate Body.

That the Appellate Body attached such seminal weight to the Doctrine of State Responsibility—that it in effect endorsed that doctrine as a critical element in the broader configuration of international economic law — is manifest, in my view, by the risk it took. By turning the issue of trademark ownership over to national law, rather than keeping it strictly within the confines of TRIPS and the other treaties, the Appellate Body knew it was opening the matter up for genuine abuse as nations would undoubtedly be tempted to craft many and novel discriminatory limitations on the recognition of foreign trademarks. Having won its victory, the United States certainly

must now keep a sharp outlook for just such opportunistic behavior. But that the Appellate Body took the risk of exposing the TRIPS regime to such a danger, is overwhelming evidence, in my view, of the importance that it assigned to preserving and expanding the international doctrine of State Responsibility for alien property.

That doctrine, of course, has long been under attack. While it has undergone something of a renaissance through the hundreds of Bilateral Investment Treaties (BITs), through NAFTA and through decisions by the Iranian-U.S. Claims Tribunal, it is still under attack, this time by the environmentalists on the left and the unilateralists on the right. Its continuing vitality will be a matter tested—perhaps sorely tested—in the negotiation of an agreement for the Free Trade Area of the Americas, a matter I would think of some interest to this Association.

But this aside, the fact remains that the principle of international law upon whose behalf the Appellate Body took such risks, is a principle critical to the continuing ability of the United States to work effectively for a free, global economy run by private enterprises operating under market disciplines for the economic benefit of all mankind; indeed for the World's political benefit as well—for a truly democratic world. As such the §211 case is one more example of how quietly, yet effectively, American power can and is everyday extended through international law. One more example of precisely how an international judicial process—the Appellate Body of the WTO—working in the best traditions of the common law to perfect a comprehensive treaty regime through the careful application of customary international law, can serve as a powerful instrument for the advance of America's vital interests. One more example of why the unilateralists caught in the trap of their own ideological premises bated so artfully by their own overwhelming arrogance, fail repeatedly to understand how disastrously they would and already have robbed this Nation of one of the most potent sources of its continuing power over the course of events in the world round us—the power of international law.

RESTORATION OF CUBAN GALLERY FORESTS, ESPECIALLY ON THE BANKS OF THE BAYAMO AND OTHER RIVERS OF THE CAUTO BASIN

Larry S. Daley

Cuba was once a land of complex forests, and these forests were a foundation of much prosperity. Not only were precious woods logged for export, but natural products, such as dye-woods, were sold as well. For example, some of the natural medicines listed in Parke, Davis & Co. manuals (1890) surely came from Cuba. However, the forests of Cuba have dwindled, and their loss is not only esthetic and environmental, but economic and climatic as well.

In the Cuba of the past century, reforestation has not been easy, and mostly unsuccessful. Given its forty plus years in power, and absolute authority, a large proportion of responsibility for these failures can be laid at the feet of the present Cuban government. As this government reaches towards its end, fossil fuel has become scarce, and demand for firewood for cooking has done critical damage to the forest environment. After all is over, restoration of the complex original forest of Cuba will be even more urgent but not much easier, since deforestation itself gives place to undesirable, difficult to reverse, climate change. Therefore, the approaches to be considered here are cautious and long term.

The intent here is to develop plans to restore one critical part of these forests: the gallery forests that once lined the streams and rivers of Cuba. Specifically this paper addresses the circumstances of the Cauto River watershed in eastern Cuba, with emphasis on restoration of the gallery forest on the now denuded banks of the Bayamo river.

One principal reason for this objective is that forests at the edges of waterways reduce air and river temperature. Those who know Cuba recall the chill of entry into these forests, living climate regulators, which evoked in the ancient Taínos the legend of the Jigüe, the water sprite. More importantly recent studies show that loss of forest severely affects climate. Approaches suggested are diverse. The important consideration is that multiple methods be tested. Then experimental results, not *dictat* by political superiors, will determine which are used.

CUBA'S RIVERSIDE GALLERY FORESTS

Borhidi (1991 p. 446, common names from Victorin and Leon, 1944; Fors, 1955; Mabberley, 1993) describes "riverside gallery forests" thus:

> the gallery forests along rivers and creeks are rich in lianes, palms and tall grasses and have only a single canopy layer. Characteristic elements are *Roystonea regia* (royal palm), *Calyptronoma dulcis* (manaca palm), *Lonchocarpus domingenesis* (guamá), *Lysiloma bahamense* (abey, bahama sabicú), *Dalbergia* (palo de rosa) *Ecastophyllum*, *Bucida buceras* (júcaro), G*inoria americana*; of the lianes *Arthrostylidium cubensis* and *A. capillifolium*, and of and of the tall grasses *Gynerium sagittatum*, the latter forming dense stands like reeds.

One should note that in Cuba speciation to the islands very diverse habitats is common. For example, there are perhaps six species of royal palm (Zona, 1991). Often selection of habitat is a strong influence (e.g. Zona, 2002).

seed dispersion which commonly involves birds, bats and other vertebrates as well as invertebrates, are fairly well understood (*e.g.* Hovestadt, *et al.* 1999). This is also true for many folivorous (leaf eating) insects and plant pathogens (*e.g.* Hochmut, 1982; Nascimento and Hay, 1994).

The forests of Cuba sustain a varied wild life, mainly birds (Garrido and Kirkconnel, 2000), amphibians, reptiles (Sepland and Schwartz, 1974; Estrada and Hedges, 1996; Rodriguez Schettino *et al*, 1999), and invertebrates (e.g. Martínez and Sánchez, 2002). Most are familiar with the need for old growth trees to provide such things as nesting holes (often in old palms) to support such birds as the Cuban parrot *Amazona leucocephala palmarum* (Forshaw and Cooper, 1977) However, there are a few strange mammals such as the—perhaps, or perhaps not, extinct—poison-fanged almiquí or *Solenodon* (Barbour, 1944; Walker, *et al.,* 1964; Ottenwalder, 1985,1991; Dufton, 1992). The wild dingo-like dogs apparently came with very early settlers perhaps with the "mammoth hunters" who preceded the Taínos (Rouse, 1992; Schwartz, 1997).

All these animals interact with the vegetation of the forest, where much of the nitrogen in the soil most probably is fixed by leguminosae trees. The rich ecology and variability of Cuban woodlands is demonstrated by the number of such legume trees. These trees include: Abey (*Lysiloma bahamensis*), Abey Blanco, Azul de sabana or Azulito, encinillo, and menudo (*Pithecellobium berterianum, P. obvale, P. discolo, P. arboreum, P. dulce* (Inga, Guamuchil), *P. glaucum, P. hystrix, P. lentiscifolium, P. nipense, P. oppositifolia, P. prehensile*), Algarrobo (*Albizzia (Samanea) saman*), Bacona (*Albizzia cubana*), Brasil, Brasilete and Guaracabuya (*Caesalpinia vesicara, C. rugeliana, C. Bonduc, C. glandulosa, C. moanensis, C. nipensis, C. pauciflora, C. pinnata, C. subglauca, C. vesicaria, C. violacea* and *C. coriaria*), Cañadonga (*Cassia grandis*) and relatives (*Cassia Bucherae, C. chrysocarpa, C. diphylla, C. Ekmaniana* (Guacamaya), *C. emarginata, C. indecora, C. ligustrina, C. lineata, C. minutiflora, C. nova, C. pilosa, C. rotundifolia, C. scleroxyla, C. Shaferi, C. stenophylla,* and *C. turquini*), Granadillo (*Byra ebenu, B. serrulatum, B. Tuerckhe-*

imii), Guabá (*Inga vera*), Guamá (*Lonchocarpus domingensis, L. longpipes, L. pentaphyllus, L. sericeus*), Guamá candelón and relatives (*Piscidia piscipula, P. cubensis, P. havanensis, P. crenata, P. Forsythiana, P. hemisphaerica, P. intermedia, P. lurida, P. mayarensis, P. micromeriaefolia, P. microphylla, P. moaensis, P. obtusangula, P. pumileoides, P. repens, P. simplex, P. spathulata, P. trianthemoides, P. uninerva*), Guacancillo (*Behaimia cubensis*), Jurabaina (*Hebestogma cubensis*), Orejas (*Enterolobium cyclocarpum*), Palo de Campeche or Blood wood tree (*Haematoxylon campechianum*), Pico de Gallo (*Tounatia (Swartzia) cubensis*) (*Cynometra cubensis*), Caguairán or Quiebra hacha (*Guibourtia (Pseudocopaiva) hymenaefolia*), Sabicú (*Lysiloma latisiliqua*), Tengue (*Poeppigia procera*), Yaba (*Andira inermis*), Yamagüey de Sabana (*Belairia mucronata, B. parvifolia, B. spinosa, B. ternata*), Yarúa (*Peltophorum brasiliensis, P. aldnatum*) (Fors, 1956; Allen and Allen, 1981; Borhidi, 1991; Mabberley, 1993).

When one sees the many colorful butterflies of Cuba, one should realize that many of their caterpillars eat tree leaves (Schwartz and Hedges, 1991; Silva Lee, 1996; Johnson and Coats, 1999). Less clearly realized is how trees are associated with fungal endophytes (*e.g.* Hoffman, *et al.* 1998; Daley, 2000); and how trees rely on the protection or nutrition supply mediated by invertebrates such as ants (Rickson, 1997; Rickson and Rickson 1986, 1998). Even the once dreaded land crabs of Cuba may play a role, as do other crabs in Ecuador (Twilley *et al.* 1997).

Background Information

To know what is unknown is as important as it is to know what is known. There is considerable information available on the botany of tree flora of Cuba, a general compilation of germination and growth rates. There are even thorough works on the associations of tree flora with soil type, location and rainfall (Borhidi, 1991). What seems missing are complete bodies of work, compendiums, covering disease resistance, nutritional, and light requirements, interaction with associated fauna and flora, etc., for all or most of the trees of Cuba. Thus, further basic research must be done to support of any project of this nature

Manpower

There are a good number of forestry scientists now in Cuba, who must make a transition from poorly paid protected status, to life as scientists in the real world. The personal trauma and waste of such scientific skills in the change to new conditions, common circumstances in Eastern Europe, could be ameliorated by such projects. These research projects, would also help give these scientist the pertinent experience, and time—with food on the table—to thus allow them to more readily adapt to a more competitive free enterprise environment.

External Support

If U.S. funding becomes available after the present circumstances in Cuba end, it will be important to set up extension and other support on the efficient applied us model (Daley, 1999).

Material and Methods

Imagery and Associated methods are described in Daley (2001)

REFERENCES CITED

Alain, Hermano (Dr. E.E. Liogier) 1962. *Flora de Cuba*, Tomo V. Rubiales, Valerianales, Cucurbitales, Campanulales, Asterales. Editorial Universitaria, Universidad de Puerto Rico, Rio Piedras.

Allen, O. N. and E. K. Allen. 1981. *The Leguminosae. A Source Book of Characteristics, Uses and Nodulation*. University of Wisconsin Press, Madison.

Areces-Mallea, Alberto E., Alan S. Weakley, Xiaojun Li, Roger G. Sayre, Jeffery D. Parrish, Camille V. Tipton, and Timothy Boucher (Edited by Nicole Panagopoulos) 2001. *A Guide to Caribbean Vegetation Types: Preliminary Classification System and Descriptions*. Web Published by The Nature Conservancy, USIAD, International Institute of Tropical Forestry At Web site: http://edcsnw3.cr.usgs.gov/ip/tnc/products/download/part1.pdf

Barbour, Thomas 1944. "The Solenodons of Cuba." *Proceedings of the New England Zoological Club*. 33, 1-8.

Borhidi, Attila 1991. *Phytogeography and Vegetation Ecology of Cuba*. Akademiai Kiado, Budapest, Hungary.

de Las Casas, Bartolomé (*circa* 1474-1566, 1995 Reprinting). *Historia de Las Indias*. Fondo de Cultura Económica, Mexico City, Vol. 2, pp. 521-522).

Daley, L. 1997. "Bioprospecting In a Post-Castro Cuba." *Cuba in Transition—Volume 7* Association for the Study of the Cuban Economy, Washington, 382-394.

Daley, L. 1999. "Preliminary Evaluation of the Needs for Agricultural Extension in a Free Cuba." *Cuba in Transition—Volume 9*. Association for the Study of the Cuban Economy, Washington, 165-172.

Daley, L. 2000. "Cuban Flora, Endophytic and Other, as a Potential Source of Bioactive Compounds: Two Technical Approaches to Bioactive Compound Discovery. *Cuba in Transition—Volume 10*. Association for the Study of the Cuban Economy, Washington, 391-398.

Daley, L. 2001. "Orographic Influences on Vegetation and Bioprospecting Potential at the Confluence of the Bayamo, Guamá and Guisa Rivers." *Cuba in Transition—Volume 11*. Association for the Study of the Cuban Economy, Washington, 179-184.

Díaz-Briquets, Sergio and Jorge F. Pérez-López 2000. *Conquering Nature: The Environmental Legacy of Socialism in Cuba*. University of Pittsburgh Press, Pittsburgh

Dufton, M. J. 1992. "Venomous mammals." *Pharmacology and Therapeutics* 53(2), 199-215.

Dunham, K.M. 1991. "Comparative Effects of *Acacia albida* and *Kigelia africana* Trees on Soil Characteristics in Zambezi Riverine Woodlands." *Journal of Tropical Ecology* 7, No. Pt.2 (May), 215-220.

Enamorado, Calixto (García-Iñiguez) 1917. *Tiempos Heroicos. Persecución*. Rambla, Bausa y Cía, Havana.

Estrada, Albert R., and S. Blair Hedges 1996. "At the lower limit in Tetrapods; a new diminutive frog from Cuba (Leptodactylidae: Eleutherodactylus)." *Copeia*, 852-859.

Fors, Albert J. 1956. *Maderas Cubanas*. Ministerio de Agricultura. Havana.

Forshaw, Joseph M., and W.T. Cooper, 1977. *Parrots of the World*. T.F.H. Press (by arrangement with Doubleday & Company), Neptune New Jersey.

Frere Marie–Victorin and Frere Leon. 1942-1944. *Itineraries Botaniques Dans L'ile de Cuba*. 2 Volumes. 1942/1944 .

Galinat, Walton C. 1971. "The Evolution of Sweet Corn." *Mass. Agric. Exp. Sta. Bull.* 591, 6-14.

Garrido, Orlando H. and Arturo Kirkconnel. *2000 Field Guide to Birds of Cuba*. Cornell University Press, Ithaca, New York.

Hochmut, R. 1982. Translated Title: "Protection of Forests against Insect Pests and Fungal Diseases In Cuba." *Silvaecultura Tropica et Subtropica*.9, 95-111.

Hovestadt, T., Yao, P., Linsenmair, K.E. 1999. "Seed Dispersal Mechanisms and the Vegetation of Forest Islands in a West African Forest-Savanna Mosaic (Comoe National Park, Ivory Coast)." *Plant Ecology*. 144, No. 1 (Sept), 1-25.

Johnson, Kurt and Steven L. Coates 1999. *Nabokov's Blues: The Scientific Odyssey of a Literary Genius*. McGraw-Hill, New York (previously Zoland Books).

Kellman, M., and Meave, J. 1997. "Fire in the Tropical Gallery Forests of Belize." *Journal of Biogeography*. 24 (1, Jan), 23-34.

Little, Elbert L. Jr. and Frank. H. Wadsworth. 1964. (Second Printing by second Author USDA Forest Service, Rio Piedras, Puerto Rico 1989). *Common Trees of Puerto Rico and The Virgin Islands*. Agricultural Handbook No. 249. U. S. Department of Agriculture, Forest Service Washington, D.C.

Mabberley, D. J. (1993 Printing). *The Plant Book. A Portable Dictionary of the Higher Plants*. Cambridge University Press. Cambridge, England.

Marrero, Leví 1981 *Geografía de Cuba*. 5th Edition. La Moderna Poesía, Coral Gables, Florida.

Martí, José (1853-1895). *Obras completas*. Edited by Jorge Quintana. Caracas, 1964.

de la Maza y Jiménez, Manuel and Juan Thomás Roig y Mesa. 1914. *Flora de Cuba. Datos Para Su Estudio*. Estacion Experimental Agronómica, Secretaría de Agricultura, Comercio y Trabajo, Bulletin 22, Havana.

Martínez, María A. and J. A. Sánchez. 2002. "Comunidades de lombrices de tierra (Annelida: Oligochaeta) en un bosque siempre verde y un pastizal de Sierra del Rosario, Cuba." *Caribbean Journal of Science*, Vol. 36, No. 1-2, 94-103

McClanahan, T. R., Young, T. P.1996. *East African Ecosystems and their Conservation*: Oxford University Press, New York.

Nascimento, M.T. and Hay, J.D. 1994. "The Impact of Simulated Folivory on Juveniles of *Metrodorea pubescens* (*Rutaceae*) in a Gallery Forest near Brasilia, Federal District, Brazil." *Journal of Tropical Ecology*. 10 (4, Nov), 611-620.

National Geophysical Data Center. http://www.ngdc.noaa.gov/mgg/image/2minsurface/1350/45N090W.jpg

Nobre, C.A., Sellers, P.J., Shukla, J. 1991. "Amazonian Deforestation and Regional Climate

Change." *Journal of Climate*. 4, (10, Oct 1991), 957-988.

Ortega Alvarez, Ana Lucía. 1999. *Iglesias de Cuba*. Agualarga Editores, S. L., Madrid.

Otsamo, R. 2000. "Secondary Forest Regeneration under Fast-Growing Forest Plantations on degraded *Imperata cylindrica* Grasslands." *New Forests* 19, (1, Jan), 69-93.

Ottenwalder, J.A. 1985. *The Distribution and Habitat of Solenodon in the Dominican Republic*. M.S. Thesis, Department of Wildlife and Range Sciences. University of Florida, Gainesville.

Ottenwalder, José Alberto 1991. *The Systematics, Biology, and Conservation of Solenodon*. University of Florida UMI Dissertation Services, Ann Arbor, Michigan.

Parke, Davis & Co. 1890. *Organic Materia Medica. Newer Material Medica*. 2nd Edition, Detroit, Michigan.

Ratter, J.A., Ribeiro, J.F., Bridgewater, S. 1997. "The Brazilian Cerrado Vegetation and Threats to Its Biodiversity." *Annals of Botany* 80, 223-230.

Rickson, F R. 1977. "Progressive Loss of [Azteca] Ant-Related Traits of *Cecropia peltata* on Selected Caribbean Islands." *Am J Bot* 64, (5, May/June 1977), 585-592

Rickson, F.R., Rickson, M.M. 1986. "Nutrient Acquisition Facilitated by Litter Collection and Ant Colonies on two Malaysian Palms." *Biotropica*.18, (4, Dec 1986), 337-343.

Rickson, F.R., Rickson, M.M. 1990. "The Cashew Nut, *Anacardium occidentale (Anacardiaceae)*, and its Perennial Association with Ants: Extrafloral Nectary Location and the Potential for Ant Defense." *American Journal of Botany*. 85, (6, June 1998), 835-849.

Rodriguez, M., Lobo, D, Simon, I. M. and Szegi, J. (Eds). 1984. "Some Aspects of the Carbon Cycle in a Tropical Thorn-Bush Forest at the Ecological Station 'El Retiro,' Santiago de Cuba." In:

Soil Biology and Conservation of the Biosphere. Akademiai Kiado; Budapest, Hungary Volume-2. 1984, pp. 637-654.

Rouse, Irving. 1992. *The Taínos. Rise and Decline of the People Who Greeted Columbus*. Yale University Press. New Haven and London.

Robineau, L. 1990 (Ed). *Towards a Caribbean pharmacopoeia*. Endo Caribe, UNAH, Santo Domingo.

Rodríguez Schettino, Lourdes, Alberto Coyo, Lourdes Otero (Editors). 1999. *The Iguanid Lizards of Cuba*. University Press of Florida, Gainesville.

Schultes, R.E. and R.F. Raffauf. 1990. *The Healing Forest. Medicinal and Toxic Plants of The Northwest Amazonia*. Dioscorides Press, Portland Oregon.

Schwartz, Albert, and S. Blair Hedges 1991. "An Elevational Transect of Lepidoptera on Pico Turquino, Cuba." *Caribbean Journal of Science* 27 (3-4): 130-138.

Schwartz, Marion. 1997. *A History of Dogs In The Early Americas*. Yale University Press, New Haven.

Sepland, B.R. and A. Schwartz. 1974. "Hispaniolan Boas of The Genus *Epicrates* (Serpentes, Boidae) and Their Antillean Relationships." *Ann. Carnegie Mus.* 45 (5), 58-143.

Shukla, J., Nobre, C., Sellers, P. 1990. "Amazon deforestation and climate change." *Science* 247 (4948, Mar 16), 1322-1325.

Silva Lee, Alfonso. 1996. *Natural Cuba*. Pangaea Press. Saint Paul, Minnesota.

Thompson, J., Proctor, J., Viana, V., Milliken, J.A. Ratter and D.A. Scott. 1992. "Ecological Studies on a Lowland Evergreen Rain Forest on Maraca Island, Roraima, Brazil. I. Physical Environment, Forest Structure and Leaf Chemistry." *Journal of Ecology*. 80 (4), 689-703.

Twilley, R.R., Pozo, M., Garcia, V.H., and Others 1997. "Litter Dynamics in Riverine Mangrove

Forests in the Guayas River Estuary, Ecuador." *Oecologia.* 111 (1), 109-122.

Walker, Ernest P., Florence Warnick, Sybil E. Hamlet, Kenneth I. Lange, Mary A. Davis, Howard E. Uible, and Patricia F. Wright. 1964. *Mammals of the World.* John Hopkins Press, Baltimore.

Wilcox, Walter D. 1908. "Among the Mahogany Forests of Cuba." *National Geographic* (July), 485-498.

Wilcox, Walter D. 1924. *Caoba. the Mahogany Tree: A Tale of the Forest.* G.P. Putnam's Sons, New York.

Woodring, W.P. and S.N. Davies. 1944. *Geology and Manganese Deposits of the Guisa-Los Negros Area of Oriente Province, Cuba.* United States Department of the Interior. Geological Survey. Bulletin 935-G.

Zayas y Alfonso, Alfredo 1914. *Lexografia Antillana.* El Siglo XX Press, Havana.

Zheng, X and E.A.B. Eltahir. 1998. The Role of Vegetation. In: "The Dynamics of West African Monsoons." *Journal of Climate.* 11, No. 8 (Aug 1998), 2078-2096.

Zona, Scott 1991. "Notes on *Roystonea in Cuba.*" *Journal of the International Palm Society 35(4).*

Zona, Scott. 1996. "*Roystonea* (Arecaceae : Arecoideae)." In: *Flora Neotropica.* No 71 : The New York Botanical Garden, Bronx. 36 pp.

Zona, Scott 2002. "Morphological and Ecological Diversity of Palms." Lecture at Fairchild Tropical Garden, Coral Gables, Florida. http://www.virtualherbarium.org/teach/zonapalmlecture.html.

RAÍCES DEL PREJUICIO NORTEAMERICANO EN CUBA

Dominga González Suárez

En un futuro próximo la comunidad internacional tendrá que enfrentarse a un proceso de tránsito de la sociedad cubana hacia la democracia y una economía de mercado. En dicho proceso intervendrán, además de los diferentes grupos que componen la población cubana actual, los países que han estado involucrados en los acontecimientos contemporáneos de la Isla. Sin duda, los Estados Unidos tendrán que jugar un papel de primer orden en dicho proceso. Para que este país pueda jugar, sin limitaciones de ningún tipo, el principalísimo papel que le corresponde, por sus relaciones históricas con Cuba y por la influencia que ejerce y ejercerá sobre la economía y la sociedad cubanas, hay que tomar medidas para erradicar (al menos paliar) los sentimientos de desconfianza y resentimiento de la población cubana (a los cuales nos referiremos como prejuicios), hacia los norteamericanos. Para poder elaborar medidas adecuadas en ese sentido, resulta imprescindible desvelar por qué y cómo surgió tal prejuicio, así como cuáles han sido los mecanismos que han hecho que perdure en la memoria de la población cubana.

LAS RELACIONES INTERGRUPALES CUBANO-NORTEAMERICANAS: DEL ESTEREOTIPO PREDOMINANTEMENTE POSITIVO AL PREDOMINANTEMENTE NEGATIVO.

Durante la ocupación militar norteamericana, la necesaria institucionalización del país, a los fines de fundar la República de Cuba, fue aprovechada por los norteamericanos para defender sus intereses en detrimento de los intereses cubanos.

Entre las leyes más dañinas encontramos la Orden Militar (OM) 155, o Ley de Inmigración; la OM 62, Ley de Deslinde de Haciendas Comuneras; la OM 139, o Ley de Ferrocarriles; y la Enmienda Platt.

La OM 155 o Ley de Inmigración

Finalizada la Guerra de Independencia la situación económica y demográfica de la isla era extremadamente crítica. Al respecto el Censo de 1899 planteaba:

> En términos generales, puede decirse que haciendo un cálculo moderado, la población de la Isla disminuyó un 12% y su riqueza las dos terceras partes (USA. War Department, p.44).

Nos encontramos conque la riqueza del país fue prácticamente aniquilada, y su población rural diezmada gracias, en gran medida, a la política de reconcentración dirigida por el General español Valeriano Weyler.

La reconstrucción del país y el rápido proceso de inversión de capitales extranjeros, básicamente norteamericanos, demandaban, según Perfecto Lacoste, hacendado cubano y por entonces Secretario de Agricultura, una política migratoria que favoreciera la importación de trabajadores.

Meses antes de la constitución y entrega de la República, el problema aún no estaba resuelto. Las discusiones sobre la política inmigratoria que debía adoptar Cuba estuvieron vinculadas directamente con las rebajas arancelarias que los Estados Unidos concederían a los productos cubanos a través del Tratado de Reciprocidad.

En los Estados Unidos existían dos grupos con intereses contrapuestos: los productores de azúcar de remolacha que abogaban por la protección arancelaria y el Trust del Azúcar, o American Refining Sugar Co., que se oponía a la misma. Las razones de sus antagonismos quedaron expuestas durante las discusiones y negociaciones que tuvieron lugar en el Congreso de los Estados Unidos para establecer los términos y condiciones del Tratado de Reciprocidad Comercial que se firmaría con la futura República de Cuba.

El periódico *La Discusión* lo planteaba en estos términos:

Mr. Henderson, presidente de la Cámara de Representantes de los Estados Unidos, al analizar las posiciones de los grupos en que se encontraba dividido en Congreso planteaba que los que tratan de ayudar a Cuba, piden una reducción en los aranceles de azúcar crudo cubano del cincuenta por ciento de derecho o su entrada libre. La defensa de estos planteamientos la basan en los intereses de este sector de la economía norteamericana, en el capital americano invertido en ferrocarriles en Cuba, en el capital americanos invertido en tierras, fincas, industrias, etc., en que los americanos residentes en Cuba ansían mayor tráfico entre Cuba y los Estados Unidos, y en la ansiedad de los cubanos por mejorar sus condiciones económicas.

En contra se presentan los argumentos siguientes. El azúcar de remolacha que se ha desarrollado tan sorprendentemente en los estados de California, Colorado, Nebraska, Wisconsin, Michigan, Iowa y todos los estados del Valle de Mississippi desean que se le aplique el principio de la protección para no ser perjudicados en la competencia; la posición del pueblo americano, que después de haber derramado su sangre y empleado millones en servicio de Cuba, ha de ver perjudicados sus propios intereses (La cuestión americana (1902, febrero 27).

La industria remolachera doméstica también estaba interesada en la implantación de una legislación inmigratoria restrictiva para evitar que Cuba pudiera abastecerse de la mano de obra suficiente que posibilitara la realización de grandes producciones de azúcar.

Sin embargo, el Trust, con importantes inversiones en el sector azucarero de Cuba y gran importador de azúcar crudo, estaba interesado en desarrollar la industria azucarera de la isla para garantizar la materia prima a sus grandes refinerías situadas en los Estados Unidos. Por esta razón, abogaba por una política inmigratoria que posibilitara la libre contratación de trabajadores extranjeros.

El control de los escaños del Congreso norteamericano por el primero de los dos grupos, fue determinante en la definición de la política inmigratoria que Cuba debía seguir. En el momento en que tiene lugar la discusión, todavía el Trust del Azúcar no había monopolizado el sector dentro de los Estados Unidos. Para satisfacer las demandas de los productores domésticos de azúcar, representados por los Republicanos, el Congreso de ese país acordó condicionar las negociaciones que derivarían en el Tratado de Reciprocidad Comercial a la adopción de las leyes inmigratorias (restrictivas y discriminatorias) vigentes en Estados Unidos y, una vez cumplido este requisito, se concedería una reducción de las tarifas arancelarias, por parte de ese gobierno, de sólo el 20% a los productos cubanos. En otras palabras, sólo se permitiría iniciar la negociación del Tratado de Reciprocidad Comercial si se le imponía a Cuba la Ley de Inmigración vigente en los Estados Unidos.[1]

El 18 de abril de 1902, la Cámara de Representantes de los Estados Unidos aprobó el proyecto de ley conocido como Bill Payne,[2] el cual concedía un 20% de rebaja arancelaria a los productos cubanos con la condición de que Cuba aceptara la Ley de Inmigración vigente en Estados Unidos.

Con relación a este problema, en la prensa aparecía una entrevista al recién electo Presidente, Don Tomás Estrada Palma, donde se mostró en total desacuerdo con la decisión adoptada por el Congreso de los Estados Unidos. Al analizar la Ley Payne, Estrada Palma declaraba que no entendía las condiciones que se le quería imponer a Cuba en lo referente a su política inmigratoria, puesto que:

en las leyes de inmigración de los Estados Unidos hay exigencias que Cuba no podrá observar necesitada como se halla de fomentar su población: pero, desde luego, desde hace muchos años, los cubanos han demostrado su oposición resuelta a la inmigración de razas inferiores (*Situación al día*, abril 19 de 1902, p. 2).

En esa misma entrevista, el Presidente Estrada Palma declaró, al explicar su oposición a la aceptación de las leyes restrictivas de inmigración de los Estados Unidos, que eso sería:

coartar a Cuba la libertad que debe tener para legislar sobre esa o cualquiera otra materia con entera independencia" (*Situación al día*, abril 19 de 1902, p. 2).

Un mes después, el 15 de mayo de 1902, y a sólo cinco días de la retirada el ejército de ocupación militar y la creación de la República, el General Leonardo Wood, Gobernador Militar de Cuba, ordenó la promulgación, a reserva de las resoluciones que el Congreso de Cuba acordara sobre la misma, de la Orden Militar No. 155 o Ley de Inmigración y su Reglamento, cuyas disposiciones eran las mismas que se encontraban vigentes en los Estados Unidos.

La Sección III de la Ley, es la que da cumplimiento a las pretensiones del Congreso de los Estados Unidos. En ella se prohibía la contratación de braceros en el país de origen, para garantizar, mediante la escasez de trabajadores en el campo, que Cuba no fuera capaz de producir grandes zafras azucareras con bajo costo de producción. Esta prohibición quedó expresada así:

Sección III: Constituirá un acto ilegal por parte de cualquier persona, razón social o compañía, pagar por anticipado, bajo cualquier forma, el importe del viaje, o de algún modo contribuir o fomentar la introducción o inmigración de cualquier extranjero o extranjeros, forastero o forasteros en Cuba, mediante contrato o convenio, de palabra o por escrito, tácito o expreso, hecho con anterioridad a la introducción o inmigración de los mencionados extranjeros o forasteros, para emplearlos en trabajos u ocupaciones de cualquier clase en Cuba.

Por su parte, la Sección IV esclarece las condenas que recibirán las personas que cometan una trasgresión de la Ley. Que en general consistía en pagar una multa de 1000 pesos por cada infracción que se cometiera.

En la Sección V, donde se establecen las excepciones de la Sección anterior, se abre una brecha, o basamento legal, que posibilitará la entrada a Cuba de miles de inmigrantes españoles, cuando se plantea:

no se entienda en estos párrafos que se cohíbe a persona alguna que auxilie a un miembro de su familia para que pueda venir del extranjero a establecerse en Cuba.

---

1. El 18 de marzo de 1902 fue votada una resolución por la Conferencia de Republicanos de la Cámara de Representantes, celebrada en Washington, la cual originó un proyecto de ley presentado a ese cuerpo. El texto íntegro expresa:

Resuelve: Que es el deseo de la Conferencia que el Comité de Medios y Arbitrios, informe favorablemente a la Cámara, un proyecto que sustancialmente diga así:

Que con el propósito de nivelar el tráfico entre los Estados Unidos y Cuba, el Presidente está debidamente autorizado, tan pronto como pueda estar constituido un gobierno independiente en Cuba, y la sanción de dicho gobierno, de las leyes de inmigración de los Estados Unidos, como si fueran sus propias leyes, a entrar en las negociaciones con dicho gobierno para el arreglo de un tratado comercial, cuyas recíprocas y equivalentes concesiones deben obtenerse en favor de los productos y manufacturas de los Estados Unidos, en la proporción de un veinte por ciento de rebaja en los aranceles sobre productos y manufacturas que no tengan cláusula más favorecida que esa, y cuando el gobierno de Cuba proclame esas leyes de inmigración, y entre en el arreglo, y haga concesiones tales a los productos y manufacturas indicados, que a juicio del Presidente sean recíprocas y equivalentes, queda autorizado a dar una proclama al efecto, en la parte a que se refiere a la ley de inmigración y al Tratado de Reciprocidad Comercial, rebajando un veinte por ciento a favor de los productos de Cuba.

El Presidente queda autorizado, para que si no se halla satisfecho del cumplimiento por parte de Cuba del acuerdo, notificar inmediatamente su suspensión.

Considerando: Que la reciente Conferencia de Bruselas ha acordado suspender todas las primas al azúcar desde el 1 de septiembre de 1903 , y desde entonces subirá el precio del dulce.

Resuelve: Que el informe del Comité recomiende que los efectos del arreglo comercial entre los Estados Unidos y Cuba, terminen el 1 de diciembre de 1903 . (Ver: Periódico *La Discusión*, La Habana, 24 de marzo de 1902).

2. El congresista Mr. Payne declaró, en relación con esta ley, que: "Es imposible que con las restricciones que se le ponen y que van comprendidas en este proyecto a la inmigración de braceros, los Hacendados cubanos puedan encontrar bastantes trabajadores para realizar esa conquista del mercado americano. (Periódico *El Mundo*, La Habana, 16 de abril de 1902, p.3.)

La Sección VI consideraba como una trasgresión el fomento de la inmigración en el extranjero mediante promesa de ocupación, por medio de "anuncios impresos y publicados." La infracción de esta disposición sería condenada con una multa de 1000 pesos.

La OM 139 o Ley de Ferrocarriles

Un ejemplo paradigmático de los conflictos de intereses tuvo lugar cuando el gobierno de la primera ocupación militar norteamericana quiso proteger la inversión de la Cuba Company, empresa presidida por Sir William Van Horne,[3] que construyó las líneas férreas que unieron la región oriental con la occidental. Para garantizar jurídicamente los privilegios que *de facto* le habían sido concedidos durante la Ocupación Militar, el Gobierno Interventor dictó la Ley de Ferrocarriles de 1902, u Orden Militar Nº139, mediante la cual se otorgaba a un privado (la Cuba Company) el derecho de expropiación, y el de crear medios propios para reprimir las huelgas.

La aprobación de la Ley de Ferrocarriles realizada al igual que la OM 155 a pocos meses de la retirada del ejército de ocupación norteamericano fue también duramente criticada por la prensa. El periódico *El Mundo* de 2 de abril de 1902 escribió al respecto:

"El Poder de la Cuba Co." Al establecerse el gobierno de la República, la intervención nos deja, por obra y gracia de Mr. Wood, un poder que puede llegar a ser tan fuerte como el ejecutivo y el legislativo, que a sus anchas legisle y ejecute conforme a sus necesidades y ambiciones y que, apoyado falsamente en la Ley Platt, pretenderá ser inviolable y pondrá el grito en el cielo cada vez que quiera la república poner coto a su poderosa fuerza... Nos referimos a la Cuba Company, para quien se ha hecho la última ley de ferrocarriles y que representa una fuerza de absorción peligrosa y desnaturalizada... Hacer, en estos días en que el poder interventor debiera concretarse a mantener el orden y a preparar la constitución al nuevo gobierno, una ley para salvar intereses extraños y consagrarlos como invulnerables e inextinguibles, es cosa que mientras más

pensemos en ella más abrumadora y atentatoria nos parece...

Dos días más tarde, el 4 de abril de 1902 apareció la siguiente información en el mismo diario:

Hemos afirmado en uno de nuestros últimos artículos que la intervención prepara las cosas, al irse, de tal modo, que seremos conquistados por la Cuba Co., y la soberanía de nuestra pobre y triste tierra llegará a pertenecerle al Sr. William Van Horne, canadiense riquísimo que ignora y le importa poco saber lo que de ello tendrá dicho la ciencia, ¿y cómo ha podido el gobierno interventor realizar ese prodigio digno de las más ilustres personalidades que de Maquiavelo a Leonardo Wood han sobresalido en la estrategia política? La Ley Platt, obra de Van Horne y Wood, en combinación con otros genios, autoriza o legaliza, por la república, todas las ilegalidades cometidas por el gobierno militar en la intervención. Dado este paso esencialísimo, y cuando ya empieza a tocar retirada el general Wood se descuelga con una ley de ferrocarriles...

Los mecanismos jurídicos utilizados por el gobierno interventor norteamericano para beneficiar unilateralmente a su grupo, fueron criticados duramente en la prensa escrita y contribuyeron al surgimiento consensuado de los rasgos negativos del estereotipo, porque ponían al descubierto el peligro de la pérdida de la personalidad política del grupo cubano y su impotencia.

La OM 62 o Ley de Deslinde de las Haciendas Comuneras

Las haciendas comuneras eran un tipo de propiedad que predominaba en la región oriental del país. Consistía en la tenencia y usufructo de una parte de la hacienda por parte de campesinos individuales. Este régimen, heredado de la colonia, imposibilitaba la compra-venta de la tierra, pues consideraba indivisible la propiedad de la hacienda y otorgaba el derecho de usufructo a través de la posesión.

Ante la necesidad de modernizar este régimen y permitir la compra-venta de la tierra, el gobierno de la

---

3. Sir William Van Horne, nació en Illinois, de origen holandés y nacionalizado súbdito británico. En 1900 desembarcó por primera vez en Cuba. Había construido el Canadian Pacific y su fama era internacional. Requirió de sólo dos años para construir el ferrocarril que uniría la región oriental de la isla con la occidental.

primera intervención norteamericana nombró una comisión de juristas cubanos para estudiar ese problema. Se rechazó la proposición de que el Gobierno asumiese la responsabilidad de la división de las tierras y se dejó a la iniciativa individual el presentar cada caso ante los tribunales creados por la Orden Militar No.62 que regulaba el deslinde y división de las haciendas comuneras.

En la aplicación de esta ley, debido a los propios procedimientos jurídicos implícitos en los procesos de deslindes, casi siempre salían perjudicados aquellos que durante generaciones habían cultivado la tierra, entre otras razones, porque la mayoría eran analfabetos y carecían de recursos para hacer las gestiones administrativas correspondientes. Esto provocó el desalojo de la gran mayoría de los guajiros de las tierras que usufructuaban. El informe de la Comisión de Asuntos Cubanos de la Foreign Policy Association, publicado en el libro *Problemas de la Nueva Cuba*, plantea al respecto:

Los cubanos criticaron la aplicación de esta orden y esta fue modificada en varios respectos por los tribunales después del cese de la Intervención Norteamericana, ya que se alegaba que los resultados de dicho decreto eran injustos, especialmente contra los pequeños propietarios que carecían de instrucción.

...Nos parece que el establecimiento de ese sistema de propiedad individual echó los cimientos para el desarrollo de la moderna corporación y de los actuales latifundios, que no habrían sido posibles de haber continuado en efecto el antiguo sistema de posesión de las tierras (Foreign Policy Association, 1935, pp. 55-56)

Al respecto señalaremos la opinión, hecha pública, del General Manuel Sanguily, prestigiosa figura de la Guerra de Independencia e intelectual íntimamente vinculado a la vida política del país, sobre la política de expansión territorial practicada por los norteamericanos. En uno de sus más conocidos discursos planteaba:

...los americanos vienen aquí como fueron a Tejas, como fueron a Hawai, como han ido a la Isla de Pinos. El mismo impulso que entonces les moviera, muévelos ahora. Llevaron a Tejas y a Hawai sus capitales, se hicieron dueños de la tierra primero, y luego del gobierno, y al fin convirtieron países extraños e in-

dependientes, aún pasando por transitoria forma republicana, en posesiones de su patria (Pichardo, 1973, p. 246).

En la memoria de los campesinos cubanos aún permanecen vivos los atropellos realizados durante los procesos de deslinde. No olvidemos que éstos son transmitidos de generación a generación y contribuyen a mantener vivo, con mayor fuerza que las informaciones proporcionadas por otras fuentes, los rasgos negativos del estereotipo del exogrupo. En uno de los testimonios obtenidos por la autora en una investigación de campo cuando se encontraba trabajando en el Atlas Etnocultural de Cuba, en Mayarí, provincia del Holguín, el campesino Rafael Calzadilla, protagonista de la rebelión que tuvo lugar en la década del treinta cuando la Compañía Hato del Medio S.A. intentó hacer el deslinde de la Hacienda Caballería de Barajagua, nos relató que:

La compañía empezó a pasarle desalojos a muchos campesinos. Logró desalojar a algunos como a Enriqueta López y Antolín Torres a quienes les botaron todas sus cosas para la guardarraya, les tumbaron las casas y a las latas de manteca le metieron cuchillos. Más tarde pasaron a la finca de José (Pepe) Hernández pero allí encontraron un grupo de campesinos que se habían reunido armados con machetes y escopetas para evitar el desalojo. Ellos pelearon contra los guardajurados, los guardias rurales, y contra un grupo de haitianos que la compañía había llevado para que les tumbaran los platanales. La pelea comenzó cuando los campesinos defendían sus plantaciones de los haitianos que venían con la guardia rural, que eran unos infelices que no sabían lo que hacían. En la riña murieron varios haitianos y varias personas resultaron heridas. En esos años la compañía no pudo realizar más desalojos (González, 1988).

La Enmienda Platt

Aún cuando la Convención Constituyente estuvo integrada por cubanos activos defensores de los intereses del país, muchos de los cuáles habían participado como combatientes en la Guerra de Independencia, el gobierno de los Estados Unidos les obligó a incluir y aceptar como apéndice a la Constitución de la República la conocida Enmienda Platt,[4] que regulaba las relaciones entre esos dos países. El principal instrumento de presión para lograr sus fines consistió en plantear que mientras no fuera aprobada la Enmienda Platt, no se consideraría pacificada la isla y continuaría en ella el ejército norteamericano de ocupación.

En una entrevista realizada al Senador norteamericano Mr. Proctor durante la visita que realizó a la Isla en marzo de 1902, para garantizar la aceptación de la Enmienda Platt por parte de los miembros de la Convención Constituyente, aparece publicado lo siguiente:

> Periodista: Pero, en la hipótesis que la Convención Constitucional cubana rechazase en absoluto la Enmienda Platt ¿Qué haría el Ejecutivo?
>
> Mr. Proctor: Pues sencillamente, que continuaría la intervención con grave perjuicio para Cuba, que no definiría su situación (Entrevista a Mr. Proctor, 1901, marzo 23).

La respuesta de los cubanos a la imposición de la Enmienda Platt fue recogida por todos los canales sociales de transmisión, en particular por toda la prensa escrita del país. Devino, como veremos, en el símbolo de la conducta de los norteamericanos y fue, y en la actualidad es, un factor esencial en el surgimiento de algunos rasgos negativos del estereotipo que del norteamericano tienen los cubanos. Ejemplo paradigmático de cómo fue transmitido, en su momento, este acontecimiento histórico es el siguiente: El periódico *La Discusión*, uno de los más importantes y de mayor circulación en el país, publicó, con relación a este hecho, una caricatura donde representaba a Cuba crucificada, y al Senador Platt como centurión romano, que le ofrecía la esponja de la enmienda clavada en una lanza (Jenks, 1960, p. 99).

Los canales de transmisión social han sido esenciales en la formación del estereotipo consensuado sobre el norteamericano. En aquella época en La Habana había 11 periódicos y 7 revistas, entre ellas *Bohemia*. También se publicaban numerosos periódicos de organizaciones anarquistas y gremiales, así como numerosos periódicos locales en el interior de la isla. El principal periódico liberal de la época era el *Heraldo de Cuba*. El periódico de los conservadores era *La Discusión*. El periódico representante de los intereses

---

4. La Enmienda Platt planteaba:

Artículo 1º. El Gobierno de Cuba nunca celebrará con ningún poder o poderes extranjeros ningún tratado u otro pacto que menoscabe o tienda a menoscabar la independencia de Cuba, ni en manera alguna autorice o permita a ningún poder o poderes extranjeros obtener por colonización o para propósitos militares o navales o de otra manera asiento o jurisdicción sobre ninguna porción de dicha isla.

Artículo 2º. Dicho Gobierno no asumirá ninguna deuda pública para el pago de cuyos intereses y amortización definitiva, después de cubiertos los gastos corrientes del Gobierno, resulten inadecuados los ingresos ordinarios..

Artículo 3º. El Gobierno de Cuba consiente que los Estados Unidos puedan ejercer el derecho de intervenir para la preservación de la independencia y el sostenimiento de un gobierno adecuado a la protección de la vida, la propiedad y la libertad individual, y al cumplimiento de las obligaciones con respecto a Cuba, impuestas a los Estados Unidos por el Tratado de París, y que deben ahora ser asumidas y cumplidas por el Gobierno de Cuba.

Artículo 4º. Todos los actos realizados por los Estados Unidos en Cuba durante su ocupación militar serán ratificados y tenidos por válidos, y todos los derechos legalmente adquiridos en virtud de aquellos serán mantenidos y protegidos.

Artículo 5º. El Gobierno de Cuba ejecutará y hasta donde fuere necesario ampliará los planes ya proyectados u otros que mutuamente se convengan para el saneamiento de las poblaciones de la Isla, con el fin de evitar la recurrencia de enfermedades epidémicas e infecciosas, protegiendo así al pueblo y al comercio de Cuba, lo mismo que al comercio y al pueblo de los puertos del sur de los Estados Unidos.

Artículo 6º. La Isla de Pinos queda omitida de los límites de Cuba, propuestos por la Constitución, dejándose para un futuro tratado la fijación de su pertenencia.

Artículo 7º. Para poner en condiciones a los Estados Unidos de mantener la independencia de Cuba y proteger al pueblo de la misma, así como para su propia defensa, el Gobierno de Cuba venderá o arrendará a los Estados Unidos las tierras necesarias para carboneras o estaciones navales en ciertos puntos determinados, que se convendrán con el presidente de los Estados Unidos..

Artículo 8º. El Gobierno de Cuba insertará las anteriores disposiciones en un Tratado Permanente con los Estados Unidos. (Jenks, 1960).

del grupo español, y también conservador, era *El Diario de la Marina* (Rivero, 2001). El papel de la prensa escrita, en este caso, fue decisivo porque las opiniones de la totalidad de las personalidades públicas aparecidas en los periódicos eran muy críticas respecto a dicha Enmienda. Entre ellas encontramos la evaluación que hizo Juan Gualberto Gómez, líder político y periodista muy respetado por el grupo cubano:

> Reservar a los Estados Unidos la facultad de decidir por sí mismos cuándo está amenazada la independencia y cuándo, por tanto, deben intervenir para preservarla, es tanto como entregarles la llave de nuestra casa para que puedan entrar a todas horas, de día y de noche, cuando se les antoje, con buenas o malas intenciones...

> Si son los Estados Unidos los llamados a decir qué gobierno cubano merece el calificativo de "adecuado," éste solamente podrá vivir contando con su benevolencia (Memoria del Senado de Cuba, 1902-1904, 26 de marzo de 1901).

La respuesta del grupo norteamericano a esta interpretación de la Enmienda Platt, no se hizo esperar. El gobierno estadounidense aclaraba las buenas intenciones que le llevó a imponer al grupo cubano, como un anexo a la constitución, la Enmienda Platt donde quedaban establecidas jurídicamente las relaciones entre ambas naciones. Con referencia a la clausula 3°, que es la que otorgaba el derecho de intervención, planteaba:

> Esta cláusula no ataca a la soberanía de Cuba: la deja independiente y soberana bajo su propia bandera. No tiene otro objeto que autorizar a los Estados Unidos para que en casos extremos puedan proteger la absoluta independencia de Cuba y quiera Dios que nunca llegue este caso. El espíritu, la tendencia, la esencia de la enmienda Platt no es otro que establecer en Cuba una nación independiente y soberana.

> Pero los Estados Unidos van más allá en favor de Cuba: quieren garantizar la subsistencia de ésta como una república libre e independiente (Memoria del Senado de Cuba 1902-1904, 29 de marzo de 1901).

Tales manifestaciones públicas, que contrastaban con lo establecido por las Órdenes Militares mencionadas más arriba, que evidentemente lesionaban los intere-

ses de los cubanos, lejos de paliar, reforzaban las consecuencias que sobre el estereotipo del norteamericano tenía la imposición de la Enmienda Platt a la incipiente República.

El nacimiento de una república castrada políticamente por el grupo norteamericano fue, indudablemente, un hecho que marcó las relaciones entre los dos grupos. Los sentimientos de frustración del grupo cubano estaban presentes en los discursos de los políticos, muchos de ellos pronunciados por connotados luchadores independentistas muy respetados por la población, como el General Manuel Sanguily o Juan Gualberto Gómez. También los periódicos, como *El Diario de la Marina*, representante de los intereses del grupo español, el *Heraldo de Cuba, La Discusión*, y *El Mundo*, los de mayor circulación en la isla, se hacían eco del malestar que causaba la política norteamericana hacia Cuba. Como en los primeros años del siglo XX en Cuba la prensa escrita constituía el principal canal de transmisión público para proporcionar información, resultaba obvio que a través de estas fuentes externas, el grupo cubano obtenía la información que posibilitaba la categorización consensuada del exogrupo norteamericano, de tal modo que este canal social de transmisión resultó esencial para la formación de los rasgos negativos del estereotipo que surgió en aquellos tiempos y que perdura en la actualidad.

El sentimiento de frustración del grupo cubano, la percepción del engaño de que había sido objeto, el sentirse discriminado al ser considerado por el exogrupo como incapaz de preservar los principios por los que se había hecho la guerra anticolonial, fueron detonantes del cambio que se produjo en el estereotipo del grupo norteamericano.

Veinte años después de la imposición de la Enmienda Platt, se hizo pública la documentación que corroboró la percepción que tuvo y tenía el grupo cubano del norteamericano. Entre esos documentos encontramos la carta del Gobernador Militar de la isla, General Wood, dirigió al Secretario de Guerra General Root, y que citamos a continuación:

> ...Estoy trabajando en la preparación de una Constitución para la Isla, análoga a la nuestra, y en integrar en dicha carta orgánica ciertas relaciones y acuerdos

específicos entre los Estados Unidos y Cuba. Este proyecto... habrá de ser sometido a la más cuidadosa consideración antes de presentarlo a la Asamblea como modelo para su adopción...

El nuevo gobierno deberá estar sometido a un residente norteamericano con facultad de veto y de mando sobre el ejército... (Roig, 1973, p. 299-300).

En otra carta de fecha 18 de octubre de 1902, comentaba Leonardo Wood a Theodoro Roosevelt, en esos años Presidente de los Estados Unidos:

...a Cuba se le ha dejado poca o ninguna independencia con la Enmienda Platt... y lo único indicado ahora es buscar la anexión... durante el período que Cuba mantenga su propio Gobierno es muy de desear que tenga uno que conduzca a su progreso y a su mejoramiento. No puede hacer ciertos tratados sin nuestro consentimiento, ni pedir prestado más allá de ciertos límites, y debe mantener las condiciones sanitarias que se le ha preceptuado, por todo lo cual es evidente que está en lo absoluto en nuestras manos y creo que no hay un gobierno europeo que la considere por un momento como otra cosa sino lo que es, una verdadera dependencia de los Estados Unidos y como tal es acreedora de nuestra consideración. Con el control que tenemos sobre Cuba, un control que sin duda pronto se convertirá en posesión, en breve controlaremos el comercio de azúcar en el mundo. Creo que es una adquisición muy deseable para los Estados Unidos. La isla se norteamericanizará gradualmente, y a su debido tiempo contaremos con una de las más ricas y deseables posesiones que haya en el mundo... (Nearing y Freeman, 1973, p.312-313).

La imposición de la Enmienda Platt, la forma en que se llevó a cabo todo ese proceso, la amplia difusión en la prensa de las percepciones de los políticos cubanos, el conocimiento posterior (hecho público dos décadas después) de los contenidos de la documentación de las negociaciones marcaron, de manera indeleble, y permanente, la actitud prejuiciosa de los cubano hacia los norteamericanos.

LA MEMORIA HISTÓRICA

Uno de los canales de transmisión que contribuye a mantener vivo los prejuicios es la memoria histórica. Juega un papel muy importante en la formación de los estereotipos grupales los textos de historia utilizados en las escuelas, tanto públicas como privadas,[5] del país. A continuación veremos como analizaba la imposición de la Enmienda Platt uno de los libros de texto más utilizado en la enseñanza del bachillerato durante las décadas de los cuarenta y cincuenta, el de *Historia de Cuba* de los Doctores Marbán y Leiva. En el análisis de este hecho histórico se exponen los criterios de diversos políticos, entre ellos, citan el siguiente juicio sobre las consecuencias del Apéndice Constitucional realizado por Juan Gualberto Gómez.

Sólo vivirían, aceptada la Enmienda Platt, los gobiernos cubanos que cuenten con el apoyo y benevolencia del Gobierno de los Estados Unidos; y lo más claro de esta situación sería que únicamente tendríamos gobiernos raquíticos y míseros conceptuados como incapaces desde su formación, condenados a vivir más atentos a obtener el beneficio de los poderes de la Unión que a servir y defender los intereses de Cuba. En una palabra, sólo tendríamos una ficción de gobierno y pronto nos convenceríamos de que era mejor no tener ninguno, y ser administrados oficial y abiertamente desde Washington que por desacreditados funcionarios cubanos dóciles instrumentos de un poder extraño e irresponsable (Marbán y Leiva, 1951, p. 606).

En este libro de texto de historia, casi siempre que se presentaba la oportunidad, se juzgaba la conducta de los norteamericanos. Así, observamos que cuando analizaba la conducta del gobierno de los Estados Unidos durante la insurrección de los Independientes de Color, en nota a pie de página, señalaba:

La intromisión de los Estados Unidos en nuestros asuntos interiores la evitó esta vez y también cuando la campaña veteranista, el gran cubano Manuel Sanguily, Secretario de Estado de José Miguel Gómez de 1910 a 1913 y mantenedor decidido de nuestra libertad, nuestra integridad territorial, nuestra indepen-

---

5. La enseñanza privada en Cuba, por ley, no tenía carácter oficial, por lo que los estudiantes de estas escuelas debían realizar los exámenes en las escuelas públicas. Por tales motivos, además de la alta calidad de la enseñanza pública en Cuba, los textos que utilizaban las escuelas privadas eran los mismos de las escuelas públicas.

dencia económica y nuestra soberanía (Marbán y Leiva, 1951, p. 622).

La imposición del Apéndice Constitucional devino en el símbolo de la conducta de los norteamericanos y en elemento esencial del contenido del estereotipo que del norteamericano tiene el cubano. En el verano del año 2000, en carta que nos envió un amigo nuestro, connotado intelectual de origen cubano residente en los Estados Unidos, éste se quejaba de que aún hoy, al discutirse acerca de las relaciones presentes y futuras entre Cuba y Estados Unidos, se pone sobre la mesa, como factor primordial, la Enmienda Platt. Un siglo después este hecho sigue siendo determinante del estereotipo norteamericano, con la inevitable consecuencia de ejercer una gran influencia en los juicios atribucionales y en las valoraciones que el grupo cubano, posiblemente, hará de las futuras relaciones intergrupales con el exogrupo norteamericano.

La percepción de la actividad empresarial de los norteamericanos

El estereotipo del norteamericano lo resumía, en su primer libro de ensayo, *Entreactos,* escrito en 1912, José Antonio Ramos, destacado literato cubano, premio nacional de literatura en 1917:

> No es cierto que los Estados Unidos sea un pueblo de cretinos ambiciosos y groseros. Neutralicemos sus armas con sus armas. Opongamos a su expansión una paz firme, una laboriosidad como la suya, infatigable y abierta a todas las corrientes...
>
> Y si a pesar de nuestros esfuerzos bien empleados, somos aniquilados y absorbidos, la Historia—esa historia que tanto parece preocuparnos—no nos acusará de haber perdido el tiempo insultando gratuitamente a los conquistadores, y tratando de echarles en cara defectos y faltas que deberíamos empezar por remediar en nosotros mismos (Ramos, 1913, p. 19-20).

Este estereotipo del grupo norteamericano que se estableció durante el primer cuarto del siglo XX estuvo marcado, de forma decisiva, por las relaciones competitivas determinadas por los conflictos de intereses que tuvieron lugar en los campos económicos y políticos.

Recién iniciada la ocupación militar, comenzó la compra de tierra por ciudadanos y empresas norte-

americanas. Ya hacia 1905, según la revista *Cuba Review*, 13 mil norteamericanos habían comprado en Cuba terrenos por valor de más de 50 millones de dólares. Sólo en la provincia de Camagüey, ubicada en la región oriental, había 7 mil propiedades estadounidenses, cuyo valor ascendía a 28 millones de dólares. Siete octavas partes de la tierras adyacentes a Sancti Spíritus eran propiedad de norteamericanos: "Los norteamericanos poseen del 7 al 10 por ciento de la superficie total de Cuba" (Jenks, 1960, p. 164). Estos nuevos propietarios de tierras se habían establecido, principalmente, en la parte oriental de la isla, donde la tierra era más barata, y donde, después de construido el ferrocarril, se trasladaría el peso de la industria azucarera, que hasta entonces se encontraba en la región occidental. Con referencia a estos hechos, en el número XXX de la revista *Louisiana Planter*, se planteaba:

> Poco a poco va pasando toda la isla a manos de ciudadanos norteamericanos, lo cual es el medio más sencillo y seguro de conseguir la anexión a los Estados Unidos (Jenks, 1960, p. 164).

Algunas de las publicaciones de la época recogen la percepción que de este fenómeno tenía el grupo cubano. Luis Felipe Rodríguez, autor del cuento "El Naranjal," expuso, en la década del veinte, el sentimiento de frustración del pueblo. En él describe el desengaño sufrido por los cubanos cuando narra los procedimientos utilizados por algunos norteamericanos para posesionarse de las tierras en una región campesina del país:

> Juan Smith, que cayó allí no se sabe como, le echó un vistazo a la tierra pobre y estéril del pobre campesino, Tranquilino Liborio, y le hizo saber, como parte de su excentricidad y rareza que lo habían llevado por esas tierras tan distantes de su hogar, su intención de comprarle las tierras por quinientos pesos. Tranquilino, al mirarlo, no pudo menos que convencerse de que estaba hablando con el mayor de los generales de los bobos. Poco tiempo después, Tranquilino vio cómo de esas tierras, antes improductivas, en virtud de la utilización de la química, brotó un naranjal. Tranquilino se puso a meditar y se dio cuenta que el yanqui de bobo no tenía un pelo. Entonces el yanqui de marras le pidió que le vendiera el resto de la finca por la que le daría otros quinientos dólares, en nombre de la civi-

lización, a la que nadie podía oponerse. A esto respondió Tranquilino: "Váyase usted a expansionarse al infierno. !Me cogiste asando maíz, americano¡" (Ibarra, 1994, pp. 117-118).

Agudización del sentimiento anti norteamericano

Los conflictos generados eran constantemente denunciados por los medios de comunicación lo que llevaba a crear entre la población de la isla un estado de opinión consensuado que, generalmente, iba en detrimento del estereotipo del grupo norteamericano.

Estos conflictos llegaron a su climax durante y después de la Primera Guerra Mundial. Durante esos años el control de la producción y del mercado del azúcar cubano devino para los Estados Unidos en una cuestión estratégica vinculada a la guerra.

El 6 de abril de 1917 el Congreso de Estados Unidos declaró la guerra a Alemania. Al día siguiente, el Presidente de la República, Mario García Menocal, con la aprobación del Congreso, le declara la guerra a Alemania. Se convertía en la primera nación del continente americano que siguió a los Estados Unidos.

El 15 de abril de 1917, en el acto de proclamación como Presidente de los Estados Unidos, Woodrow Wilson hizo mención a la escasez de reservas alimentarias en el mundo. El 9 de mayo de ese año, Herbert C. Hoover, planteó a la Comisión Senatorial de Agricultura y Montes lo siguiente:

> Me parece probable que a mediados de octubre este país haya agotado sus existencias de azúcar. La perspectiva es desconsoladora. La cosecha cubana puede ser inferior en un millón y cuarto de toneladas a los 4 000 000 normales (Jenks, 1960, p.191).

Mientras, en Cuba se iniciaron una serie de disturbios políticos causados por la reelección, considerada fraudulenta por la oposición, del entonces Presidente, Mario García Menocal. Como consecuencia de esta situación, en el mes de febrero de 1917, el partido Liberal, al que se le unió una parte del ejército, se sublevó y llegó a controlar la provincia de Oriente. Ante esta situación, los Estados Unidos, haciendo uso de la cláusula tercera de la Enmienda Platt, se pusieron al lado de Menocal.

El gobierno norteamericano hizo publicar una serie de notas dirigidas más al pueblo que al gobierno de Cuba. A continuación transcribimos la que se publicó en la prensa el 19 de febrero:

1. El gobierno de los Estados Unidos apoya y mantiene al gobierno constitucional de la República de Cuba.

2. El gobierno de los Estados Unidos considera la revolución armada contra el gobierno constitucional de Cuba como un acto ilegal y anticonstitucional que no debe fomentarse.

3. Los jefes de la revolución serán responsables de los perjuicios causados a los extranjeros y de la destrucción de las propiedades de los mismos.

4. El gobierno de los Estados Unidos estudiará con el mayor cuidado la actitud que adoptará hacia las personas interesadas en la actual perturbación de la paz en la República de Cuba" (Jenks, 1960, p. 184).

El gobierno estadounidense, alegando la defensa de sus propiedades, ordenó el desembarco de los "marines." Primero lo hicieron, el 26 de febrero, por la costa de Guantánamo; luego, el 8 de marzo, los marines norteamericanos, se apoderaron de Santiago de Cuba, a los pocos días los efectivos navales norteamericanos ocupaban Manzanillo, el Cobre, Nuevitas (Camagüey) y Preston.

La percepción que de esta situación tuvo el prestigioso historiador norteamericano de esa época, Leland H. Jenks, sobre estos acontecimientos fue reflejada en su libro *Nuestra Colonia de Cuba*, en estos términos:

> Casi parecía que los Estados Unidos, que pronto iban a entrar en guerra, no con el pueblo, sino con el gobierno de Alemania, se disponían a declararla, no al gobierno sino a una gran parte del pueblo de Cuba (Jenks, 1960, pp.184).

Los Doctores Marbán y Leiva relataban así este episodio de la historia de Cuba:

> El primero de noviembre de 1916 se efectuó la lucha comicial, que resultó reñida y el Gobierno menocalista echó mano de cuantos medios tenía a su alcance para impedir el triunfo de Zayas. Las protestas de los

partidarios de los liberales fueron numerosas y violentas. Llevado el asunto a los tribunales de justicia, éstos ordenaron la celebración de elecciones parciales; pero antes de que pudieran llevarse a efecto las mismas estalló un formidable movimiento armado dirigido por el Partido Liberal y en el que tomaron parte numerosos elementos del Ejército. La rebelión, a pesar de su importancia, fracasó, al ser condenado el movimiento por las "notas" del embajador norteamericano Míster González, que dio a conocer los propósitos de su Gobierno de no reconocer ningún Gobierno producto de una revolución; y por la caída como prisionero, en Caicaje (Santa Clara) del general José Miguel Gómez, alma de la insurrección (Marbán y Leiva, 1951, p. 625).

La crisis económica de post guerra

La crisis de post guerra. fue, como veremos a continuación, uno de los hechos más importante en el surgimiento del sentimiento antinorteamericano.

Cuando a fines de 1919 el precio del azúcar quedó libre de todo control internacional, éste comenzó a subir con rapidez y la nación alcanzó una prosperidad inimaginable. Este período económico es conocido en la historia de Cuba como el de la "Danza de los Millones."

La zafra de 1920 fue de 3.735.425 toneladas a un precio promedio de 11,95 centavos la libra. En una situación normal, ello hubiera conllevado el enriquecimiento del país y, en particular, de sus empresarios. Sin embargo, en los últimos meses del año veinte, concretamente a partir de octubre, la "Danza de los Millones" termina de forma catastrófica. El precio del azúcar que en el mes de marzo estaba en 22,5 centavos la libra comenzó a descender a partir del mes de agosto hasta llegar a 11 centavos la libra. Los especuladores, quienes compraron el azúcar a precios intermedios entre 12 y 20 centavos, quedaron arruinados. Sus resultados fueron sintetizados por Leland Jenks:

La "danza de los millones" terminó en la catástrofe del otoño de 1920, que produjo la bancarrota del pueblo y el gobierno de Cuba, trajo una nueva forma de tutela política yanqui y dio a Wall Street el control económico efectivo de la isla (Jenks, 1960, p.184).

Los banqueros, la mayoría españoles y cubanos, que habían concedidos préstamos sobre el azúcar, ingenios y cosechas se encontraron ante una crisis financiera de la que no pudieron salir. La casi totalidad de la banca de la isla se declaró en bancarrota. Una parte del azúcar no encontró mercado. Una gran parte de la población que tenía sus ahorros en los bancos, también quedó arruinada.

Para tener una idea de las consecuencias de la crisis en la concentración de capitales norteamericanos en el sector azucarero, vemos que ya en el mes de agosto de 1922, los capitales norteamericanos habían absorbido, aproximadamente, el 60% de la industria azucarera. En lo relativo a la tierra, en 1925-1926, la Cuban American Sugar Co. poseía seis ingenios con 14.867 caballerías de tierra; la Cuba Canes Sugar Co., 12 ingenios con 19.844 caballerías; la General Sugar Co., con las compañías que de ella dependían, nueve ingenios con 8.872 caballerías; y la United Fruit Co., para no hacer larga la relación, dos ingenios, con 8.578 caballerías. Sólo estas cuatro compañías juntas controlaban 29 ingenios, con 43.261 caballerías, cifra, que representa, aproximadamente, el 25% de toda la tierra que poseían los centrales azucareros de Cuba (Guerra, 1970, pp. 94-95).

En medio de la crisis financiera, en noviembre de 1920, se realizaron las elecciones presidenciales con el consecuente conflicto entre los partidos políticos (Liberal y Conservador). Según Leland Jenks, el gobierno de los Estados Unidos envió, sin que mediara solicitud por parte de alguna autoridad o personalidad de la Isla, al General Enoch H. Crowder. Numerosos técnicos norteamericanos invadieron la isla. Así comenzó una intervención que de hecho duró tres años. Durante ese período los norteamericanos decidieron en las cuestiones financieras, en las leyes de la moratoria, en la reforma constitucional, en la confección del presupuesto, en la reorganización del ejército y otros asuntos de índole puramente doméstica (Jenks, 1960).

Sobre esta intervención se hacían constantes alusiones en la prensa; en la mayoría de los casos utilizaban descalificativos y evaluaciones negativas. Todos los pasos intervencionistas dados por los norteamericanos eran comentados y criticados duramente por los diferentes canales sociales de transmisión. Uno de los casos más escandaloso fue el de los "Memorandos de

Crowder." Los Estados Unidos decidieron enviar una serie de memorandos dirigidos a Zayas, denunciando determinados hechos relativos a la corrupción del gobierno y pidiendo la adopción de soluciones para los problemas pendientes, como el ajuste de los presupuestos. Se suponía que eran secretos pero en realidad eran "vox populi" en el país. El último memorando fechado el 21 de julio de 1922 lo publicó el *Heraldo de Cuba* el 5 de agosto de ese año y el *New York Times* el 7 de agosto. El escándalo fue tan grande que dimitió todo el gabinete del gobierno (Jenks, 1960, pp. 239-240).

Una de las vías que utilizaron los cubanos para deslegitimar a los norteamericanos fue la sátira política. El semanario *La Política Cómica*, de gran circulación en el país, fue unas de sus fuentes más importante. Al comentar el escándalo de los Memorandos, el 6 de julio de 1922, apareció una caricatura titulada "Los dos presidentes," en ella figuraba Zayas firmando un documento mientras Crowder le llevaba la mano. "¿Qué pongo?—preguntaba Zayas—¿Crowder o mi nombre?" (Jenks, 1960, p. 240).

Los fuertes enfrentamientos que tuvieron lugar durante este período influenciaron grandemente en los juicios evaluativos realizados por el grupo cubano. Éstos fueron difundidos, entre otros canales de transmisión, por el ya citado libro de texto de Marbán y Leiva:

> Al mismo tiempo que encaraba la crisis económica, el doctor Zayas tuvo que afrontar las pretensiones del general Crowder, representante especial del Presidente de los Estados Unidos, de intervenir en el gobierno de la nación, invocando para ello los derechos que pretendía derivar del Tratado de Relaciones Permanentes (Enmienda Platt) entre su nación y Cuba. El General Crowder apremiaba constantemente al Gobierno de Zayas, por medio de memorándum o notas, para que pusiera en orden la administración pública y restableciera el crédito nacional.

El doctor Zayas, colocado en una difícil situación diplomática, por cuanto no podía desconocer abiertamente las indicaciones del general Crowder sin exponer al país a posibles represalias económicas por parte del gobierno norteamericano, supo dominar la injerencia del general Crowder empleando medios hábi-

les que salvaron el derecho de Cuba a regir sus propios destinos (Marbán y Leiva, 1951, p.627).

Los sentimientos de repulsa se hacían más fuertes en la misma medida en que aumentaban los conflictos de intereses. A partir de estos sentimientos negativos la mayoría de los cubanos enjuiciaba al norteamericano.

El conocido historiador norteamericano Leland Jenks plantea, en un análisis que hizo sobre el nacionalismo cubano en el acápite titulado "Aspectos antiyanquis del nacionalismo cubano" en su libro *Nuestra Colonia de Cuba*:

> Cuba, libre de la influencia española y siempre independiente del poder de la Iglesia, alimentó su celo patriótico con un resentimiento antinorteamericano.... El origen principal del sentimiento antiyanqui es la actividad de las grandes empresas norteamericanas en Cuba (Jenks, 1960, p. 254).

Y cita un editorial de la revistas *Carteles* de 5 de enero de 1926:

> Pocos países habrá en que la penetración económica y política de la plutocracia yanqui haya llegado a límites tan excesivos y consecuencias tan perjudiciales como en Cuba... Casi todos los recursos azucareros están en sus manos; y cada central administrado por una de estas compañías constituye un verdadero feudo, donde los funcionarios cubanos ocupan los puestos más inferiores, teniendo que someterse ellos, y los obreros al trato más brutal y la explotación más ilimitada, sin la protección de las leyes y las garantías constitucionales de Cuba (Jenks, 1961, p. 254).

No le falta razón al afirmar que la intensa actividad empresarial de los norteamericanos en la isla fue uno de los factores determinantes del resentimiento hacia los estadounidenses, pero también hay que considerar los factores políticos, sin olvidar la importancia que tiene en la formación del prejuicio la forma en que los hechos fueron percibidos y transmitidos, en primera instancia, por la prensa escrita, y posteriormente, por las fuentes culturales, educacionales y familiares.

CONCLUSIONES

El prejuicio hacia los norteamericanos no es fruto de la dictadura de Fidel Castro, es el resultado de los acontecimientos ocurridos casi un siglo atrás, y que aún tienen una influencia directa sobre los estereotipos actuales.

La naturaleza de las relaciones intergrupales pasadas, no se olvidan fácilmente. Guerras anteriores, intereses contrapuestos, hostilidades, o por el contrario, cooperación y amistad tienen un impacto acumulativo con el tiempo sobre la naturaleza presente de las relaciones intergrupales, y forman parte, también, de los contenidos de los estereotipos de los miembros del grupo (Bar-Tal, 1994). Los textos de historia de Cuba, de donde muchos niños y adolescentes han tomado a sus héroes que han servido de modelo de conducta, siempre han presentado un enemigo exterior (España o los Estados Unidos). Ello contribuye a exacerbar los sentimientos patrióticos y nacionalistas, y ayudan, entre otras fuentes, a mantener vivo en forma de sentimientos los acontecimientos pasados. El sentimiento antinorteamericano, basado en la historia de la naturaleza de las relaciones intergrupales, era inculcado, por esta vía, a casi toda la juventud cubana.

Los textos escolares, los periódicos, los discursos de líderes, la literatura, las representaciones teatrales fueron los canales utilizados durante el período analizado para llegar al grupo y fueron los responsables de que los cubanos tuvieran una percepción similar del exogrupo norteamericano.

Durante más de cuarenta años de gobierno, Fidel Castro ha mantenido vivo en el pueblo cubano este sentimiento antinorteamericano para consolidar la cohesión grupal en torno a su dictadura, siempre bajo la amenaza de un enemigo externo.

La existencia de tales sentimientos son un obstáculo para el tránsito de la sociedad cubana hacia la democracia. En dicho tránsito los Estados Unidos deberá jugar un papel muy importante no sólo por sus relaciones históricas con Cuba, sino también por la influencia que ejerce y ejercerá sobre la economía y la sociedad cubanas. Por tal razón hay que tomar medidas para erradicar, o al menos paliar, los sentimientos de desconfianza y resentimiento de la población cubana hacia los norteamericanos. Para poder elaborar medidas adecuadas en ese sentido, resulta imprescindible el conocimiento de las causas del surgimiento del prejuicio, así como de los mecanismos que han hecho que perdure en la memoria de la población cubana.

BIBLIOGRAFÍA

Bar-Tal, D. (1994). "Formación y cambio de estereotipos étnicos y nacionales. Un modelo integrado." En *Psicología Política*, No. 9, pp. 21-49.

Brown R.J. (1998). *Prejuicio: su Psicología Social*, Madrid: Alianza.

"El Imperio de la Cuba Co." (1902, abril 4) Editorial. *El Mundo*, p. 2.

"El Poder de la Cuba Co." (1902, abril 2) Editorial. *El Mundo*, p. 2.

"Entrevista a Mr. Proctor" (1901, marzo 23) *La Discusión*, p. 1.

Foreing Policy Association. (1935) *Problemas de la Nueva Cuba. Informe de la Comisión de Asuntos Cubanos*. La Habana: Cultural S.A. pp. 55-56.

Guerra, Ramiro (1970). *Azúcar y población en las Antillas* (5ª edición) La Habana: Ciencias Sociales.

Ibarra, Jorge (1994).*Un análisis psicosocial del cubano: 1898-1925*. La Habana: Ciencias Sociales.

Jenks, Leland H. (1960). *Nuestra Colonia de Cuba*. Buenos Aires: Palestra.

"La Cuestión Económica" (1902, febrero 27) *La Discusión*, p. 1.

"La Situación al Día" (1902, abril 19 marzo 26). Editorial. *La Discusión*, p. 2.

González, D. (1987) "La inmigración antillana en Cuba." *Economía y Desarrollo*, 100, pp. 51-61.

Marbán E. y Leiva E. (1951). *Curso de Historia de Cuba (De acuerdo con el programa vigente para el bachillerato elemental)*. La Habana: Cultural.

Memoria del Senado de Cuba, pp. 470-476.

Nearing y Freeman, (1973). *La diplomacia del dólar*. La Habana: Ciencias Sociales.

Pichardo, H. (1973). *Documentos para la Historia de Cuba*. La Habana: Ciencias Sociales.

Ramos, José Antonio (1913). *Entreactos*. La Habana: Ricardo Veloso.

Rivero Caro, A. (2001). *El período republicano intermedio y la crisis de la democracia (1920-1933)* En internet: http://www.neoliberalismo.com/republicano.htm.

Roig Leuchsering, Emilio, (1973). *Males y vicios de Cuba republicana*. La Habana: Ciencias Sociales.

USA War Department, Office Director (1900). *Census of Cuba. Report of de Census of Cuba, 1899.* Washington: United States Government Printing Office.

DEMOCRATIZATION AND MIGRATION: CUBA'S EXODUS AND THE DEVELOPMENT OF CIVIL SOCIETY—HINDRANCE OR HELP?

Silvia Pedraza[1]

The collapse of communism in the Soviet Union and the Eastern European countries ushered in a new stage in Cuba, stage which Fidel Castro himself called "a special period." In this period, we have witnessed the emergence of civil society—fragile but nonetheless real. At the same time, the 1990s and the present have also been a period of massive emigration out of Cuba—the migration of *balseros, lancheros,* and visa lottery winners, as well as Cubans who leave and arrive through third countries.

The question that frames this paper, then, is whether this new, massive Cuban exodus is a **hindrance** or a **help** to the development of this new civil society in Cuba. The question can also be posed with the analogy that Albert O. Hirschman (1970) first introduced in his book *Exit, Voice, and Loyalty: Responses to Decline in Firms, Organizations, and States.* As Hirschman noted, when there is a deterioration in the quality of the benefits or services that a firm, an organization, or a party provides, the *loyalty* of its members is threatened. To promote recuperation, they can then express themselves by using one of two options: they can choose to *exit*—simply leave—or they can use their *voice*—organize, protest. The pattern could be characterized, Hirschman (1986) underlined, as a simple hydraulic model: deterioration generates the pressure of discontent, which will be

channeled into *voice* or *exit*. The more pressure escapes through *exit*, the less is available to foment *voice*. But, Hirschman underlined, once having exited they cannot promote recuperation. Hence, the question is whether the new Cuban exodus, massive and seemingly unabated, constitutes the use of the *exit* option to such an extent that it will serve to impede the use of *voice*, which is what is necessary to develop civil society.

Let me first expand both points, regarding civil society and the Cuban exodus. Since civil society is a somewhat ambiguous concept, I follow Victor Pérez-Díaz's (1993) definition in his analysis of the return of civil society to Spain. It entails the existence of associations (whose ends may be political, economic, or purely social) that were created by and are the result of the voluntary participation of its members. Such associations occupy an intermediate position between the individual and the state—for example, the press, media, labor unions, churches, professional associations, and the like. As Pérez-Díaz (1993:57) summed it, civil society "denotes a *type* of society that combines, to one degree or another, markets, voluntary associations, and a public sphere which are outside the direct control, in a full or mitigated sense, of the state." This civil society is what Vaclav Havel (1986) called the "independent life of society."

---

1. I wish to express my gratitude to Bert Hoffman for his helpful comment on an earlier draft.

In Cuba, those intermediate associations effectively ceased to exist as they were either abolished or silenced by a government that, in the beginning years of the revolutionary process, succeeded (due to the enormous popularity of the revolutionary process as well as the enormous charisma of Fidel Castro himself) in making the state the sole arbiter, the sole owner, the sole administrator, the sole judge, and the sole political party, excluding all others from participation. Thereafter, that same government went on to organize some of the intermediate associations— such as, the professional associations, the press, the labor unions—but these lack independence from government; hence, they do not qualify as part of what is here defined as civil society. However, the crisis of the "special period"—crisis which is not only economic but is also a crisis of legitimacy—has spurred the return of civil society in Cuba.

Today, we witness in Cuba the growth of independent journalists ("independent" meaning free of government control and organization), independent professionals, efforts to create an independent labor union, a religious revival of all the churches, independent publications, independent grassroots organizations aimed to solve social problems at the local, micro level of family and town. To Cubans involved in the founding of these organizations, the effort to reconstruct civil society is a deliberate social project that entails what Dagoberto Valdés (1997:104) called moving along two paths: one, "*una renovación de los espíritus*" (a renewal of the hearts and the minds of the people) and, two, reforming the social structure of the society. To Dagoberto Valdés, this social project of reconstructing civil society issues emerges from, and is accompanied by, a Christian humanism. To others, it is a project in which they participate due to their ethical and philosophical convictions, in the absence of religious beliefs. To all in Cuba today who consciously participate in reconstructing civil society, civil society is the *sine qua non* of a democratic transition, and is also the guarantee of a democratic future in which all Cubans of all political convictions can participate (See Valdés 1997: 130).

The new Cuban exodus has been both unregulated and regulated. The unregulated exodus consisted of the exodus of the *balseros*, which peaked in the summer of 1994 when over 34,000 Cubans were rescued at sea by the U. S. Coast Guard and taken to Guantánamo to live in camps, while awaiting processing to come to the United States over a couple of years. As a consequence of this crisis, the United States and Cuba signed a new Migration Agreement, which has since allowed for the regulated and orderly departure of Cubans from the island, at the rate of 20,000 Cubans a year. An unknown but also rather sizable exodus has left for other countries— particularly Spain, Venezuela, and Costa Rica. While the regulation of the exodus certainly contributed to a decline in the number of *balseros* who risked their lives in the crossing, some continue to leave Cuba and try to enter the United States illegally—at present, occasionally as *balseros* (those who left on rafts) and, more often, as *lancheros* (those who left on speedboats operated by persons who provide such passage for pay), and through third countries in less risky ways. This new Cuban exodus is rather massive—one can easily imagine that roughly 25,000 Cubans leave Cuba now every year, or 100,000 persons every 4 years—and it shows no signs of abating.

Comparing this new Cuban exodus to the former waves of the Cuban exodus will show its proportions. Using data from the 1990 census of the United States, the largest wave of immigrants from Cuba after the revolution has been what is called the second wave—the roughly 283,000 Cuban immigrants who left the island during the 9 years from 1965 to 1974, or 41 percent of those who immigrated from 1960 to 1990 (See Pedraza 1996:Table 1). This second wave also resembled the contemporary exodus in that it was also regulated and administered by both the Cuban and the United States governments who, like now, collaborated after a major crisis, in this case the flotilla exodus out of the port of Camarioca in 1965. Like the present exodus, family reunification (though more stringently defined now) was the criteria used to allow those in Cuba to leave when claimed by their relatives in the U.S.

The major difference between the two periods, then, is that the family reunification criteria used now is extremely stringent, and, as a result, there is a visa lottery for 5,000 annual visas that is part of the annual visa total. At the rate at which Cubans are presently leaving the island, the new Cuban exodus of the 1990s and the beginning of the 21st century is a massive exodus of nearly the same dimension. However, the exodus is taking place at a very different moment in the history of the Cuban revolution—not at a time of revolutionary consolidation, as was the second wave of the exodus (after the failure of the Bay of Pigs exile invasion of Cuba, as well as the defeat of the counter-revolutionary forces in the mountains of El Escambray) but at a time when Cubans are beginning to build a civil society that is independent of government. Weak and fragile as it may be, it is real—it is now there, while it was not there earlier.

To assess the dilemma of whether the *exit* option impedes or facilitates the use of the *voice* option, I searched through the literature and found four different theses. I will first state them briefly and then comment on each.

The first thesis is Dagoberto Valdés's (1997) thesis, as stated in his book *Reconstruir la Sociedad Civil: Un Proyecto de Educación Cívica, Pluralismo, y Participación para Cuba*. Valdés clearly sees the Cuban exodus as a negative factor—a **hindrance** to the development of civil society in Cuba: "One of the causes of the impoverishment and the near disappearance of a civil society in Cuba has been the massive and permanent exodus of Cubans," and the exodus is the result of the lack of political liberty that does not allow Cubans to participate freely and responsibly in the polity and, as a consequence, of the lack of economic initiatives Cubans can undertake by themselves, which leads to dismay and to civic irresponsibility (Valdés, 1997:118-19, translation mine). Phrased in Hirschman's terms, the formulation is that which Hirschman himself postulated initially in 1970—the use of the *exit* option becomes an obstacle to the development of *voice* in the country.

The opposite thesis is that espoused by Victor Pérez-Díaz (1993) in his analysis of the transition to democracy in Spain after Franco. For many years, Spain was a periphery country in Europe that lent its labor—via a massive labor exodus—to the core Eu-

ropean countries of Germany, France, England, Switzerland, Belgium. This labor migration occurred because of the lack of job opportunities in Spain from the early 1960s to the mid-1970s, as Spain was changing from a predominantly rural, agrarian nation to a predominantly urban, industrial nation. The *émigrés* lent their labor to the industrial sector (working in factories) or the service sector (working in hotels and restaurants, for example) in these more developed European countries. In Victor Pérez-Díaz's (1993:12-13) assessment, this Spanish exodus was part of the massive flow of capital, commodities, and people that began to flow across the Spanish borders for at least 15 years, bringing with them all sorts of institutions and cultural transformations:

> Millions of tourists invaded the coasts of Mediterranean Spain, while millions of Spaniards emigrated northward, often to spend years living and working in Germany, France, Holland, or Switzerland; thousands of students and young professionals went abroad to study; entrepreneurs imported machines; foreign investors poured capital into the Spanish economy; and consumers became accustomed to buying foreign-made goods.

> As these interchanges increased in frequency, their significance soon became clear for all to see. It could be summarized as a massive, all-pervasive learning experience. Spaniards were exposed to institutions and cultures, ways of accomplishing things in all spheres of life, which were simply far more efficient than their own in achieving some of their traditional objectives as well as other objectives which they were rapidly learning to appreciate: a better, more comfortable standard of living, offering more money and resources but also increased freedom of movement, more opportunities to prosper and get ahead, less subjection to authority, more knowledge, and more varied ways of relating freely among themselves. In this way Spaniards learned from, imitated, and wound up identifying with the people of western Europe, their institutions, and their way of life (p. 13).

In this analysis, the exodus was a midwife to the development of civil society because the *émigrés* lived and worked in societies that were politically democratic and pluralistic, where groups of people were organized in institutions they themselves had created to defend them, and by living there they engaged in an *aprendizaje democrático* (a democratic apprenticeship).

It is important to note, however, that for this to have had an impact on the homeland they left, the *émigrés* had to return. They, indeed, returned to Spain and, with this know-how contributed to the development of the peaceful transition out of Franco's Spain as well as to its governability in a new, pluralistic and democratic Spain in the years that followed when democracy was consolidated and democratic institutions were institutionalized. Indeed, Felipe González was Spain's first elected prime minister to represent the opposition—the socialists; hence, to some, this election represented the key moment in which Spain could truly be said to be a democratic nation. And Felipe González was the son of a woman who had left Spain to work overseas as part of the massive labor migration that took place during those years.

To Pérez-Díaz (1993), a *successful* transition can only come about if a civil society either predates the transition or becomes established in the course of it (p. 40, emphasis his). These processes went hand in hand with what Pérez-Díaz called "the invention of a new tradition and a new identity: that of a democratic Spain in contrast to a Francoist Spain, connected in a problematic way with pre-Francoist history, from which it is cut off by the trauma of the civil war" (p. 20). According to this analysis, the exodus is a positive factor that **helped** the development of civil society. Phrased in Hirschman's terms, those who first used the *exit* option underwent a democratic apprenticeship in the countries where they migrated, and as they returned, brought what they had learned about the *voice* option with them, to exert an influence on the development of a new political culture and civil society there.

Yet a different thesis is that posed by Michel Laguerre (1998)—a Haitian social scientist who analyzed the role Haitian immigration played in the U.S. Laguerre's thesis is that the Haitian immigrants in the U.S. themselves became the civil society that Haiti lacked. Through their exercise of what Laguerre called "a transnational diasporic citizenship," Haitians became the missing political center—between the government, on the one hand, and the

atomized, inarticulate masses, on the other. In this analysis, the exodus resulted in the formation of a community that became the missing civil society. As a result of their transnationalism, Haitian *émigrés*, as individuals and as groups, crossed national boundaries to engage in productive informal interactions and dialogue:

> The diaspora is a major factor in the opening up of the political system in Haiti. By intervening at all government levels, by injecting money in various sectors of the economy, and by providing human and financial resources to grassroots and formal voluntary associations, the diaspora has infused the country widely and deeply with its democratic views (Laguerre 1998:170).

Laguerre also noted that this same transnationalism had had some negative consequences for the Haitian American community because it had diverted their energies toward their homeland, at the expense of their role and place in the receiving country. However, without doubt Laguerre saw the role of the Haitian *émigré* community towards their homeland as a positive factor, a substantial **help** in the form of an informal diplomacy carried out by civilians who traveled to Haiti and spoke not on behalf of their government but on behalf of themselves or their organizations—*"ambassadeurs du béton ou sans cravate."* Laguerre's analysis notes that they helped to establish civilian control over the military as well as funded cherished social projects back in Haiti, both of which strengthened the development of civil society there. Such informal diplomacy was not only an outcome of transnationalism but also, Laguerre underlined, was totally outside the control of both the United States and the Haitian governments, "effectively transforming the immigrant subject into a transnational citizen" (p. xx). Phrased in Hirschman's terms, it says that when the civil society in the homeland country has effectively disappeared and the people there remain too atomized and marginalized to constitute it, those who first exercised the *exit* option may end up becoming the ones who constitute its *voice*.

Yet another thesis comes from Hirschman's (1993) later work, when he applied his initial conceptual scheme to the actual case of the German Democratic Republic (GDR) in 1989, when a series of social movements developed in rapid succession in Poland, Hungary, East Germany, Czechoslovakia, Bulgaria, Romania—that resulted in the collapse of the communist world in Eastern Europe, and the demise of the GDR. While in his earlier work (1970; 1986) Hirschman had argued that a basic seesaw pattern existed between *exit* and *voice*—the more of one, the less of the other—23 years later, when he examined the GDR up close during *die Wende* (the turn, as it was generally called), he was forced to conclude that in the last year both *exit* and *voice* had "worked in tandem" and **reinforced** each other, "achieving jointly the collapse of the regime" (1993:177). This insight came from the work of the East German sociologist Detlef Pollack, who witnessed the events during 1989 at very close range.

These are the theses regarding the development of civil society and the exodus I have found to date. I will now comment on each, basing myself on my research in recent years. As some of you know, I have been working on a research project for a book to be titled *Cuba: Revolution and Exodus* that has entailed a lot of field work—participant observation, as sociologists prefer to call it—in major communities of Cuban exiles, not only Miami but also New York (in its various social worlds of the Bronx, Brooklyn, and Manhattan), New Jersey (Union City and Elizabeth), Chicago, Los Angeles, Houston, San Antonio, and Puerto Rico, as well as Spain (Madrid, Salamanca, Canary Islands). As a result of this field work, I conducted 100 very in-depth, semi-structured interviews with Cubans representative of the four major waves of the Cuban exodus.

Moreover, in recent years I have traveled to Cuba about once a year or year and a half and, not only am I old enough to remember the origins of the Cuban revolution but also since 1979 I have returned to Cuba on 10 very different trips—of different lengths and under different circumstances—in which I have made an effort to get as close to the lives of people there as I could (a social jump that at times is a leap!). These trips have taught me a great deal about the social conditions in the island as well as about the pro-

cess of change in which the Cuban people are involved. It is on the basis of this research, then, that I comment on each of these theses I identified.

A MASSIVE EXIT IMPEDES THE USE OF VOICE

Regarding Dagoberto Valdes' thesis of the exodus as a hindrance to the development of civil society, I would say that it is in line with what I myself wrote in the past regarding the functions of political and economic migration to both the societies involved (See Pedraza-Bailey 1985).

Analysts of labor migrations speak of the exodus of migrants as performing a "safety valve" function for the societies they leave (e.g., Spain, Mexico, Turkey), as it externalizes the material discontent their society could not provide for. In the same vein, I argued, a political exodus also externalizes the political discontent, the dissent, their society could not respond to. As such, the Cuban exodus always contributed to strengthening the Cuban revolution in the political sense, though at the same time it proved erosive to the development of the society because the exodus also represented an enormous brain drain of the professional and middle classes whose resources and talents the society's functioning needed.

Moreover, I found Dagoberto Valdés's thesis to be quite common in Cuba among people who, like himself, are struggling to help build that new civil society in Cuba—whether through the development of intellectual alternatives, such as his own effort in the last seven years with the magazine *Vitral* (the image is that of a stained glass window that filters the light through a many-colored prism), whose subtitle is itself indicative of its content: *la libertad de la luz* (the freedom of light), or through the strengthening of a church or synagogue as a viable alternative way to think, feel, live. When I was in Cuba a couple of years ago, I visited a friend who had been a priest in his small town for about 12 years, a community I had also visited in the past. As we drove through the small town where everyone knew everyone else, he pointed to each house where a family had left, saying "They left," then "They also left," and "Do you remember them? They are no longer here." And I felt his sense of desolation when he said: "*el país se está desangran-do*" ("the country is bleeding to death"). In this "special period," with its new Cuban exodus, there is no doubt that to those on the ground of Cuba itself who are struggling with the renewal of the minds and hearts of the Cuban people, the exodus feels like a vital loss of people who could help develop the new civil society.

Yet, despite my basic agreement with this thesis, I think one has to distinguish between those who left "in the first instance" and those who left "in the last instance." Those who leave Cuba today "in the first instance" are those who could not "translate" their evident dissatisfaction into an active search for a new political alternative, or at least another way of living and thinking. Without doubt, these are people who were disaffected from the political and economic conditions in Cuba and whose minds and hearts had grown tired of the government's empty promises, but they held their dissent close to their chest and shared it with very few intimate friends (sometimes not even with their closest family members!). They either played a public role of assenting to the conditions there—what Cubans call "*la doble moral*"—or they sought to live as uninvolved in the political process there as possible.

Some analysts have pointed out that Hirschman forgot the fourth option—*neglect*—an option that is as real a choice as those of *exit, voice,* or *loyalty.* That is to say, that most of these Cubans exercised the option of either a false *loyalty* or of a daily lived *neglect* and were unlikely to become involved in the development of civil society—even if they had remained in Cuba. They need to be distinguished from those who left Cuba "in the last instance"—Cubans who did, indeed, become involved in the dissident movement, or founded a new human rights organization, or participated in the development of a new alternative through their church or synagogue, or became an independent journalist, and the like—those who did, indeed, exercise the *voice* option. But, having done so, they then suffered its costs as they lost their jobs, many of their friends, and every door began to close behind them until they ended up either in prison or

living in conditions that were intolerable, pushing them to leave.

Those who left under those conditions, what I call "in the last instance," had, in truth, already given to the development of civil society in Cuba everything that they had to give. Their efforts to bring a democratic polity to Cuba and a sense of human rights as just that—rights—are perceived by the government and those loyal to it as going against the government there. Pushing them into a corner that they could no longer get out of certainly served as an example to many Cubans of the futility of going against the powerful government there. Yet they also became heroes to many who remained behind. Gonzalo López, for example, was a young, well-educated mulatto, who joined the independent journalists and worked in that capacity for two years before leaving for Venezuela. He explained:

> When you become an independent journalist you die socially. People in your same block look at you differently. You lose friends; you develop problems with your father in-law; you have to worry about with whom you talk; young people who hate the government viscerally come and tell you "You're young! Why are you going to do that? They'll put you in prison!" It's the result of the control they have over the society, the fear the people have inside of them, the political apathy of the young. But at the same time, it is contradictory. You feel actualized in your self, morally, as a human being. Because once you get into it people admire you, they care for you.

Another example was that of Ariel Gómez, a young man who founded a human rights organization in Camagüey. Though he was a good doctor, he ended up without a job. Even when he went to Havana to look for a job and was offered one, the municipal government back in his home town would not give him the permission to emigrate to Havana to work. Eventually, he and his wife Yolanda—who stood behind him solidly, which is not always the case—ended up sleeping in the garage of her parents' home, with two small children who went to bed every night hungry, as they ate whatever others gave them. With every door closed behind them, and the sight of children too young to understand their suffering, Ariel and his wife decided to leave Cuba, and did so with visas given not for family reunification but for political refugees. As he told it to me after he arrived in the U.S. and was resettled to Los Angeles, and I corroborated again with his old friends, when I visited Cuba, on the day he left the streets were packed with people who came out to bid them farewell—honoring them, despite the visible risk to themselves.

THOSE WHO EXITED UNDERWENT A DEMOCRATIC APPRENTICESHIP THAT HELPED VOICE DEVELOP

Regarding the thesis of *el aprendizaje democrático* (a democratic apprenticeship), I think it depends on the conditions of the exodus—the length of time the emigrants spent abroad, the nature of the access to the polity they had in the societies where they lived and worked, and—crucially—whether or not they returned, bringing their new-found political culture back with them. Ewa Morawska (2001), a Polish sociologist, has studied the recent exodus of Eastern European immigrants who went to work in Western European societies. She concluded that, for the vast majority of those *émigrés*, a democratic apprenticeship did not take place because their stay in those countries was very brief, and their participation as "guest workers" in the economy and the polity of the host countries was very delimited as they lived lives that socially were very marginal. Hence, a real change in values or behavior that was more compatible with a democratic society hardly took place.

Morawska did find a more substantial change among the more educated Eastern European immigrants who traveled overseas for professional work because though their stays were brief, the very nature of their professions allowed them greater access to the new society, from which they learned a great deal. Hence, in her analysis, since these Eastern European migrations—both the labor migrants and the professionals—were brief, the social class of the *émigrés* had a decisive impact on whether or not they could realize such a democratic apprenticeship.

However, Pérez-Díaz's analysis of the Spanish emigration to Western Europe stressed that for these working class *émigrés* such a democratic apprenticeship did take place, despite their class background— men and women who went in search of decent work

and wages at a time when Spain could not provide them. The key difference seems to be in the length of time they spent abroad—for some Spaniards I spoke with, as many as 30 years of absence—and in that they returned to Spain thereafter, at a time when Spain was growing economically and becoming part of the European Union.

On a recent trip to Spain, a Spaniard named Jesús Moguer, who was a maitre at a marvelous restaurant in Valencia, told me that he left Andalucía as a very young man, and spent 30 years in Düsseldorf, Germany, doing similar work—always in Hilton Hotels: "I lost my youth in that freezing weather!," he said. "But everything I know I learned while I was living and working there."

If Morawska and Pérez-Díaz are both correct in their assessment of the impact that living and working abroad had on these different cases of migration— the Eastern European and the Spanish, both to Western Europe—the difference should alert us to the realization that we need to take a close look at each case to see what are the conditions that impact the potential for such a democratic learning: the social class of the *émigrés*, the length of their stay abroad, and the nature of their economic and social as well as political participation there, as well as whether or not they eventually returned to their homelands or at least remained vitally linked to those who remained there, helping them.

In the Cuban case there has been such a democratic learning but time—the passage now of 42 years—as well as the economic success of a large part of the Cuban exile community go against the grain of facilitating the development of civil society in Cuba. Those who left in the early years of the exodus—say, the first two waves of the exodus, from 1959 to 1974— have already put deep roots in their adopted country, as they have seen at least one if not two generations of children and grandchildren born abroad. And, as I objected to Laguerre's analysis (Pedraza 1999), the new "transnational diasporic citizenship" may well be true of the first generation of immigrants, but can seldom true for most of their children, the second generation, most of whom will not have an interest in returning to Cuba. Due to their parents' as well as their own success, they have become very assimilated to American life, speak English rather than Spanish fluently, and from the point of view of their parents' culture, are culturally inept, finding it difficult to understand that world now and to fit back there. In general, this is true of the second generation for all immigrant groups in America. It is all the more true among Cubans at a time such as this when poverty has become so generalized among the Cuban people, irrespective of their levels of education.

Hence, while the Cuban government tells its people regularly that the Miami exiles will return and want to take their houses away (the houses where their families lived before they left the country), demographic change is an inexorable social change and I frankly see very few Cubans from those early waves of the exodus (their children, that is) returning to take anything away because they are now part of another world—perhaps better, perhaps worse, but certainly another world—where they have put new roots. Given that less time has passed, those who left more recently—the *Marielitos* and "the new Cuban exodus" of the 1990s and beyond—do have a greater potential for returning because fewer "roots" have been put out elsewhere. However, their memories of a past that for many was traumatic may impede their return.

The early exiles still to this day hold memories of *"la Cuba de ayer"* that are the happy memories of people who had a very comfortable life in a society that, at that particular time of the 1950s, was known for its splendor—music, color, gayety (see the film "Havana: Memories of Yesteryear" recently done in Miami for excellent testimonies). The recent exiles—the children of Communism—very often hold memories of their past life in Cuba that are so traumatic, so negative—not only because of the lack of all forms of material comfort, hunger, poverty, but also because of the isolation and marginality experienced by those whose *loyalty* became questioned, who often denied their real feelings and convictions—that their way of coping with a past that lacked dignity was to close the door on it, forever. Many of them, though young, will not return to

Cuba but will go on to make new futures, new lives, wherever they settled.

Moreover, Spaniards returned to Spain because, however stifling Francoism may have been to working class organizations, it did deliver economic growth and modernization as Spain underwent a transition from being a rural, agrarian society to an urban, industrial society—economic modernization that Cuba has not registered, with or without the Soviet subsidy. Still, it remains possible that if (note the if) a successful transition to a democratic society were to take place in Cuba, that were accompanied by international assistance—of the sort that the Marshall Plan after the end of World War II constituted—and economic growth could be achieved in their productive lifetimes, the more recent *émigrés* and some of the children of the early exiles might return to Cuba with the democratic learning that living and working overseas—in the United States, Spain, Venezuela, Costa Rica—entailed. But my sociological sense tells me that such a return migration would be small.

THOSE WHO EXITED BECAME ITS VOICE

Regarding the thesis of the "transnational diasporic citizenship"—that is, the *émigrés* themselves become the civil society—I think this is an underlying assumption of many exile political organizations that are situated in vastly different spaces in the political spectrum, as are the Cuban American National Foundation, at one end, and the Committee for Cuban Democracy, at the other. There are certainly ways in which the Cuban exile community, particularly that based in Miami, has sought to become the island's civil society—for example, through the development of organizations and political parties—such as the *Partido Demócrata Cristiano,* the *Partido Liberal,* and the *Partido Social Demócrata* that have ties to their homologous organizations in the dissident movement in Cuba (the *Movimiento Cristiano de Liberación,* the *Corriente Liberal,* and the *Corriente Socialista Democrática,* respectively), parties that have also joined forces and constituted themselves as *La Plataforma Democrática Cubana.* However, in my view, these groups can only be effective to the extent that they are in touch with those inside of Cuba, an effort that the Cuban government deliberately seeks to stop by making communications as difficult as possible and denying them visas.

It is also useful to examine the role that other exile groups played in other transitions to democracy—in Spain, Poland, the Czech Republic, Brazil. I believe that the historical record shows that, in general, the role of the exiles was rather delimited. One could object that the Cuban case is different in that a much greater part of the Cuban population has emigrated—estimated around 12 percent of the population—and the time span is overwhelmingly long (now 42 years). Moreover, its proximity to the island due to its concentration in Southern Florida renders it potentially a more decisive political actor than other exile communities. But I remain in doubt that it could play a leading role in such a transition unless the ties of the exile political organizations with the Cuban people in the island remain strong—as, generally, they are not.

For example, in the case of Brazil, during the political dictatorship of 1964, many Brazilian exiles—in this case, people convinced of the rightness of the communist cause—left for Europe, where they lived for many years. These Brazilian exiles did engage in a real *aprendizaje democrático*. Many were convinced communists, full of the ideals that communism was able to inspire in many. But their lived experience in the Eastern European countries—the truly existing communist societies—as well as in Italy, France, and Germany, led them to progressively change and to become true democrats of very different stripes. They returned to Brazil during the period of *la apertura* (the opening) in the early 1980s and there they became grouped in various political parties, such as that of Brizola.

But—and here is its relevance for the Cuban case— the Brazilians who remained in Brazil themselves by and large rejected political parties organized by the exiles that sought to appeal to the people there with the arguments that "We are different now—we have changed. We were not here during the years of the military dictatorship; hence, we were not corrupted by it; we are purer." To which Brazilians mostly replied: "But you were not here all those years when we

lived through and suffered the years of the dictatorship. You did not share our hardships and our suffering." As the recent incident that revolved around the custody case of Elián González, "the little *balserito*," made evident, people in Cuba did not side with what the Cuban government derisively calls "the Cuban mafia in Miami." That is a phrase that, sadly, the Cubans in the island also often use, noting the gulf that remains in understanding between those who live in Miami and are part of the dominant political organizations there, such as *Unidad Cubana, Hermanos al Rescate,* and those who live in Cuba, even when they do not side with its government. It was that segment of the organized Cuban political community in Miami that made the Elián González case into one about a child that had to be saved from returning to communism. Yet most of the people that I met with in Cuba, including those who in favor of the government, argued that the issue at stake was that a Cuban child belonged with his father back home. The gulf in understanding is much wider, longer, and deeper than the 90 miles that separate the two communities. Under such conditions, the exile community can hardly become the missing civil society.

BOTH EXIT AND VOICE INCREASED IN TANDEM

Regarding Hirschman's (1993) reformulation of his initial thesis, it is important to underline that in his analysis of the actual, historical, empirical case of the GDR, Hirschman was able to see that the course of events over the 40-year-long life of that state (1949-1989) "comprised a large variety of *exit-voice* relationships" (1993:177). While over the course of time, more often than not the easy availability of *exit* did undermine the development of *voice*, other relationships also obtained. For example, in 1961, with the building of the Berlin Wall, the authorities sought to repress both *exit* and *voice*. And in 1989, the last year of the regime, both *exit* and *voice* worked in tandem, reinforcing each other. I contend that, in recent years, both have begun to operate in tandem also in Cuba.

The cases of Cuba and the GDR hold many parallels, not the least of which was the constant availability of

255

the *exit* option to another very near place—the Federal Republic of Germany, the Miami exile community—where a measurably easier life, political liberty together with the presence of family there exerted a strong "pull." This was especially true during the years of the second wave of the exodus, when the violence of the so-called counterrevolution (to themselves, they were the real revolutionaries) came to an end and they had to lay down arms, defeated in a conflict for which thousands died and thousands more were imprisoned.

Throughout those years, the use of the *exit* option did impede the use of the *voice* option because, in the aftermath of the consolidation of the revolution, Cubans no longer believed in the chances for successful *voice*, an effective challenge to the government. Moreover, the government itself, as in the GDR, was quite conscious of the basic seesaw pattern of *exit* and *voice* and chose to consciously manipulate the *exit* option to undermine the *voice* of dissent. For example, the 1980 exodus of the *Marielitos* was largely a working-class exodus of Cubans with a visibly higher proportion of Blacks than ever before, who left from the port of Mariel. Because they were the children of communism itself, they represented a large public slap in the face of the government. Fidel Castro responded by calling them *escoria* (scum):

> Our working people are of the opinion: "Let them go, the loafers, the antisocial and lumpen elements, the criminals, and the scum!' … As always, Cuba gladly opened the doors for them, as it had done before with all the rabble that opposed socialism and the revolution (Castro 1980a).

A week later, Castro explained the benefit of externalizing dissent:

> … I think that those of them remaining here are people with whom we can work better, much better! … So we need not worry if we lose some flab. We are left with the muscle and bone of the people. We are left with the strong parts (Castro 1980b).

From the mid 1980s on, when the new dissident movement was gathering force, as in the GDR, this also took the form of a selective policy of forced *exit* that literally "pushed" certain critical *voices* out of

Cuba, while barring others from returning home. The result of this forced *exit* policy was palpable. In 1992, Amnesty International issued a special Country Report on Cuba, *Silencing the Voices of Dissent*, in which many of Cuba's most prominent dissidents then were featured. A few years later, virtually all of them were living outside of Cuba, in exile.

But the easy availability of *exit* was not the only reason why the emergence of *voice* was less likely in East Germany than elsewhere in the Soviet-dominated Eastern European countries. Hirschman noted other major reasons.

- First, East Germans had no independent institutions (more or less), like the Catholic Church of Poland, that would sustain them in a struggle for some autonomy from the all-powerful communist state. That, until very recently, was also true in Cuba.

- Second, many East Germans initially embraced the ideology of the state "for reasons intimately connected with the catastrophic historical episode they had just lived through"—Nazi Fascism. That "ideological advantage," as Hirschman (1993:182-83) called it, was also the role that Batista's dictatorship played in the initial acceptance and popularity of the Cuban revolution.

- Third, East Germany played a different role for the Soviet empire in its contest with the West during the Cold War, as evidenced by the presence of Soviet atomic missiles there. That was also true in Cuba, which played a similar role for the Soviet Union inside the Western Hemisphere and throughout the Third World, as also evidenced by the location of atomic missiles in Cuba, which led to the October Missile Crisis in 1962. In exchange for this role of exporting revolution to Latin America and Africa, and contesting the United States, the Soviet Union subsidized the Cuban economy very generously, mitigating the role of the U.S. embargo.

In sum, until the 1990s, one could arrive at the same conclusion regarding Cuba as Hirschman (1991:183) did regarding the GDR:

The direct obstacles to voice, that is, to any political movements of resistance or dissidence, were enormous. They must be added to the indirect undermining of voice by the real or imagined availability of exit to the West. Jointly these direct and indirect restraints on voice produced an exit-voice balance that was tilted far more against voice and in favor of exit than that prevailing in other Soviet-controlled East European territories, with the already noted result of substantially divergent political behavior in East Germany.

Yet throughout the 1990s, during the crisis of the "special period," we witnessed the increasing use of both the *exit* and *voice* options in Cuba, as was the case in the GDR in 1989. For example, in the summer of 1994, the dramatic *balsero* crisis took place, when over 34,000 desperate Cubans put out to sea, was the immediate result of *"el Habanazo"*—the largest *voice* event on record—when massive riots took place as Cubans ran, shouting down the streets of central Havana, protesting the economic conditions in Cuba as well as the lack of liberty. The riots themselves were set off by the detour of the small boat that regularly crossed the Bay of Havana for the town of Regla and on that day took a different course, trying to leave Cuba. The riots were also preceded by the most tragic *exit* event: the tugboat incident in mid-July. A number of Cuban families were attempting to leave the island when the Cuban Coast Guard set out to stop them and, in the process, overturned the tugboat with powerful shots of water, causing the deaths of over 40 women and children, an incident that a number of survivors lived to tell. As a result of these multiple ways in which *exit* and *voice* were expressed that summer, reinforcing each other, Fidel Castro announced that the authorities would not interfere with anyone who wanted to leave, announcement which led immediately to the massive outpouring of *balseros* to sea throughout the month of August, which in turn resulted in the signing of the Migration Agreement between Cuba and the U.S. that has now given way to the massive though orderly exodus of Cubans at present.

Even more, on September 8th, the day Cubans celebrate the national feast day of their cherished patron Saint, *La Virgen de la Caridad del Cobre* (Our Lady of Charity), Cubans witnessed yet another clear expression of the incipient use of *voice* in Cuba when Father José Conrado Rodríguez was emboldened to act by the crisis Cubans had lived through that summer. In his church in Palma Soriano, Oriente Province, that day's homily consisted of his reading a letter he had written to Fidel Castro. It is worth quoting the letter at some length:

My deep concern for the situation our people are living through moves me to write you, in the hope that you will pay attention to my reasons, and will reply accordingly.

Many humble people excuse you, saying that you do not know the truth of what we are living through, but I do not share that opinion. What is there that you do not know of the tragic situation we are living through? ...

For over 30 years, our country engaged in a politics at the base of which was violence. This politics was justified because of the presence of a powerful and tenacious enemy only 90 miles away, the United States of America. The way in which we confronted this enemy was to place ourselves under the power that for years confronted it, the Soviet Union, as we became part of the socialist block of countries that superpower led.

While the Soviet Union gave massive assistance to our economy and our arms race, Cuba gradually fell into a state of internal violence and profound repression. ... The use, within and without our country, of hatred, division, violence, suspicion and ill will, has been the main cause of our present and past misfortune.

Now we can see it clearly. The excessive growth of the state, progressively more powerful, left our people defenseless and silenced. The lack of liberty that would have allowed healthy criticism and alternative ways of thinking caused us to slide down the slippery slope of political volition and intolerance towards others. The fruits it bore were those of hypocrisy and dissimulation, insincerity and lying, and a general state of fear that affected everyone in the island. ...

We grew accustomed to not earning our daily bread with the sweat of our brow and to greatly depending for our living on the assistance others gave us. We have lived a lie, fooling others as well as ourselves. We have done wrong, and that wrong has now befallen us. We are all responsible, but no one is more responsible than you. …

I can no longer remain silent, in good conscience, which is why I speak to you, because I think we could still rectify our course and save our nation, as you have on several occasions expressed were your desires.

Right now, if you wished, it would be possible to arrive at a peaceful, negotiated agreement, through the process of a national dialogue among people representing the various tendencies within the Communist Party, the dissident groups in the island, as well as Cubans in the diaspora. A popular referendum, free and democratic, in a climate of respect and tolerance would allow the voice of all our people to be heard. If you were to be at the head of that process … it would avoid the bloodbath that our present circumstances forecast and will, unfortunately, render inevitable… (Rodríguez 1995, my translation).

Padre José Conrado's letter erupted in the Cuban scene exactly as Havel (1978) explained any sudden action that signifies a sudden coming to live in the truth, rather than the lie of the "post-totalitarian society": as an act of courage that places that person in real danger. When he began receiving threats, including death threats, the Church decided to send him to Salamanca, Spain, to study—a forced *exit* intended to protect him. After two years in Spain, he was allowed to return to Cuba, to a new parish where he continues to be what he has always wanted to be—an ordinary Cuban priest.

Due in part to the crisis of the "special period," the 1990s witnessed the rapid growth of a dissident movement the seeds of which were sown in the mid 1980s. This new dissident movement in Cuba is characterized by its being non-violent in strategy and approach, following the social movements spearheaded by Mahatma Gandhi and Martin Luther King. And it takes its inspiration from the world-wide human rights movement that found its earliest expression in the United Nation's Universal Declaration of Human Rights as well as the Czechoslovakian intellectuals' Charter 77 (Havel 1986).

That dissident movement has not only grown in size—*Concilio Cubano* (Cuban Council), the umbrella organization at one point covered over 70 different groups, albeit some with very small size—but has also grown in maturity, seeking to provide an alternative vision of a democratic society in Cuba. In recent years, among many documents, two particularly stand out: *La Patria es de Todos* (Our Nation Belongs to All of Us) and the *Proyecto Varela*. In May 2002, the *Proyecto Varela* handed the National Assembly of People's Power more than the 10,000 signatures (11,020, to be exact) that the 1976 Cuban Constitution requires for citizens to seek a Constitutional change. Though different, both projects have called for a plebiscite or a national referendum, so that Cubans can freely elect their government.

Spearheaded by one of Cuba's leading dissidents, Osvaldo Payá, founder of the *Movimiento Cristiano de Liberación* (Christian Democratic Movement for Freedom), part of the worldwide Christian Democratic Movement, the *Proyecto Varela* called for a popular referendum of the Cuban people. Such a referendum was to place five propositions on the ballot to be voted upon by the Cuban people in a free and democratic election. The five propositions are:

- the right to freedom of expression and freedom of association, so that Cubans can freely organize themselves in all sorts of associations, be they political, economic, cultural, labor, student, or religious organizations, including freedom of the press;

- amnesty for political prisoners in Cuba's jails;

- the right of Cubans to own their own enterprises, both as individuals and as members of cooperatives;

- a revision of the electoral law so that the candidates running for election are freely nominated and elected by the people in their district through the collection of their signatures supporting particular candidatures; and

- the right to a free and democratic general election.

The goal of the Project is not only to create the conditions for Cubans to participate freely in their polity, a form of participatory democracy, but also for Cubans to be able to express their *voice*: "Let no one else speak for Cubans. Let their own voices be heard in a referendum"(Payá 2001).

It is interesting to note the name of the document and project that seeks the signatures. It was named after Father Félix Varela, a Cuban priest who, in the early 19th century strove for Cuban independence from Spain. Forced to leave Cuba, he spent the rest of his life in the United States, in exile, working with Irish and Italian immigrants in a parish in New York. He also wrote prolifically, expressing his dissent, as a form of *voice*. Hence, Varela's very life holds within it the use of both the *exit* and *voice* options. Though he died in exile, long before Cuba achieved its independence, today he symbolizes the use of the *voice* option inside Cuba.

Four of Cuba's leading dissidents, each of them representing a different group, joined to write a document *La Patria es de Todos* (Our Nation Belongs to All of Us) that criticized the Communist Party's sole monopoly over power in Cuba and that called for a return to some of the principles of the 1940 Cuban Constitution, the charter that expressed the institutionalization of the short-lived Cuban Republic. Arrested in July 1997, in March 1999 the four dissidents were tried behind closed doors and sentenced to three to five years in prison for acts of sedition and for being "counterrevolutionaries" (Alfonso 1999; Tamayo 1999). The four came to be known as *El Grupo de los Cuatro* (the Group of Four); they also represented the full gamut of race and gender in Cuba. They were: Vladimiro Roca Antúñez, a former combat pilot, mulatto, and the son of the well-known communist leader Blas Roca; René Gómez Manzano, a laywer, white, who represented the Independent Lawyers; Félix Bonne Carcasés, black, an engineer who previously taught at the University; and Marta Beatriz Roque, an economist and woman, who represented the Independent Economists. Due to the pressure for their release exerted by Amnesty International, Americas Watch, Pope John Paul II, the European Union, and the governments of Canada, Mexico, and Spain (Cuba's major trading partners), they were released after serving their prison terms.

With so many obstacles to the emergent use of *voice*, how is it possible for both *exit* and *voice* to have developed in tandem, reinforcing one another? In Hirschman's analysis of Germany in the final, climatic year of 1989, the seesaw of *exit* and *voice* suddenly turned into a joint act when the inability of the government to prevent a large-scale flight of its citizens out of the country "signaled a novel, serious, and *general* decline in state authority" (Hirschman 1993:187, emphasis his), signal that proved emboldening to others. The mass exodus of some citizens— a private solution to their troubles—did feel to many then in the GDR, as today in Cuba, as a bloodletting of the country. But, as Hirschman (1993:197) underscored, it "did sufficiently impress, depress, and alert some of the more loyal citizens, those who had no thought of exiting, so that they finally decided to speak out"—a most public act.

So it was also in the Cuban case. For example, it was the *balsero* crisis of the summer of 1994 that provoked Padre José Conrado Rodríguez to write the letter to Fidel Castro and emboldened many other Cubans to join the dissident movement and to found new human human rights organizations. Hirschman underlined that the collaboration of *exit* and *voice* in the last phase can be explained by an appeal to the concept of *loyalty*. *Loyalty* delays *exit* as well as *voice* when there is a decline in the performance of an organization, party, or nation to which one belongs. But when the decline passes a certain threshold, the *voice* of the loyal members tends to become particularly vigorous. Hirschman, however, did not underline, as I think it important to do, that in this case the *loyalty* was no longer to the government, but to the nation. For Cubans, that is precisely the symbolic meaning of titling the call for a national referendum after Father Felix Varela, the 19th century hero. Quite independently, it also lent its symbolism to Father José Conrado's letter to Fidel Castro, which in its closing emphasized:

A long time ago, another Cuban priest, Father Félix Varela, wrote these wise and courageous words which I now make mine: "When the nation is in danger, ... drawing ever closer to a precipice, is it imprudent to raise our voice and to warn others of that danger? My heart does not know the prudence of the weak" (Rodríguez 1995; my translation).

CONCLUSION

My analysis of the four extant theses regarding the role of migration in the democratization effort of a society, and its implications for the Cuban case, leads me to the conclusion that clearly migration bears a relationship to democratization; but it is a highly historically-contingent one that depends on a myriad of factors we are just beginning to comprehend. Ulti-

mately, the question of whether the exodus is a **hindrance** or a **help** to the development of civil society does not have a unique answer. Rather, as Hirschman found in his last analysis, over the course of many years, a number of *exit-voice* relationships obtained. Perhaps this analysis would serve to elucidate not only the relationship of *exit* and *voice* in Cuba but also help us understand the island's present situation.

REFERENCES

Alfonso, Pablo. 1999. "Comienza el Juicio al Grupo de los Cuatro." *The Miami Herald* (27 February 1999).

Amnesty International. 1992. *Cuba: Silencing the Voices of Dissent*. New York: Amnesty International.

Castro, Fidel. 1980a. Quoted in *Granma* (13 April).

Castro, Fidel. 1980b. Quoted in *Granma* (22 April).

Laguerre, Michel S. 1998. *Diasporic Citizenship: Haitian Americans in Transnational America*. New York: St. Martin's Press.

Havel, Vaclav. 1986. "Two Notes on Charter 77." In Vaclav Havel, *Open Letters: Selected Writings 1965-1990*. New York: Vintage. (Letters selected and edited by Paul Wilson.)

Havel, Vaclav. 1978. "The Power of the Powerless." In Vaclav Havel, *Open Letters: Selected Writings 1965-1990*. New York: Vintage. (Letters selected and edited by Paul Wilson.)

Hirschman, Albert O. 1993. "Exit, Voice, and the Fate of the German Democratic Republic: An Essay in Conceptual History." *World Politics* 45:173-202.

Hirschman, Albert O. 1986. "Exit and Voice: An Expanding Sphere of Influence." In Albert O. Hir-

schman, *Rival Views of Market Society and Other Recent Essays*. New York: Viking.

Hirschman, Albert O. 1970. *Exit, Voice, and Loyalty: Responses to Decline in Firms, Organizations, and States*. Cambridge, MA: Harvard University Press.

Morawska, Ewa. 2001. "Structuring Migration: The Case of Polish Income-Seeking Travelers to the West." *Theory and Society* 30:47-80.

Payá Sardiñas, Osvaldo. 2001. *Proyecto Varela*. La Habana, Cuba: Movimiento Cristiano de Liberación.

Pedraza, Silvia. 1999. "Assimilation or Diasporic Citizenship?" Review Symposium on Immigration in America at the Turn of this Century. *Contemporary Sociology* 28:377-381.

Pedraza, Silvia. 1996. "Cuba's Refugees: Manifold Migrations." In Silvia Pedraza and Rubén G. Rumbaut, eds. *Origins and Destinies: Immigration, Race, and Ethnicity in America*. Belmont, CA: Wadsworth Press.

Pedraza-Bailey, Silvia. 1985. *Political and Economic Migrants in America: Cubans and Mexicans*. Austin, TX: University of Texas Press.

Pérez-Díaz, Victor M. 1993. *The Return of Civil Society: The Emergence of a Democratic Spain*. Cambridge, MA: Harvard University Press.

Rodríguez, José Conrado. 1995. "Cuando la Patria Peligra." *The Miami Herald* (25 March). Also my own taped interview of him in June 1998; as well as my visit to his parish in Palma Soriano, Oriente, in July 1996; to his parish in Santiago de Cuba, Oriente, in July 2001; and numerous other visits in Cuba, Miami, and Spain.

Tamayo, Juan O. 1999. "Four Cuban Dissidents Convicted." *The Miami Herald* (16 March).

United Nations.1948. *The Universal Declaration of Human Rights.* New York: United Nations.

Valdés Hernández, Dagoberto. 1997. *Reconstruir la Sociedad Civil: Un Proyecto de Educación Cívica, Pluralismo, y Participación para Cuba.* Caracas, Venezuela: Fundación Konrad Adenauer.

THE IMPACT ON THE U.S. ECONOMY OF LIFTING RESTRICTIONS ON TRAVEL TO CUBA

Dorothy Robyn, James D. Reitzes and Bryan Church

Congress currently is debating whether to lift restrictions on travel by Americans to Cuba. In connection with that debate, *The Brattle Group,* an independent economic research and consulting firm, was asked by the Center for International Policy (CIP) to estimate the impact that such a policy change would have on the U.S. economy. In response to CIP's request, we conducted an economic analysis designed to answer four questions:

- How many more Americans would travel to Cuba for overnight stay if U.S. travel restrictions were lifted?

- What would be the resulting net increase in passenger demand for travel on U.S. air carriers (*i.e.,* excluding travel diverted from other destinations)?

- How much additional economic activity would the increased demand for air travel generate?

- How many passengers would visit Cuba on U.S.-based cruise ships, and how much additional economic activity would that generate?

Our analysis focused on airline and cruise travel because increased transportation demand is the most direct way in which a decision to lift travel restrictions would affect the U.S. economy. We used our estimate of the direct increase in transportation demand to calculate the broader impact on the economy that lifting restrictions would have. This overall impact also includes "indirect" effects (*i.e.,* increased demand for labor, equipment, and other inputs to travel) and "induced" effects (*i.e.,* consumer spending by employees of airlines, cruise lines and their suppliers). We examined, but did not attempt to quantify, other economic effects of lifting travel restrictions, including inland travel and the "consumer surplus" benefits of giving Americans another travel option.

In conducting our analysis, we looked at the long-term economic impact of lifting the travel ban, rather than the impact in the first few years. Thus, we disregarded any near-term constraints in the supply of hotel rooms and other tourist infrastructure in Cuba, in the belief that supply would increase to meet demand over the long term. Similarly, we assumed that over time, Cuba would provide effectively unrestricted access to U.S. airlines in an effort to attract American travelers.

Finally, we made two assumptions about the scope of potential legislation. First, we assumed that elimination of the travel ban would not only allow Americans to go to Cuba but also enable U.S. companies to transport them there. Second, we assumed that the broader trade embargo against Cuba would remain in place.

BACKGROUND

Restrictions on Travel to Cuba

Restrictions on travel have been a key component of U.S. policy toward Cuba for most of the last 40 years.[1] In 1962, President Kennedy imposed a trade embargo on Cuba to punish the new Communist regime of Fidel Castro. A year later, the Department of the Treasury's Office of Foreign Assets Control

(OFAC) issued comprehensive regulations to carry out the embargo. Although OFAC regulations did not ban travel itself, they placed restrictions on any financial transactions related to it, effectively banning travel.

OFAC's regulations have changed many times since 1963. In 1977, President Carter lifted the ban on travel to Cuba altogether. Five years later, President Reagan reimposed restrictions on tourist and business travel but allowed continued travel by Cuban Americans visiting close relatives. President Clinton made repeated changes to the OFAC regulations in response to actions by the Cuban government. For example, after suspending flights between Cuba and the United States in 1996, Clinton in 1998 allowed resumption of charter flights from Miami to Havana, and in 1999 announced a new policy permitting direct flights to Cuba from New York and Los Angeles as well.

President Clinton's 1999 policy, designed to promote people-to-people contacts, also relaxed the OFAC rules governing who can travel to Cuba. Currently, 12 categories of travelers can visit Cuba under either a general license, which requires no written authorization, or a specific license, which requires OFAC approval.[2]

Most of the travel done under a general license consists of family visits by Cuban Americans. Specifically, U.S. residents with close relatives in Cuba can visit once every 12 months under self-defined circumstances of "humanitarian need," such as a sick or dying relative. (From 1994 to 1999, OFAC required "extreme humanitarian need.") Others who can travel under a general license include scientists, academics and researchers; fulltime journalists employed by a news organization; U.S. government officials; and non-professional athletes participating in international competitions.

Individuals who may be eligible for specific licenses include free-lance journalists, students, and business travelers arranging permitted export sales (medicine, medical equipment, and agricultural equipment and products to non-profit entities). In addition, Cuban Americans visiting close relatives for humanitarian reasons can apply to travel more than once a year. Although OFAC grants specific licenses on a case-by-case basis, an individual license may authorize more than one traveler (e.g., an entire family or the staff of a research institution) and multiple trips over an extended period of time.

Number of Americans Traveling to Cuba

Because of the nature of its licensing process (i.e., general licenses require no written approval and specific licenses can cover multiple travelers and trips), OFAC lacks precise data on how many Americans visit Cuba each year. However, the agency does track the number of Americans who travel to Cuba on (OFAC-licensed) charter flights, the only means of direct air transport from the United States. In addition, OFAC estimates the number of Americans who travel legally to Cuba (i.e., under a general or specific license) via a third country.

During 2000, the last year for which it has done an analysis, OFAC estimates that 156,000 Americans traveled to Cuba legally.[3] That is nearly double the figure for 1999 (82,000), presumably reflecting the Clinton Administration's "people-to-people" initiative. Most of those travelers—70 percent or more, according to OFAC's estimate—were Cuban Americans visiting close relatives. The vast majority of

---

1. For a detailed discussion of this issue, see Congressional Research Service Report RL31139, *Cuba: U.S. Restrictions on Travel and Legislative Initiatives in the 107th Congress*, by Mark P. Sullivan, updated March 27, 2002. Available under "Long Reports" at http://www.house.gov/markgreen/crs.htm.

2. See Prepared Statement of R. Richard Newcomb, "Restrictions on Travel to Cuba," Hearing Before the Senate Appropriations Subcommittee on Treasury and General Government, February 11, 2002, pp. 40-44.

3. Telephone interview with senior OFAC official, May 2002. Although OFAC does not issue formal statistics on travel to Cuba, the agency compiled the figures cited in this paragraph in preparation for a recent congressional hearing.

them (135,000) traveled to Cuba on direct charter flights; the rest went via a third country.

While most Americans travel legally to Cuba, some travel illegally (*i.e.,* through a third country, without a general or specific license). In response to questioning at a recent Senate hearing, the director of OFAC, Richard Newcomb, indicated that as many as one-third of all Americans traveling to Cuba do so illegally.[4]

The Government of Cuba also tracks the number of Americans who visit Cuba.[5] According to Cuban Foreign Minister Felipe Pérez Roque, some 200,000 U.S. residents visited Cuba in 2001. Pérez stated that 120,000 of them were Cuban Americans legally visiting relatives, and the rest were U.S. citizens, many traveling illegally.[6] Consistent with those figures, Cuba's official tourism statistics, which exclude most Cuban Americans, report 76,900 arrivals from the United States in 2000.[7]

ANALYSIS

Question 1: How Many More Americans Would Travel to Cuba for Overnight Stay if Travel Restrictions Were Lifted?

Estimates vary widely as to how many Americans would visit Cuba if the travel restrictions were lifted. In its 2001 report, the U.S. International Trade Commission (USITC) predicted that, absent *all* sanctions on trade with Cuba, only 100,000 to 350,000 more Americans would travel to Cuba each year, primarily as tourists.[8] By comparison, the head of the American Society of Travel Agents (ASTA) predicted in April that if the travel ban were lifted, one million Americans would visit Cuba the first year, increasing to five million annually within five years.[9] Most recently, a report issued last month by the Center for Sustainable Tourism at the University of Colorado estimated 950,000 American tourist arrivals in year one and 2.7 million arrivals in year five.[10]

The USITC's cautious estimate reflects, in part, an assumption that "the Cuban Government is not likely to grant visas in large numbers to U.S. residents with family ties to Cuba, because the Government could receive higher revenues and returns on investments from expenditures by tourists."[11] However, there is no apparent reason why Cuba would not grant entry to both American tourists *and* Cuban Americans. Stated differently, contrary to the USITC's assumption, there is no constraint that would force Cuba to favor tourists over Cuban American visitors; even a shortage of hotel rooms should not produce that result, since Cuban Americans typically stay with relatives.

Even as a forecast of tourism, the USITC estimate is conservative, reflecting the Commission's (unstated) assessment that Cuba's tourism infrastructure lacks

---

4. "Restrictions on Travel to Cuba," *op. cit.,* p. 52. Thus, using OFAC's estimate of 156,000 legal visitors, the number of Americans who traveled to Cuba in 2000 could be as high as 234,000. At the same hearing, Newcomb responded positively when asked if the number of Americans who visited Cuba in 2001 was "between 150,000 to 200,000," but he may have been referring just to those who traveled there legally.

5. The Cuban government does not recognize dual citizenship; specifically, any Cuban-born American citizen who left Cuba after 1970 is considered to be solely a Cuban citizen. Hence Cuba classifies most Cuban Americans who visit Cuba as "U.S. residents," rather than "U.S. citizens," because it still considers them Cuban citizens.

6. "U.S. Travel Association Eyes Forbidden Cuba," *Reuters*, April 6, 2002.

7. Caribbean Tourism Organization, *2000 Caribbean Tourism Statistical Report*, "Table 10: Tourist Arrivals from the United States."

8. U.S. International Trade Commission, *The Economic Impact of U.S. Sanctions With Respect to Cuba*, Publication 3398, February 2001. Available at: http://www.usitc.gov/wais/reports/arc/w3398.htm.

9. Mary Murray, "Cuba Ban Said to Hinder Travel Agents," *MSNBC*, April 6, 2002. ASTA included the same estimate as part of its written submission to the ITC study cited above (see p. D-31).

10. Ed Sanders and Patrick Long, "Economic Benefits to the United States from Lifting the Ban on Travel to Cuba," Center for Sustainable Tourism, Leeds School of Business, University of Colorado, June 2002. Available at: http://www.cubapolicyfoundation.org/pdf/CubaTravel.htm.

11. U.S. International Trade Commission, *op. cit.,* page 4-21.

the quality and quantity necessary to attract large numbers of Americans.[12] However, insofar as Cuba lacks sufficient hotel rooms to accommodate demand, American tourists may crowd out other foreign tourists more than the reverse. For example, the University of Colorado study notes that because of supply constraints, the increase in total tourist arrivals to Cuba initially would be considerably less than the increase in U.S. arrivals. This "crowding-out" scenario is consistent with the view that the United States is Cuba's "natural" tourism partner, as evidenced by the fact that Americans account for 60-70 percent of tourism in northern Caribbean islands other than Cuba.[13]

To develop our own forecast of American travel to Cuba in the absence of travel restrictions, we looked separately at three types of travel: (1) personal travel by Cuban Americans returning to see family and friends; (2) recreational travel; and (3) business travel.[14]

Personal Travel: Personal travel refers to "family visits," or what travel professionals call VFRs ("visits to friends and relatives"). The 120,000 Cuban Americans who traveled to Cuba in 2001, as reported by Cuban Foreign Minister Pérez Roque, represented about 10 percent of the 1.2 million Cuban Ameri-

cans living in the United States.[15] Because Cuban Americans can return to Cuba once a year without written approval, one might argue that lifting travel restrictions altogether would have little effect. But the spike in travel following OFAC's 1999 policy changes suggests that more Cuban Americans would visit Cuba if there were no restrictions.

To estimate the number of family visits Cuban Americans would make if travel restrictions were lifted, we looked at the frequency of such visits by other Caribbean emigrants to the United States. According to Caribbean experts, Dominican Americans, with a population of 0.9 million, are the most comparable group.[16] Among other things, Dominican Americans born in the Dominican Republic and Cuban Americans born in Cuba represent about the same fraction of their respective home country populations.[17]

The annual rate of return visits to the Dominican Republic by Dominican Americans appears to be quite high—40-45 percent, according to an unofficial estimate by the Dominican Tourism Ministry based on data on airport arrivals by Dominican non-residents.[18] Dominican experts living in the United States confirm that Dominican Americans return in large numbers to see friends and family in the Dominican Republic.

---

12. Telephone interviews with USITC staff, May 2002.

13. Ernest H. Preeg, *Feeling Good or Doing Good with Sanctions: Unilateral Economic Sanctions and the U.S. National Interest*, Center for Strategic and International Studies, Washington, D.C., 1999.

14. National statistical agencies treat any foreign visitor who stays overnight as a "tourist," even if the visit is for personal or business reasons. Because cruise passengers typically do not stay overnight, they are classified as "excursionists" rather than "tourists." We use "travel" in this section to refer to overnight visits, but in keeping with conventional usage, we reserve the term "tourist" for a recreational traveler.

15. The 2000 census reported 1,228,149 Cuban Americans living in the United States; this includes Cuban-born residents and their children. U.S. Census Bureau, Census 2000 Supplementary Survey Summary Tables, Table PCT006, "Hispanic or Latino by Specific Origin."

16. The 2000 census reported 912,501 Dominican Americans living in the United States. U.S. Census Bureau, *op. cit.*, Table PCT006.

17. In 1999, foreign-born Cuban Americans totaled nine percent of the Cuban population; for Dominican Americans, the comparable figure was eight percent. Susan Eckstein, "Dollarization and its Discontents: Remittances and the Remaking of Cuba in the Post-Soviet Era," unpublished paper, May 2002.

18. Airport arrivals by non-resident Dominicans totaled 512,966 in 2000 and 483,682 in 2001. Central Bank of the Dominican Republic, Economic and Financial Information, Tourism Sector, Tables on "Arrival of Passengers by Nationality" for 2000 and 2001. Although published statistics do not specify the country of residence, the Ministry of Tourism estimates that 75-80 percent of non-resident Dominican arrivals live in the United States. Gustavo Ricart, Analyst, Ministry of Tourism, personal communication, June 2002.

The VFR rate for Dominican Americans may well be higher than it would be for Cuban Americans. First, Dominican Americans emigrated more recently than Cuban Americans, and thus ties to the home country may be stronger.[19] Second, some "first-wave" Cuban Americans—those who emigrated before 1980—shun family visits because they oppose Castro or fear retribution from others who oppose Castro.[20] Finally, the Cuban government imposes additional travel costs on some Cuban Americans (*e.g.,* those who left after 1970 must carry a valid Cuban passport, which costs more than $200).[21]

However, other considerations suggest that Dominican Americans' VFR rate, if anything, may understate the frequency with which Cuban Americans would visit Cuba absent restrictions. First, Cuban Americans live much closer to their home country than Dominican Americans (70 percent of Cubans live in Florida, whereas 75 percent of Dominicans live in New York and New Jersey).[22] Thus, a family visit to Cuba would be significantly less expensive than one to the Dominican Republic. Second, the average income of Cuban Americans is far higher than that of Dominican Americans (although first-wave Cuban emigrants have higher incomes than other Cuban Americans).[23]

On balance, the 40-45 percent annual VFR rate for Dominican Americans is probably a reasonable predictor of the frequency with which Cuban Americans would visit Cuba absent the travel ban. However, to be conservative, we used a 33 percent rate as the basis for our subsequent calculations. At that rate, Cuban Americans would make 409,000 annual visits to Cuba—289,000 more than the current estimate of 120,000.

Recreational Travel: Existing estimates of the number of Americans tourists who would travel to Cuba absent travel restrictions rely on several predictive techniques. One approach is to examine how many Americans go to comparable Caribbean destinations such as Puerto Rico or Cancun. Another approach is to generalize from historical data—*e.g.,* by assuming that the same fraction of American tourists to the Caribbean who went to Cuba in the 1950s would do so in the future. A third approach is to estimate total tourist arrivals in Cuba and then to allocate some share of those arrivals to American tourists.

Although any technique for estimating American tourist travel to Cuba is necessarily subjective, the more direct the basis for the forecast, the better. As with personal travel, to base our estimate of tourist travel on the most direct comparison possible, we looked at groups that are like Americans in all respects except their ability to travel freely to Cuba.

The group most comparable to American tourists are Canadian tourists. Canada and the United States have similar demographic and socioeconomic profiles. Moreover, Canadians travel to the Caribbean at about the same rate as Americans. In 2000, 3.9 percent of Canadians (1.23 million) visited the Caribbean, compared to 3.5 percent of Americans (10.12 million)—a difference of only 0.38 percent. Finally,

---

19. About 43 percent of foreign-born Cuban Americans emigrated to the United States from 1980 to 2000. For Dominican Americans, the comparable figure is 70 percent (with 44 percent of all Dominican Americans admitted between 1988 and 1998). Max J. Castro and Thomas D. Boswell, "The Dominican Diaspora Revisited: Dominicans and Dominican-Americans in a New Century," Dante B. Fascell North-South Center, University of Miami, Paper No. 53, January 2002, pp. 1 and 21.

20. Susan Eckstein and Lorena Barberia, "Cuban-American Cuba Visits: Public Policy, Private Practices," Report of the Mellon-MIT Inter-University Program on Non-Governmental Organizations and Forced Migration, Center for International Studies, Massachusetts Institute of Technology, January 2001. Available at: http://web.mit.edu/cis/www/migration/eckbar.PDF.

21. Eckstein and Barberia, p.17. The Cuban government has dropped other costly requirements (*e.g.,* Cuban Americans previously had to book a hotel room, even if they were hosted by a Cuban family).

22. U.S. Census Bureau, *op. cit.*, Table PCT006.

23. Castro and Boswell, *op. cit.*, Table 4, p. 18.

Canadian and American travel patterns within the Caribbean are strikingly parallel.[24]

Canadians travel to Cuba for recreation at a surprisingly high rate. In 2000, 308,000 Canadian tourists visited Cuba.[25] That represents 25 percent of all Canadians who went to the Caribbean that year and nearly one in every hundred Canadians. The closest competitor as a destination for Canadians is the Dominican Republic. In 2000, the Dominican Republic attracted 246,000 Canadians—20 percent of all those who traveled to the Caribbean.

Because of the similarity between the two groups, the frequency with which Canadians travel to Cuba for recreation is likely to be the best predictor of the frequency with which Americans would do the same. If American tourists were to visit Cuba at the same rate as Canadians, 2.80 million Americans would travel there annually.[26] That is 2.72 million more than the number of Americans (excluding Cuban Americans) who visited Cuba in 2001.

Business Travel: According to the U.S.-Cuba Trade and Economic Council, 3,700 U.S. business representatives visited Cuba in 2001, up sharply from 500 in 1994.[27] If the United States were to lift all restrictions on trade with Cuba, business travel would no doubt skyrocket. But lifting travel restrictions while leaving the trade embargo in place may not have a significant effect on business travel. For purposes of

our analysis, we assumed there would be no increase in the number of business visits to Cuba if restrictions were lifted.

Summary: Although any estimation technique is subjective, the travel patterns of closely comparable groups provide the most direct basis for predicting how Americans would behave absent travel restrictions. Table 1 summarizes our estimates. Based on our examination of the rate at which Dominican Americans visit the Dominican Republic (40–45 percent), we estimate that at least 409,000 Cuban Americans (33 percent) would visit Cuba annually for personal reasons—289,000 more than the current number. Based on the high incidence of Canadian tourist travel to Cuba, we estimate that 2.8 million American tourists would visit there annually—2.72 million more than the current number. In all, we estimate that 3.21 million Americans would visit Cuba annually—3.01 million more than the current number.

Table 1. Estimated Travel to Cuba by Americans (thousands)

Purpose of Travel	Current Number of Travelers	Long-Run Estimate	Additional Travelers in the Long Run
Personal	120	409	289
Recreation/ Business	77	2,797	2,720
Total	197	3,206	3,009

---

24. For example, 4.4 percent of American tourists to the Caribbean visited islands within the British Commonwealth-linked Organization of Eastern Caribbean States (OECS), 32.5 percent visited other Commonwealth countries, and 1.0 percent went to the French West Indies. For Canadians, the comparable figures are 4.6 percent, 31.7 percent and 1.3 percent. (The OECS countries, a geographic cluster of former or current British Commonwealth dependent territories, include Anguilla, Antigua and Barbuda, The British Virgin Islands, Dominica, Grenada, Montserrat, St. Kitts and Nevis, St. Lucia, and St. Vincent and the Grenadines. The "other Commonwealth" countries include the Bahamas, Barbados, Belize, Bermuda, Cayman Islands, Guayana, Jamaica, Trinidad and Tobago, and the Turks and Caicos Islands. The French West Indies include Guadeloupe and Martinique.) The major difference in travel patterns within the Caribbean is that more Americans frequent U.S. territories (30.4 percent versus 4.6 percent for Canadians) and Cancun, Mexico (17.3 percent versus 7.4 percent), whereas Canadians go to Cuba and the Dominican Republic in higher numbers. Caribbean Tourism Organization, *2000 Caribbean Tourism Statistical Report,* "Table 10: Tourist Arrivals from the United States," and "Table 14: Tourist Arrivals from Canada."

25. Europeans also travel to Cuba in large numbers. In 2000, 949,000 Europeans (18 percent of all European visitors to the Caribbean) went to Cuba. The only destination more popular among Europeans was the Dominican Republic, which attracted 25 percent of all those who visited the Caribbean. *2000 Caribbean Tourism Statistical Report, op. cit.,* "Table 17: Tourist Arrivals from Europe."

26. To get this figure, we multiplied the rate at which Canadians went to Cuba for tourism in 2000 (0.97 percent) times the current U.S. population (287 million).

27. U.S.-Cuba Trade and Economic Council, Inc., "Realities of Market Cuba," p. 2. Available at: http://www.cubatrade.org/market.html.

Question 2: How Much Would Demand for U.S. Air Carriers Increase as a Result of this Additional Travel?

Travel on U.S. Airlines: Step two in our analysis was to estimate how much demand for U.S. air carriers would increase as a result of this additional travel to Cuba. We focused on U.S. airlines for two reasons. First, most people travel to the Caribbean by air. In fact, national tourism statistics such as those cited throughout this paper are based on airport arrivals. Second, absent travel restrictions, most Americans flying to Cuba would use a U.S. air carrier. Thus, the most direct and potentially significant impact on the U.S. economy of lifting the travel ban would be the increased demand for U.S. airlines.

To elaborate, if travel restrictions to Cuba were lifted, U.S. airlines would quickly set up scheduled service. According to industry experts, one or more carriers would offer shuttle service from Miami, which would become the "collection point" for Cuba-bound travelers. The current bilateral air services agreement between the United States and Cuba, signed in 1953, limits which carriers can operate, the routes they can fly, and the number of flights they can schedule. (The charter flights that U.S. carriers currently operate make use of "extra-bilateral" rights.) Thus, if Congress lifted travel restrictions, the United States and Cuba would need to renegotiate their bilateral agreement. In the short run, Cuba might limit somewhat the number of U.S. flights in an effort to promote its own international air carrier, Cubana de Aviación. But over time, Cuba would likely give U.S. carriers unrestricted access, so as to attract American travelers. [28]

To measure the value of demand for U.S. airline service, we used the price of airfare from the United States to Cuba.[29] Currently, the average roundtrip fare on a direct charter flight from Miami to Havana is $329. The fare is higher for flights to Havana from New York ($599) and Los Angeles ($670), and for flights to Cuban cities other than Havana. Since most passengers fly from Miami to Havana, we used the average fare on those flights—rounded down to $300—for purposes of our analysis.

Demand Diversion Versus Demand Creation: Many Americans who would travel to Cuba if the ban were lifted would otherwise travel to an alternative tourist destination. One indication is that officials from the Dominican Republic and Puerto Rico worry about Cuba "cannibalizing" tourism to their countries. Stated differently, much of the travel by Americans to Cuba would not create new, or incremental, demand for U.S. air carriers; it would merely divert travel from one tourist destination to another.

This distinction between "demand diversion" and "demand creation" is critical, because the impact of lifting travel restrictions on spending is limited to that share of travel that represents a genuine expansion of the market. It would not be fair to count the value of trips to Cuba by Americans who would otherwise go to Jamaica or Cancun.

Not all new trips to Cuba would represent a diversion of travel from other destinations, however. Additional family visits would be purely incremental, because the alternative for Cuban Americans would be to stay home. Moreover, some recreational travel would be market expanding. For example, some people who would otherwise stay home would travel to Cuba because of its unique characteristics. In addition, residents of South Florida would begin making incremental trips to Cuba, just as residents of Boston and Philadelphia travel to New York to attend a play or see a museum exhibit. Finally, Cuba might attract travelers who otherwise would visit a destination not served by U.S. airlines.

---

28. Cuba's treatment of Spain, which accounts for a significant share of tourism to Cuba, may provide a relevant example. The air services agreement between the two countries provides for reciprocal rights for their respective airlines. In practice, however, Spain's flagship carrier, Iberia, operates many more flights between Cuba and Spain than its Cuban counterpart. The Cuban government affords effectively open access to Iberia and other Spanish airlines, presumably because of the priority Cuba places on tourism. Personal communication with officials of Iberia Airlines, July 2002.

29. See http://www.destinationcuba.com/airfare.htm.

Alternative Methods of Estimating Increased Demand: Because the distinction between demand creation and demand diversion is so important, we use two alternative methods to estimate how much the demand for U.S. airline service would increase if restrictions on travel to Cuba were lifted. The key difference between the two methods is the way they account for demand diversion.

Estimation Method 1. Using the first method, we make an arbitrary assumption that 80 percent of additional tourist travel to Cuba would be demand-diverting and that only 20 percent would be demand-creating. Our 80-20 assumption is an educated guess, designed to err on the side of being conservative. It is one that we would apply to any Caribbean market just opening to Americans, regardless of its popularity.

Based on this conservative assumption, of the 2.72 million tourist trips to Cuba that we estimated above, only 0.544 million trips would represent incremental travel. For the reasons discussed earlier, we treat all 0.289 million of our estimated additional family visits as incremental travel. The sum of these two figures (0.833 million) is the total number of annual incremental trips that would occur absent travel restrictions.

To calculate the resulting increase in demand for U.S. air carriers, we multiply the number of incremental trips (0.833 million) by the average round-trip Miami-Cuba airfare ($300). The product, $250 million, represents the annual increase in revenues that U.S. air carriers would enjoy in the absence of restrictions on travel to Cuba.

Estimation Method 2. With the second method, we estimate incremental demand for U.S. air carrier service to Cuba directly rather than indirectly. Moreover, instead of treating Cuba the same as any other new Caribbean destination, we use market-specific information—namely, the high incidence of Canadian travel to Cuba—as an important clue in developing our estimate.

Specifically, we posit that the (small) difference in the rates at which Canadians and Americans travel to the Caribbean for recreation is due to the fact that

Canadians have Cuba as a Caribbean travel option whereas Americans do not. The fact that one in every hundred Canadians travels to Cuba is telling. It is a sufficiently high rate to suggest that the availability of Cuba may increase overall Canadian travel to the Caribbean. Although other explanations are possible, the strong similarity in demography and tastes between Canadians and Americans cancels out many alternative explanations.

Because of this strong similarity, we would expect U.S. travel activity to the Caribbean to mirror that of Canada. Stated differently, if Americans, like Canadians, were free to visit Cuba, we estimate that an additional 0.38 percent of all Americans would travel as tourists to the Caribbean. Using the current U.S. population (287 million), elimination of travel restrictions would result in 1.09 million incremental trips to Cuba by American tourists annually. This represents a 10.8 percent net increase in annual American arrivals in the Caribbean. In our judgment, this increase is a reasonable upper bound on the potential expansion of the overall air travel market as a result of lifting restrictions on travel to Cuba.

The remaining steps in method 2 are identical to those of method 1. We add incremental tourist trips (1.09 million) and additional family visits by Cuban Americans (0.289 million) to get the total number of incremental trips (1.38 million). Then we multiply that figure by the average Miami-Cuba roundtrip airfare ($300). The result—$415 million—equals our second estimate of the increased revenues that U.S. air carriers would enjoy in the absence of restrictions on travel to Cuba.

Summary: Table 2 summarizes our estimate of the net increase in demand for travel on U.S. air carriers absent restrictions on travel to Cuba. The key challenge is to distinguish between diverted travel and incremental, or market expanding, travel. Our first estimation method makes an educated but arbitrary guess that 80 percent of additional tourist travel to Cuba would be diverted from some other Caribbean destination and 20 percent would be incremental. Based on that method, and using our earlier forecast of additional travel to Cuba, we estimate that the increase in demand for U.S. air carriers absent travel re-

Table 2.   Direct Benefit to the U.S. Economy from Increased Air Travel *(thousands)*

	Increase in Tourist Trips[a]	Demand-Creating Tourist Trips[b]	Increase in Personal Trips[c]	Total Demand-Creating Trips	Increased Revenue to Airline Industry[d]
Estimation Method 1[e]	2,720	544	289	833	$250,001
Estimation Method 2[f]	N/A	1,094	289	1,384	$415,088

a.   Our estimate (from Table 1) of the number of additional recreational trips to Cuba that Americans would make if travel restrictions were lifted.

b.   Our estimate of the number of additional recreational trips to Cuba that would represent "demand creation" as opposed to "demand diversion." Demand creation refers to passengers who would travel only if travel restrictions to Cuba were lifted. Demand diversion refers to passengers who would travel to some alternative tourist destination if Cuba was not an option.

c.   Our estimate (from Table 1) of the number of additional trips to Cuba that Cuban Americans would make if travel restrictions were lifted. All of these trips represent demand creation.

d.   Assumes that U.S.-Cuba roundtrip airfare is $300.

e.   Estimation Method 1 assumes that 80 percent of increased tourist travel would be diverted from other destinations, and 20 percent would represent new travel demand.

f.   Estimation Method 2 is based on the difference between Canadian and American tourism rates to the Caribbean.

strictions would expand airline revenues by $250 million a year. Our second estimation method attributes the small difference between Canadian and American tourism rates to the Caribbean to the fact that Canadians have Cuba as an additional option—a reasonable explanation given the extremely high incidence of Canadian travel to Cuba and the strong similarity in travel tastes between Canadians and Americans. Assuming that the availability of Cuba would increase U.S. travel to the Caribbean by the same amount, U.S. air carriers would enjoy an increase in revenues of $415 million a year.

Both estimates are plausible. Thus, in the last step of our analysis below, we will treat the two estimates as a range.

Question 3: How Much Additional Economic Output and Employment Would the Increased Demand for Air Travel Generate?

As the third step in our analysis, we calculated the overall increase in economic activity that would result from the incremental demand for air travel. As we saw in the last section, lifting restrictions would have the direct effect of raising the demand for U.S. airline service by a small but significant amount. This increased demand would generate two broader economic effects. First, airlines would have to purchase additional equipment, labor, travel agent services, food and beverages, and other inputs. Airline equipment suppliers in turn would have to buy more steel, machine tools, and labor; and so on. The income and jobs created by this increased demand for inputs to air travel represent "indirect" effects. Second, employees of the airlines and their supplier firms would spend a portion of their income to buy food, clothing and other consumer goods and services, and that money in turn would get spent. The income and jobs created by this repeated spending process represent "induced" effects. In sum, the initial direct increase in demand for U.S.-Cuba air travel would ripple through the economy, increasing the income of labor and capital multiplicatively.

Economic Output: Economists have calculated a range of values with which to measure the multiplicative effects of a dollar of additional spending on airline services. Because air travel benefits the entire travel and tourism sector, sparks business activity near hub airports, and requires material inputs ranging from aircraft to eating utensils, its impact is larger than that of many other industries. Based on a forthcoming study by DRI-WEFA, we used a multiplier estimate of 2.6 to calculate the overall economic impact of our estimated increase in incremental demand for airline service.[30] Taking our first estimate ($250 million), the overall economic impact of lifting the travel restrictions would be 2.6 times that amount, or about $650 million a year. Using our second estimate ($415 million), the overall economic impact would be about $1.08 billion a year. Table 3 summarizes these results.

Employment: An alternative way to express the economic impact of increased demand for air travel to Cuba is in terms of the number of jobs that would be created in the airline industry and other sectors of the U.S. economy. This involves translating the econom-

Table 3. Overall Benefit to the U.S. Economy from Increased Air Travel (*thousands*)

	Total Demand-Creating Trips	Increased Revenue to Airline Industry	Total Increase in U.S. GDP[a]
Estimation Method 1	833	$250,001	$650,004
Estimation Method 2	1,384	$415,088	$1,079,228

a. Based on a multiplier estimate of 2.6.

Table 4. U.S. Airline Jobs Created as a Result of Increased Air Travel

	Increased Revenue to Airline Industry (thousands)	Passenger Revenue per Airline Employee[a] (thousands)	New Airline Jobs Created
Estimation Method 1	$250,001	$138	1,815
Estimation Method 2	$415,088	$138	3,014

a. *Air Transport Association Annual Report 2002*, June 2002. Passenger revenue divided by number of employees (full-time equivalents) for 2000. (http://www.airlines.org/public/industry/bin/2002ElevSum.pdf)

ic impact figures cited above into employment effects.

Specifically, to calculate the number of jobs that would be directly created in the airline industry, we divided our estimates of incremental annual airline revenue by the average annual revenue per employee in the airline industry ($138,000).[31] As reflected in Table 4 our first estimate of annual airline revenue ($250 million) is equivalent to 1,815 new jobs in the aviation industry. Our higher estimate ($415 million) is equivalent to 3,014 new airline industry jobs.

To calculate overall employment effects, we divide our estimates of the overall economic impact of in-

creased travel demand to Cuba by the average output per employee in the U.S. economy ($70,000).[32] As shown in Table 5, the overall employment effects of increased demand for air travel would range from 9,285 to 15,417 jobs created.

Table 5. Total U.S. Jobs Created as a Result of Increased Air Travel

	Total Increase in U.S. GDP (thousands)	Average GDP per Worker[a] (thousands)	Total Jobs Created
Estimation Method 1	$650,004	$70	9,285
Estimation Method 2	$1,079,228	$70	15,417

a. Equals U.S. GDP divided by the number of U.S. workers.

Summary: Because air travel benefits the entire travel and tourism industry, sparks business activity near hub airports, and increases demand for a wide range of material inputs, an increase (or decrease) in airline revenue has an effect on the economy that is a multiple of the direct impact on the airline industry. Thus, if travel restrictions were lifted, the net increase in demand for service on U.S. air carriers would generate significant additional activity throughout the economy. Using a multiplier estimate of 2.6, we calculate that this activity would expand U.S. economic output by $650 million to $1.08 billion a year. The corresponding employment effects would range from 9,285 to 15,417 new jobs.

Question 4: How many passengers would visit Cuba on U.S.-based cruise ships, and how much additional economic activity would that generate?
Industry experts are unanimous in saying that U.S.-based cruise ships will flock to Cuba if travel restrictions are lifted. U.S.-based cruise lines dominate the

---

30. DRI-WEFA, *The National Economic Impact of Civil Aviation*, forthcoming. The Bureau of Economic Analysis (BEA), in its input-output accounts, derives an output "multiplier" for air transportation of 1.84 (Table 5: Industry-by-Commodity Multipliers) to 1.92 (Table 4: Commodity-by-Commodity Multipliers). BEA, *Survey of Current Business, Annual Input-Output Accounts of the U.S. Economy, 1996*, January 2000, pp. 73-86. However, this multiplier is "conservative" because BEA is looking only at how increased aviation spending affects national output. BEA does not include induced effects that occur as increased income ripples through the economy in the form of increased spending.

31. According to the Air Transport Association (ATA), in 2000, U.S. airlines had passenger revenues of $93.62 billion and employed 679,967 full-time equivalent (FTE) workers. Thus, the average revenue per FTE was $137,686. *ATA Annual Report 2002* (June 2002). Available at: http://www.airlines.org/public/industry/bin/20002ElevSum.pdf.

32. This figure is equal to the U.S. gross domestic product (GDP) for 2000 divided by the number of workers in the U.S. economy in the same year. *Economic Report of the President*, U.S. Government Printing Office, February 2002, Tables B-1 and B-35.

Caribbean, competing for passengers who may otherwise travel to tourist destinations (*e.g.,* the Mediterranean) dominated by foreign-based cruise lines. Thus, the addition of Cuba as a Caribbean port-of-call would enhance the competitive position of U.S.-based ships. While the typical cruise would make Cuba one stop on a longer Caribbean itinerary, industry experts expect to see some 7- and 14-day cruises devoted exclusively to circumnavigating the island. Because passengers sleep on the boat, cruise lines could play a particularly important role in the initial years following the end of U.S. restrictions, when tourist demand might exceed the supply of hotel rooms.

To measure the economic impact of cruise travel to Cuba, we modified our air travel methodology in two ways. First, we did not estimate the total number of cruise passengers who would visit Cuba. Instead, we estimated directly the incremental cruise travel that would occur if U.S.-based cruises could stop in Cuba.[33] Second, we focused on industry spending in the U.S. economy rather than industry revenues. Because U.S. airlines are U.S.-owned and most of their employees live in the United States, it is reasonable to assume that airline revenues would be spent largely in the U.S. economy. By contrast, because U.S.-based cruise ships are foreign owned, foreign built, and largely foreign crewed, only a share of their revenue would be spent in the United States.

Net Increase in Caribbean Passengers: U.S.-based cruise operators carried a total of eight million passengers in 2000. Of those, roughly 3.67 million were passengers on Caribbean cruises.[34] If restrictions were lifted, hundreds of thousands of Caribbean cruise passengers would visit Cuba, but most of them would have gone on a cruise even if Cuba had not been on the itinerary. To distinguish between diverted and incremental travel, we applied estimation method 2 from our air travel analysis.

Based on the incremental difference in American and Canadian tourism rates to the Caribbean, we concluded earlier that the availability of Cuba as a travel option could lead to a 10.8 percent net expansion of American tourism to the Caribbean. Applying this estimate to Caribbean cruise traffic, we predict that 397,000 more passengers a year would take U.S.-based Caribbean cruises if Cuba were available as a port-of-call.

Spending in the U.S. Economy: The U.S.-based cruise industry accounts for about $9.4 billion a year in direct spending in the U.S. economy, according to a detailed report prepared for the International Council of Cruise Lines (ICCL).[35] In addition to $8 billion in industry spending, this figure includes about $1.4 billion in spending by cruise passengers on air transportation, lodging, and retail. To determine the value of a 10.8 percent increase in passenger demand for Caribbean travel, we did a three-step calculation.

First, using a breakdown of the $9.4 billion, we identified categories of U.S. spending by industry that are sensitive to passenger demand. Thus, we excluded "overhead" spending, which would not increase markedly with passenger demand, and spending on petroleum products, which at the margin are imported. We also excluded spending by passengers, both to be consistent with our analysis of air travel and be-

---

33. Our analysis of air travel focused exclusively on American travelers, on the theory that foreign travelers currently are free to fly to Cuba on foreign air carriers. By contrast, our analysis of cruise travel includes American and foreign passengers alike. Very few foreign-based cruise lines offer Cuba as a port-of-call due to their distance from the island; hence foreigners might well visit Cuba on U.S.-based cruises in the absence of travel restrictions. Almost 18 percent of passengers on U.S.-based cruises live outside of the United States. Business Research & Economic Advisors (BREA), *The Contribution of the North American Cruise Industry to the U.S. Economy in 2000,* October 2001, p. 12.

34. The U.S.-based cruise industry does not publish a breakdown of actual passengers by cruise destination. However, it does publish data on industry capacity by cruise destination. Our estimate of Caribbean passengers represents 45.9 percent of total passengers, which is the share of the U.S.-based cruise industry's total capacity (measured in passenger "bed days") that is devoted to Caribbean cruises.

35. BREA, *op. cit.,* Table 10, p. 34. This report covers passenger cruise lines that primarily market their cruises in North America. We treat these cruise lines as synonymous with the U.S.-based cruise industry.

Table 6.   Overall Benefit to the U.S. Economy from Increased Cruise Travel *(thousands)*

Cruise Line "Variable" Spending in the U.S.ᵃ	Spending in the U.S. Attributable to Caribbean Cruisesᵇ	Increase in Direct Spending in the U.S.	Total Increase in U.S. GDPᶜ
$5,643,000	$2,590,137	$280,146	$532,277

a. Total spending in the United States by the U.S.-based cruise industry, excluding "Air Transportation," "Passenger Retail & Lodging Spending," "Agriculture, Mining & Construction," "Printing & Publishing," "Petroleum Refining," "Business Services" and "Other Services & Government." Business Research & Economic Advisors, *The Contribution of the North American Cruise Industry to the U.S. Economy in 2000*, October 2001, "Table 10 - Direct Economic Impacts of the Cruise Industry in the U.S. - 2000."
b. Based on allocation of North American cruise ship capacity. Ibid., "Table 5 - Destination Placement of N.A. Capacity - Bed Days - Selected Years."
c. Based on a multiplier estimate of 1.9.

Table 7.   Total U.S. Jobs Created as a Result of Increased Cruise Travel

Increase in U.S. GDP (thousands)	Average GDP per Worker (thousands)	Total Jobs Created
$532,277	$70	7,603

cause it was impossible to determine how much of that spending would not have otherwise occurred.[36]

Measured in this fashion, "variable" spending by U.S.-based cruise lines totals $5.6 billion a year. Major expense items include travel agent commissions (agents receive about 16 percent of cruise fares net of port charges, taxes and fees, and on-board revenues) and payments to tour operators; salaries and wages for U.S. crew members and shoreside employees; port services (tugboat and piloting, stevedores, passenger reception and warehousing); ship maintenance and repair; and food, beverages and other supplies.[37]

Second, we estimated the amount of variable spending in the U.S. economy attributable to Caribbean passengers. Caribbean cruises account for 45.9 percent of the U.S.-based industry's passenger capacity, as measured by passenger "bed days."[38] Thus, we assumed that the amount of variable spending attribut-

able to Caribbean passengers is 45.9 percent of $5.6 billion, or $2.59 billion a year.

Third, we assumed that a 10.8 percent increase in Caribbean passenger demand would produce an equivalent increase in the U.S.-based cruise industry's Caribbean-related variable spending. That equals $280.15 million a year.

Broader Economic Impact and Job Creation: According to the ICCL report, a multiplier estimate of 1.9 is appropriate for capturing the direct, indirect and induced effects on the U.S. economy of increased spending by the U.S.-based cruise industry.[39] Applying that multiplier, the total increase in U.S. economic output as the result of cruise travel to Cuba equals $532.28 million a year. That additional output would create a total of 7,603 new jobs.[40]

Summary: Tables 6 and 7 summarize our estimate of the economic impact of lifting restrictions on cruise travel to Cuba. Based on our earlier analysis of Cuba's potential to expand the overall Caribbean travel market, we estimate that the elimination of travel restrictions would result in a 10.8 percent increase in demand for U.S.-based Caribbean cruises. As a direct impact, we estimate that U.S.-based cruise lines would spend an additional $280.15 million a year in

36. We also excluded spending by the cruise industry on air transportation to bring passengers to the port-of-embarkation so as to be consistent with our analysis of air travel.

37. BREA, *op. cit.,* pp. 33-37.

38. *Ibid.,* Table 5, p. 19.

39. *Ibid.,* Table 12, p. 40.

40. To arrive at this estimate, we used average GDP per worker in the U.S. economy, as described in footnote 32 above. We did not calculate employment effects separately for the cruise industry, as we did with air travel, since so much of the cruise industry's U.S. spending is for non-labor items.

the United States. The indirect and induced economic effects would equal another $252.13 million in spending, for a total increase in U.S. economic output of $532.28 million a year and about 7,603 new jobs.

Additional Benefits to the U.S. Economy

Our quantitative estimates were based on the most direct and easily measured benefits from lifting travel restrictions—namely, increased demand by Americans for U.S.-Cuba air services and increased demand by all passengers for U.S.-based Caribbean cruises. To avoid overstating the benefits, we excluded other potential effects that are either small or difficult to measure reliably:

- *Domestic Travel.* To reach their point of departure, Cuba-bound passengers would engage in additional travel spending beneficial to the U.S. economy. For example, airline passengers would fly to Miami or another gateway city, and cruise passengers would fly or drive to their port of embarkation.[41] Many travelers would spend one or more nights in a hotel in the gateway or port city.

- *Foreign Travelers on U.S. Airlines.* Foreign travelers, though not directly affected by the travel ban, might provide additional business for U.S. airlines if the ban were lifted. For example, European tourists visiting South Florida might add a trip to Cuba to their itinerary.[42] And U.S. carriers with extensive European operations might pick up a small amount of business from European tourists whose sole destination is Cuba.

- *High-Speed Ferries.* Industry experts believe that high-speed ferries could become a major transportation link to Cuba. Ferry service is popular in Europe and elsewhere, in part because passengers can take their cars and trucks on the boat. Although the economic benefits could be significant, the prospect remains too speculative to quantify at this point.

- *Market Growth.* Our estimates, based on recent data, do not account for the potential growth over time in travel to Cuba. As one indication, American tourist arrivals in the Caribbean grew by 37 percent from 1990 to 2000.[43] Similarly, U.S.-based cruise lines doubled their Caribbean capacity from 1990 to 2000.[44] Tourism aside, the U.S. government admits a minimum of 20,000 Cubans for permanent residency each year, and these recent emigrants are a likely source of growth in personal travel to Cuba.

- *Consumer Surplus.* In addition to the benefits to American industry, lifting travel restrictions would bring significant benefits to American tourists, by giving them a broader choice of travel destinations. Some travelers would prefer Cuba to their current best travel option. For such travelers, the ability to go to Cuba would be a significant source of value—one that we did not attempt to measure.

CONCLUSION

Elimination of restrictions on travel to Cuba would have a noticeable impact on the U.S. economy, assuming that U.S. companies were allowed to transport Americans to Cuba. The U.S. airline and U.S.-based cruise industries would benefit most directly, but other sectors would benefit as well because of the broad impact of increased travel demand on the U.S. economy.

To summarize, we estimate that an additional 3.01 million Americans would travel to Cuba annually on U.S. air carriers in the absence of travel restrictions. Of those, 2.72 million would be tourists and 289,000 would be Cuban Americans visiting friends and relatives. Excluding travel diverted from other destinations, U.S. airlines would earn from $250

---

41. Cruise passengers who fly to their port-of-embarkation have an average roundtrip airfare of $450. BREA, *op. cit.,* p. 35.

42. According to *1999 Statistical Yearbook of the Immigration and Naturalization Service* (Table 39), nearly 1.8 million European travelers arrived at the Miami and Orlando airports in 1999.

43. According to the Caribbean Tourism Organization, American arrivals in the Caribbean in 1990 totaled 7.35 million.

44. BREA, *op. cit.,* p. 20.

Table 8. Overall Impact on the U.S. Economy of Lifting Restrictions on Travel to Cuba

	Due to Increased Demand for Air Travel	Due to Increased Demand for Cruise Travel	Combined
Increase in GDP (thousands)			
Estimation Method 1	$650,004	$532,277	$1,182,281
Estimation Method 2	$1,079,228	$532,277	$1,611,505
Total Jobs Created			
Estimation Method 1	9,285	7,603	16,888
Estimation Method 2	15,417	7,603	23,020

million to $415 million a year in increased revenue as a result of this added demand. Overall, the increased demand for air travel would expand U.S. economic output by $650 million to $1.08 billion a year and create 9,285 to 15,417 new jobs.

For the U.S.-based cruise industry, we estimate that elimination of travel restrictions to Cuba would lead to a 10.8 percent net increase in demand for Caribbean cruises. To meet this demand, U.S.-based cruise lines would spend an additional $280.15 million an-

nually in the United States. Overall, this increased demand for cruise travel would expand U.S. economic output by $532.28 million annually and create 7,603 new jobs.

Looking at the total impact of lifting travel restrictions (Table 8), measured as the combined impact of increased air and cruise travel, our estimates indicate that U.S. economic output would expand annually by $1.18 billion to $1.61 billion. This expansion would create 16,888 to 23,020 new jobs.

OVERVIEW OF CUBA'S DOLLAR FOOD MARKET: AN EXPLORATION OF THE PURCHASING AND DISTRIBUTION SYSTEM

James E. Ross and Maria Antonia Fernández Mayo[1]

Cuba's purchasing and distribution system servicing the market for dollar foods[2] is decentralized and complex. It is composed of: (1) retail stores trading only with dollars, (2) hotels and restaurants catering to tourists for dollars, (3) food processing companies that sell a portion of their production within Cuba for dollars, and (4) institutions that receive imported food products. Government agencies and mixed enterprises supplying the system purchase for their own account, or for other companies, and wholesale and retail for either dollars or pesos.

SYSTEM STRUCTURE

Dollar foods purchased and sold in Cuba are both produced domestically and imported through national and foreign enterprises operating in Cuba. Domestically produced dollar foods and beverages are grown or manufactured by state-owned or controlled entities or by foreign companies operating under Foreign Investment Law No. 77. Small private farmers may also participate in the dollar food market; however, their participation in terms of dollars is relatively insignificant.

State production entities include national food manufacturers, state farms, and state-controlled agricultural cooperatives. A mixed enterprise, an entity with foreign interest, generating dollar food products may include a food manufacturer or an agricultural production unit. A mixed enterprise producing dollar foods may take the form of a joint-venture investment, an international economic association contract, or a cooperated production agreement. There are no totally foreign owned food production or manufacturing operations in Cuba.

One government agency, Alimport (Empresa Cubana Importadora de Alimentos) is Cuba's main food and feedstuff importing company. Other importing agencies of dollar foods include government-owned holding companies that supply retail dollar stores, and government-owned companies and mixed enterprises that own or operate tourist hotels, resorts and restaurants. Some joint-venture hotels have agreements under the foreign investment law to import directly, without going through a government purchasing company. Because of the foreign company's supplier contacts and expertise, government-owned hotels, at times, may import through the joint venture or contract agreement companies. The supply and quality of food products available through the

---

1. A more detailed report on Cuba's dollar food market will be available at a later date. For a copy, contact jeross@ufl.edu.

2. As used in this paper, the term "dollar foods" refers to food and beverage products, whether imported or produced domestically, that are sold to consumers, either foreign or Cuban, for dollars. Dollar foods also include ingredients purchased with dollars or sold for dollars by the food processing industry.

importing company may determine which source is used.[3]

Foods sold or made available directly to consumers and the tourist industry for dollars generally include those products classified as consumer-oriented, but may also include products classified as intermediate and bulk. Consumer-oriented products are imported under the jurisdiction of the Cuban Ministry of Public Health (Ministerio de Salud Pública—MINSAP). Imports of intermediate and bulk agricultural products are regulated by the Ministry of Agriculture (Ministerio de Agricultura—MINAGRI). [4]

Consumer-oriented foods may be imported through several different agencies and companies, while some intermediate products and all bulk commodities are imported by Alimport. Some consumer-oriented foods may also be imported by Alimport to supply ration stores and other institutions. Alimport also purchases imported food ingredients for the food industry sector. In addition, dollar stores and other government-owned companies may receive food products imported by Alimport.

Other entities involved in the dollar food chain include in-home family restaurants (restaurantes particulares), known generally as *Paladares*.[5] These restaurants are limited to family employment and may serve only 12 customers at one time. They may charge their customers in either pesos or dollars; however, most *paladares* request dollars for payment. *Paladares* do not import food products, but purchase those products through the retail dollar stores, state-operated agricultural markets, semi-private *agromercados*, and from other sources. The economic impact of the private restaurants on the dollar food market is negligible.[6]

STORES SELLING DOLLAR FOODS (TRDS)

Retail stores selling food and beverage products for dollars (*ventas minoristas en divisas*) are scattered throughout the country. The stores are owned by the Cuban government. No foreign investment in these stores has been permitted. In all of these retail stores, known as Dollar Stores or TRDs (*Tiendas de Recuperacion de Divisas*), food products that have been imported or produced domestically are sold for dollars.

In Havana there are approximately 300 dollar stores, and roughly 1,000 in the entire country. Most of the dollar stores outside Havana are located in the tourist areas of Varadero, Ciego de Avila, Holguin, Santiago de Cuba, Camagüey and Pinar de Río.

Cuba's dollar food market encompasses many semi-autonomous government-owned and operated companies. The companies are incorporated and have the Sociedad Anónima (S.A.) designation. Generally, the companies control their own hard-currency revenues and can make purchases on their own account. Sociedad Anónima companies must remit a monthly payment to the government. The amount is negotiated between the government and the company directors.[7]

The major dollar store chains and the government corporations owning them include:

- *Tiendas Panamericanas* (CIMEX S.A.)
- *Tiendas Universo* (CUBANACAN S.A.)
- *Tiendas Caracol* (HORIZONTES Hoteles S.A.)

---

3. Caribbean Basin Agricultural Trade Office of the USDA/Foreign Agricultural Service in Miami. See recent reports on food laws and the food service sector, GAIN Reports #CU2001, 2002, and 2003.

4. Ibid.

5. *Paladar*, translated means palate or taste, but the origin of the use for the Cuban family restaurants is said to be taken from a Brazilian soap opera. The main character goes to the capital and establishes a chain of small restaurants called *Paladares*.

6. Henken, Ted. "Last Resort or Bridge to the Future: Tourism and Workers in Cuba's Second Economy," *Cuba in Transition—Volume 10* (Washington: Association for the Study of the Cuban Economy, 2000), p. 331.

7. *Cuba: A Guide for Canadian Businesses*. Department of Foreign Affairs and International Trade. The Canadian Trade Commissioner Service, June 1999.

- Tiendas y Supermercados de la Sociedad Meridiano S.A. (CUBALSE Corporation—imported foodstuffs valued at $19.7 million in 2001)
- *Tiendas TRD Caribe* (GAVIOTA S.A.)
- *Tiendas de Habaguanex S.A.* (HABAGUANEX S.A.)

Priorities for supplying the stores, whether food or non-food products, are: first, products of national origin; second, mixed enterprises (companies with foreign investment, either joint ventures, international economic association contracts, or cooperative production agreements); and third, foreign sources.

For example, products of national origin (the highest priority) could be supplied by a state-owned company such as Frutas Selectas S.A. The semi-autonomous company selects the best fruits and vegetables produced by state-owned farms and state-controlled cooperatives and markets the products to the tourist hotels and restaurants. Mixed enterprises, the second highest priority, could include Sherritt Green or Tropiflora. Sherritt Green is a government joint venture with Sherritt International of Canada. Tropiflora is a joint venture with Israeli interests. Both companies produce fruit and vegetables for sale to tourist hotels and restaurants. The third priority would be food imports.

Prices of products sold in the dollar stores are normally higher than those offered in other internal food markets. The consumer may pay a price that is 200% or more above the imported price or the price in one of the internal food markets.[8] Products similar to those available in the dollar stores may be found at lower prices in other internal markets.

In addition to dollar stores, the Cuban retail food market includes: ration stores (*Mercado de Alimentos Racionados*); agricultural or farmers' markets (*Mercados Libres Agropecuarios—MLA*); Ministry of Agriculture markets (*Mercado de Productos Agrícolas a Precios Topados*); agricultural "fairs" held on the last Sunday of each month (*Las Ferias Agropecuarias*); urban garden markets (*ventas en los huertos y organopónicos*); places of sale direct to the consumer by the CPA (Cooperatives of Agricultural Production) and the EJT (Youth Work Army); and the Cadena de Tiendas Imágenes—stores selling processed foods under the jurisdiction of the Ministry of Internal Trade, MINCIN.[9]

Of all of Cuba's official internal food markets, only the dollar stores trade in dollars. The other internal food markets trade in pesos, but do compete with the dollar stores. Quality of products in the dollar stores is normally superior to those in the other internal markets.[10]

In May 2002, the Cuban government announced that prices in the dollar stores would be increased significantly; however, food prices were to remain the same or decline. In fact, many food prices did fall, only prices for chocolate products and preserved foods increased. The increase, generally, was 10 to 15 U.S. cents above the previous price.

TOURIST HOTELS AND RESTAURANTS

Cuba rates its hotels on a star basis, ranging from one to five stars. A five-star hotel is better than a four-star, etc. The rating system does not compare facilities and services to comparable stars of hotels in other countries, but is used only to compare quality of hotels within Cuba. With current standards, most international tourism and the resulting market for dollar foods, is concentrated in three, four and five-star hotels. While two-star and one-star hotels provide a limited market for imported dollar food products, the major source of food for these hotels is the domestic market.

---

8. Armando Nova González, "El mercado interno de los alimentos," *Cuba—Reflexiones Sobre su Economía*, La Habana, 2002, p. 193.

9. Ibid.

10. For detailed information on the internal markets, including price comparisons and an explanation of why consumers buy at TRDs when the same product can be purchased for less at other markets, see José Alvarez, "Rationed Products and Something Else: Food Availability and Distribution in 2000 Cuba," *Cuba in Transition—Volume 10* (Washington: Association for the Study of the Cuban Economy, 2001).

Cuba has more than 300 tourist properties with about 40,000 rooms. Less than 100 of the tourist hotels are classified as four- and five-star hotels. Four-star hotels account for approximately 40% of room occupancy, while five-star and three-star hotels each account for about 20%. Annual growth in tourism in the 1990s was more than 15%, but in 2001 the number of tourists was only slightly more than the year before, approximately 1.8 million. The slow start for tourism in 2002 could result in even fewer tourists than recorded each of the last two years.

In the early 1990s, when tourists numbered some 300,000, only 12% of the products and services required for the tourist industry were provided through national production. Almost all food products needed for tourist hotels and restaurants were imported. All of the beer and bottled water served to tourists was imported. As a result of economic reforms in the mid-1990s and pursuit of a policy of protectionism, the supply situation was reversed and Cuba now supports some 65% of the tourist hotel and restaurant needs through national production. One national brewery, a joint venture, supplies about 95% of the tourist market for beer and another joint venture supplies almost all of the bottled water.[11]

The semi-autonomous companies serving the tourist industry include: Corporación Cubanacán, Grupo Hotelero Gran Caribe, Horizontes Hoteles, Habaguanex, Grupo de Turismo Gaviota, Islazul, Grupo de Recreación y Turismo Rumbos, Companía de Marinas Puerto Sol, and the Complejo de Convenciones. To some extent, all of the companies compete with each other, but they concentrate on different segments of the tourist market. No foreign investment has been introduced in the ownership of these companies.

Corporación Cubanacán S.A. accounts for more than 40% of the tourist market. It was formed to operate four- and five-star hotels, restaurants, cafeterias, retail stores, water recreation centers, tourist health facilities, and tourist reception and other recreation centers. Cubanacán also produces and sells artisan handicrafts and operates a transportation company that provides tour buses and rents automobiles.

Many of the tourist hotels, administered as either international economic association contracts or joint ventures, involve Cubanacán. Joint investment arrangements under Foreign Investment Law No. 77 have been developed by Cubanacán with Grupo Sol Meliá (Spain), LTI (Germany), Golden Tulip (Holland), and SuperClubs (Jamaica).

Grupo Hotelero Gran Caribe S.A. operates more than 40 hotels classified as four- and five-star hotels. Gran Caribe hotels have 9,500 rooms for tourists scattered throughout the country, but are located mainly in Havana and Varadero. In addition, the group operates three primary tourist attractions in Havana, the Restaurant La Bodeguita del Medio, Bar and Restaurant La Floridita, and the Cabaret Tropicana.

Horizontes Hoteles S.A. is a hotel chain, mostly three- and four-stars, with more than 7,000 rooms. Horizontes also operates facilities with mineral water baths, treatment for stress, etc. One spa (*Centro Hospitalario que Atiende Multiples Enfermedades*) treats patients with health problems characteristic of the Caribbean.

Grupo de Recreación y Turismo Rumbos S.A., founded in 1994, has grown approximately 20% annually. It operates facilities for both national and international tourists in Cuba's major tourist cities and secondary locations. Rumbos is diversified, and has established businesses in: a travel agency; various types of restaurants, including fast food (comidas rápidas, restaurantes y parrilladas); small lodges in cities, on beaches, in the country, at golf courses, airports, and marinas; and eco-tourism. Currently, Rumbos is planning eight new golf courses to meet the standards for both international golf amateurs and professionals.

---

11. Miguel Alejandro Figueras Pérez, "El turismo internacional y la formación de clusters productivos en la economía cubana," *Cuba—Reflexiones sobre su Economía,* La Habana, 2002, pp. 111 and 112.

Companía de Marinas Puerto Sol S.A. was created to develop marinas, piers, recreational boat activities, etc. The company owns 390 rooms in two-star and local hotels to meet the needs of tourists and nationals.

Grupo de Turismo Gaviota S.A. is a tourism company controlled by the Revolutionary Armed Forces. It is dedicated to operation of four- and five-star hotels, development of marinas, restaurants and cafeterias, recreational water facilities, and health facilities for tourists. It also operates a transportation company that offers tourist buses and rental of automobiles and taxis.

Habaguanex S.A. belongs to the historical office of Havana (Oficina del Historiador de la Ciudad). It was established to develop three- and four-star hotels for international tourists in the Historic Center of Old Havana (*Centro Histórico de la Habana Vieja*). Currently, it is renovating various hotels and opening restaurants in the oldest part of the city.

Islazul S.A. was established to develop two- and three-star hotels for international tourists seeking low-cost accommodations.

Complejo de Convenciones includes operation of the Palace of Conventions (Palacio de las Convenciones), Hotel Palco, the restaurants, Rancho Palco and El Palenque, and Club Habana. It also administers the Sala de Exposiciones (PABEXPO), the *Mansión Residencial* (*Casa de Protocolo*—House of Protocol), and the auto rental agency, Palcocar. Basically, the complex specializes in the development of tourist events and conventions.

A few foreign companies have negotiated contract agreements that permit them to import food directly for their tourist facilities. Foreign companies having arrangements under Foreign Investment Law No. 77 with the Cuban companies often operate as hotel administrators and assume responsibility for food and beverage services. Some have taken equity positions in the hotels owned by the holding companies. These include, among others: Grupo Sol Meliá and Hoteles C from Spain; Accor and Club Med from France; LTI and RIU from Germany; Delta Hotels and Resorts, Commonwealth Hospitality Ltd., and Leisure Canada Inc. from Canada; Viaggi di Ventaglio and Press Tours from Italy; and SuperClubs from Jamaica. About 30% of Cuba's hotels involve investments with foreign companies. There are no totally foreign owned hotels in Cuba.

FOOD MANUFACTURERS

Food processors in Cuba import substantial amounts of food ingredients for use in the manufacture of food products. About 20% of the national production is sold for dollars, either through sales for dollars in Cuba or by exporting.

All food manufacturers in Cuba are under the jurisdiction of the Ministry of Food Industries (*Ministerio de la Industria Alimenticia*—MINAL), created in 1965. MINAL oversees industries manufacturing, principally, milk and meat products, cereals, confections, bread, biscuits and crackers, pastries, fruit and vegetable products, alcoholic beverages, water, soft drinks, and beer. Industries milling bulk commodities, such as wheat and rice, also are under the jurisdiction of MINAL.

At the time of the establishment of the Ministry of Food Industries, Cuba was importing most of the processed food consumed. In addition, most of the primary material used by the existing national food manufacturing industry was imported. There was little growth in food processing until food research centers were introduced. Between 1970 and 1975, the Food and Agricultural Organization of the United Nations and the governments of Sweden and the Netherlands provided financing for pilot plants devoted to applied research in the lactic, meat-processing, and vegetable and fruit-preserving branches.[12]

International assistance from 1975 to 1990 for research and development in Cuba's food industry led to substantial growth in food manufacturing. Production increases during this period included: canned meats, 157%; canned fruits and vegetables,

---

12. *Business Tips on Cuba*, August 1996, p. 20.

66%; cheeses, 143%; and wheat flour, 126%. The number of production lines had grown from 57 in 1975, to more than one thousand by 1989.

With the loss of Soviet and Eastern Block trade preferences in 1989 and 1990, there was a progressive decline in Cuban production in general until the mid-1990s. Food industry executives were forced to introduce products that made it possible to raise production volumes through increased use of extenders and substitutes in products destined for the domestic market. The imperative was to maintain nutritional values despite a reduction in agricultural production, especially of meat products.

Between 1989 and 1994, the worst period for the Cuban economy, the food processing industry registered a dramatic decline of 42% in the value of its output, along with a reduction of 74% in national raw-material supplies from the agricultural sector, and a 34% drop in imported raw materials.[13]

In 1994, Cuba's production of manufactured food products was 45% of the output in 1989. The output of beverages was 56%. By 2000, beverage production had increased to 81% of the 1989 level. Food manufacturing increased more slowly, reaching only 54%. While the food industry has had significant growth since 1994, production remains substantially less than the output level of more than a decade earlier.[14]

Production lines that are growing the most include: beer, soft drinks, mineral water, alcoholic beverages for export, powdered milk, pastas, flour, soft cheese, ice cream, and yogurt. Wheat flour production also showed some increase, while milled rice production decreased substantially. In 1998 the value of production among eight "Uniones" in MINAL was $1.25 billion. About $25 million was destined for dollar markets, either through the dollar stores or by exporting. Growth of production in 1998 was 27% more than the year before. (More recent data are not available to the authors at this time.)

Sixteen of Cuba's food manufacturing companies are joint ventures and 12 are Cooperated Production Agreements.[15] Each of the 16 mixed enterprises are associated with Coralsa (La Corporación Alimentaria—CORAL S.A.), a holding company constituted within MINAL in 1996. The Ministry restructured in the mid-1990s to promote increased support for food industry firms operating with foreign capital. Participation of Coralsa in the 16 enterprises ranges from 40% to 50%. Fixed assets of the companies at the time of restructing were placed at $36 million. They had $4 million in working capital and $25.5 million in the process of investment.

Enterprises associated with Coralsa produce and market sausages, candies and confections, products derived from wheat, instant beverages, wines, beers, soft drinks and mineral waters, as well as technological and refrigeration equipment for the food industry. In 1994, the mixed enterprises had a combined value of production of $20 million. By 2000, the value of production of the mixed enterprises had reached $140 million.[16]

Another area of activity of the Cuban food industries sector has been the overseas food processing operations in which there is Cuban capital and technology. A portion of the earnings from these industries is returned to Cuba. Cía. de Tasajo de Uruguay, for example, was established in Uruguay to process jerked beef and other meat products for export to Cuba and other Latin American and African countries. A Coralsa-owned company, Carnes del Mercosur S.A., located in Cuba, imports and markets the products in Cuba for the internal market.

13. Ibid, p. 18.

14. *Anuario Estadístico Cuba 2000.* Capitulo VIII, Sector Industria.

15. Omar Everleny Pérez Villanueva, "La inversión extranjera directa en Cuba: Evolución y perspectivas," *Cuba—Reflexiones Sobre su Economía,* La Habana, 2002, p. 90.

16. Pérez Villanueva, p. 90.

INSTITUTIONS AND THE ROLE OF ALIMPORT

All dollar purchases of food for use in institutions are conducted through Alimport, a government-owned company operating under the auspices of the Ministry of Foreign Trade. Alimport decides who to do business with, what quantity to buy based on end customers' needs, and negotiates and fixes prices. It also decides buying terms depending on seller, delivery terms and place, financial facilities, and freight advantages.[17]

For FAS and FOB operations, Alimport relies on a logistics group in charge of chartering vessels and monitoring the whole process of transportation from the operational standpoint. Alimport works with Cuban flag vessels, brokers, or directly with foreign flagship owners, and agrees on terms and operates with them as per international practice standards.

For CFR, CIF, CPT and CIP operations, the Alimport logistics group ensures shipping terms are in accordance with contract terms. It also follows up on shipment and carriage of goods until delivery at port of destination. Alimport negotiates and agrees on discharging terms with port terminal and stevedoring companies. According to Alimport's president, Alimport looks after needs of its end-customers and its purchasing strategy is based on such needs.[18]

In May of 2002, the Cuban government designated Alimport as the exclusive purchasing agent for U.S. based companies that want to export food products direct from the United States to Cuba. Alimport will purchase agricultural and branded food products from U.S.-based companies and re-sell, or transfer, the products to other Cuba-based companies.[19]

ESTIMATED VALUE OF THE DOLLAR FOOD MARKET

Data are not available to indicate the value of food imported or produced domestically for each of the four major areas distributing dollar foods and beverages—dollar stores, tourist hotels and restaurants, food manufacturers and institutions. Data and information that are available, however, indicate food imports amount to approximately $650 to $700 million, or about 14% of Cuba's total imports.[20]

Approximately half of the food imported by Cuba meets the classifications of intermediate and consumer-ready products. The remaining half consists of bulk commodities, such as wheat, coarse grains, pulses, and rice. Pulses and rice may enter the dollar store market direct, as well as be provided to ration stores and institutions. Most of the bulk and some of the intermediate products are resold to the food manufacturing companies. A large percentage, perhaps 50%, of the food products imported are resold through dollar stores and the tourist hotels and restaurants.

Food products sold through the Ministry of Agriculture to the tourist sector and dollar stores in 2001 totaled $167.5 million, an increase of 3.46% compared to gross revenues of US $161.7 million reported in 2000.[21] Cuba reported gross revenues from marketing agricultural commodities to the tourism sector of US $59 million in 1998 and US $70 million in 1999. Allowing for continued growth, an estimated value of food produced under the auspices of the Minister of Agriculture and sold for dollars this year could reach $170 million to $200 million.

Processed foods sold through the Ministry of Food Industries to the tourist sector and dollar stores, assuming most of the mixed enterprise production and

---

17. Presentation by Mr. Pedro Alvarez Borrego, President of Alimport, Agricultural Sales Conference, Cancún, Mexico, Jan. 30-Feb. 2, 2002.

18. Ibid.

19. On May 12, 2002, the president of Alimport reported that Alimport would be the exclusive agent in Cuba for U.S. based companies. U.S.-Cuba Trade and Economic Council.

20. Estimate by authors based on USDA/FAS data showing about $600 million in 1999 for food imports.

21. U.S.-Cuba Trade and Economic Council. March 18, 2002.

some of the national company production enter the dollar market, could range from $200 million to $300 million.

The value of products grown in Cuba by mixed enterprises is unknown, but could range from $20 to $30 million. Food from domestic production sold in Paladares for dollars is estimated to be relatively small. Combining the estimated data provides a total of all foods sold in Cuba for dollars to an estimated level ranging from $800 million to $1 billion.[22] Tourists[23] and foreign businessmen,[24] along with Cubans who receive dollars through remittances, and various means, are the sources of hard currency to buy the dollar foods.[25]

The European Union and Canada provide about half of the food imports, while Mexico, and Latin American (Argentina and Brazil for soybean products) and Asian countries (China, Thailand and Vietnam for rice imports) are also important sources of food imports. More than half of Europe's agricultural exports to Cuba, which totaled $185 million in 1999, consisted of wheat flour, vegetable oils and consumer-ready products, primarily dairy products and poultry meat. Wheat accounted for about 45% of the total. Canada's agricultural exports to Cuba, $115 million in 1999, were largely (83%) pulses and consumer-oriented products, such as red meat, poultry and dairy products.

FACTORS AFFECTING THE CURRENT MARKET

1. Cuba's purchasing and distribution system for dollar foods is an intricate network of organizations authorized to import and distribute food products in Cuba for dollars. Organizations include government agencies, state-owned companies, mixed enterprises, associated foreign firms and licensed private restaurants. They all purchase and/or sell food directly or indirectly for dollars in Cuba.

2. TRDs (dollar stores) and the tourist hotels and restaurants are the primary markets for dollar foods in Cuba. Ration stores, institutions and food industries provide the largest market for bulk commodities, and an important market for foods classified as intermediate and consumer-oriented products.

3. Alimport is the country's largest food importing company. Food imported by Alimport is distributed to Cuban consumers for pesos, or sold for dollars through various channels. Distribution of food sold for pesos is made through ration stores and government institutions. Some of the food products and beverages imported by Alimport are sold for dollars through dollar stores, tourist facilities, and food processors. Government tourist hotel and restaurant holding companies, government agencies importing for dollar stores, and mixed enterprises operating tourist facilities are also important importers of food sold in Cuba for dollars.

FACTORS AFFECTING THE FUTURE MARKET

1. The decision by the government of Cuba to make Alimport the exclusive importing agency for food and agricultural products from the United States raises questions regarding market strategy for U.S. exporters. For example:

---

22. This is a preliminary estimate by the authors. It is hoped that a more substantiated estimate can be included in the study underway. (A reminder that an estimate of value of food entering the dollar market in Cuba does not include food imported by Cuba that enters the peso and institutional markets.)

23. Tourists pay for food with hard currency at tourist hotels, and provide tips for services. Those dollars are used, largely, to make food and other purchases in the dollar stores.

24. Some mixed enterprises supplement workers' income with dollars, either through negotiated arrangements with the Cuban government or through other means. The dollars are then used by the Cuban workers to purchase dollar foods and other dollar items.

25. Remittances, money sent to Cubans by family members and other contributors living overseas, are generally estimated to range between $600 million and $1 billion annually. These dollars, while the route may not always be direct, end up primarily being used in the dollar stores.

- Will Alimport increase food imports from the United States to replenish the country's food reserves diminished by Hurricane Michelle? If so, the potential market would appear good for food products, such as rice, pulses, vegetable oil, dairy products, chicken meat, and wheat flour.

- A large number, reportedly 50 to 100[26], Cuba-based mixed enterprises, international association contract entities and government-owned companies have authorization from the Cuban government to import food products.

- Since November 2001, many of these companies have established contacts with U.S.-based companies. Will these companies be able to import the products they want through Alimport?

2. Also, will any of Cuba's authorized importing companies, other than Alimport, be permitted to import U.S.-branded products from third coun-

tries, or will Alimport be the exclusive importer of these products?

3. The growth of Cuba's dollar food market, to a large extent, is contingent on continuation of a relatively high level of remittances, and increases in tourism and foreign investment. With elevated security concern worldwide following events on September 11, 2001 in the United States, and economic recession in Canada and Europe, growth of tourism in Cuba has decreased. Foreign investment also appears to be on a descending trend. With less tourist growth and shrinkage of disposable income for tourists, as well as reduced foreign investment, Cuba's dollar food market could be affected negatively.

4. Perhaps the greatest unknown is the future of travel restrictions for U.S. tourists to Cuba. Lifting of the U.S. imposed restrictions on travel could result in a large number of tourists going to Cuba. This would create a substantial increase in demand in Cuba for dollar food and beverage products.

---

26. Caribbean Basin Trade Office, USDA/FAS. (More than 300 state-owned, but decentralized, enterprises had been licensed to import all products as of 1999 by the Ministerio del Comercio Exterior (MINCEX), Ministry of Foreign Trade, according to the Canadian Department of Foreign Affairs and International Trade.)

¿EL ESTADO PARA EL HOMBRE O EL HOMBRE PARA EL ESTADO? UN COLOQUIO CONSTITUCIONAL SOBRE LA TERCERA REPÚBLICA

Alberto Luzárraga

El viejo sistema se ha desintegrado, el nuevo aún no está construido y nuestra vida colectiva esta marcada por una incertidumbre subconsciente acerca de que tipo de sistema queremos, como construirlo y si tenemos los conocimientos para construirlo en primer lugar. (Vaclav Havel, *New York Review of Books,* 7 de marzo de 1991.)

En el futuro, Cuba enfrentará una incertidumbre similar a la citada. Aceptemos que a cortas o a largas, sea o no peligroso o imprudente (según el criterio de algunos) desembocamos en una Convención Constituyente con plenos poderes para reformar la Constitución del 40 o dictar una nueva. Es aquí donde viene a cuento la pregunta que encabeza este ensayo y que a nuestro entender se perfila como el problema constitucional del Siglo XXI. *¿El Hombre para el Estado o el Estado para el Hombre?*

En el caso cubano, después de más de cuarenta años de marxismo tiránico, parecería que la respuesta está dada. Entregarse de lleno al estado que promete renovarnos y crear el "hombre nuevo" es suicidio. El "hombre nuevo" cuando asciende al poder y hace del estado un dios al que hay que servir se parece demasiado a lo peor del "hombre viejo." Actúa como si no existieran cortapisas legales y morales, y atropella y abusa sin pudor, aunque es ducho en aducir consignas supuestamente justificativas de su conducta injusta.

El clamor por el respeto a los derechos humanos no es sino el clamor por el respeto a la ley natural, a los derechos que tiene la persona por ser persona, derechos con los que nace y que no son producto de concesión graciosa por la autoridad. Una clasificación útil es la de Carl Schmitt que divide estos derechos como sigue:

- *(a) Derechos de libertad del individuo aislado* tales como la libertad de conciencia, la propiedad privada, libertad de empresa, la inviolabilidad del domicilio, de la correspondencia y la libertad personal, tales como escoger domicilio, viajar sin permisos, etc.

- *(b) Derechos de libertad del individuo en relación a establecer relaciones y comunicarse con otros,* tales como la libertad de expresión, de prensa, de publicación sin censura previa, de manifestación, de reunión pacífica, etc

- *(c) Derechos políticos pertenecientes al ciudadano* o sea igualdad ante la ley, derecho a un sufragio en igualdad de condiciones, acceso a cargos públicos electivos o por nombramiento o elección, derecho de peticionar a las autoridades, etc.

- *(d) Derechos a prestaciones sociales dadas por el Estado* como el derecho a la educación, al trabajo, a una pensión de jubilación, al cuidado médico.

Las garantías de los puntos (a), (b) y (c) han tenido amplio desarrollo en nuestras constituciones. Plasmarlos en una nueva constitución no será difícil porque hay buenos modelos y antecedentes. Son derechos clásicos. El problema siempre es la praxis, el cómo se implementan los derechos. En términos de implementación el problema mayor surge con los derechos expuestos en (d). Sin trabajo, educación o atención médica no se puede ser ciudadano digno ni gozar de las garantías que se declaran en los derechos individuales. La dificultad estriba en lo siguiente: cuando se pide al Estado que garantice prestaciones esenciales entramos en un contrapunto difícil entre la libertad y las garantías esenciales a una vida digna. La libertad individual será el resultado del manejo adecuado de esta difícil disyuntiva: como atender al ciudadano y mantener al estado dentro de límites aceptables de modo que no asfixie al individuo y a la familia y con ello la libertad.

El pueblo cubano, como todos los que surgen de la pesadilla socialista, está acostumbrado a que le "den," aunque sea poco, malo e imprevisible. Es el sistema, y con frecuencia las personas sumidas en él no captan claramente (porque la angustia de vivir no permite meditar a fondo) la relación entre libertad y concentración del poder a través de los monopolios estatales. Este tema se ha analizado política y demagógicamente en todas partes y sistemas. Hay ideología estatista fanática y también hay exageraciones en la reacción a ese fanatismo que seguramente van a salir a relucir cuando se discuta si el sistema a seguir deberá contener gran injerencia estatal. Le pediríamos al lector cubano que ha tenido que vivir bajo el sistema, que examine cuatro temas de sentido común que cualquier observador puede constatar en su vida diaria: costos, proliferación de servicios, burocracia administrativa y control político de la burocracia.

Los costos se administran bien cuando a alguien le duele el centavo. Tienen su sistema de auto-control en la competencia. Hay que gastar lo necesario para crear un buen producto. El proveedor de bienes o servicios tacaño fracasa en la empresa privada porque acaba proveyendo productos inferiores. El ahorro en costos que degenera en codicia tiene su límite natural. Pero el estado es impersonal. Con tal de que cumpla el reglamento el burócrata se sabe seguro, y su trabajo no es mejorar el reglamento sino cumplirlo. Cómo pudiera hacer mejor y más barato el servicio es tema que no puede decidir por sí sólo y cambiar las cosas en la administración pública usualmente conlleva gran esfuerzo y riesgo personal. Pocos se atreven a enfrentar el problema. Por eso los servicios estatales tienden a ser costosos y poco eficientes. La prestación de servicios requiere administración, y así la burocracia prolifera y crea nuevos puestos por una razón también muy humana. Todos quieren progresar y en la burocracia se progresa añadiendo asistentes.

Para el político cada nuevo puesto estatal es un voto muy influenciable con lo cual se cierra el círculo del poder. Las elecciones se ganan prometiendo. ¿Y qué mejor promesa que prometer servicios "gratis" o a bajo costo que además crean empleo para sus votantes? Una vez que existen prestaciones estatales importantes surgen otras. Con las prestaciones vienen los impuestos que paga el pueblo puesto que el estado en sí no produce nada. El ciudadano descubre que nada es "gratis" y que cuando se llega a un exceso impositivo la libertad se convierte en tiranía disfrazada. La Constitución del 40 tuvo un gran acierto en este tema al intentar un sistema de presupuesto equilibrado por disposición constitucional. No permitía suprimir ingresos sin una igual supresión de gastos, ni incluir servicios cuyo costo no estuviese establecido en el presupuesto y contase con un ingreso definido.[1]

El abuso descrito es producto de la concentración del poder económico y político. Llega a su máxima cota en una tiranía socialista. Todos los sistemas políticos

---

1. Art. 257. El Congreso no podrá incluir en las leyes de presupuesto disposiciones que introduzcan reformas legislativas o administrativas de otro orden, ni podrá reducir o suprimir ingresos de carácter permanente sin establecer al mismo tiempo otros que los sustituyan, salvo el caso en que reducción o suspensión corresponda a la reducción de gastos permanentes de igual cuantía; ni asignará ninguno de los servicios que deban dotarse en el presupuesto anual cantidad mayor de la indicada en el proyecto del Gobierno. Podrá por medio de las leyes crear nuevos servicios o ampliar los existentes. Toda ley que origine gastos fuera del presupuesto, o que represente en el porvenir erogaciones de esa clase, deberá establecer, bajo pena de nulidad, el medio de cubrirlos en cualquiera de estas formas: a) Creación de nuevos ingresos. b) Supresión de erogaciones anteriores. c) Comprobación cierta de superávit o sobrante por el Tribunal de Cuentas.

son más o menos miméticos y cambian cuando es preciso. Cuando el sistema socialista se vea forzado a "democratizarse" cambiará los métodos pero no los objetivos de concentración del poder. Con facilidad podremos caer en una tiranía de facto con una cara bondadosa: "el estado niñera." Para el pueblo de Cuba el estado niñera tiene credenciales. Ha creado hábitos muy peligrosos si se aspira a lograr una sociedad libre. Es el mencionado: ¿Qué me dan? En política, el que da, cobra, y cobra en poder.

Como contrapunto del estado niñera está la teoría del mercado llevada a su máxima expresión. Según ella el estado debe ser sólo un árbitro porque supuestamente el mercado eventualmente resuelve todos los problemas y distorsiones. Los marxistas y socialistas llaman a dichas ideas neoliberalismo y lo presentan con características truculentas que no existen sino en teoría libresca. Una cosa es la teoría y otra la práctica de gobierno que no acepta costos sociales muy altos si eso es lo que produce la espera. El estado liberal bien organizado acepta sus límites y conoce los de sus gobernados. Sabe que los hombres no son ángeles y que debe vigilar ciertas actividades humanas. Y lo hace. La regulación de los mercados de valores, de los monopolios, de los conflictos laborales, son ejemplos clásicos. La intervención estatal para resolver una crisis y/o castigar a los que han delinquido es común. Es simple teoría de gobierno y el mentado neoliberalismo puro no existe en la práctica.

Los ideólogos económicos, que se dicen liberales puros y protestan contra toda acción estatal, a menudo confunden la teoría económica con la teoría de gobierno. Y lo mismo les ocurre a los ideólogos socialistas pero a la inversa. Los estatistas sistemáticos confunden su particular teoría de gobierno con el buen manejo económico.

La nueva república cubana tendrá que enfrentar una disyuntiva: o sigue arrastrando mas o menos explícitamente la cadena de la mentalidad y los lemas del socialismo o enfrenta lo que era falso y toma un rumbo nuevo. Como se resuelva la disyuntiva definirá el futuro. Más de cuarenta años de consignas y falsedades han creado una gran confusión, contradicciones internas y pésimos hábitos. El pueblo cubano quiere justicia política, económica y social, pero requiere un

cambio en su manera de pensar y actuar que tendrá que ser efectivo y no meramente retórico.

No hay que caer en "ismos inútiles" para dictar una buena constitución. Una buena constitución hace esto: divide y regula el poder para lograr un equilibrio entre los órganos de gobierno a los cuales concede funciones específicas propias de su competencia. Redactar un documento es relativamente fácil. Crear un sistema que funcione no lo es. La sociedad cubana, al considerar y discutir un nuevo proyecto de república, debe plantearse ciertas cuestiones básicas que son la semilla de la libertad actual y futura. En este coloquio intentaremos plantear algunas:

- ¿Tenemos o no suficiente madurez como nación para crear un instrumento constitucional coherente y útil?

- ¿Entiende el pueblo de Cuba porque han fracasado nuestros dos anteriores proyectos de república?

- ¿Entiende como llegar a la libertad sin caer en una transición carente de garantías?

- ¿Entiende que este intento es vital para que Cuba por fin cuaje como un país respetado por su justicia y dinamismo?

- ¿Conoce los costos y donde radican los peligros?

- ¿Entiende que es necesario dividir el poder para garantizar la libertad?

- ¿Entiende cómo protegerse de crear un sistema político inoperante? ¿Capta que es indispensable crear controles institucionales muy fuertes y apoyarlos?

CONTESTANDO LAS PREGUNTAS

¿Tenemos o no suficiente madurez como nación para crear un instrumento constitucional coherente y útil? Es hasta cierto punto una pregunta retórica porque con madurez o sin ella tendremos que bailar en este baile. Sería razonable decir que de inmediato no tendríamos la madurez necesaria porque habríamos surgido de una catástrofe y adaptarse a la normalidad requiere cierto tiempo. Pero tampoco la teníamos al acabarse la Guerra de Independencia con el agravante de que existía un alto índice de analfabetismo. Sin embargo la Constitución de 1901 fue un buen documento. Y la Constitución del 40, dictada después de una década de desórdenes, con multitud de partidos y tendencias disputándose los escaños para ir a la constituyente, fue un buen compromiso.

No debemos ser extremadamente pesimistas porque personas con capacidad de hacer un buen documento las hubo y las habrá. El problema consiste en como llegan esas personas a la constituyente. La respuesta está en la libertad de expresión y en el uso de los medios de comunicación social para informar, educar y ganar adhesiones a ideas concretas. En 1901 los electores sólo tenían periódicos pero muchos constituyentes eran libertadores bien conocidos. En el 40 había partidos políticos y medios de comunicación masiva. En el siglo XXI hay muchos más medios, pero existe gran desinformación, confusión, trauma y ansiedad.

Por ello hay que exigir al gobierno interino que estructure de inmediato un sistema de información veraz al ciudadano, abra los medios de comunicación social, y permita el discurso político sobre la esencia de la libertad. Hay que informar verazmente. No será fácil pues quien controla los medios controla el acceso a ellos. Pero podrá remediarse si se abre el sistema a la compra de estaciones de radio por personas o entidades no gubernamentales y si se permite la publicación sin restricciones de material impreso. En cuanto a la TV, la venta a grupos privados también debe estudiarse.

Pero en todos los casos, bien que el radio y la TV sean estatales o privadas, será necesario estudiar como se maneja el acceso a las diversas opiniones de modo que ninguna corriente importante de pensamiento no totalitario quede excluida. Tanto la TV como el radio en la Cuba post Castro deben tener inicialmente algunas de las características y obligaciones de un servicio público, cualesquiera sean sus dueños, por lo menos hasta que se estabilice el país y se formen corrientes de opinión independientes. Esto implica separar una cantidad de tiempo gratuito para el discurso político abierto a los partidos y no simplemente venderle tiempo a quien pueda pagarlo.

¿Entiende el pueblo de Cuba porque han fracasado nuestros dos anteriores proyectos de república? ¿En-

tiende que este intento es vital para que Cuba por fin cuaje como un país respetado por su justicia y dinamismo? Estas dos preguntas son el anverso y el reverso de la cuestión. En cuanto a si entendemos las causas de nuestro fracaso republicano me temo que solo ahora estamos empezando a meditar seriamente sobre ello. Hasta hace poco teníamos una actitud nostálgica sobre nuestro pasado. Cosa natural, pues en buena parte era una reacción a la desinformación castrista, que arremetió contra todo lo que existió antes de 1959 como si no valiese nada. Y eso no es cierto, pero tampoco lo es idealizar la historia. La realidad es que las primeras décadas de la República tuvieron sus altos y bajos pero esencialmente se intentó respetar la legalidad constitucional. No obstante, desde la prórroga de poderes de Machado (en el 1928) Cuba vivió un republicanismo constitucional de carácter irregular de 1928 a 1940 y un republicanismo normal pero deficiente del 1940 al 1952.

En este período del 28 al 52, hubo enmiendas constitucionales de dudosa legalidad, en particular la propuesta por Machado y aprobada por un congreso servil, constituciones dadas por decreto en el período post Machado y un principio de vuelta al republicanismo durante el período que siguió a la promulgación de la Constitución del 40. Sin embargo el republicanismo sufrió porque el pueblo confundió el sistema con los políticos, como inevitablemente sucede cuando buena parte de los que tienen el poder no se conducen como corresponde a sus cargos.

Nuestro republicanismo llegó escuálido y raquítico al golpe de estado de 1952 y no por falta de talento y gente de valer, pues al fin y al cabo la Constitución del 40 fue prueba de capacidad; sino porque caímos de nuevo en la manía revolucionaria que siempre nos ha consumido en mayor o menor grado.

Después de Machado la "revolución," como método de gobierno, cobró inusitada valía. El partido auténtico se llamaba Partido Revolucionario Cubano (A), los ortodoxos de Chibás se llamaban así porque alegaban tener la verdadera ortodoxia revolucionaria. Alrededor de esta doctrina y al margen de los partidos pululaban grupos con nombres truculentos que tenían más características de pandilla que de agrupación política. Castro surgió de dicho ambiente.

Carecíamos además de un número importante de asociaciones civiles no partidistas que propugnasen incansablemente el método institucional contra el revolucionario. Así las cosas, la pasividad ante el 10 de marzo no fue de extrañar. Se ha dicho que se debió al cansancio y a la propaganda devastadora de Chibás contra los auténticos y todo ello es cierto; pero lo que no se ha resaltado es que Batista hizo lo que muchos cubanos hubieran querido hacer: dar la "cañona" para ponerse él. Fue una validación cuartelera del "método revolucionario."

Y por estar harto de oírlo el pueblo concluyó que el que toma el poder en la forma que sea, manda. No sólo el pueblo, nuestro flamante Tribunal de Garantías Constitucionales y Sociales aceptó la fuerza como fuente de Derecho Constitucional y desestimó un recurso de inconstitucionalidad contra la ley constitucional decretada por Batista (otra vez constituciones por decreto) que era sólo una copia de la Constitución del 40 adaptada a la conveniencia del régimen. Y ese Tribunal constaba de magistrados nombrados por gobiernos auténticos, pero prefirieron mantenerse en el cargo a mantener la institucionalidad, aunque una minoría digna votó en contra.

El pueblo sólo tenía una idea vaga de la magnitud institucional del problema pero la intuía y la resentía. Castro, buen psicólogo, usó el sentimiento y basó su programa en el restablecimiento de la constitución y la normalidad para casi de inmediato declarar en 1959: "¿Elecciones para qué?" Y el pueblo se lo aceptó porque el modelo revolucionario era el que calaba y no el modelo institucional. Es cierto que Castro engañó pero éramos propensos al engaño y nos gustaba el invento.

El resultado lo conocemos, más de 40 años de horrible dictadura, destrucción de buena parte de la nacionalidad, confusión tremenda, materialismo de vivir solo el presente, desconfianza en el futuro, producto inevitable de tantas promesas incumplidas, y mentalidad de "resolver hoy" a como de lugar y mañana veremos.

El esfuerzo para superar esta situación será enorme pero hay que hacerlo porque ahí está la respuesta a la segunda pregunta.

¿Entiende el pueblo que este intento es vital para que Cuba por fin cuaje como un país respetado por su justicia y dinamismo? Si no lo hacemos ahora y lo hacemos bien Cuba será, tal vez por una generación entera, un país con una pobre identidad que dará tumbos hasta asentarse y cómo y en qué se asentará nadie lo sabe. Hacer las cosas bien significa crear un marco institucional serio y realista. Serio, porque debe haber compromiso ciudadano para que se cumpla, pues en eso consiste el patriotismo y no en los discursos. Realista porque hay que crear un marco institucional que garantice la libertad permanentemente, y funcione en el siglo XXI. Y por el contrario no uno que satisfaga las preferencias ideológicas de los constituyentes que enfrentarán una enorme responsabilidad.

¿Entiende el pueblo cubano como llegar a la libertad sin caer en una transición lenta y carente de garantías? Un fallo en esta etapa viciaría todo el proceso de volver al estado de derecho. No se puede aceptar un sistema que cree una "democracia formal y retórica" con poco contenido sustancial de garantías ciudadanas, ni tampoco pretender una perfección tal que haga la celebración de elecciones un evento para las calendas griegas. Hay varios remedios:

- Para empezar, derogar la "intocable" constitución castrista que es la base legal de la tiranía. Dejar de hacerlo es aceptar que el yugo es modificable. Jurídicamente no tiene remedio, es una monstruosidad como hemos demostrado en otras ocasiones.[2] Ello no significa cambiar de inmediato la organización administrativa, adefesio con el que hay que bregar, pues en realidad está plasmada en innumerables leyes y regulaciones que habrá que examinar para derogarlas y/o modificarlas con sentido común. Temporalmente podría gobernar un presidente provisional con un consejo de ministros que necesariamente tendrá facultades legislativas. Pero sujeto a la super-

---

2. Ver "Derecho Constitucional Cubano," Primera Parte. Serie de tres artículos por Alberto Luzárraga en http://www.futurodecuba.org, en la sección Constitucional.

visión del Tribunal de Garantías citado en un punto que sigue, a fin de controlar el poder e ir creando los hábitos correspondientes a un estado de derecho.

- Como medida temporal el gobierno debe dictar de inmediato una ley de garantías ciudadanas que bien pudiera recoger el contenido del título IV (Arts. 24 al 40) de la Constitución del 40. Contiene todo lo inmediatamente necesario y está redactado.

- Dado el supuesto anterior, la creación de un Tribunal de Garantías (aunque fuese sólo un adelanto provisional a un tribunal nombrado con los requisitos usuales) que amparase el ejercicio de esas libertades sería una necesidad. El tema presenta muchas aristas judiciales de difícil solución que no procede estudiar aquí, pero como medio de ir acostumbrando al pueblo al imperio de la ley es idóneo.[3]

- Depuración de los Tribunales de Justicia y creación de programas de entrenamiento para nuevos jueces. Creación de una Corte de Apelaciones o Audiencia que provisionalmente revise la actuación de los jueces que queden en funciones durante la transición. Se trata de un tema muy extenso que hemos comenzado a tratar por separado.[4]

- Dictar una ley de lustración o inhabilitación que abarque los colaboradores de importancia del régimen en los poderes ejecutivo, legislativo y judicial según se defina.

- Entrar en la democracia por etapas bien definidas a fin de "entrenar al pueblo." El pueblo cubano cuenta con más de cuarenta años no sólo de inactividad cívico/política sino, lo que es peor, de actividad política desnaturalizada.

El gobierno de transición podría marcarse hitos, con fechas a cumplir, para organizar el sistema electoral y los partidos, y convocar a elecciones municipales como primera providencia. Esto pudiera hacerse sin

tener que resolver de antemano el tema constitucional. El municipio fue nuestra primera institución importante y tenemos una excelente tradición plasmada en la antigua Ley Orgánica de los Municipios que puede adaptarse al momento. El comenzar de abajo hacia arriba tiene sus ventajas. En las comunidades más pequeñas se sabe quien es quien y es menos fácil hacer demagogia o intimidar. La creación de alcaldías independientes, con presupuesto propio y capacidad impositiva, conllevaría la necesidad de crear instituciones de inspección y control como el antiguo Tribunal de Cuentas. Esto es factible y sería otro paso hacia la restauración institucional por etapas.

Durante la primera intervención americana se efectuó primero la elección municipal que tuvo lugar el 16 de junio de 1900 y el primero de julio tomaron posesión de sus cargos los Ayuntamientos electos. El 15 de septiembre de 1900 se realizaron las elecciones para la Constituyente. Para ambas elecciones se dictó una Ley Electoral que concedía el voto solamente a los mayores de 21 años que supieran leer y escribir o tuviesen un capital de $250.00, excepto si habían sido miembros del ejército libertador lo cual eximía de cualquier requisito. Esos requisitos, y en particular el de activos mínimos, suenan fuera de lugar hoy en día pero eran otros tiempos y lo que se buscaba era que los analfabetos o desposeídos no pudieran ser explotados por los demagogos fáciles de palabra que prometen todo. Saltando un siglo adelante, tenemos hoy un problema similar pero con causas diferentes. En definitiva, la calidad de la transición y las garantías de que el proceso llegue a buen término depende de las personas electas.

¿Tienen el mismo derecho a votar y a aspirar a cargos públicos los "apparatchiks" del gobierno, los miembros de la seguridad y sus secuaces que los ciudadanos que los han sufrido por más de 40 años? ¿Es práctico y justo inhabilitarlos para el ejercicio del voto y para ocupar cargos públicos visto el cargo que ocupaban? Es lógico suponer que en algún momento resuene el

---

3. Sobre el tema de como organizar definitivamente un tribunal que mejore lo pasado ver Alberto Luzárraga, "El Tribunal Constitucional: Una Propuesta de Reforma," *Cuba in Transition—Volume 7* (1997) y http://www.futurodecuba.org sección Constitucional.

4. Ver Alberto Luzárraga, "Reflexiones sobre el Poder Judicial," http://www.futurodecuba.org, en la sección Estado de Derecho

grito solapado: "apparatchiks del mundo uníos" y que busquen militar en algún partido. La historia de Rusia y Europa Oriental indica que así ha ocurrido. Después de cierta edad las personas no quieren admitir que se equivocaron y Cuba no será diferente. Ese sector sería el que vote por el partido de los apparatchiks o quien encarne su punto de vista bajo otro nombre pues la hidra no quedará descabezada sino con trabajo.

Aunque surjan otros partidos o candidatos el inhabilitar civilmente a ciertos personas es deseable. Los países no se regeneran sin ejemplos morales. Inhabilitar no debe ser visto como una venganza contra un grupo sino como un ejemplo moral. Cuba necesita paradigmas de conducta diferentes a los que han regido por cuatro décadas.

Todos los países de Europa oriental han enfrentado este problema. Todos han dictado las llamadas leyes de "lustración," término que etimológicamente significa purificar. Un buen ejemplo es la ley checa #451 del 4 de octubre de 1991 que define los requisitos para ocupar cargos electivos por simple nombramiento o por nombramiento con aprobación por otro cuerpo del estado. Es amplia en cuanto incluye no sólo altos cargos administrativos en los ministerios sino también en empresas paraestatales, los medios de comunicación, las oficinas de apoyo al parlamento, a las academias de ciencia, y a los tribunales.

Las personas que aspiren a esos cargos no deberán haber sido oficiales de la seguridad del estado, informantes o colaboradores conscientes de la misma, o miembros con cargo importante del partido comunista. En cuanto a los servicios de seguridad inhabilita para ocupar cargos a aquéllos que figuraban con cargos de oficiales, estudiantes en las academias del servicio o colaborador o informante registrado. La ley estableció un procedimiento para verificar las circunstancias. Pensamos que el objetivo de Havel era el señalamiento social de una mala conducta, continuada e hipócrita, en las altas esferas. La medida tiene que ser bien pensada pues no se trata de marcar con la misma brocha a todas las personas. Habrá que valorar las actuaciones personales cuando proceda. Para el pueblo resultará relativamente fácil saber quienes eran los "tracatanes" del régimen y sus "cachancha-

nes," términos criollos que para el pueblo serán mejor definición que la que plasme la ley. Y el pueblo será el que reclamará y el que determine quienes se han bañado en el Jordán por su oposición al régimen.. Los de pacotilla no merece la pena inhabilitarlos para ejercer el voto. No queremos cacerías de brujas, ni certificados de "limpieza mental." Eso lo hicieron ellos. Cada cual que piense lo que quiera y lo exprese, pero organizarse para imponernos de nuevo por la fuerza su pensamiento es harina de otro costal.

¿Cómo se trata el tema partidos desde un punto de vista constitucional? ¿Se deben permitir partidos que tengan objetivos totalitarios? Una fuente que contiene valiosos antecedentes es el proceso constitucional alemán de la post guerra. Es útil para el caso cubano porque se trata de un régimen mucho más unipersonal que ideológico, como fue el de Hitler, aunque ambos tuvieran que crear una ideología con fantasmas y enemigos externos e internos para manipular a las masas. Es una verdad evidente que una sociedad que surge de una larga tiranía dedicada a la propaganda y a la agitación constante, deba tener derecho a regenerarse y vivir en paz sin que se vea constantemente asediada por agitadores organizados políticamente bajo diversos disfraces. Como hacerlo sin menoscabar la libertad personal es un problema a resolver pero una formulación útil es la de la constitución alemana que enfrentada con el mismo problema, lo resolvió así (mi subrayado):

Art. 21.2. Son inconstitucionales los partidos que por sus *fines o la conducta de sus seguidores* se propongan menoscabar o destruir el orden fundamental libre y democrático y poner en peligro la existencia de la República Federal de Alemania. Corresponde al Tribunal Constitucional declarar dicha inconstitucionalidad.

Este precepto mejora el contenido del Art. 37 de la Constitución del 40 que enfrentada a la doble amenaza del fascismo y el comunismo también consideró el problema al expresar: "Es ilícita la formación y existencia de organizaciones políticas contrarias al régimen del gobierno representativo democrático de la República, o que atenten contra la plenitud de la soberanía nacional."

Lo mejora porque se entra a considerar los fines o la conducta de los afiliados al partido y refiere la resolución del asunto al Tribunal Constitucional con lo cual convierte el problema en tema de relevancia fundamental para la sociedad en vez de lo que pudiera ser considerado como asunto meramente partidista. De esta forma se va al fondo sin entrar a perseguir al individuo por sus ideas, pues puede tener todas las ideas totalitarias que quiera y aun expresarlas por todos los medios (para eso está la libertad de expresión personal) pero organizarse políticamente para imponerlas es un evento al que una sociedad como la alemana pone coto porque el precedente fue funesto.

¿Conoce nuestro pueblo los costos de un estado democrático y donde radican los peligros? ¿Entiende que es necesario dividir el poder para garantizar la libertad? Ambas preguntas van entrelazadas porque la democracia es cara en materia de paciencia y de tolerar puntos de vista y actitudes irritantes. Ello no es lo mismo que tolerar la subversión consciente y sistematizada para imponer el totalitarismo. Ejemplo: Supongamos que una esquina del parque central en La Habana se habilita estilo Hyde Park en Londres para que los ciudadanos, desde una tribuna improvisada, digan lo que quieran. Y a diario un comunista histórico decide pararse en esa esquina y decirnos que un sólo partido, una sola opinión, un solo dueño de los medios de comunicación y producción es el sistema ideal. No hay duda de que para muchos será irritante pero hay que dejarlo hablar y el hablador tendrá que sufrir las respuestas y/o denuestos que reciba.

Es un costo de la democracia. Como también lo es la lentitud en adoptar decisiones y dictar leyes y políticas porque hay que oír a muchos. La democracia, como permite la libertad de actuación y expresión, es un sistema aparentemente "desordenado." A menudo parece andar con la cabellera suelta y desgreñada. Requiere atención, virtud ciudadana y sobre todo vocación por parte de la población. No es automática, si no se cuida desaparece y por ello el costo social es alto. Requiere, por así decirlo, un capital social de compromiso y defensa de la libertad que hay que gastar y reponer constantemente.

Es un problema bien serio para un país que surge de una tiranía sin hábitos de protesta, y con hábitos de sumisión. Aprender a protestar en forma útil y democrática es una asignatura que los cubanos tendrán que aprender. Es usar el método institucional y no el revolucionario que criticamos.

Lo cual nos da pie para contestar la pregunta sobre la división del poder. El poder se divide para que haya libertad. El Padre Varela dejo un buen sumario de la cuestión cuando en sus Cartas a Elpidio nos decía:

> Por más protestas que hagan los gobernantes, el placer de mandar es una miseria de la naturaleza humana de la que no pueden librarse. Fórmase pues un ídolo del Poder que como falsa deidad no recibe sino falsos honores y el que lo ejerce es el primer miserable a quien cautiva. Los buenos gobernantes son unos hombres justos que resisten y vencen una tentación muy poderosa y… son muy raros para desgracia del linaje humano. La generalidad de los mandarines si no son tiranos desean serlo… he aquí porque he dicho que la tiranía es el ídolo de casi todos los gobernantes.

Crear instituciones es, nada más y nada menos, que crear equilibrios y frenos al poder. Y esto en definitiva es lo que tiene que entender bien el pueblo de Cuba. Les podrán hablar de todos los "ismos" pero sólo hay dos métodos de gobierno: Los que concentran el poder y los que dividen el poder.

Los primeros inevitablemente acaban en tiranía pues la naturaleza humana no es capaz de vencer la tentación del poder. Los segundos, con sabiduría, aceptan esa condición humana y dividen las funciones en aras de la libertad. Es cierto, la división tiene sus costos. Se ha dicho muchas veces que en teoría un sistema de gobierno con un monarca absoluto brillante, justo, bueno, equitativo y humilde es mejor sistema que ninguno. Pero no ha existido dicha persona y si existiera tendría que buscar gente de igual condición a la suya para que fueran sus ministros, tarea de imposible cumplimiento. En nuestro caso ya probamos el sistema de "comandante ordene," equivalente moderno del "sí mi amo" de los tiempos de la esclavitud.

No sería necesario remachar el punto si no fuera porque los sistemas modernos de comunicación y de manipulación psicológica son tremendamente sutiles y eficaces en esconder y disimular las peores intenciones; presentando siempre como justificación causas nobles o propuestas que parecen ser razonables pero que conducen a concentraciones de poder. Es por eso que comenzamos criticando el estado niñera. De niñera se llega a madrastra en cortas etapas.

El método es simple. Ofrecer servicios simplemente porque la persona existe. Tratarla como niño y no como adulto. Esto no tiene límites. A los críticos se les acusa de ser insensibles a las necesidades del prójimo. La realidad es la que primera necesidad del prójimo es llegar a ser lo que puede ser. Una sociedad próspera no mantiene a sus hijos en dependencia perpetua. Su función debe ser proveer oportunidades. Al que se esfuerce y al que sin culpa suya sufra una desgracia, ayudarlo. Eso es ser sociedad seria y lo otro es utilizar las emociones de las personas para perpetuarse en el poder.

El pueblo cubano ha sufrido esta propaganda por décadas. La revolución es la mamá y el papá de los cubanos y Castro es su encarnación viviente. Es producto de la psicología desquiciada del tirano que no contento consigo mismo buscar difundir e imponer sus ideas a otros. El padre Varela lo definió con su habitual genio:

> ¿No ves con cuánto empeño procura obtener sufragios? Pues no es otro su objeto sino encontrar probabilidad a sus ideas por su difusión. Reconoce su debilidad....y para acallar las inquietudes que ella le causa, quiere convencerse a sí mismo que es un recelo infundado, pues no es probable que muchos entendimientos perciban del mismo modo sin que haya sólidas razones para esta unidad.

Hay una gran pobreza en el sistema castrista porque no conduce a nada que eleve al ser humano. Está basado en ser víctima desafiante y odiadora de todo y de todos los que no la complazcan y acepten la justicia absoluta de sus quejas y la virtud, también absoluta, de su actuación dañe a quien dañe. Está diseñado para difundir la psicosis de su creador y su ansia desmedida de poder. Estos lastres no deben pasar a una nueva república cubana, y a su documento constitutivo, disfrazadas de otra cosa. No pasarán si dividimos el poder y cobramos confianza en nuestra habilidad para regir nuestras vidas y producir, cosa que el cubano ha demostrado que es harto capaz de hacer en cuanto recibe la oportunidad.

¿Entiende cómo protegerse de crear un sistema político inoperante? ¿Capta que es indispensable crear controles institucionales muy fuertes y apoyarlos? Para protegernos debemos incorporar ciertos principios en un documento constitucional. Hay que meditar y no reaccionar. Varela nos dijo que debemos pensar con cabeza propia y ese es el principio básico. El pueblo cubano tiene que entrar en esa onda de pensamiento si quiere progresar con libertad. Nada más importante para volver a la normalidad que escoger bien. Saber lo que se quiere y por qué se quiere. Y quien lo propone. Si no lo hacemos no tenemos derecho a quejarnos.

A continuación una lista de temas esenciales para la construcción de la república que debe meditar el cubano votante, a fin de pensar con cabeza propia:

- El discurso político tiene que ser analizado serenamente y no sólo escuchado emotivamente. Y siempre analizado en función de libertad. Es el valor que perdimos por escuchar emotivamente y el que queremos recuperar sobre todo lo demás.

- Hay dos formas de gobiernos: los que concentran el poder y crean tiranías y los que lo dividen y crean sociedades libres. Toda reflexión debe basarse en ese simple principio.

- No es difícil desviar a la ciudadanía por otros derroteros. Basta proponer multitud de servicios a ser prestados por el estado (usualmente enunciados como derechos en la constitución) yno decir que significan carga de impuestos, burocracia y control político.

- Los principios constitucionales plasmados como derechos llegan a hacerse ley tarde o temprano. La sociedad debe ser disciplinada y exigir que lo que se propone tenga una fuente clara de pago pues de lo contrario se abre el camino a la demagogia. Si prometes debes decir cuanto cuesta y como vas a recaudar el costo.

- Los funcionarios que prestan los servicios tienen que ser remunerados adecuadamente, es decir a nivel de empresa privada, porque eso evita la corrupción. Pagar justamente nos da la medida de lo que podemos hacer y cuales son nuestros límites como sociedad.

- Las garantías constitucionales que describimos al principio de este trabajo en los puntos (a), (b), (c) y (d) tienen historia constitucional en Cuba. La preocupación constitucional por la educación, una pensión, la asistencia médica, el trabajo, la libertad sindical, la protección al trabajador, etc. tampoco son cosas nuevas. No sólo tienen antecedentes en la Constitución del 40 y en la de 1901 sino que existe abundante jurisprudencia anterior a Castro, particularmente en temas laborales. No hay duda de que esas garantías serán mantenidas y puestas al día. Este no es lugar para entrar en detalles. Lo que hay que cuidar es la implementación.

- Implementación significa respeto a los derechos garantizados por la constitución. No significa concederle a cada cual lo que le parezca adecuado. Las mayorías deciden en una democracia, pero con respeto a los derechos constitucionales de los demás que no es lo mismo que sus preferencias. En eso consiste el contrapunto mayoría / minoría.

- No hay recurso contra una mala implementación de la constitución que nos demos sin un Tribunal Constitucional de calidad que sea respetado y absolutamente independiente. De lo contrario habremos creado un documento retórico.

- El Tribunal existe para resolver disputas en cuanto al alcance de los derechos individuales frente al estado. También resuelve las disputas entre los órganos del estado. El Tribunal es en sí solo un local y unas personas. Su autoridad viene de la conciencia social de su importancia para lograr un estado de derecho.

- Si un funcionario acostumbrado al sistema arbitrario de cuatro décadas desobedece una sentencia u orden legítima del tribunal atentaría contra la libertad que se basa en el respeto y la aceptación de las instituciones. En realidad estaría desobedeciendo al pueblo de Cuba, que creó las instituciones para poder vivir en paz.

- No hay libertad civil sin compromiso ciudadano para defenderla por medios pacíficos. En casos flagrantes de irrespeto a la voluntad popular el ejercicio de todos los derechos dados por la cons-titución, o sea protesta masiva por los medios de comunicación, manifestación, petición, etc. para exigir el cumplimiento de la ley sería indispensable.

- Al igual que no hay constitución sin Tribunal Constitucional que vele por ella, no hay sociedad civil, ni estado de derecho, ni libertad sin tribunales civiles que apliquen la ley y sirvan de árbitros. El grado de civilización y viabilidad de una sociedad avanzada se mide por su capacidad de solventar conflictos pacíficamente. Los tribunales deben ser neutrales, es decir apolíticos, competentes, justos y honestos. Todo lo contrario de lo que han sido por más de cuatro décadas.

- La sociedad civil protegida por los tribunales no puede existir sin propiedad y empresa privada. Así se protege también al trabajador que labora para ser propietario o empresario particular si así lo desea. Si el estado es enorme, asfixia la sociedad civil.

- La sociedad civil necesita de libertad para ejercer las profesiones liberales. Los médicos, abogados, contables y otros profesionales no deben ser exclusivamente empleados estatales. Este principio y el anterior son indispensables para dividir el poder y dar opciones a los ciudadanos frente al estado.

- Contamos con una excelente tradición judicial y buenas leyes para su organización que datan de los comienzos de la república. Asimismo las constituciones cubanas se ocuparon de proteger los principios de independencia del poder judicial. Debemos depurar los jueces y tribunales políticos de Castro. Es un elemento esencial que debe exigir el pueblo. Sin él tendríamos solamente la apariencia de estado de derecho que estaría vacío de contenido ya que los encargados de aplicarlo serían los que lo han suprimido por más de cuatro décadas.

- No hay democracia, ni respeto al derecho ajeno, ni tribunales justos, ni honestidad en el gobierno si esas cualidades no existen en el pueblo. Todos los grandes pensadores que han tratado el tema convienen en una cosa: sin VIRTUD CIUDADANA no hay libertad.

- La virtud se inculca básicamente en la niñez y en el seno de la familia. Por eso la educación es patrimonio inalienable de los padres que tiene derecho a opinar y actuar respecto al programa de instrucción de las escuelas públicas u optar por una privada si no gustan de él.

Podremos salir adelante. Cuba cuenta con gente que ha sufrido y reflexionado. Tendrán una labor ardua frente a sí. Pero confío en que saldremos adelante con el concurso de los pocos, de los buenos, de los de siempre, palabras de ese Martí tan abusado por el régimen y los politiqueros de todas la épocas, pero que sí sabía pensar y expresarse con cabeza propia, para crear por fin una Cuba con todos y para el bien de todos.

PRIVATIZANDO EL SOCIALISMO: JUSTICIA SOCIAL CON DESARROLLO ECONÓMICO

Manuel Pérez Torres

Este trabajo propone ciertas ideas para la constitución de la Tercera República de Cuba cuyo propósito es mantener un balance entre el desarrollo económico y la justicia social, y al mismo tiempo evitar la concentración de poder dentro del estado. Estas propuestas son estratégicas y a largo plazo y tienen la intención de mantener un equilibrio entre el tamaño del estado de una Cuba futura y las necesidades de la nación.

Reconozco que he escogido un tema relativamente fácil cuando lo comparamos con los inmensos problemas de la transición política, comenzando con el monumental problema de falta de educación cívica que sufre el pueble de Cuba, ya que el más perfecto diseño de gobierno descansa sobre la conciencia de los gobernados, y que la mayor parte de estos han estado encerrados en una oscura cámara de aislamiento informativo por la totalidad de sus vidas, donde además se les alimenta con un estiércol de falsa ideología y desinformación a la manera de hongos de cultivo.

Tampoco analizo el complejísimo problema de la transición a una economía de mercado, la cual ha sido analizada por muchos mucho más capacitados y que desde el punto de vista constitucional se cubrirá en cláusulas transitorias.

UNA OPORTUNIDAD HISTÓRICA

En su ultima maniobra de movilización totalitaria, el régimen de Cuba ha declarado su constitución estalinista como "intocable," lo cual acaba de sellar su destino rumbo a la cloaca de la historia. Este asunto ya había sido analizado por varios expertos sobre el tema constitucional cubano (Manzano 1997; Luzárraga 1997; y Cuzán 2000), que concluyen que dicha constitución debe ser completamente reemplazada con una nueva.

Muchos abogan por la restitución de la constitución de 1940, pero aunque se reconoce que esta magna carta fue uno de los mayores logros políticos de la Cuba republicana, la misma contiene una serie de fallos y deficiencias, como por ejemplo la posibilidad de suspender las garantías individuales, junto con una serie de regulaciones económicas y prestaciones sociales que deben ser reexaminadas en la realidad de hoy. Además la reconstrucción de Cuba necesitará una serie de medidas transitorias que den base legal a una restitución y privatización de la propiedad estatal ordenada y sensata y que estarían en conflicto con algunas de las garantías de la constitución de 1940. Por lo tanto concluimos que esta puede servir de fuente de ideas y principios pero necesita ser reemplazada.

Todo esto nos lleva a lo que es a la vez una necesidad y una oportunidad histórica: la de *estructurar una república comenzando prácticamente desde cero.*

A los que el pueblo de Cuba le otorgue esta tarea siempre deben tener en mente que tal oportunidad es única y que deben aplicar cuanta experiencia nos ha enseñado lo que hasta ahora ha sido una dura y triste historia.

Una constitución no es más que el diseño de un "edificio político," cuyo material de construcción son los gobernados, y que así como una edificación de concreto lleva un diseño muy distinto a uno de madera o de acero, no podemos olvidar que para bien o para mal, nuestro este estará construido con cubanos, y que un plano que funciona cuando las columnas y vigas son inglesas o mejicanas debe ser adaptado a nuestras virtudes y fallas, firmezas y veleidades.

No se debe emprender esta tarea con ilusiones. Si cuarenta y tres años de totalitarismo han destrozado la estructura económica de la nación, peor es el daño cultural y moral. Además de la desinformación que sufren los cubanos y a la cual ya hemos hecho referencia, hay que tener en cuenta que los valores vigentes en la gran mayoría de los cubanos es la supervivencia a todo costo, y esto como observa Leiva (2001) es una base muy pobre sobre la cual establecer la democracia.

En un trabajo anterior (Pérez Torres 2001), he planteado ideas para el diseño de la estructura política para contrarrestar nuestra propensión al apasionamiento y al caudillismo. En este el enfoque es socioeconómico: como proteger la república de nuestras faltas respecto al manejo de los fondos públicos y de mirar al estado como fuente de riqueza, de empleo, y de solución de nuestros problemas.

EL MANEJO DEL PODER POLÍTICO Y ECONÓMICO

Antes de comenzar a hacer propuestas constitucionales, debemos sentar algunas bases históricas y filosóficas que enmarcan la mayor parte de las cartas magnas vigentes en el mundo.

Otra manera de mirar una constitución es como un contrato entre el estado y los gobernados que determina el compartimiento del poder. La libertad y el poder son conceptos equivalentes. Tener libertad significa poder actuar sin injerencias innecesarias del estado o de otros ciudadanos. Todas las desventuras que el pueblo cubano ha sufrido dentro del régimen existente emanan de la concentración del poder en manos de una persona y la casi total carencia del mismo que sufre el pueblo cubano. Las alevosas violaciones de los derechos humanos, el estado decrépito de la economía y la infraestructura, y la lamentable degeneración social son todos productos del monopolio y el abuso que Fidel Castro mantiene y ejerce sobre los instrumentos del poder.

El Contrato Social de Rousseau

En una sociedad libre, el pueblo es la fuente de todo poder y derecho, y el estado es simplemente un mecanismo por medio del cual el pueblo ejerce su voluntad común. Este concepto del estado, basado en la delegación de la soberanía popular tiene una de sus bases filosóficas originales en el "contrato social" propuesto por Jean-Jacques Rousseau (1762) con cuyo permiso parafraseamos así:

> Estado, yo el ciudadano libre te entrego mi soberano derecho a usar la fuerza para defenderme, a cambio de que tu me defiendas y me garantices el orden basado en la ley. Para que tu puedas garantizar el orden, te entrego el uso exclusivo de la violencia.

Dentro de este marco, el individuo se reserva el poder de alcanzar sus metas económicas, políticas y sociales con un nivel de intromisión y regulación por parte del estado que es el mínimo necesario para mantener las necesidades comunes tales como el orden, la salubridad y la seguridad. En dicha sociedad, el individuo posee una serie de defensas contra el uso arbitrario del poder por parte del estado, que generalmente se codifican en una carta de derechos fundamentales que a su vez, están protegidas por un poder judicial independiente.

Además de declarar y asegurar los derechos ciudadanos, las constituciones democráticas incorporan el diseño del gobierno, sus ramas y funciones, así como también la manera de elegirlo. El criterio principal en este diseño es el de prevenir por todos los medios la concentración, y el abuso del poder. La constitución de Estados Unidos fue la primera que se concentró en el diseño de separación de poderes y un sistema de mutua sujeción entre estos como medida preventiva para dicho abuso. Esta constitución ha servido bien a su nación por más de doscientos años y hasta el día de hoy los ciudadanos de Estados Unidos constantemente expresan gran admiración y gratitud por el genio previsor de sus autores

El Contrato Comunista

Según la sociedad progresaba dentro del imperio de la ley, donde la violencia estaba bajo control al menos en tiempos de paz, las contiendas entre los ciudadanos se desarrollaban en el campo económico. La fuerza de las armas dejó de ser el instrumento principal del poder y pasó a serlo el dinero.

Esta contienda económica fue evolucionando a medida que la tecnología fue avanzando y llego a un punto crítico con la revolución industrial, cuya tecnología requería concentraciones de capital, y por lo tanto a la concertación del poder económico y su consiguiente abuso.

Estos abusos produjeron corrientes intelectuales que consideraban que la sociedad había pasado de la ley del más fuerte a la ley del más rico. Una de estas era el marxismo, que proponía un modelo histórico basado en la lucha de clases entre capitalistas y proletarios.

El marxismo proponía la confiscación de los bienes de la clase capitalista a favor de una sociedad donde todos fuesen proletarios. De esta manera los "ricos" al perder su poder económico no pudieran "explotar" a los "pobres." El contrato comunista proponía lo siguiente:

> Ciudadano, yo el estado te pido que me entregues todos los medios de producción para yo manejarlos, y a cambio te ofrezco un mar de felicidad en el cual todos seremos iguales, y todas nuestras necesidades serán satisfechas.

Como bien sabemos, el resultado fue una concentración de poder aun mayor en manos del estado, que ahora, además de la violencia, controlaba todos los medios económicos. Los abusos que resultaron de este sistema han sido bien documentados por Courtois y otros (1999).

En el caso de Cuba, hemos visto que una vez que el estado controla todos los aspectos de la economía y los instrumentos de violencia, no necesita utilizar estos últimos para que más del 99% de los votantes, en humillante procesión, acudan como mansas ovejas a ratificar su sujeción al orden existente.

El Contrato Socialista

En los naciones con democracias bien establecidas que no cayeron en la trampa marxista, la lucha política también se definía mayormente en términos económicos, entre la izquierda y la derecha.

La izquierda "socialista" o "progresista" buscaba "justicia social" que traducía a "igualdad económica" por medio del gasto público, mientras que la derecha buscaba la libertad económica, con menos injerencia por el estado, y por lo tanto utilizaba el apodo de "liberal." (No confundamos el termino "liberal" como se utiliza en Estados Unidos y que se le aplica a la izquierda.)

La izquierda socialista formulaba su programa en el siguiente contrato:

> Ciudadano, quédate con los medios de producción, pero si me das el poder político, voy a instalar un sistema de impuestos y prestaciones sociales, para que todos seamos iguales y vivamos en un nuevo mar de felicidad.

El problema de este negocio es que aunque el pueblo generalmente conservaba el poder político (lo cual les permitía desmantelar el orden socialista por medio de las urnas), los incentivos económicos desaparecían y con ellos el progreso económico. Todos terminaban más iguales, pero más pobres, y con poca esperanza de superarse pues la guadaña fiscal estaba siempre dispuesta a frustrar sus intentos.

La Situación Actual

El "progresismo de izquierda" aunque ha sufrido grandes reveses a fines del siglo XX, sigue vivito y coleando, impulsado tanto por la envidia y el odio de clases, como por el genuino deseo de justicia social y de ayuda a los desposeídos y desamparados.

En la economía moderna de los países desarrollados la mayor parte del antiguo "proletariado" no tiene alguna dificultad de mantener niveles de vida decentes, y hasta confortables. La mayor problemática es la que concierne el cuidado de salud, que por razones tecnológicas tiende a ser muy caro en comparación con el ingreso promedio, y cuya demanda tiende a crecer con la edad, cuando el individuo esta generalmente en la peor situación de ingresos. Esto, junto a los efectos demográficos del desarrollo, da lugar a que el punto de contienda de este contrato social haya pasado a ser entre generaciones en lugar de entre clases.

Esta situación existe también en los Estados Unidos, cuyo presupuesto, aunque no se denomina como socialista, no es más que una gigantesca máquina de redistribución de riquezas donde el gasto social representa más de las dos terceras partes. (Ver apéndice A). En los países de Europa, el gasto social es aun mayor a pesar de que en los años noventa hubo importantes cambios para reducirlo y liberar la economía de su lastre.

El problema del gasto gubernamental tiene dos aspectos nocivos. La redistribución de ingresos de por sí es la menos dañina, aunque tiende a reducir incentivos, en particular a los beneficiarios que puedan trabajar y sostenerse por sí solos. El "welfare reform" que tuvo lugar en los Estados Unidos en los años 90 estaba dirigida a establecer un sistema de mayor responsabilidad por parte de los beneficiarios para así reducir los efectos perjudiciales a largo plazo. Cualquier constitución que garantice niveles mínimos de vivienda y sustento debe además especificar que el individuo es responsable de su propio sustento mientras tenga los medios físicos y mentales para hacerlo.

El otro aspecto nocivo es la burocracia que resulta del gasto público, su ineficiencia, su falta de responsabilidad al consumidor de sus servicios, y su tendencia a perpetuarse y a crecer. Además, el gasto público no distributivo, o sea, aquel que se gasta en actividades ejecutadas por el estado, tales como la educación pública en la Cuba republicana, tiende a convertirse en una fuente de favor político y en oportunidad de robo, ambos de los cuales fueron plaga de la república y formaron parte de la "justificación" de la llamada revolución cubana, aunque ahora desgraciada e irónicamente este régimen tiene como uno de sus logros que el robo al estado sea un modo de vida generalizado por toda la sociedad cubana.

El gasto público a su vez crea intereses en la población votante y en los políticos que manejan las riendas del fisco y que generalmente no titubean en servir con cucharón grande asistencias sociales si esto les obtiene más votos. Una vez que este proceso entra en marcha, hablando criollamente, mientras más estén chupando, más quieren chupar y el gasto público va en una sola dirección—p'arriba.

La razón fundamental de este problema es que las constituciones existentes, mientras que frenan el uso y abuso del poder violento por parte del estado, le dan rienda suelta en lo económico. Al no haber límites bien definidos, el estado tiende a lenta e imperceptiblemente introducirle la mano en el bolsillo al contribuyente, y a crecer hasta llegar a situaciones críticas que dan paso a la inestabilidad política y social.

UN CONTRATO PARA LA TERCERA REPÚBLICA

En el caso de Cuba, la contienda entre el socialismo y el liberalismo, como en otros países, será el centro del debate político. El socialismo sigue teniendo adeptos dentro de Cuba, quizás no tanto en la cúpula gobernante que es oportunista y lo que le interesa es el privilegio con socialismo o sin él, sino más bien dentro de la disidencia, que es más "idealista" y que por mucho que se oponga al régimen fue formado por éste. En mi experiencia personal me he sorprendido unas cuantas veces, hablando con cubanos que han sufrido los rigores del régimen y son opositores de convicción, oírlos plantear teorías económicas marxistas como si estas fueran axiomas. Hay que reconocer que para muchos es muy difícil el salto ideológico cuando toda su armazón intelectual fue formada por el sistema. Esto constituye un gran peligro para el desarrollo económico de la nueva república.

Por otra parte, muchos exiliados justificadamente sienten una aversión visceral a todo lo que huela a socialismo, y hay más de uno que abogan por excluir de cualquier futura carta magna las garantías sociales de la declaración universal de los derechos humanos (veáse *Delaración*, artículos 22, 23, 24, 25, 26.). Sin embargo, esta oposición filosófica en un final tiende a sucumbir ante el sentido de la caridad. Nadie quiere ver a niños o ancianos desamparados, o muriéndose de hambre o falta de cuidado medico.

Esta propuesta reconoce que las garantías sociales se han convertido en axiomas de la sociedad moderna y por lo tanto las incluye, siguiendo los esquemas establecidos sobre esta materia en la Constitución de 1940 y en la declaración universal de los derechos humanos, pero añadimos también que el individuo tiene la responsabilidad primaria de su sustento y el de su familia. Esto nos lleva al siguiente contrato:

A cambio de una porción de mis ingresos, en el caso de que yo, por motivos fuera de mi control, no pueda obtener ingresos adecuados, el estado me garantiza un nivel decente de vivienda, sustento, educación para mi prole, y cuidado de mi salud.

Este contrato no busca la igualdad sino sanar las situaciones de desamparo económico.

La prescripción constitucional de este asunto no termina aquí. Así como en el contrato social de Rousseau se vio la necesidad de restringir los poderes de coerción por parte del estado, así también es necesario restringir al estado de manera que no pueda extender su dominio económico. A continuación los frenos que proponemos.

1. **El gasto gubernamental no excederá G% del PIB:** El objetivo del este límite es impedir que el crecimiento del estado, que como vemos en Estados Unidos, responda a presiones políticas de minorías activistas. Una vez que el estado se vea obligado a operar dentro de este límite, tendrá que reestructurar o recortar programas de poco beneficio general como son los tristemente célebres "pork barrel programs" que constantemente vemos salir del congreso de Estados Unidos. Asimismo, el estado tendrá el incentivo de fomentar la economía para así poder incrementar su presupuesto. El límite de gastos puede también incentivar al estado a privatizar funciones tales como el seguro social. El número de personas empleadas por el gobierno no excederá el P% del último censo: Este límite tiene el propósito de limitar la nómina gubernamental y así eliminar al estado como fuente de empleo y de corrupción. Sólo recordemos las "botellas" y el "jamón" de la Cuba republicana.

2. **A ningún ciudadano u otra persona jurídica pagará a una tasa de impuestos en exceso del I% de sus ingresos:** La intención de este límite es evitar los impuestos confiscatorios que reducirían los incentivos económicos y pondrían en peligro el desarrollo.

3. **La deuda del estado no superará el D% del PIB:** Este límite sirve como un freno adicional en caso de que el gobierno no este dispuesto a imponer suficientes impuestos para controlar el déficit estatal.

Todos estos parámetros deben ser basados sobre estudios económicos de profundidad sobre la experiencia de otros países y sujetos al debate abierto dentro de la convención constituyente que sea elegida. Cambiar cualquiera de estos límites necesitaría una enmienda constitucional ratificada por referéndum, lo cual neutralizaría la influencia de las minorías activistas.

Una propuesta final es la que tiene implicaciones más profundas. **El gobierno no ejercerá funciones que puedan ser ejercidas por el sector privado o la sociedad civil. El gobierno se limita a planificar, regular y controlar los resultados de dichas funciones, a no ser que el sector privado y la sociedad civil no puedan ejercer dichas funciones adecuadamente.**

El apéndice B contiene una tabla que propone la división de funciones que resultaría de este principio entre el estado, la sociedad civil y el sector privado. Si nos referimos a la educación básica como ejemplo, vemos que el estado la subvenciona y controla su calidad, supuestamente por medio de exámenes uniformes, pero no tiene algún rol en construir escuelas o emplear maestros. Si por alguna razón el sector civil o privado no puede satisfacer la demanda educativa, el estado entonces tendría que emprender la construcción y manejo de escuelas, pero a largo plazo se vería obligado a privatizarlas o delegar su funcionamiento a la sociedad civil.

Hacemos una analogía deportiva. La idea central es que tanto en el ámbito económico como en el social, el estado se limite a ser árbitro y no jugador. El problema fundamental de la participación del estado en el suministro de productos y servicios es su prerrogativa exclusiva de legislar, o sea, de establecer las reglas del juego económico y social. Si el estado toma parte en el juego, su poder y sus recursos son tales que a nadie le interesaría participar y así el juego se convierte en monopolio, con sus consiguientes abusos e ineficiencias.

A diferencia del deporte, los juegos socioeconómicos tienen dos resultados. Uno es el "score" de los jugadores, y el otro es el beneficio para la sociedad en general que resulta del desempeño de la actividad. No puede haber negocio exitoso sin que este sirva una necesidad del consumidor la sociedad. El rol central del estado es de velar por el funcionamiento y bienestar de la economía y la sociedad y por esto debe definir las reglas del juego de tal forma que maximice el beneficio común, mientras que al mismo tiempo incentive la participación de los jugadores y la competición. Si el estado se incorpora al juego, se crea un conflicto entre su interés por sacar provecho como jugador, y su obligación de velar por el bien común. Generalmente este último es el que sufre.

Este concepto se aplica tanto a las actividades económicas como las sociales. El incentivo de la actividad social es la caridad, nuestro sentido innato de ayudar al prójimo. La injerencia del estado, como mismo destruye los incentivos económicos, también destruye el impulso caritativo—si el estado se ocupa de los necesitados, ¿para qué debo ocuparme yo? En esta propuesta, el estado es *garante de la seguridad social y no suministrador de servicios*. El estado entra en juego como redistribuidor de riqueza sólo cuando la economía y la sociedad civil fracasan en su misión de proporcionarle a cada ciudadano un nivel de vida decente. He ahí la privatización del socialismo.

RESUMEN

La transición en Cuba presenta una oportunidad de aplicar la experiencia nuestra y de otras naciones a un nuevo diseño constitucional.

Las constituciones existentes se concentran en limitar al estado en el uso de la fuerza, pero no prestan mucha atención a limitar su injerencia económica que en tiempos de paz es más importante aspecto del poder.

Por una parte, el pueblo de Cuba esta hastiado del sistema actual, pero por otra ha sido profundamente condicionado a esperar que el estado le resuelva todo.

Si la constitución de la nueva república no ata bien al estado en el ámbito económico, existe el peligro de que las presiones políticas, basadas en las expectativas que se han sembrado en la gran mayoría cubana nos llevaran a un estado niñera, con más libertad política que el de ahora, pero con una comparable falta de desarrollo económico y de oportunidades.

De ahí proponemos una serie de límites constitucionales a la injerencia del estado en la gestión económica y social de la Tercera República, de manera que mientras el estado es garante de último recurso de las necesidades sociales, el suministro de estas cae en manos del sector privado y la sociedad civil.

BIBLIOGRAFÍA

Courtois, Stephane, et al., *The Black Book of Communism*, Harvard University Press, 1999.

Cuzán, Alfred G., "A Constitutional Framework for a Free Cuba," *Cuba in Transition—Volume 10*, 2000.

Declaración Universal de Derechos Humanos, http://www.unhchr.ch/udhr/lang/spn.htm.

Gómez Manzano, René, "Constitución y Cambio Democrático en Cuba," *Cuba in Transition—Volume 7*, 1997.

Luzárraga, Alberto, "Privatizacion en Cuba," *Cuba in Transition—Volume 7*, 1997.

Leiva, Aldo M., "Cuban Culture and Democracy: Theory and Research Agenda," *Cuba in Transition—Volume 11*, 2001.

Pérez Torres, Manuel, "Cuba: En Busca de la Madurez Política," www.FuturodeCuba.org, 2001.

Rousseau, Jean-Jacques, *The Social Contract*, 1762, www.constitution.org/jjr/socon.htm

APÉNDICE A
Presupuesto de los Estados Unidos

Category	Actual 2001	
	Millions of Dollars	Percent
Administration of justice	30,443	
General government	15,153	
International affairs	16,601	
Natural resources and environment	26,335	
Total Basic	**88,532**	**5%**
National defense	308,533	
Veterans benefits and services	45,828	
Total Defense	**354,361**	**21%**
Agriculture	26,553	
Commerce and housing credit	6,030	
General science, space, and technology	19,896	
Transportation	55,220	
Total Miscellaneous	**107,699**	**6%**
Community and regional development	11,977	
Education, training, employment, and social services	57,302	
Health	172,634	
Income security	269,770	
Medicare	217,464	
Social security	433,129	
Total Social	**1,162,276**	**68%**
Grand Total	**1,712,868**	**100%**

Note: Excludes interest, adjustments, and emergency fund.

Fuente: OMB website.

APÉNDICE B
Propuesta de División de Funciones

	Estado	Sociedad Civil	Sector Privado
Gobierno			
Poder Judicial	Ex		
Poder Legislativo	Ex		
Ejecutivo	Ex		
Relaciones Exteriores	Ex		
Recolección de fondos	Ex		
Defensa	Ex		
Cumplimento de la Ley y Orden Publico			
Cortes	Ex		
Fiscalía	Ex		
Policía	Ex		
Defensa Civil	Ex		
Infraestructura			
Energía	P, F, R		I, M
Comunicaciones	P, F, R		I, M
Transporte	P, F, R		I, M
Agua	P, F, R		I, M
Economía			
Agricultura	P, F, R		I, M
Industria	P, F, R		I, M
Turismo	P, F, R		I, M
Medio Ambiente			
Protección	Ex		
Parques Nacionales	S, C	M	
Social			
Vivienda	P, S, R		I, M
Educación Básica	S, C	I, M	I, M
Empleo	A, En		En
Salud	S, C	I, M	I, M
Salubridad	Ex		
Tercera Edad	S, C	I, M	I, M
Educación Superior	S, F	I, M	I, M
Ciencia y Tecnología	S, F	I, M	I, M
Arte y Cultura	S, F	P	I, M

A—Aseguración	I—Inversión
C—Control de Calidad	M—Manejo
En—Entrenamiento	P—Planificación
Ex—Actividad Exclusiva	R—Regulación
F—Fomento	S—Subvención

CHALLENGES FOR A TRANSITIONAL JUDICIARY IN A POST-CASTRO CUBA

Mario Díaz-Cruz, III

Perhaps more than any other branch of government, historically the judiciary has played a critical role in protecting the individual from the awesome power of the state. Of course, that protection exists only if the judiciary operates as a legitimate and independent branch of government with sufficient power and authority to overrule legislatures and curb executives who act in violation of constitutional law. Without these characteristics, the judiciary becomes nothing more than a rubber stamp for potentially corrupt and abusive governments; it becomes a conspirator to the abuses that it should be prepared to prevent.

As accomplices to the atrocities of dictatorial governments, the judiciary faces a fundamental challenge to establishing its legitimacy, both in the eyes of the citizens whose laws it would enforce, as well as of the international community, following a transition to democratic rule. In Cuba's case, this challenge will be especially difficult given the extent to which the current regime has, for the past 43 years, decimated Cuba's legal traditions and resources. Unlike Germany, where West German judges and lawyers were able to help rebuild the East German legal system, today there are probably an insufficient number of Cubans who operated within the former legal system to replace Cuba's current judges *en masse*.

Like most Eastern European nations following their emergence from behind the Iron Curtain, Cubans will have to rely on their current judiciary—at least for the immediate term. (How long a transition will last is unknown. Let us not forget that it took Russia until 2002 to reform its criminal code.) This means,

of course, that a post-Castro transitional government will have to legitimize a judiciary that will undoubtedly continue to be operated by some of the same people that were there under the Communist regime.

In this discussion, we explore how other nations, particularly those of Eastern Europe and Latin America, went about establishing the legitimacy of their judiciary following their transitions to democracy. From their experience, we consider how a post-Castro Cuba might undertake the task of establishing the legitimacy of its judiciary.

THE CUBAN JUDICIARY: PAST AND PRESENT

Let us first review the history of Cuba's judiciary, as well as the status of the system in place today. Prior to the Revolution, Cubans lived under one of Latin America's most effective judiciaries. The island's judiciary was composed of well-educated and highly trained lawyers, judges, and law professors who enjoyed and benefited from Cuba's rich legal traditions. Most of these traditions were based on Spanish Law, which was in turn grounded on Roman legal principles and the Napoleonic Code of France, but also incorporating concepts from other systems, namely that of the U.S. In addition to this strong cultural and historical foundation, pre-Castro Cuba operated under the auspices of Cuba's 1940 Constitution, which was widely regarded as one of the most modern of its time in Latin America. In addition to international human rights concepts such as free speech, women's rights and checks and balances of governmental branches, the 1940 Constitution incorporated concepts such as *habeas corpus*, from which Fidel and many of his followers directly benefited during the pre-Castro years.

I do not, of course, mean to idealize the pre-Castro Cuban judicial system. There were no doubt faults in Cuba's pre-1959 judiciary. Like the old American cars roaming the streets of Havana, the former judicial system in Cuba was, perhaps, exemplary for its time, but it ceased to progress beyond 1959 and should most certainly not be adopted in a post-Castro Cuba without updating.

As for the current legal system, it is, of course, representative of any other communist system. The goal of the judiciary is not to act as a check on the powers of the other branches of government. Instead, its role is to preserve communism and the Revolution at the expense of individual human rights. As a most basic example, today the Cuban prosecutor and the Cuban defense attorney work together toward the common goal of preserving the Revolution and not, as you might expect, as adversaries, with one representing the might of the state and the other the rights of the individual. Needless to say, neither Cubans nor the international community are likely to attribute much legitimacy to the judiciary conceived, trained and operating in Cuba today.

ESTABLISHING THE LEGITIMACY OF POST-DICTATORIAL GOVERNMENTS

Steps taken to legitimize the governments of post-communist Eastern European and dictatorial Latin American nations can generally be divided, in order of severity, into three categories:

1. the establishment of truth commissions;

2. the establishment of laws designed to prevent former communists from holding public office in new governments. The process by which these persons are excluded from participation in a post-dictatorial government is commonly known as "lustration," from the Latin word *lustrare* meaning ceremonial purification; and

3. the criminal prosecution of former *apparatchiks*.

Truth Commissions

Truth commissions have been used in countries like Chile, Argentina, El Salvador and South Africa, where the new democratically elected governments viewed it as necessary to address the criminal allegations made against the former authoritarian governments. The purpose of these commissions is to expose the alleged crimes of the government in a public forum so that a proper investigation may be conducted and, perhaps most importantly, legitimize the claims made by the accusers. For example, the truth commissions in El Salvador, Chile, Argentina and South Africa while not having much authority to punish alleged wrongdoers, provided the victims in those countries with official recognition of their pain and anguish.

Lustration

Exclusion of former communists from participation in post-communist governments has most often been seen in the former Eastern Bloc countries, particularly in the former Czechoslovakia and in Poland.[1] Generally, the lustration laws set forth a set of standards that, if met, would exclude a person from participating in public life. The trouble with such laws, of course, is that they are subject to manipulation for political purposes. As an example, many in Poland complained that, prior to Poland's first democratically held elections, lustration was being used as a political tool to exclude political foes from office and/or tarnish their reputations. (Interestingly, claims for lustration in Poland fell precipitously following these first elections, which suggests that lustration had, in fact, been used for mere political gain.) Because of this high potential for abuse, lustration laws should be carefully implemented, with clear limitation on their powers. As with any other legal proceeding, procedures also have to be put in place to ensure that those alleged of complicity with the former government have a forum in which to proclaim their innocence, as well as a procedure for appealing any determination that they should be excluded by effect of a lustration law.

---

1. Lustration laws have also been adopted in Germany, Bulgaria, Hungary, Albania, Romania and certain former Soviet republics.

Criminal Prosecution

The method that may seem the most logical is also perhaps the most controversial. Except in extreme cases, new governments have been reluctant to pursue the criminal prosecution of former dictators, *apparatchiks* or their henchmen, especially high ranking members of the judiciary. As an example, in El Salvador, truth commissions were established to deal with the alleged misdeeds of the prior government, but criminal trials were never held. Other countries like Chile and Argentina are still struggling with their past. In Chile, it was not until very recently that General Augusto Pinochet was charged, but found to be physically unfit for prosecution. In Argentina, those accused of taking part in the "dirty war" were just recently arrested, and only after the amnesty initially granted to them was held to be unconstitutional. In some cases, nascent democracies are obviously concerned that aggressive prosecution of former leaders will encourage these former leaders and the organizations they represented to take action against the still weak civil government. Alternatively, many of these former leaders ensured that they would retain sufficient power in the new governments so as to make criminal prosecutions unlikely (*e.g.*, Gen. Pinochet was appointed a Senator-for-Life following his abdication of power, which resulted in a continuing constitutional immunity from prosecution). Either way, it is obviously difficult for newly established governments to pursue criminal prosecutions, except in connection with the most egregious examples of criminality.

ESTABLISHING THE LEGITIMACY OF A POST-CASTRO JUDICIARY

Given the precedents set forth above, let us try to determine how a post-Castro government might establish legitimacy for the judiciary.

While truth commissions are an often necessary step in national reconciliation, they serve a limited role in helping to legitimize the judiciary. Simply put, exposing the crimes of those who were part of the communist judiciary would do little to legitimize a post-communist judiciary if these same people are allowed to continue to sit in judgment. If anything, the findings of a truth commission would undermine any re-

maining legitimacy. Clearly, legitimizing the judiciary will require more than just public acknowledgment of its past failures.

If more than mere symbolic action will be required to establish the legitimacy of the judiciary, why not prosecute all of the former communist judges for their crimes? Simply put, we have already discussed how it is difficult for young democracies to prosecute all but the most virulent former communists. This type of action should perhaps be limited to circumstances where a judge is alleged to have violated human rights by rendering a sentence, or otherwise using his judicial power to cause irreparable injury or death by the state. In addition, there are other problems with criminal trials. First, criminal trials, if conducted properly so as to ensure that the accused is afforded due process of law, are costly and take a long time to complete. Criminal trials, by their nature, focus on the past; a young republic might better serve its people by focusing its limited resources on helping to secure the country's future and those of its people. Second, and perhaps most importantly, criminal trials will not capture all of those *apparatchik* judges who should be excluded from the judiciary, but whose actions may not have necessarily risen to the level of prosecutable criminal conduct.

So, if establishing the legitimacy of a post-Castro judiciary will require more force than what a truth commission can offer, but also a procedure that is more palatable and able to cast a wider net than mass criminal prosecutions, let us consider the alternative used most often in Eastern Europe: lustration. Throughout Eastern Europe, lustration laws have provided these nascent democracies with a formidable mechanism to exclude those who would undermine their democratic efforts. In the case of the Cuban judiciary, I believe lustration would provide an efficient system by which to exclude from the bench those Cuban judges whose actions under communism should absolutely preclude them from legitimate participation in a democratic government. Of course, lustration is not a perfect procedure, and such laws have had their fair share of opponents, most notably Vaclav Havel of the Czech Republic, who has in the past attempted (unsuccessfully) to limit their extension of the time they remain in effect in that country.

COULD LUSTRATION WORK IN A POST-CASTRO CUBA?

Let us focus on the key components of lustration and attempt to reach a conclusion as to the possible applicability of such laws to the judiciary of a post-Castro Cuba.

Setting a Standard

Lustration requires that the new democratic state establish "standards" to determine whether a former communist should be excluded from participation in the new government. Before establishing these standards, however, we must first define what a post-Castro Cuba is likely to accept as a "legitimate" judiciary.

Neither post-Castro Cubans nor the international community would consider legitimate a judiciary where Castro's chief judges retained their power. In fact, some would argue that all of Cuba's current judges are communist party activist who should be excluded from participation in a post-Castro judiciary. However, would a post-Castro judiciary be deemed illegitimate simply because some of these judges continued to sit on the bench? Should a few former *apparatchiks* spoil the system? Should "boot-lickers" be tolerated? Perhaps more importantly, how do you separate who are the high-ranking communist party members from those who are merely "bootlickers"?

In an attempt to answer these questions, some have made the distinction between people living under communist regimes, where every citizen is expected to participate in rallies and show support for the government (*e.g.*, East Germany), and those living in authoritarian regimes, where the ideal citizen was someone who simply stayed out of the way.[2] If we accept this distinction, those under communist rule should not be deemed to be party loyalists simply because they participated in government rallies. In contrast, those living under authoritarian regimes who have participated in pro-government activities are likely to be true government sympathizers. Unfortunately in the case of the Cuban judiciary, such bright-line tests are likely difficult to apply. Undoubtedly, communist rabble-rousers pressure Cubans to participate in pro-government rallies; there is no question of that. At the same time, however, one must consider the fact that a dictatorial regime, like Castro's, is unlikely to make someone a judge if that person is not a proven pro-government supporter.

So, does this mean that every one of Castro's current judges is a dyed-in-the-wool communist, whose participation in a post-Castro judiciary would undermine the legitimacy of the entire system? In other post-dictatorships, the question has not been directly addressed. However, a pragmatic view would suggest that these post-communist governments, as well as their constituents, have had to assume and accept that a judiciary can be legitimized, even if a percentage of its members were judges under the former dictatorial regime. There simply is no way to replace an entire bureaucracy, like the judiciary, overnight, and I suspect that Cuba will most likely be required to make the same assumption that other former communist countries have had to make. Accordingly, chances are that a Cuban lustration law would likely apply its full force only to current members of the judiciary who are also the most ardent, high-ranking members of the communist hierarchy, including those who have had involvement with Cuba's secret police.

In countries like the former Czechoslovakia, the lustration laws applied to all "conscious collaborators." In the case of the Cuban judiciary, this concept might be too broad, as most Cuban judges would probably be deemed to be "conscious collaborators." Even under a slightly narrower definition, the effects on the Cuban judiciary might be extreme. For example, the German lustration law only applied to East Germans with ties to the Stasi secret police, yet the law forced approximately 50% of the East German

---

2. See, for example, Speech given by Tina Rosenberg at the Democratic Politics and Policy Workshop, New School East & Central Europe Program, February 12, 1996 (transcript on the Internet at: http://www.newschool.edu/centers/ecep/tina.htm.)

judiciary into early retirement. As mentioned earlier in our discussion, the East German slots were filled by West German judges who also helped to educate the remaining East German judges. In Cuba, there will be no such resources. Arguably, expatriates could play a role in helping to shape the development of a post-Castro judiciary, but how likely is it that they would be available in sufficient numbers to man the Cuban judiciary ranks overnight? (As an aside, expatriates who have been naturalized in other countries may be ineligible to serve in a Cuban judiciary, unless they are willing to lose their citizenship elsewhere. For example, under U.S. law a citizen may lose his or her U.S. nationality by taking an oath or making a declaration of allegiance to, or by accepting employment in the government of, a foreign state.)

Another tool used to determine which former communists should be excluded from government has been the examination of secret police files. Presumably, if the secret police files list a person as a collaborator, this person should be considered an apparatchik and subject to exclusion under the lustrations laws. Although a seemingly reasonable approach, the procedures enacted to examine these secret files has varied widely from country to country. In Germany, citizens can apply to review the files kept on them by the Stasi (which are reputedly, in the best of German traditions, extremely detailed and voluminous). In Germany, government agencies can even run checks on their employees to make sure that they are not former Stasi agents or collaborators. According to one source, "these checks have resulted in the dismissal of thousands of judges, police officers, schoolteachers and other public employees in eastern Germany who once informed for the Stasi."[3] In the Czech Republic, access to the StB files is restricted to those who have been accused of being former collaborators, and even then, the access is restricted to relevant information only. The Romanians, by contrast, have sealed their secret police records for 40 years.

Whether post-Castro Cuba will immediately open the secret files of the Ministerio del Interior to its citizens is an obviously intriguing question. For purposes of our discussion, however, it should be made clear that if such files were to be made available for purposes of lustration, they should serve only as evidence and not as definitive proof of someone's ineligibility to participate in democratic government. The problem, as stated by the editor of a Polish newspaper asked to comment on his country's decision to open up the files of the Polish secret police, is obvious:

> I don't think it's a great idea. When you look to the past through the window of the ex-special police, you don't really look into the past, you look into the past as produced by them. They were not honest people. They were inventing people trying to use the files for their own purposes.[4]

How long should the exclusion last?

At first glance, lustration laws seem perfectly suited for short-term use during the transition from communism to democracy, while the institutions of democracy are being established and reinforced. The fear during these transitional periods is that former communists are able to undermine democratic initiatives if allowed to frustrate the efforts of nascent democratic governments to establish the laws and institutions that protect pluralism (*i.e.*, adoption of a constitution, establishment of a constitutional court and free and fair elections).

The reasoning is perhaps best summarized by the Constitutional Court of the Czech and Slovak Federal Republic in a 1992 decision upholding lustration:

> In a democratic society, it is necessary for employees of state and public bodies. . . to meet certain criteria of a civic nature, which we can characterize as loyalty to the democratic principles upon which the state is built. Such restrictions may also concern specific groups of persons without those persons being individually judged, a situation which can be found, without a great deal of difficulty, in other legal systems as

---

3. "Germans Anguish over Police Files," *The New York Times*, February 20, 1992.

4. "Poles queue for secret police files," by Douglas Herbert, *CNN.com*, posted February 15, 2001, http://europe.cnn.com/2001/WORLD/Europe/02/15/poland.files.

well (for example, in the Federal Republic of Germany, persons from the former German Democratic Republic or the east bloc may not be engaged by firms producing highly developed technology for the weapons industry).[5]

Noting that the exclusionary provisions would be in effect only during "a relatively short time period by the end of which it is foreseen that the process of democratization will have been accomplished," the court then stated in language that seems to me appropriate for a post-Castro Cuba, that:

> Each state or rather those which were compelled over a period of forty years to endure the violation of fundamental rights and basic freedoms by a totalitarian regime has the right to enthrone democratic leadership and to apply such legal measures as are apt to avert the risk of subversion or of a possible relapse into totalitarianism, or at least to limit those risks.

However, in December 2001, 44 deputies from the lower house of the Czech parliament[6] asked the Constitutional Court of the now Czech Republic to review the constitutionality of the lustration laws.[7] The deputies argued that the court's predecessor, the Constitutional Court of the Czech and Slovak Federal Republic, had held the lustration laws to be constitutional only because (1) at the time of the decision, the state had a legitimate interest in establishing the institutions of democracy without interference from former *apparatchiks*, and (2) such laws would have a limited duration (*i.e.,* only until the establishment of the institutions of democracy). The deputies argued that such institutions had been established and the lustration laws had been set to expire prior to 2001, so that an amendment indefinitely extending the validity of the lustration laws was unconstitutional.

Despite the ruling of its predecessor, which the court determined to be non-binding, and the deputies' arguments, the Constitutional Court ruled that the state had a legitimate and constitutionally valid inter-

est in continuing to exclude from government those who would undermine the institutions of democracy. The court noted that those who had consciously suppressed the rights of citizens were a danger to democratic society. Since there was no legal right to hold a position in state administration, the court upheld the state's right to exclude such people from government. The court did note, however, that lustration laws did not "restrict anyone in entering into a political office," such as becoming an elected member of parliament.

Therefore, according to precedent, particularly that of the Czech Republic, we may conclude that lustration laws may apply for an indefinite period of time. Accordingly, a post-Castro Cuba government would have discretion as to when such laws should expire, if ever.

From What Positions Should Former Communists be Excluded

Generally, lustration laws have been implemented to exclude former communists from most top level positions, such that a former communist wishing to become a bus driver would not necessarily face exclusion but one wishing to become a police officer might. For purposes of our discussion, however, it is clear that lustration laws should apply to those in every level of the judiciary, from chief appellate judges down to local magistrates. As discussed above, the difficulty for the new government will not be in determining who within the judiciary should be made subject to lustration laws, but in determining the standard by which these persons are to be excluded.

Implementation of Proper Lustration Procedures

The last but certainly most important issue to consider is the procedure by which to implement lustration.

In the Czech Republic, for example, if a person is accused of being a communist under the lustration

---

5. http://www.concourt.cz/angl_verze/doc/p-1-92.html.

6. There are presently 200 deputies in the Chamber of Deputies, as the lower house of the Czech parliament is called, so 44 deputies represented 22% of the members of the Chamber of Deputies.

7. http://www.concourt.cz.angl_verze/doc/p-9-1.html.

laws, he or she has the right to challenge the accusation and have access to any StB files used as evidence against them. The accused then has the right to appeal any such findings, and the Czech Constitutional Court has upheld these procedures as being constitutionally sound.

However, the basis upon which the Czech Constitutional Court found these lustration laws to be substantively and procedurally sound is of particular interest for purposes of our discussion because it illustrates the importance of both substance and procedure in the application of these laws.

In defending its position that lustration is a legitimate state right, the Czech court relied, in part, on the laws and judicial decisions of other European countries, as well as those of the United States. In referencing the United States, the court cited to *Adler v. Board of Education*,[8] a 1952 U.S. Supreme Court case upholding the constitutionality of a New York State law that made any person advocating, or belonging to organizations advocating, the overthrow of government by force, violence or unlawful means ineligible for employment in the New York State education system. While the *Adler* decision did uphold the New York State law, the U.S. Supreme Court did so based solely on its finding that government has the right to exclude subversives from employment. The Court did not consider the question of whether the law was constitutionally vague. In fact, the Court specifically noted that the vagueness argument had not been raised by the petitioners in the lower courts and that the Court would not "pass upon the constitutionality of a state statute before the state courts [had] an opportunity to do so."

Fifteen years later, in *Keyishian v. Board of Regents*,[9] the U.S. Supreme Court again revisited the New York statute. This time, however, the Court found the law to be unconstitutionally vague because its terms were not "susceptible of objective measurement" and because "men of common intelligence must necessarily guess at its meaning and differ as to

its application." In addition, the Court noted that "pertinent constitutional doctrines have since rejected the premises upon which [the *Adler*] conclusion rested." Specifically, the *Adler* court's premise that "public employment, including academic employment, may be conditioned upon the surrender of constitutional rights which could not be abridged by direct government action" had been rejected by later decisions as being unconstitutionally unsound. In other words, the Court found that (1) the procedures enacted to enforce the New York law were vague and incapable of being applied in a constitutionally objective manner and (2) the state could not establish criteria for exclusion from employment which necessarily infringed upon basic the constitutional rights of individuals, such as the right of free speech and association. The latter of these points directly contradicts the premise of the Czech court's argument (*i.e.*, that governments have a right to exclude subversives from employment).

Of course, our discussion of the U.S. cases and the Czech case is for illustrative purposes only. There are obvious differences between an established democracy, where democracy is entrenched in the people and their government, and a young democracy, where the fear that government will revert to a dictatorship is a real possibility. The point is that any laws enacted to legitimize a post-Castro government, particularly its judiciary, will need to ensure that that the criteria being established to exclude people from public life meet stringent constitutional scrutiny, and that the procedures established for their enforcement are also constitutionally sound. Otherwise, the process of legitimization could itself become corrupt, and we have done nothing more than replace one ill-devised system with another one.

CONCLUSION

As we have said, there is no doubt that a post-Castro government will find it difficult to establish the legitimacy of its judiciary. Based on the precedents established by other countries and given Cuba's unique

---

8. *Adler v. Board of Education*, 342 U.S. 485, 72 S.Ct. 380 (1952)

9. *Keyishian v. Board of Regents*, 385 U.S. 589, 87 S.Ct. 675 (1967)

history and present-day situation, we can conclude that this difficult task could perhaps be made easier if a post-Castro government enacted a lustration law similar to those of Eastern Europe. The goal of this "Ley de Incapacitación para el Ejercicio de Cargos Judiciales Públicos" should be to exclude from the judiciary the highest level Communist officials, members or henchmen of the Ministerio del Interior and others who were accomplices to severe violations of human rights.

Once lustration is effected, the question remains as to what to do with the remaining judges. Clearly, the very fact that they were part of a dictatorial government tarnishes their legitimacy, but as we have noted, it will be impossible to dismiss all of the judiciary, particularly not immediately. Accordingly, the new government could (1) announce that it will dismiss the entire judiciary but not state a specific date for their dismissal, which would allow the new government to dismiss judges at-will, or (2) retain judges on a provisional basis, say, for 12 months, subject to extension for further 12-month periods, for a time. However, if extended for too long, without evolution these procedures would themselves de-legitimize the judiciary, as judges eager to keep their jobs become "bootlickers" to their new bosses and forfeit their independence.

Finally, the new government might establish an independent commission to review claims arising from the process of lustration and then establish a process by which to appeal the commission's decisions. Initially, such commission could be established by decree of the new government. Thereafter, however, the functions of such committee should be passed on to the judiciary, with ultimate review by whatever is established to review constitutional issues.

REVOLUTIONARY LEADERS, IDEOLOGY AND CHANGE

Erin Ennis

Are leaders of revolutions more ideological than their successors? Does this ideological view make revolutionary leaders less open to changes not of their own making? In China, Mao Zedong created and maintained an ideology for the nation based on his own political views and led a massive upheaval of Chinese society based on ideology. Deng Xiaoping, who succeeded Mao as leader of China, moderated much of the ideological tone in politics and began to institute a regulated party apparatus and economy. In Cuba, Fidel Castro's views continue to form the basis of the ideology of the island.

The hypothesis of this study is that first-generation revolutionary leaders, men who led their nations' revolutions and became heads of state, are averse to changing the political and economic systems they create and lead. Second-generation leaders, those who succeed the revolutionary leader as head of state, who have revolutionary backgrounds similar to the original leaders, may allow changes but will still embrace the core ideology and values of the revolution within the structure of the existing system. To evaluate the hypothesis, I will consider the first and second-generation leaders of China and the current leadership of Cuba: Mao Zedong and Deng Xiaoping in China and Fidel Castro in Cuba. To provide context for recent events in both Cuba and China, I will conclude with a brief examination of China's current leadership under Jiang Zemin and a discussion of Cuba's current economic and political situations.

RESOCIALIZATION

Marx provided a useful framework for an evaluation of the actions of leaders in his work, *The Eighteenth Brumaire of Louis Bonaparte*:

> Men make their own history, but they do not make it just as they please; they do not make it under circumstances chosen by themselves, but under circumstances directly found, given and transmitted from the past.

The past creates the circumstances for men to make their own history. In social science, this process is known as resocialization.

All individuals, regardless of the political system in which they are raised, undergo socialization into the ways of that system. Each political system has its own way of doing business and pursuing its goals. People gradually learn that process beginning early in life; they observe adults and receive education in the norms of the particular political system (Hyman 1959, 19). In some cases, an individual may reject the system, perhaps because he perceives it is corrupt or because it does not address poverty, exploitation, or some other priority. In these instances, the individual may seek alternatives that better address what he perceives are the inadequacies of the present system. "Resocialization" is this rejection of the existing structure and acceptance of a new one.

An individual's quest for alternative political courses may lead to a minor change such as running for political office or changing party affiliation. Depending on the response to those efforts, however, the individual may decide that minor changes to the existing system will not address the problems he sees. If, for instance, he is imprisoned for speaking against the present order, he may determine that more radical steps are necessary and seek to fundamentally change the political system to better reflect his views of national priorities. Under the right set of circumstances—the confluence of problems in the existing system, presence of a radical opposition, and support for the opposition—a revolution is born. As Mehran Kamrava explains,

> The social and cultural context in which revolutions take place…facilitate not only the spread of revolutionary sentiments throughout society but also furnish the necessary links and bonds between revolutionary activists on the one hand and popular classes on the other (Kamrava 1990, 79).

Mao

Mao Zedong's political socialization took place during a time of significant change in China. His youthful experiences with weak political institutions stand in contrast to the strong, authoritarian system he put in place after the communist victory in 1949. This experience was molded by the Chinese Communist Party's (CCP) cooperative efforts with the Guomindang (GMD) during Japan's occupation of China but also by the GMD's betrayal of the CCP.

Considering the history of their relationship with Chiang and the GMD as well as China's domination by a foreign power, Mao and the CCP unsurprisingly viewed radical change as the only possible solution for China. As early as 1919, Mao viewed revolution as the proper path for realization of China's potential (Wu 1988, 38). This opinion probably was solidified during the republican period when political reform and coalition building had proven ineffective and deadly for the communists. As the civil war continued, the GMD was successful in forcing the CCP to retreat in what would become known as the Long March. About 100,000 troops were reported to have begun the March in 1934; only 20,000 survived (Bertsch, Clark & Wood 1991, 266). Mao's resocialization and radicalization laid the foundation for his political decisions during his leadership.

Castro

Castro came to formal communism only after he had risen to power, but his experiences during the Cuban revolution left him with indelible marks similar to those of Mao: a conviction that the existing economic and political system must be discarded in favor of one that better addressed the needs of his fellow countrymen.

Castro's experiences as the head of a rebel movement were marked by two failed attacks, one on the Moncada Barracks in 1953, and the other, his disastrous return to Cuba from Mexico in 1956. What is striking about these failures is that Castro was able to use them as propaganda for his cause. Rather than gaining a reputation as a bumbling would-be rebel, Castro's mystique only grew after each event. Castro's personal charisma clearly was an active element in the beginning as well as in and the outcome of the revolution. As K.S. Karol explains,

> Fidel succeeded, not because he was a 'Bolivar who has read Lenin,'…but because he was one of the veterans of Cayo Confites, one who had shared all the political experiences of his generation. He knew how to transcend the limits of these experiences, how to place himself one step—but only one step—in front of his countrymen, who could thus follow him without too much difficulty (Karol 1971, 177).

Castro was exposed to Marxism during his university years, but it was not the transforming experience that it had been for Mao. Rather, another element has been much more formative in his approach to politics: nationalism (Thomas 1998, 818). Castro's themes of ending exploitation of Cuba by imperialist foreign governments and improving the conditions of life for the majority of Cubans resonated with people in Cuba and thus united diverse groups opposing Batista (O'Connor 1970, 52; Bertsch, Clark & Wood 1991, 273).

Deng

Like Mao, Deng had come from a middle class background and had completed his early education in the traditional Chinese system. But Deng's resocialization and radicalization as a Marxist was very different from Mao's.

Resocialization begins with the recognition of inadequacies in the existing political system and the search for alternatives. Deng's personal resocialization began

313

while he was studying in France, when he learned of socialism and Marxism. He had a second resocialization during Mao's tenure, though this time Deng sought alternatives within the system, rather than a total rejection of it. Several reasons account for Deng's approach. Having been ousted from his party positions more than once due to disputes with Mao and his supporters, Deng knew the excesses of Stalinism. At the same time, the existing political system offered him a base of power and the apparatus to maintain it. Thus, Deng diverged from Mao in establishing his legitimacy as the leader of China. Gardner notes,

> …While personal rule has been customary, there is no constitutional or ideological justification for it, hence no principle by which personal rule can be made legitimate. In the absence of such a principle, the authority of a personal rule in a communist state cannot be transferred to another person by a regulated succession (Gardner 1982, 4).

In other words, Deng had to build alliances and support on his own, since he had neither Mao's endorsement to be China's leader nor a mechanism through which such an endorsement could have guaranteed his control. He did, however, have extensive experience in a variety of party positions and the backing of other leaders, all of which contributed to his personal legitimacy as the next leader of China,

> By virtue of his experience as past party secretary-general, finance minister, economic planner, a regional supreme leader in Southwest China, a party leader within the armed forces, a vice premier (acting during Zhao's absence, and, most important of all, the author of the blueprint for the four modernizations, [Deng] finds in the party or government no one who can claim to be his equal in policy leadership and in party politics (Chang 1988, 65).

Deng's resocialization, therefore, had an outcome different from that of Mao and Castro. Mao viewed his personal rule of China as essential to achieving the goals of his agenda for the country; Castro had a similar view for Cuba. Deng's experiences during Mao's tenure contributed to a different style of governance: one in which the leader's legitimacy was based on his achievements and his party's, rather than his personality. By changing his role from manifestation of the party to leader of the party, Deng altered how challenges to the system were viewed.

Revolutions and Resocialization

In situations where revolutions are victorious, the new regime must find ways to implement an entirely new political system with different goals and institutions, while maintaining its hold on power.

Communist revolutions have a particularly difficult task in implementing their goals, because their call to arms is the liberation of the masses, both politically and economically. The new regime must put in place a system of political resocialization to build a society of enlightened masses from a population raised in a different political system with different political goals (Bertsch, Clark & Wood 1991, 315). The regime therefore is made up of individuals who followed the path to resocialization described above and they, in turn, create the resocialization of the rest of the country. Revolutionary leaders thus go from being resocialized to being the resocializer. As Gabriel Almond explains,

> The attitudes that communist movements encounter in countries where they take power are viewed as false consciousness—whether they be nationalism, religious beliefs, liberal-pluralistic views, ethnic subcultural propensities, or attitudes toward economic interests. These attitudes are viewed as the consequences of preexisting class structure and the underlying mode of production, as transmitted by associated agents of indoctrination. Communist movements either eliminate or seek to undermine the legitimacy of these preexisting structures and processes and replace them with a quite new and thoroughly penetrative set (Almond 1983, 128).

The political resocialization of the masses also serves a more basic purpose. By creating an entirely new education system with the regime's policies at the core of the lesson plans, the new government creates propaganda departments in every school, workplace and military base, reaching every individual in the country, regardless of age. Hannah Arendt summarized this objective: "Totalitarian regimes, so long as they are in power, and the totalitarian leaders, so long as they are alive, command and rest upon mass support up to the end" (Arendt 1973, 306).[1]

Role of Political System

Once they had achieved power, Mao and Castro set about creating political systems to implement their visions for their countries. Each man chose a similar structure to realize his vision: an authoritarian system with himself as the dominant leader.

The choice of an authoritarian system may have been inherent to the circumstances. Skocpol suggests, "the logic of state-building through which social revolutions are successfully accomplished promotes both authoritarianism and popular mobilization" (Skocpol 1988, 149). Samuel Farber goes a bit further and suggests that the choice of governing systems by both Mao and Castro was both political and ideological,

…Nothing in the political upbringing of [China or Cuba's] revolutionary leaderships made them the least inclined to, or interested in, even attempting to establish pluralistic socialist democracies. Instead, they made conscious political and ideological choices favoring undemocratic political arrangements. Furthermore, these institutional arrangements were normally regarded as good in themselves and not as lesser evils imposed on their respective countries by the economic and other objective difficulties encountered at the time of, and subsequent to, the overthrow of the old order (Farber 1990, 3).

The choice of a political system to manage their newly liberated nations clearly was linked to the experiences of both men before and during their respective revolutions. Both Mao and Castro viewed authoritarian rule as necessary to achieve the goals of the revolutions. Such a system would enable the will of the victors to be more rapidly implemented in China and Cuba, all the while building a society of new socialist men (Bertsch, Clark & Wood 1991, 317). The selection of the authoritarian model, however, laid the groundwork for the leaders' future resistance to alterations of the political system.

Since Mao and Castro were the undisputed leaders of their countries, both men were in reality the embodiment of their regimes. Therefore, challenges to the policies and procedures of the governments of China and Cuba were challenges to the personal authority of Mao and Castro. And because their control of their regimes was almost total, both men were capable of stopping those challenges and reasserting their power. As Fewsmith describes,

…A major reason why reform encounters problems in Leninist systems is precisely the requisites of being a 'ruling' party (adhering to legal-rational norms and regularizing relations with society) clash with the charismatic impersonalism of Leninist systems (Fewsmith 2001, 92).

The relationship between leaders and their decisions goes back to Marx's assertion that man and his history are permanently entwined. The link can be summed up simply: political actors "replicate the patterns of behavior they have learned in the course of their own careers" (Fewsmith 2001, 87). The connection of the socialization of a leader and the choices he makes also has been called the "operational code." This code comprises the political views of leaders like Mao and Castro based on a set of general beliefs about issues of history and politics. Those beliefs shape the decisions a leader makes about strategy and tactics and are formulated with an eye to past political experience.

The paths of Mao and Castro diverged in the means they pursued to achieve that goal, but the results were the same. The combination of their radicalized political resocializations and their singular leadership of authoritarian systems made Mao and Castro resistant to challenges to their authority. Either element individually could have made them resistant to change, but combined together, resocialization and authoritarianism ensured this resistance.

---

1. The terms "authoritarian" and "totalitarian" have frequently been used interchangeably to mean a political system that concentrates power in the hands of an autocratic state. "Totalitarian," however, has a Cold War tone that implies an evaluation of the system's benevolence. Therefore, for this study, the term "authoritarian" will be used to describe the political systems created in China and Cuba because it more accurately characterizes the nature of the two systems.

By contrast, the types of reform that Deng was willing to explore remained within the structure of Marxism-Leninism, though Deng defined that structure more loosely than had his predecessor. Deng recognized that reform placed the communist leadership in a precarious situation. Movement away from the communist or socialist model could discredit the CCP's government as a whole and weaken party control of China (Fewsmith 2001, 68). Any alterations, therefore, had to reinforce the legitimacy of the party as the foundation of the state.

> A fundamental difference between Mao and Deng was their view of proposals to alter the power structure of the party. As paramount leader, Mao was able to dominate the party system on most occasions. Although he had been wary of the growing bureaucracy of the party, a concern that was manifested in the launching of the Cultural Revolution, Mao used his singular dominance of that system to continue to push his agenda. Deng, on the other hand, worked from within the party rather than attempting to replicate Mao's cult and personal dominance (Fewsmith 2001, 71).

Because he remained concerned about maintaining the party's control, Deng did not discard all elements of Mao's leadership. He maintained the authoritarian governing model that Mao had established but removed the Stalinist elements that had run amuck. Ideology was removed as the primary criterion for judging the Party's effectiveness and a new one emerged: economic performance (Fewsmith 2001, 94). Deng and his supporters included economic modernization among their primary objectives and began an aggressive plan to achieve that goal.

In addition to his economic agenda, Deng also instituted a formal governing structure for the Party that moved it away from a single, solitary political leader, further addressing the problems that Mao's Stalinist tenure had created (Lo 1999, 78). Consequently, Deng's changes moved China from the rule of man toward the rule of law, though it remained fundamentally authoritarian. Under Deng's changes, China moved toward what has been called "socialist democracy." The one-party structure remained in place and regular acknowledgements of the importance of Marxism-Leninism and the preeminence of the party continued (Lo 1999, 78).

China's political system under Deng, therefore, was more inclined to tolerate dissent than the Stalinist model pursued by Mao. Deng, however, did not lose sight of the need for a strong central authority to maintain support for and dominance of the CCP. Deng's more-open approach to China's governance also affected his approach to other types of reform.

REVOLUTIONARY LEADERS AND CHANGE

The differences in leadership styles between revolutionary leaders and their successors can best be seen by examining the responses of Mao, Castro and Deng to challenges during their tenures.

Mao: The Great Leap Forward and the Cultural Revolution

Mao's leadership of China began with an ambitious effort to modernize China's economy. After some small and relatively effective changes to the system, Mao pursued a more dramatic and rapid transformation of the Chinese economy. The Great Leap Forward, launched in 1958, sought to modernize and industrialize China in 10 to 15 years. Mao's plan built on the previous Five Year Plans, which had been moderately successful. To increase production, Mao proposed moral incentives and mass mobilization, techniques that had been used by the party in Yan'an after the Long March. Collective work projects on irrigation and farming had appeared successful during the Five Year Plans, so even larger cooperatives were included in the Great Leap's agenda. Improving rural productivity would increase industrial production, moving China forward (Spence 1990, 578).

The first year of the Great Leap Forward was blessed with a good harvest, and the initial results appeared to validate Mao's approach. However, lingering memories of the outcome of a previous political campaign against Mao's perceived detractors skewed the reporting of actual production numbers. Party cadres inflated their results out of fear of being labeled "rightists." Other problems were simply not reported (Spence 1990, 580). The unrealistic goals for production, ever more ambitious due to the illusion of progress created by cooked results, rearranged the priorities of the nation from feeding its people and modernizing its economy to meeting production goals.

Those working in the field knew of the failures; Mao either did not know that his plans were failing or chose to ignore the failures. A prominent party member attempted to end the Great Leap by suggesting to Mao privately that the policies were not working; he was removed from his position for insubordination (Smith 1987, 126). The Great Leap continued for another year, a year in which production levels continued to fall and famine took the lives of an estimated 20 million people.

Mao was not entirely opposed to changes to his agenda. When the dramatic failure of the Great Leap became undeniable, he eventually did back down. At the same time criticisms of Mao's policies were treated as criticism of Mao himself. By virtue of the system he created, Mao had the power to ensure that critics were punished and he used it.

The Cultural Revolution provides and equally compelling example of Mao's resistance to changes in his own policies. Mao's quest for constant revolution made him suspicious of the bureaucratic consolidation of the party's power. The party bureaucracy was the antithesis of revolution. Institutionalization of the party was not, in Mao's view, compatible with Mao Zedong Thought. Mao's singular leadership of both the party and the people of China, a position reaffirmed by the beginning of the Cultural Revolution, meant that no one could question his judgment on this matter.

Scholars have argued that Mao was well aware that the extreme leftists that led many of the Cultural Revolution's excesses pushed the limits but felt that they were a "lesser evil" than the Party bureaucracy he was trying to overhaul (Gittings 1989, 53). Regardless of his goals, however, Mao's actions in launching the Cultural Revolution, combined with his previous reactions to challenges to his position, show a clear pattern of aversion to reform.

Mao's resocialization and his influence on the political structure were independent factors that made him less likely to allow change to the system that guaranteed his position as unrivaled leader of China. When combined, these factors resulted in strong responses against challenges and challengers.

Castro: Market Reforms and Dollarization

While the differences in population between China and Cuba make the scale of retaliation against enemies difficult to equate, Castro has had similar extremes to Mao in his responses to challenges. Despite his late epiphany as a Communist, Castro's abhorrence for what he perceives as the excesses of capitalism is noteworthy. Market reforms in Cuba have been followed by crackdowns on capitalist activities and political reform has yet to see the light of day.

Like Mao, Castro's attempts to push the Cuban economy forward have not hit their mark. In the late 1970s and early 1980s, Castro allowed experimentation with market reform. The liberalization was in response to the failed policies of the previous decade that had set ambitious, but impossible goals for sugar production and which created shortages in other commodities.

The peasant markets that had been created manifested both the good and bad aspects of capitalism. Farmers were able to provide commodities directly to consumers, addressing the shortages that had become common. At the same time, price speculation and price gouging appeared (Black 1988, 373).

Castro's reaction to the problems that surfaced was to end the liberalizations. He condemned as "shameful" the peasant markets and accused the working class of developing a "mercenary mentality." The reforms had exposed the government's inadequacies and undermined its position with the people. In 1986, the Third Party Congress formally ended the period with a "rectification" campaign designed to bring the party firmly back in control of the island (Black 1988, 373).

The collapse of the Soviet Union in 1991 dramatically impacted Cuba's economy, which contracted by over a third in 1992-93 (Peters 1998). One tool that Castro was willing to use to improve the country's economy was to legalize the use of dollars in the domestic economy in 1993. The increased remittances from the United States, a nation that Castro continues to view as the enemy, have become a major element of restructuring the Cuban economy. The availability of U.S. dollars has increased demands for domestic products and services, creating the type of domestic growth necessary to sustain the economy (Baxter 1998, 20).

Although dollars remain legal, Cubans remain wary that the government will crack down on dollar-based transactions. Castro has spoken publicly about the criminal consequences of a dollarized economy, such as prostitution, crime and drug trading (Hammond 1999, 24). Further, in August 2001, the Cuban government announced that U.S. coins would no longer be valid currency on the island (Schweimier 2001, 4). While ending the use of U.S. coins is a minor economic change, public statements and actions of this nature remind Cubans that Castro may still pull the plug on their experiment with capitalism if it presents a real challenge to his authority.

Deng: Economic Reform and Tiananmen

Although Deng resisted fundamental ideological changes to the political and economic structure of China's system, he accepted some modifications, most importantly and broadly on the economic front. He nevertheless cracked down when he felt the authority of the party was under attack, though not nearly as strongly as Mao had.

Deng unquestionably pursued an aggressive campaign of economic reform. Deng viewed the key to China's modernization as requiring shifts away from ideology to emphasize economic performance. Even before his position was consolidated, Deng advocated proposals for improving the economy (Gardner 1982, 90). By 1978, however, economic reform became not only advisable but also necessary. China had become economically stagnant; political stability under such circumstances had become, at best, tenuous (Fewsmith 2001, 64). Thus, Deng's task was not only to find a political path that could maintain communist control but also to find an economic path that could reinforce the legitimacy of CCP rule.

Even before his position as leader had been determined, Deng advocated change. He concentrated his

reform efforts on the "Four Modernizations," which focused on agriculture, industry, defense, and science and technology. Those reforms were to be pursued under the guidance of the party, which maintained its monopoly of defining "revolution" even after Mao's passing. As the Third Plenum of the Eleventh Central Committee stated, "Socialist modernization is therefore a profound and extensive revolution" (Spence 1990, 657).

While the party endorsed Deng's modernization plans, one should keep in mind that the internal debate on this course of action was very different than it had been under Mao. Implementation of Deng's priorities was not guaranteed, and Deng was not in a position to punish those who opposed him. At the same time, Deng maintained a balance within the party with himself at the head but with input and support of others in the party (Fewsmith 2001, 50). The changes to the party's policies that Deng had supported removed the unquestioned power and judgment of the leader that Mao had enjoyed. Deng's tenure was distinguished from Mao's in this instance in its acceptance of challenges to Deng's authority. Dissent within the party did not guarantee retribution.

The Tiananmen protests of 1989 began as the celebration of an anniversary—the seventieth anniversary of the May Fourth movement, which the CCP considered a key element of its origins. Calls for political reform had begun again and were discussed in the National People's Congress (Spence 1990, 738). Then, Hu Yaobang, the former CCP General Secretary, who had fallen from grace in the years immediately before, died in April. Hu had advocated political reform but had been dismissed from his party posts in 1987 for allowing student protests to spread. Students at Beijing's universities viewed Hu's death as an opportunity to pressure the government for further economic and political reform. Sit-ins and rallies began in Beijing and soon spread to other cities (Spence 1990, 739).

By late April, Deng and the party began to display their dissatisfaction with the students. A strongly worded editorial in *People's Daily*, believed to represent Deng's views, condemned the protests and implied that continuation would result in arrest and trial. The warnings, however, only steeled the resolve of students. By May 17, crowds in Tiananmen Square reached over one million and included students, workers, and other reform supporters (Spence 1990, 741).

Deng had not taken a firm stand within the party on how to respond to the protests, but in early June, he agreed that strong action had to be taken. When the Party leadership wanted to take action, Deng sided with the hard-liners who advocated crushing the protests (Fewsmith 2001, 69). On June 3, army units dispersed the protesters with tanks and automatic weapons.

As had been the case with the Democracy Wall, Deng did not initially stop the Tiananmen protests. He waited almost two months before deciding that they must be ended after crowds had grown large enough to potentially threaten the party's hold on power. In this case, Deng went much further in stemming the criticism than he had in response to Democracy Wall. He used strong authoritarian means to maintain the party's power. Thus, while Deng differed from Mao in most of his leadership decisions, his response to the Tiananmen protests was reminiscent of Mao.

RECENT EVENTS IN CUBA AND CHINA

While Castro is the last man standing among communist revolutionary leaders in power, his actions in 2001-2002 have provided further evidence of how revolutionary leaders and their successors differ. Castro has successfully advocated a constitutional amendment making socialism "irrevocable" for Cuba. Jiang Zemin, China's second leader since Mao, has pursued further economic liberalization and has opened party membership to capitalists.

Irrevocable Socialism and Economic Difficulties

Former President Jimmy Carter brought the Varela Project to the attention of many Cubans in his remarks to the Cuban people in May 2002. Eleven thousand signatures were ultimately collected in support of a referendum to allow free speech and elections, amnesty for political prisoners and the right to own and operate private businesses. The signatures

were submitted to the Cuban National Assembly in May 2002 in accordance with the Cuban constitution's provision to allow public calls for referendum (Fritsch 2002, A2). Castro and other members of his government denounced the petition as the work of operatives of the United States and have yet to consider the petition. Instead, in a special session of the Assembly, the legislature passed a referendum, signed by 99.25 percent of eligible Cuban voters, making socialism "irrevocable" for the island (Deutsche Presse Agentur 6/24/02).

Many have cited Castro's effort on this front as a response to the Varela Project. His actions are not surprising when considered in the larger context of both his previous responses to challenges and, more importantly, the economic difficulties facing Cuba. Within days of the massive rallies led by Castro to proclaim Cuba's continued confidence in socialism came an announcement by the nation's sugar minister that half of Cuba's sugar mills would be closed permanently. While the displaced workers—an estimated 200,000—will reportedly be given alternative employment opportunities, it is difficult to imagine how the Cuban economy can create that many jobs at a time when it is struggling to meet many of its international financial commitments (Grogg 2002).

It is also not surprising that Castro proclaimed three days of holiday for ordinary Cubans to be able to watch the special parliamentary session considering the socialism petition. Cuba has been facing energy shortfalls due to the loss in April of a preferential arrangement with Venezuela that had supplied it with more than 50,000 barrels of oil a day (de Cordoba 2002). In early June, some foreign companies in joint ventures with the Cuban government reported they expected temporary closings of industrial plants due to fuel shortages (Boadle 6/10/02). Consequently, the holiday furthered Castro's political agenda without calling undue attention to the energy crisis.

Castro's recent responses to economic hardship and calls for reform have been characterized by a restatement or strengthening of the party line. These actions reinforce Castro's position as the sole leader of the nation, remind the people of Cuba that he is unwilling to entertain challenges, and allow him to place the blame for a failing economy back on his favorite scapegoat, the U.S. economic embargo of the island.

China's WTO Membership And Expanded Party Membership

China's membership in the World Trade Organization finally came to fruition in December of 2001. Implementation of many of the agreement's provisions had already begun in advance of the accession, including the initial steps to streamline and improve competitiveness of the country's multitude of state-owned enterprises.

Jiang Zemin and the CCP's party leadership are very much aware of the potential threat that a difficult transition to WTO membership might mean for their positions. Some analysts have speculated that unemployment from the streamlining of state-owned enterprises could cause 50 million workers to lose their jobs; another 78 million jobs could be lost in the agriculture sector as China's farmers begin to compete with foreign products (Wade 2001; Economist 6/15/02). The Chinese Academy of Social Sciences has suggested that unemployment rates could surge from an official estimated rate of 3.6 percent to over 15 percent (Economist 6/15/02, 13). Social unrest is a real possibility as China implements these changes.

In preparation of such possibilities, however, Jiang's government has begun to create a social safety net that would provide unemployment benefits along with job training and relocation for workers displaced by changes to the economy (BBC 3/17/02). China has come a long way from the "Iron Rice-bowl" that Mao promised—lifetime work and security for every worker in China—but the current leadership is wagering that these changes will prevent widespread unrest due to the economic changes that are planned for the country.

It is, of course, necessary to keep in mind that Jiang is not acting out of benevolence. Party rules dictate that he and most of the current leadership must retire this fall and make way for a new crop of leaders. Jiang Zemin, like Deng Xiaoping before him, is interested in maintaining his influence even in his "re-tirement," as well as securing his own place in history. The third succession in China's leadership since the founding of the People's Republic of China is expected to go smoothly. Recent reports indicate that Jiang may move up the People's Congress by a month, a suggestion that the docket of new leaders has been accepted by a majority of the party's leaders (Kynge 2002).

In retirement, Jiang seeks to maintain his role as head of China's Central Military Commission, a position that Deng also maintained after he stepped down as China's premier (Hutzler 2002). Jiang has also proposed his own set of ideological principles that he has pushed in an effort secure his place in history alongside Mao and Deng. In a speech to China's Party Congress last year, Jiang outlined his "Three Represents," his vision of how the party will maintain its position by responding to the needs of the Chinese people. Party officials have begun urging publicity and ideological departments to publicize the Three Represents to further their implementation. *The People's Daily*, China's primary paper and voice of the party, recently stated that Jiang's theory, "is the same strain as Marxism-Leninism, Mao Zedong Thought and Deng Xiaoping Theory" [BBC 6/13/02]. Jiang has also opened party membership to "capitalists," and some foreign companies have begun to allow the Party to set up organizations within their Chinese factories, all moves to broaden the appeal of the CCP (Economist 6/1/02, 40).

Like his predecessors, however, Jiang is not soft on challenges to his authority. During his watch, an internal report known in the West as the "Tiananmen Papers" became public and exposed many of the party's warts in its decision to crack down on demonstrators in 1989 and portrayed Jiang's ascension as an orchestrated coup. News reports have indicated that retaliation against suspected leakers has already been taken (Washington Post 2002). Similarly, while Jiang's government has taken steps to provide assistance to unemployed workers, demonstrations against the party are still not tolerated for long. Small protests have been reported in some areas of China, but the government has quelled them quickly by rounding up the leaders and offering others financial incentives to stem future protests (Economist 6/15/02, 13).

China's movement away from extreme responses to economic and political challenges continues. Jiang has responded to such situations in a more moderate fashion than Deng, and certainly more so than Mao had done.

CONCLUSION

The evidence presented in this paper suggests that the role of resocialization in the development of leadership style and structure is different for revolutionary leaders than it is for their successors. Revolutionary leaders maintain and dominate the systems they create. These political systems are characterized by a single strong leader who embodies both the ideals of the revolution and the new government. In the cases of China and Cuba, I have found that the combination of these elements contributes to resistance to change and reform because such changes are viewed as challenges to the leader and therefore to the regime.

Successors are more open to changes of the existing political and economic systems, though they do so within the structure of the revolution's fundamental goals. They nevertheless will still act to curtail such actions when the legitimacy of the ruling party is threatened.

As leaders of the revolutions of China and Cuba, Mao and Castro had very different revolutionary experiences. They nevertheless used similar means to achieve their goals. Both men relied upon the strategic use of history to distinguish their regimes from preceding governments. Both men found authoritarian political structures, bordering on Stalinist, to be effective in achieving their goals and maintaining their power. The combination of these factors made both Mao and Castro averse to political and economic changes that moved their countries away from their personal control.

Deng Xiaoping experienced China's revolution and the PRC's formative years under the system developed by Mao. Although he used history to distinguish his leadership from that of Mao and to identify his goals for the future of China, his distinctions were unique in that they were made in the context of the communist movement overall. He moderated the authoritarian model and the party structure but tried to maintain the overall legitimacy of the system. Deng was more willing to change China's economic and political systems but was not willing to do so blindly. Deng halted reforms of the political system when he determined the legitimacy of the CCP to be under attack.

Castro continues to follow a well-established pattern in his responses to economic and political challenges. Periods of economic or political difficulty—periods when Castro's personal authority is being challenged—are responded to with ideological rhetoric and a tightening of control.

China's leadership, however, has continued to evolve beyond the harsh responses that were common during Mao's tenure. Jiang Zemin has continued Deng's evolution away from extremist responses. His government has sought to balance economic changes with financial assistance and training. He has also begun to open party membership to capitalists, who have been barred for years from joining.

Political socialization remains at the core of these differences. Castro continues to fall back on his authoritarian habits to maintain control of Cuba. Jiang alternatively relies on political moderation as a means to maintain order and control.

BIBLIOGRAPHY

Almond, Gabriel, "Communism and Political Culture Theory," *Comparative Politics*, Vol. 15, No. 2, January 1983, pp. 127-138.

Arendt, Hannah, *The Origins of Totalitarianism*, New York: Harcourt Brace Jovanovich, 1973.

Averill, Stephen C., "The Chinese Revolution Re-evaluated," *Problems of Communism*, January-February 1989, pp. 76-84.

Baxter, Kevin, "Cuba's Suspended Revolution," *The Nation*, August, 24, 1998, Vol. 267, No. 6, p. 20.

BBC Monitoring Asia Pacific, "China's Party Daily on Changing Ideology Not Being a Negation of Marxism," June 13, 2002.

BBC Monitoring International Reports, "Xinhua Carries 'Full Text' of Report on Social, Economic Development Plan," March 17, 2002.

Bertsch, Gary, Robert Clark and David Wood, *Comparing Political Systems: Power and Policy in Three Worlds*, Fourth Edition, New York: Macmillan, 1991.

Black, George, "Cuba: The Revolution; Toward Victory Always, But When?" *The Nation*, Vol. 247, No. 11, October 23, 1988, p. 373.

Boadle, Anthony, "Cuban Economic Downturn Deepens Island's Hardship," *Reuters*, June 10, 2002.

Calbreath, Dean, "Displaced Laborers Lashing Out Against China's WTO Reforms," *San Diego Union-Tribune*, July 15, 2001, p. A1.

Chang, David Wen-Wei, *China Under Deng Xiaoping*, New York: St. Martin's Press, 1988.

De Cordoba, Jose, "Cuba's Weak Economy May be Battered Again," *Wall Street Journal*, June 6, 2002.

Deutsche Presse-Agentur, "Cuba Hastens Approval of Amendment Making Socialism 'Untouchable'," June 24, 2002.

Dominguez, Jorge I., *Cuba: Order and Revolution*, Cambridge: Belknap Press, 1978.

Economist, "Bitter Pills," June 15, 2002, p. 38.

Economist, "Out of Puff: A Survey of China," June 15, 2002, pp. 1-16.

Economist, "The Three Big Thoughts," June 15, 2000, via http:\\www.economist.com.

Economist, "Cuba's Economy: Mala Vista Social Club," October 23, 1999, p. 37.

Farber, Samuel, *Before Stalinism: The Rise and Fall of Soviet Democracy*, New York: Verso, 1990.

Fewsmith, Joseph, *Elite Politics in Contemporary China*, New York: M.E. Sharpe, 2001.

Fletcher, Pascal, "Havana seeks to soothe foreign investors over property measure," *Financial Times*, July 18, 2000, p. 5.

Frank, Marc, "Cuba will Downsize Sugar Industry by 50 Percent—Minister," *Reuters*, June 18, 2002.

Fritsch, Peter, "Cuban Activist Exploits System in Bold Petition Drive for Rights," *Wall Street Journal*, May 13, 2002, p. A1.

Gardner, John, *Chinese Politics and the Succession to Mao*, New York: Holmes & Meier, 1982.

George, Alexander L., "The 'Operational Code:' A Neglected Approach to the Study of Political Leaders and Decision-Making," *International Studies Quarterly*, Vol. 13, No. 2, June 1969, pp. 190-222.

Gittings, John, *China Changes Face: The Road from Revolution 1949-1989*, Oxford: Oxford University Press, 1989.

Grogg, Patricia, "Cuba: Workers Laid off from Sugar Industry Promised New Jobs," *Inter Press Service*, June 19, 2002.

Hammond, Jack, "The High Cost of Dollars," *NACLA Report of the Americas*, March-April 1999, Vol 32, No. 5, p. 24.

Hayward, Susana, "Castro-Fox Tape Stirs Diplomatic Tiff," *San Antonio Express News*, April 24, 2002, p. 1A.

Holsti, Ole R., "The Belief System and National Images: A Case Study," *Journal of Conflict Resolution*, Vol. 6, No. 3, 1962, pp. 244-252.

Hutzler, Charles, "A Twist in China's Succession Script," *Wall Street Journal*, July 2, 2002, www.wsj.com.

Hyman, Herbert H., *Political Socialization: A Study in the Psychology of Political Behavior*, Glencoe, IL: Free Press, 1959.

Kamrava, Mehran, "Causes and Leaders of Revolutions," *Journal of Social, Political and Economic Studies*, Vol. 15, No. 1, Spring 1990, pp. 79-89.

Karol, K.S., *Guerrillas in Power: The Course of the Cuban Revolution*, London: Jonathan Cape, 1971.

Keddie, Nikki, ed., *Debating Revolutions*, New York: New York University Press, 1995.

Kynge, James, "China's New Leaders Prepare to Take Centre Stage," *Financial Times*, July 5, 2002, p. 6.

Kynge, James, "The Leader with the Iron Face May be Getting Rusty," *Financial Times*, March 12, 2001, p. 12.

Lo, Carlos Wing-hung, "Political Liberalization in the People's Republic of China: Its Linkage to the Mainland-Taiwan Reunification," *East Asia: An International Quarterly*, Vol. 17, No. 4, Winter 1999, pp. 78-110.

Martin, Joanne, Maureen Scully and Barbara Levitt, "Injustice and Legitimation of Revolution: Damning the Past, Excusing the Present, and Neglecting the Future," *Journal of Personality and Social Psychology*, Vol. 59, No. 2, 1990, pp. 281-290.

Marx, Karl, *The Eighteenth Brumaire of Louis Bonaparte*, Peking: Foreign Language Press, 1978.

Monreal, Pedro, "Sea Changes: The New Cuban Economy," *NACLA Report on the Americas*, March-April 1999, Vol. 32, No. 5, p. 21.

O'Connor, James, *The Origins of Socialism in Cuba*, Ithaca: Cornell University Press, 1970.

Pérez-López, Jorge F., "Coveting Beijing, but Imitating Moscow: Cuba's Economic Reforms in a Comparative Perspective," *Cuba in Transition*, ASCE 1995, pp. 11-20.

Peters, Philip, "Cuba's Economic Transition and its Implications for U.S. Policy," testimony before the House Ways and Means Trade Subcommittee, May 7, 1998.

Post, Jerrold M., "Cuba's Maximal Leader under Maximal Stress," *Problems of Post-Communism*, March-April 1995, pp. 34-38.

Schweimer, Daniel, "Cuba Calls an End to the Use of US Coinage," *Financial Times*, August 30, 2001, p. 4.

Sequera, Vivian, "Summer in Cuba: As Fans and AC Switch On, Cash-Strapped Economy Feels the Energy Crunch," *Associated Press*, June 13, 2002.

Skocpol, Theda, *States and Social Revolution*, New York: Cambridge University Press, 1979.

Skocpol, Theda, "Social Revolutions and Mass Military Mobilization," *World Politics*, Vol. 40, No. 2, January 1988, pp. 147-168.

Smith, Tony, *Thinking Like a Communist: State and Legitimacy in the Soviet Union, China and Cuba*, New York: W.W. Norton, 1987.

Snow, Anita, "Millions of Workers Get Two Days Off to Watch National Assembly Session on Television," *Associated Press*, June 24, 2002.

Spence, Jonathan D., *The Search for Modern China*, New York: Norton, 1990.

Sullivan, Kevin, "Carter Urges Democracy for Cuba," *Washington Post*, May 15, 2002, p. A1.

Thomas, Hugh, *Cuba: The Pursuit of Freedom*, New York: Da Capo Press, 1998.

Wade, Christian, "Workers in China Brace for Tough Measures," *United Press International*, November 15, 2001.

Waldron, Arthur, "China's Disguised Failure," *Financial Times*, July 4, 2002, p. 11.

Washington Post, "'Tiananmen Papers' Provokes Crackdown," June 5, 2002.

Wiarda, Howard J., "Cuba, Castro and the Post-Communist World," *Problems of Post-Communism*, March-April 1995, pp. 29-33.

Wu, An-chia, "The Thought of Mao Tse-tung: A New Version of Marxism-Leninism?" in *Ideology and Politics in Twentieth Century China*, King-yuh Chang, ed., Taipei: Institute of International Relations, 1988, pp. 34-48.

AN EVALUATION OF
FOUR DECADES OF CUBAN HEALTHCARE

Felipe Eduardo Sixto[1]

In 1958, on the eve of the revolution, Cuba ranked in the first, second or third place in Latin America with respect to its healthcare indicators. However, there were notable differences between the urban and rural sectors. In the last four decades, the Cuban government has successfully reduced those gaps. For example in 1959 there was only 1 rural hospital; by 1989 there were 64. In addition, Cuba has been able to maintain and even raise many of its health indicators to levels comparable to those of industrialized nations.

Although there is no doubt that the Revolution has had a positive impact on healthcare, many gaps persist within regions, particularly with regard to availability of potable water and sanitation. Furthermore, during the economic crisis of the 1990s—during which the Cuban economy shrank by 30 to 40 percent—there were setbacks in many healthcare indicators, e.g., sanitation, food consumption, and, to a lesser degree, morbidity.

This paper is divided into four parts. The first is an overview of the evolution of the healthcare system and its organizational structure. The second describes the policy and inputs of the healthcare system. The third analyzes the performance of the system over the past four decades. And the fourth compares Cuba with other countries in Latin America with regard to

seven health indicators and evaluates Cuba's health care system.

BRIEF OVERVIEW OF THE EVOLUTION OF THE HEALTHCARE SYSTEM
Eve of the Revolution

According to many scholars, Cuba's health ideology and organization are not purely the results of the socialist nature of the revolution (Feinsilver 1993, Figueras 1998). Many precursors can be found in the pre-revolutionary health ideology. "Mutualism," a prepaid health plan much like the health maintenance organizations in the United States during the 1970s, were widespread in Cuba during the 1930s to the 1950s (Feinsilver 1993; Macdonald 1999). These mutual-aid societies provided comprehensive medical services for their members. In 1958 there were over 100 mutual aid clinics and cooperatives. However, they were mainly concentrated in Havana and other large cities like Santiago de Cuba, Cienfuegos, Camagüey and Santa Clara (Mesa-Lago 2002).

Foundation: 1959-1970

Cuba differs from other socialist countries in the way it began its allocation of health services. Other nations initially provided health services for the industrialized urban labor force. Because rural areas were neglected and suffered the worst health indicators,

---

1. This paper has been published in Spanish by the Friedrich-Ebert-Stiftung foundation and *Nueva Sociedad*. I am deeply indebted to Carmelo Mesa-Lago for assistance throughout all stages of this paper. I am also thankful to the Florida International University's Cuban Research Institute for funding my field research in Cuba.

the Cuban government initially concentrated on providing health care to the rural sector. On January 23, 1960, the Rural Health Service was established. "This service required all medical school graduates to serve for one year in the rural areas upon graduation and provided for the creation of rural health facilities. In 1961 a rural dental service was added" (Feinsilver 1993, 32). In 1961 the Ministry of Health and Welfare was replaced by the Ministry of Public Health (MINSAP). The new Ministry's role was to oversee the three types of organizations that existed in the health sector: public, mutualist, and private.

In 1960, the public health system initiated the process of providing coverage for the total population, coexisting with the mutualist and private sub-sectors. By 1961, the government had lowered the price of medicines, nationalized pharmaceutical companies, private hospitals, and mutualist cooperatives as well as expanded the network of medical institutions so that the Cuban National Healthcare System (SNS) had become totally socialized (Bravo 1998; Mesa-Lago 2002; Sixto 2000). The nationalization of mutual-aid coops and private hospital provoked the exodus of nearly two thirds of all medical professionals (2,000 out of 6,000 physicians left). This brain drain had a significant impact on many outputs of the Cuban healthcare system in the first half of the 1960s (for example the infant mortality rate increased from 33.4 in 1958 to 46.7 in 1969).

Consolidation of the System: 1970-1979

During this period, many of the policies of the previous stage were intensified and new policies implemented, specifically the establishment of policlinics (primary healthcare providers) and the creation of the Community Health Program. The goal of the Cuban government in 1959 was to "remedy the inequalities in healthcare and to establish a rapid, transitional, free, and comprehensive national service that reaches urban, rural and mountainous populations in all 6 provinces," hence, policlinics, regional medical units and provincial hospitals were developed (Danielson 1979, 130-132). By 1964, most health centers were transformed into policlinics. These policlinics were organized as the basic Cuban unit of health services, while the larger hospital units contin-

ued to be providers of second and third level care (Danielson 1979, 165).

Under the policlinic program, all residents within a given zone have the same physician (MINSAP 1999). This ideally promotes a better understanding of patients and their environment by physicians. Doctors and other healthcare professionals worked in conjunction with neighborhood communities. This "team approach" became the basis of the community health program. Cuba's system used the team approach to provide preventive and curative health care through an integrated national health system with the active participation of the communities served (Feinsilver 1993). Doctor and nurse teams had to attend patients in the policlinic, as well as at home, school, day-care, and even the workplace. In 1976, the nation was divided and organized into 14 provinces and 169 municipalities. The MINSAP was placed under the Council of Ministries and the organs of direction of the state (MINSAP 1999).

Even though the community health program was well organized, it had many setbacks. For example, care in the community was supposed to focus on prevention. According to Feinsilver, the problem was that this program did not allow medical teams to know their patients on a personal basis and often preventive care and follow-up visits were not provided. To make the situation worse, patients crowed emergency rooms at hospitals where they believed they could receive better treatment, thereby making it harder for policlinics to offer care (Feinsilver 1993, 40). In an effort to correct the problems associated with the policlinic and the community health program, the Cuban government later established the Family Doctor Program.

New Health Law and Family Doctor Program: 1980-1991

In 1983, the National Assembly enacted the Public Health Law, which laid out state activities to provide healthcare to all Cuban citizens. The law designated MINSAP as the steering agency of the national health system and specified the services it would carry out, in addition to determining the functions of local health authorities. The National Health System

Figure 1. Organization of Health System

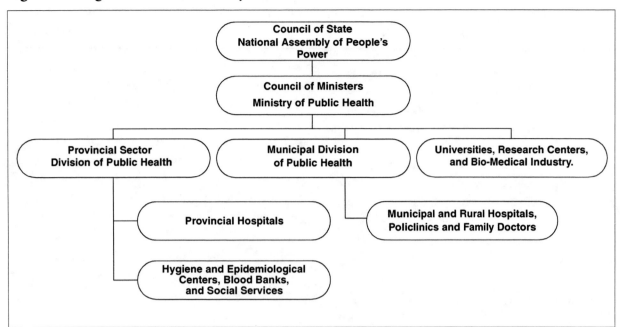

(NHS) is the only system operating in the country; it is comprehensive, regionalized and decentralized.

The NHS is organized in three levels (see Figure 1). The MINSAP represents the national, highest level, and serves as the steering agency. Directly under the MINSAP are university centers, medical research centers, and the medical-pharmaceutical production and distribution industry. The second level corresponds to "the Provincial Public Health Offices...which are under the direct financial and administrative authority of the provincial assemblies" (PAHO 1999, 3). Below the provincial governments are the provincial and inter-municipal hospitals, blood banks, provincial health and epidemiology centers, and training centers for health professionals. The third and lowest level is the municipal one. The Municipal Public Health Offices oversee policlinics, rural, local and municipal hospitals, oral health clinics, social welfare institutions for the elderly and persons with mental or physical disabilities, maternity homes and other establishments.

In 1984, Cuba initiated the Family Doctor Program, whose goal was to place a doctor and a nurse team in every neighborhood. This program was designed to project the health system's resources further into the community than the previous systems had been able

to do (MINSAP 2000). By 1985, the Family Doctor Program already served 1.3 million people. Preliminary results indicate it has reduced cost through decreased hospitalization and emergency room use. Rates of hospitalization have been cut drastically since 1985. Preventive medicine sharply reduced many diseases. "Keeping people from becoming ill cost only a tenth of treating them once they have become sick" (MacDonald 1999, 141). The family doctors are also having vast effects on rural health, however because the population is dispersed throughout the countryside, the doctor and nurse teams must continually visit homes, farms, and sugar mills, making the program costly; inefficiency has also plagued the urban areas because of well-established policlinics (Feinsilver 1993, 46).

The Family Doctor Program "has been criticized in the First World for leading to the trivialization of medical practice and for failing to provide doctors with sufficient variety and complexity of cases to maintain their medical knowledge" (Feinsilver 1993, 46). The program is also very costly and inefficient; however, it has impressed health officials, researchers, international organization personnel, and politicians from the developing world (Garfield and Sloan 1997; Garfield and Holtz 2000).

Crisis and Deterioration: 1991-Present

In 1991, with the collapse of the Soviet Union, a severe economic crisis occurred and a "Special Period in Time of Peace" began as a euphemism for an emergency crisis program. The termination of Soviet and CMEA aid as well as drastic reduction of trade led to the decrease of GDP by 35 to 40 percent. In 2000, GDP was still 18 percent below the 1989 level (Mesa-Lago 2002). The crisis had a negative impact on the importation of medical equipment, spare parts and medicines. The lack of supplies accompanied by a deterioration of basic infrastructure (potable water and sanitation) resulted in a setback of many of the previous accomplishments. The strengthening of the U.S. economic embargo in the second half of the 1990s contributed to these problems. Starting in 1997, the government implemented many austerity measures along with various organic food and herbal medicine programs. By 2000, many of the indicators that had deteriorated had seen some improvement, (e.g., the percent of children born underweight, which increased from 7.3 in 1989 to 9.0 in 1993, decreased to 6.1 in 2000.) However, many inequalities among provinces arose, particularly in income distribution (due to family remittances), food consumption and basic health indicators.

POLICIES AND INPUTS INTO THE HEALTHCARE SYSTEM

Finance

The National Health System is completely financed by state resources. It is also highly decentralized: 92.4% of expenditures for public health are financed from municipal budgets. The government's national budget allocation for health rose nearly 35 times, from 51 million pesos in 1960 to 1,857 million pesos in 2000. In the 1990s, health sector expenditures exhibited a rising trend, from 98 pesos per capita in 1990 to 166 pesos per capita in 2000, an increase of 69 percent (see Table 1). However, the real value of those expenditures was severely reduced by inflation. (The series between 1976-89 and 1989-99 cannot be technically connected because they have different base years.) Real expenditures increased from 34.7 to 91.1 pesos in 1976-1989, but declined from 65.3 to 44.4 pesos in 1989-1999 (Table 1).

In 1989 the Cuban government spent US$227.3 million in the importation of health-related products, but that amount was reduced to US$67 million in 1993; although such imports rose to US$112 million in 1997, they were still half their value before the crisis (MINSAP 1999). In 1997, 38 percent of the healthcare budget was assigned to primary care and 46 percent to hospital care. Of the total health budget, 50 to 54 percent was spent on salaries (Figueras 1998). However, since the early 1990s, there has been a sharp decline (15 percent in 1990-94; 3.1 percent in 1997) in the expenditures on the maintenance and construction of basic health sector infrastructure, as well as on hospitals and policlinics (MINSAP 1999). The lack of investment in water and sanitation has contributed to the increase of contagious diseases (see below).

Thus, "the out-of pocket expenditures assumed by families include drugs prescribed on an outpatient basis, hearing, dental, and orthopedic processes, wheelchairs, crutches, and similar devices, as well as eyeglasses" (PAHO 1999, 7). Many families spend over 400 pesos a month on these items while the average monthly salary in 2000 was 234 pesos (ONE 2001; Sixto 2001).

Since the early 1960s, Cuba has had a high dependence on external capital to finance its healthcare system. In 1960-90, the Soviet Union provided about US$65 billion in aid and loans, which allowed the release of funds for healthcare. In addition, most equipment and inputs for the health system and the production of medicines were imported from the USSR and CMEA. With the collapse of the socialist camp, a severe vacuum occurred (Mesa-Lago 2000). In 1995, the Pan American Health Organization (PAHO)/World Health Organization (WHO), the United Nations Population Fund, the United Nations Development Program (UNDP) and UNICEF lent US$3 million to Cuba; they provided another US$20 million annually in humanitarian aid during the 1990s.

Infrastructure

Basic to a healthy population are access to potable water and sanitation. The Cuban government has made a significant effort to improve the access to po-

Table 1.   Inputs to the Cuban Health-Care System: 1958-2000
    (Finances and General Indicators)

Years	Total Budget Expenditure on Health Care (Million Pesos)	Per Capita Expenditure on Health Care Nominal (Pesos)	Per Capita Expenditure on Health Care Real (Pesos)[a] Mesa-Lago	Togores	Daily Per Capita Consumption of Calories	Induced Abortions per 1,000 Women	Induced Abortion per 100 Pregnancies	% of population with Access to Safe Drinking Water	% of population with Access to Sanitation
1958	20.5	3.04	…	…	2,740	…	…	…	…
1959	25.6	3.72	…	…	2,870	…	…	…	…
1960	51.2	7.30	…	…	…	…	…	…	…
1961	77.0	10.73	…	…	2,730	…	…	…	…
1962	103.3	14.09	…	…	2,410	…	…	…	…
1963	115.7	15.47	…	…	2,320	…	…	…	…
1964	130.3	17.05	…	…	…	…	…	…	…
1965	148.8	19.07	…	…	2,665	…	…	…	…
1966	157.6	19.82	…	…	2,452	…	…	…	…
1967	158.5	19.57	…	…	…	…	…	…	…
1968	180.2	21.83	…	…	…	…	…	…	…
1969	210.9	25.07	…	…	…	…	…	…	…
1970	216.4	25.25	…	…	2,688	36.1	24.2	56	44
1971	224.4	25.89	…	…	2,657	…	…	…	…
1972	232.5	26.33	…	…	…	…	…	…	…
1973	240.5	26.72	…	…	…	…	…	…	…
1974	281.3	30.73	…	…	2,652	…	…	…	…
1975	304.1	32.73	…	…	2,726	57.4	39.5	…	…
1976	323.7	34.19	34.7	…	2,645	…	…	…	…
1977	322.1	33.58	34.2	…	2,720	…	…	…	…
1978	390.8	40.32	42.7	…	2,759	…	…	…	…
1979	409.2	41.87	42.6	…	2,866	…	…	…	…
1980	440.1	45.01	45.0	…	2,892	42.1	43.2	74	91
1981	558.9	57.29	52.8	…	2,855	43.0	44.3	…	…
1982	594.6	60.60	55.6	…	2,873	50.5	44.2	…	…
1983	668.0	67.62	61.8	…	2,910	48.7	43.4	…	…
1984	740.4	74.40	68.1	…	2,955	53.3	45.7	…	…
1985	794.2	78.97	72.9	…	2,929	55.0	43.3	…	…
1986	875.2	85.88	81.7	…	2,948	50.6	49.1	…	…
1987	922.2	89.67	85.6	…	…	47.5	45.8	…	…
1988	978.9	94.08	88.8	…	2,864	48.3	45.0	…	…
1989	1,015.6	96.66	91.1	66.9	2,845	46.8	44.7	…	…
1990	1,045.1	98.56	…	65.3	…	45.6	43.9	89	…
1991	1,038.4	97.11	…	53.0	…	38.3	43.9	…	…
1992	1,038.7	95.99	…	30.4	…	33.8	41.1	…	…
1993	1,174.9	107.57	…	16.4	1,863	26.6	36.0	…	…
1994	1,166.3	106.42	…	19.3	…	27.4	37.5	…	…
1995	1,221.9	111.31	…	37.9	2,218	25.9	36.0	91	92
1996	1,310.1	119.03	…	41.3	2,456	25.9	37.1	91	…
1997	1,382.9	125.31	…	43.2	…	24.8	34.1	93[b]	88
1998	1,473.1	132.44	…	44.4	…	22.8	32.9	93	…
1999	1,710.6	153.52	…	53.0	…	24.3	32.0	92	90
2000	1,857.0	165.99	…	…	…	23.0	34.5	…	…

Source: CEE, 1980, 1985, 1991; ONE, 1998, 1999, 2000, 2001; MINSAP, 1999, 2000, 2001; Mesa-Lago, 2000, 2002

a.   Author's calculations using Mesa-Lago's consumer price index for 1976-1989 and Togores' for 1989-1999. Technically the two series cannot be connected.
b.   Average from 1990-1997.

table water throughout the island and since the 1960s, has been successful in reducing the urban-rural gaps. In 1970, 56 percent of the total population

had access to safe drinking water; in 1980, it had increased to 74.1 percent, in 1989 to 89.0 percent, and in 1999 to 92 percent (see Table 1). However once the definition of potable water is broken down by source and quality, the urban-rural gap rises considerably. For example, in 1981, 89.8 percent of the urban population had access to safe water, while only 32.9 percent in the rural sector. In addition, the vast majority of the rural dwellings were considered as having "easy access" to water, that is, the water was available outside the dwelling. With the decline of the Cuban economy in the 1990s, the country's ability to produce chlorine declined, reducing the population covered by chlorinated water systems from 98 percent in 1988 to 26 percent in 1994. The proportion of the population without potable water increased from 10 to 12 percent in the period 1990–1994 (Garfield and Holtz 2000).

By 1994, the proportion of the population with water connections to their dwellings declined to 81 percent in urban areas and to 24 percent in rural areas (Garfield and Holtz 2000). In 2000, 83.7 percent of the urban population had access to water in the dwelling compared to only 40.5 percent of the rural population. The access to safe water through "easy access" outside the dwelling and of public service in the rural sector had been reduced by nearly 55 percent of the population (Mesa-Lago 2002). Of the total volume of water supplied to the population, "72% is of underground origin, and 28% is from surface sources; 68.3% of the population (7.5 million) receives water from aqueducts" (PAHO 1999, 216). The rest of the population is served by tank trucks and other means.

Access of the population to sanitation increased from 43.8 percent in 1970 to 90 percent in 1990. In 2000, 97 percent of the urban sector had access to sanitation, compared to 83.7 percent in the rural sector; out of the latter, 90 percent relied on septic tanks and outhouses. In 1997, the rural-urban disparity was 74 percent with respect to potable water and 80.7 percent regarding sanitation (CIEM 1997, 55 and 57 as cited by Mesa-Lago 2002, 15). These figures are relatively low compared to Latin America.

Along with the infrastructure of sanitation and potable water, healthcare facilities are fundamental for the provision of services to the population. One specific indicator of the distribution or accessibility of healthcare facilities is the number of rural hospitals and policlinics. In 1958, there was only one rural hospital on the island, while by 1997 there were 64. Many of them were very poorly equipped and maintained, however (Garfield and Holtz 2000). In 1958 there were 58 policlinics, compared to 440 in 1997 (see Table 2). Another measure of access to healthcare is the distribution of clinics. In 1970, there were 3.4 clinics per 10,000 inhabitants on the island. With various programs to distribute the number of doctors and their clinics all over the island (Family Doctor Program), the number of offices grew to 7.2 in 2000.

With more offices, clinics, and hospitals available to the population, the percentage of people born in health institutions increased from 91.5 in 1970 to nearly 100 percent in the late 1980s (see Table 2). The hospitalization rate per 100 people rose from 12.6 in 1970 to a peak of 16.0 in 1985; the rate then dropped in the next 15 years to 11.9 in 2000 (see Table 2). Some scholars attribute this decrease to the family doctor program (Feinsilver 1993; Figueras 1998; and McDonald 2000).

The number of medical hospital beds per 1000 inhabitants increased from 4.2 in 1958, to 5.3 in 1965 and 6.1 in 1995. However, many of these beds were not being occupied and were costing too much. This led the government to close down some health centers, hence, the rate of medical hospital beds per 1000 inhabitants declined to 5.2 in 2000. Mesa-Lago has estimated that the "real average number" of beds per 1,000 inhabitants rose from 4.2 in 1975 to 5.5 in 1990 and then decreased to 4.7 in 2000 (Mesa-Lago 2002). Even with the reduction of beds, the occupancy rate decreased significantly in 1980-2000, from 80.4 to 69.4 percent (Table 2). This inefficiency costs the government significant funds that can be better allocated to other areas badly in need of resources.

Personnel

Historically, the number of physicians in Cuba has been substantially high, particularly in relation to Latin American countries. Thus in 1958 there were 9.2 physicians per 10,000 inhabitants. Because of the exodus of 2,000 physicians, the rate dropped to 5.4

Table 2.   Inputs to the Cuban Health-Care System: 1958-2000 *(Hospitals)*

Years	Total Number of Hospitals	Total Number of Rural Hospitals	Total Number of Policlinics	Hospitalization Rate per 100 People	Hospitalization Rate in Maternity Centers per 100 Born Children	% of infants Born Alive in a Health Institution	Hospital Beds per 1,000		Hospital Bed Occupancy Rate (%)	Average Length of Stay (Days)
							Normal	Real		
1958	230	1	140ª	...	...	...	4.2	...	...	...
1960	...	...	...	...	...	...	4.3	...	...	...
1965	...	43	171	...	...	...	5.3	...	...	...
1970	...	...	...	12.6	...	91.5	5.0	...	...	...
1971	...	...	...	12.9	...	95.8	4.6	...	...	...
1972	...	...	...	13.1	4.9	97.6	4.4	...	...	...
1973	...	...	...	13.2	7.5	98.0	4.3	...	...	...
1974	...	...	...	13.2	10.2	97.6	4.2	...	...	...
1975	...	58	339	13.4	12.8	98.7	4.2	4.2	...	...
1976	...	...	...	12.7	13.7	98.1	4.1	...	...	...
1977	...	...	...	12.5	16.2	97.0	4.1	...	...	...
1978	...	...	...	12.6	17.7	98.2	4.2	...	...	...
1979	...	...	...	12.3	18.5	98.3	4.3	...	...	...
1980	258	53	386	13.0	19.1	98.5	4.4	4.3	80.4	9.2
1981	...	...	...	13.9	20.8	98.9	4.5	...	...	...
1982	...	...	...	14.3	18.6	98.9	4.6	...	...	...
1983	...	...	...	14.6	18.9	98.4	4.7	...	...	...
1984	...	...	...	15.1	19.1	98.7	4.7	4.7	...	...
1985	...	...	...	16.0	20.3	98.8	4.7	4.7	...	...
1986	...	...	...	15.8	23.4	99.3	4.8	4.7	...	...
1987	...	70	422	15.5	24.0	99.4	5.0	4.8	...	...
1988	264	...	...	15.5	23.2	99.8	5.1	5.0	76.9	9.9
1989	...	...	...	15.5	24.6	99.8	5.3	5.1	83.9	9.9
1990	...	65	418	15.2	24.0	99.8	6.0	5.3	78.5	10.0
1991	269	63	421	14.2	26.1	99.8	6.0	5.5	...	...
1992	272	63	423	13.5	27.9	99.8	6.0	5.5	...	...
1993	279	64	427	12.7	29.2	99.8	6.0	5.5	71.3	10.4
1994	280	64	435	12.9	32.0	99.8	6.0	5.5	...	...
1995	281	64	440	13.1	33.1	99.8	6.0	5.5	...	...
1996	281	64	442	12.9	34.9	99.8	6.0	5.4	...	...
1997	283	64	440	13.1	33.6	99.9	6.1	5.5	70.9	9.8
1998	284	64	440	12.5	34.6	99.9	6.0	5.4	...	...
1999	...	63	442	12.3	36.7	99.9	5.5	4.9	...	...
2000	270	62	440	11.9	40.3	99.9	5.2	4.7	69.4	9.4

Source: CEE, 1980, 1985, 1991; ONE, 1998, 1999, 2000, 2001; MINSAP, 1999, 2000, 2001; Mesa-Lago, 2000, 2002; Mesa-Lago and Hernández 1964.

a.   The figure is a gross underestimation of the total number of clinics when mutual-aid, cooperatives, and private practices are added. In 1958 there were 140 medical cooperatives in Cuba and 230 hospitals (Mesa-Lago y Hernández 1964: 160).

in 1962. With an increase of enrollment in medical schools at universities, the rate reached 10.0 in 1975 and 36.1 in 1990. Even in the midst of the economic crisis, the number of physicians and the rate continued to grow to 58.2 in 1999 (see Table 3). During the 1980s and until 1994, the number of medical school graduates rose, but in 1995-2000 it declined by 61 percent. While 4,780 medical students graduated in 1993, only 1,840 did so in 2000. The number of medical students enrolled also declined from 36,660 in the school year 1994/95 to 25,311 in 1997/98. To date, the decline in graduates has not affected the number of doctors; however, as rates of enrollment and graduation continue to decline, as also do mean salaries and incentives, the number of physicians is sure to diminish. Because there is a large surplus of doctors in Cuba, and they are not allowed to work in private practice, many doctors opt to find other occupations, particularly in the tourism sector and providing services such as taxi drivers.

Table 3.   Inputs to the Cuban Health-Care System: 1958-2000 *(Health Personnel)*

Years	Physicians per 10,000 inhabitants	Dentists per 10,000 inhabitants	Workers in Health Care system (thousands)a	Nurses per 10,000 inhabitants	Total Number of Medical Students Graduating
1958	9.2	...	...	1.9	728
1959	...	...	...	...	...
1960	...	...	...	...	...
1961	...	...	...	...	335
1962	5.4	...	...	5.9	434
1963	8.9	...	...	...	334
1964	8.6	...	...	...	312
1965	7.9	1.5	...	12.3	395
1966	8.7	...	...	...	380
1967	8.7	...	...	...	433
1968	7.1	...	...	...	616
1969	7.1	...	...	...	940
1970	7.2	1.6	...	13.8	700
1971	7.1	...	...	...	432
1972	7.3	...	...	...	853
1973	7.7	...	122	...	951
1974	8.8	...	131	...	1,269
1975	10.0	2.5	134	22.8	1,361
1976	11.2	...	138	...	1,477
1977	14.5	...	141	...	1,105
1978	14.8	...	149	...	579
1979	15.4	...	152	...	683
1980	15.6	3.7	158	27.8	764
1981	16.6	4.3	180	...	1,012
1982	17.2	4.1	196	...	1,087
1983	19.1	4.4	218	...	2,114
1984	20.6	4.7	233	...	1,945
1985	22.8	5.3	249	42.4	2,551
1986	25.1	5.6	264	...	3,041
1987	27.3	5.8	275	...	2,841
1988	30.0	5.9	280	...	3,401
1989	33.1	6.2	291	61.4	3,734
1990	36.5	6.6	299	65.1	4,223
1991	39.9	7.0	303	66.1	4,241
1992	43.3	7.4	311	68.0	4,583
1993	46.7	7.8	308	66.5	4,780
1994	49.3	8.1	313	65.4	4,627
1995	51.8	8.3	320	70.4	4,019
1996	54.6	8.7	329	68.9	3,534
1997	56.8	8.9	340	73.3	3,255
1998	57.1	8.9	346	74.2	2,271
1999	58.2	8.9	363	78.3	2,308
2000	59.0	8.9	360	74.3	1,840

Source: CEE, 1980, 1985, 1991; ONE, 1998, 1999, 2000, 2001; MINSAP, 1999, 2000, 2001; Mesa-Lago, 2000, 2002.

a.   Includes medical technicians and management personnel, but excludes physicians and nurses.

Cuba also improved its rates of dentists per 10,000 inhabitants over the past 40 years: from 1.5 in 1965 to 8.9 in 2000. The same trend is evident in nurses: from 1.9 in 1958 to 74.3 in 2000 (See Table 3).

Preventive Services

After Cuba and the United States ended all diplomatic relations in 1961, the Soviet Union became Cuba's primary supplier of medical equipment and medicines. The Soviet Union provided 94 percent of Cuba's imports of medical equipment in 1961-1988. After the collapse of the Soviet Union, Cuba's imports of medical equipment and medicines dropped dramatically. During the worst part of the economic crisis of the 1990s, Cuba had a severe lack of medicines. The supply of raw materials required to produce 85 percent of all drugs consumed in Cuba was halted with the collapse of the Soviet Union, resulting in the lack of 300 medicines (Mesa-Lago, 2000, 324). MINSAP began directing physicians to conserve and control the existing medicines for the neediest. The government also resorted to the use of alternative medicines. Because Cubans do not have a strong traditional reliance of herbal medicine, it was not an easy task to persuade the population to use alternative medications (Barrett 1993, 3).

The oil shortage caused by the collapse of the Soviet Union—the Soviet Union supplied 92 percent of Cuba's total fuel consumption in 1989—also affected the healthcare system. Soviet supply of crude oil fell 61 percent, from 7.8 million tons in 1987 to 3 million tons in 1995, while the supply of oil derivatives decreased by 52 percent (Mesa-Lago 2000, 332). As gasoline supplies ran low and spare parts became scarce, ambulances and other health-related transportation equipment became idle. Furthermore, the supply of electricity fell tremendously, so that the hours of laboratory and clinical operation were cut drastically. Sanitary conditions also deteriorated because of lack of gasoline needed to fuel garbage trucks. The number of operating garbage trucks declined from 200 to 99 in Havana, and infrequent pickups resulted in garbage piling up and the spread of rats (Mesa-Lago 2000). As an analyst observed, "piles of refuse were common in Havana's streets as it remained uncollected for months" (Barrett 1993, 2).

With the cut of Soviet aid and subsidies, the Cuban government also had no choice but to significantly expand food rationing: "rationing expanded to virtually all consumer goods in 1991-1994, and out of 20 products, the quotas of 17 had been cut or shifted from free distribution to rationing. A total of 28 food products and 180 consumer goods that were 'free'

became rationed. The situation deteriorated further in 1993-1994 when rationing provided only half of the monthly food minimum requirements" (Mesa-Lago 2000, 336). The per capita consumption of calories, which was at an all time high of 2,897 calories per day in 1980, severely dropped to 1,863 in 1993; it partly recovered to 2,456 in 1996, still well below the 2,740 of 1958 (See Table 1). Per capita consumption of proteins also dropped from 77.9 grams per day in 1988 to 46.0 in 1993 (Garfield and Holtz 2000). Insufficient calories and proteins contributed to an increase of the percent of children born with low weight (under 2,500 grams), from 7.3 in 1989 to 9.0 in 1993 (See Table 4).

Because of the situation explained above, the government implemented several programs in an attempt to maintain health standards. The first and most important was a reorientation toward primary healthcare and a strengthening of infant and maternal care. According to MINSAP, these two groups of the population were the two that required the most funding and care (MINSAP 1999). Between 1990 and 2000, the hospitalization rate in maternity centers per 100 born children nearly doubled from 24.0 to 40.3 (see Table 2). The same trend is evident in the rate of visits per 1,000 inhabitants under 1 year of age to pediatric doctors, which doubled from 20.8 to 42.4.

Another important achievement of the revolution has been the provision of almost universal vaccinations (95%), which began in the late 1960s. In 1970-1975 a significant increase in all vaccinations took place, but the numbers began to drop in the early 1980s and even further during the decade of the 90s (see Table 5). In 1970-1996 for BCG,[2] Duplex and Triple DPT[3] vaccinations decreased by over 50 percent. Although Cuba's vaccination program has helped eradicate many contagious diseases (polio, diphtheria, tetanus, and rubella), in 1991-1996, with the decline of vaccination and a deterioration of sanitation and the basic infrastructure, some diseases have in-

---

2. BCG is an anti-tuberculosis vaccine.

3. Triple DPT is a vaccine against diphtheria, whopping cough and tetanus.

Table 4. Outputs of the Cuban Health-Care System: 1953-2000
(General Indicators)

Years	Maternal Mortality Rate per 100,000	Infant Mortality Rate per 1,000	Under 5 Mortality Rate per 1,000	% of Children Born Under Weight	Mortality 65 Years and Above	Life Expectancy at birth	
						CEPAL[a]	Cuba
1953	...	35.0	...	...	...	...	...
1955	145.0	...	...	...	...	...	...
1956	134.0	...	...	...	...	...	...
1957	126.5	...	...	...	...	...	...
1958	125.3	33.4	...	...	...	...	...
1959	115.5	34.7	...	...	...	...	...
1960	120.1	37.3	...	...	...	...	64.0
1961	100.1	39.0	...	...	...	...	...
1962	117.9	41.7	...	...	...	...	...
1963	111.0	38.1	...	...	...	...	...
1964	112.2	37.8	...	...	...	...	...
1965	109.1	37.8	...	...	...	65.4	67.2
1966	91.3	37.2	...	...	...	...	...
1967	89.2	36.4	...	...	...	...	...
1968	83.0	38.2	...	...	...	...	...
1969	85.0	46.7	...	...	...	...	68.4
1970	70.4	38.7	43.8	...	52.9	68.6	70.0
1971	67.6	37.4	...	...	...	...	...
1972	52.0	28.3	...	...	...	...	...
1973	55.3	28.9	...	...	...	...	...
1974	58.1	29.0	...	11.7	...	...	...
1975	68.4	27.5	32.6	11.4	47.2	71.0	...
1976	47.5	23.3	...	10.8	48.4	...	...
1977	49.1	24.9	...	10.6	49.8	...	...
1978	45.2	22.4	...	10.4	48.8	...	...
1979	51.5	19.4	...	10.2	46.9	...	...
1980	52.6	19.6	24.3	9.7	47.3	73.1	73.0
1981	40.4	18.5	...	9.5	47.0	...	...
1982	48.2	17.3	...	8.7	46.3	...	...
1983	31.5	16.8	...	8.5	48.2	...	...
1984	31.3	15.0	...	7.9	48.3	...	...
1985	30.8	16.5	19.7	8.2	49.4	73.9	74.5
1986	36.7	13.6	16.7	8.0	47.8	...	...
1987	34.0	13.3	16.1	7.9	49.1	...	...
1988	26.1	11.9	14.6	7.5	49.2	...	74.7
1989	29.2	11.1	13.6	7.3	48.4	...	...
1990	36.1	10.7	13.2	7.6	52.2	74.6	74.7
1991	36.2	10.7	13.4	7.8	51.4	...	...
1992	32.5	10.2	13.1	8.6	52.6	...	...
1993	49.3	9.4	12.2	9.0	55.7	...	...
1994	65.2	9.9	12.8	8.9	54.5	...	...
1995	57.1	9.4	12.5	7.9	52.5	75.3	74.8
1996	44.9	7.9	10.7	7.3	54.9	...	...
1997	50.4	7.2	9.4	6.9	52.3	...	...
1998	47.7	7.1	9.2	6.7	50.2	...	...
1999	52.4	6.5	8.4	6.5	52.2	...	...
2000	55.7	7.2	11.1	6.1	49.7	76.0	...

Source: CEE, 1980, 1985, 1991; CEPAL, 2001; ONE, 1998, 1999, 2000, 2001; MINSAP, 1999, 2000, 2001; Mesa-Lago, 2000, 2002.

a. Five-year average.

Table 5. Inputs to the Cuban Health-Care System: 1963-2000

(Immunized Population by Type of Vaccine)

Years	Polio	BCGa	BCG Under 1 year of age	Duplex	Typhoid	Triple (DPT)a	Tetanus
1963	2,293,256a	...	128,674	355,907	708,881	432,937	882,338
1964	2,455,367a	289,917	289,917	180,312	481,560	236,439	694,645
1965	1,407,631b	368,367	368,367	213,548	458,522	284,370	1,553,966
1966	1,160,905c	338,107	338,107	166,258	439,055	215,418	976,401
1967	462,379d	370,493	370,493	191,963	438,050	255,466	959,421
1970	1,100,277	486,675	486,675	364,824	502,209	516,132	1,433,119
1971	1,080,533	356,279	356,279	316,703	649,525	437,939	1,303,827
1972	1,119,930	307,952	307,952	327,741	789,076	441,798	1,691,259
1973	1,130,271	301,958	301,958	351,012	899,750	429,367	1,858,061
1974	1,14,0519	297,174	297,174	357,944	1,003,315	467,843	2,009,679
1975	1,120,530	250,653	192,414	333,852	1,188,824	450,524	2,287,818
1976	1,077,025	305,006	173,899	295,591	177,905	395,201	1,907,447
1977	980,034	326,287	157,322	253,326	529,525	352,565	1,435,724
1978	928,608	285,089	143,614	267,375	729,534	384,902	1,528,967
1979	939,584	328,253	141,631	266,694	492,401	369,188	1,453,038
1980	852,129	372,689	135,182	305,573	762,546	298,751	1,583,275
1981	861,264	340,430	128,888	283,761	708,334	247,810	1,501,977
1982	787,522	371,912	155,933	259,417	726,159	241,527	1,402,766
1983	787,119	387,769	152,138	230,294	842,690	278,681	1,547,396
1984	777,462	382,350	161,549	196,529	971,511	305,784	1,760,182
1985	801,145	409,192	177,578	156,943	825,364	341,265	1,715,599
1986	842,963	318,226	162,303	115,522	529,546	350,139	1,269,471
1987	824,209	380,601	...	154,934	920,050	333,338	1,278,942
1988	827,983	336,451	...	155,743	691,725	341,985	1,129,262
1990	838,719	299,463	183,471	152,100	542,356	347,269	959,219
1991	816,516	308,194	170,310	179,892	558,721	347,432	925,128
1992	833,755	272,385	153,817	160,381	493,034	310,606	852,639
1993	628,033	194,198	144,728	163,915	553,792	323,300	786,401
1994	616,399	148,847	145,967	206,411	558,488	310,501	862,039
1995	602,041	146,845	146295	119,555	413,622	296,954	561,534
1996	589,544	139,490	139,269	206,004	372,513	279,130	358,361
1997	588,169	151,571	151,423	171,426	467,027	291,260	911,770
1998	604,724	149,604	149,604	169,461	517,041	306,262	1,282,712
1999	598,603	149,819	149,819	106,324	431,411	302,292	1,327,400
2000	617,323	141,596	141,596	184,955	503,647	284,594	920,327

Source: CEE, 1980, 1985, 1991; ONE, 1998, 1999, 2000, 2001; MINSAP, 1999, 2000, 2001; Mesa-Lago, 2000, 2002

a. BCG is an anti-tuberculosis vaccine, while Triple DPT is for Diphtheria and Tetanus.

creased, e.g., tuberculosis, hepatitis, acute diarrhea, and chicken pox (See Table 6).

PERFORMANCE AND OUTPUTS OF THE HEALTHCARE SYSTEM

Infant Mortality

In the 1950s, Cuba already had the lowest infant mortality rate in Latin America: 35 per 1,000 in 1953 and 33.4 in 1958 (See Table 4). In the first decade of the Revolution, the rate increased to 41.7 in 1962 and 46.7 in 1969. This increase was partly due to the exodus of thousands of doctors from the island

and the decrease in imports of medicines, which led to a raise in morbidity. Another reason for the increase was an improvement in the reporting and registration of deaths. In the 1970s, the Cuban government launched a campaign to reduce the infant mortality rate, which eventually led to a rate lower than that in the United States. This campaign was directed at maternal and prenatal care. In 1981-1994, there were 1,381,539 prenatal tests in which 1,863 defects of the neural tube and 1,056 other birth defects were diagnosed. In addition, mothers receive an average of 12 checkups during gestation

Table 6. **Outputs of the Cuban Health-Care System: 1958-2000**
(Reported Cases of Contagious Disease per 100,000 Inhabitants)

Year	Acute Diarrhea	Acute Respiratory Disease	AIDS	Chicken Pox	Diphtheria	Gonorrhea	Hepatitis
1958	...	...	*a	...	2.4	...	...
1959	...	...	*	...	4.7	...	...
1960	...	...	*	...	8.1	...	...
1961	...	...	*	...	19.1	...	5.0
1962	...	...	*	...	19.4	...	51.0
1963	...	...	*	...	12.8	...	64.4
1964	...	...	*	...	8.6	...	70.6
1965	5,707	...	*	118.6	8.2	8.9	115.8
1966	5,876	...	*	138.3	4.6	...	115.1
1967	6,165	...	*	208.2	5.5	...	139.6
1968	6,319	...	*	...	1.6	...	208.6
1969	6,417	...	*	104.6	0.6	...	85.3
1970	7,694	10,162	*	150.1	0.1	2.6	102.6
1971	7,879	...	*	76.3	*	...	151.9
1972	8,038	12,549	*	65.4	*	8.4	114.5
1973	8,286	14,219	*	93.0	*	9.7	133.6
1974	7,317	15,596	*	178.4	*	35.3	205.9
1975	6,876	15,520	*	161.7	*	47.2	217.0
1976	6,346	17,267	*	261.4	*	66.1	145.8
1977	7,358	19,348	*	144.3	*	86.4	123.2
1978	6,920	23,594	*	113.5	*	105.9	172.6
1979	6,951	21,906	*	94.8	*	141.6	225.8
1980	6,839	21,980	*	200.7	*	169.4	208.3
1981	7,836	27,595	*	425.1	*	201.8	147.2
1982	8,732	27,441	*	191.5	*	238.9	208.4
1983	8,527	33,000	*	291.1	*	294.3	101.2
1984	8,777	31,810	*	351.0	*	355.6	78.4
1985	10,487	38,160	*	820.8	*	359.6	209.2
1986	9,824	35,816	0.5	373.2	*	340.0	300.4
1987	11,436	35,452	1.1	374.9	*	352.7	238.3
1988	9,939	40,308	1.3	415.3	*	381.3	165.7
1989	8,842	36,804	1.2	365.6	*	381.3	106.1
1990	9,991	44,271	2.6	353.4	*	334.0	124.2
1991	10,982	41,965	3.4	649.3	*	298.9	323.2
1992	10,112	40,367	6.5	965.9	*	242.8	295.2
1993	10,242	35,448	7.5	397.4	*	227.4	149.5
1994	10,380	35,309	9.3	382.2	*	312.5	163.7
1995	9,261	38,873	10.6	1,137.9	*	411.7	161.1
1996	9,080	45,021	8.9	558.7	*	368.7	186.0
1997	9,122	43,981	11.5	239.8	*	307.6	222.8
1998	8,704	44,178	12.5	196.5	*	266.7	153.7
1999	8,546	46,741	15.7	288.1	*	208.4	162.6
2000	7,703	43,075	15.1	432.1	*	170.4	163.7

Source: CEE, 1980, 1985, 1991; ONE, 1998, 1999, 2000, 2001; MINSAP, 1999, 2000, 2001; Mesa-Lago, 2000, 2002.

a. * = Insignificant or null.

and more than 90% begin their medical visits by the first trimester. Additionally, 97% of children are breastfed upon their discharge from maternal centers, while 70% continue to be breast-fed for four months (Dieterich 1998). By 1984, the infant mortality rate

had decreased to 15 and was lower than in most of the third world, but Cuba continued its effort to cut the rate, which reached 10.7 in 1990. The rate increased from 9.4 in 1993 to 9.9 in 1994 "due to deteriorating social conditions and medical facilities in-

Table 6. Outputs of the Cuban Health-Care System: 1958-2000 (Continued)

(Reported Cases of Contagious Disease per 100,000 Inhabitants)

Year	Polio	Rubella	Measles	Scarlet Fever	Syphilis	Tetanus	Tuberculosis	Typhoid Fever
1958	1.6	...	2,9	2.9	0.7	...	18.0	5.1
1959	4.3	...	10,7	10.3	0.7	4.1	27.6	13.0
1960	4.3	...	5,0	10.7	8.3	4.6	27.1	17.5
1961	4.9	...	0,4	0.4	6.9	...	37.8	13.7
1962	0.7	...	22,5	22.5	11.4	9.0	38.6	14.2
1963	*a	...	94,0	94.0	23.4	6.0	38.3	5.8
1964	*	...	28,9	28.9	25.1	5.5	52.6	15.6
1965	*	...	121,6	121.6	30.4	6.7	65.0	3.1
1966	*	...	136,4	135.4	26.3	6.1	36.5	2.2
1967	*	...	165,9	165.9	13.1	5.4	37.2	2.4
1968	*	...	145,5	145.5	6.7	3.9	41.0	12.0
1969	*	...	132,2	132.2	7.1	3.5	43.3	5.5
1970	*	...	105,2	105.2	7.8	2.6	30.8	...
1971	*	...	129,7	129.7	11.1	2.0	17.9	4.8
1972	*	...	59,9	59.9	24.3	1.7	14.3	5.1
1973	*	...	78,3	78.3	48.9	1.1	15.4	3.5
1974	*	...	150,9	150.9	50.6	1.0	15.4	3.7
1975	*	...	113,4	113.4	47.6	0.7	14.2	4.0
1976	*	...	157,2	157.2	41.1	0.6	13.5	4.3
1977	*	...	263,3	263.3	39.2	0.6	13.1	4.7
1978	*	...	194,4	194.4	44.2	0.4	13.1	3.8
1979	*	...	77,3	77.3	43.6	0.3	11.6	1.8
1980	*	...	39,1	39.1	44.7	0.3	11.6	1.0
1981	*	...	190,1	190.1	36.9	0.2	8.6	1.8
1982	*	...	238,8	238.8	38.5	0.2	8.5	1.3
1983	*	...	33,2	33.2	44.3	0.2	7.7	0.6
1984	*	...	34,0	34.0	53.2	0.1	7.1	0.6
1985	*	...	28,5	28.5	62.6	0.1	6.7	0.6
1986	*	...	32,5	32.5	71.4	0.1	6.4	0.7
1987	*	...	8,3	8.3	84.2	0.1	6.2	0.7
1988	*	...	1,2	1.2	82.3	...	6.0	0.9
1989	*	...	0,1	0.1	82.1	0.1	5.5	0.5
1990	*	0.2	0,2	6.6	86.5	...	5.1	0.6
1991	*	0.2	0,2	5.7	93.4	...	4.7	0.9
1992	*	0.1	0,1	5.7	102.6	...	5.8	0.5
1993	*	*	*	3.6	91.3	*	7.2	0.2
1994	*	...	*	3.4	105.5	...	11.8	0.7
1995	*	*	*	6.1	130.6	*	14.1	1.0
1996	*	*	*	6.7	143.5	*	13.1	0.7
1997	*	*	*	7.5	142.9	*	12.2	0.4
1998	*	...	*	7.9	120.5	*	11.1	1.3
1999	*	*	*	18.6	110.1	...	10.0	1.2
2000	*	...	*	23.0	82.2	...	10.1	0.3

Source: CEE, 1980, 1985, 1991; ONE, 1998, 1999, 2000, 2001; MINSAP, 1999, 2000, 2001; Mesa-Lago, 2000, 2002.

a.   * = Insignificant or null.

fant mortality rose slightly, owing to an increase in deaths caused by respiratory and diarrhoeal diseases"(Garfield and Holtz 2000, 118). The decline was reversed by 1995 and in 1999, the rate declined to a historical low of 6.5. In 2000, there was an increase again to 7.2. Cuba's infant mortality rate was re-

duced 78 percent between 1958 and 2000 (see Table 4).

One wonders why the government did not redirect its significant expenditures to further reduce such a low infant mortality towards other areas in desperate need of resources, such as sanitation or potable water in rural areas. This inefficient allocation of resources will cost Cuba in the future and trying to lower the infant mortality rate even more will have diminishing returns. Also missing from the conventional analysis of Cuba's infant mortality reduction is its staggering abortion rate, which, because of selective termination of high-risk pregnancies, yields lower infant mortality rates. Cuba's abortion rate was 55.0 per 1,000 women in 1985 but declined to 45.6 in 1990 and 22.8 in 1998. When the abortion rate is reported per 100 pregnancies, the significance of these procedures increases. In 1970, the rate was 24.2; it increased to 49.1 in 1986 and by 1999 had declined to 32.0. Although the Cuban government has been successful in reducing the abortion rate through sexual education and contraception use, it still is among the highest in Latin America.

Life Expectancy

Cuba's life expectancy has always been one of the highest in the region, but there is not a single series for 1958-2000 published by Cuba. Table 4 shows a series from CEPAL and another from Cuba; the former is more complete than the latter. CEPAL publishes its figures in five-year intervals. According to CEPAL, in 1960-65, the life expectancy was 65.4, increasing to 73.9 in 1980-85 and to 76 in 1995-2000. Such increase can be attributed to the significant improvement in health standards in the last four decades.

Maternal Mortality Rate and Low Weight at Birth

The maternal mortality rate decreased from 125.3 in 1958 to 26.1 in 1988. During the crisis of the 1990s, the lowered level of caloric intake caused an increase in maternal mortality to a peak of 65.2 in 1994. Lack of a clear definition of reported maternal mortality rates during the late 1980s and early 1990s creates a significant inconsistency in the data. Along with maternal mortality rate, the lowered level of caloric intake caused the percent of children born under weight: to rise from 7.3 in 1988 to 9.0 in 1993, but it decreased to 6.1 in 2000 (see Table 4).

Crude Death Rate and Among Population 65 and Above

The crude death rate in Cuba has been rising over the last decade due to the aging of the population:

5.5 per 1,000 in 1976, the lowest, and 7.2 in 1994, the peak; in 2000, it was 6.8 (see Table 7). Cuba has the second oldest population in Latin America and by the next decade will surpass the leading country, which is Uruguay. The aging of the population has been caused by 3 factors among others: (1) declining birth rates: from 26.1 in 1958 to 12.8 in 2000; (2) decrease of the population growth rate, 2.6 in 1964 to 0.3 in 2000; and (3) migration of the population, mainly between ages 24 and 42. There was a decline in mortality among the population over the age of 65 from 52.9 to 46.3 in 1970-1982, an increase to 55.7 in 1993 (due to the economic crisis) and a decrease to 49.7 in 2000, still higher than in 1982 (see Table 4).

Causes of Death

The principal cause of death over the last three decades was heart disease: 147.9 deaths per 100,000 inhabitants in 1968, increasing to 180.3 in 2000 (See Table 8). The other leading causes of death in 2000 were malignant neoplasm (146.5), cerebrovascular disease (72.9), and influenza (46.2). In 1993 and 1994, mortality from infectious and parasitic disease increased dramatically due to the deterioration of quality of potable water and sanitation: from 8.7 in 1986 to 13.8 in 1993; by 2000 the outbreak had been controlled and the rate declined to 5.5.

Morbidity

Cuba has been very successful in reducing rates of many contagious diseases: polio, tetanus and diphtheria have been eradicated. However, in the 1990s many diseases that previously had been significantly reduced increased again, including acute diarrhea, chicken pox, hepatitis, tuberculosis, typhoid fever, acute respiratory diseases and sexually transmitted diseases (STDs) like syphilis, gonorrhea and AIDS (See table 6). Diseases like acute diarrhea and tuberculosis increased dramatically due to the lower levels of sanitation and clean water. Acute diarrhea jumped from 5,707 to 10,242 in 1965-1993; it decreased to 7,703 by 2000. Tuberculosis rose from 4.7 in 1991 to 14.1 in 1994; it declined to 10.1 in 2000. Acute respiratory diseases are by far the leading causes of morbidity in Cuba the rate per 100,000 inhabitants increased four-fold in 1970-2000. In 1997, respira-

Table 7.   Cuban Demographic Data: 1958-2001

Years	Population (June 30 of each year)[a]	Crude Birth Rate per 1,000	Crude Death Rate per 1,000	Migration	Population Growth Rate (%)
1958	6,824,000	26.1	6.3	-4,449	1.8
1959	6,977,000	27.7	6.4	-12,345	2.2
1960	7,028,515	30.1	6.1	-62,379	1.4
1961	7,191,000	32.5	6.4	-67,468	1.6
1962	7,318,000	34.3	7.1	-66,264	1.6
1963	7,512,000	35.1	6.7	-12,201	2.6
1964	7,713,000	35.0	6.3	-12,791	2.6
1965	7,808,291	34.3	6.4	-18,003	2.5
1966	8,064,000	33.1	6.4	-53,409	2.0
1967	8,215,000	31.7	6.3	-51,972	1.9
1968	8,353,000	30.4	6.5	-56,755	1.7
1969	8,489,000	29.2	6.6	-49,776	1.6
1970	8,572,376	27.7	6.3	-56,404	1.5
1971	8,768,000	29.5	6.2	-49,631	1.8
1972	8,951,000	28.1	5.5	-16,856	2.1
1973	9,118,000	25.1	5.7	-7,073	1.9
1974	9,232,000	22.2	5.6	-3,893	1.3
1975	9,292,104	20.8	5.4	-2,891	1.5
1976	9,493,000	19.9	5.5	-2,891	1.4
1977	9,601,000	17.7	5.8	-968	1.1
1978	9,686,000	15.4	5.7	-3,462	0.9
1979	9,754,000	14.8	5.6	-16,270	0.7
1980	9,779,795	14.1	5.7	-141,742	-0.6[a]
1981	9,756,714	14.0	5.9	-18,928	0.6
1982	9,814,114	16.3	5.8	-8,234	1.0
1983	9,879,495	16.7	5.9	-9,533	1.0
1984	9.953,699	16.7	6.0	-9,007	1.0
1985	10,058,400	18.1	6.4	-8,164	1.1
1986	10,156,800	16.3	6.2	-9,634	1.0
1987	10,288,350	17.4	6.3	-4,114	1.0
1988	10,404,900	18.1	6.5	-7,521	1.1
1989	10,506,900	17.6	6.4	-9,279	1.0
1990	10,603,200	17.6	...	-5,352	1.1
1991	10,792,923	16.3	6.7	-3,737	0.9
1992	10,869,218	14.5	7.0	-5,604	0.7
1993	10,939,714	13.9	7.2	-3,303	0.6
1994	10,960,487	13.4	7.2	-47,844	0.2[b]
1995	10,978,148	13.4	7.1	-33,648	0.4
1996	11,038,602	12.7	6.8	-20,552	0.4
1997	11,093,152	13.8	7.0	-21,000	0.5
1998	11,122,308	13.6	7.0	-26,799	0.4
1999	11,142,691	13.5	7.1	-31,224	0.4
2000	11,187,673	12.8	6.8	...	0.3
2001	11,229,688	...	...	...	...

Source: CEE, 1980, 1985, 1991; ONE, 1998, 1999, 2000, 2001; MINSAP, 1999, 2000, 2001; Mesa-Lago, 2000, 2002

... Not Available.

a. The rate declined because of massive emigration.
b. Author's estimates.

tory diseases caused about 5 million medical visits. In the past three years, the number of children and senior citizens infected with respiratory diseases has increased (PAHO 1999, 209).

Because of the increase in prostitution and lack of prevention, STDs have increased significantly. Between 1986 and 1996, 1,468 cases of HIV-positive individuals were detected; of these, 381 died and 534

Table 8. **Outputs of Cuban Health System: 1968-2000**
(Principal Causes of Death)

Causes of Death	Death Rate Per 100,000 Inhabitants										
	1968[a]	1970	1975[a]	1980	1985[a]	1990[a]	1995[a]	1997	1998	1999	2000
Heart Disease	147.9	148.2	148.9	166.7	190.0	201.3	201.3	197.5	193.0	193.2	180.3
Malignant neoplasm	147.8	98.7	99.7	106.3	117.3	128.8	133.2	137.7	141.1	147.7	146.5
Cerebrovascular Disease	93.8	60.1	51.1	55.3	62.2	65.4	70.7	69.3	71.0	74.9	72.9
Accidents	65.6	36.0	33.5	38.0	42.5	49.4	53.3	49.6	47.4	46.9	44.5
Influenza and Pneumonia	40.4	42.0	38.9	38.6	44.6	29.0	34.2	45.0	44.2	47.3	46.2
Suicides and Car Accidents	12.5	11.8	17.3	21.4	21.8	20.4	20.2	18.4	18.3	18.4	16.4
Infectious and Parasitic Diseases	...	45.4	17.0	10.1	11.4	8.3[b]	13.8[c]	9.6	8.0	7.7	5.5
Diabetes Mellitus	12.6	9.9	10.2	11.1	15.6	21.5	22.9	18.5	15.1	14.3	13.1
Homicide	...	4.1	...	3.4	...	...	...	6.8	7.3	5.5	5.3
Cirrhosis of the Liver	...	6.7	...	5.8	...	...	...	8.5	8.8	10.1	8.9

Source: CEE, 1980, 1985, 1991; ONE, 1998, 1999, 2000, 2001; MINSAP, 1999, 2000, 2001; Mesa-Lago, 2000, 2002.

a. Author's estimates.
b. 1989.
c. 1993.

developed AIDS. The 15-24 age group is the most affected; 65 percent of the infected males are homosexuals. The majority of the individuals acquired the disease in Cuba (PAHO 1999, 210). The incidence of HIV/AIDS rose from 0.5 to 15.1 per 1,000,000 inhabitants in 1986-2000.

AN EVALUATION OF CUBA'S HEALTHCARE SYSTEM

Over the past four decades, Cuba has had many accomplishments in the area of health care, including: (1) expansion of access to nearly 100 percent of the population; (2) increase of its health indicators to levels comparable with industrialized nations, with infant mortality rate among the world's lowest; (3) the creation of a large pool of health services personnel, many of whom have been exported around the world to assist foreign governments with their health problems; (4) reduction in urban-rural differences; and (5) eradication of many diseases, particularly polio, diphtheria, rubella and tetanus.

Although Cuba has performed very well in relation to other Latin American countries, its healthcare system faces many problems, including: (1) high and increasing cost in relation to GDP; (2) inefficient allocation of resources; (3) excess hospital beds and low occupancy rates; (4) excess doctors and extremely low wages; (5) deterioration of basic infrastructure; (6) scarcity of medicines and other medical inputs, as

well, equipment and spare parts; and (7) remaining urban-rural and provincial disparities.

As can be seen in Table 1 Cuba's total budget expenditures for health care have increased continuously throughout the last four decades. However, once inflation is taken into account, the purchasing power is lowered considerably: in 1976 the real per capita expenditure was 34.7 pesos and steadily rose to 91.9 in 1989. As we have noted, however, this series ends in 1989. Using a different series that begins with 1989, real per capita expenditures fell from 66.9 to 16.40 in 1989-93 due to rising inflation, climbing to 53.0 in 1999, well below the figure for 1989. In 1989-2000, the share of GDP allocated to healthcare increased from 4.3 to 6.1 percent. This was a period, however, when GDP declined from 35 to 40 percent. Since 1995 GDP has increased, however the cost of healthcare continues to grow at a much higher rate (Mesa-Lago, 2002).

Cuba has had the lowest infant mortality rate in Latin America since the 1950s. In 2000, it was one of the lowest in the world at 7.2 (see Table 4). However, the government continues to make prenatal and infant care its priority and allocates considerable resources to this program. The government should reallocate these funds into areas more in need, such as water and sanitation infrastructure, an inefficiency that misuses large resources (Mesa-Lago 2002; Sixto 2000).

Table 9.   Provincial Inputs and Outputs of the Cuban Health System: 1975 and 2000

Provinces	Infant Mortality Rate per 1,000 live births		Under 5 Mortality Rate per 1,000 live births		Maternal Mortality Rate per 100,000 live births		Percent of Children Born Under Weight		Hospital Beds per 1,000 Inhabitants		Doctors per 10,000 Inhabitant	
	1975	2000	1990	2000	1992[a]	2000	1990	2000	1976[b]	2000	1984	1999
Pinar del Río	31.5	5.9	9.4	7.7	64.8	60.8	7.6	6.2	2.1	4.8	14.0	47.5
La Habana	25.1	7.6	11.1	9.4	52.0	45.3	4.7	3.8	0.8	2.3	15.0	40.3
Ciudad Habana	24.1	7.5	12.1	9.5	53.4	71.8	7.5	6.6	18.6	9.2	48.0	90.7
Matanzas	23.0	6.4	14.3	8.3	79.0	25.5[c]	7.5	5.4	2.0	4.0	19.0	51.3
Villa Clara	18.8	5.0	10.3	7.1	54.9	30.1[c]	6.8	5.7	2.8	4.0	14.0	58.0
Cienfuegos	25.2	5.4	11.8	7.9	75.7	20.8[c]	7.1	5.7	0.9	3.7	15.0	54.8
Sancti Spíritus	20.3	6.2	9.2	7.7	83.0	54.7	6.7	5.0	1.4	4.9	13.0	55.8
Ciego de Avila	35.1	8.1	14.5	11.2	132.4	93.7	6.7	6.3	0.8	3.3	13.0	51.3
Camagüey	31.2	7.0	14.0	8.4	64.8	58.5	7.5	5.3	3.2	5.2	15.0	56.9
Las Tunas	34.5	7.0	15.3	9.1	25.2[c]	59.5	8.0	7.1	1.0	4.0	11.0	43.3
Holguín	31.2	7.3	14.5	9.0	28.4[c]	29.8[c]	8.2	6.3	3.0	4.3	11.0	45.4
Granma	26.9	8.2	16.4	10.0	39.5[c]	33.8[c]	8.8	6.5	2.1	4.4	10.0	41.3
Santiago de Cuba	28.9	8.7	14.6	10.0	75.4	81.3	8.4	7.2	4.5	5.5	16.0	60.1
Guantánamo	29.8	9.1	15.2	11.5	67.1	74.0	9.1	5.8	1.4	4.3	12.0	44.0
Isla de la Juventud	31.5	4.9	13.2	6.6	74.0	163.9	5.2	4.6	...	4.3	21.0	55.3
Total (Cuba)	27.5	7.2	13.2	9.1	59.7	55.7	7.6	6.1	4.5	5.2	20.0	58.2
Extreme Disparity[a]	1.87	1.82	1.78	1.74	2.55	3.62	1.94	1.89	23.25	4.0	4.80	2.20

Source: CEE, 1980, 1985, 1991; ONE, 1996, 1997, 1999, 2000; MINSAP, 1999, 2000, 2001; Mesa-Lago, 2000, 2002

a.   The highest figure divided by the lowest (method used following Mesa-Lago, 2002).
b.   In the late 1980s and early 1990s figures for maternal mortality lack a clear definition. Some provinces show direct, indirect or total deaths. These figures are not included in the calculation of the extreme disparity.
c.   Author estimates.

Another area to which Cuba has allocated excess resources is hospital capacity. Even with the decrease from 6.0 hospital beds per 1,000 inhabitants in 1998 to 5.2 in 2000, occupancy rates continue to be low and show a declining trend. Hospital bed occupancy has decreased since 1980 from 80.4 percent to 69.4 percent in 2000. This rate is low by international standards (See Table 2).

Since the early 1960s, Cuba has been recognized as a third world medical power for its number of doctors. The rate of doctors per 10,000 inhabitants increased dramatically since the mid-1970s to 58.2 in 1999. Cuba has a large surplus of doctors and these doctors are not allowed to practice their professions in the private sector. After the crisis of the 1990s, the purchasing power of a doctor's salary is about US$15-20 per month. Because of these conditions, many doctors opt to work in a different occupation—usually in the informal sector as taxi drivers, earning 50 to 60 times more than in practicing their profession as doctors (Garfield and Holtz 2000; Sixto 2000). The same situation is evident for dentists and nurses.

In the 1990s, the economic crisis was "associated with a reduction in the materials and products needed to ensure clean water" (Garfield and Holtz 2000). The country's sanitation and infrastructure were severely impacted. Disease associated with lack of sanitation and poor nutrition increased. Moreover, the infrastructure of facilities such as hospitals and policlinics deteriorated sharply. Ironically weakening of the hospital system resulted in more, and relatively longer, hospital stay. In 1989-1993, the average length of stay at hospitals increased from 9.9 to 10.4 days, although it decreased to 9.4 in 2000. However, this figure is still high for international standards and should have been lowered with the family doctor program and the expansion of family clinics.

As Table 9 demonstrates, gaps still exist between provinces. For example Guantánamo had an infant mortality rate of 9.1 in 2000 while Villa Clara's rate was 5. In Ciudad Habana, there were 90.7 doctors per 10,000 inhabitants in 2000 and 41.3 in Granma. Although these gaps have narrowed since previous years, the gap in maternal mortality has increased.

Table 10. Cuba's Rank in Latin America: 1959, 1980, and 2000

Infant Mortality Rate per 1,000 Live Births			Hospital Beds per 1,000 Inhabitants			Doctors per 10,000 Inhabitants			Life Expectancy			Calories Consumed per day		
1959	1980	2000	1959	1980	2000	1959	1980	2000	1959	1980	2000	1959	1980	1996
1	1	1	2	2	1	3	1	1	4	1	1	3	4	9

Source: CEE, 1980, 1985, 1991; ONE, 1996, 1997, 1999, 2000; MINSAP, 1999, 2000, 2001; Mesa-Lago, 2000, 2002; CEPAL, 1980, 1990, 1999.

The extreme disparity increased from 2.55 in 1992 to 3.62 in 2000 (see Table 9). It must be noted however, that these figures are much lower than the rest of Latin America (Mesa-Lago 2002).

When compared to the rest of Latin America, it is evident that Cuba has gone through great lengths to improve its healthcare system and its corresponding indicators. As Table 10 illustrates Cuba has increased in ranking in three of the five indicators in that table. However, for infant mortality rate, Cuba was already ahead of the region in the 1950s. As explained earlier Cuba has a surplus of hospital beds and doctors, causing inefficient utilization. Other Latin American countries have not increased the absolute numbers of doctors or of hospital beds but have been able to find equilibrium between the supply of each and the demand. The area where Cuba has declined significantly is consumption of calories. Cuba has dropped seven places.

Cuba has been praised by many for its improvements in healthcare through the last four decades. In fact, many believe that Cuba has become a world medical power providing a model for the developing world (Bravo 1998; Figueras 1998; MacDonald 1999). While much of this is true, Cuba faces several problems associated with its healthcare system. The Cuban government can significantly reduce the effects of the problems listed above if reforms are implemented. However, many of these reforms must be more market oriented.

First, the Cuban government must make the system more efficient by investing in preventive medicine. It must also allocate funds to the building and maintenance of infrastructure and sanitation. It is essential that the government close hospitals where bed occupancy rates have fallen below efficient levels.

Second, the government must establish some type of "escape valve" to permit doctors to take part in the new private sector of the economy.

Third, the remaining disparity between the urban and rural sectors and provinces should be corrected.

And fourth, reform of the finance of the system must take place to ensure its sustainability.

BIBLIOGRAPHY

Barrett, Kathleen. 1993. *The Impact of the Collapse of the Soviet Union and the Eastern Bloc on the Cuban Health System.* Washington D.C.: Master thesis, Georgetown University.

Bravo, Ernesto Mario. 1998. *Development Within Underdevelopment? New Trends in Cuban Medicine.* Insituto Cubano del Libro. Havana, Cuba.

CEPAL. 1980-2001. *Anuario Estadístico de América Latina y el Caribe.* 1980, 1990, 1999, 2000, 2001 Santiago: CEPAL

Comite Estatal de Estadísticas (CEE). 1976 to 1991. *Anuario Estadístico de Cuba,* 1975 to 1989. Havana: CEE

Danielson, Robert. 1979. *Cuban Medicine.* New Brunswick: Transaction Books.

Feinsilver, Julie Margot. 1993. *Healing the Masses: Cuban Health Politics at Home and Abroad.* Berkeley: University of California Press

Figueras, Miguel Alejandro.1998. *La Realidad de lo Imposible: La Salud Pública en Cuba*. La Habana: Editorial de Ciencias Sociales.

Garfield, Robert and S. Santana. 1997. "The Impact of the Economic Crisis and the U.S. Embargo on Health in Cuba." *American Journal of Public Health* 87: 15-20

Garfield Robert and Tim Holtz. 2000. "Health Systems Reforms in Cuba in the 1990s." In Peter Lloyd Sherlock, ed. *Healthcare Reform & Poverty in Latin America*. London: Institute of Latin American Studies.

Kirkpatrick, Anthony F. 1996. "Role of the USA in Shortage of Food and Medicine in Cuba." *TheLancet*, 348 (November 30): 1489-1491.

MacDonald, Theodore H. 1999. *A Developmental Analysis of Cuba's Health Care System Since 1959*. Queenston, England: The Edwin Mellen Press.

Mesa-Lago, Carmelo. 1968. *Social Security in Cuba*. Cuban Economic Research Project. University of Miami.

Mesa-Lago, Carmelo. 2000. *Market, Socialist, and Mixed Economies: Comparative Policy and Performance, Chile, Cuba and Costa Rica*. Baltimore, Maryland: The Johns Hopkins University Press.

Mesa-Lago, Carmelo. 2002. "La Atención de la Salud en Cuba: Diagnóstico y Sugerencias de Políticas." Forthcoming.

Ministerio de Salud Pública (MINSAP). 1995-2001. *Anuario Estadístico de Salud de Cuba* 1994, 1995, 1996, 1997, 1998, 1999, 2000. Havana: MINSAP

De Miranda Parrondo, Patricia, and Carlos J. Tabraue Castro. 2000. "Impacto Social de la Crisis Económica en la Cuba de Los Noventa." Miami: LASA Conference, March 16-18, 2000. Unpublished paper.

Oficina Nacional de Estadísticas (ONE). 1998-2001. *Anuario Estadístico de Cuba* 1996, 1997, 1999, 2000. Havana: ONE

Pan American Health Organization (PAHO). 1998. *Health in the Americas: Cuba*. Washington, D.C.: United Nations Publications: 206- 219

Pan American Health Organization (PAHO). 1999. Cuba. *Profile of the Health Services System*. Washington D.C.: Division of Health Systems and Services Development: 1-23

Sixto, Felipe. 2000. "An Analysis of Cuba's National Healthcare System." Miami: Florida International University, Unpublished paper April.

Sixto, Felipe. 2001. Log of Interviews in Cuba. May/ December 2001.

Sloan, Don. 1997. "Health-Care in Cuba." *Political Affairs* 76 (March-April): 14-18.

"VALE TODO" (ANYTHING GOES): CUBA'S *PALADARES*

Ted Henken

Today, the political, military, and ideological problem of this country is looking for food. [...] We must be clear about one thing: if there is food for the people, the risks do not matter.—Raúl Castro, September 28, 1994 (1997: 466)

As we went through the makeshift front door of Central Havana's "Paladar Las Doce Sillas" (The Twelve Chairs Restaurant),[1] I noted the owner's exasperated expression. It turned out that Gregorio, my resourceful street guide, had brought in four Spanish customers not ten minutes earlier and the owner would now have to fork out another $5 commission on top of the $20 he already owed Gregorio for his services.

Playing the fool, I inquired of Magalis, the waitress, how it was that I did not see lobster on my menu, yet noticed a large red shell lying empty on a plate nearby. She lowered her head and whispered, "You know we can't put that on the menu?" Turning toward a small, improvised service door that opened to the kitchen, she asked in a clear, confident voice, "Hey, is there any more 'L' back there?" She returned to me with a hot plate of 'L a la plancha' and continued, "If they catch us with lobster, they can confiscate all our equipment, close the *paladar*, and charge us with 'illicit sales'."

After counting the 12 chairs that filled the cramped dining room, I inquired about the name of the restaurant. Magalis admitted that it was the owner's way

of poking fun at the ridiculous restriction against having more than 12 chairs in any *paladar*. She then proudly showed me a hidden room behind the kitchen that could seat another 12 diners.

Before leaving, I spoke briefly with Orestes, the owner, who claimed, "Through this experience, I realized that I was born an entrepreneur. The only problem is that I was born in the wrong country!" As a "born entrepreneur," Orestes knows which laws he can discretely ignore. "I see you met the waitress, my 'cousin' Magalis?" he joked. "Everyone knows we're not related. On the other hand, we don't normally take the risk of serving lobster," he insisted. "If you want to know the truth, that's practically the only rule we do strictly follow."

Finally, he responded to my inquiry over the future of these private eateries by joking, "I wouldn't buy stock in any *paladar*. It's all part of the game and you have to know how to play it. The government can benefit from the positive image that the token existence of private enterprises creates, but I'm convinced that it will remain little more than that, an image."

Taking this brief anecdote as a point of departure, the following paper draws four lessons from the world of Cuba's private, speak-easy eateries—the island's infamous *paladares*. First, the policy of "legalization" of the island's private food service sector inaugurated in the summer of 1995 has been

---

1. In this paper, I make occasional references to various self-employed individuals and businesses. The names of all places and individuals have been changed to protect anonymity and descriptions of individual enterprises such as the one above are in fact composite sketches that combine the characteristics of two or more similar enterprises. Unless otherwise indicated, all translations from interviews, newspaper articles, or scholarly work were done by the author.

accompanied overtime by such a thick web of legal restrictions that, by design or default, the original aim of expansion has been lost. In fact, restrictions on private restaurants are so great and their taxes so high that they often overshadow the benefits of legal status itself, prohibiting the full development of these legal micro-enterprises and forcing them to utilize informal strategies or into outright clandestine existence, to make a living.

Second, every legal restriction put in place to control and limit the growth of these private enterprises has given rise to a corresponding (and often illegal) survival strategy. For example, restrictions against intermediaries, advertising, and employees have provoked the development of an extensive underground network of *jineteros* and fictional cousins. Menu and size restrictions have led to the proliferation of hidden rooms and forbidden foods.

Third, while often described as "islands of capitalism in a sea of socialism" (Pérez-López 1994; Jatar-Hausmann 1999), in practice these restaurants are anything but isolated from the rest of the Cuban economy. Deep and functional linkages exist between these well-known manifestations of Cuba's private economy, connecting them in various direct and indirect ways with other parts of the economy. Understandings of the economic changes introduced in Cuba over the last decade tend to give an overly dualistic image of an economy split into two isolated halves: a vibrant dollar economy and a moribund peso economy; a dynamic private economy and an inefficient socialist economy. However, since the imposition of many internal economic reforms announced in July 1993, the very real divisions in the Cuban economy have become much more complex, fluctuating, and permeable than is often assumed by outside analysts.

A fourth and final lesson that can be taken from the above anecdote is the sense that these enterprises face an unsure future. While most of the still surviving *paladar* operators doubt that they will be closed down outright by the state (especially if they have learned "how to play the game," as Orestes would say), few believe that they will ever be able to grow beyond their current small size into true small- and medium-sized businesses. The aura of illegitimacy that accompanies any independent economic activity and the government's antagonistic attitude toward self-employment effectively condemns these private restaurateurs to an informal, provisional existence.

ORIGINS AND HISTORY OF THE *PALADAR*
Birth and Premature Death (1993-1995)

Because it is one of the most visible manifestations of private enterprise to foreign visitors in Cuba, much attention has been given to the emergence of the Cuban *paladar*.[2] Literally meaning "palate" in both Spanish and Portuguese, the name's origin hints at Cubans' initial high-hopes for the potential of these private, home-grown eateries during the worst stage of the 1990s economic crisis. The name *paladar* comes from the Brazilian soap opera, *Vale Todo* (Anything Goes), which was popular in Cuba in the early 1990s. Raquel, the enterprising protagonist of the *telenovela*, was a poor migrant from the Brazilian interior who moved to Rio where she worked as an itinerant food vendor. She eventually made it big after setting up her own chain of small restaurants, christened *Paladar* (Baker 2000: 153; LaFranchi 1996).

At the time when *Vale Todo* was making Cuban mouths water, the size of the legal self-employed sector was negligible and private restaurants were forbidden by law. However, these speak-easy eateries began to pop up throughout the island in the early 1990s in response to the growing scarcity of food. Because these informal food service networks were providing an essential service to the Cuban population, they were largely tolerated. Their eventual legalization was an administrative response to a multitude of homegrown economic survival strategies (most of which were formally illegal) developed by the Cuban people (Whitefield 1993).

---

2. In addition to the many newspaper reports on the rise of these speak-easy eateries (Whitefield 1994a, 1994b; Farah 1994; Fletcher 1995; Vicent 2000; LaFranchi 1996), more scholarly studies include, Scarpaci 1995; Serge, Coyula and Scarpaci 1997; Flores Gómez 1997; Peters and Scarpaci 1998; Ritter 1998, 2000; Fernández Peláez 2000; and Duany 2001.

Essentially, the Cuban government was forced to legalize large sectors of the expanding informal economy because it had no way of preventing their growth and realized that underground activities were picking up the increasing slack left behind by the drastic contraction in state provisions, allowing Cubans (and ironically the socialist system itself) to survive (Domínguez 2001; Fernández 2000). In September 1993, the government issued a list of 117 self-employment activities. Included among the occupations were four food service activities, including what became known as the infamous "et cetera" — "producer of light snacks (refreshments, sweets, fritters, et cetera)" (Decree Law 141, 1993: 4-5; Alonso 1993; CEPAL 1997).

In the months following the September announcement, scores of Cubans who were already active in the food service sector took out licenses to begin doing legally what they had up to then been doing clandestinely. However, in early December the government reversed its decision, since many Cubans who had obtained licenses were, in fact, running full-fledged restaurants under the broadest possible interpretation of "et cetera." Debates in the late-December 1993 National Assembly meetings over the offending "et cetera" declared it a mistake due to the *paladares'* encouragement of competition, dependence on pilfered supplies, and unlawful contracting of employees (Whitefield 1994a).

The refusal of many of Cuba's fledging restaurateurs to close up shop led to the first of many crackdowns against purported "illegalities, indiscipline, and abuses" in the self-employed sector in January and February 1994 (Scarpaci 1995; Segre, et al 1997; Whitefield 1994a, 1994b). Police raided and closed down over 100 *paladares* in Havana, charging their owners with illicit enrichment despite the fact many did possess the aforementioned "producer of light snacks" licenses (Segre et al 1997: 233). Having learned the important lesson of discretion, many operators were soon back in business. In fact, despite the crackdown, the number of *paladares* was estimated at 4,000 nationwide in early 1994, with between 1,000 and 2,000 of these located in Havana (Whitefield 1994a; Farah 1994; Segre et al 1997; Pérez-López 2001).

Resurrection and Regulation (1995-1996)

The second stage in the life-cycle of the Cuban *paladar* began with the approval in June 1995 of Joint Resolution No. 4. This new law specifically addressed the previously suspended self-employment category of "producer of light snacks (et cetera)" and laid out three specific types of food service operations that would henceforth be allowed. The first category, "al detalle," was intended for street vendors and imposed a monthly tax of 100 pesos. The second category, "a domicilio," was aimed at caterers and required a 200 peso tax ($100 if business was done in dollars). The third category was true home-based, private restaurants. Monthly taxes for these full-service peso-charging *paladares* were initially set at 500 pesos, while operations that charged customers in dollars were required to pay a tax of $400 per month ("Ampliación" 1997).

While no other self-employed activity is permitted to hire salaried employees, the state recognized that *paladares* had always operated with the help of a service and kitchen staff. Therefore, the law established a peculiar regulation prohibiting "salaried employees" on the one hand, while mandating that at least two "family helpers" be employed, on the other. Thus was born the fiction that *paladares* are family businesses.

At this stage the state placed severe limitations on the size and scope of the *paladares* in order to limit competition. The most well-known restriction is the seating limit of just "doce sillas" (12 chairs). The law also indicated that each household was restricted to a single self-employment license. Operators were restricted to the expensive, retail food supplies sold in state-run dollar stores and private farmer's markets. No foods or ingredients from the state-subsidized bodegas could be resold in *paladares*. Because dollar stores were not prepared to provide customers with receipts, many entrepreneurs understood the requirement that they purchase supplies in dollar stores as the legal loophole that could be used to close them down at a future date (Segre et al 1997).

Along with the other legalized food service activities, *paladares* would be subject to unannounced visits from a number of different inspector corps. Specific prohibitions were made against the sale of seafood and horsemeat, and though later banned altogether, beef, milk, and milk derivatives would only be allowed if obtained in dollar stores. The restriction of employees to "family helpers" discriminates against those who lack kin and condemns *paladares* to continuous low productivity, forcing growth to take place through the proliferation of extremely small-scale units, wasting talent, and preventing economies of scale. Moreover, restrictions of access to credit and markets inhibit the natural growth of these businesses, while protecting state enterprises from competition (Ritter 2000; Dirmoser and Estay 1997: 485-487).

Statistics shared with the public at the time indicate that, after just one month in effect food service operations were already among the most common self-employed activities. *Granma* reported that in Havana, the five most common licenses were street vending and porch-front cafeterias, messenger, artisan, hair stylist, and private taxi drivers. Furthermore, by August 1995, Havana authorities had granted 278 *paladar* licenses out of 984 applications. However, perhaps signaling the beginning of a popular rejection of the new regulations, the overall number of registered self-employed workers in Havana dropped down to 58,000 by the end of 1995, from a peak of almost 64,000 in August. The number of registered self-employed workers in Havana would never again reach past the 60,000 mark, and by April 1997 had fallen to 35,171 (Martínez 1995: 2; Avendaño 1997; *DPPFA* 1997).

Increased Regulation and Decline (1996-2001)

Unfortunately for the operators of Cuba's *paladares*, the next two years of their existence as legal, licensed micro-enterprises coincided with a major shift in the government's policy toward self-employment. Whereas the period before December 1995 saw a gradual expansion of the number of allowed occupations from 117 to nearly 160, along with a concomitant rise in the total number of licensed operators (peaking at 208,786 in December 1995), few new occupations were legalized after that date and the issuance of new licenses in many areas was frozen indefinitely thereafter. The best gauge of the policy

change is the precipitous fall in the numbers of registered self-employed workers and the near elimination of the once ubiquitous *paladar*.

Legal and fiscal changes during these years included: (1) the announcement in February 1996 of an increase in the monthly tax rates for many occupations, including the doubling of peso *paladar* rates to 1,000 pesos and raising of dollar operations to $600, (2) the suspension of the granting of any new *paladar* licenses in Havana in April 1996, (3) a nationwide re-inscription of all self-employed workers begun in June 1996, and (4) a new comprehensive law aimed at strengthening the sanctions against the violators of self-employment regulations in June 1997 (Decree-Law #174, 1997).

Issued on April 18, 1996, Joint Resolution No. 1 mandated a nationwide re-registration of all self-employed workers and added a host of new fiscal and operational regulations for workers to follow. First, porch-front cafeterias were legally separated from roving street vendors, the former being issued the detailed regulation: "These cafeterias cannot be equipped with tables, chairs, benches, or the like; and services should be performed through direct dispensation of products without any mediating type of gastronomic service." Therefore, it bears mentioning that not only are *paladares* prohibited from having *more than* 12 chairs, but these lesser cafeterias are forbidden from having *any* chairs or tables, or engaging in any kind of customer service beyond sales ("Sobre el ejercicio…" 1996: 4; Rodríguez Cruz 1996: 5).

Second, new regulations for full-fledged *paladares* included a prohibition against having televisions, live music, or even a bar area where customers could have a drink while they wait for one of the proverbial 12 chairs to become vacant. The law reads, "When alcoholic beverages are offered, they cannot be consumed in an isolated space specifically built for that purpose." The wording here is important since the law does not prohibit bars per se. As a result, nearly all *paladares* visited by the author do have a bar and operators are simply careful about openly serving drinks to waiting customers there ("Sobre el ejercicio…" 1996: 4; Rodríguez Cruz 1996: 5).

Third, the 1996 Regulation stipulated that all "family helpers" in the private food service sector would henceforth have to take out their own self-employment license and pay a monthly personal income tax equal to 20% of the tax paid by the *paladar* itself. In practice, this tax is usually paid by *paladar* operators themselves, thus increasing their monthly tax to 1,400 pesos in the case of peso operations, and to $840 for dollar operations. The new law also prohibited advertising by *paladares* apart from a external sign for which another tax equal to 20% of their base monthly tax must be paid tax (Whitefield 1996a; Whitefield 1996b; Mayoral 1996:2; Lee 1996:2).

Harsher laws, enforcement, and calls for vigilance against crime have paid off given the precipitous drop in the number of registered *paladares*. Of the 1,562 *paladares* that had successfully become registered by 1996, the number had dropped to just 416 by August 1998 (just over half of them in Havana). Of these, only 253 were still left in 2000, two-thirds of them located in Havana. Recent articles in the international and independent Cuban press have confirmed the continuation of this downward trend, recently reporting that over 200 *paladares* were closed down in the year 2000 alone, and estimating less than 200 legal *paladar* operations left in the entire country. My own research visits to Havana and other Cuban cities during 2001 confirm this general picture (Lee 1998: 2; "No official market economy..." 2000: 4; Viño Zimerman 2001; Vicent 2000; Newman 2001; Duany 2001: 48).

In the case of *paladares*, it is ironic that enterprises that have survived to date have been forced by legal limitations and high taxes to raise their prices, charging an increasingly exclusive (and almost exclusively foreign) clientele in dollars (Holgado Fernández 2000). This is a significant change compared with the initial relatively low peso prices and decidedly domestic function of most *paladares* in the first half of the decade. Such a shift is even more unfortunate given the great difficulty most Cubans already have in procuring enough food. It seems that Raúl Castro's surprisingly bold declaration in 1994, that, "if there is food for the people, the risks do not matter," no longer applies, or at least not to the risks present-

ed by private restaurants. Indeed, the fact that *paladares* no longer serve the consumption needs of the Cuban population may be the perfect pretext for the government to continue its repressive policies against them (Scarpaci 1995; Segre et al 1997; Castro 1997: 466).

SURVIVAL STRATEGIES USED BY CUBA'S *PALADAR* OPERATORS

For every unreasonable legal restriction placed on those who engage in private food service, entrepreneurs have developed specific strategies to circumvent those restrictions. The most common strategies that micro-enterprisers have developed in the face of these legal requirements include the serving of forbidden foods, the use of hidden rooms with additional place-settings, the printing and distribution of business cards, and the increasingly common presence of *paladar* sites on the internet. Also, *paladares* make common use of intermediaries, rely on black market goods and purchase bogus receipts to account for illegally obtained goods. Due to the high commissions charged by intermediaries and to the prohibition against many foods, some *paladares* have designed two or three different menus. Diners in these establishments are offered a distinct menu based on intermediary costs, menu selections, and, sometimes, their nationality.

Because of the high retail prices and limited supplies in the dollar stores and farmer's markets, *paladar* proprietors often turn to the "wholesale" prices of the black market. According to media reports and the author's own interviewees, a source of supplies for some *paladares* is the personnel of Havana's many foreign embassies. Diplomatic status allows embassy employees to purchase goods at low rates in state stores. These employees often then resell these items to Cubans at a small profit (Stanley 2000; Fernández Peláez 2000; Reyes 1998).

In the case of the few large-scale operations, more egregious violations are common. For example, while nearly all *paladares* resort to employing non-family workers, larger-scale operations are often staffed by a small army of employees, including professional cooks, private security personnel, taxi drivers, and troupes of musicians who entertain guests with live music. Furthermore, the availability of rooms for lodging, drastic underreporting of earnings, and special arrangements with the inspector corps, are salient features of some of these high-end operations. One negative effect of the use of such strategies is that smaller operations that are unable to afford them are pushed under, while a small number of lucrative, well-connected operations thrive (Fernández Peláez 2000; Ritter 2000).

Finally, in recent years, two "last-resort" survival strategies seem to have become increasingly common in the food service sector. First, a number of entrepreneurs who have felt pressure to close their doors due to the impossibility of surviving under the maze of legal requirements put in place for *paladares*, have decided to turn in their food service license and apply for the much less onerous license to rent rooms in their homes. However, having invested much time and capital in equipping their home with the infrastructure necessary to provide quality meals, these clever operators continue to operate an unofficial *paladar* behind the legal façade of a bed and breakfast. The second "last resort" strategy is that of turning in one's license, but continuing to operate the *paladar* clandestinely ("Establecen procedimiento" 1997: 4-5).

Taken together, the common use of most of these survival strategies by licensed *paladar* operators do not support the assumption that illegality is the result of a lack of adequate top-down control or the delinquency of a few individuals deficient in proper revolutionary mentality. Instead, due to an antagonistic legal framework, in order to engage profitably in this activity, *paladar* operators have found it necessary to rely a host of informal strategies including the illicit networks of supplies in the black market.

CONCLUSION

Apart from President Fidel Castro, whose long-time ideological opposition to markets and private enterprise is well documented, other key political leaders on the island have repeatedly made open declarations against an increased role for self-employment. For example, in a November, 1997, *Granma* article, Raúl Valdés Vivo, the director of the Communist Party's ideological school and a member of the Party's Central Committee, rejected claims that it was unfair to allow for foreign investment while prohibiting domestic capitalists to participate more fully in the island's economy. Comparing the latter group to "piranhas… capable in a minimum of time of devouring a horse down to the bones" (Rice 1997), Valdés Vivo stated that the leadership had been forced to resort to capitalist investments from abroad against its will and claimed that Cuban nationals could not have provided the necessary capital, technology, or markets brought by outsiders.

However, Valdés Vivo admitted that the reasons for the restrictions against domestic capitalists are not only economic, but political and ideological as well ("Cuba will not…" 1998). Specifically, he wrote that allowing Cuban citizens to provide money to private micro-enterprises "would introduce a social force that sooner or later would serve the counterrevolution" (Rice 1997). Adding that Cuba does not desire the return of an exploitative national class propped up by foreign interests, he cited President Castro's words during the 5th Party Congress: "Cuba cannot afford the existence of a new class of rich that would later acquire great power and end up conspiring against socialism" ("Cuba will not…" 1998). Such an attitude could not contrast more with the supposed trust in the integrity and ingenuity of the Cuban people that originally permitted self-employment.

The tension between the state policies of toleration, legalization, and expansion of the private sector on the one hand, and moves toward greater control, containment, and repression on the other, reveal the revolutionary government's deep mistrust of Cuba's new entrepreneurial sector. Cuban officials and journalists continually emphasize the systematic "indiscipline, illegalities, and lack of order" that characterize the private sector, always coming to the same conclusion. Since the cause of indiscipline is the lack of strong regulation and the waning revolutionary consciousness brought on by "the individualist psychology of the private producer" (Lee 1997: 3), the only solution is greater top-down control combined with calls for greater revolutionary fervor and vigilance.

On the other hand, most Cuban social scientists who have written on the topic of self-employment are in favor of less, not more bureaucratic control.[3] Far from advocating wholesale privatization and a withdrawal of the state from the economy, these scholars recommend a proactive government approach to the private sector that would include monetary incentives, technical training, expanded opportunities to market products, and greater access to wholesale supplies. They argue that such an organic, integrated approach would allow for a greater, if still decidedly subordinate role for the non-state sector in the Cuban economy, leading to the creation of more jobs and higher standards of living for the Cuban people. However, due to the political costs and ideological compromises involved, the revolutionary leadership has refused to implement this advice.

As this study of Cuba's fledging *paladares* has shown, the Cuban state has attempted to distinguish between micro-enterprises that fall within the legal framework and those that have resisted legalization, preferring to operate underground. However, Cuba's private restaurant sector is much more heterogeneous and complex than such a legalistic distinction would indicate. While unlicensed private restaurants clearly operate outside the law, virtually all of Cuba's *paladares* find it necessary to develop illegal strategies to ensure their survival. What distinguishes one operation from another is the degree of each one's links to informality, not the fact of such a linkage itself.

The paternalism characteristic of the Cuban leadership seems determined to choke out all autonomous economic activities, seeing them as threats to its top-down control. Existing policy treats most of these entrepreneurs as an anachronism, whose role in the economy will decidedly decrease as the socialist economy recovers. Such an antagonistic policy only causes these micro-enterprises to deepen their links with informality, leading to an even greater distrust of the government and socializing these entrepreneurs further in criminality as their only means of survival. In summary, the emergence of Cuba's *paladares* over the last decade teaches the following lesson: the state's paternalistic desire to regulate and restrict their growth has transformed what was hoped to be a true expansion of the private micro-enterprise sector into another mechanism of state control over the economy.

BIBLIOGRAPHY

Alonso, José. 1993. "An Analysis of Decree 141 Regarding Cuban Small-Scale Enterprises." *La Sociedad Económica Bulletin* 35, September 20.

"Ampliación de actividades: Paladares." 1997. Joint Resolution #4, June 8, 1995. In *Economía y reforma económica en Cuba*, edited by Dietmar Dirmoser and Jaime Estay, 485-487. Caracas: Nueva Sociedad.

Avendaño, Bárbara. 1997. "Trabajadores por cuenta propia. Incremento de las cuotas fijas mensuales." *Tribuna de La Habana*, May 5, 1996. In *Economía y reforma económica en Cuba*, edited by Dietmar Dirmoser and Jaime Estay, 496-497. Caracas: Nueva Sociedad.

Baker, Christopher P. 2000. *Cuba: Moon Handbooks*. Second edition. Emeryville, CA: Avalon Travel Publishing.

Carranza Valdés, Julio, Luis Gutiérrez Urdaneta, and Pedro Monreal González. 1996. *Cuba la restruc-*

---

3. Examples include, Hernández and González 1993; Carranza Valdés et al 1996; Gutiérrez Urdaneta et al 1996; Pavón González 1996; Pérez Villanueva and Togores González 1996; Núñez Moreno 1997; Quintana Mendoza 1997; González Gutiérrez 1997; Togores González n.d.; Espina Prieto 1997; Espina Prieto et al 1998; and Fernández Peláez 2000.

turación de la economía: una propuesta para el debate. Havana: Editorial de Ciencias Sociales.

Castro, Raúl. 1997. "Si hay comida para el pueblo, no importan los riesgos." *Granma Internacional*, September 28, 1994. In *Economía y reforma económica en Cuba*, edited by Dietmar Dirmoser and Jaime Estay, 458-467. Caracas: Nueva Sociedad.

CEPAL (Comisión Económica para América Latina y el Caribe). 1997. *La economía cubana: Reformas estructurales y desempeño en los noventa*. México: Fondo de Cultura Económica.

"Cuba will not allow citizens to open businesses." 1998. *Caribbean Update*, January.

Decree-Law #141 (DL 141). 1993. "Sobre el trabajo por cuenta propia." *Granma*, September 9.

Decree-Law #174 (DL 174). 1997. "De las contravenciones personales de las regulaciones de trabajo por cuenta propia." *Gaceta Oficial*, June 30.

Dirección Provincial de Planificación Física y Arquitectura (*DPPFA*). 1997. "Diagnóstico de Población." Mimeo, Havana, July.

Dirmoser, Dietmar, and Jaime Estay, eds. 1997. *Economía y reforma económica en Cuba*. Caracas: Nueva Sociedad.

Domínguez, Jorge. 2001. "Why the Cuban Regime Has Not Fallen." In *Cuban Communism*, tenth edition, edited by Irving Louis Horowitz and Jaime Suchlicki, 533-545. New Brunswick: Transaction Publishers.

Duany, Jorge. 2001. "Redes, remesas y paladares: La diáspora cubana desde una perspectiva transnacional." *Neuva Sociedad* 174, July-August: 40-51.

Espina Prieto, Mayra Paula. 1997. "Transformaciones recientes de la estructura socioclasista cubana." *Papers* 52: 83-99.

Espina Prieto, Mayra, Lucy Martín Posada, and Lilia Núñez Moreno. 1998. "Componentes y tendencias socioestructurales de la sociedad cubana actual—resumen ejecutivo." Havana: Centro de Investigación Psicológica y Sociológica (CIPS), March.

"Establecen procedimiento para el pago del impuesto por el arrendamiento de viviendas, habitaciones o espacios." 1997. *Granma*, May 23: 4-5.

Farah, Douglas. 1994. "Speak-Easy Eateries Attract Diners with Dollars in Food-Short Havana," *Washington Post*, February 16: A9, A14.

Fernández, Damián. 2000. *Cuba and the Politics of Passion*. Austin: University of Texas Press.

Fernández Peláez, Neili. 2000. *Trabajo por cuenta propia en Cuba: Disarticulación y reacción*. Senior Thesis, Department of Sociology, University of Havana, July.

Fletcher, Pascal. 1995. "Havana permits private restaurants," *Financial Times*, June 15.

Flores Gómez, Violeta. 1997. *Género e informalidad: El caso cubano*. Master's Thesis, Social Development, FLACSO, University of Havana, July.

González Gutiérrez, Alfredo. 1997. "La economía sumergida en Cuba." In *Economía y reforma económica en Cuba*, edited by Dietmar Dirmoser and Jaime Estay, 239-256. Caracas: Editorial Nueva Sociedad.

Gutiérrez Urdaneta, Luis, Pedro Monreal González, and Julio Carranza Valdés. 1996. "La pequeña y mediana empresa en Cuba: El problema de la propiedad." Mimeo, Havana.

Hernádez, Rafael, and Maby González. 1993. "Cuba: Otros pasos en la apertura económica." In *La despenalización del dolar, trabajo por cuenta propia y coopeerativización en Cuba: Documentos y comentarios*, edited by Caridad Rodríguez and Nelson P. Valdés, 81-82. Dossier No. 3, The Latin American Institute of the University of New Mexico (Albuquerque) and the Centro de Estudios sobre América (Havana).

Holgado-Fernández, Isabel. 2000. *¡No es fácil! Mujeres cubanas y la crisis revolucionaria*. Barcelona: Icaria editorial.

Jatar-Hausmann, Ana Julia. 1999. *The Cuban Way: Communism, Capitalism, and Confrontation.* West Hartford, CT: Kumarian Press.

LaFranchi, Howard. 1996. "Cuba's Enterprising Cooks Open their Homes: Since Castro's Government Legalized Small, Private Eateries, 'paladares' Keep Popping Up," *Christian Science Monitor*, May 9.

Lee, Susana. 1996. "Entra hoy en vigor Nuevo Reglamento del Trabajo por cuenta Propia," *Granma*, June 1: 2.

Lee, Susana. 1997. "La batalla contra las ilegalidades y las indisciplinas sociales no se ganará sin los CDR," *Granma*, April 25: 3.

Lee, Susana. 1998. "El impuesto de los 'paladares'," *Granma*, November 12: 2.

Martínez, Silvia. 1995. "Regulan ejercicio del trabajo por cuenta propia," *Granma*, August 17.

Mayoral, María Julia. 1996. "Comienza reinscripción de los trabajadores por cuenta propia," *Granma*, June 21: 2.

Newman, Lucia. 2001. "Cuba squeezes private business as economy grows," *CNN*, March 12.

"No official market economy for Cuba: sharp decline in numbers of small entrepreneurs." 2000. *Latin American, Caribbean, and Central American Report*, August 22.

Núñez Moreno, Lilia. 1997. "Mas allá del cuentapropismo en Cuba," *Temas* 11.

Pavón González, Ramiro. 1996. "Estudio diagnóstico sobre el trabajo por cuenta propia en Santiago de Cuba." *Economía y Desarrollo* 120, no. 2, pp. 74-90, June.

Pérez-López, Jorge F. 1994. "Islands of Capitalism in an Ocean of Socialism: Joint Ventures in Cuba's Development Strategy." In *Cuba at a Crossroads: Politics and Economics after the Fourth Party Congress*. Gainesville: University Press of Florida.

Pérez-López, Jorge F. 2001. "Cuba's Socialist Economy: the Mid-1990s." In *Cuban Communism*, tenth edition, edited by Irving Louis Horowitz and Jaime Suchlicki, 205-236. New Brunswick: Transaction Publishers.

Pérez Villanueva, Omar Everleny, and Viviana Togores González. 1996. "Las pequeñas empresas en Cuba: Posibilidades." In *Cambios y perspectivas en la economía cubana, 1995*, edited by Elsa Barrera López, 149-153. Dossier No. 10, The Latin American Institute of the University of New Mexico (Albuquerque) and the Centro de Estudios Sobre América (Havana), February.

Peters, Phillip, and Joseph L. Scarpaci. 1998. "Cuba's New Entrepreneurs: Five Years of Small-Scale Capitalism." Arlington, VA: Alexis de Toqueville Institution (http://adti.net/html_files/cuba/TCPSAVE.htm).

Quintana Mendoza, Didio. 1997. "El sector informal urbano en Cuba: Algunos elementos para su caracterización." *Cuba, investigación económica* 3, no. 2, pp. 101-120, Havana: Instituto Nacional de Investigaciones Económicas, April-June.

Reyes, Gerardo. 1998. "Diplomats in Cuba work black market," *Miami Herald*, October 12.

Rice, John. 1997. "Cuban official signals limits on capitalism," *Miami Herald*, November 28.

Ritter, Archibald R. M. 1998. "Entrepreneurship, Micro-enterprise, and Public Policy in Cuba: Promotion, Containment, or Asphyxiation?" *Journal of International Studies and World Affairs* 40:2 (Summer): 63-94.

Ritter, Archibald R. M. 2000. "El regimen impositivo para la microempresa en Cuba." *Revista de la CEPAL* 71: 145-162, August.

Rodríguez Cruz, Francisco. 1996. "El cuenta propia también es cuenta nuestra," *Trabajadores*, June 3: 5.

Scarpaci, Joseph L. 1995. "The Emerging Food and *Paladar* Market in Havana." *Cuba in Transition—Volume 5* (ASCE): 74-84.

Serge, Roberto, Mario Coyula, and Joseph L. Scarpaci. 1997. *Havana: Two Faces of the Antillean Metropolis*. Chichester: John Wiley and Sons.

"Sobre el ejercicio del trabajo por cuenta propia." 1996. Joint Resolution #1, *Trabajadores*, June 3: 4-5.

Stanley, David. 2000. *Lonely Planet: Cuba*. Second Edition. Melbourne: Lonely Planet Publications.

Togores González, Viviana. n.d. "Consideraciones sobre el sector informal de la economía: Un estudio de su comportamiento en Cuba." Mimeo, Havana.

Vicent, Mauricio. 2000. "'Paladares' de La Habana," *El País*, December 10: 6-7.

Viño Zimerman, Luís. 2001. "Politica de exterminio de la iniciativa privada," *CubaNet News*, No. 32, April 1.

Whitefield, Mimi. 1993. "Rapid changes push Cuba into unknown: Will reforms spin out of control?" *Miami Herald*, September 27.

Whitefield, Mimi. 1994a. "Cuban home eateries refuse to close shop: Undeterred by government order," *Miami Herald*, January 7.

Whitefield, Mimi. 1994b. "Cuba tries to reign in market abuses," *Miami Herald*, January 29.

Whitefield, Mimi. 1996a. "A Taste of Capitalism," *Miami Herald*, May 19.

Whitefield, Mimi. 1996b. "The taxman comes to Cuba," *Miami Herald*, June 9.

IMPACT OF SEPTEMBER ELEVEN ON TOURISM ACTIVITIES IN CUBA AND IN THE CARIBBEAN

Nicolás Crespo and Charles Suddaby

EFFECTS OF SEPTEMBER 11 ON WORLD TOURISM

Tourism has grown almost routinely for more than 50 years and has recovered rapidly from many crises. However, the repercussions of September 11, 2001 (9/11) have threatened to end the run.

International tourism revenues have grown every year since the Second World War. Conflicts such as the 1991 Gulf War, economic crises, and ecological disasters such as Chernobyl have failed to stop the increase in international travel at any time over the past 50 years.

After an initial tidal wave of cancellations following 9/11, travel bookings have resumed but are still about 10-15 percent down from last year. Travelers planning holidays seem prepared only to book at the last minute and are reluctant to commit to long-term plans. Since the attacks, the number of tourists to France, the world's most-visited country, has fallen 20 percent. The United States, the second most-visited country suffered a reduction of 12 percent. The number of Japanese tourists leaving home—one of the world's higher spending groups—fell 22 percent during the last quarter of 2001.

The tourism industry has reacted to lower demand by cutting costs and dismissing staff. Thomas Cook, the German-based package holiday group, has reduced its 26,000 workforce by 10 percent; Walt Disney asked workers at its Orlando theme park to volunteer for a 20 percent cut in hours and salary. Worldwide 8.8 million jobs were affected. The Unit-

ed Nations estimates that the industry, one of the world's largest, employs 207 million people—equivalent to 8 percent of global employment. Business travel had experienced slower growth before 9/11 due to the U.S. economic downturn. Hotels, particularly in gateway cities in the U.S. and major European countries, reported lower occupancies last year as companies cut on travel spending.

The World Tourism Organization, the Madrid-based UN-affiliated agency, changed its forecast for 2002 several times. The prospect for 2002 is better than for 2001 but it relies heavily on improvements during the second half of the year, when European vacationers traditionally travel to tourism destinations of warmer climates. Tourism has shown a remarkable resilience to adversity, but privately, industry insiders agree that the current situation could be different from previous crises for three relevant reasons.

First, aircraft were used as weapons, which triggered a fear of flying in many people. Second, Americans, widely regarded as the most frequent international travelers, were attacked in their own country. That has led to a greater feeling of vulnerability. Third, the "war on terrorism" has the implication of being open-ended and may spill over into areas other than Afghanistan.

Even so, industry officials remain optimistic. While international tourism has slowed down in most popular destinations, it has been partially offset by an increase in short-haul and domestic travel. Many families, reluctant to venture into foreign lands and to use long-haul aircraft, have changed their vacation plans to nearby domestic resort destinations.

Travelers' confidence will have to be rebuilt through increased security and countries will have to start rekindling a desire for long-distance traveling by increasing marketing. Demand will also be affected by the extent to which the costs of additional security are passed on to the travelers.

One factor in the industry's favor is that the relentless growth in world tourism is linked to cheap transportation costs and greater disposable income and leisure time in the main demand-generating countries, such as the United States, Germany, Japan, France, United Kingdom and others. In those countries (accounting for 40 percent of international travel), a holiday is increasingly regarded not as a luxury that may be cut in strained times, but as a necessity. This trend is likely to continue and extend to other countries as a result of increases in the population's discretionary income.

EFFECTS OF SEPTEMBER 11 ON CUBAN TOURISM

The Cuban economy, as in any country that is highly dependent on international tourism, suffered the immediate impact of the attacks on the U.S. Three or more days of virtual paralysis of air transportation occurred while new security measures were established in countries that fly aircraft to the U.S. Many travelers were stranded for up to a week and no new vacation travel was initiated. Worldwide, vacations were cancelled or deferred. Even the most daring tourists stopped planning ahead and made traveling arrangements only at the last minute, taking advantage of the substantial discounts offered by airlines and resort destinations.

Like most of its Caribbean neighbors, Cuba watched as its tourism industry took a nosedive when people around the world cancelled vacations and avoided unnecessary air travel. October and November, considered part of the low season, were particularly depressed months as 30 hotels "temporarily" shut down and dozens more across the island closed off entire floors—about one third of the capacity in the coun-

try. Just two weeks after the terrorist attacks, hundreds of seasonal employees were sent home.

Tourist industry officials in Cuba had expected the year 2001 to be a landmark one, predicting a record two million visitors and US $2.2 billion in revenues. Instead 9/11 transformed an almost sure bet into a wild card.

Cuba, like other countries in the region, experienced a 25 to 30 percent decline in tourism arrivals. The slump did not stop there. Instead, it triggered a domino effect in sectors directly linked to tourism—such as construction and manufacturing.

Tourism has been described in the last ten tears as the motor of the Cuban economy. After Soviet subsidies of an estimated US $5 billion per annum dried up, Cuban planners restructured the economy and sought new trading partners. Sugar, which had ruled as the kingpin of hard currency earnings for decades, was overthrown by the leisure industry and its ability to generate quick cash returns. Last year, the tourism industry's gross revenues of US $1.9 billion outstripped Cuba's total exports of US $1.7 billion.

The events of 9/11 clearly revealed the downside of this switch. Bad times in tourism now also mean difficult times in other areas. Construction and manufacturing, including food processing—the largest branch of manufacturing in Cuba, suffered the most.

The tourism industry is credited with having helped stabilize the island's economy growth over the past ten years. An indicator of this is the high percentage of locally manufactured products, rather than imported, consumed by the tourism industry, and currently claimed to be 67 percent.

The 9/11 attacks brought more bad news to Cuba. The recession it unleashed in the U.S. left many Cuban immigrants out of work, or, at the very least, fearful of lay-offs. While not stopping them, this resulted in a reduction in the remittances to their relatives in Cuba. Last year, the UN Economic Commission for Latin America determined that family remittances to Cuba totaled somewhere between US $700 million to US $900 million a year. One way to judge the amount of US dollars floating in the Cuban market is to examine retail sales in state-run *dollar stores* catering primarily to domestic consumption. Those sales are said to be down by US $150 million.

Hurricane Michelle

Eramos pocos y parió Catana is a Cuban saying mentioned when matters continually get worse.

Nature's wrath has driven agricultural prices up even farther. Hurricane Michelle, a category four storm that ripped across the island flattening fields and homes in early November, affected half of the country and its population. But with the considerable damage to exports and the infrastructure, no Cuban has escaped Michelle's wrath. The final damage toll has yet to be calculated, but it appears it could be more than a billion dollars.

Closing of the Russian Military Post

One "minor" economic blow to the island, but a significant political casualty, was Russia's announcement in October that it would close its Lourdes military communications post on the outskirts of Havana, depriving the Cuban government of US $200 million in annual rent.

All this came when the economy was already rocky due to the global economic slowdown. Low world prices for Cuban exports of nickel, coffee and sugar are contributing to the dismal outlook making the average Cuban worry for the future. In spite of this and all the current pressure on the island's economy, the government insists that conditions will never deteriorate to the levels of 1994 again.

SIX MONTHS AFTER—THE CARIBBEAN

The Caribbean countries received US $20 billion in tourism revenue in 2001. This represents 30 percent of their overall GDP and creates employment for 30 percent of the work force. In addition, the Caribbean receives 15 million cruise ship passengers, according to the Caribbean Tourism Organization (CTO).

Hospitality industry experts anticipated that the year 2002 would be better than 2001—however, it now seems that they will only see a modest improvement. The Caribbean Tourism Organization reports data supplied by 16 Caribbean islands that we present in

Table 1. Four countries report an increase in the number of tourist arrivals, however most of the increases are small and only Bermuda experienced a significant number of arrivals. Twelve destinations report decreases in tourist arrivals. The dramatic percentage decrease (40.6%) in St. Lucia, however, represents a smaller absolute figure than the 3.6 percentage decrease for Puerto Rico.

Virtually all the Caribbean islands are launching promotional campaigns, particularly through television, the trade press, and the Internet in efforts to offset any fear of traveling still remaining since the 9/11 attacks on American soil. Package tours and cruise ship rates as well as hotel prices, have been discounted between 15 and 25 percent. Many hotel and travel enterprises have attempted to offset the loss of revenues by reducing normal expenses, sometimes to the detriment of the usual quality of service. The impact of this action is less noticeable, in hotels in the upscale market category. Within the full-service segment, those hotels operating under the all-inclusive system have initiated the deepest discounting in their rates.

Dominican Republic. The Dominican Republic reported tourism revenue decrease of US $400 million in 2001 and expects no growth in 2002.

Barbados. Barbados estimates a reduction of 18 percent in tourism revenue in 2002.

Puerto Rico. Puerto Rico has not suffered as much because of the public perception of security of this U.S. Territory. The February 2002 occupancy at 78.8 percent was slightly higher than in the same month in 2001.

SIX MONTHS AFTER — CUBA

According to Ibrahim Ferradaz, Minister of Tourism, in spite of 9/11, Cuba was able to attract 555 more tourists in 2001 than in the prior year for a total of 1,774,541 tourists. This was due to the increase in arrivals in the first half of the year before the 9/11 attacks. Compared to other countries in the Caribbean, Cuba has performed better. Total tourism revenues amounted to US $1.8 billion in 2001. However, the average tourist expenditure has decreased. In 1996 the average expenditure was US $1,474, while in 2000, it decreased to US $1,098 and to US

Table 1. Changes in Caribbean Arrivals, First Quarter 2001 vs. First Quarter 2002

Islands with Increased Arrivals			Islands with Decreased Arrivals		
Island	Period	%	Island	Period	%
Curaçao	Jan-Mar	10.5	Puerto Rico	Jan-Feb	3.2
Monserrat	Jan-Feb	12.4	St. Lucia	Jan-Feb	40.6
St. Vincent & the G.	Jan-Mar	2.7	Aruba	Jan-Apr	11.4
Bermuda	Jan-Feb	2.9	Bahamas	Jan-Apr	7.4
			Barbados	Jan-Apr	12.1
			Belize	Jan-Apr	3.8
			Cayman Is.	Jan-Apr	14.4
			Jamaica	Jan-Apr	10.7
			St. Martin	Jan-Apr	16.5
			Turks & C.	Jan-Apr	17.4
			USVI	Jan-Apr	3.8
			Cuba	Jan-Mar	14.4

$1,040 in 2001. Much of this reduction in average spending can be attributed to the declining length of stay that, in turn, has been brought about by improved access to the country.

The Minister of Tourism reported that their market strategy for 2002 would emphasize promotion of several Cuban destinations among the retailers and direct sellers targeting the European market, Canada, Brazil and Mexico. The strategy has been identified as the best means of improving the image of Cuban tourism and reducing its perception as a mass tourism/low priced destination. However no mention was made of the wholesaler trade, the "bread and butter" provider of demand in the all-inclusive segment. The impressive growth of Cuba's tourism is greatly attributed to the significant contribution of this segment. Wholesalers provide attractive packages in well-designed literature that sells the destination with exciting photography at competitive prices. Some wholesalers have joint-ventured with the Cuban government in developing and operating hotels in the island.

NEW DEVELOPMENTS — THE CARIBBEAN

The amazingly high resilience of the tourism industry is demonstrated by the abundance of new projects planned and under construction in the Caribbean. Only a few projects have been placed on hold as a result of 9/11. In the Caribbean, after the initial shock, construction has re-started, particularly in the upscale segment. Apparently, the upscale resort segment has been able to cope with the crisis better than other market segments, although most companies report

Table 2. The Caribbean—New Projects in the Upscale Market Segment, 2002-2005

Development of New Supply
Inter-Continental Cayo Largo, Puerto Rico
Four Seasons Emerald Bay, Bahamas
Fairmont Coco Beach, Puerto Rico
Ritz Carlton Pelican Island, Antigua
Mandarin Oriental Palmas, Puerto Rico
Four Seasons San Miguel, Puerto Rico

decreases in achieved rates. Table 2 lists some of the projects in the upscale category presently under development. Other new developments in the Caribbean include:

- Developers initiated the first phase of a US $3 billion project on the eastern coast of the Dominican Republic named Punta Cana. When completed, it will comprise 5,000 hotel rooms in eight properties.

- Puerto Rico's Department of Tourism announced that the island's inventory of rooms would increase by 4,000 from now until 2005.

- St. Croix, USVI expects to open a 300-room hotel and casino by 2005.

- Developers plan to build a 290-room hotel in Haiti at an estimated cost of US $40 million.

- In Cartagena, Colombia, considered part of the Caribbean, there are plans to build two hotels with 75 and 300 rooms to open in 2005 and 2007 respectively.

- A recent study on visitors arriving in cruise ships has caused several islands to budget for significant improvements in their port facilities and in the land amenities designed to cater short time visitors.

NEW DEVELOPMENTS — CUBA

The Ministry of Tourism has made several announcements regarding development of new hotels, marinas, and restaurants expected to open or start construction between 2002 and 2004. In addition, they plan to refurbish existing hotels, taking advantage of the lower occupancy and partial closing of hotels as a result of the 9/11 events.

Refurbishment of Existing Hotels

Horizontes announced that they would invest US $48 million to refurbish 79 percent of their hotels in Varadero and build some additional rooms. Horizontes owns eleven hotels with 1,900 rooms that represent 16 percent of Varadero's inventory of rooms. They plan to expend an average of US $39,350 per room in renovating 1,330 rooms.

We estimate that almost half of the existing hotels dedicated to international tourism have reached the tenth year of their life. In the hotel industry, considering the use and deterioration received as a consequence of high occupancies, it is customary to initiate a major refurbishment of the hotel property as it approaches its tenth anniversary. Cuba would need to invest about US $730 million to bring its aged international tourism rooms to competitive physical conditions. For this calculation, we have used the estimated expenditure per room as planned by Horizontes; however, it is likely that the more likely renovation cost is less than this, resulting in a total investment requirement in the order of US $500 million. Should Cuba decide to delay or defer the refurbishment of their rooms, it will run the risk of been being forced to discount room rates to offset the market demand reaction. Additionally, it might need to face the undesirable public perception of a deteriorated destination, hurting also the rest of its market.

Announcements of New Developments

During the last ten months the different corporations created to direct the development of tourism in Cuba have announced diverse projects that would increase Cuba's inventory of rooms and incorporate new hotel companies' participation in some of the projects.

Table 3 summarizes the on-going projects in Cuba as announced by the Ministry of Tourism and the Cuban hotel corporations. These projects include a mix of resort hotels and small properties located in historical buildings or resulting from restoration of architecturally important residences in the locality. There are numerous other projects, some of them very substantial in nature, that are considered still in the planning process and which have not been factored into these estimates.

Estimated Future Openings

We estimated the future opening of properties presently under development relying on the official announcements. The hotel project openings include those presently under construction and/or under contract and planning. They are expected to open during the period 2002-2005. We have also calculated the value of those hotels at an average international cost of US $110,000 per room (Table 4).

The estimated investment cost of the new projects (US $731.6 million), combined with the estimated cost of refurbishing the existing hotels that are ten years old (US $730.0 million), amounts to US $1.4616 billion.

Normally in the hospitality industry, the hotels create a reserve for replacement of furniture, fixtures and equipments calculated at 3 to 6 percent of ongoing revenues. In many cases, the reserve is timely funded so that cash is available when needed. Most probably, with the exception of a few responsible international hotel management companies, this practice is not followed on the island. Considering the decline in foreign visitors and the aggressive discounting of rates, Cuba will have to make an extraordinary effort in order to be able to fund or finance such an endeavor.

CONCLUSION

To sum up, 9/11 has affected all the islands in the Caribbean differently. The big players in the region (Dominican Republic, Cancun, Puerto Rico, Jamaica and Cuba) have a greater flexibility to take mea-

Table 3.   Cuban Tourism Projects, 2003-2005

Property	Rooms	Location	Status-Open	Owner	Operator	Stars
LTI Beaches	391	Varadero	UC 2004		LTI	5 star
Gran Lido Super Club	460	Varadero	UC 2004	Gaviota		
Blau	395	Varadero	UC 2004	Gaviota		4 star
Royal Sandals Hicacos	400	Varadero	UC 2004		Sandals	
Iberostar	384	Varadero	UP 2004	Cubanacán	Iberostar	5 star
Solymar	525	Varadero	UC 2003	Gran Caribe	Barceló	
LTI Panorama	313	Havana	UC 2004		LTI	5 star
Hospedaje Pansea	N/A	Havana	UP 2005	Cubanacán	Hotelera SA	
Paradisso	400	Cayo Largo	UP 2005		Sol Meliá	
Barcelo	N/A	Cayo Largo	UP 2005	Cubanacán	Barceló	
Hospedaje Pansea	N/A	Trinidad		Cubanacán	Hotelera SA	
Iberostar	60	Trinidad	UP 2004	Cubanacán	Iberostar	
Ancón	292	Trinidad	UC 2004	Horizontes	Mosaico	4 star
Hospedaje Pansea	60	Viñales	UP 2004	Cubanacán	Hotelera SA	
Gran Hotel	N/A	Santa Lucía	UP 2005	Cubanacán	Hotelera SA	
Barcelo	N/A	Santa Lucía	UP 2005	Gaviota	Barceló	
Hotel del Rijo	16	Sancti Spiritus	UP 2003	Cubanacán		
N/A	N/A	Bacunaya-gua	UP 2005	Cubanacán	Valle de Yumurí SA	
Barceló	N/A	Guardalavaca	UP 2005		Barceló	
Eco projects		María la Gorda				

UP Under planning
UC Under construction

Table 4.   Cuba Planned Hotel Openings, 2002-2005

Year	Hotels	Rooms	Investment in US$
2002	4	1,235	135,840,000
2003	2	541	59,510,000
2004	9	2,755	303,050,000
2005	8	2,120	233,200,000
Total	**23**	**6,651**	**731,610,000**

sures to offset the negative impact such as shifting idle workers to other jobs, anticipating vacations and leaves, accelerating regular maintenance and executing major repairs and refurbishment, increasing promotion and sales calls, etc.

Those small destinations, unless affiliated with an important hotel chain, are vulnerable for lack of some of those choices—in some cases with high social connotations.

In all, Cuba and the rest of the Caribbean are doing their best to survive until the demand for Caribbean destinations increases, forecasted to happen in the second half of 2002. Those countries that do not prohibit local people to patronize their international tourism facilities have enjoyed an increase of local demand caused by aggressive discounting, normally during the off-season months, and by their choice to enjoy their vacations in the country rather than traveling abroad. Puerto Rico and Mexico have attained local demands that represent 33% and 46%, respectively, of their total rooms occupied in 2001.

Cuba's tourism industry is not able to take advantage of this opportunity due to the current rule that precludes local people from patronizing international tourism facilities. It is rumored that Cuba is studying a change to this rule to allow the growing number of Cubans who have access to dollars and other hard currency to spend at the underutilized international tourism facilities. From the economic point of view, the tourism product will have a lower cost than the products imported and offered for sale to Cubans at the dollar stores. *An empty room today cannot be sold tomorrow.*

TRINIDAD'S TOURISM: BETWEEN "GLOCAL" HERITAGE AND NATIONAL ECONOMIC DEVELOPMENT

Joseph L. Scarpaci

Globalization studies are the 500-pound gorilla in contemporary social science research. While the meaning of "globalization" is the subject of many debates, there is no doubt that the popularity of the topic is widespread.

Once a term confined to policy analysts and scholars, the close of the 20th century quickly secured a place for "globalization" in the world's languages, practically becoming a household word thanks to a dizzying array of "gee whiz!" technologies. One metric of its usage in academic circles is its citation in the Library of Congress Card Catalog. In 1987, there were no entries for "globalization" as a keyword in the library's card catalog. In 1994, Waters (2000) found 34 entries; in August 2000, I found 884. In August 2001 there were 1,384 entries, a 57% increase in eleven months (excluding the British spelling "globalisation" n= 213). By July 2002, the number of entries had dipped to 1,273, suggesting more nuanced classifications of books at the library. While the use of the term is widespread, I contend that case-study research is one way to anchor these broad processes in micro-geographies.

If globalization is a slippery concept that has come to mean everything, then it also conveys very little meaning. I use it mainly to refer to a shrinking of time and space through the rise of information technologies. We can theorize the economic, political, and cultural dimensions of globalization to make our review of world problems more precise (Lerner and Bohli 2000). As information and commodities are exchanged at a quickening pace, the abilities of the

nation-state and its regulatory agencies diminish. That means nations slowly lose control over the flows of information, capital, and technology that pass through their boundaries. Some argue that these "new spaces of globalization" represent a victory of post-Fordist capitalism (Dicken 1999) because new types of investment are no longer based on the traditional components of economic development that included natural resources and cheap labor. Because labor unions and the conventional blocs of voters are made increasingly powerless in a globalized world, transnational capital can more easily circumvent the traditional coalitions who looked to the state for protection and support (Mishra 2000; Afshar and Pezzoli 2001; Korten 1995; Mander and Goldsmith 1996).

In this paper, I borrow the term "glocal," which is an obvious hybrid from "globalization" and "local." I wish to show the way that broader processes at foot in international tourism are tethered to local outcomes—in this case Trinidad—but filtered through the present leadership in Cuba. Globalization does not simply fill vacuums left by an eroded state or collapsed Soviet aid as in the case of Cuba. Radu (1998, 700) describes Cuban institutional behavior this way:

Because the party leadership directly controls all institutions, all-important decisions, from management to personnel to planning and production targets, are dependent upon the central policymaking apparatus, the Politburo. Hence, the ability to respond promptly to any challenge or unexpected development is severely hindered, and individual responsibility by institutional leaders is inhibited. Attempts at institutional reform–whether workers self management ... or decentralization of planning ... failed because they did not (and, by the logic of communist system, could not) escape from the party's ultimate control.

In recent years, new wealth has come to Trinidad in the form of tourism development. The Ministry of Tourism has been promoting Trinidad as a "tourist pole" along with Santiago (east), the keys and archipelagoes (north central), and Havana-Varadero (northwest). Specifically, Cuban tourism authorities seek investors to develop the Ancón peninsula, 9 kilometers south of Trinidad. However, the Ministry's five-year plan is at odds with the goals of the City Restoration Office. My research question is, then, whether a cultural heritage site with international reputation, UNESCO World Heritage Status, and articulate and passionate leadership by architects at the local level, could possibly be compromised by development of tourism at the national level.

This dilemma encapsulates the tensions inherent in "glocal" studies. Who jeopardizes Trinidad's colonial charm in the name of hard currency earnings? On the one hand, the Cuban leadership needs hard currency to sustain its social provision. On the other, local officials in Trinidad believe an unfettered international tourism market bound for its town and beaches could spoil an international heritage site. I argue that while inter-governmental collaboration among various local, regional, and national agencies is always rife with conflict, the Trinidad case study strikingly shows a top-down approach to economic development plans. In this paper, I draw on the relationship between tourism and heritage planning in Trinidad and the adjacent Sugar Mill Valley (*Valle de los Ingenios*) to make this point. The paper begins with a brief historical overview, to which we turn in the next section.

TRINIDAD: HISTORY AND GEOGRAPHY

Trinidad (pop. 42,000) is a colonial gem on the south-central coast of Cuba (Figure 1). Characterized by geographic isolation, it is tucked away at the foot of the scenic Escambray Mountains. This historic *villa* was the fourth of seven initial settlements forged in

Figure 1. Trinidad's Main Town Square

The Sánchez Iznaga house to the left is currently the Architecture Museum. The Ortíz house in the middle functions as an art gallery. At the horizon, the Caribbean Sea.

1514 by Diego de Velázquez, but it took Trinidad three centuries to reflect the opulence of sugar wealth.

Trinidad sits on the southern slopes of the Sierra de Trinidad, about 8 kilometers north of its Caribbean port, Casilda. Chronicles of the site date back to 1494 when a seaman in Columbus' crew noted hunters and gatherers in the region. They described a landscape with "fruits and bread and water and cotton, and rabbits and doves of the most different species, unknown in our lands, and [the indigenous people] sang joyfully believing that people had come from heaven" (Gutiérrez n.d, 3). Settled in 1514 by Diego Velázquez, Trinidad lost the attention of the conquistadores when Hernán Córtez, who had stopped there briefly and later, controlled the Central Valley of Mexico. Spain's interest shifted to the mineral-rich mainland at Trinidad's expense.

During the 16th and 17th centuries, the settlement remained distant and hard to reach, which led to a contraband economy. Out of the oversight of Santiago de Cuba to the east, and Havana to the west, English, French, and Dutch pirates and corsairs took advantage of Spain's frequent wars in Europe to make Trinidad one of the primary smuggling areas. Trinidad's economy benefited from events in Spain and the Caribbean. Reforms enacted during the reign of Carlos III (1759-1788) broke the privileges and monopolies that Havana enjoyed. Trinidad benefited from these Bourbon reforms and expanded trade, especially with other Caribbean islands and the South American port of Cartagena.

In the nearby island of Saint Dominique (Haiti), the 1792 slave revolt led sugar planters to resettle in Trinidad. The adjacent Sugar Mill Valley (*Valle de los Ingenios*) had fertile soils and came to house more than 50 sugar mills by the early nineteenth century. By 1825, Trinidad was producing 10% of the island's total sugar output, and all of it came out of one valley (Venegas 1973). Trinidad and its vicinity became one of the world's leading sugar producers. Several restored palaces that are now museums show the opulence of the era (Núñez Jiménez, Zerquera, and de Lara, 1986). Landed aristocrats usually spent the sugar-harvest season in country palaces, and the remainder of the year in Trinidad. The family names of the elite from that era—Brunet, Becquer, Cantero, Iznaga, and Borello—constructed elaborate residences in Trinidad that are national landmarks. The 1827 census showed 29,000 residents, 12,000 of whom lived in the urban core, with the remainder scattered throughout the countryside in sugar mills and small hamlets (Gutiérrez 1997, 29).

By the mid-1800s, however, Trinidad's traditional slave-based sugar production method could not keep pace with the newly introduced mills. The traditional *trapiche* on which the Trinidad sugar economy was based, consisting of oxen-driven grinders for crushing the cane, could not compete with modern mills (Marrero 1983). Since slavery was not abolished officially until 1878, the landed aristocracy was loath to abandon the system and modernize sugar production. Other parts of Cuba and Louisiana competed with the sugar production in Trinidad. Increased European sugar production also undercut the world price of the commodity.

In the 1820s and 1830s, investment opportunities attracted local capitalists to support railroad construction between Villa Clara and Cienfuegos, and between Puerto Principe and Nuevitas. Meanwhile, Trinidad experienced stop-and-go railroad construction and an eleborate rail network to transport sugar

cane was never fully established. Instead, plantation owners used their slaves to float cane down rivers for processing at the *trapiches*. When the rivers filled in from siltation, logistics in getting cane to the *trapiches* were complicated. Moreover, Cienfuegos, founded late (1804) in Cuban history, opened its new deepwater seaport and that siphoned off traffic from Casilda, Trinidad's port.

For all these reasons, the town and region had fallen into a deep recession by 1860. While other sugar-growing regions of Cuba—especially parts of Matanzas and Havana provinces—were connected by rail lines to sugar mills for processing, and ports for export, Trinidad remained isolated and the region stagnated. Independence wars in the late 19th centuries reduced cattle production in the valleys and coffee cultivation in the foothills and mountains around Trinidad. When American investors entered the region after the war of 1898, they bought large tracts of land cheaply and replaced some 48 smaller *ingenios* with a single, modern sugar mill (*central*) (Marín 1945).

Economic recession and geographic isolation, then, left important sections of the historic core of Trinidad in place. It was not until 1919 that a rail line made its way to Trinidad and connected the town with the national network. A paved road to Sancti Spiritus to the east, was completed in 1950 and two years later, another road was paved to Cienfuegos, to the west. All these factors of history, transportation, and technology kept Trinidad isolated and, in turn, helped ensure the antiquity of its built environment.

CONTEMPORARY OVERVIEW AND PLANNING ISSUE

In the 1980s, Trinidad's municipal government began to capitalize on that architectural resource for heritage tourism. In 1988, UNESCO declared it a World Heritage Site. Outside tourism in the historic core, the rest of the city and region has various industries such as sugar refineries, sawmills, dairies, fisheries, cigar, cattle, and cigarette factories. A small airport brings in several flights daily from the "tourist poles" of Santiago de Cuba, Camagüey, Varadero, and Havana.

The first hotel with modern tourist facilities in Trinidad was erected in 1957. Hotel Las Cuevas sits on a hillside just above the colonial core beyond the historic limits. Within the historic district, there are no hotels, and the larger facilities are a 20-minute drive to Ancón Beach, on the Caribbean Sea. Fortunately, no modern structures disrupt the colonial skyline of Trinidad's *centro histórico*. However, in 2002, more than 50 legal bed-and-breakfast facilities operated, placing serious burdens on the city's water and waste system.

In the section that follows, I discuss the Ministry of Tourism's 1998 plan to add 5,000 more hotel beds to the Ancón peninsula on the Caribbean, and the implications of such plan for the World Heritage site of Trinidad and Valle de los Ingenios.

Ancón Beach and Trinidad's Centro Histórico

Forty years ago, CIA director Richard Bissel argued that Playa Ancón should be the site of the ill-fated Bay of Pigs Invasion, and not Girón beach located to the west. Unlike the Bay of Pigs (surrounded by thick mangroves and layers of coral reefs), Ancón Beach is flat and very accessible. Today, a new invasion is expected. The Tourism Ministry seeks to add 5,000 hotel rooms to the only part of the greater Trinidad area that can handle such growth: the Ancón peninsula (Figure 2). Since the announcement in 2000, only one 300-bed facility was built, and that was done by a Cuban company, not a joint-venture. These construction figures are very different from the 5,000 units the ministry desires.

By mid-2002, only three hotels (Hotel Ancón, 279 rooms; Hotel Costa Sur, 131 rooms; Trinidad al Mar, 420 rooms) occupied the peninsula. The primary attraction is the four-kilometer beach with sugary white sand, Playa Ancón, on the Caribbean Sea (Figure 2). Hotel Ancón, located on the beach, represents the hundreds of pre-fabricated designs created during the first two decades of the Revolution. Schools, factories, office buildings, and hotels adopted a series of pre-fabricated models that were used in France, Yugoslavia, Scandinavia, and Canada (Machado 1976). Prefabrication in Cuba was economical and symbolic because it:

became reference points for the Revolution's modernization efforts...[and] spread to the most unlikely and remote corners...The enduring nature of Soviet power had been reaffirmed by victory over barbarian Nazi forces. Soviet planning sought to show new features and rights of the unfolding socialist society (Scarpaci et al 2002, 212).

To some degree, this philosophy was evident in the use of prefabrication in Cuba as well. Although prefabrication exists on the beach and in the post-colonial quarters of the city, it is not found in the historic district.

Figure 2.　Ancón Peninsula

Aerial photograph of Ancón Peninsula with Ancón Beach and the Caribbean Sea to the left (west), looking north with the Escambray Mountains in the background.

Trinidad has an underdeveloped tourist infrastructure. No hotel exists within the 1988 UNESCO-declared World Heritage district. A two-star hotel, Las Cuevas, built a few years before the Revolution and operated by the Cuban company Horizontes, sits on the side of a hill just north of the old city (Figure 3). However, there are scores of privately operated bed-and-breakfast establishments in the old city, most of them illegal, that charge between $10 and $20 daily. Although very limited private enterprise has been permitted since 1993, engineering authorities are more concerned with this type of lodging (greater water consumption, less water pressure, and more raw sewage) than is the "tax man."

Completing even half of the 5,000 desired units desired by the Ministry of Tourism may jeopardize his-

Figure 3. Location Map, Trinidad and Vicinity

Figure 4. Entrance to the non-motorized zone in historic center of Trinidad

toric preservation and will certainly place economic development interests on a collision course with architectural historians. The current water and sewage capacities in the old city have already been reached. Although standard 30-passenger buses as well as all other motorized traffic cannot enter the colonial core of Trinidad because of gated streets (Figure 4), city planners and conservators are concerned about the impact of dozens of additional buses that might bring tourists from the peninsula to the town. The Cuban- and Italian-trained Assistant Director of the City Restoration Office, architect Nancy Benítez, remarked:

> Imagine dozens of larger buses parked outside the historic center, with their air conditioning units running. The vibrations will shake the streets and buildings, while thousands of tourists flood the historic center. They're going to need restaurants and bathrooms. The pressure on the old city will be incredible.

Attracting Investors

Three major attributes may encourage tourism that, in turn, will attract investment. Foremost is the colo-

nial charm of old Trinidad. The design of elite homes reflects a blend of Spanish and French styles, especially evident in the traditional ceramic roof tiles. As noted above, the French came when sugar-cane planters fled the 1792 slave revolt in nearby Haiti (Zanetti and García 1998). With the Louisiana Purchase in 1803, more French growers resettled in this corner of the West Indies. Economic prowess grew into what historian Moreno Fraginals (1976) calls Cuba's "sugar aristocracy" or "sugar-ocracy." The result is a rich blend of Spanish, French and Creole architecture, graced by cobbled streets made out of ship ballast or rocks from nearby streams and quarries.

The City Restoration Office is the primary entity handling historic preservation in Trinidad. Formed in 1988, the office has restored dozens of mansions that have been turned into museums and cultural centers. Since 1997, the office has been renovating a

Figure 5. Residential Exterior Door

A carpenter from the City Restoration Office of Trinidad restores just the lower half of a residential exterior door in the Tres Cruces neighborhood of Trinidad. Imported cedar from Belize is costly at about $500 USD a cubic meter.

Figure 6. Iznaga Tower

Iznaga Tower on the former Manaca Sugar Plantation, located 13 kms. east of Trinidad. Built between 1835-45 for the overseer (may-ordomo) to watch over slaves in the field atop the 43-meter, seven-level structure. The staircase was in disrepair for most of the 20th century. One of the first restorations undertaken by Trinidad's Restoration Office in 1988 was to reconstruct the stairwell. Hand-sewn table clothes and other embroideries made by local women hang on clothes lines to entice tourists. Officials at the Trinidad Restoration Office believe that the vendors detract from the aesthetic value of the plantation and have tried unsuccessfully to remove the vendors from the base of the tower.

large residential quarter in the eastern part of the city called Tres Cruces (Figure 5).

Second, Trinidad is one of the few beach areas (in a region that geologically speaking has a "submerged coastline") on Cuba's south coast, in contrast to the tourist preference for the aquamarine waters and beaches that abound off the north coast. With a paved airport runway that dates back to the 1950s, the town airport receives small commercial flights several times daily from Havana, Varadero, Camagüey, and Santiago de Cuba.

Lastly, Trinidad offers tourists an attractive relative location. It serves as a departure point to explore the Escambray Mountains and the Topes de Collantes health-resort complex that sits at an elevation of about 830 meters, just one hour away. The town is also adjacent to the Sugar Mill Valley (*El Valle de los Ingenios*), which once held dozens of mills from the late 18th and early 19th centuries (Figure 6). The valley is the only natural landscape (not a town or city) designated a UNESCO World Heritage Site in Cuba (Old Havana, and, of course, Trinidad, are the other two).

Funding Small-scale Heritage Projects

Architects, planners, geographers, and engineers make up the 24 professionals of the Trinidad Restoration Office. They direct the renovation of several sugar plantations in the valley and hope to open a sugar museum in one of the former homes (Figure 7). Old slave quarters and tool sheds will be restored or reconverted for bathrooms and small restaurants. Investors are sought for reconverting specific properties in the valley both to relieve some of the tourism pressures in Trinidad, and to revive old buildings that still contain frescoes painted by Italian and French painters in the 1830s.

Restoration projects in Trinidad are now funded by a 2 percent tax that all companies operating in both dollars and pesos remit to the City Restoration Office. Architect Benítez notes that since 1998—the first year of revenue sharing—the budget has gone from a few thousand dollars to about $450,000 expected for the year 2000. The Office proposes a more modest investment strategy compared to that of the

Figure 7. Landlord's House at the former Guáimaro Plantation

Side view of the landlord's house at the former Guáimaro Plantation 21 kms. southeast of Trinidad. The original structure at the right was built in the 1830s and is covered by French-style "locking" roof tiles (versus the more common Spanish "curved" tiles). Bountiful sugar harvests in the 1840s allowed the landlord to add a colonnaded arcade to serves as a porch-gallery at the house entrance (left). The anteroom contains frescoes and murals painted by Italian masters 160 years ago. The City Restoration Office seeks investors to convert the mansion into the Museum of the Sugar Mill Valley (*El Museo del Valle de los Ingenios*) where artifacts from the slave-driven sugar economy will be displayed. Mechanization, especially stream engines and boilers, sent the Trinidad region into decline around 1860.

Figure 8. Former Iznaga residence

Former Iznaga residence, one block south of Trinidad's Plaza Mayor, awaits an investor. The property is currently managed by the Cuban tourist company, Cubanacán.

Ministry of Tourism that would encourage investors to build small hotels in restored colonial buildings. For example, a 19th century home (Figure 8) sits abandoned just two blocks south of the Plaza Mayor, and the Restoration Office has been looking for an investor for several years. "It would be the perfect five-star, small hotel," remarks Office Director and Trinidad native, Roberto "Macholo" López. To date, though, no one has come forward. "In general, hotel investors do not want to spend money on restoration," adds Benítez. "They prefer a new, clear site, where they can start fresh."

While this financing scheme for heritage preservation is innovative and serves as a window to Cuba's new political economy, some obstacles remain. Many companies that operate in either national currency (pesos) or hard currency (dollars) do not always pay. Some firms are so far in arrears with the Restoration Office, that the small group of architects has had to take the "debtors" to court and sue them for payment. Litigation drains the limited resources of the Restoration Office. Thus, not unlike market economies where cooperation is not always forthcoming, intra-governmental coordination is not always easy, even in the centrally planned economy of Cuba.

Trindad, Habana Vieja, and Santiago de Cuba serve as models for historic preservation, heritage tourism, and sustainable development in several important ways.

• First, they target specific revenues out of a larger pool of funds for upgrading the built environment of their neighborhoods. A cash-strapped state does not have to divert funds from health, education, or related public welfare sectors for this purpose. Rather, funds come from state entities that generate their own revenues. Thus, the cost sharing is minimum (2%) and widely distributed throughout the businesses that operate in the city of 42,000.

- Second, dollar-paying facilities earn their revenues from tourists, not Cubans. In that sense, one can make (and implicitly this ethos is echoed among the Trinidad community) the argument that tourists should be (indirectly) responsible for maintaining heritage sites, not the Cuban people who have seen their standard of living decline.

- Finally, the financing scheme is sustainable in that the revenues are proportional to the volume of tourists passing through. In some way, then, the Restoration Office budget will "rise and fall" with the ebb and flow of tourism. Holding constant for the moment the possible consequences of the 5,000 beds to be added on the beach, this 2% tax will allow for the constant and steady upgrading of the UNESCO site so that costly intervention is not necessary later this century.

CONCLUSION

The post-Soviet era sent shock waves throughout Eastern European nations and Cuba (Suchlicki 1998). Forced to compete without preferential prices for sugar exports, Cuba entered the global market. Since the early 1990s, it has drawn on a traditional comparative advantage, tourism, as a source of hard currency. In particular, it promotes heritage tourism as a venue to complement the traditional sun-and-surf outlets inherent in Caribbean tourism. This paper has attempted to show the ways in which a local heritage tourism setting immerses itself in the broader patterns of globalization, but with the socialist government as the intermediary force.

In contemporary Cuba, some economic development decisions made at the national level override local planning goals. In Trinidad, the City Restoration Office was notified of the 5000-bed goal after the Tourism Ministry made its decision. The differences of opinion between local and national decision-makers underscore the locals' concern with authentic heritage preservation and the latter's search for hard currency. A final determination on hotel bids, joint-venture agreements, and building construction was to be made by late 2000, but by mid-2002, there was still no word on these proposals.

E.F. Schumacher's celebrated work, *Small is Beautiful*, made a passionate plea for development projects that were locally defined, bottom-up, and small in scale. He railed against the mammoth development projects of the day: those undertaken by the Alliance for Progress in Latin America as well as a spate of World Bank-funded works in Africa, Asia, and Latin America.

Tourism planning and heritage preservation in Trinidad, Cuba embody a number of those tenets. Nevertheless, this paper has shown that firms operating in centrally planned economies are not necessarily more altruistic and cooperative than their counterparts in market economies. Opportunity comes knocking at local heritage tourism offices in ways that are serendipitous, if not tragic. Trinidad's Restoration Office currently benefits from a budget that exists in good measure because of the demise of the former USSR, and the dissolution of Cuba's traditional trading partners in Eastern Europe. No one could have anticipated the global ramifications of the events in 1989 for Trinidad, which has brought both challenges and opportunities in terms of how "glocal" processes manifest themselves in the town's built environment. Perhaps the real mettle of this new financing scheme will surface when the intragovernmental differences about beachfront development are resolved, and the residential quarters of Tres Cruces neighborhood are fully restored so that preservationists can practice their craft without policy mandates from afar.

REFERENCES

Afshar, F. and Pezzoli, K. 2001. "Globalization and Planning: Guest Editors' Introduction. Integrating globalization and planning." *Journal of Planning Education and Research* 20:277-290.

Dicken, P. 1998. *Global Shift: Transforming the World Economy.* New York: Guilford.

Gutiérrez, A. n.d. *Trinidad.* (ISBN 959-7064-02-2). Trinidad, offset.

Korten, D.C. 1995. *When Corporations Rule the World.* West Hartford, CT: Kumarian Press/Betttet-Koehler.

Mander, J. and Gildsmith, E. 1996. *The Case Against the Global Economy: And for A Turn Toward the Local.* San Francisco: Sierra Club Books.

Machado, O. 1976. *La industrialización de la construcción de la vivienda. El sistema I.M.S. en Cuba.* La Habana: DESA (mimeo).

Marín, F. 1945. *Historia de Trinidad.* Havana: Jesús Montero.

Marrero, L. 1983. *Cuba: Economía y Sociedad.* Vol. 9. Madrid: Editorial Playor.

Moreno Fraginals, M. 1976. *The Sugar Mill: The Socio-economic Complex of Sugar in Cuba, 1760-1860.* New York and London: Monthly Review Press.

Mishra, M. 2000. *Globalization and the Welfare State.* Cheltenham: Edgar Elger.

Núñez Jiménez, A. and Zerquera, C, and de Lara, F. 1986. *Trinidad de Cuba: Monumento Nacional.* Havana: Instituto Nacional de Turismo.

Radu, M. 1998. "Cuba's transition: Institutional lessons from Eastern Europe." In I.L. Horowitz and J. Suchlicki, editors, *Cuban Communism.* New Brunswick, NJ: Transaction, Chapter 37, pp. 697-718.

Scarpaci, J.L., Segre, R. and Coyula, M. 2002. *Havana: Two Faces of the Antillean Metropolis.* Chapel Hill: University of North Carolina Press.

Schumacher, E. F. 1973. *Small is Beautiful: A Study of Economics as if People Mattered.* London, Blond and Brigg.

Suchlicki, J. 1998. "Cuba without subsidies." In I.L. Horowitz and J. Suchlicki, editors, *Cuban Communism.* New Brunswick, NJ: Transaction, Chapter 36, pp. 688-696.

Venegas, H. 1973. "Apuntes sobre la decadencia trinitaria en el siglo XIX." *Islas* 46:214-23.

Zanetti, O. and García, Al. 1998. *Sugar and Railroads: A Cuban History, 1837-1959.* (Translated by F. W. Knight and Mary Todd). Chapel Hill and London: University of North Carolina Press.

IMPLICACIONES ECONÓMICAS DE LA CONSTITUCIÓN DEL 40: LECCIONES PARA EL FUTURO

Jorge A. Sanguinetty[1]

La restauración de la Constitución de 1940 como la ley principal de la República de Cuba ha sido un tema cuya vigencia ha tenido varios ciclos desde su derogación de facto por el golpe de estado del 10 de marzo de 1952. Durante los siete años de conflicto entre las diversas instancias políticas, el restablecimiento incondicional de esa constitución fue el objetivo casi universal de los distintos opositores, como lo plantean Sánchez (1996) y Carbonell Cortina (1997). En esa época no era ni siquiera pertinente discutir el contenido del texto constitucional, ni mucho menos proponer su reemplazo por otro. Parecía ser un objetivo nacional que la restauración de la democracia en Cuba y el cese de la dictadura de Batista tenía como condición *sine qua non* el restablecimiento de la Constitución del 40. De hecho, fue ese uno de los compromisos adquiridos por el movimiento dirigido por Fidel Castro durante su lucha contra la dictadura. Hoy acaso se pueda afirmar que no hay evidencia más puntual y precisa de la traición de las expectativas generadas por aquel compromiso que el que esa constitución no se haya restaurado.

Con los años, la Constitución del 40 representó para muchos cubanos el símbolo de la democracia perdida, democracia que todos sabían imperfecta pero que muchos consideraban una alternativa más deseable que lo que sucedió después de 1959. Con la caída del Muro de Berlín y su secuela de democratización en Europa Central y Oriental y la subsecuente disolución de la Unión Soviética, la restauración de la Constitución del 40 cobró nueva vigencia, no ya como símbolo sino como una posibilidad práctica que ayudaría a que Cuba entrara en una transición hacia la democracia. Y tanto como símbolo que como posibilidad, esa constitución guarda una posición cimera en el contexto de todo lo que hoy se puede considerar cubano. Fue un hito importante en la historia de la República cuando surgió de aquella Asamblea Constituyente, rigió en Cuba durante los años en que fue en gran medida respetada, ha sido portaestandarte de las luchas de ayer y de hoy y se ha mantenido vigente en la mente y en los corazones de muchos cubanos hasta nuestros días.

Desde el comienzo de la década de los noventa, cada vez que nos reunimos para discutir cómo contribuir a la democratización de Cuba, la Constitución del 40 ha vuelto a cobrar vigencia. Es obvio que el marco constitucional vigente que consagra el totalitarismo en Cuba no es compatible con una democracia y tiene que ser reemplazado por uno que consagre las libertades correspondientes. Esto habrá de suceder a pesar de los esfuerzos de Fidel Castro mientras se escriben estas líneas para eternizar su marca de socialismo en la isla. También es obvio que parezca más fácil y expedito que ese reemplazo se efectúe por medio de la Constitución del 40, pues de ese modo el país se ahorraría el enorme esfuerzo que significa definir y establecer una nueva constitución. Además, formular

1. El autor agradece los comentarios de Alberto Luzárraga, Juan Belt, Efrén Córdoba, Rolando Castañeda, Armando Ribas y Mercy Sanguinetty, pero es enteramente responsable por el contenido del trabajo.

una nueva constitución es especialmente más difícil en Cuba después de tantos años de dictadura en que los ciudadanos cubanos han estado aislados de toda corriente ideológica y filosófica que no haya sido del gusto del gobierno, además de haber estado impedidos de debatir libremente sobre cuestiones de estado y mucho menos sobre alternativas constitucionales.

Sin embargo, muy a pesar de las ventajas de restaurar la Constitución del 40 y sin querer menospreciar el valor sentimental que la misma siempre tendrá entre muchos cubanos, es necesario examinar críticamente otros aspectos prácticos de una restauración, especialmente los que se refieren a las consecuencias que tal restauración pudiera tener sobre la economía nacional. En este trabajo se presenta una análisis de las implicaciones económicas de la restauración de la Constitución del 40 y, alternativamente, de algunas de las consideranciones que deben tenerse en cuenta en caso que la población cubana opte por la promulgación de una constitución nueva.

El objetivo central de este trabajo es el de contribuir algunas ideas a este tema y estimular su discusión entre los ciudadanos que en algún momento deberán votar por alguna alternativa constitucional. En tales ocasiones debe tenerse en cuenta que cuanto más informado sea el conocimiento de los electores en el ejercicio del voto, más sólida será la democracia en que conviven. Sin que el conocimiento de los expertos llegue al ciudadano común, la estabilidad y eficacia de la democracia es una utopía y los estudiosos se hacen irrelevantes.

Este trabajo es un ejercicio limitado y modesto en lo que se ha venido desarrollando como la nueva disciplina de la economía constitucional, que aunque cuenta con una creciente bibliografía y con un número también creciente de autores y expertos, todavía se encuentra en sus etapas inciales de desarrollo. Aquí yo tomo como punto de partida a Sanguinetty (2001a, 2001b), escritos en respuesta a sendos artículos de Carbonell (2001a, 2001b). Este trabajo está dividido en tres secciones además de esta sección introductoria. La segunda sección presenta un análisis crítico de las dimensiones o implicaciones económicas de la Constitución del 40. La tercera sección trata de los elementos económicos a tener en cuenta en la

formulación de un nuevo texto constitucional. Y la cuarta sección, a manera de conclusiones, plantea algunos de los elementos logísticos y de otra índole que deben tenerse en cuenta en el caso de que se adopte una alternativa u otra.

LA CONSTITUCIÓN DEL 40 Y LA ECONOMÍA

En la misma medida que se puede suponer que una gran mayoría de cubanos prefiere vivir en un régimen democrático y no bajo la falta de libertades que sufre Cuba actualmente, debemos suponer que esos mismos cubanos preferirían disfrutar de una sistema económico más próspero y no continuar bajo la pobreza crónica que han sufrido en las últimas cuatro décadas. Y del mismo modo que la instalación de un sistema democrático de gobierno no sucederá automáticamente después del fin del castrismo o del socialismo en Cuba, tampoco será automática la instalación de una economía de mercado. Al mismo tiempo, los dos objetivos guardan una gran asimetría en cuanto a requerimientos y a condiciones para lograrse. Las libertades civiles se pueden obtener casi por decreto de un día para otro y parte de estas libertades tienen un aspecto económico, como son los derechos de propiedad y la libertad de comercio. Pero la prosperidad de una economía no es fácil de lograr. Aunque un marco constitucional dado y el sistema legal asociado al mismo pueden consagrar tanto una democracia como una economía de mercado simultáneamente, el desarrollo de la segunda requiere muchos otros elementos y mucho tiempo para lograrse.

Es un hecho que los ciudadanos de cualquier nación tienen una mayor comprensión de los requisitos legales de una democracia que de los requisitos, legales y de todo tipo, para que una economía sea capaz de crecer y elevar el nivel de vida de sus ciudadanos. Por esa razón es que en muchos casos, es más fácil promulgar leyes que fortalezcan una democracia que leyes que fortalezcan una economía. De hecho y dado el carácter contraintuitivo de la economía, es hasta más fácil que se implanten leyes que en lugar de favorecer el desarrollo económico, lo obstaculicen. Esto último muchas veces sucede como resultado de expectativas excesivamente optimistas, incluso irrealistas y hasta caprichosas, de los que promulgan las leyes, incluyendo a los que arman marcos constitucionales.

La Constitución del 40 no fue una excepción a esta regla, que fue resultado de los asambleistas que la compusieron con base en el conocimiento de aquella época y del que ellos individualmente poseían. Por supuesto que sería ingenuo suponer que el conocimiento juega un papel predominante en los diseños constitucionales. La política, la ideología y especialmente los intereses individuales de los constituyentes (y de sus representados) juegan un papel más determinante que el del conocimiento. Aquella constitución, a la que muchos le atribuyen el carácter de "avanzada" por la manera en que plantea los derechos civiles, como apunta Sánchez-Roig (1996)(calificativo que oímos con frecuencia y que es sinónimo de socialista), en realidad incluye una serie de artículos que no son congruentes con una economía de mercado. Sobre esta noción me baso para afirmar que la restauración de la Constitución del 40 no sólo impediría el pleno desarrollo de una economía de mercado en el país, si no que también haría muy difícil la recuperación de los niveles de producción necesarios para superar la crisis actual.

Hay muchos que ante tal afirmación reaccionan muy negativa y emocionalmente sin detenerse a analizar las razones de la misma. Sin embargo, aún cuando yo esté equivocado, la afirmación apunta a consecuencias que de ser ciertas son de gran gravedad para la economía cubana. Después de la devastación que ha sufrido la economía cubana en los últimos cuarenta y tres años, sería un ejercicio de gran negligencia e irresponsabilidad ciudadana invitar a la ciudadanía a votar por el establecimiento de condiciones que condenarían al país a un estancamiento crónico de su economía. La razones en que me baso para afirmar que la Constitución del 40 sería un impedimento en el desarrollo económico de Cuba, incluyendo la recuperación de los niveles de vida alcanzados antes de Castro, se exponen más abajo. Nada de lo que sigue tiene que ver con las otras virtudes que la Constitu-

ción del 40 pueda tener. Cuando propongo que la misma no se restablezca no quiero necesariamente decir que partes de la misma no sean dignas de ser rescatadas en un nuevo marco constitucional.

El espíritu intervencionista de mercado de la Constitución del 40 se pone de manifiesto cuando la misma autoriza al estado a interferir en la economía cubana de diversas maneras. Por ejemplo:

- El artículo 60 convierte al estado en un empleador de último recurso abriendo la gran caja de Pandora que ha mantenido crónicamente estancadas a las economías latinoamericanas.[2] En la medida en que la Constitución responsabiliza al estado a garantizar el empleo de todos (supuestamente Castro quizo hacerlo también con las consecuencias que todos conocemos) se facilita el descontrol del gasto público y la creación de empleo improductivo (se resucitaría la vieja institución de "la botella" o el salario que se le dá a alguien que no va a trabajar), todo lo cual lleva a los déficits fiscales que han sido la ruina de tantos países. Las frecuentes crisis fiscales que vemos en los países latinoamericanos representan dolorosos recordatorios de los límites del estado como empleador.

- El artículo 70, que "establece la colegiación oficial obligatoria para el ejercicio de las profesiones universitarias," además de lo absurdo que es que pertenezca a un texto constitucional, es incompatible con los mercados libres de trabajo. Independientemente de que ciertas profesiones requieran alguna forma de licencia, por ejemplo, la medicina, la ingeniería civil, la farmacia y la abogacía, colocar restricciones artificiales al ejercicio de las profesiones representan prácticas monopolísticas que benefician a unos pocos en detrimento de las mayorías, ya que reducen severamente la competencia entre los miembros de un mismo ramo.

- El artículo 77 desestimula la generación de empleo pues exige que antes de despedir a un traba-

---

2. Parte de dicho artículo dice: "El Estado empleará los recursos que estén a su alcance para proporcionar ocupación a todo el que carezca de ella y asegurará a todo trabajador, manual o intelectual, las condiciones económicas necesarias a una existencia digna."

jador hay que hacerle un expediente para determinar "con las demás formalidades que establezca la Ley" si el despido tiene causas justas. Este tipo de precepto se hace bajo la ilusión de proteger al trabajador empleado, pero ignora que no protege al desempleado ni al trabajador empleado de alta productividad o rendimiento. Además, reduce el estímulo para que los trabajadores más eficientes usen al máximo sus capacidades en su propio beneficio y en el de la economía en su conjunto, mientras que también reduce la capacidad de las empresas de seleccionar a los trabajadores más eficaces. A la larga, se crea una economía de poca mobilidad laboral y de poca capacidad generadora de empleo, lo cual perjudica tanto a los trabajadores como al resto de la sociedad. Todo esto reduce la capacidad del país para atraer inversiones pues cualquier inversionista nacional o extranjero lo tendrá que pensar detenidamente antes de invertir en Cuba y aún si decide hacerlo, preferirá modos de producción o tecnologías ahorrativas en mano de obra. La experiencia enseña que éste será uno de los principales obstáculos en la formación de empresas que necesiten contratar empleo y en la promoción de inversiones de las que depende críticamente la recuperación de la producción nacional.

- El artículo 79 carga al estado con la enorme responsabilidad de fomentar la creación de viviendas baratas para obreros, tarea que debe estar a cargo de las empresas privadas, aún cuando el estado pueda crear las condiciones para facilitar, más que la construcción, el financiamiento de viviendas. El mismo artículo, al indicar que "la ley determinará las empresas que, por emplear obreros fuera de los centros de población, estarán obligadas a proporcionar a los trabajadores habitaciones adecuadas, escuelas, enfermerías y demás atenciones propicias al bienestar físico y moral del trabajador, y su familia" interviene en la actividad inversionista privada y crea un elemento de incertidumbre para las empresas que además de prestarse para la corrupción, tiende a desestimular la inversión, o a crear las condiciones. En una verdadera economía de mercado, las li-

bertades de gestión y contratación, que se reflejan en las relaciones económicas de oferta y demanda, donde los obreros son libres de optar por las oportunidades disponibles de trabajo, las empresas harán todo lo posible por atraer a los trabajadores que necesiten para lograr una rentabilidad que justifique la inversión. Lo que justificaría la intervención del estado, pero no debe ser parte de un texto constitucional, es la presencia de una empresa monopsonística, o sea, que es empleadora única y por lo tanto monopolista, de manera que pueda aprovecharse de tal ventaja y dictar condiciones de trabajo inaceptables en una economía competitiva.

- El artículo 82 dificulta extraordinariamente la contratación de profesionales extranjeros que pudieran ser indispensables para el establecimiento de ciertas empresas, pues pone en manos del Congreso la promulgación de una " Ley extraordinaria, [para] acordar la suspensión temporal" del impedimento caso por caso. Este es un ejemplo del carácter coyuntural de la Constitución del 40 y su obsolecencia actual, pues este tipo de regulación corresponde a las leyes o a los decretos que respondan a los problemas de cada época. La Constitución del 40 fue diseñada todavía bajo la influencia de la elevada proporción de extranjeros que radicaban en Cuba en esos años y la necesidad de asegurar empleo a los cubanos nacidos en la isla.

- El artículo 84 complica las relaciones entre trabajadores y empleadores obligando a la creación de comisiones de conciliación para resolver "los problemas que se deriven de las relaciones entre el capital y el trabajo" recargando el trabajo del sector judicial ya que dichas comisiones tendrán que estar presididas por uno de sus funcionarios cuyas resoluciones son recurribles ante un tribunal nacional. El artículo ignora el volumen de recursos necesarios para enfrentar estas obligaciones en lugar de descansar en mecanismos privados de arbitraje capaces de resolver los problemas con recursos de las partes interesadas.

- El artículo 256 autoriza al estado a establecer asociaciones obligatorias de productores a "los efectos de la protección de los intereses comunes y nacionales," lo que abre la puerta para intervenciones en la economía que no corresponden al papel del estado en una economía de mercado. De hecho el artículo delata una desconfianza en la capacidad de una economía de mercado de desarrollarse de manera compatible con los intereses que pretende defender. Son muchos los cubanos que aunque hoy reconocen el fracaso del estado revolucionario en el manejo de la economía, todavía creen que el estado, en el marco de un régimen que concede más libertades y más comprometido con el desarrollo económico, puede jugar un papel rector en la economía. Estas creencias complementadas con la falta de comprensión que existe sobre la naturaleza de una economía de mercado conducirían al establecimiento de muchas trabas a las empresas que son las que realmente conseguirán la recuperación económica de Cuba.

- El artículo 271, posiblemente el más intervencionista de todos, presenta una amenaza para la libertad de empresas competitivas y de mercado al mandar que: "El Estado orientará la economía nacional en beneficio del pueblo para asegurar a cada individuo una existencia decorosa. Será función primordial del Estado fomentar la agricultura e industria nacionales, procurando su diversificación como fuentes de riqueza pública y beneficio colectivo." Scully (1992) nos recuerda que hace unos cuarenta años Robert Heilbroner, uno de los escritores más persuasivos del marxismo, escribió que había quedado demostrado que la propiedad colectiva y la asignación y distribución de recursos por parte del gobierno lograrían un nivel de vida y un grado de justicia social a la humanidad que no era posible bajo el capitalismo. Recientemente [hace un poco más de diez años] él dijo que la evidencia de setenta y cinco años de lucha entre el socialismo y el capitalismo era que el capitalismo ganó."[3]

- El artículo 275 es un mandato para la regulación de "la siembra y molienda de la caña por administración" en un intento de reemplazar al mercado, impidiendo toda forma de competencia entre productores e ignorando que la existencia de mercados competitivos es el motor principal del progreso económico que vemos en los países más adelantados. Este impedimento de la competencia permite que los productores más eficientes acaben subsidiando a los menos eficientes, sin cuya protección estarían forzados a producir más eficientemente o desaparecerían del mercado. Esta proposición, que puede parecer despiadada e inhumana es precisamente la base de la eficiencia de una economía y lo que le permite prosperar. En la medida que una economía protege las formas inferiores de producción, castiga a los más eficientes mediante la transferencia forzosa de recursos de los segundos a los primeros, lo cual acaba desestimulando la inversión más productiva.

Otros artículos son simplemente absurdos y no tienen sentido como parte de un marco constitucional. El artículo 52 establece una fórmula tan ridícula como arbitraria para determinar el sueldo mensual de los maestros de instrucción primaria, como si las consideraciones de oferta y demanda no tuvieran importancia. En la práctica tal artículo nunca pudo cumplirse mientras la Constitución del 40 estuvo vigente. El siguiente artículo establece la autonomía de la Universidad de La Habana, bajo el financiamiento del estado, lo cual facilita que dicha institución sirva para extraer recursos que se necesitan en la enseñanza primaria y acaben subsidiando la educación superior de los más privilegiados. Y el 56 llega al extremo de prohibir que alguien que no nació en Cuba pueda enseñar Literatura, Historia y Geografía cubanas, además de Cívica y la Constitución, en cualquier centro público o privado, lo cual tendrá que ser enseñado además mediante el uso de textos de autores cubanos por nacimiento.

---

3. Las citas son: Robert L. Heilbroner, *The Future as History* (New York: Harper, 1960) y "The Triumph of Capitalism," *New Yorker* 64 (January 23, 1989): 98-109.

Aunque a veces se reconoce que algunos de los artículos arriba mencionados son inadecuados, a la Constitución del 40 se le atribuyen efectos que no tuvo oportunidad de lograr. No se puede demostrar, por ejemplo, que "la Constitución hizo posible que Cuba antes que Castro figurase entre los tres países de Latinoamérica con el más alto estándar de vida" como arfima Carbonell (2001). Los datos disponibles en Martínez Sáenz (1959, pag. 227) indican que el crecimiento medio anual del Producto Doméstico Bruto desde 1947 hasta 1957 fue de 1.35 por ciento. En términos per cápita, dicho crecimiento se traduce en negativo si se toma en cuenta que el crecimiento de la población se puede estimar como mayor de la tasa de crecimiento del PDB. Efectivamente, de acuerdo con cálculos de Alienes y Urosa (1950, pág. 9), Cuba tuvo una tasa media anual de crecimiento de la población de 1.57 por ciento. Los únicos momentos de auge son claramente atribuíbles a factores externos, en especial a la Segunda Guerra Mundial, cuando se acumularon reservas internacionales derivadas de ventas extraordinarias de azúcar. Tales reservas fueron dedicadas a las grandes obras y otras inversiones durante la dictadura de Batista para reactivar la economía y sirvieron para crear la falsa impresión de una gran prosperidad económica.

Aunque es cierto que el ingreso per cápita de Cuba había alcanzado un nivel relativamente alto en América Latina, su economía sufría de un estancamiento crónico. Además, existía una incapacidad de atraer inversiones fuera del sector azucarero en volúmenes suficientes para reducir el alto desempleo abierto, el cual se ha estimado cercano a un 20 por ciento en el interior de la República. Si la Constitución del 40 tenía un efecto sobre la economía posiblemente era negativo pero los datos existentes no permiten demostrar una cosa o la otra.

La comparación favorable del ingreso per cápita de Cuba con el de otros países de América Latina sirve para demostrar que los cubanos venimos de un país que fue más próspero de lo que es actualmente. Sin embargo, en un análisis comparativo serio hay que tener en cuenta que cuando medimos ingreso per cápita estamos trabajando con promedios, los cuales no dicen cómo está distribuído el ingreso en la población. O sea, la prosperidad de unos no es necesariamente la prosperidad de todos. En esos años, la economía cubana estaba parcialmente subsidiada por Estados Unidos a través del mercado preferencial azucarero, mostraba graves problemas estructurales y muy poco dinamismo. Aunque se había logrado algún desarrollo, el mismo estaba muy concentrado en la capital mientras que había grandes focos de pobreza en todo el país.

Como resultado de la revolución, se puede afirmar que la economía cubana ha retrocedido varias décadas. La agenda predominantemente política e internacionalista de Castro relegó a un plano muy secundario la economía del país. Cuba perdió grandes oportunidades de desarrollo económico y tecnológico que hubiera podido aprovechar a partir de la aceleración en el desarrollo del turismo que se comenzó a experimentar en la década de los cincuenta, si no hubiera sido impedido por el gobierno revolucionario, a pesar de no tener un marco legal idóneo. Por eso es imperativo que cuando el régimen actual deje de ser un obstáculo al desarrollo del país, la economía cubana pueda rápidamente aumentar sus niveles de producción para crecer a los ritmos máximos posibles. Pero el proceso de recuperación económica no va a ser automático. Hay muchos que dan por sentada la recuperación de la economía cubana una vez que Castro desaparezca y tienden a ser los mismos que abogan por una restauración constitucional expedita. Pero aún cuando una restauración sea aconsejable, los cubanos tendrían que votar explícitamente por ella.

Muchas veces hemos oído o leído propuestas para la reconstrucción de la República de Cuba que incluyen un llamado a elecciones a pocos meses de la desaparición del gobierno actual. Sin embargo, aun cuando la desaparición del castrismo abra la posibilidad de hacer elecciones en tan corto plazo, es dudoso que la población cubana esté preparada para un proceso electoral después de más de cuatro décadas de totalitarismo. Incluso si las elecciones se hicieran bajo el manto de una restauración impuesta de la Constitución del 40, la ciudadanía no tendría tiempo de comprender el texto y las implicaciones de esa constitución y mucho menos de discutir en tan breve tiempo otras alternativas.

¿Cuántos cubanos han leído y comprenden la Constitución del 40? Los votos deben ser resultado de decisiones informadas de los electores. Democracia es mucho más que la libertad del ciudadano de votar por algo que no entiende. El acto de votar es una condición necesaria en la vida democrática de un país, pero no es suficiente. Una democracia es mucho más sólida y presumiblemente duradera cuando el votante tiene un cierto conocimiento de los funcionarios que elige y una cierta capacidad para evaluar esa información y las alternativas de política pública a las que se enfrenta. De aquí se desprende que para que el votante sepa lo que está haciendo debe tener el beneficio del conocimiento que puede derivarse del debate racional sobre aquellas cuestiones que afectan directamente tanto al interés público como al privado de los ciudadanos.

En un análisis *a priori* de la Constitución, cualquier economista al tanto de las investigaciones modernas sobre los aspectos legales e institucionales del desarrollo se daría cuenta enseguida que, por su contenido dirigista y semisocialista, tal como está redactada la del 40 le daría el tiro de gracia a una economía enferma como la cubana. Es necesario tener en cuenta que la Constitución del 40 estuvo influenciada por doctrinas económicas ya superadas como la del estado benefactor y las proposiciones de Keynes. Más de 60 años han transcurrido desde que fue concebida y su corta vigencia no le dió la oportunidad de consagrarse ni someterse a la prueba del tiempo. Antes de que los cubanos decidan restaurar la Constitución del 40 o escoger otra, deben tener la oportunidad de ponerse al día con los conceptos que se han desarrollado durante todos estos años, especialmente desde 1960. Por ejemplo, las ideas sobre contractualismo de Buchanan y Tullock, las de justicia distributiva de Rawls, las implicaciones del costo social de Coase, las investigaciones de Arrow sobre las paradojas de la votación, el análisis económico de las leyes de Posner y la lógica de la acción colectiva de Olson están entre las contribuciones contemporáneas que deben tenerse en cuenta antes de decidir sobre el marco constitucional de una nueva república.

Yo puedo comprender los sentimientos que la Constitución del 40 inspira entre algunos cubanos, pero la reconstrucción de Cuba también necesita una buena dosis de fina y precisa racionalidad. También comprendo la preocupación que muchos tienen en rescatar los aspectos sociales de la Constitución del 40, pero los mismos podrán atenderse más eficientemente fuera del texto constitucional sin obstaculizar la economía.

HACIA UNA NUEVA CONSTITUCION

La evidencia de que las libertades ciudadanas guardan una alta correlación positiva con el progreso económico de los países es ya incontrovertible. Scully (1992) por ejemplo, muestra que "las sociedades políticamente abiertas, comprometidas con un estado de derecho, la propiedad privada y la asignación de recursos por el mercado crecen tres veces más rápido y son dos veces y media más eficientes que las sociedades donde esas libertades están limitadas o prohibidas." Más recientemente, los estudios sobre el Indice de Libertad Económica de O'Driscoll, Holmes y O'Grady (2002) confirman los mismos resultados.

En esta sección suponemos que los cubanos optarán por un nuevo texto constitucional cuando existan las condiciones en Cuba para introducir reformas en la economía y que las nuevas opciones incluyen la posibilidad de construir una economía de mercado. El supuesto de que habrá una economía de mercado en Cuba después del fin del castrismo no puede darse por seguro, pues existen muchas corrientes en la isla y fuera de la isla que abogan por una forma de economía de tipo socialista o semi-socialista, con una dosis elevada de intervención estatal. Los que abogan por tal organización económica, aunque son personas con muy buenas intenciones y desean lo mejor para Cuba, desconocen la experiencia existente en esta materia y se basan más en preceptos ideológicos e ilusiones sobre el papel benefactor del estado que en el conocimiento actual sobre la materia.

Es importante tener en cuenta la experiencia de los 27 países exsocialistas en este aspecto y la proporción de la ciudadanía que esperan un papel preponderante del estado, al menos en las primeras etapas en el abandono de la planificación centralizada. Aunque muchos están convencidos que un sistema económico dirigista retrasaría la recuperación económica del país, la cuestión debe someterse a muchos debates públicos bien organizados antes de que el país entero se embarque en una u otra alternativa.

Mientras tanto, la economía no puede esperar a que se complete este debate ni mucho menos a que se instalen en el país las concepciones que emanen de un acuerdo dado. Es obvio que Cuba tendrá que funcionar por un tiempo, acaso un año o dos, con un texto constitucional provisional, hasta que se adopte uno definitivo. Es de esperar que en esa transición inicial se reinstauren las libertades ciudadanas para que Cuba pueda al menos mejorar en alguna medida su capacidad productiva y de comercio. La cuestión es entonces cómo convencer a una mayoría lo suficientemente grande, lo que pudiéramos denominar una mayoría wickselliana, para adoptar un marco constitucional que combine una democracia moderna con una economía de mercado también moderna.[4] Lo que sigue persigue ese objetivo.

¿Qué Clase de Constitución?

Aunque pudiéramos creer que se puede definir una constitución óptima para un país dado, en un cierto período de su historia, la realidad es que no existe una fórmula para calcular ese óptimo como si fuera un problema de programación matemática. Lo más probable es que Cuba llegue a una nueva constitución mediante un proceso de negociación entre las facciones que se desarrollen como parte del esfuerzo constituyente. En tal proceso, sería muy beneficioso para el país que los constituyentes y la mayor parte posible de la ciudadanía estén conscientes de que existen principios generales a ser contemplados en el diseño de una constitución, pero aún bajo esos principios, lo óptimo o simplemente la bondad de una constitución está determinada por lo que los propios constituyentes y electores crean de la misma. En este sentido es aconsejable que los electores también estén conscientes de que existen muchas alternativas, cada una de ellas con implicaciones que deben ser evaluadas *a priori*.

Cooter (2000) dice que las constituciones políticas pueden llegar a causar mucho sufrimiento o pueden servir de cimientos para construir la prosperidad y la libertad de los ciudadanos de una nación y que, por lo tanto, el diseño, las enmiendas y la interpretación de las constituciones es un juego político que puede resultar en grandes pérdidas o ganancias (stakes). Estas nociones pueden y deben ser aplicadas al diseño de una nueva constitución en la medida que un grupo de ciudadanos cubanos tomen la iniciativa y sean capaces de liderear un movimiento en ese sentido.

Tal empresa no es fácil, pero no es imposible. La alternativa de adoptar un marco constitucional mediocre o simplemente inadecuado no es nada prometedora. Cuba puede repetir la experiencia de los ciudadanos de las Trece Colonias americanas cuando después de haber ganado su libertad en el Siglo XVIII se dedicaron a reflexionar y a discutir qué clase de gobierno querían para su país y qué clase de constitución necesitaban para esos fines. En la práctica definieron en gran medida qué clase de país querían para ellos y para sus descendientes. En la formulación de una nueva constitución los cubanos se enfrentarán a la cuestión de definir cuál sería la constitución óptima o, por lo menos, cómo definir un texto que satisfaga las necesidades de una democracia estable, una economía próspera y un estado de derecho. La primera cuestión a definir es la fundamentación filosófica que una nueva constitución cubana debe tener.

En este aspecto la primera gran decisión será la de seleccionar entre las dos grandes corrientes filosóficas que rigen la política y la organización de los gobiernos en el mundo occidental y que se van haciendo evidentes después de la Revolución Gloriosa en Inglaterra en el Siglo XVII, por un lado, y el de la Revolución Francesa en el XVIII por el otro. La primera, como nos enseña Armando Ribas (1992), dió lugar al liberalismo anglosajón donde prevalece el poder del ciudadano sobre el poder del estado, mientras que la segunda supedita el individuo al estado. En el modelo anglosajón los derechos de propiedad se conside-

---

4. El concepto de mayoría o también unanimidad wickselliana proviene del economista Knut Wicksell y consiste en una proporción lo suficientemente grande de un electorado de manera que las decisiones que se tomen mediante votación sean lo suficientemente estables, o sea, difíciles de derogar por votaciones posteriores.

ran la piedra clave de las libertades individuales mientras que en el modelo europeo la búsqueda revolucionaria y violenta de la igualdad somete los derechos individuales.

Por supuesto, que hay otros factores a decidir en el diseño de una nueva constitución. Cooter, por ejemplo, no limita el objetivo de la teoría constitucional al estudio de la historia y la filosofía de los textos constitucionales, si no que lo extiende a la predicción de las concecuencias de dichos textos para informar al público y oportunamente guiar a los gobernantes y hacer que la administración de justicia llegue a mejores decisiones. En este sentido, los aspectos económicos a los que se refiere Cooter van mucho más allá de los elementos constitucionales que afectan directamente la macroeconomía, o sea, la economía nacional en su conjunto, si no aquellos otros aspectos de la constitución que son susceptibles del análisis económico moderno.

La importancia de lo que Scully (1992) llama "ambientes constitucionales" en el crecimiento de las economías es un tema que se ha venido estudiando recientemente pero que todavía no llega al público general como otras formas del conocimiento. En este aspecto, es aconsejable que se lleven a cabo preferiblemente desde ahora, o si no desde el comienzo de una transición, unas campañas sistemáticas de educación pública para elevar el nivel de comprensión de la población sobre estos temas. Tales ambientes constitucionales no son otra cosa que las "reglas del juego" que rigen los destinos de los ciudadanos mediante las economías de los diversos países del mundo y dichas reglas pueden permitir mayor o menor grados de libertad a los agentes económicos de esos países.

Todo ciudadano es un agente económico concreto e independiente y como tal toma sus decisiones en los diversos aspectos de su vida ciudadana y en la medida que las libertades establecidas se lo permitan. El ciudadano no es sólo un agente económico como consumidor, pero también como trabajador, empresario, ahorrista, inversionista, propietario, legislador, juez, etc. En conjunto, sus decisiones afectan el devenir económico de los países de manera significativa pero esas decisiones pueden estar restringidas en mayor o menor medida por las leyes de cada país. Por ejem-

plo, las leyes que impiden abrir los comercios los domingos tienden a reducir el volumen de comercio mientras que perjudican a los que desean usar los fines de semana para hacer compras, además de perjudicar a los que pudieran trabajar en esos días. Por otro lado, las leyes que facilitan las inversiones y el desarrollo de nuevas empresas tienden a estimular el ahorro y el crecimiento de las economías mediante la creación de nuevas capacidades productivas y oportunidades de empleo. Estos ejemplos ilustran las diversas formas de equilibrio que pueden existir entre las libertades del ciudadano y las del estado.

En el diseño de una nueva constitución, es de esperar que los constituyentes cubanos y posiblemente una buena parte de la población sientan la inclinación de tratar de resolver los problemas económicos y sociales del país mediante declaraciones o principios plasmados en el articulado del documento. Nada sería más riesgoso que tal tendencia. Muchos países latinoamericanos han diseñado constituciones que de hecho obstaculizan y hasta impiden el desarrollo económico de los países correspondientes. Los casos son muy numerosos y requerirían un estudio de más envergadura que éste.

Un punto de partida para el diseño de una constitución moderna puede ser el estudio de la propia constitución de Estados Unidos, su historia, su desarrollo y sus enmiendas. ¿Por qué? Porque como apunta Belt (2002) en un trabajo simultáneo a éste, dicha constitución es la más vieja del mundo de entre todas las que están vigentes y es la ley principal del país más próspero y poderoso del mundo con una conocida trayectoria de respeto a las libertades civiles y a los derechos de sus ciudadanos. Que se estudie, no quiere decir que se copie, sino que se use como marco de referencia al igual que otras constituciones. Una de las características de esa constitución que puede ser de particular interés para los constituyentes cubanos, especialmente después de varias décadas de gobierno en que el estado cubano ha tenido un poder aplastante sobre el ciudadano, es el de limitar el poder del gobierno a la producción y administración de bienes públicos, o sea bienes y servicios que benefician a toda la población sin que se pueda excluir a nadie. Típicamente, estos bienes incluyen la defensa o seguridad de la nación, la sanidad pública, la administración de justicia, la estabilidad de la moneda de curso legal y otros. En lo económico propiamente dicho, la constitución debe limitarse a garantizar las libertades necesarias para que la economía se desarrolle en manos de agentes privados, aunque deben crearse los instrumentos para mantener igualdad de oportunidades de competir y evitar las prácticas monopolísticas que puedan surgir.

¿Cómo se Logra?

La constitución es el compromiso de una sociedad para cumplir sus partes componentes. Es generalmente el contrato más serio o sacrosanto que los ciudadanos de una sociedad hacen. Independientemente de las virtudes de su contenido, una constitución es un contrato que debe cumplirse o modificarse de acuerdo a métodos acordados previamente y plasmados en el texto constitucional. Cuando los firmantes de un acuerdo lo hacen libremente es porque esperan obtener algunos beneficios del mismo. Si el acuerdo se incumple acarrea el costo de perder los beneficios esperados.[5] Los beneficios que los ciudadanos de un país pueden recibir de una constitución son muchos y de mucho valor, entre los más importantes las garantías de sus libertades, el derecho a perseguir su felicidad y que propicie gobiernos que garanticen esos derechos. Los incumplimientos de la Constitución del 40 durante los 12 años escasos que estuvo vigente y los incumplimientos de las constituciones anteriores se suman a la violación flagrante de la del 40, el 10 de marzo de 1952 y los incumplimientos del acuerdo implícito de Fidel Castro de restaurarla como la evidencia histórica del costo que ha pagado la sociedad cubana por no tener la capacidad de mantener sus compromisos. Nada puede incluirse en el texto de una constitución que impida o haga más difícil su incumplimiento. Los factores que determinan el respeto a la constitución están fuera de ella misma y radican en primer lugar en los valores que los ciudadanos portan para hacer que se cumplan los compromisos que se adquieren.

La capacidad de una sociedad de mantener ese compromiso dice mucho sobre ella. De hecho, esa capacidad es una medida del grado de civilización que esa sociedad ha alcanzado. Pueden ser muchas las dudas que se puedan esgrimir para evitar el esfuerzo de diseñar una nueva constitución y simplemente adoptar la del 40, siguiendo la ley del menor esfuerzo. Del mismo modo, el debate sobre una nueva constitución puede ser lo suficientemente prolongado que la instauración de una ley fundamental pudiera demorarse. Esto último no estaría sin precedentes pues Israel, por ejemplo, funciona sin una constitución porque sus ciudadanos no se han podido poner de acuerdo sobre un texto dado. Por otro lado, existen ejemplos dignos de emular sobre cómo una sociedad superó grandes diferencias para llegar a un acuerdo y comprometerse en cumplirlo. Como nos relata Sunstein (2001), "el asombroso éxito del diseño constitucional de Africa del Sur fue en gran medida posible porque los que tenían un punto de vista estaban en discusión constante con los que tenían puntos de vista opuestos. El respeto por desacuerdos razonables puede producir resultados aceptables para todos."

Con base en estas consideraciones es que deben evitarse cronogramas de trabajo muy estrechos e inflexibles para establecer una nueva constitución. Muchas veces oimos decir o leemos que tan pronto las condiciones lo permitan Cuba debe adoptar un marco constitucional y llamar a elecciones en plazos tan perentorios como de seis meses. Tal modo de actuar improvisadamente sería un mal comienzo para una nueva república. Es cierto que muchos cubanos dudan de la capacidad del país de iniciar una acción colectiva organizada y sostenida por un largo período de tiempo y que además alcance un final feliz. Esto es parte de la pobreza que Cuba sufre de lo que ahora se llama capital social y una de cuyas dimensiones es el grado de confianza en que los miembros de una sociedad tienen sobre las formas de conducta y las capacidades y valores de los otros miembros.

---

5. En una reunión en que discutíamos cuáles podían ser los elementos necesarios para una constitución óptima, Leonel de la Cuesta dijo que lo más importante era que la constitución se cumpliera. Para un estudio de las constituciones cubanas véase a de la Cuesta (1974).

¿Será esa la causa principal o una de las causas que expliquen por qué los cubanos no han podido formular un plan de nación para gobernar el país después que desaparezca el sistema totalitario que hoy lo rige? Olson (1965) nos enseñó que los grupos grandes de individuos no son capaces de actuar colectivamente y de manera voluntaria en función de sus intereses a menos que existan incentivos adecuados para ello. Es indudable que contar con una buena constitución puede ser congruente con el interés común de los cubanos. Pero, ¿qué incentivos tendrían que aplicarse para que los cubanos comiencen a pensar en el futuro después de Castro y por lo menos bosquejen el tipo de país en que quieren vivir? Es obvio que los cubanos residentes en la isla no cuentan con las libertades necesarias para realizar muchas formas de acción colectiva. Las dificultades para llevar a cabo el Plan Varela es un ejemplo de estas dificultades. Sin embargo, los cubanos en el exterior sí han tenido esas libertades pero no han sido utilizadas en planear un futuro. Su comportamiento con relación a alguna acción colectiva que cree una economía de mercado y una democracia es la del "que viaja de gratis" o *free rider* en la terminología de la Nueva Economía Institucional. O sea, se espera que sean otros los que resuelvan esos problemas. En tales condiciones, el futuro se presenta como una gran incógnita desde el punto de vista de las perspectivas que Cuba después de Castro consiga regresar a una democracia e instale una economía de mercado.

CONCLUSIONES

Es difícil creer que Cuba pueda pasar de un régimen de despotismo absoluto hacia una democracia plena, después de más de cuatro décadas en que los ciudadanos han estado completamente marginalizados de toda forma de participación en el gobierno. Muchos serán los caminos posibles de esa transición y ninguno ha de ser fácil. Si aplicamos el análisis de Olson (2000), sobre los factores que inciden en la acción colectiva de los grandes grupos humanos, vemos que son bajas las probabilidades de que la democracia deseada por muchos para Cuba reemplace el régimen actual. Yo soy de opinión que tales probabilidades pueden mejorar en la medida que la ciudadanía tenga un grado de comprensión más elevado de las cuestiones de una transición.

La transición tendrá muchos aspectos, entre los más importantes habrá uno político que definirá los cambios de poderes en el gobierno; uno legal, que podrá legitimizar o no los cambios políticos y de otra índole y los cambios económicos. Los tres irán estrechamente ligados pero en la medida que se pueda esperar que el poder que suceda al régimen actual se legitimice, los cambios de tipo legal serán críticos pues de ahí se definirán las condiciones de los cambios en las demás dimensiones de la sociedad. Algunos de estos aspectos se han estudiado para Cuba en los últimos años y es importante tenerlos presentes. Acosta (1992) escribió sobre algunos aspectos jurídicos de un gobierno provisional en Cuba y opina que desde un punto de vista estrictamente técnico-jurídico la Constitución del 40 todavía está vigente en Cuba, pues nunca fue "válidamente derogada ni modificada." Carbonell Cortina (1997) es de la misma opinión.

Otro trabajo de importancia para comprender la logística jurídica de la transición hacia una economía de mercado es el de Travieso-Díaz y Escobar (1994). Estos autores plantean los cambios necesarios en leyes e instituciones legales, legislativas y administrativas que se requieren o que facilitarían no sólo la instalación de un nuevo sistema económico si no la reactivación de la economía nacional bajo una mayor participación ciudadana. El estudio incluye una visión de los períodos pre y post constitucionales y brinda suficiente material para que oportunamente las partes interesadas puedan definir sus contribuciones a la organización de un nuevo orden político y económico.

Si adoptamos una visión más optimista y pensamos que Castro representa un nudo gordiano que una vez que se desate permitirá que se creen los incentivos a las acciones colectivas necesarias para establecer una democracia y una economía de mercado. En ese momento, muchos cubanos se enfrentarán a una gran disyuntiva, "la de preservar un pasado idealizado o señalar un futuro ideal" para usar las palabras de Sunstein (2001, pag. 68) en su libro sobre diseño constitucional. El pasado idealizado sin duda está representado por la Constitución del 40 y cuya restauración parece proponerse más por motivos sentimentales que racionales. Por otro lado, es concebible que una transición constitucional se realice en dos etapas buscando una solución ecléctica. La misma consistiría en la reinstauración provisional de la Constitución del 40 seguida de la derogación de los artículos incongruentes con una economía de mercado y quizás algunas otras enmiendas como lo ha propuesto Gómez Manzano (1997).

El futuro ideal es el que puede lograrse mediante un diseño constitucional racional en función de las libertades que otorgan las constituciones de los países más prósperos. La cuestión es si los cubanos o una masa crítica de los mismos podrán tener confianza en: a) su capacidad para llegar a un diseño constitucional que pueda contar con el apoyo de una mayoría wickselliana y b) la capacidad de la ciudadanía de respetar esa constitución por un tiempo indefinido.

Es difícil definir fórmulas que propicien ambos resultados. Creo que lo que mejor podemos hacer para propiciar las acciones correspondientes es la de darle una amplia divulgación a las ideas modernas sobre economía de mercado, estados de derecho y diseños constitucionales entre la mayor cantidad posible de cubanos en la isla y en el exterior. Aunque existen algunas iniciativas en este sentido, parece que las mismas todavía no llegan a cubrir segmentos importantes de la población en la isla. Creo que el aumento de la cobertura de estas ideas debía ser una primera prioridad para propiciar una transición eficiente dentro de un marco legal adecuado.

REFERENCIAS BIBLIOGRÁFICAS

Acosta, José D., "El marco jurídico-institucional de un Gobierno Provisional de Unidad Nacional en Cuba" en *Cuba in Transition—Volume 2*, ASCE, Miami, Florida, 1992.

Alienes y Urosa, Julián, *Características Fundamentales de la Economía Cubana*, Banco Nacional de Cuba, La Habana, 1950.

Belt, Juan A. B., "The U.S. Constitution and Private Property: Reflections for Cuba," in this volume.

Carbonell-Cortina, Néstor, *Grandes Debates de la Constituyente Cubana de 1940*, Ediciones Universal, Miami, Florida, 2001.

Carbonell-Cortina, Néstor, "Redescubrimiento de la Constitución" en *El Nuevo Herald*. Miami, Florida, septiembre 2001.

Carbonell-Cortina, Néstor, "Y sin Embargo Pervive" en *El Nuevo Herald*, Miami, Florida, octubre 2001.

Carbonell-Cortina, Néstor, "La Constitución de 1940: Simbolismo y Vigencia" en *Cuba in Transition—Volume 7*, ASCE, Washington, D.C. 1997.

Cooter, Robert D., *The Strategic Constitution*, Princeton University Press, Princeton, New Jersey, 2000.

De la Cuesta, Leonel, *Constituciones Cubanas: Desde 1812 hasta nuestros días*, Ediciones Exilio, New York, 1974.

Gómez Manzano, René, "Constitución y Cambio Democrático en Cuba" en *Cuba in Transition—Volume 7*, ASCE, Washington, D.C. 1997.

Martínez Sáenz, Joaquín, *Por la Independencia Económica de Cuba: Mi Gestión en el Banco Nacional*, Editorial Cenit, La Habana, 1959.

O'Driscoll, Jr., Gerald. P.; Holmes, Kim R.; & O'Grady, Mary Anastasia, *2002 Index of Economic Freedom*, The Heritage Foundation, Washington, D.C. y *The Wall Street Journal*, New York, 2002.

Olson, Mancur, *The Logic of Collective Action: Public Goods and the Theory of Groups*, Harvard University Press, Cambridge, Massachusetts, 1965.

Olson, Mancur, *Power and Prosperity: Outgrowing Capitalist and Communist Dictatorships*, Basic Books, New York, 2000.

Ribas, Armando, *Entre la Libertad y la Servidumbre*, Editorial Sudamericana, Buenos Aires, 1992.

Sánchez, Ignacio E., "Constitutional Protection of Cuban Property Rigths" en *Cuba in Transition—Volume 6*, ASCE, Washington, D.C. 1996

Sánchez-Roig, Rebeca, "Cuban Constitutionalism and Rights: An Overview of the Constitutions of 1901 and 1940" en *Cuba in Transition—Volume 6*, ASCE, Washington, D.C., 1996.

Sanguinetty, Jorge A., "El Fetiche de la Constitución del 40" en *El Nuevo Herald*, Miami, Florida, 9 de septiembre de 2001.

Sanguinetty, Jorge A., "Los Nuevos Debates sobre la Constitución del 40" en www.cubafuturo.net, 25 de octubre de 2001.

Scully, Gerald W., *Constitutional Environments and Economic Growth*, Princeton University Press, Princeton, New Jersey, 1992.

Sunstein, Cass R., *Designing Democracy: What Constitutions Do*, Oxford University Press, Oxford y New York, 2001.

Travieso-Díaz, Matías F., y Escobar, Steven R., "Overview of Required Changes in Cuba's Laws and Legal Institutions During its Transition to a Free-Market Democracy" in *Cuba in Transition—Volume 4*, ASCE, Washington, D.C., 1994.

THE U.S. CONSTITUTION AND PRIVATE PROPERTY: REFLECTIONS FOR CUBA

Juan A. B. Belt[1]

This paper is not meant to be a scholarly treatise on such a momentous topic. Pretending to do that would be arrogant. Among its purposes are:

- to remind the reader of the key role natural law principles played in the drafting of the Declaration of Independence and the U.S. Constitution, with emphasis on the importance of private property rights; and

- to argue that there are numerous U.S. citizens, many in high positions, who either do not know about this or act as if they did not know about it, and that some of these are "Washington mandarins" and seem to believe that private property is a type of luxury only suitable for countries that are developed rather than a necessity for the future welfare of a country, regardless of its level of development.

I am sure many would say: "who cares what these 'Washington mandarins' think?" My answer is that whether you like it or not, such people often play a role in "transition processes" and that these deficiencies of knowledge or understanding could be harmful to the future welfare of Cuba. If you do not believe what I am saying, ask a Nicaraguan who is still suffering from Jimmy Carter's ill-fated mediation in that country and his tacit support for the "piñata."

I believe it is inevitable that there will be a transition to democracy in Cuba. The final and most important purpose of this paper is to make a plea to Cubans who may be involved in a transition process to remain vigilant so that important principles of natural law are not traded away by some mediator.

INTELLECTUAL ORIGINS OF THE DECLARATION OF INDEPENDENCE AND THE U.S. CONSTITUTION AND SOME IMPORTANT PRINCIPLES THAT EMERGED FROM THOSE ORIGINS

To understand better the principles that underlie the U.S. Constitution one has to begin with the Declaration of Independence, promulgated July 4, 1776. The immediate aim of the Declaration of Independence was to justify to the world at large the decision to declare independence. To achieve this, the signers set forth a theory of legitimate government that was influenced by Natural Law theorists such as Burlamaqui and Vattel, but primarily by John Locke, and his *Two Treatises on Government,*" written in 1679-1680 and first published in 1690. It can be said that John Locke was the intellectual father of the United States, as he probably had a greater influence on Thomas Jefferson, author of the Declaration of Independence, than any other writer.

---

1. The opinions expressed in this paper are the author's, and they do not necessarily reflect the point of views of the Inter-American Development Bank or its Board of Directors. Some of the ideas presented here are from an article Jorge Sanguinetty and I wrote in May 2002.

The political philosophy of Locke was based on natural law. Men were presumed to be born with natural rights and not receive them from the government. According to Locke, men unite in a society "for the mutual preservation of their lives, liberties, and estates, which I call by the general name 'property'" (Locke, *op cit*, pp. 356-368). He also said: "Man being born, as has been proved, with a title to perfect freedom and an uncontrolled enjoyment of all the rights and privileges of the law of Nature, equally with any other man, or number of men in the world, hath by nature a power not only to preserve his property—that is, his life, liberty, and estate, against the injuries and attempts of other men, but to be a judge of and punish the breaches of that law." In summary, John Locke believed that property rights are the basis of human freedom and that the Government exists to protect them. These "Lockean" principles were reflected in the Declaration of Independence.

Later, during the Constitutional Convention, the "Framers of the Constitution" agreed with the importance of protecting private property.[2] Madison said "the primary objectives of civil society are the security of property and public safety." Hamilton stated that "one great objective of Government is personal protection and the security of property." According to Forrest Mc Donald, George Mason and Luther Martin concurred. Additionally, "Gouvernor Morris, John Rutledge and Rufus King put the protection of property ahead of liberty as the primary object of society."[3]

John Adams spoke eloquently on the subject. He said:

> The moment is admitted into society, that property is not as sacred as the laws of God, and there is not a force of law and public justice to protect it, anarchy and tyranny commence. If thou shall not covet and

thou shall not steal were not commandments of Heaven, they must be made inviolable precepts of every society, before it can be civilized or made free.[4]

Another thinker that influenced the Framers of the Constitution was Adam Smith, particularly with respect to the limits of Government action. Adam Smith wrote:

> According to the system of natural liberty, the sovereign has only three duties to attend to; three duties of great importance indeed, but plain and intelligible to common understandings: first, the duty of protecting society from the violence and invasion of other independent states; secondly, the duty of protecting, as far as possible, every member of society from the injustice or oppression of every other member of it, or the duty of establishing an exact administration of justice; and thirdly, the duty of erecting and maintaining certain publick works and publick institutions, which can never be for the interest of any individual or small number of individuals, to erect and maintain, because the profit could never repay the expense to any individual or small number of individuals, though it may frequently do much more than repay it to a great society.[5]

Putting Adam Smith in the language of modern public finance, the Government should be limited to national defense, to the administration of justice and to the provision of public goods.

Section 8 of Article I of the U.S. Constitution enumerates the powers of Congress, and follows closely the principles established in the Adam Smith passage quoted above.[6] An indication of how strongly the Framers believed in the strength of Section 8 is the debate on the necessity of having a Bill of Rights (Amendments 1 to 10 of the Constitution). Alexander Hamilton, for example, argued that it was not necessary, because Section 8 did not explicitly give Congress the power to establish a religion, or to restrain the freedom of the press, and that therefore the

---

2. This paragraph and the quotes are from Forrest McDonald, *Novus Ordo Seclorum*.

3. Forrest McDonald, *op. cit.*

4. John Adams, *The Works of John Adams*, Volume 6.

5. Adam Smith, *An Inquiry into the Nature and Causes of the Wealth of Nations*, 1776.

6. The text of Section 8 is reproduced in Annex A.

Bill of Rights was superfluous and perhaps even dangerous, as it could actually weaken that Section.

The Constitution of the United States, drafted by the Constitutional Convention that met in Philadelphia between May 25 and September 25, 1787, is the world's oldest written constitution still in effect. Besides limiting the scope of Government action, and protecting private property, it has a number of important features:

- The U.S. Constitution essentially codifies the rules to access power, it details how officials can be removed from office, and specifies the ways in which the Constitution can be modified.

- The U.S. Constitution does not mandate special benefits to citizens, as do some constitutions in Latin America. For example, a fairly recent constitution in Latin America states that all citizens have the right to a "dignified dwelling," and that the "rights of all persons to recreation, to engaging in sports and to the enjoyment of leisure time is recognized." In this particular country, property rights are not well protected, and the value of a human life is, *de facto*, negligible, but the constitution "guarantees" the right to engage is sports!

- The U.S. Constitution is simple and practical and has been able to meet extraordinary needs by changes in emphasis and arrangement without loss of essential form.

An important feature of the Constitution is the separation of power and the system of "checks and balances," something the Framers learned from Montesquieu. John Adams listed eight balancing mechanisms contained in the Constitution. These were:

- the states vs. the central government;

- the House vs. the Senate;

- the president vs. Congress;

- the courts vs. Congress;

- the Senate vs. the president (with regard to appointments and treaties);

- the people vs. their representatives;

- the state legislatures vs. the Senate (in the original election of senators); and

- the Electoral College vs. the people.

Natural law, property rights, limited Government, and checks and balances were important principles embedded in the Declaration of Independence and the U.S. Constitution. The next section discusses the treatment of private property in the U.S. Constitution.

PROTECTION OF PRIVATE PROPERTY IN THE U.S.

The protection of property is enshrined in the Fifth Amendment of the U.S. Constitution. It reads:

> No person shall be held to answer for a capital, or otherwise infamous crime, unless on a presentment or indictment of a grand jury, except in cases arising in the land or naval forces, or in the militia, when in actual service in time of war or public danger; nor shall any person be subject for the same offense to be twice put in jeopardy of life or limb; nor shall be compelled in any criminal case to be a witness against himself, nor be deprived of life, liberty, or property, without due process of law; nor shall private property be taken for public use, without just compensation.

The Fourteenth Amendment, approved in 1868, after the Civil War, was initially enacted to protect freed slaves from the abrogation of their rights by the Southern states. One of its main effects, however, has been to protect private property against state regulatory legislation in the years after 1880. Section 1 of the Amendment reads:

> All persons born or naturalized in the United States, and subject to the jurisdiction thereof, are citizens of the United States and of the state wherein they reside. No state shall make or enforce any law which shall abridge the privileges or immunities of citizens of the United States; nor shall any state deprive any person of life, liberty, or property, without due process of law; nor deny to any person within its jurisdiction the equal protection of the laws.

The protection of private property, and a commitment to economic freedom, remained very important features of the U.S. Government during more than a century and a half, and one could argue that this permitted the U.S. to grow rapidly. Forrest McDonald concludes that the more basic changes came during the presidency of Lyndon Johnson and the chief justiceship of Earl Warren, when the Supreme Court began to legislate rather than adjudicate and a growing bureaucracy attempted to run economic activity through a myriad of regulations. Some of these regulations clearly "take" property without compensation by reducing the value of assets such as real estate. In any case, the century and a half of relative economic freedom that the U.S. enjoyed permitted the country to grow rapidly and to reach unprecedented levels of welfare. And recently, the courts have begun to give greater importance to the protection of property rights.

EXAMPLES OF LACK OF COMMITMENT TO THE PRINCIPLES OF THE FOUNDING FATHERS BY AMERICANS

The most obvious case of case of a prominent American acting as if property rights were not important is Jimmy Carter's ill-fated intervention in the transition to democracy in Nicaragua. Mark Falcoff, of the American Enterprise Institute, documents Carter's intervention in Nicaragua in an article in which he says:[7]

> Once ejected by popular vote, they (the Sandinistas) rushed with indecent haste to 'privatize' the vast property holdings they had confiscated after 1979, with themselves as the beneficiaries. But not even this looting expedition—a huge *piñata*, as it was called— was enough to unmask them once and for all in the eyes of their well-wishers. Immediately after the elections of 1990, former President Jimmy Carter rushed to Violeta Chamorro's house in the capital city of Managua to urge her, in the name of 'national reconciliation,' to retain for the Sandinistas a measure of power in the new government. She graciously, but mistakenly, concurred: until very recently, the Nicaraguan army remained the Sandinista army, and its commander, General Humberto Ortega, was the same man who had commanded it in the 1980's. The result has been truly lamentable: neither genuine na-

tional reconciliation nor, thanks largely to unresolved claims to expropriated property, a serious recovery of Nicaragua's economy.

Jimmy Carter is a politician, and was not an U.S. Government official when he visited Nicaragua. In the rest of this section I will give two other examples of U.S. Government career officials who also seem to disregard the teachings of the Founding Fathers. One example is documented in *The Wall Street Journal* and the other is something from my own experience as a member of the U.S. Senior Foreign Service.

- *The Wall Street Journal* documents the bizarre and unwarranted attacks by the U.S. Embassy in Guatemala against the Francisco Marroquín University and its founder, Manuel Ayau.[8] Essentially, the U.S. Embassy circulated to several ambassadors accredited to Guatemala a cable drafted by an Embassy official labeling Mr. Ayau and the University as enemies of freedom. This is quite strange, given the commitment of this University to the ideals of freedom enshrined in the U.S. Constitution. As Ms O'Grady, the author of the article puts it, "classic Marroquin teaching, … argues that the foundation of a free society is a rule of law prohibiting arbitrary government intervention." My own experience, teaching at the University and having professional contact with its graduates, would lead me to conclude that the University adheres much more closely to the principles of the "founding fathers" than most universities in the United States.

- During my career in the U.S. Foreign Service, I encountered many colleagues who did not seem to believe very strongly in the principles of the "founding fathers." I could give a number of examples but will not as I do not want to personalize this paper.

LESSONS FOR CUBA

Cuba will some day be free. I am sure of it. Hopefully, the people and their representatives will choose to

---

7. Mark Falcoff, "Nicaragua on the Brink—of What," *AEI Latin American Outlook* (October 2001).

8. Mary Anastasia O'Grady, "A Guatemalan Free-Market Reformer is Under Fire form the U.S.," *The Wall Street Journal,* August 3, 2001.

establish a political and economic system based on natural law, including a strong emphasis on the protection of property rights. It is important to note that the protection of property rights and political freedom go together. For example, protecting freedom of speech is meaningless without protecting property, as the threat to take your property is a powerful silencer.

I believe ASCE and other institutions interested in the welfare of Cuba should make every effort to distribute in Cuba the writings of the great thinkers of natural law, including Locke and others. Other interesting books to distribute would be Adam Smith's *An Inquiry into the Nature and Causes of the Wealth of Nations* and *The Theory of Moral Sentiments*. Books by more modern writers, such as Milton and Rose Friedman, should also be distributed.[9]

My main recommendation is for any Cuban who would be involved in a transition to democracy process to remain vigilant of foreign mediators who may be seeking Nobel Peace Prizes, or promotions in the U.S. State Department, or other types of benefits that would result from participation in the transition process. These individuals can afford, a lá Carter, to negotiate a reduction in economic freedom and in the protection of property rights, knowing that in the end, their assets, peanut farms or whatever are in the U.S. and protected by the Fifth and Fourteenth Amendments of the U.S. Constitution.

ANNEX A
U.S. CONSTITUTION—SECTION 8, ARTICLE I

The Congress shall have power to lay and collect taxes, duties, imposts, and excises, to pay the debts and provide for the common defense and general welfare of the United States; but all duties, imposts, and excises shall be uniform throughout the United States:

- To borrow money on the credit of the United States;

- To regulate commerce with foreign nations, and among the several states, and with the Indian tribes;

- To establish a uniform rule of naturalization, and uniform laws on the subject of bankruptcies throughout the United States;

- To coin money, regulate the value thereof, and of foreign coin, and fix the standard of weights and measures;

- To provide for the punishment of counterfeiting the securities and current coin of the United States;

- To establish post offices and post roads;

- To promote the progress of science and useful arts, by securing for limited times to authors and inventors the exclusive right to their respective writings and discoveries;

- To constitute tribunals inferior to the Supreme Court;

- To define and punish piracies and felonies committed on the high seas, and offenses against the law of nations;

- To declare war, grant letters of marque and reprisal, and make rules concerning captures on land and water;

- To raise and support armies, but no appropriation of money to that use shall be for a longer term than two years;

- To provide and maintain a navy;

- To make rules for the government and regulation of the land and naval forces;

9. A member of the Board of the Francisco Marroquín University visited Cuba once and showed a Spanish version of "Free to Choose," the documentary about Milton Friedman's book. Additionally, they provided scholarships to students from the University of Havana.

- To provide for calling forth the militia to execute the laws of the union, suppress insurrections, and repel invasions;

- To provide for organizing, arming, and disciplining the militia, and for governing such part of them as may be employed in the service of the United States, reserving to the states respectively, the appointment of the officers, and the authority of training the militia according to the discipline prescribed by Congress;

- To exercise legislations in all cases whatsoever, over such district (not exceeding ten miles square) as may, by cession of particular states, and the acceptance of Congress, become the seat of the government of the United States, and to exercise like authority over all places purchased by the consent of the legislature of the state in which the same shall be, for the erection of forts, magazines, arsenals, dock-yards, and other needful buildings; and

- To make all laws which shall be necessary and proper for carrying into execution the foregoing powers, and all other powers vested by this Constitution in the government of the United States, or in any department or officer thereof.

ANNEX B
FOURTEENTH AMENDMENT, ADOPTED JULY 28, 1868

SECTION 1

All persons born or naturalized in the United States, and subject to the jurisdiction thereof, are citizens of the United States and of the state wherein they reside. No state shall make or enforce any law which shall abridge the privileges or immunities of citizens of the United States; nor shall any state deprive any person of life, liberty, or property, without due process of law; nor deny to any person within its jurisdiction the equal protection of the laws.

SECTION 2

Representatives shall be apportioned among the several states according to their respective numbers, counting the whole number of persons in each state, excluding Indians not taxed. But when the right to vote at any election for the choice of electors for president and vice president of the United States, representatives in Congress, the executive and judicial officers of a state, or the members of the legislature thereof, is denied to any of the male inhabitants of such state, being twenty-one years of age, and citizens of the United States, or in any way abridged, except for participation in rebellion, or other crime, the basis of representation therein shall be reduced in proportion which the number of such male citizens shall bear to the whole number of male citizens twenty-one years of age in such state.

SECTION 3

No person shall be a senator or representative in Congress, or elector of president and vice president, or hold any office, civil or military, under the United States, or under any state, who, having previously taken an oath, as a member of Congress, or as an officer of the United States, or as a member of any state legislature, or as an executive or judicial officer of any state, to support the Constitution of the United States, shall have engaged in insurrection against the same, or given aid or comfort to the enemies thereof. But Congress may by a vote of two-thirds of each house, remove such disability.

SECTION 4

The validity of the public debt of the United States, authorized by law, including debts incurred for payment of pensions and bounties for services in suppressing insurrection or rebellion, shall not be questioned. But neither the United States nor any state shall assume or pay any debt or obligation incurred in aid of insurrection or rebellion against the United States, or any claim for the loss or emancipation of any slave; but all such debts, obligations, and claims shall be held illegal and void.

SECTION 5

The Congress shall have power to enforce, by appropriate legislation, the provisions of this article.

CASTRO'S CHOICES: THE ECONOMICS
OF ECONOMIC SANCTIONS

Gary M. Shiffman[1]

A reader of debates taking place in the U.S. Congress might justly conclude that U.S. sanctions have had a significant effect on the performance of the Cuban economy. Opponents of sanctions argue that sanctions have impoverished the island and therefore caused innocent Cubans to suffer. Supporters of sanctions argue that sanctions have kept valuable resources from Fidel Castro, rendering him unable to build his military and extend his security forces and domestic control. Both sides in the debate assume that sanctions prevent wealth from entering the sanctioned economy. The argument is only about who feels the brunt of the impact: the dictator or the people.

But what if the sanctions actually have negligible impact on Cuba's domestic economic performance? In fact, a detailed analysis of the Cuban economy during the 1990s provides compelling evidence that sanctions may not have the economic impact usually assumed. Instead, it is Castro's internal policies—the lack of freedoms, property rights, and the rule of law; the use of repression, fear, and other totalitarian tools to maintain the regime in power—that account for Cuba's poor economic performance.

Let me quickly clarify what I am *not* arguing. I am not arguing that Castro's actions are responsible for the current impoverishment of Cuba *because his repressions caused the United States to sanction Cuba.*

Those who put this argument forward see sanctions policy as a response to dictatorship, arguing that sanctions seek (successfully or unsuccessfully) to sow the seeds of discontent and insurrection by impoverishing the island. Such an analysis would shift responsibility, moral or political, for Cuba's impoverishment to Castro's regime; yet, ultimately, it too assumes that the direct cause of Cuba's poor *economic* performance is an external policy—the economic sanctions of the United States, the world's largest economy.

I argue the opposite. Empirical evidence demonstrates that the choices and actions of Fidel Castro have contributed to the island's impoverishment, including its failure to attract foreign direct investment, to a far greater extent than any external market event, including U.S. sanctions. This evidence closely tracks the predictions of a Public Choice model of the economic incentives facing the totalitarian dictator.

TRENDS IN THE 1990S:
A BRIEF ECONOMIC HISTORY

To examine the impact of internal versus external events on Cuban economic performance, I examined the Cuban economy beginning in the early 1990s, to coincide with the time when Cuba re-entered the world economy absent significant dependency on the Soviet Union. The data from that analysis indicates

---

1. This paper received valuable input from Mark Crain, Roger Congleton, Vivien Ravdin, Jorge Pérez-López, and many others too numerous to list. All errors are my own.

388

that the impact of U.S. policies is dwarfed by the impact of Cuba's domestic policies.

By the early 1990s, Cuba had been ruled by Fidel Castro for some 33 years. It is perhaps worth recalling that when he came to power in 1959, Cuba had a per capita income among the highest in Latin America (U.N. Monthly Bulletin of Statistics 1961). However, shortly after the revolution that overthrew Batista in 1959, Castro nationalized nearly all property. From the first Agrarian Reform Law of May 1959 and the second Agrarian Reform Law of October 1963, his government actively worked to liquidate the capitalist system, eliminating Cuba's market-oriented institutions and supplanting them with institutions that support a centrally planned economy.

The resulting Marxist-Leninist command economy ran production into the ground. Cuba survived as the Soviet Union's largest aid-receiving state, absorbing an annual Soviet subsidy of approximately $5 billion.[2] In the early 1990s, upon the collapse of the Soviet Union, subsidies ended. The Cuban economy entered a period of crisis, when for the first time it faced market pressures.

From 1990 to 1993, the country's imports and exports dropped precipitously as the Soviet subsidies ended. Cuba's fixed capital and inventories began to degrade and diminish. Merchandise imports fell by 75 percent from 1989 to 1993 (Pérez-López 1996). According to some estimates, up to 80 percent of the factories were unable to operate because of lack of fuel, machinery, raw materials, and spare parts (Pérez-López 1996). As the Cuban government maintained fixed prices and continued its priority of keeping state-run enterprises in business, the budget deficit increased from 9.4 percent of GDP in 1990 to 30.4

percent in 1993 (Hernández-Catá 2000). Since prices were fixed, real balances increased, which further exacerbated shortages and depleted inventories. In the small black market for some agricultural products, inflation increased from 2 percent in 1990 to more than 200 percent in 1993 (Hernández-Catá 2000).

In the mid-1990s the Cuban government instituted a series of reforms. The major legal changes that impacted the Cuban economy during the "Special Period"[3] were:

- The Constitution of 1992 [(Aug 1, 1992)]

- The Law on Foreign Investment [Law No. 77 (1995)]

- Decree-Law No. 165: Duty-Free Zones and Industrial Parks [(1996)]

- Decree-Law No. 173: Banks and Non-Banking Financial Institutions [(1997)]

These actions, with associated expectations of continued reform, caused the Cuban economy to level off and begin to grow toward the end of this period. Foreign investment rose. The fiscal deficit dropped, reaching 2.5 percent in 1996. With monetary tightening, inflation returned to lower levels and national savings increased.

However, as many observers have noted, Castro had instituted his reforms to invite capitalists without the capitalism.[4] Although Cuban officials extolled the freedom with which foreign-owned enterprises were able to operate in the island, in fact there remained significant restraints stemming from the government's determination to maintain control over the conduct of economic activity in the country (Travieso-Díaz and Ferraté 1995). Four important mani-

---

2. Subsidies averaged $4.3 billion per year from 1986-1990, or 15% of Cuba's GDP at official exchange rates. This number would be much higher if converted at market exchange rates (Hernández-Catá, 2000).

3. Kimmerling, Stephen J. 2000.

4. Paraphrased from Vogel, 1995, *The Wall Street Journal,* as quoted in Pérez-López (1996): "And this is Cuba, land of vast possibilities and murky probabilities. Money managers who visited Cuba for three days earlier this summer with LatInvest Securities Ltd., a London-based investment bank, found themselves in an economic twilight zone. They discovered a country that wants capitalists, but not capitalism."

festations of that control have been identified by Jorge Pérez-López:

- FDI must be "individually authorized" by the Cuban government.[5]

- Important sectors of the Cuban economy are off limits to foreign investors.

- Foreign investors must use the Cuban government to hire, fire, and pay workers; they cannot manage their own personnel.[6]

- The Cuban government can terminate a joint venture at will, claiming as national property any capital and assets in Cuba. With no guarantee that the Cuban government will not seize everything, and a few cases of this type of seizure actually happening, the disincentive to invest in Cuba is apparent (Travieso-Díaz and Ferraté).

In addition, Cuba's government wanted the benefits of liberalizing the economy without paying the cost of losing political control. When the middle class began to grow and civil society started to develop, Castro responded by retreating from some of the reforms and increasing repression. In early 1996, he cracked down on *Concilio Cubano*, an umbrella group, created in November 1995, that consisted of 108 dissident factions. They had petitioned the government to meet in Havana from February 24 to February 27, 1996: the meeting never took place and many leaders were subsequently jailed.

In the late 1990s, economic growth began to slow, and foreign investment in Cuba fell. But what really explains the decline? The quality of the Cuban workforce did not diminish. Cuban workers remained competitive among the economies against which Cuba competed for foreign investment. Infrastructure was not deteriorating at an appreciably greater rate. The possibility of some demand shock has been investigated and dismissed by Hernández-Catá (2000). Nor does Cuba's poverty *per se* help explain the shift: for, while the island's economic performance remained significantly below its 1989 levels (Hernández-Catá, 2000), by the late 1990s, it had nonetheless improved dramatically from its earlier lows, an improvement that might have tended to boost investors' expectations that it would continue to grow.

Of course, the literature contains ample explanation of why foreigners might have invested in Cuba in the mid-1990s but then reduced their rate of investment and even pulled out of Cuba in the late 1990s. The slide in Cuba's economic performance had leveled off in 1993, likely due to the Cuban government's economic reforms and its concerted effort to attract foreign investment. Thus began a virtuous cycle, however brief, where investment led to economic growth, which inspired additional investment based upon expectations of additional economic growth. In reality, however, the government was not prepared to give up monopoly power over the sources of wealth on the island. This gradually became more evident as economic reforms were slowed or reversed, and political repression grew. Thus, in spite of the early rhetoric, the practical value of the reforms began to diminish, the pace of structural reforms began to slow, and by 1995 fears of policies being reversed became apparent.

---

5. Note that private property is outlawed in Cuba, although individuals may operate self-employment businesses such as government-licensed restaurants from private homes (*paladares*). Until the mid-1990s it was illegal for anyone other than the government to own real property, including a home or a business. All foreign investors, therefore, were forced to partner with the Cuban government through joint ventures, production agreements, and joint accounts. This law changed during in September 1995 (Decree Law 77) with the intent to increase foreign investment. In practice, however, there has been no change in the implementation of ownership rights under Cuban law. The Cuban government in effect is still the partner in all significant foreign investments in Cuba (Pérez-López 1996).

6. Because the Cuban government controls employment, salaries, benefits, and other personnel decisions, the foreign investor's ability to improve the workers' wealth and quality of life is limited by the government's willingness to accept such improvements. This is not the case in some other dictatorships. For example, an investment in the People's Republic of China in 2000 could have dramatically impacted the lives of workers as Western companies set wages, working and safety conditions, and even provided housing and medical care. In Cuba, however, no such power exists for the foreign investor. The government, in fact, controls the flow of income and assets to the Cuban people.

Indeed, the unwillingness of Cuban authorities (either in Law-decree No. 50 or in Law No. 77) to permit foreign investors to acquire title to the properties in which they invest, and statements by Cuban officials that reinforced Cuba's commitment to maintain its socialist economic and political structure, negated some of the positive climate created by the investment protection policies (Pérez-López 1996). So, sufficient research and literature exists to conclude that, during the 1990s, Cuba's internal policies were sufficient to both initially attract and then deter foreign direct investment.

THE IMPACT OF SANCTIONS

However, this summary history begs the question regarding U.S. sanctions. If the external policies of the United States towards Cuba caused the economic downturn, then internal political decisions would not be the primary perpetrator.

To answer that question, we need to evaluate the impact of U.S. sanctions on the Cuban economy vis-à-vis the impact of Cuba's domestic policies on its economy. Using an event study, I have compared the performance of the Cuban foreign investment portfolio to a general market portfolio over the period of foreign direct investment in Cuba during the period 1994-2000 (the period in which the Soviet subsidy ended and the Cuban government could have been expected to seek foreign investment to supplant the lost income).

To assess the impact of external and internal policy events, I looked at significant policy changes that could reasonably be expected to alter Cuban economic performance and the risks associated with foreign investment in Cuba. This included a close examination of international press coverage of internal and external events, reporting that would have been widely available to foreign investors and could reasonably be expected to inform their decision making.

If external policies such as sanctions have an important or decisive impact on the Cuban economy, then

events related to changes or anticipated changes in such policies should be reflected in significant changes in the Cuba portfolio relative to the benchmark, general market portfolio. At the same time, events related to Cuban domestic policies should have relatively little impact on the Cuban stock portfolio when compared to the general portfolio. In contrast, if Cuban domestic policies are decisive, then we might expect to see that changes or anticipated changes in Cuban policy change the Cuba portfolio relative to the world benchmark, and U.S. sanctions policies have relatively little impact.

The main difficulty in any empirical analysis lies in the scarcity of reliable data. The Cuban economy has operated as an independent entity only since the end of the Soviet subsidy. It took several years after that for the government to implement and adopt accounting standards. The numbers once reported, moreover, contain inconsistencies and inaccuracies.[7]

To overcome these difficulties in using Cuba's internally-generated data, I used the stock price of companies outside of Cuba that made investments in Cuba. This approach provides two specific advantages.

- First, this study is concerned with the impact of foreign direct investment in Cuba. Analyzing the micro-level data on companies that made such investments gets directly at the relevant issues.

- Second, the indicator metrics, daily stock prices, are determined by a well functioning global capital market, specifically the NASDAQ, and prices are not subject to government manipulation.

To measure the benchmark, general market portfolio, I use the FTSE All World Actuaries Index.[8] This index assigns a daily value to a portfolio designed to proxy for the entire world market, a composite of stock performance throughout the world. To proxy for foreign investment in Cuba I use the Herzfeld Caribbean Basin Fund, a mutual fund traded on the NASDAQ exchange under the ticker symbol "CUBA." This fund's managers characterize the fund as

---

7. For detailed examples of the problems with Cuban government data see Werlau 1998 and Pérez-López 2000.

8. Source: www.ftse.com

an opportunity to invest in Cuba indirectly by investing in companies that either currently invest in Cuba or are poised to benefit from investment in Cuba. They therefore bypass U.S. restrictions on current direct investment in Cuba while maintaining a focus on the foreign direct investment market of Cuba.[9]

THE EVENT STUDY: CAUSES OF CUBA'S ECONOMIC PERFORMANCE

In the six-and-one-half years of data, it appears that only during six brief time periods did the market portfolio fail to predict the CUBA foreign investment portfolio, using the two-standard-error criterion.[10] The task now becomes the examination of these six periods to determine what might have caused Cuba's performance to diverge from the expected. (See Figure 1)

The figure may be most revealing when looking at the two most important events: Cuba's Law on Foreign Investment of September 1995, and the U.S. Helms-Burton Law of March 1996. Cuba's Law on

Foreign Investment is arguably the most important piece of domestic legislation passed in Cuba during the 1990s. This law sought to entice foreign investment into the Cuban economy, promising to allow free-trade zones, permitting limited foreign business and property ownership, and promising administrative changes that would streamline and speed government approval processes.

The United States' Helms-Burton law of 1996 is the most important U.S. legislation specifically directed at Cuba during the sample period. Helms-Burton, known formally as the Cuban Liberty and Democratic Solidarity (LIBERTAD) Act of 1996,[11] codified the previous laws and executive orders currently in effect toward Cuba. Under its provisions, only the Congress can lift sanctions; since Congress was considered to be more "hard line" toward Cuba, this can be, and was, considered a significant tightening of existing sanctions. In addition, Helms-Burton sought to place new and significant disincentives to foreign investment in Cuba, providing for recourse in U.S.

---

9. Each of these data series is non-stationary, and to correct for detected serial autocorrelation in these data I employ a recursive least squares technique. Specifically, the dependent variable is CUBA and the independent variable is the market portfolio (World), and the equation is estimated by repeatedly adding a daily value to the set with each estimate until all observations are used. At each step the last estimate of the coefficient vector, b, can be used to predict the next value of the dependent variable. The one-step forecast error is defined to be the *recursive residual*. The recursive residual w_t is formally described as follows:

$$w_t = \frac{y_t - x'_t \, b_{t-1}}{\sqrt{1 + x'_t \, (X'_{t-1} \, X_{t-1})^{-1} \, x'_t}}$$

where:

y_t = the dependent variable CUBA
x_t = the regressor variable, World
X_{t-1} = the t-1 by k matrix of the World variable.

The residual from the recursive model, w_t, is independent and normally distributed with mean equal to zero and variance equal to 6^2. The residuals thus reflect random "shocks," or unanticipated deviations from the time series pattern. The analysis focuses on the significant variations when the World portfolio fails to predict the CUBA portfolio to within two standard deviations.

This recursive residual is measured on the vertical axis in Figure 1. In addition, lines representing two standard errors from the residual are also plotted. Points falling outside of two standard errors indicate a time of instability when the World portfolio failed to predict the Cuba portfolio. Moving forward in time, the outlying values will be incorporated into the model for the next least squares prediction, so the mean would again be expected to go to zero.

10. This criterion comes from the literature on recursive regression (Green 2000) and the E Views software package and users guide.

11. P.L. 104-114 of March 12, 1996.

Figure 1.   Date: Recursive Residuals ± 2 S.E

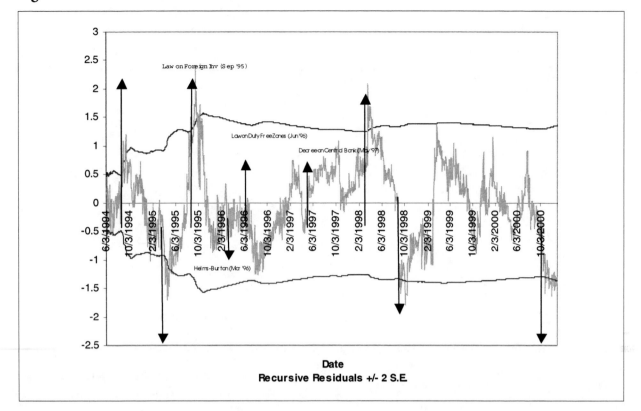

courts for any American who has property in Cuba that is being trafficked in by foreign investors.[12]

The figure highlights these two events on the timeline. It can be seen that the Helms-Burton Act, the single largest U.S. policy change during the observed period, did *not* significantly impact the Cuban foreign investment market, especially when compared to the magnitude of the change from the Cuban Law on Foreign Investment. Indeed, March 1996, or the months leading up to or following it, does not even appear in the list of six significant economic periods discovered in our benchmark comparison.

If the most significant U.S. sanctions effort of the 1990s is not reflected among the most significant upturns or downturns in Cuba's economic perfor-

mance, what events are? The six events, in chronological order, are as follows:

September 1994

The period around September 1994 is one of marked economic improvement, the first after the end of Soviet subsidies, followed Cuba's introduction of legal "farmer's markets"—farmers were allowed to sell their surplus crops to Cuban citizens willing to pay, and for any price they could obtain. Similar types of market reforms instituted in the People's Republic of China in the 1980s led to significant increases in productivity and improvement in the economy. Perhaps, in the autumn of 1994, investors expected Cuba to follow China's model. Whatever the case, a review of world and U.S. policy events during or leading up to

---

12. The lack of significant impact of the Helm-Burton law may be attributable to market expectations. If the market expected the eventual passage of this law, then the daily stock prices would have already incorporated this law. However, this bill had been introduced in Congress with no action for a considerable amount of time with no action and clear opposition. It passed immediately following Castro's shoot-down of the Brothers to the Rescue aircraft in the Florida straits. Therefore, this act's final passage into law was a surprise to many of the Members of Congress who had advocated its passage for the previous year, so it is reasonable to assume that it was a surprise to the market.

September 1994 finds no significant external occurrences that might have caused Cuba's upturn.

Spring of 1995

During this period, in which the Cuba portfolio under-performed the world portfolio, a close review of the international press finds no external events related to Cuba. In contrast, on May 28, 1995, the Cuban government shows signs of retreating from its newly implemented, relatively open investment policies when, in violation of what should have been legally binding contracts, it unexpectedly expelled the Spanish managers of four joint-ventured Cuban hotels.

In a country such as Cuba, where the government is subject to little or no oversight—no checks and balances—what matters to foreign investors may be how investors are actually treated rather than what the laws say.[13] Although the world seemed to react with enthusiasm to domestic statements designed to attract foreign investment, this first public act of abrogating an otherwise enforceable agreement probably sent shivers down the spines of current and would-be investors.

Summer and Autumn of 1995

This period, which shows the largest variation from the world portfolio, comprised the months leading up to and including the September 1995 landmark Law on Foreign Investment, in which Castro instituted changes in policy, law, and rhetoric. This was the time in Cuba's special period of transformation when the government was experimenting with market openings, an event heavily covered in the international press. In contrast, no significant external policy changes are reported during this period.

February 23, 1998 to June 11, 1998

During this period, the CUBA portfolio significantly outperformed that predicted by the model. No significant Cuban domestic events were reported during this time period. On the international scene, the

United States and the European Union reached an agreement on the implementation of the Helms-Burton law. Specifically, the United States agreed not to take retaliatory action against foreign firms operating in Cuba, while European governments agreed to prohibit aid to companies doing business in Cuba.[14]

As such, this period could be the exception to the rule that external events have less impact on Cuban economic performance than domestic ones. However, it is important to note that these events do not answer our question about the impact of (unilateral) sanctions policy, but rather respond to multilateral events. It appears worthwhile to investigate in another venue the relative impact of unilateral versus multilateral sanctions on the economy of a totalitarian dictator.

August 31, 1998 to December 11, 1998

No significant relevant events external or internal to Cuba appeared in the international press during this period. This deviation from the predicted values for the CUBA portfolio cannot be explained by the methods employed in the events study.

October 12, 2000 to December 29, 2000

This period of underperformance occurred as the international press was reporting that the Cuban government was actively pursuing policies of domestic repression. In contrast, no relevant events external to Cuba appeared in the international press during this period.

WHAT DOES CASTRO WANT? THE PUBLIC CHOICE MODEL

In summary, during the six years following the end of the Soviet subsidy and subsequent pressures on Castro to open his economy to foreign investment, it appears that the policies of the Cuban government, and not those of the United States or other external powers, are responsible for Cuba's economic successes or failures.

---

13. We know that some of the most democratic and egalitarian constitutions in the world are and were those of the People's Republic of China and the Soviet Union. The implementation of these documents, however, was far from rigorous and the world understood the governments based upon their deeds.

14. For a detailed discussion of this agreement see Roy 2000.

Clearly, two factors diminish the importance of U.S. sanctions on the Cuban economy. First, Castro himself limits the amount of foreign direct investment based upon his selection of internal policies in Cuba—his political choices as absolute ruler. Second, the sanctions are unilateral—the rest of the world can trade with Cuba. If the United States cannot influence the flow of FDI from other countries (Canada, Mexico, and Europe were the largest investors in Cuba in the 1990s), the reasons these countries reduced their rate of investment in the late 1990s must lie elsewhere—beyond the continuing U.S. sanctions. Indeed, the data shows that the Helms-Burton law did not significantly impact foreign investment performance in the Cuba portfolio until the European Union agreed on implementation measures with the United States.

It appears that Castro himself is responsible for the poor economic performance of his economy. He has the entire world except the United States to trade with now. He had the opportunity to open the economy to a much higher level of foreign investment but made policy decisions that limit further investment.

Without the U.S. embargo, would Castro let the Cuban economy flourish? A public choice economic model of the impact of sanctions on a totalitarian dictator suggests he would not (see Appendix).

The totalitarian dictator is an income-maximizer whose economic constraints are synonymous with those of the entire economy. Characteristics include: control of government spending, taxation, monetary policy, trade and foreign investment, an infinite time horizon, lack of political legitimacy, rule by force and coercion, the need for a costly system of internal security, including police and military forces, to prevent insurrection and overthrow, and the need for a system of rewards for the elite to engender their loyalty. Power is an economic good which Castro must purchase at a cost.[15]

Castro's rule reflects each of these characteristics. He has totally controlled the Cuban government since shortly after coming to power in January 1959. He controls government policy over wages and working standards, tax rates, monetary policy, government spending, and foreign investment. He controls the police and the all-powerful Committees for the Defense of the Revolution (CDR)—the neighborhood watch network that prevents ordinary Cubans from communicating freely or organizing within their communities.[16] Nor does Castro have the Cuban people's consent to rule. Shortly after seizing power in 1959, however, he rejected elections; on May 16, 1961, he declared Cuba a Socialist country, and he has ruled Cuba ever since.

Castro's rule exhibits another important characteristic of totalitarian dictatorships: an unlimited time horizon. He came to power as a revolutionary and never gave up that persona. He has always fought the Yanqui enemy and the capitalistic imperialists. After spending so much of his adult life fighting against his chosen enemy, it can be argued that he wants more than simply to live well. He wants his life to have long-lasting meaning for the world—he wants his ideology to be continued beyond his lifetime. "I trust in what we've done, I trust ideas, I trust all those children, those young people. Nobody can change these people. Not even me with the level of authority I have, could lead these people away from the Revolution."[17]

It is plausible to assume that Castro wants to maximize his power for the reasons described above. In particular, given his lack of legitimacy, he needs to maintain his military and security forces, needs to maintain the appearances of strength and power, and needs to keep society's elites convinced that any attempt at overthrow is futile. To do all this he must continue to monopolize the nation's sources of wealth.

---

15. See "The Iron Fist and the Invisible Hand: A Case Study in the Economics of Totalitarianism," by Gary Shiffman, unpublished dissertation.

16. The CDRs were formed on September 28, 1960, inaugurated by Castro in a speech given at the Plaza of the Revolution.

17. To a Chicago Tribune reporter, Havana, March 2001.

If Castro seeks simply to maximize his revenues, the Cuban government would provide the profit-maximizing marginal tax rate and level of government spending. However, a vital element in the budget constraints of a totalitarian dictator is the cost of maintaining his power, such as the CDR and military police. In addition, stability and wealth are not necessarily complementary goals for the dictator. In fact, wealth above a theoretical level can promote instability and below a theoretical level promote stability.

Thus, Castro's legitimacy and his survival in office both depend upon his successful management of the national budget to maximize his revenues while minimizing his security costs—which will tend to rise as the middle class grows and civil society develops. He will provide a regular system of taxation and ensure his monopolization of this power, and he will provide for public services to enhance the productive capacities of his economy. He will accept foreign direct investment to the extent that he can control it, and he will accept unlimited amounts of direct investment through the government.

The expectations of the model suggest that the dictator does not want unlimited economic growth in Cuba. The unifying element of his behavior is control: the totalitarian dictator will seek to monopolize all sources of wealth. It became apparent from the model that he needs economic control because the diffusion of economic wealth increases his costs of maintaining political power.

CONCLUSIONS

Regardless of his rhetoric in Congressional debates in Washington, DC, Castro in fact prohibits the flow of private investment into Cuba through rigid policies detrimental to foreign investment. Castro chooses the poverty in Cuba, because this suffering of the Cuban people corresponds to his optimum level of economic performance given the constraints modeled above.

In the end, one may conclude that sanctions amount to symbolism—a condemnation by one country of another. Many argue that public condemnation by the United States has meaning in the world in 2002. U.S. Presidents and the Congress may choose sanctions exactly because they are symbolic. Significant in this analysis is the point that the sanctions do not harm the innocents, and so the moral cost associated with the "purchase" of these sanctions may be acceptable to the policy maker. That policy maker, however, may also reject unilateral sanctions as a tool because of the inability to also inflict any economic harm on the dictator. Regardless of the decision within the United States, the debates regarding these policies should be based upon a realistic understanding of the extent to which sanctions actually produce economic results in Cuba.

If U.S. import and export embargoes do not affect Cuba's economic performance, then U.S. sanctions neither harm the Cuban people nor prevent the strengthening of Castro's security forces. In this case, policy analysts might ask two questions: what does the *United States* gain and lose from its sanctions, and why do the Cuban people suffer in poverty?

The answer to the first question is for another day and another forum. This study, however, seeks to set out the framework for a new, hopefully cogent policy debate. The debate over "who the United States is harming, the dictator or the people" must end. It is time to address the causes of poverty and the constraints placed upon a totalitarian dictator by the circumstances of his power.

REFERENCES

Betancourt, Roger R. 1999. "Cuba's Economic 'Reforms': Waiting for Fidel on the Eve of the Twenty-First Century." In *Cuba in Transition—* *Volume 9.* Washington: Association for the Study of the Cuban Economy.

Green, William H. 2000. *Econometric Analysis*, 4th edition. New Jersey: Prentice Hall.

Hernández-Catá Ernesto. 2000. "The Fall and Recovery of the Cuban Economy in the 1990s: Mirage or Reality." In *Cuba in Transition—Volume 10*. Washington: Association for the Study of the Cuban Economy.

Illán, José M. 1964. *Cuba: Facts and Figures of an Economy in Ruins*. Miami: Agencia Interamericana de Publicaciones.

Kimmerling, Stephen J. 2000. "A Survey of Significant Legal Changes During Cuba's Special Period: Setting Parameters for Change." In *Cuba in Transition—Volume 10*. Washington: Association for the Study of the Cuban Economy.

Maybarduk, Gary H. 1999. "The State of the Cuban Economy 1998-1999." In *Cuba in Transition—Volume 9*. Washington: Association for the Study of the Cuban Economy.

Mesa-Lago, Carmelo. 1998. "The Cuban Economy in 1997-1998: Performance and Policies." In *Cuba in Transition—Volume 8*. Washington: Association for the Study of the Cuban Economy.

Mesa-Lago, Carmelo. 2001. "Assessing Economic and Social Performance in the Cuban Transition of the 1990s." in Horowitz, Irving Louis, and Jaime Suchlicki, editors, *Cuban Communism*, 10th edition, New Brunswick: Transaction Publishers.

Pérez-López, Jorge. 1995. "Coveting Beijing, but Imitating Moscow: Cuba's Economic Reforms in a Comparative Perspective," In *Cuba in Transition—Volume 5*. Washington: Association for the Study of the Cuban Economy.

Pérez-López, Jorge. 1996. "Foreign Direct Investment in the Cuban Economy: A Critical Look." Unpublished.

Pérez-López, Jorge. 1998. "The Cuban Economic Crisis of the 1990s and the External Sector." In *Cuba in Transition—Volume 8*. Washington: Association for the Study of the Cuban Economy.

Pérez-López, Jorge. 2000. "Cuba's Balance of Payments Statistics." In *Cuba in Transition—Volume 10*. Washington: Association for the Study of the Cuban Economy.

Roy, Joaquín. 2000. "The 'Understanding' Between the European Union and the United States Over Investment in Cuba." In *Cuba in Transition—Volume 10*. Washington: Association for the Study of the Cuban Economy.

Travieso-Díaz, Matías F. and Alejandro Ferraté. 1995. "Recommended Features of a Foreign Investment Code for Cuba's Free-Market Transition." In *Cuba in Transition—Volume 5*. Washington: Association for the Study of the Cuban Economy.

Werlau, Maria C. 1998. "Update on Foreign Investment in Cuba 1997-98 and Focus on the Energy Sector." In *Cuba in Transition—Volume 8*. Washington: Association for the Study of the Cuban Economy.

APPENDIX
THE PUBLIC CHOICE MODEL

THE BASIC MODEL

The production function for this dictator in a closed economy without foreign trade is a function of government spending and tax revenues. $Q = q(G, t)$, where Q is national output (or GDP), G is government spending, and t is the average marginal tax rate. By assumption, tax revenue (T) is proportional to Q: $T = tQ$.

The dictator's cost function includes both the costs of providing public goods and services (C) as well as the maintenance of internal security (S) to protect his power. Total costs, therefore, can be characterized as both a function of the total government spending as well as a function of the size of the GDP, where **C** is a function of government spending, and **S** is a function of GDP.

$$C = c(G) \text{ and } S = s(Q).$$

This dictator's net income (**Y**) therefore equals tax revenues (**T**) minus the cost of governing and providing public goods and stability (**C**) and minus the cost of maintaining a hold on power through security forces and payments to the elites (**S**).

$$Y = T - C - S$$
$$Y = t * q(G,t) - c(G) - s(q(G,t))$$

Taking the first order condition with respect to *t* and G reveals the net income-maximizing rate of taxation (*t**), and the net income-maximizing level of government spending on infrastructure and services (**G***).

Investment

Opening the model, investment is broken down into two categories: foreign investment strictly limited to investment through the government (I_g) and foreign investment directly into private hands (I_d). I_g imposes no direct costs on and poses no risks to this dictator. Further this dictator can successfully insulate the domestic economy from foreign investment that goes directly into privately held properties or ventures (I_d). Foreign investors must partner with the government. The dictator then pays the local workers—the foreign investor does not get to control the wages or working conditions. The impact, therefore, of I_g investment on tax revenue (**T**) is very small and here assumed to be zero. All of the direct benefits to foreign investment (I_g) accrue to the government-as-business-partner.

This is not the case, however, with I_d. FDI invested directly in the productive factors of the economy and not directed through the government will likely increase GDP. It will therefore increase security costs (**S**). If the dictator can limit investment to I_g, and he takes a percentage of this investment, kI_g such that $0 < k < 1$, where **k** is the effective tax rate on I_g, as net

profits from the investment, then the revised net income equation can be characterized as follows:

$$Y = T + kI_g - C - S$$
$$Y = tQ + kI_g - C - S$$
$$Y = t^* q(G,t) + kI_g - c(G) - s(q(G,t))$$

Of significance, the income-maximizing level of I_g is unlimited. Taking the derivative of Y with respect to kI_g yields a positive constant. $\dfrac{dY}{dI_g} = k$. The slope of the relationship is linear and positive, therefore there should be no limit to the amount of direct investment through the government for this dictator.

Since the economic impact of I_d directly benefits the economy, it cannot be segregated from **Q**, and the dictator's benefit from this investment derives only from the marginal tax rate on the production of the economy.

$$Y = t^* q(G,t,I_d) + kI_g - c(G) - s(q(G,t,I_d))$$

Foreign Direct Investment (I_d) benefits the dictator, but not without also increasing the cost of maintaining power (**S**).

Dynamics

A dictator may be tempted to at least partially open his economy to foreign direct investment (I_d). The probability that the dictator loses control (**P**) is equal to some function of the amount of I_d direct foreign investment: **P** = **p**(I_d). The probability that he keeps control while opening the economy to direct foreign investment is one minus the probability the dictator loses control (**1 − P**). Assuming the dictator is risk-neutral and hopes to perpetuate his regime forever, his decision regarding taxes, services and FDI can be characterized as follows:

$$Y^e = \frac{P(0) + (1-P)Y}{r}$$

$$Y^e = \frac{(1-p(I_d))[t^* q(G,t,I_d) + kI_g - c(G) - s(q(G,t,I_d))]}{r}$$

Expected income (Y^e) equals the probability of being deposed (**P**) multiplied by the wealth received if deposed (zero), plus the probably he remains in power multiplied by the wealth received if he remains in power (**Y**). Since his time horizon is assumed infinite, the entire equation is divided by the interest rate (**r**), which for simplicity is assumed to be a constant rate.

A rational, risk-neutral dictator chooses the net income maximizing tax rate t^*, net income maximizing level of government spending **G***, and as much $\mathbf{I_g}$ as he can attract (there is no maximum level as discussed above). There also exists a net income maximizing level of direct investment into the economy, $\mathbf{I_d}^*$.

$$\frac{\partial Y^e}{\partial t} = (1-P)\left(Q + t\frac{\partial q}{\partial t}\right) - \frac{\partial s}{\partial q}\frac{\partial q}{\partial t} = 0 \text{ at max, } t^* = t(G, I_d)$$

$$\frac{\partial Y^e}{\partial G} = (1-P)\left(t\frac{\partial q}{\partial G}\right) - \frac{\partial s}{\partial q}\frac{\partial q}{\partial G} = 0 \text{ at max, } G^* = g(t, I_d)$$

$$\frac{dY^e}{dI_g} = k > 0$$

$$\frac{\partial Y^e}{\partial I_d} = \left(\frac{\partial p}{\partial I_d}tQ\right) + (1-P)t\left(\frac{\partial q}{\partial I_d}\right) - \frac{\partial s}{\partial q}\frac{\partial q}{\partial I_d} = 0, \ I_d^* = i_d(G, t)$$

CUBA'S FUTURE ECONOMIC CRISIS: THE AGEING POPULATION AND THE SOCIAL SAFETY NET

Sergio Díaz-Briquets

In this paper I examine the impact demographic trends are having on the evolution of Cuba's population age structure. The analysis is conducted within a comparative perspective and focuses on the most significant demographic development of the late twentieth century and the first half of the twenty-first, the ageing of the world's population. The analyses suggests that Cuba will confront serious difficulties in years to come as a result of these demographic trends. Their impact will be so profound and pervasive as to interfere with the country's prospects for long-term economic development, even after Cuba discards its current economic system and becomes fully integrated into the international economy.

A GLOBAL OVERVIEW

Two major turning points in world demographic history will mark the period from 1750 to 2050. The first was a gradual but eventual explosive growth in human population. This was accompanied by the emergence of population age structures largely dominated by the young. With the onset of gradual mortality declines, population growth rates began to increase, in some cases dramatically. The world's population rose from about 800 million in 1750 to 1.7 billion in 1900. Following the Second World War, the pace of growth accelerated further, particularly in the developing world, with global population reaching 4 billion by 1975 (Caldwell and Schindlmayr 2002). By 2000, 6 billion humans inhabited the earth; current population projections suggest that the number may well reach 9.3 billion by 2050 (United Nations 2002).

Despite continuous growth, the global population growth rate has begun to slow down due to declines in fertility rates. Sustained fertility declines and continued mortality declines at the older ages on a global scale are giving rise to another equally momentous demographic transformation: the rapid ageing of the world's population. While population projections may only imperfectly capture the magnitude of the transformation—particularly as such projections seek to anticipate distant demographic developments fifty years into the future—the trends they suggest are credible enough to warrant a great deal of concern.

So significant is the projected change that by 2050, for the world population as a whole, the share of the young population (under 15 years of age)—formerly dominant—is expected to attain rough parity with that of the older population (above age 60), about 21% each. The world's median population age, consequently, is expected to rise from 27 years in 2000 to 36 years by 2050 (Population Division 2002a: 15 and 17). These changes, however, will not impact all countries equally, as mortality and fertility differentials across countries are quite wide and prevalent. Some countries, in fact, still evidence relatively high mortality and fertility rates. Irrespective of these gaps, and occasional setbacks such as that resulting from the current HIV/AIDS pandemic, the secular trend is for rates to converge as medical and public health advances continue to be diffused around the globe. Preferences for smaller family size, increasing female labor force participation rates, and the growing availability of modern contraceptives, among other factors, are contributing factors behind continued fertility declines.

Other significant demographic developments are impacting the characteristics of the elderly population. The various segments of the elderly population are increasing at different rates. Growth rates for the older-old population (above 80 years of age) are higher than for the old (the population above age 60) or the young-old (between 60 and 79 years of age). Women, barring exceptions in a few countries, have achieved more significant life expectancy increases than males, both at birth and at older ages. Across the age distribution (except at birth), but progressively more so at older ages, the number of women exceeds that of males.

These demographic trends have important economic and social implications. Since people are surviving to older ages, they are expending a growing number of years economically inactive. Thus, they are more likely to rely on pensions, personal savings, or family support to cover living expenses after retirement, as well as surviving into ages at which chronic diseases and disabilities are more frequent, acute and costly to treat. Major societal and financial adjustments will be in order to accommodate the needs of the old, at the same time as the number of economically active workers proportionally contracts. Pension and health care systems will be hard pressed as their client base experiences substantial growth, just as the number of active contributors to these systems contracts relatively and, in many countries, absolutely. More vulnerable are those retiree programs financed through active worker contributions (pay as you go systems) than those with substantial reserves accumulated over time through government or privately-sponsored trust funds or via individual beneficiary retirement accounts. In the United States, for example, concerns about the long-term viability and financial soundness of programs such as Social Security and Medicare are

driving an intense policy debate. Many other countries are tackling similar issues.

THE CUBAN CASE

Cuba generally conforms to the global demographic trends described above. In some important respects, however, the situation in Cuba differs from that in most other developing countries, while approximating that of the economically wealthier nations.

First, Cuba's demographic transition—the decline from high death and birth rates to low death and birth rates—began earlier than in most other developing countries (notable exceptions in Latin America were Argentina and Uruguay). Second, during the 1960s and early 1970s, the country experienced a brief baby boom followed by a rapid and sustained birth rate decline that within a few years brought fertility below replacement level, or the level at which population growth will eventually cease (discounting the potential population momentum associated with age structure features, or immigration) as the number of deaths eventually equals or exceeds the number of births. At Cuba's current mortality level, replacement fertility roughly corresponds to a total fertility rate (TFR) of 2.1.[1]

Several factors contributed to the 1960s baby boom, a generally rare phenomenon only infrequently observed internationally. By the late 1950s, Cuba had already attained a fertility level low enough to allow for increases within normal demographic boundaries. But a number of social, economic and regulatory determinants associated with the profound changes produced by the revolution immediately after 1959 came together to produce the fertility increase. Policies to redistribute wealth; reforms in various social areas, including job creation; a favorable economic performance facilitated by a surge in aggregate demand and economic disinvestments; and popular expectations for a bountiful future fed by wildly exaggerated leadership promises of economic prosperity, led many Cuban couples to establish families or have additional children. At the same time, and for a few

---

1. The total fertility rate could be interpreted as the number of children the average women has over her reproductive lifetime. The fraction represents an allowance for the replacement of dead offspring.

Figure 1. Total Fertility Rates in Cuba: 1970–2000

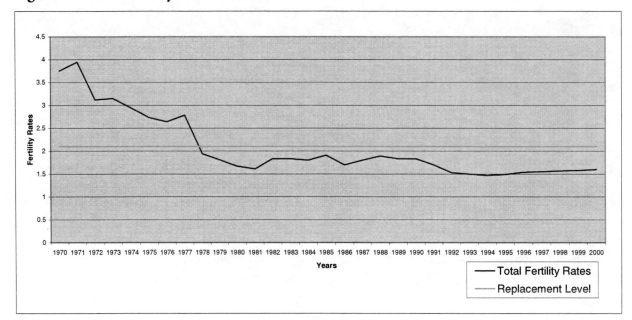

years, the revolutionary authorities enforced laws that proscribed induced abortions, just as consumer goods shortages, including contraceptive supplies, began to be felt (for a discussion, see Díaz-Briquets and Pérez 1982:517-523).

As a result, the crude birth rate rose by 35% between 1958 and 1963, only to gradually resume its prior secular decline. By 1974, the fertility decline was rapid, as shown by the trend in annual TFRs depicted in Figure 1, Cuba reaching below replacement fertility in 1978. Since then, the TFR has fluctuated within a narrow band, reaching its lowest historical level in the early 1990s, notably 1994, during the depth of the Special Period's economic crises. That the lowest TFR on record was in 1994, following the year when the economy contracted the most, is a testimony to the responsiveness of Cuba's fertility to economic conditions.

Cuba's Population Pyramid in 2000

The annual number of births in a population is not simply a function of age-specific fertility rates, the number of births produced by a given female age cohort (individuals sharing a common year or time interval when they were born). It is also influenced by the relative size of each age cohort within a population's age structure. An age-sex pyramid graphically describes the age and sex structure of a population.

Conventionally, the right side of the pyramid portrays the female population, with each bar representing a given age group (usually arranged in five-year intervals). The youngest cohort is the base, with progressively older age cohorts following, the oldest topping the pyramid. A high fertility/high mortality population pyramid has a broad base that peters out gradually as age cohorts become older and die, thus the figure's traditional name.

A population pyramid is a very effective devise to assess the effects of fertility and mortality fluctuations in a population's age-sex composition. As shown in the upper left panel of Figure 2, Cuba's age-sex pyramid in the year 2000 (U.S. Bureau of the Census 2002) presented an irregular shape, although still retaining the pyramidal outline associated with gradual fertility and mortality decline. Four indentations are apparent. Most prominent is that between 25 and 39 years of age—corresponding to the 1960s baby boom generation—followed by another indentation at ages 5 to 14, the offspring of the baby boom cohorts. Notice that the size of the 5 to 9 and 10 to 14 birth cohorts was larger than for birth cohorts preceding or following them, although TFR levels were nearly constant throughout the 1980s. This is a consequence of the larger absolute size of the potential pool of mothers born during the baby boom of the

Figure 2. Population Pyramids: Cuba and the United States

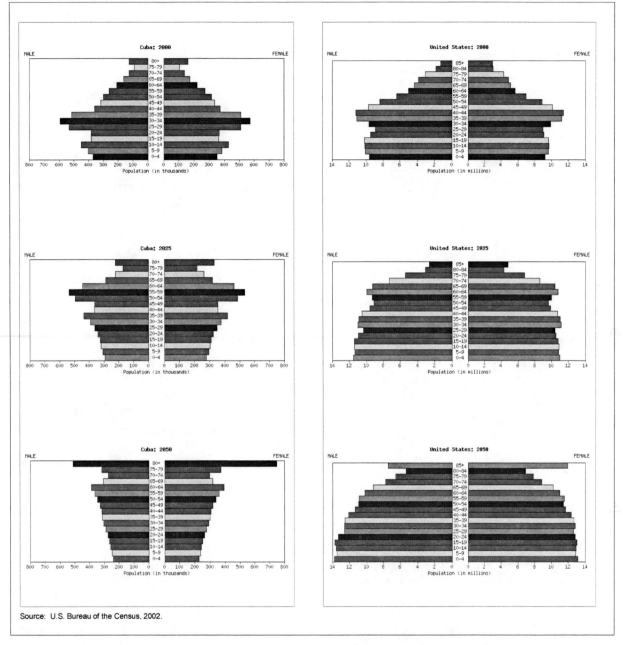

Source: U.S. Bureau of the Census, 2002.

1960s. The reduced numbers at ages 5 to 9 and 0 to 4 are consistent with the 1990s fertility decline and the increasing age of baby boom mothers. Finally, the disproportionately large birth cohort shown at the top of the pyramid is partly a statistical artifact since it includes all birth cohorts beyond 80 years of age. One last point is that at the oldest ages, most evident past 80 years of age, the relative share of the female population exceeds the male share by a considerable margin. This pattern is consistent with higher female life expectancies at all ages, but especially among the elderly.

The Ageing of Cuba's Population

The demographic picture provided above (together with emigration) will bring to a halt Cuba's population growth. This may have already occurred, or will happen in the not-too-distant future. Another consequence is the rapid ageing of Cuba's population. The country's median age has risen from 23.4 years in 1960 to 32.9 in 2000; it is projected to increase to

43.1 by 2025, rising even further by 2050, the end of the projection period.

The results of the ageing process can be appreciated in the middle and lower left-hand panels of Figure 2, where population pyramids for Cuba in 2025 and 2050 appear. By 2025, just about two decades from now, the number of individuals reaching retirement age will be increasing rapidly, and just as significantly, the size of the older-old age cohort (above 80 years of age) will be almost twice as large as in 2000. Large-scale emigration, underway since the mid-1990s, further accentuates the aging trend since emigrants are generally drawn from the pool of the economically active.

The relative size of the older-old age cohort is projected to expand dramatically by 2050. In unison with this development, as the baby boom cohorts approach the end of life, Cuba's age-sex structure begins to resemble an inverted pyramid. The elderly, including the older-old, attains disproportionate importance within the overall population age structure. As the baby boom cohorts eventually die out, the proportional significance of the elderly population in Cuba's demography will diminish in relative terms, but the country will still have, if current projections hold, a much older population by the second half of this century than it is the case today, a pattern common to Cuba and many other countries.

Ageing Indicators

The concerns associated with an ageing population are manifold and primarily reflect the social and economic demands than an elderly population beyond its productive years places on a nation's resources. The satisfaction of these demands is determined, in part, by the ability of countries to accumulate or generate wealth to fulfill the needs of the elderly population. To some extent this is a function, in turn, of the relative numerical balance between generations.

Several demographic indicators can be used to assess these relationships, as shown in Table 1 for the world, world regions according to level of development, and selected countries in 2002 and 2050 (Population Division 2002b). For several of these indicators (e.g., percent of the population above age 60,

percent of the elderly population 80 years of age and over), in 2002 Cuba occupied an intermediate position between developed and developing regions. In contrast, by 2050, Cuba's indicators are projected to be at parity with those of developed regions. In fact, by mid-century, only a few other countries, notably Italy, Japan, Singapore and Spain, are projected to have older-old population shares higher than Cuba, these countries then having among the oldest populations in the world.

Particularly germane are the statistics shown under the "Potential Support Ratio" rubric, or PSR. This ratio—the inverse of the old-age dependency ratio (the population 65 years of age and over to the 15 to 64 working age population)—signals the number of individuals in working ages for every person above age 65. In 2002, when the country had 1.6 million elderly, the PSR in Cuba was 7, a relatively favorable ratio. By 2050, as the number of elderly is projected to reach 3.7 million, with a relatively unchanged overall population size, the PSR is expected to decline to 2 potential workers per retiree. This ratio will be typical for developed countries but about half that for the world as a whole. For some of the countries in Table 1, such as Chile and the United States, the PSR will be about 50% higher than in Cuba, with three working age people for every person above age 65.

Another factor to consider is the average retirement age for workers in different countries. As can be ascertained in Table 1, retirement ages for Cuban workers are generally lower than for other countries included in the table, particularly for females. This is reflected in lower percentages of older Cuban workers (past 60 years of age) in the labor force compared to other countries, the difference being generally quite substantial among females. Finally, Table 1 also shows the considerable life expectancy differential separating the sexes at age 60, alluded to above.

The patterns, in the aggregate, together with other data sets, suggest that Cuba's ageing population will act as a major brake on the country's economic development in years to come for reasons examined below. To substantiate this conclusion the next section

Table 1. **Ageing Indicators, Cuba and Comparison Countries and Regions, 2002**

	Percentage of Total Population 60 Years of Age and Over		Percentage 80 Years or Older of the Population 60 years and over		Sex Ratios		Potential Support Ratio		Statutory Retirement Age		Percentage 60+ in Labor Force		Life Expectancy at Age 60 (2000-2005)	
	2002	2050	2002	2050	2002	2050	2002	2050	2002	2050	2002	2050	Males	Females
Cuba	14	34	16	29	91	84	7	2	60	55	20	3	20	22
United States	16	27	21	28	76	50	5	3	65	65	23	13	19	24
Mexico	7	24	12	19	85	70	13	3	65	65	60	15	20	22
Dominican Republic	7	21	8	17	93	89	14	4	60	60	76	16	17	19
Chile	11	24	13	23	76	53	9	3	65	60	37	7	19	22
Spain	22	44	18	30	75	51	4	1	65	65	13	4	20	25
World Total	10	21	12	19	81	53	9	4			40	15	17	20
More Developed	20	33	17	29	71	44	5	2			21	10	18	23
Less Developed	8	19	9	17	88	64	12	5			50	19	16	19

Source: Population Division 2000b

compares Cuba's projected age structure evolution with those projected for other countries.

SOCIAL AND ECONOMIC IMPLICATIONS: AN INTERNATIONAL PERSPECTIVE

The second panel of Figure 2, and Figures 3 and 4 present, respectively, age-sex pyramids for several countries, namely the United States (Figure 2), Mexico and the Dominican Republic (Figure 3), and Chile and Spain (Figure 4). Selection was dictated by several considerations:

- The United States was included since the ongoing policy debate surrounding what to do about the Social Security and Medicare programs will be familiar to most readers.

- Mexico and the Dominican Republic were included because they are neighboring countries with less advanced demographic regimes than Cuba, but where economic growth is occurring rapidly.

- Chile is a particularly interesting case, not only because of its sustained economic growth and rising per capita incomes but, more importantly, because this country has led the way in devising market-oriented approaches to cope with the pressures of financing the elderly social safety net, including a series of pension reform initia-

tives designed to accumulate reserves and ensure the system's sustainability (see Mesa-Lago and others 2000). Chile is also considering introducing market driven reforms to make more viable and efficient the health care system. These initiatives have been part of broader strategies designed to diversify the national economy and make it more internationally competitive, thus far with very successful results.

- Spain is included since it is projected that by 2050 it will be among the countries with the oldest populations in the world.

The most striking demographic feature of the U.S. population pyramid is that it retains its triangular shape by 2025, and even by 2050 (Figure 2). Although fertility in the United States has been below replacement for several decades, population growth continues unabated due to high immigration and above-average fertility among immigrant women. This means that for the next 50 years, assuming population projections hold, the PSR in the United States will be more favorable than in Cuba. Despite growing concern about the long-term financial viability of Social Security and Medicare (a detailed review of issues surrounding the Medicare program may be found in Reischauer, Butler and Lave 1998), in comparison with Cuba, the United States is in an enviable position given its substantial trust reserves (and availability of private pensions funds and accounts) and the dynamism of its economy.

The long-term viability of the American elderly safety net is far more manageable than Cuba's, not only because of demographic trends, but also because Cuba is bankrupt, devoid of financial reserves, and pays for pensions and health care costs exclusively from current government revenues. Making the

long-term situation worse, the Cuban economic system impedes growth, while the country is only partially integrated into the global economy. These conditions interfere with the country's ability to accumulate financial reserves to address the future needs of the old. Cuba's situation is further aggravated by early retirement ages, as low as 55 years for women (Mesa-Lago and others 2000; Donate-Armada 2001).

Figure 3. Population Pyramids: Mexico and the Dominican Republic

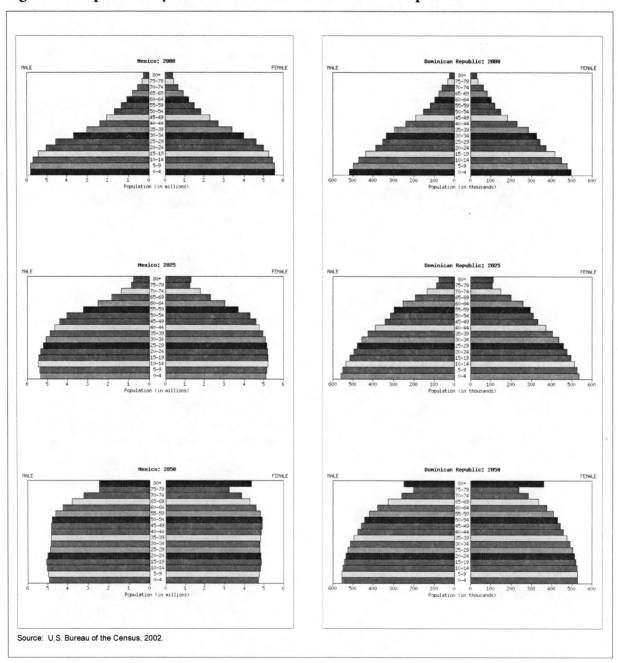

Source: U.S. Bureau of the Census, 2002.

From a demographic point of view, the long-term picture in Mexico and the Dominican Republic (Figure 3) resembles more the United States situation than it does Cuba's. Currently both countries' population pyramids have characteristics typical of countries still undergoing demographic transition. Relatively youthful age structures are symptomatic of countries with dependency burdens still dominated by the young. A youthful dependency burden, however, is far less onerous than an elderly one, as noted by the United Nations (Population Division 2002a:33). However, due to anticipated gradual fertility declines and life expectancy gains, these countries will eventually attain age structures that should make more sustainable, on demographic grounds exclusively, the elderly safety net, as suggested by the percent of the older-old population and the PSR. I already noted that the economies of these two countries have grown appreciably during the last two decades; this economic growth and more favorable age structures may provide breathing room for these two countries to build financial reserves in anticipation of the ageing of their populations.

Chile's age-sex pyramid in 2002 (Figure 4) was fairly typical of a country well along its demographic transition, already acquiring the inverse pyramidal shape being projected for low fertility populations later in this century. Yet, by 2050, the older-old population is projected to only account for 23% of the elderly population and Chile's PSR will be a relatively robust 3.

In Spain, close to half (44%) of the population is projected to be above age 60 by 2050 and the PSR will be well below 2 (projected at 1.5). It is instructive to compare Spain and Cuba's age structures, as they are quite similar. The major differences are that in 2050 the share of the older-old in Cuba—due to

the baby boom cohorts reaching the oldest ages—is projected to be even higher than in Spain, just as the base of the pyramid will be narrower in the former than in the latter country. The implications are easy to draw when it is recalled that Spain's prosperity is related to its membership in the European Community.

CONCLUDING OBSERVATIONS

The conclusion to be drawn from this analysis is that, barring some unforeseen and dramatic demographic developments—such as a major and sustained fertility increase or large-scale immigration—or unprecedented economic growth in decades to come, Cuba's elderly safety net will face a sustainability crisis of major proportions. The Cuban elderly are already feeling the strains of the 1990s economic debacle, receiving average monthly pensions worth but a few dollars, while being subjected to substandard care in a poorly-financed health care system. A miraculous economic recovery in the next few years could well improve the situation over the short- to medium-term, but long-term prospects are rather gloomy.

How to finance the retirement and health care needs of the Cuban elderly under the projected demographic scenario will preoccupy several generations of Cuban leaders, regardless of economic system. Equally worrisome is that the provision of the elderly safety net is likely to exact a heavy economic cost that may imperil the country's economic development since financing pension and health care programs will consume a disproportionate share of national resources. Paying for elderly services will be a major drag on the economy, placing a heavy tax burden on individuals and businesses. The tax burden may even be so onerous as to make Cuba less than attractive as an international investment destination.

Figure 4.   Population Pyramids: Chile and Spain

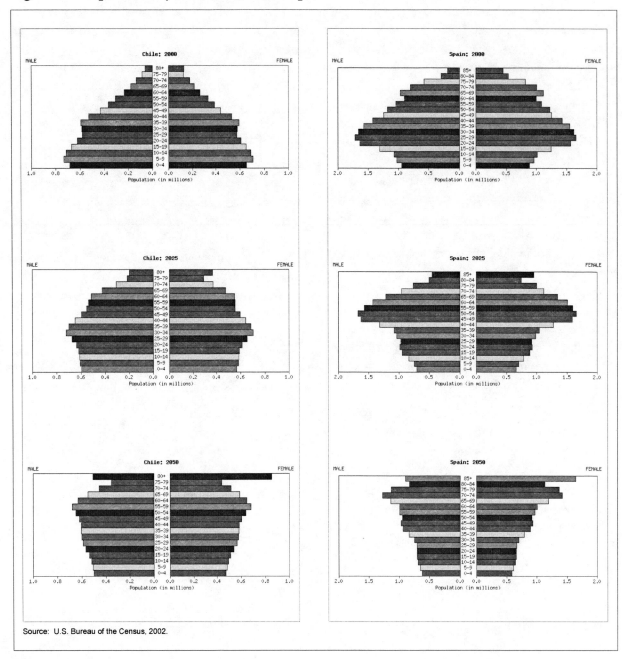

Source: U.S. Bureau of the Census, 2002.

REFERENCES

Caldwell, John C. and Thomas Schindlmayr, "Historical Population Estimates: Unraveling the Consensus," *Population and Development Review*, 28:2, pp. 183-204, 2002.

Díaz-Briquets, Sergio and Lisandro Pérez, "Fertility Decline in Cuba: A Socioeconomic Interpretation," *Population and Development Review*, 8:3, pp. 513-537, 1982.

Donate-Armada, Ricardo A., "The Aging of the Cuban Population." *Cuba in Transition—Volume 11*, 2001.

Mesa-Lago, Carmelo (and others), *Market. Socialist, and Mixed Economies: Comparative Policy and Performance, Chile, Cuba and Costa Rica*, The Johns Hopkins University Press, Baltimore, 2000.

Population Division, *World Population Ageing: 1950-2050*, www.un.org/esa/population/publications/world ageing19502050/index.htm, United Nations, New York, 2002a.

Population Division, *Population Ageing 2002 Wallchart*, United Nations, New York, 2002b.

Reischauer, Robert D., Stuart Butler and Judith R. Lave, editors, *Medicare: Preparing for the Challenges of the 21st Century*, National Academy of Social Insurance, Washington, D.C., 1998.

U.S. Bureau of the Census, International Data Base, http://www.census.gov/cgi-bin/ipc/idbsprd, Washington, D.C., 2002.

A GENERAL EQUILIBRIUM MODEL OF FAMILY REMITTANCES TO CUBA: OR WHY IS IT SO EXPENSIVE TO SEND MONEY TO THE ISLAND?

Luis Locay[1]

The question of remittances from persons of Cuban descent living outside of Cuba to their relatives on the Island is one of the most contentious in the Cuban-American community. Even if the economic and political impact on Cuba of remittances were not significant—and I believe they are—the important role they play in the international debate on policy toward the Island would make them worthy of study.

Much of the debate on remittances to Cuba revolves around their magnitude. In the 1990s the Cuban government resumed publishing balance of payments statistics (Pérez-López (2000)). The category *net current transfers*, which includes remittances, showed a substantial increase from $263 million in 1993 to $828 million in 1999 (Morris (2000)). More recently the figure of one billion dollars has been bandied about. These numbers are often used as measures of remittances. To see the importance of these magnitudes, consider that gross tourism earnings for 1999 were $1,901 million (Morris (2000)). Since only about 30% of this is net hard currency earnings, that would make remittances the single biggest source of hard currency in 1999.

These large magnitudes have been used by opponents of the U.S. embargo on trade with Cuba to argue in favor of lifting sanctions (Betancourt (2000)). The argument has been that the Cuban-American community is being hypocritical by opposing the lifting of the embargo, while at the same time providing financial support to the Cuban regime to the tune of upwards of $800 million per annum. This is a specious argument, for there is nothing contradictory about being in favor of maintaining the embargo and sending money to one's relatives in Cuba. This is an example of a situation where individual maximizing behavior (on the part of opponents of the embargo) will likely not lead to the optimal choice for the group. Each individual Cuban-American will see his or her remittances as helping his relatives directly, while having an insignificant effect on the regime's survival. We have here an example of the "tragedy of the commons," where individual action leads to excessive transfers to Cuba. The argument would be analogous to saying that because I contribute to air pollution by driving a car I cannot be in favor of tougher air quality standards.

Regardless of how these numbers are abused in political debate, the question of their accuracy still remains. Betancourt (2000) charges that the $800 million figure of the late 1990s is grossly inflated, and that the inflation is a means by which to disguise earnings from drug trafficking by the Cuban government. A closer look at how net current transfers were calculated, however, suggests that the numbers may be accurate, but they simply are not a measure of re-

1. I would like to thank Roger Betancourt for comments on an earlier draft of this paper.

mittances. According to Morris (2000) the "figures are calculated as the turnover of dollar shops minus dollar earnings accounted for by official payment of dollars." As Morris points out, net current transfers includes earnings from the informal tourist sector, which may explain why the category grew so rapidly in the 1990s. If we assume that the informal tourist sector was small in 1993, then that year's figure of $263 million could serve as an estimate of remittances. [2]

An alternative to the balance of payment figures can be found in Díaz-Briquets (1994). His approach is to use U.S. Census data on persons of Cuban descent to essentially simulate levels of remittances based on a range of parameter assumptions. Referring to 1994, he opines that "remittances do not exceed $300 to $400 million annually," numbers that are consistent with the figure mentioned above based on the balance of payments statistics for 1993. Such simulations are useful in checking the plausibility of a given estimate, but not to obtain an accurate estimate of remittances, since the results are sensitive to the assumptions made. A good example is Díaz-Briquets' assumption, in what he considers his more reasonable estimates, that U.S.-born persons of Cuban descent do not remit money to their relatives in Cuba. While this may be true, they may provide financial support to their older Cuban-born relatives in the United States, freeing up the latter's resources to send to relatives on the Island. An older Cuban who appears to have meager resources of his own, may send a large fraction of those resources to relatives in Cuba if he is supported in the United States by a younger relative. Ignoring the resources of those born in the U.S., therefore, may significantly underestimate remittances.

Persons with strong prior beliefs are unlikely to be persuaded by simulated estimates supporting a different view. The best way to estimate remittances would

appear to be to conduct a survey for this purpose among persons of Cuban descent living in the United States.[3] It would be very valuable to be able to conduct such a survey soon so as to be able to evaluate the impact of September 11 and the U.S. recession before time blurs people's memories of what they remitted before these events.

The lack of accurate numbers on remittances to Cuba precludes doing any econometric work on the subject at this time. So instead I am focusing on exploring a specific qualitative feature of remittances to Cuba: why is it so expensive to send money to the Island? The reader may think that the answer to this question is obvious: the Cuban government is in a monopolistic position and charges monopoly prices to remit money to Cuba. I will argue below that this argument is too simplistic. It ignores the interrelationship between remittances and purchases at dollar stores. The real question is not why the Cuban government should charge monopoly prices, but why its monopoly prices should take the form that they do. More specifically, I will be asking under what circumstances does it make sense for the Cuban government to charge high prices for both remittances and for goods sold at dollar stores. In doing this, the government is essentially treating dollars from remittances differently from other sources of dollars (remittance fees on top of high prices at dollar stores), and it is not evident why it would want to do so. To address this question I develop below a model of remittances to Cuba that I hope may serve as the starting point of a research program to accurately measure remittances to Cuba, to analyze their place in Cuban policies, and to investigate their impact on Cuba's economy and on a future transition. First, however, I provide a brief discussion of the role that remittances played in the process of economic "reform" in Cuba following the collapse of the Soviet Union and a critique of the simple monopoly pricing explanation for

---

2. If the only source of dollars used in dollar stores were remittances, transactions at such stores would underestimate remittances. Remittances can also go to increase holdings of dollars, which could be substantial in an economy with a growing black market financed at least in part by dollars. The fees the government charges for sending funds to Cuba would also not appear as dollar sales.

3. This would ignore Cubans living outside of Cuba and the United States, but results from the U.S. could be extrapolated for other countries to at least obtain an upper bound.

why sending money to Cuba is so expensive. These first two sections provide motivation for the model. I conclude with a brief summary and some suggestions for future work.

REMITTANCES AND THE COLLAPSE OF THE SOVIET BLOC

Remittances to Cuba obviously provide the regime with much-needed hard currency. The regime "captures" remittances through the direct fees it charges for sending money to Cuba and through high prices for goods at dollar stores. This clear benefit to the government raises the question of why have remittances not always been allowed or encouraged. There must be a downside to remittances, and the tradeoff between the beneficial and harmful effects of remittances to the Cuban regime must have been altered after 1989.

One clear undesirable effect of remittances from the point of view of the Cuban government is that they can lead to severe skewing of the distribution of income on the Island. Many Cubans either have no relatives in the United States or are not on sufficiently good terms to receive remittances from them. The problem is made worse by the fact that the recipients of remittances tend to be those persons most hostile to the regime, and that remittances reduce reliance on the government. Such considerations were the major reason leading Betancourt (2000) to argue that remittances could not possibly be as high as $800 million.

These considerations would lead to the following interpretation of the Cuban government's policy change concerning remittances following the collapse of the Soviet Union. When Cuba was receiving Soviet subsidies, high levels of remittances were not worth the social and political problems they would cause. This cost-benefit calculation was reversed by the end of Soviet subsidies. According to official figures, Cuba's real GDP fell 35% during 1990-93 from an already low level. The relative and absolute importance of remittances naturally rose, making it acceptable to incur the accompanying risks in allowing and encouraging them.

The change in remittances policy was closely connected to dollarization. Allowing the dollar to circulate not only encouraged remittances, but also created a mechanism—the dollar stores—to capture them (Locay (1998)). The Cuban government also imposed high tariff barriers on goods brought into Cuba. Prior to dollarization, remittances often took the form of this sort of in-kind transfer. The objective of these high tariffs seems not to have been the raising of revenue, but rather to force remittances to be in dollars. Again, this is consistent with the downsides to remittances discussed above. The benefit of in-kind transfers accrue entirely to the recipient, but part of the benefit of dollar transfers is captured by the government through high prices at dollar stores (Locay (1998)).

THE CUBAN GOVERNMENT AS MONOPOLIST

Sending money to Cuba through legal channels is much costlier than sending money to other countries in Latin America. Wiring funds abroad is probably characterized by a small fixed cost and zero (or very close to zero) marginal cost. I contacted two local companies in Miami that wire funds to Nicaragua and Colombia, and their pricing policies reflect this hypothesized cost structure. Both charged a small fee to send $100, and no additional fee for larger amounts. I contacted two companies that send money to Cuba, and both quoted me higher fees for a $100 remittance. Furthermore, the fee increased with the amount sent. To send $500 to Cuba both companies charged around 10% ($50 and $52).

Higher fees for Cuba are common for other services. A recent ad for overseas telephone service to 23 cities or countries in Latin America, excluding Cuba, showed an average rate of $0.21 per minute. The charge for Cuba was $0.95 per minute. This would appear to be standard monopoly pricing.

Let us consider the case of remittances more formally. To keep things simple let us assume that the marginal cost is indeed zero. Let r be the rate charged per dollar, and define $X(r)$ to be the amount remitted as a function of r. X is what is received in Cuba, and $(1+r)X$ is the total amount of money spent. $X(r)$ is the demand to remit, and consequently it is a decreasing function of r. If the Cuban government behaves as a simple monopolist interested in maximizing profits, it will set r so as to maximize $r X(r)$. This occurs where the demand elasticity equals -1, which apparently is around $r = 0.10$. This is the standard textbook solution for a monopolist to maximize profit when marginal cost is zero, i.e., maximize revenue. Notice that not only does this explain why it is expensive to remit money to Cuba, but also why the expense rises with the amount sent.

At best, however, this simple explanation has to be incomplete. The reason is that the Cuban government also sets prices at dollar stores. In setting r the Cuban government will want to take into account that remittances eventually find their way to dollar stores where they are captured through high prices. Could the government do better, for example, by setting r equal to zero, encouraging more remittances, and taking its profits through high prices at dollar stores?

To explore this question let us expand the model to take into account purchases at dollar stores. To keep things simple let us think of a single good, which sells at dollar stores for a price in dollars of P. The cost of this good to Cuba is normalized to $1, which is the price in the United States. Let us further assume that all remittances make their way to the dollar stores. In this case the revenue from remittances and dollar store sales is given by:

$$R(r) = rX(r) + X(r) \tag{1}$$

$X(r)$ remittances will purchase $X(r)/P$ units of the good at dollars stores. Since each unit has a cost of $1, net revenue, or profit, to the government is given by:

$$H(r,P) = R(r) X(r)/P \tag{2}$$

The Cuban government's objective is to maximize (2) with respect to r and P. Inspection of (2), however, shows an immediate problem. Since remittances are assumed to be insensitive to the price at dollar

stores, P, it is optimal for the government to set that price infinitely high and sell an infinitesimally small quantity.[4] Clearly we need to make purchases from dollar stores sensitive to the price at such stores. One way to do that is to allow remittances to depend on P, and the best way to do that is to formally model the decision of how much to remit. I turn to that in the next section.

A FORMAL MODEL OF REMITTANCES

It is not difficult to construct an ad hoc model that can "account" for a positive remittance fee. One can assume, for example, that there are demand functions for remittances and sales at dollar stores that are functions of r and P and that have the necessary elasticities. Such a model would be of little or no value, however, as it would simply embellish with a theoretical apparatus what we already know: that it is expensive to send money to Cuba and that dollar store prices are high. It would add nothing to our understanding of why this is so. Furthermore, such a model would likely not be useful in explaining other features of remittances. The model I construct in this section will therefore be based on full rationality. It is a model where each group of decision makers is assumed to be composed of identical individuals. Each group of identical persons is represented by a representative agent. The model is a general equilibrium one, in the sense that it includes the decisions of individuals or households in Cuba and the United States, and the Cuban government, and all three groups are connected through their budget constraints. Such general equilibrium, rational agent models tend to be complex, and this one is no exception, despite my efforts to keep it simple. Before developing the full model let us begin with a simpler version that will illustrate some of the difficulties of deriving the desired results.

I begin by modeling the behavior of a typical Cuban person or household. Let the budget constraint of a representative person in Cuba be given by:

$$c_C = g + (x+t)/P \tag{3}$$

---

4. The elasticity of demand for goods from dollar stores here is -1. It is well known that for an interior solution when marginal costs are positive requires demand to be elastic.

where c_C is per capita real consumption in Cuba, g is per capita real government transfers, x is per capita remittances in dollars, and t is per capita income in dollars received from other sources (e.g., employment in the informal tourist industry). Recall that the price of goods in dollar stores is P. Let us further assume that everyone in Cuba has a relative in the US who sends him money. The budget constraint of the representative Cuban-American is

$$c_A + (1+r)x = m \qquad (4)$$

where c_A is real per capita consumption and m is real per capita income of the Cuban-American relative. In constraint (4) U.S. prices are normalized to one. Substituting (3) into (4), the representative Cuban-American's constraint can be rewritten as follows:

$$c_A + q\, c_C = F \qquad (5)$$

where $q = (1+r)P$ is the "full price" faced by the Cuban-American for consumption by his Cuban relative, and $F = m+q(g+t/P)$ is his "full income."

The representative Cuban has no real decision problem to speak of here. He simply spends whatever dollars he receives at dollar stores at whatever price is set by the government. The representative Cuban-American is the only one with a choice to make. He cares about his own well-being and that of his Cuban relative, and he must decide how much to transfer to him through remittances. I assume that the Cuban-American's preferences are represented by a standard utility function, $u(c_A, c_C)$. His objective is to maximize $u(c_A, c_C)$ subject to constraint (5). This maximization yields a consumption function for his Cuban relative of $c_C(q, F)$. Notice that the representative Cuban-American chooses his relatives level of consumption through his choice of how much to remit.[5]

The solution to the representative Cuban-Americans problem is depicted in Figure 1. The "*" on a variable indicates the optimal value. Figure 1 makes it clear that what the Cuban-American is choosing is his relative's consumption level. This means that

changes in other sources of income will to some extent be offset by remittances. From this it follows that remittances cause the government to lose some of its control over the consumption level, i.e., well-being, of its subjects.

Figure 1.

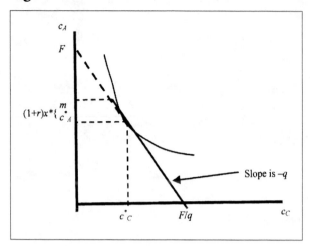

Substituting $c_C(q, F)$ into constraint (3) and rewriting yields the level of remittances as:

$$x(q, F, P, g, t) = P(c_C(q, F) - g) - t \qquad (6)$$

Equation (1) giving the Cuban government's revenue in dollars, is now given by the following:

$$R(q, F, P, g, t) = N(rx + x + t) = rX + X + T \qquad (7)$$

where N is the population of Cuba, $T = Nt$, and the terms of x have been suppressed for simplicity. The first term in (7), $Nrx = rX$, is the revenue from the fee on remittances. The sum of the next two terms, $N(x + t) = X + T$, makes up total expenditure in dollar stores. Under the normalization that the marginal cost of goods to the government in dollar stores is one (the U.S. price), the combined "profit" to the Cuban government from remittances and sales at dollar stores (given in (2) previously) now becomes:

$$H(r, P) = R - (X + T)/P \qquad (8)$$

The government's objective is to maximize (8) with respect to the remittance fee, r, and the price at dollar

---

5. This does not mean that remittances make up the bulk, or even a major part, of Cuban income. The Cuban-American relative determines the marginal dollar received by his relative in Cuba, so he determines the Cuban's precise income or consumption level.

stores, P, and subject to (6). From (8) the partial derivatives of H with respect to r and P can be written as follows:

$$H_r = X + NP(q-1)c_{Cq}$$
$$H_P = (1+r)[X+T+NP(q-1)c_{Cq}] \qquad (9)$$

where subscripts represent partial derivatives. Let us begin by interpreting the first equation, the marginal profit of the remittance fee. Increasing the remittance fee, r, raises revenue directly depending on the amount being remitted. This is captured by the term X in the first equation of (9). Revenue from remittances is reduced, however, because remittances fall, and because lower remittances translate into lower dollar store sales. This is somewhat offset by the cost savings from reduced sales. These combined effects are captured in the second term of the first equation, $NP(q-1)c_{Cq} < 0$. The second equation in (9), the marginal profit of the dollar store price, is more complicated to interpret, but the end result is that raising P has the added marginal benefit of increasing profit from non-remittance financed dollar store sales.

Inspection of (9) shows that making remittances a function of P is not enough to obtain the result that $r > 0$. If there exists a finite solution for P, which means that $H_P = 0$, then $H_r < 0$. That is, it would be optimal to reduce r to its lowest possible value. It would actually be in the government's interest to pay Cuban-Americans to remit funds to Cuba if that was possible. For an interior solution for r—this does *not* necessarily mean that $r > 0$—it is required that $H_r = 0$, so that $H_P > 0$. This implies that the dollar store price should be infinite. But even before the price at dollar stores becomes infinite Cuban-Americans would cease sending their relatives funds. This can be seen by letting P go to infinity in Figure 1. The constraint faced with an infinite price and the choice made by the representative Cuban-American is depicted in Figure 2. As can be seen, the representative Cuban-American spends his entire income on himself.

Figure 2.

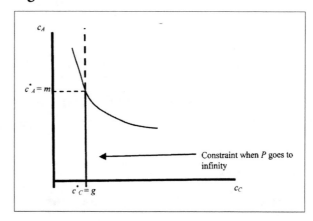

In the model presented above the government makes no distinction between a dollar raised through dollar stores and a dollar raised through the remittance fee. Since raising the dollar store price has the added benefit of generating profit from non-remittance financed dollar store sales, it is better to encourage remittances with a low fee (below zero if possible). I now develop a model based on the discussion in sections 1 and 2 that drops these assumptions.

Suppose that there are three types of Cubans: those that receive remittances, those that have informal dollar earnings, and those that depend exclusively on the government for support. I assume that those who receive remittances do not also have other sources of dollars. This assumption is not important and is made simply to reduce the number of groups that have to be dealt with.[6] Those who have informal dollar earnings are self-employed, so the government knows who they are. The government, however, does not distinguish between those who receive remittances and those who do not.

The budget constraint of each representative Cuban, given in (3) before, now becomes the following:

$c_C = g_0$ government support only
$c_C = g_0 + x$ government and remittances
$c_C = g_0 + t$ government and self-employment   (10)

As before, Cuban individuals have no choice problem to speak of. They simply spend at dollar stores

---

6. It is important, however, that those who receive remittances not be exactly the same people who have other sources of dollars. That is, the two groups can overlap, but cannot be identical.

what they receive in remittances or through self-employment.

The representative Cuban-American still faces budget constraint (5), except that now the recipient of his remittances has $t = 0$ and $g = g_0$. In order to simplify the analysis I assume that the Cuban-American's utility function is log-linear. That is, it is given by the following:

$$u(c_A, c_C) = c_A + b\ln(c_C) \quad (11)$$

Like all specific functional forms, this utility function is restrictive, but the restrictions it imposes on this analysis do not significantly affect my main concerns.[7] It certainly makes the exposition easier. Maximization of (11) subject to constraint (5) yields the following demand for remittances:

$$x(r, P, g_0) = b/(1+r) - Pg_0 \quad (12)$$

In real terms the demand for remittances becomes:

$$z(q, g_0) = x/P = b/P - g_0 \quad (13)$$

Notice that the demand for "real" remittances depends only on the full price, q, and not on the remittance fee and the price at dollar stores separately.

The Cuban government's objective is no longer to maximize profit, but rather political support. Before looking at the government's objective function more closely, we need to derive the government's budget constraint. Let s_X be the fraction of Cubans that receive remittances from abroad and s_T be the fraction with dollar earnings from self-employment. Let G_O and G_T be government spending on those without self-employment dollar earnings and on those who have such earnings, respectively. Then the government's budget constraint is given by the following:

$$G_O + G_T = K + rX + (P - 1)(X+T)/P \quad (14)$$

where K are the resources available to the government other than remittance fees and sales at dollar

stores (domestic production, Soviet subsidies, etc.). In per capita terms (14) becomes:

$$(1 - s_T)g_0 + s_T g_T = k + s_X(q-1)z + s_T(P-1)y \quad (15)$$

where $y = t/P$ is real per capita dollar earnings by those who have such earnings, and $k = K/N$. We can turn now to the government's objective function.

One of the problems of the earlier model is that the government cared only about profit, and it was more profitable to have a zero or negative remittance fee and a high dollar store price. I now assume a more general objective function for the government. The discussion in previous sections suggests that remittances may directly erode the government's political support, but they provide funds with which such support can be "purchased." Dollar earnings from self-employment should have similar effects to remittances. Furthermore, since the source of both self-employment earnings and remittances is not the government, they may purchase less political support than government expenditures. A political support function that reflects these general considerations is the following:

$$\begin{aligned} S(g_O, g_T, z, y, s_X, s_T) &= (1 - s_T - s_X)v(g_O) \\ &+ s_X[\, v(g_O + z) - az^2 \,] + s_T[\, v(g_T + y) \\ &- a(g_T + y - g_0)^2 \,] \end{aligned} \quad (16)$$

where v is an increasing, concave function, and a is a positive constant.

Let us interpret the function given in (16): $v(g_O)$ is the support received per individual whose consumption comes completely from the government. This support increases with g_0, but does so at a decreasing rate. To obtain the aggregate support from this group, $v(g_O)$ is weighted by the fraction of the population, $(1 - s_T - s_X)$, whose consumption comes completely from the government. The support received from an individual who receives remittances is given by $v(g_O + z) - az^2$. The support here has two parts. Individuals in this group have real consumption, $(g_O + z)$, which should have the same effect as g_O. Remit-

---

7. The primary restriction this utility function imposes is that there are no income effects in the demand for remittances. That is, changes in the income of Cuban-Americans have no effect on the amount remitted. Obviously this would not be a suitable utility function if that were the focus of this paper.

tances, however, have a separate effect, reflecting the fact that they do not come from the government and that they worsen the distribution of income. Once again the aggregate support from this group is weighted by the fraction of people that compose it.[8] The support from the self-employed group is similar, except that the detrimental effect of dollar income, $-a(g_T +y - g_O)$,[2] depends on the income differential between them and those that receive all of their support from the government, rather than y. For the recipients of remittances z played both of these roles. Notice that the detrimental effects from dollar earnings also exist if the self-employed have the lower level of consumption.

The government's decision problem is now to maximize (16) with respect to prices r and P, government expenditures g_O and g_T, and real remittances, z, subject to its budget constraint, (15), the constraint imposed by the demand for remittances by Cuban-Americans, (13), and $y = t/P$. From of the first order conditions to this maximization problem we get the following two insightful results:

$$s_T[v(g_T +y) - 2a(g_T +y - g_O)] = ls_T > 0$$
$$s_X[v(g_O +z) - 2az] = ls_X[1 - qg_O/(g_O +z)] \qquad (17)$$

where $l > 0$ is a the Lagrange multiplier associated with the government's budget constraint. It is the marginal support of income, i.e., how much more support can the government purchase with an additional dollar. The left hand side of the first equation in (17) has three interpretations. It is the marginal support from spending an additional dollar on those with self-employment dollar income. It is also the marginal support from an additional dollar of self-employment income, or what amounts to the same thing, the marginal support from allowing those with self-employment dollar income to keep an additional dollar through lower prices at dollar stores. Notice that (17) requires that for any interior solution such marginal supports be positive. At the margin the government gains support from an additional dollar

earned. The situation can be considerably different for remittances. The marginal support from remittances is given by the left hand side of the second equation in (17). Notice that this quantity may well be negative. Despite considerable symmetry in the treatment of informal dollar income and remittances, remittances can end up being a "bad" for the government at the margin.

What accounts for the different treatment of these two sources of dollars in this model? The difference arises because the government can adjust its expenditures on those that earn dollars, but not on those that receive remittances. Those that work in the informal sector are assumed not to work for the government, and therefore they receive less from the government. Such an adjustment is not possible for the recipients of remittances.

So at the margin remittances may well reduce political support (they are a "bad"), implying that the government will wish to discourage them relative to informal dollar earnings. If the government further increases the price at dollar stores it will reduce the real value of informal dollar earnings, which is equivalent to reducing the government's income. Instead the government charges a direct remittance fee that is above marginal cost. Here, then, is a complete and consistent explanation.

To illustrate the model, I have computed the results for the following parameterized example:

$$v(g) = g^{0.835}, k = 1700, b = 3250, s_X = 0.2,$$
$$s_T = 0.1, a = 0.0016, t = 450 \qquad (18)$$

The parameter k in (18) corresponds to per capita GDP in purchasing power parity, which *The World Factbook 2001* sets at $1700 for the year 2000. The fractions of persons receiving remittances and with informal dollar income I set at values that seemed reasonable to me, but I do not know if they are even approximately correct. I set dollar earnings at $450 per capita for persons with such income.[9] Assuming a

---

8. It is not clear that the detrimental effect on support from remittances, az should be weighted simply by the fraction of people receiving remittances. I do not explore the possibilities here, since I do nothing with the relative sizes of the various groups.

9. Keep in mind that this figure is per person. A single person in a family of four with informal dollar income, for example, would have to earn $1800 a year for each member of the family to have a per capita dollar income of $450.

population of 11 million, this generates aggregate informal dollar earnings of $495 million, which is consistent with the balance of payments statistics cited previously. These parameter values generate a remittance fee (assuming a marginal cost of zero) of 11%, and a dollar price that is 55% above marginal cost. The remittance fee is close to the rates that I was quoted. I do not know what is the average markup at dollar stores.

The implied aggregate remittances come to $413 million. The income (consumption) differential between someone receiving remittances and someone dependent completely on the government for support is $121. The income (consumption) differential between someone with informal dollar earnings and someone dependent completely on the government for support is only about $2. The difference $g_O - g_T$, which is essentially the average government salary, is $287.[10] Finally, at the margin remittances are a "bad", i.e., they reduce political support, but dollar earnings increase it.

CONCLUSIONS AND FUTURE WORK

I have argued in this paper that the popular explanation for why it is expensive to remit money to Cuba —monopoly pricing on the part of the Cuban government—is incomplete because it ignores the interrelationship that exists between remittances and purchases at dollar stores. A rational monopolistic Cuban government would not ignore such connections in designing its pricing policies. I originally thought that a fairly simple model with fully rational decision-making could account for a positive remittance fee. The model I eventually developed, and that I have presented here, is surprisingly complicated. If a simpler rational general equilibrium model exists, I have not been able to discover it.

The model in this paper built on the idea that resources that do not originate with the government,

and that therefore the government does not directly control, can pose political problems for it. The government will, of course, try to capture and control those resources. But this it can do through the prices at dollar stores. To charge a remittance fee above marginal cost is to treat dollars from different sources differently. But why should the government wish to make such a distinction? The answer given here is that one fundamental difference between those receiving remittances and those earning dollars through employment in the informal tourist sector is that the government can identify and compensate the latter differently from the general population. People who work in the informal sector do not work for the government, so via government salaries those working in the informal sector will receive fewer resources from the government. The government can, at least to some extent, neutralize the politically harmful effects of dollar earnings. Essentially, dollar earnings can be turned into the government's income. This is not possible with remittances. Because of their politically harmful effects that cannot be neutralized, the government will wish to raise the cost of remittances, which it does through a positive remittance fee.

I hope the model will prove useful in exploring other aspects of remittances. As can be seen in the numerical example above, the model can be calibrated to generate reasonable numbers. With better estimates, a better calibration should be possible. In the future I would like to explore the implications of the elimination of the Soviet subsidies. The elimination of those subsidies would be modeled as a reduction in k. Some preliminary calculations with the example used above resulted in increased remittances. However, the end of Soviet subsidies was accompanied by other changes, such as dollarization and the legalization of self-employment, that I have not explicitly modeled here. In future work I would like to extend the model to be able to account for these other policy changes.

---

10. Again, this is a per capita figure. It would be higher per worker.

REFERENCES

Betancourt, Ernesto F., 2000. "Cuba's Balance of Payments Gap, the Remittances Scam, Drug Trafficking and Money Laundering." *Cuba in Transition—Volume 10.* Association for the Study of the Cuban Economy, Washington, D.C.

CIA. *The World Factbook 2001.* http://www.cia.gov/cia/publications/factbook/

Hernández-Catá, Ernesto, 2000. "The Fall and Recovery of the Cuban Economy in the 1990s: Mirage or Reality." *Cuba in Transition—Volume 10.* Association for the Study of the Cuban Economy, Washington, D.C.

Morris, Emily, 2000. "Interpreting Cuba's External Accounts." *Cuba in Transition—Volume 10.* Association for the Study of the Cuban Economy, Washington, D.C.

Locay, Luis, 1998. "Toward a Market Economy or Tinkering with Socialism," in Pérez-López and Travieso-Díaz (eds.) *Perspectives on Cuban Economic Reforms.* Tempe: Arizona State University Press.

Pérez-López, Jorge F., 2000. "Cuba's Balance of Payments Statistics." *Cuba in Transition Volume—10.* Association for the Study of the Cuban Economy, Washington, D.C.

A BIAS FOR HOPE—MIGRATION, OPPORTUNITY COST, AND DEMOCRATIC COALITIONS

Enrique S. Pumar

These brief comments address several pointed ideas raised in Silvia Pedraza's provocative paper, "Democratization and Migration: Cuba's Exodus and the Development of Civil Society—Hindrance or Help?,"[1] and offer a far-reaching, but nonetheless possible scenario, for a future democratic transition in Cuba. Before I develop these points, I must confess that I regard myself as a very sympathetic student of Silvia's work as well as that of Albert O. Hirschman, the theorist she wittingly utilizes in her paper.

Following the framework in Hirschman's seminal *Exit, Voice, and Loyalty,* Silvia argues that awkward institutional arrangements and a sustained desire to regain a relative high standard of living lost after the revolution motivates many Cubans to exit the island. She careful assesses four different scenarios about the relation between exit (migration) and the prospects for democracy.

1. Massive exit further undermines the articulation of voice (or internal dissent).

2. Exit embraces democracy abroad and assists voice to develop internally.

3. Those who exit become voice.

4. Exit and voice increase in tandem.

After a careful analysis of each possibility, she argues convincingly for the latter. Migration and the inter-

nal opposition have progressively developed and are increasingly networked.

Recent events in Cuba support this conclusion. Cubans who visit the island reconnect with family, neighbors, and friends. Opposition groups have an increasing number of allies abroad in part because of the narrow-minded policy the island government has adopted, which offers former dissidents the option of serving jail time or migrating north. More significantly, the development of the internet makes political isolation virtually impossible. Thus, today dissident journalists publish their stories regularly in the web, opposition groups also have a presence there, and email communications have become almost the norm. All in all, I see a time in the future when researchers will give due credit to how increasing channels of communications between the Cuban community abroad and at home contributed to a more pluralistic and open society. After all, many scholars are doing just that now when they study the downfall of authoritarian regimes in the Southern Cone. One of the credits of this paper is to pioneer this line of research in the context of Cuba. In short, Silvia concludes that there is hope for the future of democracy in Cuba since both the Cuban exile community and civil society internally are pushing for pluralism.

This circumstance assumes that exile indeed reinforces democratic values. I think this has generally been the case. However, the jury is still out on the effects

---

1. Included in this volume.

some counter-democratic events have had on the souls and minds of the Miami enclave where the majority of the Cuban-American community resides. In addition, many recent immigrants do not enjoy the same living standards and opportunities of previous immigration waves and it is entirely possible these immigrants may be somewhat disillusioned with the brand of market capitalism they have gotten to know.

These concerns aside, the paper offers many insightful points and a thorough analysis of migration. For instance, Silvia rightfully argues that Cuban migration is generically different from others. She interviewed a Spaniard restaurant owner in Valencia who confessed he lost his youth in the cold German winters while in exile. We Cubans, on the other hand, have Miami and when we grow tired of Dade County, have the option to move to Miramar—in Broward County, a few miles to the north.

Also, following Hirschman, my bias for hope unfolds from a different perspective. I would like to ask the question, can exit (migration) permit an alliance between the voice left behind and loyalty or the skeptical supporters of the regime? This possibility may sound far fetched to some. However, it is entirely possible if we consider three assumptions: (1) hardcore opposition leaders may migrate, leaving behind those more willingly to compromise; (2) for any successful transition to take place, supporters of the regime will have to play a role, as painful as it may seem; and (3) there may be no way out for the opposition and supporters but to bargain a transition. After all, coalition building has been an essential component in previous transitions. Hirschman himself describes, in another essay, how European migration once facilitated democracy in the continent[2]. There is also the element of demography here. The generation that follows those who carried the insurgency is always more eager to compromise.

In short, while not contradicting Silvia's exceptional analysis, I vote for the inclusion of the loyalty in any future democratic scenarios in the island.

---

2. Albert O. Hirschman, "Exit, Voice, and the State," *World Politics,* 1978.

ENERGY IN CUBA

Amy Myers Jaffe and Ronald Soligo[1]

Cuba is considered a promising growth energy market in the Americas. Domestic supply increases are expected in the coming years. In addition, rising local demand and trading opportunities could also be attractive to energy companies. However, political factors may be as important as economic forces in the coming years. United States economic sanctions against Cuba limit for now the country's potential as both an energy supplier and growth user market. Were these sanctions eased, Cuba's energy sector would benefit greatly from its strategic proximity to the important U.S. market.

The Cuban economy is still suffering from the aftermath of the collapse of the Soviet Union, which provided generous economic subsidies including cheap energy supplies. To alleviate the economic downturn that began in the early 1990s, Cuba has introduced some market-oriented reforms to supplement its command economy structure. The reforms, which include opening the economy to tourism, decentralizing agriculture and authorizing self-employment in 150 occupations, are likely to pave the way for both increased energy use and a shift in distribution of energy use by sector.

Cuba has invited foreign private investment in a variety of industries including its energy sector. Several firms have explored for oil and gas off Cuba's coastline but with only limited success. Cuba's refining sector is also in need of investment and upgrading. Despite U.S. sanctions, several European, Canadian and South American energy firms have investigated the possibility of making investments in Cuba's energy sector, anticipating an expanding market even without exports to nearby U.S. markets. Were U.S. economic sanctions to be eased, the growth potential of the Cuban energy sector would be even greater.

This paper investigates the state of Cuba's energy sector and its future trends. Attention is given to the impact that an easing of U.S. sanctions against Cuba could have on its energy sector.

ENERGY DEMAND TRENDS IN CUBA

Total primary Cuban energy supply (TPES), that is total energy used including process losses, rose from 10,934 thousand tons of oil equivalent (KTOE) in 1971 to a peak of 16,877 KTOE in 1989 before beginning a general descent following the cut-off of Soviet aid (see Table 1). After hitting a 20 year low in 1993, total primary Cuban energy supply recovered to 12,464 KTOE in 1999. In addition to hydrocarbons, renewables and waste such as sugar cane biomass, windmills, solar and small hydro-powered generators have accounted for a substantial, although declining share of energy supply. Their share of TPES declined from 32.9% in 1971 to 22.8% in 1999.

Some 60% of total primary energy supply is imported. Production of oil has steadily increased but in 1999, 80% of petroleum and petroleum products were imported. According to the U.S. Department of

1. The authors thank the Cuba Policy Foundation for support of this research, and Kenneth Medlock for helpful comments and assistance.

Energy (U.S. DOE, June 2002), Cuba generated 13.3 quadrillion BTUs of electricity in 1998, of which 94% came from thermal powered generators. Hydroelectric power is miniscule, accounting for less than 1%. Almost all Cuban households (95%) have electricity, accounting for 36% of total electricity consumption in 1999. Approximately 100 thousand cubic meters of natural gas were also consumed by households (in Havana) in 1997 (Werlau, 1998).

Table 1 shows *net* energy imports rather than total imports. For most years there is little difference. However, during the 1980s Cuba re-exported Soviet oil. In 1985, these exports amounted to roughly 3,500 KTOE. Exports declined to 2,700 KTOE in 1989 and then ceased in 1990.

The collapse of the Soviet Union and the end of Soviet aid to Cuba have had a dramatic impact on Cuba's economy in general and on its energy sector in particular. Energy demand was curtailed to the largest extent in the sectors involving private usage such as the transportation sector and to a lesser extent, the residential electricity sector. Electricity blackouts were common during the transition period.

Table 1 shows the effect of the collapse of the Soviet Union and end of Soviet aid on energy imports and supply. Net imports fell sharply from 13,626 KTOE in 1989 to 8,184 KTOE in 1991—almost 40%. TPES fell only 20%, reflecting the importance of renewables and waste products in Cuban energy supply. Imports dropped a further 23% from 1991-93 while TPES decreased another 20%. TPES regained some of that loss by 1996. However, TPES in 1999 was essentially the same as it was in 1996.

PATTERNS OF END-USE ENERGY DEMAND

Medlock and Soligo (2001) have examined the patterns of end-use sector energy demand as a function of the level of economic development as measured by per capita GDP. Allowing for country-specific heterogeneity, the Medlock-Soligo model permits the forecasting of per capita end-use energy demand us-ing the assumption that countries tend to follow similar patterns of economic development. Although the resulting forecast assumes the energy intensity of various countries will follow similar patterns, it ignores future technological changes that may improve energy efficiency. Hence, forecasts of future energy may tend to be biased upward.[2]

Figure 1 shows the typical pattern of end use energy demand estimated by Medlock/Soligo using data from Latin American countries plus Canada and the U.S. (Although the data are from different countries, the pattern is similar to that for a data set of non-Latin American countries). Per capita energy use (KTOE per thousand persons) is plotted against per capita income measured in 1995 PPP dollars. In the early stages of development, energy use by the industrial sector rises rapidly as countries begin to industrialize. At some stage of development, this process slows down and energy use in the industrial sector levels off. However, per capita energy use in the transport and commercial/residential sectors continues to increase, eventually overtaking consumption in the industrial sector.

In the long run, the demand for energy is inelastic with respect to changes in per capita GDP. That is, the demand for energy, per capita, rises at a slower rate than output. However, at low levels of per capita income, this elasticity is greater that unity. Countries at specific levels of per capita income will deviate from the predicted level of energy use to the extent that there are differences in climate, population density, energy taxes and other policies that affect energy prices and investments in transportation infrastructure.

Forecasts of Energy Demand

The Medlock/Soligo model has been estimated using data from market economies. Placing Cuba into this framework requires some adjustment because Cuba has been and generally remains a "command" economy. As such, the level and composition of energy use has not followed the pattern of development experi-

---

2. Because income is highly correlated with time (in most countries), use of a time trend to account for technological change produced statistically insignificant coefficients for either the time trend or income variable.

Table 1. Cuban Energy Production and Imports (KTOE)

	Domestic Production	Net Imports	TPES	Production Renewables	Renewables Share	Net Imports Share
1971	3739	7436	10934	3593	32.9%	68.0%
1972	3351	7360	10651	3207	30.1%	69.1%
1973	3563	8804	11918	3391	28.5%	73.9%
1974	3694	9307	12839	3481	27.1%	72.5%
1975	3809	9390	13119	3535	26.9%	71.6%
1976	3811	9959	13781	3524	25.6%	72.3%
1977	3931	9655	13708	3622	26.4%	70.4%
1978	4554	10349	14765	4214	28.5%	70.1%
1979	4683	10393	15126	4335	28.7%	68.7%
1980	4227	10438	14910	3896	26.1%	70.0%
1981	4534	11020	15464	4230	27.4%	71.3%
1982	4881	11395	15992	4261	26.6%	71.3%
1983	5038	11018	16115	4192	26.0%	68.4%
1984	5075	9651	14708	4309	29.3%	65.6%
1985	4890	10159	14525	4018	27.7%	69.9%
1986	5168	9804	14654	4227	28.8%	66.9%
1987	5187	10397	15377	4276	27.8%	67.6%
1988	5349	10946	15954	4613	28.9%	68.6%
1989	5893	10955	16877	5144	30.5%	64.9%
1990	6271	10198	16524	5576	33.7%	61.7%
1991	5459	8184	13530	4908	36.3%	60.5%
1992	5792	6932	12456	4901	39.3%	55.7%
1993	4636	6323	10839	3521	32.5%	58.3%
1994	4741	6591	11264	3443	30.6%	58.5%
1995	4285	7030	11149	2819	25.3%	63.1%
1996	4799	7687	12222	3324	27.2%	62.9%
1997	4613	7901	12186	3134	25.7%	64.8%
1998	4448	7669	11816	2689	22.8%	64.9%
1999	5242	7428	12464	2837	22.8%	59.6%

Note: Domestic production plus net imports do not add up to TPES because of stock changes. TPES is net of energy exports

Source: IEA Energy Balances: 1971-1999

enced by more market-oriented economies. In particular, private motor vehicle ownership is substantially lower in Cuba than in other countries with comparable per capita incomes, reflecting the different priorities of the planning authorities and possibly, the more equal distribution of income.

Given the energy use characteristics of the Cuban economy, how do we estimate future Cuban energy

consumption? Will Cuba be able to hold energy intensity relatively constant as GDP continues to grow? In our opinion, this latter possibility is unlikely in the non-manufacturing sectors. Energy consumption has been severely repressed during the past decade. As per capita income grows, the public will demand better public, if not increasing access to private, transportation and more consumer durables. Also, as tourism, the primary engine of growth, continues to

Figure 1. Hypothetical Country Total Final Consumption

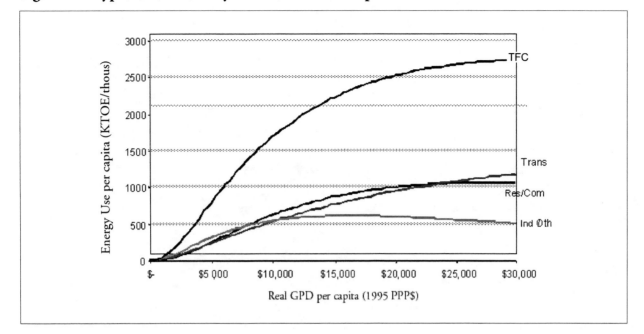

increase, demand for transportation fuels and electricity will similarly grow. Tourists will demand access to air conditioned hotels and restaurants (especially important given Cuba's climate) and rental cars or transportation by taxi.

Tourism to Cuba has been growing rapidly as appropriate infrastructure has been built. The number of hotel rooms increased from 10,000 in 1988 to over 32,000 in 1999 (Crespo and Suddaby, 2000, p. 353). In nominal terms, revenues from tourism have grown fromUS$243 million in 1990 to US$2 billion in 2000, an increase of over 700%.

During 1999-2000, gross income from tourism to Cuba grew by 8.1% (ECLAC, 1999-2000) despite the restriction on travel by U.S. citizens. In 1998, U.S. tourists accounted for 60% of all tourists to other Caribbean islands. Without the embargo, ordinary Americans would be free to travel to Cuba possibly adding an additional $1 billion to Cuban tourist earnings within a few years (Preeg, 1998).

In generating some estimates of future energy demand in Cuba, we use the Medlock/Soligo model, mindful that this model has been estimated using data from market- economies. In forecasting future energy demand for Cuba a critical assumption concerns whether or not Cuba will move towards a more

market oriented economy where investment and output decisions reflect consumer preferences to a greater degree than in the past. At this point, significant reforms towards a more open, market-oriented economy do not appear to be imminent. On the other hand, it does seem reasonable to assume that the Cuban economic model will eventually evolve towards at least a market economy, be it socialist or capitalist, where consumer preferences will have a larger effect on resource allocation.

In applying the Medlock/Soligo modeling approach to Cuba, it is necessary to make some assumptions about future growth rates in per capita income. Cuban GDP growth has recently averaged about 4 per cent per annum, equivalent to a per capita growth of roughly 3.5%. If per capita income were to continue to grow at this rate, per capita income in 2010 will increase from 1999 levels by 46% and in 2015, by 74%. By 2010, Cuban per capita income in 1995 PPP dollars would be only 76% of the 1999 level for the Dominican Republic. By 2015, it would be $4862, still only 97% of the 1999 Costa Rican level of $7731.

Clearly, the future growth rate for Cuba will depend on a number of factors including future U.S. policy towards the island. Removal of sanctions will in-

Table 2. Energy Consumption Forecasts for Cuba (in KTOE)

	Historical	Projected			Projected			Projected		
	1999	2005			2010			2015		
Per Capita GDP growth Rate		0.005	0.02	0.035	0.005	0.02	0.035	0.005	0.02	0.035
Consuming Sector										
Residential and Commercial	989	1337	1626	1956	1450	2053	2822	1570	2569	3954
Transportation	1062	2150	2487	2858	2297	2983	3808	2454	3561	4996
Industrial and Other	7480	7718	8894	10153	8240	10584	13214	8793	12479	16718
Total Final Consumption	9531	11206	13006	14967	11987	15621	19843	12816	18608	25668
Total Primary Consumption (a)	12697	14926	17325	19936	15967	20807	26431	17071	24786	34190
Thousands barrels/day equivalent (b)	254	299	346	399	319	416	529	341	496	684
Less Biomass (c)	58	54	62	72	48	62	79	41	59	82
	196	245	284	327	271	354	449	300	436	602
Increase over 1999 thousands b/d		49	88	131	75	158	253	104	240	406
Real GDP per capita	2804	2889	3157	3446	2962	3699	4093	3037	3849	4862

Notes: Population is assumed to grow at a rate of 0.5% per annum.

(a) Transformation losses in 1999 were 29.3%. Thus, to obtain Primary, we assume this value.

(b) Conversion used for tons to barrels is 7.30 barrels/ton.

(c) Share of Biomass assumed to be 18% in 2005; 15% in 2010 and 12% in 2020.

crease the rate of growth, more so if the Cuban government encourages trade and investment with the U.S. Growth prospects are higher if sanctions are removed and foreign relations are normalized within the context of the current political regime so that property claims and other contentious issues can be dealt with in a stable and orderly manner. A chaotic transition accompanied by civil strife and a struggle to assert old property claims could seriously set back growth and development. We have used 3.5% as the upper bound on future per capita income growth rates. This is a fairly high rate compared with experience in other Latin American cases. It is equivalent to the 4% growth rate that Cuba has experienced in the latter half of the 1990s (with population growth at .5%) but that growth rate might reflect the fact that Cuba was rebounding from the repressed levels of GDP experienced in the early 1990s. A more realistic per capita growth rate is 2%, especially over a longer period of time. As a lower bound, we assume a growth rate of 0.5%.

Table 2 shows projections for total energy consumption by end-use sector, total primary energy demand and, finally, total primary energy less biomass, as projected by the Medlock/Soligo model. This final number represents the energy that must be supplied by hydrocarbon sources, mainly oil and to a lesser extent, natural gas.

For all of the scenarios studied, it is assumed that the Cuban population will increase by a total of 8% between 1998 and 2015, roughly the same rate of growth (about 0.5% per annum) as experienced in the 1990s.

Projections yield estimates for 2015 of between 300 and 602 thousand barrels a day of (b/d) oil equivalent, an increase in consumption over 1999 levels of 104 to 406 thousand of b/d of oil equivalent. This is the energy requirement that would have to be supplied by non-biomass sources, principally oil and natural gas. Forecasts of future energy consumption also indicate a significant change in the composition of demand by end-sector (see Table 3). In particular, demand from the transport sector will grow much more rapidly than in other sectors. Assuming an annual per capita growth of 2%, the industry/other sector shows the largest increase in consumption but its share of total final consumption declines from 78.5% to 67.1%. The transportation sector shows the second largest absolute increase in demand but experiences an increase in its share of TFC from 11.1% to 19.1%. The residential/commercial sector shows the smallest increase in demand but its share also increases. It should be emphasized that these are conservative estimates in the sense that they do not assume a rapid adjustment of the structure of the Cuban economy that might accompany a change in the economic model. Rather, the projection take the existing structure of demand and assumes that demand will *change* over time, in response to increases in per capita income, following the pattern of other developing economies.

Table 3. Composition of Sector Energy in Total Primary Consumption

Consuming Sector	1999	2015	Increase (KTOE) 1999-2015
Residential and Commercial	10.4%	13.8%	1580
Transportation	11.1%	19.1%	2499
Industrial and Other	78.5%	67.1%	4999

Source: Assuming annual per capita GDP growth of 2%

To summarize, we project that Cuban energy needs will increase by 104,000 b/d-406, 000 b/d by 2015. With a per capita income growth rate of 2%, the additional requirements would be 240,000 b/d. This increase will have to be met by additional imports or increases in domestic production of crude or natural gas. In absolute terms, the industrial and other sector will show the largest increase in consumption. But in relative terms, it is the transport sector that will show the greatest increase in demand.

CUBA'S ENERGY INDUSTRY: PRESENT CONDITIONS

To meet Cuba's rising energy needs, its current industry will need to be significantly expanded. Otherwise, the country's import bill will increase substantially. Cuba has proven crude oil reserves of about 750 million barrels, while its proven natural gas reserves total 2,500 billion cubic feet (U.S.

DOE, June 2002). Due to its limited natural resources, Cuba is dependent upon oil imports to meet about two-thirds of its 190,000 b/d domestic needs. In 2000, Cuba produced about 46,500 b/d of crude oil, mostly from the north central coast in the state of Matanzas, and 600 million cubic meters of natural gas. State oil firm Cubapetróleo (Cupet) has also recently suggested that it plans to boost output to 120,000 b/d by 2005, though those figures appear speculative in light of recent exploration disappointments.

Between 1991 and 1999, foreign investment in oil exploration and production in Cuba increased by about $600 million. Roughly half a dozen foreign companies are currently active in Cuban waters, either exploring for or producing oil, despite the threat posed by the Helms-Burton Act. Industry experts believe that the Cuban sector of the Gulf of Mexico could contain as much as 3 to 4 billion barrels of recoverable reserves, mainly in deeper waters. One of Cuba's largest oil fields, the Varadero field, has an estimated 2 billion barrels of oil in place.

Opportunities for the Future in Cuba's Energy Sector

The benefits of a successful Cuban oil and gas offshore sector to the U.S. are large given its proximity to Florida markets. If the introduction of superior drilling technology and methods by the U.S. industry or large supermajors could increase the chances for increased exploration success in Cuba, it would enhance U.S. energy security and supplement an increasingly downgraded outlook for other Latin American supplies.

At present, Florida can purchase natural gas supplies from the U.S. Gulf of Mexico via Florida Gas Transmission (FGT), an existing pipeline system running from Texas. The capacity of this onland Gulf coast pipeline is being expanded and is expected to grow to 2.2 billion cubic feet/day (bcf/d) by the end of 2003, up from 1.66 bcf/d currently.

The U.S. Federal Energy Regulatory Commission (FERC) has also given its final certification for the $1.6 billion, Duke Energy/Williams Gulfstream pipeline project that will carry 1.13 bcf/d from sup-

Table 4.   Sample Costs for Natural Gas Supplies to Florida

Source	Average Production Costs[a]	Liquefaction Costs	Pipeline/Tanker Costs	Regasification Costs	Total Costs
Cuba	$2.50		$0.40		$2.90
Trinidad	$0.75	$1.00	$0.45	$0.60	$2.80
FGT[b]	$2.50		$0.40		$2.90
Gulfstream	$2.50		$0.35		$2.85

a.   Estimated for deepwater gas production and does not include liquids credit or savings from oil related infrastructure.
b.   Actual pipeline tariffs are 80 cents but prevailing spot market for transportation costs is 40 cents.

ply areas in Alabama and the Gulf coast to the Tampa area via a 744 mile underwater pipeline. The Tampa landing point will connect by pipeline across the state to Palm Beach. An LNG terminal at Elba Island, Georgia, is also slated to reopen shortly, with a pipeline connection to Florida through the Cypress Pipeline.

The new projects do not appear to be oversubscribed with customers at the moment. Demand for natural gas in Florida is expected to grow significantly in coming years from just under 1.5 bcf/d in recent years to 2 to 4 bcf/d between 2005 and 2015, according to industry estimates. Much of the seasonal rise in energy use in Florida is now met by imports of refined oil products but this could change over time as more natural gas could be made available to the state, potentially lowering energy costs during periods when international oil prices are rising.

If a significant level of natural gas supply could be made available from Cuban waters by pipeline into Florida, the Cuban supply would enhance competition in the Florida market. The addition of additional Cuban sellers with the incentive to market the bulk of their supply to Florida will prompt a lowering of prices so that these additional sellers can find a market for their supplies by increasing the quantity demanded.

The economics for Cuban natural gas supplies are not likely to be all that different from Texas and Alabama gas. Drilling and other finding costs will likely be similar to deepwater plays along the U.S. Gulf of Mexico and could be lower if Cuba offers more attractive fiscal and royalty terms, depending on the size of any finds and the amount of liquids associated with the natural gas. Pipeline costs to Florida are un-

likely to exceed 40 to 50 cents per mcf even for a relatively small discovery of 200 mmcf/d, assuming a 15% rate of return over a 20-year operating period with operating costs of 3% capital cost. This is in line with transportation costs for existing pipeline infrastructure from natural gas trading hub and storage area Henry Hub and amortized costs for the Gulfstream project.

Table 4 shows how average Cuban costs might stake up against the costs of competing supplies to Florida. The costs in Table 4, however, do not fully reflect the competitiveness of Cuban natural gas. That's because Cuban supplies would likely to be "associated" gas and therefore could presumably be priced to the market. Revenue from related oil production from Cuban fields would offset the fixed costs of drilling and producing any associated natural gas, allowing Cuban producers to price natural gas closer to marginal production costs. Cuban sellers, having transportation linked solely to the Florida market, would be likely to undercut other suppliers to maintain market share, creating a competitive market structure and contributing to lower prices to the state.

Other Aspects of Energy Sector Growth: Cuba as a Trading Entrepot

The Cuban energy market continues to be of interest to European and Latin American energy firms. While the growth potential is not considered large, the country's geographic position near to expanding markets in the U.S. and Mexico make it an interesting possible entrepot for energy project development.

Overall growth possibilities of around 104,000 to 406,000 b/d of oil equivalent by 2015 still represent a solid business opportunity for regional players. There will also be opportunities for investment in the electric power industry. Electricity use in the residential/commercial/public service sector alone is expected to grow by 47% by 2010 and 59% by 2015 under the 0.5% per annum per capita growth scenario. With 2% growth, electricity demand would increase by 108% and 160% respectively. In 1999, the sector consumed over 61% of total electricity consumed. Of the 4.34 gigawatts of installed capacity, some 2.65 were devoted to satisfying demand for this sector. Hence, expected growth in demand from this sector alone could require the addition of from 1.2 to 2.9 gigawatts of additional capacity by 2010, depending on whether per capita income growth were 0.5% or 2% per annum. By 2015, the required additional capacity would range from 1.6 to 4.2 GW.

The Cuban government has been working to upgrade its refining system to be able to accommodate a blend of imported and domestic crudes. The country has four refineries with nameplate capacity of about 301,000 b/d, with two units, one in Havana (122,000 b/d) and the other in Santiago de Cuba (100,000 b/d), accounting for the bulk of that capacity. A smaller refinery in the Ciego de Avila province produces about 2,000 b/d of lubricants for the local market.

The 76,000 b/d Russian-built Cienfuegos plant, designed in the early 1990s to handle Russian shipments, was not brought on stream due to the collapse in supplies from the former Soviet Union. An estimated $250 million is required to bring it into service. A number of foreign oil firms have been in on-again, off-again discussions with Cuba about establishing joint ventures to reactivate the unit.

Were U.S. restrictions to be lifted, Cuba would be an ideal entrepot for energy trading, in refined oil products, natural gas processing and distribution facilities and crude oil storage for shipments to the U.S. and possibly Mexico. Already, several Caribbean islands play this transshipment role. The Caribbean currently houses independent petroleum storage facilities with a capacity of approximately 100 million barrels of crude oil and refined products tankage.

The U.S. imported over 580,000 b/d from the Caribbean in 2001, almost 90% of which was refined products from the Virgin Islands, the Netherland Antilles, Trinidad and Tobago and Puerto Rico. With U.S. refining capacity reaching its limits to meet rising U.S. demand for oil products, and with environmental restrictions making construction of new U.S. domestic facilities unlikely, Caribbean refining ventures remain a promising option for supplying growing future U.S. refined products demand.

CONCLUSION

The changing pattern in energy demand in Cuba reflects both shifting economic policies as well as the consequences of an end to economic assistance from the USSR. Given recent growth rates and the rapid development of a tourist industry, we believe that per capita income growth of 0.5% per annum is possible into the future. A 2% growth rate is probably at the upper end of the spectrum unless there is rapid change in the policy/economic environment in which Cuba operates.

At a conservative 0.5% per capita growth rate, total final energy consumption is expected to grow by 3,270 KTOE by 2010 and by 4,374 KTOE by 2015. Making some assumptions regarding the role of biomass in future energy supply, this increase translates into 75,000 b/d of oil by 2010 and 104,000 b/d by 2015. This could be met with even modest success in the exploration and development of Cuba's energy sector. Greater expansion of Cuba's own oil industry could mean that further production increases could result in a reduction in the amount of oil imported.

Cuban waters also house natural gas resources. There may be significant amounts of additional gas in offshore areas adjacent to areas off the southwest coast of Florida. The gas is in deep water and would require the expertise of international, and mostly U.S. oil companies to be developed. If this gas is developed, Cuba could substitute some natural gas for oil imports if investments were made in the industrial and electricity sector to burn gas. Moreover, depending on how much natural gas is found and developed, Cuba could become a source of gas exports to Florida, competing there with imports of LNG.

Even given a modest growth in per capita income, Cuba will need to invest in additional electricity production and refineries. Both of these areas represent potential opportunities for foreign investors.

Finally, Cuba is well situated to become a storage and distribution entrepot for oil and natural gas coming into the U.S., Mexico and Latin America. Thus, Cuba's energy sector would likely see higher growth as well as attract increased foreign investment, were U.S. economic sanctions to be eased. Such ties would enhance US energy security by diversifying regional sources for petroleum product and oil and gas export supply.

REFERENCES

Crespo, Nicolas and Charles Suddaby, "A Comparison of Cuba's Tourism Industry with the Dominican Republic and Cancun, 1988-1999," *Cuba in Transition—Volume 10*, Association for the Study of the Cuban Economy (ASCE), 2000.

ECLAC, "Economic Survey of Latin America and the Caribbean, 1999-2000."

IEA, "Energy Balances for Non OECD Countries," CD, 2001.

Medlock III, Kenneth and Ronald Soligo, "Economic Development and End-Use Energy Demand," *Energy Journal*, April 2001.

Pérez, Guillermo H. and Jon Frederic Blickwede, "Cuba Deepwater exploration Opportunities," *Oil and Gas Journal*, December 11, 2000.

Preeg, Ernest H., Testimony Before the Subcommittee on Trade, House Committee on Ways and Means, May 7, 1998.

U.S. Department of Energy, Energy Information Agency, "Caribbean Fact Sheet," June 2002.

Werlau, Maria C., "Update on Foreign Investment in Cuba 1997-98 and Focus on the Energy Sector," *Cuba in Transition—Volume 8*, Association for the Study of the Cuban Economy (ASCE), 1998.

ACTION PLAN FOR THE RECONSTRUCTION OF THE CUBAN SUGAR INDUSTRY

Pablo A. Carreño

The purpose of this paper is to present the point of view of the National Association of Sugar Mill Owners of Cuba (Asociación Nacional de Hacendados de Cuba, ANDHAC), for the reconstruction of the sugar industry in a free and democratic Cuba. Members of the Association have written extensively about this matter in conferences and articles.

Many civic organizations and individuals have also expressed their ideas on the reconstruction of the Cuban economy, but to complete this task, the individual branches of the industrial sector have to develop their own plan of action.

Our plan is based upon the establishment in Cuba of a provisional government during the transition period that will bring about a free election as soon as possible. The Constitution of 1940 that was abolished by the communist regime during its takeover of the island should be enforced immediately. The ANDHAC has to be established in Cuba to hastily work in the reconstruction of the sugar industry so that it can contribute toward an economic recovery that will benefit the country as a whole. The Association would work together with the government through the necessary committees to address the basic problems that will face the industry and the Cuban economy at large.

All industrial properties should be returned to their legitimate owners in an orderly manner in the shortest period or time. All functional mills should start operation under their rightful owners, in order to avoid losing any crop, which is badly needed for the economic recovery of the country. There will be another group of mills that will be in need of major repairs; these repairs should be accomplished as soon as possible to put these mills back in operation.

A very important matter is to seek the necessary funds to finance the needs of the whole sugar operations (repairs, grinding operation, farming, etc.) from the international banking community (International Monetary Fund, World Bank), and from private banks directly to private industry or through loans guaranteed by the provisional government (government-to-government loans, etc.). A preliminary estimate of the cost has already been made and updated based on information gathered from the island and from international sources. It gives an idea of the magnitude of this problem, but the estimate has to be replaced as soon as possible by an on-site study that should include not only the industrial sector (mills) but also the related industries (e.g., distilleries) and also the farming operations which is primordial for a good crop.

The estimates in Table 1 should not be taken as the amount that the Cuban sugar industry needs to borrow, but as a guideline for the financial help that would be most needed during the first five years. Afterwards, the mills should be able to generate the necessary funds to take care of their operations and repayments of loans; thus the need for financial help will be lower than expressed. This study is for the reconstruction of 157 mills; however, we do not know how many of those that are presently not in operation will be functional.

Table 1. Financing Needs of the Cuban Sugar Industry (in million U.S. dollars)

	First Year	Next Four Years	First Five Years	Next Five Years	Total
Equipment	427.4	639.8	1067.2	831.0	1898.2
Operations	362.8	2324.2	2687.0	3230.5	5917.5
Farm	195.4	1154.6	1350.0	1523.0	2733.2
Mill	150.1	1060.1	1210.2	1523.0	2733.2
Others	17.3	109.5	126.8	154.0	280.8
Total	790.2	2964.0	3754.2	4061.5	7815.7

The assumptions considered for the development of the financing estimates follow:

- Equipment is based on U.S cost.

- Labor cost is based on those provided in the "Ley de Coordinación Azucarera" (Agricultural Coordination Law). At a price of 12 cents/lb for raw sugar in the world market (contract No. 11), the minimum wage for industrial workers would be $12.88/day and $7.46/day for agricultural workers. The average has been calculated at $18.18/day ($2.77/hr) and $10.51/day ($1.31/hr), respectively, based on research in some sugar producing where governments set minimum wages but actual wages are always higher. Prices of sugar under contract No.14 for a possible U.S. market has not been taken into account to compute the average labor cost.

- Performance is based on U.S. standards, adjusted for deficiencies during the first five years of operation.

- Land under cane production for milling: 1.3 million hectares (3.2 million acres).

- Additional land for a 7-year rotation: 184,000 hectares (455,000 acres).

- Total land under cane cultivation: 1.48 million hectares (3.655 million acres).

- Cane production: 38.0 MT/ha. (15.4/acre), with a goal of 76.0 MT/ha (30.8/acre) after the 5th year of operations, freeing up approximately 650,000 ha for other uses.

- Average yield: 12.88%, the average for 3 last pre-Castro crop less a reduction in yield correction for mechanical harvesting of 0.75 points = 12.13%

- Grinding correction factor for mechanical harvested cane: 0.95%

- Estimated lost time: 10% (20% for the 1st year, 15% for the 2nd and thereafter at 10%.

- Cane to be ground: 1st year 26.8; 2nd year 35.8; 3rd year 44.7; 4th year and thereafter 54.4 millions of short tons.

- Actual rated grinding capacity for existing 157 mills: 547,000 MTC/day

If all mills could be placed back in their normal operations, they would be capable of producing 7.4 million metric tons of 96% sugar.

The reconstruction and revitalization of the sugar industry in Cuba, as shown in this paper, will take time and will not come cheap. But the land, the climate, and most importantly, the people, will contribute to the success of this effort. More detailed information about the capital needs is shown in Annexes A and B.

It is a must to consolidate the existing market for 4 million metric tons of sugar and promote additional sales to the U.S. market (return to the pre-communist quota; expand the TRQ; assign to Cuba U.S. consumption increments or amounts to cover diminished U.S. production; same treatment as Mexico under NAFTA; or a combination of these and other options), and to the world market. Taking into consideration local sugar consumption estimated to be in the range of 0.5 million metric tons, there is an initial availability of sugar for export of 4.5 million metric tons that progressively goes up to 6.0 million during the first 5 years of operation. Our estimates take into consideration HFCS, not only for internal consumption but also for the future effect in the world market. We should not depend only on the sugar market, but should also actively pursue the production and sales of by-products like alcohol, paper and board, co-generation of electricity, wax, chemicals from molasses, etc. There are vivid examples of these products in sugar producing areas around the world.

The "Ley de Coordinación Azucarera" that was in force prior to the communist takeover, has to be reestablished. This law, among other things, set the bases for the relations between farmers, managers and labor, including salary compensation that varied in accordance with the overall price of the sugar. Programs should be established to improve the working conditions in the industry, which means safety and environmental issues and other incentives.

A program should be developed to improve the agricultural sector that will comprise new varieties of cane (experimental stations), proper cultivation (fer-

tilization, etc.), harvesting and hauling. To mechanize the harvesting economically, the harvesters should be utilized in large and mostly flat areas. This could be accomplished by the sharing of equipment among several farmers. It is estimated that one-half of the existing area will be needed for sugar cane, and two-thirds of this area would be fit for mechanical harvesting.

This action plan has to be coordinated with farmers, labor, and the provisional government.

APPENDIX A
Equipment Costs (million U.S. dollars)

	1st Year	2nd Year	3rd Year	4th Year	5th Year	6th to 10th (each year)
Total	427.4	177.2	186.2	211.6	64.6	166.2
(1) Land preparation	70.9	23.9	23.5	28.0		18.0
(2) Planting	37.7	12.8	12.6	13.7		9.6
(3) Harvesting	192.7	64.7	64.1	69.7		49.0
(4) Hauling	71.2	23.9	23.6	25.8		18.0
(5) Normal capital expenditures	427.4	177.2	186.2	211.8	64.6	11.6

Notes:

(1) Equipment needed to replace all sugar cane in five years. However, better utilization of the existing equipment should shorten this period. Afterward, a normal rotation of seven years is estimated. The remaining old equipment should be used as spare, and replaced as needed after the first five-year period. A replacement program of the equipment to follow after the fifth year consisting of 1/3 of the mechanical system to be substituted first and the hand labor equipment with a replacement value estimated at 1/2 of the mechanical system. Life expectancy of the equipment to be between 10 and 15 years.

(2) Same as (1) above.

(3) Two-thirds (2/3) of the cane to be cut by mechanical harvesters and one-third (1/3) by hand. One half of the mechanically-harvested cane will be cut by new harversters and the other half by existing harvesters. Scrapped harvesters will be used for parts for the existing ones. The replacement of machinery to follow the same schedule as for (1) and (2) above. Also considered in this calculation were the type of soil and slope of the terrain in Cuba.

(4) Equipment needed to haul one-third (1/3) of the total cane to be cut in areas and at distances where this type of transportation is economically feasible. The existing equipment—railroad facilities and other means of transportation—are to be utilized for the remaining two-thirds (2/3) of the total haul. Replacement schedule the same as (1)–(3) above.

(5) Capital expenditures likely to be more towards replacement during the first five years and then additions and replacements as needed. During the first year of operation, there will not be enough time to put in place a capital program in each mill because the priority will be repairs, but later on it will progressively increase to normal levels. For farms, during the first year, there is only the extraordinary expenditure noted above and nothing additional is contemplated. Only minor additions are taken into consideration in this line item because the replacements are outlined in the equipment replacement program. This item comprises what is needed for upgrading and/or setting up mill and farm research stations and for minor replacement of railroad facilities. Rail transportation to be substituted by ground transportation as much as feasibly possible.

APPENDIX B
Operating Costs (million U.S. dollars)

	1st Year	2nd Year	3rd Year	4th to 10th (each year)
(1) Farm	195.4	241.1	290.1	310.7
(2) Land preparation & planting	22.6	22.6	22.6	9.7
(3) Cultivation—plant cane	13.4	13.4	13.4	5.7
—stubble cane	17.7	17.7	17.7	7.6
(4) Harvesting	61.0	81.6	101.9	124.0
(5) Hauling	62.2	83.1	103.7	126.2
(6) General farm expenses	18.5	24.7	30.8	37.5
Mill	150.1	200.5	250.4	304.6
(7) Crop season operation	83.1	111.0	138.6	168.6
(8) Idle season repairs	67.0	89.5	111.8	304.6
(9) Other	17.3	20.9	27.0	30.8

Notes:

(1) Cost figures include shop allocation for equipment repairs.

(2) Based on three years' total cane replacement to accelerate the cane production. It should be accomplished by utilizing, during this period, the old equipment that has been replaced.

(3) Based on the schedule for land preparation and planting in (2) above, and assuming cane production during the first five-year period of 28.8 million short tons per annum in the first year; 35.8 in the second; 44.7 in the third; and 54.4 in the fourth and subsequent years.

(4) Based on the schedule for cane cultivation in (3) above. One-third (1/3) of the cane to be harversted with the new equipment acquired; one-third (1/3) to utilize the existing equipment; and the remaining one-third (1/3) to be cut by hand. Replaced equipment to be used as spare.

(5) Same as (4) above.

(6) Includes pest control, irrigation, road and rail maintenance, research, farm overhead, etc.

(7) Crop season to last the following number of days/year: 59 in the first year; 74 in the second; 87; in the third; and 106 in the fourth and subsequent years. The daily rated capacity is 547,000 MTC/day corrected for the mechanical harvester factor of 0.95 and a down time of 20% (1st year); 15% (2nd) and stabilized at 10% afterwards.

(8) For the following season, with the necessary days for repairs and installation of new equipment.

(9) To cover direct administrative expenses.

THEORETICAL AND EMPIRICAL REFLECTIONS ON THE FUTURE OF CUBAN AGRICULTURE

José Alvarez[1]

It is not farfetched to believe that, sooner or later, Cuban agriculture will be centered on a free enterprise system.[2] That transition, which many believe has already started with the breakup of the state monopoly on land and the creation of cooperatives in 1993 and of free agricultural markets in 1994, will rest on theoretical characteristics specific to the Cuban situation. Issues of special importance for Cuba will include the feasibility of coexistence of plan and market, the potential importance of property rights in increasing production and conserving the natural resources, and the role of government.

Most dictionaries define transition as "a passing from one condition, form, stage, activity, place, etc., to another." The words "passing from one condition" and "to another" have different meanings and imply diverse scenarios for different people. That is, there exist several opinions on what is the current stage of Cuban agriculture and what it should be once the "transition" has taken place. For that reason, before exploring the three issues of special importance referenced in the previous paragraph, it is necessary to delve into the theory upon which the collectivization

of Cuban agriculture and the reforms of the 1990s are based.

THE CURRENT SITUATION

The Theory Behind Collectivization

Collectivization[3] is mostly defined as the pooling of small, privately held parcels into larger-scale agricultural enterprises (Pryor, 1992, p. 3; Meurs, 1999, p. 4). Most of the collectivization processes are based on so-called scientific socialism. That theory originated in the works of Karl Marx[4] (hence the word "Marxism"), later expanded and first applied first in Russia by Vladimir Lenin (hence "Leninism" and "Marxism-Leninism").

Marxist-Leninist theory states that the socialization of production is a continuous process that has been developing since the beginnings of humanity. It is important to distinguish between capitalist socialization, encompassing only the production phase, and socialist socialization, which encompasses both the production and distribution phases. In the latter case, production results are aimed at satisfying the necessities of the entire population (Vilariño Ruiz, 1997, p.

---

1. I would like to thank René Costales for his valuable comments and suggestions on an earlier draft. The usual caveats apply.

2. This reminds me of the remarks I heard several years ago in relation to reforms in U.S. agricultural legislation that, although announced, had not materialized. "Those changes," said the speaker, "are similar to the second coming of Christ: Most Christians know it's coming but nobody knows when."

3. The words to describe this process, although defining the same phenomenon, are many and varied. In addition to "collectivization" and "collective agriculture" one finds "planned" and "centrally-planned," "Marxist" and "Marxist-Leninist," "command," "socialist," and others. In this article they are used indistinctly depending on the source.

4. It is interesting to note that Marx conducted most of his work in collaboration with F. Engels. Despite his important contributions, his name was not used at the time of "baptizing" the new doctrine.

7; Pérez Marín, 1990, p. 5). Those premises, along with the resulting implications for the elimination of private property, gave birth to the process of organizing production along socialist lines. Those theoretical principles have been applied in Cuban agriculture since the outset of the revolution in 1959.

According to Deere et al. (1992, p. 116), Cuba's collectivization efforts departed from the experience of most socialist countries, where collectivization was achieved through the use of force. These authors emphasize the voluntary nature of that process in Cuba.[5] It has been voluntary in that some real choice has always existed for peasants. The response of most peasants was to continue farming individually; even many cooperative members abandoned their participation in the collectivization drive through cooperatives to search for other type of employment.

Whether by force or by choice, collectivization was encouraged and carried out until the state controlled most of Cuba's farm land. Pérez Marín (1990) contains a summary of the implementation of such doctrine. According to him, Cuba's agrarian policy derives from the principles of the Cuban Communist Party. Such policy encompasses a series of important linkages, the main one being the establishment, on a scientific basis, of the agricultural development ideas for both the short and long run. Under socialism, planning is the law and it is the main link of all processes and socioeconomic aspects of the country. The scientific elaboration of the plan and forecasts based on the plan is a requirement in the building of socialism and it becomes more important as production and the interdependency of the agricultural sector with the remaining sectors of the economy grows (pp. 1-3). The above principles engendered the large state farms, considered for more than thirty years the "superior form of agricultural production" (p. 20).

The logic of large farms appears to be supported by basic economic theory. This is simply the principle of economies of scale or economies of size arising from phenomena which cause unit costs to decrease as size of business (farm in our case) and output are expanded. Internal economies (generally derived from the decisions of the manager) are reflected by a negative slope of a firm's long-run average cost curve. External economies (generally beyond the manager's control) are reflected by downward shifts of the cost curve itself. This principle is of special importance to future agricultural organizations in Cuba.

Recent research has shed doubts on Marx's explanation that the larger farms have lower costs and gradually drive the smaller farms out of business. Empirical studies in general and production function research in particular have not revealed at a single point in time either important economies of scale or size for most crops. Even the case for economies of scale or size for traditional plantation crops is now open to question. Furthermore, economies of scale in agriculture seem to occur in economically developed countries but not in developing countries (Pryor, 1992, pp. 372-373).

Since one of the objectives of this paper is to relate theories of agricultural development to the future of Cuban agriculture, it is important to evaluate very briefly the performance of collective agriculture. Meurs' evaluation contains both positive and negative features:

> Like its organization, the performance of collective agriculture has also varied greatly across time and place. There is no doubt that collectivization and collective agriculture resulted in significant losses of productivity, output, and living standards in some periods and some places. In the cases of China and Russia, declines resulted in widespread famine. At the same time ... collectivization sometimes also contributed to rapid growth in agricultural output. In so doing, the collectives contributed to the government goal of rapid industrialization and sometimes to substantial improvements in living standards (1999, p. 18).

---

5. To reinforce the concept of the voluntary nature of that process in Cuba, Deere et al. (1992) state that "collectivization was not encouraged until almost twenty years into the Revolution" (p. 117). These authors, however, seem to forget that most of the land distributed after the 1959 agrarian reform law had been converted into state farms by 1962.

When discussing the reasons for the negative performance of agriculture in Marxist regimes, Pryor (1992, pp. 119, 120, 220, 222, 232) differentiates between two groups: (a) some structural features of agriculture; and (b) a number of governmental economic policies, often tied to the organization of agriculture.

The structural factors include the large size of the farms, their imperfect vertical linkages with other parts of the agro-industrial complex, and the peculiar incentive structure established not only by higher administrative authorities for the managers of state and collective farms, but also by the managers of these farms for the workers.

Pryor divides the governmental policies into four groups. In the first group, he places those related to transition problems such as overvalued exchange rates, transformation of the systems for supplying agricultural inputs and buying farm output, and restructuring farms and their production. His second group relates to the bimodal development pattern[6] where the government focuses its resources either on a particular subsector such as the plantation, rather than the smallholder economy, or on a particular group of farmers. In the third group he places those policies derived from the political interference in farm operations which arises from the principle that the economic sphere is no longer autonomous, but subordinated to the political sphere. The last group of governmental policies relates to the administrative allocation system. When the agricultural sector is an integral part of the centrally-administered economy, production units are subject to plans and quotas, and, according to plan directives, the state trading agencies purchase and transfer rural products to the cities and urban products to the countryside.

Based on an analysis of a number of country experiences, Pryor concludes:

> In sum, much remains to be done before a final evaluation of the performance of collectivized agriculture can be made. These preliminary results suggest, however, that this grand experiment in the organization of agriculture cannot be considered an economic success, particularly with regard to the long-term growth of total factor productivity (1992, p. 261).

After surveying previous studies on different measures of performance, Pryor (1992, pp. 241-242) describes the results of comparisons between the socialist and private agricultural sectors of a single country for a single factor of production. Data on land productivity differences between the private and socialist sectors in a number of Marxist regimes seem to indicate higher productivity for the private sector when compared with the socialist sector. Examples include China and the Soviet Union.

In Cuba, Deere et al. (1992) consider that the collectivization process was a success in the cooperative sector. They recognize the lack of adequate data "to evaluate conclusively the costs and benefits of promoting production cooperatives rather than individual private farms" (p. 116). They also state that it was impossible for them "to reach any definitive conclusions about the relative productivity or efficiency of the state, cooperative, and peasant sectors in Cuban agriculture" (p. 116).

Such research for the state and nonstate sectors, however, was conducted in 1994 and 2001. Studies on land productivity, similar to those described above by Pryor for the socialist and private sectors, were performed by Alvarez and Puerta (1994) and Alvarez (2001). Results show that the nonstate sector outproduced the state sector in almost all crops studied in all years under consideration. Research has not only shown differences in productivity between the state and nonstate sectors, but also disparities in income levels among workers in farms with different agricultural organizations. For example, Deere et al. (1995) show that peasant households generated the highest income levels in the agricultural sector. Moreover, private sector incomes were considerably higher than those of households of state farm wage workers. According to Deere et al. (1995) the relatively high in-

---

6. In a unimodal development pattern, the government spreads its resources to agriculture across the entire sector, so that all subsectors benefit (Pryor, 1992, p. 199).

comes earned by members of Agricultural Production Cooperatives are indicative of the higher profitability and, hence, productivity of Cuba's production cooperatives as compared to the state farms (p. 231).

The inefficiency inherent to the agricultural socialist model was one of the reasons that led the Cuban leadership to look for alternative forms of agricultural organization and incentives. The new ideas translated into the economic reform of the 1990s.

The Theory Behind the Reforms of the 1990s

The explicit recognition of the failure of the old economic model, especially the state extensive growth model applied in agriculture, has been suggested as the basis for the economic reform of the 1990s. Arias Guevara and Hernández Benítez (1998) explain it in the following manner:

> The [old] model was more and more in contradiction with the objective need to develop the productive forces, which demanded a real democratization of the economic management. The old model, viable within the framework of the economic relations established by the CAME, became nonfunctional and in crisis in the nineties after the crumbling of eastern-European socialism and the demise of the USSR; therefore, neither the old mechanisms of leadership nor the former features for participation could be efficient under the new circumstances. The country did not have other alternative than to go toward new forms of economic management. It was under these conditions that the Basic Units of Cooperative Production appear (p. 110).

Theoreticians studying changes in the economies of the former members of the socialist bloc that have not completely abandoned the socialist ideas but have implemented some market-oriented reforms, such as Cuba, China, and Vietnam, have been involved in the search for a name for the mixed economic systems emerging in such countries. Vilariño Ruiz (1997, pp. 74, 76) believes that a growing consensus seems to indicate that the new economic system should be called "socialist market economy." The name appears to be appropriate since it combines the system of public property with the market economy. According to him, several features are important for the development of the new system. With respect to agriculture, the main objective is "to stabilize the basic production relations in rural areas and to establish a rural economic structure appropriate to the socialist market economy." The specific actions required are:

- to continue with the multiform system of property and responsibility that combines the unified management with the individual and collective ones;

- to develop the socialized services in rural areas;

- to promote specialization, commercialization, and socialization of agriculture;

- to impel the development of rural enterprises and of other non-agricultural industries; and

- to readjust the rural industrial structure with the goal of generating more employment to surplus workers of rural areas and to satisfy the needs of the population.

The theoreticians of the new economic system, however, insist in the difference between action and regulation of the market. The market can act without being necessarily the regulator of the economy, since the latter is really incompatible with any socialist economic model (Hidalgo-Gato Rodríguez, 1995, p. 81).

The economic system based on Marxist-Leninist theory has failed in most countries where it has been implemented. Cuba is not an exception. The inability of that model to develop Cuba's agricultural economy forced the Cuban leadership to look for alternative forms of agricultural organization. Theoreticians have baptized the new economic system emerging in a few countries as a socialist market economy since it contains elements of both planning and the market. The process is a modest, albeit important, step toward a market economy.

THE TRANSITION TO A MARKET ECONOMY

The process of transition from a centrally-planned to a market economy has attracted the attention of numerous scholars since the demise of socialism in the eastern and central European countries.[7] What appears to be an intermediate step between a command and a market economy, called a socialist market economy, has emerged in some countries. One of those countries is Cuba. Our task here is to reflect on the potential transition from the current system to a market economy.

Can Plan and Market Coexist?

The socialist market economy, as explained above, is a mix of economic planning tools and market forces. One wonders if these two can coexist or if they will be incompatible features in the present and future economic systems.

The dilemma, although gaining in importance since the crumbling of the European socialist countries and the reforms in China and Vietnam, is not new. A theoretical debate about the issue had already taken place in the 1920s. On the one side, the Austrian school of economic thought was represented by Ludwig von Mises. He argued that "the socialist system is incompatible with the market mechanism and, therefore, cannot rationally allocate resources and organize economic activities" (Shan, 1990, p. 17). On the other side, socialist reformer economists such as Oskar Lange and Abba Lerner, "demonstrated that in theory the socialist system could also make use of the market principle" (Shan, 1990, p. 17). According to most economists involved in the debate, the theoretical question was basically resolved. It was now time to prove that it could be applied successfully.

That was the other aspect of the debate. The Austrian school, Friedrich Hayek and Milton Friedman to some extent, argued that "although the socialist system could in theory make use of the market mechanisms, public enterprises lack the incentive to observe the market principles and, therefore, cannot respond effectively to market pressures" (Shan, 1990, p. 17). The practical problem remains unresolved. The reason is that no socialist country has yet had a completely successful experience in making use of the

market. The issue has regained importance after the reform movements in China, Vietnam, and Cuba.

China began its latest process of economic reforms at the end of 1978 with a radical market-oriented group of policies tied to the abandoning of collectivization in the agricultural sector. Some of the early measures included the "responsibility system linking remuneration to production." In the next few years, the communes were dismantled, household agriculture made a comeback (although, as is the case of the Basic Units of Cooperative Production in Cuba, the peasants did not receive formal ownership of the land), the system of sales to monopolistic state enterprises was eliminated, and large subsectors of agriculture were impacted by market-oriented reforms. The Chinese, however, have not abandoned planning completely, and the extensive privatization of state enterprises is not part of their objectives. Therefore, China's direction is toward the development of a planned-market economy that is based on socialist public ownership and not toward a market economy.

Vietnam presents a different case. While implementing a series of economic reforms in the 1980s, the Vietnamese were not concerned with the issue of the coexistence of plan and market. The real economic transformation started with the announcement in 1986 that central planning was to be dismantled. In just two years, according to Utting (1992), "Vietnam moved further and faster than any other Third-World socialist country in adopting market-oriented reforms" (p. 98). Despite its differences with China, both countries share a common political strategy: the hegemony of the Communist Party can not be challenged and no political concessions appear to be realistic in the near future.

The first issue that has been addressed by Cuban theoreticians is the importance of convincing the population that their belief of the incompatibility of economic planning and market forces in a socialist system, held during more than thirty years of indoc-

---

7. For example, to mention just a few general studies, Bromley (1993) describes the path from a command to a market economy, while Infanger (1995) studies the same for Russian agriculture emphasizing the sluggishness of the process. In addition, Linz and Stepan (1996) present a thorough analysis from a political perspective.

trination, is wrong. Vilariño Ruiz (1997, p. 100) states that planning was considered as a synonym of socialism and the market as synonym of capitalism. Steps, as many as necessary, were taken to bridle the development of the market and the monetary-mercantile relations. Despite its nationalistic character, it was based on the theory of the so-called real socialism. The failure of the latter in the socialist bloc became a strong call of alert to the Cuban leadership.

The Chinese and Vietnamese experiences, according to Vilariño Ruiz (1997, pp. 100-101), became reference points to evaluate Cuba's own innovations. The "absolute truth" that plan and market are two opposing phenomena began to crumble. The understanding of the need for some gradual development of the market gave room to the understanding of the inevitability of its many-sided development. The Cuban leadership began to realize that some initial market reforms would generate the need for additional transformations. Those two countries have come to the conclusion that it is necessary to build a socialist market economy based on each country's own special conditions. For example, prior experiences with small private property in the countryside would dictate the speed at which large state farms can be broken up and to what extent.

Cuban and foreign theoreticians have produced abundant literature on plan versus market. Some examples include:

- The Cuban agrarian case suggests it is too simplistic to equate the market with efficiency and democratization; but it also suggests the need to rethink state controls and market mechanisms (Stubbs, 1991, p. 164).

- The market is not in contrast with the principles of planning which should orient and ensure a balanced development in order to avoid the damages that could arise from the spontaneity and the lack of organization (Nova González, 1995, p. 87).

For almost all Cuban writers, the problem is solved. Two foreign scholars are the only ones, that I know of, alerting about the potential difficulties of utilizing market mechanisms to perfect central planning.

Deere and Meurs (1992, p. 827) enumerate two of them:

- markets must take a specific form for their allocational benefits to work; that is, prices of inputs and products must be mutually responsive in a system of interrelated, competitive markets, and where those prices are the source of information about scarcity and consumer wants. If an input or product is not allocated through competitive markets, they will not benefit from the allocation of resources where there is scarcity; and

- market mechanisms consistently generate tensions with central planning. When lack of inputs for market production slows supply response to price increases market prices remain consistently high. If an effective tax system is not in place, the result will be a large increase in income inequality. More important than that is the fact that the high prices will provoke the illegal channeling of both inputs and outputs from the state sector into the market sector.

I have observed the former problems in Cuba. A good example is the use of fertilizer and other inputs allocated to the Basic Units of Cooperative Production used in the self-provisioning plots of the cooperatives. Another example is the hiding of production from private farms to be sold in the black market or, since 1994, in the free agricultural markets. The abundance of fruits, vegetables, grains, and some processed products in those two markets, and their scarcity or nonexistence in the rationed market, is proof that quota production is not delivered to the state collection agency but redirected to those markets.

In summary, the problem of the incompatibility of central planning and market forces has been solved in theory. The empirical part, however, is yet to be solved.

The Role of Property Rights

A growing field in the economics literature is the study of the different stages from production to consumption trying to relate bottlenecks or inefficiencies to property rights. Several terms are used in studying this process. Austrian economists call it "structure of production" (Skousen, 1990). Harvard Professor Michael Porter prefers the term "value chain." Professor Shank uses "strategic cost management" (Shank and Govidarajan, 1993), while marketing specialists (the last step of the chain) refer to this methodology as "channels of distribution."

Regardless of the name, one has to consider an aspect of the issue of property rights that has been neglected by the literature.[8] I am referring to the concept of social property over agricultural production. The reason for this dereliction might rest on the emphasis always given to the concept of property rights over the means of production and not to the social ownership of goods and services derived from those means such as agricultural output. The two concepts are entirely different as are their implications. The lack of empirical examples from which theoretical concepts can be developed has also been responsible for this gap.

One of the rare exceptions appears to be the Peruvian experience. When a military coup lead by General Juan Velasco Alvarado overthrew the government of President Belaúnde Terry in 1968, a process of reform was carried out in the agricultural sector. Expropriated landlords were reluctant to invest using as collateral the bonds received as compensation. Such reluctance was not surprising since the government was creating a sector of social property in which the state controlled all important industrial and commercial enterprises and allowed the workers a degree of participation. This experience, however, was short-lived, lasting until 1975.

It is startling that, after more than forty years, Cuban theoreticians have ignored the concept of social property over production. The failure to consider this important aspect might lead to undisputed income inequalities. Cuba presents a good example. During the early years of the economic reforms started in 1993, and also thereafter, a good number of individuals took advantage of the opportunities generated by the free farmers' markets and the black market to accu-

mulate large sums of money. Some of them derived from legal and others came from illegal activities. This wealth prompted the irritable authorities to launch a campaign of persecution and harassment against the so-called *macetas*[9] some of whom were incarcerated and almost all of them saw their money and properties confiscated. Cuban theoreticians, however, never questioned the social-property nature of that wealth.

Despite an apparent growing consensus that lack of clarity and enforcement of property rights remains a key impediment to investment and production, research results on the issue of property rights and productivity are different in several areas of the world. For example, a direct relationship was found in Thailand (Feder and Onchan, 1987), Sub-Saharan Africa (Place and Hazell, 1993), Uganda (Roth et al., 1994), and Gambia (Hayes et al., 1997), to mention just a few. Interestingly enough, a study in Kenya (Place and Migot-Adholla, 1998) found a weak relationship between registration, titles, perceived land rights of farmers, credit used and crop yields. The same was found in Honduras (López, 1995; Montaner-Larson, 1995). The study by Foltz et al. (2000) shows both positive and negative relationships between property rights and several variables related to investment and productivity in Nicaragua.

The issue of the relationship between property rights and productivity, therefore, has not been settled. Variations exist between countries and even between regions of a country. Those findings dictate thorough research before major decisions on this issue are made in Cuba.

Equally important is the potential relationship between property rights, productivity, and the conservation of natural resources. This issue has been researched in socialist Cuba (Sáez, 1997). After presenting data on increasing private sector output in contrast with declining trends in state farms during the Special Period, Sáez states:

---

8. I thank René Costales for alerting me about this fact and for his help in the development of this concept.

9. The term *maceta* comes from the word *mazo* (bunch; bundle) used to describe the huge amounts of Cuban pesos and U.S. dollars held by these individuals.

The evidence presented... shows that, in the case of [the municipality of] Santo Domingo, private family farmers have conserved and developed their natural resource base, which allowed them to respond to the economic crisis. On the other hand, the state failed to foster resource conservation. The decline of output in state farms is explained in part by the degradation of natural resources in the area (p. 130).

Among the reasons he identifies as promoting conservation are selective use of organic and commercial fertilizers, intercropping, and fallow periods. Sáez also found that laws and regulations aimed at conserving the environment enacted by the Cuban government are not enforced in the study area in state farms while private farmers apply environment-conserving practices in their operations.

Research results from other areas of the world seem to confirm the previous findings. Ramírez and Shults (2000) used an econometric model to analyze factors (land tenure, among others) influencing the adoption of Integrated Pest Management (IPM), agro forestry, and soil conservation techniques among small farmers in Costa Rica, Panama, and El Salvador. Farm ownership is predicted to have a positive effect on the levels of adoption of both IPM technologies and soil conservation practices.

The Role of Government

The third issue studied in this section is that of the role of government in the transition from a planned to a market economy.[10] Jones et al. (2000, p. 36) believe the latter to be very difficult and the former not well understood by the populace of countries in transition. And they add: "For a market economy to work, the government must play a strong role in areas such as contract law and defining property rights. Moreover, the government, which sets up and supports these institutions, must be trusted" (p. 36).

Finding the proper role for government in a transition economy is extremely difficult. In the emerging market economies of eastern and central Europe, international organizations and western advisors have not fully understood the large differences between the existing institutional structures of these economies and those required for a market economy. That fact has led to an underestimation of the magnitude and timing of the transformation process. In many instances, advice from consultants conflicts with basic historical and cultural institutions in the target countries.

Jones et al., state that a particular market economy results from the interaction of economic, institutional, legal, and cultural factors:

- Economics. In centrally planned economies efficiency is not an objective. Success is measured by physical output, and input and output prices are largely set by the government. In a market economy, individuals generate signals that guide economic activity. Market transactions are protected by the institutional framework, while in socialist economies it is done by the government with considerable protection for labor. The transition requires a shift to business managers with less protection for labor.

- Institutional framework. Stability is required for the formation of institutions that provide the backbone of a market economy. Institutions endure only if they are based on shared values.

- Legal institutions. Under socialist civil law, a person can act as long as the act is permitted by the statutes, which is similar to the behavior allowed by civil law in western countries. Participation of the populace during the transition is hindered by the perceived need for permission from the government, which in many cases may be required. A frequently heard complaint about the privatization process in emerging market economies is that the elites (called "mafia businessmen") have "taken" ownership of assets without waiting for permission. The black market culture which existed previously operated outside the legal framework. Legal mechanisms for buying and selling exist in small-scale form.

---

10. This section on the role of government is mostly based on Jones et al. (2000).

- Culture. Historical and current cultural factors influence the development and operation of market institutions. Because institutions are defined by the aggregate set of rights, cultural expectations about rights will influence the new "rules of the market." Some time will have to elapse before the new institutional structure can outweigh the influence on choices and actions of the coercion that was prevalent under central planning.

Jones et al. have a few final thoughts that summarize and put in perspective the issues previously discussed:

Creating an exchange economy requires a set of legal and economic institutions that are transparent to participants and overseen by an impartial third party. Limiting government to the role of oversight in a previously state-trading system requires considerable behavioral change on the part of the government and cultural change on the part of market participants. Approximately 50 years of central planning have created a cultural response of distrusting government. Unless an alternative, credible third party can be designated, the ultimate constraint to creating a market system may be the ability to generate trust in the government (2000, p. 40).

REFERENCES

Alvarez, José. "Differences in Agricultural Productivity in Cuba's State and Nonstate Sectors: Further Evidence." *Cuba in Transition—Volume 10.* Washington: Association for the Study of the Cuban Economy, 2000, pp. 98-107.

Alvarez, José and Ricardo A. Puerta. "State Intervention in Cuban Agriculture: Impact on Organization and Performance." *World Development* 22:11 (1994), pp. 1663-1675.

Arias Guevara, María de los Angeles and Raciel Hernández Benítez. "Cooperación y Participación." In Niurka Pérez Rojas, Ernel González Mastrapa and Miriam García Aguilar (Comp.) *Campesinado y Participación Social.* La Habana: Equipo de Estudios Rurales, Universidad de la Habana, 1998, pp. 108-112.

Bromley, Daniel W. "Creating Market Economies from Command Economies." *Economic Issues* No. 121, Department of Agricultural Economics, University of Wisconsin, Madison, March 1993.

Deere, Carmen Diana and Mieke Meurs. "Markets, Markets Everywhere? Understanding the Cuban Anomaly." *World Development* 20:6 (1992), pp. 825-839.

Deere, Carmen Diana, Mieke Meurs and Niurka Pérez. "Toward a Periodization of the Cuban Collectivization Process: Changing Incentives and Peasant Response." *Cuban Studies* 22 (1992), pp. 115-149.

Deere, Carmen Diana, Ernel González, Niurka Pérez and Gustavo Rodríguez. "Household Incomes in Cuban Agriculture: A Comparison of State, Cooperative, and Peasant Sectors." *Development and Change* 26:2 (April 1995), pp. 209-234.

Feder, G. and T. Onchan. "Land Ownership Security and Farm Productivity: Evidence from Thailand." *Journal of Development Economics* 24 (1987), pp. 16-30.

Foltz, Jeremy, Bruce A. Larson and Rigoberto Lopez. "Land Tenure, Investment, and Agricultural Production in Nicaragua." Development Discussion Paper No. 738, Harvard Institute for International Development, February 2000.

Hayes, Joseph, Michael Roth and Lydia Zepeda. "Tenure Security, Investment and Productivity in Gambian Agriculture: A Generalized Probit Analysis." *American Journal of Agricultural Economics* 79 (1997), pp. 369-382.

Hidalgo-Gato Rodríguez, Francisco. "Perfecciona-miento del Modelo Económico Cubano: Un En-foque Teórico." *Economía y Desarrollo* 95:1 (September 1995), pp. 54-84.

Infanger, Craig L. "Reforming Russia's Agriculture—The Slow Path from Plan to Mar-ket." *Choices* (Second Quarter, 1995).

Jones, Eluned, Judith I. Stallmann and Craig In-fanger. "Free Markets at a Price." *Choices* 15:1 (First Quarter, 2000), pp. 36-40.

Linz, Juan J. and Alfred Stepan. *Problems of Demo-cratic Transition and Consolidation.* Baltimore, MD: The Johns Hopkins University Press, 1996.

López, R. "Land Titles and Farm Productivity in Honduras," University of Maryland, College Park, July 31, 1995. Unpublished Manuscript.

Meurs, Mieke. "The Continuing Importance of Col-lectivization." In Mieke Meurs (Ed.) *Many Shades of Red—State Policy and Collective Agri-culture.* Lanham, MD: Rowman & Littlefield Publishers, 1999, pp. 1-33.

Montaner-Larson, J.B. "An Economic Analysis of Land Titling in Honduras." Ph.D. Dissertation, University of Oxford, Worcester College, 1995.

Nova González, Armando. "La Reactivación Económica del Sector Agropecuario Cubano." *Economía y Desarrollo* 95:1 (September 1995), pp. 85-90.

Pérez Marín, Enrique. *Agropecuaria—Desarrollo Económico.* La Habana: Editorial de Ciencias So-ciales, 1990.

Place, F. and P. Hazell. "Productivity of Indigenous Land Tenure System in Sub-Saharan Africa." *American Journal of Agricultural Economics* 75 (1993), pp. 10-19.

Place, F. and S.E. Migot-Adholla. "The Economic Effects of Land Restoration on Small Holder Farms in Kenya: Evidence from Nyeri and Kaka-mega Districts." *Land Economics* 74 (1998), pp. 360-373.

Pryor, Frederic L. *The Red and the Green—The Rise and Fall of Collectivized Agriculture in Marxist Regimes.* Princeton, NJ: Princeton University Press, 1992.

Ramírez, Octavio A. and Steven D. Shultz. "Poisson Count Models to Explain the Adoption of Agri-cultural and Natural Resource Management Technologies by Small Farmers in Central American Countries." *Agricultural and Applied Economics* 32:1 (April 2000), pp. 21-33.

Roth, M., J. Cochrane and W.W. Kisamba-Muger-wa. "Tenure Security, Credit Use, and Farm In-vestment in the Rujumbura Pilot Land Registra-tion Scheme, Uganda." In J. Bruce and S.E. Migot-Adhulla (Eds.) *Searching for Security of Tenure in Africa.* Dubuque, IA: Kendall/Hunt, 1994.

Sáez, Héctor R. "Property Regimes, Technology, and Environmental Degradation in Cuban Agricul-ture," Ph.D. Dissertation, University of Massa-chusetts, May 1997.

Shan, Pu. "Planning and the Market." In Janes A. Dorn and Wang Xi (Eds.) *Economic Reform in China: Problems and Prospects.* Chicago, IL: The University of Chicago Press, 1990, pp. 17-20.

Shank, John K. and Vijay Govindarajan. *Strategic Cost Management - The New Tool for Competitive Advantage.* New York, NY: The Free Press, 1993.

Skousen, Mark. *The Structure of Production.* New York, NY: New York University Press, 1990.

Stubbs, Jean. "State Versus Grass-Roots Strategies for Rural Democratization Among the Cuban Peasantry." *Cuban Studies* 21 (1991), pp. 149-168.

Utting, Peter. *Economic Reform and Third-World So-cialism - A Political Economy of Food Policy in Post-Revolutionary Societies.* London, UK: The Macmillan Press, 1992.

Vilariño Ruiz, Evelio. *Cuba: Reforma y Moderniza-ción Socialistas.* La Habana: Editorial de Ciencias Sociales, 1997.

HEALTH CARE IN CUBA AND IN THE UNITED STATES OF AMERICA: AN ECLECTIC APPROACH

Gloria Casal, Antonio A. Fernández, Pedro Melchor González and Pedro F. Pellet

"No hay dinero que pague una buena atención médica" or *"La medicina es un sacerdocio."* These colloquial phrases used in Cuba many years ago refer to medical services as an almost divine vocation. Things are different now in most highly industrialized societies. Why has reality changed so dramatically? It seems that when monetary compensation is included in the economic provision of health care, significant problems arise.

In reference to economics, healthcare is highly price-inelastic. In other words, when price increases, quantity demanded decreases by a lesser extent. In some instances, however, and as a result of treatment being very specific, it is said that demand is perfectly inelastic: as long as the patient or a third party is capable of paying, the quantity demanded will not decrease no matter the increase in prices. Economists call this service a "necessity" or an "essential." In addition, most economic principles do not fully apply the provision of health care in a market economy. Therefore, it is irrelevant to try to uphold consumer sovereignty in a context where asymmetry, lack of information, irrationality and contradictions between market and religious-philosophical values prevail. In other words, the benefits of the market are not applicable to the health care industry in the U.S. and other market oriented economies.

HEALTH CARE IN CUBA BEFORE THE REVOLUTION

Before 1959, Cuba was able to find partial solutions for most health problems. Cuban physicians and healthcare institutions were internationally recognized and accepted as offering high-standard and reliable services. Physicians, nurses and allied-health science professionals in every field were trained in Europe, the United States, and Cuba. Some of Cuba's most adept and venerable physicians volunteered their expertise and time in teaching hospitals. In addition, doctors with successful practices frequently maintained beds in public hospitals, and paid all expenses with their own resources.

During that time, the health care system in Cuba consisted of the traditional fee-for-service private practice and the free public health system, financed by the State, which oversees hospitals, and research facilities. Not to mention, some of the most advanced medical technology was available, including the use of recently developed antibiotics.

An additional system, widely used by a significant segment of the country's population, was the *"Sistema de Clínicas Mutualistas y Regionales."* This system consisted of independent organizations capable of providing for their associates comprehensive health care packages with particular emphasis on the development of specializations, full hospitalization, outpatient clinics, medications and urgent care. The state initially implemented the system as a way to provide affordable health care for members of regional associations—in this case, for people born in different "regions" of Spain or their descendants. For example, people coming from Galicia and their descendants typically joined the Association of the Galician Center (*Asociación del Centro Gallego, Hijas de Galicia*) for a modest monthly fee of 2 to 3 pesos per family. Similarly, those coming from Asturia joined the *Centro Asturiano, Quinta Covadonga,* and those from the Canary Islands joined the *Quinta Canaria.*

Each of these regional associations owned its own hospitals where all medical specialty services were available. All these services were included in the health package, which typically covered the cost of the patient visit to the urgent care facilities or scheduled specialist, completing all indicated lab tests, X-rays, microbiology, etc. Hospitalization, surgery (emergency and elective), urgent care and physiotherapy were also offered. Hospital staff also provided house calls. When the diagnosis was completed, the center's pharmacy provided the prescribed drugs. There were no out-of-pocket expenses for patients. They only had to prove that their membership was in good-standing by presenting the updated payment receipt. The monthly fee for these services was very low, around 2-3% of the household income.

This system proved so effective that it was later copied and implemented in the same manner by other organizations and trade unions (*Clínica de Dependientes*). Additionally, that could be joined with no requirement other than payment of the monthly fee adapted the system. Prior to 1959, Kaiser Permanente sent researchers to Cuba to study this system.

HEALTH CARE UNDER THE REVOLUTION

The Cuban revolution in 1959 marked a significant change in the way Cubans received health care. The Revolutionists promised free access to healthcare for all Cubans. The MINSAP (Cuban Ministry of Public Health) began to own and control every activity related to health care in the country. Furthermore, the authorities banned new graduates from private practice and gradually they confiscated the private clinics and hospitals. By 1968, only a handful of private practices remained.

Today, no professional can enter or leave the health care field without approval from MINSAP. The MINSAP decides where and when things will be implemented in the country's health care system, from the introduction of new instruments and diagnostic machines to the implementation and application of new therapeutical approaches. Everything related to

healthcare, except for ambulatory drugs, is free because there is no health insurance system in the country.

This system was purported as universally egalitarian, where everybody would have the same access to existing facilities and resources available in the country. However, the system was corrupted from the very beginning and special hospital and clinics were created for high-level governmental officials and their families. Thus, this healthcare system has evolved into several sub-systems. For the general population, there is a sub-system whose quality and availability of resources and supplies varies according to the country's general economic situation. There is a much better sub-system for high-ranked civil servants, party officials and military personnel. In addition, when the number of foreign visitors started to increase, some extremely well maintained and equipped facilities were established, providing excellent health care services paid in foreign currency. Both pathological and non-pathological conditions were treated, including cosmetic surgery under the general umbrella of health tourism. The sub-system catering to foreign tourists raised many bio-ethical issues, such as aborted fetal brain tissue transplant, obtained without parental consent, which was advertised abroad with false promises, as a cure for neurological disorders.

The healthcare system available to the population has experienced a precipitous decline over the years to the point where patients must provide many supplies for themselves. An extraordinary economic gulf divides Cuba into two classes, people with access to U.S. dollars and people without dollars. This rendered devastating consequences to the healthcare system, because the general population, those who have the US dollars can access better healthcare than those without the "enemy's money." It seems that in Castro's Cuba the circle has been completed and, people with hard currency can get much better health care than without.

BIOETHICS IN CUBA AND IN THE USA

Physicians in Cuba face a perplexing situation. They have to juggle conflicting interests—their obligations to the revolution, their own patient's welfare, and their own conscience. For instance, if a pacemaker is required but not available, a physician is forced to obfuscate the situation ("shuffle the deck of cards") so patients' relatives do not complain to the administrators. Interventions, such as abortions of high-risk pregnancies, are practiced upon patients without proper "informed and due" consent. Added factors, such as legal concerns and expected good revolutionary behavior, exacerbate these embarrassing conflicting situations and make mutual tolerance and communication quite difficult.

The U.S. is not free from bioethical dilemmas. Physicians must also juggle patients' values when suggesting appropriate treatment with what is suitable from the patients' perspectives, what is medically appropriate and by the physician's conscience. Patients, however, do have the right to refuse a given course of treatment. They often request that their physicians perform or omit a given procedure, when said actions or omissions will violate the physician's values or medical protocol.

U.S. liberal constitutionalism (which stresses a utilitarian, individualist, expressivist philosophy), posits equality and openness with minimal state interference; on the other hand, Cuba's practice, institutionalizes deceit and concealment. In order to enhance appropriate decision-making both countries need to work with bioethics consultants and committees to provide equal and efficient care.

HEALTH CARE IN THE UNITED STATES OF AMERICA

Thirty-seven years ago, President Johnson presented the first Medicare benefits card to Harry Truman, the former president. Medicare was signed into law with the hope of providing low-cost quality healthcare to senior Americans, but Medicare finances were based on wrong assumptions. Seniors enrolled in Medicare today are responsible to cover a large deductible.

A recent study by the National Coalition on Health Care predicted a 20% increase in premiums for small business. Recession, rising unemployment, increases in premiums, and the aftermath of the terrorist attacks is expected to result in close to 45 million Americans lacking health insurance coverage. The

money spent on health care in the United States today, is officially around 14% of the Gross Domestic Product (GDP). The U.S. expenditure in healthcare as a percentage of GDP is greater than that of most European countries (between 7 and 10%), Canada (9.5%), Japan (7.6%), and New Zealand (8.1%). This disparity began in the 1980's and has been broadening since.

Health Maintenance Organizations (HMOs) were created as an alternative to control the increase cost of health services, and work differently from the traditional health insurance plans by actually providing both health insurance and medical treatments to the insured. An HMO is usually a for-profit corporation with responsibilities to its stockholders and controls the amount of health care that the doctor is allowed to provide. In the 1990's a new trend known as Managed Care Organization (MCO) emerged as a combination of HMO and other insurance plans, where patients are kept in the organization despite their changing needs. Capitation is a system where the basis of payment to physicians is the number of people covered, and not the service actually provided. A conflict of interests was created between good health care and financial interests when MCOs offered incentives to physician for reducing costs. This resulted in physicians endangering optimal clinical outcomes under the guise of efficient and optimal care. This was finally solved in 1996 when the American Medical Association (AMA) Council on Ethical and Judicial Affairs declared this practice unethical.

With the current state of affairs, both patients and physicians feel that a healthcare reform is long overdue in the United States. Last year, President Bush acknowledged that Medicare needs to expand its coverage, improves its services and strengthen its finances, giving seniors more control over their health care. He announced a national drug discount for seniors. The idea of the administration was to protect seniors without overtaxing their children.

The question remains whether citizens are able to reconcile values like efficiency and equity with the realities of a budget. Governments and their health care reform consultants have to struggle with a very human experience because of technological advances.

It is evident that health care delivery deals with individuals, family members, (their norms, mores, values), and their moment of confrontation with life and death. It is about the individual, their family and the collectivity. Unfortunately there is a trade-off and sacrifice to improve imperfect systems of health care delivery.

HEALTH CARE IN CUBA AFTER THE REVOLUTION

After a period of propitious political and economic changes in Cuba, many Cubans living overseas may want to return to their motherland. This event will create tremendous developments in the health care system. While in the U.S., the Congress is considering reforming private insurance, encouraging medical savings, providing financial assistance and reforming medical malpractice some Americans want to be able to use the free market to choose the care that suits their needs. Congressional actions in the US may eventually amend the Social Security Act of 1965, allowing the Medicare services to be provided outside its borders (See Díaz-Briquets, 2001). Currently, the pharmaceutical industry in Cuba is a state monopoly where workers make a nickel an hour and

quality control is not subject to reliable scrutiny. Our research indicates that a transition toward a mixed economy (returning to a modern version of the *Clínicas Mutualistas*) could provide an acceptable way to deliver health care in a post-revolutionary Cuba. If the situation changes, some Congressional actions in the U.S. may create the conditions for a rapid transformation of the health care sector in Cuba, providing services in Cuba to Cubans living abroad and to U.S. citizens. This change of health care policy in the United States could lower the price of this service in America and would create an incentive for economic development in Cuba, providing unemployed and underemployed healthcare workers in Cuba the opportunity to become highly productive and restore and augment their medical tradition.

A long-term universally accessible, publicly and/or privately funded healthcare system, with adequate resources and sustainable foundations, should be able to secure future access to high quality and continuity of care. The long-term goal for the highest quality healthcare should be patients and provider's satisfaction, adequate supplies of human resources, and efficient delivery systems at a reasonable price.

BIBLIOGRAPHY

Anderson, G & Wiest, Axel (1998). *Multinational Comparisons of Health Care: Expenditures, Coverage, and Outcomes.* The Commonwealth Fund.

Capper, S. A., Ginter, P. M., and Swayn L.E. (2002) *Public Health Leadership and Management: Cases and Context* (www.SAGEPUB.COM). Sage Publications, Thousand Oaks, CA.

Díaz-Briquets, Sergio (1991). "MEDICARE: A Potential Income-Generating Activity for Cuba in the Future," *Cuba in Transition—Volume 11.*

Easterling, D., Gallagher, K. & Lodwick, D. (2002). *Promoting Health at the Community Level* (www.SAGEPUB.COM). Sage Publication, Thousand Oaks, CA.

Friedman, Milton (2001). "How to Cure Health Care," http://www.thepublicinterest.com/archives/2001.

Herzlinger, Regina (1999). *Market-Driven Healthcare: Who Wins, Who Loses in the Transformation of America's Largest Service Industry.* Perseus Publishing, Cambridge, MA.

Jackson, J.L. (1997). "The German health system: Lessons for reform in the United States." *Archival of Internal Medicine*, Arch Int Med. 157:155-160.

Piturro, Marlene, (2002). *Managed Care* (April).

Qadeer, I., Sen, K. & Nayar, K. R. (2001). *Public Health and the Poverty of Reforms.* (www.SAGE-

PUB.COM). Sage Publications, University of Cambridge, UK.

Rice, R. E. & Katz, J. E. (2001). *The Internet and Health Communication: Experiences and Expectations*. (www.SAGEPUB.COM). Sage Publications, Thousand Oaks, CA.

Rodwin, V.G. & Sandier S. (1993). "Health care under French national health insurance." *Health Affairs*, Fall, 1993.

Slass, L. (1998). *Premium Pay: Compensation in America's HMOs*. Families USA Foundation. Washington, DC.

Sidel, V.W. (2000). "Britain's health care, and ours." Letter to the Editor, *The New York Times*, February 14, 2000.

Snehendu, B.K., Alcalay, R. & Alex, S. (2000). *Health Communication: A Multicultural Perspective* (www.SAGEPUB.COM). Sage Publications. Thousand Oaks, CA.

"Some Lessons to be Learned From Canadian Health System" (2002). *Managed Care* (April).

Spiegel, Henry William (1983). *The Growth of Economic Thought*, Revised and Expanded Edition. Durham, North Carolina, Duke University Press.

Starfield, B. (1998). *Primary Care: Balancing health needs, services, and technology*. N. Y., Oxford University Press.

Wahner-Roedler, D.L., Knuth, P. & Juchems, R.H. (1997). "The German health care system." *Mayo Clinic Proceedings*.

Witte, K., Martell, D. & Meyer, G. (2001). *Effective Health Risk Messages: A Step-By-Step Guide*. (www.SAGEPUB.COM). Sage Publications, Thousand Oaks, CA.

CUBA IN THE HUMAN DEVELOPMENT INDEX IN THE 1990s: DECLINE, REBOUND AND EXCLUSION

Carmelo Mesa-Lago[1]

For more than a decade, the United Nations Development Program (UNDP) has annually published the important *Human Development Report* (hereafter the *Report*). The most consulted aspect of this widely used international report is the *Human Development Index (HDI)*, which at its peak ranked 174 countries in the world, including Cuba, based on socio-economic indicators.

Due to the severe crisis of the 1990s, Cuba's HDI ranking fell from 61st to 89th place in the world, and from 9th to 12th place in Latin America. In two previous publications I pointed out that it was impossible to estimate the crucial economic indicator of the HDI for Cuba because of the lack of essential statistics. In the 1999 edition of the *Report* (based on 1997 data), there was a change in the methodology which resulted in Cuba jumping from 85th to 58th place in the world and from 11th to 9th in the region; moreover, in the 2000 edition, Cuba climbed to 56th and 6th places, respectively. This miraculous leap could not be justified given the incomplete process of economic recovery in the island. In the latest edition of the *Report* (2001), however, Cuba was partly excluded from the HDI due to the lack of reliable data.

This paper follows the evolution of Cuba in the HDI: that nation's ranking in the world and the re-gion, identifies problems in the social indicators as well as in the problematic economic indicator, and explains how the miraculous jump occurred because of statistical inaccuracies and the methodology change.

THE RANKING OF DEVELOPMENT BY THE WORLD BANK AND CUBA

The most internationally used indicator to measure the development level of a country is its GDP, which annually estimates the value of all goods and services generated in the economy. To correct for inflation, GDP is adjusted with a consumer price index based on the price variations of a basket of the essential commodities and services. In order to properly compare GDP among countries with diverse populations, it is divided by the number of inhabitants to obtain GDP per capita. To address the problem of the diverse currencies that are used to measure national GDP and allow for international comparison, each nation's GDP is converted to U.S. dollars, either based on the official exchange rate or according to the "purchasing power parities" (PPP) of currencies. The latter measures the diverse purchasing power of currencies based on the national prices of a large number of goods and services, comparing each of them with the corresponding prices in the United

1. The author gratefully acknowledges valuable comments on a preliminary version of this paper from Sergio Díaz-Briquets, Manuel Madrid-Aris, Manuel Pastor Jr., Jorge Pérez-López, and the Human Development Report Office in New York, as well as in the editing of the final version by Jorge Perez-López. In addition, Kristin Kleinjans helped in the evaluation of the methodological change in the economic index, and Jorge Gorostiaga in the formatting of the final version of the paper. The author is only responsible for what is said herein.

States in order to make the conversion to the dollar ("international dollar").

The World Bank, in its *World Development Report*, annually ranks all the countries of the world using their GDP per capita, adjusted for inflation and converted to U.S. dollars based on the official exchange rate and the PPP (hereafter GDP p/c PPP US$). Countries are classified in three groups: high, medium and low (the most recent edition is World Bank 2000/2001). In the decades of the 1960s and 1970s, the Bank included Cuba in its *World Development Report*. But at that time Cubans used the so-called "material product system" (MPS), typical of the USSR and socialist countries, while the rest of the world used the system of national accounts (SNA). The two accounting systems were not comparable for two reasons. On the one hand, the MPS counted many times the value of a product in its different stages of processing instead of counting only the "value added" at each stage of production or transformation as the SNA does. For instance, cotton is successively transformed into thread, fabric and clothing; the MPS counted the value of cotton four times, while the SNA only counted the value added at each stage of garment production. On the other hand, as a legacy of Karl Marx, the MPS excluded the value of all "non productive" services (not directly related to material production), such as education, health care, social security, defense, etc., underestimating the value of GDP (actually it was called "global social product," GSP). This second distortion was not favorable for Cuba due to the importance of its social services and defense in GDP. Therefore, the MPS overestimated GDP for one set of reasons and underestimated it for another.

In addition, Cubans changed four times the formula of calculation of the MPS, resulting in four series that could not be connected. Even worse, Cuban statisticians have not revealed how they determine the basket for adjusting GDP to inflation or how they measured inflation. On top of that, the conversion of the Cuban peso to the dollar was made at par, that is, at the official exchange rate of one peso for one dollar, even though the black market rate was several pesos to one dollar. Finally, Cuba did not—and does not—publish the necessary information about goods and services prices, as well as many other elements that are needed to make the conversion to PPP. Therefore, the comparison of the Cuban GSP with GDP in the rest of Latin America and other capitalist countries in the world was like matching up elephants with peanuts.[2]

At the beginning of the 1980s, the World Bank put together an international team of experts to evaluate the MPS in the socialists countries with the goal of converting MPS measures to the SNA, and make feasible a proper comparison of GDP in all countries—capitalist as well as socialist—included in its *World Development Report*. An extensive study of the Cuban case demonstrated that it was impossible to estimate its GDP due to the deficiencies noted above (Mesa-Lago and Pérez-López 1985). As a result, the World Bank excluded Cuba from its comparisons.

WHY THE HDI IS MORE THOROUGH THAN THE SIMPLE GDP AND IT FAVORS CUBA

The ranking of countries based solely on their GDP per capita presupposes that development is measured only with that single indicator. But let's consider a country with a highly unequal income distribution, where the richest 10% of the population receives 40% of GDP, and the poorest 40%, just 10%. That country's GDP per capita would be a deceptive average, since the income of a small minority of the population would be considerably above the national average, and the income of a large majority would be considerably below the average. Moreover, countries like Costa Rica, Cuba and Uruguay have reached higher standards in their social indicators (health care, education, social security) than in their GDP levels, while the opposite is true in other countries

---

2. Nevertheless, ECLAC published for many years Cuban GSP comparing it with GDP in the rest of the region. Only a footnote in fine print warned that the Cuban figure was GSP, without any explanation of the implications of using one concept or the other.

that have seriously neglected their social services despite significant GDP growth.

In order to cope with the problem discussed above, the UNDP constructed the HDI, combining an economic indicator with two social indicators. The economic indicator is GDP p/c PPP US$, based on estimates by the World Bank and the International Comparative Program.

The two social indicators are: (1) life expectancy at birth (to measure health standards); and (2) a combination of the adult literacy rate and the enrollment rates at primary, secondary and tertiary education (to measure educational levels).

The values of the three indicators cannot be merged because they are expressed in different units: PPP dollars, years of life expectancy and percentages in education, respectively. In order to overcome this difficulty and interrelate the values of all countries, an index is estimated for each of the three indicators, with a maximum and a minimum value derived from all the countries included, hence, the index's range is from 1 for the best to 0 for the worst. Each index contributes one-third to the HDI value, which is calculated by adding the three indices, and then dividing the result by three (equal weights). Based on the HDI, countries are classified in three groups (high, medium and low) and numerically ranked from the best performer (1, the highest) to the worst (174, the lowest).

The HDI favors Cuba because the island has performed quite well in the social indicators (health care and education), which have double weight, compared with the economic indicator on which Cuba has not had a good performance and has a single weight. Of course, this also applies to other countries in the region, like Costa Rica and Uruguay, which, as pointed out above, have invested considerable resources in developing their social services. The crisis of the 1990s, however, not only caused a sharp decline in Cuba's GDP, but also harmed several social indicators (Mesa-Lago 1998, 2000, 2001b).

THE DECLINE AND JUMP OF CUBA IN THE HDI RANKING

Table 1 shows Cuba's rank in the HDI, among all countries in the world and among Latin American countries. The first column of the table indicates the publication year, and the second column, the information year of the HDI.[3] In 1989, before the crisis, Cuba occupied the 61st place among 160 countries in the world, and the 9th place among the 20 Latin American countries. In 1991, when the economic crisis began, Cuba fell to the 89th place among 174 countries, and to the 12th place in the region. Even though the crisis worsened in 1992 and 1993, Cuba climbed, according to the HDI, to the 72nd and 79th places in the world, and the 11th in the region. In 1994, the decline of Cuba's GDP stopped, and in 1995 Cuba began a slight economic recovery, prompted by modest market-oriented reforms initiated in 1993. However, the HDI had Cuba falling to the 85th/86th places in the world, and remaining in the 11th place in the region. During the decade of 1990s, Cuba's GDP growth rate peaked in 1996, but there is not HDI for that year.[4] In 1997-1998 Cuban economic growth decelerated but nevertheless, in 1997, Cuba's HDI jumped to 58th place in the world and to 9th place in the region, and in 1998 to 56th and 6th places, respectively. (It should be noted, nevertheless, that the values of the HDI and ranking before and after 1997 are not technically comparable due to a change in methodology, as will be explained in detail later). Cuba's HDI ranking in 1998 was significantly higher than in 1989. However, in 1998 Cuba's GDP was still 33% below the 1989 level, and

---

3. The first edition of the *Report*, published in 1990 with figures for 1985-1988, ranked the countries from lower to higher level of human development, while the second edition, published in 1991 with figures for 1980-1990, inverted the ranking from higher to lower level of human development, and also introduced other changes. The third edition used more standardized figures (1989-1990) and the following editions standardized all the figures in the same year. As this paper analyzes the changes for Cuba on the eve of and during the 1990 crisis, its tables start with the third edition of the *Report*.

4. Until 1998 there was a gap of three years between the publication of the HDI and the information used. Starting with the 1999 edition, that gap was reduced to two years, which led to the elimination of the year 1996.

a similar pattern applied to production of goods and services, with very few exceptions (Mesa-Lago 2001b). How did this miraculous jump occur? In order to explain that phenomenon it is necessary to analyze the three indicators that comprise the HDI.

Table 1. HDI Rank of Cuba in the World and Latin America: 1989-1999[a]

Human Development Index (Years)[b]		Number of countries in the world	Ranking[c]	
				Latin
Publication	Data		World	America
1992	1989	160	61	9
1993	1990	173	75	10
1994	1991	173	89	12
1995	1992	174	72	11
1996	1993	174	79	11
1997	1994	175	86	11
1998	1995	174	85	11
1999	1997	174	58	9
2000	1998	174	56	6
2001	1999	162	50-51[d]	5[d]

Source: UNDP 1991-2001a, 2001b.

a. Years refer to HDI data.
b. The ranking for the years 1989-1995 and 1997-1999 are not technically comparable due to a change in methodology in the 1999 *Report*.
c. The lower the rank number, the better the country's performance.
d. Unofficial rank (HDI website).

THE EXPLANATION OF THE CUBAN JUMP

Doubts on the Social Indicators

The first indicator (which contributes a third of the HDI value) is health care and it is measured by life expectancy at birth. In Latin America, Cuba has always ranked among the two or three leaders regarding this indicator and, in the 1990s, occupied the second place (after Costa Rica). Usually, life expectancy changes, though very slowly, from year to year, and this has occurred in Cuba (see ECLAC 2001b), therefore, this indicator cannot explain the jump in 1997. Moreover, the HDI series on life expectancy for Cuba shows various contradictions:

- for 1990 it reported 75.4 years in three consecutive editions;

- for 1992, it gave two different figures: 75.6 and 75.3. Based on the first one, there was an increase compared to 1990, but based on the second figure there was a decline;

- for 1993, it reported 75.4, which suggests that life expectancy stagnated at the 1990 level;

- for 1994, it reported 75.6, which can be interpreted either as stagnation or as a rise in relation to 1992, depending on what figure is used for 1992; and

- for 1995-1999, it showed a slight increase from 75.7 to 75.8.

For 1995 and 1997 the figure was the same (75.7)[5] and this indicator index (for Cuba related to all the countries) remained unchanged at 0.84 (UNDP 1991-2000). This last point confirms that this indicator cannot explain the 1997 miraculous jump.

The Human Development Report Office in New York (HDRO 2002) disagreed with my conclusion for the following reasons: (1) "it is not correct to compare data estimated with refined methodologies;" (2) "lack of data for Cuba didn't allow enough adjustment through the years," and (3) "fluctuations is not a sign of data contradiction neither of doubt upon their accuracy." I do agree with the last comment but my analysis shows significant contradiction in HDI estimates for 1992, and the most important point (not addressed by the HDRO) is that there was no increase of life expectancy in 1995-1997 hence this indicator could not explain Cuba's jump in the HDI value for 1997. Actually a comparison of the years 1995 and 1997 done in the 1999 *Report* showed a *decline* of 2 points between these years (UNDP 1999: 165).

The second indicator—which contributes another third of the HDI value—is education. This indicator combines two variables, the first of which is the adult literacy rate (population older than 15 years); this variable contributes two thirds of the value of the education indicator. In the 1990s, Cuba ranked third

5. A study of the HDI conducted in Cuba gives a life expectancy of 74.7 in 1998 (CIEM 2001:146) compared to 75.8 given by the HDI (UNDP 2000).

in the region (after Uruguay and Argentina) on this variable and yet, only about 4% of the population is illiterate and it is very difficult to reduce this level, particularly in single years. For the year 1985 the HDI rating for Cuba was 96% later reduced to 92.4%; based on the first figure there was stagnation by 1998 (96.4%) but based on the second figure there was an increase (deterioration) of 4 percentage points. Since 1990 (94%) there was constant growth in this variable, but the increase in 1995-1997 was only two tenths of a percentage point: from 95.7% to 95.9% (UNDP 1990-1999), which does not seem to explain Cuba's great leap forward in 1997. The HDRO (2002) repeated the first argument summarized on the life expectancy indicator but, once again, did not address the major point: the minute increase in literacy in 1995-1997 could not explain the jump of Cuba in the HDI in 1997. (The comparison between 1995 and 1997 showed no change in these years; UNDP 1999: 165).

The second variable of the education indicator is the percentage of school-age population enrolled in the three educational levels (see first three columns of Table 2). In Cuba, elementary instruction was already available to the whole population since the end of the 1960s and, based on official data the gross enrollment rate was 100% in 1989.[6] Since 1990-1991, however, that rate began to decrease and was 99.3% in 1992 and 99.1% in 1999 (ONE 1998, 2000). According to UNESCO (2001), Cuba reached the highest percentage of coverage at the secondary level in 1989 with 90.2%, then decreased to 74.5% in 1994 and increased to 80% in 1996-1997, still 10 percentage points below the 1989 level.[7] Enrollment in higher education dropped 56% in 1989-1999 (CEE 1991, ONE 2000); the gross rate was 20.5% in 1989 (21.8% in 1987; UNESCO 2001) and de-

clined to 12.4% in 1996-1997 (this continuing decline is acknowledged by CIEM 2000). Given that primary and higher education gross enrollment rates fell almost without interruption in 1989-1997, and that the rate of secondary education in 1997 was well below the 1989 level, the combined rate of the three levels must have fallen in that period.

Table 2. Enrollment in the Three Levels of Education According to Cuba/UNESCO and the HDI: 1989-1999[a]

Information Year	Cuba Primary	UNESCO Secondary	UNESCO Higher	HDI: 3 levels combined
1989	100.0	90.2	20.5	a
1990	99.7	88.9	20.9	a
1991	99.8	85.7	19.8	a
1992	99.3	81.8	18.1	65
1993	99.5	76.7	16.7	65
1994	99.2	74.5	13.9	63
1995	99.7	79.8	12.7	66
1996	99.4	80.8	12.4	n.a.
1997	99.3	80.0	12.4	72
1998	99.3	n.a.	n.a.	73
1999	99.1	n.a.	n.a.	76

Source: HDI from UNDP 1992-2001a. Cuba: primary from ONE 1998-1999, secondary and higher years 1989-1999 from UNESCO 1999, 2001; the year 1997 is an estimate of the author (based on ONE 1998) to allow for a comparison with the same year from the HDI.

a. In these years, a different indicator was used (average years of schooling) that cannot be connected with the subsequent indicator.

Unfortunately, the HDI does not have a consistent series on the three combined educational levels for 1989-1999: in the first three years it used average years of schooling, but since 1992 it shifted to the school enrollment rate and the two cannot be connected.[8] The last column of Table 2 shows the decline of the combined gross enrollment rate for the three levels of education in 1992-1994, estimated by

6. In fact, in 1970-1985 the percentage exceeded 100% since there was not a perfect matching between enrollment and school-age population at the primary level (UNESCO 2001).

7. A study of the HDI done in Cuba acknowledges that "the secondary level is the most problematic of the Cuban educational system" and there was "a slight decline in the 1993-94 and 1994-95 years, but recovered in the following two years" (CIEM 2000: 82; author's translation). However, the 1989 level had not been recovered by 1997.

8. It is not possible to compare HDI and Cuba/UNESCO figures because the *Report* of the HDI does not publish gross enrollment rates separately but the combined rate of the three levels. The study of the HDI done in Cuba does not offer separate series of those rates, either, but only the rates of two levels for a year (CIEM 2000).

the HDI, which agree with the figures from Cuba and UNESCO. The HDI, however, shows an enormous jump in the combined rate between 1995 and 1999—from 66% to 76%—in contrast with the official data from Cuba for primary education, which show a decrease from 99.7% to 91.1% (due to its two-third weight, the primary level enrollment variable largely determines the trend of the enrollment variable within the education indicator). There is also a contradiction between the increase in the combined enrollment rate and the decline of the higher education enrollment rate: from 12.7% to 12.4% in 1995-1997 according to UNESCO. With regard to the secondary enrollment, it is true that there was an increase in 1995-1997, according to UNESCO, but the 1997 level was 10 points below the 1989 level. The HDRO (2002) concurred with this conclusion: "The combined education ratio does not confirm the Cuban official data. This is a very important issue that we are continuously facing."

In summary, the health care indicator (life expectancy) shows remarkable contradictions that raise doubts about its reliability. Within the education indicator, the literacy variable is rather consistent but cannot explain Cuba's miraculous jump in the HDI ranking in 1997. Finally, the combined enrollment rate data used in the HDI for the three educational levels conflicts with the official figures from Cuba and UNESCO.

The Questionable Calculations of the Economic Indicator

The economic indicator, which contributes one third to the HDI, is the GDP p/c PPP US$. It is the most complex and difficult to analyze. In 1995 Cuba shifted from the MPS to the SNA, and began publishing GDP adjusted by inflation (with 1981 as the base year) going back to 1985, so that there is a GDP series for 1989-2000. This change corrected some of the explained problems of the MPS (overestimation, underestimation and impossibility of connecting di-

verse series), but did not solve the adjustment to inflation and the conversion to PPP dollars.

Cuba's two main statistical agencies (ONE and BCC) have never released information about the way GDP is adjusted to inflation, including the methodology for the elaboration of the consumer price index (CPI), the GDP deflator, the basket of goods and services used to measure inflation, and the weights assigned to price changes of the latter. In addition, after two decades, the year 1981 is still used as the base for the series of GDP in constant prices, in spite of the criticisms made about the anomaly of that year, and the universal practice of periodically updating the base year.[9] Moreover, in 1992-1994 inflation escalated (reaching a historical record of 25.7% in 1993), which might have affected the series. Last but not least, the adjustment does not take into account the very high prices of goods sold in state dollar shops, parallel official markets, free agricultural markets and black market. According to a Cuban estimate, the CPI increased 1,552% in those markets in 1989-1993 (CIEM 2000) and therefore inflation must have been much higher than the official estimates.

With regard to the conversion from peso to dollars, Cuba's official exchange rate is one peso for one dollar, but the exchange rate in the black market reached 95 pesos for one dollar in 1994, while the state exchange agencies (CADECA) established in 1995 paid 32 pesos for one dollar in that year and 21 pesos in 1998 (see Table 3, last column). The worst problem is how to calculate the purchasing power parity (PPP) of the peso, since Cuba does not publish the statistics that are necessary to estimate such value. It should be noted that *Investigación sobre desarrollo humano y equidad en Cuba 1999,* a long and impressive study on human development made in Cuba under UNDP sponsorship, simply reproduced the HDI figures, and did not explain how Cuba's GDP p/c PPP US$ was estimated (CIEM 2000).

---

9. ECLAC's recently-released note on Cuba for 2001 (ECLAC 2002) published GDP at constant prices of 1997, but only for 2001, making impossible to connect that year with the previous series at 1981 prices.

In conclusion, based on the discussion above and my experience accumulated over 40 years of studying and analyzing Cuban statistics (see Mesa-Lago 2001a), I believe that it is impossible to estimate Cuba's GDP p/c PPP US$. So, how did the HDI calculate it?

Table 3. Estimates of GDP per Capita in Dollars in the HDI and Cuba: 1989-1999

Information Year	HDI[a]	Cuba Official[b]	Unofficial[c]
1989	2,500	1,976	6
1990	2,200	1,787	7
1991	2,000	1,580	20
1992	3,412	1,386	35
1993	3,000	1,172	78
1994	3,000	1,175	95
1995	3,100	1,201	32
1997	3,100	1,317	23
1998	3,967	1,327	21
1999	4,224	1,405	20

Source: HDI from UNDP 1992-2001a. Cuba official from CCE 1991, ONE 1998 and 2000, BNC 2001; unofficial from ECLAC 2001a.

a. GDP p/c PPP US$; the years before and since 1997 may not be comparable.
b. GDP p/c adjusted for inflation and converted to dollars at the official exchange rate of one peso per one dollar (not PPP).
c. Annual average. For 1990-1994, refers to black market rates; for 1995-1999, refers to rates in state-operated exchange houses.

The first column of Table 3 shows estimates of GDP p/c PPP US$ from the HDI while the second column exhibits the corresponding Cuban figures (GDP p/c, adjusted for inflation and converted to dollars based on the official exchange rate—one peso equal to one dollar); it must be noted, nevertheless, that these two sets are not technically equal. Furthermore, the HDRO (2002) warns: "it is not correct to present the progress of HDI by collecting data from different reports and build a table for evaluation. Should a comparison be possible, it is by using Table 2 of the *Report* where the HDI is computed with the same methodology through years." And yet this recommendation is unfeasible because the tables of the *Report* that show trends with the same methodology in various years (1975, 1980, 1985, 1990 and 1997/98) don't offer any data on Cuba (UNDP 1999:151-158; 2000:178-185; and 2001a:145-148). The *Report* for 1999 is the only one that offers a partial comparison, giving the HDI values for 1995 (old) and 1997 (new), as well as the changes in points of all indicators and Cuba's ranking for those two years (but not the values). The HDI value for 1995 based on the old methodology (1998 *Report*) is repeated, but no figure is provided for said value in 1995 under the new methodology, as it is done in most countries including the large majority in Latin America (UNDP 1999: 165).[10] Granted that Table 3 is affected by the explained problem, still it offers the only available comparison and shows significant differences between the two estimates.[11]

The HDI shows a decline in the economic indicator of 20% in 1989-1991, corresponding to the economic crisis, but an increase of 71% in 1992 when the crisis was worsening, as well as a decrease of 12% in 1993 when the crisis reached its worst point. For 1989-1993 the HDI figures indicate an *increase* (improvement) of 20%, while the Cuban figures indicate a *decrease* of 41%. For 1993 the Cuban figure was 61% lower than the HDI figure. In 1989-1999, according to the HDI, there was an *increase* of 69% in the economic indicator but, based on Cuban data, there was a *decrease* of 29%. For 1999, Cuba's figure was 67% lower than the HDI figure. All previous Cuban figures are based on the official exchange rate. Although is not technically appropriate to estimate Cuba's GDP based on the unofficial exchange rate, it is obvious that if that conversion were made, GDP would be substantially lower than if based on the of-

---

10. Another anomaly in the HDI comparison is the change in rank: in the year 1995 Cuba was ranked in the 85th place and in the year 1997 was ranked in 58th place, for an improvement of 27 positions, but the 1999 *Report* gave an improvement of 26 positions (UNDP 1999: 165).

11. It should be noted that the 1990-1996 Cuban figures were not published until 1998, because Cuba's statistical yearbook (*Anuario Estadístico de Cuba*) suspended its publication in 1991 (the 1989 issue) and did not resume it until 1998 (CCE 1991 and ONE 1998). Therefore, the 1992-1997 editions of the *Report*, which gave figures for the years 1990-1994, did not have available published Cuban data for those years.

ficial exchange rate of one peso equal to one dollar. The last column of Table 3 shows the unofficial exchange rate, which differs significantly from the official rate.

Could the differences between the HDI and the Cuban data be explained based on the purchasing power parity (PPP) of the peso? Leaving aside that currently it is impossible to estimate Cuba's PPP, in my opinion the answer to that question is negative, due to three reasons: (1) the large gap between both figures; (2) the depreciation of the peso vis-à-vis the dollar (at the unofficial exchange); and (3) the loss of purchasing power of the pesos due to high inflation. The Cuban Central Bank argued in 1996, however, that the value of the free social services provided to the population (health care, education, social security) combined with subsidized prices of rationed goods equaled 50% of the monetary value of GDP. If we accept this argument for the sake of the comparison, GDP would be 2,108 in 1999 at the official exchange rate, that is, half the HDI figure.

How did the HDI estimate GDP p/c PPP US$ without having the needed essential statistics from Cuba? To answer that question it is necessary to undertake a tedious exercise referring to the notes that appear in several editions of the *Report* explaining how the estimate was done. In the 1995 edition the note reads: "Preliminary update of the Penn World Tables using an expanded set of international comparisons, as described in Summers and Heston 1991."[12] When that source is checked, however, a serious omission and two unsolvable obstacles are found:

- Cuba does not appear among the 138 countries (including the other 19 Latin American countries) for which the authors did the estimate of GDP p/c PPP US$;

- the PPP methodology requires prices of between 400 and 700 goods, services and labor inputs, as well as expenses for 150 detailed GDP categories, which do not appear in Cuba's statistical publications (there are no surveys done by foreign experts either); and

- the estimates presented by Summers and Heston refer to the period 1970-1988, when Cuba used the MPS instead of the SNA, which makes even more difficult the estimation (these problems were noted in Mesa-Lago 1998).

In the 1996 edition, the corresponding footnote in the *Report* gave as a source for the GDP p/c PPP US$: the World Bank, *World Bank Atlas 1995* (Washington D.C., 1994:18-19). This source, however, did not show a figure for Cuba in the referenced table; a footnote, however, gave a broad range of between $696 and $2,785. The HDI settled for $3,000, that is, a figure outside the range but arguably the result of rounding upward the figure at the top of the range, but it does not explain how that was done.[13] In the 1997 edition, the explanation given in the footnote was the same as in 1995. The 1998 and 1999 editions gave as general source "calculated on the basis of estimates from World Bank" (1997 and 1999 respectively) but excluded Cuba with the following footnote: "Human Development Report Office estimates" (UNDP 1998:129-130; 1999:135-137). In those two years it was decided by the HDRO not to give an external source and take the responsibility for the estimate, but without explaining how it was done. This was revealed in the 2000 edition, where a specific note said: "As GDP per capita (PPP US$) is not available for Cuba, the sub-regional weighted average of the Caribbean was used" (UNDP 2000:160).

12. The complete citation is Robert Summers and Alan Heston, "Penn World Tables (Mark 5): An Expanded Set of International Comparisons, 1950-1988," *Quarterly Journal of Economics*, 106 (1991): 327-368.

13. The World Bank, *World Atlas 1996* (Washington D.C., 1996:19) gave a range from 726 to 2,895 for Cuba in 1994, and the HDI estimated 3,000. The *World Atlas 1997* (Washington D.C., 1997: 36-37) gave a range from 766 to 3,035 for Cuba in 1995, and the HDI estimated 3,100. In both cases the HDI estimate was higher than the higher figure of the World Bank's range for Cuban GDP p/c PPP US$.

Not only the average used is absurd because of the differences between Cuba and the rest of the Caribbean, but also it is not specified which countries were included in the estimate. In 1998, five English-speaking Caribbean countries (Bahamas, Barbados, Saint Kitts and Nevis, Antigua and Barbuda, and Trinidad and Tobago) had a GDP p/c PPP US$ that ranged from 12,000 to 7,500, which situated them in the high or medium superior groups of the HDI, and, therefore, much higher than Cuba's 3,967. Moreover, six other countries of this group (Suriname, Dominica, Grenada, Belize, Saint Vincent and Saint Lucia) had a GDP p/c PPP US$ higher than Cuba's (from 5,161 to 4,566), and only two had a slightly lower GDP p/c PPP US$: Guyana (3,403) and Jamaica (3,389). The Dominican Republic also had a GDP p/c PPP US$ higher than Cuba's (4,589) and only Haiti, the poorest country in the region and the only one in the lowest group, had a GDP p/c PPP US$ lower than Cuba's (1,389). The arithmetic average of the GDP for these 15 countries was 6,586, that is, 66% higher than the estimate for Cuba. The HDI used a weighted average, probably based on the population size of the countries, to make the 3,967 estimate for Cuba. This average resulted from the fact that almost all of the Caribbean countries have very small populations (from 38,000 to 307,000 inhabitants), except three: Jamaica (2.6 million), Haiti (8.4 million) and Dominican Republic (8.5 million), so that the higher relative weight of these three countries determined to a great extent the "Caribbean" average that was used to impute a value for Cuba.

Summing up, the doubts about the two social indicators explained in the previous section paled compared to the problems with the economic indicator, and both discussions demonstrate that Cuba's HDI has been estimated in a faulty manner.

THE PARTIAL EXCLUSION OF CUBA FROM THE HDI

Perhaps as a result of the shortcomings analyzed in the previous two sections, the 2001 edition of the *Report* excluded Cuba (together with 11 other countries) from the HDI master table, as well as from other key tables, due to the "lack of reliable data." Table 28 of the *Report* included Cuba in "Basic Indicators

for other UN Member Countries" not included in the master and other tables, and gave ten social indicators, excluding GDP p/c PPP US$. The website version of the *Report* also provided in one table in an addendum, socioeconomic statistics on Cuba and the other countries excluded from the HDI, but warned that these data "may be of varying quality and may not be directly comparable to those presented in the Report" (UNDP 2001b; this statement does not appear in the printed version UNDP 2001a). The addendum table did not show the GDP p/c PPP US$ either, but a footnote stated that "the Human Development Report Office estimate of the sub-regional weighted average of the Caribbean of $2,224(PPP US$) was used." Based on those indicators, the HDRO then proceeded to calculate Cuba's HDI and ranked that country between the 50th and the 51st places in the world (UNDP 2001b, website version), although Cuba and its ranking were excluded in the master table. This implied another advance in relation to 1998, and unofficially ranked Cuba in fifth place in Latin America. Surprisingly, all this information did not appear in the printed version of the *Report*.

After more than a decade, the *Report* acknowledges that Cuba's GDP p/c PPP US$ "is not available" and that its estimate is not comparable with data for the countries included in the HDI. This is done, however, for the years 1998-1999, when Cuba was already publishing extensive statistics (although still insufficient to do this estimate). It logically follows that all previous HDI estimates on Cuba's economic indicator were even more invalid, as either there were no statistics or the existing ones were less reliable. In fact, the 1999 and 2000 *Reports* published a series of GDP p/c in US$ for 1975-1997/98 that included all Latin American countries but excluded Cuba (UNDP 1999: 152; 2000: 179). Finally, the estimate of an average GDP for the Caribbean as proxy for Cuba does not specify which countries were included and appears as an artifice. If Cuban economic data are not reliable, why was a rugged, unfeasible and unreal estimate of the GDP p/c PPP US$ and Cuba's HDI world and regional ranks repeated for two years?

A METHODOLOGICAL CHANGE IN THE ECONOMIC INDEX CAUSED CUBA'S JUMP

We have discussed the deficiencies in the estimation of Cuba's social and economic indicators. But that nation's jump in the HDI ranking in 1997-1999 was essentially caused by a crucial change in the methodology used to estimate the economic index, which resulted in notable alterations in both the HDI values and the ranking of countries.

For the entire period 1989-1999, Cuba was never in the HDI high group: Argentina, Chile, Costa Rica and Uruguay consistently ranked in the high group, while Mexico, Venezuela, Colombia, Panama and Brazil were in the high or medium group depending on the year.[14] At the other end, Haiti was consistently in the low group, while Bolivia, Guatemala, Honduras, El Salvador and Nicaragua occasionally fell into that group or climbed to the medium group.[15] Cuba, Ecuador, Paraguay, Peru and the Dominican Republic consistently ranked in the medium group. In 1989-1995, Cuba was below Venezuela, Panama, Mexico and Colombia and, in 1991-1994, also below Ecuador. With the miraculous jump of 1997-1999, however, Cuba surpassed Ecuador and Brazil first, then Panama, Venezuela and Colombia, and finally, tied or surpassed Mexico. According to the 1999 tentative ranking, Cuba was in the upper edge of the medium group, only surpassed by the four countries in the high group. Next, we analyze the methodological change and its impact on the HDI and on Cuba's rank.

The estimation methodology of the GDP p/c PPP US$ index has been modified several times. In the 1994 to 1998 editions (1998 with information for 1995) the index was estimated with a formula that distinguished whether countries were below or above an income threshold that was the world average. Be-

ginning with the 1999 edition (with information for 1997), the estimation formula was changed, and this affected the values of the HDI and the ranking of the countries.[16] The 1999 *Report* stated in this regard: "Because of these changes, this year's HDI is not comparable with last year's. The improvements in methodology and data affect the HDI ranks of almost all countries ... A drop or rise in rank could be attributed to the change in methodology or data" (UNDP 1999:129).

This paper does not pass judgment on the merits or shortcomings of the new methodology, but only focuses on its impact on the estimates for Cuba. Assuming there were no changes in the two social indicators and as a result of the methodological change for the economic index, the countries with the highest GDP p/c PPP US$ (those in the high group) dropped in the economic index, and this negatively affected their HDI value and rank; countries in the medium-high group also fell in the economic index, as well as in the HDI value and rank. However, countries in the medium-middle, medium-low and low groups climbed in the economic index and the HDI value and rank. The HDI study done in Cuba concluded, after analyzing in detail the methodological change, that: "the new approach for treating income relatively favors, in the HDI estimate, the poorest countries, and penalizes the richest countries" (CIEM 2000:128; author's translation). Cuba benefited from this change, since in 1995 it was in the medium-middle group and the new formula caused a rise in its GDP p/c PPP US$ index, its HDI value, and its world and regional rankings.

The information for 1997 compared to that for 1995 (there are no data for 1996) shows that all Latin American countries increased their GDP p/c PPP US$ in *absolute* value, except Cuba, whose value stag-

---

14. In 1989-1995, when the high group was expanded in the HDI, but not in 1997-1999, when that group was considerably reduced.

15. In 1989-1990, when that group was larger.

16. This is a technical and complex aspect that cannot be analyzed in this article. With the 1994-1998 formula, if the GDP p/c PPP US$ of a country was below the average threshold, it was not adjusted. If it was above the average, it was adjusted with a discount. As income rose, the adjustment and the discount increased. Beginning with the 1999 edition (data from 1997 on), the threshold was eliminated, an income logarithm was used, and the discount decreased. For the differences between the two formulas see UNDP 1998: 107, and UNDP 1999: 127-130.

Table 4. **Opposite Impact of the Methodology Change on the HDI Indices, Value and Ranking of Brazil and Cuba: 1995 and 1997**

| Country | Year | Indices | | | | Rank | Absolute GDP p/c PPP US$ |
		Health	Education	GDP p/c PPP US$	HDI	World LA	
Brazil	1995	0.69	0.80	0.94	0.809	62 9	5.928
	1997	0.70	0.83	0.70	0.739	79 11	6.480
Cuba	1995	0.85	0.86	0.48	0.729	85 11	3.100
	1997	0.84	0.88	0.57	0.765	58 9	3.100

Source: UNDP 1998 and 1999.

nated, but ten countries declined in the corresponding economic *index* (i.e., the relative position of the countries vis-à-vis each other), while Cuba ascended. The four Latin American countries in the high group (Chile, Argentina, Uruguay and Costa Rica) considerably increased their GDP p/c PPP US$, but fell in the index, their HDI values and in their world rank, even though most of those countries also improved or maintained the level of their indices on the social indicators.[17] The same occurred with regard to the four Latin American countries in the medium group (Venezuela, Panama, Mexico and Colombia). On the contrary, Cuba slightly fell in the life expectancy index, slightly rose in the education index (incorrectly, as we have seen), and *did not change its absolute* GDP p/c PPP US$ but had a *significant jump in this index* and considerably improved its HDI value, hence leaped from 85th to 56th in world rank. Because of this, Cuba leapt over Brazil and Ecuador, which had increased their absolute GDP p/c PPP US$ but had markedly fallen in their economic index.

The opposite impact that the methodology change had on Brazil and Cuba is shown in Table 4, which compares—for 1995 and 1997—the three indices: health care (life expectancy, first column), education (literacy rates and enrollment in the three educational levels, second column), and economic (GDP p/c PPP US$, third column). To understand this table, three important aspects must be recalled: (1) indices interrelate all countries among each other (the best performer would score close to 1 and the worst close

to 0); (2) each of the three indices contributes a third to the HDI value; and (3) the higher the HDI index, the better the country and the higher its rank. For instance, in 1997, the top performing country (Canada, 1st) had a HDI index of 0.932 while the lowest country (Sierra Leone,174th) had 0.254. The *Report* warned that the years 1995 and 1997 should not be compared due to the methodological change of the economic index and UNRO also cautioned against comparing indices of various years, but there are no standardized indices for Brazil and Cuba in 1995 and 1997. Table 4, albeit affected by the methodological shift, offers the only feasible comparison available, which indicates the differing effect of the methodological change in the ranking of the two countries.

Comparing the health index in 1995 and 1997, Brazil improved (+0.01) and Cuba declined (-0.01), while in the education index both improved, Brazil slightly more (+0.03) than Cuba (+0.02). Therefore, in the two social indices, Brazil performed better than Cuba. In the economic index, however, Brazil notably declined (-0.24) while Cuba improved (+0.09), and these changes were the most important for the two countries. Brazil's drop and Cuba's rise in the economic *index*, however, are at odds with their *absolute* value, which is shown in the last column of Table 4: Brazil's GDP p/c PPP US$ increased 9% (from 5,928 to 6,480) while Cuba's remained the same (3,100 for both years). Therefore, the methodology change in the estimate of the economic index determined that Brazil's HDI value declined (-0.07)

17. Surprisingly, life expectancy at birth in 1995-1997 slightly declined in Chile, and a little bit more in Costa Rica, apparently due to a revision of previous estimates, but all the information available for both countries confirms that their life expectancy showed an increasing rise in 1980-2000 (ECLAC 2001a:12-13).

while Cuba's increased (+0.04). At the same time, this resulted in a drop of 17 positions in the world ranking of Brazil (from 62nd to 79th place) and a jump of 27 positions for Cuba (from 85th to 58th place), as well as in an inversion in their position in Latin America: Brazil fell from 9th to 11th place, while Cuba leaped from 11th to 9th.

The HDI study done in Cuba offers a serious and comprehensive analysis of the impact of the methodological change in the economic index on the ranking of the Latin America and Caribbean countries, separating such change from the effects that variations in other indicators may have had. That study concludes: "Cuba presents the largest positive difference (26 positions), exclusively explained by the change in the methodology to estimate the income" (CIEM 2000:128; author's translation). In other words, Cuba's jump from 85th to 58th place (the largest among 33 countries) was solely the result of the methodological change. Conversely, Brazil fell 17 points in the HDI ranking, and the Cuban study estimates that its descent from 62nd to 79th place occurred in spite of improvements in the social indicators, so that the methodology change was responsible for the drop of 19 positions (CIEM 2000:134).[18] The 1999 *Report* acknowledges that Cuba's improvement of 26 points and Brazil's decline of 19 points were "rank changes due to the refined methodology" (UNDP 1999: 165).

In 1998, the crises in Asia, Russia and other emerging economies, negatively affected economic growth in Latin America, and the vast majority of countries in the region suffered a decline in GDP p/c PPP US$, its index, the HDI values and the world rank. This happened in Panama, Venezuela and Colombia, countries that for many years were above Cuba in the HDI. Cuba, however, was one of the few countries that, according to the 2000 edition of the *Report*, experienced growth of its GDP p/c PPP US$—28% growth—a true miracle, particularly if we take into account that, according to official data, GDP p/c in-

creased only 0.8% (ONE 2001). Due to this anomaly, Cuba ascended in the economic index, the HDI value and its world rank, surpassing the three Latin American countries mentioned above. In the 2001 edition of the *Report*, although Cuba did not have a precise rank, it ascended even higher (the website version of the *Report* showed Cuba's position between the 50th and 51st places in the world), tying or leaving behind Mexico.

CONCLUSION

This paper demonstrates that the HDI estimate for Cuba in 1989-1999, as well as Cuba's rank in the world and Latin America, have been flawed for the following reasons: (1) the health indicator was based on a series on life expectancy that is inconsistent and contradictory; (2) the education indicator showed an ascending gross enrollment rate when its three components (i.e., educational levels) showed enrollments lower in 1991-1999 than in 1989; (3) the economic indicator was estimated despite the lack of the essential statistics, using spurious sources and, more recently, based on an inappropriate Caribbean average (the HDI estimated a GDP p/c PPP US$ increase of 69% in 1989-1999, while Cuban official GDP p/c adjusted for inflation and converted to US$ based on the official exchange rate decreased 29%); and (4) the methodological change for the estimation of the economic index in 1997 was solely responsible of Cuba's rise of 26 positions in the world ranking, even though in that year it was the only country in Latin America with a stagnant GDP p/c PPP US$ (for 1998, the HDI estimated a 28% growth in the GDP p/c PPP US$ even though the official GDP p/c adjusted for inflation increased only 0.8%).

The flawed data and methodology result in indexes that show Cuba surpassing Panama, Venezuela, Colombia and Brazil in the HDI ranking, countries that for many years were above Cuba in the world and regional rankings. In 2001 the *Report* excluded Cuba from the HDI, acknowledging that it does not offer reliable data and that its GDP p/c PPP US$ is not

---

18. It should be noted that the CIEM study defends Cuba's advances, criticizes the HDI methodology and proposes to replace it with a new Index of Human Development and Equity, in which Cuba would rank second among 23 countries of Latin America and the Caribbean.

available. Despite of this, the *Report* estimated Cuba's GDP p/c PPP US$ in 1999 (based on the Caribbean average) and raised Cuba in the ranking again, placing at the same level or above Mexico, and close to the upper edge of the medium group, only surpassed by the four countries in the high group.

The UNDP intends in the future "to include all UN member countries in the HDI exercise" (2001a:136). The HDRO (2002) made an effort, for the *Report* 2001 edition (joining forces with the World Bank and the University of Pennsylvania), to estimate Cuban GDP p/c PPP US$ but "it proved extremely difficult" and was unsuccessful. And yet HDRO reports

that for 2002 "we are again using our own estimate," which can be interpreted as repeating the faulty Caribbean average approach.

It is my hope that this paper makes UNDP officials more aware of the problems in Cuba's social indicators and helps to correct them. It would be advisable also to suspend the publication of all estimates of Cuba's GDP p/c PPP US$ until the necessary and reliable data become available. Last but not least, until those problems are solved, Cuba's HDI should not be calculated and that nation should not ranked within the world and within Latin America.

REFERENCES

Banco Central de Cuba (BCC). 2001. *Informe económico 2000*. La Habana: May.

Castañeda, Rolando. 2000. "Cuba y América Latina: Consideraciones sobre el nivel y la evolución del Índice de Desarrollo Humano y el gasto social ...", *Cuba in Transition—Volume 10*. Washington D.C.: ASCE, 234-253.

Centro de Investigaciones de la Economía Mundial (CIEM). 2000. *Investigación sobre el desarrollo y la equidad en Cuba 1999*. La Habana: Sponsored by UNDP.

Economic Commission for Latin America and the Caribbean (ECLAC). 2001a, 2002. *Cuba: Evolución económica durante 2000* and *2001*. México: LC/MEX/L/.465 and 525, May 21 and June 6.

Economic Commission for Latin America and the Caribbean (ECLAC). 2001b. *Statistical Yearbook for Latin America and the Caribbean 2000*. Santiago.

Comité Estatal de Estadística (CEE). 1991. *Anuario Estadístico de Cuba 1989*. La Habana.

Mesa-Lago, Carmelo. 1998. "Assessing Economic and Social Performance in the Cuban Transition of the 1990s," *World Development* 26: 5 (May 1998): 857-876.

Mesa-Lago, Carmelo. 2000. *Market, Socialist and Mixed Economies: Comparative Policy and Performance—Chile, Cuba and Costa Rica*. Baltimore: Johns Hopkins University Press.

Mesa-Lago, Carmelo.. 2001a. "The Resurrection of Cuban Statistics," *Cuban Studies*, 31: 139-150.

Mesa-Lago, Carmelo. 2001b. "The Cuban Economy in 1999-2001: Evaluation of Performance and Debate on the Future", *Cuba in Transition*. Washington D.C.: ASCE, 11: 1-17.

Mesa-Lago, Carmelo and Jorge Pérez-López. 1985. *A Study of Cuba's National Product System, its Conversion to the System of National Accounts, and Estimation of GDP Per Capita and Growth Rates*. Washington D.C.: World Bank Staff Working Papers, 770.

Oficina Nacional de Estadística (ONE). 1998, 1999, 2000, 2001. *Anuario Estadístico de Cuba 1996, 1997, 1999, 2000*. La Habana.

UNESCO. 2001. http://unescostat.unesco.org/en/stats/stats0.htm.

United Nations Human Development Report Office (HDRO). 2002. New York: Correspondence with the author, May 22.

United Nations Development Programme (UNDP). 1990 to 2001a. *Human Development Report 1990* to *2001*. New York: Oxford University Press.

United Nations Development Programme (UNDP). 2001b. *Human Development Report 2001* (web-site version). http://www.undp.org/hdr2001/Addendum4.pdf.

World Bank. 2001. World Development Report 2000/2001. New York: Oxford University Press.

A MODEL FOR THE ESTABLISHMENT OF A MARKET-DRIVEN SOFTWARE INDUSTRY IN A POST SOCIALIST CUBA

Joel C. Font

I have been involved in the computer industry in the United States for more than 12 years, ten of which have been as president of a company that has undergone three major metamorphic changes, from hardware distribution to networking and communications support, to software and Internet development. Recently, I began to think about how a viable market-driven software industry may be developed in Cuba after the departure of totalitarian socialism. Following are my very personal observations.

In 1916 my grandfather, Pedro Nolasco Font, a hard working Quaker and a recent accounting graduate, applied for a job with the Royal Bank of Canada, in one of its new branches in Oriente province, Cuba. Unsure of my grandfather's credentials, the branch manager instead offered him a position as "barrendero" or floor sweeper, with the stipulation that if he proved himself to be honest, timely, and good with numbers, he would be considered for the position. Needing to make money and not insulted by the Canadians, my grandfather accepted the job, which paid U.S. $24.00 dollars per month. After a short period, he proved his skills and went on to a career with the Royal Bank of Canada where in the 1920's he became a manager in the very same place he had started as floor sweeper.

This family story helps to bring perspective to the subject of this paper. First, it focuses attention to the incredible fact that the wages of a 1916 capitalist Cuban floor sweeper were higher than those of a worker in a state-run enterprise in modern day socialist Cuba. The political, social, and economic implications of this retardation have been widely discussed by objective scholars for quite some time now and you will find some of these in my reference materials. Secondly, it shows that in a competitive environment, an honest and hard working well-educated man, just like a business with good products and a rational business plan, usually succeed regardless of adversity. Finally, it clearly shows that before you can run, you have to take a few clumsy steps. This paper summarizes from the perspective of a businessman and a technologist, not an academician, some of the issues that may be faced if an internationally competitive software industry is to be established in a post socialist Cuba. It accepts that the potential exists for this phenomenon to occur even though the required social, political, and economic conditions needed are currently absent, and may not be in place for a while.[1]

COMPUTER SCIENTISTS ALONE ARE NOT ENOUGH

Before I begin to discuss Cuba, I will take you to Asia—India in particular. The experience of India in this context is important because it succeeded in lifting itself from a quasi-socialist technologically backward existence into a technologically advanced capi-

---

1. Betancourt, Roger R., 1999, "Cuba's Economic 'Reforms': Waiting for Fidel on the Eve of the 21st Century." *Cuba in Transition—Volume 9.* Washington: Association for the Study of the Cuban Economy, 276–281.

talist economy in about fifteen years. And, yes I see a connection to Cuba. Let me elaborate.

During a business trip to India in 1984, I noticed the effects of that country's maladjusted economic practices due to its enamorament with socialism. During this time, India's economy was in a strange socialist/capitalist transition. Those elements of its economy that brought in foreign exchange ran smoothly, based on a capitalist model, while most of its internal economy and domestic services where clearly socialist and stagnant. Bajaj motor scooters sold in the internal market were available to those who ordered them, paid for them, and then waited four years to receive them, since this was the "normal" production backlog that resulted from the government's centrally planned scheme. In the black market, Bajaj motor scooters could be obtained rapidly. The state-owned telephone system was ancient and still used obsolete equipment left over from the time of the British, ending in 1948. The average factory worker earned less than $60 per month.

Upon arriving at Delhi International Airport, all electronic equipment such as VCR's, Sony Walkmans, or electronic calculators were either taken by corrupt customs officials, or you where hit with "import" fees sometimes exceeding 400% of the value of the product. The most sought after electronic equipment in the major cities were portable electric generators because the power grid was antiquated and power generation insufficient, producing chronic power failures, spikes, and blackouts. This dilemma wreaked havoc with any type of industry that depended on steady electrical power. Indians lived with a maze of monetary laws designed to restrict the flow of capital, and discouraged the "encroachment" of domestic industries by foreign competitors. Respect by a large segment of the business community for foreign copyrights, patents, trademarks, and intellectual property was generally ignored, and most manufacturing concerns operated with great pride in their ability to copy or reverse engineer any product they could get their hands on. In response to these anomalies, the Indian government used to recite its laws, participation in international business forums, and commercial code, all of which, on paper, made India

a very appealing and rational place to do business. For those who wished to ignore reality, socialists or western visitors not responsible for dealing with the bureaucracy, Indian public relations and the romantic appeal of the Taj Mahal generally succeeded in making the place appear as an attractive environment for business. This dislocation with the facts on the ground reminded me of Cuba, where on paper the "socialist paradise" and the "eradication of inequality" gives it the appearance of being the most advanced and well balanced society on earth.

It was in this environment that a group of friends and I had dinner at the U.S. Embassy in New Delhi, with a group of Indian business people, engineers and government officials. The discussions centered on textile industry issues, which were my main focus at the time, and then it moved on to technology and computers, which to my surprise turned out to be their main interest. These far-sighted individuals had a good pulse on their country's movement towards full-fledged capitalism, upcoming trends in the global economy and the eventual bankruptcy of socialism—and believed in these things so strongly that they where about to resign their positions in government to start an entrepreneurial company importing computers from the United States.

Their business plan as outlined to us focused on the following: (1) India was at least ten years behind the rest of the world in computer technology. This meant that if they were to import foreign technology that was five years old by Western standards, their company would still be considered "cutting edge" in their domestic market; (2) Since their government had protectionist policies in place to keep out foreign companies, they would incorporate as an Indian company, although most of their operations were to occur in overseas "branches" whose operating costs were to be kept as high as possible in order to legally transfer profits out of the country; (3) Since the government had import duties and a tax system discouraging to their plans and focused on consumer electronics, they planned to disassemble computers in Abu Dhabi (in the Persian Gulf), then import the components to India at a lower tariff to be later reassembled using local labor as needed; (4) Immediately begin to cultivate local spheres of influence in academia and selected key local governments that would support the development of future educational programs generating the trained technicians needed to support the influx of software and hardware products brought in by their company; (5) Lobby their government for the establishment of liberal foreign investment laws and securities laws that would allow them to raise overseas venture capital to expand their operations in India in the future.

Of all the points discussed, I asked my Indian friends which one they considered to be the most important for the future of technology in their country. Without hesitation, they said it was the liberalization of foreign investment regulations, specifically the ability of Indian companies to attract and compete for foreign capital without fear of government intervention or the imposition of "centrally planned" policies in the technology sector. In other words, they wanted to operate in a classical capitalist open market environment, generate as much wealth as possible regardless of where in the world they had to do it, constantly adjust strategies in order to avoid excessive tariffs or taxation, and seek foreign capital to do it—period. To my surprise, the answer had little to do with computer programming, networking technology, or the acquisition of compilers or microprocessors. They felt technicians and programmers were important issues, but not a central concern because their assessment of India's private technical schools and English speaking curriculums at the University level led them to conclude that within five years the country would be producing large numbers of highly trained computer scientists who would then react to the market "appropriately."

There is no need to outline for the reader the indisputable success of today's India as a world class intellectual and technology power, especially in the field of software. It is also clear that this leap from third world to first world technology only began to exert

itself after India abandoned its socialist pretensions, interestingly done after the fall of the Soviet Union, and after an analysis of globalization found a niche that could be attacked based on its already existing institutions and human capital. Before India became a computer science contender it had to substantially change its socio-political structures to the point where international investors could begin to think of its markets and legal systems as worthy of confidence and a place where returns on investments could be calculated without the perpetual Latin American question of "what will the next government do?" In the end, India's elites and its government understood the forces of globalization and became active partners in the development of a modern economic infrastructure, giving the technology sector all the prerequisites needed to succeed.[2]

Early in the transition from socialism to capitalism, Cuba will find itself with the rare opportunity India had in the mid-1980's. The way Cuba's elites and government analyze the global marketplace, the way they decide to channel existing intellectual capital, and how they re-structure the commercial, legal and monetary systems will determine whether the country can become a serious contender in the global software industry and technology in general. Like in India, if the right decisions are made, a transformation of the economic landscape can occur in a relatively short time.

The nature of the technology sector demands quick decisions and actions. The technology world is re-invented every seven to 12 months, and the exchange of ideas across national boundaries is instantaneous due to the Internet. The flow of capital towards "worthy" projects is no longer tightly controlled by bankers with political agendas, but by venture capitalists with an eye for first mover positions and maximum returns.[3] A successful software development industry needs competition, the unencumbered flow of information, people, ideas, capital, and products—

---

2. American University, Washington D.C. 2001. Information Technology Landscape in Nations. http://www.american.edu/academic.depts/ksb/mogit/country.html

3. Milken, Michael, 2000. "The Democratization of Capital." *California Lawyer* (July, 2000).

things not associated with socialism or the current government of Cuba. Therefore, trying to analyze the potential for a software industry in Cuba, based only on technology issues, is the wrong approach. The challenge for the future is not so much whether Cuba can create 100,000 software programmers, 50,000 networking engineers, or 25,000 systems analysts.[4] The challenge for Cuba is what to do with them. How does the society compete internationally for their loyalty? How does it stimulate their creativity, and how can it generate confidence with those international investors and venture capitalists whose money will be needed to fuel the growth of the technology sector?

WHERE IS THE OPPORTUNITY FOR CUBA?

Cuba's opportunity in software lies in these four areas: First, by exploiting the inefficiencies and lack of technology infrastructure endemic in Latin America. Second, by exploiting the demand that is developing for Spanish language software in the U.S. market, created by the growing Hispanic population. Third, as an offshore Spanish and English language software development center for established world-class technology companies. And fourth, by exploiting the existing business connections held by Cuban exiles in the U.S. Cuba's goal should be no less than to become the premier software development center of Latin America.

Such pretentious goals from a small non-English speaking country so far behind the rest of the world in technology can be achieved due to the following reasons:

- the competition from other Latin American countries is poor, inconsistent and disorganized, and not likely to improve in the future. Countries like Argentina, Peru, Chile, and Brazil, have software industries, but aside from Chile, lack consistency and sophistication in their efforts.[5] I hold this view as a businessman, and I realize a great many people, especially natives of these

countries, will disagree with me. But my interest in writing this paper is not to win a popularity contest;

- Even though Cuba's intellectual and technical cadres are not experienced in market economics, there may already exist enough of an elite to staff a good number of seed companies that will "spawn" self-sustaining viable enterprises;

- The demand for Spanish language software is growing steadily in Latin America as the use of computers in the Hispanic world increases, and this trend is not likely to decrease;

- Just like there is "market segmentation" for television, radio, and mass media in the U.S. market focusing products on the "Hispanic market", segmentation for software, Internet, and other technology products and services will likely occur;

- There exists a sizable Cuban exiled population with experience in "capitalism" in the United States, Latin America, and Europe that can serve as future conduits for capital, ideas, technical expertise, and distribution channels for these new companies;

- It is likely that there will be strong demand in the domestic Cuban market for vertical software solutions after the departure of socialism, opening the door for home grown developers to "practice" or launch many "version 1.0" type products prior to venturing into the international arena;

- It is very likely that software development costs and associated expenses in Cuba will be substantially lower than those of the developed world, including places like India;

- The physical proximity of Cuba to the United States, and the quality of life benefits of the tropics may facilitate the attraction of high quality

4. Valdés, Nelson P. and Rivera, Mario A., 1999. "The Political Economy of the Internet in Cuba." *Cuba in Transition—Volume 9.* Washington: Association for the Study of the Cuban Economy, 141–154 .

5. World Information Technology and Services Alliance, 2002. Official Website. http://www.witsa.org

young foreign talent to Cuba, needed to create the dynamism of the technology sector;

- The post socialist Cuban government may continue to support "incubator" programs matching up promising young entrepreneurs with sales and marketing expertise, and seed capital;

- Foreign venture capital may be attracted by establishing venture capital brokerages in Cuba, the U.S., and other countries devoted to raising capital for the Cuban technology sector; and

The Cuban diplomatic network can be used as an instrument of world commerce, similar to the Japanese model, which gathers market intelligence, product samples, consumer behaviors, and merger and acquisition targets in a rational program to acquire new markets and increase share in newly created ones. Since Cubans have proven to be good political spies, they may also turn out to be good business spies.

Some of these things can be done by the private sector alone; some have to be done by the government, while others will require a private/public partnership. The opportunity for "Cuba, Inc." is there. It just has to be taken when the right time comes.

WHAT WILL THE CUBAN SOFTWARE INDUSTRY LOOK LIKE IN A CAPITALIST ENVIRONMENT?

Cuban software companies in a post socialist Cuba will hopefully look like their counterparts everywhere else in the world. Software development companies do not require conveyor belts, 300 lbs per square inch floors, loading docks, or chimneys in their facilities. A well-lit pleasant room with a personal computer network, access to the Internet, some technical manuals, and proximity to some pizza and soft drinks are all that is needed. In Cuba, of course, the pizza will be substituted with "tamales" and "croquetas." Two or three proficient developers can work on a multimillion-dollar project for six to eight months, and, in the end, their only environmental impact is the crunched up paper they leave behind, some floppies, some Styrofoam cups, and a hole in the wall created by the fist of one of the developers when he got frustrated after accidentally deleting two weeks worth of work.

Most software development companies in the United States and the world are classified as small to mid-sized businesses, in terms of the number of people employed. There are of course giants, like Microsoft, Computer Associates, Lotus, Adobe, etc., employing hundreds or thousands of developers, but generally most software companies operate with less than 25 people. In the vertical software area, the trend is towards even smaller companies with six to ten people being the norm. Valuing or trying to understand a software company by the number of employees is spurious. The importance and value of the economic activity undertaken by a software company is completely disproportional to the number of people involved in it. After the product is created, its sales and marketing are further divorced from the development process, often creating great fluctuations in the number of people involved in the cycle. It is often described as an "accordion strategy" in personnel management, where you bring in specific expertise for a defined period of time. When the project is done, certain people leave and others may come. To clarify for those unfamiliar with this process, let me just say that there are no labor unions involved in the software industry and none are likely to appear in the near future. Both employee and employer recognize the need to cross-pollinate, and maintain free agent status in order to increase the value of one's work, although this has eroded the remnants of the old concept of "corporate allegiance" that existed during our parents' generation.

The culture of the software industry around the world is very similar, and not likely to develop differently in a post socialist Cuba. It is generally non-political, youth-oriented, challenging of authority, and viciously focused on the pursuit of intellectual problem solving. It is a meritocracy that is used to making a lot of money, doing things that make others a lot of money, and living in a cocoon where most things are judged based on their importance to technology. Twenty-four year old U.S.-based developers earning $65.00 to $150.00 per hour with expense accounts, operate with an incredible amount of mobility and make decisions about taking on projects in Los Angeles, London, Toronto, or Sydney, with incredible speed. Respect among your peers is judged by your proficiency in C++, Visual Basic, Java, Lotus Script, .Net, SQL, BizTalk, HTML, or XML. The culture of software development is refreshingly based on an individual's ability to deliver regardless of his/her social or ethnic origin, with little room for "faking" knowledge. And, its casualness seems to repel individuals with presumptuous personalities. The Cuban male character depicted in popular culture, with his "macho" and "simpatico womanizer" skills, doesn't fit in very well.

After a short period of time, the Cuban software industry will begin to mimic and catch up with the rest of the world. Cuban nerds will look like American nerds, Irish nerds and Indian nerds. A Cuban software company will have six to ten people in a loft building in Havana, or Holguín, near a technical school or college, or in an area of attraction to intellectually inclined youth—and this company will be part of a small hub of other companies that will feed each other with new ideas, fear of competition, and talent. There will be sales and marketing companies who may act as exclusive agents to these software companies in certain vertical markets, advertising companies, graphics companies, and an active venture capital marketplace keeping an eye open for new products and aggressive growth opportunities.

Most software development companies will also be working in the Internet development area since the two areas are about to merge and the differences will soon blur. Many of these companies will simply do contract work for U.S.-based software companies who will act as ladders for local developers who want to enter the U.S. market. There will be many free agents whose skills will allow them to work for several companies at the same time without conflicts. Slowly, a legal and accounting specialty will develop to support the special needs of these active elite. Freelancers may work for $10 to $20 dollars an hour, with contract houses subbing out talent to overseas clients at $15 to $45 per hour, the current range in places like India, with certain specialties fetching more.

Because of the nature of the industry, the average software company will be more in tune with globalization issues and the needs of the international mar-

ketplace than most other sectors of the Cuban economy, including the government. And because of the industry's mobility and its relative high level of education, its members are likely to exert strong influence over certain segments of the political structure. After the industry is established, any perceptions viewed as detrimental to its technical and merit based subculture and economic stability are not likely to be welcomed. The technology sector in Cuba may become one of the pillars of capitalism and a deterrent against bad government. The speed in which a laptop with code for a $25 million dollar product can be folded and moved to Miami or Barcelona by its owner should restrain future Cuban policy makers from acting in ways that will disturb Cuba's integration in the global economy. Fold ten laptops and an entire industry is gone. Confiscate the laptops, and there's always the Internet. It is unlikely that there will be many other sectors of the Cuban economy with the potential promised by the software industry. It will also be a bit of a novelty for the average Cuban used to the socialist concept of production and industry to adjust to a group of people whose schedules will be erratic, compensations will be based on non-standard formulas, and their main activity and products disappear when a switch is turned off. Unlike anything Cubans have experienced during the Castro years, the software industry in Cuba will have to function based on open market pressures, and supply and demand.

VERTICAL SOFTWARE OR RETAIL

Vertical software is the most direct way to start the industry in Cuba. The retail market is too costly to crack, it requires a huge investment in time, and worldwide consumer electronics companies that squash small competitors like they were flies dominate it. It is better to get started by not competing against Microsoft. As the industry matures it will inevitably find its way to the world's software retail markets.

Vertical software development and sales is a business-to-business activity where a client/server software application (software developed to run on a computer network) or an Internet service is custom-developed for a particular company or industry with the plan of reselling it to others with similar need. This type of product usually fulfills a particular niche or high value workflow that cannot be easily resolved by off-the-shelf or retail software. Because of this, most vertical software in the United States is very expensive ranging in price from $25,000 to $100,000 per client—and often exceeding $250,000 for multi-site installations. These expenditures are justifiable in light of the fact that these products' use often releases dozens of employees, who are paid an average of $40,000 per year, to handle similar workflows manually or using antiquated systems.

The future of vertical software around the world will be highly impacted by the Internet and the Application Service Provider model (ASP), which brings to customers a rental approach to software rather than the current licensed sales model mentioned above. This model promises greater mass distribution due to lower prices and the reach of the Internet. The ASP business model is of benefit to both developer and client and should slowly replace the current model. The ASP model holds great promise in Latin America, especially in light of the fact that currently more than 80% of the software in use there is stolen or pirated. Encrypted ASP software running on a web browser is very difficult to steal.

The process of pricing vertical software products often has little to do with the costs of development. Profits of several hundred percent are normal since price is driven by demand, and the fact that such a product has to be customized signifies that there is likely to be no other like it anywhere else. In Latin America, wages are lower and vertical software sells for less; nevertheless, the profit ratios are similar and the formula for success is the same.

Developing vertical software is easier said than done. It is something that requires a lot of work, an understanding of the markets in question, and a special sales and marketing approach unique to the vertical sales cycle which is often very long. A particular type of intellectual mix needs to exist within the software development company, strong technical support, an ability to establish long-term relationships with clients who expect high quality consistent support, and enough reserved capital to hold the company together through the long sales cycles. Some of these practices require a mindset contrary to the values instilled in people by the socialist system, which again brings to focus that the challenge in establishing a viable software industry in Cuba is less technical than behavioral and political. Having the programmers and the centrally planned incubators, as is the case now, is not enough.

Successful vertical software companies focus on a major industry, like hospitals for example, and analyze the workflow processes of greatest value determining if these can be automated, if there are competing products addressing these tasks, determining costs and a sustainable price matrix, and finding out if at least one client in their market will be interested in buying their solution at the set price. Having identified a potential client, they then set out to build the solution generously asking for ideas and product improvements from the client, and anybody else who can help. If the developer is established, he/she hires a product specialist and puts together a focus group to regularly critique and fine-tune the product along the way. After a rigorous quality assurance program, whose length of time is often difficult to determine, the product is released. After several years in this process, the company gains reputation and market share becoming the leader in the chosen "niche" as it expands into other related workflows. With one to three products, some companies reach tens of millions of dollars in sales yearly.

In what industries should the nascent free market oriented Cuban vertical software industry concentrate? The market for Spanish language vertical software is practically virgin territory. There are opportunities in almost every industry imaginable. And like the Indians did in the 1990's, they should promote themselves and search for work as offshore "low cost" development alternatives to other more established places. Each offshore project they get will forward their skills allowing them to move up the "complexity ladder." As the population of English speaking Cuban software developers increases, Cuban vertical software companies should set their sights on penetrating niche markets in the USA.

WHICH TECHNOLOGIES SHOULD BE CONSIDERED?

Cuba has a generation of developers trained in Eastern bloc development techniques that are antiquated and clumsy by today's standards. The ones I've met have explained the use of tools that get the job done, sometimes in a creative manner not done by American programmers. At other times, they seemed unaware of components and shortcuts that can save hours or days of programming time. Nevertheless, they are programmers whose brains are accustomed to dealing with problems systematically and logically. Like many Eastern European programmers, they are likely to quickly adjust to Western methods after a year or two of experimentation with new tools. However, practicality should rule when deciding how an individual or a country's policies should be made regarding a decision of this magnitude. Time should not be spent on anything other than technologies that produce the highest return, the most international portability, and the quickest entry point. For vertical software development and Internet applications, currently only Microsoft development tools meet these criteria although other companies will make strong claims to this effect. Energy and resources should not be spent on Unix-based systems and mainframe technologies. Linux, although offering a cheap entry point and having a strong following in academia, should also be disqualified due to its miniscule market and its never changing "experimental" state.

The source for talent, tools, and business inspiration in the technology field is the United States. Although other countries have strong software industries, they are all clearly second rate players who acknowledge the central role of the United States when pressed. It makes little sense for Cuba, or Cuban computer scientists, to seek expertise anywhere else but at the source. Studying computer technology in Mexico, Poland, Spain, Canada, India, Argentina, or Taiwan will be short-sighted and is a strategy guaranteed to produce second-rate results. The integration of future private and public technical schools in Cuba into a system that closely resembles the technical curriculum of their peers in the United States is of critical importance for Cuba's success in the software field. Every effort for cross-pollination with U.S.-based businesses should be made to allow Cuban developers to shed their Eastern European shadows and gain the lingo and habits of their North American counterparts. The rest will take care of itself. Market forces and individual pride will force Cubans to choose the appropriate tools to succeed, and this evaluation will automatically occur every seven to 12 months.

A successful Cuban software development company will be able to create Internet products with the same ease as it develops client/server products. Those development companies that do not transition into the Internet space will go out of business. The ability to create ASP products, integrate wireless systems, exploit the promise of XML, develop secure encrypted communications, and bring products quickly to market will determine who flourishes and who doesn't.

SEEDING A FEW ENTREPRENURIAL SOFTWARE COMPANIES

Starting a software development company from scratch takes courage and patience, and at a certain stage it takes substantial money. Most companies composed of highly technical people tend to have high failure rates. Companies controlled by sales people do not attract the best technical talent, and companies controlled by finance people rarely develop trend-setting products and become farms where new developers gain experience before moving on to the big time. Government-sponsored companies have the attractiveness of the plague and are usually avoided by most experienced programmers from developed countries.

Achieving a balance where the right personalities come together is something not taught in business schools and an art approaching black magic. This mix is critical to success and something experienced venture capitalists look for as a prerequisite to funding. From my experience, the ideal mix for a successful software company is the following:

- One individual whose high intellect and addiction to technology is so severe that he/she constantly forgets to wear socks because he/she is too consumed with ideas for improving his/her code or adding a new component to a new product;

- One individual who is a great talker, an idealist whose understanding of technology comes from popular magazines and has sold his mothers' underwear to the Salvation Army, and is capable of surviving a five minute conversation with Mr. Nerd in order to understand why Mr. Nerd does not sleep at night, and the flashing little box on the screen has the potential to generate $15 million dollars within two years. (This individual is called the pain-in-the-neck salesman and his value is important but never as much as he would like);

- One individual who is a normal person has enough patience to put up with Mr. Nerd, and the salesman, has some artistic flair, and/or book keeping skills and shows up consistently every morning. This person handles the general administration of the business, and makes sure clients and business partners don't get too upset at the antics of either Mr. Nerd or the pain in the neck salesman;

- A general-purpose technical support person who knows enough about the products to install them, train clients, and provide technical support to the salesman if needed;

- A sales support person to help the salesman find prospects via telemarketing, mass mailers, cold calls, the Internet, advertising and product presentations; and

- A software development consultant (freelancer) with complimentary skills to Mr. Nerd who can be called on short notice to assist Mr. Nerd in the event of work overflows or emergencies.

This type of organization tends to build up over a period of time with Mr. Nerd and the salesman as the core drivers. They enslave themselves as they develop the key products, working at below market compen-

sation and borrowing from family and friends to keep things going until the first few sales come in. Rarely does this type of enterprise start with a finished product and at full speed with all five or six employees. After several sales, the founders usually look for expansion capital to hire the rest of the team and expand sales to new territories. This is a crucial time, since most teams at this stage are still inexperienced and lack the financial expertise or a well-devised business plan of the caliber that appeals to venture capitalist or investment bankers. Rarely do traditional banks provide financing at this level. Many companies that survive to this stage do not obtain the required capital needed to move on to the next stage because of this problem and they wither away due to the pressures of under capitalization.

No matter how great a product, vertical software reaches a point where it needs an infusion of capital greater than what their developing companies have been able to accumulate. Without it, they can not break out into the major leagues. For the future software industry in Cuba, finding these types of companies and helping them jump over this hurdle is going to be crucial. Having a mechanism to provide the critical $250,000 to $500,000 in first stage financing is exactly the type of thing the Indian businessmen I met in New Delhi were talking about in 1984. How many of these types of companies will reach this stage each year in Cuba? No one can tell at this point. With a yearly capital investment of only $5 million dollars, it may be possible to seed as many as 20 such companies whose potential return by the third or fourth years can be in the hundreds of millions of dollars. Cuba has little experience with venture capital markets, investment banking, securities and stock transactions, or private placements, and raising local capital even a miserly $5 million per year will not be easy. This dearth of capital formation infrastructure will open the door to entrepreneurs with the ability, contacts, and experience to formally, legally, and consistently broker investors with worthy needy enterprises.[6]

---

6. Sanginetty, Jorge A., 1999. "Macroeconomic Policy Issues for a Free Market Cuba." *Cuba in Transition—Volume 9.* Washington: Association for the Study of the Cuban Economy, 204–216.

It is my belief, based on personal conversations with recently-arrived Cuban software developers and Cuba's future ability to create large numbers of technically proficient young people, that such small companies may be easily created, and that there are many individuals who currently have many of the required skills for these enterprises— but the socio-economic, and political environment of the country does not allow it. In many ways, Cuba is well positioned to start this process soon after the departure of socialism.

CHOOSING BETWEEN PLANTING PAPAYAS AND DEVELOPING SOFTWARE

The wage of a typical Cuban worker today is about $10 U.S. dollars per month; this may double or quadruple in a post socialist Cuba to about U.S. $40 dollars per month. While, a Cuban software developer during this time may earn $10 to $20 per hour; we need to acknowledge that the software industry will create an elite group and an anomaly similar to what exists today between people who work in the tourism sector (the dollar economy) and the rest of Cuban society. The situation will be exacerbated because software is not labor intensive and requires substantial capital in relation to other endeavors. For example, $5 million dollars may seed 20 software companies per year employing 120 people, with trickle down effects that may employ an additional several hundred people, while the same $5 million could employ more than 10,400 papaya planters per year at a wage of $40 per month each. The 120 people may generate several hundred million dollars within five years creating hundreds of future high paying jobs whose impact on the general economy will be great But during that time, what do the 10,400 papaya planters do to survive if the resources don't exist to fund both endeavors? [7]

Should the venture capitalists and private investment bankers focus on raising investment dollars for improving sugar production, expanding rum distilleries, building tobacco factories, building new music recording studios or more cabarets for tourism? Should government investments for power plants, cellular communications, transportation, biotechnology, the film industry, and the restoration of old historic buildings take precedence over computer software and computer technology? Certainly all are important, and private and public investments will flow to all these sectors, but decisions on priorities cannot be avoided. The current socialist government clearly understands the importance of diversifying the economy and focusing precious resources, and within the scope of its Marxist model, is attempting to create a software industry. They have decided that Cuban software is not a fantasy dream, and have created incubators attached to several universities with the goal of attracting partners from Canada and Europe. It appears that socialist policy makers have looked at the future of sugar and other traditional Cuban industries and they do not like what they see. Morality and ethics aside, the socialists seem to have decided to place bets on software and technology and are lessening their bets on papayas. [8]

In a free market system, these important resource allocation and political questions are outside the scope of the average private entrepreneur. Hopefully, these issues will hopefully be debated and decisions will be based on the best interests of the citizens of Cuban public opinion and the social contract that evolves in the country after the departure of socialism. Entrepreneurs will interpret the laws, the competition, and the opportunities to make a profit, deciding to act based on what they perceive as the action that will expose them to the fewest risks and the highest profits. The social, moral, ethical, and religious questions of the society in a post socialist Cuba will be the responsibility of politicians, priests, academicians, sociologist, philosophers, lobbyist, labor unions, and political parties who will hopefully exercise their democratic responsibilities to argue and disagree. The technology sector will have its own professional

7. Smith, Benjamin, 1999. "The Self Employed in Cuba: A Street Level View." *Cuba in Transition—Volume 9.* Washington: Association for the Study of the Cuban Economy, 49–59.

8. Echevarría, Oscar, 1995. "Cuba and the International Sugar Market." *Cuba in Transition—Volume 5.* Washington: Association for the Study of the Cuban Economy, 363–373.

associations (its lobbyist) and will try to compete for public and private resources just like everyone else agreeing and disagreeing in the process.

RISKS AND CHALLENGES

The 2001 dot.com collapse in the U.S. taught everyone that the new tech economy is not based on thin air principles and that breakeven points still matter. The thing that makes software development an attractive economic activity is the very thing that makes it un-attractive. It lacks substance in the old-fashioned sense. It is difficult to collaterize software. Valuations of software companies and products are notoriously difficult and volatile. Often the most valuable asset of a software company is the brain of its founder or main developer, who recklessly enjoys parachute jumping. Since technological innovations rapidly change and client expectations are affected by variables out of anyone's direct control, market dominance can be and is usually challenged every 24 months. Products need to be regularly upgraded and major marketing/advertising campaigns have to be re-conceptualized. For the majority of Cubans, these conditions are unfamiliar and a likely cause for abstinence from participating significantly as investors in these new software ventures. For the software industry, this is likely to create and maintain an environment where foreign capital will be the driving force and eventually the major equity partners in most successful enterprises. Furthermore, it is not likely that in a resource poor post socialist Cuba with strong socialist ideological leftovers, risky venture capital will be raised for anything but the most simple and traditional of industries even though most of these will have limited potential or little long-term impact. When re-established in Cuba, little can be expected from the traditional banking sector and its risk adverse culture.

In addition to a deficit of capital, the Cuban software industry will have to face the question of competition with the U.S. software industry. The question that some American software companies will ask themselves when they notice the emergence of Cuba as a competitor will be, do we partner up, do we buy them out, or should we put them out of business? But in reality, the capture by Cuban software companies of several hundred million dollars worth of business each year from the type of activity described in this paper is not likely to cause industry-wide concern in the U.S. because of the enormity of the one trillion dollar per year U.S. information technology industry.[9]

Because of factors outside the scope of this paper, the U.S. software industry has not focused on the Spanish speaking market, and this is not likely to change. By default, this gives the Cubans a relatively large market to exploit. Many U.S. companies will find synergies with Cuban vertical software companies and will form partnerships, invest in them, and may buy them outright. Given the expected shortage of capital in which the Cuban software industry will operate, this will not be too bad. The major competition factor and human dynamic with the U.S., though, will not be in mergers and acquisitions, but in the "brain drain" of talent to U.S. companies with the ability to pay higher compensations. After a few years of experience, Cuban developers will reach a proficiency level that will make them competitive on a worldwide level. This challenge is faced by every developing country in the world and it cannot be avoided.

The brain drain however, will have a positive side effect, in the sense that highly paid young Cuban developers employed overseas will have economic ties to family and friends back in Cuba, sending them valuable remittances. They will also serve as bridges between Cuba and the worldwide technology sector, allowing those same Cuban technicians and developers to become a future source of capital, industry stimulus, and talent for new enterprises in Cuba. At one point, policy decisions will have to be made regarding whether Cuban schools should train high numbers of youth in the technology sector in order to create a large pool of computer talent in highly paid and high demand areas overseas, simply to ex-

---

9. Information Technology Association of America (ITAA), 2001. Official Website. http://www.itaa.org

port them. India has adopted this policy with great success, and H-1B visas (professional workers) for software programmers in the U.S. will be easily obtained. Serious efforts will have to be made to assure that once a computer scientist leaves Cuba for overseas work, his cultural, family, and economic links to Cuba remain strong so he/she can provide benefits to the national economy, although in seemingly indirect ways. As large numbers of these "high tech" workers establish themselves in advanced wealthy markets, they will establish businesses in those markets whose benefits to Cuba will be significant, but difficult to measure.

Professor AnnaLee Saxenian of Harvard University has studied these types of activities and technology transfers. Her lectures on "Brain Drain or Brain Circulation? The Silicon Valley-Asia Connection" help shed light on the multi-dimensional aspects that will likely play themselves out in a post socialist Cuba.[10] If Professor Saxenian is correct, the "Brain Circulation" that will occur during and after the transition away from socialism in Cuba will provide great economic benefits. This is not difficult to see in a country that has been kept isolated and under a totalitarian regime for more than 43 years. Since globalization has eroded national frontiers, there is no reason why Cuban software companies cannot operate anywhere in the world where economic conditions make most sense. In a post socialist environment, travel restrictions will not be an issue.[11] California, for example, is now spotted with Taiwanese, Indian, Korean and Chinese high tech companies.

Another unavoidable problem facing the Cuban software industry is the so-called "Miami" problem. Over the years, Cuban exiles in Miami have succeeded in creating a vibrant "Cuban" economy whose diversity goes well beyond the sale of guayaberas and hot tamales in Little Havana.

There exist in Miami a sufficient number of software programmers, trained in Cuba and the U.S., capable of quickly exploiting the conditions outlined in this paper. Their only impediment to executing this type of strategy is that they already have access to the most lucrative software market in the world and they view a diversion of time and money towards the Spanish speaking market as an effort that will yield relatively small returns. Some recent arrivals have the desire but lack the capital to jump past the first stage hurdle, and most are discouraged by the high piracy rate and disrespect for intellectual property in Latin America. These exiled programmers from Miami and other parts of the U.S. may become the primary recruiters for Cuban programmers and the catalysts for the brain drain described. It is likely that such U.S.-based Cuban exile-owned technology companies will greatly benefit by the opening of the software industry in Cuba. It is also likely that many of these firms will expand their services in the U.S. market by becoming agents to Cuban firms, setting up limited partnerships, and in many cases providing the sales and marketing expertise needed by the Cubans to jump start their industry.

The risk in this, from a purely nationalistic Cuban perspective, is that Miami may end up becoming the center of the Cuban software industry. In many ways, from a strictly software centered perspective; Miami has greater potential than Havana in achieving this. It already has the communications and energy infrastructure, the laws, the economic stability, the academic institutions, the international links, and a mass of Cuban capitalists whose focus can be easily turned to this task. Using the Indian model, Cuban exiles may be able to use the deficiencies of a post socialist Cuba to take advantage of the disparities that will exist between the two economies and their ability to attract capital to the task. Whether you view this possibility as a risk and a challenge, of course, depends on whether you live in Cuba or Miami.

---

10. Saxenian, AnnaLee, 2002. "Local and Global Networks of Immigrant Professionals in Silicon Valley." Public Policy Institute of California.

11. Travieso-Díaz, Matías F., 1998. "Cuban Immigration: Challenges and Opportunities." *Cuba in Transition—Volume 8*. Washington: Association for the Study of the Cuban Economy, 65–84.

One of the major decisions that post socialist Cuba will have to make pertaining to laying out the groundwork for the development of a viable market driven software industry will be how to best leverage the value of Miami, and whether the best return on investment will come from investing one dollar in Miami or one dollar in Havana. This Cuba/Miami dynamic holds great promise if properly coordinated by the politicians at both ends. Although large differences have evolved between the Miami Cubans and the "New Cubans" of Castro's "Socialist Paradise," both parties have more to gain by bridging these differences than by amplifying them. A transitional Cuba will need all the help it can get from anyone willing to help it. Its most immediate natural ally is Miami. If market forces favor establishing Miami as the center of the Cuban technology sector, no amount of government intervention by the Cubans will stop it. Instead, it should ride the wave and learn what the Indians and most Asians learned a while ago —study the market and profit by it!

So, it may come to pass that after seeding a good number of software companies, bringing them beyond the critical first stage of growth, and seeing many of them reach the $15 to $50 million dollar a year sales mark, they will begin to feel a brain drain, become targets of mergers and acquisitions by foreigners, and some may decide to setup "branches" in Guatemala or Peru because developers there are cheaper. It may also come to pass that most corporate offices will be in Miami, and programmers will work in Santiago from Monday through Wednesday, and then in Miami on Thursday and Friday. When Cuba finds itself with this type of problem, it should interpret it as a sign that it has succeeded in becoming a contender in the international software industry and this problem will make a lot of Cubans (private individuals and private companies, not state owned or controlled enterprises) happy and rich. It will also indicate that the country has finally transitioned out of the restrictive grip of totalitarian socialism.

SMALL CLUMSY STEPS

Like my grandfather, we all have to take a few clumsy steps before we can run. And, there must be a clear starting point with specifics.

Socialist Cuba has already taken the steps to create the technology culture (computer scientists) required for the eventual creation of a capitalist software industry. During the last seven to eight years, it has laid out a rudimentary legal framework that may, if the other reforms mentioned here take place, support the structures needed to kick-start the software industry when the political transition occurs.[12] In the surreal environment of Cuban politics, this means after the death of Fidel Castro. At that point, it will not be difficult to retrain a sufficient number of highly educated technologists and computer programmers in modern software development techniques to form the core of a competitive market driven industry. Currently, these programmers' best contribution to this transition is to continue improving their skills, learn about the international software market and the weaknesses of Latin America (the vertical software industry in particular), and by becoming proficient in Internet technologies.

If the Cuban exiled community in the United States is to play a role in this challenging transition, it has to take action in two very important areas. The first one is the establishment of a small network of private investment intermediaries whose focus will be to raise venture capital to fuel the kind of activity outlined in this paper. These intermediaries should be registered with the U.S. Securities and Exchange Commission. When the political climate allows, appropriate similar Cuban government agencies should be established to offer investors the protection of the law and exclude unscrupulous and criminal activity. Such intermediaries will be responsible for brokering private placement memorandums, limited partnerships, stocks, and other legal investment tools needed for the accumulation and transfer of capital to Cuba.

---

12. Asociación Nacional de Economistas Independientes de Cuba. 2001. Sumario de Leyes de Comercio Internacional de Cuba. Official Website: http://www.geo.unipr.it/~davide/cuba/economy/

There are currently some Cuban-American investment brokers and American investment organizations that may fit this role. They may be able to dominate the market because large American brokerages and venture capitalists will find the overall size of the Cuban market too small for their involvement. With 1.2 million people, the exiled community, which currently sends remittances to Cuba in excess of $700 million per year and whose GDP is greater than that of the Republic of Cuba, may be able to finance the entire effort as outlined in this paper.[13] Secondly, Cuban-American computer technologists should form a U.S.-based professional association capable of participating in and taking advantage of the transition discussed here.

There are sufficient numbers of exiled computer businesses to warrant this activity and the numbers are growing steadily. Working closely together with the venture capitalists, this professional association will be able to make significant contributions to the future. It should lay the foundation by first organizing and strengthening the exiled computer technology sector, building an awareness of the importance of this endeavor, and creating important alliances for the future. Its focus should be on the here and now, bringing tangible organizational and economic benefits to its members and making it a valuable asset for growing the industry here in the United States. Its appeal should be from a purely business perspective, not focused on political issues that lay outside of its control, such as the overthrow of the Castro regime. By becoming successful, this Cuban-American Information Technology "Council" or "Association" will indirectly add strength to the exile community and will serve as a stimulus to young exiles as they enter the technology sector. If the Cuban exiled community does not aggressively take these opportunities soon, it may be too late later when the political changes actually occur in Cuba, and by then others may be better positioned to control the future of the technology sector in Cuba, Latin America, and indirectly in Miami. [14]

CONCLUSIONS

In the software industry and many sectors of technology, India leapfrogged from the status of a Third World country to a first world powerhouse in 15 years. A post socialist Cuba will have the potential to do the same. The pre-requisites for such a change, however, have more to do with political, social, and finance sector reforms, than in the creation of a technical culture or the acquisition of software and hardware tools. Once these structural issues are solved, the biggest challenge will be in obtaining and consistently channeling foreign venture capital to competitive young firms. Cuba's greatest market potential lies in the exploitation of the Latin American market and the development of vertical software and ASP offerings for niche markets in both the Spanish and English speaking world, and as an offshore development center for U.S. based companies.

Cuba is likely to face little competition in the Spanish-speaking marketplace, and its gradual success is likely to attract U.S.-based partners and much needed capital for future projects. Because of the existence of a large Cuban exile community in Miami, its superior infrastructure, and access to capital and markets, Miami may become the de-facto center for the "Cuban" software industry. If venture capital averaging only $5 million dollars per year can be raised, as many as 20 software companies can be seeded annually. This model lends itself to other "new economy" industries and should be considered alongside other more traditional methods of redevelopment.

However, after discussing this proposal with many Cubans and exchanging correspondence with countless others in the Cuban-American business community, there appears to be little indication that the exiled community has a strong interest in pursuing this type of coordinated effort. The simple fact that all

---

13. Díaz-Briquets, Sergio, 1999. "Emigrant Remittances in the Cuban Economy: Their Significance During and After the Castro Regime." *Cuba in Transition—Volume 9.* Washington: Association for the Study of the Cuban Economy.

14. LatinTrade.Com Internet Newsletter, 2002. "Trade Information for Cuba. General Investment and Trade Policies." http://www.latintrade.com

the ingredients needed to set the elements in motion are present does not mean that the challenge will be taken. After 43 years of false starts and dashed hopes for a change in Cuba, exhaustion and apathy towards schemes to "rebuild Cuba" are not uncommon. It may be that this undertaking will not find mass appeal until the day after Fidel Castro dies. As previously indicated, this sort of timing may be off.

Those that are not apathetic and are from the technology sector, investment banking, academia, and business should consider organizing the infrastructure mentioned here. The upsize rewards are much greater than the rewards of inactivity. Rarely does a country go through the convulsions that Cuba will go through during the expected transition away from totalitarian socialism, creating opportunities for well-organized groups to fashion entire industries and major sectors of a new economy. Hopefully, this will happen with less pain, less criminality, and less waste than in the former Soviet Union. As crazy as it may sound to some, the future of Cuba will no longer be in sugar, papayas, or rum, but in technology.

SOCIAL MECHANISMS AND POLITICAL ORDER

Enrique S. Pumar

"Actions are caused by desires and opportunities."

— Jon Elster[1]

Can social mechanisms sustain political order in autocratic-authoritarian regimes? Does the use of mechanisms tell us something significant about how these regimes govern? In many ways, these questions are more than rhetorical. Despite the indiscriminative repression against its opponents, citizens continue to find innovating mechanism to resist state policies. In the case of the velvet revolution and others like it, these tactics ultimately contributed to the debilitation of the regime and their eventual downfall. In the end, autocracies continue to be more prone to experience revolutionary uprisings during the succession period than any other polities.

Alienation gives us another reason for examining mechanisms. Some institutionalized vehicles to foster political allegiance tend to alienate significant numbers of supporters. For example, capricious recruitment of party membership or rotation within the political elite often erodes support for these regimes. The secrecy around the rise and demise of key state figures from the public sphere gives way to widespread speculation about the inner workings of official circles. States recur to social mechanisms, then, because these provide deceptive maneuvers to manage state-society relations.

Conversely, mechanisms are also a strategy of popular survival and perseverance, especially among the

dissatisfied in non-democratic societies. In the absence of institutions to channel or articulate discontent, individuals resort to innovative manifestations against the existing political order. In Franco's Spain, for instance, many workers participated in work slow-downs since strikes were harshly punished. Opposition newspapers were also disguised inside official publications to avoid repression. The use of regional dialects, known to be a form of protest against the central administration in Madrid, became a mechanism to rally support for regional identity. Many economists cogitate whether sluggish productivity is a manifestation of popular disgruntlement in Cuba lately.

In this paper I propose to examine non-institutional manifestation of authority and resistance in non-democratic societies. In particular, I examine instances of preference falsification as mechanisms. My argument is that social mechanisms provide a unique opportunity to govern in situations such as the one we witness in Cuba today where the Castro regime faces a paradoxical situation. After the breakdown of its ideological bedfellows, Castro needs to promote a benign image abroad to avoid jeopardizing the inflow of venture capital and counter the persistent advocacy for political reforms while his government insists in marginalizing any organized dissent. Some informal mechanisms, such as market reforms, can reconcile these two contradictory needs by providing a deceiving sense of regime moderation and tolerance.

---

1. Jon Elster, "A plea for mechanisms," in Peter Hedstrom and Richard Swedberg eds., *Social Mechanisms* (New York: Cambridge University Press, 1998), 58.

While Cuba today has implemented many reforms, the state continues to hold the arbitrary power to allocate resources, determine the legality of transactions, and decide when and to what extent enforce its autocratic decisions, among others.

The Cuban quagmire today resembles the final days of the former Soviet-style communism in Eastern Europe. From all these cases one can conclude that the longer these non-democratic regimes manage to rule, the more they will resort to mechanisms to maintain authority and bogus legitimacy. The longer an authoritarian situation persists, the more individuals too would resort to resistance mechanisms to survive the hardships imposed by these regimes. This assertion is almost paradoxical. One would expect that regime longevity might foster favorable conditions for Weberian institutional authority to prevail. Many authoritarian rulers set up political institutions but these do not operate autonomously. Prevailing lack of accountability and transparency and the disproportionate concentration of power in a handful of top government officials discourage institutionalization.

I plan to proceed as follows. After briefly surveying the literature on mechanisms, I plan to discuss the taxonomy of mechanisms people use in everyday situations and the range of state responses to sustain political order. I close the essay with a few observations about the *Projecto Varela* and the *cuentapropistas* movement which are recently evident in the island. Since the Varela Project is the most formable recent attempt by the opposition to liberalize the political sphere, it serves as an important case to illustrate the interplay of social mechanisms between the regime and its foes. *Cuentapropistas* are viewed by some to be a hopeful sign of progressive market reforms.

A CALL FOR MECHANISMS

A significant motivating factor for examining mechanisms is the invigorating claim by Juan Linz about the "low specificity of political institutions" among authoritarian regimes.[2] Under the political conditions described by Linz, mechanisms provide a false sense of legitimacy for authoritarian rule. In addition to re-enforcing an authoritarian situation, mechanisms may also foster a lingering continuity from the past. This is particularly the case when an authoritarian regime succeeds another and the former resorts to similar patterns of *clientelismo* and *personalismo* to assure political order.

In fact, there are several additional reasons to further investigate the low degree of rationalization and institutionalization in autocratic regimes. First, the notion of rationality embeds more political autonomy for bureaucrats than the autocratic leader is willing to tolerate—witness the lack of legislative autonomy of the *Poder Popular* in Cuba, for instance. Rational decision-making requires a number of available choices and alternatives and independent judgment to determine choices which undermines the regime demand for secrecy and orthodoxy. Institutionalization opens opportunities for citizens to challenge a regime's rulings, something autocracy abhors. Adherence to constitutional law undermines the revolutionary aura the regime publicly likes to promote or perpetuate itself. Constitutionalism also implies stability and conformity. The persistent articulation of revolutionary rhetoric and appearance is a crucial strategy for political mobilization and recruitment among non-democratic governments. The use of social mechanisms, finally, could promote a fictitious appearance of regime unity and detachment from some of its most vulgar forms of political repression as was the case after the several attempts by the Cuban regime to disassociate itself from "*los actos de repudio*" against those seeking to leave the island during the early 1980s.

In short, mechanisms seem to cement political authority. In rare occasions, mechanisms are the only available tool to exercise political power, however. In most instances they form part of the repertoire of political maneuvers and strategies to sustain the ruling elite. In the case of Cuba, one finds simultaneously both institutions and mechanisms juxtaposed in many issue-areas and the looming threat of repres-

---

2. Juan J. Linz, *Totalitarian and Authoritarian Regimes* (Boulder, Colorado: Rienner, 2000), 160-161.

sion on the background. With regards to labor relations, for instance, there is a fairly institutionalized process to file labor grievances and seek compensation, but in the areas of hiring and recruitment, there is ample evidence that individuals rely on informal networks of acquaintances and friends more often than not.

DEFINING SOCIAL MECHANISMS

The concept of mechanisms has a long and grueling trajectory in the social sciences. Economists, for instance, spend a great deal of time theorizing about market mechanisms. Recently, Albert O. Hirschman and Thomas Schelling have resorted to mechanisms to explain purposive action.[3] Jon Elster describes the political impact generated by the tension between adaptive preferences and counter-adaptive preferences.[4] Other political scientists examine mechanisms of repression and cooptation as political maneuvers. Many sociologists revisited the notion of mechanisms after World War II as part of a movement promoting middle-range theorizing spearheaded by Merton and the Columbia School.

In *Social Theory and Social Structure,* Robert Merton defines mechanisms as "social processes having designated consequences for designated parts of the social structure."[5] Following Merton, I designate as social mechanisms state sanctions designed to internalize social order and the voluntary, informal, and extra-legal strategies to cope with the intricacies of governance. Mechanisms exist under every regime type. Industrial nations have witnessed the resort to symbolic manipulation and displays as vehicles for public protest and articulation by anti-globalization movements. Military coups, on the other extreme, could be regarded as mechanisms to engulf political power by the military.

Evidence of informal mechanisms in authoritarian regimes suggests that despite the overriding control these regimes exercise, popular ingenuity cannot be crushed. Referring to Cuban society in a recent interview, the writer David Chavarría stated: "There are injustices, but the country has survived. This is the kingdom of improvisation. Everything here has to be invented."[6] The last part of Chavarría's comment suggests that perhaps one of the reasons why informal mechanisms flourish in non-democratic societies is the basic necessity to make sense of everyday situations, what is popularly referred in Cuba as *resolver.* What makes this desire and others like it politically relevant are a persistence stream of state intrusive and measureless policies that categorize most social events political.

Further, in Cuba there is evidence of spontaneous instincts of everyday resistance in many spheres of society—witness, for instance, the art of hustling or *jinetear* as is known in the popular lexicon.[7] Yet, in this paper I am more interested in exploring instances of preference falsification as mechanisms, or how most people publicly support a policy that few favor privately, and attempts by the state to regulate and sanction manifestations of organized popular resistance.[8] Before proceeding, it is first important to mention the obvious. The widespread practice of preference falsification is most politically relevant among autocratic-authoritarianism and other non-democratic political types because it may be the most cost effective recourse to express popular discontent.

---

3. See particularly, Albert O. Hirschman, *Exit, Voice, and Loyalty: Responses to the Decline of Firms, Organizations, and States* (Cambridge: Harvard University Press, 1970) and Thomas Schelling, *Micromotive and Macrobehavior* (New York: W. W. Norton, 1978).

4. Jon Elster, *Sour Grapes* (New York: Cambridge University Press, 1983).

5. Robert Merton, *Social Theory and Social Structure* (New York: Free Press, 1968), 43-44.

6. *New York Times,* July 4, 2002, E14.

7. For this an many others terms that capture popular survival strategies, see Carlos Paz Pérez, *Diccionario Cubano de Términos Populares y Vulgares,* (La Habana: Editorial de Ciencias Sociales, 1994).

8. The most elaborate treatment of this topic can be found in Timur Kuran, *Private Truths, Public Lies* (Cambridge: Harvard University Press, 1995).

In this sense, falsification manifests itself indescribably. A survey conducted in 1999 presents examples of the widespread practice of falsification. Recent émigrés were asked in the United States after their arrival about the reaction of government sympathizers to the decision to invite the Pope to Cuba and 47% responded that the followers accepted the decision despite their disagreement with the visit. Later, when asked about how the average citizen reacts toward official repudiation against dissidents, 43% said they would assist the dissidence but privately. Of the same group, 35% said they participated in the Committees for the Defense of the Revolution or CDRs.[9]

Each of these responses gives us a glimpse of the complexity involved in finding sufficient empirical evidence to demonstrate the political effects of mechanism. Significantly, it is evident that close to half of the respondents feared state reprisals when engaging in any manifestation of political behavior while residing in the island since they insisted they would assist dissidents only privately. Close to half of regime supporters did not even feel confident enough to simply disagree with the regime publicly on matters of policy. About one third of all the émigrés had belonged to a mass organization while contemplating leaving the country.

These numbers also shed some light on the limitations of explanatory and predictive powers of models that attempted to analyze the downfall of communism in the former Eastern Europe and elsewhere. In many cases the patterns of resistance and dissatisfaction is disguised under social norms and symbols not easily captured by the kind of factual evidence required for empirical political analysis. Inter-subjective, interpretative evidence of falsification is difficult to grasp at first hand. In the pointed words of Kuran "preferences are imperfectly observable."[10]

TAXONOMY OF MECHANISMS

As stated earlier, the use of mechanisms in the political arena generally falls into the categories of individuals and official maneuvers. Within this dichotomy, I find it useful to categorize mechanisms into the political, the economic, the social and the ideological spheres. The first category captures those strategies related to the question of political authority. One obvious one is the ridiculous manipulation of judicial criteria to incarcerate and censor emerging adversarial voices. A more conspicuous shroud is the constant reference to the situation rather than any particular institution or individual when condemning policy failures. It is usual these days to hear state officials and other Cubans state matter of factually "*la situación no es fácil*" or "*se cometieron errores.*"

These references to an impersonal situation can be interpreted in many ways. Regime officials could save face by alluding to external constrains supposedly imposed by the embargo or the situation could also refer to other extraneous, uncontrollable forces. In any case, blaming hardships on the situation deflect any responsibility from individuals responsible for the situation. And since alluding to situations connotes ambiguity, it will be absurd and paranoid for the state to repress anyone who interprets state failures in such imprecise terms. This mechanism of falsification then permits state officials and other individuals to air differences without incrimination. In fact, references to "the situation" support the regime's public deception of portraying itself as trapped by a hostile international environment. What makes this particular strategy anti-democratic is that it permits the state to take credit for any achievements while deflecting responsibilities for its failures. Notice that in pluralistic societies the opposite tendency is the norm. Particular public servants are generally blamed for all state failures, voluntary or not, during their mandate.

Economic mechanisms encompass bottlenecks imposed by the state to maintain its monopolistic grip on the economy, on the one hand, and the irresistible instinct to get around these bottlenecks, on the other. The juxtaposition of a dual market economy, con-

9. Churchill Roberts, Ernesto Betancourt, Guillermo Grenier, and Richard Scheaffer, *Measuring Cuban Public Opinion. Project Report* (Washington, DC: USAID, 1999), Table 38, p. 73, Table 43, p. 79, Table 70, p. 96.

10. Kuran (1995), 332.

sisting of official egalitarian rations and the perilous parallel market, has been a constant feature of the revolution almost since its beginning. More recently, along with the new restrictive market initiatives sponsored by the regime to cope with the necessities generated by the Special Period, the state has also devised more sophisticated vehicles of state control. The dollarization of the economy and the required exchange mechanism offers us one such illustration. While the official exchange rate is artificially set taking political considerations in mind, people have set up a more real second tier exchange unofficially to reflect true market value.

In other instances, *paladares* owners purchase receipts for merchandise bought at the so- called "diplo-stores" from neighbors and friends to show proof of purchase for goods bought in unofficial markets to protect themselves against an eventual visit by state inspectors. Moreover, *paladares* owners also do not include in their menu those dishes prohibited for sale by the state, rather they verbally communicate their availability to trusted clients.

Social and ideological mechanisms refer to inter-subjective norms, conventions, and principles that govern every day social relations. Two obvious illustration of this realm are the reconstructed meaning of the words *compañero* and *revolucionario*. To identify supporters and to characterize political allegiance, revolutionary officials popularized these two terms during the early days of the revolution.[11] Initially, the first conceptual implication of these terms was intended to depict a general sense of popular egalitarianism.

Today these terms have a much broader and binary connotation. Everyone calls each other a *compañero*

regardless of their feelings towards the regime, particularly in situations involving either a hierarchy of status or when people do not know one another. This implies a more cautious meaning of the term from what was originally intended. *Revolucionario* today practically describes any manifestation of social behavior that does not directly threaten the dictates of the regime. So, to march in support of one of the government's initiatives and to engage in capitalist self-employment are simultaneously revolutionary under the current popular connotation.

It is clear that the transgression of meaning of these two norms imply an apparent culture of conformity or *habitus*.[12] Yet, a closer look at these practices reveals a distinct evidence of another manifestation of falsification identified by Timur Kuran as moral dissonance.[13] Moral dissonance suggests evidence of a certain tension between the popular and the official. On the one hand, it indicates that social actions evolve within a framework of possibilities determined undemocratically from above. But on the other, it also reveals how social agents manipulate and negotiate the range of public spaces to justify new practices of social action.

The stage provided by formal mechanisms of socialization has not been spared from falsification. Conversations with recent émigrés indicate that the once-feared Committees for the Defense of the Revolution (CDRs) in many blocks have become social gatherings where participants exchange information about opportunities or seek services to satisfy immediate necessities. Here again, non-institutional patterns of dominance devised by the regime have been turned socially to survival. The result is a very dynamic constant negotiated social construction of reality.

---

11. In the words of Jon Elster, "Identification is one major mechanism whereby norms are internalized." In Elster's *The Cement of Society. A Study of Social Order* (New York: Cambridge University Press, 1989), 132.

12. Pierre Bourdieu, *Outline of a Theory of Practice* (Cambridge: Cambridge University Press, 1977).

13. According to Kuran, "Moral dissonance arises when one's value are impractical or infeasible. One feels obligated to achieve a goal, satisfy a limit, or abide by a standard; yet, one preferences steers one away from these objectives." Timur Kuran, "Social Mechanism of Dissonance Reduction" in Peter Hedstrom and Richard Swedberg, eds, *Social Mechanisms* (Cambridge: Cambridge University Press, 1998), 154.

Table 1 intends to summarize some of the behavioral manifestations of the taxonomy of falsification mechanisms discussed here.

Table 1.

	Official	Popular
Political	Social order	Resistance survival
Economic	Bottlenecks and sanctions	Parallel economic activities
Social/ Ideological	Hegemonic discourse	Moral dissonance

PROJECTO VARELA AND *CUENTAPROPISTAS*

Two recent developments that reveal the increasing meaningful negotiated social order in Cuba are the Varela Project, organized by opposing human rights organizations, and the widespread practice of self-employment or *cuentapropistas*. Although these two illustrations show few things in common, they do share an ongoing tension between being granted official accreditation and their own quest for survival. For opponents, accreditation will probably mean adopting the semi-official status of "soft opposition." A political plebiscite is an apparent indictment against state officials but not necessarily against the revolution. Ironically, allowing the opposition to operate under terms outlined by the Varela Project could in essence afford the regime an opportunity to restraint this bourgeoning movement at a very marginal cost. Also, the revolutionary state stands to gain most from this reform since it would deprive opponents of a chance to continue to wave the dismal human rights record against the Castro regime. But once again, autocracy considerations stand on the way of political reforms in Cuba.

The composition and development of the Varela Project has been well documented by others and there is no need to recapitulate its history here. Rather, I simply would like to discuss two aspects of this development that illustrate the thesis of this paper. First, while it is clear what the public demands of the opposition really are, there is a deep seated and indis-

tinct hope that the revolution will be radically transformed once its current leaders are deposed. In the words of Oswaldo Payá, one of the key figures behind the Varela drive, "the key to the Varela Project is the personal and spiritual liberation of people. No more masks. The regime did not respond. It fled."[14] Thus, again, the call for reforms manifests itself as the only falsification strategy of survival in the face of regime intransigence.

The second aspect of this incident that deserves consideration is the nature of state response. In the early years of the revolution not only would projects like Varela be deemed unthinkable, but the state would surely have responded with indiscriminate violence against it. Today, the state response has been more tamed and definably sophisticated. After briefly jailing some key figures involved in the project, government officials have resorted to discredit the effort and, up to date, have chosen not to officially respond to the specific demands of a plebiscite. A dissident characterized the government falsification strategy in the following terms. "We believe they will not reply to the project, and once again violate the Constitution. They do not hear us. We are not part of that public which has the right to intervene in the affairs of the homeland."[15]

The other illustration I would like to briefly discuss stems from a recent a series of in-depth interviews I conducted with *cuentapropistas* visiting relatives in the United States. Many of the self-employed I interviewed described themselves as "passive sympathetic" with the revolution. In their minds, this means that they are not active in political organizations but have served the revolution in a number of capacities. One interviewee saw a lot of good deeds performed by the regime. For instance, when asked about her most defiant criticisms of the revolution, she replied calmly that leaders were usually not aware of abuses committed by lower levels bureaucrats and when they become aware, she said, they will immediately correct these situations.

---

14. "Cuba can't ignore a dissident it calls insignificant," *The New York Times*, October 13, 2002, A4.

15. "Cuba can't ignore a dissident...," *The New York Times*, October 13, 2002, A4.

Another interviewee organized a group of artists primarily composed of other people with similar political orientations. In her opinion, the main difficulty her group faces is the lack of accreditation by the state artistic agencies. The denominated official stamp of approval by the state would facilitate many of the routine business activities faced by her group, she assured me. Most prominently, state endorsement would permit her to sell her craft legally in state conventions and several hotels at a fair price in dollars. She was particularly interested in selling her art outside Cuba too, something that without state approval becomes officially impossible because of difficulties with transferring payments, shipping, marketing, or storage facilities without the legal infrastructure. Faced with no accreditation, my interviewee resorts to selling her trade to state own enterprises and foreigners through informal channels of friends and relatives both in and outside the island at heavily discounted prices.

Curiously, the inability to obtain official accreditation by these artists also demonstrates the sophisticated repressive tactics by the state. As with the Varela Project, the state capriciously decides the extent of permissible popular activities. However, instead of contemplating challenging the accreditation process to make it more open and transparent, the interviewees and others like them continues to promote their trade at the margins. Sometimes legally and others illegally, they engage in the very capitalist commercial enterprise the regime condemns. In the

minds of this group, engaging in this kind of commercial activity is revolutionary.

CONCLUDING THOUGHTS

In response to the two concerns at the start of this paper, it is clear that social mechanisms are another more sophisticated practice instituted by authoritarian-autocratic regimes to maintain their social dominance and by others to resist it. These mechanisms provide a corrupting façade of reform. They also offer a possible explanation for Elizardo Sánchez and others' observation that the regime has become more ruthless despite recent instituted chances. The increased sophistication of state-sponsored mechanisms demonstrates the maturity of the state apparatus. In this regard, the current situation in Cuba seems to support the keen observation by José Joaquín Brunner some time ago when he said "Pensamos que la represión y el efecto temor no son mecanismos capaces de crear y mantener un orden social; se necesita mucho más para asegurar el dominio de una clase y el funcionamiento integrado de una sociedad."[16]

Ultimately, this analysis also indicates some cause for optimism. The Cuban condition is not a one-sided, dead-end situation as the state proclaims. Social actors have remarkably retained their capacity to re-invent and negotiate spaces by manipulating their own mechanisms and reacting against those utilized by the state. History, as Marx once remarked, is made by individuals according to circumstances given. Social mechanisms are the vehicle to govern state/society relations in Cuba today.

---

16. José Joaquín Brunner, "La cultura en una sociedad autoritaria," FLACSO, SCL/10879/083 (1983).

THE STABILITY OF THE INSTITUTIONS OF
THE CUBAN STATE DURING THE TRANSITION

B. E. Aguirre

The author makes the assumption that there *will not be* a rapid political transition in Cuba immediately after the death of Mr. Fidel Castro. It is also assumed that democracy, constitutional guarantees and liberties, and the rule of law will not be established over a short period of time. Instead, it is argued here that at the death of Mr. Castro, the one-party political regime in place today will continue to govern the island for the foreseeable future. The author's cited articles on the reasons for the stability of Cuba's political system (Aguirre, 1999), the nature of the culture of opposition in the island (Aguirre, 1998; 2001), the effectiveness of social control systems (Aguirre, 2002), and the nature of the Cuban elite provide the rationale for this perspective on political change in Cuba.

OUTLOOK

It is the author's view is that there *will not be* a rapid political transition in Cuba immediately after the death of Mr. Castro. Instead, the present-day one-party political regime and the absence of constitutional guarantees will continue during the first five years following his death. This forecast is based on the following reasons:

First Reason: The legitimacy of the Castro-led government, if legitimacy is understood not as a population's agreement with the government about its programs and policies but as hegemonic control by the government of the interpretative schemes people use to make sense of their worlds (Aguirre, 1999). Such legitimacy is based in large part on the presence of a cultural system producing social control rather than

primarily on sheer force and terror. As I have written elsewhere (Aguirre, 2002), the basic quality of the system of social control in Cuba is its combination of both formal and informal processes that simultaneously emphasize openness and rigidity. Both formal and informal systems are guided by an ideology, a reigning political culture, and the operations of a centrally planned society. Elements of the informal system are propaganda, education, residential patterns, humor, myths and rituals, and charismatic authority. The formal system is one geared to block all anti-hegemonic acts of individuals and organizations, particularly those acts that if left unchecked could become symbolic acts encouraging similar patterns of behaviors perceived as undesirable by the authorities. Comparatively greater importance is given nowadays to reactive rather than proactive formal social control mechanisms—as exemplified by the Cuban government's rapid action brigades.

There are too many empirically verifiable examples of the effectiveness of this system of domination to give an inclusive account here. A critical dimension is the near absence of knowledge among the Cuban people of actors and actions and events that reflect a culture of opposition to the present-day regime. In an earlier paper (Aguirre, unpublished), the author created a culture of opposition (CO) scale based on information collected during December 1998 to April 1999 from 1,023 recently arrived Cuban immigrants who had been in the United States for 90 days or less (for the methodology used in the original survey, see Roberts et al., 1999, 11ff.; Roberts, 1999;

Betancourt and Grenier, 1999). The Knowledge of culture of opposition scale is a seven-item scale that includes information on explicit acts of dissent and on leaders and organizations of the dissidence:

- Whether respondents had knowledge of independent union leaders;

- Personally knew Cuban dissidents;

- Knew about the "Support for a Democratic Transition in Cuba" document released by the Clinton administration in 1994;

- Knew the substance of "The Fatherland Belongs to All" declaration by four prominent Cuban dissidents;

- Knew about the 1998 street demonstration in support of dissident Reinaldo Alfaro;

- Could identify eight major leaders of the dissident movement in the island; and

- Knew of the existence of the "Cuban Council," an organized, peaceful, important effort to bring about political and social change.

Figure 1. Knowledge of the Culture of Opposition

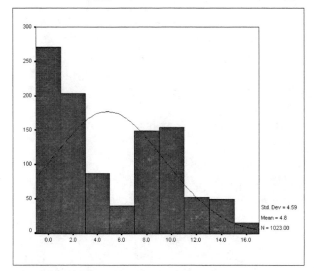

As shown in Figure 1, the distribution of the Cuban respondents in the scale is negatively skewed. The vast majority of respondents had a rather incomplete knowledge of the CO; 26.5 percent had no knowledge whatsoever of the CO, while 50 percent scored

3. Only 87 respondents scored 12 or more in this scale. This state of generalized ignorance of the culture of opposition can be hypothesized to be partly the result of the great effectiveness of the systems of social control in Cuba as well as of a generalized sense of disinterestedness in public affairs and distrust of public institutions in the population.

This generalized state of ignorance and cynicism is produced by government policies and programs and would continue to be an important contributor to the political stability and continuity of the regime at the death of Mr. Castro. This is the case since the prevailing contemporary view in the social sciences regarding the preconditions for the occurrence of political change in national political systems agree that such change depends not only on structural opportunities and the presence of social movement organizations clamoring for change, but on the availability to populations of competing frames of interpretation which are at present insufficiently developed in Cuba.

The stability of the political system in Cuba is in part the result of the political alienation of the Cuban people, their indifference towards the public good. It is a generalized sense of alienation produced by the system of social control of the Cuban state that during decades has channeled, controlled and frustrated the aspirations of the Cuban people. They cannot change it so they try to ignore it, showing in their indifference their lack of hope and their skepticism. Their quietude is a key foundational element of the present day domination of the Cuban state by the Castro brothers and their followers.

State-sponsored collective behavior in Cuba illustrates the legitimacy-building mechanisms used by the regime. It is in this context that the vote of 100 percent of the population in favor of the government's initiative in the last plebiscite cannot be assumed to reflect the wishes and the opinions of the people of Cuba, but rather is a wonderful example of the effectiveness of the hegemonic control by the government of the rhetorical interpretations available to Cubans which shape their behavior in public. It is not proof of their unanimity of opinion in favor of the government.

Swidler (1986) calls our attention to the value of thinking about culture as external to the person. She identifies culture in terms of semiotic codes, rhetorical contexts, and the institutional networks impacting people's lives. Using her framework to understand the Cuban case, we can say that governmental social control materializes in Cuba in institutional terms in the absence of civil society. All of the institutions present in people's lives reflect the interpretative scheme and follow the guidelines of the state, so people, to get along in their institutionally-based relations must also act within government's stipulations.

Rhetorical control comes from the restriction of the interpretative schemes available to people, so that the only rhetoric that takes place in Cuba in public occasions is the rhetoric of the state. The alternative rhetoric of the enemy, of the other, of the dissidence, of the Yankee, are always second hand, as it were, always fictional messages mediated by the government's interpretations. They are in fact made part of the officially sanctioned reigning rhetoric. These alternative rhetorical schemes constructed by the government and made part of its own rhetoric are thus examples of hyper reality, for they suppose the existence of a reality that never existed, of presumed "enemies" that are never allowed to act in Cuba.

Controls based on semiotic codes come from the person's perception of what others will interpret and say about the person's actions. They come from "del que dirán," from doing what needs to be done to not attract attention to oneself. People do what they do not because they want to do it or think it is appropriate or the right thing to do, but because they worry about how others are going to interpret their actions. I would suggest that these three types of cultural dynamics identified by Swidler help us understand the system of social control that makes possible a vote of 100 percent in favor of a government initiative.

Second Reason: A second matter is the absence of an important type of political opportunity, namely splits and severe conflicts among members of the Cuban political elite and lack of control over the key institutions through which power is exercised, namely the armed forces and the Cuban Communist Party (CCP) (del Aguila, 1999). It is an elite that has been in power more than forty years, which gives it a great deal of cultural and political coherence. This longevity makes possible and implies similarities among elite members of experiences of socialization, styles of living, expectations, and sense of responsibility in the exercise of public office. It is an elite united by:

- Endogamy;

- Racial homogeneity;

- The economic interdependence of its members and their recognition that their privileges are tied to the economic and political system established during the Castro regime;

- The widespread complicity of the elite in the multiple and variegated crimes of the regime. Much can be understood about this process if we study the sentencing to death of General Arnaldo Ochoa in 1989 and the participation in this crime of the most important members of the Cuban elite.

In sum, the Cuban elite is a political elite unified by traditions, similarities in life experiences, family relations, economic interests, and odious political acts. These various elements strengthen each other and form a strong community of interests: the elite will not disappear at the death of its leader. Nor can we find evidence of chronic and unresolved conflict among different segments of the key institutions of the state.

Third Reason: The third matter to consider is that the Cuban government limits very effectively the growth of civil society. Moreover, the dissident movements and the isolated opposition to Castro's government are ineffective and weak and suffer extensive persecution by government social control systems. The opposition lacks political opportunities at present and does not have the resources, such as access to the mass media, the right to assemble and to organize and petition the authorities, and other tactical matters necessary to advance programmatic alternatives that would have a chance of gaining a degree of acceptance by the Cuban people at the death of Mr. Castro. It will take time, probably a few years, and an opening of the political system for the opposition to begin to transform the political landscape in the island.

The author's intent is not to dismiss the great courage and unremitting effort of the many patriots in Cuba that at great personal costs carry peaceful opposition to the regime. Instead, we can expedite change in Cuba not only by supporting the opposition, but also by helping diminish the cultural domination of the regime, the unity of the reigning elite, and by propitiating conflict in the armed forces and the CCP. To paraphrase Doug McAdam's argument (1996), we need to foster the cognitive liberation of the Cuban people and divisions within the political elite. In my view, neither of these preconditions exists in Cuba today to the extent that they would bring about a rapid change of the political system at the death of Mr. Castro.

A number of analysts of Cuba argue for a quick political transition in Cuba in the aftermath of Mr. Castro's death. I concede that this is probably the majority opinion. Partly supporting their reasoning is the experience of former Soviet republics and countries like East Germany and Czechoslovakia. There is also the perception among many Cuba watchers that the political regime is much less in control of events in Cuba than I have portrayed it and that its domination is undermined by corruption and cynicism. I do not agree with either of these lines of reasoning. Cuba is not Eastern Europe. The links of the Cuban revolution to nationalist feelings and resentment towards the USA is very different from the domination of the communist parties in Eastern Europe in the aftermath of World War II and their dependence on the threat of invasion by the Russian Army. Mr. Castro's regime has much greater legitimacy. I also do not agree with the perception that his regime is a paper tiger, waiting to collapse on its own weight. Obviously unexpected events could change the outcome I outline. These can be either internal or external events. Internally, there could be a military putsch. Externally, there could be an invasion by United States military. Both scenarios would mean a great deal of bloodshed with very uncertain outcomes. I do not believe that either present viable, much less desirable, political alternatives at this time.

FIVE TO TEN YEARS AFTER THE DEATH OF MR. CASTRO

The long-term prognosis of what would happen in Cuba at the death of Mr. Castro depends on national and international dynamics too complex to discuss at length here but which, at any rate, would take five to ten years to develop after the death of Mr. Castro. It will probably take that much time for new patterns to come into being. The elite will change after his death, most probably to a Chinese-type system in which there is the commingling of the continued totalitarian political control of the state by the ruling political elite and the CCP, with the emergence and public acceptability of a capitalist elite which would act as intermediary between the state and the agents of international capitalism in Cuba.

The entrepreneurial activity of segments of the political elite will become more marked in the years to come, particularly after the death of Mr. Castro, at which time it can be expected that the Cuban state will relax access to the economy by international capital, particularly from the United States of America. The opportunity for corruption at all levels will increase exponentially during this time (for an extended analysis of corruption in Cuba see Puerta, 2002). It is conceivable that the Cuban state will allow the emergence of Cuban oligarchs, duplicating, to some extent, the experience of Boris Berezovsky, Vladimir Gusinsky, and Alexander Smolensky, among others, in Russia in the aftermath of the disappearance of the U.S.S.R.

The most important task for the Cuban government during this time of transition will be to negotiate this opening to capitalism and the transformation of segments of the ruling elite into a capitalist class in such a way that it will not endanger its continued political control. The success of this project will mean the establishment of severe and ruthless capitalist exploitation of the Cuban people under the intermediary auspices and patronage of a new Cuban capitalist class allied to the state. The present day incorporation of officers from the security services, the armed forces, and other adepts to the government into advanced training in economics and managerial activities can be understood as an exploratory attempt by the regime to set the limits that will be enforced during the economic transformation to come. It is also in this context that the recent, historic visit of President J. Carter to Cuba can be understood. With it, Mr. Castro anticipates his own death and tries to influence the terms of the rapprochement between the Cuban state and American capitalist firms in a future without him.

Thus, my sense is that, absent some other opposing set of forces, in the immediate future we will see a Cuban state that favors the transformation of a political elite into an economic elite that in turn acts as the conduit between international capital and the government and enriches itself in the process. This is, I am afraid, the real nature of the transition that everyone awaits so impatiently thinking, erroneously I believe, that it will be a political transition.

AN ALTERNATIVE

One final question: What can stop this process? What can create the opportunity for democracy and equality of opportunities and the rule of law and constitutional guarantees in Cuba? If it comes, it will not come primarily or initially from the United States of America, the exile community in Miami, or from capitalist firms. Capitalists require political stability to guarantee their investments. They do not require either freedom or democracy. It is true that most capitalist developed countries have democratic political systems, but this happy coincidence is not the case in the periphery of the world, in the developing world, and in Communist China.

We must look inward for an answer. Poverty is widespread on the island, and, if the literature on the social science of protest is any guide, the poor, to the extent that they are not organized and mobilized, are not political actors. Thus, it is not poverty per se but the social organization of aggrieved populations that allows us to guess about the nature of post-transitional political dynamics. What will be the political mobilization of aggrieved communities? What sectors of the public will likely be important political actors or, expressed differently, what groups likely will become mobilized and place demands on the political system and limits on capitalist exploitation?

For many decades, interest group politics have been suppressed very effectively by the Castro-led government even as it created a sense of entitlement in the population. This seemingly contradictory process typifies the regime: it cannot provide for the most elemental needs of the people and yet it portrays itself as their champion and benefactor, always blaming the United States government for every problem it cannot solve. But that system of justifications will not be as successful when the very state becomes the main underwriter of capital and when the contradictions allowing for the new capitalist class begins to play an ever increasing role in the daily lives of the people. An inescapable contradiction in the process of capitalist class emergence and the presence of international capitalist firms operating in Cuba is also the growth of civil society and the loss of control by the state of the institutional life ways. The economic change will bring with it increasing contacts between Cubans in and out of Cuba as well as increasing opportunities for social movement organizations to coordinate activities in and out of Cuba. It is obvious to me that it will also mean the reactivation of aggrieved populations in the island.

Old and new political claimants will become active and will organize under an emergent capitalist economic system. Many of these constituencies were active in the pre-1959 Republican period. Others are products of the post 1959 period. Probable candidates for active public participation are: university students, the labor movement [Grenier (1996) writes that in the future we can expect many independent labor unions rather than one major labor union such as the Cuban Workers' Central (Central de Trabajadores de Cuba—CTC)], agricultural cooperatives, environmentalists, ethnic and racial minorities, women, homosexual and bisexual minorities, and professional associations.

Before Castro took power in 1959, active social movements of university students and a powerful labor union movement existed in Cuba (Magnusen and Rodríguez, 1998). Also active in the defense of the interest of their members were a number of very effective voluntary organizations in the black community (Aguirre, 1976; Aguirre and Bonilla Silva, 2002), as well as professional organizations of lawyers, doctors, architects, newspaper writers, and other occupational groups. Since 1959, other groups, particularly small agriculturists, private agricultural cooperatives (Alvarez, 1999), independent women's organizations, and environmentalists, have emerged in Cuba and suffered varying degrees of repression.

Nevertheless, they are part of civil society and can be expected to participate vigorously in the future life of the country. It is these forces of the Cuban nation assisted by the exile community, the European community, the international labor movement, and other organizations throughout the world that are the only hope for equality and democracy in the island and for bringing to justice those who have robbed the nation.

BIBLIOGRAPHY

Aguirre, B. E. "A Test of Culture of Opposition Power Grid." Unpublished manuscript, work in progress.

Aguirre, B. E., and E. Bonilla Silva. "Does Race Matter Among Cuban Immigrants? An Analysis of the Racial Characteristics of Recent Cuban Immigrants," *Journal of Latin American Studies*, 34, no. 2 (2002): 311–24.

Aguirre, B. E. "A Test of Culture of Opposition Theory." Pages 404–17 in *Cuba in Transition—Volume 11*. Washington: Association for the Study of the Cuban Economy, 2001.

Aguirre, B. E. "The Internationalization of Collective Behavior: Lessons from Elian." Pages 254–64 in *Cuba in Transition—Volume 10*. Washington: Association for the Study of the Cuban Economy, 2000.

Aguirre, B. E. "The Stability of Cuba's Political System." Pages 273–78 in E. Linger and J. Cotman, eds., *Cuban Transitions at the Millennium*. Maryland: International Development Options, 1999 (reprint).

Aguirre, B. E. "Culture of Opposition in Cuba." Pages 326–43 in *Cuba in Transition—Volume 8*. Washington: Association for the Study of the Cuban Economy, 1998.

Aguirre, B. E. "Differential Migration of Cuban Social Races," *Latin American Research Review*, 12 (1976): 103–24.

Betancourt, E. F. and G. Grenier. "Measuring Cuban Public Opinion: Economic, Social and Political Issues." Pages 251–69 in *Cuba in Transition—Volume 9*. Washington: Association for the Study of the Cuban Economy, 1999.

del Aguila, Juan M. "Reflections on a Non-Transition in Cuba: Comments on Elites." Pages 192–200 in *Cuba in Transition—Volume 9*. Washington: Association for the Study of the Cuban Economy, 1999.

Grenier, Guillermo J. "The Changing Nature of Labor Organizations in Post Communist Europe and the Implications for Labor in Cuba." Pages 346–57 in *Cuba in Transition—Volume 6*. Washington: Association for the Study of the Cuban Economy, 1996.

Magnusen, Karl O., and Leonardo Rodríguez. "Cuba, Labor and Change," *Labor Studies Journal*, 23, no. 2 (1998): 21–41

McAdams, Doug. "Conceptual Origins, Current Problems, Future Directions." Pp. 23-40 in D. McAdams, J. D. McCarthy, and Mayer N. Zald, editors. *Comparative Perspectives on Social Movements*. Cambridge, Cambridge University Press, 1996.

Puerta, Ricardo. "Corrupción Actual en Cuba: Herencia y Vicio," in this volume.

Roberts, Churchill, Ernesto Betancourt, Guillermo Grenier, Richard Scheaffer. *Measuring Cuban Public Opinion: Project Report*. Gainesville: The University of Florida, United States Agency for International Development, Agency Contract LAG-G-00-98-00021-01, September 1999.

Roberts, Churchill. "Measuring Public Opinion: Methodology." Pages 245–48 in *Cuba in Transition—Volume 9*. Washington: Association for the Study of the Cuban Economy, 1999.

Swidler, Ann. "Culture in Action: Symbols and Strategies," *American Sociological Review* 15 (April 1986): 273-286.

THE SURVIVAL OF THE CUBAN REGIME: A POLITICAL ECONOMY PERSPECTIVE

Javier Corrales[1]

The Cuban regime has survived three major pressures for change in the last two decades: the democratic wave that swept both left- and right-wing dictatorships in Latin America in the 1980s; the demise of the Soviet Bloc in the late 1980s; and a major economic depression at home in the 1989-1994 period. The continuity of the political regime (see Suchlicki 2000, Domínguez 1993) has amazed most Cubanologists.

Although politics in Cuba changed little in the 1990s, the economy on the other hand changed a lot. Between 1993 and 1996, the Cuban government opened several sectors to foreign direct investment, liberalized farm markets, legalized dollar-holding and some forms of self-employment, and reduced the fiscal deficits by cutting spending. Compared to reforms elsewhere in Latin America, the Cuban reforms were timid in scope. Cuba fell short of privatizing any state-owned enterprise, permitting full-scale profit making, and liberalizing many markets to domestic investors, as many Latin American nations did in the early 1990s. But compared to the Revolution's own past, the reforms were profound. The few sectors that were targeted for reform actually underwent profound change.

Economically, therefore, the Cuban regime displayed a combination of both deep reform and reform avoidance. It introduced substantial change in some areas, but it also acted cautiously by exempting many sectors from reform.

This paper seeks to provide an explanation for these two puzzles—the survival of Cuban regime, and the combination of change-seeking and change-avoidance in economic policy in the 1990s. It makes two central points. First, the dual nature of reform in Cuba is explained by the interplay between hard-liners and soft-liners at the top level of government. Castro in 1994 faced competing, mutually exclusive political demands: important sectors of the ruling party demanded reform, whereas others demanded no reform at all. The dual outcome of the reforms is the result of an Executive Branch seeking to carry out a balancing act between these two groups.

Second, and more important, the dual nature of economic reforms helps explain the survival of the regime, for two reasons. First, the reforms served to deflate, in fact, completely fool those actors that in the early 1990s were pressuring for deeper economic and political opening. The reforms allowed the state to give the impression that the regime was moving toward the market—a type signal that was necessary to placate the pressures coming from reform demanders—when in fact, the government never intended to move in that direction. Instead, the government intended to side with the hard-liners, but this was only possible after sufficiently placating those pressuring for change. The reforms allowed the

1. This paper is part of a larger book manuscript on "The Politics of Economic Crises in Latin America in the 1990s" (in progress).

state to fool the reformers while simultaneously boosting the hard-liners.

The second reason is that the reforms, however limited, actually magnified the power of the state by enhancing its capacity to dispense inducements and constraints. It is normally believed that economic openings hurt incumbent politicians, and in the end, undermine authoritarian states in general. In Cuba, the opposite happened. The reforms were carried out in a manner that enlarged the leverage of Cuba's incumbents over society. They allowed the state to become the gatekeeper of a new and highly valuable commodity in the economy: the private, externally-connected sector. By becoming the gatekeeper, the state has increased the payoff of cooperating with it: loyalty is rewarded by receiving access to this sector. In many ways, the Cuban state has transformed the way it interacts with society: while the number of winners is decreasing, the reward that actors obtain for endorsing the state is becoming more valuable.

THE RESILIENCE OF (ONE-PARTY) AUTHORITARIAN REGIMES

Incumbents in authoritarian regimes in general, especially in one-party authoritarian regimes, stand a better chance of surviving internal and external shocks than in democracies. Bueno de Mesquita, Morrow, Siverson and Smith (2000) argue that this phenomenon is explained by the differences in size of the winning coalition, defined as the members of the population whose support is essential for the survival of the regime (see also Geddes 1999). Incumbents in democracies require, by definition, large winning coalitions, at least large enough to win the necessary votes over those of their rivals. Incumbents in authoritarian regimes, by definition, do not require large winning coalitions to stay in office. They are sustained by a small size of the population.

To stay in office, incumbents in both democracies and authoritarian regimes must do the same: please or reward their winning coalition with "things of value." Precisely because winning coalitions in authoritarian regimes are smaller, pleasing them is easier, or less costly to the incumbents. So, in the context of a huge crisis, the incumbents in authoritarian regimes will still find enough pork to please the small winning coalition. In one-party dominant authoritarian regimes, the incumbents enjoy "greater political resources": they can use bureaucratic privileges for recruiting a minimal number of subordinates (Haggard and Kaufman 1995:13). If the winning coalition were larger, as is the case in every democracy, it would be harder to find sufficient "things of value" for the entire coalition.

In principle, therefore, it is easier for authoritarian regimes to maintain the loyalty of the core group during economic crisis than it is for democracies. With fewer favors, they can achieve far greater loyalty among the reduced number of actors that support them.

Cuba certainly qualifies as an example of small winning coalition regime. The pillar of the regime includes three selective groups: the party (with a membership of 600,000 in a country of 11 million), the top echelon of the military, and the security apparatus (Suchlicki 2000). As long as enough "things of value" can be provided to these actors, which is not too costly given that this is not a large group, the loyalty of this core group can be preserved, even during harsh times.

PRESSURE FOR REFORM

In their model about the survivability of authoritarian regimes, Bueno de Mesquita et al. fail to consider the possibility of internal splits within the winning coalition. Other theorists have convincingly shown that deep economic crises in general tend to create divisions among incumbent forces, whether democratic or authoritarian. The incumbent leadership will split regarding how best to respond to the crisis. Essentially, the split occurs between soft-liners (pro-reform) and hard-liners (reform-adverse) (see Przeworski 1991, Haggard and Kaufman 1995; Corrales 2000). In authoritarian regimes, the split can occur along yet another dimension: what to do politically? Again, the incumbents will split between those favoring political opening and those seeking hardening (O'Donnell et al. 1986). Although the incidence of splits is less likely in single-party authoritarian regimes as opposed to military or personalistic regimes (see Geddes 1999; Haggard and Kaufman 1995:11-13), these splits have nonetheless occurred in one-party states such as Mexico, Korea, Taiwan, leading to regime change (Solinger 2001).

In the 1990s, Cuba's winning coalition did not split over the issue of politics—a consensus on preserving single-party dominance seems to have prevailed. Yet, it split significantly over economics. An important part of the Cuban leadership lobbied Castro on behalf of significant market opening. At the 1991 party congress, which took place shortly after the demise of the Soviet bloc and in the midst of recession, these pro-reformers achieved more vocal and prominent positions of power (see *Miami Herald* 9/28/92:12A), constituting an internal focus of pressure.

Pressure for economic reform also came from external actors. The literature on economic reform stresses that in conditions of economic crises, incumbents are desperate to recruit new external allies or favors. Cuba's potentially new external allies became all the more insistent on the need for economic reform. One such set of allies included countries in Western Europe (see Roy 2002), and to a lesser extent, Latin America. Some of these external actors themselves were engaged in deep market reforms (e.g., Spain and Mexico) and wanted Cuba, at the very least, to do the same. They were eager to invest in Cuba, provided more market facilities were granted. Foreign investors—another set of sought-after allies whom Cuba desperately needed to lure in order to ease the island's investment deficit—were also clamoring for economic reforms. Cuba desperately needed capital: its capital stock depreciated over a decade and no new investment had taken place nor was possible (Zimbalist 2000:21-22). Hungry for diplomatic allies and, increasingly, external investors, Castro simply could not afford to disregard the view of these external actors.

Finally, pressure also came from society at large. In the early 1990s, Cuba entered into a severe depression, which took a heavy toll on citizens' livelihoods. Food consumption levels, to mention one indicator, plummeted from 3,109 calories a day in 1989 to 2,357 by 1996, a dramatic 24 percent drop in calories in a space of a few years (Cubanalysis n.d.). The regime had justifiable reasons to fear urban riots. Offering some relief to society was imperative.

Thus, by 1993, Fidel Castro faced two competing and mutually exclusive sets of political pressures. On the one hand, a majority within the winning coalition wanted to entrench the status quo (the hard-liners). On the other hand, a not insignificant part of the winning coalition (including both domestic and external actors) and societal groups, called for reforms (the pro-reform group). How did the Cuban state react?

THE DILEMMA OF MARKET REFORMS FOR AUTHORITARIAN REGIMES

The Cuban state faced a dilemma. Reforms were necessary to please a growing component of the domestic winning coalition, to court a large component of external actors, and to placate domestic anguish. Yet, reforms risked alienating the largest sector of the winning coalition, the hard-liners.

This alienation could occur in three ways. First, hard-liners could feel politically abandoned, seeing their views ignored by Castro. Second, hard-liners would feel the costs of reforms more profoundly. Liberalization entailed shrinking the size and prominence of the state, an this meant reduced prerogatives to those who managed state offices, mostly hard-liners (Pérez-Stable 1999). Third, the reforms would increase the power of political rivals by promoting the rise of new, possibly wealthier, societal actors (self-employed, new capitalists, new business groups, new labor associations, new savers). By empowering civil society, reformers can undermine the monopoly of political power held by hard-liners in authoritarian contexts (see Feng 2000:204).

The *duros* thus hated *glasnost* and *perestroika*, in vogue in the Soviet world in the 1980s. They possibly gave Castro a warning along these lines: "if you liberalize, compañero Fidel, your political base, tenuous as it is, will become even shakier. You will unleash unpredictable forces, and worse, we will abandon you." For Castro, it was risky to dismiss the *duros*. The *duros* were, after all, the most die-hard loyalists of his regime. Castro simply could not afford to forgo their support at a time when every other pillar of the regime was crumbling.

The dilemma confronted by the authoritarian state is that reforming was necessary as a way to soften the crisis and placate the ever-larger political pressure for change, but it undermined the very same group that acted as the most reliable pillar of the regime. Castro needed to make a decision, and a quick one: by 1993, the economy continued to plunge, showing no signs of recovery. Pro-reformers argued that reforms were urgently needed to prevent the ship from sinking; the *duros* argued that the time was not right to loosen things up.

EVIDENCE OF THE SPLIT: A LOOK AT CUBA'S CABINET IN 1996

It is not easy to gauge the political divisions within the top echelon of the Cuban government, a regime that is well known for its hermetic internal politics. Assessing internal politics is even harder in a country that lacks a free press and whose government is keen on always portraying an image of unity. Yet, theoretical analysis and anecdotal evidence suggests that the economic crisis and the process of economic reforms produced internal divisions within the Cuban cabinet.

Albeit imperfect, one way to discern this is to examine the number of new entrants into the cabinet. Most theorists of presidential politics agree that new policies come with new ministers. This is so because new policies require new leaders with new convictions and new energy to promote the changes (Domínguez 1997). There is no question that the 1993-96 period—unquestionably the most policy dynamic in years—was characterized by a significant degree of new entrants into the Executive branch. Up until then, changes in the Cuban cabinet were for the most part modest. Between 1987 and 1992, for instance, there were a total of 20 cabinet changes,

amounting to approximately 3.33 changes per year (in a cabinet that included 33-34 positions).[2] In terms of economic policy orientation, this period was characterized by one of the most hard-line in Cuba, which some analysts have described as the return to totalitarianism after a brief transition into a softer post-totalitarian regime (Mujal-León and Busby 2001).[3] This cabinet stability ends in 1993-96, coinciding with the period of major policy change.[4] Between 1993 and 1996, there were 25 cabinet changes, peaking in 1994/95, with 10 changes in that year alone.

The result of these changes is that Cuba's Executive branch was transformed in the 1993-96 period: 17 newcomers were incorporated, coming very close to matching the number of the old guards (those who entered prior 1992, some going as far back as the 1970s). By 1996, the number of the old guard was 21 (see Table 1). I will call this group the "pre-1992 class."

Two points are clear. During the high reform period of 1993-96, Castro did not hand over the cabinet entirely to newcomers. The cabinet remained under the control of the pre-1992 class." Nevertheless, the space provided to newcomers was not miniscule either. Newcomers captured almost half of the cabinet, including crucial positions (e.g., foreign relations, economy and planning).

It is possible to assume that the balance between the "pre-1992 class" and the newcomers represent a rough estimate of the balance between the *duros* and the reformers. I recognize the risks behind this assumption. It is conceivable that some of the newcomers were not that much more committed to reforms than the old guards, or that the some of the old-guards might have been pragmatists amenable to

---

2. All data of cabinet changes drawn from *Europa World Year Book* (various years).

3. Mujal-León and Busby (2001) argue that during 1971-85 Cuba seemed to have been moving gradually toward to "post-totalitarianism." Politically, there was greater institutionalization of political organizations such as the party and lesser dependence on Fidel Castro (see also Bengelsdorff 1994). Economically, the regime experimented in 1970s with Soviet-style forms of economic organization that granted more decision-making power to state enterprises, and in 1980-1985 went as far as to create farmer's markets (see Mesa-Lago 2000).

4. In 1994, the government underwent a deep reform: some ministries and agencies were abolished or merged; others were created (Cubanalysis 2000).

accepting the new changes.[5] Some reports suggest that these are indeed new technocrats, or perhaps, "communist technocrats" (Cubanalysis 2000). The only way to confirm this is to conduct interviews. In the absence of that, I will need to rely on a well accepted theoretical assumption. The policy orientation of hired ministers ought to reflect the policy direction of the period of recruitment. It is unlikely for an Executive chief to recruit newcomers whose views go against the official policy. Cuba's official policy in 1993-96 was precisely the pursuit of some market-friendly reforms. Thus, the class of 1993-96 must have been quite sympathetic, or at least comfortable with, such a policy stand. Otherwise they would not have been appointed.

One can now conclude that the Cuban cabinet became severely split in the 1993-96 period between reformers (the newcomers) and *duros* (the pre-1992 class). Which side did the Chief Executive take?

The common view is that, at least during this period, Castro sided with many of the reformers, who were believed to have had the upper hand, at least until the 1996. A closer look at the reform process reveals that quite the contrary, the *duros* were probably achieving the greatest influence

One can hypothesize that a government that is siding with the hard-liners will display the following features in its reform process:

- Economic reforms are delayed as long as possible for reasons that are hard to justify economically.

- Once reforms are unavoidable, the authorities proceed to reform by simultaneously creating "power reserves" for the hard-liners. Power reserves means domains of policy that remain under control of the hard-liners.

- As soon as the economy begins to show signs of improvement, the Executive discontinues (rather than deepens) the reform process.

Fidel Castro's approach to economic reforms meets each of these patterns. I discuss each in turn.

DELAYING REFORMS: THE 1991 DECISION NOT TO REFORM

Pressure for reform peaked by 1990-91. At that point, it was clear that the economy was in a tailspin and that external aid from the collapsing Soviet Union would not be forthcoming. There is evidence that at the 1991 party congress, members of the politburo ardently debated the need for reforms.

Yet, the Party Congress decided not to make any major economic changes. Other than announcing austerity (i.e., more rationing of food), what came to be called as the "Special period," and approving a few symbolic political changes in 1992, no major reform initiatives were launched (Font 1997).[6] The hard-line policy of 1986, in which self-employment and property-transactions were limited and street vendors were banned, was continued. Although the government recognized the need for private foreign investments (allowed by law since 1982), very few important foreign investments took place.

POWER RESERVES FOR THE HARD-LINERS: OPENING AND RESTRICTING IN 1993-96

In mid 1993, when Cuba hit its fourth consecutive annual GDP contraction and deepest economic trough yet, the government realized that it had no option but to begin to liberalize. At this point, the pressure for reform was at its highest, both economically and politically. The economic numbers showed no signs of improving, and the domestic and external actors demanding change became all the more insistent. Bowing to this pressure, Cuba launched far

---

5. One hypothesis could be that these cabinet changes were nothing more than a technical downgrading: i.e., an effort by Fidel to replace competent people with younger, easier to manipulate yes-men. On the possibility that the Castro brothers might be surrounding themselves with less-technocratic, more-acquiescent advisers, see declarations by Cuban defector Alcibíades Hidalgo, former adviser to Raúl Castro (*El Nuevo Herald*, July 28 and 30, 2002).

6. The most important symbolic political changes was reforming, or rather, rewording the constitution. References to Soviet-era terms such as the "Soviet Union," "socialist community," "scientific materialism," etc. were replaced with less loaded and more Cuban-like terms such as nationalism, regional solidarity, social justice, Latin America and the Caribbean, José Martí, etc.

Table 1. Cuba's Cabinet, 1996–2002

	Cuba's Cabinet in 1996			Cuba's Cabinet in 2002
Class of pre 1992	**Ministry**	**Entry**	**Born**	
Amat Flores, Carlos	Justice	1991		X
Cabrisas Ruiz, Ricardo	Foreign Trade, Minister of Government	pre 1980	1937	Yes
Cañete Alvarez, José M.	Construction Materials Industry	1990		X
Castro Ruz, Raúl	Armed Forces	pre 1980	1931	Yes
Cienfuegos Gorriarán, Osmany	Tourism			Yes
Colomé Ibarra, Abelardo (Gen.)	Interior	1990	1939	Yes
Dávalos, Arnando Hart	Culture	pre 1980		X
Diarias Rodés, Ramón	S.C. for Standardization	1980		Yes
Gómez Gutiérrez, Luis Ignacio	Education	1991	1943	Yes
Portal León, Marcos J.	Heavy Industry, Basic Industries	1984	1945	Yes
Regueiro, Senén Casas (Gen)	Transport	1990		X
Roca Iglesias, Alejandro	Food Industry	1981	1936	Yes
Rodríguez Cardona, Sonia	S.C. for Tech. And Material Supplies	1987		Yes
Simeón Negrín, Rosa Elena	Pres. of the Ac. of Sci./ Sci, Tech, Env	1986	1943	Yes
Vascos González, Fidel Emilio	S.C. of Statistics	1980-2002		Yes
Vecino Alegret, Fernando	Higher Education	pre 1980	1938	Yes
Fernández Alvarez, José Ramon	VP	pre 1980		Yes
Hernández-Baquero, Jaime Crombet	VP	1991		X
Díaz Suárez, Adolfo	VP	1991		X
Rodríguez Rodríguez, Carlos Rafael	VP	pre 1980		X
Esquivel Yebra, Antonio	VP	1983		X
Retirement rate (8 retired of 21)				38%
		1985		Miret Prieto, Pedro
		pre 1980		Prieto Jiménez, Abel
Modified retirement rate (6 of 21)[a]				29%
Class of 1993-1996				
Castillo Cuesta, Bárbara	Domestic Trade	1995	1946	Yes
Colas Sánchez, Silvano (Gen.)	Communications	1994		Yes
Dotres Martinez, Carlos	Public Health	1996	1948	X
Ferradaz García, Ibrahim	Foreign Invest. and Econ. Coop., Tourism	1996	1949	Yes
González Planas, Roberto Ignacio	Iron/Steel/Metallurigical Industries	1993		X
Jordán Morales, Alfredo	Agriculture	1994		Yes
Junco del Pino, Juan Mario	Construction	1996	1957	Yes
Lage Dávila, Carlos	Secretary of the Council of Ministers	1993	1951	Yes
López Rodríguez, Wilfredo	Without Portfolio	1995	1951	Yes
Millares Rodríguez, José Manuel	Finance and Prices	1996	1934	Yes
Pérez Othon, Jesús D.	Light Industry	1995	1942	Yes
Robaina González, Roberto	Foreign Affairs	1994		X
Rodríguez Garcia, José Luis	Economy and Planning	1996	1946	Yes
Rodríguez Romay, Orlando Felipe	Fishing Industry	1995		X
Soberón Valdés, Francisco	Pres. of the National Bank of Cuba	1995	1944	Yes
Torres Pérez, Nelson	Sugar Industry	1994		X
Valdés Mesa, Salvador	S.C for Labor and Social Security	1995		X
Retirement rate (6 of 17)				35%
				Class of 1997-2002
		2001	1961	Acosta Santana, Fernando
		1997	1953	Díaz Sotolongo, Roberto
		2000	1950	Lomas Morales, Marta
		2001	1951	López Valdés, Alfredo
		2000	1948	Morales Cartaya, Alfredo
		2000	1955	Pedraza Rodríguez, Lina O.
		1997	1948	Pérez Morales, Alvaro
		2000	1965	Pérez Roque, Felipe R.
		1998	1942	Rosales del Toro, Ulises

a. Two of the retirees in 1996-2002 were replaced by old guardians.

reaching reforms starting in mid 1993. Yet, the pattern of liberalization conformed with the "power reserve" hypothesis. Efforts were done to please the hard-liners by guaranteeing them new sources of power.

In reviewing Cuba's economic policy in the 1980s, Cruz and Seleny (2002) argue that a crucial objective of the government was to assert the power of the party-state, over that of technocrats and market actors. The few market openings that occurred in the late 1970s came to an abrupt close in 1986, despite the economic gains achieved. The reasoning was: if the market were allowed to determine everything, Castro wondered, what would be left for the party to administer. Thus, despite the economic stagnation that ensued from 1986-90 (Roque Cabello and Sánchez Herrero 1998), the state maintained its anti-market policy until 1993.

By 1993, as the reform pressures peaked, Castro was compelled to do something. The optimum strategy, from his point of view, was to introduce the least amount of reform in order to placate reform-demanders and still not alienate hard-liners. The solution was to introduce an uneven process of market reform: liberalize selectively, and in those sectors that were liberalized, introduce substantial state-based restrictions. This led to an odd pattern of reform. Some areas were opened, in order to please the pressure group that most actively called for this change, but in the end creating sufficient restrictions, in order to please the non-reformers (See Pastor 2000). Appendix 1 provides detailed examples of the restrictions in agriculture, foreign trade, monetary policy (dollarization), self-employment, the private sector, and telecommunications. These are the areas typically considered subject to the largest degree of opening. Yet, the restrictions imposed were quite substantial.

Cruz and Seleny (2002) label this "segmented marketization." I propose instead: stealth statism. Behind the pretense of market reforms, the Cuban government managed to introduce new opportunities for the state to impose penalties.

The point of this opening and restricting style of economic reform was twofold. First, the government managed to create the illusion in 1993-96 that Cuba was indeed committed to market change. This was necessary in order to alleviate the pressure for change. The reforms served as a fooling device. Economists and political scientists agree that economic policy can often be used by governments to issue signals. Governments can announce audacious policies ("overshooting") for no reason other than to send a signal of commitment: the more audacious the policy announcement, the more likely it is that skeptics will begin to think that this government is serious. The higher the credibility deficit faced by the government, the more likely it will rely on signaling devices. Latin American presidents in the early 1990s did this precisely because investors did not believe their intentions to enact reform. Likewise, reform-demanders were skeptical of Castro's intentions. Castro needed to change those expectations. Hence, it was necessary to take bold steps, or at least, appear to be doing so.

A clear example of this occurred in November 1993, during a visit of Rosa Diez, a trade representative from Spain and a leading figure in the ruling PSOE. Castro said: Cuba "must adapt to the reality of today's world; the reforms are 'irreversible,'" and "we're creating an opening and we're making it as broad as possible" (*The Miami Herald*, 11/5/93:18A). In reality, this was nothing more than an illusion. Cuba did not intend to go far on the reforms. Indeed, even as the reforms were being announced, enormous restrictions on each reform were being created. Thus, Cuba's reforms differ from those of Latin America in the early 1990s in that the Executive never intended to pursue liberalization at all. The reforms were nothing more than a way to create the illusion that the government was going to reform, in order to placate a source of political pressure, and gain some political space.

The second objective was to reward the *duros* within the government. The *duros* were opposed to change. The restrictions placated their opposition. It persuaded them that the reforms would not go too far. And more important, it gave the *duros* a privileged new role: gatekeepers to the "new economy." I develop this point later.

ONCE OUT OF THE WOODS...

Another indicator that the Chief Executive favored the *duros* was the pace of reform after recovery. A true reform-minded administration, in which reforming technocrats have the upper hand, normally deepens the reforms once there has been some degree of economic recovery. Pro-reform sectors of the ruling party will use the recovery to argue that the reforms are working, and thus, it is necessary to do more. In contrast, an Executive committed to pleasing the hard-liners does the opposite, doing everything possible to decelerate, and maybe even discontinue some of the reform accomplishments.

This is precisely what happened in Cuba. Once the economy began to recover (mid 1996), the government slowed down the reform process, reversed some existing policies, and never considered again seriously the most profound reforms (legalizing private property, liberalizing the labor market, privatizing state-owned enterprises) (see Pérez-López 2001). By January 1996, for instance, one of the hard-liners in the Central Committee declared: the party cadre "must form an ideological trench, impenetrable and indomitable, from which the Marxist ideology ... can be defended and from which diversionist ideology can be countered" (*The Miami Herald*, 1/16/96). In the Spring of 1996, the government launched attacks against the intellectual community and political dissidents (*The Miami Herald* 5/2/96). Raúl Castro strongly criticized both the reforms implemented and even the Communist analysts advocating more reforms (Pérez-López 2001:51). In 1997, the size of the winning coalition is reduced further: the Central Committee of the Cuban Communist Party was purged, reducing its size from 225 to 150 members (Inter-Press Service, 10/13/97). And by 2000, the pace of approved foreign direct investments slowed down considerably, with the government increasing the amount of "trabas," or bureaucratic obstacles, to the approval of new joint ventures (Travieso-Díaz and Trumbull 2002). Vice President Lage has also criticized the foreign trade zones, and efforts are being made to grant contracts to domestic state-owned enterprises rather than foreign corporations.

THE NEW "GATEKEEPER" STATE

The economic reforms transformed Cuba from a centrally planned economy to a state-capitalist economy. Students of Latin America's political development should recognize this term. State-capitalism was the term used to describe the situation in Latin America prior to the 1980s, in which the state achieved dominance by maintaining a mixed economy. In Latin America, it became customary to speak of the triple-alliance: an alliance of the state, international capital, and domestic capital. More than at any other point since the 1930s, Cuba is now closer to this model, with one modification: there is no private domestic capital. Rather than a triple alliance, there is a double alliance between the state and international capital.

Essentially, this has magnified the power of the Cuban state. To see this, it is important to look at the way in which the reforms have fragmented the Cuban economy. As Zimbalist and others point out, the Cuban economy is fragmented into three sectors, in increasing order of profitability: the old-fashioned statist sector, a growing informal market, and a joint state-private external sector (Zimbalist 2000). The old-fashioned statist sector is stagnant and contracting. The informal sector is growing, but as is the case with all informal sectors where property rights are not specified, its growth prospects are circumscribed. The joint state-external sector is truly thriving. A comparison of growth rates between industries in the statist sector (e.g., sugar) and in the state-private sector (nickel, tourism) shows how dramatic this divergence is. Whereas sugar production has essentially collapsed, nickel and tourism are thriving (see Table 2). Nickel and tourism are two of the most important recipients of FDI.

The state is profiting from this arrangement in two ways. First, there is an economic gain (Jatar-Hausmann 1999; Kaufman Purcell 2000): the statist economy is living off of the profits of the state-external sector. The other gain is political, and it is more important. The state has emerged as the gatekeeper of the external sector. It, and only it, gets to decide which Cuban citizens have access to this sector. Access is reserved to core members of the winning coali-

Table 2.   Growth Differential: State vs. FDI sectors

	1992/93 (a)	1999 (b)
State Sector:		
A. Sugar (Production, thousand tons raw value)	4,300	3,700
Sector with FDI:		
A. Nickel (tons)	35,000	68,000
B. Tourist Arrivals (thousands)	326	1,603

Sources: (a) EIU Country Profile (1993/94:17, 22).
(b) EIU Country Report June 2000.

tion. Only friends of the communist party get recommended for jobs in hotels. The state keeps all Cubans away from tourist facilities, but rewards well behaved Cubans with packages in these resorts. The military, considered by some to be the most important pillar of the winning coalition, has been the primary beneficiary of this thriving sector. The military owns properties in the tourist sector, owns many joint ventures, controls key cabinet positions connected to the external sector such as telecommunications, and is in charge of reforms in the state-owned sectors (see Espinosa 2001).

In addition, the state uses access to the state sector as a way to reward important citizens. Tourism supports 100,000 jobs in Cuba (Figueras 2001). Those in that sector can earn *bonos* or *estímulos*. The Cuban government gets to decide which Cubans can seek employment in these jobs, and can influence which Cubans get fired from those jobs.

The Cuban state also manages to gain from the other two sectors, and to use them as a way to reward citizens. If you want to drive a modern car, have access to the Internet, travel freely and enjoy other pleasures, it pays to have a state job, since these amenities are only available in the formal state economy.

Citizens who do not want to accept the low wages of state jobs and are not qualified to enter the external sector, can operate in the informal market. But even these citizens cannot escape the power of the state fully. First, as mentioned, the government retains monopoly over banks, exchange houses, and retail trade. Sooner or later, dollars transacted in the informal economy reach the state. Second, and most important, the government can hold citizens participating in the informal/illegal market hostages by being a selective enforcer of strict rules. Most informal mar-

ket activities are illegal. Most of the time, as with prostitution, the state allows those informal/illegal activities to take place, but always reserving the right to enforce the law at any given moment, thus catching them by surprise. Citizens operating in informal markets can never discount the possibility of a crack down, and thus, live in constant fear. And they use resources in order to bribe representatives of the state, including members of the CDRs, to look the other way. Either way, the state manages to dominate citizens: by allowing informal activities while simultaneously threatening to intervene against them, state officials obtain enormous leverage over ordinary citizens. And because citizens now are somewhat better off than in the 1989-94 period (they have access, for the first time ever, to consumer goods through state-run stores, have the opportunity to try to get a job in the external sector, are free to have more contact with tourists and Miami relatives), they tolerate their misery better. The state succeeded in placating pressures for reform within and outside the ruling coalition, and still managed to the hard-liners in charge.

THE VICTORY OF THE OLD GUARD: THE CABINET IN 2002

There is no question that the reformers have been politically weakened, not just in terms of the extent to which their policies were watered down, rejected or reversed, but also in terms of their presence in the cabinet. A look at retirements during the post 1996 period makes this clear.[7] By 2002, six of the 17 members of the 1993-96 class were retired, a retirement rate of 35 percent. In contrast, eight of the 21 old-guards holding office in 1996 retired by 2002, a retirement rate of 38 percent. Furthermore, three of these retiring old-guards were replaced by old-guardians themselves. If you include the number of old-guards who were replaced by old-guardians, the retirement rate of the old guard drops to 29 percent.

One would expect that with time, older cabinet members would occupy fewer positions in any cabinet. In the Cuban cabinet by 2002, however, this is not the case. Due to their lower retirement rates, old-timers predominate. The pre-1992 class holds 14 positions, including three of the four vice presidencies. The 1993-96 class holds 11 positions, and the remaining 9 are newcomers (i.e., individuals who entered in the 1997-2002 period). This cabinet continues to lean heavily toward the old timers. And if the suppositions of these papers are correct, by extension, it leans toward anti-reform ideas. The survival of old timers in the Cuban cabinet is simply remarkable, as remarkable as the survival of the regime itself.

CONCLUSION: THE NEW CUBAN STATE, ITS NATURE AND POWER

What kind of state is the Cuban state today? Rather than more open, the Cuban state is arguably more repressive, or perhaps, more capable of eliciting cooperation from society through the manipulation of inducements and constraints. Essentially, the Cuban state has created a new racket in the way it governs. This is how it works.

The State is the entity that creates small market-oriented sectors, mostly those sectors open to FDI or transacted in dollars. These have become small pockets of wealth and growth in an island of relative poverty and economic stagnation. The state has become the sole gatekeeper of such markets, getting to decide who has access to them. Since 1989, US$1.3 billion in investments have moved in. This is a small figure relative to Cuba's needs, but it is a significant amount of money when only one small entity, the Cuban Communist Party, gets to privatize most of it. The value of retail sales in dollars, all owned by the government, is not insignificant: it is estimated at 73.6 percent of the GDP (Ritter and Rowe

2002:107), perhaps one of the most dollarized economies in the Western Hemisphere.

The state has also become the sole privatizer of the wealth generated or captured by these small market pockets (FDI, remittances, tourism, illegal cash bonuses to employees in tourism, fees for legal transactions, etc). And despite these huge earnings, the state remains as unaccountable as ever, due to the absence of mechanisms of horizontal and vertical accountability typical of non-democratic regimes. An important source of external accountability, the one provided by the IMF and the World Bank, is also inoperative because Cuba does not belong to either institution. Consequently, nobody really knows how large the dollar economy is.

In some ways, therefore, this new state is more powerful than the centrally planned state prevailing from late 1960s to early 1990s. Under the previous model, there was only one economy: the state sector. All non-dissidents were guaranteed access to it. Because it was the "only pie" to be distributed among many, the value of each piece of the pie was significantly discounted. In the new economy, in contrast, the state distributes pieces from three different pies. The most valuable pie, the private-state export economy, is the one that is distributed among the smallest portion of the population: the winning coalition, and those members of the selectorate willing to be loyal. Hence, the state can offer a more valuable reward to loyalists than before—access to the most valuable aspect of the economy. It can also offer a more onerous punishment against dissidents—exclusion from the most desirable pie. The predominant incentive is for people "to leave the state peso economy" (Ritter and Rowe 2002:109). One exit is Miami. The other is to befriend a government official who controls access to the dollar economy.

There is no question that Cuba's new economic model is neither market nor socialist. It is not market economy because there is no freedom of association

---

7. For a different view, suggesting that "there has been an almost complete changing of the guard a the ministerial level," see Cubanalysis (2000). This report is impressed by the newcomers. I, on the other hand, focus on the resilience of the old guard, despite the passage of time.

and property rights for citizens. You cannot have capitalists in the absence of a system of property rights, a labor market, and price freedom. It is not socialist economy either because the state is now the guarantor, in fact, the generator, of enormous inequalities: those with access to the thriving external market sector; everyone else is either a loser or merely a survivor. Because the state has taken for itself the role of deciding who gets to go into these sectors, it is directly responsible for the rise of inequality in Cuba.

We can now understand the two puzzles with which the paper began. The combination of risk-taking and risk aversion is explained by the split in preferences within the winning coalition at the start of the reforms. The survival of the regime is explained by the state's newly acquired capacity to distribute inducements and constraints by way of regulating access to small market pockets. More so than ever before, the payoff of being loyal to the state far outweighs the payoff of turning against the state.

It is no wonder why Fidel Castro reiterates, as vociferously as he does, that he will not give up socialism in Cuba. He is reaffirming a commitment to a system that however unequal and inefficient, is quite efficient in generating loyalty and rewards within the winning coalition. It is easy to understand also why Fidel is not alone in Cuba in displaying preference for keeping things the way they are. Few Cubans gain from it, but those who count politically for the regime, gain the most.

BIBLIOGRAPHY

Bengelsdorff. 1994. *The Problem of Democracy in Cuba*. New York: Oxford University Press.

Boas, Taylor C. 2000. "The Dictator's Dilemma: The Internet and U.S. Policy Toward Cuba." *The Washington Quarterly* 23, 3:57-67.

Bueno de Mesquita, Bruce, James D. Morrow, Randolph M. Siverson, and Alastair Smith. 2000. "Political Institutions, Political Survival, and Policy Success." In Bruce Bueno de Mesquita and Hilton L. Root, eds. *Governing for Prosperity*. New Haven: Yale University Press.

CEPAL. 2000. *La economía cubana: reformas estructurales y desempeño en los noventa*. Santiago: CEPAL.

Corrales, Javier. 2000. "Presidents, Ruling Parties and Party Rules. A Theory on the Politics of Economic Reform in Latin America." *Comparative Politics* 32, 2 (January).

Corrales, Javier. 2002. "Lessons from Latin America." In Leslie Simon, Javier Corrales, Don Wolfenson, eds., *Democracy and the Internet*. Washington, DC: The Woodrow Wilson Center Press.

Cruz, Consuelo and Anna Seleny. 2002. "Reform and Counterreform: The Path to Market in Hungary and Cuba." *Comparative Politics* 34, 2 (January).

Cubanalysis. n.d. "Learned, Healthy... and Skinny." No. 13 (mimeo).

Cubanalysis. 2000. "Almost Invisible Changes." No. 29 (mimeo).

Espinosa, Juan Carlos. 2001. "'Vanguard of the State': The Cuban Armed Forces in Transition." *Problems of Post-Communism* 48, 6 (November/December):19-30.

Europa World Year Book (various years). London, England : Europa Publications Limited.

Feng, Yi (with Margaret Huckeba, Son Nguyen T., and Aaron Williams). 2000. "Political Institutions, Economic Growth, and Democratic Evolution: The Pacific Asian Scenario." In Bruce Bueno de Mesquita and Hilton L. Root, eds. *Governing for Prosperity*. New Haven: Yale University Press.

Figueras, Miguel Alejandro. 2001. "Cuba's Tourism Sector." Talk at Smith College, Northampton, MA, September 10.

Font, Mauricio. 1997. "Crisis and Reform in Cuba." In Miguel Ángel Centeno and Mauricio Font, eds. *Toward a New Cuba*. Boulder: Lynne Rienner.

Geddes, Barbara. 1999. "What Do We Know About Democratization After Twenty Years." *Annual Review of Political Science* 2:115-144.

Haggard, Stephan and Robert Kaufman. 1995. *The Political Economy of Democratic Transitions*. Princeton, NJ: Princeton University Press.

Jatar-Hausmann, Ana Julia. 1999. *The Cuban Way*. West Hartford, CT: Kumarian Press.

Kaufman Purcell, Susan. 2000. "Why the Cuban Embargo Makes Sense in a Post-Cold War World." In Susan Kaufman Purcell and David Rothkopf, eds., *Cuba: The Contours of Change*. Boulder, CO: Lynne Rienner.

Maybarduk, Gary H. 1999. "The State of the Cuban Economy 1998-1999." *Cuba in Transition— Volume 9*. Washington: Association for the Study of the Cuban Economy, 1999.

Mesa-Lago, Carmelo. 2000. "Un ajiaco cubano-alemán sobre la tercera reforma agraria de Cuba." *Encuentro* (Madrid) 18 (Fall):254-258.

Mujal-León, Eusebio and Joshua W. Busby. 2001. "Much Ado About Something? Regime Change in Cuba." *Problems of Post-Communism* 48, 6 (November-December):6-18

O'Donnell, Guillermo and Philippe C. Schmitter. 1986. *Transitions from Authoritarian Rule. Tentative Conclusions About Uncertain Democracies*. Baltimore : Johns Hopkins University Press.

Pastor, Manuel Jr. 2000. "After the Deluge? Cuba's Potential as a Market Economy." In Susan Kaufman Purcell and David Rothkopf, eds., *Cuba: The Contours of Change*. Boulder, CO: Lynne Rienner.

Pérez-López, Jorge F. "Waiting for Godot: Cuba's Stalled Reforms and Continuing Economic Crisis." *Problems of Post-Communism* 48, 6 (November/December):43-55.

Pérez-Stable, Marifeli. 1999. "Caught in a Contradiction: Cuban Socialism Between Mobilization and Normalization." *Comparative Politics* 32, 1 (October):63-82.

Placencia, Sergio. 2000. Presentation by the President of the Central Bank of Cuba, the Inter-American Dialogue, Washington, DC.

Przeworski, Adam. 1991. *Democracy and the Market*. New York: Cambridge University Press.

Ritter, Archibald R.M. and Nicholas Rowe. 2002. "Cuba: From 'Dollarization' to 'Euroization' or 'Peso Reconsolidation'?" *Latin American Politics and Society* 44, 2 (Summer):99-124.

Roque Cabello, Marta Beatriz and Manuel Sánchez Herrero. 1998. "Background: Cuba's Economic Reforms: An Overview." In Jorge F. Pérez-López and Matías F. Travieso-Díaz, eds., *Perspectives on Cuban Economic Reforms* (Special Studies, No. 30). Arizona State University Center for Latin American Studies.

Roy, Joaquín. 2002. "The European Anchoring of Cuba: From Persuasion and Good Intentions to Contradiction and Frustration." University of Miami (mimeo).

Solinger, Dorothy J. 2001. "Ending One-Party Dominance: Korea, Taiwan, Mexico." *Journal of Democracy* 12, 1 (January):30-42.

Suchlicki, Jaime. 2000. "Castro's Cuba: Continuity Instead of Change." In Susan Kaufman Purcell and David Rothkopf, eds., *Cuba: The Contours of Change*. Boulder, CO: Lynne Rienner.

Travieso-Díaz, Matías F. and Charles P. Trumbull IV. 2002. "Foreign Investment in Cuba: Prospects and Perils." In this volume.

Zimbalist, Andrew. 2000. "Wither the Cuban Economy?" In Susan Kaufman Purcell and David Rothkopf, eds., *Cuba: The Contours of Change*. Boulder, CO: Lynne Rienner.

APPENDIX 1:
OPENINGS AND RESTRICTIONS IN CUBA'S ECONOMIC REFORMS, 1993-97

Agriculture

Opening: The state permitted transforming state farms into cooperatives, Unidades de Básicas de Producción Cooperativa (September 1993) and the emergence of farmers' markets (October 1994).

Restriction: The proportion of privately-owned land did not increase, staying at around 15 percent throughout the decade (Jatar-Hausmann 1999:73). What changed was the composition of the non-private agricultural sector. By 1997, 42.1 percent of land was controlled by UBPCs. UBPCs lack autonomy: the state still determines production plans, sets the price of products, and maintains a monopoly over the distribution of goods. State also retains monopoly over, and charges high prices for, inputs (e.g., fertilizers, fuels, pesticides, equipment, etc.) (See Mesa-Lago 2000:256). The state must approve which farmers can form or join a cooperative.

External Sector

Opening: Allow foreign direct investment (FDI) up to 100 percent (September 1995). By 1995 there were 200 joint ventures. More recently, the government has reported 370 entities with foreign capital (Placencia 2000).

Restriction: Although foreigners are allowed 100 percent ownership, only one firm is 100 percent foreign owned. The rest of FDI occurs as joint ventures with the state. The state is keen on ensuring its own participation in these investments. The state explicitly bans ownership by Cuban nationals. States hold monopoly over hiring lists. Joint ventures can only hire from a list of candidates provided by the state. Marcos Portal, Minister of Basic Industry, declared shortly after the approval of the 1995 FDI law that hard currency salaries will go directly to the state for redistribution and assure fair job practices, with workers approved by organizations linked to the Communist Party (Associated Press, 9/6/95). Joint ventures are required to pay wages to the state (in dollars); the state then pays the workers in undervalued pesos, thereby realizing a huge profit as a result of this exchange rate distortion. These agencies retain approxi-

mately 90-95 percent of the payment received in dollars from the foreign joint venture and remunerate the workers in Cuban pesos. This violates Article 2 of Convention 87 of the International Labor Organization, banning the confiscation of wages and the interference with labor rights to choose employment (Travieso-Díaz and Trumbull 2002). In practice, private owners invest 50 percent and often lend the Cuban government 35 percent of the initial capital of a joint venture (Maybarduk 1999). A law decentralizing foreign trade allows state-owned enterprises to engage in import-export activities.

Dollarization

Opening: De-penalization of dollar-holding (derogation of Article 140 of the Penal Code), legalization of formerly black-market operations; loosening of restrictions for Cuban citizens to receive dollars from the U.S. (July 1993).

Restriction: State holds monopoly over dollar-transacted retail trade and exchange rate houses. The government opened approximately 275 shops where dollar holders can buy goods, thus capturing most of the dollars, especially those circulating in informal markets (Zimbalist 2000:18). Dollar-retail stores charge a sales tax of 140 percent on most products (Ritter and Rowe 2002). Very few goods are channeled to the peso/rationing based economy.

Domestic Private Sector

Opening: Allow self-employment (Decree 141, September 1993).

Restriction: From the start, the self-employed were banned from hiring labor, setting huge brakes in the capacity of these initiatives to expand. Further, the government restricted the type of sectors and professionals that could engage in self-employment. Cubans are still not allowed to buy and sell real estate or any other property. Concern about the boom in self-employment began immediately (*The Miami Herald* 1/29/94). Already in January 1994, the Cuban government began to crack down on the self-employed: the government ordered closing of hundreds of private restaurants (*paladares*) and reduced licenses issued to run taxis and other vendors (*The Miami Herald*1/29/94). Fidel Castro said: "I do not really think one or two tables (at a private restaurant) will affect socialism...However, the man with 25 tables and 100 chairs is something else...imagine what it would be like if we gave him some space to fly." Restaurants are permitted only 12 chairs and cannot advertise. Inputs have to be acquired from state stores. *Paladares* are banned from serving beef, fish, shellfish unless purchased in a state store, where prices are 20-40 higher (*Miami Herald*, March 27, 1997). Inspectors were imposing fines of up to 1000 pesos for each chair over the limit (*The Miami Herald* 3/27/97). Private restauranters pay a tax of 50 percent on all revenues after deducting 10 percent for cost, amounting to an effective tax rate of 90 percent (Zimbalist 2000:22). Consequently, after peaking in mid 1990s, self-employed is a stagnant sector.

Telecommunications

Opening: The government proclaimed interest in promoting the "massive use of services and products related to information technology, communications, and computing" (http://www.cubagob.cu/). It even created a special ministry for this (Ministry of Computing and Communications, Decree Law 204).

Restriction: Access to the Internet has been permitted "only where it directly benefits the regime" (Boas 2000:62). Email access is only permitted in the workplace, users typically share a single account, disallowing Internet cafes or connections in public libraries, no Internet Service Providers (ISPs). Only NGOs that are neutral or loyal to the regime are allowed access (ibid, p. 63). Cuba thus had one of the lowest levels of Interconnectivity in the Americas, despite its levels of socioeconomic development (53.6 users per 10,000 inhabitants, compared to 293.2 in Brazil and 1,155.31 in Chile) (see Corrales 2002).

THE CUBAN ECONOMY IN AN UNENDING SPECIAL PERIOD

Jorge F. Pérez-López[1]

Speaking to the Cuban nation on November 2, 2001, President Fidel Castro described at length the ongoing world economic crisis, worsened by the September 11 terrorist attacks on New York City and Washington. Castro spoke about its impact on Cuba's economy, particularly on the external sector, as world market prices for the island's commodity exports declined and tourists postponed or cancelled vacations because of the slowdown and fear from terrorist attacks. Castro concluded that further belt tightening would be needed, as Cuba had financial obligations that had to be met despite the worsening economic situation: "We will confront the economic crisis and we will win. No sacrifice frightens us, not even giving up our lives. This is very well known. We have withstood sacrifices for many years. Those who thought that the revolution would only last weeks today admire our heroic capacity to resist and move ahead."[2]

Barely three days after these sobering remarks, Cuba suffered another blow: Hurricane Michelle, a category four storm, directly struck Cuba, crossing the island from south to north through the central provinces. Michelle affected 45 percent of the territory and 53 percent of the population, damaging the nation's agriculture, transportation, communications and industrial sectors, as well as the already-deteriorated housing stock.[3]

The one-two punch of the world economic slowdown and hurricane Michelle pummeled a Cuban economy already weakened by the loss a decade earlier of trade and economic assistance from the former Soviet Union and the socialist countries. In the early 1990s, Cuba plunged into a deep economic crisis that affected nearly all sectors of the economy and sharply reduced population consumption levels. Consistent with its proclivity to use military symbols to rally the population, the Cuban leadership referred to this economic crisis as "a special period in time of peace," a national emergency occurring in peacetime but with potential consequences for the survival of the regime as serious as those of a war. After four consecutive years of economic contraction, the Cuban economy began to record positive growth in 1994, a trend that continued through 2001. Nevertheless, Cuban gross domestic product and many other economic indicators have yet to reach their pre-crisis levels.

The fragile recovery of the Cuban economy in the second half of the 1990s is seriously threatened in mid-2002 by several exogenous shocks that have added pressure to an already-stressed external sector, pre-

---

1. This paper is a revised and updated version of "El período especial interminable de la economía cubana," presented at a conference on Cuba sponsored by the Center for International Studies, El Colegio de Mexico, March 15, 2002, forthcoming in *Foro Internacional*. The paper expresses only the views of the author.

2. Fidel Castro, "Estamos más unidos y fuertes que nunca y mucho mejor preparados para enfrentar esta situación," *Granma* (4 November 2001), www.granma.cubaweb.cu/2001/11/04/nacional/articulo16.html.

3. Carlos Lage, ¡Un pueblo unido puede vencer las mayores adversidades!," *Granma* (11 November 2001), www.granma.cubaweb.cu/2001/11/11/nacional/articulo05.html.

Table 1.   Selected Cuban Economic Indicators, 1989-2000
(in million pesos unless otherwise indicated)

	1989	1993	1994	1995	1996	1997	1998	1999	2000	2000/ 1989 (%)
Macroeconomic										
GDP at constant prices	19578	12768	12868	13185	14218	14572	14754	15674	16556	-15.4
GDP growth rate (%)	1.5	-14.9	0.7	2.5	7.8	2.5	1.2	6.2	5.6	—
GDP per capita (at constant prices)	1851	1172	1175	1201	1290	1317	1327	1405	1478	-20.5
GDP/capita growth rate	1.0	-15.4	0.3	2.2	7.4	2.1	0.8	5.9	5.3	—
Gross domestic investment/GDP (%)	26.7	5.4	5.5	7.2	8.2	9.5	10.9	10.4	10.8	—
Monetary liquidity/GDP (%)	21.6	73.2	51.8	42.6	41.8	41.1	40.6	38.8	38.0	—
Budget balance/GDP (%)	-7.3	-33.5	-7.4	-3.5	-2.5	-2.0	-2.3	-2.4	-2.4	—
External Sector										
Merchandise exports	5400	1137	1381	1507	1866	1819	1512	1496	1676	-69.0
Merchandise imports	8140	1984	2353	2883	3659	3987	4181	4349	4849	-40.7
Foreign debt (US $ billion)	6.2	8.8	9.1	10.5	10.5	10.2	11.2	11.1	11.0	77.4
Physical Production										
Sugar cane (000 metric tons)	81000	43700	43200	33600	41300	38900	32800	34000	36400	-55.1
Fresh vegetables (000 metric tons)	610	393	322	402	494	472	643	1015	1461	139.5
Cereals (000 metric tons)	584	226	300	304	473	545	391	554	509	-12.8
Citrus (000 metric tons)	1016	645	505	564	662	808	713	710	898	-11.6
Fish catch (000 metric tons)	192	94	88	102	121	136	134	145	162	-15.6
Milk (000 metric tons)	762	328	296	268	273	270	272	291	305	-60.0
Sugar (000 metric tons)	7579	4246	4017	3259	4259	4318	3291	3875	4057	-46.4
Nickel (000 metric tons)	46.6	30.2	27.0	42.7	53.7	61.6	67.7	66.5	71.4	53.2
Oil (000 metric tons)	718	1108	1299	1471	1476	1462	1678	2136	2695	275.3
Electricity (billion kwh)	15.2	11.0	12.0	12.5	13.2	14.1	14.1	14.5	15.0	-1.3
Cement (000 metric tons)	3759	1049	1085	1456	1438	1701	1713	1785	1633	-56.6
Steel (000 metric tons)	314	98	148	203	229	335	283	303	327	4.1
Paper (000 metric tons)	102.0	11.0	17.0	12.1	11.4	7.9	7.3	6.1	8.6	-91.6
Beer (000 hectoliters)	3333	1304	1201	1330	1504	1639	1759	2009	2136	-35.9
Rum (000 hectoliters)	514	388	592	529	476	499	540	603	592	15.2
Cigarettes (billion units)	16.5	12.2	14.5	12.6	10.7	10.7	11.7	13.4	12.1	-26.7
Cigars (000 units)	304	208	186	192	194	215	264	285	241	-20.7

Sources: 1989: Comité Estatal de Estadísticas, *Anuario Estadístico de Cuba 1989* (La Habana: Comité Estatal de Estadísticas, 1991), and author's extrapolations.

1993-2000: Oficina Nacional de Estadísticas, *Anuario Estadístico de Cuba 1996* (La Habana, 1998), *Anuario Estadístico de Cuba 1999* (La Habana, 2000), and *Anuario Estadístico de Cuba 2000* (La Habana, 2001).

saging the continuation of the special period for the foreseeable future. The first part of the paper reviews very briefly the performance of the Cuban economy in the 1990s. The second part summarizes the Cuban government's tentative and inadequate policy responses. The third part discusses developments that have complicated Cuba's economic situation in 2002 and support the proposition that there is no end in sight for the special period.

TEN YEARS OF SPECIAL PERIOD: A LOST ECONOMIC GROWTH DECADE

In August 1990, President Castro declared that Cuba had entered a "special period in time of peace"

(*período especial en tiempos de paz*), a severe economic crisis triggered by disruptions in trade with the socialist community. These disruptions manifested themselves in delays and shortfalls in imports of oil, raw materials and machinery from the Soviet Union and the former socialist countries of Eastern Europe and loss of financial assistance from, and markets in, these countries for Cuban exports. As is clear from the data in Table 1, the crisis affected nearly all aspects of the economy. Thus, between 1989 and 1993:

• The gross domestic product (GDP) contracted by 34.8 percent, probably the largest decline over

Figure 1. Cuban GDP Growth Rates, 1989–2000

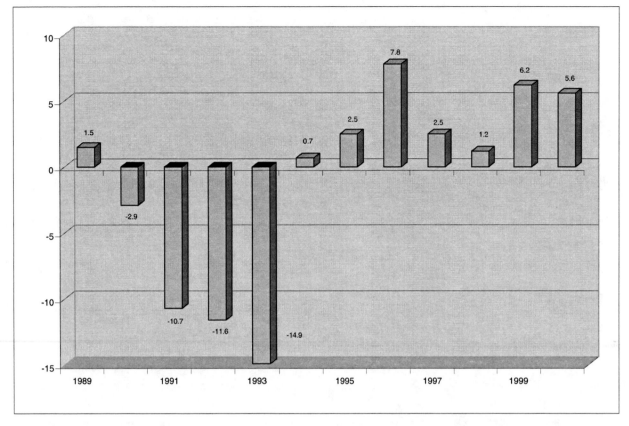

a four-year period in twentieth-century Cuba;

• GDP per capita contracted even more sharply, by 36.7 percent;

• Gross domestic investment fell from 26.7 percent to an abysmally low 5.4 percent of GDP;

• Monetary liquidity (cash balances in the hands of the population plus demand deposits) rose from 21.6 percent of GDP to 73.2 percent of GDP as citizens were not able to spend their cash holdings in consumption activities;

• The fiscal deficit mushroomed from 7.3 percent to 33.5 percent of GDP, as losses of state enterprises mounted and the government maintained social services expenditures close to pre-crisis levels;

• Merchandise exports contracted by 78.9 percent and imports by 75.6 percent; and

• The hard currency international debt increased by nearly 42 percent.

Physical production of all key agricultural and industrial products reported in Table 1 (with the exception of crude oil production) fell between 1989 and 1993, translating into sharp reductions in consumption and population standard of living. Of the products listed in the table, particularly significant were the declines in output of paper (89 percent), cement (72 percent), steel (69 percent), beer (61 percent), cereals (61 percent), milk (57 percent) and fish catch (51 percent); production of sugar cane (agriculture) fell by 43 percent and of sugar (industry) by 44 percent.

The economic slide apparently ended sometime around mid-1994, and according to official Cuban statistics, GDP grew by 0.7 percent in 1994. Cuba has recorded positive growth in every year since 1994, although the growth rate has fluctuated significantly from year to year (see Figure 1). Over the period 1993-2000, GDP grew by 29.7 percent, or at an annual average growth rate of 3.8 percent; over a like period, GDP per capita grew by 26.1 percent, or at an average annual rate of 3.4 percent. In 2000, however, Cuban GDP was still 15.4 percent below its

Table 2.   Composition of Imports, 1989-2000
    (in million pesos)

	1989	1990	1991	1992	1993	1994	1995	1996	1997	1998	1999	2000
Total Imports	8140	7417	4234	2315	2008	2017	2883	3569	3987	4181	4323	4829
Percent	100.0	100.0	100.0	100.0	100.0	100.0	100.0	100.0	100.0	100.0	100.0	100.0
Consumer goods	845	803	654	395	420	381	549	718	764	909	1010	1040
Percent	10.4	10.8	15.4	17.1	20.9	18.9	19.0	20.1	19.2	21.7	23.2	21.5
Intermediate goods	5438	4649	2661	1735	1512	1571	2135	2508	2788	2745	2753	3133
Percent	66.8	62.7	62.8	74.9	75.3	77.9	74.1	70.3	69.9	65.7	63.3	64.9
Capital goods	1856	1965	919	185	76	65	198	344	435	528	587	656
Percent	22.8	26.5	21.7	8.0	3.8	3.2	6.9	9.6	10.9	12.6	13.5	13.6
Memo: Oil and oil products	2604	1994	1253	811	699	743	851	95.8	970	665	710	1137
Percent	38.0	26.9	29.6	35.0	34.8	36.8	29.5	26.8	24.3	15.9	16.4	23.5

Sources: 1989-1994: Comisión Económica para América Latina y el Caribe, *La economía cubana: Reformas estructurales y desempeño en los noventa*, Revised Edition (Mexico: Fondo de Cultura Económica, 2000), Statistical Annex; Oficina Nacional de Estadísticas (ONE), *Anuario Estadístico de Cuba 1998* (La Habana, 1999), *Anuario Estadístico de Cuba 1999* (La Habana, 2000), and *Anuario Estadístico de Cuba 2000* (La Habana, 2001).

level in 1989—the last year before the economic crisis struck—and GDP per capita 20.5 percent below.

Therefore, the 1990s—the first decade of the special period—was a lost decade for Cuban economic growth and for the standard of living of the Cuban population. As Brundenius and Monreal write: "Even with official projected rates of growth of around 4 per cent per year, the Cuban economy would be back to its pre-crisis levels only by the year 2005. Thus the economic impasse of the 1990s would represent 15 years of lost economic growth for the country."[4]

The gross domestic investment to GDP ratio, a key indicator of future output growth, also recovered in the second half of the 1990s, climbing from 5.4 percent of GDP in 1993 to 10.8 percent of GDP in 2000. While this was a significant improvement, this ratio's level in 2000 was significantly lower—by two and one-half times—than its level in 1989 (Table 1 and Figure 2). For comparison, the ratio of gross investment to GDP in 2000 for Latin American and Caribbean countries as a group was 21 percent; for Mexico, 23 percent; for Chile, 22 percent; and for China, 38 percent.[5]

To further illustrate the sharp decline in investment, Table 2 shows the composition of merchandise imports in 1989-2000 by end use categories. In 1989, 10.4 percent of imports were consumption goods, 66.8 percent were intermediate goods for further processing and 22.8 percent were capital goods (investment goods) to support future production capabilities. During 1993-94, the peak years of the economic crisis, the share of consumer goods imports doubled to about 20 percent while the share of capital goods shrank to 3-5 percent. By 1999-2000, capital goods' share of total imports had risen to over 13 percent, but was still significantly below its 1989 share, while consumer goods' share was very high at over 20 percent.

In May 1994, the National Assembly of People's Power adopted a resolution calling for strict discipline in the implementation of the budget law and for reductions in expenditures and increases in revenues at all levels of government. On the expenditures side, the National Assembly directed the Executive to take concrete steps to limit spending across the board, but particularly by reducing subsidies to cover enterprise losses. On the revenue side, the government increased prices of cigarettes and alcoholic bev-

---

4. Claes Brundenius and Pedro Monreal González, "The Future of the Cuban Model: The Longer View," p. 130. In Claes Brundenius and John Weeks, editors, *Globalization and Third World Socialism* (Houndmills, Great Britain: Palgrave, 2001).

5. World Bank, *Building Institutions for Markets: World Development Report 2002* (New York: Oxford University Press for the World Bank, 2001), pp. 235-237.

Figure 2. Selected Macroeconomic Indicators, 1989–2000

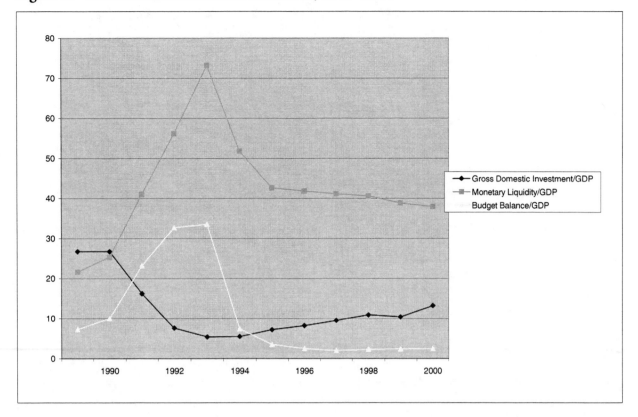

erages, gasoline, electricity, public transportation and of sending mail and telegrams; effectively increased prices of meals at workplace cafeterias by eliminating subsidies; and began to charge for services formerly provided free, such as school lunches, some medications, and admission to sports and cultural events. Two macroeconomic indicators in Table 1 suggest that the stabilization program instituted in the first half of the 1990s had some success:

- Monetary liquidity declined from the mentioned 73.2 percent of GDP in 1993 to 51.8 percent in 1994, and steadily thereafter, reaching 38.0 percent of GDP in 2000; and

- The budget deficit fell from 33.5 percent of GDP in 1993 to 7.4 percent of GDP 1994— reflecting a remarkable reduction in government spending—and decreased subsequently to 2.0 percent of GDP in 1996, inching up to 2.4 percent of GDP in 1999 and 2000.

Merchandise exports and imports recovered during the second half of the 1990s, with exports growing by 47.4 percent between 1993 and 2000, and im-

ports by 144.4 percent during a like period. The much faster growth of imports relative to exports means that the merchandise trade deficit expanded significantly during this period, from 847 million pesos in 1993 to nearly 3.2 billion pesos in 2000. Although Cuba had very limited access to international credit markets in the 1990s (recall that Cuba defaulted on its hard currency debt in 1986 and credit has been limited to supplier loans and other instruments with very short maturity), the hard currency debt grew from $8.8 billion in 1993 to $11.0 billion in 2000 as a result of the accumulation of interest and shifts in the relative value of currencies in which the debt was contracted.

Turning to specific sectors of the economy, physical production of most items in Table 1 recovered in the second half of the 1990s. Notable exceptions were sugar cane (agriculture), milk, sugar and paper production. Nickel and citrus, two sectors that received foreign capital (in the form of joint ventures between foreign investors and domestic enterprises), showed significant increases in production after 1993, with

Table 3.   International Tourism Industry Indicators, 1990-2000

	1990	1991	1992	1993	1994	1995	1996	1997	1998	1999	2000
Tourist arrivals (000)	340	424	461	546	619	745	1004	1170	1416	1603	1774
Growth rate (%)	—	24.8	8.7	18.4	13.4	20.4	34.8	16.5	21.0	13.2	10.7
Convertible currency revenue (million USD)	243	402	550	720	850	1100	1333	1515	1759	1901	1948
Growth rate (%)	—	65.4	36.8	30.9	18.1	29.4	21.2	13.7	16.1	8.1	2.5
Occupancy rate (%)	NA	NA	NA	57.9	59.1	62.9	64.9	75.4	76.1	71.7	74.2
Employment (000)	39.7	43.0	41.9	43.9	46.1	52.3	56.2	53.6	62.8	66.0	68.0
Share of total employment (%)	1.1	1.1	1.1	1.2	1.2	1.5	1.6	1.5	1.7	1.7	1.7
No. of hotels and motels	328	347	346	356	331	348	375	400	412	424	431
Growth rate (%)	—	5.8	0.0	2.9	-7.0	5.1	7.8	6.7	3.0	2.9	1.7
No. of rooms in hotels and motels	18565	20816	23221	24262	24884	27236	29161	31043	34891	36252	37178
Growth rate (%)	—	12.1	11.6	4.5	2.6	9.5	7.1	6.5	12.3	3.9	2.6
Daily lodging capacity in hotels and motels	37740	41633	44956	49433	50410	50562	59350	62674	70222	74620	75869
Growth rate (%)	—	10.3	8.0	10.0	2.0	0.3	17.4	5.6	12.0	6.3	1.7

Note: Employment statistics are from Comisión Económica plara América Latina y el Caribe, *La economía cubana: Reformas estructurales y desempeño en los noventa*, Revised Edition (Mexico: Fondo de Cultura Económica, 2000). The statistics for 1998, 1999 and 2000 are estimates given by this source.

Sources: 1990-92: Statistical Annex, Comisión Económica plara América Latina y el Caribe, *La economía cubana: Reformas estructurales y desempeño en los noventa*, Revised Edition (Mexico: Fondo de Cultura Económica, 2000); 1993-2000: Oficina Nacional de Estadísticas (ONE), *Anuario estadístico de Cuba 2000* (La Habana, 2001).

nickel output increasing by 136.4 percent—and reaching an all-time high in 2000 of 71,400 metric tons (MT)—and citrus by 39.2 percent. Oil production, another sector that has received foreign investment, continued to set records, reaching an all-time high output level of 2.7 million MT in 2000.

For many of the products in Table 1, however, although production levels in 1999-2000 were higher than in 1993, they were still lower than in the pre-crisis year of 1989. This is the case, for example, for cement (2000 level of output was 56.6 percent below 1989), beer (39.7 percent below), and cigarettes (25.5 percent below).

The most successful sector of the Cuban economy in the 1990s has been international tourism. In 1990, 340,000 foreign tourists visited the island, generating $243 million in convertible currency revenue[6] (Table 3). While other sectors of the Cuban economy struggled in the early 1990s, the number of international tourist arrivals and tourism revenues increased steadi-

ly, with the number of international tourists more than doubling and revenues more than quadrupling between 1990 and 1995. Double-digit annual growth rates in both international tourist arrivals and revenue from tourism were the rule through 1998, albeit starting from a low base. Figure 3 compares the value of exports of the sugar industry (principally raw sugar and molasses) and revenue from international tourism for the period 1990-2000. The figure shows the precipitous drop in the value of exports of the sugar industry in the early 1990s as preferential relations with the former Soviet Union and the Eastern European socialist countries came to an end and the continuing downward trend, at the same time that revenue from tourism expanded steadily. In 1993-94, tourism revenue overtook the sugar industry as the main generator of export revenue.

The tourism infrastructure expanded substantially in the 1990s, with the number of hotel and motel rooms suitable for international tourists nearly doubling between 1990 and 2000 (Table 3). Joint ven-

---

6. Cuba produces two series of tourism revenue figures, one that should be more properly called gross revenue from tourism and includes, in addition to visitors' receipts, revenue from other activities related to tourism such as international communications, aviation, and so on. The second series, more properly called net revenue from tourism, excludes the additional activities. Cuban government officials and some analysts use the series interchangeably, often resulting in incorrect analysis of the situation. See María Dolores Espino, "Cuban Tourism: A Critique of the CEPAL 2000 Report," in *Cuba in Transition—Volume 11* (Washington: Association for the Study of the Cuban Economy, 2001), especially pp. 344-346.

Figure 3. Sugar Exports and Tourism Revenues, 1990–99 *(million pesos)*

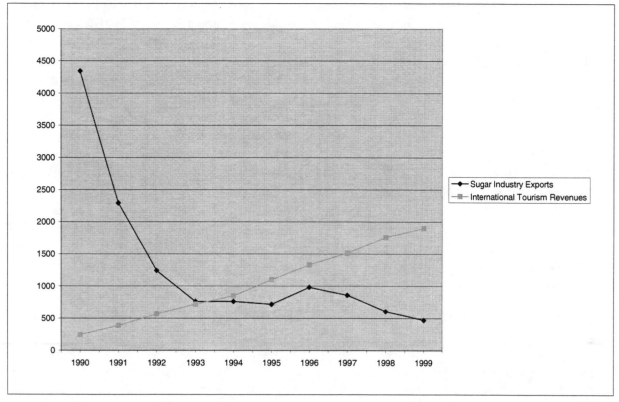

tures with foreign investors have been a key source of capital, management and markets for the international tourism industry. According to statistics of Cuba's Ministry of Foreign Investment and Economic Cooperation, out of 392 joint ventures between foreign investors and Cuban enterprises active at the end of 2000, 70 (or about 18 percent) were in the tourism industry.[7]

ECONOMIC REFORMS—OR LACK THEREOF?

Cuba's macroeconomic situation in the early 1990s was dismal: large government budget deficits, very high levels of repressed inflation (expressed through physical shortages and rampant black markets, including a hard currency black market), large mone-

tary balances in the hands of the population, serious balance of payment imbalances, and inability to borrow in international markets.

The Cuban government's initial response to the economic crisis brought on by the disruption of economic relations with the socialist countries was an economic austerity program to conserve energy and raw materials; a national program to increase food production; renewed efforts to secure new markets for exports; a campaign to attract foreign investment, particularly in the tourism industry; and some management reforms.[8] At that point in time (1990), the Cuban leadership could not come to terms with the proposition that the political and economic changes that were occurring with lightning speed in Eastern

---

7. Paolo Spadoni, "The Impact of the Helms-Burton Legislation on Foreign Investment in Cuba," in *Cuba in Transition—Volume 11* (Washington: Association for the Study of the Cuban Economy, 2001), p. 21.

8. For a description and evaluation of the Cuban economic strategy of the early 1990s, see *Cuba at a Crossroads: Politics and Economics after the Fourth Party Congress*, edited by Jorge F. Pérez-López (Gainesville: University Press of Florida, 1994), particularly: Sergio G. Roca, "Reflections on Economic Policy: Cuba's Food Program"; María Dolores Espino, "Tourism in Cuba: A Development Strategy for the 1990s?"; Jorge F. Pérez-López, "Islands of Capitalism in an Ocean of Socialism: Joint Ventures in Cuba's Development Strategy"; and Andrew Zimbalist, "Reforming Cuba's Economic System from Within."

Europe and the former Soviet Union were irreversible, and still harbored the illusion that the *status quo ante* of trade and economic support from the socialist bloc would be reestablished. The inadequacy of the initial Cuban government response—which lacked any meaningful policy reforms—is evident from the official statistics reported in the previous section.

Reform Measures

In the summer of 1993, the Cuban government began to take some policy actions to stabilize the economy, selectively liberalize segments of the economy and introduce some structural changes. Additional actions were taken the following year, but the pace of change slowed down subsequently. The policy reform actions taken during the 1990s are described briefly below more or less in chronological order.[9]

Legalization of the Holding and Use of Foreign Currencies: In the summer of 1993, Cuba decriminalized the holding and use of hard currency by Cuban citizens. The purpose of this action was two-fold: (1) to stem the booming hard currency black market; and (2) to stimulate hard currency remittances to Cuban citizens by relatives and friends living abroad in order to close the balance of payments gap. To give concrete meaning to this so-called "dollarization" policy, the government created special stores at which individuals holding hard currencies could shop for items not available to Cubans holding pesos and liberalized travel to the island by relatives and friends of Cuban citizens. Later, the government created foreign currency exchange houses (*Casas de Cambio*, CADECA) at which Cuban citizens could exchange hard currencies for pesos at rates close to those prevailing in the hard currency black market and facilitated remittances by easing the procedures for receiving foreign funds and allowing private foreign companies to carry out some of the transactions.

Self-Employment: In September 1993 the Cuban government authorized self-employment in over 100 occupations, subject to some restrictions. The authorized occupations spanned home repair and transportation, agricultural and personal services. Among the restrictions on self-employment were, for example, that professionals holding a university degree could not become self-employed; similarly, since education and public health services continued to be supplied by the state, physicians, dentists, teachers, professors and researchers were excluded from self-employment altogether. Candidates for self-employment had to request a license, could not hire others, had to pay fees and taxes to the government, and were restricted how they sold the goods or services they produced. The list of occupations amenable to self-employment was expanded in October 1993 and in June 1995, bringing the total number of authorized occupations to 140.

Agricultural Cooperatives: Also in September 1993, the Council of State approved breaking up large state farms into Basic Units of Cooperative Production (*Unidades Básicas de Producción Cooperativa*, UBPC). These UBPCs would have the use of the land they worked for an indefinite period of time, own the output they produced, have the ability to sell their output to the state through the state procurement system (*acopio*) or through other means, have their own bank accounts and be able to elect their own management. The rationale for the policy change was that the shift from state farms to cooperatives would give workers greater incentives to increase production with the least expenditure of material resources.

Tax Code: In August 1994, the National Assembly approved a new and very broad tax code, to be implemented gradually beginning in October 1994. The new system levies taxes on the income of enterprises, including joint ventures with foreign investors, as well as on the value of assets owned; earned income; sales; consumption of products such as cigarettes, alcoholic beverages, electro-domestic appliances and

---

9. For full description and evaluation of the measures see Carmelo Mesa-Lago, *Are Economic Reforms Propelling Cuba to the Market?* (Coral Gables, Florida: North-South Center, University of Miami, 1994) and Omar Everleny Pérez Villanueva, "Cuba's Economic Reforms: An Overview," in Jorge Pérez-López and Matías Travieso-Díaz, editors, *Perspectives on Cuban Economic Reforms* (Tempe, Arizona: Arizona State University Center for Latin American Studies Press, 1998).

other luxury goods; public services such as electricity, water and sewer, telephone, telegrams, transportation, restaurants and lodging; real estate holdings; gasoline- or draft animal-powered transportation vehicles; transfer of property, including inheritances; public documents issued; payrolls; and use of natural resources. The law also foresees employer contributions to social security, user fees on roads (tolls) and airport services, and charges for advertising of products or services.

Agricultural Markets: Complementing the creation of the UBPCs, in late September 1994, Cuba authorized the creation of agricultural markets, locations at which producers of selected agricultural products could sell a portion of their output at prices set by demand and supply. In most respects, the agricultural markets authorized in September 1994 are similar to the farmers' free markets (*mercados libres campesinos*, MLC) that were created in 1980 and scuttled in 1986. In October 1994 the Cuban government announced that it would also allow the free sale of a wider range of consumer products through a network of artisan and manufactured products markets.

Foreign Investment Facilitation: In September 1995, the National Assembly adopted a new foreign investment law that codified the *de facto* rules under which joint ventures had been operating and introduced some innovations to the legal framework for foreign investment. For example, pursuant to the new law, 100 percent foreign ownership of investments would be permitted, up from the 49 percent allowed by the earlier statute. The new law also simplified the process for screening foreign investment, explicitly allowed foreign investment in real estate, and authorized the establishment of export processing zones. In June 1996 the Council of State implementing legislation creating export processing zones (*zonas francas y parques industriales*).

Banking Reform: Long-expected legislation to reform the banking system was finally passed by the Council of State in May 1997. Decree-law No. 172

established the Cuban Central Bank (*Banco Central de Cuba*, BCC) as an autonomous and independent entity and assigned to it traditional central banking functions; the BNC was restructured to perform strictly commercial banking functions. Decree-law No. 173, passed at the same time, set out the legal framework for registration and operation of commercial banks and financial institutions under the supervision of the BCC.

Are the Reforms Adequate?

To summarize, in 1993 and 1994, Cuba took some steps to reduce the state's role in the economy by legalizing the use of foreign currencies, liberalizing and expanding self-employment, reforming the structure of agricultural production and allowing the creation of some private marketplaces. In 1995-96 it liberalized foreign investment and created export processing zones. The Cuban government also took some tentative steps to restructure the economy, establishing a tax code in 1994 and reforming the banking system in 1997. Cuba has not undertaken liberalization measures since 1996, and those in 1995 and 1996 were tightly focused on foreign investment.

The combination of stabilization measures and policy reforms that Cuba implemented in the 1990s has been successful in keeping Cuba's socialist government in power and permitting it to maintain a tight grip on the polity of the nation. But the patchwork of reforms has been inadequate to return the population to the already-meager levels of income and consumption of the late 1980s and to lay the groundwork for sustainable future economic growth. Ominously, the relative economic improvement in the second half of the 1990s strengthened the hand of those who favored maintaining the political and economic status quo and paralyzed essential structural reforms. Ritter argued in 1998 that the reform process, in the sense of further liberalization of institutions and policies, had ceased and a case could be made that the process not only had been aborted but had in fact been put into reverse.[10]

---

10. Archibald R.M. Ritter, *Cuba's Economic Reform Process, 1998: Paralysis and Stagnation?*, Department of Economics and School of International Affairs, Carleton University, mimeo (July 8, 1998).

Rather than following a blue print to reform its economy to improve efficiency and compatibility with the world economy, the Cuban government has instead followed a piece meal approach, seemingly only adopting policy changes reluctantly when faced with crisis, and undermining their application by contradictory actions and reversals. The Cuban government has postponed politically-sensitive measures such as restructuring of state enterprises, authorization of the creation of small businesses, liberalization of prices, and labor market reforms that although beneficial for the economy would also arguably either create unemployment and dissatisfaction among the population or reduce the grip of the state on productive resources.[11]

SPECIAL PERIOD IN TIME OF UNCERTAINTY

At the end of 2000, the Cuban leadership could look back to seven consecutive years of positive economic growth, a nearly-miraculous turnaround for an economy widely believed to be on the ropes in the early 1990s. For 2000, Cuba reported a GDP growth rate of 5.6 percent and an average GDP growth rate of 4.6 percent for 1996-2000, a very respectable performance within Latin America. Cuban journalists highlighted the broadness and stability of the recovery,[12] as did also a report by the Banco Central de Cuba.[13] The latter report hinted that the special period might be over:

> The Cuban economy has, therefore, followed an intense path of transformations during the last decade in order to achieve a substantial increase of efficiency, the opening to and insertion into the world economy, the creation of spaces for new economic players, the correction of the internal and external imbalance and entrepreneurial improvement. … After these years of Special Period, and with the end of the decade, there is a steady trend toward economic recovery begun at the end of 1994, with an average growth of 4.7 percent, higher than the 3.0 percent achieved by Latin America.[14]

Writing in April 2001, a journalist was more definitive, attributing the overcoming of the economic crisis to the Cuban people's "discipline, pride and mass consciousness."[15]

For 2001, according to Minister of Finance and Planning José Luis Rodríguez, the GDP growth target was 5.0 percent; while recognizing the positive economic performance during 1995-2000, Rodríguez warned that the recovery was entering a new phase in which the emphasis would be on increasing efficiency in an adverse external economic environment.[16] Other economic targets for 2001 were a 20 percent increase in merchandise exports; a 4 percent increase in merchandise imports; arrival of 2 million foreign tourists and a 14 percent increase in revenue generated by tourism; a sugar harvest of 4 million tons; growth of 5.7 percent in nickel output; a 26 percent in oil production (to 3.4 million MT); and a 10 percent growth in non-sugar agriculture.[17]

Preliminary results suggest that most of the 2001 goals were not met:[18]

---

11. Some of these reforms have been advocated by economists within the island. See, e.g., Julio Carranza Valdés, Luis Gutiérrez Urdaneta and Pedro Monreal González, "Reforming the Cuban Economy: A Proposal," in Jorge F. Pérez-López and Matías F. Travieso-Díaz, editors, *Perspectives on Cuban Economic Reforms* (Tempe, Arizona: Arizona State University Center for Latin American Studies Press, 1998).

12. E.g., Raisa Pagés, "Estabilidad económica en los últimos cinco años," *Granma Internacional Digital* (22 December 2000), www.granma.cu.

13. Banco Central de Cuba, *Cuban Economy in the Special Period 1990-2000* (La Habana, n.d.).

14. Banco Central de Cuba, *Cuban Economy in the Special Period 1990-2000* (La Habana, n.d.), p. 10.

15. Domingo Alberto Rangel, "Cómo superó Cuba una crisis," *Granma Internacional Digital* (20 April 2001), www.granma.cu.

16. José Alejandro Rodríguez, "Crece la economía," *Juventud Rebelde* (8 January 2001), www.jrebelde.cubaweb.cu.

17. These targets are taken from Carmelo Mesa-Lago, "The Cuban Economy in 1999-2001: Evaluation of Performance and Debate on the Future," in *Cuba in Transtion—Volume 11* (Washington: Association for the Study of the Cuban Economy, 2001), p. 12.

18. These results come from Comisión Económica para América Latina y el Caribe, *Cuba: Evolución Económica Durante 2001*, LC/MEX/L.525. México (6 June 2002).

- GDP grew at a rate of 3.0 percent, compared with a projected 5 percent growth rate, and GDP per capita grew by 2.6 percent;

- Value of merchandise exports fell by 1.5 percent (compared to a projected 20 percent growth) and imports fell by 1.7 percent (compared to a 4 percent projected growth rate);

- International tourist arrivals were essentially flat in 2001 (compared to a projected growth rate of 12.7 percent) and gross tourism revenue declined by 10 percent (compared to projected growth of 14 percent);

- Sugar production was 3.5 million MT, a 500,000 MT or 12.5 percent shortfall from projections;

- Crude oil production was 2.9 million MT, another historical high, and 7.5 percent above 2001 level, but short of the projection;

- Nickel production was 76,500 MT, a new record high, 7.1 percent above the 2000 level of 71,400 MT (the projected growth rate had been 5.7 percent); and

- Output of the agricultural sector overall declined by 1.7 percent (a 10 percent growth in non-sugar agriculture had been projected).

The disappointing performance of the economy in 2001 can be attributed to the inefficiency of Cuba's socialist economy compounded by a severely worsened external economic environment: a global economic slowdown, the terrorist attacks of September 11 and the war against international terrorism waged by the United States and its coalition of allies, and a major hurricane that affected a large portion of the national territory. Cuba may well have entered a "special period in time of uncertainty": a continuation of the special period in time of peace but in an environment fraught with uncertainty.[19]

The Global Economic Slowdown

Even before the tragic September 11 events, the World Tourism Organization had revised down its estimates of industry growth to 2-3 percent as a result of the deceleration of the world economy and waning consumer confidence.[20] World market prices for sugar and nickel, Cuba's main export commodities, also weakened markedly in 2001: sugar world market prices, which had been around 10 cents/pound in the second half of 2000 and first quarter of 2001, fell to about 9 cents/pound in the second quarter of 2001, 8 cents/pound in the third, and 7 cents/pound in the fourth; nickel prices, which averaged $8638/metric ton in 2000, declined to $6551/metric ton in the first quarter of 2001, $6677 in the second quarter, $5495 in the third quarter, and $5056 in the fourth quarter.

The global economic slowdown also affected foreign direct investment (FDI). Worldwide FDI fell sharply in 2001, declining by 40 percent from $1,271 billion in 2000 to $760 billion in 2001. FDI into Latin America and the Caribbean fell for the second consecutive year, to $80 billion in 2001 from $88 billion in 2000 and $105 billion in 1999.[21] According to journalists who have had access to an unpublished report by the Banco Central de Cuba, FDI in Cuba amounted to $38.9 million in 2001, compared to $488 million in 2000, a 92 percent decline.[22]

The Post-September 11 Shocks

Further Reductions in Tourism: The aftermath of the terrorist attacks compounded the woes of Cuba's

---

19. Analyst Pablo Alfonso suggested in October 2001 that a new special period may be in the offing. See Pablo Alfonso, "A las puertas de otro período especial," *El Nuevo Herald Digital* (31 October 2001), www.elherald.com.

20. World Tourism Organization, *The impact of the attacks in the United States on international tourism: An initial analysis* (Madrid, September 18, 2001), at www.world-tourism.org.

21. "Cae inversión extranjera en América Latina," Comunicado de Prensa, Comisión Económica para América Latina y el Caribe (17 June 2002).

22. MSNBC/Reuters, "Foreign investment in Cuba falls, EU wants reforms," (8 July 2002), http://famulus.msnbc.com/FamulusIntl/reuters07-08-090224.asp?reg=AMERICAS.

tourism industry, particularly coming at a time when the island was preparing for the high tourist season, the time of the year when it receives the largest number of tourists. Gross revenue from tourism in 2000 was over $1.9 billion based on 1.774 million tourists and in 2001 about $1.8 billion based on 1.775 million tourists. The projected two million tourist arrivals would have meant revenue of about $2.2 billion (assuming the same expenditures per tourist as in 2000) and therefore actual revenues in 2001 were about $400 million off from the projection.

Slowdown in Remittances: Unrequited transfers to Cuba amounted to $799 million in 1999, $842 million in 2000 and an estimated $850 million in 2001.[23] The bulk of these transfers—about 85 percent, according to estimates by the Comisión Económica para América Latina y el Caribe (CEPAL)[24]—and the fastest growing segment are private remittances from the United States. Even before the September 11 attacks, the slowdown in the U.S. economy had affected the flow of remittances. As U.S. companies adjusted to slower demand for their goods and services, cutting back on overtime and laying off workers, income of the remittance-sending population declined. This tendency became even sharper after September 11 for two reasons: (1) the slowdown of the U.S. economy intensified; and (2) particularly hard hit was the U.S. tourism industry, a significant industry in South Florida, where the bulk of the remitters are believed to reside. CEPAL estimates that remittances actually turned down in 2001, to $730 million from $740 million in 2000.[25]

The importance for Cuba of family remittances is evident in the public commitments President Castro made on November 2—as he prepared the population for more belt-tightening—when he pledged that despite the economic difficulties facing the nation: (1) the currency exchange outlets (CADECAS) would not be shut down; (2) all deposits in the banking system, whether denominated in pesos, convertible pesos or dollars would be absolutely respected; (3) hard currency stores would not be shut down; and (4) agricultural markets would continue to operate.[26] With these commitments, Castro hoped to raise the confidence of the remittances-sending community that recipients in the island would continue to be able to make use of the funds they received from abroad to gain access to products and services not available in peso-denominated markets.

Enhanced Controls on International Financial Flows: One of the elements of the global campaign to root out international terrorism is to deny it financial means. The United States has taken a number of steps to freeze assets that terrorist organizations held in U.S. financial institutions. Several multilateral initiatives are also under way. While these actions do not directly involve Cuba, increased surveillance and control of international financial flows could have an adverse indirect impact on the island since they might affect investments of questionable origin.

Through 1995, 31 of the 212 joint ventures with foreign investors (15 percent) were reported by the Cuban government to involve capital originating from so-called "tax havens,"[27] nations whose financial systems are not transparent and where the identity of depositors and the source of their deposits are safeguarded by banks and financial institutions. Drug traffickers and other criminals are believed to use tax

---

23. The 1999 and 2000 figures are from Oficina Nacional de Estadísticas (ONE), *Anuario Estadístico de Cuba 2000* (La Habana: ONE, 2001), p. 128. The estimate for 2001 is from Comisión Económica para América Latina y el Caribe, *Cuba: Evolución Económica Durante 2001*.

24. Comisión Económica para América Latina y el Caribe, *La economía cubana: Reformas estructurales y desempeño en los noventa* (Mexico: Fondo de Cultura Económica, 2000). Based on the ratio of remittances to transfers for each of the years 1995-98.

25. Comisión Económica para América Latina y el Caribe, *Cuba: Evolución Económica Durante 2001*, Table 17. For earlier years, CEPAL estimated the following flow of remittances: $537 million in 1995, $630 in 1996, $670 in 1997, $690 in 1998, and $700 in 1999.

26. "Estamos más unidos y fuertes que nunca y mucho mejor preparados para enfrentar esta situación," *Granma* (4 November 2001), www.granma.cubaweb.cu/2001/11/04/nacional/articulo16.html.

27. Consultores Asociados, S.A., *Cuba: Inversiones y Negocios, 1995-1996* (La Habana: CONAS, 1995), p. 18.

havens to "launder" illicitly-generated funds and direct them to legal operations. There is scattered information that suggests that some of the foreign capital flowing to the island and invested there has originated from illicit sources.[28]

Russian Withdrawal from Lourdes Base: In mid-October 2001, Russian President Putin announced that Russsia would close down its electronic eavesdropping center in Cuba before the end of the year.[29] In addition to the political implications for Cuba-Russia relations of the unilateral Russian withdrawal, it also had financial implications, as Russia reportedly paid Cuba about $200 million per annum for the use of the facilities. This represented a significant inflow of foreign exchange to the island and its termination "obviously has an [adverse] impact" for the nation, according to Cuban economist and National Assembly member Osvaldo Martínez.[30]

Hurricane Michelle

In the afternoon of November 4, Hurricane Michelle made landfall near Soplillar, a small town in the southern coast of Matanzas province near the Bay of Pigs. After landing, Michelle turned east and crossed the island at a slow pace, exiting on Monday morning, November 5, through the northern coast of Matanzas-Villaclara provinces, near the town of Corralillo.

According to Vice President Carlos Lage, Hurricane Michelle pummeled Cuba with sustained winds of 130 mph, with gusts of 155 mph. The diameter of the hurricane was about 310 miles. It affected eight western provinces (Pinar del Río, Ciudad de la Habana, La Habana, Matanzas, Cienfuegos, Sancti Spíritus, Villa Clara and Ciego de Avila) plus the special municipality of the Island of Youth. The affected provinces account for 45 percent of the territory and 53 percent of the population of the nation.[31] The hurricane caused significant damage to the sugar industry, non-sugar agriculture, industry, housing and infrastructure. In mid-December 2001, President Castro reported that the losses to the nation caused by Michelle amounted to 1,866 million pesos, [32] or about 6 percent of GDP in 2001.[33]

Sugar industry: Hurricane Michelle's strong winds affected over 590,000 hectares of sugarcane plantings, or 54 percent of total sugarcane plantings.[34] Sugar crop losses associated with the hurricane have been estimated at 120 million pesos.[35] Fidel Castro has stated that sugar exports would decline by 400,000 tons, valued at $60 million.[36] There is no systematic information on damages to sugar mills and other sugar industry facilities resulting from Michelle, but there are reports that the roofs of 99 of

---

28. See, e.g., Gerardo Reyes, "Un poderoso narco pagó millones a Cuba," *El Nuevo Herald* (10 December 2001), p. 29A, referring to activities of Mexican drug trafficker Amado Carrillo Fuentes. See also allegations of activities in Cuba by Russian organized criminals in Robert I. Friedman, *Red Mafiya* (Boston: Little, Brown and Co., 2000), p. 169.

29. Susan B. Glasser, "Russia to Dismantle Spy Facility in Cuba," *The Washington Post* (18 October 2001), p. A34; Nancy Sar Martin, "Russia closing huge eavesdropping site in Cuba," *The Miami Herald* (18 October 2001), pp. 1A, 2A; Pablo Alfonso, "Moscú retira su base de Cuba," *El Nuevo Herald* (18 October 2001), pp. 1A, 2A.

30. "El embajador ruso en La Habana ratifica cierre de base de escucha," *El Nuevo Herald* (24 October 2001), www.miami.com/elnuevoherald.

31. "¡Un pueblo unido puede vencer las mayores adversidades! ¡Lo haremos,!" *Granma* (11 November 2001), www.granma.cubaweb.cu/2001/11/11/nacional.articulo5.html.

32. "Tenemos soluciones para cada situación," *Granma* (19 December 2001), www.granma.cubaweb.cu/2001/12/20/nacional/articulo12.html.

33. Comisión Económica para América Latina y el Caribe, *Cuba: Evolución Económica Durante 2001*, p. 8.

34. "Michelle dañó más de la mitad de la caña," *El Nuevo Herald* (10 December 2001), p. 28A.

35. "Adelantan el inicio de la próxima zafra," *El Nuevo Herald* (21 November 2001), www.elherald.com.

36. "Tenemos soluciones para cada situación," *Granma* (19 December 2001), www.granma.cubaweb.cu/2001/12/20/nacional/articulo12.html.

the 100 sugar mills in the provinces affected by the hurricane were damaged.[37]

Non-sugar agriculture: Hurricane Michelle damaged citrus production areas in the Isle of Youth before squarely hitting Jagüey Grande, in Matanzas province, the nation's premier citrus production area. Michelle also flattened plantain plantings and affected other crops and agricultural equipment. Losses to the agricultural sector inflicted by Hurricane Michelle amounted to 260 million pesos, and the costs of remediating the effects of the storm to 317 million pesos.[38]

Industry: In all, 780 industrial plants were damaged throughout the country.[39] The electricity distribution and communications systems were also severely affected by the hurricane. Michelle brought down 125 high-voltage electricity transmission towers in the center of the island, a large microwave retransmission tower associated with the telephone and television systems located near Jovellanos and two television towers, one in Cienfuegos and the other in Santa Cruz del Norte.

Housing: The already deteriorated housing stock was severely affected by the hurricane. President Castro has reported that the hurricane damaged 166,515 housing units, totally destroying 12,579 of them.[40]

Infrastructure: About 500 schools and over 80 public health centers were damaged.[41]

Prospects for 2002 and Beyond

The economic picture for 2002 and beyond is not a promising one for the average Cuban citizen. The growth rate goal for 2000 has been set at 3 percent, the same rate reached in 2001. There is every indication that it will be a challenge to achieve even this relatively low growth rate given the aftermath of Hurricane Michelle and the very serious hard currency crisis facing the nation. As President Castro stated in an intervention before the National Assembly in December 2001,

> The most serious problem that our country will face in 2002 will be convertible currency revenue. This is not a new problem—we have been facing convertible currency deficits for the last decade of special period, but today we face a very different international situation, a world dominated by a single super power and numerous risks and dangers that threaten humanity.[42]

Vice President Carlos Lage reported to the December 2001 session of the National Assembly that the factors that were pressuring the external sector were heavy indebtedness associated with the borrowing of funds in previous years to finance oil imports and the unfavorable performance of the five principal sources of foreign exchange: (1) tourism (reduced tourist arrivals); (2) sugar (damage to sugar cane crop from Hurricane Michelle and low world market prices); (3) nickel (low world market prices); and (4) tobacco (reduced world demand).[43] The fifth source of income—not mentioned in the article—was undoubtedly family remittances.

Another source of pressure on the Cuban balance of payments is the rise in the price of oil in the world market and the apparent breakdown of the bilateral agreement between Cuba and Venezuela, signed in October 2000, that provided the island with 53,000 barrels per day of Venezuelan crude under preferential terms. After falling to $19 to $21 per barrel in the fourth quarter of 2001 and first quarter of 2002,

---

37. "Adelantan el inicio de la próxima zafra," *El Nuevo Herald* (21 November 2001), www.elherald.com.

38. "Tenemos soluciones para cada situación," *Granma* (19 December 2001), www.granma.cubaweb.cu/2001/12/20/nacional/articulo12.html.

39. Pablo Alfonso, "Cuba: El duro azote del huracán," *El Nuevo Herald* (9 November 2001), p. 1A.

40. "Tenemos soluciones para cada situación," *Granma* (19 December 2001), www.granma.cubaweb.cu/2001/12/20/nacional/articulo12.html.

41. Pablo Alfonso, "Cuba: El duro azote del huracán," *El Nuevo Herald* (9 November 2001), pp. 1A.

42. Fidel Castro, intervention before the National Assembly, as given in María Julia Mayoral, Félix López and Juan Varela Pérez, "Lidiaremos con éxito contra todas las tempestades," *Granma Digital* (22 December 2001), www.granma.cubaweb.cu.

43. Mayoral López and Varela Pérez, "Lidiaremos con éxito contra todas las tempestades."

international oil prices climbed in the second quarter again to over $25 per barrel. In April 2002, Venezuela's state owned oil company, Petróleos de Venezuela, S.A. (PDVSA), reportedly suspended oil sales to Cuba because of the island's failure to pay for earlier deliveries. According to press reports, Cuba's debt to PDVSA in April 2002 amounted to nearly $130 million. Indications were that PDVSA was prepared to continue to sell oil to Cuba, but was considering asking for payment in advance of the deliveries to prevent Cuba from running up the unpaid oil debt.[44]

Finally, as a result of the shortages of foreign exchange, the value of the Cuban peso in official exchange markets deteriorated by 22.7 percent in 2001, falling to 26 to 27 pesos to the dollar at the end of 2001 from 21-22 pesos to the dollar at the beginning of the year.[45] In late May 2002, Cuba announced a general increase in prices of products sold at government stores that use hard currencies (*Tiendas Recaudadoras de Divisas*) ranging from 10 to 30 percent. This action was taken to soak up dollars from the population and presumably also to stimulate additional family remittances.[46]

The long-term prospects of the Cuban economy hinge on whether the current economic model is maintained or is reformed to bring it closer to a market economy. The current economic model is simply not capable of generating sustained economic growth in the medium and long term.[47] Further liberalization and restructuring of the economy are essential for generating vigorous and sustained future economic growth.

CONCLUDING REMARKS

The decade of the 1990s was a challenging one for the Cuban economy, weaned suddenly from the subsidies and preferential economic relations it had enjoyed with the former Soviet Union and the socialist countries for three decades. In 1990, Cuba entered what the leadership called a special period in time of peace as it tried to stop a free falling economy. Cuba began to generate positive economic growth in 1994 and has done so for the last eight consecutive years. By the end of the decade, most economic indicators showed improvement from 1993-94 levels, although they were considerably below their 1989 levels. Thus, the 1990s were a lost decade for Cuba in terms of economic growth.

During the economic crisis of the 1990s, Cuba neglected investment in favor of consumption. This priority is readily observable in the low share of capital goods' imports relative to consumption goods. The insufficient levels of investment will redoubt in low growth rates in the future and the inability to pull the economy out of the low-growth trap in which it currently operates.

In 2002, Cuba faces an economic conundrum: a weak recovery after a deep economic crisis and very tight constraints on external resources, worsened by external shocks such as the world economic slowdown, the September 11 terrorist attacks, the Russian withdrawal from the Lourdes Radar Base and Hurricane Michelle. Absent meaningful reforms that liberalize and restructure the economy, there is no end in sight for the special period. Until such reforms take place, the Cuban population will continue to experience economic hardships.

---

44. Pablo Alfonso, "Cuba tendrá que pagar por adelantado el crudo de Venezuela," *El Nuevo Herald* (7 July 2002).

45. Marc Frank, "Cuban Peso Under Increasing Pressure," Reuters (10 July 2002).

46. Pablo Alfonso, "Castro necesita más dólares del exilio," *El Nuevo Herald* (23 June 2002).

47. This point is also made by Brundenius and Monreal: "...in the absence of economic reforms directed towards the development of a sizable domestic non-state productive sector, sustained high economic growth should not be expected in Cuba." Claes Brundenius and Pedro Monreal González, "The Future of the Cuban Model: The Longer View," p. 148.

THE CUBAN TRANSITION IN THE LIGHT OF THE LESSONS OF TEN YEARS OF EXPERIENCE IN THE FORMER SOVIET BLOC

Ernesto F. Betancourt[1]

This paper is on the assistance that may be required from various international organizations to support the Cuban transition after Castro's demise in the light of the experience accumulated by these organizations in the last decade. Therefore, it is assumed that a Transition Government has replaced the present regime. Furthermore, it is also assumed that this Transition Government is committed to restore democratic rule and a market economy and that it has attained the minimum legitimacy required to rule the country in pursuit of such objectives. In making these assumptions, it is also recognized that there are other possible contextual situations for the transition. It is just impossible to approach this task under a multiplicity of scenarios. Therefore, the paper is written as mere suggestions to be submitted to whatever transitional authority emerges to provide a starting point or agenda to define the assistance required from international organizations for the transition.

One point made by Anders Aslund on the Soviet bloc transitions is critical to keep in mind throughout the paper:

> The central drama of postcommunist economic transformation has been an intense struggle between liber-al reformers, who wanted to build a normal democracy and market economy, and rent seeking businessmen and officials, who desired to make money at the expense of the state and society in transition.[2]

The truth is that the transition in Cuba will have to face such a struggle. Because the Special Period started after the collapse of the Soviet Union constitutes in itself a transition from the old Stalinist system that prevailed in Cuba at that time, mostly in relation to how the economy is managed, while retaining a single party system. As will be seen later on, insiders within the *nomenklatura* have taken advantage of the Special Period to create a rent seeking managerial oligarchy that controls state enterprises under decentralized management and in partnership with foreign investors in mixed ownership enterprises. This insider oligarchy will resist any effort to move towards a free market economy, not to mention democratic rule.

Surprisingly, these regime insiders count with the support of a group of retired U.S. generals who support a succession, rather than a transition, under the leadership of Raúl Castro. Fortunately, they may not prevail. For the dissidence has taken advantage of some hesitation in repression, as well as increasing in-

---

1. This paper is based on *International Organizations and Post-Castro Cuba*, prepared for the Cuba Transition Project, University of Miami. I wish to express my gratitude to José Alvarez, Rolando Castañeda, Armando Linde, Joaquín Pujol and Carlos Quijano for their comments and suggestions, as well as to Eugenio Pons for providing the data on the U.S. Bureau of the Census survey of Cuban American business. Needless to say, I am fully responsible for the contents in this paper.

2. Aslund, Anders. *Building Capitalism: The Transformation of the Former Soviet Bloc* (Cambridge: Cambridge University Press, 2002), p. 4.

522

ternational recognition and support, to expand from the initial human rights groups into independent journalists, libraries, professional associations, agricultural cooperatives and labor unions. This, despite being denied freedom of expression and rights of assembly and association. Cuba's emergent civil society cannot be ignored. It is a force to be reckoned with in Cuba's future.

Fortunately, as the research for this paper was starting, the World Bank released its comprehensive report on a decade of experience with transition in the former Soviet Bloc.[3] The lessons of those transitions are most relevant to the Cuban situation, although requiring adaptation to its peculiarities. In fact, they offer a rationale to address one important peculiarity of the Cuban context: the existence of a Cuban diaspora that owns 30,000 U.S. enterprises with yearly sales of US$24 billion, and, with Castro still in power, has become the most important net source of foreign exchange for the island. A situation not faced by any of the other former members of the Soviet Bloc, perhaps with the exception of Armenia.[4]

The World Bank found that the most successful approach to attain economic success was to privatize while encouraging competitive new enterprises and discouraging continuation of former state enterprises, prone to corruption, asset stripping, tunneling and rent seeking practices. Such an approach requires privatization combined with financial discipline and encouragement of new enterprises. This approach provided a solid base for the rule of competitive democracies in Eastern Europe. It also provides the transition model for Cuba.

In the first section of this paper, the findings of the World Bank report are summarized and reinforced, where relevant, with findings from other sources. In the second section, an attempt is made to fit the Cuban situation into the paradigm resulting from the

lessons of ten years of transition in the former Soviet Bloc. Finally, in the third section, the assistance program that will be required from various international organizations is outlined and then summarized in a matrix linking its elements with potential international aid sources.

It is assumed that a Consultative Group on Cuba will be formed. In view of The World Bank's rich experience in assisting systemic transitions, it is also assumed that this agency will be entrusted with the basic responsibility for coordinating the assistance effort through the Consultative Group. Since Cuba is not a member of the International Monetary Fund (IMF), the World Bank or the Inter-American Development Bank (IDB), it is suggested that preparatory work be started before the actual transition starts to cut the time lag in securing access to urgent financial resources for Cuba's reconstruction.

LESSONS FROM SOVIET BLOC TRANSITIONS
Parallel Political/Economic Transitions
Transition processes are grouped in the mentioned World Bank report, according to the political systems under which they were undertaken, under four categories:[5]

- **Competitive democracies,** that have maintained a high level of political rights to compete in multiparty democratic elections and an extensive range of civil liberties.

- **Concentrated political regimes,** conduct multiparty elections, but for some period they have either curtailed full rights or limited political competition through constraints on civil liberties.

- **Non-competitive political regimes,** constraint entry of potential opposition parties into the political process and sharply restrict political participation, having few limitations on their executives branches.

3. The World Bank, *Transition: The First Ten Years, Analysis and Lessons for Eastern Europe and the Former Soviet Union* (Washington, 2002).

4. Freinkman, Lev M. "Role of the Diasporas in Transition Economies: Lessons from Armenia." In *Cuba in Transition—Volume 11* (Washington: Association for the Study of the Cuban Economy, 2001), pp. 332-342.

5. The World Bank, *Transition: The First Ten Years,* p. 97.

- **War-torn regimes,** these countries had to face internal or external violence during the transition period, causing severe strains on the respective states.

Recognizing that no two countries are identical, in this paper we will consider mostly experiences related to **competitive democracies,** a group that includes the Czech Republic, Slovenia, Hungary, Poland, Lithuania, Estonia and Latvia. This is the most desirable group to consider as a model under which to undertake the post-Castro transition from the political point of view; and, it is also the one that includes the countries most successful in their economic transitions. In the post-Castro transition, it is a given that political rights must prevail, that a multiparty democratic system is imperative and that civil liberties must be guaranteed under the rule of law. One characteristic of the competitive democracies is that they generate substantial contestability and a high government turnover and, contrary to usual assumptions, this has not prevented them from attaining significant systemic reform and high rates of economic growth. Therefore, as a group, they offer a model that is most consistent with the desired outcome of the Cuban transition.

However, it can be argued that the reform that has taken place in Cuba under the so-called Special Period falls broadly under the third group of non-competitive political regimes. In Cuba, the Communist Party retains a monopoly of political activity and the executive branch reigns supreme over the other two branches of government. In the absence of any competition and transparency, there is a continuation of rule by an oligarchy of insiders from the *nomenklatura* who have taken over control of state enterprises or state representation in mixed joint ventures with foreign investors. The regime has already arranged for a succession of this system under Raúl Castro with the support of retired American generals.[6] A situation that the experience of the former Soviet Bloc

states has shown is conducive to lack of competition and corruption, resulting in asset stripping, tunneling, increasing economic inequality and economic stagnation. This option competes with the one being advanced in this paper.

Role of New Enterprises vs. Control by Oligarchs and Insiders

Central to the synergy between the political systems and economic reform and growth in the competitive democracies has been the creation of new enterprises. In a circular effect, the resulting broader inclusion of stakeholders in society reinforces the bases of democratic rule and provides a form of insurance against a return to past statist practices.

By opening access to new entrants into the economic and, therefore, the political system, there is a tendency to wean enterprise management coming from the previous regime's oligarchy from rent seeking arrangements to which they became addicted under state interventionism. A key factor pushing for this competitive enterprise environment has been "the pull of European accession" that strengthened the need to attain both democratic rule and market competition.[7] A similar pull, but with much smaller economic benefits, will be generated in the case of Cuba by the possibility of access to the Free Trade Area of the Americas (FTAA), with its contingent demand for democratic rule explicitly required in the Democratic Charter approved on September 11, 2001, in Lima, Peru. This will entail a substantial effort for Cuban enterprises, since the country is not a full member of any of the sub-regional integration agreements already existing in the Hemisphere and their plants are still saddled with obsolete Soviet technology.

This brings us to the key finding in this report on the lessons learned from transition in the former Soviet Bloc: not only is it necessary to pursue policies that encourage the privatization of state enterprises, but

---

6. Strategic Forecasting, *Succession Plan in Place for a Post-Castro Cuba*, in Center for Defense Information (CDI) Webpage, www.us-cubasecurity.org, 2/28/02. This succession option has been advocated by some retired U.S. generals, such as Wilhelm, Asketon and McCaffrey, all associated with the CDI, who have traveled on various occasions to meet with the Castro brothers.

7. The World Bank, *Transition: The First Ten Years*, p. 107.

also to encourage the emergence of new small enterprises until they cross a critical threshold set, on an empirical basis, at 40 percent in employment and value added.[8] There is ample evidence of a correlation between reliance on small and medium enterprises, instead of state enterprises, whether restructured or not, in attaining higher levels of growth.

During the initial decline in output that resulted from the systemic transition, the countries in Southeastern Europe and the Baltics (CSB), which include all the **competitive democracies,** showed a smaller cumulative output decline (22.6%) and a shorter duration of the recession (3.8 years) than the countries of the Commonwealth of Independent States (CIS), in which the other political modalities prevailed, with a larger (50.5%) average decline in output and a longer average duration of the recession (6.5 years). Obviously, the policies pursued in the CSB countries resulted in a shorter and more moderate initial recession.[9] They also behaved better than other groups with regard to the growth of the private sector's share of economic activity and growth of exports, factors essential to success in a transition effort. As Cuba has undertaken some economic reforms already, mostly to decentralize enterprise management and reduce budgetary subsidies, the transition recession may be even milder and shorter and the recovery start sooner. However, if chaos and conflict prevail, it may be deeper and last longer. Cuba may fall under the **war-torn** category of transitions.

Accepting that intact transfers of experiences are not feasible among countries, whoever is in charge of the Cuban transition in the post-Castro era should look at the **competitive democracies** for the model to follow, with the pertinent adaptations. How was it done? What are the policies involved and what are the institutional changes required? It is evident that there is a lot more involved than a mere change in macroeconomic policy or lip service statements about the changed role of the state. A very complicated carpentry, including societal and bureaucratic attitudes, has to be dismantled and a new carpentry has to be designed and installed.

This is a complex task, requiring not only external assistance from international organizations, but, more so, a sense of ownership from an understanding and committed domestic leadership. This cannot be an international organization led effort but one that emerges from the conviction of national leaders who realize that such a transformation is essential to meet the needs and aspirations of the Cuban people.

Transition Policy Environment: Pursuit of Financial Discipline and Encouragement of Small Enterprise Development

According to the broad consensus that emerges from a decade of World Bank transition experience, it is agreed that, with adaptations to individual circumstances, reforms should include: [10]

- Macroeconomic stabilization;

- Price and trade liberalization;

- Imposition of hard budget constraints on banks and enterprises;

- Enabling environment for private sector development;

- Reform of the tax system and restructuring of public expenditure;

- Legal and judicial reform; and

- Reform of public sector institutions.

This is quite a tall order to fill. Decisions on sequencing are flexible to a certain extent but there is no question that one of the first tasks of the national counterpart will be to work out with the Consultative Group a timetable for these multiple reforms, some of which will have to precede others or at least be undertaken in a well coordinated parallel effort. The preparatory task force, discussed in greater detail below, could assume the task of preparing a tentative scheduling sequence to be submitted for review and

---

8. The World Bank, *Transition: The First Ten Years*, p. 42.

9. The World Bank, *Transition: The First Ten Years*, p. 6.

10. The World Bank, *Transition: The First Ten Years*, p. 14.

approval to transition authorities. This will require a multi-week joint planning session using a computerized PERT program to manage implementation coordination and monitoring.

Success in the transition, according to the lessons learned, is measured in terms of being able to generate economic growth and this success, in turn, is dependent on creating an environment conducive to creating new enterprises, not only in a process of privatization of state enterprises. This requires the pursuit of policies of financial discipline in dealing with old enterprises, privatized or not, and of encouragement of the entry of new enterprises to create a competitive market. This goal is more complex than a mere privatization effort and the time dimension is crucial for its success.

There are no magic formulas offering instant reforms. And regressive forces within the system may be at work to undermine, for selfish reasons, the required discipline. Old regime insiders, in control of former state enterprises, whether restructured or not, as well as even some newcomers, can be expected to resist being deprived of the rents and subsidies that prevailed in the previous regime.

Within the group of **competitive democracies**, in countries like the Czech Republic, Hungary, Lithuania and Poland, the growth of total employment and value added contributed by small enterprises, which are considered a proxy of new enterprises, was higher. They now account for more than 50% of employment and for between 55 and 65% of value added. Meanwhile, in **concentrated** or in **non-competitive political regimes**, like Russia, Kazakhstan and Ukraine, the share of new enterprise employment has stayed below 20% and valued added between 20 and 30%.[11]

This is the result of differences in financial discipline and encouragement policies pursued, as well as in the political origin of the respective transition regimes.

Political institutions in **competitive democracies** "emerged" from round table negotiations among broadly representative popular fronts and a wide range of other organized interests. This, together with the links with Western and Northern Europe and the pull of potential access to the European Union, produced a combination of endogenous and exogenous variables creating the climate for the consensus on the reforms needed. It is this paper's assumption that a similar combination of variables will prevail during the Cuban transition. The process of interaction between political system and economic policies and institutions is too complex to discuss in this brief paper, the reader is referred to the full World Bank report for that discussion and to my book, *De la Patria de Uno a la Patria de Todos*,[12] for a discussion of political, legal and institutional changes required in Cuba during the transition.

Suffice it to say that financial discipline involves "imposing hard budget constraints on enterprises, providing exit mechanisms for insolvent enterprises, monitoring and influencing managerial behavior to reward efficient stewardship of assets and to discourage tunneling and theft, increasing product market competition, transferring social assets from enterprises to local governments, and using the social safety net as a cushion for displaced workers and other losers from reform." Of these, only the transfer of social assets does not apply in general, since in Cuba social services have remained basically a state responsibility at the national or local level, although some enterprises—such as the Canadian company Sherritt International—have assumed some responsibilities for those services. As to encouragement, it involves creating a favorable investment climate for domestic and foreign investors, including: "establishing secure property and contract rights and providing basic infrastructure, reducing excessive marginal tax rates, simplifying regulatory and licensing procedures, and developing a competitive and efficient banking system."[13] In the Cuban case, encouragement may also

11. The World Bank, *Transition: The First Ten Years*, p. xviii.

12. Betancourt, Ernesto F. *De la Patria de Uno a la Patria de Todos* (Miami: Ediciones Universal, 2001).

13. The World Bank, *Transition: The First Ten years*, Annex 1. pp xxix-xxxi.

require specific consideration of the unique situation resulting from the existence of an overseas Cuban community that is already the largest source of net foreign exchange revenues and could make a significant contribution to the process of establishing new small and medium enterprises.

Lessons from Political Transition in Eastern Europe

The process of political transition in Eastern Europe offers interesting lessons that apply to the post-Castro transition in Cuba. Here it is feasible only to present a broad outline. Studies made of those transitions have revealed that they really started ahead of the collapse of the Soviet Bloc and that the factors influencing the shape they took can be expected also to be present in the case of Cuba.[14] It was established that three factors influenced that process: (1) the history of each country; (2) the communist political system; and (3) the conjuncture that resulted in the transition. Of these, history and conjuncture led to variations in outcomes, while the communist system promoted commonality of outcomes due to its impact on the behavior of political elites.

Two important common factors to consider in terms of the political system are: (1) that resulting from the application of Leninist principles of political rule, autonomous political associations were weak mostly because people became accustomed to receiving orders from the *nomenklatura* in the party apparatus and there was an atrophy of the initiative to seek protection for group's interests through advocacy associations; and (2) that the party, through the *nomenklatura* and the monopoly of power granted by the system, was the only organization with capacity to act. Waller concludes that these factors explain, among other things, the continuation of the role of the party beyond the end of its monopoly power.[15] These two characteristics are also present in Cuba and it is likely they will lead to similar outcomes.

In terms of the phases of the process, in the already-quoted Waller paper, a distinction is made of three phases: (1) the heroic phase of defying the monopoly of the party; (2) the actual moment of transfer of power, when the Soviet Bloc collapsed; and (3) the period beyond the first election.[16] For purposes of this paper we will consider only the first two.

In East Germany, autonomous groups emerged around issues related to the environment and with the support of churches; in Poland, the issues were related mostly to nationalist responses to the Soviet presence and labor issues promoted by Solidarity and the Catholic Church; and, in Czechoslovakia, to a general challenge to the system by intellectuals under the Prague Spring movement that was crushed by the Soviet invasion of 1968. In Hungary, the roots went back to the 1956 uprising. In general, these were initiatives, outside the control of the party monopoly, that somehow were tolerated, although in the face of various degrees of repressive actions. A similar situation is presented by the Cuban dissidence since 1990 and the beginning of the Special Period, with results similar to those in Eastern Europe.

Another source of ideas outside the formal authority of the parties, although subordinated to them in diverse ways, was research centers that enjoyed some autonomy in developing ideas and proposals related to national problems and possible reforms to solve them. A similar emergence of research centers has taken place in Cuba, leading to incidents such as Raúl Castro's 1996 attack on the Center for the Study of the Americas (CEA), which ended in CEA's eventual dissolution, or the dismissal and harassment of Dr. Miriam Grass of the Political Science Group at the School of History and Philosophy at Havana University for her monograph *El Sistema de Gobierno Cubano: Control vs Autonomía.*

In the second phase of the Eastern European transition, the work of the more autonomous groups that

---

14. Waller, Michael, "Groups, parties and political change in Eastern Europe from 1977." In Pridham, Geoffrey and Vanhanen, Tatu, *Democratization in Eastern Europe* (London: Routledge, 1994), pp. 38-61.

15. Waller, "Groups, parties ...," p. 45.

16. Waller, "Groups, parties ...," pp. 45-58.

had been leading a precarious existence suddenly acquired legitimacy and provided the seeds for political parties and political leaders such as Walesa in Poland and Havel in Czechoslovakia. The communist party was able to survive in most cases under a diversity of names and without the monopoly of power it had enjoyed up to that time. And the managing of the transition itself was undertaken by ad-hoc temporary institutional arrangements in so-called round tables in which the previous dissident groups, elements from the party and, in some cases, from the military, agreed on the steps to be taken to facilitate an orderly and peaceful transition. In most cases, the resulting transition governments incorporated representatives of the groups composing the round tables until elections brought to power authorities elected by the people.

The outcome of these round tables in general fell under four categories:

1. The negotiation of the transfer;

2. The formal abolition of the party's monopoly power;

3. The passing of laws legalizing political associations; and,

4. The establishment of an electoral process and the holding of a free election.[17]

This is in a nutshell the best analogy available to the political process that would be faced in Cuba during the first phase of the post-Castro transition.

The Role of Labor Unions

One would think that labor unions would enjoy a privileged status and significant power in a system that is supposed to be based on the working class. However, this is not so. The main reason is the political domination of society by the party and the setting of policy from above. Labor unions in capitalist societies emerged in response to the need to represent the working class in the defense of their interests against employers. In Communist societies, the role of the labor unions is to act as a conveyor belt for transmission of party directives to the working class. They are just another mass mobilization instrument of the party. The notion of autonomous labor unions representing the interests of the working class and demanding their rights is anathema for the *nomenklatura*. Labor leaders learn to behave accordingly.

The experience of the Eastern European countries in the atrophy of this representational role of the interests of workers is very revealing. With the exception of Solidarity in Poland, which as was mentioned above emerged in response to nationalist anti-Soviet feelings more than exclusively labor issues, the labor unions in most of these countries came down as part of the collapse of the Communist regimes. The various unions enjoyed a significant membership but did not seem to have acquired the more aggressive behavioral stance of unions in traditional capitalistic societies. Therefore, with the exception of Poland and Yugoslavia, workers have not played a significant role in gaining ownership shares in privatized enterprises. Neither have they played a decisive role in the political process. In fact, even Solidarity in Poland has seen its political influence decline. It is expected that with the passage of time this will change. A new leadership will emerge free of the behavioral atrophy caused by the overpowering domination the party exerted on the previous labor leadership.[18]

In the case of Cuba, the situation is quite different. Labor unions were very prominent and influential in the vigorous civic society that prevailed before Castro. Cuban labor union membership was equal to that of Brazil in absolute numbers, while Cuba had 10% of Brazil's population. The leadership of Cuba's unions included many members of the old communist party, the Partido Socialista Popular (PSP), which had been granted control of labor unions by Batista in 1940 in exchange for their support of his presidential candidacy. Afterwards, they were displaced by anti-communist leaders under the presidencies of Ramón Grau San Martín and Carlos Prío

---

17. Waller, "Groups, parties...," p. 53.
18. Waller, "Groups, parties...," p. 42 and 58-59.

Socarrás. Castro restored control of the labor federation to the old PSP as part of his alliance with the Soviet Union. However, PSP labor leaders were used to represent labor before employers and their patterns of behavior were totally different from what the traditional communist party in power expected from its union leaders. With the passage of time the old leaders have retired or passed away and today the Cuban labor unions are as submissive as were those of Eastern Europe, with the exception of Poland, of course. In a survey of Cuban public opinion among recent arrivals it was found that a whopping 97% reported that being a member of a labor union did not provide them any benefits.[19] It will be interesting to see if, in the absence of party control, behavior consistent with the culture of previous labor leaders in defense of workers demands and interests will reappear earlier in Cuba's transition than in Eastern Europe.

Privatization as the Central Process of the Transition

The above-described lessons from the transitions in the former Soviet Bloc also include those related to the various privatization processes. One significant finding from the political process is that behavior of party *nomenklatura* is not expected to change until there is a change in property relations.[20] As to the lessons from the various privatization efforts, experiences are not clustered so clearly as in relation to other issues. Learning from those experiences will require a very precise matching of context and objectives.

The mentioned World Bank report reaches conclusions less favorable to the use of voucher systems and so-called Mass Privatization Programs (MPP) than earlier studies of the Eastern Bloc experience in privatization. However, it recognizes that these methods could be considered in the context of additional criteria beyond economic growth. In fact, the change in perception of the success of privatization efforts from the mid-1990s to date led the World Bank to commission an evaluation of those efforts with special emphasis on Russia, Poland and the Czech Republic. Evaluation findings are less categoric than some privatization critics have posited, first, because of the lack of workable alternatives offered by the critics and, second, because the initial objective of mass privatization was to depoliticize enterprise management and improved corporate governance was added as an objective ex-post facto. Two important lessons emerge, though: (1) it is necessary to create an institutional framework to protect the public interest before a mass privatization is undertaken; and (2) the quality of the resulting corporate governance must be taken into account as one of the objectives of privatization.[21]

Therefore, although mass privatization should be designed taking precautions in the light of the experiences in Eastern Europe and the Soviet Bloc, it is still worth considering as an option in view of the lack of valid alternatives, but blending it with other approaches. Privatization was an answer to a two-fold situation. First, although enterprises were state-owned, their control was in the hands of managers or, in the case of Poland the workers, leading to asset stripping and tunneling; and, second, that it was necessary to quickly depoliticize the enterprise sector.[22] These conditions are likely to be present in Cuba.

Therefore, it is advisable to consider MPPs as a privatization option, taking into account the relevance to Cuba of the three basic objectives they pursue:

- to get the population in general involved in the process of economic transformation;

19. Roberts, Churchill; Betancourt, Ernesto; Grenier, Guillermo; and Schaeffer, Richard. *Measuring Cuban Public Opinion: Project Report* (Gainesville: University of Florida, September, 1999), Table 74, p. 98.

20. Waller, "Groups, parties ...," p. 45.

21. Nellis, John. *The World Bank, Privatization and Enterprise Reform in Transition Economies: A Retrospective Analysis* (Washington: Center for Global Development, The World Bank, 2002).

22. Hare, Paul; Batt, Judy; and Estrin, Saul, Editors. *Reconstituting the Market: The Political Economy of Microeconomic Transformation* (Amsterdam, The Netherlands: Overseas Publishers Association, 1999), pp. 14-15.

- to attain some degree of distributive equity by making everybody an owner of part of the national productive capacity; and

- to quickly privatize a large number of firms and productive assets to deepen the roots of market forces and competition in the economic environment.[23]

Of course, based on the experience of countries like Russia, Poland, Hungary, the Czech Republic and Lithuania in undertaking a voucher process or MPP, measures should be included to avoid the difficulties experienced by those countries.

The lessons learned in relation to privatization indicate that success in the next phase—that is, pursuing economic growth—is very much contingent on the quality of the corporate governance that prevails under the new ownership.[24] And that quality is heavily influenced by whether ownership is diffuse or concentrated and whether the selection of investors was made by auctions or transparent tenders instead of through purely administrative actions, which make insider deals more feasible. It was also found that selection of foreign investors to take over related industries is the formula providing the most favorable results, although this is applicable in limited instances and may generate resistance and some negative political repercussions due to nationalistic feelings. This is a factor of great weight in Cuba.

One aspect that becomes evident is that institutional capacity to oversee enterprises in the privatization stage is essential to avoid asset stripping and tunneling that depletes their assets to the detriment of minority stockholders. Also, the experience with workers taking over enterprise management has resulted much too frequently in depletion of assets through pay and benefit increases rather than increasing the investment capacity of the enterprise. The use of investment funds in the mass privatization scheme in the Czech Republic failed to attain its objectives in

some cases due to lack of managerial competence and also interlocking relationships with the banks that held the enterprises' debts.

Finally, a comment is necessary on the issue of restitution, which is closely related to privatization. In Aslund's analysis, restitution is discussed in the case of East Germany and it reveals that the impact on economic growth was extremely negative. The main reason was that a very legalistic notion of justice prevailed, while economic growth was given a lower priority. As a result of very complicated legal issues going back to Nazi Germany, "some two million claims were presented, clogging the courts for years and stopping thousands of construction projects and enterprises because of uncertain legal claims."[25] Besides the moral and justice motivations that justify including restitution in a privatization effort, a key point to keep in mind is that the process should be designed so that it does not interfere with the ability to restore production and economic growth. This will be critical in the case of Cuba.

In summary, without excluding the Mass Privatization option, the following agenda is suggested for the Cuban case by the experiences documented by the World Bank:

- Privatization should be part of an overall strategy of discipline and encouragement.

- Small enterprises should be sold quickly and directly to new owners;

- Medium-size and large enterprises should be targeted for possible sale to strategic outside investors. In doing this, due consideration should be given to the many mixed enterprises already established with foreign partners by the present regime.

- Investor protection should be enshrined in the legal system and enforced, covering rules to protect minority stockholders; rules against insider dealings and conflicts of interest; creditor surveil-

---

23. Betancourt, Ernesto F. *De la Patria de Uno a la Patria de Todos*, p. 21.

24. The World Bank, *Transition: The First Ten years* …. This discussion draws on pp. 71-72.

25. Aslund, *Building Capitalism*, p. 259.

lance, accounting, auditing, and disclosure standards; and takeover, insolvency and collateral legislation.

- Privatization should be accompanied by increasing competition and enforcement of competition policy.

- The cash flow and property rights of the state should be clarified when the state continues as partial owner.

- Divesting enterprises in natural monopoly or oligopoly sectors should include provisions for regulatory supervision.[26]

APPLYING TRANSITION LESSONS TO CUBA

The transition started in Cuba before the collapse of the Soviet Bloc and was given a tremendous push by the Special Period caused by that collapse. As far back as the 1980 Mariel exodus, the regime was forced to introduce economic reforms which were the start of an economic opening. And the dissident movement, started in the mid and late seventies, is the seed of the political opening feeding an incipient civil society. *Glasnost* and *Perestroika* challenged Castro's Stalinism, which had already regressed into harsher totalitarian rule in response to the initial threat poised by the dissidence and the farmers' markets of the early eighties.

The Special Period in the early nineties forced an initial economic opening that Castro started to brake as soon as the worst of the economic collapse passed around 1996. But Cuba's Special Period was not a transition into a competitive democracy situation with a free market. Instead, the regime moved to a non-competitive political regime, insisting on perpetuating one party rule under Castro, with the most significant economic change being legalization of tenure of dollars, while maintaining a *dirigiste* economy along with an opening to foreign investment and decentralized management of state enterprises.

In order to make itself more attractive to foreign investment, and perhaps even to gain access to eco-

nomic assistance from the European Union, the regime kept repression at a low level, reducing harassment of opponents and harsh reprisals and imprisonment. The result has been that opposition to the regime has expanded with the dissidence movement blooming from human rights denunciation to independent journalists, libraries, professional associations, labor unions and agricultural cooperatives. This, despite denial of universal rights of assembly and association, which are formally recognized in the Cuban Constitution. But the result in political terms is similar to the World Bank experience reported mostly in the former Soviet Bloc in the case of the CIS: a **non-competitive political regime.**

Moving to the economic side of the reforms introduced during the Special Period in Cuba, the results have also been similar to those found by the World Bank in the CIS. An oligarchy from within the Cuban *nomenklatura* has emerged as rent-seeking insiders who control state enterprises under decentralized management and in partnership with foreign investors. Perhaps the largest and most influential, but certainly not the only one, GAESA, is centered in the Ministry of the Armed Forces (MINFAR) and is headed by General Julio Casas Regueiro, with Raúl Castro's son-in-law as general manager. Basic Industries Minister, Marcos Portal, married to a niece of Raúl and Fidel Castro, is described as a power to be dealt with in the succession promoted by the regime.[27]

These rent-seeking managers are trying to increase internal enterprise efficiency with the introduction of modern management methods in a nationwide effort called "Perfeccionamiento Empresarial." A pointless exercise, because economic efficiency at the micro or enterprise level, besides being hindered by external diseconomies, is made meaningless at the macro level by a context in which prices are set administratively, there is no free access of new entrepreneurs and no market allocation of capital to investment to ensure a competitive market environment. This is precisely

---

26. The World Bank, *Transition: The First Ten Years ...*, Chapter 7, pp. 79-80.

27. Strategic Forecasting, *Succession Plan*.

the type of situation that led Aslund to reach the conclusion that a privatization effort is essential to ensure a successful transition to a market economy.[28]

Needless to say that the insiders' oligarchy within Cuba's current regime with access to dollars shows manifestations of the same corrupt practices identified within the **non-competitive political regimes** in the CIS, such as asset stripping, tunneling and blocking of reforms that may threaten their privileged status. The regime even established a new Ministry of Audit and Control in 2001 to cope with fraud. In Cuba, accounting systems were severely hurt by Castro's high-handed decision against the practice of the profession, including banning it for years from university curricula. In the last few years, there has been an effort to restore it as an integral part of enterprise management, but with limited success. In fact, it is the main reason why the majority of enterprises have not qualified for the process of "Perfeccionamiento Empresarial." At the annual meeting to assess its accomplishments for 2001, the Ministry of Finance and Prices reported that only 180 out of 382 accounting and internal control systems submitted for approval under the "Perfeccionamiento Empresarial" program were considered satisfactory, with 202 rejected.[29] Insider managers are not interested in improving accounting records that could reveal asset stripping and tunneling actions related to their corrupt practices.

The Cuban Political Transition

At some point in the Cuban transition process, there will emerge the need to create a forum similar to the round tables that emerged in Eastern Europe. There is no way to predict the dynamics of the process that will generate the need for such an instrument. It could be some health problem faced by Castro or even his passing away. It could be a policy split between insiders favoring more economic liberalization to calm popular unrest and hardliners advocating harsher repression to deter that unrest. It could be a

coup d'etat by younger unknown elements in the armed forces.

A Round Table in Cuba will have to include representatives of the four groups of stakeholders mentioned above. In the Cuba case, the main difference will be the presence of representatives of overseas Cubans. The agenda would be similar to the one mentioned earlier under the subsection "Lessons from political transition in Eastern Europe."

However, it will have to address issues such as the freeing of political prisoners and the abolition of mass organizations, like the Committees for the Defense of the Revolution, that have become associated with regime repression. In the survey of Cuban public opinion undertaken in 1999 by the University of Florida, based on interviews of over one thousand recent arrivals, it was found that the Communist Party had a most hated rating of 77% and the Committees for the Defense of the Revolution of 71%.[30] The repressive agencies are equally unpopular and the problem of their abolition will have to be contemplated under the light of the public order situation at the time. Such levels of unpopularity with the opposition will have to be taken into account at the time of transition by the Round Table, not only in the determination of its composition, but also in the priorities of its agenda for action. The Organization of American States (OAS), through its Inter-American Commissions on Human Rights and the regional body of jurists could provide assistance, with ample participation of overseas and national Cuban lawyers, to deal with the actions required from the round table in restoring the rule of law.

Then, there is the issue of calling for elections. The International Federation of Electoral Systems (IFES) could be asked by the U.S. Agency for International Development (USAID) to update a study they prepared for them years ago with suggestions on the Cuban electoral system. The OAS has ample experience

---

28. Aslund, *Building Capitalism* .., p. 261.

29. "Balance Anual del Ministerio de Finanzas y Precios," *Granma* (March 16, 2002).

30. Roberts, Betancourt, Grenier, and Scheaffer, *Measuring Cuban Public Opinion: Project Report.*

in supervising elections, so it could be called to provide technical assistance in this respect.

As to the overall creation of the Round Table itself, the experience of countries such as the Czech Republic and Poland, could be extremely useful in this respect. They themselves benefitted from the lessons of the Spanish transition at the time of Franco's death. When transitions were taking place in Eastern Europe, "Madrid became the Mecca for transition actors from Eastern Europe with visits by figures such as Havel, Roman, Mazowiecki and Yeltsin to talk to Spanish political leaders."[31] The European Union or the respective national assistance programs would certainly be happy, when the time comes, to facilitate access to Cuban round table leaders to the experiences of those who worked in European transitions, including, of course, the Spanish.

Privatization as the Central Transition Process

Therefore, the transition to a post-Castro regime should be defined as a process of moving from a **noncompetitive political** regime into a **competitive political** regime, centered in a process of privatization that allows for the emergence of new enterprises as quickly as possible to provide the overwhelming majority of employment and value added. As stakeholders in the post-Castro's Cuba, the following groups should be represented in the Round Table and Transition Government, which means their interest and aspirations should be recognized:

- All Cuban citizens residing in the island;

- Insiders from the *nomenklatura* of the current regime and its supporters who are willing to accept the end of the party monopoly of power;

- Dissidents, victims of regime repression and oppositionists in general; and

- Overseas Cubans willing to continue engaged in Cuba, particularly in the reconstruction of Cuba's economy.

It is suggested that the Round Table or the Transition Government request advice from the World Bank on how to set up a privatization scheme to attain in as short a period of time as possible the transfer of ownership of the productive capacity of the nation to private owners. The scheme will have to satisfy certain criteria. Citizens should be able to acquire a share of their places of work in the case of small enterprises. The agricultural cooperatives (UBPC and others) should be sold to their members, offering special credit facilities if necessary. Medium size enterprises should be placed in the market to be acquired by management and workers or sold to the highest bidder. Large enterprises, already in joint ventures, should be privatized following transparent bidding processes. But nothing should be given for free.

Consideration should be given to alloting additional rights for acquisition of enterprises to those: (1) whose properties were confiscated without compensation; (2) who were victims of regime repression; and, (3) who were sent to fight overseas by the regime and did not get any assistance in reintegrating to Cuban society at the end of their internationalist service.

In view of the Eastern Europe experience, how to do that should be left to the technical expertise of the advisory team. It is evident that a preparatory phase will be required: (1) to strengthen the ability of the banking system to provide effective lending and supervision for new and restructured enterprises; (2) to establish open access procedures for the creation of new enterprises; and, (3) to enforce hard financial discipline to eliminate rents and subsidies.

As the Eastern European experience suggests, privatization should be the central process of the transition effort in Cuba. Substantial technical and financial assistance will be required to undertake the design and implementation of such privatization effort. That effort should include transitory measures to reinforce governmental institutional capacity to avoid, to the extent possible, asset stripping and tunneling. In order to ensure that production is activated and not paralyzed by the complex process involved, enterprise

---

31. Pridham, Geoffrey, "Democratic Transitions in Theory and Practice," in Pridham and Vanhanen, *Democratization ...*, p. 29.

governance should be included as a specific objective of the privatization effort. It is suggested that the steps enumerated at the end of the earlier subsection titled "Privatization as the Central Process of the Transition" be considered as the starting agenda for adaptation to Cuban conditions. This, in turn, should be considered in the agenda for assistance from international organizations as a priority topic. If at all possible, work should be started by the suggested preparatory work task force or working group.

Assistance to Reform National Policies

As discussed above, Cuba will require massive technical assistance to transform the present **non-competitive political regime** economic policies and institutions into those of a **competitive democracy**. This will involve changes in macroeconomic, monetary, banking, and fiscal policies. Learning from the experience of previous transitions,[32] attention will have to be paid to the parallel changes required in institutions, in sociological and organizational terms, as well as in the training of cadres from the new public administration that is required and of the emerging private sector, who will need to change their behaviors in order to work in the new competitive environment.

This effort will involve the largest component of international organization: assistance Cuba will require. This will be more so as the assistance is directed at sectors such as private banking, trade and services, not to mention agriculture and small and medium enterprise, all of which face serious market distortions in the current Cuban economic environment. The assistance for fiscal and monetary policy and stabilization will have to be requested from the International Monetary Fund. The assistance for other policies related to what is called structural adjustment, as well as other sectoral efforts is usually split among the World Bank, IDB, the European Community and country efforts. This will have to be

one of the first assignments for the joint staff working in preparation for the convening of the Consultative Group.

It is in this respect that the role of overseas Cubans could become critical to transition success thanks to a felicitous convergence of the Eastern Europe experience and unique conditions peculiar to the Cuban situation. As mentioned before, one of the lessons from the successful transitions linked new enterprises with the attainment of the highest levels of economic growth, while shortening the recession caused by the initial systemic changes. Cuba has access to a very rich source of entrepreneurs for small and medium enterprises, which usually are ignored by the multinational corporations, yet have been found to be the biggest source of employment and value added.

This is reflected in the impact of remittances within Cuba's current balance of payments. Writing in the journal *Encuentro*, Cuban economist Pedro Monreal estimates the flow of remittances to be around $500 million per year and suggests that encouraging investments by overseas Cubans "could be one of the most efficient ways of obtaining access to investment resources."[33]

But overseas Cubans can be more than a mere source of investment capital, important as that is: they can also be a very significant source of entrepreneurship, technological, managerial and marketing know-how. To realize the magnitude of that potential, it is worth considering the summary information from the 1997 U.S. Economic Census.[34] It must be kept in mind that this refers only to domestic U.S. enterprises and does not include the many Cuban-owned enterprises in countries such as Venezuela, Spain, Mexico, South and Central America, nor the thousands of Cuban managers and technical staffers working throughout the world in multinational corporations.

---

32. Nunberg, Barbara. *The State After Communism: Administrative Transition in Central and Eastern Europe* (Washington: The World Bank, 1999).

33. Monreal, Pedro, "Las remesas familiares en la economía cubana," *Encuentro*, Issue 14 (Fall 1999), p. 61.

34. U.S. Bureau of the Census. *1997 Economic Census: Minority - and Women-owned Businesses*, http://www.census.gov/csd/mwb/

According to the 1997 U.S. Economic Census, there were 125,273 Cuban-owned firms in the United States, of which 89,682 (around 70%) were located in Florida. For purposes of our study, we will limit ourselves to firms with paid employees, of which there were 30,203 nationally, 21,033 (again around 70%) located in Florida. If only a fraction of the owners of these firms can be encouraged to enter into partnerships with relatives or friends in Cuba with some experience as self-employed entrepreneurs, or make direct investments in totally new enterprises, Cuba could experience a much more significant recovery than if they are ignored, or, even worse, discouraged from participating in the transition. Overseas Cuban entrepreneurs represent a most powerful source of know-how and resources that, if encouraged properly to participate in the Cuban reconstruction, could make the Cuban case an exceptional transition success story.

OUTLINE OF INTERNATIONAL ASSISTANCE PROGRAM

The assistance program required from international agencies in the Cuban transition should be started in the pre-transition period. This has already been commented in a previous paper.[35] In essence, what is suggested is that the U.S. Government, as the largest contributor to the IMF, the World Bank and the IDB, request from these agencies the formation of a preparatory working group or task force to start formulating a tentative program of assistance to Cuba during the transition. This request must be made by the U.S. Treasury and the related costs financed through a grant from USAID. Since the present Cuban Government is not an active member of any of these organizations, there can be no formal objection from them to such a request.

At present, the Inter-American Dialogue is promoting cooperation between these agencies and the present Cuban Government, with a grant from the Ford Foundation. This cooperation is heavily influenced by the whims of the present Cuban Government, that allows or denies representatives from these agencies entrance to Cuba depending on the willingness of the Dialogue to submit to Cuban vetoes on who they may contact in other activities. For example, the project was suspended when the Dialogue invited Cuban American National Foundation (CANF) President Jorge Mas Santos to address one of its meetings. Under such a coercive atmosphere, it is unlikely that any serious research work can be undertaken. Much less related to a post-Castro Cuba.

But, even worse, there is a basic philosophical disagreement with the World Bank and the IMF that was clearly expressed by Castro himself during his speech at the Monterrey Summit on March 22, 2002, when he accused these organizations of promoting genocidal policies and added that "their prestige is below zero." The fact is that Castro rejects both neo-liberalism and globalization, two basic tenets of the policies of these agencies. Therefore, under present unofficial arrangements, the staffers from these agencies going to Cuba end up being mere props for Cuban propaganda efforts. Or, if they do any planning for assistance, they may have to renounce the principles that guide the stabilization and structural adjustment efforts of their agencies. In either case, what they are doing does not advance one iota the preparation for transition assistance.

Pre-Transition Assistance

Even under expedited procedures, it takes easily a year from the moment a country decides to apply for membership in the international financial institutions to the moment disbursements start.[36] Therefore, it would be advisable to consider other organizational options for these institutions to start the preparatory work required so that the time frame is collapsed as much as is feasible. The Helms-Burton legislation, under Section 202 (e) provides the basis

---

35. Betancourt, Ernesto F., "Selected Technical Assistance Needs for Democratic and Institutional Transformation during the Cuban Transition," *Studies in Comparative International Development*, Vol. 34, No. 4 (Winter 2000), pp. 60-61.

36. Quijano, Carlos N. "The Role of International Organizations in Cuba's Transition," paper presented at the Cuba Transition Workshop, sponsored jointly by Shaw, Pittman, Potts, and Trowbridge and the Association for the Study of the Cuban Economy (January 1994), p. 5. This section will draw at large from this paper.

for the U.S. Government, through its directors at these agencies, to request that planning for assistance to a Transition Government in Cuba be started by creating a joint preparatory working group or task force. If the statutes or policies of these agencies forbid using their financial resources in any work related to non-member countries, USAID can provide a grant to sustain such efforts.

The results of the preparatory work should be tentative plans contingent on the decisions to be made, at the proper time, by the authorities that emerge in a Transition Government in Cuba. The setting up of a flexible roll-over plan, properly sequenced in a computerized PERT system, should be one of the basic outputs of the preparatory stage.

Emergency Assistance

The first task that will require attention is the emergency assistance that will be needed to restore, from whatever is their deteriorated state, ports, highways, railroads, bridges, and telecommunications and power generation systems. At this stage, supplies of food, medicines and spare parts to compensate for shortages in domestic output or imports will also be required.[37] The World Food Program may also have to be involved but, since Cuba is a UN member and at present a recipient of food assistance, it is not feasible for that agency to participate before an actual transition starts. Depending on how much progress is attained in preparatory work, USAID and other country donors are likely to have to provide financing for initial emergency assistance. The World Bank could schedule rapid disbursement balance of payment adjustment loans to reach effectiveness, or disbursement stage, as early as possible and emergency social fund programs to alleviate poverty and generate employment. The IDB would also need to schedule emergency program loans, preferably jointly with the World Bank and other donors for early disbursement. The Transition Government should proceed to finalize access to the Cotonú Agreement and to establish a Framework Agreement for cooperation with the European Union, if they are still pending at the moment of the transition.

Assistance will be required in setting up the Round Table for transition preparation. This aid could be requested from the European Union, at the proper time, or from the Czech, Hungarian, or Polish Governments, as well as from Spain. If at all feasible, this should start during the preparatory stage. Cuba will also need assistance from the OAS in meeting democracy and human rights requirements as demanded by the Democratic Charter approved on September 11, 2001 in Lima, Perú.

Monetary Stabilization

In these endeavors, the main focus will be on necessary changes in monetary and fiscal policies to move to a market economy, as well as to secure the financial assistance necessary to ensure currency and price stability, while undertaking structural reforms. The IMF is the leading agency in such efforts, and membership in this organization is also a pre-requisite for being a member of the World Bank. The IMF is the source of financing for stabilization agreements and also provides assistance in the formulation and administration of fiscal policies, including tax, customs and budget, and of monetary policies, including the setting of an independent central bank, as well as bank supervision regulations and agency. It also assists in restructuring foreign debt; developing policies and procedures for conducting transparent open market operations; organizing an efficient payments clearance system among commercial banks; and, regulating the operations of the exchange market.

The Paris Club could play a role in helping the Transition Government deal with the foreign debt. Cuba's debt with the West (except with the United States, which has none thanks to the embargo) has been reported by Carmelo Mesa-Lago to have reached US$11 billion by the end of 2001.[38] Cuba also has a very large debt with the former Soviet

---

37. Betancourt, "Selected Technical Assistance," p. 49 provides a discussion and recommendations on this matter.

38. Mesa-Lago, Carmelo. "The Cuban Economy in 1999-2001: Evaluation of Performance and Debate on the Future." In *Cuba in Transition—Volume 11* (Washington: Associations for the Study of the Cuban Economy, 2001), Table 3, p. 4.

Union that was surrogated to Russia and which Cuba has rejected. Failure to solve this disagreement is one of the factors preventing progress in Cuba's efforts to reach an agreement with the Paris Club.

Parallel to these efforts, and complementing them to attain sound macro-economic management, would be those related to structural adjustment. The World Bank is usually the leading institution providing the policy and financial assistance related to the structural adjustment of an economy at the macro-economic level. An effort which, in the case of Cuba, will have enormous ramifications. The IDB, as the leading source of international financial assistance in the Hemisphere, should share this effort with the World Bank. This means that Cuba will also have to join this agency, of which it has never been a member, and IDB membership requires the country to be a member of the OAS, from which Cuba's present government is suspended. So, the Transition Government will have to apply first to be reinstated at the OAS.

Structural Adjustment

In line with the lessons of transition in Eastern Europe, the central focus of the structural adjustment program will be attainment of a successful privatization that provides the framework for encouraging the emergence of a competitive market in which new enterprises flourish. It must satisfy the aspirations of all stakeholders previously identified in the future of Cuba: the people at large, those around Castro at present willing to join the future, the dissidence, and the overseas Cubans. This will be the central issue around which to build a Cuba for all.

Structural adjustment will also require the enactment of new policies to ensure financial and market discipline and encouragement of entrance of new enterprises as discussed in the first section of this paper. In targeting poverty pockets and unemployment, the creation of a social emergency fund and complementary loans to it would be necessary. Assistance to social emergency funds usually involves other sources of financial assistance beyond the international lending organizations, and it might include the European Union and country programs.

Productive and Social Sectors

At this stage, there will be some overlapping of assistance. Structural adjustment efforts will require, depending on the situation prevailing in the country at that time, that assistance be provided to cope with both productive and sectoral sector problems facing the country. The IDB and the World Bank have developed many joint efforts in these areas in the hemisphere and their joint experience will have to be drawn upon by the Transition Government. Therefore, both the World Bank and the IDB would be the leading lending institutions providing both, technical assistance for policy guidance and financing, for sectoral, productive and social rehabilitations or restructuring necessary to attain the required goals.

State Reform

Learning from the experience of the transitions in Eastern Europe, parallel to the policy changes there will have to be a massive reorganization of the public sector, as well as of the legislative and judicial apparatus, along with retraining of cadres in both the public and private sector. The organizational culture associated with the present regime will have to be replaced by a new one, as happened in Singapore after independence, and was discussed in the previous study on selected technical assistance needs.[39]

A meeting of a Consultative Group should be convened to mobilize resources from external donors willing to participate in assisting the country, as well as private sector international banks. Cuba would be likely to attract many donors interested in participating in its reconstruction. As mentioned before, the World Bank, due to the wealth of experience it has accumulated on systemic transitions, would be the logical agency to prepare and manage the Consultative Group. However, the IDB, as the largest source of financial assistance in the hemisphere, may be preferred by the Transition Government.

---

39. Betancourt, "Selected Technical Assistance," p. 70.

To provide a map of all potential participants in the provision of assistance to the Transition Government in this extraordinary undertaking, a matrix attached to this paper has been prepared indicating the outline of the reform effort required in the Transitional Assistance Program and the potential role of the various international actors. Taking advantage of the lessons learned, institutional assistance for state reform, as well as training activities, should be scheduled parallel or preceding the proposed assistance for policy reforms. This will ensure that organizational structure and culture change along with the desired policy changes.

The Role of the Cuban Nation

In the end, all the international assistance here identified, and much more that has not been covered, must be complementary to the national effort. It is upon the shoulders of the Cuban people and its Transition Government that will fall the responsibility for the future of Cuba.

The proposals in this paper represent a synthesis of the lessons learned by others in similar efforts at systemic transitions from command economies and totalitarian rule into market economies and democratic rule. These examples cannot be transferred intact: they merely provide guidance, very useful indeed, about the experience of other nations facing similar challenges. It will be up to Cuban society to free the creative capacity of its citizens, organized in a vigorous civil society and with an effective and committed state leadership, to ensure success. International agency assistance is a necessary but not sufficient condition for success.

The potential is there but it will require a new spirit to ensure that in this new century, Cuba learns from the lessons of the past two centuries and takes the road of tolerance and hard work that will provide its people with the freedom, peace and prosperity it hopes for and deserves.

ATTACHMENT
Potential International Actors in a Cuban Transition and their Roles

Transition Assistance Program Element	IMF	World Bank	IDB	OAS	UN	European
EMERGENCY AID						
Pre-transition planning	Participates	Leads task force	Participates			
Infrastructure rebuilding and food, drugs and parts needs					World Food Program	May particip:
Round Table	Cuba rejoins	Cuba rejoins, requires IMF membership	Cuba applies to join, requires OAS membership	Cuba rejoins, assists on Democratic Charter		Cuba joins C and framewc
STABILIZATION						
Monetary and fiscal policy revamping consistent w/ market economy and macro-economic stability as well as Paris Club debt restructuring / reorganization of banking system	Leads policy and management reform T/A advice/provide short term financing/ debt rescheduling w/ Paris Club	Participates and may provide loans for financial system restructuring	Participates and may provide loans for financial system restructuring			
STRUCTURAL ADJUSTMENT						
Advice on privatization policy, discipline and encouragement	Participates in reference to issues related to stability	Leads advice work based on transition experience and provides structural adjustment loans	May share with the Wold Bank advice work and structural lending		UNDP or CEPAL may participate in advice work	May particip: under Cotoni Framework Agreements
Social emergency fund created		Leads or shares design advice and financing	Leads or shares design advice and financing			May particip:
PRODUCTIVE SECTORS						
Assistance in restructuring under a privatized market economy, including advice and lending, for infrastructure, agriculture, small and medium enterprises, mining, domestic and foreign trade, etc.	May provide advice on banking reorganization and regulation	Provides sectoral adjustment. loans, alone or jointly with IDB.. Others	Provides sectoral loans, alone or jointly with World Bank and others		May provide assistance through UNDP, CEPAL or UN agencies	May provide assistance ul Cotonú or Framework Agreements
SOCIAL SECTORS						
Assistance in restructuring, in accordance with a market economy, provision of health, education, housing, etc.		Similar role to the one on productive sector reform	Similar role to the one on productive sector reform		Similar role to the one on productive sector reform	Similar role t one on produc sector reform
STATE REFORM						
Consistent with above policy revamping, assistance for a massive change in public sector organizational structure and culture, including executive, legislative and judicial branches	May provide assistance in fiscal policy formulation and management	Assistance in modernization of the state and the judiciary	May take lead in assistance f/ modernization of the state, the legislature and the judiciary	May provide assistance in human rights, legal reform, w/ Democratic Charter and elections	May provide assistance through UNDP and CEPAL	May provide assistance th the Cotonú o Framework Agreements
Organization of Consultative Group Meeting to ensure effort coordination and pledges of resources.	Shall participate	Should lead due to transition experience	Shall participate, lead alternative	Shall participate	Shall participate	Shall particip

VALORACIONES SOBRE EL DOCUMENTO:

"The Cuban Transition in the Light of the Lessons of Ten Years of Experience in the Former Soviet Bloc" de Ernesto F. Betancourt

Marta Beatriz Roque Cabello[1]

El supuesto básico de que un Gobierno de Transición ha reemplazado al actual régimen y que está legitimizado—al menos al mínimo—es importante. Otros documentos en que los que se han expuesto soluciones para la transición, no consideran un escenario preliminar, y ¿cómo proponer alternativas sin tener una base inicial?

Aunque no se detalla como se va a alcanzar esta situación—ya que es imposible predeterminarla—no sería igual diseñar una estrategia para construir una sociedad democrática y de libre mercado, que para hacer algunas restauraciones a esta en que vivimos, como algunos sugieren.

Es importante dejar sentada la opinión, de que no ha habido, no hay, ni habrá una transición con Fidel Castro en el poder; algo que él se ha cansado de repetir. No obstante queda la interrogante de si podría haber un **castrismo** sin Castro.

Sin la figura física de Fidel Castro, su poder unipersonal, su carisma—lo que hay que reconocer—el castrismo no significa nada desde el punto de vista ideológico, ni institucional. Detrás, no quedará, ni siquiera una clase o un aparato burocrático; ya que,

con su afán absolutista, él mismo se ha encargado de impedirlo. Pero sí, deja muchos intereses, sobre todo en los grupos próximos al poder, que desearán que lo inevitable transcurra sin grandes daños físicos y económicos para ellos y su familia.

Una transición, sin Castro y sin caos, posiblemente tendrá que ser producto de un pacto, entre los que asumirán como único fin salvar lo que puedan—evitando un vacío inicial de poder—y las fuerzas democráticas que deberán a la larga producir la transición.

El escenario actual que tiene el país, permite afirmar que aquellos **"nuevos ricos"**—nombre con que los designa el pueblo—que han sido ubicados por la jerarquía gubernamental en altos puestos gerenciales, no se desplazarán fácilmente para ceder su lugar en una transición a los que aspiran a reformas liberales. Este **"estrato social"** está muy bien determinado y desde ya, son los que se pasean por la ciudad en los autos recién adquiridos por las empresas extranjeras —que forman parte de los convenios mixtos con el Gobierno—y poseen suficientes divisas para tener una vida muy por encima del ciudadano medio. Ade-

---

1. Este documento no constituye una ponencia opuesta a los apuntes de Ernesto Betancourt "The Cuban Transition in the Light of the Lessons of Ten Years of Experience in the Former Soviet Bloc." Después de haber estudiado profundamente sus sugerencias, se puede definir como un complemento a lo que él escribió—aunque no coincidamos en todos los aspectos—basado en las experiencias que tenemos los economistas independientes dentro de la Isla. Es por eso que no hay respuestas a cada punto, sino comentarios hechos a lo largo de todo el escrito. Espero que ayuden a los propósitos que tiene la reunión de ASCE.

más, tienen prerrogativas importantes, como poder visitar Varadero y otros lugares prohibidos para el resto de los cubanos, así como viajar al extranjero con pasaporte oficial, y los gastos pagos por parte del Estado. Los más encumbrados deben disponer además de otros recursos, como pueden ser cuentas en bancos foráneos y negocios en otros países.

Hay que considerar, que en estos momentos ellos significan la aceleración de la transición social, aunque estén apoyando al régimen, no comparten sus ideas de cómo debe desarrollarse la existencia del cubano, las comodidades que tienen actualmente, forman parte de la vida que quieren para sus hijos y nietos. Esta **"nueva clase"** es muy sensible a los cambios, ya que una vez acomodada como está, no va a permitirle nunca un retroceso al Gobierno.

Por otra parte, los altos oficiales desmovilizados de los Ministerios de las Fuerzas Armadas y del Interior, no serán los que formen parte del Consejo de Defensa Nacional (con 7 integrantes), que se supone tome el poder en caso de alguna emergencia, según la Ley de Defensa Nacional, No. 75/94.

En estos momentos hay una transición social que es inaplazable, que hace cierto el hecho de que la sociedad civil no puede ser ignorada. En la medida en que tome más fuerza, con o sin la desaparición física del Presidente Fidel Castro, dará al traste con la dictadura y permitirá alcanzar la libertad del país.

Esta transición social, comenzó al iniciar la década de los 90, el pasado siglo y se manifestaba de una forma muy lenta, pero factores de índole político y económico han hecho que tome un ritmo más acelerado y en el presente, es el centro de preocupación de la elite gobernante, que constantemente toma el pulso a la sociedad y trata de combatirla con la llamada "batalla de ideas."

El ejemplo de las transiciones que se han llevado a cabo en el ex bloque soviético, es algo a tener en consideración. Es muy inteligente imaginar que no se puede llevar a Cuba exactamente por ese mismo contorno, ya que las circunstancias que prevalecen en la Isla son diferentes. Además de las características especiales de la sociedad cubana, las cuales hay que tener en cuenta, el cambio se puede efectuar más rápidamente, ya que prácticamente en los últimos años se ha aplicado una terapia de choque, con una rebaja del salario real y del nivel de vida, quedando únicamente pendiente el desempleo masivo, que se ha evitado a toda costa, inventando, entre otras cosas nuevos puestos burocráticos de trabajo, que sólo están diseñados para tratar de sostener el régimen y que no producen bienes materiales.

Un factor que hay que tener en cuenta durante la transición es la disidencia cubana, que también es innegable ha ganado espacios, ha tenido poco a poco, reconocimiento y ayuda internacional, lo que ha pagado muy caro, con años de cárcel, mucha represión y ante todo con el sufrimiento y las necesidades que pasa la familia.

La diáspora cubana, a través de su exilio en Miami, ha demostrado su deseo de participar en la reconstrucción del país, por lo que no sólo hay que tener en consideración el hecho de que existe, sino su voluntad de cooperar y la experiencia en el conocimiento empresarial que ha logrado acumular durante todos estos años y por supuesto los recursos financieros de que dispone, ya que una de las limitantes en esa época será la falta de capital.

El llevar a cabo la formación de un Grupo Consultivo sobre Cuba, es una estupenda idea, pero no así, si se ve a largo plazo. Es necesario seguir paso a paso las incidencias que la crisis política actual tiene sobre la economía y la sociedad, por lo que este Grupo es totalmente necesario en la presente situación. En estos momentos el Gobierno Cubano trabaja en la total destrucción de la agro-industria azucarera. Esto significa que parcialmente, la producción de azúcar ha decaído de tal forma que cualquier intento de reducirla no es más que la manera de eliminarla, situación que se hace necesario seguir de cerca y desde ahora.

El grupo de las **democracias competitivas,** clasificado así por el Banco Mundial, es efectivamente el que ha tenido más éxitos en la transición económica, y como grupo ofrece también el modelo más consistente con el deseo, pero cada uno de los otros tres grupos tiene experiencias que transmitir a la transición, por lo que no se puede tomar un solo modelo para la transición, por el contrario, deben analizarse los fac-

541

tores positivos y negativos de todos para poder racionalizarla.

No obstante las "reformas" que se llevaron a cabo durante el llamado Período Especial, no encajan en el **grupo de regímenes con políticas no competitivas,** ya que en Cuba en ningún momento ha habido una idea de transición política, sino un inmovilismo total. Los actores institucionales que pueden vetar las decisiones políticas no concurren en Cuba, sólo hay una persona que alcanza hacerlo: Fidel Castro.

No existe división alguna de poderes en ramas, el poder está concentrado en una sola persona. Entre una reunión y otra de la Asamblea Nacional del Poder Popular, se gobierna por *decreto*. Con un solo ejemplo, se puede apreciar esto: El Ministro de Justicia es el Jefe de la Comisión Electoral.

Resultaría importante, que la sociedad cubana se preparara para poder participar en el ALCA. En estos momentos, para la población lo único que se sabe de esta asociación es que es "un monstruo" que exhiben como tal por la televisión. No parece que haya nadie preparado, dentro del país, para poder afrontar la posibilidad de acceso a este sistema. Hay que recordar que los Estados Unidos son el socio comercial por excelencia de Cuba, dado su posición geográfica.

Indiscutiblemente, la incorporación de Cuba a diversos acuerdos de integración, ya sean regionales, o sub regionales, dentro del hemisferio y también con los países de la Unión Europea sería sumamente importante para la transición. Aunque no sea un requisito indispensable, la inserción en estas organizaciones internacionales, aceleraría el proceso. No quiere decir que lideren ellas la transición, ésta tendrá sus propios líderes nacionales que respondan indudablemente a las necesidades y aspiraciones que el pueblo ha visto frustradas en estos momentos por más de 43 años, debido a la mal llamada Revolución, que se convirtió en un **Robo ilusión.**

Alentar la construcción de nuevas empresas, en la etapa de la transición, tendrá un gran valor económico y social, aunque si se trabaja desde ahora las bases empíricas pueden estar reforzadas. Por lo que el Instituto Cubano de Economistas Independientes "Manuel Sánchez Herrero" se ha afanado en organizar dentro

de la disidencia interna la "Asamblea para Promover la Sociedad Civil," que tiene entre sus fines la educación del pueblo sobre la democracia. Indiscutiblemente esto lleva incluido las libertades económicas y las posibilidades de crear pequeñas empresas, incluso que den trabajo al núcleo familiar y a otras personas relacionadas con ellos. Hay que borrar de la mente del pueblo lo que se ha hecho una costumbre, **"no tener."**

La disidencia trabaja en estos momentos fuertemente con la sociedad civil y sobre todo en promover las ideas de la democracia y los derechos humanos. Solamente en un mes la Asamblea para Promover la Sociedad Civil repartió al pueblo 12 000 declaraciones universales de los derechos humanos, en parques, iglesias y hasta en las propias casas.

A los indicadores del PIB, que se puedan mostrar, habría que añadir siempre, la economía subterránea. Hay que dudar de los números oficiales, porque aquí no existen controles de ningún tipo. El Instituto Cubano de Economistas Independientes, ha realizado un estudio para la Universidad de Princeton sobre la economía informal, en el cual se destaca la cifra de que un 50% del PIB ocurre en el mercado negro y el Estado no está en condiciones de controlarlo. En estos momentos existen negocios que toman como base la propiedad estatal, y para el segmento poblacional más rico, hay un mercado sofisticado.

Para la transición, esta economía informal sirve como una especie de práctica, una forma de entrenamiento para actuar de acuerdo a las reglas del mercado y en ese sentido ha sido provechoso. Pero la costumbre masiva de proceder al margen de la ley en ésta y en muchas otras actividades, resulta perniciosa y constituirá uno de los males a combatir desde el primer momento, ya que la corrupción está generalizada.

De esta experiencia que se vive en el escenario actual, se puede concluir que hay que llevar a cabo una profunda desregulación, que permita adaptar la inexistencia de un sistema económico a una serie de preceptos que inicialmente ayuden a la instauración de procedimientos para el funcionamiento de la economía.

Si bien es cierto que las reformas deben incluir los siete aspectos que fueron sacados del consenso del Banco Mundial y su experiencia en la transición, hay que analizar el escenario especial que tiene Cuba. En el punto de la estabilización macroeconómica, caben muchos aspectos, ya que es muy global, no obstante existen problemas macrofinancieros. Entre ellos la circulación de tres monedas a nivel nacional (el dólar, el peso cubano convertible y el peso) y en estos momentos una cuarta en la playa de Varadero (el euro).

Por eso la creación de nuevas políticas financieras en todo el proceso de transición se hace importante e incluso imprescindible y también la disciplina en ese sentido, tomando en consideración que las empresas no estarán todas privatizadas y que lo que se hereda del sector estatal referente al orden financiero es bastante negativo.

Las nuevas empresas pequeñas que puedan fundarse e incluso las que se privaticen, deben acceder a una disciplina financiera diferente, lo que permitirá que nazcan otras fuentes de trabajo, que es fundamental para el desarrollo social.

En la situación actual, en que 71 centrales azucareros van a ser cerrados, se reducen en 100 mil los empleos. El Gobierno "trata" de solucionar esto enviando a estudiar a los trabajadores, lo que crea empleos ficticios (subempleos).

El cierre de estos centrales es una medida tomada con atraso y bruscamente, ante una situación de caos, para tratar de salvar parte de la industria y hacerla competitiva, pero si la transición se demora, el colapso de la industria será inevitable. En alrededor de 100 municipios de los 169 existentes, se asientan los 156 centrales actuales, por lo que el problema social que se generará se esparcirá por todo el país. La reubicación de esas personas agravará, entre otras cosas el agudo problema actual de la vivienda.

Para cualquier estudio sobre las posibilidades de fuentes de trabajo, hay que tener en cuenta la formación por edades de la Población Económicamente Activa, tanto en estos momentos como en el futuro, para los próximos 20 años, donde habrá un gran envejecimiento en la composición poblacional.

Las organizaciones sindicales independientes, que se encuentran formando parte de la Asamblea para Promover la Sociedad Civil, están pensando en el futuro de algunos trabajadores y se han dado a la tarea de diseñar unos formularios que le permitan recopilar información de todos aquellos que han sido expulsados de sus centros laborales y que no tendrán la oportunidad de jubilarse o contar con esos años de trabajo para su pensión; así como los cuentapropistas que no tienen derecho a retirarse por no estar vinculados al Estado. El resultado de esta recopilación se presentará, en su oportunidad, al Gobierno de Transición.

Los grupos sindicales dentro de la disidencia (unos 15 en total), tuvieron su período de mayor auge en los años 1996-98. Algunos de ellos hacen informes para diferentes organizaciones en el mundo. Estos sindicatos independientes deben aprender, en particular, sobre los convenios internacionales que existen, incluyendo aquellos a los que Cuba no pertenece, por no haberlos firmado. Tienen que adquirir toda una cultura sindical, que ciertamente no todos poseen. La Asamblea está trabajando en ello, en particular con la mayoría de los que residen en Ciudad de La Habana.

Cómo es indiscutible que se va a llevar a cabo la transición, se necesita de una entidad conciliadora, que ayude a enlazar a los diferentes sectores. La Asamblea para promover la Sociedad Civil es quizás una semilla, ya que trata de poner de acuerdo, en estos momentos, a más de 260 organizaciones dentro de la Isla.

Cuando se liberen algunas políticas restrictivas, los trabajadores tendrán alicientes para producir, cosa que no sucede ahora, por lo que en un inicio hay que considerar mecanismos que permitan a las empresas estatales que no obtienen ganancias, resolver sus problemas, hasta que puedan ser privatizadas.

El exilio jugará un papel importante, los cubanos de adentro, cuentan con la contribución que pueda hacer al establecimiento de pequeñas y medianas empresas, para agilizar la reconciliación nacional.

Ahora bien, la transición política, es otra cosa, será mucho más fácil de llevar a cabo. El pueblo en estos momentos, no sólo está acostumbrado a recibir órdenes de la nomenclatura y del aparato partidista, sino que absorbe una gran cantidad de propaganda de la llamada "batalla de ideas," que envuelve su desarrollo diario. Cuando se ponga fin a los medios de información unipartidistas y a toda la actividad que despliega el sistema buscando una ideología que tiene perdida, será muy fácil conseguir esta transición.

Si queremos construir una sociedad democrática, puede haber un partido comunista, ya que el pluripartidismo es una de las cualidades que ésta ofrece; lo que habría que ver cuantos simpatizantes alcanzará a tener y si se mantendrá como un partido elitista, donde se seleccionan sus miembros.

Aunque no se sabe como va a ser la transición hacia la democracia, sí tiene que tenerse en consideración la formación de una Asamblea Constituyente. Es imposible un proceso electoral basado en la actual Constitución que hace al *sistema socialista* **"irreversible,"** y que tiene como modo de Gobierno, la Asamblea Nacional del Poder Popular, que fue creada atendiendo a los intereses del sistema totalitario, tratando de buscar una forma institucional que se le acomodara, para poder entrar a ser parte del CAME (Consejo de Ayuda Mutua Económica).

Algunos piensan en el restablecimiento de la Constitución de 1940, esto es prácticamente imposible, los abogados independientes han explicado los pormenores que dificultan retomar completamente esta Carta Magna, no obstante podría ser la base de la nueva.

En el caso de Cuba las semillas de los partidos políticos están sembradas, tanto aquí dentro como en el exterior, habrá que asegurarse solamente de que en la transición se le permita también participar a la parte del exilio que así lo desee.

Con el grupo de la población más pobre, habrá que ser bien cuidadoso. Los alimentos que se venden por la libreta de racionamiento, no pueden ser eliminados de una sola vez por la privatización, sin antes tener la seguridad de que podrán tener acceso a ellos. Esto sería fatal para la parte anciana de la sociedad, hay que recordar que aunque lo que se adquiere de esta forma no alcanza ni para una tercera parte del

mes, es algo que tienen asegurado, y a lo que han estado acostumbrados por casi 40 años.

Hay varias preguntas que caben hacerse, entre ellas: ¿participarán en la privatización todas las empresas que han estado apoyando al Gobierno actual, que han formado con él sociedades mixtas, y que han estado explotando a los trabajadores?

¿Cómo se considerarán las reclamaciones que se han hecho en los Estados Unidos, de empresas que fueron nacionalizadas por el gobierno cubano?

En el primer cuestionamiento se podría oir la opinión del pueblo. Son muchos los trabajadores que conocen el verdadero salario que ganan, y sencillamente se les paga en moneda nacional, resolviendo la diferencia, en algunos casos con una moneda llamada "dura," pero sin ningún respaldo, que es el peso convertible; en otros con una "jaba" con algunos productos de aseo personal y no en pocos con una tarjeta para comprar en tiendas donde los precios están sumamente elevados.

Con respecto a la segunda pregunta, el régimen ha hecho una gran divulgación negativa con respecto a los que tenían posesiones en el país antes de 1959. La que más afecta la opinión popular, es la referida a que los que están en los Estados Unidos de América quieren que les retornen las casas, las escuelas y los círculos infantiles. Muchas de estas construcciones, son prácticamente inhabitables, están totalmente deterioradas, pero no obstante la propaganda crea una confrontación con la sociedad.

Si bien es cierto que el período especial hizo que se realizaran algunas "reformas" económicas, también lo es que se han dado tres pasos hacia atrás con ello. Los **"paladares,"** que fueron el termómetro que medía esta pequeña apertura, han ido desapareciendo poco a poco, el mercado campesino también y los trabajadores por cuenta propia son cada vez menos, el gobierno no está dando más licencias. Esto no fue una transición, en ningún momento, fue un escape a la situación existente y ahora es una vuelta atrás.

La descentralización de las empresas ha sido sólo nominal. Por ejemplo, cada vez que hay una actividad política, se moviliza su transporte, el personal y también se hace para otras acciones tales como: las prácticas de las milicias, de los ciclones, etc., las empresas no tienen autonomía para decidir sobre si lo hacen o no y todo esto va contra sus gastos. Recientemente el país se paralizó 4 días, para la firma y aprobación de la irrevocabilidad. ¿Es esto autonomía empresarial? Existen reportes, por ejemplo de Moa (provincia de Holguín) donde los disidentes son acosados en autos de la firma Sherritt.

El llamado "Perfeccionamiento Empresarial" es algo ilusorio, porque no se ha logrado establecer, la mayoría de las empresas siguen con la nombrada **"contabilidad no confiable,"** una forma de decir que no hay control. El rescate de los registros es algo que se hace como de diente para fuera, porque no lleva toda la autoridad y seriedad necesaria, ya que el sistema tiene que sobrevivir con la corrupción y el mercado negro; y eliminar el descontrol, implica excluir ambas cosas.

Actualmente sólo el 20% de la producción mercantil se realiza en las empresas en perfeccionamiento, por lo que cuatro quintas partes se efectúa por entidades sin control contable, que constituye la limitante fundamental para su implantación.

Un problema que no se resolvería fácilmente es el de la tierra. Vender a los cooperativistas sus tierras, algunas de ellas reclamadas por sus dueños, crearía más malestar que soluciones. Existen también, grandes plantaciones como las de cítricos, o grandes empresas arroceras (el sur del Jíbaro), donde se aplica una elevada mecanización, que no parece conveniente dividir en pequeñas parcelas, pero que sería positivo privatizar.

Si una solución fuera darle facilidades adicionales para la adquisición de empresas a aquellos que les fueron confiscadas sin compensación (extranjeros o cubanos), y/o a las víctimas de la represión del régimen, y/o a los que están en el extranjero luchando por cambiar el sistema, hay que tomar en consideración todo lo que le fue quitado a la gente, en particular las tierras. Un equipo de expertos debe estudiar todas estas situaciones.

Es bien cierto que en el período pre transición deben hacerse algunas cosas, como por ejemplo determinar los programas de asistencia internacional que se requieren, pero es importante que tanto entes del exilio como de la disidencia interna participen en estos programas.

El Diálogo Inter-Americano vino a Cuba, se entrevistó con el Gobierno Cubano y con la disidencia, pero no hemos visto más progresos al efecto. Señalamos en esa oportunidad que era necesario un análisis del escenario cubano para poder elaborar un documento como el que se había hecho, ya que se escaparon aspectos de lo que ocurría en esos momentos.

La asistencia de emergencia es algo que debe tenerse en consideración, ya que el deterioro nacional es muy grande, en todos los sentidos. El PNUD tiene programas en Cuba, pero es tanta la necesidad que no son suficientes. Esta ayuda de emergencia es algo que no debe faltar en cualquier programa de transición, pero hay que empezar desde ahora a pensar en ella. La ayuda de la OEA también sería importante.

La deuda externa cubana en el Club de París asciende a más de 12 mil millones de dólares y a ella hay que sumar la de los ex países socialistas por más de 35 mil millones de dólares. Por lo que en la etapa de transición habría que encontrar acuerdos con el Club de París y en particular con Rusia. La gravedad de esto, sólo puede aquilatarse cuando se compara con la pobre capacidad del país para generar y gestionar recursos financieros, determinada en primer término por el menguado volumen de las ventas al exterior. La situación es tal que si se destinaran todas las exportaciones—al nivel de la realizadas en el 2001— a amortizar la deuda, se demoraría un cuarto de siglo en lograrlo.

Al destacar la capacidad de exportación, hay que referirse en primer lugar a la industria azucarera, otrora la primera del país y virtualmente arruinada en la actualidad, ya que a los altos costos que exceden en casi tres veces los precios actuales en el mercado internacional, se suma la imposibilidad de alcanzar niveles de producción superiores a los que se lograban 60 años atrás.

Hay que tener en cuenta que cuando ese sector deje de constituir un factor económico, se convertirá en un gravísimo problema social.

El otro renglón exportable de envergadura es el níquel, que requeriría capital y tecnología para reducir sus altos índices de consumo de energía, que lo hace muy vulnerable a las oscilaciones de los precios internacionales, pero sobre todo sería necesario la adquisición de tecnologías para separar el cobalto y profundizar en la refinación.

En los primeros años de la transición, el turismo pudiera convertirse en la primera fuente de ingresos, para lo cual los primeros esfuerzos en esta etapa, deberán dedicarse a negociar el fin del embargo de Estados Unidos, para propiciar el arribo masivo de turistas de ese país y sobre todo de capitales para ampliar las capacidades de alojamiento, diversión y la infraestructura turística.

La agricultura deberá ser objeto de atención preferente, no sólo como fuente de empleo, sino mayormente para el abastecimiento a la población y a la industria alimentaria, que propicie que las importaciones se destinen preponderantemente a materias primas y maquinarias.

El sector de la construcción además de fuente de empleo en ese período deberá encargarse de restituir, modernizar y ampliar las redes de la infraestructura vial, de comunicaciones, de acueductos alcantarillados y de otros servicios comunales y en especial las viviendas.

El sector público tiene que ser reorganizado totalmente. Para ayudar en los ajustes estructurales debe consultarse tanto a la disidencia interna como al exilio, en dependencia de la situación que prevalezca en el país en el momento de la transición.

La llamada "batalla de ideas" tiene que quedar bien atrás, debe removerse la cultura, para poder permitir la crítica en broma y todo lo que hasta el momento está prohibido. El pueblo debe retomar sus aspectos éticos y volver a la identidad nacional. Esas son las circunstancias más deseables en que debe darse la transición, la variante que deje el protagonismo al pueblo cubano.

Si la transición comenzara pronto se enfrentaría con un escenario muy complejo, el cual se agravaría de forma muy acelerada en la medida que ésta se demore. Desde el punto de vista social habría que destacar que más del 86 % de la población—que es la totalidad de su parte activa—entraría en ese proceso sin experiencia democrática, con instituciones en formación, con una pésima formación laboral y sin preparación para encarar la vida en una sociedad competitiva.

En lo político e institucional, todo deberá variarse, por lo que sólo los más jóvenes podrán encarar con facilidad las enormes y rápidas transformaciones que habrán de realizarse.

El trasfondo económico, determinará el ritmo a que podrán ejecutarse las modificaciones y ello dependerá tanto de la situación económica interna, como de la magnitud de la cooperación internacional.

Todo lo hasta aquí detallado no sería suficiente, si paralelamente no se instaura un régimen democrático y transparente donde se impida la corrupción, que ha hundido la economía de naciones con una situación menos comprometida que a la que Cuba deberá enfrentarse.

Appendix A
Authors and Discussants

B. E. Aguirre is Professor, Department of Sociology and Criminal Justice, University of Delaware.

Pablo Alfonso is a journalist with *El Nuevo Herald*, Miami, Florida, where he writes the column "Cuba por Dentro."

José Alvarez is Professor, Food and Research Economics Department, Institute of Food and Agricultural Sciences, University of Florida, where he works as the Area Economist at the Everglades Research and Education Center, Belle Glade, Florida. He has traveled to Cuba in the last few years as one of the principal investigators in two grants from John D. and Catherine T. MacArthur Foundation to study Cuban agriculture and the potential economic impact on the agricultural economies of Florida and Cuba after lifting the U.S. economic embargo. He earned a B.A. in economics (1971) and M.S. (1974) and Ph.D. (1977) in Food and Resource Economics from the University of Florida.

Juan A. B. Belt is a Senior economist with the Inter-American Development Bank. He works on finance and infrastructure projects, with particular emphasis on telecommunications and information technology. Before joining the IDB, he was the Chief Economist of the Global Bureau of USAID, Deputy Director of USAID Guatemala, and Chief economist of USAID Missions in Panama, Costa Rica and El Salvador. Before working for USAID he was an economist at the World Bank.

Ernesto Betancourt is a consultant on government reforms. He has an MPA from the University of Pittsburgh and studied Advertising and Marketing at American University. He was the first Director of Radio Martí and represented Castro in Washington in 1957-58. He has written extensively on the Cuban Revolution.

Pablo A. Carreño is Vice President of the National Association of Sugar Mill Owners of Cuba (Asociación Nacional de Hacendados de Cuba, ANDHAC). He holds a degree in agricultural engineering and sugar chemistry from the Univeridad de la Habana and has done graduate work in this field at Louisiana State University and in business administration at the Alexander Hamilton Institute in New York. He has worked for several corporations in technical and administrative positions and is currently an engineering consultant.

Gloria Casal, M.D., is a Diplomat of the American Board of Internal Medicine. She is presently working for Leon Medical Centers, Miami-Dade County, Florida.

Rolando H. Castañeda is an economic consultant. He retired from the Inter-American Development Bank, where he worked for 27 years. His last assignment with the IDB was as Principal Project Specialist in Santiago, Chile, in 1996-2001.

Javier Corrales specializes in comparative and international politics of Latin America. He is the author *of Presidents Without Parties: Economic Reforms in Argentina and Venezuela in the 1990s* (Penn State University Press, 2002) and several articles in academic journals. In 2000-01, he was a fellow at the Woodrow Wilson International Center for Scholars in Washington, DC. He holds a Ph.D. in Political Science from Harvard University awarded in 1996.

Nicolás Crespo is President, The Phoenix Hospitality and Consulting Corporation, Miami, Florida.

Graciella Cruz-Taura is Associate Professor of History at the Dorothy F. Schmidt College of Arts and Letters, Florida Atlantic University. Her presentation during ASCE's 12th Annual Meeting is part of the study she prepared on Cuban education for the *Cuba Transition Project* based at the University of Miami's Institute for Cuban and Cuban American Studies.

Larry Daley (García-Iñiguez Enamorado) holds BSA and MSA degrees from the University of Florida and a Ph.D. from the University of California, Davis. He is currently Professor of Biophysics and Biochemistry of Plant Germplasm at the Department of Horticulture, Oregon State University, Corvallis, Oregon.

Sergio Díaz-Briquets is Vice President of Casals & Associates, Inc. (C&A), a Washington area-based consulting firm. For the seven years, C&A has conducted, under contract to the U.S. Agency for International Development, the America's Accountability and Anti-Corruption (AAA) project. Other C&A projects address similar concerns in specific countries and on a global basis.

Erin Ennis holds a Masters degree in International Affairs from The Catholic University of America. She currently works for Kissinger McLarty Associates in Washington, D.C.

Oscar Espinosa Chepe is an independent journalist residing in Cuba.

Antonio A. Fernández, M.D., is Associate Professor of Barry University, Miami-Dade County and Adjunct Professor at Nova Southeastern University, Fort Lauderdale, Florida.

María Antonia Fernández Mayo is Co-Researcher, International Agricultural Trade and Development Center, Department of Food and Resource Economics, Institute of Food and Agricultural Sciences, University of Florida.

Joel Cirilo Font is the founder and President of Envision Technologies, a New Jersey based software and Internet applications development company. Insurance companies, third party administrators and labor unions throughout the United States use his software products. His interests outside the technology sector are in business development and mass commu-

nications. He is a member of the Association for the Study of the Cuban Economy, and Executive Director of the Cuban-American Technology Group. He is a native of Holguín, Cuba.

Manuel García Díaz is Professor in the Department of Applied Economics, Universidd de Granada, Spain. He holds a Licenciatura in Economics from the Universidad de La Habana and a Doctorate in Economic Sciences from Moscow State University, M. V. Lomonosov.

Andy S. Gomez is Special Assistant to the Provost at the University of Miami. He is also Senior Fellow at the Institute for Cuban and Cuban-American Studies at UM. From 2000-2002 he served as Dean of the School of International Studies at UM.

Pedro Melchor González, M.D., is a Psychiatrist at the Veterans Administration Hospital, Clinical Assistant Professor at University of Miami Medical School, and Adjunct Professor at Albizú University, Miami-Dade County, Florida.

Dominga González Suárez is Professor in the Department of Social Psychology and Methodology of the Behavioral Sciences, Faculty of Psychology, Universidad de Granada, Spain. She received a Licenciatura in History from the Universidad de La Habana and a Doctorate in Psychology from the Universidad de Granada.

Ted Henken worked in Cuba for Tulane University's Cuban and Caribbean Studies Institute as the in-country liaison and program coordinator during the spring of 2001. He successfully defended his dissertation in March 2002, and received his Ph.D. in Latin American Studies from Tulane University in May. He is currently an adjunct professor of Latin American Studies at Tulane. His research on Cuba's "second economy" has been published in *Cuba in Transition* and in an article forthcoming in volume 33 (2003) of *Cuban Studies*.

Amy Myers Jaffe is Energy Research Coordinator, Baker Institute for Public Policy, Rice University.

Francisco León is a consultant to CEPAL and to the University of Giessen project "Relations between the European Union and Latin America: Bi-regionalism in a Changing Global System," in the framework of Volkswagen-Stiftung's Priority Area "Global Structures and Governance." He was a Senior Visiting Fellow, Institute for European-Latin American Relations, Madrid, during 2000. From 1971 to 2000, he was Social Research Officer, UN Economic Commission for Latin America and the Caribbean (CEPAL). He earned degrees in Economic Sociology from the University of Louvain, Belgium.

Roberto Orro is an economist with the H. Calero Consulting Group, San Juan, Puerto Rico.

Silvia Pedraza is Associate Professor of Sociology at the University of Michigan, Ann Arbor. She is the author of numerous articles in professional journals and two books, *Origins and Destinations: Immigration, Race and Ethnicity in America* (Wadsworth, 1996), co-edited with Rubén G. Rumbaut, and *Political and Economic Migrants in America: Cubans and Mexicans* (University of Texas Press, 1985). Her research interests are in the areas of the sociology of immigration, race and ethnicity in America, as well as the sociology of Cuba's revolution and exodus. She holds a Ph.D. in Sociology from the University of Chicago.

Pedro F. Pellet, Ph.D., is Professor of Economics and Statistics at Nova Southeastern University, Fort Lauderdale, Florida.

Jorge F. Pérez-López is an international economist with the Bureau of International Labor Affairs, U.S. Department of Labor. He is the author of *Cuba's Second Economy: From Behind the Scenes to Center Stage* (Transaction Publishers, 1995), co-editor of *Perspectives on Cuban Economic Reforms* (Arizona State University Press, 1998), and co-author of *Conquering Nature: The Environmental Legacy of Socialism in Cuba* (University of Pittsburgh Press, 2000). He received a Ph.D. in Economics from the State University of New York at Albany.

Guy Pfeffermann is Director and Chief Economist at the International Finance Corporation.

Enrique S. Pumar, Ph.D., is Assistant Professor of Sociology and Latin American Studies at the William Paterson University of New Jersey where he teaches courses on research methods, comparative national development, and economic sociology and is the Director of the university's MOST Program.

Dorothy Robyn is a Senior Advisor to The Brattle Group, a Boston-based economic research and consulting firm, where she focuses on aviation, transportation and trade. She was a senior economic adviser to President Clinton, on the staff of the White House National Economic Council. Previously, she was an assistant professor at Harvard's John F. Kennedy School of Government, and a visiting scholar at the Brookings Institution.

Marta Beatriz Roque is President of the Instituto Cubano de Economistas Independientes, La Habana, Cuba.

James E. Ross is Courtesy Professor and Program Advisor, International Agricultural Trade and Development Center, Department of Food and Resource Economics, Institute of Food and Agricultural Sciences, University of Florida.

Jesús (Jay) Sanchelima is an attorney and the founder of Sanchelima & Associates, P.A., a law firm specializing in intellectual property, commercial law, and international business law. Mr. Sanchelima is an expert on Cuban intellectual property law. He is a member of the Florida Bar, the American Bar Association, the Cuban American Bar Association, the American Arbitration Association, and the International Trade Association.

Joseph L. Scarpaci is Professor of Urban Affairs and Planning in Virginia Tech's College of Architecture and Urban Studies.

Miguel Schloss is Executive Director of Transparency International.

Gary Shiffman is Adjunct Senior Fellow, Institute for Cuban and Cuban-American Studies at the University of Miami (2001-2002), Adjunct Faculty, Georgetown University, School of Foreign Service, Security Studies Program, and Director, Governmental Affairs, Greenberg Traurig.

Ronald Soligo is Professor of Economics, Rice University.

Paolo Spadoni is a PhD student in the Department of Political Science at the University of Florida. He holds a Master in Latin American Studies from the Center for Latin American Studies at the University of Florida.

Mary Speck, a former correspondent in Latin America, is completing a dissertation on business and bureaucracy in the Republic of Cuba for Stanford University.

Alan C. Swan, is Professor of Law, University of Miami School of Law. He teaches international business transactions, international economic law, federal courts, administrative law, commercial law, constitutional law, and contracts. He currently serves as director of the University of Miami School of Law's Master of Laws in International Law program. Professor Swan served as an associate at Milbank, Tweed, as assistant general counsel of the Agency for International Development, and as assistant vice-

president, programs and projects, at the University of Chicago.

Matías F. Travieso-Díaz is a partner in Shaw Pittman LLP, a law firm with offices in Washington, D.C., London, New York City, Los Angeles and Northern Virginia. He is the author of *The Laws and Legal System of a Free-Market Cuba* (Quorum Books, 1996) and numerous law review articles, papers and newspaper columns on matters related to Cuba's transition to a free-market, democratic society. He holds B.S. and M.S. degrees in Electrical Engineering from the University of Miami and a Ph.D. in Electrical Engineering from Ohio State University. He earned a J.D. degree from Columbia Law School.

Charles Trumbull is a recent graduate of Dartmouth College. He has traveled to Cuba several times to conduct research on Cuban economic reforms and their impact on society.

Appendix B
Acknowledgements

We want to take the opportunity to acknowledge the continued financial support provided to ASCE's activities by the following sponsoring members:

Alvarez, José
Asociación Nacional de Hacendados de
    Cuba
Barquín, Ramón C.
Batista, Víctor
Betancourt, Ernesto F.
Betancourt, Roger R.
Busto, Luis
Carbonell-Cortina, Néstor
Cosío, Alberto
Crespo, Nicolás
Cuzán, Alfred G.
De Lasa, José M.
Espino, María Dolores
Falcoff, Mark
Fernández, Matías A.
Fernández-Pujals, Leopoldo
Gayoso, Antonio
Giral, Juan A.
Gutiérrez, Alfredo D.
Gutiérrez, Ariel E. and Enrique H.
Hernández-Catá, Ernesto
Juncadella, Salvador J.

Locay, Luis
Luis, Luis R.
Luzárraga, Alberto
Maidique, Modesto A.
Miranda, Norma
Monserrat, René
O'Connell, Richard
Palomares, Carlos
Pérez, Lorenzo
Pérez-Lópex, Jorge F.
Perry, Joseph
Pujol, Joaquín
Rasco, José Ignacio
Ricardo, José M.
Roca, Rubén A.
Sánchez, Nicolás
Sanguinetty, Jorge
Scarpaci, Joseph L., Jr.
Tarajano, Beatriz S.
Vázquez, Manuel
Villalón, Manuel F.
Werlau, María C.
Zayas-Bazán, Eduardo